Common Symbols and Notation (continued)

P_E	price of common stock
P_i	price of security i
P_{pfd}	price of preferred stock
P_{rep}	stock price with share repurchase
P_T	pre-merger share price of target
P_t	stock price at the end of year t, price on date t
$Pr(\cdot)$	probability of
$P\%$	fraction of the firm financed with preferred stock
PV	present value
PV_t	present value on date t
r	interest rate, discount rate or projected cost of capital
r_n	interest rate or discount rate for an n-year term, interest rate or discount rate for a cash flow that arrives in period n
r_E, r_D	equity and debt costs of capital
r_f	risk-free interest rate
r_{FOC}	foreign currency risk-free interest rate
r_L	cost of capital for an insured loss
r_{pfd}	preferred stock cost of capital
$\tilde{r}_t$	floating interest rate on date t
r_U	unlevered cost of capital
r_{wacc}	weighted average cost of capital
r^*_{HOC}	home currency cost of capital
r^*_{HOC}	home currency risk-free interest rate
r^*_{FOC}	foreign currency cost of capital
$\bar{R}$	average return
R_P	return on portfolio P
R_t	realized or total return of a security from date t-1 to t
S	spot exchange rate, value of all synergies
SD(R)	standard deviation of return R
$SD(R_i)$	standard deviation (volatility) of the return of security i
T	pre-merger total value of target
T_c	marginal corporate tax rate
U	market value of unlevered equity
UCC	undepreciated capital cost
V^L	value of firm with leverage
V^L_0	initial levered value
V_t	enterprise value on date t
V^u	value of the unlevered firm
$Var(R)$	variance of return R
$Var(Ri)$	variance of the return of security i
w_i	fraction of the portfolio invested in security i (its relative *weight* in the portfolio)
x	number of new shares issued by acquirer to pay for target
y	yield to maturity
YTC	yield to call on a callable bond
YTM	yield to maturity on a bond
YTM_n	yield to maturity on a bond with n periods to maturity
β_i	beta of a security i with respect to market portfolio
β_L	beta of an insured loss

P9-CKB-264

THIRD CANADIAN EDITION

FUNDAMENTALS OF CORPORATE FINANCE

Jonathan **Berk**
Stanford University

Peter **DeMarzo**
Stanford University

Jarrad **Harford**
University of Washington

David **Stangeland**
University of Manitoba

András **Marosi**
University of Alberta

Pearson

Pearson Canada Inc., 26 Prince Andrew Place, North York, Ontario M3C 2H4.

Copyright © 2020, 2017, 2013 Pearson Canada Inc. All rights reserved.

Printed in the United States of America. This publication is protected by copyright, and permission should be obtained from the publisher prior to any prohibited reproduction, storage in a retrieval system, or transmission in any form or by any means, electronic, mechanical, photocopying, recording, or otherwise. For information regarding permissions, request forms, and the appropriate contacts, please contact Pearson Canada's Rights and Permissions Department by visiting www.pearson.com/ca/en/contact-us/permissions.html.

Authorized adaptation from Fundamentals of Corporate Finance, Fourth Edition, Copyright © 2018, Pearson Education, Inc. Used by permission. All rights reserved. This edition is authorized for sale only in Canada.

Attributions of third-party content appear on the appropriate page within the text. Cover Image: © Gemenacom/ Shutterstock.

PEARSON and ALWAYS LEARNING are exclusive trademarks owned by Pearson Education Inc. or its affiliates in the United States and/or other countries.

Unless otherwise indicated herein, any third party trademarks that may appear in this work are the property of their respective owners and any references to third party trademarks, logos, or other trade dress are for demonstrative or descriptive purposes only. Such references are not intended to imply any sponsorship, endorsement, authorization, or promotion of Pearson Canada products by the owners of such marks, or any relationship between the owner and Pearson Canada or its affiliates, authors, licensees, or distributors.

If you purchased this book outside the United States or Canada, you should be aware that it has been imported without the approval of the publisher or the author.

9780134735313

Library and Archives Canada Cataloguing in Publication

Berk, Jonathan B., 1962-, author
Fundamentals of corporate finance/Jonathan Berk, Stanford University, Peter Marzo, Stanford University, Jarrad Harford, University of Washington, David Stangeland, University of Manitoba, András Marosi, University of Alberta. -- Third Canadian edition.

Includes bibliographical references and index.
ISBN 978-0-13-473531-3 (hardcover)

1. Corporations--Finance--Textbooks. 2. Textbooks. I. DeMarzo, Peter M., author II. Harford, Jarrad V. T., author III. Stangeland, David, 1964-, author IV. Marosi, András, author V. Title.

HG4026.B485 2019 658.15 C2018-903974-4

To my family, friends, colleagues, and God for all the love, support, and encouragement, and to our country, Canada, where we can take for granted all the freedoms that are sought after, but often denied, around the world.

—David Stangeland

To my family for all their love and support.

—András Marosi

Brief Contents

PART 1 Introduction 1

CHAPTER 1 Corporate Finance and the Financial Manager 2
CHAPTER 2 Introduction to Financial Statement Analysis 27

PART 2 Interest Rates and Valuing Cash Flows 71

CHAPTER 3 The Valuation Principle: The Foundation of Financial Decision Making 72
CHAPTER 4 The Time Value of Money 95
CHAPTER 5 Interest Rates 134
CHAPTER 6 Bonds 162
CHAPTER 7 Valuing Stocks 202

PART 3 Investment Decisions 259

CHAPTER 8 Investment Decision Rules 260
CHAPTER 9 Fundamentals of Capital Budgeting 301

PART 4 Return, Risk, and the Cost of Capital 347

CHAPTER 10 Risk and Return in Capital Markets 348
CHAPTER 11 Systematic Risk and the Equity Risk Premium 381
CHAPTER 12 Determining the Cost of Capital 425
CHAPTER 13 Risk and the Pricing of Options 454

PART 5 Financing Decisions 483

CHAPTER 14 Raising Equity Capital 484
CHAPTER 15 Debt Financing 519
CHAPTER 16 Capital Structure 549
CHAPTER 17 Payout Policy 592

PART 6 Financial Planning and Forecasting 629

CHAPTER 18 Financial Modelling and Pro Forma Analysis 630
CHAPTER 19 Working Capital Management 661
CHAPTER 20 Short-Term Financial Planning 688

PART 7 Special Topics 719

CHAPTER 21 Risk Management 720
CHAPTER 22 International Corporate Finance 750
CHAPTER 23 Leasing 787
CHAPTER 24 Mergers and Acquisitions 814
CHAPTER 25 Corporate Governance 848

Detailed Contents

PART 1
Introduction 1

1 Corporate Finance and the Financial Manager 2

1.1 **Why Study Finance? 3**

1.2 **The Three Types of Firms 3**
Sole Proprietorships 4
Partnerships 5
Corporations 5
Tax Implications for Corporate Entities 7

CORPORATE TAXATION AROUND THE WORLD 9

1.3 **The Financial Manager 10**
Making Investment Decisions 11
Making Financing Decisions 11
Managing Short-Term Cash Needs 11
The Goal of the Financial Manager 11

1.4 **The Financial Manager's Place in the Corporation 12**
The Corporate Management Team 12
Ethics and Incentives in Corporations 13

1.5 **The Stock Market 16**
The Largest Stock Markets 16
NYSE 18
New Competition and Market Changes 18
Listing Standards 19
Other Financial Markets 19

1.6 **Financial Institutions 19**
The Financial Cycle 19
Types of Financial Institutions 20
Role of Financial Institutions 21

MyLabFinance SUMMARY 21 • PROBLEMS 23

2 Introduction to Financial Statement Analysis 27

2.1 **Firms' Disclosure of Financial Information 28**
Types of Financial Statements 28

PREPARATION OF FINANCIAL STATEMENTS 28

INTERNATIONAL FINANCIAL REPORTING STANDARDS 29

2.2 **The Statement of Financial Position or Balance Sheet 29**
Assets 31
Liabilities 31
Shareholders' Equity 32
Market Value versus Book Value 32
Market-to-Book Ratio 33
Enterprise Value 34

2.3 **The Statement of Comprehensive Income and Income Statement 35**
Earnings Calculations 35
EBITDA 37

2.4 **The Statement of Cash Flows 37**
Operating Activity 39
Investment Activity 40
Financing Activity 40

2.5 **Other Financial Statement Information 41**
Statement of Shareholders' Equity 41
Management Discussion and Analysis 42
Notes to the Financial Statements 42

2.6 **Financial Statement Analysis 42**
Profitability Ratios 42
Liquidity Ratios 43
Asset Efficiency 45
Working Capital Ratios 45
Interest Coverage Ratios 46
Leverage Ratios 47
Valuation Ratios 48

COMMON MISTAKE MISMATCHED RATIOS 49
Operating Returns 50
The DuPont Identity 51

2.7 **Financial Reporting in Practice 55**
Enron 55
The Sarbanes-Oxley Act 55
The Financial Statements: A Useful Starting Point 57

MyLab Finance SUMMARY 58 • REVIEW QUESTIONS 61 • PROBLEMS 61 • DATA CASE 69

PART 2
Interest Rates and Valuing Cash Flows 71

3 The Valuation Principle: The Foundation of Financial Decision Making 72

3.1 Cost-Benefit Analysis 73
Role of the Financial Manager 73

YOUR PERSONAL FINANCIAL DECISIONS 73
Quantifying Costs and Benefits 74
Role of Competitive Market Prices 74

3.2 Market Prices and the Valuation Principle 75
The Valuation Principle 76
Why There Can Be Only One Competitive Price for a Good 77

3.3 The Time Value of Money and Interest Rates 78
The Time Value of Money 78
The Interest Rate: Converting Cash across Time 79
Timelines 82
Constructing a Timeline 82
Identifying Dates on a Timeline 82
Distinguishing Cash Inflows from Outflows 83
Representing Various Time Periods 83

3.4 Valuing Cash Flows at Different Points in Time 83

COMMON MISTAKE SUMMING CASH FLOWS ACROSS TIME 84
Rule 1: Comparing and Combining Values 84
Rule 2: Compounding 84

RULE OF 72 85
Rule 3: Discounting 86

USING A FINANCIAL CALCULATOR 88

MyLab Finance SUMMARY 89 • REVIEW QUESTION 91 • PROBLEMS 91

4 The Time Value of Money 95

4.1 Valuing a Stream of Cash Flows 96
Applying the Rules of Valuing Cash Flows 96

4.2 Perpetuities and Annuities 101
Perpetuities 101

HISTORICAL EXAMPLES OF PERPETUITIES 102

COMMON MISTAKE DISCOUNTING ONE TOO MANY TIMES 103
Annuities 104

USING A FINANCIAL CALCULATOR OR EXCEL: SOLVING FOR PRESENT AND FUTURE VALUES OF CASH FLOW STREAMS 106

4.3 Solving for Variables Other Than Present Value or Future Value 110
Solving for the Cash Flows 110
Rate of Return 112
Solving for n, the Number of Periods 115

SOLVING FOR N USING LOGARITHMS 116

4.4 Growing Cash Flows 118

MyLab Finance SUMMARY 122 • REVIEW QUESTIONS 123 • PROBLEMS 124 • DATA CASE 129

CHAPTER 4 APPENDIX: USING A FINANCIAL CALCULATOR 131

5 Interest Rates 134

5.1 Interest Rate Quotes and Adjustments 135
The Effective Annual Rate 135
Adjusting the Effective Annual Rate to an Effective Rate over Different Time Periods 136
Annual Percentage Rates 137

COMMON MISTAKE USING THE APR OR EAR IN THE ANNUITY FORMULA 140

5.2 Application: Discount Rates and Loans 140
Computing Loan Payments 140

Computing Canadian Mortgage Payments 143
Computing the Outstanding Loan Balance 143

5.3 The Determinants of Interest Rates 144
Inflation and Real versus Nominal Rates 145
Investment and Interest Rate Policy 146
The Yield Curve and Discount Rates 147

COMMON MISTAKE USING THE ANNUITY FORMULA WHEN DISCOUNT RATES VARY 150
The Yield Curve and the Economy 150

5.4 The Opportunity Cost of Capital 153

INTEREST RATES, DISCOUNT RATES, AND THE COST OF CAPITAL 153

MyLab Finance SUMMARY 155 • REVIEW QUESTIONS 157 • PROBLEMS 157

6 Bonds 162

6.1 Bond Terminology 163

6.2 Zero-Coupon Bonds 164
Zero-Coupon Bond Cash Flows 164
Price and Yield to Maturity of a Zero-Coupon Bond 164
Risk-Free Interest Rates 166

GLOBAL FINANCIAL CRISIS: NEGATIVE BOND YIELDS 167

6.3 Coupon Bonds 169
Coupon Bond Cash Flows 169
Price and Yield to Maturity of a Coupon Bond 170
Coupon Bond Price Quotes 171

6.4 Why Bond Prices Change 173

FINDING BOND PRICES ON THE WEB 173
Interest Rate Changes and Bond Prices 174
Time and Bond Prices 176
Interest Rate Risk and Bond Prices 178
Bond Prices in Practice 179

6.5 Corporate Bonds 182
Credit Risk 182
Corporate Bond Yields 183
Bond Ratings 183
Corporate and Provincial Yield Curves 185

THE CREDIT CRISIS AND BOND YIELDS 188

MyLab Finance SUMMARY 189 • REVIEW QUESTIONS 191 • PROBLEMS 191 • DATA CASE 195

CHAPTER 6 APPENDIX A: SOLVING FOR THE YIELD TO MATURITY OF A BOND USING A FINANCIAL CALCULATOR 196

CHAPTER 6 APPENDIX B: THE YIELD CURVE AND THE LAW OF ONE PRICE 197

CHAPTER 6 APPENDIX C: INTEREST RATE RISK MEASUREMENT: DURATION ONLINE

7 Valuing Stocks 202

7.1 Stock Basics 203
Stock Market Reporting: Stock Quotes 203
Common Stock 205
Preferred Stock 206

7.2 The Dividend-Discount Model 206
A One-Year Investor 207
Dividend Yields, Capital Gains, and Total Returns 207
A Multi-Year Investor 209
Dividend-Discount Model Equation 210

7.3 Estimating Dividends in the Dividend-Discount Model 211
Constant Dividend Growth 211
Dividends versus Investment and Growth 212
Changing Growth Rates 215

COMMON MISTAKE THE FIRST DIVIDEND 216
Value Drivers and the Dividend-Discount Model 217

7.4 Limitations of the Dividend-Discount Model 218
Uncertain Dividend Forecasts 218
Non-Dividend-Paying Stocks 219

7.5 Share Repurchases and the Total Payout Model 220

7.6 The Discounted Free Cash Flow Model 221

7.7 Valuation Based on Comparable Firms 226
Valuation Multiples 227
Limitations of Multiples 230
Comparison with Discounted Cash Flow Methods 231
Stock Valuation Techniques: The Final Word 232

7.8 Information, Competition, and Stock Prices 234
Information in Stock Prices 234
Competition and Efficient Markets 236
Lessons for Investors and Corporate Managers 239

The Efficient Markets Hypothesis versus No Arbitrage 240

7.9 **Individual Biases and Trading 240**
Excessive Trading and Overconfidence 240
Hanging on to Losers and the Disposition Effect 241
Investor Attention, Mood, and Experience 242

MyLab Finance SUMMARY 243 • REVIEW QUESTIONS 247 • PROBLEMS 247 • DATA CASE 255

PART 2 INTEGRATIVE CASE 257

PART 3
Investment Decisions 259

8 Investment Decision Rules 260

8.1 **The NPV Rule 261**
Net Present Value 261
Making Decisions: The NPV Rule 262

8.2 **Using the NPV Rule 263**
Organizing the Cash Flows and Computing the NPV 263
The NPV Profile 264
Measuring Sensitivity with IRR 264
Alternative Rules versus the NPV Rule 265

USING EXCEL: COMPUTING NPV AND IRR 266

8.3 **Alternative Decision Rules 267**
The Payback Rule 268
The Internal Rate of Return Rule 269

COMMON MISTAKE IRR VERSUS THE IRR RULE 272

WHY DO RULES OTHER THAN THE NPV RULE PERSIST? 273

8.4 **Choosing Between Projects 274**
Differences in Scale 274
Timing of the Cash Flows 281

8.5 **Evaluating Projects with Different Lives 282**
Important Considerations When Using the Equivalent Annual Annuity 284

8.6 **Choosing Among Projects When Resources Are Limited 285**
Evaluating Projects with Different Resource Requirements 285

8.7 **Putting It All Together 288**

MyLab Finance • SUMMARY 289 • REVIEW QUESTIONS 290 • PROBLEMS 291 • DATA CASE 297

CHAPTER 8 APPENDIX: USING EXCEL TO MAKE AN NPV PROFILE 299

9 Fundamentals of Capital Budgeting 301

9.1 **The Capital Budgeting Process 302**

9.2 **Forecasting Incremental Earnings 303**
Revenue and Cost Estimates 303

COMMON MISTAKE USING THE WRONG CCA ASSET CLASS 305
Incremental Revenue and Cost Estimates 306

9.3 **Determining Incremental Free Cash Flow 309**
Calculating Free Cash Flow from Earnings 309
Calculating Free Cash Flow Directly 313
Calculating the NPV 314

9.4 **Other Effects on Incremental Free Cash Flows 315**
Opportunity Costs 315

COMMON MISTAKE THE OPPORTUNITY COST OF AN IDLE ASSET 315
Project Externalities 316
Sunk Costs 316

COMMON MISTAKE THE SUNK COST FALLACY 317
Adjusting Free Cash Flow 317
Replacement Decisions 323

9.5 **Analyzing the Project 325**
Sensitivity Analysis 325
Break-Even Analysis 327
Scenario Analysis 327

9.6 **Real Options in Capital Budgeting 329**
Option to Delay 330
Option to Expand 330
Option to Abandon 330

MyLab Finance SUMMARY 331 • REVIEW QUESTIONS 332 • PROBLEMS 333 • DATA CASE 338

CHAPTER 9 APPENDIX: USING EXCEL FOR CAPITAL BUDGETING 340

PART 3 INTEGRATIVE CASE 345

PART 4
Return, Risk, and the Cost of Capital 347

10 Risk and Return in Capital Markets 348

10.1 A First Look at Risk and Return 349

10.2 Historical Risks and Returns of Stocks 351
Computing Historical Returns 351
Average Annual Returns 355
The Variance and Volatility of Returns 357

ARITHMETIC AVERAGE RETURNS VERSUS COMPOUND ANNUAL RETURNS 358

COMMON MISTAKE MISTAKES WHEN COMPUTING STANDARD DEVIATION 360

USING EXCEL: COMPUTING THE STANDARD DEVIATION OF HISTORICAL RETURNS 360
The Normal Distribution 361

10.3 The Historical Trade-Off between Risk and Return 363
The Returns of Large Portfolios 363
The Returns of Individual Stocks 363

10.4 Common versus Independent Risk 365
Theft versus Earthquake Insurance: An Example 365
Types of Risk 366

10.5 Diversification in Stock Portfolios 367
Unsystematic versus Systematic Risk 367
Diversifiable Risk and the Risk Premium 370
The Importance of Systematic Risk 370

COMMON MISTAKE A FALLACY OF LONG-RUN DIVERSIFICATION 371

MyLab Finance SUMMARY 373 • REVIEW QUESTIONS 374 • PROBLEMS 375 • DATA CASE 379

11 Systematic Risk and the Equity Risk Premium 381

11.1 The Expected Return of a Portfolio 382
Portfolio Weights 382
Portfolio Returns 382
Expected Portfolio Return 384

11.2 The Volatility of a Portfolio 385
Diversifying Risks 385
Measuring Stocks' Co-movement: Correlation 386

USING EXCEL: CALCULATING THE CORRELATION BETWEEN TWO SETS OF RETURNS 390
Computing a Portfolio's Variance and Standard Deviation 390
Risk versus Return: Choosing an Efficient Portfolio with Two Stocks 392
The Effect of Correlation 395
The Volatility of a Large Portfolio 395

NOBEL PRIZE HARRY MARKOWITZ 396

11.3 Measuring Systematic Risk 397
Role of the Market Portfolio 397
Stock Market Indexes as the Market Portfolio 398

INDEX FUNDS AND EXCHANGE TRADED FUNDS 399
Market Risk and Beta 399

COMMON MISTAKE STANDARD DEVIATION VERSUS BETA 401
Estimating Beta from Historical Returns 403

USING EXCEL: CALCULATING A STOCK'S BETA 405

11.4 Putting It All Together: The Capital Asset Pricing Model 406
The CAPM Equation Relating Risk to Expected Return 407

WHY NOT ESTIMATE EXPECTED RETURNS DIRECTLY? 408
The Security Market Line 409
The CAPM and Portfolios 409
Summary of the Capital Asset Pricing Model 412
The Big Picture 412
Problems with the CAPM in Practice 412

NOBEL PRIZE WILLIAM SHARPE 413

MyLab Finance SUMMARY 414 • REVIEW QUESTIONS 416 • PROBLEMS 416

CHAPTER 11 APPENDIX: ALTERNATIVE MODELS OF SYSTEMATIC RISK 422

12 Determining the Cost of Capital 425

12.1 A First Look at the Weighted Average Cost of Capital 426
The Firm's Capital Structure 426

Opportunity Cost and the Overall Cost of Capital 427
Weighted Averages and the Overall Cost of Capital 427
Weighted Average Cost of Capital Calculations 428

12.2 The Firm's Costs of Debt and Equity Capital 430
Cost of Debt Capital 430

COMMON MISTAKE USING THE COUPON RATE AS THE COST OF DEBT 431
Cost of Preferred Stock Capital 432
Cost of Common Stock Capital 432

12.3 A Second Look at the Weighted Average Cost of Capital 435
WACC Equation 435
Weighted Average Cost of Capital in Practice 436
Methods in Practice 436

12.4 Using the WACC to Value a Project 439
Key Assumptions 440
WACC Method Application: Extending the Life of Facilities at BCE 440
Summary of the WACC Method 441

12.5 Project-Based Costs of Capital 442

COMMON MISTAKE USING A SINGLE COST OF CAPITAL IN MULTIDIVISIONAL FIRMS 442
Cost of Capital for a New Acquisition 442
Divisional Costs of Capital 443

12.6 When Raising External Capital Is Costly 445

MyLab Finance SUMMARY 446 • REVIEW QUESTIONS 448 • PROBLEMS 449 • DATA CASE 452

13 Risk and the Pricing of Options 454

13.1 Option Basics 455
Option Contracts 455
Stock Option Quotations 456
Options on Other Financial Securities 458

OPTIONS ARE FOR MORE THAN JUST STOCKS 459

13.2 Option Payoffs and Profits at Expiration 459
The Long Position in an Option Contract 459
The Short Position in an Option Contract 461
Profit from Holding an Option to Expiration 463
Short Sales 464

13.3 Factors Affecting Option Prices 466
Strike Price and Stock Price 466
Option Prices and the Expiration Date 466
Option Prices and the Risk-Free Rate 466
Option Prices and Volatility 466

13.4 The Binomial Option Pricing Model 468
The Two-State Single-Period Model: An Example 468
The Binomial Pricing Formula 469

13.5 The Black-Scholes Option Pricing Formula 470

13.6 Put-Call Parity 472
Portfolio Insurance 472

13.7 Options and Corporate Finance 475

MyLab Finance SUMMARY 477 • REVIEW QUESTIONS 479 • PROBLEMS 479 • DATA CASE 481

PART 5 Financing Decisions 483

14 Raising Equity Capital 484

14.1 Equity Financing for Private Companies 485
Sources of Funding 485
Crowdfunding: The Wave of the Future? 488
Securities and Valuation 489
Exiting an Investment in a Private Company 491

14.2 Taking Your Firm Public: The Initial Public Offering 492
Advantages and Disadvantages of Going Public 492
Primary and Secondary IPO Offerings 494
Other IPO Types 499

GOOGLE'S IPO 502

14.3 IPO Puzzles 503
Underpriced IPOs 503
"Hot" and "Cold" IPO Markets 503

GLOBAL FINANCIAL CRISIS 2008–2009: A VERY COLD IPO MARKET 505
High Cost of Issuing an IPO 506
Poor Post-IPO Long-Run Stock Performance 507

14.4 Raising Additional Capital: The Seasoned Equity Offering 507

SEO Process 508
SEO Price Reaction 510
SEO Costs 511

MyLab Finance SUMMARY 512 • REVIEW QUESTIONS 514 • PROBLEMS 514 • DATA CASE 517

15 Debt Financing 519

15.1 Corporate Debt 520
Private Debt 520

DEBT FINANCING AT HERTZ: BANK LOANS 520
Public Debt 521

DEBT FINANCING AT HERTZ: PRIVATE PLACEMENTS 521

DEBT FINANCING AT HERTZ: PUBLIC DEBT 523

15.2 Other Types of Debt 525
Sovereign Debt 525
Agency Securities 527
Provincial and Municipal Bonds 527

FINANCIAL CRISIS 528

15.3 Bond Covenants 529
Types of Covenants 529
Advantages of Covenants 530
Application: Hertz's Covenants 530

15.4 Repayment Provisions 530
Call Provisions 530
The Canada Call or Make-Whole Call Provision 533
Sinking Funds 534
Convertible Provisions 534

MyLab Finance SUMMARY 538 • REVIEW QUESTIONS 540 • PROBLEMS 541 • DATA CASE 542

CHAPTER 15 APPENDIX: USING A FINANCIAL CALCULATOR TO CALCULATE YIELD TO CALL 544

PART 5 INTEGRATIVE CASE 545

16 Capital Structure 549

16.1 Capital Structure Choices 550
Capital Structure Choices across Industries 550
Capital Structure Choices within Industries 551

16.2 Capital Structure in Perfect Capital Markets 553
Application: Financing a New Business 553
Leverage and Firm Value 554
The Effect of Leverage on Risk and Return 556
Homemade Leverage 558
Leverage and the Cost of Capital 558
M&M and the Real World 560

COMMON MISTAKE CAPITAL STRUCTURE FALLACIES 561

NOBEL PRIZE FRANCO MODIGLIANI AND MERTON MILLER 562

GLOBAL FINANCIAL CRISIS 563

16.3 Debt and Taxes 564
The Interest Tax Deduction and Firm Value 564
Value of the Interest Tax Shield 566
The Interest Tax Shield with Permanent Debt 567
Leverage and the WACC with Taxes 569
Debt and Taxes: The Bottom Line 569

16.4 The Costs of Bankruptcy and Financial Distress 570
Direct Costs of Bankruptcy 570
Indirect Costs of Financial Distress 571

BANKRUPTCY CAN BE EXPENSIVE 571

16.5 Optimal Capital Structure: The Trade-Off Theory 572
Differences across Firms 573
Optimal Leverage 573

16.6 Additional Consequences of Leverage: Agency Costs and Information 574
Agency Costs 575

AIRLINES USE FINANCIAL DISTRESS TO THEIR ADVANTAGE 575

MORAL HAZARD AND GOVERNMENT BAILOUTS 577
Debt and Information 577

16.7 Capital Structure: Putting It All Together 580

MyLab Finance SUMMARY 581 • REVIEW QUESTIONS 583 • PROBLEMS 584

CHAPTER 16 APPENDIX: THE BANKRUPTCY CODE 591

17 Payout Policy 592

17.1 Distributions to Shareholders 593
Dividends 594
Share Repurchases 595

17.2 Dividends versus Share Repurchases in a Perfect Capital Market 596
Alternative Policy 1: Pay a Dividend with Excess Cash 597
Alternative Policy 2: Share Repurchase (No Dividend) 598

COMMON MISTAKE REPURCHASES AND THE SUPPLY OF SHARES 599
Modigliani and Miller and Dividend Policy Irrelevance 600

COMMON MISTAKE THE BIRD IN THE HAND FALLACY 601
Dividend Policy with Perfect Capital Markets 602

17.3 The Tax Disadvantage of Dividends 602
Taxes on Dividends and Capital Gains 602
Optimal Dividend Policy with Taxes 603
Tax Differences across Investors 607

17.4 Payout versus Retention of Cash 608
Retaining Cash with Perfect Capital Markets 608
Retaining Cash with Imperfect Capital Markets 609

17.5 Signalling with Payout Policy 613
Dividend Smoothing 613
Dividend Signalling 614
Signalling and Share Repurchases 615

ROYAL & SUNALLIANCE'S DIVIDEND CUT 615

17.6 Stock Dividends, Splits, and Spinoffs 617
Stock Dividends and Splits 617

BERKSHIRE HATHAWAY'S A AND B SHARES 618
Spinoffs 619

17.7 Advice for the Financial Manager 619

MyLab Finance SUMMARY 620 • REVIEW QUESTIONS 623 • PROBLEMS 623 • DATA CASE 626

PART 5 INTEGRATIVE CASE 628

PART 6
Financial Planning and Forecasting 629

18 Financial Modelling and Pro Forma Analysis 630

18.1 Goals of Long-Term Financial Planning 631
Identify Important Linkages 631
Analyze the Impact of Potential Business Plans 631
Plan for Future Funding Needs 631

18.2 Forecasting Financial Statements: The Percent of Sales Method 632
Percent of Sales Method 632
Pro Forma Income Statement 632
Pro Forma Balance Sheet 634

COMMON MISTAKE CONFUSING STOCKHOLDERS' EQUITY WITH RETAINED EARNINGS 636
Making the Balance Sheet Balance: Net New Financing 636
Choosing a Forecast Target 638

18.3 Forecasting a Planned Expansion 638
KXS Design's Expansion: Financing Needs 639
KXS Design's Expansion: Pro Forma Income Statement 640

COMMON MISTAKE TREATING FORECASTS AS FACT 642
Forecasting the Balance Sheet 642

18.4 Growth and Firm Value 644
Sustainable Growth Rate and External Financing 644

18.5 Valuing the Expansion 647
Forecasting Free Cash Flows 648

COMMON MISTAKE CONFUSING TOTAL AND INCREMENTAL NET WORKING CAPITAL 649
KXS Design's Expansion: Effect on Firm Value 649
Optimal Timing and the Option to Delay 652

MyLab Finance SUMMARY 653 • REVIEW QUESTIONS 655 • PROBLEMS 655

CHAPTER 18 APPENDIX: THE BALANCE SHEET AND STATEMENT OF CASH FLOWS 659

19 Working Capital Management 661

19.1 Overview of Working Capital 662
The Cash Cycle 662
Working Capital Needs by Industry 664
Firm Value and Working Capital 665

19.2 Trade Credit 667
Trade Credit Terms 667

COMMON MISTAKE USING APR INSTEAD OF EAR TO COMPUTE THE COST OF TRADE CREDIT 668
Trade Credit and Market Frictions 668
Managing Float 669

19.3 Receivables Management 671
Determining the Credit Policy 671

THE 5 C'S OF CREDIT 671
Monitoring Accounts Receivable 673

19.4 Payables Management 675
Determining Accounts Payable Days Outstanding 675
Stretching Accounts Payable 676

19.5 Inventory Management 677
Benefits of Holding Inventory 677

INVENTORY MANAGEMENT ADDS TO THE BOTTOM LINE AT GAP 678
Costs of Holding Inventory 678

19.6 Cash Management 679
Motivation for Holding Cash 679

CASH BALANCES 680
Alternative Investments 680

MyLab Finance SUMMARY 682 • REVIEW QUESTIONS 683 • PROBLEMS 684

20 Short-Term Financial Planning 688

20.1 Forecasting Short-Term Financing Needs 689
Application: Whistler Snowboards Inc. 689
Negative Cash Flow Shocks 690
Positive Cash Flow Shocks 690
Seasonalities 691
The Cash Budget 691

20.2 The Matching Principle 694
Permanent Working Capital 694
Temporary Working Capital 694
Permanent versus Temporary Working Capital 695
Financing Policy Choices 695

20.3 Short-Term Financing with Bank Loans 697
Single End-of-Period-Payment Loan 697
Line of Credit 698
Bridge Loan 698
Common Loan Stipulations and Fees 699

20.4 Short-Term Financing with Commercial Paper 701

20.5 Short-Term Financing with Secured Financing 702
Accounts Receivable as Collateral 702

A SEVENTEENTH-CENTURY FINANCING SOLUTION 703
Inventory as Collateral 703

20.6 Putting It All Together: Creating a Short-Term Financial Plan 705

MyLab Finance SUMMARY 706 • REVIEW QUESTIONS 708 • PROBLEMS 709

PART 6 INTEGRATIVE CASE 713

PART 7 Special Topics 719

21 Risk Management 720

21.1 Insurance 721
The Role of Insurance: A Simplified Example 721
Insurance Pricing in a Perfect Market 722
The Value of Insurance 724
The Costs of Insurance 726
The Insurance Decision 728

21.2 Commodity Price Risk 728
Hedging with Vertical Integration and Storage 729

HEDGING STRATEGY LEADS TO PROMOTION . . . SOMETIMES 730
Hedging with Long-Term Contracts 730
Hedging with Futures Contracts 732
Hedging with Options Contracts 735

Comparing Futures Hedging with Options Hedging 736
Deciding to Hedge Commodity Price Risk 739

COMMON MISTAKE MISTAKES WHEN HEDGING RISK 739

DIFFERING HEDGING STRATEGIES AT U.S. AIRLINES 740

21.3 Interest Rate Risk 740
Interest Rate Risk Measurement: Duration 741
Duration-Based Hedging 741
Swap-Based Hedging 741

MyLab Finance SUMMARY 744 • REVIEW QUESTIONS 745 • PROBLEMS 745

22 International Corporate Finance 750

22.1 Currency Exchange Rates 751
The Foreign Exchange Market 752
Exchange Rates 752

22.2 Exchange Rate Risk 756
Exchange Rate Fluctuations 756
Hedging with Forward Contracts 758
Cash-and-Carry and the Pricing of Currency Forwards 759
Hedging Exchange Rate Risk with Options 762

22.3 Internationally Integrated Capital Markets 764

22.4 Valuation of Foreign Currency Cash Flows 766
Application: Ityesi Inc. 767
The Law of One Price as a Robustness Check 769

22.5 Valuation and International Taxation 771
A Single Foreign Project with Immediate Repatriation of Earnings 771
Multiple Foreign Projects and Deferral of Earnings Repatriation 772

22.6 Internationally Segmented Capital Markets 772
Differential Access to Markets 773
Macro-Level Distortions 774
Implications of Internationally Segmented Capital Markets 776

22.7 Capital Budgeting with Exchange Rate Risk 776
Application: Ityesi Inc. 776
Conclusion 778

MyLab Finance SUMMARY 778 • REVIEW QUESTIONS 781 • PROBLEMS 781 • DATA CASE 785

23 Leasing 787

23.1 The Basics of Leasing 788
Examples of Lease Transactions 788
Lease Payments and Residual Values 789
Leases versus Loans 790

CALCULATING AUTO LEASE PAYMENTS 791
End-of-Term Lease Options 792
Other Lease Provisions 793

23.2 Accounting, Tax, and Legal Consequences of Leasing 794
Lease Accounting 794
The Tax Treatment of Leases 797
Leases and Bankruptcy 798

SYNTHETIC LEASES 798

23.3 The Leasing Decision 799
Cash Flows for a True Tax Lease 800
Lease versus Buy (an Unfair Comparison) 801
Lease versus Borrow (the Right Comparison) 802
Evaluating a True Tax Lease 805
Evaluating a Non-tax Lease 805

23.4 Reasons for Leasing 806
Valid Arguments for Leasing 806
Suspect Arguments for Leasing 809

MyLab Finance SUMMARY 810 • REVIEW QUESTIONS 811 • PROBLEMS 812

24 Mergers and Acquisitions 814

24.1 Background and Historical Trends 815
Merger Waves 815
Types of Mergers 817

24.2 Market Reaction to a Takeover 817

24.3 Reasons to Acquire 818
Economies of Scale and Scope 819
Vertical Integration 819
Expertise 819
Monopoly Gains 820
Efficiency Gains 820
Tax Savings from Operating Losses 821
Diversification 822
Earnings Growth 823
Managerial Motives to Merge 825

24.4 Valuation and The Takeover Process 826
Valuation 826
The Offer 827
Merger "Arbitrage" 828
Tax and Accounting Issues 830
Board and Shareholder Approval 831

24.5 Takeover Defences 832
Poison Pills 832
Staggered Boards 833
White Knights 834
Golden Parachutes 834
Recapitalization 834
Other Defensive Strategies 835
Regulatory Approval 835

WEYERHAEUSER'S HOSTILE BID FOR WILLAMETTE INDUSTRIES 836

24.6 Who Gets the Value Added from a Takeover? 837
The Free Rider Problem 837
Toeholds 838
The Leveraged Buyout 838

THE LEVERAGED BUYOUT OF RJR NABISCO BY KKR 841
The Freezeout Merger 841
Competition 842

MyLab Finance SUMMARY 842 • REVIEW QUESTIONS 845 • PROBLEMS 845

25 Corporate Governance 848

25.1 Corporate Governance and Agency Costs 849

25.2 Monitoring by the Board of Directors and Others 850
Types of Directors 850
Board Independence 851
Board Size and Performance 852
Other Monitors 852

25.3 Compensation Policies 853
Stock and Options 853
Pay and Performance Sensitivity 854

25.4 Managing Agency Conflicts 855
Direct Action by Shareholders 856
Management Entrenchment 858
The Threat of Takeover 859

25.5 Regulation 859
The Sarbanes-Oxley Act 859
The Cadbury Commission 860
Dodd-Frank Act 861
Insider Trading 862

MARTHA STEWART AND IMCLONE 864

25.6 Corporate Governance Around the World 864
Protection of Shareholder Rights 864
Controlling Owners and Pyramids 865
The Stakeholder Model 867
Cross Holdings 868

25.7 The Trade-off of Corporate Governance 868

MyLab Finance SUMMARY 869 • REVIEW QUESTIONS 872 • PROBLEMS 872

Index I1

About the Authors

Jonathan Berk, Peter DeMarzo, and Jarrad Harford

Jonathan Berk is the A.P. Giannini Professor of Finance at the Graduate School of Business, Stanford University, and is a Research Associate at the National Bureau of Economic Research. Before coming to Stanford, he was the Sylvan Coleman Professor of Finance at Haas School of Business at the University of California, Berkeley. Prior to earning his PhD, he worked as an Associate at Goldman Sachs (where his education in finance really began).

Professor Berk's research interests in finance include corporate valuation, capital structure, mutual funds, asset pricing, experimental economics, and labour economics. His work has won a number of research awards, including the TIAA-CREF Paul A. Samuelson Award, the Smith Breeden Prize, Best Paper of the Year in *The Review of Financial Studies*, and the FAME Research Prize. His paper, "A Critique of Size-Related Anomalies," was selected as one of the two best papers ever published in *The Review of Financial Studies*. In recognition of his influence on the practice of finance he has received the Bernstein-Fabozzi/Jacobs Levy Award, the Graham and Dodd Award of Excellence, and the Roger F. Murray Prize. He served two terms as an associate editor of the *Journal of Finance* and a term as a Director of the American Finance Association, the Western Finance Association, and the academic director of the Financial Management Association. He is a Fellow of the Financial Management Association and a member of the advisory board of the *Journal of Portfolio Management*.

Born in Johannesburg, South Africa, Professor Berk is married, has two daughters, and is an avid skier and biker.

Peter DeMarzo is the Mizuho Financial Group Professor of Finance at the Graduate School of Business, Stanford University. He is the current Vice President of the American Finance Association and a Research Associate at the National Bureau of Economic Research. He teaches MBA and PhD courses in Corporate Finance and Financial Modelling. In addition to his experience at the Stanford Graduate School of Business, Professor DeMarzo has taught at the Haas School of Business and the Kellogg Graduate School of Management, and he was a National Fellow at the Hoover Institution.

Professor DeMarzo received the Sloan Teaching Excellence Award at Stanford, and the Earl F. Cheit Outstanding Teaching Award at U.C. Berkeley. Professor DeMarzo has served as an associate editor for *The Review of Financial Studies*, *Financial Management*, and the *B.E. Journals in Economic Analysis and Policy* as well as a Director of the American Finance Association. He has served as Vice President and President of the Western Finance Association. Professor DeMarzo's research is in the area of corporate investment and financing, asset securitization, and contracting, as well as market structure and regulation. His recent work has examined issues of the optimal design of contracts and securities, leverage dynamics and the role of bank capital regulation, and the influence of information asymmetries on stock prices and corporate investment. He has received numerous awards, including the Western Finance Association Corporate Finance Award and the Barclays Global Investors/Michael Brennan best-paper award from *The Review of Financial Studies*.

Professor DeMarzo was born in Whitestone, New York, and is married with three boys. He and his family enjoy hiking, biking, and skiing.

Jarrad Harford is the Paul Pigott - PACCAR Professor of Finance at the University of Washington. Prior to Washington, Professor Harford taught at the Lundquist College of Business at the University of Oregon. He received his PhD in Finance with a minor in Organizations and Markets from the University of Rochester. Professor Harford has taught the core undergraduate finance course, Business Finance, for over nineteen years, as well as an elective in Mergers and Acquisitions, and "Finance for Non-financial Executives" in the executive education program. He has won numerous awards for his teaching, including the UW Finance Professor of the Year (2010, 2012, 2016), Panhellenic/Interfraternity Council Business Professor of the Year Award (2011, 2013), ISMBA Excellence in Teaching Award (2006), and the Wells Fargo Faculty Award for Undergraduate Teaching (2005). Professor Harford is currently a managing editor of the *Journal of Financial and Quantitative Analysis*, and serves as an associate editor for the *Journal of Financial Economics* and the *Journal of Corporate Finance*. His main research interests are understanding the dynamics of merger and acquisition activity as well as the interaction of corporate cash management policy with governance, payout, and global tax considerations. Professor Harford was born in Pennsylvania, is married, and has two sons. He and his family enjoy travelling, hiking, and skiing.

David Stangeland, PhD, BComm (Distinction), CPA, CMA, did his undergraduate and graduate university education at the University of Alberta in Edmonton. In 1991 he moved to Winnipeg, where he joined the Accounting and Finance Department at the I. H. Asper School of Business at the University of Manitoba. Dr. Stangeland is a Professor of Finance and Associate Dean for Professional Programs. Over his career, he was the Associate Dean responsible for the following programs: undergraduate, MBA, Co-op, and International Exchange; he was Head of the Department of Accounting and Finance for nine years (until 2009), and he was reappointed Head of the Department of Accounting and Finance effective July 1, 2015.

Professor Stangeland teaches finance courses at the University of Manitoba and in the Canadian Executive MBA program at the Warsaw School of Economics in Poland. His teaching spans undergraduate, MBA, and PhD courses in corporate finance, investment banking, and international finance.

Professor Stangeland's research interests are in the areas of corporate governance, corporate control, and corporate finance. His work is well cited and has been published in several journals, including the *Journal of Financial and Quantitative Analysis*, the *Journal of Banking and Finance*, the *Journal of Corporate Finance*, *Financial Management*, the *Stanford Journal of Law, Business and Finance*, and numerous others.

Dr. Stangeland served on the Board of Directors of CMA Canada and he chaired CMA Canada's Pension Committee. He is a member of the Pension Committee and the Investment Committee for the University of Manitoba Pension Plans and is a member of the Investment Committee for the Teachers Retirement Allowances Fund (the pension fund for Manitoba teachers). He has also served on the Independent Review Committees for two mutual fund companies. Professor Stangeland is a two-time recipient of the CMA Canada Academic Merit Award for Teaching and Research, a four-time winner of the University of Manitoba Teaching Services Award, and a recipient of the Associates Award for Research.

Professor Stangeland was born and raised in Edmonton, Alberta, where he learned to appreciate the outdoors through activities, including running, cycling, hiking, and skiing, and in the winter travelling to warmer climates—Puerto Vallarta is his favourite warm-weather destination.

András Marosi is Executive Professor of Finance at the University of Alberta and Associate Dean, undergraduate programs. He received his PhD in Finance from the University of Texas at Austin and MPhil in Finance from the University of Cambridge. Professor Marosi has taught introductory and elective corporate finance courses for several years to undergraduate, MBA, Executive MBA, and Master of Financial Management students. He has won several teaching awards, including the MBA Association Award for Excellence in Teaching (2015 and 2016), the MBA MacKenzie Teaching Award (2014), and the undergraduate Business Student Association MacKenzie Teaching Award (2004 and 2018). Professor Marosi's research has been published in the *Journal of Finance* and the *Journal of Financial and Quantitative Analysis*, and he received the Jean Perrien Award at the 2012 Administrative Sciences Association of Canada (ASAC) Conference. Professor Marosi was born in Hungary and is married, with one daughter. He is a passionate runner and triathlete.

Preface

Finance professors are united by their commitment to shaping future generations of financial professionals as well as instilling financial awareness and skills in non-majors. Our goal with *Fundamentals of Corporate Finance* is to provide an accessible presentation for both finance and nonfinance majors.

We know that countless undergraduate students have felt that corporate finance is challenging. It is tempting to make the subject more accessible by de-emphasizing the core principles and instead concentrating on the results. In our over 90 years of combined teaching experience, we have found that this approach actually makes the subject matter less accessible. The core concepts in finance are clear and intuitive. What makes the subject challenging is that it is often difficult for a novice to distinguish between these core ideas and other intuitively appealing approaches that, if used in financial decision making, will lead to incorrect decisions. Therefore, our primary motivation is to equip students with a solid grounding in the core financial concepts and tools needed to make good decisions. Such grounding will serve these students well, whether this is their only course in finance or it is the foundation of their major.

The field of finance has undergone significant change in the past 30 years. Yet much of the empirical evidence in financial economics amassed over this period supports the existing theory and strengthens the importance of understanding and applying corporate financial principles. The 2007–2009 financial crisis was fuelled in part by many practitioners' poor decision making when they did not understand—or chose to ignore—the core concepts that underlie finance and the pedagogy in this book. With this point in mind, we present finance as one unified whole based on two simple, powerful ideas: (1) valuation drives decision making—the firm should take projects for which the value of the benefits exceeds the value of the costs—and (2) in a competitive market, market prices (rather than individual preferences) determine values. We combine these two ideas with what we call the Valuation Principle, and from it we establish all the key ideas in corporate finance.

With the increasing focus on finance in the news, today's undergraduate students arrive in the classroom with a greater interest in finance than many of their predecessors. The challenge is to use that natural interest and motivation to overcome their fear of the subject and communicate these time-tested core principles. Again, we take what has worked in the classroom and apply it to the text: by providing examples involving familiar companies such as Starbucks, Air Canada, and Apple; making consistent use of real-world data; and demonstrating personal finance applications of core concepts, we strive to keep even nonfinance majors engaged.

Our commitment to setting a new standard for undergraduate corporate finance textbooks extends beyond the printed page.

Core Concepts

Fundamentals of Corporate Finance provides thorough coverage of core finance topics to provide students with a comprehensive—but manageable—introduction to the topic.

Valuation as the Unifying Framework

In our experience, students learn best when the material in a course is presented as one unified whole rather than a series of separate ideas. As such, this book presents corporate finance as an application of a subset of simple, powerful ideas. The first is that valuation drives decision making—the firm should take projects for which the value of the benefits exceeds the value of the costs. The second is that in a competitive market, market prices (rather than individual preferences) determine values. The combination of these two ideas is what we call the *Valuation Principle*, and from it we establish all the key ideas in corporate finance, including the *NPV* rule, security pricing, the relation between risk and return, and the tradeoffs associated with capital structure and payout policies.

We use the Valuation Principle as a compass; it keeps financial decision makers on the right track. We introduce it in Chapter 3 along with direct applications. Each part opener relates the topics in that part to the Valuation Principle running theme.

Emphasis on Application

Applying the Valuation Principle provides skills to make the types of comparisons—among loan options, investments, and projects—that will turn students into knowledgeable, confident financial consumers and managers. When students see how to apply finance to their personal lives and future careers, they grasp that finance is more than abstract, mathematically based concepts.

Reinforcement of the Basic Tools

Mastering the tools for discounting cash flows is central to students' success in the introductory course. As always, mastery comes with practice and by approaching complex topics in manageable units. To this end, we focus on time value of money basics in Part 2. Chapter 3 introduces the time value of money for single cash flows as a critical component of the Valuation Principle. Chapter 4 then focuses on the time value of money for cash flows over several periods. Finally, Chapter 5 demonstrates how interest rates are quoted and determined. We present a methodical approach to the cash flows in each problem within this framework:

- Introduce timelines in Chapter 3 and stress the importance of creating timelines for every problem that involves cash flows.
- Include a timeline as the critical first step in each example involving cash flows.
- Incorporate financial calculator keystrokes and Excel techniques into the presentation.

Focus on Capital Budgeting

The capital budgeting decision is one of the most important decisions in corporate finance. We emphasize it early in the textbook, by comparing benefits and costs in Chapter 3. Building on this, we formally introduce the *NPV* rule in Chapter 8 and evaluate it with respect to other investment decision rules. In Chapter 9 on capital budgeting, we examine the valuation of projects within a firm and provide a clear and systematic presentation of the difference between earnings and free cash flow. This early introduction to capital budgeting allows us to present the idea of the cost of capital conceptually, which then motivates the risk and return coverage in Chapters 10 and 11. In Chapter 12, we calculate and use the firm's overall cost of capital with the WACC method.

New Ideas

Fundamentals of Corporate Finance carefully balances the latest advancements in research and practice with thorough coverage of core finance topics. Innovations that distinguish this textbook include the following:

- Chapter 7 on stock valuation values a firm's equity by considering its future dividends, free cash flows, or how its value compares to that of similar, publicly traded companies.
- Chapter 13 on the pricing of options lays the foundations for important topics such as the valuation of convertible securities, the conflict of interest between equity holders and creditors, and the ability to implement risk management strategies. The early placement of the options material in the book allows options knowledge to be used in latter parts—particularly in the discussion of capital structure and the agency costs of debt.
- Chapter 17 on payout policy examines the role of asymmetric information between managers and investors and how payout decisions may signal this information.
- Chapter 18 distinguishes between sustainable and value-increasing growth with a focus on determining whether "growth" will increase or decrease the value of the firm.

The Tools Your Students Need to Succeed

Problem-Solving Methodology Guided Problem Solutions (GPS) of worked examples appear alongside every important concept. Finance is about much more than the numerical solution: to be successful, students must understand the underlying intuition and interpret the mathematical solution. To foster this mindset, after the problem statement a three-step solution process—Plan, Execute, Evaluate—aids students' comprehension and models the process they should follow when tackling problems and cases on their own. We also identify the seminal errors our students have made over the years in Common Mistake boxes within each chapter.

Applied Approach References to well-known companies, such as Apple, Air Canada, and Starbucks, add colour and interest to each chapter. We even include two case-based chapters (14 and 15) that profile Facebook and Hertz. Chapter conclusions offer bottom-line advice on the key take-away points for financial managers. Interviews with notable professionals such as John Connors, former Microsoft CFO, support this practical perspective.

An applied approach also involves presenting the tools on which practitioners rely. Excel boxes and chapter-ending appendices teach students Excel techniques, whereas designated Spreadsheet Tables available online enable students to enter their own inputs and formulas.

New to the Third Canadian Edition

A Canadian text should reflect Canadian realities and show how they fit in the bigger world picture. For instance, the institutional environment in Canada is different. While Canadian banks came out of the financial crisis with great admiration for their performance relative to banks around the world, Canada's success at corporate law enforcement (laws relating to competition, insider trading, options backdating, and other aspects of corporate governance) is sometimes criticized relative to other developed countries. The Canadian tax system also differs from the United States and other countries. It would be a pity if students were exposed only to the U.S. tax system and missed the realities of capital cost allowance, capital gains taxes, tax free savings accounts, and registered retirement savings plan accounts—all of which are very important for Canadian investors. We feel it is important for students to understand the Canadian system but to also be able to understand that other systems exist too. Other countries' institutional systems may be better or worse than what exists in Canada. We believe it is especially important to point out where other systems seem better than what exists in Canada because our students will go on to be business and political leaders and may be the instruments to push for change in Canada that will make us stronger.

David Stangeland and András Marosi are also proud Canadians, and we celebrate the great success stories that have emerged in Canadian business. We also recognize some stories of failure and rebirth that have taken place. As such, we feature Canadian businesses in the text when they make suitable examples. A side benefit for students of this is that they can learn about some Canadian corporate history and become more familiar with the firms that may eventually be their employers. We do not exclude non-Canadian businesses. For example, when we want to look at the dominance of the corporate form in terms of business revenue in the world, there is only one largest company by revenue, Walmart (in 2017), so it has its place in the text. Again, though, when appropriate, we bring in Canadian corporations and their relative position for comparative purposes. Many firms not headquartered in Canada are so familiar and important to Canadians that it would be foolish to exclude them when they make good examples. Apple and Starbucks are two of such firms.

An additional advantage of a Canadian text is that because Canada is a smaller player on the world scene than the United States, Canadians must think more internationally. Thus, the Canadian edition has more of an international focus than the original U.S. edition.

Fundamentals of Corporate Finance offers coverage of the major topical areas for introductory-level undergraduate courses. Our focus is on financial decision making related to the corporation's choice of which investments to make or how to raise the capital required to fund an investment. We designed the book with the need for flexibility and with consideration of time pressures throughout the semester in mind.

In response to reviewer's feedback we retained the sequence of chapters first introduced in the 2nd Canadian edition.

Chapters 3 through 13 focus on valuation and risk, and progress from relatively easier material to more difficult topics, starting with the Valuation Principle and time value of money in Chapters 3 and 4 and concluding with the challenging options topic in Chapter 13. Subsequently, Chapters 14 through 17 examine various aspects of corporate finance, from raising funds to payoff policy, and make extensive use of the lessons learned in the preceding valuation and risk chapters. In addition, by bringing forward the discussion of options we can use such knowledge in other areas of the text that can be viewed in an options context.

In addition to reorganizing the contents, we have thoroughly updated each of the chapters in the book.

Chapter 1 Corporate Finance and the Financial Manager includes updates on Canadian taxes and corporate tax around the world. We also introduced a new table showing the largest Canadian corporations so students have a better understanding of the big players in the Canadian economy. We updated the information on stock exchanges and added information on dark pools. We have included a new hypothetical case in the end-of-chapter problems that facilitate discussion of shareholder wealth maximization and the principal-agent problem, as well as stakeholder satisfaction and corporate social responsibility.

Chapter 2 Introduction to Financial Statement Analysis includes discussion of the impact of the Sarbanes-Oxley Act, specifically how changes in Canada are different from those in the United States. We also discuss International Financial Reporting Standards

(IFRS) and how convergence toward IFRS has been progressing. Several new end-of-chapter problems and a new Data Case are also added.

Chapter 3 The Valuation Principle: The Foundation of Financial Decision Making has been refined in its discussion of the Valuation Principle, and we added four additional end-of-chapter problems.

Chapter 4 The Time Value of Money has been revised to improve clarity for students. A new and improved financial calculator appendix has been included. An additional eight end-of-chapter problems were added, too.

Chapter 5 Interest Rates includes a new summary of how to do interest rate conversions, and we revised the box on the cost of capital. We have also updated data and figures with respect to inflation, interest rates, and yield curves. An additional eight end-of-chapter problems have been included.

Chapter 6 Bonds includes updates on Canada's national debt and new summary on how interest rates and other factors affect bond prices. Chapter 6 is accompanied by a **new appendix—Appendix C—Interest Rate Risk Measurement: Duration**.

Chapter 7 Valuing Stocks includes updates on how the forecasts on stock prices related to what actually occurred. Five new end-of-chapter problems were added, including one that relates back to the Chapter 1 end-of-chapter hypothetical case so that further discussion can be accompanied by detailed calculations; this new problem ties together the principal-agent problem, shareholder wealth maximization, managerial incentives, and informational efficiency.

We introduce *NPV* and *IRR* in **Chapter 8 Investment Decision Rules** and have included additional information on profitability index. In addition, four new end-of-chapter problems are added.

Chapter 9 Fundamentals of Capital Budgeting now includes a new discussion of sunk costs and unavoidable competitive effects. Further explanations regarding capital cost allowance (CCA) asset classes are included.

Chapter 10 Risk and Return in Capital Markets contains new end-of-chapter problems, updated Excel instructions, and a new Data Case.

Chapter 11 Systematic Risk and the Equity Risk Premium benefits from new end-of-chapter problems.

The BCE example has been updated throughout **Chapter 12 Determining the Cost of Capital** and a new Common Mistake Box and a practitioner interview have been added as well.

Chapter 13 Risk and the Pricing of Options now refers students to the online option pricing calculator of the Montreal Exchange (MX). The MX website is a great resource for those wanting to learn about derivatives.

Chapter 14 Raising Equity Capital includes new information on crowdfunding in Canada, and has two new end-of-chapter problems included.

Chapter 15 Debt Financing includes standard debt coverage plus references to option features and to the options chapter to enrich the discussion of callable and convertible bonds. New material on sovereign debt, agency debt, and provincial and municipal bonds is added. In addition to new end-of-chapter problems, a new Data Case and Integrative Case are included.

Chapter 16 Capital Structure contains a new General Interest Box discussing bank capital regulation and the ROE fallacy in the context of the 2008 global financial crisis. Example 16.4 has been replaced; the new example illustrates the calculation the value of the levered firm rather than just the present value of tax savings. Three new end-of-chapter problems have also been added.

Chapters 17 Payout Policy and 18 Financial Modelling and Pro Forma Analysis contain updates to tax rates, data, and figures throughout and more information on Canadian and U.S. companies that hold large cash balances.

Chapter 19 Working Capital Management includes company and data updates.

Chapter 22 International Corporate Finance includes the updates on taxation of foreign income for Canadian multinationals and constrasts this to the most recent and significant changes U.S.–based firms have faced regarding their foreign-sourced income.

And we have thoroughly updated the figures and data in the remaining chapters of the book.

Part-by-Part Overview

Parts 1 and 2 lay the foundation for our study of corporate finance. In **Chapter 1**, we introduce the corporation and related business forms. We then examine the role of financial managers and outside investors in decision making for the firm. **Chapter 2** reviews basic corporate accounting principles and the financial statements on which the financial manager relies.

Part 2 presents the basic tools that are the cornerstones of corporate finance. **Chapter 3** introduces the Valuation Principle, which underlies all of finance and links all of the ideas throughout this book. **Chapter 4** on the time value of money analyzes cash flow streams lasting several periods. We explain how to value a series of future cash flows and derive shortcuts for computing the present value of annuities and perpetuities. We focus on how interest rates are quoted and determined in **Chapter 5**, with an emphasis on how to use market interest rates to determine the appropriate discount rate for a set of cash flows. In **Chapter 6**, we demonstrate an application of the time value of money tools using interest rates: valuing the bonds issued by corporations and governments. The **Appendix C to Chapter 6** discusses interest rate risk and duration. In **Chapter 7**, we extend the valuation framework to determining stock prices. After valuing a firm's equity with various methods, we discuss market efficiency and its implications for financial managers.

Part 3 addresses the most important decision financial managers face: the choice of which investments the corporation should make, driving the value of the firm. **Chapter 8** presents the investment decision rules that guide a financial manager's decision making. In **Chapter 9** on capital budgeting, we outline estimating a project's incremental cash flows, which then become the inputs to the *NPV* decision rule.

Part 4 looks at the critical concept of risk and return. We explain how to measure and compare risks across investment opportunities to determine the cost of capital for each investment opportunity. **Chapter 10** introduces the key insight that investors demand a risk premium only for nondiversifiable risk. In **Chapter 11**, we quantify this idea, leading to the Capital Asset Pricing Model (CAPM). In **Chapter 12**, we apply what we've learned to estimate a company's overall weighted average cost of capital. In **Chapter 13**, we discuss options, their pricing, and what affects their value.

Part 5 shows how the firm raises the funds it needs to undertake its investments. We explain the mechanics of raising equity in **Chapter 14** and debt markets in **Chapter 15** (where we also continue the institutional overview of bond markets that began in Chapter 6). Following the discussions on equity and debt financing, we turn to capital structure and examine the impact of financing choices on the value of the firm. **Chapter 16** on capital structure opens by intuitively establishing the Modigliani and Miller result and then turns to the impact of important market imperfections. Payout policy is the focus of **Chapter 17**.

Part 6 turns to the details of running the financial side of a corporation on both a long-term and a day-to-day basis. **Chapter 18** develops the tools to forecast the cash flows and long-term financing needs of a firm. In **Chapter 19**, we discuss how firms manage their working capital requirements, whereas **Chapter 20** explains how firms finance their short-term cash needs.

Part 7 addresses select special topics in corporate finance. **Chapter 21** focuses on the corporation's use of options, futures, forwards, insurance, and other methods to manage risk. **Chapter 22** examines the issues a firm faces when making a foreign investment, including exchange rate risk, and addresses the valuation of foreign projects. **Chapter 23** introduces an alternative to long-term debt financing—leasing. By presenting leasing as a financing alternative, we apply the Law of One Price to determine that the benefits of leasing must derive from the tax differences, incentive effects, or other market imperfections. The Law of One Price continues to provide a unifying framework as we consider the topics of mergers and acquisitions in **Chapter 24** and corporate governance in **Chapter 25**.

Features: Bridging Theory and Practice

Study Aids with a Practical Focus

To be successful, students need to master the core concepts and learn to identify and solve problems that today's practitioners face.

- The **Valuation Principle** is presented as the foundation of all financial decision making: The central idea is that a firm should take projects or make investments that increase the value of the firm. The tools of finance determine the impact of a project or investment on the firm's value by comparing the costs and benefits in equivalent terms. The Valuation Principle is first introduced in Chapter 3, revisited in the part openers, and integrated throughout the text.
- **Guided Problem Solutions (GPS)** are examples that accompany every important concept using a consistent problem-solving methodology that breaks the solution process into three steps: *Plan, Execute,* and *Evaluate*. This approach aids student comprehension, enhances their ability to model the solution process when tackling problems on their own, and demonstrates the importance of interpreting the mathematical solution.
- **Personal Finance GPS** examples showcase the use of financial analysis in everyday life by setting problems in scenarios such as purchasing a new car or house and saving for retirement.
- **Common Mistake** boxes alert students to frequently made mistakes stemming from misunderstanding core concepts and calculations—in the classroom and in the field.
- **Using Excel** boxes describe Excel techniques and include screenshots to serve as a guide for students using this technology.

Applications That Reflect Real Practice

Fundamentals of Corporate Finance features actual companies and practitioners in the field.

- **Practitioner Interviews** from notable professionals featured in many chapters highlight leaders in the field and address the effects of the financial crisis.
- **General Interest** boxes highlight timely material from financial publications that shed light on business problems and real company practices.

Teaching Every Student to Think Finance

With consistency in presentation and an innovative set of learning aids, *Fundamentals of Corporate Finance* simultaneously meets the needs of both finance majors and nonfinance business majors. This textbook truly shows every student how to "think finance."

Simplified Presentation of Mathematics

Because one of the hardest parts of learning finance is mastering the jargon, math, and nonstandardized notation, *Fundamentals of Corporate Finance* systematically uses

- **Notation Boxes.** Each chapter begins with a Notation box that defines the variables and the acronyms used in the chapter and serves as a "legend" for students' reference.
- **Numbered and Labelled Equations.** The first time a full equation is given in notation form it is numbered. Key equations are titled and revisited in the summary and in end papers.
- **Financial Calculator** instructions, including a box in Chapter 4 on solving for future and present values, and appendices to Chapters 4, 6, and 15 with keystrokes for HP-10BII and TI BAII Plus Professional, highlight this problem-solving tool.
- **Spreadsheet Tables.** Select tables are available on the MyLab Finance as Excel files, enabling students to change inputs and manipulate the underlying calculations.
- **Using Excel** boxes describe Excel techniques and include screenshots to serve as a guide for students using this technology.

Practice Finance to Learn Finance

Working problems is the proven way to cement and demonstrate an understanding of finance.

- **Concept Check questions** at the end of each section enable students to test their understanding and target areas in which they need further review.
- **End-of-chapter problems written personally by Jonathan Berk, Peter DeMarzo, Jarrad Harford, David Stangeland, and Andras Marosi** offer instructors the opportunity to assign first-rate materials to students for homework and practice with the confidence that the problems are consistent with the chapter content. All end-of-chapter problems are available in MyLab Finance, the fully integrated homework and tutorial system. Both the problems and solutions, which were also written by the authors, have been class tested and accuracy checked to ensure quality. Selected end-of-chapter problems are also accompanied by Excel spreadsheets with different icons indicating what the spreadsheets are for, and where they can be found:

Indicates that the problem is accompanied by an Excel Solution, which is found in the Instructor's Solutions Manual. Blank templates for these Excel Solutions are available for students on the MyLab Finance.

Indicates that the problem is accompanied by an **Auto-Graded Excel Project** on Pearson's MyLab Finance. Using proven, field-tested technology, these new auto-graded Excel Projects allow instructors to seamlessly integrate Excel content into their course.

End-of-Chapter Materials Reinforce Learning

Testing understanding of central concepts is crucial to learning finance.

- **MyLab Finance Chapter Summary** presents the key points and conclusions from each chapter, provides a list of key terms with page numbers, and indicates online practice opportunities.
- **Data Cases** present in-depth scenarios in a business setting, with questions designed to guide students' analysis. Many questions involve the use of internet resources.
- **Integrative Cases** occur at the end of some parts and present a capstone extended problem with a scenario and data for students to analyze based on that subset of chapters.

Acknowledgments

Given the scope of this project, identifying the many people who made it happen is a tall order. This textbook was the product of the expertise and hard work of many talented colleagues. Professor Stangeland would like to thank Hayden Ng for his excellent research and editing support. Professor Marosi would like to thank Marc McCoy for excellent research assistance.

We are especially gratified with the work of those who developed the array of print supplements that accompany the book: **David Birkett of the University of Guelph-Humber** for the Test Bank; **Therese Trainor** for the Instructor's Manual; and **Cleusa Yamamoto of Douglas College** for the PowerPoint lecture notes.

At Pearson Education Canada, we would like to thank

- Vice President, Editorial, Anne Williams
- Director of Marketing, Leigh-Anne Graham
- Sr. Portfolio Manager, Keara Emmett
- Marketing Manager, Darcey Pepper
- Content Developer, Toni Chahley
- Content Managers, Emily Dill, Nicole Mellow
- Project Manager, Pippa Kennard
- Production Editor, Suzanne Simpson Millar
- Designer, Anthony Leung
- Copyeditor, Julie VanTol
- Proofreader, Simpson Editorial Group

We are indebted to our colleagues for the time and expertise invested as manuscript reviewers. The sound guidance from these trusted advisors throughout the writing process was truly invaluable. We strived to incorporate every contributor's input and are truly grateful for each comment and suggestion. The book has benefited enormously from this input.

Reviewers for the Third Canadian Edition

Gavin Blair, *University of Waterloo*
Reza H. Chowdhury, *University of Northern British Columbia*
Sheri Christie, *Northern Alberta Institute of Technology*
Merlyn Foo, *Athabasca University*
Karolina Krystyniak, *University of Ontario Institute of Technology*
Egor Matveyev, *University of Alberta*
Danny L. Morrison, *Western University*
Patrick J. O'Meara, *Southern Alberta Institute of Technology*
Isaac Otchere, *Carleton University*
Bill Ross, *Southern Alberta Institute of Technology*
Santoso Sugianto, *University of Ontario Institute of Technology*
Pan Zhang, *Northern Alberta Institute of Technology*

Reviewers for the Second Canadian Edition

David Birkett, *University of Guelph-Humber*
Reza H. Chowdhury, *University of Northern British Columbia*
Merlyn Foo, *Athabasca University*
Caren Lombard, *Kwantlen Polytechnic University*
Colin F. Mang, *Nipissing University*
Isaac Otchere, *Carleton University*
Rahul Ravi, *Concordia University*
Traven Reed, *Canadore College*
David Roberts, *Southern Alberta Institute of Technology*
Cleusa Sachiko Yamamoto, *Douglas College*
Charles Schell, *Vancouver Island University*
Mark Weaver, *Sheridan College*
Allen Zhu, *Capilano University*
Patricia Zima, *Mohawk College*

Reviewers for the First Canadian Edition

Trevor Chamberlain, *McMaster University*
Bin Cheng, *University of Ontario Institute of Technology*
Kirk Collins, *St. Francis Xavier University*
Bill Fletcher, *St. Mary's University*
Yi Feng, *Ryerson University*
Merlyn Foo, *Athabasca University*
Larbi Hammabi, *McGill University*
Robert Ironside, *Kwantlen University*
Raad Jassim, *McGill University*
Garth Jensen, *Laurentian University*
Lew Johnson, *Queen's University*
Keith Christian Jensen, *Vancouver Island University*
Vic Kariappa, *Carleton University*
Dave Kennedy, *Lethbridge College*
Kai Li, *University of British Columbia*
Audrey Lowry, *Grant MacEwan*
András Marosi, *University of Alberta*
Isaac Otchere, *Carleton University*
Eloisa Perez, *Grant MacEwan*
Ian Rakita, *Concordia University*
Shishir Singh, *University of Manitoba*
Jun Yang, *Acadia University*

Get $500,000 in Virtual Cash, Apply the Concepts Learned in Class, and Test Your Trading Skills Against Your Classmates!

Manage a portfolio of stocks, bonds, and mutual funds.

With the purchase of this book, you are entitled to a **50% discount** to StockTrak.com, the leading portfolio simulation for the university market!

To take advantage of this offer, ask your professor to register on StockTrak.com and create a custom trading challenge for your class. When you receive an HTML link from your professor, you will be asked to enter this code to receive your discount:

BCF-919

If your professor is not using StockTrak.com as part of the class, you can still register as an individual and **save 50%**!

STOCK|TRAK
GLOBAL PORTFOLIO SIMULATIONS

PART

Introduction

1

CHAPTER 1 Corporate Finance and the Financial Manager
CHAPTER 2 Introduction to Financial Statement Analysis

Valuation Principle Connection. What is corporate finance? No matter what your role in a corporation, an understanding of why and how financial decisions are made is essential. The focus of this book is how to make optimal corporate financial decisions. In this part of the book, we lay the foundation for our study of corporate finance. In Chapter 1, we begin by introducing the corporation and related business forms. We then examine the role of financial managers and outside investors in decision making for the firm. To make optimal decisions, a decision maker needs information. Therefore, in Chapter 2 we review and analyze an important source of information for corporate decision making—the firm's accounting statements. These chapters will introduce us to the role and objective of the financial manager and some of the information the financial manager uses in applying the Valuation Principle to make optimal decisions. In the next section of the book, we will introduce and begin applying the Valuation Principle.

CHAPTER

1 Corporate Finance and the Financial Manager

LEARNING OBJECTIVES

- Grasp the importance of financial information in both your personal and business lives
- Understand the important features of the three main types of firms and see why the advantages of the corporate form have led it to dominate economic activity
- Explain the goal of the financial manager and the reasoning behind that goal, as well as understand the three main types of decisions a financial manager makes
- Know how a corporation is managed and controlled, the financial manager's place in it, and some of the ethical issues financial managers face
- Understand the importance of financial markets, such as stock markets, to a corporation and the financial manager's role as liaison to those markets
- Recognize the role that financial institutions play in the financial cycle of the economy

Corporations have existed in Canada since before Canada was a nation. One of the oldest and most recognized corporations in Canada is the Hudson's Bay Company (HBC). HBC was given its charter in 1670 and still continues its operation today. In 1970, the head office of HBC moved from London, England, to Winnipeg; it is now in Toronto. Ownership and control of the HBC has changed location over the years too, from England, where it was originally, to Canada and then to the United States. Corporations are arguably the most important business organizations in Canada and around the world because of their dominance in terms of products produced, revenues and profits generated, and people employed.

This book focuses on how people in corporations make financial decisions. Although the subject of this book is *corporate* finance, much of what we discuss applies to the financial decisions made within any organization, including not-for-profit entities, such as charities and universities. In this chapter, we introduce the corporation and alternative business organizational forms common in Canada. We also highlight the financial manager's critical role inside any business enterprise. What products to launch, how to pay to develop those products, what profits to keep, and how to return profits to investors—all of these decisions and many more fall within corporate finance. The financial manager makes these decisions with the goal of maximizing the value of the business, which is determined in the financial markets. In this chapter and throughout the book, we will expand on this goal, provide you with the tools to make financial management decisions, and show you how the financial markets provide funds to a corporation and produce market prices that are key inputs to any financial manager's investment analysis.

1.1 Why Study Finance?

Finance and financial thinking are everywhere in our daily lives. Consider your decision to go to university. You surely weighed alternatives, such as starting a full-time job immediately, and then decided that university provided you with the greatest net benefit. More and more, individuals are taking charge of their personal finances with decisions such as these:

- When to start saving and how much to save for retirement.
- Whether a car loan or lease is more advantageous.
- Whether a particular stock is a good investment.
- How to evaluate the terms for a home mortgage.

Our career paths have become less predictable and more dynamic. In previous generations, it was common to work for one employer your entire career. Today, that would be highly unusual. Most of us will instead change jobs, and possibly even careers, many times. With each new opportunity, we must weigh all the costs and benefits, financial and otherwise.

Some financial decisions, such as whether to pay $2.00 for your morning espresso, are simple, but most are more complex. In your business career, whether you are in finance or another field, you may face such questions as these:

- Should your firm launch a new product?
- Should a marketing plan be undertaken?
- Which supplier should your firm choose?
- Should your firm upgrade its information systems?
- Is a new staff training initiative worth its cost?
- Should your firm produce a part of the product or outsource production?
- Should your firm issue new stock or borrow money instead?
- How can you raise money for your start-up firm?

In this book, you will learn how all of these decisions in your personal life and inside a business are tied together by one powerful concept, the *Valuation Principle*. It shows how to make the costs and benefits of a decision comparable so that we can weigh them properly. Learning to apply the Valuation Principle will give you the skills to make the types of comparisons—among loan options, investments, and projects—that will turn you into a knowledgeable, confident consumer and manager.

Whether you plan to major in finance or simply take this one course, you will find the fundamental financial knowledge gained here to be essential in your personal and business lives.

1.2 The Three Types of Firms

We begin by introducing the three major types of firms: sole proprietorships, partnerships, and corporations. We explain each organizational form in turn, but our primary focus is on the most important form—the corporation. Although the number of proprietorships and partnerships in the Canadian economy is greater than the number of corporations, corporations tend to be much larger and are the most significant business organizations in Canada, as demonstrated by their dominance in terms of business income generated (see Figure 1.1). In addition to describing what a corporation is, we also provide an overview of why corporations are so successful.

FIGURE 1.1 Sources of Profit Generation in Canada for 2011

Although there are many more unincorporated businesses in Canada than there are corporations, non-corporate private enterprises (including all proprietorships and partnerships) account for only 33% of profit generation whereas corporations account for 62% of profit generation in the Canadian economy. The remaining 5% of profit generation is from government business enterprises, including Crown corporations.

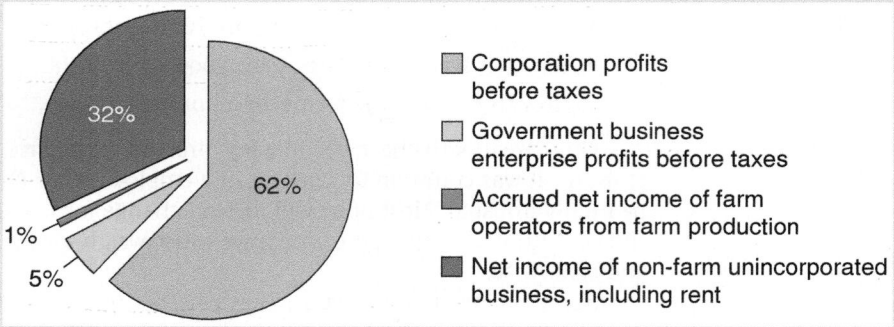

Source: Statistics Canada, CANSIM Table 3800016. This does not constitute an endorsement by Statistics Canada of this product. Note, Statistics Canada stopped updating this data series after 2011, so more current data is not available.

Sole Proprietorships

sole proprietorship A business owned and run by one person.

A **sole proprietorship** is a business owned and run by one person. Sole proprietorships are usually very small with few, if any, employees. Although they are the most common type of business unit in the economy, sole proprietorships are relatively small in terms of revenues and profits produced and people employed.

We now consider the key features of a sole proprietorship.

1. Sole proprietorships have the advantage of being straightforward to set up. Consequently, many new businesses use this organizational form.
2. The principal limitation of a sole proprietorship is that there is no separation between the firm and the owner—the firm can have only one owner who runs the business, and the business income is taxed as personal income of the owner. If there are other investors, they cannot hold an ownership stake in the firm; this limits the ability of the owner to raise additional money for the business.
3. The owner has unlimited personal liability for any of the firm's debts. That is, if the firm defaults on any debt payment, the lender can (and will) require the owner to repay the loan from personal assets. An owner who cannot afford to repay a loan for which he or she is personally liable must declare personal bankruptcy.
4. The life of a sole proprietorship is limited to the life of the owner. It is also difficult to transfer ownership of a sole proprietorship.

For most growing businesses, the disadvantages of a sole proprietorship outweigh the advantages. As soon as the firm reaches the point at which it can borrow without the owner agreeing to be personally liable, the owner typically converts the business into another form. Conversion also has other benefits that we will consider as we discuss the other forms below.

gen

Partnerships

Partnerships can be organized as general partnerships or limited partnerships. The common feature of all partnerships is that income from the partnership is taxed at the personal level. The income is split among partners according to their ownership in the partnership.

general partnership An unincorporated business owned and run by more than one owner.

A **general partnership** is a partnership owned and run by more than one owner—each called a general partner. Key features include the following:

1. *All general partners have unlimited liability.* That is, a lender can require *any* partner to repay *all* the firm's outstanding debts. Similarly, in a legal judgment against the partnership, each partner is fully liable; thus, partners must be chosen carefully, as any single partner's actions can affect the exposure of all the partners.
2. The partnership ends in the event of the death or withdrawal of any single partner. Partners can avoid liquidation if the partnership agreement provides for alternatives, such as a buyout of a deceased or withdrawn partner.

Some old and established businesses around the world remain as general partnerships or sole proprietorships. Often, these firms are the types of businesses in which the owners' personal reputations are the basis for the businesses. For example, law firms and accounting firms in some countries are organized as general partnerships. For such enterprises, the partners' personal liability increases the confidence of the firm's clients that the partners will strive to maintain the firm's reputation.

limited partnership A partnership with two kinds of owners: general partners and limited partners.

limited liability Liability that is limited to an owner's initial investment.

A **limited partnership** is a partnership with two kinds of owners: general partners and limited partners. In this case, the general partners have the same rights and privileges as partners in any general partnership—they are personally liable for the firm's obligations. Limited partners, however, have **limited liability**—that is, their liability is limited to their investment. Their private property cannot be seized to pay off the firm's outstanding debts. Furthermore, the death or withdrawal of a limited partner does not dissolve the partnership, and a limited partner's interest is transferable. However, a limited partner has no management authority and cannot legally be involved in the managerial decision making for the business.

limited liability partnership (LLP) A form of partnership used in Canada for law and accounting firms that provides partial limitation of a partner's liability.

In Canada, a special type of partnership called a **limited liability partnership (LLP)** can be used in the legal and accounting professions. An LLP is similar to a general partnership in that the partners can be active in the management of the firm, and they do have a degree of unlimited liability. The limitation on a partner's liability is only in cases related to actions of negligence of other partners or those supervised by other partners. In all other respects, including a particular partner's own negligence or the negligence of those supervised by the particular partner, that partner has unlimited personal liability. In addition, the assets of the business are potentially at risk of seizure due to the actions of anyone within the partnership. Thus, while a partner's personal assets are protected from the negligent actions of other partners, the investment in the overall partnership may be lost.

Corporations

- separate from owners, partners and shareholders

corporation A business form that is a legally-defined artificial being, separate from its owners.

A **corporation** is a business form that is a legally-defined artificial being (a legal entity) that is separate from its owners. As such, it has many of the legal powers that people have. It can enter into contracts, acquire assets, incur obligations, and receive similar protection against the seizure of its property as that received by an individual. Because a corporation is a legal entity, separate and distinct from its owners, it is solely responsible for its own obligations. Consequently, the owners of a corporation (its shareholders) are not liable for any obligations the corporation enters into. Similarly, the corporation is not liable for any personal obligations of its owners.

Formation of a Corporation. In most provinces, corporations are defined under the provincial Business Corporations Act or the Canada Business Corporations Act. Corporations must be legally formed, which means that the articles of incorporation must be filed with the relevant registrar of corporations. The articles of incorporation, sometimes referred to as the corporate charter, are like a corporate constitution that sets out the terms of the corporation's ownership and existence. Setting up a corporation is therefore considerably more costly than setting up a sole proprietorship. Most firms hire lawyers to create the formal articles of incorporation and a set of bylaws.

Ownership of a Corporation. There is no limit on the number of owners a corporation can have. Because most corporations have many owners, each owner owns only a fraction of the corporation. The entire ownership stake of a corporation is divided into shares known as **stock**. The collection of all the outstanding shares of a corporation is known as the **equity** of the corporation. An owner of a share of stock in the corporation is known as a **shareholder, stockholder,** or **equity holder**. Shareholders are entitled to **dividend payments**; that is, payments made at the discretion of the corporation's board of directors to the equity holders. Shareholders usually receive voting rights and dividend rights that are proportional to the amount of stock they own. For example, a shareholder who owns 30% of the firm's shares will be entitled to 30% of the votes at an annual meeting and 30% of the total dividend payment. In Canada, many corporations have a dominant shareholder (controlling in excess of 25% of the equity); in the United States, more corporations are considered widely held (with the largest shareholder holding less than 5% of the equity). About 19% of Canadian corporations listed on the Toronto Stock Exchange (TSX) have multiple classes of stock such that some classes may have more voting rights than others even though they have the same rights to dividends.

stock The ownership or equity of a corporation divided into shares.

equity The collection of all the outstanding shares of a corporation.

shareholder, stockholder, or **equity holder** An owner of a share of stock or equity in a corporation.

dividend payments Payments to the corporation's equity holders made at the discretion of the corporation's board of directors.

A unique feature of a corporation is that there is no limitation on who can own its stock. That is, an owner of a corporation need not have any special expertise or qualification. This feature allows free trade in the shares of the corporation and provides one of the most important advantages of organizing a firm as a corporation rather than as a sole proprietorship or partnership. Corporations can raise substantial amounts of capital because they can sell ownership shares to anonymous outside investors.

As shown in Figure 1.1, the availability of outside funding has enabled corporations to dominate the economy compared to unincorporated businesses. Let's take the world's largest corporation ranked by total revenue in the 2017 Fortune Global 500 survey, Walmart (Wal-Mart Stores, Inc.), headquartered in Bentonville, Arkansas. For the fiscal year ended January 31, 2017, Walmart's annual report indicated revenue was about $486 billion and profit was about $14 billion. Walmart's **market capitalization** (or **market cap**—the wealth in the company the owners collectively owned or the total value of all shares outstanding) was over $203 billion. It employed about 2.3 million people. Let's put these numbers into perspective. According to the World Bank, a country with $486 billion gross domestic product (GDP) in 2016 would rank just before Poland as the 23rd richest country (out of more than 200).[1] Poland has about 38 million people, more than 16 times as many people as employees at Walmart. Indeed, if the number of employees were used as the "population" of Walmart, it would rank as the 143rd largest country, just behind Namibia whose GDP in 2016 was about $10.9 billion. To put Walmart's numbers in a Canadian perspective, for the fiscal year ending October 31, 2017, the Royal Bank of Canada (RBC) had revenues of about $40.7 billion. While revenues were less than one-tenth of Walmart's revenues, RBC also had the highest profits of any Canadian firm at about $11.4 billion. In February 2018, RBC was also the most valuable firm in Canada with market capitalization of about $146.1 billion. Table 1.1 shows Canada's top 10 firms ranked by profit and their

market capitalization (or market cap) The total value of all shares outstanding of a company, calculated by multiplying the price per share by the number of shares outstanding.

[1]*Source*: World Development Indicators, The World Bank.

TABLE 1.1 **Total Revenues of Canada's Top 10 Corporations Ranked by Profit (amounts in $billions)**

Profit Ranking	Stock Ticker	Company Name	Revenues	Net Income	Market Cap
1	RY	Royal Bank of Canada	$40.7	$11.4	$146.1
2	TD	Toronto-Dominion Bank	$36.1	$10.4	$133.3
3	BNS	Bank of Nova Scotia	$27.2	$8.0	$93.3
4	CNR	Canadian National Railway	$13.0	$5.5	$71.4
5	BMO	Bank of Montreal	$22.3	$5.3	$63.0
6	CM	Canadian Imperial Bank of Commerce	$16.3	$4.7	$51.1
7	SU	Suncor Energy	$32.1	$4.5	$69.8
8	CVE	Cenovus Energy	$12.3	$3.4	$12.1
9	BCE	BCE Inc.	$22.7	$2.9	$50.1
10	TECK.B	Teck Resources	$12.0	$2.5	$21.8
		Sum (in Canadian Dollars)	$234.7	$58.6	$711.9
		Sum (in US Dollars @ 0.77 USD per CAD)	$183.1	$45.7	$555.3

Source: Company data is based on data available February 15, 2018, from Bloomberg and company filings. The exchange rate is based on the average exchange rate for 2017 as reported by the Bank of Canada. Numbers shown also reflect author's calculations.

first corporation pay tax and then shareholders pay tax

corresponding revenue, net income, and market cap numbers. You can see that for the top 10 Canadian firms, the sum of the revenues is less than half of the revenues of Walmart, the sum of net incomes is about 3.3 times Walmart's net income, and the sum of the market caps is about 2.7 times Walmart's market cap.

Tax Implications for Corporate Entities

An important difference between the types of corporate organizational forms is the way they are taxed. Because a corporation is a separate legal entity, a corporation's profits are subject to taxation separate from its owners' tax obligations. In effect, shareholders of a corporation pay taxes twice. First, the corporation pays tax on its profits, and then, when the remaining profits are distributed to the shareholders as dividends, the shareholders pay their own personal income tax on this income. This system is sometimes referred to as double taxation.

EXAMPLE 1.1 Taxation of Corporate Earnings

PROBLEM

You are a shareholder in a corporation. Some of your shares are held inside your tax-free savings account (TFSA), so any earnings there are not taxed; income from shares held outside your TFSA is taxable.[2] The corporation earns $5.00 per share before taxes. After the corporation has paid taxes, it will distribute the rest of its earnings to you as a dividend. The corporate tax rate is 35% and your tax ▶

35%

[2]Income earned within a registered retirement savings account (RRSP) is not taxed, but when money is withdrawn from an RRSP it is fully taxable. Other tax-sheltered investments include a registered education savings plan (RESP), a registered retirement income fund (RRIF), and a pension plan.

rate on dividend income outside your TFSA is 24%.[3] How much of the earnings remains after all taxes are paid?

SOLUTION

■ **Plan**

CORPORATE INFORMATION

Earnings before taxes: $5.00 Corporate tax rate: 35%

PERSONAL TAX RATES ON DIVIDENDS

From shares held inside your TFSA: 0% From shares held outside your TFSA: 24%

We first need to calculate the corporation's earnings after taxes by subtracting the taxes paid from the pre-tax earnings of $5.00. The taxes paid will be 35% (the corporate tax rate) of $5.00. Since all of the after-tax earnings per share will be paid to you as a dividend, you will pay taxes of 0% on the dividend for the shares inside your TFSA and 24% on the dividend for the shares outside your TFSA. The amount left over is what remains after all taxes are paid.

■ **Execute**

$5.00 per share × 0.35 = $1.75 in taxes at the corporate level, leaving $5.00 − $1.75 = $3.25 in after-tax earnings per share to distribute as a dividend.

For each share within your TFSA, you will pay no tax at the personal level for the dividend, leaving you with the full $3.25 dividend. For each dividend from the shares outside your TFSA, you will pay $3.25 × 0.24 = $0.78 in taxes on that dividend, leaving you with $2.47 from the original $5.00 after all taxes.

■ **Evaluate**

Each of your shares within your TFSA allows you to keep $3.25 of the original $5.00 in earnings; only the corporate tax of $1.75 is paid, and your total effective tax rate is just the corporate tax rate of 35%.

Each of your shares outside your TFSA allows you to keep $2.47 of the original $5.00 in earnings; the remaining $1.75 + $0.78 = $2.53 is paid as taxes. Thus, your total effective tax rate is 2.53/5 = 50.6%.

flow-through entities Businesses in which all income produced flows to the investors and virtually no earnings are retained within the business.

income trust A trust that holds income-producing assets directly or holds all the debt and equity securities of an income-producing corporation within the trust.

While the corporate organizational structure is subject to double taxation, Canada Revenue Agency allowed an exemption from double taxation for certain **flow-through entities** where all income produced by the business flows to the investors and virtually no earnings are retained within the business. This type of entity is an **income trust** and comes in three forms. A **business income trust** holds all the debt and equity securities of a corporation (the underlying business) in trust for the trust's owners, called the **unit holders**. An **energy trust** either holds resource properties directly or holds all the debt and equity securities of a resource corporation within the trust. A **real estate investment trust (REIT)** either holds real estate properties directly or holds all the debt and equity securities of a corporation that owns real estate properties. For income trusts formed before November 2006, there was no tax

[3]Your tax on dividend income from a Canadian corporation is determined by Canada Revenue Agency (CRA) requirements. In 2017, the CRA required you to "increase" or gross up the dividend amount by 38%, apply your federal and provincial tax rates to the grossed-up amount, then receive a federal dividend tax credit of 15.0198% of the actual dividend and finally receive a provincial dividend tax credit that ranged from 5.4% to 15% depending on the province or territory. For taxpayers in the highest tax bracket in the 2017 tax year, this resulted in combined federal and provincial tax rates on dividends that ranged from 24.8% in Yukon to 42.6% in Newfoundland and Labrador; the average across all provinces and territories was about 34.5%.

business income trust
An income trust that holds all the debt and equity securities of a corporation (the underlying business).

at the business level until 2011. REITs continue to have no tax at the business level beyond 2011, but the other forms of income trusts are now taxed. Due to the loss of this tax advantage, many of these other income trusts have now converted back to corporations.

EXAMPLE 1.2 Taxation of a Real Estate Investment Trust (REIT)

PROBLEM

Rework Example 1.1 assuming the corporation in that example was actually a REIT and flowed through all earnings to trust unit owners. Again, assume you hold some of the trust units within your TFSA so they are not subject to personal taxes. For the trust units held outside your TFSA, suppose you pay tax at a rate of 46% (equal to the tax rate on regular income).

SOLUTION

■ **Plan**

REIT INFORMATION

Earnings before taxes: $5.00 Tax at the business level: 0%

PERSONAL TAX RATES ON REGULAR INCOME

From units held inside your TFSA: 0% From units held outside your TFSA: 46%

Since there is no tax at the business level, the entire $5.00 of earnings is passed through to the unit holders. The $5.00 received is taxed as ordinary income at the personal level. However, for the units held within your TFSA, you will pay no tax. For the units held outside your TFSA, you will pay tax at a rate of 46% on the REIT distribution. The amount left over is what remains after all taxes are paid.

■ **Execute**

$5.00 per unit is distributed to each unit holder.

For each unit within your TFSA, you will pay no tax at the personal level, leaving you the full $5.00 amount. For each distribution from the units outside your TFSA, you will pay $5.00 × 0.46 = $2.30 in taxes on that distribution, leaving you with $2.70 from the original $5.00 after all taxes.

■ **Evaluate**

Each of your shares within your TFSA allows you to keep the full $5.00 in earnings, so your total effective tax rate is 0%.

Each of your shares outside your TFSA allows you to keep $2.70 of the original $5.00 in earnings; the remaining $2.30 is paid as taxes. Thus, your total effective tax rate is 46% (the rate of tax you pay on regular income).

CORPORATE TAXATION AROUND THE WORLD

In most countries there is some relief from double taxation. Thirty countries make up the Organisation for Economic Co-operation and Development (OECD), and of these countries, only Ireland offers no relief from double taxation. In Canada, the dividend tax credit gives some relief by effectively giving a lower tax rate on dividend income than on other sources of income. In the 2017 tax year, for most provinces, dividend income was taxed at a rate about 15% less than ordinary income; for example, in Ontario the effective personal tax rates (combined provincial and federal) were 39.34% for dividends and 53.5% for regular income for individuals in the top tax bracket. A few countries, including Australia, Finland, Mexico, New Zealand, and Norway, offer complete relief by effectively not taxing dividend income.

unit holders The owners of an income trust.

energy trust An income trust that holds resource properties directly or holds all the debt and equity securities of a resource corporation within the trust.

real estate investment trust (REIT) An income trust that holds real estate properties directly or holds all the debt and equity securities of a corporation that owns real estate properties.

TABLE 1.2 Characteristics of Different Types of Firms

	Number of Owners	Liability for Firm's Debts	Owners Manage the Firm	Ownership Change Dissolves the Firm	Taxation
Sole proprietorship	One	Yes	Yes	Yes	Personal
General partnership	Unlimited	Yes	Yes	Yes	Personal
Limited partnership	At least one general partner, no limit on number of limited partners	General partners: yes Limited partners: no	General partners: yes Limited partners: no	General partners: yes Limited partners: no	Personal
Corporation	Unlimited	No	No (but they may legally)	No	Business and personal
REIT	Unlimited	No	No	No	Personal

As we have discussed, there are three main types of firms: sole proprietorships, partnerships (general and limited), and corporations. In addition, a business or particular assets may be held within an income trust for tax purposes. Table 1.2 compares and contrasts the main characteristics of each.

CONCEPT CHECK

1. What are the advantages and disadvantages of organizing a business as a corporation?
2. What is a limited liability partnership (LLP)? How does it differ from a limited partnership?
3. What is an income trust? Which type of trust still gets preferential tax treatment after 2011?

1.3 The Financial Manager

As of October 20, 2017, Apple Inc. had more than 5 *billion* shares of stock held by 25,333 owners.[4] Because a corporation has many owners, each of whom can freely trade his or her stock, often it is not feasible for the owners of a corporation to have direct control of the firm. The financial manager has responsibility for making the financial decisions of the business for the stockholders. Within the corporation, the financial manager has three main tasks:

1. Make investment decisions.
2. Make financing decisions.
3. Manage short-term cash needs.

We will discuss each of these in turn, along with the financial manager's overarching goal.

[4]Apple Inc., 10-K Form for fiscal year ended September 30, 2017.

Making Investment Decisions

The financial manager's most important job is to make the firm's investment decisions. The financial manager must weigh the costs and benefits of each investment or project and decide which of them qualify as good uses of the money stockholders have invested in the firm. These investment decisions fundamentally shape what the firm does and whether it will add value for its owners. For example, it may seem hard to imagine now, but there was a time when Apple's financial managers were evaluating whether to invest in the development of the first iPod. They had to weigh the substantial development and production costs against uncertain future sales. Their analysis indicated that it was a good investment, and the rest is history. In this book, we will develop all the tools necessary to make these investment decisions.

Making Financing Decisions

Once the financial manager has decided which investments to make, he or she also decides how to pay for them. Large investments may require the corporation to raise additional money. The financial manager must decide whether to raise more money from new and existing owners by selling more shares of stock (equity) or to borrow the money instead (debt). In this book, we will discuss the characteristics of each source of money and how to decide which one to use in the context of the corporation's overall mix of debt and equity.

Managing Short-Term Cash Needs

The financial manager must ensure that the firm has enough cash on hand to meet its obligations from day to day. This job, also commonly known as managing working capital,[5] may seem straightforward, but in a young or growing company it can mean the difference between success and failure. Even companies with great products require a lot of money to develop and bring those products to market. Consider the costs to Apple of launching the iPhone, which included developing the technology and creating a huge marketing campaign, or the costs to Boeing of producing the 787—billions of dollars were spent before the first 787 left the ground. A company typically burns through a significant amount of cash before the sales of the product generate income. The financial manager's job is to make sure that access to cash does not hinder the firm's success.

The Goal of the Financial Manager

shareholder wealth maximization The overriding corporate objective that seeks to maximize the financial benefit to all persons holding stock in the corporation by maximizing the current value of the company's share price.

The financial manager makes all these decisions within the context of the overriding goal of a firm's management—**shareholder wealth maximization**. The stockholders have invested in the corporation, putting their money at risk to become the owners of the corporation. Thus, the firm's management is a caretaker of the money stockholders have invested and makes decisions in their interests. Many corporations have thousands of owners (shareholders). These shareholders vary from large institutions to small first-time investors, from retirees living off their investments to young employees just starting to save for retirement. Each owner is likely to have different

[5]Working capital refers to things such as cash on hand, inventories, raw materials, loans to suppliers, and payments from customers—the grease that keeps the wheels of production moving. We will discuss working capital in more detail in the next chapter and devote all of Chapter 19 to working capital management.

interests and priorities. Whose interests and priorities determine the goals of the firm? You might be surprised to learn that the interests of shareholders are aligned for many, if not most, important decisions. Regardless of their own personal financial position and stage in life, all shareholders will agree that they are better off if the value of their investment in the corporation is maximized. For example, suppose the decision concerns whether to develop a new product that will be a profitable investment for the corporation. All shareholders will probably agree that developing this product is a good idea. Returning to our iPod example, by the end of January 2018, Apple shares were worth about over 150 times as much as they were in the beginning of October 2001, when the first iPod was introduced. All Apple shareholders at the time of the development of the first iPod are clearly much better off because of it, whether they have since sold their shares of Apple to pay for retirement or are still watching those shares appreciate in their retirement accounts.

Even when all the owners of a corporation agree on the goals of the corporation, these goals must be implemented. In the next section, we discuss the financial manager's place in the corporation and how owners exert control over the corporation.

CONCEPT CHECK

4. What are the main types of decisions that a financial manager makes?

5. What is the goal of the financial manager?

↳ max profit

↳ Investment

↳ finance

↳ day to day

1.4 The Financial Manager's Place in the Corporation

We have established that the stockholders own the corporation but rely on the firm's managers to actively manage the corporation. The *board of directors* and the management team headed by the *chief executive officer* have direct control of the corporation. In this section, we explain how the responsibilities for the corporation are divided between these two entities and describe conflicts that arise between stockholders and the management team.

The Corporate Management Team

board of directors A group of people elected by shareholders who have the ultimate decision-making authority in the corporation.

The shareholders of a corporation exercise their control by electing a **board of directors**, a group of people who have the ultimate decision-making authority in the corporation. In most corporations, each share of stock gives a shareholder one vote in the election of the board of directors, so investors with more shares have more influence. When one or two shareholders own a very large proportion of the outstanding stock, these shareholders might either be on the board of directors themselves, or they may have the right to appoint a number of directors.

chief executive officer (CEO) The person charged with running the corporation by instituting the rules and policies set by the board of directors.

The board of directors makes rules on how the corporation should be run (including how the top managers in the corporation are compensated), sets policy, and monitors the performance of the company. The board of directors delegates most decisions that involve the day-to-day running of the corporation to its management. The **chief executive officer (CEO)** is charged with running the corporation by implementing the rules and policies set by the board of directors. The size of the rest of the management team varies from corporation to corporation. In some corporations, the separation of powers between the board of directors and CEO is not always distinct. In fact, the CEO can also be the chair of the board of directors. The most senior financial manager is the chief financial officer (CFO), who often reports directly to the CEO. Figure 1.2 presents

FIGURE 1.2 The Financial Functions within a Corporation

The board of directors, representing the stockholders, controls the corporation and hires the top management team. A financial manager might hold any of the green-shaded positions, including that of chief financial officer (CFO). The controller oversees accounting and tax functions. The treasurer oversees more traditional finance functions, such as capital budgeting (making investment decisions), risk management (managing the firm's exposure to movements in the financial markets), and credit management (managing the terms and policies of any credit the firm extends to its suppliers and customers).

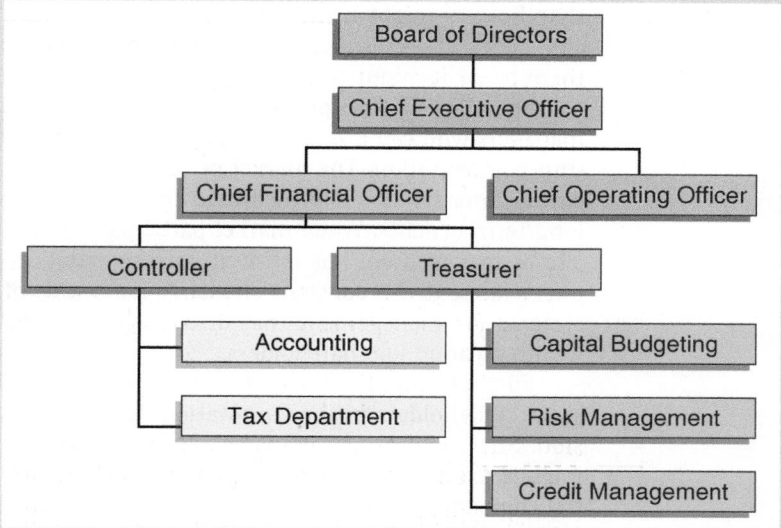

part of a typical organizational chart for a corporation, highlighting the positions a financial manager may take.

Ethics and Incentives in Corporations

A corporation is run by a management team, separate from its owners. How can the owners of a corporation ensure that the management team will implement their goals?

shirking Neglecting the responsibilities of managing the business.

perquisites Benefits provided free of charge to the managers of a corporation.

principal-agent problem When managers, despite being hired as the agents of shareholders, put their own self-interest ahead of the interests of the shareholders (the principals).

Principal-Agent Problem. Many people claim that because of the separation of ownership and control in a corporation, managers have little incentive to work in the interests of the shareholders when this means working against their own self-interest. As a manager, wouldn't it be more fun to relax all day and freely eat in the company's gourmet dining room? Unfortunately for shareholders, they benefit little by managers' **shirking** or consuming **perquisites**, which of course benefit managers considerably. Economists call this the **principal-agent problem**—when managers, despite being hired as the agents of shareholders, put their own interests ahead of the interests of those shareholders (also called the principals). Managers face the ethical dilemma of whether to do what is in their own best interests or adhere to their responsibility to put the interests of shareholders first. The downfall of many corporations can ultimately be blamed on management acting in their own interests at the expense of shareholders. A criticism of management teams in failing firms in the financial sector during the financial crisis of 2008 was that managements' prior decisions maximized their own well-being (through short-term bonuses and compensation) at the expense of the long-term viability of their companies.

The most common way the principal-agent problem is addressed in practice is by minimizing the number of decisions managers must make for which their own self-interest substantially differs from the interests of the shareholders. For example, managers' compensation contracts should be designed to ensure that most decisions in the shareholders' interests are also in the managers' interests; shareholders often tie the compensation of top managers to the corporation's profits or perhaps to its stock price. Thus, if managers shirk or consume too many perquisites, the corporation's profit and stock price will drop and managers' compensation will decline. This encourages managers not to shirk or consume too many perquisites. There are, however, two important limitations to this strategy. One, by tying compensation too closely to performance, the shareholders might be asking managers to take on more risk than they are comfortable taking. As a result, managers may not make decisions that the shareholders want them to, or it might be hard to find talented managers willing to accept the job. Two, compensation tied to profits or share price may lead to short-sighted behaviour by managers who can pursue a strategy that may artificially boost short-term results and thus compensation. The market price of the firm may rise on such a strategy if market participants are less informed than management and believe the strategy will provide long-term benefits. When market participants eventually learn the truth, it may be too late as management has received its compensation and may have cashed out of their own shares. It is a constant challenge for boards of directors to design compensation systems for management that discourage short-sighted strategies and promote true wealth creation for shareholders.

Further potential for conflicts of interest and ethical considerations arise when some stakeholders in the corporation benefit from and others lose because of a decision. Shareholders and managers are two stakeholders in the corporation, but others include the regular employees, customers, suppliers, and the communities in which the company operates. Managers may decide to take the interests of other stakeholders into account in their decisions, such as keeping a loss-generating factory open because it is the main provider of jobs in a small town, paying above local market wages to factory workers in a developing country, or operating a plant at a higher environmental standard than local law mandates. In Japan and some European countries, this **stakeholder satisfaction** view seems to be more highly regarded than the shareholder wealth maximization view. Tied with the stakeholder satisfaction view is the idea of corporate social responsibility. Investopedia defines **corporate social responsibility** (CSR) as "a corporation's initiatives to assess and take responsibility for the company's effects on environmental and social wellbeing." Investopedia expands on this as follows: "The term generally applies to efforts that go beyond what may be required by regulators or environmental protection groups. CSR may also be referred to as "corporate citizenship" and can involve incurring short-term costs that do not provide an immediate financial benefit to the company, but instead promote positive social and environmental change." (Investopedia, retrieved from www.investopedia.com/terms/c/corp-social-responsibility.asp).

stakeholder satisfaction A corporate objective of seeking to meet the interests of all stakeholders of the corporation.

corporate social responsibility "Corporate initiative to assess and take responsibility for the company's effects on the environment and impact on social welfare" (Investopedia).

In many cases, though, actions that benefit other stakeholders and corporate social responsibility initiatives may also benefit the firm's shareholders by creating a more dedicated workforce, generating positive publicity with customers, enhancing the firm's reputation or brand, or other indirect effects. Thus, for the most part, stakeholder satisfaction and corporate social responsibility can be consistent with shareholder wealth maximization. In other instances, when these decisions benefit other stakeholders at shareholders' expense, they represent a form of corporate charity. Indeed, many if not most corporations explicitly donate (on behalf of their shareholders) to local and global causes. Shareholders often approve of such actions, even though they are costly.

Whether such donations increase the reputation and goodwill of the firm and thus increase shareholder wealth or cost more than the benefits and so reduce shareholder wealth is an open question. While it is the manager's job to make decisions that maximize shareholder value, shareholders—who own the firm—also want the firm's actions to reflect their moral and ethical values and enhance the long-term reputation of the corporation. Of course, shareholders may not have identical preferences in these matters, leading to potential sources of conflict.

The CEO's Performance. Another way shareholders can encourage managers to work in the interests of shareholders is to discipline them if they do not. If shareholders are unhappy with a CEO's performance, they could, in principle, pressure the board to oust the CEO. Despite a few high-profile examples, directors and top executives are rarely replaced through a grassroots shareholder uprising. Instead, dissatisfied investors often choose to sell their shares. Of course, somebody must be willing to buy the shares from the dissatisfied shareholders. If enough shareholders are dissatisfied, the only way to entice investors to buy (or hold) the shares is to offer them a low price. Similarly, investors who see a well-managed corporation will want to purchase shares, which drives the stock price up. Thus, the stock price of the corporation is a barometer for corporate leaders that continuously gives them feedback on the shareholders' opinion of their performance.

When the stock performs poorly, the board of directors might react by replacing the CEO. In some corporations, however, the senior executives might be entrenched because boards of directors do not have the independence or motivation to replace them. Often the reluctance to fire results when the board is composed of people who are close friends of the CEO and lack objectivity. In corporations in which the CEO is entrenched and doing a poor job, the expectation of continued poor performance will cause the stock price to be low. Low stock prices create a profit opportunity. In a **hostile takeover**, an individual or organization—sometimes known as a corporate raider—can purchase a large fraction of the company's stock and in doing so get enough votes to replace the board of directors and the CEO. With a new, superior management team, the stock is a much more attractive investment, which would probably result in a price rise and a profit for the corporate raider and the other shareholders. Although the words "hostile" and "raider" have negative connotations, corporate raiders themselves provide an important service to shareholders. The mere threat of being removed as a result of a hostile takeover is often enough to discipline bad managers and motivate boards of directors to make difficult decisions. Consequently, the fact that a corporation's shares can be publicly traded creates a "market for corporate control" that encourages managers and boards of directors to act in the interests of their shareholders. If there is a dominant shareholder or a shareholder that owns a class of shares with multiple votes, it may be impossible for the market for corporate control to work as desired, because not enough shares can be purchased on the market to accumulate enough votes to change control. Shareholder rights activists point out this problem for many Canadian firms that have multiple voting classes or a dominant shareholder tied to management, so as investors we might want to reconsider investing in such firms.

hostile takeover A situation in which an individual or organization, sometimes referred to as a corporate raider, purchases a large fraction of a target corporation's stock and in doing so gets enough votes to replace the target's board of directors and its CEO.

CONCEPT CHECK

6. How do shareholders control a corporation?
7. What types of jobs would a financial manager have in a corporation?
8. What ethical issues could confront a financial manager?

1.5 The Stock Market

In Section 1.3, we established the goal of the financial manager—shareholder wealth maximization: to maximize the wealth of the owners, the stockholders. The value of the owners' investments in the corporation is determined by the price of a share of the corporation's stock. Corporations can be private or public. A private corporation has a limited number of owners and there is no organized market for its shares, making it hard to determine the market price of its shares at any point in time. A public corporation has many owners and its shares trade on an organized market, called a **stock market (**or **stock exchange** or **bourse)**. These markets provide *liquidity* for a company's shares and determine the market price for those shares. An investment is said to be **liquid** if it can easily be turned into cash by selling it immediately at a price at which it could be contemporaneously bought. An investor in a public company values the ability to turn his investment into cash easily and quickly by simply selling his shares on one of these markets. In this section, we provide an overview of the functioning of the major stock markets. The analysis and trading by participants in these markets provide an evaluation of financial managers' decisions that not only determine the stock price, but also provide feedback to the managers on their decisions.

stock market (or **stock exchange** or **bourse**) An organized market on which the shares of many corporations are traded.

liquid In reference to an investment, one that can easily be turned into cash because it can be sold immediately at a competitive market price.

The Largest Stock Markets

The largest stock market in the world is the New York Stock Exchange (NYSE). Billions of dollars of stock are exchanged every day on the NYSE. Based on 2017 year-end domestic market capitalization, the TMX Group (owner of the Toronto Stock Exchange or TSX, the TSX Venture Exchange, and the Montreal Exchange) was the ninth largest exchange in the world. Figure 1.3 ranks the world's largest stock exchanges by domestic market capitalization and value of trades for 2017.

All of these markets are *secondary markets.* The term **primary market** refers to a corporation issuing new shares of stock and selling them to investors. After this initial transaction between the corporation and investors, the shares continue to trade in a **secondary market** between investors without the involvement of the corporation. For example, if you wish to buy 100 shares of the Suncor Energy Inc., you could place an order on the TSX, where Suncor trades under the ticker symbol SU. You would buy your shares from someone who already held shares of Suncor, not from Suncor itself. Because firms only occasionally issue new shares, secondary market trading accounts for the vast majority of trading in the stock market.

primary market The market where new shares of stock are issued by a corporation and sold to investors.

secondary market Markets, such as the TSX, NYSE, or NASDAQ, where shares of a corporation are traded between investors without the involvement of the corporation.

LovePhy/Fotolia

FIGURE 1.3 Worldwide Stock Markets Ranked by Two Common Measures

The largest stock markets in the world ranked on (a) the total value of all domestic corporations on the market as of the end of 2017 and on (b) the total value of the volume of shares traded on the electronic order book during the year 2017.

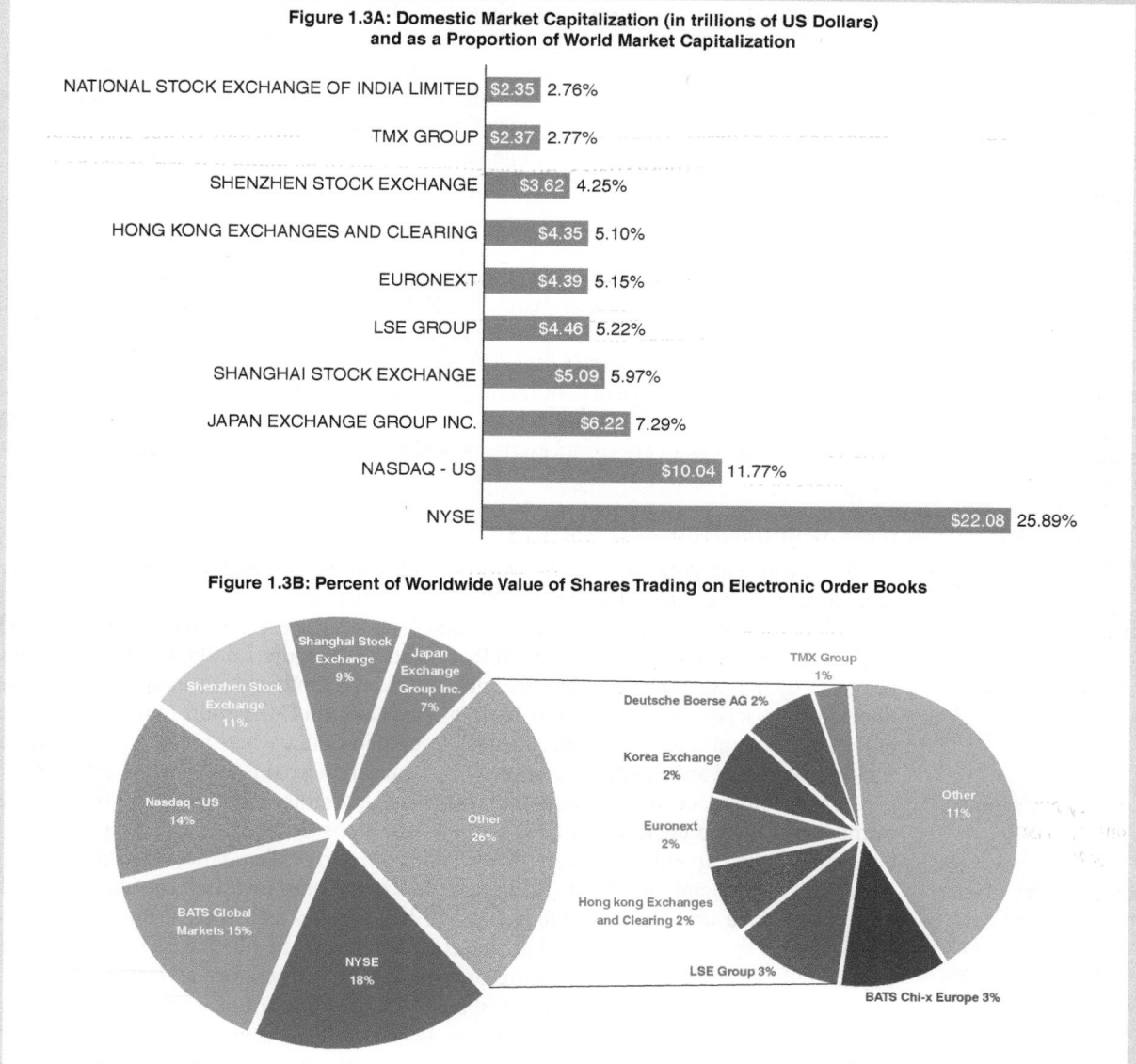

Source: Based on World Federation of Exchanges members, affiliates, correspondents, and non-members.

bid price The highest price in a market for which someone is willing to purchase a security.

ask (or offer) price The lowest price in a market for which someone is willing to sell a security.

The TSX is an electronic exchange. Investors (individuals and institutions) can post orders onto the TSX trading system from anywhere. The highest price being quoted to buy a stock is called the **bid price**. The lowest price being quoted to sell a stock is called the **ask** (or **offer**) **price**. When the bid and ask prices are at the same price, the trade is completed; then the next highest bid and next lowest ask become the quoted bid and ask prices, respectively.

Posted ask prices exceed the posted bid prices. This difference between the ask price and bid price is called the **bid-ask spread**. If you enter the market wanting to buy a stock, you can post a **limit order** to buy at a specified price, but until your order matches the ask

bid-ask spread The amount by which the ask price exceeds the bid price.

limit order An order to buy or sell a stock at a specified price.

market order An order to buy or sell a stock at the currently available ask or bid price quoted on the market.

transaction cost In most markets, an expense, a broker commission and the bid-ask spread, investors must pay in order to trade securities.

thinly traded In reference to a security, one that is infrequently traded.

specialists (or **market makers)** Individuals on the trading floor of a stock exchange who match buyers with sellers. These specialists are given preferential access to orders but must also stand ready to buy or sell shares on their own account at their posted bid and ask prices.

dark pools Trading venues in which the size and price of orders are not disclosed to participants. Prices are within the best bid and ask prices available in public markets, but traders face the risk their orders may not be filled if an excess of either buy or sell orders is received.

price (the amount for which someone will sell the stock to you), no trade will take place. Alternatively, a **market order** to buy will transact immediately because it automatically takes the best ask price already posted. However, with market orders, customers end up always buying at the ask (the higher price) and selling at the bid (the lower price); the bid-ask spread is an implicit **transaction cost** investors have to pay in order to trade quickly. Companies that are more interesting to investors are frequently traded, and many investors put in orders to buy and sell the stock. In these cases, the bid-ask spread is generally quite small. Other companies that attract fewer investors' interest are said to be **thinly traded.** Because not many investors want to trade these stocks, the bid-ask spreads tend to be much larger. Stocks that trade on the TSX tend to have lower bid-ask spreads than those that trade on the TSX Venture Exchange (an exchange for relatively small companies).

NYSE

The NYSE is one of the last major stock exchanges to have an active trading floor to which orders are routed for the trading of shares. The NYSE also has **specialists (**or **market makers)** who are given preferential access to orders but who must also stand ready to buy or sell shares at their posted bid and ask prices. The NYSE has combined electronic trading with the trading on the floor. The role of floor trading and the importance of the specialist will decline as the need for a specialist to make a market in a company's stock is replaced by the ability of investors to access an electronic exchange and post their own bid and ask prices directly.

New Competition and Market Changes

Stock markets have gone through enormous changes in the last decade. In 2006, the market capitalization of the shares listed on the NYSE accounted for about 30.5% of the world stock market capitalization while Shanghai accounted for only 1.8% and the Shenzhen Stock Exchange was less than 0.5%. As seen in the top panel of Figure 1.3, the NYSE has dropped below 26%, but we have seen the Shanghai Stock Exchange rise to almost 6% and the Shenzhen Stock Exchange rise to over 4% to surpass Canada's TMX Group. In the second panel of Figure 1.3, we also see the significant stock trading in China, where the U.S. dollar value of trades in Shanghai and Shenzhen combined is greater than what is observed on the NYSE.

When trading on an exchange, investors are guaranteed the opportunity to trade immediately at the current bid or ask price, and transactions are visible to all traders when they occur. In contrast, alternative trading systems called dark pools do not make their limit order books visible. Instead, these **dark pools** offer investors the ability to trade at a better price (for example, the average of the bid and ask, thus saving the bid-ask spread), with the trade-off being that the order might not be filled if an excess of either buy or sell orders is received. Trading on a dark pool is therefore attractive to traders who do not want to reveal their demand and who are willing to sacrifice the guarantee of immediacy for a potentially better price. When dark pools are included, researchers estimate that in the U.S. alone there could be as many as 50 venues in which to trade stocks. These venues compete with one another for order volume. Because traders value liquid markets, an important area of competition is liquidity—exchanges try to ensure that their limit order books are deep; that is, that they contain many orders. As a result, exchanges have been experimenting with different rules designed to encourage traders who provide liquidity and discourage traders who take advantage of stale limit orders. For example, some trading venues pay traders to post limit orders and charge traders who place market orders. Others pay for orders from retail investors and impose additional charges on high-frequency trading. The proliferation of exchange venues has generated a wide variety of compensation schemes. Indeed, BATS, the second largest exchange in terms of value of share trading, shown in the bottom panel of Figure 1.3, operates different markets with different rules, essentially tailoring markets to the perceived needs of customers. It is highly unlikely that we have seen the end of these changes. Stock markets remain in a state of flux, and only time will tell what the eventual shake out will look like.

Listing Standards

listing standards The requirements a company must meet to be traded on an exchange.

Each exchange has its own **listing standards** that outline the requirements a company must meet to be traded on the exchange. These standards usually require that the company have enough shares outstanding for shareholders to have a liquid market and to be of interest to a broad set of investors. The NYSE's standards are more stringent than the TSX's standards, which are more stringent than the standards for listing on the TSX Venture Exchange. Traditionally, there has been a certain pride in being listed on the NYSE, and many Canadian companies list on the NYSE in addition to the TSX as a signal of their higher quality. Exchanges around the world compete actively over listings of companies, and the decision of where to list often comes down to which exchange the company's board believes will give its stockholders the best execution and liquidity for their trades. For example, the TSX is popular for energy-related companies while the NASDAQ is popular for technology-related companies (although many companies in many different industries trade on all these exchanges).

Other Financial Markets

Of course, stock markets are not the only financial markets. There are markets to trade practically anything. Two of the largest financial markets in the world, the bond market and the foreign exchange market, are simply networks of dealers connected by phone and computer. We will discuss each of these in more detail in later chapters (bonds in Chapters 6 and 15 and foreign exchange in Chapter 22). Commodities like oil, wheat, and canola are traded on commodity markets. *Derivative securities,* which are complicated financial products used to hedge risks, are traded in locations such as the Chicago Board Options Exchange and the Montreal Exchange (discussed in Chapters 13 and 21).

CONCEPT CHECK

9. What advantage does a stock market provide to corporate investors?

10. What is the importance of a stock market to a financial manager?

1.6 Financial Institutions

financial institutions Entities that provide financial services, such as taking deposits, managing investments, brokering financial transactions, or making loans.

The spread of the financial crisis from subprime mortgages in the United States, to stock markets, and to traditional banks and businesses drew everyone's attention to *financial institutions* and their role in the economy. In general, **financial institutions** are entities that provide financial services, such as taking deposits, managing investments, brokering financial transactions, or making loans. In this section, we describe the key types of financial institutions and their function.

The Financial Cycle

Keeping straight the names and roles of the different types of financial institutions can be challenging. It is helpful to keep in mind the basic financial cycle, depicted in Figure 1.4, as context. In the financial cycle, (1) people invest and save their money; (2) that money, through loans and stock, flows to companies that use it to fund growth

FIGURE 1.4 The Financial Cycle

This figure depicts the basic financial cycle, which matches funds from savers to companies that have projects requiring funds and then returns the profits from those projects to the savers.

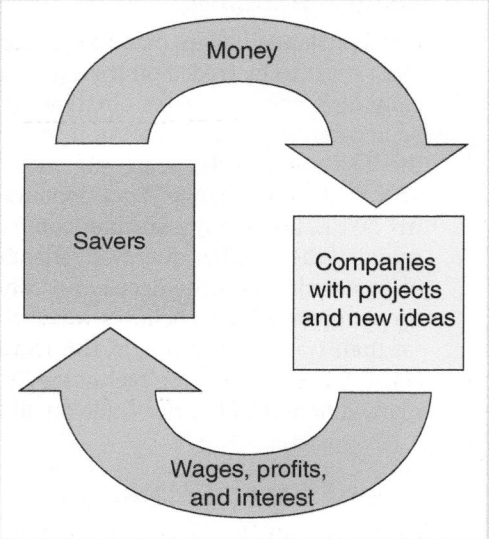

through new products, generating profits and wages; and (3) the money then flows back to the savers and investors. All financial institutions play a role at some point in this cycle of connecting money with ideas and returning the profits to the investors.

Types of Financial Institutions

Table 1.3 summarizes the major categories of financial institutions, provides examples of representative firms, and details the institutions' sources and uses of funds.

TABLE 1.3 Financial Institutions and Their Role in the Financial Cycle

Institution	Money Source	Money Use
Banks and Credit Unions *CIBC, Royal Bank*	Deposits (savings)	Loans to people and businesses
Insurance Companies *Great West Life, Manulife Financial*	Premiums and investment earnings	Invests mostly in bonds and some stocks, using the investment income to pay claims
Mutual Funds *AGF Investments, CI Investments*	People's investments (savings)	Buys stocks, bonds, and other financial instruments on behalf of its investors
Pension Funds *Ontario Teachers Pension Plan, Caisse de dépôt et placement du Québec*	Retirement savings contributed through the workplace	Similar to mutual funds, except with the purpose of providing retirement income
Hedge Funds *Bridgewater, Soros Fund*	Investments by wealthy individuals and endowments	Invests in any kind of investment with an attempt to maximize returns for relatively low risk
Venture Capital Funds *Covington Capital, GrowthWorks*	Investments by wealthy individuals and endowments	Invests in start-up, entrepreneurial firms
Private Equity Funds *KKR, Onex*	Investments by wealthy individuals and endowments	Purchases whole companies by using a small amount of equity and borrowing the rest

One major financial institution not listed in the table is an investment bank, because it is involved in many different aspects of the financial cycle. Investment banks operate as the "grease for the wheels" of the financial system, brokering many of the transactions that take place between institutions and between companies and institutions. Finally, financial conglomerates, sometimes referred to as financial services firms, combine more than one type of institution. Examples include the largest Canadian banks, which operate in commercial banking, insurance, mutual funds, investment banking, and other areas.

Role of Financial Institutions

Financial institutions have a role beyond moving funds from those who have extra funds (savers) to those who need funds (borrowers and firms): they also move funds through time. Suppose you need a $20,000 car loan. You need $20,000 now but do not have it. However, you will have it in the future, as you earn a salary. The financial institution, in this case a bank or credit union, helps transfer your future salary into funds today by issuing you a loan.

Financial institutions also help spread out risk bearing. Insurance companies essentially pool premiums together from policyholders and pay the claims of those who have an accident, fire, or medical need, or who die. This process spreads the financial risk of these events out across a large pool of policyholders and the investors in the insurance company. Similarly, mutual funds and pension funds take your savings and spread them out among the stocks and bonds of many different companies, limiting your risk exposure to any one company.

While you may have seen coverage of the stock markets and discussion of financial institutions on the news, it is unlikely that you have had any exposure to the finance function within the firm. In this chapter, we provided a sense of what corporate finance is all about, what a financial manager does, and the importance of stock markets and financial institutions. In the coming chapters, you will learn how to make financial management decisions and how to use financial market information. We will develop the tools of financial analysis and a clear understanding of when to apply them and why they work.

CONCEPT CHECK

11. What is the basic financial cycle? – Bank Invest → give company funds ↓ money flow back

12. What are the three main roles financial institutions play?

↳ anything with money
deposit loans

MyLab Finance

Here is what you should know after reading this chapter. MyLab™ Finance will help you identify what you know, and where to go when you need to practice.

KEY POINTS AND EQUATIONS	TERMS	ONLINE PRACTICE OPPORTUNITIES
1.1 Why Study Finance? ■ Finance and financial decisions are everywhere in our daily lives. ■ Many financial decisions are simple, but others are complex. All are tied together by the Valuation Principle—the foundation for financial decision making—which you will learn in this book.		

KEY POINTS AND EQUATIONS	TERMS	ONLINE PRACTICE OPPORTUNITIES
1.2 The Three Types of Firms ■ There are three types of firms in Canada: sole proprietorships, partnerships, and corporations. ■ Firms with unlimited personal liability include sole proprietorships and partnerships (for general partners). ■ Firms with limited liability include limited partnerships (for limited partners but not for general partners) and corporations. ■ A corporation is a legally defined artificial being (a judicial person or legal entity) that has many of the legal powers people have. It can enter into contracts, acquire assets, and incur obligations, and it enjoys protection against the seizure of its property. ■ The shareholders in a corporation effectively must pay tax twice. The corporation pays tax once and then investors must pay personal tax on any funds that are distributed. A REIT does not pay tax at the business level. ■ The ownership of a corporation is divided into shares of stock collectively known as equity. Investors in these shares are called shareholders, stockholders, or equity holders.	business income trust, p. 8 corporation, p. 5 dividend payments, p. 6 energy trust, p. 8 equity, p. 6 equity holder, p. 6 flow-through entities, p. 8 general partnership, p. 5 income trust, p. 8 limited liability, p. 5 limited liability partnership (LLP) p. 5 limited partnership, p. 5 market capitalization (or market cap), p. 6 real estate investment trust (REIT), p. 8 shareholder, p. 6 sole proprietorship, p. 4 stock, p. 6 stockholder, p. 6 unit holders, p. 8	MyLab Study Plan 1.2
1.3 The Financial Manager ■ The financial manager makes investing, financing, and cash-flow management decisions. ■ The goal of the financial manager is to maximize the wealth of the shareholders (maximize the stock price).	shareholder wealth maximization, p. 11	MyLab Study Plan 1.3
1.4 The Financial Manager's Place in the Corporation ■ The ownership and control of a corporation are separate. Shareholders exercise their control indirectly through the board of directors.	board of directors, p. 12 chief executive officer (CEO), p. 12 hostile takeover, p. 15 perquisites, p. 13 principal-agent problem, p. 13 shirking, p. 13 stakeholder satisfaction, p. 14 corporate social responsibility, p. 14	MyLab Study Plan 1.4

KEY POINTS AND EQUATIONS	TERMS	ONLINE PRACTICE OPPORTUNITIES
1.5 The Stock Market ■ The shares of public corporations are traded on stock markets. The shares of private corporations do not trade on a stock market. ■ When a firm sells shares to investors, that is a primary market transaction. Stock exchanges, such as the TSX and NYSE, are secondary markets where investors trade shares among each other.	ask (or offer) price, p. 17 bid-ask spread, p. 17 bid price, p. 17 dark pools, p. 18 limit order, p. 18 liquid, p. 16 listing standards, p. 19 market order, p. 18 primary market, p. 16 secondary market, p. 16 specialists (or market makers), p. 18 stock market (or stock exchange or bourse), p. 16 thinly traded, p. 18 transaction cost, p. 18	MyLab Study Plan 1.5
1.6 Financial Institutions ■ In the basic financial cycle, money flows from savers and investors to companies and entrepreneurs with ideas, and then back to the savers and investors in the form of profits and interest. ■ Financial institutions all play some role in this cycle. ■ Financial institutions also help move money through time (e.g., loans against future wages) and spread risk across large investor bases.	financial institutions, p. 19	MyLab Study Plan 1.6

PROBLEMS

All problems in this chapter are available in MyLab Finance. An asterisk (*) indicates problems with a higher level of difficulty.

The Three Types of Firms

1. What is the most important difference between a corporation and *all* other organization forms?
2. What does the phrase *limited liability* mean in a corporate context?
3. Which organizational forms give their owners limited liability?
4. What are the main advantages and disadvantages of organizing a firm as a corporation?
5. Explain the difference between a real estate corporation and a REIT.

6. You are a shareholder in a corporation. The corporation earns $2.00 per share before taxes. Once it has paid taxes, it will distribute the rest of its earnings to

you as a dividend. The corporate tax rate is 34%, the personal tax rate on dividend income is 18%, and the personal tax rate on ordinary income is 40%. How much is left for you after all taxes are paid?

7. Repeat Problem 6 except assume the corporation is now a REIT and you own units in the trust.

The Financial Manager

8. What is the most important type of decision that the financial manager makes?

9. Why do all shareholders agree on the same goal for the financial manager?

The Financial Manager's Place in the Corporation

10. Corporate managers work for the owners of the corporation. Consequently, corporate managers should make decisions that are in the interests of the owners, rather than in their own interests. What strategies are available to shareholders to help ensure that managers are motivated to act this way?

11. Think back to the last time you ate at an expensive restaurant where you paid the bill. Now think about the last time you ate at a similar restaurant, but your parents paid the bill. Did you order more food (or more-expensive food) when your parents paid? Explain how this relates to the principal-agent problem in corporations.

12. Suppose you are considering renting an apartment. You, the renter, can be viewed as an agent, while the company that owns the apartment can be viewed as the principal. What principal-agent conflicts do you anticipate? Suppose, instead, that you work for the apartment company. What features would you put into the lease agreement that would give the renter incentives to take good care of the apartment?

13. You are the CEO of a company and are considering entering into an agreement to have your company buy another company. You think the price might be too high, but you will be the CEO of the combined, much larger company. You know that when the company gets bigger, your pay and prestige will increase. What is the nature of the principal-agent problem here, and how is it related to ethical considerations?

***14.** You are the CEO of a company and are considering a new project that, if accepted, would add $1 million to the value of the company's equity. If you decide to proceed with the project, you realize that you will have to work eight extra hours each week for one year; the value to you of losing this leisure time is $51,000. Assume that your salary will not be adjusted to reflect this extra work and that the net benefit to you is your only consideration in deciding whether or not to proceed with the project.

a. What would your decision be if you owned 100% of the company's equity?
b. What would your decision be if you owned 1% of the company's equity?
c. What would your decision be if you owned 3% of the company's equity and the board of directors promised you a bonus of $25,000 if the company's equity value was increased by $50,000 or more?
d. Suppose you owned 3% of the company's equity and the board of directors promised you a bonus of $25,000 if the company's equity value was increased by $50,000 or more. Assume that accepting the project no longer adds $1 million to the company's equity value, but rather increases the equity value by $X. How high must X be for you to accept the project?
e. Evaluate your results in parts (a) to (d) in the context of the principal-agent problem.

15. Consider the case of a local supermarket manager who decides that, to increase profit, milk held in the store's storage room will no longer be refrigerated. Milk on the display shelf will still be refrigerated. What stakeholders might this affect? Will the impact of this decision be positive or negative for the stakeholders? Will it be positive or negative for the shareholders? Explain.

***16.** Consider the case of SPB Ltd., a solar panel and battery manufacturing company. You are the CEO of SPB. In producing solar panels and batteries, certain toxic chemical waste is generated and proper disposal is very expensive. A recently hired engineer has brought to you a project code named "Stealth Disposal" or SD for short. SD involves constructing underground chambers in which the toxic waste would be dumped. Since your company is in a remote location, it is unlikely that regulators will discover the unconventional disposal method. The engineer has designed a chamber to contain the hazardous waste underground and projects that there is less than a 25% chance that it will leak into ground water used for the drinking water of the nearest city. There is an up-front cost to constructing SD, but projected cost savings from using SD rather than normal disposal look very significant each year for the next 10 years – this could have an extremely positive impact on your performance bonus each year. After 10 years, the SD site would be full and other disposal methods would need to be considered. What considerations are important for your decision to accept SD or reject it? Consider how accepting this might affect you personally and how it might affect SPB. How might this tie into the principal-agent problem?

The Stock Market

17. What is the difference between a public and a private corporation?

18. What is the difference between a primary and a secondary market?

19. Explain why the bid-ask spread is a transaction cost.

20. The following quotes were observed for Buffin Corp. (ticker: BUFN) on the two dates indicated.

Buffin Corp.	BUFN
	September 14
Bid	$14.56
Ask	$14.60

Buffin Corp.	BUFN
	September 15
Bid	$15.04
Ask	$15.10

a. Suppose you decide to use a market order to buy 500 shares of BUFN on September 14 and then sell the 500 shares using a market order on September 15. Assuming no brokerage commissions, how much of a gain or loss did you make?

b. Suppose you decide to use limit orders instead of market orders. On September 14 you put in a limit order to buy 500 shares of BUFN at $14.58 per share. On September 15 you put in a limit order to sell 500 shares of BUFN at $15.08 per share. Both orders were executed on their respective days. Assuming no brokerage commissions, how much of a gain or loss did you make?

c. What are the trade-offs between using market orders and limit orders?

21. The following quotes were observed for Buffin Corp. (ticker: BUFN) on the two dates indicated.

Buffin Corp.	BUFN
	September 16
Bid	15.05
Ask	15.14

Buffin Corp.	BUFN
	September 17
Bid	15.12
Ask	15.20

a. Suppose you decide to use a market order to buy 1000 shares of BUFN on September 16 and then sell the 1000 shares using a market order on September 17. Assuming no brokerage commissions, how much of a gain or loss did you make?
b. Suppose you decide to use limit orders instead of market orders. On September 16 you put in a limit order to buy 1000 shares of BUFN at $15.08 per share. On September 17 you put in a limit order to sell 1000 shares of BUFN at $15.18 per share. Both orders were executed on their respective days. Assuming no brokerage commissions, how much of a gain or loss did you make?
c. What are the trade-offs between using market orders and limit orders?

CHAPTER

Introduction to Financial Statement Analysis

2

LEARNING OBJECTIVES

- Know why the disclosure of financial information through financial statements is critical to investors
- Understand the function of the statement of financial position
- Understand how the income statement is used
- Interpret a statement of cash flows
- Know what management's discussion and analysis and the statement of shareholders' equity are
- Use financial statement information to analyze a company's profitability, liquidity, asset efficiency, working capital, interest coverage, leverage, valuation, and operating returns
- Understand the main purpose and aspects of the Sarbanes-Oxley reforms following Enron and other financial scandals

As we discussed in Chapter 1, anyone with money to invest is a potential investor who can own shares in a corporation. As a result, corporations are often widely held, with investors ranging from individuals who hold one share to large financial institutions that own millions of shares. For example, in 2018, International Business Machines Corporation (ticker symbol: IBM) had about 921 million shares outstanding held by over 500,000 shareholders. Although the corporate organizational structure greatly facilitates the firm's access to investment capital, it also means that stock ownership is most investors' sole tie to the company. How, then, do investors learn enough about a company to know whether or not they should invest in it? One way firms evaluate their performance and communicate this information to investors is through their *financial statements*. Financial statements also enable financial managers to assess the success of their own firm and compare it to competitors.

Firms regularly issue financial statements to communicate financial information to the investment community. A detailed description of the preparation and analysis of these statements is sufficiently complicated that to do it justice would require an entire book. In this chapter, we briefly review the subject, emphasizing only the material that investors and corporate financial managers need in order to make the corporate finance decisions we discuss in the text.

We review the four main types of financial statements, present examples of these statements for a firm, and discuss where an investor or manager might find various types of information about the company. We also discuss some of the financial ratios used to assess a firm's performance and value. We close the chapter with a look at highly publicized financial reporting abuses at Enron.

2.1 Firms' Disclosure of Financial Information

financial statements Accounting reports issued by a firm quarterly and/or annually that present past performance information and a snapshot of the firm's assets and financing of those assets.

annual reports The yearly summary of business sent by public companies to their shareholders; accompanies or includes the financial statements.

Generally Accepted Accounting Principles (GAAP) A common set of rules and a standard format for companies to use when they prepare their financial reports.

auditor A neutral third party, which corporations are required to hire, that checks a firm's annual financial statements to ensure they are prepared according to GAAP and provide evidence to support the reliability of the information.

Financial statements are accounting reports issued by a firm periodically (usually quarterly and annually) that present past performance information and a snapshot of the firm's assets and the financing of those assets. Canadian public companies are required to file these reports (called interim financial statements and **annual reports**) with their provincial securities commissions. This process is centralized nationally through the System for Electronic Document Analysis and Retrieval (SEDAR). At www.sedar.com, Canadian company filings can be easily accessed. U.S. public companies are required to file their financial statements with the U.S. Securities and Exchange Commission (SEC) on a quarterly basis on form 10-Q and annually on form 10-K.[1] Companies in Canada and the United States must also send an annual report with their financial statements to their shareholders each year. Often, private companies also prepare financial statements, but they usually do not have to disclose these reports to the public. Financial statements are important tools with which investors, financial analysts, and other interested outside parties (such as creditors) obtain information about a corporation. They are also useful for managers within the firm as a source of information for the corporate financial decisions we discussed in the previous chapter. In this section, we examine the guidelines for preparing financial statements and introduce the different types of financial statements.

Types of Financial Statements

Under IFRS, every public company is required to produce a *statement of financial position* (also known as a *balance sheet*), *statement of comprehensive income* (which includes the *income statement*), *statement of cash flows*, *statement of changes in equity*, and *notes including accounting policies*. These financial statements provide investors and creditors with an overview of the firm's financial performance. In the sections that follow, we take a close look at the content of these financial statements.

PREPARATION OF FINANCIAL STATEMENTS

Reports about a company's performance must be understandable and accurate. **Generally Accepted Accounting Principles (GAAP)** provide a framework including a common set of rules and a standard format for public companies to use when they prepare their reports. This standardization also makes it easier to compare the financial results of different firms. The Accounting Standards Board of Canada has adopted International Financial Reporting Standards (IFRS) for GAAP in Canada for publicly accountable enterprises. Using IFRS makes financial statements for Canadian companies comparable to those for companies in other countries that have adopted IFRS.

Investors also need some assurance that the financial statements are prepared accurately. Corporations are required to hire a neutral third party, known as an **auditor**, to check the annual financial statements, ensure they are prepared according to GAAP, and verify that the information is reliable.

[1]The SEC was established by Congress in 1934 to regulate securities (e.g., stocks and bonds) issued to the public and the financial markets (exchanges) on which those securities trade.

INTERNATIONAL FINANCIAL REPORTING STANDARDS

Because GAAP differ among countries, companies face tremendous accounting complexities when they operate internationally. Investors also face difficulty interpreting financial statements of foreign companies, which is often considered a major barrier to international capital mobility. As companies and capital markets become more global, however, interest in harmonization of accounting standards across countries has increased.

The most important harmonization project began in 1973 when representatives of 10 countries (including Canada) established the International Accounting Standards Committee. This effort led to the creation of the International Accounting Standards Board (IASB) in 2001, with headquarters in London. Now the IASB has issued a set of International Financial Reporting Standards (IFRS).

The IFRS are taking root throughout the world. The European Union (EU) approved an accounting regulation in 2002 requiring all publicly traded EU companies to follow IFRS in their consolidated financial statements starting in 2005. Canadian publicly accountable enterprises (we will simply refer to them as public companies from this point on) must follow IFRS in their financial statements for fiscal years beginning January 1, 2011, or later. Many other countries have adopted IFRS for all listed companies, including Australia and several countries in Latin America and Africa. Indeed, all major stock exchanges around the world accept IFRS except the United States and Japan, which maintain their local GAAP. In November 2007, the United States' SEC allowed foreign companies listed on U.S. exchanges to use IFRS rather than U.S. GAAP. This will be important for Canadian companies, as they will no longer have to reconcile their statements with U.S. GAAP if their filings correspond to IFRS.

The main conceptual difference between U.S. GAAP and IFRS is that U.S. GAAP are based primarily on accounting rules with specific guidance in applying them, whereas IFRS are based more on principles requiring professional judgment by accountants, and specific guidance in application is limited. In implementation, the main difference is how assets and liabilities are valued. Whereas U.S. GAAP are based primarily on historical cost accounting, IFRS places more emphasis on "fair value" of assets and liabilities, or estimates of market values. Effort to achieve convergence between U.S. GAAP and IFRS was spurred by the Sarbanes-Oxley Act (SOX) of 2002 in the United States. It included a provision that U.S. accounting standards move toward international convergence on high-quality accounting standards. This process is still ongoing in 2018 and it is not clear if there will ever be full convergence.

CONCEPT CHECK

1. What is the role of an auditor?
2. What are the four financial statements that all public companies must produce?

2.2 The Statement of Financial Position or Balance Sheet

statement of financial position or **balance sheet**
A list of a firm's assets, liabilities, and equity that provides a snapshot of the firm's financial position at a given point in time.

The **statement of financial position** or **balance sheet**,[2] lists the firm's *assets, liabilities, and equity,* providing a snapshot of the firm's financial position at a given point in time. Table 2.1 shows the statement of financial position for a fictitious company, Global Corporation. Notice that the statement of financial position is divided into two parts, with one part including the assets and the other part including the liabilities and equity.

[2]In IFRS, the balance sheet is referred to as the *statement of financial position*; however, some companies still use the balance sheet terminology in their statements.

assets The cash, inventory, property, plant and equipment, and other investments a company has made.

liabilities A firm's obligations to its creditors.

shareholders' equity An accounting measure of a firm's net worth that represents the difference between the firm's assets and its liabilities.

common stock The amount that shareholders have directly invested in the firm through purchasing stock from the company.

1. The **assets** list the firm's cash, inventory, property, plant and equipment, and any other investments the company has made.
2. The **liabilities** show the firm's obligations to its creditors.
3. Also shown with liabilities on the right side of the statement of financial position is the *shareholders' equity.* **Shareholders' equity**, the difference between the firm's assets and liabilities, is an accounting measure of the firm's net worth. For Global, the shareholders' equity has two parts: (1) **common stock**, the amount that shareholders have directly invested in the firm through purchasing stock from the company and (2) *retained earnings*, which are profits made by the firm but retained within the firm and reinvested in assets or held as cash. We will take a more detailed look at retained earnings in our discussion of the statement of cash flows later in this chapter.

The assets on the left side show how the firm uses its capital (its investments), and the information on the right side summarizes the sources of capital, or how the firm raises the money it needs. Because of the way shareholders' equity is calculated, the left and right sides must balance:

The Statement of Financial Position Identity

$$\text{Assets} = \text{Liabilities} + \text{Shareholders' Equity} \tag{2.1}$$

In Table 2.1, total assets for 2018 ($170.1 million) are equal to total liabilities ($147.9 million) plus shareholders' equity ($22.2 million).

TABLE 2.1 Global Corporation Statement of Financial Position for 2018 and 2017

Assets	2018	2017	Liabilities	2018	2017
Current Assets			Current Liabilities		
Cash	23.2	20.5	Accounts payable	29.2	26.5
Accounts receivable	18.5	13.2	Notes payable/ short-term debt	5.5	3.2
Inventories	15.3	14.3			
Total current assets	57.0	48.0	Total current liabilities	34.7	29.7
Long-Term Assets			Long-Term Liabilities		
Net property, plant, and equipment	113.1	80.9	Long-term debt	113.2	78.0
Total long-term assets	113.1	80.9	Total long-term liabilities	113.2	78.0
			Total Liabilities	**147.9**	**107.7**
			Shareholders' Equity		
			Common stock	8.0	8.0
			Retained earnings	14.2	13.2
			Total Shareholders' Equity	**22.2**	**21.2**
Total Assets	**170.1**	**128.9**	**Total Liabilities and Shareholders' Equity**	**170.1**	**128.9**

We now examine the firm's assets, liabilities, and shareholders' equity in more detail. Finally, we evaluate the firm's financial standing by analyzing the information contained in the statement of financial position.

Assets

current assets Cash or assets that could be converted into cash within one year.

marketable securities Short-term, low-risk investments that can be easily sold and converted to cash.

accounts receivable Amounts owed to a firm by customers who have purchased goods or services on credit.

inventories A firm's raw materials as well as its work in progress and finished goods.

In Table 2.1, Global's assets are divided into *current* and *long-term assets*. We discuss each in turn.

Current Assets. **Current assets** are either cash or assets that could be converted into cash within one year. This category includes the following:

1. Cash and other **marketable securities**, which are short-term, low-risk investments that can be easily sold and converted to cash (such as money market investments, like government debt, that mature within a year).
2. **Accounts receivable**, which are amounts owed to the firm by customers who have purchased goods or services on credit.
3. **Inventories**, which are composed of raw materials as well as work in progress and finished goods.
4. Other current assets, which is a catch-all category that includes items such as prepaid expenses (expenses that have been paid in advance, such as rent or insurance).

long-term assets Assets that produce tangible benefits for more than one year.

depreciation A yearly deduction a firm makes from the value of its fixed assets (other than land) over time, according to a depreciation schedule that depends on an asset's life span.

book value The acquisition cost of an asset less its accumulated depreciation.

Long-Term Assets. Assets, such as real estate or machinery, that produce tangible benefits for more than one year are called **long-term assets**. If Global spends $2 million on new equipment, this $2 million will be included with net property, plant, and equipment under long-term assets on the statement of financial position. Because equipment tends to wear out or become obsolete over time, Global will reduce the value recorded for this equipment through a yearly deduction called **depreciation** according to a depreciation schedule that depends on an asset's life span. Depreciation is not an actual cash expense that the firm pays; it is a way of recognizing that buildings and equipment wear out and, thus, become less valuable the older they get. The **book value** of an asset is equal to its acquisition cost less accumulated depreciation. The figures for net property, plant, and equipment show the total book value of these assets.

Other long-term assets can include such items as property not used in business operations, start-up costs in connection with a new business, trademarks and patents, property held for sale, and goodwill. The sum of all the firm's assets is the total assets at the bottom of the left side of the statement of financial position in Table 2.1.

Liabilities

current liabilities Liabilities that will be satisfied within one year.

accounts payable The amounts owed to creditors for products or services purchased with credit.

notes payable and **short-term debt** Loans that must be repaid in the next year.

We now examine the liabilities shown on the right side of the statement of financial position, which are divided into *current* and *long-term liabilities*.

Current Liabilities. Liabilities that will be satisfied within one year are known as **current liabilities**. They include the following:

1. **Accounts payable**, the amounts owed to suppliers for products or services purchased with credit.
2. **Notes payable** and **short-term debt**, loans that must be repaid in the next year. Any repayment of long-term debt that will occur within the next year would also be listed here as current maturities of long-term debt.

3. Accrual items, such as salary or taxes, that are owed but have not yet been paid, and deferred or unearned revenue, which is revenue that has been received for products that have not yet been delivered.

net working capital The difference between a firm's current assets and current liabilities that represents the capital available in the short term to run the business.

The difference between current assets and current liabilities is the firm's **net working capital**, the capital available in the short term to run the business:

$$\text{Net Working Capital} = \text{Current Assets} - \text{Current Liabilities} \tag{2.2}$$

For example, in 2018, Global's net working capital totalled $22.3 million ($57.0 million in current assets − $34.7 million in current liabilities). Firms with low (or negative) net working capital may face a shortage of funds. In such cases, the liabilities due in the short term exceed the company's cash and expected payments on receivables.

Long-Term Liabilities. Long-term liabilities are liabilities that extend beyond one year. When a firm needs to raise funds to purchase an asset or make an investment, it may borrow those funds through a long-term loan. That loan would appear on the statement of financial position as **long-term debt**, which is any loan or debt obligation with a maturity of more than a year.

long-term debt Any loan or debt obligation with a maturity of more than a year.

Shareholders' Equity

The sum of the current liabilities and long-term liabilities is total liabilities. The difference between the firm's assets and liabilities is the *shareholders' equity*; it is also called the **book value of equity**. As we stated earlier, it represents the net worth of the firm from an accounting perspective.

book value of equity The difference between the book value of a firm's assets and its liabilities; also called shareholders' equity, it represents the net worth of a firm from an accounting perspective.

Ideally, the statement of financial position would provide us with an accurate assessment of the true value of the firm's equity. Unfortunately, this is unlikely to be the case. First, many of the assets listed on the statement of financial position are valued based on their historical cost rather than their true value today. For example, an office building is listed on the statement of financial position according to its historical cost less its accumulated depreciation. But the actual value of the office building today may be very different than this amount; in fact, it may be much *more* than the amount the firm paid for it years ago. The same is true for other property, plant, and equipment: the true value today of an asset may be very different from, and even exceed, its book value. A second, and probably more important, problem is that *many of the firm's valuable assets are not captured on the statement of financial position.* Consider, for example, the expertise of the firm's employees, the firm's reputation in the marketplace, the relationships with customers and suppliers, and the quality of the management team. All these assets add to the value of the firm but do not appear on the statement of financial position. Although the book value of a firm's equity is not a good estimate of its true value as an ongoing firm, it is sometimes used as an estimate of the **liquidation value** of the firm—the value that would be left after its assets were sold and liabilities paid.

liquidation value The value of a firm after its assets are sold and liabilities paid.

Market Value versus Book Value

For these reasons, the book value of equity is an inaccurate assessment of the actual value of the firm's equity. Thus, it is not surprising that the book value of equity will often differ substantially from the amount investors are willing to pay for the equity. The total market value of a firm's equity equals the market price per share times the number of shares, referred to as the company's **market capitalization**. The market value of a stock does not depend on the historical cost of the firm's assets; instead, it depends on what investors expect those assets to produce in the future. To see the difference, think about what happens when a company like Bombardier unveils a new plane. If investors

market capitalization The total market value of equity; equals the market price per share times the number of shares.

have favourable expectations about future cash flows from selling those planes, the stock price will increase immediately, elevating Bombardier's market value. However, the revenue from selling the planes will be reflected in Bombardier's financial statements only when the company actually sells them.

EXAMPLE 2.1 Market versus Book Value

PROBLEM

If Global has 3.6 million shares outstanding, and these shares are trading for a price of $10.00 per share, what is Global's market capitalization? How does the market capitalization compare to Global's book value of equity?

SOLUTION

Plan

Market capitalization is equal to price per share times shares outstanding. We can find Global's book value of equity at the bottom of the right side of its statement of financial position.

Execute

Global's market capitalization is 3.6 million shares × 10.00/share = $36 million. This market capitalization is significantly higher than Global's book value of equity of $22.2 million.

Evaluate

Global must have sources of value that do not appear on the statement of financial position. These include potential opportunities for growth, the quality of the management team, relationships with suppliers and customers, etc.

Finally, we note that the book value of equity can be negative (liabilities exceed assets) and that a negative book value of equity is not necessarily an indication of poor performance. Successful firms are often able to borrow in excess of the book value of their assets because creditors recognize that the market value of the assets is far higher. For example, in June 2005, Amazon.com had total liabilities of $2.6 billion and a book value of equity of –$64 million. At the same time, the market value of its equity was over $15 billion. Clearly, investors recognized that Amazon's assets were worth far more than the book value reported on the balance sheet. By March 2018, several years of strong growth had brought its book value of equity to over $27 billion and its market value of equity to more than $737 billion!

Market-to-Book Ratio

market-to-book ratio (price-to-book [P/B] ratio) The ratio of a firm's market (equity) capitalization to the book value of its shareholders' equity.

In Example 2.1, we compared the market and book values of Global's equity. A common way to make this comparison is to compute the **market-to-book ratio (price-to-book [P/B] ratio)**, which is the ratio of a firm's market capitalization to the book value of shareholders' equity:

$$\text{Market-to-Book Ratio} = \frac{\text{Market Value of Equity}}{\text{Book Value of Equity}} \tag{2.3}$$

It is one of many financial ratios used to evaluate a firm. The market-to-book ratio for most successful firms substantially exceeds 1, indicating that the value of the firm's assets when put to use exceeds their historical cost (or liquidation value). The ratio will vary across firms due to differences in fundamental firm characteristics as well as the value added by management. Thus, this ratio is one way a company's stock price provides feedback to its managers on the market's assessment of their decisions.

In mid-2006, Ford Motor Company (ticker symbol: F) had a market-to-book ratio of 0.89, a reflection of investors' assessment that many of Ford's plants and other assets were unlikely to be profitable and were worth less than their book value. In the following years, Ford had such large losses that its book value of equity fell below zero and the market-to-book ratio fell to −35.57 by late 2010. In 2010, the average market-to-book ratio for large U.S. firms was close to 4.0. By March 2018 Ford's market-to-book ratio was about 1.2 and the average for large U.S. firms was about 7.4. Analysts often classify firms with low market-to-book ratios as **value stocks**, and those with high market-to-book ratios as **growth stocks**. Negative market-to-book ratios (like Ford's in 2010) are not considered meaningful, because we normally associate a higher ratio with a better assessment of a firm's future performance. With a negative market-to-book ratio, a higher ratio (close to zero) can occur when the market value of a firm is close to zero or when the book value of equity is far below zero. A near-zero market-to-book value is consistent with expectations that the firm will probably not survive. In contrast, a firm with a book value of equity far below zero may be a turnaround prospect and its future may be quite bright. The implication of a negative market-to-book value ratio is simply not clear.

value stocks Firms with low market-to-book ratios.

growth stocks Firms with high market-to-book ratios.

Enterprise Value

A firm's market capitalization measures the market value of the firm's equity, or the value that remains after the firm has paid its debts. But what is the value of the business itself? The **enterprise value** of a firm assesses the value of the underlying business assets, unencumbered by debt and separate from any cash and marketable securities. We compute it as follows:

$$\text{Enterprise Value} = \text{Market Value of Equity} + \text{Debt} - \text{Cash} \tag{2.4}$$

For example, given its market capitalization from Example 2.1, Global's enterprise value in 2018 is 36 + 118.7 − 23.2 = \$131.5 million. We can interpret the enterprise value as the cost to take over the business. That is, it would cost 36 + 118.7 = \$154.7 million to buy all of Global's equity and pay off its debts. Because we would acquire Global's \$23.2 million in cash, the net cost is only 154.7 − 23.2 = \$131.5 million.

enterprise value The total market value of a firm's equity and debt, less the value of its cash and marketable securities; a measure of the value of the firm's underlying business.

EXAMPLE 2.2 Computing Enterprise Value

PROBLEM

In March 2018, BCE Inc. had a share price of \$56.50 and 901 million shares outstanding. BCE had a market-to-book ratio of 2.61, a book debt-equity ratio of 1.42, and cash of \$600 million. What was BCE's market capitalization? What was its enterprise value?

SOLUTION

Plan

We will solve the problem using Equation 2.5: Enterprise Value = Market Value of Equity + Debt − Cash. We can compute the market capitalization by multiplying the share price by the shares outstanding. We are given the amount of cash. We are not given the debt directly, but we are given the book debt-equity ratio. If we knew the book value of equity, we could use the ratio to infer the value of the debt. Since we can compute the market value of equity (market capitalization) and we ▶

have the market-to-book ratio, we can compute the book value of equity, so that is the last piece of information we will need.

■ Execute

BCE had a market capitalization of \$56.50/share × 901 million shares = \$50.9065 billion.

We divide the market value of equity by BCE's market-to-book ratio to calculate BCE's book value of equity as 50.9065/2.61 = \$19.504406 billion. Given a book debt-equity ratio of 1.42, BCE had total debt of 1.42 × 19.504406 = \$27.696257 billion. Thus, BCE's enterprise value was 50.9065 + 27.696257 − 0.6 = \$78.002757 billion.

■ Evaluate

As you can see, BCE's enterprise value is larger than its market capitalization. This is because enterprise value shows the value of all assets (not including cash) financed by all sources. These assets are not just financed with equity; a significant portion of the assets are financed with debt.

CONCEPT CHECK

3. What is depreciation designed to capture?
4. The book value of a company's assets usually does not equal the market value of those assets. What are some reasons for this difference?

2.3 The Statement of Comprehensive Income and Income Statement

income statement A list of a firm's revenues and expenses over a period of time.

net income or **earnings** The last or "bottom" line of a firm's income statement that is a measure of the firm's income over a period of time.

When you want someone to get to the point, you might ask them for the "bottom line." This expression comes from the *income statement*. The **income statement** lists the firm's revenues and expenses over a period of time. The last, or bottom, line of the income statement shows the firm's **net income** or **earnings**, which is a measure of its profitability during the period. The income statement is sometimes called a *statement of profit and loss*, or *"P&L"* statement. Under IFRS, the statement of comprehensive income includes the income statement and adds "other comprehensive income" to get overall comprehensive income. This other comprehensive income includes unrealized gains or losses that result from applying fair value accounting (or marking to market) of various financial instruments. In this section, we examine the components of the income statement in detail and introduce ratios we can use to analyze this data.

Table 2.2 shows Global's income statement for 2018 and 2017.

Earnings Calculations

Whereas the statement of financial position shows the firm's assets and liabilities at a given point in time, the income statement shows the flow of revenues and expenses generated by those assets and liabilities between two dates. We examine each category on Global's statement.

TABLE 2.2 Global Corporation

GLOBAL CORPORATION Income Statement Year ended December 31 (in $ millions)		
	2018	**2017**
Net sales	186.7	176.1
Cost of sales	–153.4	–147.3
Gross Profit	**33.3**	**28.8**
Selling, general, and administrative expenses	–13.5	–13
Research and development	–8.2	–7.6
Depreciation and amortization	–1.2	–1.1
Operating Income	**10.4**	**7.1**
Other income	—	—
Earnings Before Interest and Taxes (EBIT)	**10.4**	**7.1**
Interest income (expense)	–7.7	–4.6
Pre-tax Income	**2.7**	**2.5**
Taxes	–0.7	–0.6
Net Income	**2.0**	**1.9**
Earnings per share:	$0.56	$0.53
Diluted earnings per share:	$0.53	$0.50

Gross Profit. The first two lines of the income statement list the revenues from sales of products and the costs incurred to make and sell the products. Note that, in accounting terms, *revenues* and *net sales* are often used interchangeably. Net sales is simply gross sales minus any returns, discounts, and allowances. We will simply use the term *sales* from here on. The third line is **gross profit**, the difference between sales revenues and the costs.

gross profit The third line of an income statement that represents the difference between a firm's sales revenues and its costs.

Operating Expenses. The next group of items is operating expenses. These are expenses from the ordinary course of running the business that are not directly related to producing the goods or services being sold. They include administrative expenses and overhead, salaries, marketing costs, and research and development expenses. The third type of operating expense, depreciation and amortization (a charge that captures the change in value of acquired assets), is not an actual cash expense but represents an estimate of the costs that arise from wear and tear or obsolescence of the firm's assets.[3] The firm's gross profit net of operating expenses is called **operating income**.

operating income A firm's gross profit less its operating expenses.

Earnings Before Interest and Taxes. We next include other sources of income or expenses that arise from activities that are not the central part of a company's business.

[3]Depreciation and amortization are not deductible for tax purposes. Instead, the Canada Revenue Agency (CRA) uses capital cost allowance (CCA) for tax purposes. CCA rates vary depending on the asset type (or class) and cover tangible and intangible (e.g., patents) assets.

Cash flows from the firm's financial investments are one example of other income that would be listed here. After we have adjusted for other sources of income or expenses, we have the firm's earnings before interest and taxes, or **EBIT**.

EBIT A firm's earnings before interest and taxes are deducted.

Pre-tax and Net Income. From EBIT, we deduct the interest paid on outstanding debt to compute Global's pre-tax income, and then we deduct corporate taxes to determine the firm's net income.

Net income represents the total earnings of the firm's equity holders. It is often reported on a per-share basis as the firm's **earnings per share (EPS)**, which we compute by dividing net income by the total number of shares outstanding:

earnings per share (EPS) A firm's net income divided by the total number of shares outstanding.

$$\text{EPS} = \frac{\text{Net Income}}{\text{Shares Outstanding}} = \frac{\$2.0 \text{ million}}{3.6 \text{ million shares}} = 0.56 \text{ per share} \tag{2.5}$$

Although Global has only 3.6 million shares outstanding as of the end of 2018, the number of shares outstanding may grow if Global has made commitments that would cause it to issue more shares. Consider these two examples:

1. Suppose Global compensates its employees or executives with **stock options** that give the holder the right to buy a certain number of shares by a specific date at a specific price. If employees "exercise" these options, the company issues new stock and the number of shares outstanding will grow.
2. The number of shares may also grow if the firm issues **convertible bonds**, a form of debt that can be converted to shares of common stock.

stock options Right to buy a certain number of shares of stock by a specific date at a specific price.

convertible bonds Corporate bonds with a provision that gives the bondholder an option to convert each bond owned into a fixed number of shares of common stock.

In the cases of stock options and convertible bonds, because there will be more total shares to divide the same earnings, this growth in the number of shares is referred to as **dilution**. Firms disclose the potential for dilution from options they have awarded by reporting **diluted EPS**, which shows the earnings per share the company would have if the stock options were exercised. For example, if Global has awarded options for 200,000 shares of stock to its key executives, its diluted EPS is \$2.0 million/3.8 million shares = \$0.53.

dilution An increase in the total number of shares that will divide a fixed amount of earnings.

diluted EPS A firm's disclosure of its potential for dilution from options it has awarded.

EBITDA

As will become clear when we discuss the statement of cash flows in the next section, neither EBIT nor net income are the same as the firm's cash flow. So, financial analysts often compute a firm's earnings before interest, taxes, depreciation, and amortization, or **EBITDA**. Because depreciation and amortization are not cash expenses for the firm, EBITDA reflects the cash a firm has earned from its operations. Global's EBITDA in 2018 was 10.4 + 1.2 = \$11.6 million.

EBITDA A computation of a firm's earnings before interest, taxes, depreciation, and amortization are deducted.

CONCEPT CHECK

5. What do a firm's earnings measure?
6. What is meant by dilution?

2.4 The Statement of Cash Flows

The income statement provides a measure of the firm's profit over a given time period. However, it does not indicate the amount of *cash* the firm has earned. There are two reasons that net income does not correspond to cash earned. First, there are non-cash entries on the income statement, such as depreciation and amortization. Second, certain uses, such as the purchase of a building or expenditures on inventory, and sources of cash,

statement of cash flows
An accounting statement that shows how a firm has used the cash it earned during a set period.

such as the collection of accounts receivable, are not reported on the income statement. The firm's **statement of cash flows** uses the information from the income statement and statement of financial position to determine how much cash the firm has generated and how that cash has been allocated during a set period. Cash is important because it is needed to pay bills and maintain operations and is the source of any return of investment for investors. Thus, from the perspective of an investor attempting to value the firm or a financial manager concerned about cash flows (vs. earnings), the statement of cash flows provides what may be the most important information of the four financial statements.

The statement of cash flows is divided into three sections: operating activities, investment activities, and financing activities. These sections roughly correspond to the three major jobs of the financial manager.

1. Operating activity starts with net income from the income statement. It then adjusts this number by adding back all non-cash entries related to the firm's operating activities.
2. Investment activity lists the cash used for investment.
3. Financing activity shows the flow of cash between the firm and its investors.

Global's statement of cash flows is shown in Table 2.3. In this section, we take a close look at each component of the statement of cash flows.

TABLE 2.3 Global Corporation's Statement of Cash Flows for 2018 and 2017

GLOBAL CORPORATION Statement of Cash Flows Year ended December 31 (in $ millions)		
	2018	**2017**
Operating activities		
Net income	2.0	1.9
Depreciation and amortization	1.2	1.1
Cash effect of changes in		
Accounts receivable	–5.3	–0.3
Accounts payable	2.7	–0.5
Inventory	–1.0	–1.0
Cash from operating activities	–0.4	1.2
Investment activities		
Capital expenditures	–33.4	–4.0
Acquisitions and other investing activity		
Cash from investing activities	–33.4	–4.0
Financing activities		
Dividends paid	–1.0	–1.0
Sale or purchase of stock	—	—
Increase in short-term borrowing	2.3	3.0
Increase in long-term borrowing	35.2	2.5
Cash from financing activities	36.5	4.5
Change in cash and cash equivalents	2.7	1.7

Operating Activity

The first section of Global's statement of cash flows adjusts net income by all non-cash items related to operating activity. For instance, depreciation is deducted when computing net income, but it is not an actual cash expense. Thus, we add it back to net income when determining the amount of cash the firm has generated. Similarly, we add back any other non-cash expenses (e.g., future income taxes).

Next, we adjust for changes to net working capital that arise from changes to accounts receivable, accounts payable, or inventory. When a firm sells a product, it records the revenue as income even though it may not receive the cash from that sale immediately. Instead, it may grant the customer credit and let the customer pay in the future. The customer's obligation adds to the firm's accounts receivable. We use the following guidelines to adjust for changes in working capital:

1. Accounts receivable: When a sale is recorded as part of net income, but the cash has not yet been received from the customer, we must adjust the cash flows by *deducting* the increases in accounts receivable. These increases represent additional lending by the firm to its customers and it reduces the cash available to the firm.
2. Accounts payable: Similarly, we *add* increases in accounts payable. Accounts payable represents borrowing by the firm from its suppliers. This borrowing increases the cash available to the firm.
3. Inventory: Finally, we *deduct* increases in inventory. Increases in inventory are not recorded as an expense and do not contribute to net income. (The cost of the goods are included in net income only when the goods are actually sold.) However, the cost of increasing inventory is a cash expense for the firm and must be deducted.

Working capital adjustments address the difference between the time when sales and costs are recorded on the income statement and when the cash actually goes in and out of the firm. For example, in 2018, we subtracted the $5.3 million increase in accounts receivable from net income as part of the operating cash flow calculation. What happened? From Table 2.2, we see that Global had $10.6 million more in sales in 2018 than in 2017. However, from Table 2.1, we also see that Global's accounts receivable increased to $18.5 million in 2018 from $13.2 million in 2017. So, even though Global's sales were up considerably, the company has not yet collected all the cash flow for those sales; instead, Global's customers owe the company $5.3 million more at the end of 2018 than they did at the end of 2017. Because the statement of cash flows starts with net income, which includes sales for which Global has not yet been paid, we deduct the additional $5.3 million in sales that Global is still owed when computing the actual cash flows it generated.

We must make a similar adjustment for inventory. Global does not record the cost of the inventory until it is sold, when it is in cost of goods sold. However, when the company actually pays for the inventory, cash has flowed out of Global, decreasing operating cash flow. The opposite is true for accounts payable—Global has recorded additional expenses without actually paying for them yet. Those expenses reduce net income but do not represent cash outflows.

Finally, we add depreciation to net income before calculating operating cash flow. Depreciation is an accounting adjustment to book value that is an expense but not a cash outflow; that is, when Global's property, plant, and equipment depreciate by $1.2 million, the loss does not literally cost Global $1.2 million in cash flow. Because this is an expense that reduces net income but is not an actual cash outflow, we must add it back to calculate cash flow. We will talk more about depreciation when we do capital budgeting in Chapter 9. All these adjustments mean that cash flows can be very different from net income. Although Global showed positive net income on the income statement, it actually had a negative $0.4 million cash flow from operating activity, in large part because of the increase in accounts receivable.

Investment Activity

capital expenditures Purchases of new property, plant, and equipment.

The next section of the statement of cash flows shows the cash required for investment activities. Purchases of new property, plant, and equipment are referred to as **capital expenditures**. Recall that capital expenditures do not appear immediately as expenses on the income statement. Instead, the firm depreciates these assets and deducts depreciation expenses over time. To determine the firm's cash flow, we have already added back depreciation, because it is not an actual cash expense. Now, we subtract the actual capital expenditure that the firm made. Similarly, we also deduct other assets purchased or investments made by the firm, such as acquisitions. In Table 2.3, we see that in 2018 Global spent $33.4 million in cash on investing activities.

Financing Activity

The last section of the statement of cash flows shows the cash flows from financing activities. Dividends paid to shareholders are a cash outflow. Global paid $1 million to its shareholders as dividends in 2018.

retained earnings The difference between a firm's net income and the amount it spends on dividends.

payout ratio The ratio of a firm's dividends to its net income.

The difference between a firm's net income and the amount it spends on dividends is referred to as the firm's **retained earnings** for that year:

$$\text{Retained Earnings} = \text{Net Income} - \text{Dividends} \tag{2.6}$$

Global retained $2 million − $1 million = $1 million, or 50% of its earnings in 2018. This makes its *payout ratio* for 2018 equal to 50%. A firm's **payout ratio** is the ratio of its dividends to its net income:

$$\text{Payout Ratio} = \frac{\text{Dividends}}{\text{Net Income}} \tag{2.7}$$

Also listed under financing activity is any cash the company received from the sale of its own stock, or cash spent buying (repurchasing) its own stock. Global did not issue or repurchase stock during this period.

The last items to include in this section result from changes to Global's short-term and long-term borrowing. Global raised money by issuing debt, so the increases in short-term and long-term borrowing represent cash inflows. The last line of the statement of cash flows combines the cash flows from these three activities to calculate the overall change in the firm's cash balance over the period of the statement. In this case, Global had cash inflows of $2.7 million. By looking at the statement in Table 2.3 as a whole, we can determine that Global chose to borrow (mainly in the form of long-term debt) to cover the cost of its investment and operating activities. Although the firm's cash balance has increased, Global's negative operating cash flows and relatively high expenditures on investment activities might give investors some reasons for concern. If that pattern continues, Global will need to continue to borrow to remain in business.

EXAMPLE 2.3 The Impact of Depreciation on Cash Flow

PROBLEM

Suppose Global had an additional $1 million depreciation expense in 2018. If Global's tax rate on pre-tax income is 26%, what would be the impact of this expense on Global's earnings? How would it impact Global's cash at the end of the year?

SOLUTION

Plan

Depreciation is an operating expense, so Global's operating income, EBIT, and pre-tax income would be affected. With a tax rate of 26%, Global's tax bill will decrease by 26 cents for every dollar that pre-tax income is reduced. In order to determine how Global's cash would be affected, we have to determine the effect of the additional depreciation on cash flows. Recall that depreciation is not an actual cash outflow, even though it is treated as an expense, so the only effect on cash flow is through the reduction in taxes.

Execute

Global's operating income, EBIT, and pre-tax income would fall by \$1 million because of the \$1 million in additional operating expense due to depreciation.

This \$1 million decrease in pre-tax income would reduce Global's tax bill by 26% $\times$ \$1 million = \$0.26 million. Therefore, net income would fall by 1 − 0.26 = \$0.74 million.

On the statement of cash flows, net income would fall by \$0.74 million, but we would add back the additional depreciation of \$1 million, because it is not a cash expense. Thus, cash from operating activities would rise by −0.74 + 1 = \$0.26 million. Therefore, Global's cash balance at the end of the year would increase by \$0.26 million, the amount of the tax savings that resulted from the additional depreciation deduction.

Evaluate

The increase in cash balance comes completely from the reduction in taxes. Because Global pays \$0.26 million less in taxes even though its cash expenses have not increased, it has \$0.26 million more in cash at the end of the year.

CONCEPT CHECK

7. Why does a firm's net income not correspond to cash earned?
8. What are the components of the statement of cash flows?

2.5 Other Financial Statement Information

The most important elements of a firm's financial statements are the statement of financial position, income statement, and the statement of cash flows, which we have already discussed. Several other pieces of information contained in the financial statements warrant brief mention: the *management discussion and analysis, the statement of shareholders' equity*, and *notes to the financial statements*.

statement of shareholders' equity
An accounting statement that breaks down the shareholders' equity computed on the statement of financial position into the amount that came from issuing new shares versus retained earnings.

Statement of Shareholders' Equity

The **statement of shareholders' equity** breaks down the shareholders' equity computed on the statement of financial position into the amount that came from issuing new shares versus retained earnings. Because the book value of shareholders' equity is not a useful assessment of value for financial purposes, the information contained in the statement of shareholders' equity is also not particularly revealing, so we do not spend time on the statement here.

Management Discussion and Analysis

management discussion and analysis (MD&A) A preface to the financial statements in which a company's management discusses the recent year (or quarter), providing a background on the company and any significant events that may have occurred.

off-balance sheet transactions Transactions or arrangements that can have a material impact on a firm's future performance yet do not appear on the statement of financial position.

The **management discussion and analysis (MD&A)** is a preface to the financial statements in which the company's management discusses the recent year (or quarter), providing a background on the company and any significant events that may have occurred. Management may also discuss the coming year and outline goals and new projects.

Management must also discuss any important risks that the firm faces or issues that may affect the firm's liquidity or resources. Management is also required to disclose any **off-balance sheet transactions**, which are transactions or arrangements that can have a material impact on the firm's future performance yet do not appear on the statement of financial position. For example, if a firm has made guarantees that it will compensate a buyer for losses related to an asset purchased from the firm, these guarantees represent a potential future liability for the firm that must be disclosed as part of the MD&A.

Notes to the Financial Statements

In addition to the four financial statements, companies provide extensive notes with additional details on the information provided in the statements. For example, the notes document important accounting assumptions that were used in preparing the statements. They often provide information specific to a firm's subsidiaries or its separate product lines. They show the details of the firm's stock-based compensation plans for employees and the different types of debt the firm has outstanding. Details of acquisitions, spinoffs, leases, taxes, and risk management activities are also given. The information provided in the notes is often very important to a full interpretation of the firm's financial statements.

CONCEPT CHECK

9. Where do off-balance sheet transactions appear in a firm's financial statements?
10. What information does the notes to financial statements provide?

2.6 Financial Statement Analysis

Investors often use accounting statements to evaluate a firm in one of two ways:

1. Compare the firm with itself by analyzing how the firm has changed over time.
2. Compare the firm to other similar firms using a common set of financial ratios.

In this section we will describe the most commonly used ratios—those related to profitability, liquidity, asset efficiency, working capital, interest coverage, leverage, valuation, and operating returns—and explain how each one is used in practice.

Profitability Ratios

We introduce three profitability ratios: *gross margin, operating margin,* and *net profit margin.*

gross margin The ratio of gross profit to revenues (sales); it reflects the ability of the company to sell a product for more than the sum of the direct costs of making it.

Gross Margin. The **gross margin** of a firm is the ratio of gross profit to revenues (sales):

$$\text{Gross Margin} = \frac{\text{Gross Profit}}{\text{Sales}} \tag{2.8}$$

The gross margin simply reflects the ability of the company to sell a product for more than the sum of the direct costs of making it. All the firm's other expenses of doing business (those not directly related to producing the goods sold) must be covered by this margin. In 2018, Global's gross profit was $33.3 million and its sales were $186.7 million, for a gross margin of 33.3/186.7 = 17.84%.

operating margin The ratio of operating income to revenues; it reveals how much a company has earned from each dollar of sales before interest and taxes are deducted.

Operating Margin. Because operating income reflects all of the expenses of doing business, another important profitability ratio is the **operating margin**, the ratio of operating income to revenues:

$$\text{Operating Margin} = \frac{\text{Operating Income}}{\text{Total Sales}} \tag{2.9}$$

The operating margin reveals how much a company earns before interest and taxes from each dollar of sales. Global's operating margin in 2018 was 10.4/186.7 = 5.57%, an increase from its 2017 operating margin of 7.1/176.1 = 4.03%. By comparing operating margins across firms within an industry, we can assess the relative efficiency of firms' operations. For example, for the fiscal year ending in 2017, Air Canada (ticker symbol: AC) had an operating margin of 8.39%. However, competitor WestJet (ticker symbol: WJA) had an operating margin of 9.75%.

Differences in operating margins can also result from differences in strategy. For example, for the fiscal year ending in 2017, Canadian Tire Corporation (ticker symbol: CTC.A) had an operating margin of 9.12% while Lululemon Athletica Inc. (ticker symbol: LULU) had an operating margin of 17.96%. In this case, Canadian Tire's lower operating margin is not a result of its inefficiency but is part of its strategy of offering lower prices to sell common products in high volume. Indeed, Canadian Tire's sales were about 4.3 times higher than those of Lululemon.

net profit margin The ratio of net income to revenues; it shows the fraction of each dollar in revenues that is available to equity holders after the firm pays its expenses, plus interest and taxes.

Net Profit Margin. A firm's **net profit margin** is the ratio of net income to revenues:

$$\text{Net Profit Margin} = \frac{\text{Net Income}}{\text{Total Sales}} \tag{2.10}$$

The net profit margin shows the fraction of each dollar in revenues that is available to equity holders after the firm pays its expenses, plus interest and taxes. Global's net profit margin in 2018 was 2.0/186.7 = 1.07%. Differences in net profit margins can be due to differences in efficiency, but they can also result from differences in leverage (the firm's reliance on debt financing), which determines the amount of interest payments.

Liquidity Ratios

current ratio The ratio of current assets to current liabilities.

quick ratio ("acid-test" ratio) The ratio of current assets other than inventory to current liabilities.

Creditors often compare a firm's current assets and current liabilities to assess whether the firm has sufficient working capital to meet its short-term needs. This comparison is sometimes summarized in the firm's **current ratio**, the ratio of current assets to current liabilities, or its **quick ratio ("acid-test" ratio)**, the ratio of current assets other than inventory to current liabilities. A higher current or quick ratio implies better liquidity for the firm in that there is less risk of the firm experiencing a cash shortfall in the near future:

$$\text{Current Ratio} = \frac{\text{Current Assets}}{\text{Current Liabilities}} \tag{2.11}$$

$$\text{Quick Ratio} = \frac{\text{Current Assets} - \text{Inventory}}{\text{Current Liabilities}} \tag{2.12}$$

The quick ratio may be better to use than the current ratio as a measure of liquidity when there is concern the firm may not be able to easily liquidate its inventory. Example 2.4 illustrates the use of these ratios.

EXAMPLE 2.4 Analyzing Liquidity

PROBLEM

You are considering buying the stock of two companies, Highlev Corp. (HC) and Stabilizer Products Corp. (SPC), and as part of your analysis of the companies you want to ensure their short-term viability by looking at their liquidity ratios. The following financial information is available about the two companies:

Selected data from the most recent quarterly report ($ millions)	Highlev Corp.	Stabilizer Products Corp.
Current Assets		
Cash	25.6	42.9
Accounts Receivable	17.3	31.4
Inventories	48.1	39.6
Total Current Assets	91.0	113.9
Current Liabilities		
Accounts Payable	29.2	35.8
Notes payable/short-term debt	19.7	11.6
Total Current Liabilities	48.9	47.4

Calculate the current and quick ratios for the two companies and indicate whether there are concerns about their short-term viability.

SOLUTION

Plan

We will use Equations 2.11 and 2.12 for each of the two firms. Lower ratios indicate a greater concern about short-term viability.

Execute

The ratios are calculated as follows:

$$\text{Current Ratio}_{HC} = \frac{91.0}{48.9} = 1.86$$

$$\text{Current Ratio}_{SPC} = \frac{113.9}{47.4} = 2.40$$

$$\text{Quick Ratio}_{HC} = \frac{91.0 - 48.1}{48.9} = 0.88$$

$$\text{Quick Ratio}_{SPC} = \frac{113.9 - 39.6}{47.4} = 1.57$$

Evaluate

Stabilizer Products Corp. would not cause you concern regarding short-term viability because both the current and quick ratios are substantially above 1.0, and this indicates that there would be enough liquid assets to pay off upcoming liabilities. Highlev Corp. also has a current ratio above 1.0, and this would be reassuring as long as the inventory it holds could be expected to sell. However, its quick ratio is only 0.88, so if Highlev's inventories could not be sold, then Highlev would not have enough liquid assets to pay off upcoming liabilities—this would cause concern about Highlev's short-term viability.

Asset Efficiency

A financial manager can use the combined information in the firm's income statement and statement of financial position to gauge how efficiently his or her firm is using its assets. A first broad measure of efficiency is asset turnover, the ratio of sales to total assets:

$$\text{Asset Turnover} = \frac{\text{Sales}}{\text{Total Assets}} \tag{2.13}$$

Low values of asset turnover indicate that the firm is not generating much revenue (sales) per dollar of assets. In 2018, Global's $170.1 million in assets generated $186.7 million in sales, for an asset turnover ratio of 1.1. Since total assets includes assets, such as cash, that are not directly involved in generating sales, Global's manager might also look at Global's fixed asset turnover, which is equal to sales divided by fixed assets:

$$\text{Fixed Asset Turnover} = \frac{\text{Sales}}{\text{Fixed Assets}} \tag{2.14}$$

Global's fixed assets in 2018 were $113.1 million worth of property, plant, and equipment, yielding a fixed asset turnover of 1.7 (= $186.7/$113.1). Low asset turnover ratios indicate that the firm is generating relatively few sales given the amount of assets it employs.

Working Capital Ratios

accounts receivable days (average collection period or **days sales outstanding)** An expression of a firm's accounts receivable in terms of the number of days' worth of sales that the accounts receivable represents.

accounts payable days An expression of a firm's accounts payable in terms of the number of days' worth of cost of goods sold that the accounts payable represents.

inventory days An expression of a firm's inventory in terms of the number of days' worth of cost of goods sold that the inventory represents.

inventory turnover ratio Sales divided by either the latest cost of inventory or the average inventory over the year; it shows how efficiently companies turn their inventory into sales.

Global's managers might be further interested in how efficiently they are managing their net working capital. We can express the firm's accounts receivable in terms of the number of days' worth of sales that it represents, called the **accounts receivable days (average collection period** or **days sales outstanding)**:[4]

$$\text{Accounts Receivable Days} = \frac{\text{Accounts Receivable}}{\text{Average Daily Sales}} \tag{2.15}$$

Given average daily sales of $186.7 million/365 = $0.51 million in 2018, Global's receivables of $18.5 million represent 18.5/0.51 = 36 days' worth of sales. In other words, Global takes a little over one month to collect payment from its customers, on average. In 2017, Global's accounts receivable represented only 27 days' worth of sales. Although the number of receivable days can fluctuate seasonally, a significant unexplained increase could be a cause for concern (perhaps indicating the firm is doing a poor job collecting from its customers or is trying to boost sales by offering generous credit terms). Similar ratios exist for accounts payable and inventory. Those ratios are called **accounts payable days** (accounts payable divided by average daily cost of goods sold) and **inventory days** (inventory divided by average daily cost of goods sold).

We can also compute how efficiently firms use inventory. The **inventory turnover ratio** is equal to cost of goods sold divided by the average inventory over the year:

$$\text{Inventory Turnover} = \frac{\text{Cost of Goods Sold}}{\text{Average Inventory}} \tag{2.16}$$

[4]Accounts receivable days can also be calculated based on the average accounts receivable at the end of the current and prior years. This is generally an acceptable approach whenever a ratio compares an income statement figure to a statement of financial position figure. Since the income statement figure is measured over a period of time, taking the simple average of the statement of financial position figure can approximate its amount over the same period of time.

A normal level for this ratio, similar to the others in this section, can vary substantially for different industries, although a higher level (more dollars of sales per dollar of inventory) is generally better.

EXAMPLE 2.5 Computing Working Capital Ratios

PROBLEM

Compute Global's accounts payable days, inventory days, and inventory turnover for 2018.

SOLUTION

Plan

Working capital ratios require information from both the statement of financial position and the income statement. For these ratios, we need inventory and accounts payable from the statement of financial position, and cost of goods sold from the income statement (often listed as cost of sales). Inventory = 15.3, Accounts payable = 29.2, Cost of goods sold (Cost of sales) = 153.4

Execute

$$\text{Accounts Payble days} = \frac{\text{Accounts Payable}}{\text{Average Daily Cost of Goods Sold}} = \frac{29.2}{(153.4/365)} = 69.48$$

$$\text{Inventory Days} = \frac{\text{Inventory}}{\text{Average Daily Cost of Goods Sold}} = \frac{15.3}{(153.4/365)} = 36.40$$

$$\text{Inventory Turnover} = \frac{\text{Cost of Goods Sold}}{\text{Inventory}} = \frac{153.4}{15.3} = 10.03$$

Evaluate

Assuming that Global's accounts payable at year end on its statement of financial position is representative of the normal amount during the year, Global is able, on average, to take about 69.5 days to pay its suppliers. This compares with the 27.5 days we calculated that it waits on average to be paid (its accounts receivable days). Global typically takes 36 days to sell its inventory. Note that inventory turnover and inventory days tell us the same thing in different ways—if it takes Global about 36 days to sell its inventory, then it turns over its inventory about 10 times per 365-day year. In Chapter 19 on working capital management, we'll see how a company's receivable, inventory, and payable days make up its operating cycle.

Interest Coverage Ratios

interest coverage ratio or **times interest earned (TIE) ratio** An assessment by lenders of a firm's leverage, it is equal to a measure of earnings divided by interest.

Lenders often assess a firm's leverage by computing an **interest coverage ratio** or **times interest earned (TIE) ratio**, which is equal to a measure of earnings divided by interest. Financial managers watch these ratios carefully, using them to assess how easily the firm will be able to cover its interest payments. There is no single accepted measure of earnings for these ratios; it is common to consider operating income, EBIT, or EBITDA as a multiple of the firm's interest expenses. When this ratio is high, it indicates that the firm is earning much more than is necessary to meet its required interest payments.

EXAMPLE 2.6 Computing Interest Coverage Ratios

PROBLEM

Assess Global's ability to meet its interest obligations by calculating interest coverage ratios using both EBIT and EBITDA.

SOLUTION

Plan

Gather the EBIT, depreciation, and amortization and interest expense for each year from Global's income statement.

2017: EBIT = 7.1, EBITDA = 7.1 + 1.1, Interest expense = 4.6

2018: EBIT = 10.4, EBITDA = 10.4 + 1.2, Interest expense = 7.7

Execute

In 2017 and 2018, Global had the following interest coverage ratios:

$$2017: \frac{\text{EBIT}}{\text{Interest}} = \frac{7.1}{4.6} = 1.54 \quad \textit{and} \quad \frac{\text{EBITDA}}{\text{Interest}} = \frac{7.1 + 1.1}{4.6} = 1.78$$

$$2018: \frac{\text{EBIT}}{\text{Interest}} = \frac{10.4}{7.7} = 1.35 \quad \textit{and} \quad \frac{\text{EBITDA}}{\text{Interest}} = \frac{10.4 + 1.2}{7.7} = 1.51$$

Evaluate

The coverage ratios indicate that Global is generating enough cash to cover its interest obligations. However, Global's low—and declining—interest coverage could be a source of concern for its creditors.

Leverage Ratios

leverage A measure of the extent to which a firm relies on debt as a source of financing.

debt-equity ratio The ratio of a firm's total amount of short- and long-term debt (including current maturities) to the value of its equity, which may be calculated based on market or book values.

Another important piece of information that we can learn from a firm's statement of financial position is the firm's **leverage**, or the extent to which it relies on debt as a source of financing. The **debt-equity ratio** is a common ratio used to assess a firm's leverage, which we calculate by dividing the total amount of short- and long-term debt (including current maturities) by the total stockholders' equity:

$$\text{Debt-Equity Ratio} = \frac{\text{Total Debt}}{\text{Total Equity}} \tag{2.17}$$

We can calculate this ratio using either book or market value for equity and debt. From Table 2.1, Global's debt in 2018 includes notes payable of $5.5 million and long-term debt of $113.2 million, for a total of $118.7 million. Therefore, using the book value of equity, its *book* debt-equity ratio is 118.7/22.2 = 5.3. Note the large increase from 2017, when the book debt-equity ratio was only (3.2 + 78)/21.2 = 3.8.

Because of the difficulty interpreting the book value of equity, the book debt-equity ratio is not especially useful. It is more informative to compare the firm's debt to the market value of its equity. Global's debt-equity ratio in 2018, using the market value of equity (from Example 2.1), is 118.7/36 = 3.3, which means Global's debt is a bit more than triple the market value of its equity.[5] As we will see later in the text, a firm's *market* debt-equity ratio has important consequences for the risk and return of its stock.

[5]In this calculation, we have compared the market value of equity to the book value of debt. Strictly speaking, it would be best to use the market value of debt. But because the market value of debt is generally not very different from its book value, this distinction is often ignored in practice.

debt-to-capital ratio The ratio of total debt to total debt plus total equity.

We can also calculate the fraction of the firm financed by debt in terms of its **debt-to-capital ratio**:

$$\text{Debt-to-Capital Ratio} = \frac{\text{Total Debt}}{\text{Total Equity} + \text{Total Debt}} \tag{2.18}$$

Again, this ratio can be computed using book or market value.

While leverage increases the risk to the firm's equity holders, firms may also hold cash reserves in order to reduce risk. Thus, another useful measure to consider is the firm's **net debt**, or debt in excess of its cash reserves:

net debt Debt in excess of a firm's cash reserves.

$$\text{Net Debt} = \text{Total Debt} - \text{Excess Cash \& Short-Term Investments} \tag{2.19}$$

To understand why net debt may be a more relevant measure of leverage, consider a firm with more cash than debt outstanding. Because such a firm could pay off its debts immediately using its available cash, it has not increased its risk and has no effective leverage.

Analogous to the debt-to-capital ratio is the concept of net debt, which we can use to compute the firm's **debt-to-enterprise value ratio**:

debt-to-enterprise value ratio The ratio of a firm's net debt to its enterprise value.

$$\text{Debt-to-Enterprise Value Ratio} = \frac{\text{Net Debt}}{\text{Market Value of Equity} + \text{Net Debt}} = \frac{\text{Net Debt}}{\text{Enterprise Value}} \tag{2.20}$$

Given Global's 2018 cash balance of \$23.2 million, and total long- and short-term debt of \$118.7 million, its net debt is 118.7 − 23.2 = \$95.5 million.[6] Given its market value of equity of \$36.0 million, Global's enterprise value in 2018 is 36.0 + 95.5 = \$131.5 million, and thus its debt-to-enterprise value ratio is 95.5/131.5 = 72.6%. That is, 72.6% of Global's underlying business activity is financed via debt.

equity multiplier A measure of leverage equal to total assets divided by total equity.

A final measure of leverage is a firm's **equity multiplier**, measured in book value terms as Total Assets/Book Value of Equity. As we will see shortly, this measure captures the amplification of the firm's accounting returns that results from leverage. The market value equity multiplier, which is generally measured as Enterprise Value/Market Value of Equity, indicates the amplification of shareholders' financial risk that results from leverage.

Valuation Ratios

price-earnings (P/E) ratio The ratio of the market value of equity to the firm's earnings, or of its share price to its earnings per share.

Analysts and investors use a number of ratios to gauge the market value of the firm. The most important is the firm's **price-earnings (P/E) ratio**:

$$\text{P/E Ratio} = \frac{\text{Market Capitalization}}{\text{Net Income}} = \frac{\text{Share Price}}{\text{Earnings per Share}} \tag{2.21}$$

That is, the P/E ratio is the ratio of the value of equity to the firm's earnings, either on a total basis or on a per-share basis. For example, Global's P/E ratio in 2018 was 36/2.0 = 10/0.56 = 18. The P/E ratio is a simple measure that is used to assess whether a stock is over- or under-valued, based on the idea that the value of a stock should be proportional to the level of earnings it can generate for its shareholders. P/E ratios can vary widely across industries and tend to be higher for industries with high growth rates.

[6]While net debt should ideally be calculated by deducting cash in excess of the firm's operating needs, absent additional information, it is typical in practice to deduct all cash on the statement of financial position.

COMMON MISTAKE

Mismatched Ratios

When considering valuation (and other) ratios, be sure that the items you are comparing both represent amounts related to the entire firm or that both represent amounts related solely to equity holders. For example, a firm's share price and market capitalization are values associated with the firm's equity. Thus, it makes sense to compare them to the firm's earnings per share or net income, which are amounts paid out to equity holders after interest has been paid to debt holders. We must be careful, however, if we compare a firm's market capitalization to its revenues, operating income, or EBITDA. These amounts are related to the whole firm, and both debt and equity holders have a claim to them. Therefore, it is better to compare revenues, operating income, or EBITDA to the enterprise value of the firm, which includes both debt and equity.

PEG ratio The ratio of a firm's P/E to its expected earnings growth rate.

One way to capture the idea that a higher P/E ratio can be justified by a higher growth rate is to compare it to the company's expected earnings growth rate. For example, if Global's expected growth rate is 18%, then it would have a P/E to Growth, or **PEG ratio**, of 1. Some investors consider PEG ratios of one or below as indicating the stock is fairly priced, but would question whether the company is potentially overvalued if the PEG is higher than 1. P/E ratios also vary widely across time and tend to be low when the economy is headed for a downturn but high when an economy starts rebounding.

The P/E ratio considers the value of the firm's equity and so depends on its leverage. Recall that the amount of assets controlled by the equity holders can be increased through the use of leverage. To assess the market value of the underlying business, it is common to consider valuation ratios based on the firm's enterprise value. Typical ratios include the ratio of enterprise value to revenue, or enterprise value to operating income or EBITDA. These ratios compare the value of the business to its sales, operating profits, or cash flow. Similar to the P/E ratio, these ratios are used to make intra-industry comparisons of how firms are priced in the market.

The P/E ratio is not useful when the firm's earnings are negative. In this case, it is common to look at the firm's enterprise value relative to sales. The risk in doing so, however, is that earnings might be negative because the firm's underlying business model is fundamentally flawed, as was the case for many internet firms in the late 1990s.

EXAMPLE 2.7 Computing Profitability and Valuation Ratios

PROBLEM

Consider the following data for Canadian Pacific Railway (ticker symbol: CP) and Canadian National Railway (ticker symbol: CNR):

	Canadian Pacific Railway Limited (CP) ($ millions)	Canadian National Railway Company (CNR) ($ millions)
Sales	4303	7367
Operating Income	900	2406
Net Income	612	1854
Market Capitalization	9569	25,604
Cash	679	352
Debt	4495	6461

Compare CP's and CN's operating margin, net profit margin, P/E ratio, and the ratio of enterprise value to operating income and sales.

SOLUTION

Plan

The table contains all of the raw data, but we need to compute the ratios using the inputs in the table.

Operating Margin = Operating Income / Sales
Net Profit Margin = Net Income / Sales P/E ratio = Price / Earnings
Enterprise Value to Operating Income = Enterprise Value / Operating Income
Enterprise Value to Sales = Enterprise Value / Sales

Execute

CP had an operating margin of 900/4303 = 20.9%, a net profit margin of 612/4303 = 14.2%, and a P/E ratio of 9569/612 = 15.6. Its enterprise value was 9569 + 4495 – 679 = $13,385 million, which has a ratio of 13,385/900 = 14.9 to operating income and 13,385/4303 = 3.1 to sales.

CN had an operating margin of 2406/7367 = 32.7%, a net profit margin of 1854/7367 = 25.2%, and a P/E ratio of 25,604/1854 = 13.8. Its enterprise value was 25,604 + 6461 − 352 = $31,713 million, which has a ratio of 31,713/2406 = 13.2 to operating income and 31,713/7367 = 4.3 to sales.

Evaluate

Note that despite their large difference in size, CP's and CN's P/E and enterprise value to operating income ratios were similar, with CP's results slightly higher in both cases. CN's profitability was somewhat higher than CP's, however, explaining the difference in the ratio of enterprise value to sales.

Operating Returns

return on equity (ROE) The ratio of a firm's net income to the book value of its equity.

Analysts and financial managers often evaluate the firm's return on investment by comparing its income to its investment using ratios such as the firm's **return on equity (ROE)**[7]:

$$\text{Return on Equity} = \frac{\text{Net Income}}{\text{Book Value of Equity}} \tag{2.22}$$

Global's ROE in 2018 was 2.0/22.2 = 9.0%. The ROE provides a measure of the return that the firm has earned on its past investments. A high ROE may indicate the firm is able to find investment opportunities that are very profitable. Of course, one weakness of this measure is the difficulty in interpreting the book value of equity.

return on assets (ROA) The ratio of net income to the total book value of the firm's assets.

Another common measure is the **return on assets (ROA)**, which is net income divided by the total assets. A firm must earn both a positive ROE and ROA to grow.

As a performance measure, ROA has the benefit that it is less sensitive to leverage than ROE. However, it is sensitive to working capital—for example, an equal increase in the firm's receivables and payables will increase total assets and, thus, lower ROA. To avoid this problem, we can consider the firm's **return on invested capital (ROIC)**:

return on invested capital (ROIC) The ratio of the after-tax profit before interest to the book value of invested capital not being held as cash (book equity plus net debt).

$$\text{Return on Invested Capital} = \frac{\text{EBIT}\ (1 - \text{tax rate})}{\text{Book Value of Equity} + \text{Net Debt}} \tag{2.23}$$

[7]As indicated earlier, because net income is measured over the year, the ROE can also be calculated based on the average book value of equity at the end of the current and prior years.

The ROIC measures the after-tax profit generated by the business itself, excluding any interest expenses (or interest income), and compares it to the capital raised from equity and debt holders that has already been deployed (i.e., is not held as cash). Of the three measures of operating returns, ROIC is the most useful in assessing the performance of the underlying business.

EXAMPLE 2.8 Computing Operating Returns

PROBLEM

Assess how Global's ability to use its assets effectively has changed in the last year by computing the change in its ROA.

SOLUTION

Plan and Organize

In order to compute ROA, we need net income, interest expense and total assets.

	2017	2018
Net Income	1.9	2.0
Interest Expense	4.6	7.7
Total Assets	128.9	170.1

Execute

In 2018, Global's ROA was (2.0 + 7.7)/170.1 = 5.7%, compared to an ROA in 2017 of (1.9 + 4.6)/128.9 = 5.0%.

Evaluate

The improvement in Global's ROA from 2017 to 2018 suggests that Global was able to use its assets more effectively and increase its return over this period.

The DuPont Identity

DuPont Identity Expresses return on equity as the product of profit margin, asset turnover, and a measure of leverage.

Global's financial manager will need to know that its ROE is 9%, but that financial manager would also need to understand the drivers of his or her firm's ROE. High margins, efficient use of assets, or even simply high leverage could all lead to a higher ROE. By delving deeper into the sources of ROE, the financial manager can gain a clear sense of the firm's financial picture. One common tool for doing so is the **DuPont Identity**, named for the company that popularized it, which expresses ROE as the product of profit margin, asset turnover, and a measure of leverage.

To understand the DuPont Identity, we start with ROE and decompose it in steps into the drivers identified in the identity. First, we simply multiply ROE by (sales/sales), which is just 1, and rearrange terms:

$$\text{ROE} = \left(\frac{\text{Net Income}}{\text{Total Equity}}\right)\left(\frac{\text{Sales}}{\text{Sales}}\right) = \left(\frac{\text{Net Income}}{\text{Sales}}\right)\left(\frac{\text{Sales}}{\text{Total Equity}}\right) \tag{2.24}$$

This expression says that ROE can be thought of as net income per dollar of sales (profit margin) times the amount of sales per dollar of equity. For example, Global's ROE comes from its profit margin of 1.1% multiplied by its sales per dollar of equity of

(186.7/22.2 = 8.41), so we have 1.1% × 8.41 = 9%.[8] While this can be a useful insight into ROE, we can take the decomposition further by multiplying Equation 2.17 by assets/assets, which again is just 1, and rearranging the terms:

$$\text{ROE} = \left(\frac{\text{Net Income}}{\text{Sales}}\right)\left(\frac{\text{Sales}}{\text{Total Equity}}\right)\left(\frac{\text{Total Assets}}{\text{Total Assets}}\right)$$

$$= \left(\frac{\text{Net Income}}{\text{Sales}}\right)\left(\frac{\text{Sales}}{\text{Total Assets}}\right)\left(\frac{\text{Total Assets}}{\text{Total Equity}}\right) \tag{2.25}$$

This final expression says that ROE is equal to net income per dollar of sales (profit margin) times sales per dollar of assets (asset turnover) times assets per dollar of equity (equity multiplier). Equation 2.25 is the DuPont Identity, expressing ROE as the product of profit margin, asset turnover, and the equity multiplier. Turning to Global, its equity multiplier is 7.7 (= 170.1/22.2). A financial manager at Global looking for ways to increase ROE could turn to the DuPont Identity to assess the drivers behind its current ROE. With a profit margin of 1.1%, asset turnover of 1.1, and an equity multiplier of 7.7, we have

$$\text{ROE} = 9\% = (1.1\%)(1.1)(7.7)$$

This decomposition of ROE shows that leverage is already high (confirmed by the fact that the book debt-equity ratio shows that Global's debt is more than five times its equity). However, Global is operating with only 1% profit margins and relatively low asset turnover. Thus, Global's manager could pursue lowering costs to increase profit margin and utilizing the firm's existing assets more efficiently.[9]

EXAMPLE 2.9 DuPont Analysis

PROBLEM

The following table contains hypothetical information about Canadian Tire (ticker symbol: CTC.A) and Lululemon Athletica (ticker symbol: LULU). Compute their respective ROEs and then determine how much Canadian Tire would need to increase its profit margin in order to match Lululemon's ROE.

	Profit Margin	Asset Turnover	Equity Multiplier
Canadian Tire	3.9%	0.99	2.38
Lululemon	12.9%	1.47	1.32

SOLUTION

■ Plan

The table contains all the relevant information to use the DuPont Identity to compute the ROE. We can compute the ROE of each company by multiplying together its profit margin, asset turnover, and equity multiplier. In order to determine how much Canadian Tire would need to increase its margin ▶

[8]Due to rounding to two decimal places in the financial statements and our calculations, the calculations for Global will not exactly match the ROE we computed.

[9]Although the DuPont Identity gives the impression that you can increase ROE just by increasing leverage, it is not quite that simple. An increase in leverage will increase your interest expense, decreasing your profit margin.

to match Lululemon's ROE, we can set Canadian Tire's ROE equal to Lululemon's, keep its turnover and equity multiplier fixed, and solve for the profit margin.

Execute

Using the DuPont Identity, we have:

$ROE_{CTC.A} = 3.9\% \times 0.99 \times 2.38 = 9.2\%$
$ROE_{LULU} = 12.9\% \times 1.47 \times 1.32 = 25.0\%$
Now, using Lululemon's ROE but Canadian Tire's asset turnover and equity multiplier, we can solve for the margin that Canadian Tire needs to achieve Lululemon's ROE:
$25.0\% = \text{Margin} \times 0.99 \times 2.38$

$$\text{Margin} = \frac{25.0\%}{2.36} = 10.6\%$$

Evaluate

Canadian Tire would have to increase its profit margin from 3.9% to 10.6% in order to match Lululemon's ROE. It would be able to achieve Lululemon's ROE even with a lower margin than Lululemon (10.6% vs. 12.9%) and lower turnover (0.99 vs. 1.47) because of its higher leverage.

Table 2.4 summarizes financial ratios and provides typical values of those ratios for the manufacturing, retail, and service sectors along with the 500 firms in the S&P 500 index.

TABLE 2.4 A Summary of Key Financial Ratios

Ratio	Formula	Manufacturing	Retail	Service	S&P 500
Profitability Ratios					
Gross Margin	$\frac{\text{Gross Profit}}{\text{Sales}}$	33.8%	30.1%	51.4%	39.0%
Operating Margin	$\frac{\text{Operating Income}}{\text{Sales}}$	8.1%	7.3%	12.2%	16.2%
Net Profit Margin	$\frac{\text{Net Income}}{\text{Sales}}$	1.3%	2.6%	2.5%	4.5%
Liquidity Ratios					
Current Ratio	$\frac{\text{Current Assets}}{\text{Current Liabilities}}$	2.6	1.5	1.8	2.1
Quick Ratio	$\frac{\text{Current Assets} - \text{Inventory}}{\text{Current Liabilities}}$	1.9	0.8	1.7	1.6
Efficiency and Working Capital Ratios					
Accounts Receivable Days	$\frac{\text{Accounts Receivable}}{\text{Average Daily Sales}}$	57.6	7.8	63.0	60.2
Fixed Asset Turnover	$\frac{\text{Sales}}{\text{Fixed Assets}}$	5.4	6.6	10.6	4.8
Total Asset Turnover	$\frac{\text{Sales}}{\text{Total Assets}}$	0.7	1.7	0.6	0.5

(continued)

TABLE 2.4 *(Continued)*

Ratio	Formula	Manufacturing	Retail	Service	S&P 500
Inventory Turnover	$\frac{\text{Cost of Goods Sold}}{\text{Inventory}}$	4.2	6.9	26.9	5.7
Interest Coverage Ratios					
EBIT/Interest Coverage	$\frac{\text{EBIT}}{\text{Interest Expense}}$	3.2	5.5	2.3	3.9
EBITDA/Interest Coverage	$\frac{\text{EBITDA}}{\text{Interest Expense}}$	6.0	9.3	5.3	6.7
Leverage Ratios					
Book Debt-to-Equity Ratio	$\frac{\text{Total Debt}}{\text{Book Value of Total Equity}}$	27.1%	44.2%	21.5%	46.6%
Market Debt-to-Equity Ratio	$\frac{\text{Total Debt}}{\text{Market Value of Total Equity}}$	10.0%	17.2%	6.2%	21.8%
Debt-to-Capital Ratio	$\frac{\text{Total Debt}}{\text{Total Equity} + \text{Total Debt}}$	20.9%	30.6%	17.6%	32.0%
Debt-to-Enterprise Value	$\frac{\text{Net Debt}}{\text{Enterprise Value}}$	0.0%	4.7%	0.0%	2.0%
Equity Multiplier	$\frac{\text{Total Assets}}{\text{Total Equity}}$	1.8	2.4	1.98	2.4
Operating Returns					
Return on Equity	$\frac{\text{Net Income}}{\text{Book Value of Equity}}$	4.2%	10.4%	3.6%	7.1%
Return on Assets	$\frac{\text{Net Income} + \text{Interest Expense}}{\text{Total Assets}}$	3.6%	5.8%	3.3%	4.1%
Return on Invested Capital (ROIC)	$\frac{\text{EBIT}(1 - \text{Tax Rate})}{\text{Book Value of Equity} + \text{Net Debt}}$	18.0%	20.1%	18.3%	17.0%
Valuation Ratios					
Market-to-Book Ratio	$\frac{\text{Market Value of Equity}}{\text{Book Value of Equity}}$	2.7	2.7	3.5	2.1
Price-to-Earnings Ratio	$\frac{\text{Share Price}}{\text{Earnings per Share}}$	21.5	21.6	28.8	21.2
Enterprise Value Ratio (typical values shown are based on EV/EBITDA)	$\frac{\text{Enterprise Value}}{\text{EBIT or EBITDA or Sales}}$	8.3	11.7	10.5	12.1

Source: Standard and Poors' Compustat based on averages of fiscal years 2012 to 2015.

CONCEPT CHECK

11. What does a high debt-to-equity ratio tell you?

12. What is a firm's enterprise value?

13. How can a financial manager use the DuPont Identity to assess the firm's ROE?

14. How do you use the price-earnings (P/E) ratio to gauge the market value of a firm?

2.7 Financial Reporting in Practice

The various financial statements we have examined are of critical importance to investors and financial managers alike. Even with safeguards such as GAAP and auditors, financial reporting abuses unfortunately do take place. We now review one of the most infamous recent examples and offer some concluding thoughts to guide financial managers through the complexities of financial statements.

Enron

Enron is the most well-known of the accounting scandals of the early 2000s. Enron started as an operator of natural gas pipelines but evolved into a global trader dealing in a range of products including gas, oil, electricity, and even broadband internet capacity. A series of events unfolded that led Enron to file the largest bankruptcy filing in U.S. history in December 2001. By the end of 2001, the market value of Enron's shares had fallen by over $60 billion.

Interestingly, throughout the 1990s and up to late 2001, Enron was touted as one of the most successful and profitable companies in the United States. *Fortune* magazine rated Enron "The Most Innovative Company in America" for six straight years, from 1995 to 2000. But while many aspects of Enron's business were successful, subsequent investigations suggest that Enron executives had been manipulating Enron's financial statements to mislead investors and artificially inflate the price of Enron's stock and to maintain its credit rating. In 2000, for example, 96% of Enron's reported earnings were the result of accounting manipulation.[10]

Although the accounting manipulations that Enron used were quite sophisticated, the essence of most of the deceptive transactions was surprisingly simple. Enron sold assets at inflated prices to other firms (or, in many cases, business entities that Enron's CFO Andrew Fastow had created) together with a promise to buy back those assets at an even higher future price. Thus, Enron was effectively borrowing money, receiving cash today in exchange for a promise to pay more cash in the future. But Enron recorded the incoming cash as revenue and then, in a variety of ways, hid the promises to buy the assets back.[11] In the end, much of Enron's revenue growth and profits in the late 1990s were the result of this type of manipulation.

The Sarbanes-Oxley Act

The Enron case highlights the importance to investors of accurate and up-to-date financial statements for firms they choose to invest in. Many of the problems at Enron and elsewhere were kept hidden from boards and shareholders until it was too late. In the wake of these scandals, many people felt that the accounting statements of these companies, while often remaining true to the letter of GAAP, did not present an accurate picture of the financial health of a company. In 2002, the United States Congress passed the **Sarbanes-Oxley Act (SOX)** that requires, among other things, that CEOs and CFOs certify the accuracy and appropriateness of their firm's financial statements, and increases the penalties against them if the financial statements later prove to be fraudulent.

Sarbanes-Oxley Act (SOX) Legislation passed by the U.S. Congress in 2002, intended to improve the accuracy of financial information given to both boards and shareholders.

---

[10]John R. Kroger, "Enron, Fraud and Securities Reform: An Enron Prosecutor's Perspective," *University of Colorado Law Review,* December, 2005, pp. 57–138.

[11]In some cases, these promises were called "price risk management liabilities" and hidden with other trading activities; in other cases, they were off-balance sheet transactions that were not fully disclosed.

Auditing firms are supposed to ensure that a company's financial statements accurately reflect the financial state of the firm. In reality, most auditors have a long-standing relationship with their audit clients; this extended relationship and the auditors' desire to keep the lucrative auditing fees make auditors less willing to challenge management. More importantly perhaps, most accounting firms have developed large and extremely profitable consulting divisions. Obviously, if an audit team refuses to accommodate a request by a client's management, that client will be less likely to choose the accounting firm's consulting division for its next consulting contract. SOX addressed this concern by putting strict limits on the amount of non-audit fees (consulting or otherwise) that an accounting firm can earn from the same firm that it audits. It also required that audit partners rotate every five years to limit the likelihood that auditing relationships become too cozy over long periods of time. Finally, SOX called on the SEC to force companies to have audit committees that are dominated by outside directors, and required that at least one outside director have a financial background.

Following the Sarbanes-Oxley Act in the United States, Canada adopted similar measures through Bill C198 that came into effect in 2005. In Canada, the response and implementation of changes were somewhat measured in comparison with those in the United States, partly due to the fact that the same scale of corporate fraud had yet to be experienced in Canada. Additional differences between Canada and the United States also contributed to differences in adoption. For example, Canada does not have a national securities commission, whereas the United States does. Creating uniform change across Canada is problematic, as agreement among 13 different authorities would be needed. Canada also has a much larger percentage of public firms with a controlling shareholder. Implementing SOX requirements such as increasing the proportion of independent directors might be unworkable in Canada, as many controlling shareholders may desire to name board representatives. Finally, Canadian companies tend to have lower market capitalization compared to U.S. firms. Forcing companies to validate their financial control processes, another measure introduced in SOX, in a more formalized way can increase costs significantly, putting a greater burden on smaller firms than on larger ones.

INTERVIEW WITH SUE FRIEDEN

Sue Frieden

Sue Frieden is Ernst & Young's Global Managing Partner, Quality & Risk Management. A member of the Global Executive board, she is responsible for Every aspect of quality and risk management—employees, services, procedures, and clients.

Q Do today's financial statements give the investing public what they need?

A Globally, we are seeing an effort to provide more forward-looking information to investors. But fundamental questions remain, such as how fully do investors understand financial statements and how fully do they read them? Research shows that most individual investors don't rely on financial statements much at all. We need to determine how the financial statements can be improved. To do that we will need a dialogue involving investors, regulators, analysts, auditors, stock exchanges, academics, and others to ensure that financial statements are as relevant as they can be.

Q Ernst & Young is a global organization. How do accounting standards in the U.S. compare to those elsewhere?

A In January of 2005, 100 countries outside the United States began the process of adopting new accounting standards (International Financial Reporting Standards) that would in large measure be based on principles rather than rules. As global markets become more complex, we all need to be playing by the same set of rules. As a first step we need consistency from country to country. There are definite challenges to overcome in reconciling principle-based and rules-based systems, but we are optimistic that these challenges will inevitably get resolved. At the same time, there are efforts under way to ensure that auditing standards are globally consistent. Ultimately, financial statements prepared under global standards and audited under consistent global auditing standards will better serve investors.

Q What role does the audit firm play in our financial markets, and how has that changed since the collapse of Arthur Andersen?

A The accounting profession has seen unprecedented change in the past few years as well. The passage of Sarbanes-Oxley and other changes are helping to restore public trust. We're now engaging on a regular basis with a wider range of stakeholders—companies, boards, policymakers, opinion leaders, investors, and academia. And we've had the chance to step back and ask ourselves why we do what we do as accounting professionals, and why it matters. In terms of the services we offer, much of what we do helps companies comply with regulations, guard against undue risks, and implement sound transactions. Part of the value in what we do is providing the basis to all stakeholders to understand whether companies are playing by the rules—whether it is accounting rules, financial reporting rules, or tax rules. The public may not fully understand precisely what auditors do or how we do it, but they care that we exist because it provides them the confidence they so badly need and want.

Q Accounting standards seem to be shifting from historical cost-based methods to methods that rely on current market values of assets. During the financial crisis, however, many financial institutions complained that "mark-to-market" rules exacerbated their financial difficulties. Do you believe accounting professionals should rethink the wisdom of moving to market-based accounting methods?

A Fair value accounting can certainly be improved, particularly in light of the difficulty in applying fair value in illiquid markets, which the financial crisis highlighted, and because of some of the anomalies that fair value accounting can produce. But by and large, fair value accounting provided transparency into reality for investors. It is the most transparent way to reflect the economic reality of prevailing market conditions and provide investors and companies with current financial information on which they can base investment and management decisions. Fair value accounting did not cause the economic crisis; it simply kept a fair scorecard.

The Financial Statements: A Useful Starting Point

In this chapter, we have highlighted the role of the financial statements in informing outside analysts, investors, and the financial managers themselves about the performance, position, and financial condition of the firm. However, especially from the financial manager's perspective, financial statements are only a starting point. For example, we have emphasized the importance of market values over book values. We have also shown that while much can be learned through ratio analysis, these ratios are only markers that point the financial manager toward areas where the firm is doing well or where he or she needs to focus effort for improvement. No single ratio tells the whole story. However, by studying all of the financial statements and considering ratios that assess profitability, leverage, and efficiency, you should be able to develop a clear sense of the health and performance of the firm. Finally, using the case of Enron, we emphasize that the usefulness of the financial statements to investors relies on the ethics of those constructing them. Even in these cases of deception, however, an informed reader of the financial statements could have spotted the warning signs by focusing on the statement of cash flows and carefully reading the notes to the financial statements.

CONCEPT CHECK

15. Describe the transactions Enron used to increase its reported earnings.

16. What is the Sarbanes-Oxley Act?

MyLab Finance

Here is what you should know after reading this chapter. MyLab™ Finance will help you identify what you know, and where to go when you need to practice.

KEY POINTS AND EQUATIONS	TERMS	ONLINE PRACTICE OPPORTUNITIES
2.1 Firms' Disclosure of Financial Information ■ Financial statements are accounting reports that a firm issues periodically to describe its past performance. ■ Investors, financial analysts, managers, and other interested parties, such as creditors, rely on financial statements to obtain reliable information about a corporation. ■ The main types of financial statements are the statement of financial position, the income statement, the statement of cash flows, and the statement of stockholders' equity. ■ Most countries in the world are standardizing their accounting systems around International Financial Reporting Standards.	annual reports, p. 28 auditor, p. 28 financial statements, p. 28 Generally Accepted Accounting Principles (GAAP), p. 28	MyLab Study Plan 2.1
2.2 The Statement of Financial Position or Balance Sheet ■ The statement of financial position shows the current financial position (assets, liabilities, and stockholders' equity) of the firm at a single point in time. ■ The two sides of the statement of financial position must balance: Assets = Liabilities + Stockholders' Equity (2.1) ■ Stockholders' equity is the book value of the firm's equity. It differs from the market value of the firm's equity, its market capitalization, because of the way assets and liabilities are recorded for accounting purposes. ■ A successful firm's market-to-book ratio typically exceeds 1. ■ The enterprise value of a firm is the total value of its underlying business operations: Enterprise Value = Market Value of Equity + Debt − Cash (2.4)	accounts payable, p. 31 accounts receivable, p. 31 assets, p. 30 book value, p. 31 book value of equity, p. 32 common stock, p. 30 current assets, p. 31 current liabilities, p. 31 depreciation, p. 31 enterprise value, p.34 growth stocks, p. 34 inventories, p. 31 liabilities, p. 30 liquidation value, p. 32 long-term assets, p. 31 long-term debt, p. 32 market capitalization, p. 32 marketable securities, p. 31 market-to-book ratio (price-to-book [P/B] ratio), p. 33 net working capital, p. 32 notes payable and short-term debt, p. 31	MyLab Study Plan 2.2

KEY POINTS AND EQUATIONS	TERMS	ONLINE PRACTICE OPPORTUNITIES
	shareholders' equity, p. 30 statement of financial position or balance sheet, p. 29 value stocks, p. 34	
2.3 The Statement of Comprehensive Income and Income Statement ■ The income statement reports the firm's revenues and expenses, and it computes the firm's bottom line of net income, or earnings. ■ Net income is often reported on a per-share basis as the firm's earnings per share: Earnings per Share (EPS) = Net Income/Shares Outstanding (2.5) ■ We compute diluted EPS by adding to the number of shares outstanding the possible increase in the number of shares from the exercise of stock options the firm has awarded.	convertible bonds, p. 37 diluted EPS, p. 37 dilution, p. 37 earnings per share (EPS), p. 37 EBIT, p. 37 EBITDA, p. 37 gross profit, p. 36 income statement, p. 35 net income or earnings, p. 35 operating income, p. 36 stock options, p. 37	MyLab Study Plan 2.3
2.4 The Statement of Cash Flows ■ The statement of cash flows reports the sources and uses of the firm's cash. It shows the adjustments to net income for non-cash expenses and changes to net working capital, as well as the cash used (or provided) from investing and financing activities.	capital expenditures, p. 40 payout ratio, p. 40 retained earnings, p. 40 statement of cash flows, p. 38	MyLab Study Plan 2.4
2.5 Other Financial Statement Information ■ The management discussion and analysis section of the financial statement contains management's overview of the firm's performance, as well as disclosure of risks the firm faces, including those from off-balance sheet transactions. ■ The statement of stockholders' equity breaks down the stockholders' equity computed on the statement of financial position into the amount that came from issuing new shares versus retained earnings. It is not particularly useful for financial valuation purposes. ■ The notes to a firm's financial statements generally contain important details regarding the numbers used in the main statements.	management discussion and analysis (MD&A), p. 42 off-balance sheet transactions, p. 42 statement of shareholders' equity, p. 41	MyLab Study Plan 2.5
2.6 Financial Statement Analysis ■ Profitability ratios show the firm's operating or net income as a fraction of sales, and they are an indication of a firm's efficiency and its pricing strategy.	accounts payable days, p. 45 accounts receivable days (average collection	MyLab Study Plan 2.6

KEY POINTS AND EQUATIONS	TERMS	ONLINE PRACTICE OPPORTUNITIES
■ Liquidity ratios help creditors assess whether the firm has enough cash to meet its short-term needs. ■ Asset efficiency ratios assess how efficiently the firm is using its assets by showing how many dollars of revenues the firm produces per dollar of assets. ■ Working capital ratios express the firm's working capital as a number of days of sales (for receivables) or cost of sales (for inventory or payables). ■ Interest coverage ratios indicate the ratio of the firm's income or cash flows to its interest expenses, and they are a measure of financial strength. ■ A common ratio used to assess a firm's leverage is $$\text{Debt-Equity Ratio} = \frac{\text{Total Debt}}{\text{Total Equity}} \quad (2.17)$$ ■ This ratio is most informative when computed using the market value of equity. It indicates the degree of leverage of the firm. ■ Valuation ratios compute market capitalization, or enterprise value of the firm, relative to its earnings or operating income. ■ The P/E ratio computes the value of a share of stock relative to the firm's EPS. P/E ratios tend to be high for fast-growing firms. ■ When comparing valuation ratios, it is important to be sure both the numerator and denominator match in terms of whether they include debt. ■ ROE and ROA are typical operating return ratios. ROE express the firm's net income as a return on the book value of its equity. ROA expresses net income plus interest as a return on total assets. ■ The DuPont Identity says that $$\text{ROE} = \left(\frac{\text{Net Income}}{\text{Sales}}\right)\left(\frac{\text{Sales}}{\text{Total Assets}}\right)\left(\frac{\text{Total Assets}}{\text{Total Equity}}\right) \quad (2.25)$$	period or days sales outstanding), p. 45 current ratio, p. 43 debt-equity ratio, p. 47 debt-to-capital ratio, p. 48 debt-to-enterprise value ratio, p. 48 DuPont Identity, p. 51 equity multiplier, p. 48 gross margin, p. 42 interest coverage ratio or times interest earned (TIE) ratio, p. 46 inventory days, p. 45 inventory turnover ratio, p. 45 leverage, p. 47 net debt, p. 48 net profit margin, p. 43 operating margin, p. 43 PEG ratio, p. 49 price-earnings (P/E) ratio, p. 48 quick ratio ("acid-test" ratio), p. 43 return on assets (ROA), p. 50 return on equity (ROE), p. 50 return on invested capital (ROIC), p. 50	
2.7 Financial Reporting in Practice ■ Recent accounting scandals have drawn attention to the importance of financial statements. New legislation has increased the penalties for fraud and tightened the procedures that firms must use to ensure that statements are accurate.	Sarbanes-Oxley Act (SOX), p. 55	MyLab Study Plan 2.7

REVIEW QUESTIONS

1. Why do firms disclose financial information?
2. Who reads financial statements? List at least three different categories of people. For each category, provide an example of the type of information they might be interested in and discuss why.
3. What four financial statements can be found in a firm's filing with its provincial securities commission? What checks exist to ensure the accuracy of these statements?
4. What is the purpose of the statement of financial position?
5. How can you use the statement of financial position to assess the health of the firm?
6. What is the purpose of the income statement?
7. How are the statement of financial position and the income statement related?
8. What is the DuPont Identity and how can a financial manager use it?
9. How does the statement of cash flows differ from the income statement?
10. Can a firm with positive net income run out of cash? Explain.
11. What can you learn from management's discussion or the notes to the financial statements?
12. How did accounting fraud contribute to the collapse of Enron?

PROBLEMS

All problems in this chapter are available in MyLab Finance. An asterisk (*) indicates problems with a higher level of difficulty.

Firms' Disclosure of Financial Information

1. What financial statements can be found in a firm's annual report? What checks exist to ensure the accuracy of these statements?
2. Find the most recent financial statements for Starbuck's Corporation (ticker symbol: SBUX) using the following sources:
   a. From the company's webpage (*Hint:* Search for "investor relations").
   b. From the SEC website, www.sec.gov (*Hint:* Search for company filings in the EDGAR database).
   c. From the Yahoo! Finance website, http://finance.yahoo.com.
   d. From at least one other source (*Hint:* Enter "SBUX 10K" at www.google.com).
3. Repeat the analysis for Tim Hortons (www.timhortons.com). In addition to the EDGAR site, check www.sedar.com for Canadian filings.

The Statement of Financial Position or Balance Sheet

4. Consider the following potential events that might have occurred at Global on December 30, 2018. For each one, indicate which line items in Global's statement of financial position would be affected and by how much. Also indicate the change to Global's book value of equity.

a. Global used $20 million of its available cash to repay $20 million of its long-term debt.
b. A warehouse fire destroyed $5 million worth of uninsured inventory.
c. Global used $5 million in cash and $5 million in new long-term debt to purchase a $10 million building.
d. A large customer owing $3 million for products it already received declared bankruptcy, leaving no possibility that Global would ever receive payment.
e. Global's engineers discover a new manufacturing process that will cut the cost of its flagship product by over 50%.
f. A key competitor announces a radical new pricing policy that will drastically undercut Global's prices.

5. What was the change in Global's book value of equity from 2017 to 2018 according to Table 2.1? Does this imply that the market price of Global's shares increased in 2018? Explain.

6. Use Yahoo! Finance (https://finance.yahoo.com/) to find the statement of financial position data for Qualcomm as of the end of September 2014.
a. How much did Qualcomm have in cash and short-term investments?
b. What were Qualcomm's total accounts receivable?
c. What were Qualcomm's total assets?
d. What were Qualcomm's total liabilities? How much of this was long-term debt?
e. What was the book value of Qualcomm's equity?

7. Find the annual 10-K report for Costco Wholesale Corporation (COST) for fiscal year 2015 (filed in October 2015). Answer the following questions from its balance sheet:
a. How much cash did Costco have?
b. What were Costco's total assets?
c. What were Costco's total liabilities? How much debt did Costco have?
d. What was the book value of Costco equity?

The Statement of Comprehensive Income and Income Statement

8. Find online the annual 10-K report for Costco Wholesale Corporation (COST) for fiscal year 2015 (filed in October 2015). Answer the following questions from the income statement:
a. What were Costco's revenues for 2015? By what percentage did revenues grow from the prior year?
b. What were Costco's operating and net profit margins in 2015? How do they compare with its margins in the prior year?
c. What were Costco's diluted earnings per share in 2015? What number of shares is this EPS based on?

TABLE 2.5 2014–2018 Financial Statement Data and Stock Price Data for Mydeco Corp.

Mydeco Corp. 2014–2018 (All data as of fiscal year end; $ in millions)

Income Statement	2014	2015	2016	2017	2018
Revenue	404.3	363.8	424.6	510.7	604.1
Cost of Goods Sold	(188.3)	(173.8)	(206.2)	(246.8)	(293.4)
Gross Profit	215.9	190.0	218.3	263.9	310.7
Sales and Marketing	(66.7)	(66.4)	(82.8)	(102.1)	(120.8)
Administration	(60.6)	(59.1)	(59.4)	(66.4)	(78.5)
Depreciation & Amortization	(27.3)	(27.0)	(34.3)	(38.4)	(38.6)
EBIT	61.4	37.5	41.9	57.0	72.8

(continued)

TABLE 2.5 *(continued)*

Interest Income (Expense)	(33.7)	(32.9)	(32.2)	(37.4)	(39.4)
Pre-tax Income	27.7	4.6	9.7	19.6	33.4
Income Tax	(9.7)	(1.6)	(3.4)	(6.9)	(11.7)
Net Income	18.0	3.0	6.3	12.7	21.7
Share outstanding (millions)	55.0	55.0	55.0	55.0	55.0
Earnings per share	$0.33	$0.05	$0.11	$0.23	$0.39
Balance Sheet	**2014**	**2015**	**2016**	**2017**	**2018**
Assets					
Cash	48.8	68.9	86.3	77.5	85.0
Accounts Receivable	88.6	69.8	69.8	76.9	86.1
Inventory	33.7	30.9	28.4	31.7	35.3
Total Current Assets	171.1	169.6	184.5	186.1	206.4
Net Property, Plant & Equip.	245.3	243.2	309.0	345.5	347.0
Goodwill & Intangibles	361.7	361.7	361.7	361.7	361.7
Total Assets	778.1	774.6	855.2	893.3	915.0
Liabilities					
Accounts Payable	18.7	17.9	22.0	26.8	31.7
Accrued Compensation	6.7	6.4	7.0	8.1	9.7
Total Current Liabilities	25.4	24.3	29.0	34.9	41.4
Long-Term Debt	500.0	500.0	575.0	600.0	600.0
Total Liabilities	525.4	524.3	604.0	634.9	641.4
Stockholders' Equity	252.7	250.3	251.2	258.5	273.7
Total Liabilities & Stockholders' Equity	778.1	774.6	855.2	893.4	915.1
Statement of Cash Flows	**2014**	**2015**	**2016**	**2017**	**2018**
Net Income	18.0	3.0	6.3	12.7	21.7
Depreciation & Amortization	27.3	27.0	34.3	38.4	38.6
Chg. in Accounts Receivable	3.9	18.8	(0.0)	(7.1)	(9.2)
Chg. in Inventory	(2.9)	2.8	2.5	(3.3)	(3.6)
Chg. in Payables & Accrued Comp.	2.2	(1.1)	4.7	5.9	6.5
Cash from Operations	48.5	50.5	47.8	46.6	54.0
Capital Expenditures	(25.0)	(25.0)	(100.0)	(75.0)	(40.0)
Cash from Investing Activities	(25.0)	(25.0)	(100.0)	(75.0)	(40.0)
Dividends Paid	(5.4)	(5.4)	(5.4)	(5.4)	(6.5)
Sale (or purchse) of Stock	–	–	–	–	–
Debt Issuance (Pay Down)	–	–	75.0	25.0	–
Cash from Financing Activities	(5.4)	(5.4)	69.6	19.6	(6.5)
Change in Cash	18.1	20.1	17.4	(8.8)	7.5
Mydeco Stock Price	*$7.92*	*$3.30*	*$5.25*	*$8.71*	*$10.89*

9. See Table 2.5 showing financial statement data and stock price data for Mydeco Corp.
   a. By what percentage did Mydeco's revenues grow each year from 2015 to 2018?
   b. By what percentage did net income grow each year?
   c. Why might the growth rates of revenues and net income differ?

10. See Table 2.5 showing financial statement data and stock price data for Mydeco Corp. Suppose Mydeco repurchases 2 million shares each year from 2015 to 2018. What would its earnings per share be in 2018?

11. See Table 2.5 showing financial statement data and stock price data for Mydeco Corp. Suppose Mydeco had purchased additional equipment for $12 million at the end of 2015, and this equipment was depreciated by $4 million per year in 2016, 2017, and 2018. Given Mydeco's tax rate of 35%, what impact would this additional purchase have had on Mydeco's net income in years 2015–2018?

12. See Table 2.5 showing financial statement data and stock price data for Mydeco Corp. Suppose Mydeco's costs and expenses had been the same fraction of revenues in 2015–2018 as they were in 2014. What would Mydeco's EPS have been each year in this case?

13. Suppose a firm's tax rate is 35%.
   a. What effect would a $10 million operating expense have on this year's earnings? What effect would it have on next year's earnings?
   b. What effect would a $10 million capital expense have on this year's earnings if the capital is depreciated at a rate of $2 million per year for five years? What effect would it have on next year's earnings?

*14. Quisco Systems has 6.5 billion shares outstanding and a share price of $18. Quisco is considering developing a new networking product in-house at a cost of $500 million. Alternatively, Quisco can acquire a firm that already has the technology for $900 million worth (at the current price) of Quisco stock. Suppose that, absent the expense of the new technology, Quisco will have EPS of $0.80.
   a. Suppose Quisco develops the product in-house. What impact would the development cost have on Quisco's EPS? Assume all costs are incurred this year and are treated as an R&D expense, Quisco's tax rate is 35%, and the number of shares outstanding is unchanged.
   b. Suppose Quisco does not develop the product in-house but instead acquires the technology. What effect would the acquisition have on Quisco's EPS this year? (Note that acquisition expenses do not appear directly on the income statement. Assume the firm was acquired at the start of the year and has no revenues or expenses of its own so that the only effect on EPS is due to the change in the number of shares outstanding.)
   c. Which method of acquiring the technology has a smaller impact on earnings? Is this method cheaper? Explain.

The Statement of Cash Flows

15. Find online the annual 10-K report for Costco Wholesale Corporation (COST) for fiscal year 2015 (filed in October 2015). Answer the following questions from its cash flow statement:
   a. How much cash did Costco generate from operating activities in 2015?
   b. What was Costco's depreciation expense in 2015?
   c. How much cash was invested in new property and equipment (net of any sales) in 2015?
   d. How much did Costco raise from the sale of shares of its stock (net of any purchases) in 2015?

16. See the cash flow statement below (all values in thousands of dollars). (*See MyLab Finance for the data in Excel format.*):

a. What were the company's cumulative earnings over these four quarters? What were its cumulative cash flows from operating activities?

Quarter	4	3	2	1
Operating Activities, Cash Flows Provided By or Used In				
Net Income	276,710	228,964	194,062	218,532
Depreciation	69,997	75,733	74,570	73,173
Adjustments to net income	14,359	(13,142)	48,826	(47,993)
Changes in accounts receivables	(38,869)	(53,218)	100,732	(84,711)
Changes in liabilities	82,816	(111,577)	201,725	39,949
Changes in inventories	(195,186)	(114,121)	85,028	57,681
Changes in other operating activities	17,675	(26,574)	12,692	(2,097)
Total Cash Flow from Operating Activities	**227,502**	**(13,935)**	**717,635**	**254,534**
Investing Activities, Cash Flows Provided By or Used In				
Capital expenditures	(82,584)	(41,634)	(100,109)	(69,170)
Investments	(5465)	5465	(93,153)	(48,330)
Other cash flows from investing activities	(108,903)	732	(58,069)	20,652
Total Cash Flows from Investing Activities	**(196,952)**	**(35,437)**	**(251,331)**	**(96,848)**
Financing Activities, Cash Flows Provided By or Used In				
Dividends paid	(131,483)	(131,333)	(119,452)	(121,404)
Sale purchase of stock	78,774	1,210	(76,807)	(79,288)
Net borrowings	515,709	114,766	(283,696)	64,885
Other cash flows from financing activities	(282)	2000	(46,234)	39,763
Total Cash Flows from Financing Activities	**462,718**	**(13,357)**	**(526,189)**	**(96,044)**
Effect of exchange rate changes	(119,960)	(610)	32,807	6,890
Change in Cash and Cash Equivalents	**$373,308**	**(63,339)**	**(27,078)**	**$68,532**

b. What fraction of the cash from operating activities was used for investment over the four quarters?

c. What fraction of the cash from operating activities was used for financing activities over the four quarters?

17. Suppose your firm receives a $5 million order on the last day of the year. You fill the order with $2 million worth of inventory. The customer picks up the entire order the same day and pays $1 million up front in cash; you also issue a bill for the customer to pay the remaining balance of $4 million within 40 days. Suppose your firm's tax rate is 0% (i.e., ignore taxes). Determine the consequences of this transaction for each of the following:

a. Revenues
b. Earnings
c. Receivables
d. Inventory
e. Cash

18. Nokela Industries purchases a $40 million cyclo-converter. The cyclo-converter will be depreciated by $10 million per year over four years, starting this year. Suppose Nokela's tax rate is 40%.

a. What impact will the cost of the purchase have on earnings for each of the next four years?

b. What impact will the cost of the purchase have on the firm's cash flow for the next four years?

Financial Statement Analysis

19. In December 2015, General Electric (GE) had a book value of equity of $98 billion, 9.4 billion shares outstanding, and a market price of $31 per share. GE also had cash of $102 billion, and total debt of $199 billion.

a. What was GE's market capitalization? What was GE's market-to-book ratio?

b. What was GE's book debt-equity ratio? What was GE's market debt-equity ratio?

c. What was GE's enterprise value?

20. In December 2015, Apple had cash of $38.07 billion, current assets of $76.22 billion, and current liabilities of $76.09 billion. It also had inventories of $2.45 billion.

a. What was Apple's current ratio?

b. What was Apple's quick ratio?

c. In January 2016, Hewlett-Packard had a quick ratio of 0.66 and a current ratio of 0.90. What can you say about the asset liquidity of Apple relative to Hewlett-Packard?

21. In early 2016, the following information was true about Abercrombie & Fitch (ANF) and The Gap (GPS), both clothing retailers. Values (except price per share) are in millions of dollars.

	Book Equity	Price per Share	Number of Shares (millions)
ANF	1,291	26.35	67.59
GPS	2,545	24.74	397.14

a. What is the market-to-book ratio of each company?

b. What conclusions do you draw from comparing the two ratios?

22. In fiscal year 2015, Walmart Stores. (WMT) had revenue of $485.65 billion, gross profit of $120.57 billion, and net income of $16.36 billion. Costco Wholesale Corporation (COST) had revenue of $116.20 billion, gross profit of $15.13 billion, and net income of $2.38 billion.

a. Compare the gross margins for Walmart and Costco.

b. Compare the net profit margins for Walmart and Costco.

c. Which firm was more profitable in 2015?

23. Local Co. has sales of $10 million and cost of sales of $6 million. Its selling, general, and administrative expenses are $500,000 and its research and development is $1 million. It has annual depreciation charges of $1 million and a tax rate of 35%.

a. What is Local's gross margin?

b. What is Local's operating margin?

c. What is Local's net profit margin?

24. If Local Co., the company in Problem 23, had an increase in selling expenses of $300,000, how would that affect each of its margins?

25. If Local Co., the company in Problem 23, had interest expense of $800,000, how would that affect each of its margins?

26. Chutes & Co. has interest expense of $1 million and an operating margin of 10% on total sales of $30 million. What is Chutes' interest coverage ratio?

27. Ladders Inc. has a net profit margin of 5% on sales of $50 million. It has book value of equity of $40 million and total liabilities with a book value of $30 million. What is Ladders' ROE? ROA?

28. JPJ Corp has sales of $1 million, accounts receivable of $50,000, total assets of $5 million (of which $3 million are fixed assets), inventory of $150,000, and cost of goods sold of $600,000. What is JPJ's accounts receivable days? Fixed asset turnover? Total asset turnover? Inventory turnover?

29. If JPJ Corp (the company from Problem 28) is able to increase sales by 10% but keep its total and fixed asset growth to only 5%, what will its new asset turnover ratios be?

***30.** Suppose that in 2018, Global launched an aggressive marketing campaign that boosted sales by 15%. However, its operating margin fell from 5.57% to 4.50%. Suppose that the company had no other income, interest expenses were unchanged, and the corporate tax rate for 2018 is 25%.

a. What was Global's EBIT in 2018?
b. What was Global's income in 2018?
c. If Global's P/E ratio and number of shares outstanding remained unchanged, what was Global's share price in 2018?

31. You are analyzing the leverage of two firms and you note the following (all values in millions of dollars):

	Debt	Book Equity	Market Equity	Operating Income	Interest Expense
Firm A	500	300	400	100	50
Firm B	80	35	40	8	7

a. What is the market debt-to-equity ratio of each firm?
b. What is the book debt-to-equity ratio of each firm?
c. What is the interest coverage ratio of each firm?
d. Which firm will have more difficulty meeting its debt obligations?

32. For 2015, Walmart and Target had the following information (all values are in millions of dollars):

	Sales (Income Statement)	Cost of Goods Sold (Income Statement)	Accounts Receivable (Balance Sheet)	Inventory (Balance Sheet)
Walmart	482,130	360,984	5,624	44,469
Target	73,785	51,997	779	8,601

a. What is each company's accounts receivable days?
b. What is each company's inventory turnover?
c. Which company is managing its accounts receivable and inventory more efficiently?

33. In January 2016, United Airlines (UAL) had a market capitalization of $20.6 billion, debt of $11.9 billion, and cash of $5.2 billion. United Airlines had revenues of $37.9 billion. Southwest Airlines (LUV) had a market capitalization of $27.5 billion, debt of $3.2 billion, cash of $3.0 billion, and revenues of $19.8 billion.

a. Compare the market capitalization-to-revenue ratio (also called the price-to-sales ratio) for United Airlines and Southwest Airlines.

b. Compare the enterprise value-to-revenue ratio for United Airlines and Southwest Airlines.

c. Which of these comparisons is more meaningful? Explain.

34. Consider a retail firm with a net profit margin of 3.5%, a total asset turnover of 1.8, total assets of $44 million, and a book value of equity of $18 million.

a. What is the firm's current ROE?

b. If the firm increased its net profit margin to 4%, what would its ROE be?

c. If, in addition, the firm increased its revenues by 20% (while maintaining this higher profit margin and without changing its assets or liabilities), what would its ROE be?

***35.** Find online the annual 10-K report for Costco Wholesale Corporation (COST) for fiscal year 2015 (to ensure your numbers are what were actually reported in 2015, be sure to use the 10-K that was filed in October 2015 and not a more recent 10-K as sometimes numbers are revised in subsequent filings).

a. Compute Costco's net profit margin, total asset turnover, and equity multiplier.

b. Verify the DuPont Identity for Costco's ROE.

c. If Costco managers wanted to increase its ROE by 1 percentage point, how much higher would their asset turnover need to be?

36. Repeat the analysis from parts (a) and (b) in Problem 35 using Walmart Stores (WMT) instead. Specifically, use Walmart's 2015 fiscal data, (to ensure your numbers are what were actually reported in 2015, be sure to use the 10-K that was filed in October 2015 and not a more recent 10-K as sometimes numbers are revised in subsequent filings). Based on the DuPont Identity, what explains the difference between the two firms' ROEs?

Other Financial Statement Information

37. Some statement of financial position information is shown here (all values in millions of dollars). (*See MyLab Finance for the data in Excel format.*):

Statement of Financial Position:	2018	2017	2016	2015
Assets				
Current Assets				
Cash and cash equivalents	293	300	255	232
Net receivables	401	362	385	460
Inventory	374	342	437	306
Other current assets	60	43	53	45
Total Current Assets	**1128**	**1047**	**1130**	**1043**
Long-term investments	128	97	—	200
Property, plant, and equipment	979	991	995	1052
Goodwill	744	748	736	742
Other assets	777	827	911	797
Total Assets	**3756**	**3710**	**3772**	**3834**

Liabilities				
Current Liabilities				
Accounts payable	876	1467	922	980
Short/current long-term debt	410	2	173	288
Other current liabilities	—	—	—	—
Total Current Liabilities	**1286**	**1469**	**1095**	**1268**
Long-term debt	2381	2124	474	475
Other liabilities	435	574	559	551
Total Liabilities	**4102**	**4167**	**2128**	**2294**
Total Stockholder Equity	**–346**	**–457**	**1644**	**1540**
Total Liabilities and Stockholder Equity	**$3756**	**$3710**	**$3772**	**$3834**

a. What change in the book value of the company's equity took place at the end of 2017?
b. For 2017 and 2018, is the company's market-to-book ratio meaningful? Is its book debt-equity ratio meaningful? Explain.
c. Does the company's book value of equity in 2018 imply that it is unprofitable? Explain.

Financial Reporting in Practice

38. Find online the annual 10-K report for Costco Wholesale Corporation (COST) for fiscal year 2015 (filed in October 2015).
a. Which auditing firm certified the financial statements?
b. Which officers of Costco certified the financial statements?

DATA CASE

This is your second interview with a prestigious brokerage firm for a job as an equity analyst. You survived the morning interviews with the department manager and the vice-president of equity. Everything has gone so well that they want to test your ability as an analyst. You are seated in a room with a computer and a list with the names of two companies—Ford (F) and Microsoft (MSFT). You have 90 minutes to complete the following tasks:

1. Download the annual income statements, balance sheets, and cash flow statements for the last four fiscal years from Morningstar (www.morningstar.com). Enter each company's stock symbol and then go to "financials." Copy and paste the financial statements into Excel.

2. Collect historical stock prices for each firm from Yahoo! Finance (https://finance.yahoo.com). Enter the stock symbol and hit enter. On the page for that stock, click "Historical Data" and enter the proper date range to cover the last day of the month corresponding to the date of each financial statement. Use the closing stock prices (not the adjusted close). To calculate the firm's market capitalization at each date, multiply the number of shares outstanding by the firm's historic stock price. You can find the number of shares by using "Basic" under "Weighted average shares outstanding" at the bottom of the Income Statement.

3. Obtain industry averages for each firm from Reuters (www.reuters.com/finance/stocks). Enter the stock symbol at the top of the page in the "Symbol lookup" and then click the "Financials" button, and then click "Search."
   a. Scroll down to "Valuation Ratios," and compare each firm's ratios to the available industry ratios for the most recent year. (Ignore the "Company" column as your calculations will be different.)
   b. Analyze the performance of each firm versus the industry and comment on any trends in each individual firm's performance. Identify any strengths or weaknesses you find in each firm.
4. Examine the market-to-book ratios you calculated for each firm. Which, if either, of the two firms can be considered "growth firms" and which, if either, can be considered "value firms"?
5. Compare the valuation ratios across the two firms. How do you interpret the difference between them?
6. Consider the enterprise value of both firms for each of the four years. How have the values of both firms changed over the time period?

PART

Interest Rates and Valuing Cash Flows

2

CHAPTER 3 The Valuation Principle: The Foundation of Financial Decision Making
CHAPTER 4 The Time Value of Money
CHAPTER 5 Interest Rates
CHAPTER 6 Bonds
CHAPTER 7 Valuing Stocks

Valuation Principle Connection. In this part of the text, we introduce the basic tools for making financial decisions. Chapter 3 presents the most important idea in this book, the Valuation Principle. The Valuation Principle states that we can use market prices to determine the value of an investment opportunity to the firm. As we progress through our study of corporate finance, we will demonstrate that the Valuation Principle is the one unifying principle that underlies all of finance and links all of the ideas throughout this book.

For a financial manager, evaluating financial decisions involves computing the net present value of a project's future cash flows. We use the Valuation Principle's Law of One Price to derive a central concept in financial economics—the time value of money. In Chapter 4, we explain how to value any series of future cash flows and derive a few useful shortcuts for valuing various types of cash flow patterns. Chapter 5 discusses how interest rates are quoted in the market and how to handle interest rates that compound more frequently than once per year. We apply the Valuation Principle to demonstrate that the return required from an investment will depend on the rate of return of investments with maturity and risk similar to the cash flows being valued. This observation leads to the important concept of the cost of capital of an investment decision. In Chapter 6, we demonstrate an application of the time value of money tools using interest rates: valuing the bonds issued by corporations and governments. In Chapter 7, we apply the time value of money tools to valuing stocks and get our first glimpse at the equity cost of capital.

CHAPTER

3 The Valuation Principle: The Foundation of Financial Decision Making

LEARNING OBJECTIVES

- Identify the role of financial managers in decision making
- Recognize the role competitive markets play in determining the value of a good
- Understand the Valuation Principle and how it can be used to identify decisions that increase the value of the firm
- Assess the effect of interest rates on today's value of future cash flows
- Understand the Law of One Price

NOTATION

r	interest rate
PV	present value
FV	future value
C	cash flow
n	number of periods

In November 2013, the Hudson's Bay Company (HBC) acquired Saks Inc. (owner of the luxury department store chain Saks Fifth Avenue). How did HBC's managers decide this was the right decision for the company?

Every decision has future consequences that will affect the value of the firm. These consequences will generally include both benefits and costs. For example, in addition to the upfront cost of buying Saks, HBC will also incur ongoing costs associated with future store openings, marketing efforts, and e-commerce upgrades. The benefits to HBC include the revenues from Saks stores and also the reduced costs of merchandise by being able to negotiate volume discounts with suppliers. This decision will increase HBC's value if these benefits outweigh the costs.

More generally, a decision is good for the firm's investors if it increases the firm's value by providing benefits whose value exceeds the costs. But how do we compare costs and benefits that occur at different points in time, or are in different currencies, or have different risks associated with them? To make a valid comparison, we must use the tools of finance to express all costs and benefits in common terms. We convert all costs and benefits into a common currency and common point of time, such as dollars today. In this chapter, we learn (1) the *Valuation Principle*, which demonstrates how to use market information to evaluate costs and benefits, and (2) the *Law of One Price*, which explains why market prices are so important. Then, we will start to build the critical tools relating to the time value of money. These tools will allow you to correctly compare the costs and benefits of a decision no matter when they occur.

3.1 Cost-Benefit Analysis

The first step in decision making is to identify the costs and benefits of a decision. In this section, we look at the role of financial managers in evaluating costs and benefits and the tools they use to quantify them.

Role of the Financial Manager

A financial manager's job is to make decisions on behalf of the firm's investors. Our objective in this book is to explain how to make decisions that increase the value of the firm to its investors. In principle, the idea is simple and intuitive: for good decisions, the benefits exceed the costs. Of course, real-world opportunities are usually complex, so the costs and benefits are often difficult to quantify. Quantifying them often involves using skills from other management disciplines, as in the following examples:

Marketing: to determine the increase in revenues resulting from an advertising campaign

Economics: to determine the increase in demand from lowering the price of a product

Organizational behaviour: to determine the effect of changes in management structure on productivity

Strategy: to determine a competitor's response to a price increase

Operations: to determine production costs after the modernization of a manufacturing plant

For the remainder of this text, we will assume that we can rely on experts in these different areas to provide this information so that the costs and benefits associated with

YOUR PERSONAL FINANCIAL DECISIONS

While the focus of this text is on the decisions a financial manager makes in a business setting, you will soon see that concepts and skills you will learn here apply to personal decisions as well. As a normal part of life, we all make decisions that trade off benefits and costs across time. Going to university, purchasing this book, saving for a new car or house down payment, taking out a car loan or home loan, buying shares of stock, and deciding between jobs are just a few examples of such decisions that you have faced or could face in the near future. As you read through this book, you will see that the *Valuation Principle* is the foundation of all financial decision making—whether in a business or in a personal context.

a decision have already been identified. With that task done, the financial manager's job is to compare the costs and benefits and determine the best decision to make for the value of the firm.

Quantifying Costs and Benefits

The first step in decision making is to identify the costs and benefits of a decision. The next step is quantifying these costs and benefits. To evaluate the costs and benefits of a decision, we must value the effects in the same terms—cash today. Let's make this concrete with a simple example.

Suppose a jewellery manufacturer has the opportunity to trade 600 ounces of silver for 10 ounces of gold today. An ounce of silver differs in value from an ounce of gold. Consequently, it is incorrect to compare 600 ounces to 10 ounces and conclude that the larger quantity is better. Instead, to compare the costs of the silver and benefit of the gold, we first need to quantify their values in equivalent terms—cash today.

Consider the silver. What is its cash value today? Suppose silver can be bought and sold for a current market price of $20 per ounce. Then the 600 ounces of silver we give up has a cash value of [1]

$$(600 \text{ ounces of silver}) \times (\$20/\text{ounce of silver}) = \$12{,}000$$

If the current market price for gold is $1500 per ounce, then for the 10 ounces of gold we receive a cash value of

$$(10 \text{ ounces of gold}) \times (\$1500/\text{ounce of gold}) = \$15{,}000$$

We have now quantified the decision. The jeweller's opportunity has a benefit of $15,000 and a cost of $12,000. The net benefit of the decision is $15,000 − $12,000 = $3000 today. The net value of the decision is positive, so by accepting the trade, the jewellery firm will be richer by $3000.

Role of Competitive Market Prices

Suppose the jeweller works exclusively on silver jewellery or thinks the price of silver should be higher. Should his decision change? The answer is no—he can always make the trade and then buy silver at the current market price. Even if he has no use for the gold, he can immediately sell it for $15,000, buy back the 600 ounces of silver at the current market price of $12,000, and pocket the remaining $3000. Thus, independent of his own views or preferences, the value of the silver to the jeweller is $12,000.

Because the jeweller can both buy and sell silver at its current market price, his personal preferences or use for silver and his opinion of the fair price are irrelevant in evaluating the value of this opportunity. This observation highlights an important general principle related to goods trading in a **competitive market**, a market in which a good can be bought and sold at the same price. Whenever a good trades in a competitive market, that price determines the value of the good. This point is one of the central and most powerful ideas in finance. It will underlie almost every concept we develop throughout the text.

competitive market A market in which a good can be bought *and* sold at the same price.

[1]You might worry about commissions or other transaction costs (such as transportation costs) that are incurred when buying or selling silver, in addition to the market price. For simplicity, we will ignore transaction costs.

EXAMPLE 3.1 Competitive Market Prices Determine Value

PROBLEM

You have just won a radio contest and are disappointed to find out that the prize is four tickets to the Celine Dion concert (face value $100 each). Not being a fan of Celine (as you were traumatized by having to watch the movie *Titanic* several times when you were younger), you have no intention of going to the show. However, it turns out that there is a second choice: two tickets to Justin Bieber's sold-out show (face value $150 each). You notice that on eBay, tickets to the Celine Dion show are being bought and sold for $70 each and tickets to Justin Bieber's show are being bought and sold at $180 each. What should you do?

SOLUTION

Plan

Market prices, not your personal preferences (nor the face value of the tickets), are relevant here:

4 Celine Dion tickets at $70 each
2 Justin Bieber tickets at $180 each

You need to compare the market value of each option and choose the one with the highest market value.

Execute

The Celine Dion tickets have a total market value of $280 (4 × $70) versus the $360 total market value of the Justin Bieber tickets (2 × $180). You should take the tickets to Justin Bieber even though their face value (2 × $150 = $300) is lower than the Celine Dion tickets' face value (4 × $100 = $400).

Evaluate

As we emphasized earlier, competitive market prices determine value and should guide your decision. You should take the Justin Bieber tickets even if you don't want to go to his show. You can always sell the tickets on eBay for their market value of $360, which is more than you would get if you took the Celine Dion tickets and tried to sell them. If you changed your mind and decided you and three friends did want to go to Celine Dion's show, you should still take the Justin Bieber tickets, sell them for $360, buy the Celine Dion tickets for $280 and pocket the remaining $80.

CONCEPT CHECK

1. When costs and benefits are in different units or goods, how can we compare them?
2. If canola trades in a competitive market, would a canola oil producer that has a use for the canola value it differently than another investor would?

3.2 Market Prices and the Valuation Principle

In the previous examples, the right decisions were clear because the costs and benefits were easy to evaluate and compare. They were easy to evaluate because we were able to use current market prices to convert them into equivalent cash values. Once we can express costs and benefits in terms of "cash today," it is a straightforward process to compare them and determine whether the decision will increase the firm's value. When using market prices to evaluate the costs and benefits of a decision in terms of cash today, it is then a simple matter to determine the best decision for the firm. The best decision makes the firm and its investors wealthier, because the value of its benefits exceeds the value of its costs. We call this idea the Valuation Principle.

The Valuation Principle

Our discussion so far establishes competitive market prices as the way to evaluate the costs and benefits of a decision in terms of cash today. Once we do this, it is a simple matter to determine the best decision for the firm, the decision that makes the firm and its investors wealthier through the value of its benefits exceeding the value of its costs. This is the Valuation Principle:

Valuation Principle The value of a commodity or an asset to the firm or its investors is determined by its competitive market price. The benefits and costs of a decision should be evaluated using those market prices. When the value of the benefits exceeds the value of the costs, the decision will increase the market value of the firm.

> **The Valuation Principle:**
>
> *The value of a commodity or an asset to the firm or its investors is determined by its competitive market price. The benefits and costs of a decision should be evaluated using those market prices. When the value of the benefits exceeds the value of the costs, the decision will increase the market value of the firm.*

The **Valuation Principle** provides the basis for decision making throughout this text. In the remainder of this chapter, we apply it to decisions whose costs and benefits occur at different points in time. We then consider its consequences for the prices of assets in the market and develop the concept of the *Law of One Price.*

EXAMPLE 3.2 Applying the Valuation Principle

PROBLEM

You are the operations manager at your firm. Due to a pre-existing contract, you have the opportunity to acquire 200 barrels of oil and 3000 pounds of copper for a total of $25,000. The current market price of oil is $90 per barrel, and copper is $3.50 per pound. You are not sure that you need all of the oil and copper, so you are wondering if you should take this opportunity. How valuable is it? Would your decision change if you believed the value of oil or copper would plummet over the next month?

SOLUTION

Plan

We need to quantify the costs and benefits using market prices. We are comparing $25,000 with

200 barrels of oil at $90 per barrel
3000 pounds of copper at $3.50 per pound

Execute

Using the competitive market prices we have

$$(3000 \text{ pounds of copper}) \times (\$3.50/\text{pound today}) = \$10{,}500 \text{ today}$$
$$(200 \text{ barrels}) \times (\$90/\text{barrel today}) = \$18{,}000 \text{ today}$$

The value of the opportunity is the value of the oil plus the value of the copper less the cost of the opportunity, or $18,000 + $10,500 – $25,000 = $3500 today. Because the value is positive, we should take it. This value depends only on the *current* market prices for oil and copper. If we do not need all of the oil and copper, we can sell the excess at current market prices. Even if we thought the value of oil or copper was about to plummet, the value of this investment would be unchanged. (We can always exchange them for dollars immediately at the current market prices.)

Evaluate

Since we are transacting today, only the current prices in a competitive market matter. Our own use for or opinion about the future prospects of oil or copper does not alter the value of the decision today. This decision is good for the firm and will increase its value by $3500.

Why There Can Be Only One Competitive Price for a Good

Law of One Price In competitive markets the same goods must have the same price; financial securities that produce exactly the same cash flows must have the same price.

arbitrage The practice of buying and selling equivalent goods or portfolios to take advantage of a price difference.

arbitrage opportunity Any situation in which it is possible to make a profit without taking any risk or making any investment.

Principle of No Arbitrage In normal competitive markets, supply and demand forces cause prices to adjust so that arbitrage opportunities are eliminated.

The Valuation Principle and finance in general rely on using a competitive market price to value a cost or benefit. We cannot have two different competitive market prices for the same good—otherwise, we would arrive at two different values. Fortunately, powerful market forces keep competitive prices the same. To illustrate, imagine what you would do if you saw gold simultaneously trading for two different prices. You and everyone else who noticed the difference would buy at the low price and sell at the high price for as many ounces of gold as possible, making instant risk-free profits. A flood of buy and sell orders would push the two prices together until the profit was eliminated. These forces establish the **Law of One Price**, which states that in competitive markets the same goods must have the same price. More generally, financial securities that produce exactly the same cash flows must have the same price.

In general, the practice of buying and selling equivalent goods in different markets to take advantage of a price difference is known as **arbitrage**. We refer to any situation in which it is possible to make a profit without taking any risk or making any investment as an **arbitrage opportunity**. Because an arbitrage opportunity's benefits are more valuable than its costs, whenever an arbitrage opportunity appears in financial markets, investors will race to take advantage of it. Supply and demand forces, influenced by their trades, will cause prices to equalize across competitive markets and eliminate the arbitrage opportunity. Arbitrage opportunities are like money lying in the street; once spotted, they will quickly disappear. Thus, the normal state of affairs in competitive markets should be that no arbitrage opportunities exist—this is known as the **Principle of No Arbitrage**.

Retail stores often quote different prices for the same item in different markets. *The Economist* magazine has long compared prices for a McDonald's Big Mac around the world. In Table 3.1, we show Big Mac prices from January 2018.

TABLE 3.1 **The prices of McDonald's Big Mac around the world in January 2018.**

Shown are prices in the local currency, the name of the local currency, and prices converted to U.S. dollars.

Country	Local Price	Local Currency	Price in U.S. Dollars
Ukraine	47	hryvnia	$1.64
Russia	130	ruble	$2.29
Mexico	48	peso	$2.57
Hong Kong	20.5	HK dollar	$2.62
India	180	rupee	$2.82
Vietnam	65,000	đồng	$2.86
Poland	10.1	złoty	$2.97
China	20.4	yuan	$3.17
Japan	380	yen	$3.43
Czech Republic	79	koruna	$3.81
Greece	3.35	euro	$4.10
Britain	3.19	pound	$4.41
New Zealand	6.2	NZ dollar	$4.51
Germany	3.9	euro	$4.77

(continued)

TABLE 3.1 *(continued)*

Country	Local Price	Local Currency	Price in U.S. Dollars
Israel	16.5	new shekel	$4.80
Brazil	16.5	real	$5.11
Canada	6.55	dollar	$5.26
United States	5.28	US dollar	$5.28
Norway	49	krone	$6.24
Switzerland	6.5	franc	$6.76

Sources: IMF; McDonald's; Thomson Reuters; *The Economist;* author's calculations

Of course, these are not examples of competitive market prices because you can only buy a Big Mac at these prices but you are not able to sell at these prices (only McDonald's has the right to sell a Big Mac). Hence, these price differences across markets do not present an arbitrage opportunity.

CONCEPT CHECK

3. How do investors' profit motives keep competitive market prices correct?
4. How do we determine whether a decision increases the value of the firm?

3.3 The Time Value of Money and Interest Rates

Unlike in the examples presented so far, most financial decisions have costs and benefits that occur at different points in time. For example, typical investment projects incur costs up front and provide benefits in the future. In this section, we show how to account for this time difference when using the Valuation Principle to make a decision.

Time value of money: The diff between dollar today der Tom

The Time Value of Money

Consider a firm's investment opportunity with the following cash flows:

Cost: $100,000 today
Benefit: $105,000 in one year

Because both are expressed in dollar terms, are the cost and benefit directly comparable? Calculating the project's net value as $105,000 – $100,000 = $5000 is incorrect because it ignores the *timing* of the costs and benefits. That is, it treats money today as equivalent to money in one year. In general, a dollar today is worth *more* than a dollar in one year. To see why, note that if you have $1 today, you can invest it. For example, if you deposit it in a bank account paying 7% interest, you will have $1.07 at the end of one year. We call the difference in value between money today and money in the future the **time value of money**.

time value of money
The difference in value between money today and money in the future; also, the observation that two cash flows at two different points in time have different values.

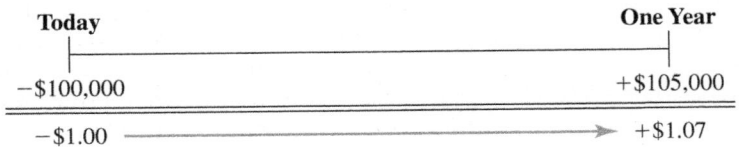

FIGURE 3.1 Converting between Dollars Today and Gold or Dollars in the Future

We can convert dollars today to different goods or points in time by using the competitive market price or interest rate. Once values are in equivalent terms, we can use the Valuation Principle to make a decision.

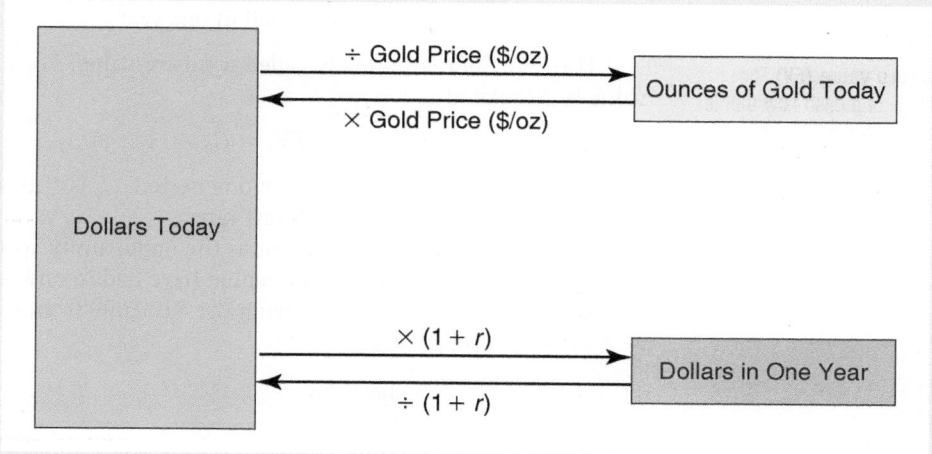

Figure 3.1 illustrates how we use competitive market prices and interest rates to convert between dollars today and other goods, or dollars in the future. Just like silver and gold, money today and money tomorrow are not the same thing. We compare them just like we did silver and gold—using competitive market prices. But in the case of money, what is the price? It is the interest rate: the price for exchanging money today for money in a year. We can use the interest rate to determine values in the same way we used competitive market prices. Once we quantify all the costs and benefits of an investment in terms of dollars today, we can rely on the Valuation Principle to determine whether the investment will increase the firm's value.

The Interest Rate: Converting Cash across Time

We now develop the tools needed to value our $100,000 investment opportunity correctly. By depositing money into a savings account, we can convert money today into money in the future with no risk. Similarly, by borrowing money from the bank, we can exchange money in the future for money today. Suppose the current annual interest rate is 7%. By investing $1 today, we can convert this $1 into $1.07 in one year. Similarly, by borrowing at this rate, we can exchange $1.07 in one year for $1 today. More generally, we define the **interest rate**, r, for a given period as the interest rate at which money can be borrowed or lent over that period. In our example, the interest rate is 7% and we can exchange $1 today for $(1 + 0.7)$ dollars in one year. In general, we can exchange $1 today for $(1 + r)$ dollars in the future, and vice versa. We refer to $(1 + r)$ as the **interest rate factor** for cash flows; it defines how we convert cash flows across time, and has units of "$ in one year/$ today."

interest rate The rate at which money can be borrowed or lent over a given period.

interest rate factor One plus the interest rate. It is the rate of exchange between dollars today and dollars in the future; it has units of "$ in one year/$ today."

As with other market prices, the interest rate ultimately depends on supply and demand. In particular, at the market-determined interest rate, the supply of savings equals the demand for borrowing. Regardless of how it is determined, once we know the interest rate, we can apply the Valuation Principle and use it to evaluate other decisions in which costs and benefits are separated in time.

Value of $100,000 Investment in One Year. Let's reevaluate the investment we considered earlier, this time taking into account the time value of money. If the interest rate is 7%, then we can express the cost of the investment as

$$\text{Cost} = (\$100{,}000 \text{ today}) \times \left(\frac{\$1.07 \text{ in one year}}{\$1 \text{ today}}\right)$$

$$= \$107{,}000 \text{ in one year}$$

future value (FV) The value of a cash flow that is moved forward in time.

This $107,000 amount is called a **future value**. For a one-period case, the future value is calculated as follows:

$$FV_1 = C_0 \times (1 + r) \tag{3.1}$$

where FV_1 is the future value after one period, C_0 is the amount invested or borrowed now (at time 0), and r is the interest rate.

Think of this $107,000 amount as the opportunity cost of spending $100,000 today. The firm gives up the $107,000 it would have had in one year if it had left the money in the bank. Alternatively, by borrowing the $100,000 from the same bank, the firm would owe $107,000 in one year.

	Today	One Year
Investment	−$100,000	+$105,000
Bank	−$100,000	+$107,000

We have used a market price, the interest rate, to put both the costs and benefits in terms of "dollars in one year," so now we can use the Valuation Principle to compare them and compute the investment's net value by subtracting the cost of the investment from the benefit in one year:

$$\$105{,}000 - \$107{,}000 = -\$2000 \text{ in one year}$$

In other words, the firm could earn $2000 more in one year by putting the $100,000 in the bank rather than making this investment. Because the net value is negative, we should reject the investment; if we took it, the firm would be $2000 poorer in one year than if we did not.

Value of $100,000 Investment Today. The previous calculation expressed the value of the costs and benefits in terms of a future value amount: dollars in one year. Alternatively, we can use the interest rate factor to convert to a present value amount: dollars today. Consider the benefit of $105,000 in one year. What is the equivalent amount in terms of dollars today? That is, how much would we need to have in the bank today so that we would end up with $105,000 in the bank in one year? We find this amount by dividing by the interest rate factor:

$$\text{Benefit} = (\$105{,}000 \text{ in one year}) \div \left(\frac{\$1.07 \text{ in one year}}{\$1 \text{ today}}\right)$$

$$= \$98{,}130.84 \text{ today}$$

present value (PV) The value of a cost or benefit computed in terms of cash today.

This $98,130.84 amount is called a **present value (PV)**. For a one-period case, the present value is calculated as follows:

$$PV_0 = C_1 \div (1 + r) = \frac{C_1}{(1 + r)} = C_1 \times \frac{1}{(1 + r)} \tag{3.2}$$

where PV_0 is the present value now (at time 0), C_1 is the cash flow in one year (at time 1), and r is the interest rate.

This \$98,130.84 is also the amount the bank would lend to us today if we promised to repay \$105,000 in one year.[2] Thus, it is the competitive market price at which we can "buy" or "sell" a cash flow of \$105,000 that occurs in one year.

	Today		One Year
Value of Cost Today	−\$100,000		+\$105,000
Value of Benefit Today	+\$98,130.84 ←	$\frac{105{,}000}{1.07}$	←

Now we are ready to compute the net value of the investment by subtracting the cost from the benefit:

$$\$98{,}130.84 - \$100{,}000 = -\$1869.16 \text{ today}$$

Once again, the negative result indicates that we should reject the investment. Taking the investment would make the firm \$1869.16 poorer today because it gave up \$100,000 for something worth only \$98,130.84.

Present versus Future Value. This calculation demonstrates that our decision is the same whether we express the value of the investment in terms of the future value amount (dollars in one year) or the present value amount (dollars today): we should reject the investment. Indeed, if we convert from dollars today to dollars in one year,

$$(-\$1869.16 \text{ today}) \times (1.07\ \$ \text{ in one year}/\$ \text{ today}) = -\$2000 \text{ in one year}$$

we see that the two results for the net benefit minus cost are equivalent but expressed as values at different points in time.

discount factor $1/(1+r)$ or the inverse of the interest rate factor. It is used to move cash flows one period back in time along the timeline and has units of "\$ today/\$ in the future."

Discount Factors and Rates. In the preceding calculation, we can interpret

$$\frac{1}{1+r} = \frac{1}{1.07} = 0.93458$$

as the *price* today of \$1 in one year. In other words, for just under 93.5 cents, you can "buy" \$1 to be delivered in one year. Note that the value is less than \$1; money in the future is worth less today, and so its price reflects a discount. Because it provides the discount at which we can purchase money in the future, the amount $\frac{1}{1+r}$ is called the one-year **discount factor**. The interest rate is also referred to as the **discount rate** for an investment.

discount rate The appropriate rate to discount cash flows to determine their value at an earlier time.

[2]We are assuming the bank is willing to lend at the same 7% interest rate, which would be the case if there were no risk associated with the cash flow.

EXAMPLE 3.3 Comparing Revenues at Different Points in Time

PROBLEM

The launch of Sony's PlayStation 3 was delayed until November 2006, giving Microsoft's Xbox 360 a full year on the market without competition. Sony did not repeat this mistake in 2013 when PS4 launched at the same time as Xbox One. Imagine that it is November 2005 and you are the marketing manager for the PlayStation. You estimate that if PlayStation 3 were ready to be launched immediately, you could sell \$2 billion worth of the console in its first year. However, if your launch is delayed a year, you believe that Microsoft's head start will reduce your first-year sales by 20% to \$1.6 billion. If the interest rate is 8%, what is the cost of a delay of the first year's revenues in terms of dollars in 2005?

SOLUTION

Plan

Revenues if released today: $2 billion. Revenue if delayed: $1.6 billion. Interest rate: 8%.

We need to compute the revenues if the launch is delayed and compare them to the revenues from launching immediately (in 2005). In order to make a fair comparison, however, we need to convert the future revenues of the PlayStation if they are delayed into an equivalent present value of those revenues.

Execute

If the launch is delayed to 2006, revenues will drop to $1.6 billion. To compare this amount to revenues of $2 billion if launched in 2005, we must convert it using the interest rate of 8%:

$$\$1.6 \text{ billion in } 2006 \div \left(\frac{\$1.08 \text{ in } 2006}{\$1 \text{ in } 2005}\right) = \$1.481 \text{ billion in } 2005$$

Therefore, the cost of a delay of one year is

$2 billion 2 $1.481 billion 5 $0.519 billion 5 $519 million

Evaluate

Delaying the project for one year was equivalent to giving up $519 million in revenue. In this example, we focused only on the effect on the first year's revenues. However, delaying the launch delays the entire revenue stream by one year, so the total cost would be calculated in the same way by summing the cost of delay for each year of revenues.

Timelines

timeline A linear representation of the timing of (potential) cash flows.

Our visual representation of the cost and benefit of the $100,000 investment in this section is an example of a **timeline**, a linear representation of the timing of the expected cash flows. Timelines are an important first step in organizing and then solving a financial problem. We use them throughout this text.

Constructing a Timeline

To illustrate how to construct a timeline, assume that a friend owes you money. He has agreed to repay the loan by making two payments of $10,000 at the end of each of the next two years. We represent this information on a timeline as follows:

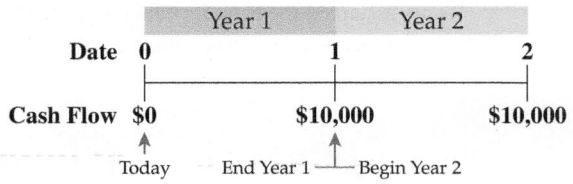

Identifying Dates on a Timeline

Date 0 represents the present. Date 1 is one year later and represents the end of the first year. The $10,000 cash flow below date 1 is the payment you will receive at the end of the first year. Date 2 is two years from now; it represents the end of the second year. The $10,000 cash flow below date 2 is the payment you will receive at the end of the second year.

To track cash flows, we interpret each point on the timeline as a specific date. The space between Date 0 and Date 1 then represents the time period between these dates—in this case, the first year of the loan. Date 0 is the beginning of the first year, and Date 1 is the end of the first year. Similarly, Date 1 is the beginning of the second year, and Date 2 is the end of the second year. By denoting time in this way, Date 1 signifies *both* the end of Year 1 and the beginning of Year 2, which makes sense since those dates are effectively the same point in time.[3]

Distinguishing Cash Inflows from Outflows

In this example, both cash flows are inflows. In many cases, however, a financial decision will involve both inflows and outflows. To differentiate between the two types of cash flows, we assign a different sign to each: inflows (cash flows received) are positive cash flows, whereas outflows (cash flows paid out) are negative cash flows.

To illustrate, suppose you have agreed to lend your brother $10,000 today. Your brother has agreed to repay this loan in two instalments of $6000 at the end of each of the next two years. The timeline is

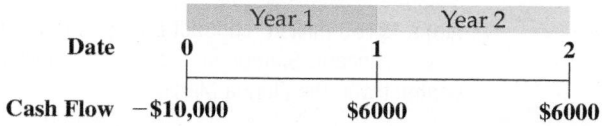

Notice that the first cash flow at Date 0 (today) is represented as −$10,000 because it is an outflow. The subsequent cash flows of $6000 are positive because they are inflows.

Representing Various Time Periods

So far, we have used timelines to show the cash flows that occur at the end of each year. Actually, timelines can represent cash flows that take place at any point in time. For example, if you pay rent each month, you could use a timeline, such as the one in our first example, to represent two rental payments, but you would replace the "year" label with "month."

Many of the timelines included in this chapter are very simple. Consequently, you may feel that it is not worth the time or trouble to construct them. As you progress to more difficult problems, however, you will find that timelines identify events in a transaction or investment that are easy to overlook. If you fail to recognize these cash flows, you will make flawed financial decisions. Therefore, approach *every* problem by drawing the timeline as we do in this chapter.

CONCEPT CHECK

5. How is an interest rate like a price? – give you more money
6. Is the value today of money to be received in one year higher when interest rates are high or when interest rates are low?

3.4 Valuing Cash Flows at Different Points in Time

The example of the $100,000 investment in the previous section laid the groundwork for how we will compare cash flows that happen at different points in time. In this section, we will generalize from the example by introducing three important rules central to financial decision making that allow us to compare or combine values across time.

[3]That is, there is no real time difference between a cash flow paid at 11:59 p.m. on December 31 and one paid at 12:01 a.m. on January 1, although there may be some other differences, such as taxation, that we will overlook for now.

COMMON MISTAKE

Summing Cash Flows Across Time

Once you understand the time value of money, our first rule may seem straightforward. However, it is very common, especially for those who have not studied finance, to violate this rule, simply treating all cash flows as comparable regardless of when they are received. One example is in sports contracts. In 2011, Albert Pujols signed a contract with the Los Angeles Angels that was repeatedly referred to as a "$240 million" contract. The $240 million comes from simply adding up all the payments Pujols would receive over the 10 years of the contract—treating dollars received in 10 years the same as dollars received today. The same thing occurred when Lionel Messi signed a contract extension with FC Barcelona in 2013, giving him a "$150 million" contract through 2018, and in 2015 when Giancarlo Stanton signed a "$325 million" 13-year contract with the Florida Marlins.

Xavier Subias/age fotostock/Alamy Stock Photo

Lionel Messi, FC Barcelona

Rule 1: Comparing and Combining Values

Our first rule is that it is possible to compare or combine values only at the same point in time. This rule restates a conclusion from the last section—only cash flows in the same units can be compared or combined. A dollar today and a dollar in one year are not equivalent. Having money now is more valuable than having money in the future; if you have the money today you can invest it and earn interest on it.

To compare or combine cash flows that occur at different points in time, you first need to convert the cash flows into the same units by moving them to the same point in time. The next two rules show how to move the cash flows on the timeline.

Rule 2: Compounding

Suppose we have $1000 today, and we wish to determine the equivalent amount in one year's time. As we saw earlier in this chapter, if the current market interest rate is $r = 10\%$, we can use the interest rate factor $(1 + r) = 1.10$ as an exchange rate, meaning the rate at which we exchange money today for money in one year, to move the cash flow forward in time. That is,

$$(\$1000 \text{ today}) \times \left(\frac{\$1.10 \text{ in one year}}{\$1 \text{ today}}\right) = \$1100 \text{ in one year}$$

In general, if the market interest rate for the year is r, then we multiply by the interest rate factor $(1 + r)$ to move the cash flow from the beginning to the end of the year. We multiply by $(1 + r)$ because at the end of the year you will have ($1 \times$ your original investment) plus interest in the amount of ($r \times$ your original investment). This process of moving forward along the timeline to determine a cash flow's value in the future (its future value) is known as **compounding**. *Our second rule stipulates that to calculate a cash flow's future value, you must compound it.*

compounding Computing the future value of a cash flow over a long horizon by multiplying by the interest rate factors associated with each intervening period.

We can apply this rule repeatedly. Suppose we want to know how much the $1000 is worth in two years' time. If the interest rate for year 2 is also 10%, then we convert as we just did:

$$(\$1100 \text{ in one year}) \times \left(\frac{\$1.10 \text{ in two years}}{\$1 \text{ in one year}}\right) = \$1210 \text{ in two years}$$

Let's represent this calculation on a timeline:

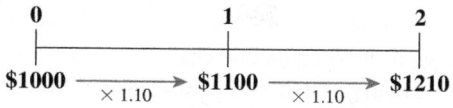

Given a 10% interest rate, all of the cash flows—$1000 at date 0, $1100 at date 1, and $1210 at date 2—are equivalent. They have the same value to us but are expressed in different units (dollars at different points in time). An arrow that points to the right indicates that the value is being moved forward in time—that is, it is being compounded.

In the preceding example, $1210 is the future value of $1000 two years from today. Note that the value grows as we move the cash flow further in the future. In the last section, we defined the time value of money as the difference in value between money today and money in the future. Here, we can say that $1210 in two years is equivalent to $1000 today. The reason money is more valuable to you today is that you have opportunities to invest it. As in this example, by having money sooner, you can invest it (here at a 10% return) so that it will grow to a larger amount of money in the future. Note also that the equivalent amount grows by $100 the first year, but by $110 the second year. In the second year, we earn interest on our original $1000, plus we earn interest on the $100 interest we received in the first year. This effect of earning interest both on the original principal and on the accrued interest is known as **compound interest**. Figure 3.2 shows how over time the amount of money you earn from interest on interest grows so that it will eventually exceed the amount of money that you earn as interest on your original deposit.

compound interest The combination of earning interest on the original principal and earning interest on accrued interest.

How does the future value change in the third year? Continuing to use the same approach, we compound the cash flow a third time. Assuming the competitive market interest rate is fixed at 10%, we get

$$\$1000 \times (1.10) \times (1.10) \times (1.10) = \$1000 \times (1.10)^3 \times \$1331$$

In general, if we have a cash flow now, C_0, to compute its value n periods into the future, we must compound it by the n intervening interest rate factors. If the interest rate r is constant, this calculation yields,

Future Value of a Cash Flow

$$FV_n = C_0 \times \underbrace{(1 + r) \times (1 + r) \times \cdots \times (1 + r)}_{n \text{ times}} = C_0 \times (1 + r)^n \tag{3.3}$$

RULE OF 72

Another way to think about the effect of compounding is to consider how long it will take your money to double, given different interest rates. Suppose you want to know how many years it will take for $1 to grow to a future value of $2. You want the number of years, n, to solve

$$FV_n = \$1 \times (1 + r)^n = \$2$$

If you solve this formula for different interest rates, you will find the following approximation:

Years to double ≈72 ÷ (interest rate in percent)

This simple "Rule of 72" is fairly accurate (i.e., within one year of the exact doubling time) for interest rates higher than 2%. For example, if the interest rate is 9%, the doubling time should be about 72 ÷ 9 = 8 years. Indeed, $1.09^8 = 1.99$! So, given a 9% interest rate, your money will approximately double every eight years.

FIGURE 3.2 The Composition of Interest over Time

This bar graph shows how the account balance and the composition of the interest change over time when an investor starts with an original deposit of $1000 (represented by the red area) in an account earning 10% interest over a 20-year period. Note that the turquoise area representing interest on interest grows and by year 15 has become larger than the interest on the original deposit, shown in green. Over the 20 years of the investment, the interest on interest the investor earned is $3727.50, while the interest earned on the original $1000 principal is $2000. The total compound interest over the 20 years is $5727.50 (the sum of the interest on interest and the interest on principal). Combining the original principal of $1000 with the total compound interest gives the future value after 20 years of $6727.50.

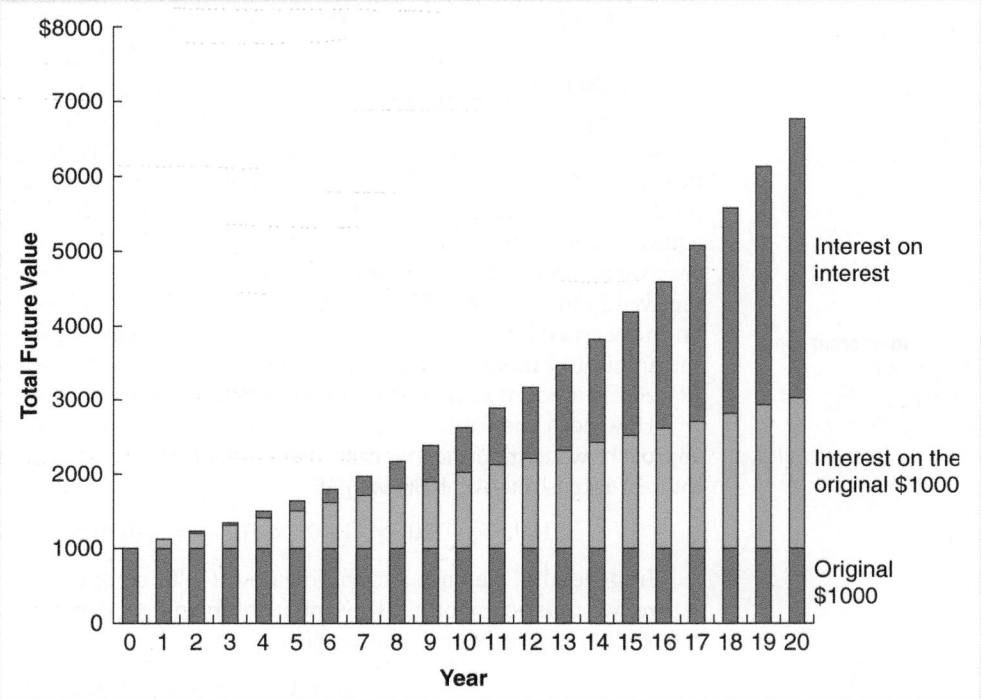

Rule 3: Discounting

The third rule describes how to put a value today on a cash flow that comes in the future. Suppose you would like to compute the value today of $1000 that you anticipate receiving in one year. If the current market interest rate is 10%, you can compute this value by converting units as we did earlier in this chapter:

$$(\$1000 \text{ in one year}) \div \left(\frac{\$1.10 \text{ in one year}}{\$1 \text{ today}}\right) = \$909.09 \text{ today}$$

That is, to move the cash flow back along the timeline, we divide it by the interest rate factor $(1 + r)$ where r is the interest rate. The discount factor, defined earlier, is the inverse of the interest rate factor and is as follows:

$$\text{Discount Factor} = \frac{1}{(1 + r)}$$

discounting Finding the equivalent value today of a future cash flow by multiplying by a discount factor, or equivalently, dividing by 1 plus the discount rate.

The discount factor has units of "$ today/$ in the future," so by multiplying a future amount by the discount factor (or equivalently dividing by the interest rate factor) we move a cash flow back in time along the timeline. This process of finding the equivalent value today of a future cash flow is known as **discounting**. *Our third rule stipulates that to calculate the value of a future cash flow at an earlier point in time, we must discount it.*

Suppose that you anticipate receiving the $1000 two years from today rather than in one year. If the interest rate for both years is 10%, you can prepare the following timeline:

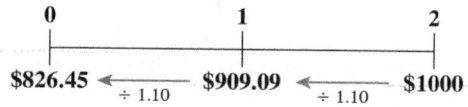

When the interest rate is 10%, all of the cash flows—$826.45 at date 0, $909.09 at date 1, and $1000 at date 2—are equivalent. They represent the same value to us but in different units (different points in time). The arrow points to the left to indicate that the value is being moved backward in time, or discounted. Note that the value decreases the further in the future is the original cash flow.

The value of a future cash flow at an earlier point on the timeline is its present value at the earlier point in time. That is, $826.45 is the present value at date 0 of $1000 in two years. The present value is the "do-it-yourself" price to produce a future cash flow. Thus, if we invested $826.45 today for two years at 10% interest, we would have a future value of $1000, using the second rule of valuing cash flows:

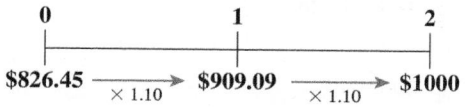

Suppose the $1000 were three years away and you wanted to compute the present value. Again, if the interest rate is 10%, we have,

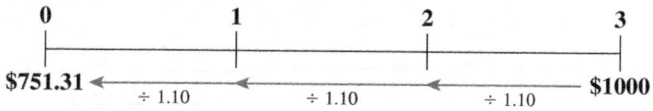

That is, the present value today of a cash flow of $1000 in three years is given by

$$\$1000 \div (1.10) \div (1.10) \div (1.10) = \$1000 \div (1.10)^3 = \$751.31$$

In general, to compute the present value today (date 0) of a cash flow, Cn, that comes n periods from now, we must discount it by dividing by the n intervening interest rate factors or, equivalently, multiplying by the n intervening discount factors. If the interest rate, r, is constant, this yields

Present Value of a Cash Flow

$$PV_0 = \underbrace{C_n \div (1 + r)^n}_{\text{divide by the interest rate factor to the power } n}$$

$$= \underbrace{C_n \times \frac{1}{(1 + r)^n}}_{\text{or multiply by the discount factor to the power } n}$$

$$= \frac{C_n}{(1 + r)^n} \tag{3.4}$$

EXAMPLE 3.4 Present Value of a Single Future Cash Flow

PROBLEM

You are considering investing in a Government of Canada bond that will pay $15,000 in 10 years. If the competitive market interest rate is fixed at 6% per year, what is the bond worth today?

SOLUTION

Plan

First set up your timeline. The cash flows for this bond are represented by the following timeline:

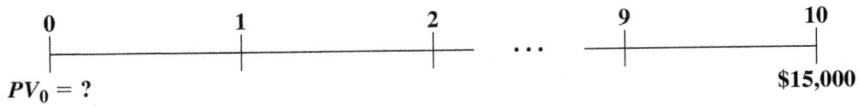

Thus, the bond is worth $15,000 in 10 years. To determine the value today, PV_0, we compute the present value using Equation 3.4 with our interest rate of 6%.

Execute

$$PV_0 = \frac{15{,}000}{1.06^{10}} = \$8375.92 \text{ today}$$

Evaluate

The bond is worth much less today than its final payoff because of the time value of money.

USING A FINANCIAL CALCULATOR

Financial calculators are programmed to perform most present and future value calculations. However, we recommend that you develop an understanding of the formulas before using the shortcuts. We provide a more extensive discussion of financial calculators on page 106 and in the Appendix to Chapter 4, but we'll cover the relevant functions for this chapter here. To use financial calculator functions, you always enter the known values first and then the calculator solves for the unknown.

To answer Example 3.4 with a financial calculator, do the following:

Concept	Number of Periods	Interest Rate per Period	Recurring Payments	Future Value
Calculator Key	N	I/Y	PMT	FV
Enter	10	6	0	15000

Because you are solving for the present value (PV), press the PV key last (on an HP calculator), or press CPT then the PV key FV on a TI calculator. The calculator will return −8375.92. Note that the calculator balances inflows with outflows, so because the FV is positive (an inflow), it returns the PV as a negative (an outflow).

If you were solving for the future value instead, you would enter

N	I/Y	PV	PMT
10	6	−8375.92	0

And finally, on an HP press the FV key or on a TI press CPT and then the FV key.

As we have seen in this section, we can compare cash flows at different points in time as long as we follow the Three Rules of Valuing Cash Flows, summarized in Table 3.2. Armed with these three rules, a financial manager can compare an investment's costs and benefits that are spread out over time and apply the Valuation Principle to make the right decision. In Chapter 4, we will show you how to apply these rules to situations involving multiple cash flows at different points in time.

TABLE 3.2 The Three Rules of Valuing Cash Flows

Rule	Formula
1: Only values at the same point in time can be compared or combined.	None
2: To calculate a cash flow's future value, we must compound it.	Future value of a cash flow: $FV_n = C_0 \times (1 + r)^n$
3: To calculate the present value of a future cash flow, we must discount it.	Present value of a cash flow: $PV_0 = \dfrac{C_n}{(1 + r)^n}$

$C_n \div (1 + r)^0$

CONCEPT CHECK

7. How do you compare costs at different points in time?
8. What do you need to know to compute a cash flow's present or future value?

MyLab Finance

Here is what you should know after reading this chapter. MyLab™ Finance will help you identify what you know, and where to go when you need to practice.

KEY POINTS AND EQUATIONS	TERMS	ONLINE PRACTICE OPPORTUNITIES
3.1 Cost-Benefit Analysis ■ To evaluate a decision, we must value the incremental costs and benefits associated with that decision. A good decision is one for which the value of the benefits exceeds the value of the costs. ■ To compare costs and benefits that occur at different points in time, we must put all costs and benefits in common terms. Typically, we convert costs and benefits into cash today. ■ A competitive market is one in which a good can be bought and sold at the same price. We use prices from competitive markets to determine the cash value of a good.	competitive market, p. 74	MyLab Study Plan 3.1

KEY POINTS AND EQUATIONS	TERMS	ONLINE PRACTICE OPPORTUNITIES
3.2 Market Prices and the Valuation Principle ■ Arbitrage is the process of trading to take advantage of equivalent goods that have different prices in different competitive markets. ■ The Law of One Price states that if equivalent goods or securities trade simultaneously in different competitive markets, they will trade for the same price in each market. This law is equivalent to saying that no arbitrage opportunities should exist. ■ The Valuation Principle states that the value of a commodity or an asset to the firm or its investors is determined by its competitive market price. The benefits and costs of a decision should be evaluated using those market prices. When the value of the benefits exceeds the value of the costs, the decision will increase the market value of the firm.	arbitrage, p. 77 arbitrage opportunity, p. 77 Principle of No Arbitrage, p. 77 Law of One Price, p. 77 Valuation Principle, p. 76	MyLab Study Plan 3.2
3.3 The Time Value of Money and Interest Rates ■ The time value of money is the difference in value between money today and money in the future. ■ The rate at which we can exchange money today for money in the future by borrowing or investing is the current market interest rate. ■ The present value (PV) of a cash flow is its value in terms of cash today. ■ Timelines are a critical first step in organizing the cash flows in a financial problem.	discount factor, p. 81 discount rate, p. 81 future value (FV), p. 80 interest rate, p. 79 interest rate factor, p. 79 present value (PV), p. 80 time value of money, p. 78 timeline, p. 82	MyLab Study Plan 3.3
3.4 Valuing Cash Flows at Different Points in Time ■ There are three rules of valuing cash flows: a. Only cash flows that occur at the same point in time can be compared or combined. b. To calculate a cash flow's future value, you must compound it. c. To calculate a cash flow's present value, you must discount it. ■ The future value in n years of a cash flow, C, today is $$FV_n = C_0 \times (1 + r)^n \quad (3.3)$$ ■ The present value today of a cash flow, C, received in n years is $$PV_0 = \frac{C_n}{(1 + r)^n} \quad (3.4)$$	compounding, p. 84 compound interest, p. 85 discounting, p. 87	MyLab Study Plan 3.4

REVIEW QUESTIONS

1. What makes an investment decision a good one?
2. How important are our personal preferences in valuing an investment decision?
3. Why are market prices useful to a financial manager?
4. What is the relation between the Law of One Price and the Principle of No Arbitrage?
5. How does the Valuation Principle help a financial manager make decisions?
6. Can we directly compare dollar amounts received at different points in time?

PROBLEMS

All problems in this chapter are available in MyLab Finance. An asterisk (*) indicates problems with a higher level of difficulty.

Cost-Benefit Analysis

1. Honda Motor Company is considering offering a $2000 rebate on its minivan, lowering the vehicle's price from $30,000 to $28,000. The marketing group estimates that this rebate will increase sales over the next year from 40,000 to 55,000 vehicles. Suppose Honda's profit margin with the rebate is $6000 per vehicle. If the change in sales is the only consequence of this decision, what are its costs and benefits? Is it a good idea?
2. You are an international shrimp trader located in New Orleans. A food producer in the Czech Republic offers to pay you 2 million Czech koruna (CZK) today in exchange for a year's supply of frozen shrimp. Your Thai supplier will provide you with the same supply for 3 million Thai baht (THB) today. If the current competitive market exchange rates are 25.50 CZK per U.S. dollar (USD) and 41.25 THB per USD, what is the value of this deal?
3. Suppose your employer offers you a choice between a $5000 bonus and 100 shares of the company's stock. Whichever one you choose will be awarded today. The stock is currently trading at $63 per share.
   a. Suppose that if you receive the stock bonus, you are free to trade it. Which form of the bonus should you choose? What is its value?
   b. Suppose that if you receive the stock bonus you are required to hold it for at least one year. What can you say about the value of the stock bonus now? What will your decision depend on?
4. Suppose Bank One offers an interest rate of 5.5% on both savings and loans, and Bank Two offers an interest rate of 6% on both savings and loans.
   a. What arbitrage opportunity is available?
   b. Which bank would experience a surge in the demand for loans? Which bank would receive a surge in deposits?
   c. What would you expect to happen to the interest rates the two banks are offering?
5. If the cost of buying a CD and ripping the tracks to your iPod (including your time) is $25, what is the most Apple could charge on iTunes for a whole 15-track CD?

6. Some companies cross-list their shares, meaning that their stock trades on more than one stock exchange. For example, BlackBerry (BB) trades on both the TSX and NASDAQ. If its price in Toronto is 10 Canadian dollars per share and anyone can exchange Canadian dollars (CAD) for U.S. dollars (USD) at the rate of 0.95 USD/CAD, what must BB's price be on NASDAQ?

Market Prices and the Valuation Principle

7. Bubba is a shrimp farmer. In an ironic twist, Bubba is allergic to shellfish, so he cannot eat any shrimp. Each day he has a one-tonne supply of shrimp. The market price of shrimp is $10,000 per tonne.
   a. What is the value of a tonne of shrimp to him?
   b. Would this value change if he were not allergic to shrimp? Why or why not?
8. Brett has almond orchards, but he is sick of almonds and prefers to eat walnuts instead. The owner of the walnut orchard next door has offered to swap this year's crop with him in an even exchange. Assume he produces 1000 tonnes of almonds and his neighbour produces 800 tonnes of walnuts. If the market price of almonds is $100 per tonne and the market price of walnuts is $1.10 per tonne,
   a. Should he make the exchange?
   b. Does it matter whether he prefers almonds or walnuts? Why or why not?

The Time Value of Money and Interest Rates

9. You have $100 and a bank is offering 5% interest on deposits. If you deposit the money in the bank, how much will you have in one year?
10. You expect to have $1000 in one year. A bank is offering loans at 6% interest per year. How much can you borrow today?
11. Due to your good credit, your bank reduces the interest rate on your $12,000 loan from 9% to 7.5% per year. Thanks to the change, how much will you save in interest this year?
12. A friend asks to borrow $55 from you and in return will pay you $58 in one year. If your bank is offering a 6% interest rate on deposits and loans,
    a. How much would you have in one year if you deposited the $55 instead?
    b. How much money could you borrow today if you pay the bank $58 in one year?
    c. Should you lend the money to your friend or deposit it in the bank?
13. What is the discount factor that is equivalent to a 6% discount rate?
14. If your discount factor is 0.9009, what is your discount rate?
15. You plan to borrow $1000 from a bank. In exchange for $1000 today, you promise to pay $1080 in one year. What does the cash flow timeline look like from your perspective? What does it look like from the bank's perspective?
16. The local electronics store is offering a promotion, "one year: same as cash," meaning that you can buy a TV now, and wait a year to pay (with no interest). So, if you take home a $1000 TV today, you will owe them $1000 in one year. If your bank is offering 4% interest, what is the true cost of the TV to you today?

17. You are purchasing a new TV at Visions Electronics and the salesperson is trying to convince you to buy a five-year extended warranty. The cost of the warranty to you today will be $399. However, if there is no claim against the warranty, you will get a store credit for $399 to spend five years from now. Assume you won't have any problems with your TV and you plan on buying more electronics at Visions in five years (so you would be certain to use the store credit). Also assume the interest rate is 6% per year.
a. What is the value to you today of the promised store credit?
b. Given your answer to (a), what is the net cost of the extended warranty?

Valuing Cash Flows at Different Points in Time

18. Suppose the interest rate is 4%.
a. Having $200 today is equivalent to having what amount in one year?
b. Having $200 in one year is equivalent to having what amount today?
c. Which would you prefer, $200 today or $200 in one year? Does your answer depend on when you need the money? Why or why not?

19. You are considering a savings bond that will pay $100 in 10 years. If the interest rate is 2%, what should you pay today for the bond?

20. If your bank pays you 1.5% interest and you deposit $500 today, what will your balance be in five years?

21. Consider the following alternatives:
i. $100 received in 1 year
ii. $200 received in 5 years
iii. $300 received in 10 years
a. Rank the alternatives from most valuable to least valuable if the interest rate is 10% per year.
b. What is your ranking if the interest rate is only 5% per year?
c. What is your ranking if the interest rate is 20% per year?

***22.** Suppose you invest $1000 in an account paying 8% interest per year.
a. What is the balance in the account after 3 years? How much of this balance corresponds to "interest on interest"?
b. What is the balance in the account after 25 years? How much of this balance corresponds to interest on interest?

23. Calculate the future value of $2000 in
a. 5 years at an interest rate of 5% per year.
b. 10 years at an interest rate of 5% per year.
c. 5 years at an interest rate of 10% per year.
*d. Why is the amount of interest earned in part (a) less than half the amount of interest earned in part (b)?

24. What is the present value of $10,000 received
a. 12 years from today when the interest rate is 4% per year?
b. 20 years from today when the interest rate is 8% per year?
c. 6 years from today when the interest rate is 2% per year?

25. Your brother has offered to give you either $5000 today or $10,000 in 10 years. If the interest rate is 7% per year, which option is preferable?

26. Your bank pays 2.5% interest per year. You put $1000 in the bank today and $500 more in the bank in one year. How much will you have in the bank in two years?

27. Your cousin is currently 12 years old. She will be going to college in six years. Your aunt and uncle would like to have $100,000 in a savings account to fund her education at that time. If the account promises to pay a fixed interest rate of 4% per year, how much money do they need to put into the account today to ensure that they will have $100,000 in six years?

28. Your mom is thinking of retiring. Her retirement plan will pay her either $250,000 immediately on retirement or $350,000 five years after the date of her retirement. Which alternative should she choose if the interest rate is

a. 0% per year?
b. 8% per year?
c. 20% per year?

29. You just won a prize that comes with two payout choices. The first option is to get $100,000 right now and nothing thereafter. The second option is to get $94,000 right now and $10,000 three years from now (and nothing after that). If your discount rate is 8%, which should you take?

30. You are planning to invest $5000 in an account earning 9% per year for retirement.

a. If you put the $5000 in an account at age 23, and withdraw it 42 years later, how much will you have?
b. If you wait 10 years before making the deposit, so that it stays in the account for only 32 years, how much will you have at the end?

***31.** Your grandfather put some money in an account for you on the day you were born. You are now 18 years old and are allowed to withdraw the money for the first time. The account currently has $3996 in it and pays an 8% interest rate.

a. How much money would be in the account if you left the money there until your 25th birthday?
b. What if you left the money until your 65th birthday?
c. How much money did your grandfather originally put in the account?

***32.** Your computer manufacturing firm must purchase 10,000 keyboards from a supplier. One supplier demands a payment of $100,000 today plus $10 per keyboard payable in one year. Another supplier will charge $21 per keyboard, also payable in one year. The interest rate is 6%.

a. What is the difference in their offers in terms of dollars today? Which offer should your firm take?
b. Suppose your firm does not want to spend cash today. How can it take the first offer and not spend $100,000 of its own cash today?

CHAPTER

The Time Value of Money

4

LEARNING OBJECTIVES

- Value a series of many cash flows
- Apply shortcuts to value special sets of regular cash flows called *perpetuities* and *annuities*
- Compute the number of periods, cash flow, or rate of return in a loan or investment

NOTATION

C	cash flow
C_t	cash flow at date t
FV	future value
FV_t	future value on date t
g	growth rate
n	number of periods for time value calculations
P	initial principal or deposit, or equivalent present value
PV	present value
PV_t	present value on date t
r	interest rate

As we discussed in Chapter 3, to evaluate a project, a financial manager must compare its costs and benefits. In most cases, the cash flows in financial investments involve more than one future period. Thus, the financial manager is faced with the task of trading off a known up-front cost against a series of uncertain future benefits. We learned to value those costs and benefits by computing their cash value today—their present values.

In financial management, as well as in your personal finances, you will need to evaluate series of cash flows occurring across time. In this chapter, we build on the tools we developed in Chapter 3 to value any series of cash flows. We will develop shortcuts for valuing *annuities, perpetuities*, and other special cases of assets with cash flows that follow regular patterns.

In Chapter 5, we will learn how interest rates are quoted and determined. Once we understand how interest rates are quoted, it will be straightforward to extend the tools of this chapter to cash flows that occur more frequently than once per year.

4.1 Valuing a Stream of Cash Flows

stream of cash flows A series of cash flows lasting several periods.

We refer to a series of cash flows lasting several periods as a **stream of cash flows**. As with single cash flows, we can represent a stream of cash flows on a timeline. In this chapter, we will continue to use timelines and the rules of cash flow valuation introduced in Chapter 3 to organize and then solve financial problems.

Applying the Rules of Valuing Cash Flows

Most investment opportunities have multiple cash flows that occur at different points in time. In Chapter 3, we learned the rules to value such cash flows:

Rule 1: Only values at the same point in time can be compared or combined.

Rule 2: To calculate a cash flow's future value, we must compound it using Equation 3.3 from Chapter 3.

$$FV_n = C_0 \times (1 + r)^n \tag{4.1}$$

Rule 3: To calculate the present value of a future cash flow, we must discount it using Equation 3.4 of Chapter 3.

$$PV_0 = \frac{C_n}{(1 + r)^n} \tag{4.2}$$

The rules of cash flow valuation allow us to compare and combine cash flows that occur at different points in time. Suppose we plan to deposit into our Simplii Financial bank account $1000 at the end of each of the next three years. If we earn a fixed 10% interest rate on our savings, how much will we have three years from today (just after the last deposit)?

Again, we start with a timeline:

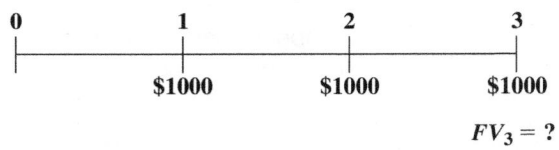

The timeline shows the three deposits we plan to make. We need to compute their value at the end of three years.

We can use the cash flow valuation rules in a number of ways to solve this problem. First, we can take the deposit at Date 1 and move it forward to Date 2. Because it is then in the same time period as the Date 2 deposit, we can combine the two amounts to find out the total in the bank on Date 2:

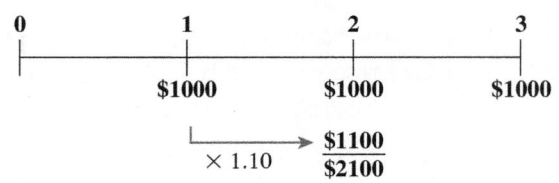

Using the first two rules, we find that our total savings on Date 2 will be $2100. Continuing in this fashion, we can solve the problem as follows:

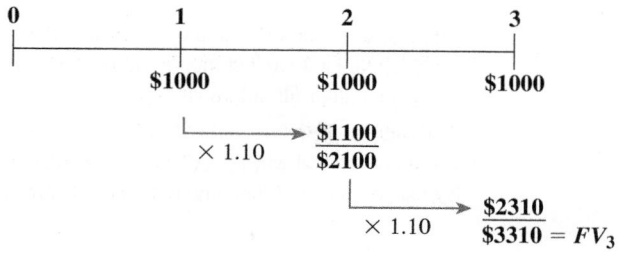

The total amount we will have in the Simplii Financial bank account at the end of three years is $3310. This amount is the future value of our three $1000 savings deposits.

Another approach to the problem is to compute the future value in year 3 of each cash flow separately. Once all three amounts are in year-3 dollars, we can then combine them.

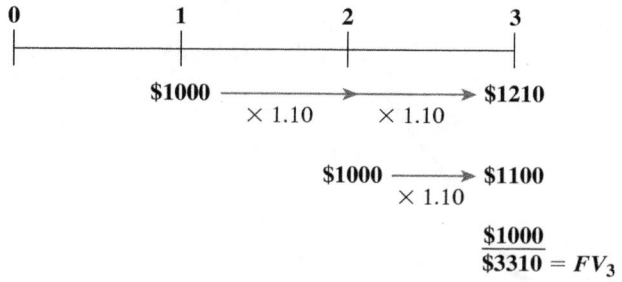

Both calculations give the same future value of $3310. As long as we follow the rules, we get the same result. The order in which we apply the rules does not matter. The calculation we choose depends on which is more convenient for the problem at hand. In Chapter 3, Table 3.2 summarizes the three rules of valuing cash flows and their associated formulas.

EXAMPLE 4.1 Personal Finance: Computing the Future Value

PROBLEM

Let's revisit the savings plan we considered earlier: We plan to save $1000 at the end of each of the next three years. At a fixed 10% interest rate, how much will we have in the Simplii Financial bank account three years from today?

SOLUTION

■ **Plan**

We'll start with the timeline for this savings plan:

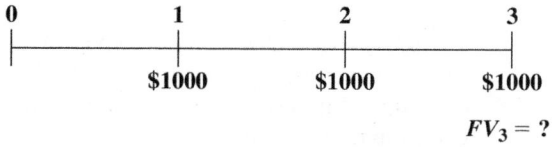

Let's solve this problem in a different way than we did in the text, while still following the rules we established. First we'll compute the present value of the cash flows. Then we'll compute its value three years later (its future value).

Execute

There are several ways to calculate the present value of the cash flows. Here, we treat each cash flow separately and then combine the present values.

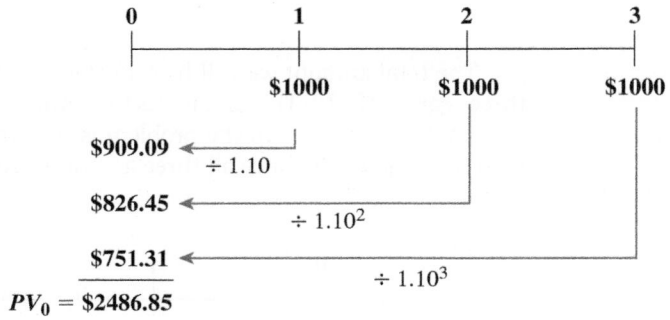

Saving $2486.85 today is equivalent to saving $1000 per year for three years. Now let's compute the future value in year 3 of that $2486.85:

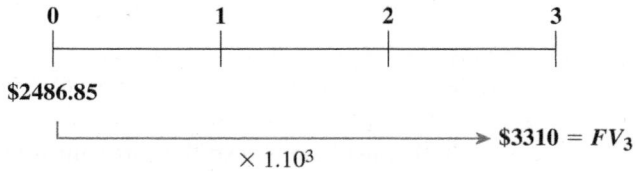

Evaluate

This answer of $FV_3 = \$3310$ is precisely the same result we found earlier. As long as we apply the three rules of valuing cash flows, we will always get the correct answer.

Now we formalize this approach by deriving a general formula for valuing a stream of cash flows.

Consider a stream of cash flows: C_0 at date 0, C_1 at date 1, and so on, up to C_n at date n. We represent this cash flow stream on a timeline as follows:

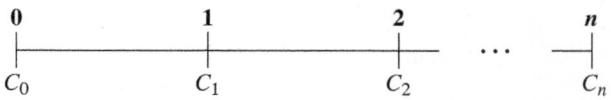

Using the rules of cash flow valuation, we compute the present value of this cash flow stream in two steps. First, we compute the present value of each individual cash flow. Then, once the cash flows are in common units of dollars today, we can combine them.

For a given interest rate r, we represent this process on the timeline as follows:

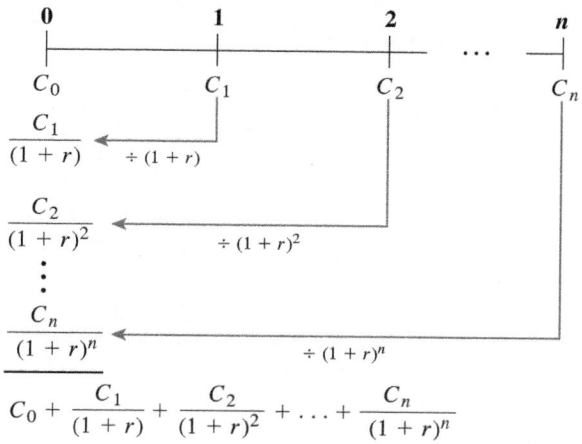

This equation provides the general formula for the present value of a cash flow stream:

$$PV_0 = C_0 + \frac{C_1}{(1+r)} + \frac{C_2}{(1+r)^2} + \cdots + \frac{C_n}{(1+r)^n} \tag{4.3}$$

That is, the present value of the cash flow stream is the sum of the present values of each cash flow. Recall from Chapter 3 that we defined the present value as the dollar amount you would need to invest today to produce the single cash flow in the future. The same idea holds in this context. The present value is the amount you need to invest today to generate the cash flows stream $C_0, C_1, \ldots, C_n$. That is, receiving those cash flows is equivalent to having their present value in the bank today.

EXAMPLE 4.2 Personal Finance: Present Value of a Stream of Cash Flows

PROBLEM

You have just graduated and need money to buy a new car. Your rich Uncle Henry will lend you the money as long as you agree to pay him back within four years, and you offer to pay him the rate of interest that he would otherwise get by putting his money in a savings account. Based on your earnings and living expenses, you think you will be able to pay him $5000 in one year, and then $8000 each year for the next three years. If Uncle Henry would otherwise earn 6% per year on his savings, how much can you borrow from him?

SOLUTION

■ Plan

The cash flows you can promise Uncle Henry are as follows:

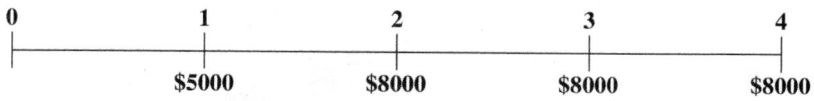

How much money should Uncle Henry be willing to give you today in return for your promise of these payments? He should be willing to give you an amount that is equivalent to these payments in present value terms. This is the amount of money that it would take him to produce these same ▶

cash flows. We will (1) solve the problem using Equation 4.6 and then (2) verify our answer by calculating the future value of this amount.

Execute

1. We can calculate the PV as follows:

$$
\begin{aligned}
PV &= \frac{5000}{1.06} + \frac{8000}{1.06^2} + \frac{8000}{1.06^3} + \frac{8000}{1.06^4} \\
&= 4716.98 + 7119.97 + 6716.95 + 6336.75 \\
&= \$24{,}890.65
\end{aligned}
$$

Now suppose that Uncle Henry gives you the money and then deposits your payments to him in the bank each year. How much will he have four years from now?

We need to compute the future value of the annual deposits. One way to do so is to compute the bank balance each year:

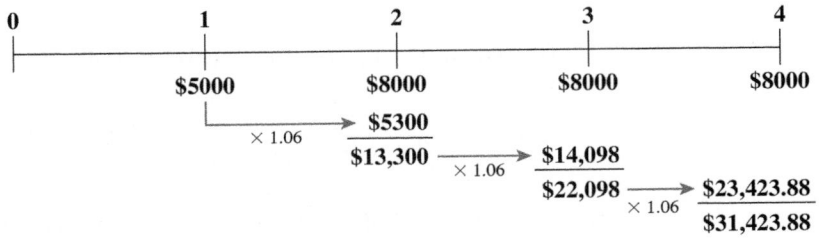

2. To verify our answer, suppose your uncle kept his $24,890.65 in the bank today earning 6% interest. In four years he would have

$$FV_4 = \$24{,}890.65 \times (1.06)^4 = \$31{,}423.87 \text{ in four years}$$

We get the same answer both ways (within a penny, which is because of rounding).

Evaluate

Thus, Uncle Henry should be willing to lend you $24,890.65 in exchange for your promised payments. This amount is less than the total you will pay him ($5000 + $8000 + $8000 + $8000 = $29,000) due to the time value of money.

Example 4.2 illustrates that if you want to compute the future value of a stream of cash flows, you can do it directly (the first approach used in Example 4.2), or you can first compute the present value and then move it to the future (the second approach). As always, we use Equation 4.1 to calculate the future value of any present value. Because we obey the rules of valuing cash flows in both cases, we get the same result.

CONCEPT CHECK

1. How do you calculate the present value of a cash flow stream?
2. How do you calculate the future value of a cash flow stream?

4.2 Perpetuities and Annuities

The formulas we have developed so far allow us to compute the present or future value of any cash flow stream. In this section, we consider two types of cash flow streams, *perpetuities* and *annuities,* and learn shortcuts for valuing them. These shortcuts are possible because the cash flows follow a regular pattern.

Perpetuities

perpetuity A stream of equal cash flows that occurs at regular intervals and lasts forever.

consol A bond that promises its owner a fixed cash flow every year, forever.

A **perpetuity** is a stream of equal cash flows that occur at regular intervals and last forever. One example is the British government bond called a **consol** (or perpetual bond). Consol bonds promise the owner a fixed cash flow every year, forever.

Here is the timeline for a perpetuity:

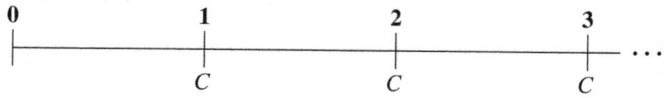

Note from the timeline that the first cash flow does not occur immediately; *it arrives at the end of the first period.* This timing is sometimes referred to as payment *in arrears* and is a standard convention in loan payment calculations and elsewhere, so we adopt it throughout this text.

Using the formula for the present value, the present value of a perpetuity with payment C and interest rate r is given by

$$PV = \frac{C}{(1+r)} + \frac{C}{(1+r)^2} + \frac{C}{(1+r)^3} + \cdots$$

Notice that all of the cash flows (C in the formula) are the same because the cash flow for a perpetuity is constant; thus, we do not need a time subscript on each one. Also, because the first cash flow is in one period, there is no cash flow at time 0 ($C_0 = 0$).

To find the value of a perpetuity by discounting one cash flow at a time would take forever—literally! You might wonder how, even with a shortcut, the sum of an infinite number of positive terms could be finite. The answer is that the cash flows in the future are discounted for an ever-increasing number of periods, so their contribution to the sum eventually becomes negligible.

To derive the shortcut, we calculate the value of a perpetuity by creating our own perpetuity. The Valuation Principle tells us that the value of a perpetuity must be the same as the cost we incurred to create our own identical perpetuity. To illustrate, suppose you could invest $100 in a bank account paying 5% interest per year forever. At the end of one year, you will have $105 in the bank—your original $100 plus $5 in interest. Suppose you withdraw the $5 interest and reinvest the $100 for a second year. Again, you will have $105 after one year, and you can withdraw $5 and reinvest $100 for another year. By doing this year after year, you can withdraw $5 every year in perpetuity:

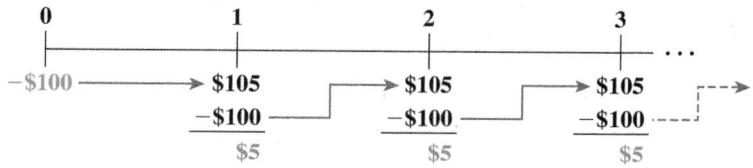

By investing $100 in the bank today, you can, in effect, create a perpetuity paying $5 per year. Recall from Chapter 3 that the Law of One Price tells us that equivalent cash flows must have the same price in every market. Because the bank will "sell" us

HISTORICAL EXAMPLES OF PERPETUITIES

Perpetual bonds were some of the first bonds ever issued. The oldest perpetuities that are still making interest payments were issued by the *Hoogheemraadschap Lekdijk Bovendams,* a seventeenth-century Dutch water board responsible for upkeep of the local dikes. The oldest bond dates from 1624. Two finance professors at Yale University, William Goetzmann and Geert Rouwenhorst, personally verified that these bonds continue to pay interest. On behalf of Yale, they purchased one of these bonds on July 1, 2003, and collected 26 years of back interest. On its issue date in 1648, this bond originally paid interest in Carolus guilders. Over the next 355 years, the currency of payment changed to Flemish pounds, Dutch guilders, and most recently euros. Currently, the bond pays interest of €11.34 annually.

Although the Dutch bonds are the oldest perpetuities in existence, the first perpetuities date from much earlier times. For example, *census agreements* and *rentes,* which were forms of perpetuities and annuities, were issued in the twelfth century in Italy, France, and Spain. They were initially designed to circumvent the usury laws of the Catholic Church; because they did not require the repayment of principal, in the eyes of the church they were not considered loans.

(allow us to create) the perpetuity for \$100, the present value of the \$5 per year in perpetuity is this "do-it-yourself" cost of \$100.

Now let's generalize this argument. Suppose we invest an amount P in a bank account with an interest rate r. Every year we can withdraw the interest we have earned, $C = r \times P$, leaving the principal, P, in the bank. Because our cost for creating the perpetuity is only the initial investment of principal (P), the value of receiving C in perpetuity is therefore the upfront cost P. Rearranging $C = r \times P$ to solve for P we have $P = C/r$. Therefore,

Present Value of a Perpetuity with Constant Cash Flows, *C*, and Discount Rate, *r*

$$PV_0 = \frac{C}{r} \tag{4.4}$$

By depositing the amount $\frac{C}{r}$ today, we can withdraw interest of $\frac{C}{r} \times r = C$ each period in perpetuity. Note, the first cash flow of C is received one period after the deposit is made. Thus it is important to remember that the PV calculated is one period before the first cash flow.

Our methodology can be summarized as follows. To determine the present value of a cash flow stream, we computed the "do-it-yourself" cost of creating those same cash flows at the bank. This is an extremely useful and powerful approach—and is much simpler and faster than summing those infinite terms!

EXAMPLE 4.3 Personal Finance: Endowing a Perpetuity

PROBLEM

You want to endow an annual graduation party at your university. You want the event to be a memorable one, so you budget \$30,000 per year forever for the party. If the university earns 8% per year on its investments, and if the first party is in one year's time, how much will you need to donate to endow the party?

SOLUTION

■ **Plan**

The timeline of the cash flows you want to provide is

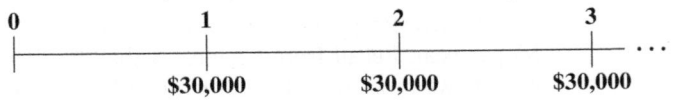

This is a standard perpetuity of $30,000 per year. The funding you would need to give the university in perpetuity is the present value of this cash flow stream.

Execute

Use the formula for a perpetuity:

$$PV_0 = C/r = \$30{,}000/0.08 = \$375{,}000 \text{ today}$$

Evaluate

If you donate $375,000 today, and if the university invests it at 8% per year forever, then the graduates will have $30,000 every year for their graduation party.

COMMON MISTAKE

Discounting One Too Many Times

The perpetuity formula assumes that the first payment occurs at the end of the first period (at date 1). Sometimes perpetuities have cash flows that start later in the future. In this case, we can adapt the perpetuity formula to compute the present value, but we need to do so carefully to avoid a common mistake.

To illustrate, consider the graduation party described in Example 4.3. Rather than starting in one year, suppose that the first party will be held two years from today. How would this delay change the amount of the donation required?

Now the timeline looks like this:

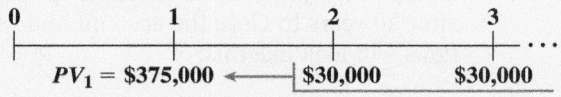

We need to determine the present value of these cash flows, as it tells us the amount of money in the bank needed today to finance the future parties. We cannot apply the perpetuity formula directly, however, because these cash flows are not *exactly* a perpetuity as we defined it. Specifically, the cash flow in the first period is "missing." But consider the situation on date 1—at that point, the first party is one period away and then the cash flows occur regularly. From the perspective of date 1, this *is* a perpetuity, and we can apply the formula (effectively getting PV_1). From the preceding calculation, we know we need $375,000 on date 1 to have enough to start the parties on date 2. We rewrite the timeline as follows:

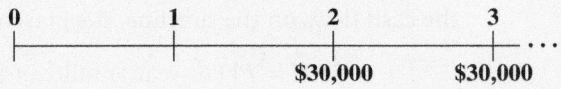

Our goal can now be restated more simply: How much do we need to invest today to have $PV_1 = \$375{,}000$ in one year? This is a simple present value calculation:

$$PV_0 = \frac{PV_1}{(1 + r)}$$

$$PV_0 = \$375{,}000/1.08 = \$347{,}222 \text{ today}$$

A common mistake is to discount the $375,000 twice because the first party is in two periods. *Remember—the present value formula for the perpetuity already discounts the cash flows to one period prior to the first cash flow.* Keep in mind that this common mistake may be made with perpetuities, annuities, and all of the other special cases discussed in this section. All of these formulas discount the cash flows to one period prior to the first cash flow.

Annuities

annuity A stream of equal cash flows arriving at a regular interval over a specified time period.

An **annuity** is a stream of n equal cash flows paid at regular intervals. The difference between an annuity and a perpetuity is that an annuity ends after some fixed number of payments. Most car loans, mortgages, and some bonds are annuities. We represent the cash flows of an annuity on a timeline as follows:

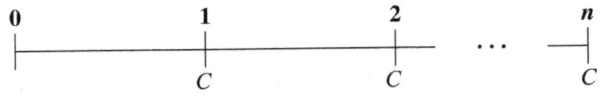

Note that just as with the perpetuity, we adopt the convention that the first payment takes place at date 1, one period from today. The present value of an n-period annuity with payment C and interest rate r is

$$PV_0 = \frac{C}{(1+r)} + \frac{C}{(1+r)^2} + \frac{C}{(1+r)^3} + \cdots + \frac{C}{(1+r)^n}$$

Present Value of an Annuity. To find a simpler formula, we use the same approach we followed with the perpetuity: find a way to create your own annuity. To illustrate, suppose you invest \$100 in a bank account paying 5% interest. At the end of one year, you will have \$105 in the bank—your original \$100 plus \$5 in interest. Using the same strategy as you did for calculating the value of a perpetuity, suppose you withdraw the \$5 interest and reinvest the \$100 for a second year. Once again you will have \$105 after one year. You can repeat the process, withdrawing \$5 and reinvesting \$100, every year. For a perpetuity, you left the principal in the bank forever. Alternatively, you might decide after 20 years to close the account and withdraw the principal. In that case, your cash flows will look like this:

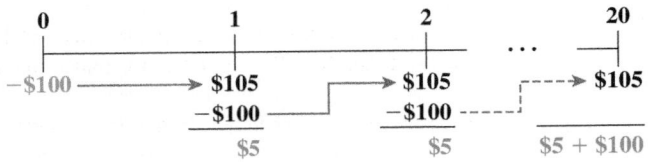

With your initial \$100 investment, you have created a 20-year annuity of \$5 per year, plus you will receive an extra \$100 at the end of 20 years. Again, the Valuation Principle's Law of One Price tells us that because it only took an initial investment of \$100 to create the cash flows on the timeline, the present value of these cash flows is \$100, or

$$\$100 = PV(\text{20-year annuity of \$5 per year}) + PV(\$100 \text{ in 20 years})$$

So if we invest \$100 now, we can receive \$5 per year for 20 years as well as \$100 in the 20th year, representing the following cash flows:

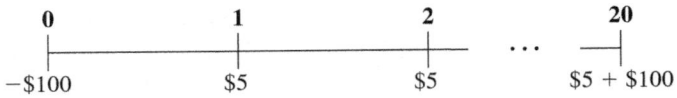

Rearranging the equation above shows that the cost of a 20-year annuity of \$5 per year is \$100 minus the present value of \$100 in 20 years.

$$\begin{aligned} PV(\text{20-year annuity of \$5 per year}) &= \$100 - PV(\$100 \text{ in 20 years}) \\ &= \$100 - \frac{\$100}{(1.05)^{20}} = \$100 - \$37.69 = \$62.31 \end{aligned}$$

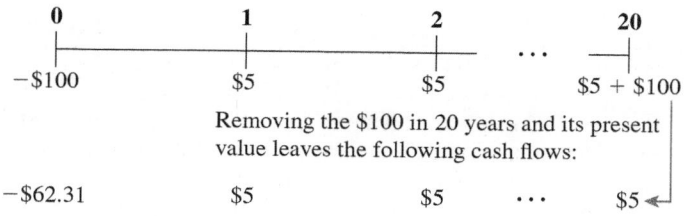

So the present value of $5 for 20 years is $62.31. Intuitively, the value of the annuity is the initial investment in the bank account minus the present value of the principal that will be left in the account after 20 years.

The $5 we receive every year is the interest on the $100 and can be written as $100(.05) = $5. Rearranging, we have $100 = $5/.05. If we substitute $5/.05 into our formula above, we can represent the PV of the annuity as a function of its cash flow ($5), the discount rate (5%), and the number of years (20):[1]

$$PV(\text{20-year annuity of \$5 per year}) = \frac{\$5}{.05} - \frac{\frac{\$5}{.05}}{(1.05)^{20}} = \frac{\overset{C}{\$5}}{.05}\left(1 - \frac{1}{(1.05)^{\overset{n}{20}}}\right)$$

$$= \$5 \times \frac{1}{\underset{r}{.05}}\left(1 - \frac{1}{(1.05)^{20}}\right)$$

This method is very useful because we will most often want to know the *PV* of the annuity given its cash flow, discount rate, and number of years. We can write this as a general formula for the present value of an annuity of *C* for *n* periods:

Present Value of an *n*-Period Annuity with Constant Cash Flows, *C*, and Discount Rate, *r*

$$PV_0 = C \times \frac{1}{r}\left(1 - \frac{1}{(1 + r)^n}\right) \tag{4.5}$$

Let's revisit the cash flows presented in Example 4.1 ($1000 invested at the end of each of the next three years). Using Equation 4.5, we get the following:

$$PV_0 = \$1000 \times \frac{1}{.10}\left(1 - \frac{1}{(1 + .10)^3}\right) = \$2486.85$$

As you can see, this is the same result we obtained when discounting the cash flows individually. Equation 4.5, though, does the calculation in one step instead of having to do calculations for each cash flow as we did in Example 4.1. Using the present value of an annuity formula can save a lot of time when analyzing annuities that have many cash flows.

---

[1]An early derivation of this formula is attributed to the astronomer Edmond Halley in *Of Compound Interest*, published after Halley's death by Henry Sherwin, Sherwin's Mathematical Tables (London: W. and J. Mount, T. Page and Son, 1761).

USING A FINANCIAL CALCULATOR OR EXCEL: SOLVING FOR PRESENT AND FUTURE VALUES OF CASH FLOW STREAMS

So far, we have used formulas to compute present values of cash flow streams. As we discussed at the end of Chapter 3, both financial calculators and spreadsheets have time value formulas pre-programmed to quicken the process. In this box, we focus on financial calculators, but spreadsheets such as Excel have very similar shortcut functions.

Financial calculators have a set of functions that perform the calculations that finance professionals do most often. The functions are all based on the following timeline, which among other things can handle most types of loans:

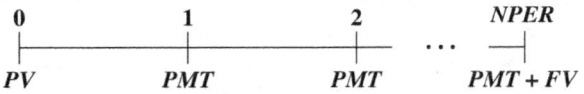

There are a total of five variables: number of periods (*N* or NPER), present value (PV), cash flow or "payment" (PMT), future value (FV), and the interest rate (*I/Y* or *I/YR* or RATE). Each function takes four of these variables as inputs and returns the value of the fifth one that ensures that the sum of the present value of all the cash flows is zero.

By setting the recurring payments equal to 0, you could compute present and future values of single cash flows such as we have done in Chapter 3. We will now consider the situation when there are non-zero recurring equal cash flows. The best way to learn to use a financial calculator is by practising. We present one example below. We will also show the calculator buttons for any additional examples in this chapter that can be solved with financial calculator functions. Finally, the appendix to this chapter contains step-by-step instructions for using the two most popular financial calculators.

Example

Let's return to Example 4.1 where you will invest $1000 at the end of each year for three years. The interest rate is 10% per year. What is the present value of those cash flows today and how much will you have in the account in three years? The following timeline represents our situation.

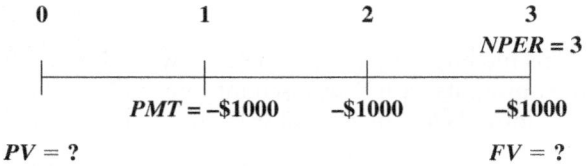

To compute the PV, we enter the four variables we know, $N = 3$, $I/Y = 10$, PMT $= -\$1000$, and, for now, FV $= 0$ as you are not depositing an additional cash flow at the end of the third period. We can then solve for the PV amount. Specifically, for the HP-10BII or TI-BAII Plus calculators,

1. Enter 3 and press the **N** button.
2. Enter 10 and press the **I/Y** button (**CPT** for the HP calculator).
3. Enter 0 and press the **FV** button.
4. Enter –$1000 and press the **PMT** button.
5. Press the **PV** button (for the Texas Instruments calculator, press **CPT** and then **PV**).

	N	I/Y	PV	PMT	FV
Given:	3	10		–1000	0
Solve for:			2486.85		
Excel Formula: $=PV(RATE,NPER,PMT,FV)=PV(0.10,3,-1000,0)$					

The calculator then shows a present value of $2486.85.

To compute the FV, we enter the four variables we know, $N = 3$, $I/Y = 10$, $PMT = -\$1000$ and, for now, PV $= 0$ as you are not depositing an additional cash flow now (at date 0 on the timeline). We can then solve for the FV amount.

1. Enter 3 and press the **N** button.
2. Enter 10 and press the **I/Y** button (**I/YR** for the HP calculator).
3. Enter 0 and press the **PV** button.
4. Enter –$1000 and press the **PMT** button.
5. Press the **FV** button (for the Texas Instruments calculator, press **CPT** and then **FV**).

USING A FINANCIAL CALCULATOR OR EXCEL (*continued*)

	N	I/Y	PV	PMT	FV
Given:	3	10	0	−1,000	
Solve for:					**3310.00**

Excel Formula: $=FV(RATE,NPER,PMT,PV)=FV(0.10,3,-1000,0)$

The calculator then shows a future value of $3310.00.

Note that we entered PMT as a negative number (the amounts you are putting *into* the bank), and the calculated PV or FV amounts are shown as positive numbers. The interpretation of the FV is that it would be a positive cash flow for you ($3300 is the amount you could take *out* of the bank in three years). Similarly, the PV is positive because you could take out its amount today if you were to promise to repay $1000 each year for three years (so $2486.85 is how much you could borrow today that would be repaid by you with the loan payments of $1000 for three years). It is important to use signs correctly to indicate the direction in which the money is flowing when using the calculator functions. You will see more examples of getting the sign of the cash flows correct throughout the chapter.

Excel has the same functions, but it calls "N," "NPER" and "I/Y," "RATE". ***Also, it is important to note that you enter an interest rate of 10% as "10" in a financial calculator, but as "0.10" in Excel.***

EXAMPLE 4.4 Personal Finance: Present Value of a Lottery Prize Annuity

PROBLEM

While vacationing in the United States, you purchased a state lottery ticket, and now you are the lucky winner of the $30 million prize. Upon reading the fine print, though, you find that you can take your prize money either as (a) 30 payments of $1 million per year (starting today), or (b) $15 million paid today. If the interest rate is 8%, which option should you take?

SOLUTION

■ Plan

Option (a) provides $30 million in prize money but paid over time. To evaluate it correctly, we must convert it to a present value. Here is the timeline:

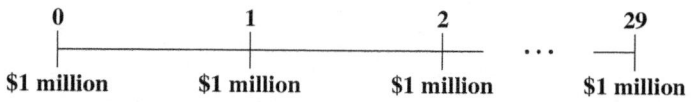

Because the first payment starts today, the last payment will occur in 29 years (for a total of 30 payments).[2] The $1 million at date 0 is already stated in present value terms, but we need to compute the present value of the remaining payments. Fortunately, this case looks like a 29-year annuity of $1 million per year, so we can use the annuity formula.

■ Execute

We use the annuity formula:

$$PV(\text{29-year annuity of \$1 million}) = \$1\text{ million} \times \frac{1}{0.08}\left(1 - \frac{1}{1.08^{29}}\right)$$
$$= \$11{,}158{,}406.01 \text{ today}$$

[2]An annuity in which the first payment occurs immediately is sometimes called an *annuity due*. Throughout this text, we always use the term "annuity" to mean one that is paid in arrears (i.e., at the end of each period).

Thus, the total present value of the cash flows is \$1 million + \$11,158,406.01 = \$12,158,406.01. In timeline form,

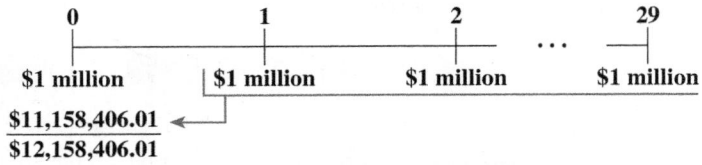

Option (b), \$15 million up front, is more valuable—even though the total amount of money paid is half that of option (a).

Financial calculators or Excel can handle annuities easily—just enter the cash flow in the annuity as the PMT:

	N	I/Y	PV	PMT	FV
Given:	29	8		1,000,000	0
Solve for:			−11,158,406.01		
Excel Formula: =*PV(RATE,NPER,PMT,FV)*=*PV*(0.08,29,1000000,0)					

Both the financial calculator and Excel will give you the PV of the 29 payments (\$11.16 million) to which you must add the first payment of \$1 million just as above.

■ Evaluate

The reason for the difference is the time value of money. If you have the \$15 million today, you can use \$1 million immediately and invest the remaining \$14 million at an 8% interest rate. This strategy will give you \$14 million × 8% = \$1.12 million per year in perpetuity! Alternatively, you can spend \$15 million − \$11.16 million = \$3.84 million today, and invest the remaining \$11.16 million, which will still allow you to withdraw \$1 million each year for the next 29 years before your account is depleted.

Future Value of an Annuity. Now that we have derived a simple formula for the present value of an annuity, it is easy to find a simple formula for the future value. If we want to know the value n years in the future, we move the present value n periods forward on the timeline.

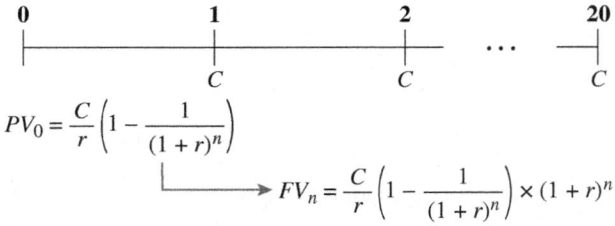

As the timeline shows, we compound the present value for n periods at interest rate r:

Future Value of an n-Period Annuity with Constant Cash Flows, C, and Interest Rate, r

$$\begin{aligned} FV_n &= PV_0 \times (1+r)^n \\ &= \frac{C}{r}\left(1 - \frac{1}{(1+r)^n}\right) \times (1+r)^n \\ &= C \times \frac{1}{r}\left((1+r)^n - 1\right) \end{aligned} \tag{4.6}$$

This formula is useful if we want to know how a savings account will grow over time and the investor deposits the same amount every period. We can re-evaluate the cash flows in Example 4.1 ($1000 invested at the end of each of three years) to get their future value using Equation 4.6.

$$FV_3 = \$1000 \times \frac{1}{0.10}\left((1 + 0.10)^3 - 1\right) = \$3310$$

As you can see, this gives the same result, in one step, as the three calculations used in Example 4.1.

EXAMPLE 4.5 Personal Finance: Retirement Savings Plan Annuity

PROBLEM

Ellen is 35 years old and she has decided it is time to plan seriously for her retirement. At the end of each year until she is 65, she will save $10,000 in a registered retirement savings account (RRSP). If the account earns 10% per year, how much will Ellen have saved at age 65?

SOLUTION

■ Plan

As always, we begin with a timeline. In this case, it is helpful to keep track of both the dates and Ellen's age:

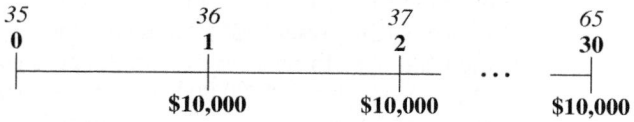

Ellen's savings plan looks like an annuity of $10,000 per year for 30 years. (*Hint:* It is easy to become confused when you just look at age, rather than at both dates and age. A common error is to think there are only 65 − 36 = 29 payments. Writing down both dates and age avoids this problem.)

To determine the amount Ellen will have in the bank at age 65, we'll need to compute the future value of this annuity.

■ Execute

$$FV = \$10{,}000 \times \frac{1}{0.10}(1.10^{30} - 1)$$

$$= \$1{,}644{,}940.23 \text{ million at age 65}$$

Using a financial calculator or Excel:

	N	I/Y	PV	PMT	FV
Given:	30	10	0	−10,000	
Solve for:					1,644,940

Excel Formula: =*FV*(*RATE,NPER,PMT,PV*)=*FV*(0.10,30,−10000,0)

■ Evaluate

By investing $10,000 per year for 30 years (a total of $300,000) and earning interest on those investments, the compounding will allow her to retire with about $1.645 million in her RRSP.

CONCEPT CHECK

3. How do you calculate the present value of
   a. a perpetuity?
   b. an annuity?
4. How do you calculate the future value of an annuity?

4.3 Solving for Variables Other Than Present Value or Future Value

So far, we have calculated the present value or future value of a stream of cash flows. Sometimes, however, we know the present value or future value, but do not know one of the variables that so far we have been given as an input. For example, when you take out a loan, you may know the amount you would like to borrow, but may not know the loan payments that will be required to repay it. Or, if you make a deposit into a bank account, you may want to calculate how long it will take before your balance reaches a certain level. In such situations, we use the present and/or future values as inputs, and solve for the variable we are interested in. We examine several special cases in this section.

Solving for the Cash Flows

Let's consider an example where we know the present value of an investment, but do not know the cash flows. The best example is a loan—you know how much you want to borrow (the present value) and you know the interest rate, but you do not know how much you need to repay each year. Suppose you are opening a business that requires an initial investment of $100,000. Your bank manager has agreed to lend you this money. The terms of the loan state that you will make equal annual payments for the next 10 years and will pay an interest rate of 8% with the first payment due one year from today. What is your annual payment?

From the bank's perspective, the timeline looks like this:

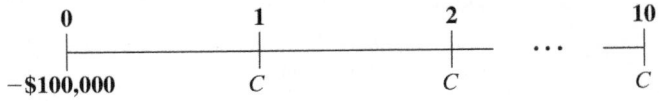

The bank will give you $100,000 today in exchange for 10 equal payments over the next decade. You need to determine the size of the payment C that the bank will require. For the bank to be willing to lend you $100,000, the loan cash flows must have a present value of $100,000 when evaluated at the bank's interest rate of 8%. That is,

$$100{,}000 = PV\text{ (10-year annuity of } C \text{ per year, evaluated at the loan rate)}$$

Using the formula for the present value of an annuity,

$$100{,}000 = C \times \frac{1}{0.08}\left(1 - \frac{1}{1.08^{10}}\right) = C \times 6.71$$

solving this equation for C gives

$$C = \frac{100{,}000}{6.71} = \$14{,}903$$

You will be required to make 10 annual payments of $14,903 in exchange for $100,000 today.

We can also solve this problem with a financial calculator or Excel:

	N	I/Y	PV	PMT	FV
Given:	10	8	100,000		0
Solve for:				**−14,903**	
Excel Formula: $=PMT(RATE,NPER,PV,FV)=PMT(0.08,10,100000,0)$					

In general, when solving for a loan payment, think of the amount borrowed (the loan principal) as the present value of the payments. If the payments of the loan are an annuity, we can solve for the payment of the loan by inverting the annuity formula. Writing the equation for the payments formally for a loan with principal P, requiring n periodic payments of C and interest rate r, we have

Loan Payment

$$C = \frac{P}{\frac{1}{r}\left(1 - \frac{1}{(1+r)^n}\right)} \tag{4.7}$$

EXAMPLE 4.6 Personal Finance: Computing a Loan Payment

PROBLEM

Your firm plans to buy a warehouse for $100,000. The bank offers you a 30-year loan with equal annual payments and an interest rate of 8% per year. The bank requires that your firm pay 20% of the purchase price as a down payment, so you can borrow only $80,000. What is the annual loan payment?

SOLUTION

■ Plan

We start with the timeline (from the bank's perspective):

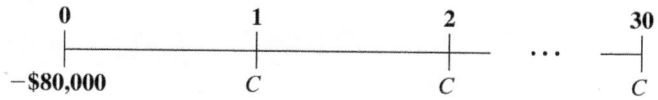

Using Equation 4.7, we can solve for the loan payment, C, given $n = 30$, $r = 8\%$ (0.08) and $P = \$80{,}000$.

■ Execute

Equation 4.10 gives the following payment (cash flow):

$$C = \frac{P}{\frac{1}{r}\left(1 - \frac{1}{(1+r)^n}\right)} = \frac{80{,}000}{\frac{1}{0.08}\left(1 - \frac{1}{(1.08)^{30}}\right)}$$

$$= \$7106.19$$

Using a financial calculator or Excel:

	N	I/Y	PV	PMT	FV
Given:	30	8	−80,000		0
Solve for:				**7106.19**	
Excel Formula: $=PMT(RATE,NPER,PV,FV)=PMT(0.08,30,-80000,0)$					

▶

Evaluate

Your firm will need to pay $7106.19 each year to repay the loan. The bank is willing to accept these payments because the PV of 30 annual payments of $7106.19 at 8% interest rate per year is exactly equal to the $80,000 it is giving you today.

We can use this same idea to solve for the cash flows when we know the future value rather than the present value. As an example, suppose you have just graduated from college and you decide to be prudent and start saving for a down payment on a house. You would like to have $60,000 saved 10 years from now. If you can earn 7% per year on your savings, how much do you need to save each year to meet your goal?

The timeline for this example is

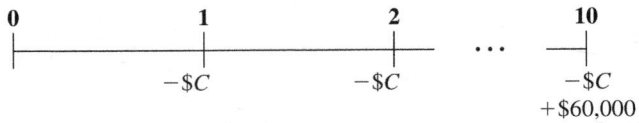

That is, you plan to save some amount C per year, and then withdraw $60,000 from the bank in 10 years. Therefore, we need to find the annuity payment that has a future value of $60,000 in 10 years. Use the formula for the future value of an annuity from Equation 4.6:

$$60{,}000 = FV(\text{annuity}) = C \times \frac{1}{0.07}(1.07^{10} - 1) = C \times 13.816448$$

Therefore, $C = \frac{60{,}000}{13.816448} = \$4342.65$. Thus, you need to save $4342.65 per year. If you do, then at a 7% interest rate your savings will grow to $60,000 in 10 years, when you are ready to buy a house.

Now let's solve this problem using a financial calculator or Excel:

	N	I/Y	PV	PMT	FV
Given:	10	7	0		60,000
Solve for:				−4343	
	Excel Formula: $=PMT(RATE,NPER,PV,FV)=PMT(0.07,10,0,60000)$				

Once again, we find that you need to save $4343 for 10 years to accumulate $60,000.

Rate of Return

rate of return The rate at which the value of an amount invested grows to exactly fund the future cash flows received by the investment.

In some situations, you know the present value and cash flows of an investment opportunity but you do not know the interest rate that equates them. The **rate of return** on an investment is the rate at which the value of the amount invested grows to exactly fund the future cash flows received by the investment.

For example, suppose that you have an investment opportunity that requires a $1000 investment today and will have a $2000 payoff in six years. This would appear on a timeline as

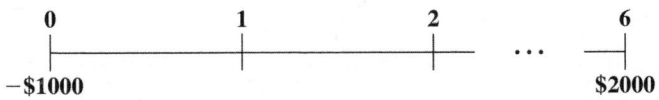

One way to analyze this investment is to ask the question, what interest rate, r, would you need so that the present value of what you get is exactly equal to the present value of what you give up?

$$1000 = \frac{2000}{(1 + r)^6}$$

Rearranging this calculation gives the following:

$$1000 \times (1 + r)^6 = 2000$$

That is, r is the rate of return you would need to earn on your \$1000 to have a future value of \$2000 in six years. We can solve for r as follows:

$$1 + r = \left(\frac{2000}{1000}\right)^{1/6} = 1.1225$$

Or, $r = 12.25\%$. This rate is the rate of return of this investment opportunity. Making this investment is like earning 12.25% per year on your money for six years.

When there are just two cash flows, as in the preceding example, it is easy to compute the rate of return. Consider the general case in which you invest an amount P today, and receive FV in n years:

$$P \times (1 + r)^n = FV$$

$$1 + r = (FV/P)^{1/n}$$

Now, let's consider a more sophisticated example. Suppose your firm needs to purchase a new forklift. The dealer gives you two options: (1) a price for the forklift if you pay cash and (2) the annual payments if you take out a loan from the dealer. To evaluate the loan that the dealer is offering you, you will want to compare the interest rate on the dealer's loan with the rate that your bank is willing to offer you. Given the dealer's quoted loan payment, how do you compute the interest rate charged by the dealer?

In this case, we need to compute the rate of return of the dealer's loan. Suppose the cash price of the forklift is \$40,000, and the dealer offers financing with no down payment and four annual payments of \$15,000. This loan has the following timeline:

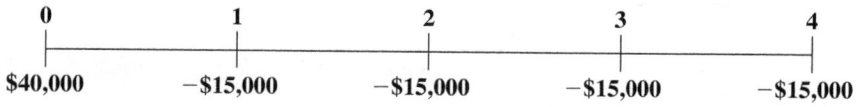

From the timeline, it is clear that the loan is a four-year annuity with a payment of \$15,000 per year and a present value of \$40,000. Setting the present value of the payments equal to the purchase price, we can write the equation as follows:

$$40{,}000 = 15{,}000 \times \frac{1}{r}\left(1 - \frac{1}{(1 + r)^4}\right)$$

The value of r that solves this equation is the interest rate charged on the loan. Unfortunately, in this case there is no simple way to solve for the interest rate r.[3] The only way to solve this equation is to guess at values of r until you find the right one.

[3]In general, with five or more periods, there is *no* formula to solve for r; trial and error and interpolation (by hand or computer) is the *only* way to compute r.

Start by guessing $r = 10\%$ In this case, the value of the annuity is

$$15{,}000 \times \frac{1}{0.10}\left(1 - \frac{1}{(1.10)^4}\right) = 47{,}548$$

The present value of the payments is too large. To lower it, we need to use a higher interest rate. We guess 20% this time:

$$15{,}000 \times \frac{1}{0.20}\left(1 - \frac{1}{(1.20)^4}\right) = 38{,}831$$

Now the present value of the payments is too low, so we must pick a rate between 10% and 20%. We continue to guess until we find the right rate. Let's try 18.45%:

$$15{,}000 \times \frac{1}{0.1845}\left(1 - \frac{1}{(1.1845)^4}\right) = 40{,}000$$

The interest rate charged by the dealer is 18.45%.

An easier solution than guessing the rate of return and manually calculating values is to use a spreadsheet or financial calculator to automate the guessing process. When the cash flows are an annuity, as in this example, we can use a financial calculator or Excel to compute the rate of return on an investment or the interest rate on a loan (RATE). Both Excel and the financial calculator solve (with slightly varying notation) the following equation:

$$PV + PMT \times \frac{1}{RATE}\left(1 - \frac{1}{(1 + RATE)^{NPER}}\right) + \frac{FV}{(1 + RATE)^{NPER}} = 0$$

The equation ensures that the present value of all outflows equals the present value of all inflows. So for a loan, the present value of repayments equals the amount borrowed. For an investment, the future value accumulated is equal to the future value of deposits (and since their future values are the same, so are their present values). When the unknown variable is RATE, it will solve for the interest rate on the loan or the rate of return on an investment. For this case, you could use a financial calculator or Excel as follows:

	N	I/Y	PV	PMT	FV
Given:	4		40,000	−15,000	0
Solve for:		18.45			
	Excel Formula: =RATE(*NPER,PMT,PV,FV*)=RATE(4,−15000,40000,0)				

Both the financial calculator and Excel correctly compute a rate of return of 18.45%. Note that the calculator returns I/Y as 18.45, but it should be read as 18.45%, which is 0.1845, the number that Excel returns.

EXAMPLE 4.7 Personal Finance: Computing the Rate of Return with a Financial Calculator

PROBLEM

Let's return to the lottery prize in Example 4.6. How high a rate of return do you need to earn investing on your own in order to prefer the $15 million payout? ▶

SOLUTION

■ **Plan**

Recall that the lottery offers you the following deal: take either (a) $15 million lump-sum payment immediately, or (b) 30 payments of $1 million per year starting immediately. This second option is an annuity of 29 payments of $1 million plus an initial $1 million payment.

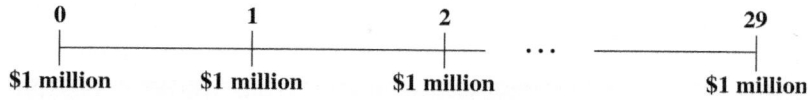

We need to solve for the rate of return that makes the two offers equivalent. Anything above that rate of return would make the present value of the annuity lower than the $15 million lump-sum payment, and anything below that rate of return would make it greater than the $15 million.

■ **Execute**

First, we set the present value of option (b) equal to option (a), which is already in present value since it is an immediate payment of $15 million:

$$\$15 \text{ million} = \$1 \text{ million} + \$1 \text{ million} \times \frac{1}{r}\left(1 - \frac{1}{(1+r)^{29}}\right)$$

$$\$14 \text{ million} = \$1 \text{ million} \times \frac{1}{r}\left(1 - \frac{1}{(1+r)^{29}}\right)$$

Using a financial calculator to solve for r:

	N	I/Y	PV	PMT	FV
Given:	29		−14,000,000	1,000,000	0
Solve for:		5.72			

Excel Formula: =RATE(*NPER,PMT,PV,FV*)=RATE(29,1000000,−14000000,0)

The rate of return equating the two options is 5.72%.

■ **Evaluate**

A rate of 5.72% makes giving up the $15 million payment and taking the 30 instalments of $1 million exactly equal in present value terms. If, you could earn more than 5.72% investing on your own, then you could take the $15 million, invest it, and generate 30 instalments that are each more than $1 million. If you could not earn at least 5.72% on your investments, you would be unable to replicate the $1 million instalments on your own and would be better off taking the instalment plan.

Solving for *n*, the Number of Periods

In addition to solving for cash flows or the interest rate, we can solve for the amount of time it will take a sum of money to grow to a known value. In this case, the interest rate, present value, and future value are all known. We need to compute how long it will take for the present value to grow to the future value.

Suppose we invest $10,000 in an account paying 10% interest, and we want to know how long it will take for the amount to grow to $20,000.

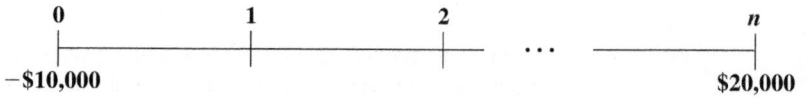

SOLVING FOR *N* USING LOGARITHMS

The problem of solving for the number of periods can be solved mathematically as well. We had $\$10{,}000 \times 1.10^n = \$20{,}000$. Dividing both sides by \$10,000, we have

$$1.10^n = 20{,}000/10{,}000 = 2$$

To solve for an exponent, we take the logarithm of both sides, and use the fact that $\ln(X^y) = y\ln(X)$:

$$\ln(1.10^n) = \ln(2)$$
$$n\ln(1.10) = \ln(2)$$
$$n = \ln(2)/\ln(1.10) = 0.6931/0.0953 \approx 7.27 \text{ years}$$

We want to determine n.

In terms of our formulas, we need to find n so that the future value of our investment equals \$20,000:

$$FV_n = \$10{,}000 \times 1.10^n = \$20{,}000$$

One approach is to use trial and error to find n. For example, with $n = 7$ years, FV = \$19,487, so it will take longer than 7 years. With $n = 8$ years, FV = \$21,436, so it will take between 7 and 8 years.

Alternatively, this problem can be solved on a financial calculator or Excel. In this case, we solve for n:

	N	I/Y	PV	PMT	FV
Given:		10	−10,000	0	20,000
Solve for:	7.27				

Excel Formula: =NPER(RATE,*PMT*,*PV*,*FV*)=NPER(0.10,0,−10000,20000)

It will take about 7.27 years for our savings to grow to \$20,000.

EXAMPLE 4.8 Personal Finance: Solving for the Number of Periods in a Savings Plan

PROBLEM

Let's return to your savings for a down payment on a house. Imagine that some time has passed and you have \$10,050 saved already, and you can now afford to save \$5000 per year at the end of each year. Also, interest rates have increased so that you now earn 7.25% per year on your savings. How long will it take you to get to your goal of \$60,000?

SOLUTION

■ Plan

The timeline for this problem is

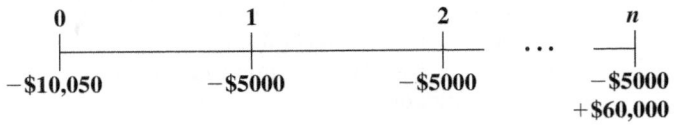

We need to find n so that the future value of your current savings plus the future value of your planned additional savings (which is an annuity consisting of n payments) equals your desired amount. There are two contributors to the future value: the initial lump sum of \$10,050 that will continue to earn interest, and the annuity contributions of \$5000 per year that will earn interest as ▶

they are contributed. Thus, we need to find the future value of the lump sum plus the future value of the annuity.

■ **Execute**

We can solve this problem using a financial calculator or Excel:

	N	I/Y	PV	PMT	FV
Given:		7.25	−10,050	−5000	60,000
Solve for:	7.00				

Excel Formula: =NPER(RATE, *PMT*, *PV*, *FV*)=NPER(0.0725, −5000, −10050, 60000)

There is also a mathematical solution. We can calculate the future value of the initial cash flow by using Equation 4.1 and the future value of the annuity using Equation 4.6:

$$10{,}050 \times 1.0725^n + 5000 \times \frac{1}{0.0725}(1.0725^n - 1) = 60{,}000$$

Rearranging the equation to solve for n,

$$1.0725^n = \frac{60{,}000 \times 0.0725 + 5000}{10{,}050 \times 0.0725 + 5000} = 1.632$$

we can then solve for n:

$$n = \frac{\ln(1.632)}{\ln(1.0725)} = 7 \text{ years}$$

■ **Evaluate**

It will take seven years to save the down payment.

We began this chapter with the goal of developing the tools a financial manager needs to be able to apply the Valuation Principle by computing the net present value of a decision. Starting from the fundamental concept of the time value of money—a dollar today is worth more than a dollar tomorrow—we learned how to calculate the equivalent value of future cash flows today and today's cash flows in the future. We then learned some shortcuts for handling common sets of regular cash flows, such as those found in perpetuities and loans. As we have seen, the discount rate is a critical input to any of our present value or future value calculations. Throughout this chapter, we have taken the discount rate as given.

What determines these discount rates? The Valuation Principle shows us that we must rely on market information to assess the value of cash flows across time. In the next chapter, we will learn the drivers of market interest rates as well as how they are quoted. Understanding interest rate quoting conventions will also allow us to extend the tools we developed in this chapter to situations where the interest rate is compounded more frequently than once per year.

CONCEPT CHECK

5. How do you calculate the cash flow of an annuity?
6. What is the rate of return on an investment or the interest rate on a loan, and how do you calculate the rate?
7. How do you solve for the number of periods for an investment or loan?

4.4 Growing Cash Flows

So far, we have considered only cash flow streams that have the same cash flow every period. If, instead, the cash flows are expected to grow at a constant rate in each period, we can also derive a simple formula for the present value of the future stream.

growing perpetuity A stream of cash flows that occurs at regular intervals and grows at a constant rate forever.

Growing Perpetuity. A **growing perpetuity** is a stream of cash flows that occurs at regular intervals and grows at a constant rate forever. For example, a growing perpetuity with a first payment of $100 that grows at a rate of 3% has the following timeline:

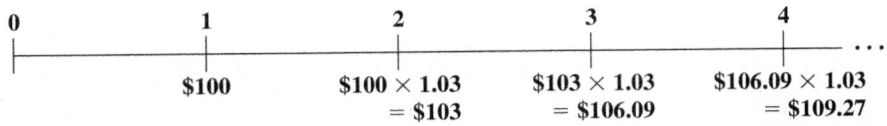

To derive the formula for the present value of a growing perpetuity, we follow the same logic used for a regular perpetuity: Compute the amount you would need to deposit today to create the perpetuity yourself. In the case of a regular perpetuity, we created a constant payment forever by withdrawing the interest earned each year and reinvesting the principal. To increase the amount we can withdraw each year, the principal that we reinvest each year must grow. We therefore withdraw less than the full amount of interest earned each period, using the remaining interest to increase our principal.

Let's consider a specific case. Suppose you want to create a perpetuity growing at 2%, so you invest $100 in a bank account that pays 5% interest. At the end of one year, you will have $105 in the bank—your original $100 plus $5 in interest. If you withdraw only $3, you will have $102 to reinvest—2% more than the amount you had initially.

This amount will then grow to $102 × 1.05 = $107.10 in the following year, and you can withdraw $3 × 1.02 = $3.06, which will leave you with principal of $107.10 − $3.06 = $104.04. Note that $102 × 1.02 = $104.04. That is, both the amount you withdraw and the principal you reinvest grow by 2% each year. On a timeline, these cash flows look like this:

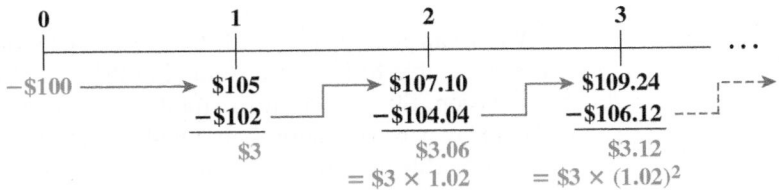

By following this strategy, you have created a growing perpetuity that starts at $3 and grows 2% per year. This growing perpetuity must have a present value equal to the cost of $100.

We can generalize this argument. If we want to increase the amount we withdraw from the bank each year by g, then the principal in the bank will have to grow by the same factor g. That is, instead of reinvesting P in the second year, we should reinvest $P(1 + g) = P + gP$. In order to increase our principal by gP, we need to leave gP of the interest in the account, so of the total interest of rP, we can only withdraw $rP - gP = P(r - g)$. We demonstrate this for the first year of our example:

Initial amount deposited	$100	P
Interest earned	(0.05) ($100)	rP
Amount needed to increase principal	(0.02) ($100)	gP
Amount withdrawn	(0.05) ($100) − (0.02) ($100)	$rP - gP$
	= $100 (0.05 − 0.02)	$= P(r - g)$

Denoting our first withdrawal as C_1, we have $C_1 = P(r - g)$. Solving this equation for P, the initial amount deposited in the bank account, gives the present value of a growing perpetuity with C_1 as the initial cash flow.[4]

Present Value of a Growing Perpetuity with First Cash Flow, C_1, and Growth Rate, g

$$PV_0 = \frac{C_1}{r - g} \tag{4.8}$$

EXAMPLE 4.9 Personal Finance: Endowing a Growing Perpetuity

PROBLEM

In Example 4.3, you planned to donate money to your university to fund an annual $30,000 graduation party. Given an interest rate of 8% per year, the required donation was the present value of

$$PV_0 = \$30{,}000/0.08 = \$375{,}000 \text{ today}$$

Before accepting the money, however, the student association has asked that you increase the donation to account for the effect of inflation on the cost of the party in future years. Although $30,000 is adequate for next year's party, the students estimate that the party's cost will rise by 4% per year thereafter. To satisfy their request, how much do you need to donate now?

SOLUTION

■ **Plan**

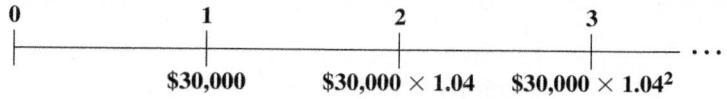

The cost of the party next year is $30,000, and the cost then increases 4% per year forever. From the timeline, we recognize the form of a growing perpetuity and can value it that way.

■ **Execute**

To finance the growing cost, you need to provide the present value today of

$$PV_0 = \$30{,}000/(0.08 - 0.04) = \$750{,}000 \text{ today}$$

■ **Evaluate**

You need to double the size of your gift!

---

[4]Suppose $g \geq r$. Then the cash flows grow even faster than they are discounted; each term in the sum gets larger, rather than smaller. In this case, the sum is infinite! What does an infinite present value mean? Remember that the present value is the "do-it-yourself" cost of creating the cash flows. An infinite present value means that no matter how much money you start with, it is *impossible* to reproduce those cash flows on your own. Growing perpetuities of this sort cannot exist in practice because no one would be willing to offer one at any finite price. A promise to pay an amount that forever grew faster than the interest rate is also unlikely to be kept (or believed by any savvy buyer). The only viable growing perpetuities are those where the growth rate is less than the interest rate, so we assume that $g < r$ for a growing perpetuity.

growing annuity A stream of n growing cash flows, paid at regular intervals.

Growing Annuity. A **growing annuity** is a stream of n growing cash flows, paid at regular intervals. It is a growing perpetuity that eventually comes to an end. The following timeline shows a growing annuity with initial cash flow C_1, growing at rate g every period until period n:

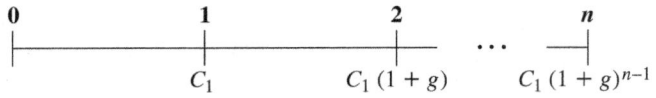

As with growing perpetuities discussed earlier, we adopt the convention that the first payment occurs at date 1. Since the first payment, C_1, occurs at date 1 and the nth payment, Cn, occurs at date n, there are only $n - 1$ periods of growth between these payments.

The present value of an n-period growing annuity with initial cash flow C_1, growth rate g, and interest rate r is given by

Present Value of a Growing Annuity

$$PV_0 = C_1 \times \frac{1}{r-g}\left(1 - \left(\frac{1+g}{1+r}\right)^n\right) \tag{4.9}$$

Because the annuity has only a finite number of terms, Equation 4.9 also works when $g > r$[7]. The process of deriving this simple expression for the present value of a

EXAMPLE 4.10 Personal Finance: Retirement Savings with a Growing Annuity

PROBLEM

In Example 4.5, Ellen considered saving $10,000 per year for her retirement. Although $10,000 is the most she can save in the first year, she expects her salary to increase each year so that she will be able to increase her savings by 5% per year. With this plan, if she earns 10% per year in her RRSP, what is the present value of her planned savings, and how much will Ellen have saved at age 65?

SOLUTION

■ Plan

As always, we begin with a timeline. It is helpful to keep track of both the dates and Ellen's age:

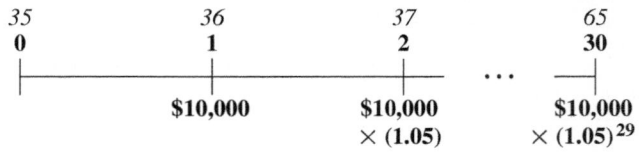

This example involves a 30-year growing annuity, with a growth rate of 5% and an initial cash flow of $10,000.

■ Execute

The present value of this growing annuity is given by

$$\begin{aligned} PV &= \$10{,}000 \times \frac{1}{0.10 - 0.05}\left(1 - \left(\frac{1.05}{1.10}\right)^{30}\right) \\ &= \$10{,}000 \times 15.0463 \\ &= \$150{,}463 \text{ today} \end{aligned}$$

▶

To determine the amount she will have at age 65, we need to move this amount forward 30 years:

$$FV = \$150{,}463 \times 1.10^{30}$$
$$= \$2.625 \text{ million in 30 years}$$

Unfortunately, your financial calculator and Excel do not have pre-programmed functions to handle growing annuities.

Evaluate

By investing the growing amounts (starting with $10,000) each year for 30 years, Ellen's proposed savings plan is equivalent to having $150,463 in the bank *today*.

Ellen will have saved $2.625 million at age 65 using the new savings plan. This sum is almost $1 million more than she would have had in her RRSP without the additional annual increases in savings (as shown in Example 4.5).

growing annuity is the same as for a regular annuity. Interested readers may consult the online appendix for details.

Finding a simple formula for the future value of a growing annuity is easy, just as we saw for regular annuities. If we want to know the value n years in the future, we move the present value n periods forward on the timeline; that is, we compound the present value for n periods at interest rate r:

Future Value of a Growing Annuity

$$PV_0 = C_1 \times \frac{1}{r-g}\left(1 - \left(\frac{1+g}{1+r}\right)^n\right)$$

$$FV_n = PV_0 \times (1+r)^n = C_1 \times \frac{1}{r-g}\left(1 - \left(\frac{1+g}{1+r}\right)^n\right) \times (1+r)^n$$

$$FV_n = C_1 \times \frac{1}{r-g}\left((1+r)^n - (1+g)^n\right) \tag{4.10}$$

Try using this formula in Example 4.10 to get the future value of Ellen's savings when she is 65.

CONCEPT CHECK

8. What is the reasoning behind the fact that an infinite stream of cash flows has a finite present value?
9. How do you calculate the present value of a
   a. growing perpetuity?
   b. growing annuity?
10. How do you calculate the future value of a growing annuity?

MyLab Finance

Here is what you should know after reading this chapter. MyLab™ Finance will help you identify what you know, and where to go when you need to practice.

KEY POINTS AND EQUATIONS	TERMS	ONLINE PRACTICE OPPORTUNITIES
4.1 Valuing a Stream of Cash Flows ■ The present value of a cash flow stream is $PV_0 = C_0 + \frac{C_1}{(1+r)} + \frac{C_2}{(1+r)^2} + \cdots + \frac{C_n}{(1+r)^n}$ (4.3)	stream of cash flows, p. 96	MyLab Study Plan 4.1
4.2 Perpetuities and Annuities ■ A perpetuity is a constant cash flow paid every period, forever. The present value of a perpetuity is $PV_0 = \frac{C}{r}$ (4.4) ■ An annuity is a constant cash flow, C, paid every period for n periods. The present value of an annuity is $PV_0 = C \times \frac{1}{r}\left(1 - \frac{1}{(1+r)^n}\right)$ (4.5) ■ The future value of an annuity at the end of the annuity is $FV_n = C \times \frac{1}{r}\left((1+r)^n - 1\right)$ (4.6)	annuity, p. 104 consol, p. 101 perpetuity, p. 101	MyLab Study Plan 4.2 Interactive Annuity Calculator
4.3 Solving for Variables Other Than Present Value or Future Value ■ The annuity and perpetuity formulas can be used to solve for the annuity payments when either the present value or the future value is known. ■ The periodic payment on an n-period loan with principal P and interest rate r is $C = \frac{P}{\frac{1}{r}\left(1 - \frac{1}{(1+r)^n}\right)}$ (4.7) ■ The rate of return of an investment opportunity is the interest rate at which the PV of the benefits of the investment opportunity exactly offset the PV of the costs. ■ The annuity formulas can be used to solve for the number of periods it takes to save a fixed amount of money.	rate of return, p. 112	MyLab Study Plan 4.3

KEY POINTS AND EQUATIONS	TERMS	ONLINE PRACTICE OPPORTUNITIES
4.4 Growing Cash Flows ■ In a growing perpetuity, the cash flows grow at a constant rate, g, each period. The present value of a growing perpetuity is $$PV_0 = \frac{C_1}{r - g} \quad (4.8)$$ ■ A growing annuity is a growing series of cash flows, starting with C_1 paid every year for n years. The present value of a growing annuity is $$PV_0 = C_1 \times \frac{1}{r - g}\left(1 - \left(\frac{1 + g}{1 + r}\right)^n\right) \quad (4.9)$$ ■ The future value of a growing annuity is $$FV_n = C_1 \times \frac{1}{r - g}\left((1 + r)^n - (1 + g)^n\right) \quad (4.10)$$	growing perpetuity, p. 118 growing annuity, p. 120	

REVIEW QUESTIONS

1. What is the intuition behind the fact that the present value of a stream of cash flows is just the sum of the present values of each individual cash flow?
2. What must be true about a cash flow stream in order for us to be able to use the shortcut formulas?
3. What is the difference between an annuity and a perpetuity?
4. What are some examples of perpetuities?
5. How can a perpetuity have a finite value?
6. What are some examples of annuities?
7. What must be true about the growth rate in order for a growing perpetuity to have a finite value?
8. In what types of situations would it be useful to solve for the number of periods or the rate of return?

PROBLEMS

All problems in this chapter are available in MyLab Finance. An asterisk (*) indicates problems with a higher level of difficulty.

Valuing a Stream of Cash Flows

1. a. What is the present value of the following set of cash flows, discounted at 10% per year?

Year	1	2	3	4	5
CF	10	20	30	40	50

b. What is the present value of the following set of cash flows, discounted at 10% per year?

Year	1	2	3	4	5
CF	50	40	30	20	10

c. Each set contains the same cash flows (10, 20, 30, 40, 50), so why is the present value different?

2. What is the present value of the following set of cash flows, discounted at 15% per year?

Year	1	2	3	4
CF	100	–100	200	–200

3. You want to borrow $10,000. You figure that you can make the following payments. If the interest rate on the loan is 8.5% per year, will your payments be enough to pay off the $10,000 loan?

Year	1	2	3	4
Payment	2000	3000	3500	3975

4. You have a balance of $5000 on your credit card, which charges an interest rate of 1.5% per month. Looking at your budget, you figure you can make the following payments. Will they be enough to pay off your credit card?

Month	1	2	3	4	5	6	7	8
Payment	500	550	600	650	700	750	800	850

5. You have just taken out a five-year loan from a bank to buy an engagement ring. The ring costs $5000. You plan to put down $1000 and borrow $4000. You will need to make annual payments of $1000 at the end of each year. Show the timeline of the loan from your perspective. How would the timeline differ if you created it from the bank's perspective?

6. You currently have a one-year-old loan outstanding on your car. You make monthly payments of $300. You have just made a payment. The loan has four years to go (i.e., it had an original term of five years). Show the timeline from your perspective. How would the timeline differ if you created it from the bank's perspective?

7. You plan to deposit $500 in a bank account now and $300 at the end of one year. If the account earns 3% interest per year, what will the balance be in the account right after you make the second deposit?

8. You have just received a windfall from an investment you made in a friend's business. She will be paying you $10,000 at the end of this year, $20,000 at the end of the following year, and $30,000 at the end of the year after that (three years from today). The interest rate is 3.5% per year.
   a. What is the present value of your windfall?
   b. What is the future value of your windfall in three years (on the date of the last payment)?

9. Suppose you receive $100 at the end of each year for the next three years.
   a. If the interest rate is 8%, what is the present value of these cash flows?
   b. What is the future value in three years of the present value you computed in (a)?
   c. Suppose you deposit the cash flows in a bank account that pays 8% interest per year. What is the balance in the account at the end of each of the next three years (after your deposit is made)? How does the final bank balance compare with your answer in (b)?

10. You have a loan outstanding. It requires making three annual payments of $1000 each at the end of the next three years. Your bank has offered to allow you to skip making the next two payments in lieu of making one large payment at the end of the loan's term in three years. If the interest rate on the loan is 5%, what final payment will the bank require you to make so that it is indifferent to the two forms of payment?

11. Assume you can earn 9% per year on your investments.
   a. If you invest $100,000 for retirement at age 30, how much will you have 35 years later for retirement?
   b. If you wait until age 40 to invest the $100,000, how much will you have 25 years later for retirement?
   c. Why is the difference so large?

Perpetuities and Annuities

12. You want to endow a scholarship that will pay $10,000 per year forever, starting one year from now. If the school's endowment discount rate is 7%, what amount must you donate to endow the scholarship?

13. How would your answer to Problem 12 change if you endow it now, but it makes the first award to a student 10 years from today?

14. The British government has a consol bond outstanding paying £100 per year, forever. Assume the current interest rate is 4% per year.
   a. What is the value of the bond immediately after a payment is made?
   b. What is the value of the bond immediately before a payment is made?

15. You are offered the opportunity to receive $1000 per year forever, starting in one year. If your discount rate is 5%, what is this offer worth to you?

16. You have $100,000 to donate to your university. You want to endow a perpetual scholarship that makes its first payment in one year. If the university's discount rate is 4%, how large will be the annual scholarship payment?

17. If you still donate the $100,000 from Problem 16 today, but ask the university to delay the scholarship payment so that the first scholarship payment is made 10 years from today, then how large will the annual payment be?

18. What is the present value of $1000 paid at the end of each of the next 100 years if the interest rate is 7% per year?

19. Your grandmother has been putting $1000 into a savings account on every birthday since your first (that is, when you turned one). The account pays an interest rate of 3%. How much money will be in the account immediately after your grandmother makes the deposit on your 18th birthday?

PROJECT **20.** Assume that your parents wanted to have $160,000 saved for university by your 18th birthday and they started saving on your first birthday. They saved the same amount each year on your birthday and earned 8% per year on their investments.

a. How much would they have to save each year to reach their goal?

b. If they think you will take five years instead of four to graduate and decide to have $200,000 saved, just in case, how much more would they have to save each year to reach their new goal?

PROJECT ***21.** When you purchased your car, you took out a five-year annual-payment loan with an interest rate of 6% per year. The annual payment on the car is $5000. You have just made a payment and have now decided to pay the loan off by repaying the outstanding balance. Assuming there are no penalties for early payment, what is the payoff amount if

a. you have owned the car for one year (so there are four years left on the loan)?

b. you have owned the car for four years (so there is one year left on the loan)?

22. You figure that the total cost of university will be $100,000 per year 18 years from today. If your discount rate is 8% compounded annually, what is the present value today of four years of university costs starting 18 years from today?

PROJECT **23.** Assume that the Canada Pension Plan promises you $40,000 per year starting when you retire 45 years from today (the first $40,000 will come 45 years from now). If your discount rate is 7%, compounded annually, and you plan to live for 15 years after retiring (so that you will get a total of 16 payments, including the first one), what is the value today of Canada Pension Plan's promise? (*See MyLab Finance for the data in Excel Format.*)

***24.** When Alex Rodriguez moved to the Texas Rangers in 2001, he received a lot of attention for his "$252 million" contract (the total of the payments promised was $252 million). Assume the following about the contract:

Rodriguez earns $16 million in the first year, $17 million in years 2 through 4, $19 million in years 5 and 6, $23 million in year 7, and $27 million in years 8 through 10. He would also receive his $10 million signing bonus spread equally over the first five years ($2 million per year). His deferred payments begin in 2011. The deferred payment amounts total $33 million and are $5 million, then $4 million, then eight amounts of $3 million (ending in 2020). However, the actual payouts will be different. All of the deferred payments will earn 3% per year until they are paid. For example, the $5 million is deferred from 2001 to 2011, or 10 years, meaning that it will actually be $6.7196 million when paid. Assume that the $4 million payment deferred to 2012 is deferred from 2002 (each payment is deferred 10 years).

The contract is a 10-year contract, but each year has a deferred component so that cash flows are paid out over a total of 20 years. The contractual payments, signing bonus, and deferred components are given below. Note that, by contract, the deferred components are not paid in the year they are earned, but instead are paid (plus interest) 10 years later.

2001	2002	2003	2004	2005	2006	2007	2008	2009	2010
$16M	$17M	$17M	$17M	$19M	$19M	$23M	$27M	$27M	$27M
$2M	$2M	$2M	$2M	$2M					
Deferred									
$5M	$4M	$3M	$3M	$3M	$3M	$3M	$3M	$3M	$3M

Assume that an appropriate discount rate for A-Rod to apply to the contract payments is 7% per year.

a. Calculate the true promised payments under this contract, including the deferred payments with interest.

b. Draw a timeline of all of the payments.

c. Calculate the present value of the contract.
d. Compare the present value of the contract to the quoted value of $252 million. What explains the difference?

PROJECT

***25.** You are trying to decide how much to save for retirement. Assume you plan to save $5000 per year with the first investment made one year from now. You think you can earn 10% per year on your investments and you plan to retire in 43 years, immediately after making your last $5000 investment.
a. How much will you have in your retirement account on the day you retire?
b. If, instead of investing $5000 per year, you wanted to make one lump sum investment today for your retirement that will result in the same retirement saving, how much would that lump sum need to be?
c. If you hope to live for 20 years in retirement, how much can you withdraw every year in retirement (starting one year after retirement) so that you will just exhaust your savings with the 20th withdrawal (assume your savings will continue to earn 10% in retirement)?
d. If, instead, you decide to withdraw $300,000 per year in retirement (again with the first withdrawal one year after retiring), how many years will it take until you exhaust your savings?
e. Assuming the most you can afford to save is $1000 per year, but you want to retire with $1 million in your investment account, how high a return do you need to earn on your investments?

Solving for Variables Other Than Present Value or Future Value

26. You are thinking about buying a savings bond. The bond costs $50 today and will mature in 10 years with a value of $100. What annual interest rate will the bond earn?

27. You started an investment account 10 years ago with $1000 and it now has grown to $5000.
a. What annual rate of return have you earned (you have made no additional contributions to the account)?
b. If the investment account earns 15% per year from now on, what will the account's value be 10 years from now?

28. You have an investment opportunity that requires an initial investment of $5000 today and will pay $6000 in one year. What is the rate of return of this opportunity?

29. You have decided to buy a perpetual bond. The bond makes one payment at the end of every year forever and has an interest rate of 5%. If the bond initially costs $1000, what is the payment every year?

30. You are thinking of purchasing a house. The house costs $350,000. You have $50,000 in cash that you can use as a down payment on the house, but you need to borrow the rest of the purchase price. The bank is offering a 30-year mortgage that requires annual payments and has an interest rate of 7% per year. What will your annual payment be if you sign up for this mortgage?

31. You are shopping for a car and read the following advertisement in the newspaper: "Own a new Spitfire! No money down. Four annual payments of just $10,000." You have shopped around and know that you can buy a Spitfire for cash for $32,500. What is the interest rate the dealer is advertising (what is the internal rate of return (IRR) of the loan in the advertisement)? Assume that you must make the annual payments at the end of each year.

***32.** Your grandmother bought an annuity from Great-West Life Insurance Company for $200,000 when she retired. In exchange for the $200,000, Great-West Life will pay her $25,000 per year until she dies. The interest rate is 5%. How long must she live after the day she retired to come out ahead (that is, to get more in value than what she paid in)?

*33. You would like to buy the house and take the mortgage described in Problem 30. You can afford to pay only $23,500 per year. The bank agrees to allow you to pay this amount each year, yet still borrow $300,000. At the end of the mortgage (in 30 years), you must make a balloon payment; that is, you must repay the remaining balance on the mortgage. How much will this balloon payment be?

*34. You are saving for retirement. To live comfortably, you decide you will need to save $2 million by the time you are 65. Today is your 22nd birthday, and you decide that, starting today and continuing on every birthday up to and including your 65th birthday, you will put the same amount into a savings account. If the interest rate is 5%, how much must you set aside each year to make sure that you will have $2 million in the account on your 65th birthday?

35. You graduate and get a $10,000 cheque from your grandparents. You decide to save it toward a down payment on a house. You invest it, earning 10% per year, and you think you will need to have $20,000 saved for the down payment. How long will it be before the $10,000 has grown to $20,000?

36. A local bank is running the following advertisement in the newspaper: "For just $1000 we will pay you $100 forever!" The fine print in the ad says that for a $1000 deposit, the bank will pay $100 every year in perpetuity, starting one year after the deposit is made. What interest rate is the bank advertising (what is the rate of return of this investment)?

*37. You are thinking of making an investment in a new plant. The plant will generate revenues of $1 million per year for as long as you maintain it. You expect that the maintenance costs will start at $50,000 per year and will increase 5% per year thereafter. Assume that all revenue and maintenance costs occur at the end of the year. You intend to run the plant as long as it continues to make a positive cash flow (as long as the cash generated by the plant exceeds the maintenance costs). The plant can be built and become operational immediately and the interest rate is 6% per year.

a. What is the present value of the revenues?
b. What is the present value of the maintenance costs?
c. If the plant costs $10 million to build, should you invest in the plant?

*38. You have just turned 22 years old, have just received your bachelor's degree, and have accepted your first job. Now you must decide how much money to put into your retirement plan. The plan works as follows: Every dollar in the plan earns 7% per year. You cannot make withdrawals until you retire on your 65th birthday. After that point, you can make withdrawals as you see fit. You decide that you will plan to live to 100 and work until you turn 65. You estimate that to live comfortably in retirement, you will need $100,000 per year, starting at the end of the first year of retirement and ending on your 100th birthday. You will contribute the same amount to the plan at the end of every year that you work. How much do you need to contribute each year to fund your retirement?

Growing Cash Flows

39. A rich relative has bequeathed you a growing perpetuity. The first payment will occur in a year and will be $1000. Each year after that, you will receive a payment on the anniversary of the last payment that is 8% larger than the last payment. This pattern of payments will go on forever. If the interest rate is 12% per year,

a. what is today's value of the bequest?
b. what is the value of the bequest immediately after the first payment is made?

PROJECT

***40.** You are thinking of building a new machine that will save you $1000 in the first year. The machine will then begin to wear out so that the savings decline at a rate of 2% per year forever. What is the present value of the savings if the interest rate is 5% per year?

41. When Alfred Nobel died, he left the majority of his estate to fund five prizes, each to be awarded annually in perpetuity starting one year after he died. (The sixth one, in economics, was added later.)

a. If he wanted the cash award of each of the five prizes to be $45,000 and his estate could earn 7% per year, how much would he need to fund his prizes?

b. If he wanted the value of each prize to grow by 4% per year (perhaps to keep up with inflation), how much would he need to leave? Assume that the first amount was still $45,000.

c. His heirs were surprised by his will and fought it. If they had been able to keep the amount of money you calculated in (b), and had invested it at 7% per year, how much would they have in 2014, 118 years after he died?

42. You work for a pharmaceutical company that has developed a new drug. The patent on the drug will last 17 years. You expect that the drug's profits will be $2 million in its first year and that this amount will grow at a rate of 5% per year for the next 17 years. Once the patent expires, other pharmaceutical companies will be able to produce the same drug and competition will likely drive profits to zero. What is the present value of the new drug if the interest rate is 10% per year?

43. A rich aunt has promised you $5000 one year from today. In addition, each year after that, she has promised you a payment (on the anniversary of the last payment) that is 3% larger than the last payment. She will continue to show this generosity for 20 years, giving a total of 20 payments. If the interest rate is 5%, what is her promise worth today?

***44.** You have just turned 22 years old, have just received your bachelor's degree, and have accepted your first job. Now you must decide how much money to put into your registered retirement savings plan (RRSP). The RRSP works as follows: Every dollar in the RRSP earns 7% per year. You will not make withdrawals until you retire on your 65th birthday. After that point, you can make withdrawals as you see fit. You decide that you will plan to live to 100 and work until you turn 65. You estimate that to live comfortably in retirement, you will need $100,000 at the end of the first year of retirement (i.e., when you turn 66) and that the annual amount should grow with inflation at 3% per year ending on your 100th birthday. Your first contribution to your RRSP will be when you turn 23; you will increase your contributions by 5% per year (your expectation for salary increases); and you will make these contributions at the end of every year that you work. How much do you need to contribute on your 23rd birthday to begin funding your retirement?

DATA CASE

Assume today is February 28, 2018. Natasha Kingery is 30 years old and has a bachelor of science degree in computer science. She is currently employed at Open Text Corporation in Ottawa and earns $38,000 a year that she anticipates will grow at 3% per year. Natasha hopes to retire at age 65 and has just begun to think about the future.

Natasha has $75,000 that she recently inherited from her aunt. She invested this money in 10-year Government of Canada bonds. She is considering whether she should further her education and would use her inheritance to pay for it.

She has investigated a couple of options and is asking for your help as a financial planning intern to determine the financial consequences associated with each option. Natasha has already been accepted to both of these programs, and could start either one soon.

One alternative that Natasha is considering is attaining a certification in network design. This certification would automatically promote her to a new position and give her a raise of $10,000. This salary differential will grow at a rate of 3% per year as long as she keeps working. The certification program requires the completion of 20 web-based courses and a score of 80% or better on an exam at the end of the course work. She has learned that the average amount of time necessary to finish the program is one year. The total cost of the program is $5000, due when she enrolls in the program. Because she will do all the work for the certification on her own time, Natasha does not expect to lose any income during the certification.

Another option is going back to school for an MBA degree. With an MBA degree, Natasha expects to be promoted to a managerial position at Open Text. The managerial position pays $20,000 a year more than her current position. She expects that this salary differential will also grow at a rate of 3% per year for as long as she keeps working. The evening program, which will take three years to complete, costs $25,000 per year, due at the beginning of each of her three years in school. Because she will attend classes in the evening, Natasha doesn't expect to lose any income while she is earning her MBA if she chooses to undertake the MBA.

1. Determine the interest rate she is currently earning on her inheritance by going to the Bank of Canada website (http://www.bankofcanada.ca/) and clicking on the "Statistics" page. On the page, choose the "Interest Rates" link and then click on "Bond Yields." Then, where it indicates "Related Pages," click on "Canadian Bond Yields 10-year lookup." Enter the appropriate date you want (February 28, 2018) and check off the desired bond, "10 year" (daily prices), to obtain the average yield or interest rate that she is earning. Use this interest rate as the discount rate for the remainder of this problem.

2. Create a timeline in Excel for her current situation, as well as the certification program and MBA degree options, using the following assumptions:
   a. Salaries for the year are paid only once, at the end of each year of your timeline.
   b. The salary increase becomes effective immediately upon graduating from the MBA program or being certified. That is, because the increases become effective immediately but salaries are paid at the end of the year, the first salary increase will be paid exactly one year after graduation or certification.

3. Calculate the present value of the salary differential for completing the certification program. Subtract the cost of the program to get the net value of undertaking the certification program.

4. Calculate the present value of the salary differential for completing the MBA degree. Calculate the present value of the cost of the MBA program. Based on your calculations, determine the net value of undertaking the MBA.

5. Based on your answers to Questions 3 and 4, what advice would you give to Natasha? What if the two programs are mutually exclusive? If Natasha undertakes one of the programs, there is no further benefit to undertaking the other program. Would your advice change?

Specifying Decimal Places

Make sure you always have plenty of decimal places displayed!

HP-10BII

TI BAII PLUS PROFESSIONAL

Toggling between the Beginning and End of a Period

You should always make sure that your calculator is in *end-of-period* mode.

HP-10BII

TI BAII PLUS PROFESSIONAL

Set the Number of Periods per Year

You will avoid a lot of confusion later if you always set your periods per year "P/Y" to 1:

HP-10BII

TI BAII PLUS PROFESSIONAL

General TVM Buttons

HP-10BII

TI BAII PLUS PROFESSIONAL

Solving for the Present Value of a Single Future Cash Flow (Example 3.4)

You are considering investing in a Government of Canada bond that will make one payment of $15,000 in 10 years. If the competitive market interest rate is fixed at 6% per year, what is the bond worth today? [Answer: $8375.92]

HP-10BII

[Orange Shift] C CALL	Press [Orange Shift] and then the [C] button to clear all previous entries.
1 0 N	Enter the Number of periods.
6 I/YR	Enter the market annual interest rate.
1 5 0 0 0 FV	Enter the Value you will receive in 10 periods.
0 PMT	Indicate that there are no payments.
PV	Solve for the Present Value.

TI BAII PLUS PROFESSIONAL

2ND FV	Press [2ND] and then the [FV] button to clear all previous entries.
1 0 N	Enter the Number of periods.
6 I/Y	Enter the market annual interest rate.
1 5 0 0 0 FV	Enter the Value you will receive in 10 periods.
0 PMT	Indicate that there are no payments.
CPT PV	Solve for the Present Value.

Solving for the Future Value of an Annuity (Example 4.5)

Ellen is 35 years old, and she has decided it is time to plan seriously for her retirement. At the end of each year until she is 65, she will save $10,000 in a retirement account. If the account earns 10% per year, how much will Ellen have saved at age 65? [Answer: $1,644,940]

HP-10BII

[Orange Shift] C CALL	Press [Orange Shift] and then the [C] button to clear all previous entries.
3 0 N	Enter the Number of periods.
1 0 I/YR	Enter the market annual interest rate.
1 0 0 0 0 PMT	Enter the Payment amount per period.
0 PV	Indicate that there is no initial amount in the retirement account.
FV	Solve for the Present Value.

TI BAII PLUS PROFESSIONAL

2ND FV	Press [2ND] and then the [FV] button to clear all previous entries.
3 0 N	Enter the Number of periods.
1 0 I/Y	Enter the market annual interest rate.
1 0 0 0 0 PMT	Enter the payment amount per period.
0 PV	Indicate that there is no initial amount in the retirement account.
CPT FV	Solve for the Future Value.

Solving for the Internal Rate of Return

If you have an initial cash outflow of $2000 and one cash inflow per year for the following four years of $1000, $400, $400, and $800, what is the rate of return on the project per year? [Answer: 12.12%]

HP-10BII

C CALL	Press [Orange Shift] and then the [C] button to clear all previous entries.
2 0 0 0 +/– CF_j	Enter the initial cash of outflow.
1 0 0 0 CF_j	Enter the first cash inflow.
4 0 0 CF_j	Enter the Second cash inflow.
2 CF_j N_j	Enter the number of consecutive periods the second cash inflow occurs.
8 0 0 CF_j	Enter the fourth cash inflow.
CST IRR/YR	Press [Orange Shift] and then the [CST] button to calculate the IRR/year.

TI BAII PLUS PROFESSIONAL

CF	Access Cash Flow Worksheet.
2ND CE/C	Press [2ND] and then the [CE/C] button to clear all previous entries.
2 0 0 0 +/– ENTER	Enter the initial cash of outflow.
↓ 1 0 0 0 ENTER	Enter the first cash inflow.
↓	Leave the frequency of the initial cash inflow at 1 (Default Setting).
↓ 4 0 0 ENTER	Enter the second cash inflow.
↓ 2 ENTER	Enter the frequency of the second cash inflow as 2.
↓ 8 0 0 ENTER	Enter the fourth cash inflow.
↓	Leave the frequency of the fourth cash inflow at 1 (Default Setting).
IRR CPT	Solve for the IRR.

CHAPTER

5 Interest Rates

LEARNING OBJECTIVES

- Understand the different ways interest rates are quoted
- Use quoted rates to calculate loan payments and balances
- Know how inflation, expectations, and risk combine to determine interest rates
- Be exposed to the term structure of interest rates and yield curves
- See the link between interest rates in the market and a firm's opportunity cost of capital

NOTATION

APR	annual percentage rate
APY	annual percentage yield
C	cash flow
C_n	cash flow that arrives in period n
EAR	effective annual rate
FV	future value
m	compounding frequency of a quoted interest rate
n	number of periods
PV	present value
r	interest rate or discount rate
r_n	interest rate or discount rate for an n-year term

In Chapter 4, we explored the mechanics of computing present values and future values given a market interest rate. Recall that an interest rate allows us to convert money at one point in time to another. But how do we determine that interest rate? In this chapter, we consider the factors that affect interest rates and discuss how to determine the appropriate discount rate for a set of cash flows. We begin by looking at the way interest is paid and interest rates are quoted, and we show how to calculate the effective interest paid in one year given different quoting conventions. We then consider some of the main determinants of interest rates—namely, inflation and economic growth. Because interest rates tend to change over time, investors will demand different interest rates for different investment horizons, based on their expectations and the risk involved in longer time horizons.

5.1 Interest Rate Quotes and Adjustments

If you spend some time looking through a newspaper, you will find literally dozens of interest rates discussed and advertised, from savings deposit rates to auto loan rates to interest rates being paid on the government's debt. Interest rates are clearly central to the functioning of any financial system. To understand interest rates, it's important to think of interest rates as a price—the price of using money. When you borrow money to buy a car, you are using the bank's money now to get the car and paying the money back over time. The interest rate on your loan is the price you pay to be able to convert your future loan payments into the money needed to buy a car today. Similarly, when you deposit money into a savings account, you are letting the bank use your money until you withdraw it later. The interest the bank pays you on your deposit is the price it pays to have the use of your money (for things like making car loans).

Just like any other price, interest rates are set by market forces, in particular the supply of and demand for funds. When the supply (savings) is high and the demand (borrowing) is low, interest rates are low, other things being equal. Additionally, as we discuss later in the chapter, interest rates are also influenced by expected inflation and risk.

To be able to study and use interest rates, we have to understand how they are quoted. In practice, interest is paid and interest rates are quoted in different ways. For example, on March 11, 2018, Tangerine offered a 5-year guaranteed investment certificate (GIC) with an interest rate of 3% per year with annual compounding, while Simplii Financial offered an interest rate of 2.423% per year, but with the interest compounded on a monthly basis. Interest rates can also change through time and differ depending on the investment horizon. On January 31, 1990, investors earned about 11% on 1-year risk-free (Government of Canada) investments but earned only about 9.3% on 20-year risk-free investments. This is in sharp contrast to February 16, 2010, when investors earned only 0.63% on 1-year risk-free investments but 4.06% on 20-year risk-free investments. Interest rates can also vary due to risk. For example, the Canadian government is able to borrow at a much lower interest rate than Molson Coors Brewing Company.

Because interest rates may be quoted for different time intervals, such as monthly, semi-anually, or annually, it is often necessary to adjust the interest rate to a time period that matches that of our cash flows. We explore these mechanics of interest rates in this section.

The Effective Annual Rate

effective annual rate (EAR) The total amount of interest that will be earned at the end of one year expressed as a proportion of the amount invested at the beginning of the year.

Interest rates are sometimes reported as an **effective annual rate (EAR)**, which indicates the total amount of interest that will be earned at the end of one year, expressed as a proportion of the amount invested at the beginning of the year. We have used this method of quoting the interest rate thus far in this book, and in Chapter 4 we used the EAR as the discount rate, r, in our time value of money calculations. For example, with an EAR of 5%, a $100 investment grows to

$$\$100 \times (1 + r) = \$100 \times (1.05) = \$105$$

in one year. After two years it will grow as follows:

$$\$100 \times (1 + r)^2 = \$100 \times (1.05)^2 = \$110.25$$

Year:	**0**		**1**		**2**
Cash flow:	$100	× (1.05)	= $105	× (1.05)	= $110.25
	$100	×	$(1.05)^2$	=	$110.25
	$100	×	(1.1025)	=	$110.25

Adjusting the Effective Annual Rate to an Effective Rate over Different Time Periods

The preceding example shows that earning an EAR of 5% for two years is equivalent to earning 10.25% in total interest over the entire period:

$$\$100 \times (1.05)^2 = \$100 \times 1.1025 = \$110.25$$

In general, by raising the interest rate factor $(1 + r)$ to the appropriate power, we can compute an equivalent effective interest rate for a longer time period.

We can use the same method to find the equivalent effective interest rate for periods shorter than one year. In this case, we raise the interest rate factor $(1 + r)$ to the appropriate fractional power. For example, earning 5% interest in one year is equivalent to receiving

$$(1 + r)^{0.5} = (1.05)^{0.5} = \$1.0247$$

for each \$1 invested every six months (0.5 years). That is, a 5% EAR is equivalent to an interest rate of approximately 2.47% earned every six months—this would be an effective six-month rate. We can verify this result by computing the interest we would earn in one year by investing for two six-month periods at this rate:

$$(1 + r)^2 = (1.0247)^2 = \$1.05$$

Year:	**0**		**$\frac{1}{2}$**		**1**
Cash flow:	\$1	$\times(1.0247)$	$= \$1.0247$	$\times(1.0247)$	$= \$1.05$
	\$1	$\times$	$(1.0247)^2$	$=$	\$1.05
	\$1	$\times$	(1.05)	$=$	\$1.05

In general, we can convert an effective discount rate of r for one period to an equivalent effective discount rate for n periods using the following formula:

$$\begin{aligned}&(1 + \text{Equivalent } n\text{-Period Effective Rate}) = (1 + r)^n \\ &\text{and thus, the Equivalent } n\text{-Period Effective Rate} = (1 + r)^n - 1\end{aligned} \tag{5.1}$$

In this formula, n can be larger than 1 (to compute an effective rate over more than one period) or smaller than 1 (to compute an effective rate over a fraction of a period). In the above examples, we started with an EAR and used $n = 2$ to calculate the effective two-year interest rate and $n = 0.5$ to find the effective half-year (i.e. six-month) rate.

When computing present or future values, you should adjust the discount rate to match the time period of the cash flows.

This adjustment is necessary to apply the perpetuity or annuity formulas to non-annual cash flows, as in the following example.

EXAMPLE 5.1 Personal Finance: Valuing Monthly Cash Flows

PROBLEM

Suppose your bank account pays interest monthly with an *EAR* of 6%. What amount of interest will you earn each month?

If you have no money in the bank today, how much will you need to save at the end of each month to accumulate \$100,000 in 10 years?

SOLUTION

■ **Plan**

We can use Equation 5.1 to convert the *EAR* to an effective monthly rate, answering the first part of the question. The second part of the question is a future value of an annuity question. It is asking how big a monthly annuity we would have to deposit to end up with $100,000 in 10 years. However, to do this problem, we need to write the timeline in terms of *monthly* periods, because our cash flows (deposits) will be monthly:

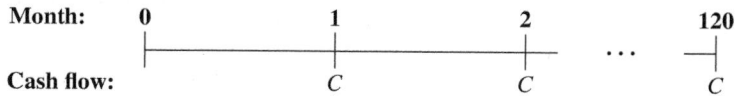

That is, we can view the savings plan as a monthly annuity with $10 \times 12 = 120$ monthly payments. We have the future value of the annuity ($100,000) and the length of time (120 months), and we will have the monthly interest rate from the first part of the question. We can then use the future value of an annuity formula (Equation 4.6) to solve for the monthly deposit.

■ **Execute**

From Equation 5.1, a 6% EAR is equivalent to earning $(1.06)^{1/12} - 1 = 0.4868\%$ as the effective rate per month. The exponent in this equation is 1/12 because the period is 1/12 of a year (a month).

Now that we have all of the inputs in terms of months (monthly payment, effective monthly interest rate, and total number of months), we use the future value of annuity formula from Chapter 4 to solve for the amount to save each month:

$$FV(\text{annuity}) = C \times \tfrac{1}{r}[(1 + r)^n - 1]$$

We solve for the amount to save each month, C, using the equivalent effective monthly interest rate $r = 0.4868\%$, and $n = 120$ months:

$$C = \frac{FV(annuity)}{\frac{1}{r}[(1 + r)^n - 1]} = \frac{\$100{,}000}{\frac{1}{0.004868}[(1.004868)^{120} - 1]} = \$615.47 \text{ per month}$$

We can also compute this result using a financial calculator:

	N	I/Y	PV	PMT	FV
Given:	120	0.4868	0		100,000
Solve for:				−615.47	
Excel Formula: = *PMT*(*RATE*,*NPER*,*PV*,*FV*) = *PMT*(0.004868,120,0,100000)					

■ **Evaluate**

Thus, if we save $615.47 per month and we earn interest monthly at an *EAR* of 6%, we will have $100,000 in 10 years. Notice that the timing in the annuity formula must be consistent for all of the inputs. In this case, we had a monthly deposit, so we needed to convert our interest rate to an effective monthly interest rate and then use total number of months (120) instead of years.

annual percentage rate (APR) The amount of simple interest earned in one year without considering the effects of compounding that may occur.

Annual Percentage Rates

The most common way to quote interest rates is in terms of an **annual percentage rate (APR)**, which indicates the amount of **simple interest** earned in one year; that is, the amount of interest earned *without* the effect of compounding, even though compounding may occur. Because it does not include the effect of compounding, the APR quote

simple interest Interest earned only on the original principal amount without considering compounding of interest or interest earned on accrued interest.

is typically less than the actual amount of interest that you will earn. To compute the actual amount that you will earn in one year, you must first convert the APR to an EAR.

For example, suppose Scotiabank advertises savings accounts with an interest rate of "6% APR with monthly compounding." By convention, this rate quote implies you will earn an effective monthly rate of 6%/12 = 0.5% every month. So, an APR with monthly compounding is actually a way of indirectly quoting an *effective monthly* interest rate, rather than an effective annual interest rate. In other words, the APR with monthly compounding is the effective monthly interest rate multiplied by the number of months per year: APR = 12 × 0.5% = 6%. Because the interest compounds each month, each dollar you invest will grow to

$$\$1 \times (1.005)^{12} = \$1.061678$$

by the end of one year, for an EAR of 6.1678%. The 6.1678% that you earn on your deposit is higher than the quoted 6% APR due to compounding within the year; in later months, you earn interest on the interest paid in earlier months. To summarize, an actual rate of 0.5% *per month* can be stated in either of the following ways:

- 6% APR, compounded monthly
- EAR of 6.1678%, which indicates the total amount of interest earned *per year*

It is important to remember that, because the APR does not reflect the true amount you will earn over one year, *the* APR *itself cannot be used as a discount rate.* Generalizing the earlier example, the APR is the effective interest rate per compounding period multiplied by the number of compounding periods per year. If m is the number of compounding periods per year, then APR = m × Effective Interest Rate per Compounding Period. Therefore, an APR quote is an indirect way of quoting the actual interest earned each compounding period:

$$\text{Implied Effective Interest Rate per Compounding Period} = \frac{APR}{m} \tag{5.2}$$

(m = number of compounding periods per year, also known as the compounding frequency)

We call this rate an implied effective rate because it shows the actual interest earned over the compounding period and, by convention, it is what is implied from an APR quote. In our example of 6% APR with monthly compounding, the 0.5% equivalent will be the implied effective rate per month. Once we have computed the implied effective rate per compounding period from Equation 5.2, we can compute the equivalent effective rate for any other time interval using Equation 5.1. The EAR corresponding to an APR with m compounding periods per year is given by the following conversion formula:

Converting an APR to an EAR

$$(1 + EAR) = \left(1 + \frac{APR}{m}\right)^m \text{ and thus the } EAR = \left(1 + \frac{APR}{m}\right)^m - 1 \tag{5.3}$$

Table 5.1 shows the *EAR*s that correspond to an APR of 6% with different compounding intervals. The EAR increases with the frequency of compounding because of the ability to earn interest on interest sooner. Investments can compound even more frequently than daily. In principle, the compounding interval could be hourly or every second. As a practical matter, compounding more frequently than daily has a negligible impact on the effective annual rate and is rarely observed.

TABLE 5.1 Effective Annual Rates for a 6% APR with Different Compounding Periods

Compounding Interval	Effective Annual Rate
Annual	$\left(1+\frac{0.06}{1}\right)^{1}-1=6\%$
Semi-annual	$\left(1+\frac{0.06}{2}\right)^{2}-1=6.09\%$
Monthly	$\left(1+\frac{0.06}{12}\right)^{12}-1=6.1678\%$
Daily	$\left(1+\frac{0.06}{365}\right)^{365}-1=6.1831\%$

To summarize, when working with APRs, we must first convert the APR to an implied effective discount rate per compounding interval using Equation 5.2. We can then use Equation 5.1 to convert the effective rate per compounding period to an equivalent effective rate per *different* compounding period. If we need to convert our APR to an effective rate per year—that is, an APR—we can use Equation 5.3 (which is a special case of applying both Equations 5.2 and 5.1 simultaneously).

EXAMPLE 5.2 Converting the APR to a Discount Rate

PROBLEM

Your firm is purchasing a new telephone system that will last for four years. You can purchase the system for an upfront cost of $150,000, or you can lease the system from the manufacturer for $4000 paid at the end of each month. The lease price is offered for a 48-month lease with no early termination—you cannot end the lease early. Your firm can borrow at an interest rate of 6% APR with monthly compounding. Should you purchase the system outright or pay $4000 per month?

SOLUTION

Plan

The cost of leasing the system is a 48-month annuity of $4000 per month:

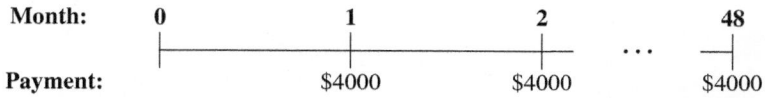

We can compute the present value of the lease cash flows using the annuity formula, but first we need to compute the effective discount rate that corresponds to a period length of one month. To do so, we convert the borrowing cost of 6% APR with monthly compounding to an implied effective monthly discount rate using Equation 5.2. Once we have a monthly rate, we can use the present value of annuity formula (Equation 4.5) to compute the present value of the monthly payments and compare it to the cost of buying the system.

Execute

As Equation 5.2 shows, the 6% APR with monthly compounding implies 6%/12 = 0.5% every month. We know that $m = 12$ since there are 12 monthly compounding periods per year. Now that we have ▶

the implied effective monthly rate corresponding to the quoted APR, we can use that as the discount rate in the annuity formula (Equation 4.5) to compute the present value of the monthly payments:

$$PV = 4000 \times \frac{1}{0.005}\left(1 - \frac{1}{1.005^{48}}\right) = \$170{,}321.27$$

Using a financial calculator or Excel:

	N	I/Y	PV	PMT	FV
Given:	48	0.5		−4000	0
Solve for:			170,321.27		
Excel Formula: = *PV*(*RATE,NPER,PMT,FV*) = *PV*(0.005,48,−4000,0)					

■ **Evaluate**

Thus, paying $4000 per month for 48 months is equivalent to paying a present value of $170,321.27 today. This cost is $170,321.27 − $150,000 = $20,321.27 higher than the cost of purchasing the system, so it is better to pay $150,000 for the system rather than lease it.

COMMON MISTAKE

Using the APR or EAR in the Annuity Formula

At this point, many students make the mistake of trying to use the APR or EAR in the annuity formula. The interest rate in the annuity formula must match the length of time between cash flows. That's why in Example 5.1 we first converted the EAR into a monthly rate and then used the annuity formula to compute the monthly loan payments. The common mistake in this case would be to use an APR or an EAR in the annuity formula to obtain annual cash flows, and then divide those cash flows by 12 to obtain the monthly payments.

This process will produce the wrong answer. To see why, consider the timing of the first deposit in Example 5.1. With a monthly rate and monthly payments, the annuity formula assumes that the first payment will be made one month from now. It then assumes that you will be making 11 more monthly deposits before the end of the first year. Each of those deposits will start earning interest as soon you make it. In contrast, if you use an annual rate and calculate an annual cash flow, the formula assumes that you will make your first deposit one *year* from now, so that you will forgo a whole year of interest before you start earning anything. Thus, you can see that using an annual rate misses the fact that you are making deposits earlier and more often than annually, so you are adding to your interest-earning principal more frequently than once per year.

CONCEPT CHECK

1. What is the difference between an EAR and an APR quote?
2. Why can't the APR be used as a discount rate?

5.2 Application: Discount Rates and Loans

Now that we have explained how to compute the proper discount rate to use from a given interest rate quote, let's apply the concept to solve two common financial problems: calculating a loan payment and calculating the remaining balance on a loan.

amortizing loan A loan on which the borrower makes monthly payments that include interest on the loan plus some part of the loan balance.

Computing Loan Payments

Many loans, such as personal and car loans, have monthly payments and are quoted in terms of an APR with monthly compounding. This type of loan is an **amortizing loan,** which means that each month you pay interest on the loan plus some part of the loan balance. Each monthly payment is the same, and the loan is fully repaid with the final payment. Typical terms for a new car loan might be "6.75% APR for 60 months." Most provinces in Canada have harmonized their cost of credit disclosure requirements so that when the compounding interval for the APR is not stated explicitly, it is equal to the interval between the payments, or one month in this case.[1] Thus, this quote means that the loan will be repaid with 60 equal monthly payments, computed using a 6.75% APR with monthly compounding. Let's look at the cash flows associated with this loan. The bank will give you $30,000 in cash today to use to buy the car. In return, you will give the bank 60 equal payments each month for 60 months, starting one month from now. For the bank to be willing to accept this exchange, it must be true that the present value of what you will give the bank, discounted at the loan's interest rate, is equal to the amount of cash the bank is giving you now. Here is the timeline for a $30,000 car loan with these terms:

Month:	**0**	**1**	**2**	...	**60**
Cash flow:	$30,000	$-C$	$-C$		$-C$

The payment, C, is set so that the present value of the cash flows, evaluated using the loan interest rate, equals the original principal amount of $30,000. In this case, the 6.75% APR with monthly compounding corresponds to a one-month discount rate of $6.75\%/12 = 0.5625\%$. It is important that the discount rate match the frequency of the cash flows—here we have a monthly discount rate and a monthly loan payment, so we can proceed. Because the loan payments are an annuity, we can use Equation 4.10 to find C:

$$C = \frac{P}{\frac{1}{r}\left(1 - \frac{1}{(1+r)^n}\right)} = \frac{30{,}000}{\frac{1}{0.005625}\left(1 - \frac{1}{(1+0.005625)^{60}}\right)} = \$590.50$$

Alternatively, we can solve for the payment C using a financial calculator or a spreadsheet:

	N	I/Y	PV	PMT	FV
Given:	60	0.5625	30,000		0
Solve for:				−590.50	

Excel Formula: = *PMT*(*RATE,NPER,PV,FV*) = *PMT*(0.005625,60,30000,0)

Your loan payment each month includes interest and repayment of part of the principal, reducing the amount you still owe. Because the loan balance (amount you still owe) is decreasing each month, the interest that accrues on that balance is decreasing. As a result, even though your payment stays the same over the entire 60-month life of the loan, the part of that payment needed to cover interest each month is constantly decreasing and the part left over to reduce the principal further is constantly increasing. We illustrate this effect in panel (a) of Figure 5.1, which shows the proportion of each monthly loan payment that covers interest (red) and the portion left over to reduce the principal (turquoise). As you can see, $168.75 of your first $590.50 payment is needed just to cover interest accrued over the first month ($30,000 × 0.005625 = $168.75). However, this amount steadily decreases so that by the end of the loan, nearly all of your payment is going toward principal.

Panel (b) of Figure 5.1 shows the effect of your payments on the loan balance. When you make your first payment of $590.50, $168.75 covers interest on the loan, leaving

[1]An important exception is Canadian mortgages. These are quoted with APRs using semi-annual compounding even though payments are usually monthly.

FIGURE 5.1 Amortizing Loan

Panel (a) shows how the interest (red) and principal portions (turquoise) of the monthly payment on the $30,000 car loan change over the life of the loan. Panel (b) illustrates the effect on the outstanding balance (principal) of the loan. Note that as the balance decreases, the amount of the payment needed to cover interest on that balance decreases, allowing more of the payment to be used to reduce the principal.

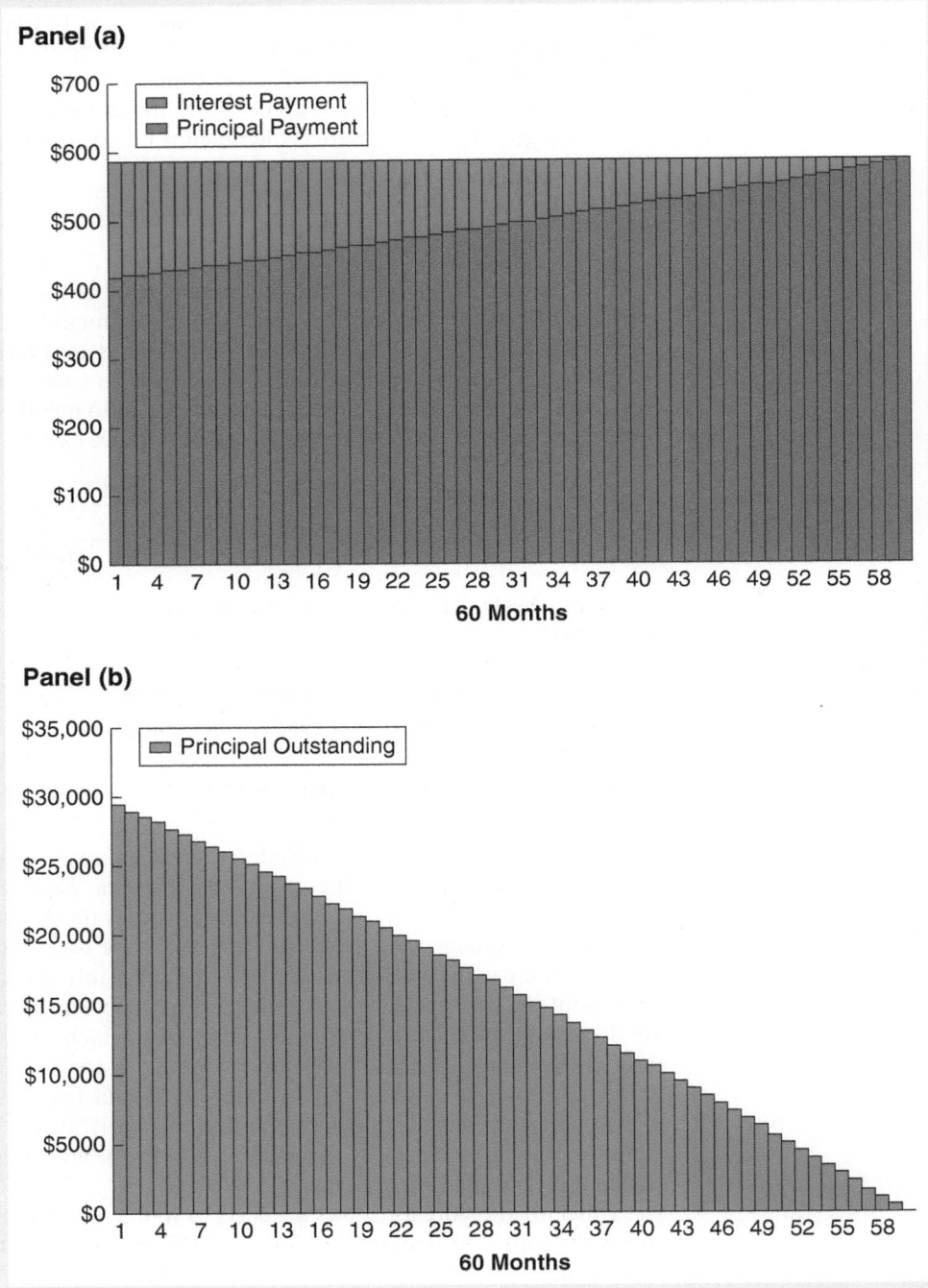

$421.75 to reduce the principal to $30,000 – $421.75 = $29,578.25. The next month, you owe interest only on the $29,578.25 loan balance, which is $166.38, leaving more of your $590.50 payment to reduce the principal further. This effect continues so that each month more of your payment is available to reduce the principal, causing the principal to decrease rapidly toward the end of the loan as you are paying off bigger and bigger amounts of the balance.

Computing Canadian Mortgage Payments

mortgage A loan for which the borrower offers property as security for the lender.

When you buy a home, you usually need to borrow money. This is done using a **mortgage**, which is a loan for which the borrower offers property as security for the lender. Rates for Canadian mortgages are typically quoted in the form of an APR with semi-annual compounding even though the mortgage has monthly payments. Suppose you need to borrow $400,000 and the Bank of Montreal offers you a 5-year term for a mortgage with a rate of 7.252% to be amortized over 25 years of monthly payments. To determine your monthly payments, you need to convert the 7.252% APR with semi-annual compounding into an equivalent effective rate per month. This requires two steps. First, you can use Equation 5.2 to get the implied effective interest rate per semi-annual period:

$$\frac{7.252\%}{2} = 3.626\% \text{ per semi-annual period}$$

Then, noting that each semi-annual period consists of six months, you can use Equation 5.1 to convert the effective semi-annual rate to the equivalent effective monthly rate:

$$(1.03626)^{1/6} - 1 = 0.005954 \text{ or } 0.5954\% \text{ per month}$$

You can calculate the monthly payments using the same method as shown above for loan payments. However, you might get confused by the terms of the mortgage. It is a 5-year mortgage but amortized over 25 years of monthly payments. What does this mean? The 5-year term of the mortgage means that the quoted rate is fixed for the 5 years. At the end of the 5 years, you must renegotiate the mortgage at prevailing rates or pay off the outstanding balance. The amortization over 25 years means that your payments are calculated as though the interest rate will stay at the quoted APR for the full 25 years and the same 300 monthly payments will be made over this entire time. So, using Equation 4.10, we can solve for the monthly mortgage payments, C:

$$C = \frac{P}{\frac{1}{r}\left(1 - \frac{1}{(1+r)^n}\right)} = \frac{400{,}000}{\frac{1}{0.005954}\left(1 - \frac{1}{(1+0.005954)^{300}}\right)} = \$2{,}864.17$$

Although the payments are calculated as though 300 monthly payments will be made, they are paid only over the term of the mortgage (5 years, or 60 months). When the term of the mortgage is over, you can either repay the outstanding balance in full or you can refinance it (usually by renewing your mortgage).

Computing the Outstanding Loan Balance

As Figure 5.1 shows, the outstanding balance on an amortizing loan is different each month. The amount you owe at any point in time can be calculated as the present value of your future obligations on the loan. So, the outstanding balance, also called the outstanding principal, is equal to the present value of the remaining future loan payments, again evaluated using the loan interest rate. We calculate the outstanding loan balance by determining the present value of the remaining loan payments using the loan rate as the discount rate.

EXAMPLE 5.3 Personal Finance: Computing the Outstanding Loan Balance on a Canadian Mortgage

PROBLEM

Returning to our previous hypothetical Bank of Montreal mortgage example, we are interested in what your outstanding balance will be at the end of the mortgage's initial five-year term.

SOLUTION

Plan

We have already determined that the monthly payments on the mortgage are $2864.17. At the end of the mortgage's 5-year term, there are 20 years of monthly payments remaining (or 240 monthly payments). The remaining balance on the loan is the present value of the remaining 240 months of payments. Thus, we can just use the annuity formula with the monthly rate of 0.5954%, a monthly payment of $2864.17, and 240 months remaining.

Execute

$$\text{Balance after five years} = \$2864.17 \times \frac{1}{0.005954}\left(1 - \frac{1}{1.005954^{240}}\right) = \$365{,}321.11$$

Thus, after five years, you owe $365,321.11 on the loan.
Using a financial calculator or Excel:

	N	I/Y	PV	PMT	FV
Given:	240	0.5954		−2864.17	0
Solve for:			365,321.11		

Excel Formula: = *PV*(*RATE,NPER,PMT,FV*) = *PV*(0.005954,240,−2864.17,0)

Evaluate

At any point in time, including when you first take out the loan, you can calculate the balance of the loan as the present value of your remaining payments. Since your initial principal was $400,000 and your outstanding balance at the end of the mortgage's term is $365,321.11, you paid a total of $34,678.89 toward principal. Since you paid 60 payments of $2864.17 summing to $171,850.20, the amount of your payments that went to interest charges is $171,850.20 − $34,678.89 = $137,171.31.

CONCEPT CHECK

3. How is the principal repaid in an amortizing loan?
4. Why does the part of your loan payment covering interest change over time?

5.3 The Determinants of Interest Rates

Now that we understand how interest rates are quoted and used in loans, we turn to a broader question: how are interest rates determined? Fundamentally, interest rates are determined by market forces based on the relative supply and demand of funds. This supply and demand is in turn determined by the willingness of individuals, banks, and firms to borrow, save, and lend. Changes in interest rates affect consumer decisions, such as how much you can borrow for a car loan or mortgage. Because they change the present value of future cash flows, changes in interest rates also have a broad impact on capital budgeting decisions within a firm. In this section, we look at some of the factors that may influence interest rates, such as inflation, current economic activity, and expectations of future growth.

Inflation and Real versus Nominal Rates

Inflation measures how the purchasing power of a given amount of currency declines due to increasing prices. How many times have you heard the expression, "A dollar just doesn't buy what it used to"? We've all witnessed the steady upward climb of prices—for example, your morning coffee probably costs a little more today than it did five years ago. Inflation affects how we evaluate the interest rates being quoted by banks and other financial institutions. Those interest rates, and the ones we have used for discounting cash flows in this book, are **nominal interest rates**, which indicate the rate at which your money will grow if invested for a certain period. Of course, if prices in the economy are also increasing due to inflation, the nominal interest rate does not represent the true increase in purchasing power that will result from investing.

nominal interest rates Interest rates quoted by banks and other financial institutions that indicate the rate at which money will grow if invested for a certain period of time.

For example, let's say that a cup of coffee costs \$1 this year. If you have \$100, you could buy 100 coffees. Instead, if you put that \$100 in a bank account earning 5.06% per year, you will have \$105.06 at the end of the year. But how much better off will you really be? That depends on how much prices have increased over the same year. If inflation was 3% over the year, then that cup of coffee would cost 3% more, or \$1.03 at the end of the year. Thus, you could take your \$105.06 and buy \$105.06/\$1.03 = 102 coffees, so you're really only 2% better off.

That 2% is your **real interest rate**—the rate of growth of your purchasing power, after adjusting for inflation. Just as in the example, we can calculate the rate of growth of purchasing power as follows:

real interest rate The rate of growth of purchasing power after adjusting for inflation.

$$1 + \text{Growth in Purchasing Power} = 1 + \text{real rate} = \frac{1 + \text{nominal rate}}{1 + \text{inflation rate}}$$

$$= \frac{\text{Growth of Money}}{\text{Growth of Prices}} \tag{5.4}$$

We can rearrange Equation 5.4 to find the following formula for the real interest rate, together with a convenient approximation for the real interest rate when inflation rates are low:

The Real Interest Rate

$$\text{real rate} = \frac{\text{nominal rate} - \text{inflation rate}}{1 + \text{inflation rate}} \approx \text{nominal rate} - \text{inflation rate} \tag{5.5}$$

That is, the real interest rate is approximately equal to the nominal interest rate less the rate of inflation.[2]

[2] The real interest rate should not be used as a discount rate for future cash flows. It can be used as a discount rate only if the cash flows are not the expected cash flows that will be paid but are the equivalent cash flows before being adjusted for growth due to inflation. (In that case, we say the cash flows are in real terms.) This approach is error prone, however, so throughout this book we will always forecast cash flows including any growth due to inflation, and discount using nominal interest rates.

EXAMPLE 5.4 Calculating the Real Interest Rate

PROBLEM

In the year 2000, short-term Canadian government bond rates were about 5.8% and the rate of inflation was about 3%. In 2003, interest rates were about 2.7% and inflation was about 3.1%. What was the real interest rate in 2000 and 2003?

SOLUTION

Plan

The bond rates tell us the nominal rates. Given the nominal rates and inflation for each year, we can use Equation 5.5 to calculate the real interest rate.

Execute

Equation 5.5 says

$$\text{real rate} = \frac{\text{nominal rate} - \text{inflation rate}}{1 + \text{inflation rate}}$$

Thus, the real interest rate in 2000 was (0.058 – 0.03)/(1.03) = 0.0272, or 2.72% (which is approximately equal to the difference between the nominal rate and inflation: 5.8% – 3% = 2.8%). In 2003, the real interest rate was (0.027 – 0.031)/(1.031) = –0.0039 or –0.39%.

Evaluate

Note that the real interest rate was negative in 2003, indicating that interest rates were insufficient to keep up with inflation. As a result, investors in Canadian government bonds were able to buy less at the end of the year than they could have purchased at the start of the year.

Figure 5.2 shows the history of nominal interest rates and inflation rates in Canada since 1962. Note that the nominal interest rate tends to move with inflation. Individuals' willingness to save will depend on the growth in purchasing power they can expect (given by the real interest rate). Thus, when the inflation rate is high, a higher nominal interest rate is needed to induce individuals to save.

Investment and Interest Rate Policy

Interest rates affect not only individuals' propensity to save, but also firms' incentive to raise capital and invest. Consider an opportunity that requires an upfront investment of \$10 million and generates a cash flow of \$3 million per year for four years. If the interest rate is 5%, this investment generates cash inflows with a present value (PV) of

$$PV_{\text{inflows}} = \frac{3}{1.05} + \frac{3}{1.05^2} + \frac{3}{1.05^3} + \frac{3}{1.05^4} = \$10.638 \text{ million}$$

Since the PV of the cash inflows exceeds the \$10 million upfront cost of the investment, the firm would have an incentive to raise capital and make the investment. However, if the interest rate is 9%, the PV of the cash inflows falls to

$$PV_{\text{inflows}} = \frac{3}{1.09} + \frac{3}{1.09^2} + \frac{3}{1.09^3} + \frac{3}{1.09^4} = \$9.719 \text{ million}$$

Since the PV of the cash inflows is less than the \$10 million upfront cost of the investment, the firm would have no incentive to raise capital and make the investment. The reason, of course, is that we are discounting the cash inflows (that occur in

FIGURE 5.2 Canadian Interest Rates and Inflation Rates, 1960–2016

Interest rates are average three-month treasury bill rates, and inflation rates are based on year-to-year changes in the Consumer Price Index (CPI) compiled by Statistics Canada.

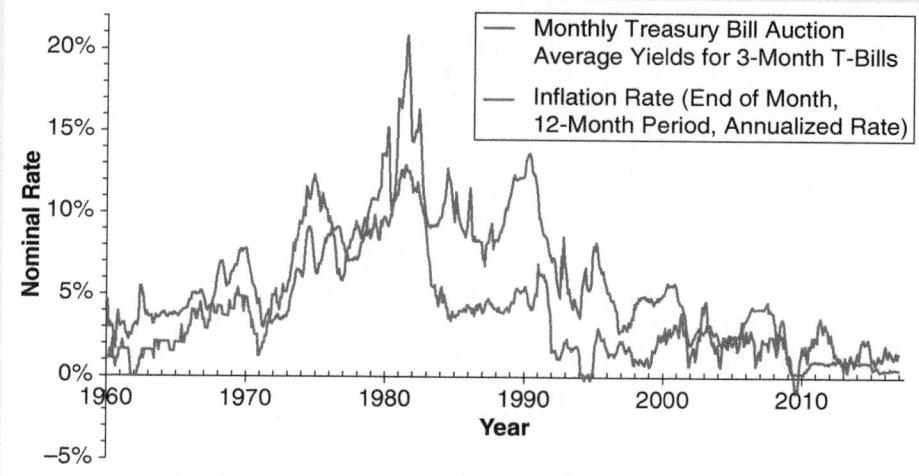

Source: Adapted from the Statistics Canada CANSIM database, http://cansim2.statcan.gc.ca, Table 176 - 0043 and Table 326 - 0020, extracted January 17, 2017. This does not constitute an endorsement by Statistics Canada of this product.

the future) at a higher rate, which reduces their present value. The cost of $10 million occurs today, however, so its present value is independent of the discount rate.

More generally, when the costs of an investment precede the benefits, an increase in the interest rate will decrease the net value created by an investment. All else being equal, higher interest rates will therefore tend to shrink the set of attractive investments available to firms. The Bank of Canada and central banks in other countries attempt to use this relationship between interest rates and investment incentives when trying to guide the economy. They will often lower interest rates in attempts to stimulate investment if the economy is slowing, and they will raise interest rates to reduce investment if the economy is "overheating" and inflation is on the rise.

The Yield Curve and Discount Rates

term structure The relationship between the investment term and the interest rate.

yield curve A plot of bond yields as a function of the bonds' maturity dates.

risk-free interest rate The interest rate at which money can be borrowed or lent without risk over a given period.

The interest rates that banks offer on investments or charge on loans depend on the horizon, or *term*, of the investment or loan. For example, a bank may offer you a higher rate of interest on a two-year locked-in guaranteed investment certificate (GIC) than it will offer for a GIC that is locked in for only one year. The relationship between the investment term and the interest rate is called the **term structure** of interest rates. We can plot this relationship on a graph called the **yield curve**. Figure 5.3 shows the term structure and corresponding yield curve of risk-free Canadian interest rates that were available to investors in January of 2004, 2008, 2009, 2010, and 2016. In each case, note that the interest rate depends on the horizon, and that the difference between short-term and long-term interest rates was especially pronounced in 2010. The rates plotted are interest rates for Canadian government debt securities, which are considered to be free of any risk of default (the Canadian government will not default on its loans). Thus, each of these rates is a **risk-free interest rate**, which is the interest rate at which money can be borrowed or lent without risk over a given period.

FIGURE 5.3 **Term Structure of Risk-Free Canadian Interest Rates, January 2004, 2008, 2009, 2010, and 2016**

Term	Date				
(Years)	Jan. 2004	Jan. 2008	Jan. 2009	Jan. 2010	Jan. 2016
0.25	2.6990	3.8327	0.8310	0.1597	0.49059
1	2.5875	3.6641	0.8908	0.7381	0.4957
2	3.0484	3.6220	1.1881	1.5069	0.44741
3	3.4756	3.6651	1.5043	2.0958	0.51657
4	3.8278	3.7159	1.7811	2.5152	0.64751
5	4.1399	3.7588	2.0239	2.8189	0.80171
6	4.4059	3.7942	2.2449	3.0579	0.96071
7	4.6099	3.8252	2.4539	3.2665	1.11676
8	4.7494	3.8545	2.6571	3.4624	1.26704
9	4.8379	3.8843	2.8571	3.6513	1.41048
10	4.8969	3.9157	3.0533	3.8315	1.54639
11	4.9469	3.9485	3.2424	3.9981	1.67386
12	5.0023	3.9819	3.4191	4.1453	1.79171
13	5.0696	4.0145	3.5779	4.2682	1.89864
14	5.1490	4.0444	3.7135	4.3637	1.9934
15	5.2363	4.0701	3.8218	4.4307	2.07497
16	5.3252	4.0902	3.9007	4.4701	2.14277
17	5.4089	4.1041	3.9500	4.4845	2.19667
18	5.4815	4.1113	3.9713	4.4776	2.23709
19	5.5385	4.1123	3.9681	4.4540	2.26495
20	5.5774	4.1078	3.9448	4.4181	2.28161
21	5.5973	4.0988	3.9065	4.3746	2.28874
22	5.5993	4.0866	3.8584	4.3272	2.28823
23	5.5855	4.0724	3.8050	4.2794	2.28205
24	5.5590	4.0577	3.7507	4.2337	2.2721
25	5.5232	4.0435	3.6986	4.1920	2.26016
26	5.4814	4.0308	3.6514	4.1556	2.24778
27	5.4368	4.0205	3.6107	4.1251	2.23625
28	5.3922	4.0132	3.5778	4.1010	2.22658
29	5.3497	4.0092	3.5531	4.0832	2.21945
30	5.3109	4.0089	3.5368	4.0714	2.21528

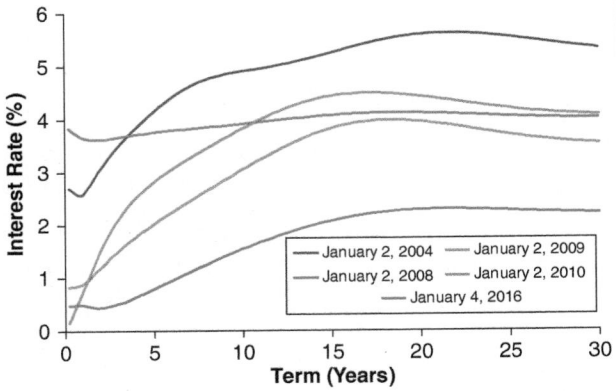

Source: Bank of Canada.

We can use the term structure to compute the present and future values of a risk-free cash flow over different investment horizons. For example, \$100 invested for 1 year at the 1-year interest rate in January 2004 would grow to a future value of

$$\$100 \times 1.025875 = \$102.59$$

at the end of 1 year, and \$100 invested for 10 years at the 10-year interest rate in January 2004 would grow to[3]

$$\$100 \times (1.048969)^{10} = \$161.30$$

We can apply the same logic when computing the present value of cash flows with different maturities. A risk-free cash flow received in 2 years should be discounted at the 2-year interest rate, and a cash flow received in 10 years should be discounted at the 10-year interest rate. In general, a risk-free cash flow of Cn received in n years has the present value

$$PV = \frac{C_n}{(1 + r_n)^n} \tag{5.6}$$

[3] We could also invest for 10 years by investing at the 1-year interest rate for 10 years in a row. However, because we do not know what future interest rates will be when we start our investment, our ultimate payoff would not be risk free.

where r_n is the risk-free interest rate only applicable for an n-year term. (Sometimes this is called an n-year spot rate of interest.) In other words, when computing a present value, we must match the term of the cash flow with the term of the discount rate.

Combining Equation 5.6 for cash flows in different years leads to the general formula for the present value of a cash flow stream:

Present Value of a Cash Flow Stream Using a Term Structure of Discount Rates

$$PV = \frac{C_1}{1 + r_1} + \frac{C_2}{(1 + r_2)^2} + \cdots + \frac{C_n}{(1 + r_n)^n} \tag{5.7}$$

Note the difference between Equation 5.7 and Equation 4.3. Here, we use a different discount rate for each cash flow, based on the rate from the yield curve with the same term. When interest rates are very similar across maturities, we say that the yield curve is flat, because it is close to a flat line. When the yield curve is relatively flat, as it was in January 2008, the distinction of using different rates for each cash flow is relatively minor and is often ignored by discounting using a single "average" interest rate, r. But when short-term and long-term interest rates vary widely, as they did in January 2010, Equation 5.7 should be used.

Warning: All of our shortcuts for computing present values (annuity and perpetuity formulas, and financial calculators) are based on discounting all of the cash flows *at the same rate*. They *cannot* be used in situations in which cash flows need to be discounted at different rates.

EXAMPLE 5.5 Using the Term Structure to Compute Present Values

PROBLEM

Compute the present value of a risk-free, 5-year annuity of $1000 per year, given the yield curve data for January 2010 in Figure 5.3.

SOLUTION

Plan

The timeline of the cash flows of the annuity is

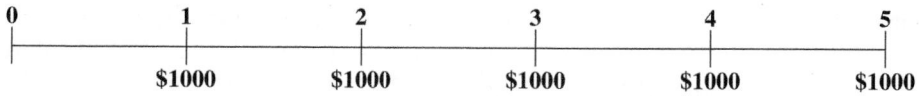

We can use the table next to the yield curve to identify the interest rate corresponding to each length of time: 1, 2, 3, 4, and 5 years. With the cash flows and those interest rates, we can compute the PV.

Execute

From Figure 5.3, we see that the interest rates are 0.7381%, 1.5069%, 2.0958%, 2.5152%, and 2.8189% for terms of 1, 2, 3, 4, and 5 years, respectively.

To compute the present value, we discount each cash flow by the corresponding interest rate:

$$PV = \frac{1000}{1.007381} + \frac{1000}{1.015069^2} + \frac{1000}{1.020958^3} + \frac{1000}{1.025152^4} + \frac{1000}{1.028189^5} = \$4678.52$$

Evaluate

The yield curve tells us the market interest rate per year for each different maturity. To correctly calculate the PV of cash flows from five different maturities, we need to use the five different interest rates corresponding to those maturities. Note that we cannot use the annuity formula here because the discount rates differ for each cash flow.

COMMON MISTAKE

Using the Annuity Formula When Discount Rates Vary

When computing the present value of an annuity, a common mistake is to use the annuity formula with a single interest rate even though interest rates vary with the investment horizon. For example, we *cannot* compute the present value of the five-year annuity in Example 5.5 using the five-year interest rate from January 2005:

$$PV \neq \$1000 \times \frac{1}{0.028189}\left(1 - \frac{1}{1.028189^5}\right) = \$4603.48$$

If we want to find the single interest rate that we could use to value the annuity, we must first compute the present value of the annuity using Equation 5.7 and then use the methodology from Chapter 4 to solve for its rate of return. For the annuity in Example 5.5, we use a financial calculator or spreadsheet to find its rate of return of 2.2569%. The rate of return of the annuity is always between the highest and lowest discount rates used to calculate its present value, as is the case in this example.

	N	I/Y	PV	PMT	FV
Given:	5		−4678.52	1000	0
Solve for:		2.2569			

Excel Formula: = *RATE(NPER,PMT,PV,FV)*
= *RATE* (5,1000,−4678.52,0)

The Yield Curve and the Economy

As Figure 5.3 illustrates, the yield curve changes over time. Sometimes, short-term rates are close to long-term rates (as in 2008), and at other times they may be very different (as in 2010). What accounts for the changing shape of the yield curve?

overnight rate The rate at which banks can borrow cash reserves on an overnight basis from the Bank of Canada.

Interest Rate Determination. The Bank of Canada determines very short-term interest rates through its influence on the **overnight rate**, which is the rate at which banks can borrow cash reserves on an overnight basis. All other interest rates on the yield curve are set in the market and are adjusted until the supply of lending matches the demand for borrowing at each loan term. As we shall see in a moment, expectations of future interest rate changes have a major effect on investors' willingness to lend or borrow for longer terms and, therefore, on the shape of the yield curve.

Suppose short-term interest rates are equal to long-term interest rates. If interest rates are expected to rise in the future, investors would not want to make long-term investments. Instead, they could do better by investing on a short-term basis and then reinvesting after interest rates rose. Thus, if interest rates are expected to rise, long-term interest rates will tend to be higher than short-term rates to attract investors.

Similarly, if interest rates are expected to fall in the future, then borrowers would not wish to borrow at long-term rates that are equal to short-term rates. They would do better by borrowing on a short-term basis and then taking out a new loan after rates fall. So, if interest rates are expected to fall, long-term rates will tend to be lower than short-term rates to attract borrowers.

Yield Curve Shape. These arguments indicate that the shape of the yield curve will be strongly influenced by interest rate expectations. A sharply increasing (*steep*) yield curve, with long-term rates much higher than short-term rates, generally indicates that interest rates are expected to rise in the future. A decreasing (*inverted*) yield curve, with long-term rates lower than short-term rates, generally signals an expected decline in future interest rates. Because interest rates tend to drop in response to a slowdown in the economy, an inverted yield curve is often interpreted as a negative forecast for economic growth. Conversely, the yield curve tends to be steep as the economy comes out of a recession and interest rates are expected to rise.

The normal shape of the yield curve is moderately upward sloping. This would be the case if investors almost always believed that interest rates were going to rise in the future. But that is unlikely, so there have to be other forces at work to cause long-term interest rates normally to be higher than short-term rates. The most commonly cited reason is that, for the most part, investors have a preference for liquidity, and they would probably want to be able to have their investment mature (or to be able to sell it) in a shorter time frame than that covered by the term of a longer-term bond. Thus, long-term investments, such as lending money to the government by buying a long-term Government of Canada bond, are riskier for most investors than short-term investments (such as buying a Government of Canada bond with one year left until maturity). Suppose you would like to liquidate your investment in one year. If you invest in a 30-year bond today and lock in the interest rate, you know exactly what you will get if you hold the bond for the entire 30 years. However, in one year, given that interest rates may have changed, the price (which equals the present value of the remaining bond payments discounted using the new, currently unknown interest rate) may be much different than you anticipated. In fact, the present value of the payments you receive from a bond is very sensitive to even small changes in market interest rates, and this sensitivity is higher for longer-term bonds. If, instead, you had invested in a one-year bond, then at the time you liquidate your investment, you know exactly what you will have as the bond matures at that time and pays you its face value with no risk. This increased sensitivity of bond prices for longer-maturity bonds is due to the effect of compounding a change in interest rates over a longer period. To see this effect, consider the following example.

EXAMPLE 5.6 Long-Term versus Short-Term Lending

PROBLEM

Suppose it is January 2019, and you are considering lending $10,000 to the Government of Canada, as a form of investing, and you need to choose between buying a bond that gives you a single payment in 5 years or in 30 years. Assume the term structure is flat and both terms have an interest rate of 4%. You intend to liquidate your investment after one year and are concerned about the risk associated with the price you will receive when you sell the claim to your loan to the Government of Canada. Consider what will happen if market interest rates on these loans stay the same or either rise or fall by 1% by the time you sell your investment.

SOLUTION

■ Plan

Each of these loans has only one repayment cash flow at the end of the loan. They differ only by the time to repayment. You need to figure out what these locked-in repayments will be and then you can consider what happens in January 2020 to the present value of these repayments, given the different possible interest rates. That will let you see how risky your own cash flow will be in January 2020 and also how risky your return will be by holding the investment from January 2019 to January 2020. ▶

Execute

The 5-year loan locks in a payment of

$$\$10{,}000 \times (1 + .04)^5 = \$12{,}166.53 \text{ to be paid in January, 2024.}$$

The 30-year loan locks in a payment of

$$\$10{,}000 \times (1 + .04)^{30} = \$32{,}433.98 \text{ to be paid in January, 2049.}$$

Now calculate the present value of these payments as of January 2020, given the possible changes in interest rates. For the loan that matures in 2024, its present value will be

$$PV_{2020} = \frac{\$12{,}166.53}{(1 + r)^4}$$

and for the loan that matures in 2049, its present value will be

$$PV_{2020} = \frac{\$32{,}433.98}{(1 + r)^{29}}$$

The following table shows the present values calculated for different interest rates.

Prices in 2020 given new rates	2024 Maturity Loan		2049 Maturity Loan	
	Rate	PV in 2020	Rate	PV in 2020
Rates rise 1%	5%	$10,009.43	5%	$7879.71
Rates constant	4%	$10,400.00	4%	$10,400.00
Rates drop 1%	3%	$10,809.80	3%	$13,763.24

To determine your rate of return by holding your investment from 2019 to 2020 (one year), you can do the following calculation:

$$\frac{\text{2020 Price} - \$10{,}000}{\$10{,}000} = \text{return}$$

The following table shows the returns calculated based on the 2020 prices shown above

Returns from 2019 to 2020 given new rates	2024 Maturity Loan		2049 Maturity Loan	
	New Rate	Return	New Rate	Return
Rates rise 1%	5%	0.0943%	5%	–21.2029%
Rates constant	4%	4.0000%	4%	4.0000%
Rates drop 1%	3%	8.0980%	3%	37.6324%

Evaluate

Depending on the new interest rates after 1 year, the value of the 5-year loan ranged from $10,009.43 to $10,809.80, giving a 1-year realized return of from 0.0943% to 8.0980%, but the value of the 30-year loan ranged from only $7879.71 to $13,763.24, giving a 1-year realized return of from –21.2029% to 37.6324%. The small change in market interest rates, compounded over a longer period, resulted in a much larger change in the present value of the loan repayment and the possible return realized by the investor. You can see why investors who have a liquidity preference (a preference for shorter-term investments) view longer-term loans as being riskier than short-term loans.

In addition to specifying the discount rates for risk-free cash flows that occur at different horizons, the yield curve provides information about future interest rate expectations and is also a potential leading indicator of future economic growth. Due to these qualities, the yield curve provides extremely important information for a business manager.

CONCEPT CHECK

5. What is the difference between a nominal and a real interest rate?
6. How are interest rates and the level of investment made by businesses related?

5.4 The Opportunity Cost of Capital

As we have seen in this chapter, the interest rates we observe in the market will vary based on quoting conventions, the term of the investment, and risk. In this chapter, we have developed the tools to account for these differences and gained some insights into how interest rates are determined. This knowledge will provide the foundation for our study of bonds in the next chapter.

In Chapter 3, we argued that the Valuation Principle tells us to use the "market interest rate" to compute present values and evaluate an investment opportunity. But with so many interest rates to choose from, the term "market interest rate" is inherently ambiguous. Therefore, going forward in the textbook, we will base the discount rate that we use to evaluate cash flows on the investor's **opportunity cost of capital** or **cost of capital**, which is *the best available expected return offered in the market on an investment of comparable risk and term to the cash flow being discounted.*

opportunity cost of capital or **cost of capital** The best available expected return offered in the market on an investment of comparable risk and term to the cash flow being discounted; the return the investor forgoes on an alternative investment of equivalent risk and term when the investor takes on a new investment.

In order to understand the definition of opportunity cost of capital, it helps to think of yourself as a financial manager competing with financial managers at other firms to attract investors' funds (capital). To attract investors to invest in your firm or creditors to lend to your firm, you have to be able to offer them an expected return at least as good as what they could get elsewhere in the market for the same risk and length of investment. Now it is easier to see where the term (opportunity) cost of capital comes from—investors in your firm are giving up the opportunity to invest their funds elsewhere. This is an opportunity cost to them, and to overcome it you must offer them a return equal to or better than their opportunity cost of capital. Even if you already have the funds internally in the firm to invest, the logic still applies. You could either return the funds to your shareholders to invest elsewhere or reinvest the funds in a new project; however, you should reinvest them only if doing so provides a better return than the shareholders' other opportunities.

INTEREST RATES, DISCOUNT RATES, AND THE COST OF CAPITAL

By now, you may have noticed that we are using three terms to refer to rates of return. While many people use these three terms interchangeably, they are distinct. Throughout this book, we will use "interest rate" to mean a quoted rate in the market. A "discount rate" is the appropriate rate for discounting a given cash flow, *matched to the frequency of the cash flow.* Finally, we use "cost of capital" to indicate the rate of return on an investment opportunity of similar risk.

The opportunity cost of capital is the return the investor forgoes when taking on a new investment. For a risk-free project, the opportunity cost of capital will typically correspond to the interest rate on Government of Canada securities with a similar term. But the opportunity cost of capital is a much more general concept that can be applied to risky investments as well.

EXAMPLE 5.7 The Opportunity Cost of Capital

PROBLEM

Suppose a friend offers to borrow $100 from you today and in return pay you $110 one year from today. Looking in the market for other options for investing the $100, you find your best alternative option, which you view as equally risky as lending it to your friend. That option has an expected return of 8%. What should you do?

SOLUTION

Plan

Your decision depends on what the opportunity cost is of lending your money to your friend. If you lend her the $100, then you cannot invest it in the alternative with an 8% expected return. Thus, by making the loan, you are giving up the opportunity to invest for an 8% expected return. You can make your decision by using your 8% opportunity cost of capital to value the $110 in one year.

Execute

The value of the $110 in one year is its present value, discounted at 8%:

$$PV = \frac{\$110}{(1.08)^1} = \$101.85$$

The $100 loan is worth $101.85 to you today, so you make the loan.

Evaluate

The Valuation Principle tells us that we can determine the value of an investment by using market prices to value the benefits net of the costs. As this example shows, market prices determine what our best alternative opportunities are so that we can decide whether an investment is worth the cost.

Chapter 3 introduced the Valuation Principle as a unifying theme in finance. In this and the preceding chapter, we have developed the fundamental tools a financial manager needs to value cash flows at different points in time. In this last section, we have reiterated the importance of using market information to determine the opportunity cost of capital, which is your discount rate in valuation calculations. In the next chapter, we will study bonds and how they are priced, which provides us with an immediate application of the knowledge we have built so far.

CONCEPT CHECK

7. What is the opportunity cost of capital?
8. Can you ignore the cost of capital if you already have the funds inside the firm?

MyLab Finance

Here is what you should know after reading this chapter. MyLab™ Finance will help you identify what you know, and where to go when you need to practice.

KEY POINTS AND EQUATIONS	TERMS	ONLINE PRACTICE OPPORTUNITIES
5.1 Interest Rate Quotes and Adjustments ■ Just like any other price, interest rates are set by market forces, in particular the supply and demand of funds. ■ The EAR indicates the actual amount of interest earned in one year. The EAR can be used as a discount rate for annual cash flows. ■ Given an EAR, r, the equivalent effective rate for an n-year time interval, where n may be more than one year or less than or equal to one year (a fraction), is Equivalent n-period Effective Rate $= (1 + r)^n - 1$ (5.1) ■ An APR is a common way of quoting interest rates. It indicates the amount of simple interest per year and does not consider the effects of compounding. ■ An APR quote gives an Implied Effective Interest Rate per Compounding Period $= APR/m$ (5.2) (m = number of compounding periods per year, also known as the compounding frequency). ■ We need to know the compounding frequency of an APR to determine the EAR: $1 + EAR = \left(1 + \frac{APR}{m}\right)^m$ (5.3) ■ For a given APR, the EAR increases with the compounding frequency.	annual percentage rate (APR), p. 137 effective annual rate (EAR), p. 135 simple interest, p. 137	MyLab Study Plan 5.1
5.2 Application: Discount Rates and Loans ■ Loan rates are, typically, stated as APRs. The outstanding balance of a loan is equal to the present value of the loan cash flows, when evaluated using the actual interest rate per payment interval based on the loan rate. ■ In each loan payment on an amortizing loan, you pay interest on the loan plus some part of the loan balance.	amortizing loan, p. 140 mortgage, p. 143	MyLab Study Plan 5.2

KEY POINTS AND EQUATIONS	TERMS	ONLINE PRACTICE OPPORTUNITIES
5.3 The Determinants of Interest Rates ■ Quoted interest rates are nominal interest rates, which indicate the rate of growth of the money invested. The real interest rate indicates the rate of growth of one's purchasing power after adjusting for inflation. ■ Given a nominal interest rate and an inflation rate, the real interest rate is $\text{Real Rate} = \frac{\text{Nominal Rate} - \text{Inflation Rate}}{1 + \text{Inflation Rate}}$ $\approx \text{Nominal Rate} - \text{Inflation Rate}$ (5.5) ■ Nominal interest rates tend to be high when inflation is high and low when inflation is low. ■ Higher interest rates tend to reduce the attractiveness of typical investment projects. The Bank of Canada raises interest rates to moderate investment and combat inflation, and lowers interest rates to stimulate investment and economic growth. ■ Interest rates differ with the investment horizon according to the term structure of interest rates. The graph plotting interest rates as a function of the horizon is called the yield curve. ■ Cash flows should be discounted using the discount rate that is appropriate for their horizon. Thus, the PV of a cash flow stream is $PV = \frac{C_1}{1 + r_1} + \frac{C_2}{(1 + r_2)^2} + \ldots + \frac{C_n}{(1 + r_n)^n}$ (5.7) ■ Annuity and perpetuity formulas cannot be applied when discount rates vary with the horizon. ■ The shape of the yield curve tends to vary with investors' expectations of future economic growth and interest rates. It tends to be inverted prior to recessions and to be steep coming out of a recession. Because investors have a liquidity preference and, thus, view long-term loans as riskier, long-term rates are generally higher than short-term rates.	overnight rate, p. 150 nominal interest rates, p. 145 real interest rate, p. 145 risk-free interest rate, p. 147 term structure, p. 147 yield curve, p. 147	MyLab Study Plan 5.3 Interactive Yield Curve
5.4 The Opportunity Cost of Capital ■ An investor's opportunity cost of capital (or simply, the cost of capital) is the best available expected return offered in the market on an investment of comparable risk and term to the cash flow being discounted.	opportunity cost of capital or cost of capital, p. 153	MyLab Study Plan 5.4

REVIEW QUESTIONS

1. Explain how an interest rate is just a price.
2. Why is the EAR for 6% APR, with semi-annual compounding, higher than 6%?
3. Why is it so important to match the frequency of the interest rate to the frequency of the cash flows?
4. Why aren't the payments for a 15-year mortgage twice the payments for a 30-year mortgage at the same rate?
5. What mistake do you make when you discount real cash flows with nominal discount rates?
6. How do changes in inflation expectations affect interest rates?
7. Can the nominal interest rate available to an investor be negative? (*Hint:* Consider the interest rate earned from saving cash "under the mattress.") Can the real interest rate be negative?
8. In the early 1980s, inflation was in the double digits and the yield curve sloped sharply downward. What did the yield curve say about investors' expectations about future inflation rates?
9. What do we mean when we refer to the "opportunity cost" of capital?

PROBLEMS

All problems in this chapter are available in MyLab Finance. An asterisk (*) indicates problems with a higher level of difficulty.

Interest Rate Quotes and Adjustments

1. Your bank is offering you an account that will pay 20% interest in total for a two-year deposit. Determine the equivalent discount rate for a period length of
   a. six months.
   b. one year.
   c. one month.

2. Do the relevant calculations so you can indicate which you prefer: a bank account that pays 5% per year (EAR) for 3 years or
   a. an account that pays 2.5% every 6 months for 3 years?
   b. an account that pays 7.5% every 18 months for 3 years?
   c. an account that pays 0.5% per month for 3 years?

3. You have been offered a job with an unusual bonus structure. As long as you stay with the firm, you will get an extra $70,000 every 7 years, starting 7 years from now. What is the present value of this incentive if you plan to work for the company for a total of 42 years and the interest rate is 6% (EAR)?

4. You have found three investment choices for a one-year deposit: 10% APR compounded monthly, 10% APR compounded annually, and 9% APR compounded daily. Compute the EAR for each investment choice. (Assume that there are 365 days in the year.)

5. Your bank account pays interest with an EAR of 5%. What is the APR quote for this account based on semi-annual compounding? What is the APR with monthly compounding?

6. Suppose the interest rate is 8% APR with monthly compounding. What is the present value of an annuity that pays $100 every six months for five years?

7. You have been accepted into university. The university guarantees that your tuition will not increase for the four years you attend. The first $10,000 tuition payment is due in six months. After that, the same payment is due every six months until you have made a total of eight payments. The university offers a bank account that allows you to withdraw money every six months and has a fixed APR of 4% (semi-annual) guaranteed to remain the same over the next four years. How much money must you deposit today if you intend to make no further deposits and would like to make all the tuition payments from this account, leaving the account empty when the last payment is made?

8. You are considering buying an Audi for $50,000 and your financing is quoted at 6% APR with monthly compounding.
   a. What rate do you need in order to use the annuity formulas (Equations 4.5 or 4.7) to find the monthly payments?
   b. What is the effective annual rate of interest for this financing?

9. Your friends are going to Puerto Vallarta, Mexico, over Reading Week and you want to go too. Unfortunately, you haven't been good at saving, so you need to borrow $2000 to pay for the trip. You can finance the trip on your credit card at a rate of 21% APR with daily compounding. Alternatively, your parents (who are both bankers) are willing to lend you the money at a rate of 10% per six months compounded every six months.
   a. What is the EAR of borrowing with your credit card? (Assume 365 days in a year.)
   b. What is the EAR of borrowing from your parents?
   c. If you plan to repay the $2000 in equal monthly instalments, what would be the rates to use in the annuity formulas (Equations 4.5 or 4.7) to calculate your monthly payments?
      i. Assume you borrowed with the credit card.
      ii. Assume you borrowed from your parents.

10. Suppose for its deposit accounts Simplii Financial is offering to pay interest at a rate of 0.25% per month with monthly compounding, but Tangerine is offering to pay interest at a rate of 0.75% per quarter with quarterly compounding. (One quarter is equal to three months.) Which financial institution is offering the higher rate?

Application: Discount Rates and Loans

11. You make monthly payments on your car loan. It has a quoted APR of 5% (monthly compounding). What percentage of the outstanding principal do you pay in interest each month?

PROJECT 12. Suppose Capital One is advertising a 60-month, 5.99% APR motorcycle loan. If you need to borrow $8000 to purchase your dream Harley-Davidson, what will your monthly payment be?

13. Suppose the Bank of Montreal is offering a 30-year mortgage with an EAR of 6.80%. If you plan to borrow $150,000, what will your monthly payment be?

14. You have decided to refinance your mortgage. You plan to borrow whatever is outstanding on your current mortgage. The current monthly payment is $2356, and you have made every payment on time. The original term of the mortgage was 30 years, and the mortgage is exactly 4 years and 8 months old. You have just made your monthly payment. The mortgage interest rate is 6.2% (APR with semi-annual compounding). How much do you owe on the mortgage today?

15. You have just sold your house for $1,000,000 in cash. Your mortgage was originally a 30-year mortgage with monthly payments and an initial balance of $800,000. The mortgage is currently exactly 18.5 years old, and you have just made a payment. If the interest rate on the mortgage is 7.75% (APR with semi-annual compounding), how much cash will you have from the sale once you pay off the mortgage?

16. You have just purchased a home and taken out a $500,000 mortgage. The mortgage has a 30-year term with monthly payments and an APR (with semi-annual compounding) of 6.5%.

a. How much will you pay in interest, and how much will you pay in principal, during the first year?

b. How much will you pay in interest, and how much will you pay in principal, during the 20th year (i.e., between 19 and 20 years from now)?

17. You have just purchased your Audi and taken out a $50,000 loan. The loan has a five-year term with monthly payments and an APR of 6% (with monthly compounding).

a. How much will you pay in interest and how much will you pay in principal during the first month, second month, and first year? (*Hint:* Compute the loan balance after one month, two months, and one year.)

b. How much will you pay in interest and how much will you pay in principal during the fourth year (i.e., between three and four years from now)?

***18.** Consider the loan from the previous question: a 60-month, $50,000 car loan with a 6% APR, compounded monthly. Assume that right after you make your 50th payment, the balance on the loan is $9405.81. How much of your next payment goes toward principal and how much goes toward interest? Compare this with your answers in the last question—what is happening?

***19.** You have some extra cash this month and are considering putting it toward your car loan. Your interest rate is 7%, your loan payments are $600 per month, and you have 36 months left on your loan. If you pay an additional $1000 with your next regular $600 payment (due in one month), how much will it reduce the amount of time left to pay off your loan?

20. Assume you graduate from university with a $30,000 student loan. If your interest rate is fixed at 4.66% APR with monthly compounding and you will repay the loan over a 10-year period, what will be your monthly payment?

***21.** You have an outstanding student loan with required payments of $500 per month for the next four years. The interest rate on the loan is 9% APR (monthly). You are considering making an extra payment of $100 today (i.e., you will pay an extra $100 that you are not required to pay). If you are required to continue to make payments of $500 per month until the loan is paid off, what is the amount of your final payment? What effective rate of return (expressed as an APR with monthly compounding) have you earned on the $100?

PROJECT

***22.** Consider again the situation in Problem 21. Now that you realize your best investment is to prepay your student loan, you decide to prepay as much as you can each month. Looking at your budget, you can afford to pay an extra $250 per month in addition to your required monthly payments of $500, or $750 in total each month. How long will it take you to pay off the loan?

***23.** If you decide to take the mortgage described in Problem 13, the Bank of Montreal will offer you the following deal: instead of making the monthly payment you computed in that problem every month, you can make half the payment every two weeks (so that you will make 52/2 = 26 payments per year). How long will it take to pay off the mortgage if the EAR remains the same at 6.80%?

***24.** Your friend tells you he has a very simple trick for taking one-third off the time it takes to repay your mortgage: use your year-end bonus to make an extra payment on January 1 of each year (that is, pay your monthly payment due on that day twice). If you take out your mortgage on July 1, so that your first monthly payment is due August 1, and you make an extra payment every January 1, how long will it take to pay off the mortgage? Assume that the mortgage has an original term of 30 years and an APR (with semi-annual compounding) of 12%.

***25.** The mortgage on your house in Winnipeg is 5 years old. It required monthly payments of $1402, had an original term of 30 years, and had an interest rate of 9% (APR with semi-annual compounding). In the intervening 5 years, interest rates have fallen, housing prices in the United States have fallen, and you have decided to retire to Florida. You have decided to sell your house in Winnipeg and use your equity for the down payment on a condo in Florida. You will roll over the outstanding balance of your old mortgage into a new mortgage in Florida. The new mortgage has a 30-year term, requires monthly payments, and has an interest rate of 6.625% (APR with monthly compounding, which is typical for U.S. mortgages).

a. What monthly repayments will be required with the new loan?
b. If you still want to pay off the mortgage in 25 years, what monthly payment should you make on your new mortgage?
c. Suppose you are willing to continue making monthly payments of $1402. How long will it take you to pay off the new mortgage?
d. Suppose you are willing to continue making monthly payments of $1402 and want to pay off the new mortgage in 25 years. How much additional cash can you borrow today as part of the new financing?

PROJECT **26.** You have credit card debt of $25,000 that has an APR (monthly compounding) of 15%. Each month you pay a minimum monthly payment only. You are required to pay only the outstanding interest. You have received an offer in the mail for an otherwise identical credit card with an APR of 12%. After considering all your alternatives, you decide to switch cards, roll over the outstanding balance on the old card into the new card, and borrow additional money as well. How much can you borrow today on the new card without changing the minimum monthly payment you will be required to pay?

27. Your firm has taken out a $500,000 loan with 9% APR (compounded monthly) for some commercial property. As is common in commercial real estate, the loan *is a* 5-year loan based on a 15-year amortization. This means that your loan payments *will be* calculated as if you will take 15 years to pay off the loan, but you actually must do so in 5 years. To do this, you will make 59 equal payments based on the 15-year amortization schedule and then make a final 60th payment to pay the remaining balance.

a. What will your monthly payments be?
b. What will your final payment be?

The Determinants of Interest Rates

28. In 1974, interest rates were 7.782% and the rate of inflation was 12.299% in Canada. What was the real interest rate in 1974? How would the purchasing power of your savings have changed over the year?

PROJECT **29.** If the rate of inflation is 5%, what nominal interest rate is necessary for you to earn a 3% real interest rate on your investment?

30. You have $100,000 and the basket of goods and services that Statistics Canada uses to track inflation (the basket) currently costs $100. You have the opportunity to invest your $100,000 and earn a return on your funds of 19%, however you expect the basket to cost $116 in one year.

a. How many baskets can you buy today if you don't do the investing?
b. If you invest, how much money will you have in one year?
c. What is the expected inflation rate over the coming year?
d. How many baskets do you expect to buy in one year if you invest? By how much do you expect your purchasing power to change if you invest? What do you expect to earn as the real rate of return by investing?
e. Relate the nominal interest rate, real interest rate, and inflation rate to each other. Do these results match what you found in the previous parts of this question?

31. Suppose the term structure of risk-free interest rates is as shown below:

Term	1 year	2 years	3 years	5 years	7 years	10 years	20 years
Rate (EAR, %)	1.99	2.41	2.74	3.32	3.76	4.13	4.93

What is the present value of an investment that pays $100 at the end of each of years 1, 2, and 3? If you wanted to value this investment correctly using the annuity formula, which discount rate should you use?

32. What is the shape of the yield curve given in the term structure from Question 25? What expectations are investors likely to have about future interest rates?

The Opportunity Cost of Capital

33. You are thinking about investing $5000 in your friend's landscaping business. Even though you know the investment is risky and you can't be sure of the outcome, you expect your investment to be worth $5750 next year. You notice that the rate for one-year treasury bills is 1%. However, you feel that other investments of equal risk to your friend's landscape business offer a 10% expected return for the year. What should you do?

34. You have invested in a business that proudly reports that it is profitable. Your investment of $5000 has produced a profit of $300. The managers think that if you leave your $5000 invested with them, they should be able to generate $300 per year in profits for you in perpetuity. Evaluating other investment opportunities, you note that other long-term investments of similar risk offer an expected return of 8%. Should you remain invested in this firm?

CHAPTER

6 Bonds

LEARNING OBJECTIVES

- Understand bond terminology
- Compute the price and yield to maturity of a zero-coupon bond
- Compute the price and yield to maturity of a coupon bond
- Analyze why bond prices change over time
- Know how credit risk affects the expected return from holding a corporate bond

NOTATION

CPN	coupon payment
FV	face value of a bond
n	number of periods
P	initial price of a bond
PV	present value
r_n	interest rate or discount rate for a cash flow that arrives in period n
YTM_n	yield to maturity on a bond with n periods to maturity

In this chapter, we introduce bonds and apply our tools for valuing cash flows to them. Bonds are simply loans. When an investor buys a bond from an issuer, the investor is lending money to the bond issuer. Who are the issuers of bonds? Federal, provincial, and local governments issue bonds to finance long-term projects, and many companies issue bonds as part of their debt financing. The bond markets are very large and very liquid. Canada's Department of Finance reported that by the end of January 2018, the total interest-paying debt of the Canadian Federal Government surpassed $1 trillion for the first time in history. Bonds comprise a significant portion of outstanding debt. The Bank of Canada reported that, as of the end of 2017, there were over $3.3 trillion of outstanding bonds issued by Canadian entities. About $1.4 trillion of these bonds were issued by various governments (federal, provincial, and municipal), and over $1.3 trillion of these bonds were issued by corporations.

Understanding bonds and their pricing is useful for several reasons. First, we can use the prices of risk-free government bonds to determine the risk-free interest rates that produce the yield curve discussed in Chapter 5. As we saw there, the yield curve provides important information for valuing risk-free cash flows and assessing expectations of inflation and economic growth. Second, firms often issue bonds to fund their own investments. The return that investors receive on those bonds is the cost of debt that borrowers pay and is thus one factor determining a firm's cost of capital. Finally, bonds provide an opportunity to begin our study of how securities are priced in a competitive market because, like shares, they can be traded in secondary markets. Further, the ideas we develop in this chapter will be helpful when we turn to the topic of valuing stocks in Chapter 7.

Pricing bonds gives us an opportunity to apply what we have learned in the last three chapters about valuing cash flows using competitive market prices. As we explained in Chapter 3, the Valuation Principle implies that the price of a security in a competitive market should be the present value of the cash flows an investor will receive from owning it. Thus, we begin the chapter by evaluating the promised cash flows for different types of bonds. If a bond is risk free, so that the promised cash flows will be paid with certainty, we can use the Law of One Price to directly relate the return of a bond and its price. We then discuss how and why bond prices change over time. Once we have a firm understanding of the pricing of bonds in the absence of risk, we add the risk of default, where cash flows are not known with certainty. The risk of default and its implications are important considerations for a financial manager who is considering issuing corporate bonds. (In Chapter 15, we will discuss the details of issuing debt financing and cover some additional corporate bond features.)

6.1 Bond Terminology

bond indenture A statement of the terms of a bond, as well as the amounts and dates of all payments to be made.

maturity date The final repayment date of a bond.

term The time remaining until the final repayment date of a bond.

face value or **par value** The notional amount of a bond paid to the holder at maturity. Also called the principal amount.

coupons The promised interest payments of a bond, paid periodically until the maturity date of the bond.

coupon rate The rate that determines the amount of each coupon payment of a bond. The coupon rate indicates the percentage of the face value paid out as coupons each year.

Recall from Chapter 3 that a bond is a security sold by governments and corporations to raise money from investors today in exchange for a promised future payment. The terms of the bond are described as part of the **bond indenture**, which indicates the amounts and dates of all payments to be made. Payments on the bond are made until a final repayment date, called the **maturity date** of the bond. The time remaining until the repayment date is known as the **term** of the bond.

Bonds typically make two types of payments to their holders. The principal or **face value** (also known as **par value**) of a bond is the notional amount we use to compute the interest payments. Typically, the face value is repaid at maturity. It is generally denominated in standard increments such as $1000. A bond with a $1000 face value, for example, is often referred to as a "$1000 bond."

In addition to the face value, most bonds also promise additional payments called **coupons.** The bond indenture typically specifies that the coupons will be paid periodically (e.g., semi-annually) until the maturity date of the bond. Historically, on a payment date, the holder of the bond would clip off the next coupon and present it for payment. It follows that the interest payments on the bond are called coupon payments. Today, the majority of bonds are registered electronically but the term remains.

The amount of each coupon payment is determined by the **coupon rate** of the bond. This coupon rate is set by the issuer and stated on the bond indenture. By convention, the coupon rate indicates the percentage of face value paid out as coupons each year; thus, each coupon payment, CPN, can be calculated as follows:

Coupon Payment

$$CPN = \frac{\text{Coupon Rate} \times \text{Face Value}}{\text{Number of Coupon Payments per Year}} \tag{6.1}$$

For example, a "$1000 bond with a 10% coupon rate and semi-annual payments" will pay coupon payments of $\$1000 \times 10\%/2 = \$50$ every six months.

Table 6.1 summarizes the bond terminology we have presented thus far.

TABLE 6.1 Review of Bond Terminology

Maturity Date	Final repayment date of the bond. Payments continue until this date.
Term	The time remaining until the final repayment date.
Coupons	The promised interest payments of a bond. Usually they are paid semi-annually, but the frequency is specified in the bond indenture. The amount paid is equal to $\frac{\text{Coupon Rate} \times \text{Face Value}}{\text{Number of Coupon Payments per Year}}$
Principal, Par Value, or Face Value	The notional amount used to compute the interest payment. It is usually repaid on the maturity date.

CONCEPT CHECK

1. What types of cash flows does a bond buyer receive?
2. How are the periodic coupon payments on a bond determined?

6.2 Zero-Coupon Bonds

zero-coupon bond A bond with its only payment occurring at maturity.

treasury bills Zero-coupon bonds, with a maturity of up to one year, issued by a national government such as the Government of Canada or the U.S. government.

Not all bonds have coupon payments. A bond without coupons is called a **zero-coupon bond**. As these are the simplest type of bond, we will analyze them first. The only cash payment an investor in a zero-coupon bond receives is the face value of the bond on the maturity date. **Treasury bills**, which are bonds issued by a national government (such as the Government of Canada or the U.S. government) are zero-coupon bonds with a maturity of up to one year.

Zero-Coupon Bond Cash Flows

There are only two cash flows if we purchase and hold a zero-coupon bond. First, we pay the bond's current market price at the time we make the purchase. Then, at the maturity date, we receive the bond's face value. For example, suppose that a one-year, risk-free, zero-coupon bond with a $100,000 face value has an initial price of $96,618.36. If you purchased this bond and held it to maturity, you would have the following cash flows:

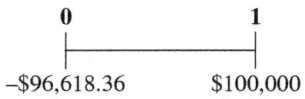

Note that although the bond pays no "interest" directly, as an investor you are compensated for the time value of your money by purchasing the bond at a discount to its face value. Recall from Chapter 3 that the present value of a future cash flow is less than the cash flow itself. As a result, prior to its maturity date, the price of a zero-coupon bond is always less than its face value. That is, zero-coupon bonds always trade at a **discount** (a price lower than the face value), so they are also called **pure discount bonds**.

discount A bond pricing term that means the price at which the bond trades is less than its face value.

pure discount bonds Zero-coupon bonds.

Price and Yield to Maturity of a Zero-Coupon Bond

Now that we understand the cash flows associated with a zero-coupon bond, we can calculate the rate of return of buying a bond and holding it until maturity. Recall from Chapter 4 that we can always find the rate of return of an investment opportunity as the rate at which the value of the amount invested grows to exactly fund the future cash flows received by the investment. So the rate of return on the zero-coupon bond is the discount rate that equates the cost of the bond with the present value of the future cash flow received. We can extend this concept to a coupon bond: the rate of return is the discount rate at which the present value of all future cash flows from the bond equals the price of the bond. The rate of return of an investment in a bond is given a special name, the **yield to maturity (YTM)**, or just the *yield*: *the yield to maturity of a bond is the discount rate that sets the present value of the promised bond payments equal to the current market price of the bond.*

yield to maturity (YTM) The rate of return of an investment in a bond that is held to its maturity date. The YTM is the discount rate that sets the present value of the promised bond payments equal to the current market price for the bond.

Intuitively, the yield to maturity for a zero-coupon bond is the return you will earn as an investor by buying the bond at its current market price, holding the bond to maturity, and receiving the promised face value payment.

Let's determine the yield to maturity of the one-year zero-coupon bond discussed earlier in this chapter. According to the definition, the yield to maturity of the one-year bond solves the following equation:

$$96{,}618.36 = \frac{100{,}000}{1 + YTM_1}$$

In this case,

$$1 + YTM_1 = \frac{100{,}000}{96{,}618.36} = 1.035 \therefore YTM_1 = 0.035 = 3.5\%$$

That is, the yield to maturity for this bond is 3.5%. Because the bond is risk free, investing in this bond and holding it to maturity is equivalent to earning 3.5% interest on your initial investment with certainty:

$$\$96{,}618.36 \times 1.035 = \$100{,}000$$

We can use a similar method to find the yield to maturity for any maturity zero-coupon bond. Setting up the pricing equation for a zero-coupon bond, we have

Price (P) of a zero-coupon bond with face value (FV) paid in *n* periods

$$P = \underbrace{\frac{FV}{(1 + YTM_n)^n}}_{\substack{\text{Present Value of the} \\ \text{Face Value repayment} \\ \text{using the } YTM_n}} \tag{6.2}$$

Solving for the YTM, we get

YTM of a zero-coupon bond with price (P) and face value (FV) paid in *n* periods

$$1 + YTM_n = \left(\frac{FV}{P}\right)^{1/n} \therefore YTM_n = \left(\frac{FV}{P}\right)^{1/n} - 1 \tag{6.3}$$

The yield to maturity (YTM_n) in Equation 6.3 is the effective rate of return per period for holding the bond from today until maturity *n periods in the future*. It is important to note that if n is not in years, then the YTM_n calculated in Equation 6.3 will not be an effective rate per year. For example, if n is 20 semi-annual periods, then YTM_{20} is an effective rate per semi-annual period for a bond held for 20 semi-annual periods or 10 years. This peculiarity of the notation is not so important for zero-coupon bonds, as n is normally in years; it becomes more important further on in this chapter when we learn how to calculate and quote the YTM for a coupon-paying bond.

Risk-Free Interest Rates

Above, we calculated the yield to maturity of the one-year risk-free bond as 3.5%. But recall that the Valuation Principle's Law of One Price implies that all one-year risk-free investments must earn this same return of 3.5%. That is, 3.5% must be *the* competitive market risk-free interest rate.

More generally, in the last chapter we discussed the competitive market interest rate, r_n, available from today until date n for risk-free cash flows. Recall that we used this interest rate as the cost of capital for a risk-free cash flow that occurs on date n. A default-free zero-coupon bond that matures on date n provides a risk-free return over the same period. So the Law of One Price guarantees that the risk-free interest rate equals the yield to maturity on such a bond. Consequently, we will often refer to the yield to maturity of the appropriate maturity, zero-coupon risk-free bond as *the* risk-free interest rate. Some financial professionals also use the term **spot interest rates** to refer to these default-free zero-coupon yields, because these rates are offered "on the spot" at that point in time.

spot interest rates The current default-free, zero-coupon yields.

In Chapter 5, we introduced the yield curve, which plots the risk-free interest rate for different maturities. These risk-free interest rates correspond to the yields of risk-free zero-coupon bonds. Thus, the yield curve we introduced in Chapter 5 is also referred to as the **zero-coupon yield curve**. Figure 6.1 illustrates the yield curve consistent with the zero-coupon bond prices in Example 6.1.

zero-coupon yield curve A plot of the yields of risk-free zero-coupon bonds as a function of the bonds' maturity dates.

FIGURE 6.1 Zero-Coupon Yield Curve Consistent with the Bond Prices in Example 6.1

Recall from Chapter 5 that a yield curve simply plots the yield to maturity of investments of different maturities. This figure shows the yield curve that would be produced by plotting the yields to maturity determined by the bond prices in Example 6.1. Note that, as in this figure, the longer maturities generally have higher yields.

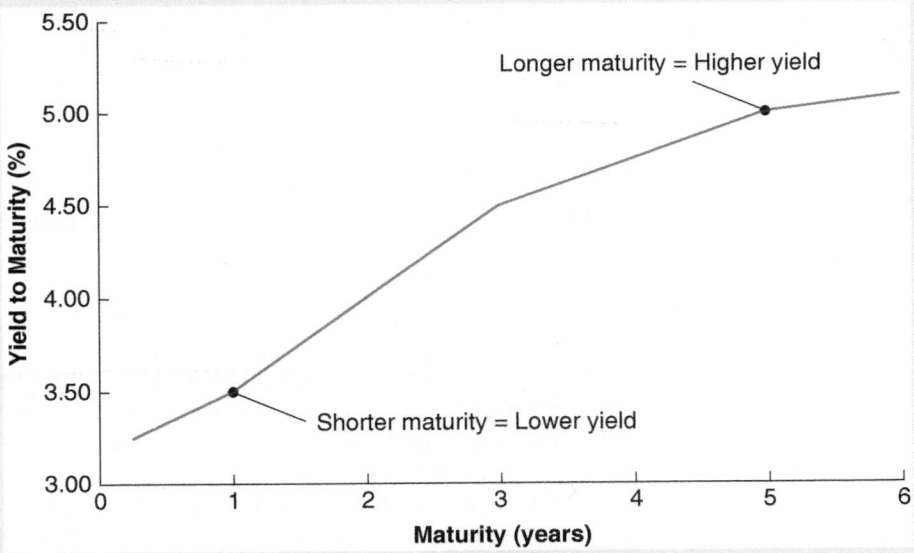

In that example, we use the bond's price to compute its yield to maturity. But from the definition of the yield to maturity, we can also use a bond's yield to compute its price. In the case of a zero-coupon bond, the price is simply equal to the present value of the bond's face value, discounted at the bond's yield to maturity.

GLOBAL FINANCIAL CRISIS: NEGATIVE BOND YIELDS

On December 9, 2008, in the midst of one of the worst financial crises in history, the unthinkable happened: For the first time since the Great Depression, U.S. Treasury Bills traded at a negative yield. That is, these risk-free pure discount bonds traded at premium. As Bloomberg.com reported, "If you invested $1 million in three-month bills at today's negative discount rate of 0.01%, for a price of 100.002556, at maturity you would receive the par value for a loss of $25.56."

A negative yield on a Treasury bill implies that investors have an arbitrage opportunity: By selling the bill, and holding the proceeds in cash, they would have a risk-free profit of $25.56. Why did investors not rush to take advantage of the arbitrage opportunity and thereby eliminate it?

Well, first, the negative yields did not last very long, suggesting that, in fact, investors did rush to take advantage of this opportunity. But, second, after closer consideration, the opportunity might not have been a sure risk-free arbitrage. When selling a Treasury security, the investor must choose where to invest, or at least hold, the proceeds. In normal times, investors would be happy to deposit the proceeds with a bank and consider this deposit to be risk free. But these were not normal times—many investors had great concerns about the financial stability of banks and other financial intermediaries. Perhaps investors shied away from this "arbitrage" opportunity because they were worried that the cash they would receive could not be held safely anywhere (even putting it "under the mattress" has a risk of theft!). Thus, we can view the $25.56 as the price investors were willing to pay to have the U.S. Treasury hold their money safely for them at a time when no other investments seemed truly safe.

This phenomenon repeated itself in Europe starting in mid-2012. In this case, negative yields emerged due to concerns about both the safety of European banks and the stability of the euro as a currency. As investors in Greece or other countries began to worry that their economies might depart from the euro, they were willing to hold German and Swiss government bonds even at negative yields as a way to protect themselves against unravelling of the eurozone. By mid-2015, almost 25% of European government bonds had negative yields, with some Swiss bonds having yields close to -1%!

These persistent and significantly negative yields are challenging to explain. Most of the holders of these bonds are institutions and pension funds which are restricted to hold very safe assets. And, while they could hold currency instead, obtaining, storing, and securing large quantities of cash would also be very costly. (Indeed, Swiss banks have reportedly refused large currency withdrawals by hedge funds attempting to exploit the arbitrage opportunity.) Bonds are also much easier to trade, and use as collateral, than are giant vaults of cash. Together, the safety and convenience of these bonds must be worth the nearly 1% per year these investors are willing to sacrifice.

CONCEPT CHECK

3. Why would you want to know the yield to maturity of a bond?

4. What is the relationship between a bond's price and its yield to maturity?

EXAMPLE 6.1 Yields for Different Maturities

PROBLEM

Suppose the following zero-coupon bonds are trading at the prices shown below per $100 face value. Determine the corresponding yield to maturity for each bond.

Maturity	1 year	2 years	3 years	4 years
Price	$96.62	$92.45	$87.63	$83.06

SOLUTION

Plan

We can use Equation 6.3 to solve for the YTM of the bonds. The table gives the prices and number of years to maturity, and the face value is $100 per bond.

Execute

Using Equation 6.3, we have

$$YTM_1 = (100/96.62)^{1/1} - 1 = 3.50\%$$

$$YTM_2 = (100/92.45)^{1/2} - 1 = 4.00\%$$

$$YTM_3 = (100/87.63)^{1/3} - 1 = 4.50\%$$

$$YTM_4 = (100/83.06)^{1/4} - 1 = 4.75\%$$

Evaluate

Solving for the YTM of a zero-coupon bond is the same process we used to solve for the rate of return in Chapter 4. Indeed, the YTM is the rate of return of buying the bond.

EXAMPLE 6.2 Computing the Price of a Zero-Coupon Bond

PROBLEM

Given the yield curve shown in Figure 6.1, what is the price of a five-year risk-free zero-coupon bond with a face value of $100?

SOLUTION

Plan

We can compute the bond's price as the present value of its face amount using Equation 6.2, where the discount rate is the bond's yield to maturity. From the yield curve, the yield to maturity for five-year risk-free zero-coupon bonds is 5.0%.

Execute

$$P = \frac{100}{(1.05)^5} = 78.35$$

Evaluate

We can compute the price of a zero-coupon bond simply by computing the present value of the face amount using the bond's yield to maturity. Note that the price of the five-year zero-coupon bond is even lower than the price of the other zero-coupon bonds in Example 6.1, because the face amount is the same but we must wait longer to receive it.

6.3 Coupon Bonds

coupon bonds Bonds that pay regular coupon interest payments up to maturity, when the face value is also paid.

Government of Canada bonds A bond issued by the Government of Canada.

Like zero-coupon bonds, **coupon bonds** pay investors the face value at maturity. In addition, these bonds make regular coupon interest payments. As of the end of 2013, the Government of Canada had bonds outstanding with maturities from one month to 34 years into the future. Normally, at issue, the **Government of Canada bonds** are sold with maturities of 2, 5, 10, or 30 years.

Coupon Bond Cash Flows

While an investor's return on a zero-coupon bond comes from buying it at a discount to its face value, the return on a coupon bond comes from two sources: (1) any difference between the purchase price and the face value and (2) its periodic coupon payments. Before we can compute the yield to maturity of a coupon bond, we need to know all of its cash flows, including the coupon interest payments and when they are paid. In Example 6.3, we translate a bond description into the bond's cash flows.

EXAMPLE 6.3 The Cash Flows of a Coupon Bond

PROBLEM

Assume that it is May 15, 2020, and the Government of Canada has just issued bonds with a May 2025 maturity, $1000 par value, and a 5% coupon rate with semi-annual coupons. The first coupon payment will be paid on November 15, 2020. What cash flows will you receive if you hold this bond until maturity?

SOLUTION

■ **Plan**

The description of the bond should be sufficient to determine all of its cash flows. The phrase "May 2025 maturity, $1000 par value" tells us that this is a bond with a face value of $1000 and five years to maturity. The phrase "5% coupon rate with semi-annual coupons" tells us that the bond pays a total of 5% of its face value each year in two equal semi-annual instalments. Finally, we know that the first coupon is paid on November 15, 2020.

■ **Execute**

The face value of this bond is $1000. Because this bond pays coupons semi-annually, using Equation 6.1, you determine that you will receive a coupon payment every six months of CPN = $1000 × 5%/2 = $25. Here is the timeline based on a six-month period, and there are a total of 10 cash flows:

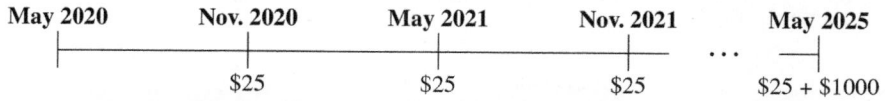

Note that the last payment occurs five years (10 six-month periods) from now and is composed of both a coupon payment of $25 and the face value payment of $1000.

■ **Evaluate**

Since a bond is just a package of cash flows, we need to know those cash flows in order to value the bond. That is why the description of the bond contains all of the information we would need to construct its cash flow timeline.

Price and Yield to Maturity of a Coupon Bond

Once we have determined the coupon bond's cash flows, given its market price we can determine its yield to maturity. The yield to maturity for a bond is the rate of return of investing in the bond and holding it to maturity. This investment has the cash flows shown in the timeline below:

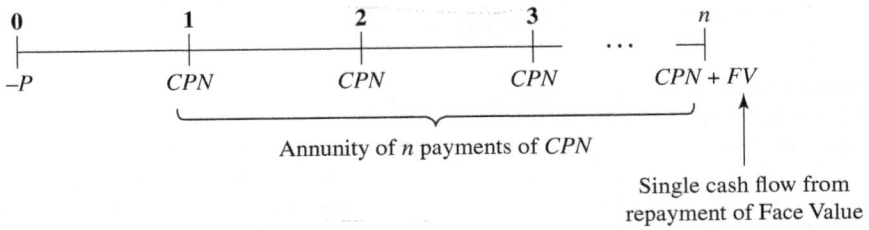

The yield to maturity of the bond is the *single* discount rate, YTM_n, that equates the present value of the bond's remaining cash flows to its current price. For zero-coupon bonds, there were only two cash flows, but coupon bonds have many cash flows, complicating the yield to maturity calculation. From the timeline, we see that the coupon payments represent an annuity, so the yield to maturity is the interest rate, YTM_n, that equates the bond's price, P, to the present value of an annuity of coupons plus the present value of the bond's face value, FV:

Price and YTM of a coupon bond with *n* coupon payments

$$P = \underbrace{CPN \times \overbrace{\frac{1}{YTM_n}\left(1 - \frac{1}{(1 + YTM_n)^n}\right)}^{\text{Annuity Factor using the } YTM_n}}_{\text{Present Value of all of the periodic coupon payments}} + \underbrace{\left(\frac{FV}{(1 + YTM_n)^n}\right)}_{\text{Present Value of the Face Value repayment using the } YTM_n} \tag{6.4}$$

If we know the values of each variable except the price, Equation 6.4 can easily be used to compute the price. However, if we know each of the variables except YTM, it is not possible to solve for YTM from Equation 6.4 directly. Instead, we need to use a financial calculator or a spreadsheet (using Excel's *RATE* function), introduced in Chapter 4.

When we calculate a bond's yield to maturity by solving Equation 6.4, the yield we compute will be an effective rate *per coupon interval*. However, yields are typically quoted as annual percentage rates (APRs), so we multiply by the number of coupons per year, thereby converting the answer into an APR quote compounded over the same time as the time period between coupons.

EXAMPLE 6.4 Computing the Yield to Maturity of a Coupon Bond

PROBLEM

Consider the five-year, $1000 bond with a 5% coupon rate and semi-annual coupons described in Example 6.3. If this bond is currently trading for a price of $957.35, what is the bond's yield to maturity?

SOLUTION

■ **Plan**

We worked out the bond's cash flows in Example 6.3. From the cash flow timeline, we can see that the bond consists of an annuity of 10 payments of $25, paid every six months, and one lump-sum payment of $1000 in five years (10 six-month periods). We can use Equation 6.4 to solve for the yield to maturity. However, we must use six-month intervals consistently throughout the equation.

■ **Execute**

Because the bond has 10 remaining coupon payments, we compute its YTM_{10} by solving Equation 6.4 for this bond:

$$957.35 = 25 \times \frac{1}{YTM_{10}}\left(1 - \frac{1}{(1 + YTM_{10})^{10}}\right) + \frac{1000}{(1 + YTM_{10})^{10}}$$

We can solve it by using a financial calculator or a spreadsheet. To use a financial calculator, we enter the price we pay as a negative number for the present value (PV) (it is a cash outflow), the coupon payments as the PMT, and the bond's par value as its FV. Finally, we enter the number of coupon payments remaining (10) as *N*.

	N	I/Y	PV	PMT	FV
Given:	10		−957.35	25	1000
Solve for:		**3.00**			

Excel Formula: = *RATE*(*NPER*,*PMT*,*PV*,*FV*) = *RATE*(10,25,−957.35,1000)

Therefore, $YTM_{10} = 3\%$. Because the bond pays coupons semi-annually, YTM_{10} is an effective rate for a six-month period. As coupon-paying bond yields are normally quoted as an APR with semi-annual compounding, we must do an interest rate conversion by manipulating Equation 5.2 to get the APR with semi-annual compounding. Therefore, we multiply the 3% by two (i.e., we multiply by the number of coupon payments per year). Thus, this five-year bond has a quoted yield to maturity, YTM_5 (where five is the number of years), equal to a 6% APR with semi-annual compounding.

■ **Evaluate**

As the equation shows, the yield to maturity is the discount rate that equates the present value of the bond's cash flows with its price. Bonds with semi-annual payments normally have their yields to maturity quoted as an APR with semi-annual compounding.

We can also use Equation 6.4 to compute a bond's price based on its yield to maturity. We simply discount the cash flows using the yield, as in Example 6.5.

Coupon Bond Price Quotes

Because we can convert any price into a yield, and vice versa, prices and yields are often used interchangeably. For example, the bond in Example 6.5 could be quoted as having a yield of 4.50% or a price of $1022.17 per $1000 face value. Indeed, bond traders

EXAMPLE 6.5 Computing a Bond Price from Its Yield to Maturity

PROBLEM

Consider again the five-year, $1000 bond with a 5% coupon rate and semi-annual coupons in Example 6.4. Suppose interest rates drop and the bond's yield to maturity decreases to 4.50% (expressed as an APR with semi-annual compounding). For what price is the bond trading now? Compare this bond's yield to maturity to the effective annual rate of interest (EAR) earned by the bond.

SOLUTION

Plan

Given the yield, we can compute the price using Equation 6.4. First, note that a 4.50% APR with semi-annual compounding gives an implied effective semi-annual rate of 2.25% (see Equation 5.2). Also, recall that the cash flows of this bond are an annuity of 10 payments of $25, paid every six months, and one lump-sum cash flow of $1000 (the face value), paid in five years (10 six-month periods). Given the implied effective semi-annual rate of 2.25%, we can convert this into another equivalent effective rate using Equation 5.1. This will allow us to convert the bond's yield to maturity to an EAR.

Execute

Using Equation 6.4 and the six-month yield of 2.25%, the bond price must be

$$P = 25 \times \frac{1}{0.0225}\left(1 - \frac{1}{1.0225^{10}}\right) + \frac{1000}{1.0225^{10}} = \$1022.17$$

To convert the bond's YTM to an effective annual rate, we first note that most YTMs are quoted as APRs with semi-annual compounding; the implied effective rate per six-month period is obtained by dividing the APR by two (see Equation 5.2). This gives 2.25% per six months. Then, using Equation 5.1, we convert the effective six-month rate to an equivalent EAR as follows:

$$EAR = (1 + 0.0225)^2 = 0.04550625 = 4.550625\%$$

We can also use a financial calculator to determine the bond price:

	N	I/Y	PV	PMT	FV
Given:	10	2.25		25	1000
Solve for:			−1022.17		
Excel Formula: = *PV*(*RATE,NPER,PMT,FV*) = *PV*(.0225,10,25,1000)					

Evaluate

The bond's price has risen to $1022.17, lowering the return from investing in it from 3% to 2.25% per six-month period or providing the new YTM of 4.5%, which is in line with the lower competitive rates being offered for bonds of similar risk and maturity elsewhere in the market. Comparing the YTM to the EAR, we see that the YTM is lower than the EAR because, like most quoted bond yields, the YTM is quoted with semi-annual compounding.

generally quote bond yields rather than bond prices. One advantage of quoting the yield to maturity rather than the price is that the yield is independent of the face value of the bond. When prices are quoted in the bond market, they are conventionally quoted per $100 face value. Thus, the bond in Example 6.5 would be quoted as having a price of

$102.217 (per $100 face value), which would imply an actual price of $1022.17, given the $1000 face value of the bond.

CONCEPT CHECK

5. What cash flows does a company pay to investors holding its coupon bonds?
6. What do we need in order to value a coupon bond?

(1) change in market IR
(2) Time, get closer to its
Interest rate

6.4 Why Bond Prices Change

As we mentioned earlier, zero-coupon bonds always trade at a discount—that is, prior to maturity, their price is less than their face value. But, as shown in Examples 6.4 and 6.5, coupon bonds may trade at a discount or at a **premium** (a price greater than their face value). In this section, we identify when a bond will trade at a discount or premium, as well as how the bond's price will change due to the passage of time and fluctuations in interest rates.

premium A price at which coupon bonds trade that is greater than their face value.

Most issuers of coupon bonds choose a coupon rate so that the bonds will *initially* trade at, or very close to, **par** (that is, at the bond's face value). For example, the Government of Canada sets the coupon rates on its bonds in this way. After the issue date, the market price of a bond generally changes over time for two reasons. First, as time passes, the bond gets closer to its maturity date. Holding fixed the bond's yield to maturity, the present value of the bond's remaining cash flows changes as the time to maturity decreases. Second, at any point in time, changes in market interest rates affect the bond's yield to maturity and its price (the present value of the remaining cash flows). We explore these two effects in the remainder of this section.

par A price at which coupon bonds trade that is equal to their face value.

FINDING BOND PRICES ON THE WEB

Unlike the TSX or NYSE, where many stocks are traded, there is no particular physical location where bonds are traded. Instead, they are traded electronically. In the United States, the Financial Industry Regulatory Authority (FINRA) has made an effort to make bond prices more widely available. FINRA's website allows anyone to search for the most recent trades and quotes for bonds (www.finra-markets.morningstar.com/BondCenter). In Canada, institutional investors use two electronic platforms to trade bonds (in addition to directly trading with each other): CanDeal and CBID. Here we show a screen shot from the CBID website (www.CanadianFixedIncome.ca) displaying the pricing information for some provincial and corporate bonds on March 28, 2018. Consider, for example, the Alberta bond shown. The information displayed indicates the bond's coupon is 2.9% and it matures in September 2029. Its price is $100.13 based on a $100 face value (so a typical $1000 face value bond would be priced at $1001.30) and its YTM is 2.89% (APR with semi-annual compounding).

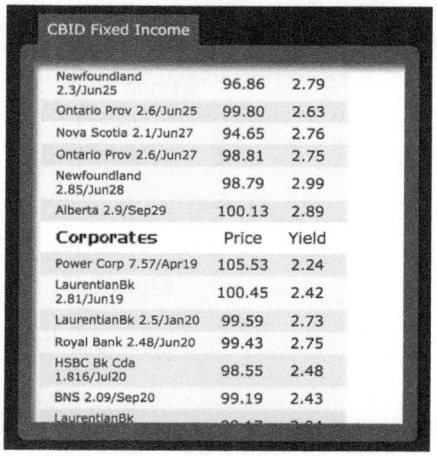

CBID Fixed Income

Newfoundland 2.3/Jun25	96.86	2.79
Ontario Prov 2.6/Jun25	99.80	2.63
Nova Scotia 2.1/Jun27	94.65	2.76
Ontario Prov 2.6/Jun27	98.81	2.75
Newfoundland 2.85/Jun28	98.79	2.99
Alberta 2.9/Sep29	100.13	2.89
Corporates	Price	Yield
Power Corp 7.57/Apr19	105.53	2.24
LaurentianBk 2.81/Jun19	100.45	2.42
LaurentianBk 2.5/Jan20	99.59	2.73
Royal Bank 2.48/Jun20	99.43	2.75
HSBC Bk Cda 1.816/Jul20	98.55	2.48
BNS 2.09/Sep20	99.19	2.43
LaurentianBk		

Source: http://www.canadianfixedincome.ca/
Screen capture March 28, 2018 @ 8:55 a.m. CDT.

Interest Rate Changes and Bond Prices

If a bond sells at par (at its face value), the only return investors will earn is from the coupons that the bond pays. Therefore, the bond's coupon rate will exactly equal its yield to maturity. As interest rates in the economy fluctuate, the yields that investors demand to invest in bonds will also change. Consider the Government of Canada bond of Examples 6.3 to 6.5; suppose that the government issued the bond when market interest rates implied a YTM of 5%, and thus they set the coupon rate to be 5%. Suppose interest rates then rise so that new bonds have a YTM of 9%. These new bonds would have a coupon rate of 9% and sell for $1000. So, for $1000, an investor would get $90 per year until the bond matured. The 5% coupon-rate bond was issued when rates were lower such that its coupon is fixed at 5%, so it offers payments of $50 per year until maturity. Because its cash flows are lower, the 5% coupon-rate bond must have a lower price than the 9% coupon-rate bond.[1] Thus, the price of the 5% bond will fall until the investor is indifferent between buying the 5% bond and buying the 9% bond. Figure 6.2 illustrates the relationship between the bond's price and its yield to maturity.

In our example, the price of the 5% bond will drop to below face value ($1000), so it will be trading at a discount (also called trading *below par*). If the bond trades at a discount, an investor who buys the bond will earn a return both from receiving the

FIGURE 6.2 Bond's Price versus Its Yield to Maturity

At a price of $1000, the 5% coupon-rate bond (from Examples 6.3 to 6.5) offers a 5% YTM. If rates have risen to 9%, in order for the 5% coupon-rate bond to offer a competitive yield to maturity, its price must fall until its yield to maturity rises to the 9% yield being offered by otherwise similar bonds. In the example depicted here, for a bond with five years left to maturity, its price must fall to $841.75 before investors will be indifferent between buying it and the 9% coupon-rate bond priced at $1000. The higher the required yield to maturity, the more a bond's cash flows are discounted, and in the graph we can see the corresponding lower prices at which the bond will be valued.

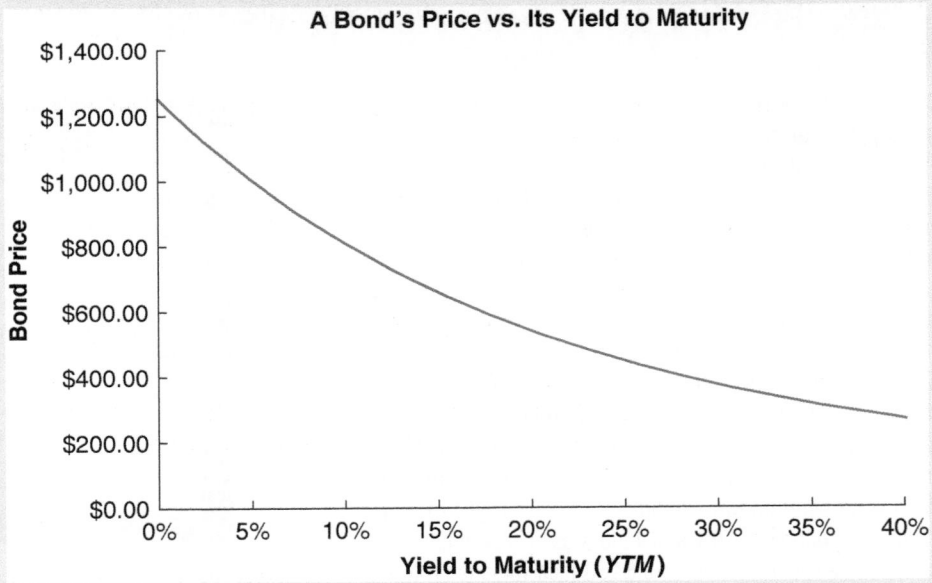

[1]Otherwise, if the 5% bond had the same or higher price, there would be an arbitrage opportunity—one could sell the 5% bond and buy the 9% bond, receiving cash today and higher coupons going forward.

coupons and from receiving a face value that exceeds the price paid for the bond. As a result, if a bond trades at a discount, its yield to maturity will exceed its coupon rate.

A bond that pays a coupon can also trade at a premium to its face value (trading *above par*). Imagine what would have happened in our example if interest rates had gone down to 3% instead of up to 9%. Then, the holder of the existing 5% bond would not part with it for $1000. Instead, its price would have to rise until the yield to maturity from buying it at that price would be 3%. In this case, an investor's return from the coupons is diminished by receiving a face value less than the price paid for the bond. *Thus, a bond trades at a premium whenever its yield to maturity is less than its coupon rate.*[2]

This example illustrates a general phenomenon. A higher yield to maturity means that investors demand a higher return for investing. They apply a higher discount rate for a bond's remaining cash flows, reducing their present value and hence the bond's price. The reverse holds when interest rates fall. Investors then demand a lower yield to maturity, reducing the discount rate applied to the bond's cash flows and raising the price. Therefore, *as interest rates and bond yields rise, bond prices will fall, and vice versa, so that interest rates and bond prices always move in the opposite direction.*

Table 6.2 summarizes the relationship between interest rates and bond prices.

TABLE 6.2 Bond Prices Immediately after a Coupon Payment

When the bond price is . . .	greater than the face value	equal to the face value	less than the face value
We say the bond trades . . .	"above par" or "at a premium"	"at par"	"below par" or "at a discount"
This occurs when the . . .	Coupon Rate > Yield to Maturity	Coupon Rate = Yield to Maturity	Coupon Rate < Yield to Maturity

EXAMPLE 6.6 Determining the Discount or Premium of a Coupon Bond

PROBLEM

Consider three 30-year bonds with annual coupon payments. One bond has a 10% coupon rate, one has a 5% coupon rate, and one has a 3% coupon rate. If the yield to maturity of each bond is 5%, what is the price of each bond per $100 face value? Which bond trades at a premium, which trades at a discount, and which trades at par?

SOLUTION

■ Plan

From the description of the bonds, we can determine their cash flows. Each bond has 30 years to maturity and pays its coupons annually. Therefore, each bond has an annuity of coupon payments, paid annually for 30 years, and then the face value paid as a lump sum in 30 years. They are all priced so that their yield to maturity is 5%, meaning that 5% is the discount rate that equates the present value of the cash flows to the price of the bond. Therefore, we can use Equation 6.4 to compute the price of each bond as the PV of its cash flows, discounted at 5%. ▶

[2]The terms "discount" and "premium" are simply descriptive and are not meant to imply that you should try to buy bonds at a discount and avoid buying bonds at a premium. In a competitive market, the Law of One Price ensures that all similar bonds are priced to earn the same return. That is why buying a discount or premium bond is still a fair transaction: the price exactly equals the present value of the bond's cash flows, so you earn a fair rate of return but not an abnormally good (or bad) return.

◀

■ **Execute**

For the 10% coupon bond, the annuity cash flows are $10 per year (10% of each $100 face value). Similarly, the annuity cash flows for the 5% and 3% bonds are $5 and $3 per year. We use a $100 face value for all of the bonds.

Using Equation 6.4 and these cash flows, the bond prices are

$$P(10\%\text{ coupon}) = 10 \times \frac{1}{0.05}\left(1 - \frac{1}{1.05^{30}}\right) + \frac{100}{1.05^{30}} = \$176.86 \text{ (trades at a premium)}$$

$$P(5\%\text{ coupon}) = 5 \times \frac{1}{0.05}\left(1 - \frac{1}{1.05^{30}}\right) + \frac{100}{1.05^{30}} = \$100.00 \text{ (trades at a par)}$$

$$P(3\%\text{ coupon}) = 3 \times \frac{1}{0.05}\left(1 - \frac{1}{1.05^{30}}\right) + \frac{100}{1.05^{30}} = \$69.26 \text{ (trades at a discount)}$$

■ **Evaluate**

The prices reveal that when the coupon rate of the bond is higher than its yield to maturity, it trades at a premium. When its coupon rate equals its yield to maturity, it trades at par. When its coupon rate is lower than its yield to maturity, it trades at a discount.

Time and Bond Prices

Let's consider the effect of time on the price of a bond. As the next payment from a bond grows nearer, the price of the bond increases to reflect the increasing present value of that cash flow. Take a bond paying semi-annual coupons of $50 and imagine tracking the price of the bond starting on the day after the last coupon payment was made. The price will slowly rise over the following six months as the next $50 coupon payment grows closer and closer. It will peak right before the coupon payment is made, when buying the bond still entitles you to receive the $50 payment immediately. If you buy the bond right after the coupon payment is made, you do not have the right to receive that $50 coupon. The price you are willing to pay for the bond will therefore be $50 less than it was right before the coupon was paid. This pattern—the price slowly rising as a coupon payment nears and then dropping abruptly after the payment is made—continues for the life of the bond. Figure 6.3 illustrates this phenomenon.

EXAMPLE 6.7 The Effect of Time on the Price of a Bond

PROBLEM

Suppose you purchase a 30-year zero-coupon bond with a yield to maturity of 5%. For a face value of $100, the bond will initially trade for

$$P(30\text{ years to maturity}) = \frac{100}{1.05^{30}} = \$23.14$$

If the bond's yield to maturity remains at 5%, what will its price be 5 years later? If you purchased the bond at $23.14 and sold it 5 years later, what would be the rate of return of your investment?

SOLUTION

■ **Plan**

If the bond was originally a 30-year bond and 5 years have passed, then it has 25 years left to maturity. If the yield to maturity does not change, then you can compute the price of the bond ▶

with 25 years left exactly as we did for 30 years, but using 25 years of discounting instead of 30. Once you have the price in 5 years, you can compute the rate of return of your investment just as we did in Chapter 4. The FV is the price in 5 years, the PV is the initial price ($23.14), and the number of years is 5.

Execute

$$P(\text{25 years to maturity}) = \frac{100}{1.05^{25}} = \$29.53$$

If you purchased the bond for $23.14 and then sold it after 5 years for $29.53, the rate of return of your investment would be as follows:

$$\left(\frac{29.53}{23.14}\right)^{1/5} - 1 = 5.0\%$$

That is, your return is the same as the yield to maturity of the bond.

Evaluate

Note that the bond price is higher, and hence the discount from its face value is smaller, when there is less time to maturity. The discount shrinks because the yield has not changed, but there is less time until the face value will be received. This example illustrates a more general property for bonds: *If a bond's yield to maturity does not change, then the rate of return of an investment in the bond equals its yield to maturity even if you sell the bond early.*

FIGURE 6.3 **The Effect of Time on Bond Prices**

The graph illustrates the effects of the passage of time on bond prices when the yield remains constant (in this case, 5%). The price of a zero-coupon bond rises smoothly. The prices of the coupon bonds are indicated by the zigzag lines. Notice that the prices rise between coupon payments but tumble on the coupon date, reflecting the amount of the coupon payment. For each coupon bond, the grey line shows the trend of the bond price just after each coupon is paid.

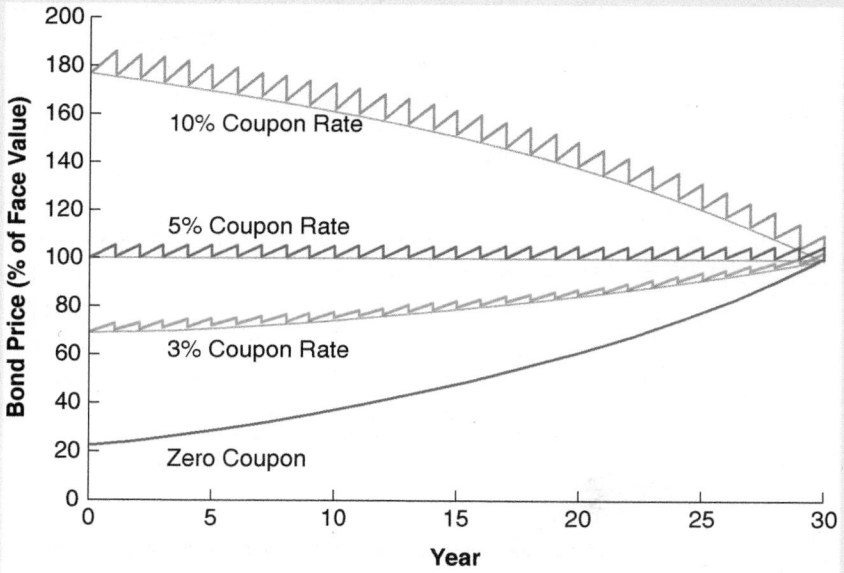

Interest Rate Risk and Bond Prices

While the effect of time on bond prices is predictable, unpredictable changes in interest rates will also affect bond prices. Further, bonds with different characteristics will respond differently to changes in interest rates—some bonds will react more strongly than others. We showed in Chapter 5 that investors view long-term loans to be riskier than short-term loans. Because bonds are just loans, the same is true of short-term versus long-term bonds.

The example illustrates how bonds of different maturity will have different sensitivities to interest rate changes. However, even bonds with the same maturity will differ in interest rate sensitivity if their coupon rates are different. Because they pay higher cash flows up front, bonds with higher coupon rates are less sensitive to interest rate changes than otherwise identical bonds with lower coupon rates. Interest rate sensitivity is often measured by a bond's duration.[3] (See online Chapter 6 Appendix C for the formal definition and calculations.) Table 6.3 summarizes this conclusion.

TABLE 6.3 Bond Features and Interest Rate Risk

Bond Feature (holding all else equal)	Effect on Interest Rate Risk
Longer Term to Maturity	Increases Interest Rate Risk
Shorter Term to Maturity	Decreases Interest Rate Risk
Lower Coupon Rate	Increases Interest Rate Risk
Higher Coupon Rate	Decreases Interest Rate Risk

EXAMPLE 6.8 The Interest Rate Sensitivity of Bonds

PROBLEM

Consider a 10-year coupon bond and a 30-year coupon bond, both with 10% annual coupons. By what percentage will the price of each bond change if its yield to maturity increases from 5% to 6%?

SOLUTION

Plan

We need to compute the price of each bond for each yield to maturity and then calculate the percentage change in the prices. For both bonds, the cash flows are \$10 per year for \$100 in face value and then the \$100 face value repaid at maturity. The only difference is the maturity: 10 years and 30 years. With those cash flows, we can use Equation 6.4 to compute the prices.

Execute

YTM	10-Year, 10% Annual Coupon Bond	30-Year, 10% Annual Coupon Bond
5%	$10 \times \frac{1}{0.05}\left(1 - \frac{1}{1.05^{10}}\right) + \frac{100}{1.05^{10}} = \$138.61$	$10 \times \frac{1}{1.05}\left(1 - \frac{1}{1.05^{30}}\right) + \frac{100}{1.05^{30}} = \$176.86$
6%	$10 \times \frac{1}{0.06}\left(1 - \frac{1}{1.06^{10}}\right) + \frac{100}{1.06^{10}} = \$129.44$	$10 \times \frac{1}{0.06}\left(1 - \frac{1}{1.06^{30}}\right) + \frac{100}{1.06^{30}} = \$155.06$

The price of the 10-year bond changes by $(129.44 - 138.61)/138.61 = -6.6\%$ if its yield to maturity increases from 5% to 6%. For the 30-year bond, the price change is $(155.06 - 176.86)/176.86 = -12.3\%$. ▶

[3]Duration is a bond characteristic that combines the effect of a bond's maturity and the size of its coupon payments to give the average maturity of all the bond's cash flows. Longer-duration bonds are more sensitive to interest rate changes.

■ **Evaluate**

The 30-year bond is almost twice as sensitive as the 10-year bond to a change in the yield. In fact, if we graph the price and yields of the two bonds, we can see that the line for the 30-year bond, shown in blue, is steeper throughout than the green line for the 10-year bond, reflecting its heightened sensitivity to interest rate changes.

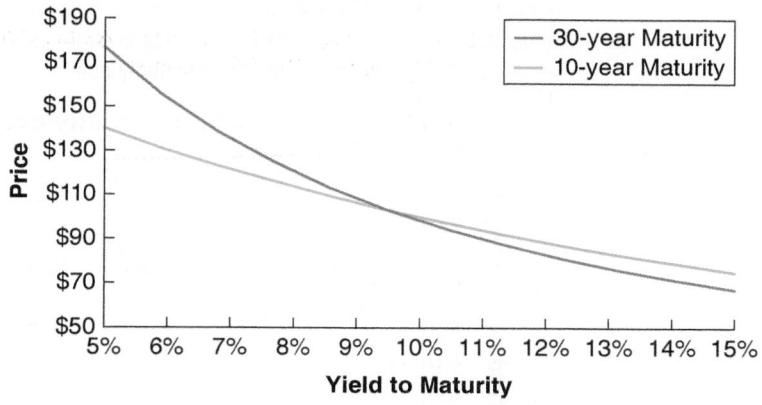

Bond Prices in Practice

In actuality, bond prices are subject to the effects of both the passage of time and changes in interest rates. Bond prices converge to the bond's face value due to the time effect. (See the grey lines in Figure 6.3.) However, bond prices also move up and down due to unpredictable changes in bond yields; Figure 6.4 illustrates this behaviour by demonstrating how the price of the 30-year zero-coupon bond might change over its life. Note that the bond price tends to converge to the face value as the bond approaches the maturity date but also moves higher when its yield falls and lower when its yield rises.

As the fluctuating price in Figure 6.4 demonstrates, prior to maturity the bond is exposed to interest rate risk. If an investor chooses to sell and the bond's yield to maturity has decreased, then the investor will receive a high price and earn a high return. If the yield to maturity has increased, the bond price is low at the time of sale and the investor will earn a low return.

Due to the impact of compounding over time, the later the investor receives payments from an investment, the more sensitive the value of that investment will be to changes in the discount rate. This is why, as demonstrated by Examples 6.8 and 6.9, bonds with a longer maturity as well as bonds with a lower coupon rate are more interest rate sensitive (remember that both lengthening the maturity and lowering the coupon rate will cause the investor to receive a greater fraction of the bond's cash flows at a later date). This is also shown in Figure 6.4, where we see that as the bond gets closer to maturity, there are smaller fluctuations of the bond's price due to interest rate changes. Again, the concept of duration, discussed in the online Chapter 6 Appendix C, can be used to provide a more formal analysis if this phenomenon.

FIGURE 6.4 Yield to Maturity and Bond Price Fluctuations over Time

The graphs illustrate changes in price and yield for a 30-year zero-coupon bond over its life. Panel (a) illustrates the changes in the bond's YTM over its life. In Panel (b), the actual bond price is shown in blue. Because the YTM does not remain constant over the bond's life, the bond's price fluctuates as it converges to the face value over time. Also shown is the price if the YTM remained fixed at 4%, 5%, or 6%. Panel (a) shows that the bond's YTM mostly remained between 4% and 6%. The broken lines in Panel (b) show the price of the bond if its YTM had remained constant at those levels. Note that in all cases, the bond's price must eventually converge to 100% of its face value on its maturity date.

Panel (a) The Bond's Yield to Maturity over Time

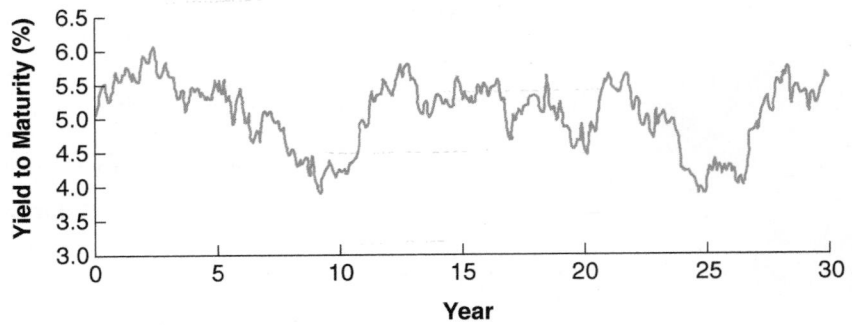

Panel (b) The Bond's Price over Time (Price = $100 on Maturity Date)

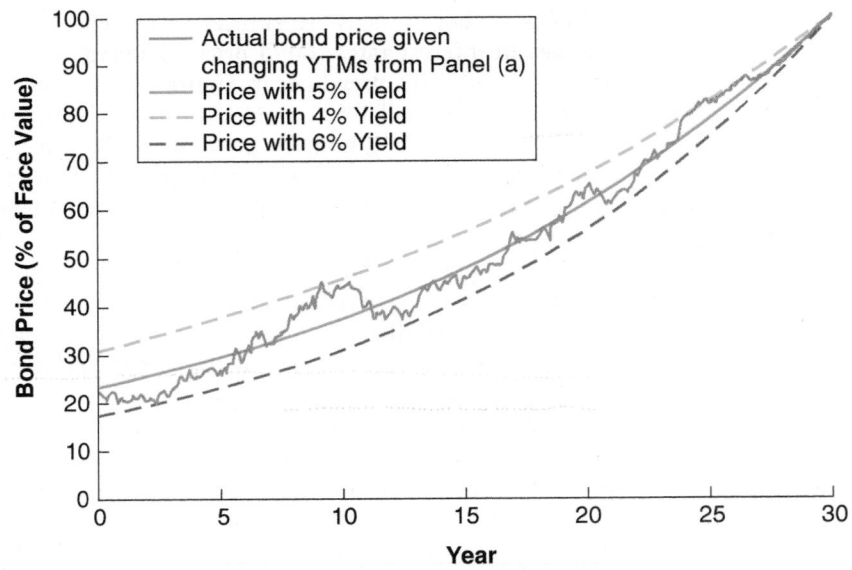

EXAMPLE 6.9 Coupons and Interest Rate Sensitivity

PROBLEM

Consider two bonds, each of which pays semi-annual coupons and has five years left until maturity. One has a coupon rate of 5% and the other has a coupon rate of 10%, but both currently have a yield to maturity of 8%. How much will the price of each bond change if its yield to maturity decreases from 8% to 7%?

SOLUTION

Plan

As in Example 6.8, we need to compute the price of each bond at 8% and 7% yield to maturities and then compute the percentage change in price. Each bond has 10 semi-annual coupon payments remaining, along with the repayment of par value at maturity. The cash flows per $100 of face value for the first bond are $2.50 every six months and then $100 at maturity. The cash flows per $100 of face value for the second bond are $5 at six months and then $100 at maturity. Since the cash flows are semi-annual, the yield to maturity is quoted as a semi-annually compounded APR, so we convert the yields to match the frequency of the cash flows by dividing by two. With semi-annual rates of 4% and 3.5%, we can use Equation 6.4 to compute the prices.

Execute

YTM	5-Year, 5% Coupon Bond	5-Year, 10% Coupon Bond
8%	$2.50 \times \frac{1}{1.04}\left(1 - \frac{1}{1.04^{10}}\right) + \frac{100}{1.04^{10}} = \$87.83$	$5 \times \frac{1}{1.04}\left(1 - \frac{1}{1.04^{10}}\right) + \frac{100}{1.04^{10}} = \$108.11$
7%	$2.50 \times \frac{1}{1.035}\left(1 - \frac{1}{1.035^{10}}\right) + \frac{100}{1.035^{10}} = \$91.68$	$5 \times \frac{1}{1.035}\left(1 - \frac{1}{1.035^{10}}\right) + \frac{100}{1.035^{10}} = \$112.47$

The 5% coupon bond's price changed from $87.83 to $91.68, or 4.4%, but the 10% coupon bond's price changed from $108.11 to $112.47, or 4.0%. You can calculate the price change very quickly with a financial calculator. Take the 5% coupon bond for example:

	N	I/Y	PV	PMT	FV
Given:	10	4		2.50	100
Solve for:			−87.83		

Excel Formula: = *PV*(*RATE*,*NPER*,*PMT*,*FV*) = *PV*(.04,10,2.5,100)

With all of the basic bond information entered, you can simply change the *I/Y* by entering 3.5 and pressing *I/Y* and then solve for PV again. So, with just a few keystrokes, you will have the new price of $91.68.

Evaluate

The bond with the smaller coupon payments is more sensitive to changes in interest rates. Because its coupons are smaller relative to its par value, a larger fraction of its cash flows is received later. As we learned in Example 6.8, later cash flows are affected more greatly by changes in interest rates, so compared to the 10% coupon bond, the effect of the interest change is greater for the cash flows of the 5% bond.

CONCEPT CHECK

7. Why do interest rates and bond prices move in opposite directions?
8. If a bond's yield to maturity does not change, how does its cash price change between coupon payments?

6.5 Corporate Bonds

- Bonds issued by corporation

corporate bonds Bonds issued by a corporation.

In the previous sections, we developed the basics of bond pricing in the context of Government of Canada bonds, which have no risk of default. In this section, our focus is on **corporate bonds**, which are bonds issued by corporations. We will examine the role of default risk in the price and yield to maturity of corporate bonds. As we will see, corporations with higher default risk will need to provide higher yields to attract buyers to their bonds.

Credit Risk

- The risk of default

Table 6.4 lists the interest rates paid for three-year bonds from a number of different borrowers on March 28, 2018. Why do these interest rates vary so widely? The lowest interest rate is the 1.93% rate paid on Government of Canada bonds. Government of Canada securities are widely regarded to be risk free, because there is virtually no chance the government will fail to pay the interest and default on these bonds. Thus, as we noted in Section 6.1, when we refer to the risk-free interest rate, we mean the rate on Government of Canada bills or bonds.

credit risk The risk of default by the issuer of any bond that is not default free; it is an indication that the bond's cash flows are not known with certainty.

The remaining bonds are all corporate bonds. The issuer of a corporate bond may default—that is, it might not pay back the full amount promised in the bond prospectus. For example, a company with financial difficulties may be unable to fully repay the loan. This risk of default, which is known as the **credit risk** of the bond, means that the bond's cash flows are not known with certainty. To compensate for the risk that the firm may default, investors demand a higher interest rate than the rate on Government of Canada bonds.[4] The difference between the interest rate of the loan and the Government of Canada bond rate will depend on investors' assessment of the likelihood that the firm will default. For example, investors place a higher probability of default on Sherritt International than on Canadian Utilities, forcing Sherritt to pay a higher interest rate due to its higher credit risk. The second column of Table 6.4 indicates how the various bonds were rated by Dominion Bond Rating Service (DBRS). AAA is the highest rating a bond can have, followed by AA, A, BBB,BB, B and so on. Sometimes ratings agencies indicate where in a particular range a bond is rated. We see that Bell Canada is in the high end of the range for BBB-rated bonds compared to Fairfax Financial which is in the middle of the range for BBB-rated bonds.

TABLE 6.4 Interest Rates on Three-Year Bonds for Various Borrowers as of March 28, 2018

Borrower	Bond Rating (DBRS)	YTM
Government of Canada	AAA	1.93%
TD Bank	AA	2.59%
Canadian Utilities	AA	2.64%
Bell Canada	BBB high	2.80%
RioCan REIT	BBB high	2.97%
Fairfax Financial	BBB middle	3.11%
Cominair REIT	BB high	4.12%
Sherritt International	B low	10.10%

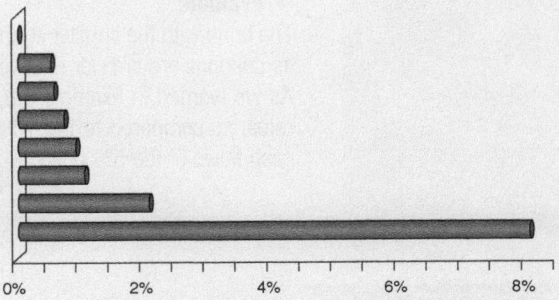

Source: webbroker.td.com and author's calculations.

[4]Because trading in corporate bonds is much less liquid than trading in government bonds, part of the increased interest rate is to compensate investors for this lack of liquidity.

Corporate Bond Yields

How does the credit risk of default affect bond prices and yields? The cash flows promised by the bond are the most that bondholders can hope to receive. Due to credit risk, the cash flows that a purchaser of a corporate bond actually *expects* to receive are less than that amount. For example, General Motors (GM) was struggling financially in 2006 and 2007, substantially increasing the chance that it would default on its bonds. Realizing this, in 2007, investors in GM bonds incorporated an increased probability that the bond payments would not be made as promised, and prices of the bonds fell. Because the yield to maturity of GM's bonds is computed by comparing the price to the *promised* cash flows, the yield to maturity in 2007 and 2008 *increased* as the probability of being paid as promised decreased. This example highlights the following general truths:

1. Investors pay less for bonds with credit risk than they would for an otherwise identical default-free bond.
2. Because the yield to maturity for a bond is calculated using the promised cash flows instead of the *expected* cash flows, the yield of bonds with credit risk will be higher than that of otherwise identical default-free bonds.
3. Because the expected return includes the possibility that the bond will pay as promised and the possibility that the bond will pay less due to default, if the bond of a corporation at risk of bankruptcy actually does default, the actual return to an investor in the bond will be lower than the return expected when the bond was purchased.

These three points lead us to an important conclusion: *the yield to maturity of a defaultable bond is not equal to the expected return of investing in the bond.* The promised cash flows used to determine the yield to maturity are always higher than the expected cash flows investors use to calculate the expected return. As a result, the yield to maturity will always be higher than the expected return of investing in the bond. *Moreover, while a higher yield to maturity may imply a higher expected return (associated with a bond that is risky), this does not imply the actual return earned by investors is higher. In the case of GM, the actual return to bondholders was substantially less than both the promised yield and the expected return when investors bought the bonds in 2007, as GM filed for bankruptcy on June 1, 2009.*

→ Investment grade bond - low credit risk

Bond Ratings

→ Junk bond - high risk, high maturity

The probability of default clearly affects the price you are willing to pay for a corporate bond. How do you assess a firm's likelihood of default? Several companies rate the creditworthiness of bonds and make this information available to investors. By consulting these ratings, investors can assess the creditworthiness of a particular bond issue. The ratings therefore encourage widespread investor participation and relatively liquid markets. The three best-known bond rating companies in Canada are the Dominion Bond Rating Service (DBRS), a privately held Canadian firm; Standard & Poor's (which acquired the Canadian Bond Rating Service); and Moody's Investors Service. Table 6.5 summarizes the equivalent ratings classes each company uses and indicates their meanings. Going back to Table 6.4, you can see the bond ratings from DBRS for each of the bonds presented; notice how the higher-rated bonds have lower YTMs and lower credit spreads; this is because they are judged to have a lower probability of default.

investment-grade bonds Bonds in the top four categories of creditworthiness, with a low risk of default.

speculative bonds (junk bonds or **high-yield bonds)** Bonds in one of the bottom five categories of creditworthiness (below investment grade) that have a high risk of default.

Bonds in the top four categories are often referred to as **investment-grade bonds** because of their low default risk. Bonds in the bottom five categories are often called **speculative bonds (junk bonds** or **high-yield bonds)**, because the likelihood of their default is high and so they promise higher yields. The rating depends on the risk of bankruptcy, as well as the bondholders' ability to lay claim to the firm's assets in the event of such a bankruptcy. Thus, debt issues with a low-priority claim in bankruptcy

TABLE 6.5 Bond Ratings in Canada

Dominion Bond Rating Service (DBRS)	Moody's	Standard & Poor's	Description (Moody's)
Investment-Grade Debt			
AAA	Aaa	AAA	Judged to be of the best quality. They carry the smallest degree of investment risk and are generally referred to as "gilt edged." Interest payments are protected by a large or an exceptionally stable margin, and principal is secure. While the various protective elements are likely to change, such changes as can be visualized are most unlikely to impair the fundamentally strong position of such issues.
AA	Aa	AA	Judged to be of high quality by all standards. Together with the AAA group, they constitute what are generally known as high-grade bonds. They are rated lower than the best bonds because margins of protection may not be as large as in AAA securities, or fluctuation of protective elements may be of greater amplitude, or there may be other elements present that make the long-term risk appear somewhat larger than for the AAA securities.
A	A	A	Possess many favourable investment attributes and are considered as upper-medium-grade obligations. Factors giving security to principal and interest are considered adequate, but elements may be present that suggest a susceptibility to impairment some time in the future.
BBB	Baa	BBB	Are considered as medium-grade obligations (i.e., they are neither highly protected nor poorly secured). Interest payments and principal security appear adequate for the present, but certain protective elements may be lacking or may be characteristically unreliable over any great length of time. Such bonds lack outstanding investment characteristics and, in fact, have speculative characteristics as well.
Speculative Bonds			
BB	Ba	BB	Judged to have speculative elements; their future cannot be considered as well assured. Often the protection of interest and principal payments may be very moderate and thereby not well safeguarded during both good and bad times over the future. Uncertainty of position characterizes bonds in this class.
B	B	B	Generally lack characteristics of the desirable investment. Assurance of interest and principal payments of maintenance of other terms of the contract over any long period of time may be small.
CCC	Caa	CCC	Are of poor standing. Such issues may be in default, or there may be present elements of danger with respect to principal or interest.
CC	Ca	CC	Are speculative in a high degree. Such issues are often in default or have other marked shortcomings.
C, D	C	C, D	Lowest-rated class of bonds, and issues so rated can be regarded as having extremely poor prospects of ever attaining any real investment standing.

Sources: Based on Moody's, DBRS, TD Waterhouse Canada Inc.

strip bonds Coupon-paying bonds purchased by a financial intermediary where the claims to the coupon payments have been separated and sold to other investors and the remaining "stripped" bonds available to be purchased by investors just consist of the claim to the final face value (zero-coupon) payment.

default spread or **credit spread** The difference between the risk-free interest rate on Government of Canada bonds and the interest rates on all other loans. The magnitude of the credit spread will depend on investors' assessment of the likelihood that a particular bond issuer will default.

will have a lower rating than issues from the same company that have a high priority in bankruptcy or that are backed by a specific asset, such as a building or a plant.

Corporate and Provincial Yield Curves

Just as we can construct a yield curve from risk-free Government of Canada securities, we can plot a similar yield curve for provincial and corporate bonds. Ideally, **strip bonds** should be used to compare yields across different maturities because, without coupons, differences in coupon rates do not influence the yield calculation. See Appendix B, Example 6B.1 for how bonds with different coupon rates will have different yields. Since strip bond data was not available, Figure 6.5 shows yield curves for coupon-paying bonds. Included is Bell Canada Enterprises (BCE) debt, which has a BBB-high DBRS credit rating for senior unsecured corporate debentures. Figure 6.5 also shows yield curves for Province of British Columbia and Government of Canada bonds. We refer to the difference between the yields of the various bonds and the Government of Canada yields as the **default spread** or **credit spread**. Credit spreads fluctuate as investors' perceptions regarding the probability of default change. Note that the credit spread is higher for bonds with lower ratings and, therefore, a greater likelihood of default. The British Columbia bonds have a positive credit spread of between 0.15%

FIGURE 6.5 Corporate and Provincial Yield Curves for Feb. 16, 2017

This figure shows the coupon-paying yield curve for bonds from the Government of Canada, the province of British Columbia, and Bell Canada on February 16, 2017. Note how the yield to maturity is higher for lower-rated bonds, which have a higher probability of default.

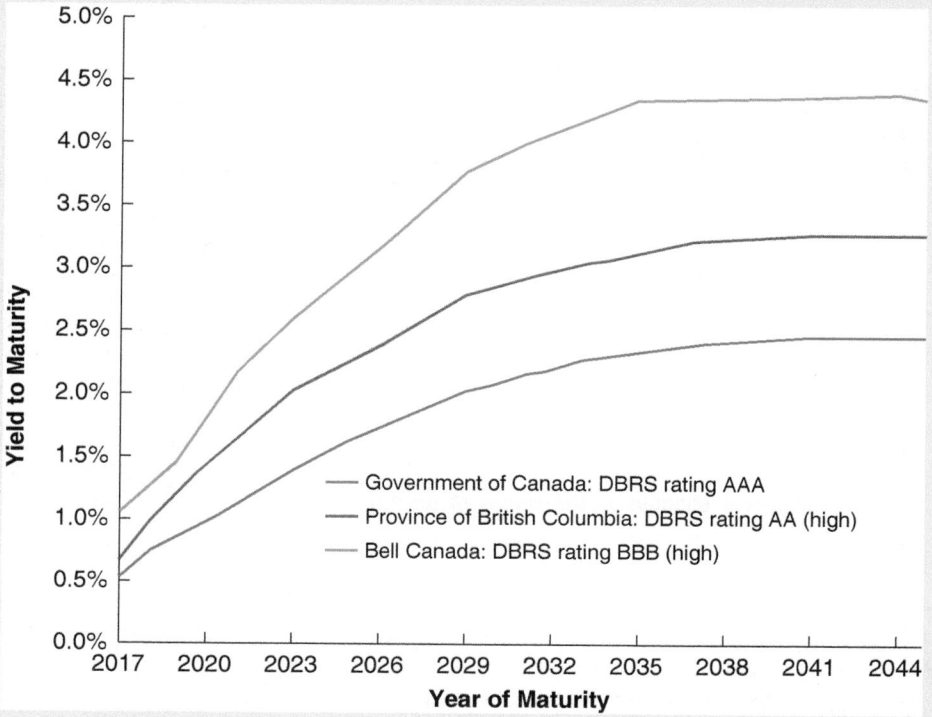

Sources: Based on www.moodys.com, www.dbrs.com, TD Waterhouse Canada Inc., and author's calculations. Note: missing data is interpolated

INTERVIEW WITH LISA BLACK

Lisa Black

Lisa Black is managing director at Teachers Insurance and Annuity Association (TIAA-CREF), a major financial services company. A chartered financial analyst, she oversees a variety of fixed income funds, including money market, intermediate bond, high-yield, emerging market debt, and inflation-linked bond funds.

Q When many people think about the financial markets, they picture the equity markets. How big and how active are the bond markets compared to the equity markets?

A The dollar volume of bonds traded daily is about 10 times that of equity markets. For example, a single $15 billion issue of 10-year U.S. Treasury bonds will sell in one day. The market value of the Barclays Capital U.S. Universal Bond Index of dollar-denominated debt as of June 30, 2009, was $13.8 trillion, with the U.S. Aggregate Index (investment-grade debt) accounting for almost 90%. It includes treasuries, agencies, corporate bonds, and mortgage-backed securities. Other major sectors of the Universal Index include corporate high-yield bonds, Eurodollar bonds, emerging markets, and private placements.

Q How do the bond markets operate?

A Firms and governments turn to bond markets when they need to borrow money to fund new construction projects, to finance acquisitions, and to serve general corporate purposes. On the other side, institutions like TIAA-CREF, endowments, and foundations have funds to invest. Investment bankers serve as intermediaries, matching borrowers with creditors in terms of maturity needs and risk appetite. Because we provide annuities for professors, for example, we invest money for longer periods of time than an insurance company that needs funds to pay claims. In the institutional world, bond funds typically trade in blocks of bonds ranging from $5 million to $50 million at a time.

Q What drives changes in the values of government bonds?

A The simple answer is that when interest rates rise, bond prices fall. The key is to dig below that reality to see why interest rates rise and fall. A major factor is investors' expectations for inflation and economic growth. Interest rates generally rise when the expectation is that growth will accelerate, because inflation won't be far behind. During the 2008–09 recession, interest rates dropped as the U.S. Federal Reserve and other central banks around the world injected liquidity into the system. There was also a flight to quality after the bankruptcy of Lehman Brothers. The value of The Reserve Fund (a U.S. money market fund) fell drastically as its holdings of about $785 million of Lehman's short-term debt securities became all but worthless. Worried retail and institutional investors sold their money market funds and purchased U.S. Treasury bills and notes to protect their principal. With increased demand, interest rates on risk-free U.S. Treasury securities fell sharply. At one point T-bills even had a negative yield.

Q What impact did the 2008–09 financial crisis have on the bond market? What changes do you anticipate going forward as a result?

A While the effects of the crisis on equity markets have been widely discussed, the effects on the bond market have been just as profound. Particularly noteworthy is the role governments and central bankers have played—and likely will continue to play—to stabilize financial institutions deemed too big or important to fail. The U.S. Federal Reserve introduced an unprecedented number of stimulus programs to unfreeze credit markets, including programs to guarantee money funds. The challenge will be how and when the various support programs and financial infusions will end and/or be paid back. In addition, the rating agencies' role and ratings methodologies will likely be subject to greater scrutiny, both from regulators and investors.

In the corporate sector, many borrowers—the automotive industries, for example—could not raise debt financing during the crisis. Credit spreads widened dramatically as investors shunned even AAA- and AA-rated credits. Major institutional investors sat on the sidelines for several months, and the corporate bond new issue market was essentially nonexistent. Not until federal governments announced programs to increase liquidity did institutional investors re-enter the market, first buying only the highest-credit-quality instruments, such as first mortgage bonds issued by utilities and government-guaranteed mortgage-backed securities. Investors then began to move down the credit quality chain, selectively focusing on issuers that could weather an economic downtown.

DISCUSSION QUESTIONS

1. In what ways might you as a financial manager make use of the information in interest rate changes and the yield curve?
2. How do you think financial managers will prepare the companies for future credit market crises?

and 0.81% (as of February 16, 2017), but BCE has a larger credit spread ranging from 0.53% to 1.9%. The credit spreads are higher for longer terms to maturity. You might wonder why there would be any credit spread for British Columbia, as it seems unimaginable that a province would default on its debt. In fact, the province with the lowest current credit spread, Alberta, is also the only province to have defaulted on its debt; this occurred in 1936.

As we indicated at the beginning of this chapter, the bond market, while less well known than the stock markets, is large and important. Because debt is a substantial part of the financing of most corporations, a financial manager needs to understand bonds and how investors price the company's bonds. In this chapter, we have introduced you to the major types of bonds, how bonds repay investors, and how bonds are priced. In Chapter 15, we will discuss the bond markets further, including the process a firm goes through to issue debt.

EXAMPLE 6.10 Credit Spreads and Bond Prices

PROBLEM

Your firm has a credit rating of AA. You notice that the credit spread for five-year maturity AA-rated debt is 90 basis points (0.90%). Your firm's five-year debt has a coupon rate of 5%. You see that new five-year Government of Canada bonds are being issued at par with a coupon rate of 4.5%. What should the price of your outstanding five-year bonds be?

SOLUTION

Plan

If the credit spread is 90 basis points, then the YTM on your debt should be the YTM on similar Government of Canada bonds plus 0.9%. The fact that new five-year Government of Canada bonds are being issued at par with coupons of 4.5% means that, with a coupon rate of 4.5%, these bonds are selling for \$100 per \$100 face value. Thus, their YTM is 4.5% and your debt's YTM should be 4.5% + 0.9% = 5.4%. The cash flows on your bonds are \$5 per year for every \$100 face value, paid as \$2.50 every six months (for a total of 10 coupon payments). The implied effective six-month rate corresponding to a 5.4% yield (APR with semi-annual compounding) is 5.4%/2 = 2.7%. Armed with this information, you can use Equation 6.4 to compute the price of your bonds.

Execute

$$2.50 \times \frac{1}{0.027}\left(1 - \frac{1}{1.027^{10}}\right) + \frac{100}{1.027^{10}} = \$98.27$$

Evaluate

Your bonds offer a higher coupon (5% vs. 4.5%) than Government of Canada bonds of the same maturity but sell for a lower price (\$98.27 vs. \$100). The reason is the credit spread. Your firm's higher probability of default leads investors to demand a higher YTM on your debt. To provide a higher YTM, the purchase price for the debt must be lower. If your debt paid a 5.4% coupon rate, it would sell at \$100, the same as the Government of Canada bonds. But to get that price, you would have to offer coupons that are 90 basis points higher than those on the Government of Canada bonds—exactly enough to offset the credit spread.

THE CREDIT CRISIS AND BOND YIELDS

The financial crisis that engulfed the world's economies in 2008 originated as a credit crisis that first emerged in August 2007. At that time, problems in the U.S. mortgage market had led to the bankruptcy of several large mortgage lenders there. The default of these firms, and the downgrading of much of the short-term commercial paper and long-term bonds backed by mortgages these firms had made, caused many investors to reassess the risk of commercial paper, bankers' acceptances, and other bonds in their portfolios.[5] In Canada and around the world, fear spread that debt securities might be exposed to the same problem, as it was not clear whether the debt issuers held claims to U.S. mortgages as part of their assets. As perceptions of risk increased, and investors attempted to move into safer government securities, the prices of corporate debt fell, and so their credit spreads rose relative to riskless debt (such as Government of Canada treasury bills). Figure 6.6 shows how the credit spreads of bankers' acceptances (the highest-rated short-term corporate debt) rose dramatically over this time period. The normal credit spread prior to the crisis was less than 20 basis points (or 0.2%); credit spreads jumped dramatically to over 150 basis points during the crisis and peaked at 269 basis points in October of 2008. The effect was even more pronounced for commercial paper and long-term corporate debt. In some cases, it became impossible for corporations to borrow new money or to refinance current obligations coming due. This problem with borrowing costs and feasibility made it extremely difficult for firms to raise the capital needed for new investment and, in the case of some firms that were not able to refinance, led to bankruptcy. The net result was a dramatic slowing in economic growth that turned into an economic contraction in most countries around the world. The decline in these credit spreads in early 2009 (facilitated by central banks like the U.S. Federal Reserve and the Bank of Canada keeping their lending rates low and buying corporate debt) was viewed by many people as an important first step in mitigating the ongoing impact of the financial crisis on the rest of the economy. You can see lingering effects of the credit crisis as credit spreads seemed to have normalized above 30 basis points compared to less than 20 basis points prior to the crisis.

FIGURE 6.6 **Credit Spreads on Three-Month Canadian Bankers' Acceptances: Weekly (Wednesday) Series: 2004-04-14 to 2018-05-02**

Credit spreads before, during, and after the financial crisis

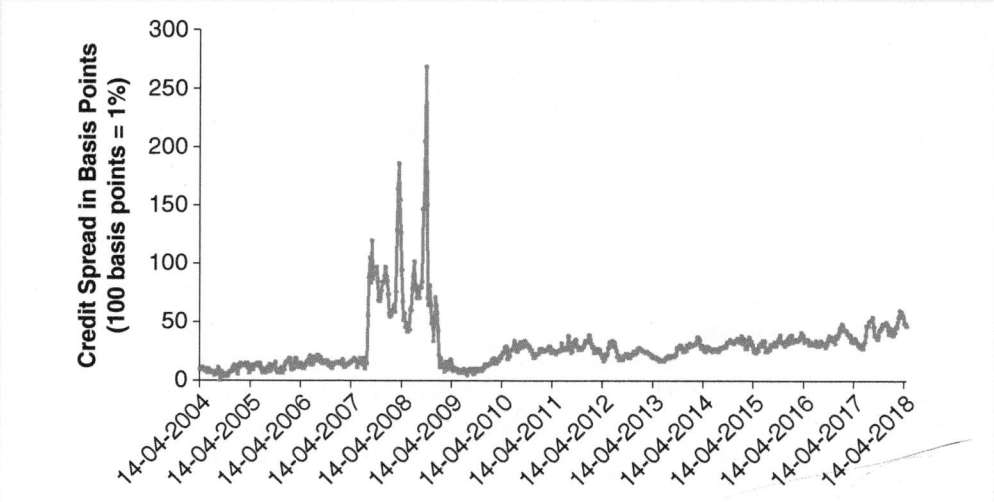

[5]Commercial paper is short-term debt usually issued by large firms with high credit ratings. Bankers' acceptances are commercial paper guaranteed by a bank.

CONCEPT CHECK

9. What is a junk bond?

10. How will the yield to maturity of a bond vary with the bond's risk of default?

MyLab Finance

Here is what you should know after reading this chapter. MyLab™ Finance will help you identify what you know, and where to go when you need to practice.

KEY POINTS AND EQUATIONS	TERMS	ONLINE PRACTICE OPPORTUNITIES
6.1 Bond Terminology ■ Bonds pay both coupon and principal, or face value, payments to investors. By convention, the coupon rate of a bond is the percentage of face value paid out as coupons each year; thus, each coupon payment, CPN, is $CPN = \frac{\text{Coupon Rate} \times \text{Face Value}}{\text{Number of Coupon Payments per Year}}$ (6.1)	bond indenture, p. 163 coupon rate, p. 163 coupons, p. 163 face value or par value, p. 163 maturity date, p. 163 term, p. 163	MyLab Study Plan 6.1
6.2 Zero-Coupon Bonds ■ Zero-coupon bonds make no coupon payments, so investors receive only the bond's face value. ■ The rate of return of a bond is called its yield to maturity (or yield). The yield to maturity of a bond is the discount rate that sets the present value of the promised bond payments equal to the current market price of the bond. ■ The price for a zero-coupon bond is given by $P = \frac{FV}{(1 + YTM_n)^n}$ (6.2) ■ The yield to maturity for a zero-coupon bond is given by $1 + YTM_n = \left(\frac{FV}{P}\right)^{1/n}$ (6.3) ■ The risk-free interest rate for an investment until date n equals the yield to maturity of a risk-free zero-coupon bond that matures on date n. A plot of these rates against maturity is called the zero-coupon yield curve.	discount, p. 164 pure discount bonds, p. 164 spot interest rates, p. 166 treasury bills, p. 164 yield to maturity (*YTM*), p. 165 zero-coupon bond, p. 164 zero-coupon yield curve, p. 166	MyLab Study Plan 6.2

KEY POINTS AND EQUATIONS	TERMS	ONLINE PRACTICE OPPORTUNITIES
6.3 Coupon Bonds ■ The yield to maturity for a coupon bond (expressed as an effective rate compounded over the same time period as the time between coupon payments) is the discount rate, *YTMn*, that equates the present value of the bond's future cash flows with its price: $P = CPN \times \frac{1}{YTM_n}\left(1 - \frac{1}{(1 + YTM_n)^n}\right) + \frac{FV}{(1 + YTM_n)^n}$ (6.4)	coupon bonds, p. 169 Government of Canada bonds, p. 169	MyLab Study Plan 6.3
6.4 Why Bond Prices Change ■ A bond will trade at a premium if its coupon rate exceeds its yield to maturity. It will trade at a discount if its coupon rate is less than its yield to maturity. If a bond's coupon rate equals its yield to maturity, it trades at par. ■ As a bond approaches maturity, the price of the bond approaches its face value. ■ Bond prices change as interest rates change. When interest rates rise, bond prices fall, and vice versa. ■ Long-term zero-coupon bonds are more sensitive to changes in interest rates than are short-term zero-coupon bonds. ■ Bonds with low coupon rates are more sensitive to changes in interest rates than are bonds with similar maturity and high coupon rates.	par, p. 173 premium, p. 173	MyLab Study Plan 6.4 Interactive Interest Rate Sensitivity Analysis
6.5 Corporate Bonds ■ When a bond issuer does not make a bond payment in full, the issuer has defaulted. ■ The risk that default can occur is called default or credit risk. Government of Canada securities are free of default risk. ■ The expected return of a corporate bond, which is the firm's debt cost of capital, equals the risk-free rate of interest plus a risk premium. The expected return is less than the bond's yield to maturity, because the yield to maturity of a bond is calculated using the promised cash flows, not the expected cash flows. ■ Bond ratings summarize the creditworthiness of bonds for investors. ■ The difference between yields on Government of Canada securities and yields on corporate bonds is called the credit spread or default spread. The credit spread compensates investors for the difference between promised and expected cash flows and for the risk of default.	corporate bonds, p. 182 credit risk, p. 182 default spread or credit spread, p. 185 investment-grade bonds, p. 183 speculative bonds (junk bonds or high-yield bonds), p. 183 strip bonds, p. 185	MyLab Study Plan 6.5

REVIEW QUESTIONS

1. How is a bond like a loan?
2. How does an investor receive a return from buying a bond?
3. How is yield to maturity related to the concept of rate of return?
4. Does a bond's yield to maturity determine its price, or does the price determine the yield to maturity?
5. Explain why the yield of a bond that trades at a discount exceeds the bond's coupon rate.
6. Explain the relationship between interest rates and bond prices.
7. Why are longer-term bonds more sensitive to changes in interest rates than shorter-term bonds?
8. Explain why the expected return of a corporate bond does not equal its yield to maturity.

PROBLEMS

All problems in this chapter are available in MyLabFinance. An asterisk (*) indicates problems with a higher level of difficulty.

Bond Terminology

1. Consider a 10-year Government of Canada bond with a face value of $1000 that has a coupon rate of 5.5%, with semi-annual payments.
   a. What is the coupon payment for this bond?
   b. Draw the cash flows for the bond on a timeline.
2. Assume that a bond will make payments every six months as shown on the following timeline (using six-month periods):

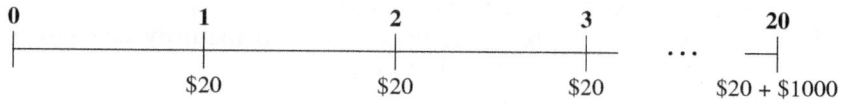

   a. What is the maturity of the bond (in years)?
   b. What is the coupon rate (as a percentage)?
   c. What is the face value?

Zero-Coupon Bonds

3. Your company wants to raise $10 million by issuing 20-year zero-coupon bonds. If the yield to maturity on the bonds will be 6% (EAR), what total face value amount of bonds must you issue? 10 mill

4. The following table summarizes prices of various default-free zero-coupon bonds (expressed as a percentage of the face value):

Maturity (years)	1	2	3	4	5
Price (per $100 face value)	$95.51	$91.05	$86.38	$81.65	$76.51

a. Compute the yield to maturity for each bond.
b. Plot the zero-coupon yield curve (for the first five years).
c. Is the yield curve upward sloping, downward sloping, or flat?

Use the following information for Problems 5 to 7. The current zero-coupon yield curve for risk-free Government of Canada bonds is as follows:

Maturity (years)	1	2	3	4	5
YTM	5%	5.5%	5.75%	5.95%	6.05%

5. What is the price per $100 face value of a two-year, zero-coupon, risk-free bond?

6. What is the price per $100 face value of a four-year, zero-coupon, risk-free bond?

7. What is the risk-free interest rate for a five-year maturity?

Coupon Bonds

8. For each of the following pairs of Government of Canada bonds, identify which will have the higher price as a percentage of the face value.
a. A three-year zero-coupon bond or a five-year zero-coupon bond
b. A three-year zero-coupon bond or a three-year 4% coupon bond
c. A two-year 5% coupon bond or a two-year 6% coupon bond

9. The yield to maturity of a $1000 bond with a 7% coupon rate, semi-annual coupons, and two years to maturity is 7.6% APR, compounded semi-annually. What must its price be?

10. Assume the current yield curve shows that the spot rates for six months, one year, and one and a half years are 1%, 1.1%, and 1.3%, respectively, all quoted as semi-annually compounded APRs. What is the price of a $1000 par, 4% coupon bond maturing in one and a half years? (The next coupon is exactly six months from now.)

PROJECT **11.** Suppose a 10-year, $1000 bond with an 8% coupon rate and semi-annual coupons is trading for a price of $1034.74.
a. What is the bond's yield to maturity (expressed as an APR with semi-annual compounding)?
b. If the bond's yield to maturity changes to 9% APR, what will the bond's price be?

12. Suppose a five-year, $1000 bond with annual coupons has a price of $900 and a yield to maturity of 6%. What is the bond's coupon rate?

Why Bond Prices Change

13. The prices of several bonds with face values of $1000 are summarized in the following table:

	Discount	P	P	Par
Bond	A	B	C	D
Price	$972.50	$1040.75	$1150.00	$1000.00

For each bond, state whether it trades at a discount, at par, or at a premium.

14. You have purchased a 10% coupon bond for $1040. What will happen to the bond's price if market interest rates rise?

15. Suppose a seven-year, $1000 bond with an 8% coupon rate and semi-annual coupons is trading with a yield to maturity of 6.75%.

a. Is this bond currently trading at a discount, at par, or at a premium? Explain.

b. If the yield to maturity of the bond rises to 7.00% (APR with semi-annual compounding), what price will the bond trade for?

Suppose that General Motors Acceptance Corporation issued a bond with 10 years until maturity, a face value of $1000, and a coupon rate of 7% (annual payments). The yield to maturity on this bond when it was issued was 6%. Use this information for Problems 16 to 18.

PROJECT **16.** What was the price of this bond when it was issued?

PROJECT **17.** Assuming the yield to maturity remains constant, what is the price of the bond immediately before it makes its first coupon payment?

PROJECT **18.** Assuming the yield to maturity remains constant, what is the price of the bond immediately after it makes its first coupon payment?

19. Your company currently has 6% coupon-rate bonds (coupons are paid semi-annually) with 10 years to maturity and a price of $1078. If you want to issue new 10-year coupon bonds at par, what coupon rate do you need to set?

***20.** Suppose you purchase a 10-year bond with 6% annual coupons. You hold the bond for four years, and sell it immediately after receiving the fourth coupon. If the bond's yield to maturity was 5% when you purchased and sold the bond,

a. What cash flows will you pay and receive from your investment in the bond per $100 face value?

b. What is the rate of return of your investment?

Consider the following bonds for Problems 21 and 22:

Bond	Coupon Rate (annual payments)	Maturity (years)
A	0%	15
B	0%	10
C	4%	15
D	8%	10

PROJECT **21.** What is the percentage change in the price of each bond if its yield to maturity falls from 6% to 5%?

22. Which of the bonds A to D is most sensitive to a 1% drop in interest rates from 6% to 5% and why? Which bond is least sensitive? Provide an intuitive explanation for your answer.

PROJECT **23.** Suppose you purchase a 30-year zero-coupon bond with a yield to maturity of 6%. You hold the bond for five years before selling it.

a. If the bond's yield to maturity is 6% when you sell it, what is the rate of return of your investment?

b. If the bond's yield to maturity is 7% when you sell it, what is the rate of return of your investment?

c. If the bond's yield to maturity is 5% when you sell it, what is the rate of return of your investment?

d. Even if a bond has no chance of default, is your investment risk free if you plan to sell it before it matures? Explain.

Corporate Bonds

24. The following table summarizes the yields to maturity on several one-year zero-coupon securities:

Security	Yield (%)
Government of Canada	3.1
AAA corporate	3.2
BBB corporate	4.2
B corporate	4.9

a. What is the price (expressed as a percentage of the face value) of a one-year zero-coupon corporate bond with an AAA rating?
b. What is the credit spread on AAA-rated corporate bonds?
c. What is the credit spread on B-rated corporate bonds?
d. How does the credit spread change with the bond rating? Why?

25. Andrew Industries is contemplating issuing a 30-year bond with a coupon rate of 7% (annual coupon payments) and a face value of $1000. Andrew believes it can get a rating of A from Standard & Poor's. However, due to recent financial difficulties at the company, Standard & Poor's is warning that it may downgrade Andrew Industries bonds to BBB. Yields on A-rated long-term bonds are currently 6.5%, and yields on BBB-rated bonds are 6.9%.
a. What is the price of the bond if Andrew maintains the A rating for the bond issue?
b. What will the price of the bond be if it is downgraded?

26. HMK Enterprises would like to raise $10 million to invest in capital expenditures. The company plans to issue five-year bonds with a face value of $1000 and a coupon rate of 6.5% (annual payments). The following table summarizes the yield to maturity for five-year (annual-payment) coupon corporate bonds of various ratings:

Rating	AAA	AA	A	BBB	BB
YTM	6.20%	6.30%	6.50%	6.90%	7.50%

a. Assuming the bonds will be rated AA, what will the price of the bonds be?
b. How much of the total principal amount of these bonds must HMK issue to raise $10 million today, assuming the bonds are AA rated? (Because HMK cannot issue a fraction of a bond, assume that all fractions are rounded to the nearest whole number.)
c. What must the rating of the bonds be for them to sell at par?
d. Suppose that when the bonds are issued, the price of each bond is $959.54. What is the likely rating of the bonds? Are they junk bonds?

27. A BBB-rated corporate bond has a yield to maturity of 8.2%. A U.S. Treasury security has a yield to maturity of 6.5%. These yields are quoted as APRs with semi-annual compounding. Both bonds pay semi-annual coupons at a rate of 7% and have five years to maturity.
a. What is the price (expressed as a percentage of the face value) of the Treasury bond?
b. What is the price (expressed as a percentage of the face value) of the BBB-rated corporate bond?
c. What is the credit spread on the BBB bonds?

28. Your firm has a credit rating of A. You notice that the credit spread for five-year maturity A debt is 85 basis points (0.85%). Your firm's five-year debt has semi-annual coupons and a coupon rate of 6%. You see that new five-year Government of Canada bonds are being issued with a YTM of 2.0%. What should the price of your outstanding five-year bonds be?

DATA CASE

You are an intern with Ford Motor Company in its corporate finance division. The firm is planning to issue $50 million of 12% annual coupon bonds with a 10-year maturity. The firm anticipates an increase in its bond rating. Your boss wants you to determine the gain in the proceeds of the new issue if it is rated above the firm's current bond rating. To prepare this information, you will have to determine Ford's current debt rating and the yield curve for its particular rating.

1. Begin by finding the current U.S. Treasury yield curve. At the U.S. Treasury website (www.treas.gov), search using the term "yield curve" and select "US Treasury—Daily Treasury Yield Curve." *Beware*: There will probably be two links with the same title. Look at the description below the link and select the one that does *not* say "Real Yield"; you want the nominal rates. Copy the table into an Excel file.
2. Find the current yield spreads for the various bond ratings. Unfortunately, the current spreads are available only for a fee, so you will use old ones. Go to Bonds-Online (www.bondsonline.com) and click on "Today's Market." Next, click on "US Corporate Bond Spreads." Copy this table to the Excel file into which you copied the U.S. Treasury yields.
3. Find the current bond rating for Ford Motor Co. Go to Standard & Poor's website (www.standardandpoors.com). Select your country. Look for the "Find a Rating" box under "Ratings" and enter "Ford Motor Co." and select "Ford Motor Co." from the list it returns. At this point you will have to register (free of charge) or enter the username and password provided by your instructor. Use the issuer credit rating for "local long term."
4. Return to Excel and create a timeline with the cash flows and discount rates you will need to value the new bond issue.
   - **a.** To create the required spot rates for Ford's issue, add the appropriate spread to the treasury yield of the same maturity.
   - **b.** The yield curve and spread rates you have found do not cover every year that you will need for the new bonds. Specifically, you do not have yields or spreads for 4-, 6-, 8-, and 9-year maturities. Fill these in by linearly interpolating the given yields and spreads. For example, the 4-year spot rate and spread will be the average of the 3- and 5-year rates. The 6-year rate and spread will be the average of the 5- and 7-year rates. For years 8 and 9, you will have to spread the difference between years 7 and 10 across the 2 years.
   - **c.** To compute the spot rates for Ford's current debt rating, add the yield spread to the treasury rate for each maturity. However, note that the spread is in basis points, which are 1/100th of a percentage point.
   - **d.** Compute the cash flows that would be paid to bondholders each year and add them to the timeline.
5. Use the spot rates to calculate the present value of each cash flow paid to the bondholders.
6. Compute the issue price of the bond and its initial yield to maturity.
7. Repeat steps 4 to 6 based on the assumption that Ford is able to raise its bond rating by one level. Compute the new yield based on the higher rating and the new bond price that would result.
8. Compute the additional cash proceeds that could be raised from the issue if the rating were improved.

CHAPTER 6 APPENDIX A SOLVING FOR THE YIELD TO MATURITY OF A BOND USING A FINANCIAL CALCULATOR

You are looking to purchase a three-year, $1000 par, 10% annual coupon bond. Payments begin one year from now in. The price of the bond is $1074.51 per $1000 par value. What is the yield to maturity of the bond? [answer: 7.15%]

HP-10BII

[ ] [C]	Press [Orange Shift] and then the [C] button to clear all previous entries.
[3] [N]	Enter the Number of periods.
[1] [0] [0] [PMT]	Enter the payment amount per period.
[1] [0] [0] [0] [FV]	Enter the par value of the bond you will receive in year 3.
[1] [0] [7] [4] [•] [5] [1] [+/−] [PV]	Enter present value or price of the bond you solved for earlier.
[I/YR]	Solves for the yield to maturity.

TI-BAII Plus Professional

[2ND] [FV]	Press [2ND] and then the [FV] button to clear all previous entries.
[3] [N]	Enter the Number of periods.
[1] [0] [0] [PMT]	Enter the payment amount per period.
[1] [0] [0] [0] [FV]	Enter the par value of the bond you will receive in year 3.
[1] [0] [7] [4] [•] [5] [1] [+/−] [PV]	Enter present value or price of the bond you solved for earlier.
[CPT] [I/Y]	Solves for the yield to maturity.

Thus far, we have focused on the relationship between the price of an individual bond and its yield to maturity. In this section, we explore the relationship between the prices and yields of different bonds. In Chapter 3, we saw how market forces keep the same asset from having two prices at the same time; we call this the Law of One Price. Using the Law of One Price, we show that, given the spot interest rates, which are the yields of default-free zero-coupon bonds, we can determine the price and yield of any other default-free bond. As a result, the yield curve provides sufficient information to evaluate all such bonds.

Valuing a Coupon Bond with Zero-Coupon Prices

We begin with the observation that it is possible to replicate the cash flows of a coupon bond using zero-coupon bonds. Therefore, we can use the Valuation Principle's Law of One Price to compute the price of a coupon bond from the prices of zero-coupon bonds. For example, we can replicate a three-year, $1000 bond that pays 10% annual coupons using three zero-coupon bonds as follows:

	0	1	2	3
Coupon Bond:		$100	$100	$1100
1-year zero:		$100		
2-year zero:			$100	
3-year zero:				$1100
Zero-Coupon Bond portfolio:		$100	$100	$1100

We match each coupon payment to a zero-coupon bond with a face value equal to the coupon payment and a term equal to the time remaining to the coupon date. Similarly, we match the final bond payment (final coupon plus return of face value) in three years to a three-year zero-coupon bond with a corresponding face value of $1100. Because the coupon bond cash flows are identical to the cash flows of the portfolio of zero-coupon bonds, the Law of One Price states that the price of the portfolio of zero-coupon bonds must be the same as the price of the coupon bond.

To illustrate, assume that current zero-coupon bond yields and prices are as shown in Table 6B.1. (They are the same as in Example 6B.1.)

TABLE 6B.1 Yields and Prices (per $100 Face Value) for Zero-Coupon Bonds

Maturity	1 Year	2 Years	3 Years	4 Years
YTM	3.50%	4.00%	4.50%	4.75%
Price	$96.62	$92.46	$87.63	$83.06

We can calculate the cost of the zero-coupon bond portfolio that replicates the three-year coupon bond as follows:

Zero-Coupon Bond	Face Value Required	Cost
1 Year	100	96.62
2 Years	100	92.46
3 Years	1100	$11 \times 87.63 = 963.93$
		Total Cost: $1153.00

By the Law of One Price, the three-year coupon bond must trade for a price of $1153. If the price of the coupon bond were higher, you could earn an arbitrage profit by selling the coupon bond and buying the zero-coupon bond portfolio. If the price of the coupon bond were lower, you could earn an arbitrage profit by buying the coupon bond and selling the zero-coupon bonds.

Valuing a Coupon Bond Using Zero-Coupon Yields

To this point, we have used the zero-coupon bond *prices* to derive the price of the coupon bond. Alternatively, we can use the zero-coupon bond *yields*. Recall that the yield to maturity of a zero-coupon bond is the competitive market interest rate for a risk-free investment with a term equal to the term of the zero-coupon bond. Since the cash flows of the bond are its coupon payments and face value repayment, the price of a coupon bond must equal the present value of its coupon payments and face value discounted at the competitive market interest rates (see Equation 5.7 in Chapter 5):

Price of a Coupon Bond

$$\begin{aligned} P &= PV\,(\text{Bond Cash Flows}) \\ &= \frac{CPN}{1 + YTM_1} + \frac{CPN}{(1 + YTM_2)^2} + \cdots + \frac{CPN + FV}{(1 + YTM_n)^n} \end{aligned} \tag{6B.1}$$

where CPN is the bond coupon payment, YTM_n is the yield to maturity of a *zero-coupon* bond that matures at the same time as the nth coupon payment, and FV is the face value of the bond. For the three-year, $1000 bond with 10% annual coupons considered earlier, we can use Equation 6B.1 to calculate its price using the zero-coupon yields in Table 6B.1:

$$P = \frac{100}{1.035} + \frac{100}{1.04^2} + \frac{100 + 1000}{1.045^3} = \$1153$$

This price is identical to the price we computed earlier by replicating the bond. Thus, we can determine the no-arbitrage price of a coupon bond by discounting its cash flows using the zero-coupon yields. In other words, the information in the zero-coupon yield curve is sufficient to price all other risk-free bonds.

Coupon Bond Yields

Given the yields for zero-coupon bonds, we can use Equation 6B.1 to price a coupon bond. In Section 6.1, we saw how to compute the yield to maturity of a coupon bond from its price. Combining these results, we can determine the relationship between the yields of zero-coupon bonds and coupon-paying bonds.

Consider again the three-year, $1000 bond with 10% annual coupons. Given the zero-coupon yields in Table 6B.1, we calculate a price for this bond of $1153. From Equation 6.4, the yield to maturity of this bond is the rate YTM_3 that satisfies

$$P = 1153 = \frac{100}{(1 + YTM_3)} + \frac{100}{(1 + YTM_3)^2} + \frac{100 + 100}{(1 + YTM_3)^3}$$

We can solve for the yield by using a financial calculator:

	N	I/Y	PV	PMT	FV
Given:	3		−1153	100	1000
Solve for:		4.44			

Excel Formula: = *RATE(NPER,PMT,PV,FV)* = *RATE*(3,100,−1153,1000)

Therefore, the yield to maturity of the bond is 4.44%. We can check this result directly as follows:

$$P = \frac{100}{1.0444} + \frac{100}{1.0444^2} + \frac{100 + 1000}{1.0444^3} = \$1153$$

Because the coupon bond provides cash flows at different points in time, the yield to maturity of a coupon bond is a weighted average of the yields of the zero-coupon bonds of equal and shorter maturities. The weights depend (in a complex way) on the magnitude of the cash flows each period. In this example, the zero-coupon bonds yields were 3.5%, 4.0%, and 4.5%. For this coupon bond, most of the value in the present value calculation comes from the present value of the third cash flow, because it includes the principal, so the yield is closest to the three-year zero-coupon yield of 4.5%.

Example 6B.1 Yields on Bonds with the Same Maturity

PROBLEM

Given the following zero-coupon yields, compare the yield to maturity for a three-year zero-coupon bond; a three-year coupon bond with 4% annual coupons; and a three-year coupon bond with 10% annual coupons. All of these bonds are default free.

Maturity	1 Year	2 Years	3 Years
Zero-coupon	3.50%	4.00%	4.50%

SOLUTION

■ **Plan**

From the information provided, the yield to maturity of the three-year zero-coupon bond is 4.50%. Also, because the yields match those in Table 6B.1, we already calculated the yield to maturity for the 10% coupon bond as 4.44%. To compute the yield for the 4% coupon bond, we first need to ▶

calculate its price, which we can do using Equation 6B.1. Since the coupons are 4%, paid annually, they are $40 per year for three years. The $1000 face value will be repaid at that time. Once we have the price, we can use Equation 6.4 to compute the yield to maturity.

■ **Execute**

Using Equation 6B.1, we have

$$P = \frac{40}{1.035} + \frac{40}{1.04^2} + \frac{40 + 1000}{1.045^3} = \$986.98$$

The price of the bond with a 4% coupon is $986.98. From Equation 6.4

$$\$986.98 = \frac{40}{(1 + YTM_3)} + \frac{40}{(1 + YTM_3)^2} + \frac{40 + 1000}{(1 + YTM_3)^3}$$

We can calculate the yield to maturity using a financial calculator or spreadsheet:

	N	I/Y	PV	PMT	FV
Given:	3		−986.98	40	1000
Solve for:		**4.47**			

Excel Formula: = *RATE(NPER,PMT,PV,FV)* = *RATE*(3,40,−986.98,1000)

To summarize, for the three-year bonds considered,

Coupon Rate	0%	4%	10%
YTM_3	4.50%	4.47%	4.44%

■ **Evaluate**

Note that even though the bonds all have the same maturity, they have different yields. In fact, holding constant the maturity, the yield decreases as the coupon rate increases. We discuss why below.

Example 6B.1 shows that coupon bonds with the same maturity can have different yields depending on their coupon rates. The yield to maturity of a coupon bond is a weighted average of the yields on the zero-coupon bonds. As the coupon increases, earlier cash flows become relatively more important than later cash flows in the calculation of the present value. The shape of the yield curve keys us in on trends with the yield to maturity:

1. If the yield curve is upward sloping (as it is for the yields in Example 6B.1), the resulting yield to maturity decreases with the coupon rate of the bond.
2. When the zero-coupon yield curve is downward sloping, the yield to maturity will increase with the coupon rate.
3. With a flat yield curve, all zero-coupon and coupon-paying bonds will have the same yield, independent of their maturities and coupon rates.

Government of Canada Yield Curves

As we have shown in this section, we can use the zero-coupon yield curve to determine the price and yield to maturity of other risk-free bonds. The plot of the yields of coupon bonds of different maturities is called the coupon-paying yield curve. When Canadian bond traders refer to "the yield curve," they are often referring to the coupon-paying Government of Canada bond yield curve. As we show in Example 6B.1, two coupon-paying bonds with the same maturity may have different yields. By convention, practitioners always plot the yield of the most recently issued bonds, termed the on-the-run bonds. Using similar methods to those employed in this section, we can apply the Law of One Price to determine the zero-coupon bond yields using the coupon-paying yield curve. Thus, either type of yield curve provides enough information to value all other risk-free bonds.

Appendix on The Web

This Online Appendix is on MyLab Finance at
www.mylabfinance.com

Chapter 6 Appendix C — Interest Rate Risk Measurement: Duration

CHAPTER

7 Valuing Stocks

LEARNING OBJECTIVES

- Describe the basics of common stock, preferred stock, and stock quotes
- Value a stock as the present value of its expected future dividends
- Understand the trade-off between dividends and growth in stock valuation
- Appreciate the limitations of valuing a stock based on expected dividends
- Value a stock as the present value of either the company's total payout or its free cash flows
- Value a stock by applying common multiples based on the values of comparable firms
- Understand how information is incorporated into stock prices through competition in efficient markets
- Describe some behavioural biases that influence the way individual investors trade

NOTATION

Div_t	dividends paid in year t
EBIT	earnings before interest and taxes
EBITDA	earnings before interest, taxes, depreciation, and amortization
EPS_t	earnings per share on date t
FCF_t	free cash flow on date t
g	expected dividend growth rate
g_{FCF}	expected free cash flow growth rate
n	terminal date or forecast horizon
P_t	stock price at the end of year t
PV	present value
r_E	equity cost of capital
r_{wacc}	weighted average cost of capital
V_t	enterprise value on date t

On February 19, 2014, Sherritt International, a world leader in nickel mining and an oil & gas and power producer, announced an annual adjusted loss of 21 cents per share for its 2013 fiscal year, compared to annual profit of 35 cents per share in 2012. The fourth quarter result, a loss of

13 cents per share, was significantly worse than all analysts' expectations. Sherritt also announced that it was slashing its dividends by 77%. Sherritt's stock dropped 12% in trading on the TSX that day following the announcement and closed at a value of $3.02 per share.

How might an investor decide whether to buy or sell a stock such as Sherritt International at this price? Why would the stock suddenly be worth 12% less after the announcement of this news? What actions can Sherritt's managers take to increase the stock price?

To answer these questions, we turn to the Valuation Principle. It indicates that the price of a security should equal the present value of the expected cash flows an investor will receive from owning it. In this chapter, we apply this idea to stocks. Thus, to value a stock, we need to know the expected cash flows an investor will receive and the appropriate cost of capital with which to discount those cash flows. Both of these quantities can be challenging to estimate, and we will discuss many of the details needed to do so throughout the remainder of this text. In this chapter, we begin our study of stock valuation by identifying the relevant cash flows and developing the main tools that practitioners use to evaluate them.

Our analysis opens with a consideration of the dividends and capital gains received by investors who hold the stock for different periods, from which we develop the *dividend-discount model* of stock valuation. Next, we apply the tools to value stocks based on the free cash flows generated by the firm. Having developed these stock valuation methods based on discounted cash flows, we then relate them to the practice of using valuation multiples based on those of comparable firms. We conclude the chapter by discussing the role of competition in the information contained in stock prices and its implications for investors and corporate managers.

7.1 Stock Basics

As discussed in Chapter 1, the ownership of a corporation is divided into shares of stock. A public corporation has many owners, and its shares trade on a stock market that provides liquidity for a company's shares and determines the market price for those shares. In this section, we explain what a stock market quote is and introduce the two types of stocks, *common* and *preferred.*

common stock A share of ownership in the corporation, which confers rights to any common dividends as well as rights to vote on election of directors, mergers, and other major events.

ticker symbol A unique abbreviation assigned to a publicly traded company.

Stock Market Reporting: Stock Quotes

Figure 7.1 shows a stock quote with basic information about Nike's stock from Google Finance (www.google.com/finance) for June 25, 2013.[1] Nike's stock is **common stock,** which means a share of ownership in the corporation gives its owner rights to any common dividends as well as rights to vote on the election of directors, mergers, and other major events. The webpage notes that the company is a public corporation (its shares are widely held and traded in a market) and that its shares trade on the NYSE (New York Stock Exchange) under the ticker symbol NKE. A **ticker symbol** is a unique abbreviation assigned to a publicly traded company and used when its trades are reported on the ticker (a real-time electronic display of trading activity).

[1]There are many places on the internet to get free stock information, such as the websites of the TMX Group (tmx.com), the NYSE (nyse.com), and the NASDAQ (nasdaq.com). Detailed stock data is also reported by many news sites such as those found on Bloomberg, Google, Yahoo, BNN, and others.

FIGURE 7.1 Stock Price Quote for Nike (NKE)

This screenshot from Google Finance shows the basic stock price information and price history charting for the common stock of Nike. The historical price chart covers the period mid-February through late June 2013. The price of $60.39 is for June 25, 2013.

Source: www.google.com/finance?q=NYSE:NKE. Google and the Google logo are registered trademarks of Google Inc., used with permission.

During the period mid-February through late June 2013, Nike paid two quarterly dividends to its common shareholders: on February 28, and May 30. The dividends are marked by a "D" and show the amount of the dividend. In this case, the dividend was 21 cents per share. Thus, if you owned 1000 shares of NKE, you would have received $0.21 \times 1000 = \$210$ when Nike paid each dividend.

Finally, the webpage displays some basic information about the performance of NKE stock. Notice the price of the last trade of NKE shares in the market ($60.39), the price that shares started at when the market opened that day ($60.42), the range of low to high prices reached during trading that day ($59.95 to $60.99), and the volume of trading for the day (5.45 million shares). The total value of all the equity of NKE is its market capitalization, equal to the price per share multiplied by the number of shares

market capitalization = Price per share × number of outstanding shares outstanding: on June 25, 2013, it was \$60.39 × 893.61 million = \$53.97 billion. Over the preceding 52 weeks, NKE achieved a high price of \$66.07 and a low price of \$42.55 and had an average daily volume of shares traded of 3.54 million shares. Also, note some basic information about the company: the price-earnings (P/E) ratio and earnings per share (EPS), both of which we discussed in Chapter 2. The webpage also notes that NKE's beta is 0.88.[2]

Common Stock

We now examine the rights of common stockholders, including their voice in the running of the corporation. All rights accruing to the shareholders are in proportion to the number of shares they hold.

Shareholder Voting. To illustrate the shareholder voting process, consider an election of 10 directors at a company with only two shareholders: Donna and Jonathan. Donna has 600 shares and Jonathan has 400, but they have very different views on how the company should be run. If the company has **straight voting**, each shareholder has as many votes for each director as shares held. That is, for each director, Donna will have 600 votes and Jonathan 400, so Jonathan will lose every vote and have no representation on the board. If the company has **cumulative voting**, each shareholder's total vote allocation for all directors is equal to the number of open spots multiplied by his or her number of shares. With 10 directors up for election, Jonathan is allocated a total of 10 times 400 votes (4000 votes) and Donna is allocated 10 times 600 votes (6000 votes) to use across the 10 director spots. Rather than unsuccessfully trying to get his director candidates elected for all 10 spots, Jonathan could allocate all his votes to just four directors, ensuring that he has four directors representing his views on the board. Donna would do the same for six directors, ensuring her representation. With cumulative voting, even shareholders with minority blocks (less than 50%) have a chance at representation on the board.

straight voting Voting for directors during which shareholders must vote for each director separately, with each shareholder having as many votes as shares held.

cumulative voting Voting for directors during which each shareholder is allocated votes equal to the number of open spots multiplied by his or her number of shares.

This example is based on the concept of one share, one vote. Some companies have different types of common stock, called *classes*, which carry different voting rights. This is typical in companies that are family run, or where the founder is still active. For example, Nike has Class A and Class B stock. Phil Knight, Nike's founder, owns almost all the Class A stock, which carries the rights to elect nine of the company's 12 directors. Google also has Class A and Class B stock. Class A stock has been sold to the public, while Google's founders and managers hold all the Class B stock, each share of which carries 10 times the voting power of a share of Class A stock.

Shareholder Rights. Each year, companies hold an **annual meeting** at which managers and directors answer questions from shareholders, and shareholders vote on the election of directors and other proposals. All shareholders have the right to attend the annual meeting and cast their votes directly. In practice, though, most either allow the board to vote for them or direct that their shares be voted for them via **proxy**, or explicit instructions on how they should be voted. Typically, matters at the annual meeting are uncontested, but occasionally a dissident shareholder group will propose an alternative slate of directors or oppose a management proposal. In that case, each side will actively solicit the proxies of all the shareholders so they may win the vote in a **proxy contest**.

annual meeting Meetings held once per year at which shareholders vote on directors and other proposals, as well as ask managers questions.

proxy A written authorization for someone else to vote your shares.

proxy contest A contest between two or more groups competing to collect proxies to prevail in the matter up for shareholder vote (such as election of directors).

As an ownership claim, common stock carries the right to share in the profits of the corporation through dividend payments. Recall from Chapter 1 that dividends are periodic payments, usually in the form of cash, which firms make to shareholders as a partial return on their investment in the corporation. The board of directors decides the

[2]Beta is a measure of risk that we will discuss in Chapter 11.

timing and amount of each dividend. Shareholders are paid dividends in proportion to the amount of shares they own. If the company is liquidated through bankruptcy and there are assets left over after satisfying the claims of the bondholders, shareholders divide the remaining assets proportionally based on each shareholder's number of shares.

Preferred Stock

preferred stock Stock with preference over common shares in payment of dividends and in liquidation.

Some companies have an additional issue of stock called **preferred stock**, which has preference over common shares in the distribution of dividends or liquidation. While the directors can at their discretion choose not to pay the preferred dividend, they may not pay a dividend to common stockholders unless they pay the promised dividend to preferred shareholders first. For example, Nike has preferred shares that pay a $0.10 dividend per share each year. The firm must pay this dividend before common shareholders can receive a dividend.

cumulative preferred stock Preferred stock for which all missed preferred dividends must be paid before any common dividends may be paid.

non-cumulative preferred stock Preferred stock for which missed preferred dividends do not accumulate. Only the current dividend is owed before common dividends may be paid.

Cumulative versus Non-Cumulative Preferred Stock. There are two types of preferred stock: *cumulative* and *non-cumulative*. With **cumulative preferred stock**, any unpaid dividends are carried forward. For example, if DuPont fails to pay its preferred dividend for several years, its obligation to its cumulative preferred shareholders accumulates, and it cannot pay any dividends to common shareholders until it has paid all the unpaid preferred dividends. With **non-cumulative preferred stock**, missed dividends do not accumulate, and the firm can pay current dividend payments first to preferred and then to common stock shareholders. Many Canadian banks (e.g., Canadian Imperial Bank of Commerce [CIBC]) have non-cumulative preferred stock outstanding. Some companies provide preferred stockholders with additional features such as the right to elect a director to the board if the firm is substantially in arrears on preferred dividends.

Preferred Stock: Equity or Debt? You may have wondered how to think about preferred stock—is it equity or is it debt? Economically, it is like a perpetual bond. It has a promised constant periodic cash flow to holders, and there are consequences if these cash flows are not paid. However, preferred shareholders cannot force the firm into bankruptcy. Preferred shareholders stand in line in front of common shareholders for annual dividends but behind regular bondholders, whose interest payments come first. If the firm is bankrupt, the same priority is followed in settling claims: bondholders, preferred shareholders, and then common shareholders. Finally, as long as the firm is meeting its preferred dividend obligations, the preferred shareholders have none of the control rights of owners, such as voting on directors or other important matters. However, despite all these similarities to debt, preferred shares are, for all tax and legal purposes, treated as equity.

- ownership in a company, dividends payment for equity

CONCEPT CHECK

1. What is a share of stock and what are dividends?
2. What are some key differences between preferred and common stock?

↳ Preferred shares are giving priority in payments of dividends and liquidation

7.2 The Dividend-Discount Model

The Valuation Principle implies that to value any security, we must determine the expected cash flows that an investor will receive from owning it. We begin our analysis of stock valuation by considering the cash flows for an investor with a one-year investment horizon. We will show how the stock's price and the investor's return from the investment are related. We then consider the perspective of investors with long investment horizons. Finally, we will reach our goal of establishing the first stock valuation method: the *dividend-discount model*.

A One-Year Investor

There are two potential sources of cash flows from owning a stock:

1. The firm might pay out cash to its shareholders in the form of a dividend.
2. The investor might generate cash by selling the shares at some future date.

The total amount received in dividends and from selling the stock will depend on the investor's investment horizon. Let's begin by considering the perspective of a one-year investor.

When an investor buys a stock, she will pay the current market price for a share, P_0. While she continues to hold the stock, she will be entitled to any dividends the stock pays. Let Div_1 be the total dividends paid per share during the year. At the end of the year, the investor will sell her share at the new market price. Let P_1 be the price the investor expects to sell her share for at the end of the year. Assuming for simplicity that all dividends are paid at the end of the year, we have the following timeline for this investment:

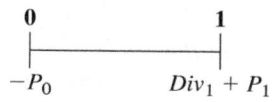

Of course, the future dividend payment and stock price in this timeline are not known with certainty. Rather, these values are based on the investor's expectations at the time the stock is purchased. Given these expectations, the investor will be willing to pay a price today up to the point that the benefits equal the costs—that is, up to the point at which the current price equals the present value of the expected future dividend and sale price.

Because these cash flows are risky, we cannot discount them using the risk-free interest rate, but instead must use the cost of capital for the firm's equity. We have previously defined the cost of capital of any investment to be the expected return that investors could earn on their best alternative investment with similar risk and maturity. Thus we must discount the equity cash flows based on the **equity cost of capital**, r_E, for the stock, which is the expected return of other investments available in the market with risk equivalent to that of the firm's shares. Doing so leads to the following equation for the stock price:

equity cost of capital
The expected rate of return available in the market on other investments that have risk equivalent to that associated with the firm's shares.

$$P_0 = \frac{Div_1 + P_1}{1 + r_E} \tag{7.1}$$

If the current stock price were less than this amount, the cost would be less than the PV of the benefits, so investors would rush in and buy it, driving up the stock's price. If the stock price exceeded this amount, selling it would be attractive and the stock price would quickly fall.

Dividend Yields, Capital Gains, and Total Returns

A critical part of Equation 7.1 for determining the stock price is the firm's equity cost of capital, r_E. At the beginning of this section, we pointed out that an investor's return from holding a stock comes from dividends and cash generated from selling the stock.

We can rewrite Equation 7.1 to show these two return components. If we multiply by $(1 + r_E)$, divide by P_0, and subtract 1 from both sides, we have

Total Return

$$r_E = \frac{Div_1 + P_1}{P_0} - 1 = \underbrace{\frac{Div_1}{P_0}}_{\text{Dividend Yield}} + \underbrace{\frac{P_1 - P_0}{P_0}}_{\text{Capital Gain Rate}} \tag{7.2}$$

dividend yield The expected annual dividend of a stock divided by its current price; the percentage return an investor expects to earn from the dividend paid by the stock.

capital gain The amount by which the selling price of an asset exceeds its initial purchase price.

capital gain rate An expression of capital gain as a percentage of the initial price of the asset.

total return The sum of a stock's dividend yield and its capital gain rate.

The first term on the right side of Equation 7.2 is the stock's **dividend yield**, which is the expected annual dividend of the stock divided by its current price. The dividend yield is the percentage return the investor expects to earn from the dividend paid by the stock. The second term on the right side of Equation 7.2 reflects the **capital gain** the investor will earn on the stock, which is the difference between the expected sale price and the original purchase price for the stock: $P_1 - P_0$. We divide the capital gain by the current stock price to express the capital gain as a percentage return, called the **capital gain rate**.

The sum of the dividend yield and the capital gain rate is called the **total return** of the stock. The total return is the expected return that the investor will earn for a one-year investment in the stock. Equation 7.2 states that the stock's total return should equal the equity cost of capital. In other words, *the expected total return of the stock should equal the expected return of other investments with equivalent risk that are available in the market.*

This result is exactly what we would expect: the firm must pay its shareholders a return commensurate with the return they can earn elsewhere while taking the same risk. If the stock offered a higher return than other securities with the same risk, investors would sell those other investments and buy the stock instead. This activity would then drive up the stock's current price, lowering its dividend yield and capital gain rate until Equation 7.2 holds true. If the stock offered a lower expected return, investors would sell the stock and drive down its price until Equation 7.2 was again satisfied.

EXAMPLE 7.1 Stock Prices and Returns

PROBLEM

Suppose you expect Loblaw Companies Ltd. (ticker symbol: L on the TSX) to pay an annual dividend of $0.56 per share in the coming year and to trade for $45.50 per share at the end of the year. If investments with risk equivalent to that of Loblaw's stock have an expected return of 6.80%, what is the most you would pay today for Loblaw's stock? What dividend yield and capital gain rate would you expect at this price?

SOLUTION

■ Plan

We can use Equation 7.1 to solve for the beginning price we would pay now (P_0), given our expectations about dividends ($Div_1 = 0.56$) and future price ($P_1 = \$45.50$) and the return we need to expect to earn to be willing to invest ($r_E = 6.8\%$). We can then use Equation 7.2 to calculate the dividend yield and capital gain.

▶

■ **Execute**

Using Equation 7.1, we have

$$P_0 = \frac{Div_1 + P_1}{1 + r_E} = \frac{0.56 + 45.50}{1.0680} = \$43.13$$

Referring to Equation 7.2, we see that at this price, Loblaw's dividend yield is $Div_1/P_0 = 0.56/43.13 = 1.30\%$. The expected capital gain is \$45.50 − \$43.13 = \$2.37 per share, for a capital gain rate of $2.37/43.13 = 5.50\%$.

■ **Evaluate**

At a price of \$43.13, Loblaw's expected total return is 1.30% + 5.50% = 6.80%, which is equal to its equity cost of capital (the return being paid by investments with equivalent risk to Loblaw). This amount is the most we would be willing to pay for Loblaw's stock. If we paid more, our expected return would be less than 6.8% and we would rather invest elsewhere.

A Multi-Year Investor

We now extend the reasoning we developed for the one-year investor's return to a multi-year investor. Equation 7.1 depends on the expected stock price in one year, P_1. But suppose we planned to hold the stock for two years. Then we would receive dividends in both year one and year two before selling the stock, as shown in the following timeline:

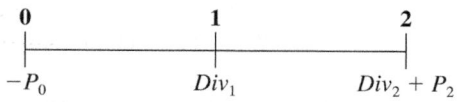

Setting the stock price equal to the present value of the future cash flows in this case implies the following:[3]

$$P_0 = \frac{Div_1}{1 + r_E} + \frac{Div_2 + P_2}{(1 + r_E)^2} \tag{7.3}$$

Equations 7.1 and 7.3 are different: as two-year investors, we care about the dividend and stock price in year two, but these terms do not appear in Equation 7.1. Does this difference imply that a two-year investor will value the stock differently than a one-year investor?

The answer to this question is no. A one-year investor does not care about the dividend and stock price in year two directly. She will care about them indirectly, however, because they will affect the price for which she can sell the stock at the end of year one. For example, suppose the investor sells the stock to another one-year investor with the

[3]In using the same equity cost of capital for both periods, we are assuming that the equity cost of capital does not depend on the term of the cash flows; that is, r_E is not different for year two (or any other year). Otherwise, we would need to adjust for the term structure of the equity cost of capital (as we did with the yield curve for risk-free cash flows in Chapter 5). This step would complicate the analysis but would not change its results.

same expectations. The new investor will expect to receive the dividend and stock price at the end of year two, so he will be willing to pay

$$P_1 = \frac{Div_2 + P_2}{1 + r_E}$$

for the stock. Substituting this expression for P_1 into Equation 7.1, we get the same result as in Equation 7.3:

$$P_0 = \frac{Div_1 + P_1}{1 + r_E} = \frac{Div_1}{1 + r_E} + \frac{1}{1 + r_E}\overbrace{\left(\frac{Div_2 + P_2}{1 + r_E}\right)}^{P_1}$$

$$= \frac{Div_1}{1 + r_E} + \frac{Div_2 + P_2}{(1 + r_E)^2}$$

Thus, the formula for the stock price for a two-year investor is the same as that for a sequence of two one-year investors.

Dividend-Discount Model Equation

We can continue this process for any number of years by replacing the final stock price with the value that the next holder of the stock would be willing to pay. Doing so leads to the general **dividend-discount model** for the stock price, where the horizon, n, is arbitrary:

dividend-discount model
A model that values shares of a firm according to the present value of the future dividends the firm will pay.

Dividend-Discount Model

$$P_0 = \frac{Div_1}{1 + r_E} + \frac{Div_2}{(1 + r_E)^2} + \cdots + \frac{Div_n}{(1 + r_E)^n} + \frac{P_n}{(1 + r_E)^n} \tag{7.4}$$

Equation 7.4 applies to a single n-year investor, who will collect dividends for n years and then sell the stock, or to a series of investors who hold the stock for shorter periods and then resell it. Note that Equation 7.4 holds for any horizon, n. As a consequence, all investors (with the same expectations) will attach the same value to the stock, independent of their investment horizons. How long they intend to hold the stock and whether they collect their return in the form of dividends or capital gains is irrelevant. For the special case in which the firm eventually pays dividends and is never acquired or liquidated, it is possible to hold the shares forever. In this scenario, rather than having a stopping point where we sell the shares, we rewrite Equation 7.4 to show that the dividends go on into the future:

$$P_0 = \frac{Div_1}{1 + r_E} + \frac{Div_2}{(1 + r_E)^2} + \frac{Div_3}{(1 + r_E)^3} + \cdots \tag{7.5}$$

That is, *the price of the stock is equal to the present value of all of the expected future dividends it will pay.*

$P_0 = P_1 + D$

CONCEPT CHECK

3. How do you calculate the total return of a stock?

4. What discount rate do you use to discount the future cash flows of a stock?

RRR

7.3 Estimating Dividends in the Dividend-Discount Model

Equation 7.5 expresses the value of a stock in terms of the expected future dividends the firm will pay. Of course, estimating these dividends—especially for the distant future—is difficult. A commonly used approximation is to assume that, in the long run, dividends will grow at a constant rate. In this section, we consider the implications of this assumption for stock prices and explore the trade-off between dividends and growth.

Constant Dividend Growth

The simplest forecast for the firm's future dividends states that they will grow at a constant rate, g, forever. That case yields the following timeline for the cash flows for an investor who buys the stock today and holds it:

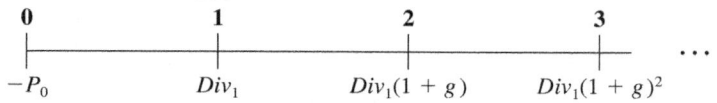

Because the expected dividends are a constant growth perpetuity, we can use Equation 4.9 to calculate their present value. We then obtain the following simple formula for the stock price:[4]

Constant Dividend Growth Model

$$P_0 = \frac{Div_1}{r_E - g} \tag{7.6}$$

constant dividend growth model A model for valuing a stock by viewing its dividends as a constant growth perpetuity.

According to the **constant dividend growth model**, the value of the firm depends on the dividend level next year, divided by the equity cost of capital adjusted by the growth rate. Note, for preferred shares $g = 0$, as the dividends are set at a constant periodic amount, and thus the valuation simplifies to valuing a constant perpetuity of dividends, so Equation 7.6 simplifies to $P_0 = Div/r$.

For another interpretation of Equation 7.6, note that we can rearrange it as follows:

$$r_E = \frac{Div}{P_0} + g \tag{7.7}$$

Comparing Equation 7.7 with Equation 7.2, we see that g equals the expected capital gain rate. In other words, with constant expected dividend growth, the expected growth rate of the share price matches the growth rate of the dividends.

[4]As discussed in Chapter 4, this formula requires that $g < r_E$. Otherwise, the present value of the growing perpetuity is infinite. The implication here is that it is impossible for a stock's dividends to grow at a rate $g > r_E$ *forever*. If the growth rate does exceed r_E, the situation must be temporary, and the constant growth model cannot be applied in such a case.

EXAMPLE 7.2 Valuing a Firm with Constant Dividend Growth

PROBLEM

Hydro One is a regulated utility company that provides transmission and distribution of electricity in Ontario. Suppose Hydro plans to pay $2.30 per share in dividends in the coming year. If its equity cost of capital is 7% and dividends are expected to grow by 2% per year in the future, estimate the value of Hydro's stock.

SOLUTION

■ **Plan**

Because the dividends are expected to grow perpetually at a constant rate, we can use Equation 7.6 to value Hydro. The next dividend (Div_1) is expected to be $2.30, the growth rate ($g$) is 2%, and the equity cost of capital (r_E) is 7%.

■ **Execute**

$$P_0 = \frac{Div_1}{r_E - g} = \frac{\$2.30}{0.07 - 0.02} = \$46.00$$

■ **Evaluate**

You would be willing to pay 20 times this year's dividend of $2.30 to own Hydro One stock because you are buying a claim to this year's dividend *and* to an infinite growing series of future dividends.

Dividends versus Investment and Growth

In Equation 7.6, the firm's share price increases with the current dividend level, Div_1, and the expected growth rate, g. To maximize its share price, a firm would like to increase both these quantities. Often, however, the firm faces a trade-off: increasing growth may require investment, and money spent on investment cannot be used to pay dividends. The constant dividend growth model provides insight into this trade-off.

dividend payout rate The fraction of a firm's earnings that the firm pays out as dividends each year.

A Simple Model of Growth. What determines the rate of growth of a firm's dividends? If we define a firm's **dividend payout rate** as the fraction of its earnings that the firm pays as dividends each year, then we can write the firm's dividend per share at date t as follows:

$$Div_t = \underbrace{\frac{\text{Earnings}_t}{\text{Share Outstanding}_t}}_{EPS_t} \times \text{Dividend Payout Rate}_t \tag{7.8}$$

That is, the dividend each year is equal to the firm's earnings per share (EPS) multiplied by its dividend payout rate. The firm can, therefore, increase its dividend in three ways:

1. It can increase its earnings (net income).
2. It can increase its dividend payout rate.
3. It can decrease its number of shares outstanding.

Suppose for now that the firm does not issue new shares (or buy back its existing shares), so that the number of shares outstanding remains fixed. We can then explore the trade-off between options 1 and 2.

A firm can do one of two things with its earnings: it can pay them out to investors, or it can retain and reinvest them. By investing cash today, a firm can increase its future dividends. For simplicity, let's assume that if no investment is made, the firm does not grow, so the current level of earnings generated by the firm remains constant. If all increases in future earnings result exclusively from new investment made with retained earnings, then

$$\text{Change in Earnings} = \text{New Investment} \times \text{Return on New Investment} \tag{7.9}$$

retention rate The fraction of a firm's current earnings that the firm retains.

New investment equals the firm's earnings multiplied by its **retention rate**, or the fraction of current earnings that the firm retains:

$$\text{New Investment} = \text{Earnings} \times \text{Retention Rate} \tag{7.10}$$

Substituting Equation 7.10 into Equation 7.9 and dividing by earnings gives an expression for the growth rate of earnings:

$$\begin{aligned}\text{Earnings Growth Rate} &= \frac{\text{Change in Earnings}}{\text{Earnings}} \\ &= \text{Retention Rate} \times \text{Return on New Investment} \qquad (7.11)\end{aligned}$$

If the firm chooses to keep its dividend payout rate constant, then the growth in its dividends will equal the growth in its earnings:

$$g = \text{Retention Rate} \times \text{Return on New Investment} \tag{7.12}$$

Profitable Growth. Equation 7.12 shows that a firm can increase its growth rate by retaining more of its earnings. However, if the firm retains more earnings, it will be able to pay out less of those earnings; according to Equation 7.8, the firm will then have to reduce its dividend. If a firm wants to increase its share price, should it cut its dividend and invest more, or should it cut its investments and increase its dividend? Not surprisingly, the answer to this question will depend on the profitability of the firm's investments. Let's consider an example.

In Example 7.3, cutting the firm's dividend in favour of growth raised the firm's stock price. This is not always the case, however, as Example 7.4 demonstrates.

EXAMPLE 7.3 Cutting Dividends for Profitable Growth

PROBLEM

Suppose Canadian Tire Corporation Ltd (ticker symbol: CTC.A on the TSX) expects to have earnings per share of $6 in the coming year. Rather than reinvest these earnings and grow, the firm plans to pay out all of its earnings as a dividend. With these expectations of no growth, Canadian Tire's current share price is $60.

Suppose Canadian Tire could cut its dividend payout rate to 75% for the foreseeable future and use the retained earnings to open new stores. The return on its investment in these stores is expected to be 12%. If we assume that the risk of these new investments is the same as the risk of its existing investments, then the firm's equity cost of capital is unchanged. What effect would this new policy have on Canadian Tire's stock price?

SOLUTION

■ Plan

To figure out the effect of this policy on Canadian Tire's stock price, we need to know several things. First, we need to compute its equity cost of capital. Next, we must determine Canadian Tire's dividend and growth rate under the new policy.

Because we know that Canadian Tire currently has a growth rate of 0 ($g = 0$), a dividend of $6, and a price of $60, we can use Equation 7.7 to estimate r_E. Next, the new dividend will simply be 75% of the old dividend of $6. Finally, given a retention rate of 25% and a return on new investment of 12%, we can use Equation 7.12 to compute the new growth rate (g). Finally, armed with the new dividend, Canadian Tire's equity cost of capital, and its new growth rate, we can use Equation 7.6 to compute the price of Canadian Tire's shares if it institutes the new policy. ▶

Execute

Using Equation 7.7 to estimate r_E, we have

$$r_E = \frac{Div_1}{P_0} + g = 10\% + 0\% = 10\%$$

In other words, to justify Canadian Tire's stock price under its current policy, the expected return of other stocks in the market with equivalent risk must be 10%.

Next, we consider the consequences of the new policy. If Canadian Tire reduces its dividend payout rate to 75%, then, from Equation 7.8, its dividend this coming year will fall to $Div_1 = EPS_1 \times 75\% = \$6 \times 75\% = \$4.50$.

At the same time, because the firm will now retain 25% of its earnings to invest in new stores, from Equation 7.12, its growth rate will increase to

$$g = \text{Retention Rate} \times \text{Return on New Investment} = 25\% \times 12\% = 3\%$$

Assuming Canadian Tire can continue to grow at this rate, we can compute its share price under the new policy using the constant dividend growth model of Equation 7.6:

$$P_0 = \frac{Div_1}{r_E - g} = \frac{\$4.50}{0.10 - 0.03} = \$64.29$$

Evaluate

Canadian Tire's share price should rise from \$60 to \$64.29 if the company cuts its dividend in order to increase its investment and growth, implying that the investment has a positive net present value (NPV). By using its earnings to invest in projects that offer a rate of return (12%) greater than its equity cost of capital (10%), Canadian Tire has created value for its shareholders.

EXAMPLE 7.4 Unprofitable Growth

PROBLEM

Suppose Canadian Tire decides to cut its dividend payout rate to 75% to invest in new stores, as in Example 7.3. But now suppose that the return on these new investments is 8%, rather than 12%. Given its expected earnings per share this year of \$6 and its equity cost of capital of 10% (we again assume that the risk of the new investments is the same as that of its existing investments), what will happen to Canadian Tire's current share price in this case?

SOLUTION

Plan

We will follow the steps in Example 7.3, except that in this case, we assume a return on new investments of 8% when computing the new growth rate (g) instead of 12% as in Example 7.3.

Execute

Just as in Example 7.3, Canadian Tire's dividend will fall to $\$6 \times 75\% = \$4.50$. Its growth rate under the new policy, given the lower return on new investment, will now be $g = 25\% \times 8\% = 2\%$. The new share price is therefore

$$P_0 = \frac{Div_1}{r_E - g} = \frac{\$4.50}{0.10 - 0.02} = \$56.25$$

■ **Evaluate**

Even though Canadian Tire will grow under the new policy, the new investments have a negative NPV. The company's share price will fall if it cuts its dividend to make new investments with a return of only 8%. By reinvesting its earnings at a rate (8%) that is lower than its equity cost of capital (10%), Canadian Tire has reduced shareholder value.

Comparing Example 7.3 with Example 7.4, we see that the effect of cutting the firm's dividend to grow depends, crucially, on the value of the new investments the firm plans to make. In Example 7.3, the return on new investment of 12% exceeds the firm's equity cost of capital of 10%, so the investment is a good one. In Example 7.4, however, the return on new investment is only 8%, so the new investment's return is below the firm's cost of capital. In that case, the new investment is not worthwhile even though it will lead to earnings growth. In this example, we can check that cutting the firm's dividend to increase investment will create value and raise the stock price if, and only if, the new investments generate a greater return than their cost of capital. In the next chapter, we will consider more generally how to identify projects that create value and thus increase stock price.

Changing Growth Rates

Successful young firms often have very high initial earnings growth rates. During this period of high growth, firms often retain 100% of their earnings to exploit profitable investment opportunities. As they mature, their growth slows to rates more typical of established companies. At that point, their earnings exceed their investment needs and they begin to pay dividends.

We cannot use the constant dividend growth model to value the stock of such a firm for two reasons:

1. These firms often pay *no* dividends when they are young.
2. Their growth rate continues to change over time until they mature.

However, we can use the general form of the dividend-discount model to value such a firm by applying the constant growth model to calculate the future share price of the stock, P_n, once the firm matures and its expected growth rate stabilizes:

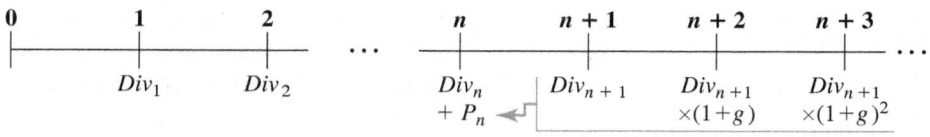

Specifically, if the firm is expected to grow at a long-term rate g after year $n + 1$, then from the constant dividend growth model,

$$P_n = \frac{Div_{n+1}}{r_E - g} \tag{7.13}$$

We can then use this estimate of P_n as a final cash flow in the dividend-discount model. Intuitively, we value the stock as the present value of the dividends we will receive plus the present value of the price we expect to be able to sell the stock for in the future. For example, consider a company with expected dividends of \$2.00, \$2.50, and \$3.00

COMMON MISTAKE

The First Dividend

The most common mistake in handling growing dividends is to use the current period's dividend in the numerator of the growing perpetuity formula. In the example just discussed in the text, the dividends reached $3 in year three, and then grew by 5% per year thereafter. A common mistake is to calculate the growing stream of dividends as $\frac{3.00}{.12 - .05}$, and forgetting that next year's dividend (the numerator) has already grown by 5%! As we show in the example, the correct calculation is $\frac{3.00 \times (1.05)}{.12 - .05} = \$45$. Also, remember to avoid the common mistake from Chapter 4: the growing perpetuity formula gives the value in year n for dividends starting in year $n + 1$. In the example above, the formula gives the value in year three of the growing dividend stream starting in year four. That is why we discount the $45 back only three years.

in each of the next three years. After that point, its dividends are expected to grow at a constant rate of 5%. If its equity cost of capital is 12%, we can find the stock's price. Using Equation 7.13, we can compute the price in year three:

$$P_n = \frac{Div_{n+1}}{r_E - g} \quad \text{so} \quad P_3 = \left(\frac{\$3.00(1.05)}{0.12 - 0.05}\right) = \$45.00$$

Now, using Equation 7.4, we can calculate the current price as the PV of the first three years' dividends and then the price at the end of year three:

$$P_0 = \frac{\$2.00}{1.12} + \frac{\$2.50}{(1.12)^2} + \frac{\$3.00}{(1.12)^3} + \frac{\$45.00}{(1.12)^3} = \$37.94$$

This example also reinforces an important point: the constant growth dividend model (Equation 7.13) is just a special case of the general dividend-discount formula (Equation 7.4). We can always value all the stream of dividends using Equation 7.4. However, if we assume constant growth, we can apply the growing perpetuity shortcut to all or part of the dividend stream, depending on whether the constant growth starts now or at some point in the future.[5]

EXAMPLE 7.5 Valuing a Firm with Two Different Growth Rates

PROBLEM

Small Fry Inc. has just invented a potato chip that looks and tastes like a French fry. Given the phenomenal market response to this product, Small Fry is reinvesting all of its earnings to expand its operations. Earnings were $2 per share this past year and are expected to grow at a rate of 20% per year until the end of year four. At that point, other companies are likely to bring out competing products. Analysts project that at the end of year four, Small Fry will cut its investment and begin paying 60% of its earnings as dividends. Its growth will also slow to a long-run rate of 4%. If Small Fry's equity cost of capital is 8%, what is the value of a share today? ▶

[5]If the dividends grew at an initial constant rate over the near term and then a second constant rate over the long term, rather than discounting the near-term dividends one by one as we just did above, we could use the present value of a growing annuity for the near dividends and then use the present value of a growing perpetuity for the long-term dividends (being careful to discount the growing perpetuity's PV back to time 0).

SOLUTION

Plan

We can use Small Fry's projected earnings growth rate and payout rate to forecast its future earnings and dividends. After year four, Small Fry's dividends will grow at a constant 4%, so we can use the constant dividend growth model (Equation 7.13) to value all dividends after that point. Finally, we can pull everything together with the dividend-discount model (Equation 7.4).

Execute

The following spreadsheet projects Small Fry's earnings and dividends:

1	Year	0	1	2	3	4	5	6
2	**Earnings**							
3	EPS Growth Rate (versus prior year)		20%	20%	20%	20%	4%	4%
4	EPS	$2.00	$2.40	$2.88	$3.46	$4.15	$4.31	$4.49
5	**Dividends**							
6	Dividend Payout Rate		0%	0%	0%	60%	60%	60%
7	*Div*		$—	$—	$—	$2.49	$2.59	$2.69

Starting from $2.00 in year zero, EPS grows by 20% per year until year four, after which growth slows to 4%. Small Fry's dividend payout rate is zero until year four, when competition reduces its investment opportunities and its payout rate rises to 60%. Multiplying EPS by the dividend payout ratio, we project Small Fry's future dividends in line 4.

After year four, Small Fry's dividends will grow at the expected long-run rate of 4% per year. Thus, we can use the year four dividend as the first dividend in a constant dividend growth model ($g = 4\%$) to project Small Fry's share price at the end of year three. Given its equity cost of capital of 8%,

$$P_3 = \frac{Div_4}{r_E - g} = \frac{\$2.49}{0.08 - 0.04} = \$62.25$$

We then apply the dividend-discount model (Equation 7.4) with this terminal value:

$$P_0 = \frac{Div_1}{1 + r_E} + \frac{Div_2}{(1 + r_E)^2} + \frac{Div_3}{(1 + r_E)^3} + \frac{P_3}{(1 + r_E)^3} = \frac{\$62.25}{(1.08)^3} = \$49.42$$

Evaluate

The dividend-discount model is flexible enough to handle any forecasted pattern of dividends. Here, the dividends were zero for three years and then settled into a constant growth rate, allowing us to use the constant growth rate model as a shortcut.

Table 7.1 summarizes the dividend-discount model, including how to apply the shortcut for constant growth.

Value Drivers and the Dividend-Discount Model

Now that we have fully developed the dividend-discount model, it is worth assessing how well it does in capturing the intuitive drivers of stock value. When we think about how valuable a company is, we usually focus on how profitable it is now and

TABLE 7.1 The Dividend-Discount Model

General formula	$P_0 = \frac{Div_1}{1 + r_E} + \frac{Div_2}{(1 + r_E)^2} + \cdots + \frac{Div_n}{(1 + r_E)^n} + \frac{P_n}{(1 + r_E)^n}$
If dividend growth is constant	$P_0 = \frac{Div_1}{r_E - g}$
If dividends are constant (no growth), such as with preferred stock	$P_0 = \frac{Div}{r_E}$
If early growth is variable, followed by constant growth	$P_0 = \frac{Div_1}{1 + r_E} + \frac{Div_2}{(1 + r_E)^2} + \cdots + \frac{Div_n}{(1 + r_E)^n} + \left(\frac{1}{(1 + r_E)^n}\right)\frac{Div_n(1 + g)}{r_E - g}$

how that profitability will grow or decline in the future, along with the risk of investing in the company. Where are these measures captured in the dividend-discount model? Profitability determines the company's ability to pay dividends, so implicitly, in the forecasted dividend stream, we are forecasting the company's profitability. As for the risk, that is captured in the equity cost of capital we use to discount those forecasted dividends. Riskier investments require higher expected returns, which enter the dividend-discount model as higher equity cost of capital.

CONCEPT CHECK

5. What are three ways that a firm can increase the amount of its future dividends per share?
6. Under what circumstances can a firm increase its share price by cutting its dividend and investing more?

7.4 Limitations of the Dividend-Discount Model

The dividend-discount model has two fundamental limitations that we will now address: its reliance on dividend forecasts and lack of applicability to non-dividend-paying stocks.

Uncertain Dividend Forecasts

The dividend-discount model values a stock based on a forecast of the future dividends paid to shareholders. But, unlike a Government of Canada bond whose cash flows are known with virtual certainty, a tremendous amount of uncertainty is associated with any forecast of a firm's future dividends.

Let's consider the example of Nike (ticker symbol: NKE on the NYSE). In 2013, NKE paid annual dividends of \$0.84 (by paying four quarterly dividends of \$0.21 each). If we assume an equity cost of capital of 10% and expected dividend growth of 8.5%, the constant dividend growth model implies a share price for NKE of

$$P_0 = \frac{Div_1}{r_E - g} = \frac{\$0.84(1 + 0.085)}{0.10 - 0.085} = \$60.76$$

which is quite close to the \$60.39 share price that the stock had at the time. With a 9% dividend growth rate, however, this estimate would rise to more than \$91 per share; with a 6% dividend growth rate, the estimate falls to less than \$23 per share. As we see in Figure 7.2, even small changes in the assumed dividend growth rate can lead to large changes in the estimated stock price.

FIGURE 7.2 Implied NKE Stock Prices for Different Expected Growth Rates

The figure shows what the price of Nike would be in 2013 for different dividend growth expectations. Stock prices are based on the constant dividend growth model. We assume a dividend in 2013 of $0.84 and an equity cost of capital of 10%. The expected dividend growth rate varies from 0% to 9%. Note how even a small change in the expected growth rate produces a large change in the stock price, especially at higher growth rates.

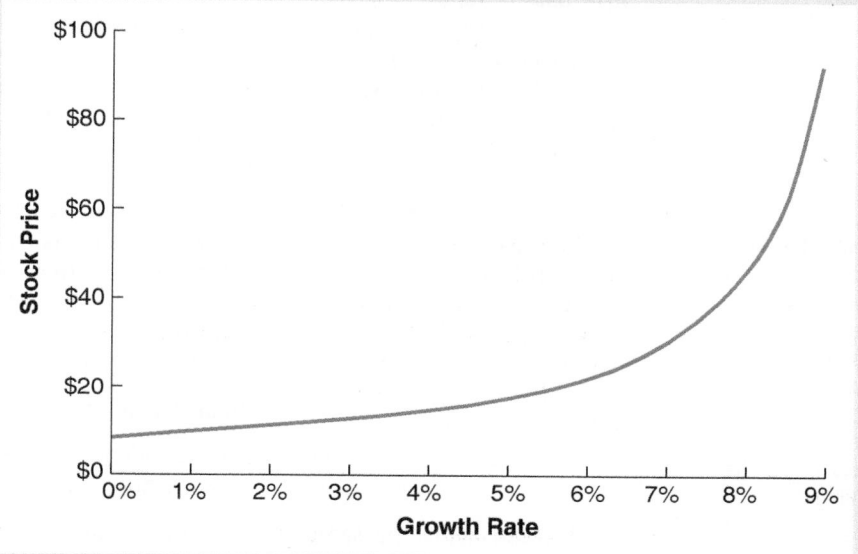

Furthermore, it is difficult to know which estimate of the dividend growth rate is more reasonable. NKE more than doubled its dividend between 2005 and 2010, but its earnings growth rate then moderated. Consequently, this rate of increase is not sustainable. From Equation 7.8, forecasting dividends requires forecasting the firm's earnings, dividend payout rate, and future share count. Future earnings, however, will depend on interest expenses (which, in turn, depend on how much the firm borrows), and the firm's share count and dividend payout rate will depend on whether NKE uses a portion of its earnings to repurchase shares. Because borrowing and repurchase decisions are at management's discretion (discussed in Part 5), they can be more difficult to forecast reliably than other, more fundamental aspects of the firm's cash flows.

Non-Dividend-Paying Stocks

Many companies do not pay cash dividends—BlackBerry, Air Canada, Facebook, and Alphabet (Google) are just a few examples. How then do we value those stocks? In the next section, we discuss a small modification to the dividend-discount model to capture total payouts to shareholders, whether the payouts are dividends or not. We will then discuss other valuation approaches that do not rely on payouts. Those approaches will be more meaningful once we have covered how financial managers create value within the firm through decisions about which projects to approve. So, in the next two chapters, we will cover investment decision rules and project evaluation.

CONCEPT CHECK

7. What are the main limitations of the dividend-discount model?
8. What pieces of information are needed to forecast dividends?

7.5 Share Repurchases and the Total Payout Model

share repurchase A firm's use of cash to buy back its own stock.

In our discussion of the dividend-discount model, we implicitly assumed that any cash paid out by the firm to shareholders takes the form of a dividend. In recent years, an increasing number of firms have replaced dividend payouts with *share repurchases*. In a **share repurchase**, the firm uses excess cash to buy back its own stock. Share repurchases have two consequences for the dividend-discount model. First, the more cash the firm uses to repurchase shares, the less cash it has available to pay dividends. Second, by repurchasing shares, the firm decreases its share count, which increases its earnings and dividends on a per-share basis.

In the dividend-discount model, we valued a share from the perspective of a single shareholder, discounting the dividends the shareholder will receive:

$$P_0 = PV(\text{Future Dividends per Share}) \tag{7.14}$$

total payout model A method that values shares of a firm by discounting the firm's total payouts to equity holders (i.e., all the cash distributed as dividends and stock repurchases) and then dividing by the current number of shares outstanding.

An alternative method that may be more reliable when a firm repurchases shares is the **total payout model**, which values *all* of the firm's equity rather than a single share. To use this model, we discount the total payouts that the firm makes to shareholders, which is the total amount spent on both dividends *and* share repurchases (net of new share issuance).[6] This gives the total value of the firm's equity. We then divide by the current number of shares outstanding to determine the share price:

Total Payout Model

$$P_0 = \frac{PV(\text{Future Total Dividends and Repurchases})}{\text{Shares Outstanding}_0} \tag{7.15}$$

We can apply the same simplifications that we obtained by assuming constant growth in Section 7.2 to the total payout method. The only change is that *we discount total dividends and share repurchases and use the growth rate of earnings (rather than earnings per share) when forecasting the growth of the firm's total payouts.* When the firm uses share repurchases, this method can be more reliable and easier to apply than the dividend-discount model.

EXAMPLE 7.6 Valuation with Share Repurchases

PROBLEM

Suppose Buhler Industries (ticker symbol: BUI on the TSX) has 217 million shares outstanding and expects earnings at the end of this year of $860 million. Buhler plans to pay out 30% of its earnings as a dividend and 20% of its earnings through share repurchases. If Buhler's earnings are expected to grow by 7.5% per year and these payout rates remain constant, determine Buhler's share price assuming an equity cost of capital of 10%.

SOLUTION

■ **Plan**

Based on the equity cost of capital of 10% and an expected earnings growth rate of 7.5%, we can compute the present value of Buhler's future payouts as a constant growth perpetuity. The only ▶

[6]You can think of the total payouts as the amount you would receive if you owned 100% of the firm's shares; you would receive all of the dividends, plus the proceeds from selling shares back to the firm in the share repurchase.

input missing here is Buhler's total payouts this year, which we can calculate as 50% of its earnings (30% by dividends plus 20% by repurchases). The present value of all of Buhler's future payouts is the value of its total equity. To obtain the price of a share, we divide the total value by the number of shares outstanding (217 million).

■ **Execute**

Buhler will have total payouts this year of 50% × \$860 million = \$430 million. Using the constant growth perpetuity formula, we have

$$PV(\text{Future Total Dividends and Repurchases}) = \frac{\$430 \text{ million}}{0.10 - 0.075} = \$17.2 \text{ billion}$$

This present value represents the total value of Buhler's equity (i.e., its market capitalization). To compute the share price, we divide by the current number of shares outstanding:

$$P_0 = \frac{\$17.2 \text{ billion}}{217 \text{ million shares}} = \$79.26 \text{ per share}$$

■ **Evaluate**

Using the total payout method, we did not need to know the firm's split between dividends and share repurchases. To compare this method with the dividend-discount model, note that Buhler will pay a dividend of 30% × \$860 million/(217 million shares) = \$1.19 per share, for a dividend yield of 1.19/79.26 = 1.50%. From Equation 7.7, Buhler's expected EPS, dividend, and share price growth rate is $g = r_E - Div_1/P0 = 8.50\%$. This growth rate exceeds the 7.50% growth rate of earnings because Buhler's share count will decline over time owing to its share repurchases.[7]

7.6 The Discounted Free Cash Flow Model

discounted free cash flow model A method for estimating a firm's enterprise value by discounting its future free cash flow.

In the total payout model, we first value the firm's equity, rather than just a single share. The **discounted free cash flow model** goes one step further and begins by determining the total value of the firm's productive assets to all of its investors—both equity holders *and* debt holders. That is, we begin by estimating the firm's enterprise value as follows:

$$\text{Enterprise Value} = \text{Market Value of Equity} + \text{Debt} - \text{Cash} \tag{7.16}$$

Because the enterprise value is the value of the firm's underlying productive assets, unencumbered by debt and separate from any cash[8] (included with cash may be other assets that do not contribute to the firm's free cash flows and are thus sometimes called non-productive assets), it is also the value of the underlying business to all investors. We can interpret the enterprise value as the net cost of acquiring the firm's equity, taking

[7]We can check that an 8.5% EPS growth rate is consistent with 7.5% earnings growth and Buhler's repurchase plans as follows. Given an expected share price of \$79.26 × 1.085 = \$86.00 next year, Buhler will repurchase 20% × \$860 million ÷ (\$86.00 per share) = 2 million shares next year. With the decline in the number of shares from 217 million to 215 million, EPS grows by a factor of 1.075 × (217/215) = 1.085 or 8.5%.

[8]To be precise, when we say "cash," we are referring to the firm's cash in excess of its working capital needs.

its cash (and any other non-productive assets), and paying off all debt; in essence, it is equivalent to owning the unlevered productive assets of the business. The advantage of the discounted free cash flow model is that it allows us to value a firm without explicitly forecasting its dividends, share repurchases, or use of debt.

Valuing the Enterprise. How can we estimate a firm's enterprise value? To estimate the value of the firm's equity, we compute the present value of the firm's total payouts to equity holders. Likewise, to estimate a firm's enterprise value, we compute the present value of the *free cash flow* (FCF) that the firm has available to pay all investors, both debt and equity holders. We now define FCF explicitly for the entire firm. (Further development and explanation of the components of FCF are discussed in detail in Chapter 9.)

$$\begin{aligned}\text{Free Cash Flow} = {} & EBIT \times (1 - \text{tax rate}) + \text{Depreciation} \\ & - \text{Capital Expenditures} - \text{Increases in Net Working Capital}\end{aligned} \tag{7.17}$$

Note: If, for tax purposes, capital cost allowance (CCA, introduced in Chapter 2) replaces depreciation, then CCA would be used in the calculation of EBIT and would replace depreciation in Equation 7.17. We subtract changes in net working capital to undo non-cash accruals that may impact EBIT and to include other changes in balance sheet current assets and liabilities that may not be reflected in EBIT.

Free cash flow measures the cash generated by the firm before any payments to debt or equity holders are considered. We estimate a firm's current enterprise value, V_0, by computing the present value of the firm's free cash flow:

Discounted Free Cash Flow Model

$$V_0 = PV(\text{Future Free Cash Flow of Firm}) \tag{7.18}$$

Given the enterprise value, we can estimate the share price by using Equation 7.16 to solve for the value of equity and then divide by the total number of shares outstanding:

$$P_0 = \frac{V_0 + \text{Cash}_0 - \text{Debt}_0}{\text{Shares Outstanding}_0} \tag{7.19}$$

In the dividend-discount model, the firm's cash and debt are included indirectly through the effect of interest income and expenses on earnings. By contrast, in the discounted free cash flow model, we ignore interest income and expenses because free cash flow is based on EBIT (earnings *before* interest and taxes), but we then adjust for cash and debt directly (in Equation 7.19).

Implementing the Model. A key difference between the discounted free cash flow model and the earlier models we have considered is the discount rate. In previous calculations, we used the firm's equity cost of capital, r_E, because we were discounting the cash flows to equity holders. Here, we are discounting the free cash flow that will be paid to both debt and equity holders. Thus, we should use the firm's **weighted average cost of capital (WACC)**, denoted by r_{wacc}; it is the cost of capital that reflects the risk of the overall business, which is the combined risk of the firm's equity *and* debt. We interpret r_{wacc} as the expected return the firm must pay to investors to compensate them for the risk of holding the firm's debt and equity together. If the firm has no debt, then $r_{wacc} = r_E$.[9] We will develop methods to calculate the WACC explicitly in Part 4 of this text.

weighted average cost of capital (WACC) The cost of capital that reflects the risk of the overall business, which is the combined risk of the firm's equity and debt.

[9]We can also interpret the firm's WACC as the average cost of capital associated with all of the firm's projects. In that sense, the WACC is the expected return associated with the average risk of the firm's investments.

Given the firm's WACC, we implement the discounted free cash flow model in much the same way as we did the dividend-discount model. That is, we forecast the firm's free cash flow up to some horizon, together with a terminal (continuation) value of the enterprise:

$$V_0 = \frac{FCF_1}{1 + r_{wacc}} + \frac{FCF_2}{(1 + r_{wacc})^2} + \cdots + \frac{FCF_n}{(1 + r_{wacc})^n} + \frac{V_n}{(1 + r_{wacc})^n} \tag{7.20}$$

Often, we estimate the terminal value by assuming a constant long-run growth rate, g_{FCF}, for free cash flows beyond year n, so that

$$V_n = \frac{FCF_{n+1}}{r_{wacc} - g_{FCF}} = \left(\frac{1 + g_{FCF}}{r_{wacc} - g_{FCF}}\right) \times FCF_n \tag{7.21}$$

The long-run growth rate g_{FCF} is typically based on the expected long-run growth rate of the firm's revenues.

EXAMPLE 7.7 Valuing Nike, Inc., Stock Using Free Cash Flow

PROBLEM

Recall our earlier example of Nike. Nike had sales of $25.3 billion in 2012. Suppose you expect its sales to grow at a rate of 10% in 2013, but then slow by 1% per year to the long-run growth rate that is characteristic of the apparel industry, 5%, by 2018. Based on Nike's past profitability and investment needs, you expect EBIT to be 10% of sales, increases in net working capital requirements to be 10% of any increase in sales, and capital expenditures to equal depreciation expenses. If Nike has $3.3 billion in cash, $1.2 billion in debt, 893.6 million shares outstanding, a tax rate of 24%, and a WACC of 10%, what would have been your estimate of the value of Nike stock in early 2013?

SOLUTION

■ Plan

We can estimate Nike's future free cash flow by constructing a pro forma statement. Furthermore, we need to calculate a terminal (or continuation) value for Nike at the end of our explicit projections. Because we expect Nike's free cash flow to grow at a constant rate after 2018, we can use Equation 7.21 to compute a terminal enterprise value. The present value of the free cash flows during the years 2013–2018 and the terminal value will be the total enterprise value for Nike. From that value, we can subtract the debt, add the cash, and divide by the number of shares outstanding to compute the price per share (Equation 7.19).

■ Execute

The following spreadsheet presents a simplified pro forma for Nike based on the information we have:

1	**Year**	**2012**	**2013**	**2014**	**2015**	**2016**	**2017**	**2018**
2	**FCF Forecast ($ million)**							
3	Sales	25,300.0	27,830.0	30,334.7	32,761.5	35,054.8	37,158.1	39,016.0
4	*Growth versus Prior Year*		*10.0%*	*9.0%*	*8.0%*	*7.0%*	*6.0%*	*5.0%*
5	**EBIT** (10% of sales)		2,783.0	3,033.5	3,276.1	3,505.5	3,715.8	3,901.6
6	Less: Income Tax (24%)		667.9	728.0	786.3	841.3	891.8	936.4
7	Plus: Depreciation		–	–	–	–	–	–
8	Less: Capital Expenditures		–	–	–	–	–	–
9	Less: Increase in NWC (10% ΔSales)		253.0	250.5	242.7	229.3	210.3	185.8
10	**Free Cash Flow**		1,862.1	2,055.0	2,247.2	2,434.8	2,613.7	2,779.4

Because capital expenditures are expected to equal depreciation, lines 7 and 8 in the spreadsheet cancel out. We can set them both to zero rather than explicitly forecast them.

Given our assumption of constant 5% growth in free cash flows after 2018 and a WACC of 10%, we can use Equation 7.21 to compute a terminal enterprise value:

$$V_{2018} = \left(\frac{1 + g_{FCF}}{r_{wacc} - g_{FCF}}\right) \times FCF_{2018} = \left(\frac{1.05}{0.10 - 0.05}\right) \times 2{,}779.4 = \$58{,}367.9 \text{ million}$$

From Equation 7.20, Nike's current enterprise value is the present value of its free cash flows plus the present value of the firm's terminal value:

$$V_0 = \frac{1{,}862.1}{1.10} + \frac{2{,}055.0}{1.10^2} + \frac{2{,}247.2}{1.10^3} + \frac{2{,}434.8}{1.10^4} + \frac{2{,}613.7}{1.10^5} + \frac{2{,}779.4}{1.10^6} + \frac{58{,}367.9}{1.10^6}$$
$$= \$42{,}881.5 \text{ million}$$

We can now estimate the value of a share of Nike stock using Equation 7.19:

$$P_0 = \frac{\$42{,}881.5 + \$3{,}300 - \$1{,}200}{893.6} = \$50.34$$

■ **Evaluate**

The total value of all of the claims, both debt and equity, on the firm must equal the total present value of all cash flows generated by the firm, in addition to any cash it currently has. The total present value of all cash flows to be generated by Nike is $42,881.5 million, and it has $3300 million in cash. Subtracting the value of the debt claims ($1200 million) leaves us with the total value of the equity claims, and dividing by the number of shares produces the value per share. It is important to remember two things about valuation models: (1) They are only good at the time they are made; as time goes by, the data and assumptions used in the valuation model will change and, thus, so will the value, and (2) they use projections of what will happen, but these projections are subject to a lot of error. In the case of Nike, its projected enterprise value for 2018 was around $58 billion. In reality, by May 7, 2018, Nike's enterprise value was just over $110 billion.

Connection to Capital Budgeting. There is an important connection between the discounted free cash flow model for the firm and how we evaluate individual investment projects to be undertaken by the firm. In Chapter 3, we learned that decisions should be evaluated based on the costs and benefits, and if the value of the benefits outweighs the value of the costs the decision to proceed should be accepted. In Chapters 8 and 9, we will introduce and use the NPV criterion for evaluating projects. Essentially, the NPV criterion takes the present value of all expected future free cash flows of the project (the present value of the benefits) and compares it to the cost of undertaking the project. Because the firm's future free cash flow in any particular year is equal to the sum of that year's free cash flows from the firm's current and future investment projects, we can interpret the firm's enterprise value as the total value that the firm will generate from continuing its existing projects and initiating new ones. Hence, the NPV of any new project represents its contribution to the firm's enterprise value. To maximize the firm's share price, we should accept those projects that have a positive NPV (or, as we said in Chapter 3, make decisions that result in the value of the benefits being greater than the value of the costs).

Many forecasts and estimates are necessary to calculate the free cash flows of a project and, consequently, the free cash flows of the firm. We must forecast future sales, operating expenses, taxes, capital requirements, and other factors. On the one hand, estimating free cash flow in this way gives us flexibility to incorporate many specific details about the future prospects of the firm. On the other hand, some uncertainty inevitably surrounds each assumption. A sensitivity analysis shows how our final calculated value changes with respect to changes in one of the input variables in our model. Example 7.8 shows two sensitivity analyses: how the valuation changes with a change in revenue growth and how the valuation changes with a change in EBIT margin. We explore sensitivity analysis more fully in Chapter 9.

EXAMPLE 7.8 Sensitivity Analysis for Stock Valuation

PROBLEM

In Example 7.7, Nike's EBIT was assumed to be 10% of sales. If Nike can reduce its operating expenses and raise its EBIT to 11% of sales, how would the estimate of the stock's value change?

SOLUTION

■ Plan

In this scenario, EBIT will increase by 1% of sales compared to Example 7.7. From there, we can use the tax rate (24%) to compute the effect on the free cash flow for each year. Once we have the new free cash flows, we repeat the approach in Example 7.7 to arrive at a new stock price.

■ Execute

In year 1, EBIT will be 1% × \$27,830 million = \$278.3 million higher. After taxes, this increase will raise the firm's free cash flow in year 1 by (1 − 0.242) × \$278.3 = \$211.5 million, to \$2073.6 million. Doing the same calculation for each year, we get the following revised FCF estimates:

Year	2013	2014	2015	2016	2017	2018
FCF	2,073.6	2,285.5	2,496.2	2,701.2	2,896.1	3,075.9

We can now re-estimate the stock price as in Example 7.7. The terminal value is

$$V_{2018} = [1.05/(0.10 - 0.05)] \times 3{,}075.9 = \$64{,}594.80 \text{ million, so}$$

$$V_0 = \frac{2{,}073.6}{1.10} + \frac{2{,}285.5}{1.10^2} + \frac{2{,}496.2}{1.10^3} + \frac{2{,}701.2}{1.10^4} + \frac{2{,}896.1}{1.10^5} + \frac{3{,}075.9}{1.10^6} + \frac{64{,}594.8}{1.10^6}$$
$$= \$47{,}491 \text{ million}$$

The new estimate for the value of the stock is $P_0 = (47{,}491 + 3{,}300 - 1{,}200)/893.6 =$ \$55.50 per share, a difference of about 10% compared to the result found in Example 7.7.

■ Evaluate

Nike's stock price is fairly sensitive to changes in the assumptions about its profitability. A 1% permanent change in its margins affects the firm's stock price by 10%.

Figure 7.3 summarizes the different valuation methods we have discussed so far. The value of the stock is determined by the present value of its future dividends. We can estimate the total market capitalization of the firm's equity from the present value of the firm's total payouts, which includes dividends and share repurchases. Finally, the present value of the firm's free cash flow, which is the amount of cash the firm has available to make payments to equity or debt holders, determines the firm's enterprise value.

FIGURE 7.3 A Comparison of Discounted Cash Flow Models of Stock Valuation

By computing the present value of the firm's dividends, total payouts, or free cash flows, we can estimate the value of the stock, the total value of the firm's equity, or the firm's enterprise value. The final column details what adjustment is necessary to obtain the stock price.

Present Value of...	Determines the...	To Get Stock Price Estimate...
Dividend Payments	Stock Price	No adjustment necessary
Total Payouts (all dividends and repurchases)	Equity Value	Divide by shares oustanding
Free Cash Flow (cash available to pay all security holders)	Enterprise Value	Subtract what does not belong to equity holders (debt and preferred stock) and add back cash or other non-performing assets that do not contribute to the firm's free cash flows. Then divide by shares outstanding.

CONCEPT CHECK

9. What is the relation between capital budgeting and the discounted free cash flow model?
10. Why do we ignore interest payments on the firm's debt in the discounted free cash flow model?

7.7 Valuation Based on Comparable Firms

So far, we have valued a firm or its stock by considering the expected future cash flows it will provide to its owner. The Valuation Principle then tells us that its value is the present value of its future cash flows, because the present value is the amount we would need to invest elsewhere in the market to replicate the cash flows with the same risk.

method of comparables An estimate of the value of a firm based on the value of other, comparable, firms or other investments that are expected to generate very similar cash flows in the future.

Another application of the Law of One Price is the method of comparables. In the **method of comparables** (or "comps"), rather than value the firm's cash flows directly, we estimate the value of the firm based on the value of other, comparable, firms or investments that we expect will generate very similar cash flows in the future. For example, consider the case of a new firm that is *identical* to an existing publicly traded company. Recall that from competitive market prices, the Valuation Principle implies that two securities with identical cash flows must have the same price. Thus, if firms will generate identical cash flows, we can use the market value of the existing company to determine the value of the new firm.

Of course, identical companies do not really exist. Even two firms in the same industry selling the same types of products, while similar in many respects, are likely to be of a different size or scale. For example, Hewlett-Packard and Dell both sell personal computers directly to consumers using the internet. In 2009, Hewlett-Packard had sales of $115 billion, whereas Dell had sales of approximately $53 billion. In this section, we consider ways to adjust for scale differences to use comparables to value firms with similar businesses and then discuss the strengths and weaknesses of this approach.

Valuation Multiples

valuation multiple A ratio of a firm's value to some measure of the firm's scale or cash flow.

We can adjust for differences in scale between firms by expressing their value in terms of a **valuation multiple**, which is a ratio of the value to some measure of the firm's scale. As an analogy, consider valuing an office building. A natural measure to consider would be the price per square foot for other buildings recently sold in the area. Multiplying the size of the office building under consideration by the average price per square foot would typically provide a reasonable estimate of the building's value. We can apply this same idea to stocks, replacing square footage with some more appropriate measure of the firm's scale.

The Price-Earnings Ratio. The most common valuation multiple is the price-earnings (P/E) ratio, which we introduced in Chapter 2. The P/E ratio is so common that it is almost always part of the basic statistics computed for a stock (as shown in Figure 7.1, the screenshot from the Google Finance website for Nike). A firm's P/E ratio is equal to the share price divided by its earnings per share. The reasoning behind its use is that when you buy a stock you are in a sense buying the rights to the firm's future earnings. If differences in the scale of firms' earnings are likely to persist, you should be willing to pay proportionally more for a stock with higher current earnings. Using this idea, we can estimate the value of a firm's share by multiplying its current earnings per share by the average P/E ratio of comparable firms.

trailing earnings A firm's earnings over the prior 12 months.

forward earnings A firm's anticipated earnings over the coming 12 months.

trailing P/E A firm's P/E ratio calculated using its trailing earnings.

forward P/E A firm's P/E ratio calculated using its forward earnings.

We can compute a firm's P/E ratio by using either **trailing earnings** (earnings over the prior 12 months) or **forward earnings** (expected earnings over the coming 12 months), with the resulting ratios being called the **trailing P/E** or the **forward P/E**, respectively. For valuation purposes, the forward P/E is generally preferred, as we are most concerned about future earnings.

To understand how P/E ratios relate to other valuation techniques we have discussed, consider the dividend-discount model introduced earlier in the chapter.[10] For example, in the case of constant dividend growth, dividing through Equation 7.6 we had

$$P_0 = \frac{Div_1}{r_E - g}$$

Dividing through by EPS_1, we find that

$$\text{Forward P/E} = \frac{P_0}{EPS_1} = \frac{Div_1/EPS_1}{r_E - g} = \frac{\text{Dividend Payout Rate}}{r_E - g} \tag{7.22}$$

Earlier, we showed that Nike's price was consistent with an equity cost of capital of 10% and an expected dividend growth rate of 8.5%. From the Nike quote, we can also see that Nike had EPS of $2.52 and a dividend of $0.21 per quarter, or $0.84 per year, which

[10]We use the dividend-discount model rather than discounted cash flows because price and earnings are variables associated exclusively with equity.

gives a dividend payout rate of $0.84/2.52 = 0.333$. Assuming that earnings growth and payout rates remain at this level for the foreseeable future, then we could compute the forward P/E as

$$\text{Forward P/E} = \frac{0.84/2.52}{.10 - 0.085} = 22.22, \text{ which is not far off its reported P/E of 24.00.}$$

Equation 7.22 suggests that firms and industries that have high growth rates, and that generate cash well in excess of their investment needs so that they can maintain high payout rates, should have high P/E multiples. In the Nike example, we showed that at an expected growth rate of 8.5%, it would have a P/E ratio of 22.22. If our growth expectations were lower, its P/E would drop. Holding current earnings, dividends, and equity cost of capital constant, but decreasing the growth rate to 5%, we would have

$$\text{Forward P/E} = \frac{0.84/2.52}{.10 - 0.05} = 6.67$$

This result is much lower than its current P/E of 24.00, making it clear that simply comparing P/E ratios without taking into account growth prospects can be highly misleading.

Figure 7.4 shows the relationship between expected earnings growth and P/E ratios.

FIGURE 7.4 Relating the P/E Ratio to Expected Future Growth

The graph shows the expected growth in earnings under two growth scenarios for Nike: 8.5% and 5% in 2013. Current earnings per share is $2.52. Higher growth increases the PV of the earnings stream, which means that the price increases. The result is that the higher price divided by current earnings yields a higher P/E ratio. We found that a growth rate of 8.5% implied a P/E ratio of 22.22, while a growth rate of 5% implied a P/E ratio of 6.67. The graph shows how higher expected growth translates into a higher P/E.

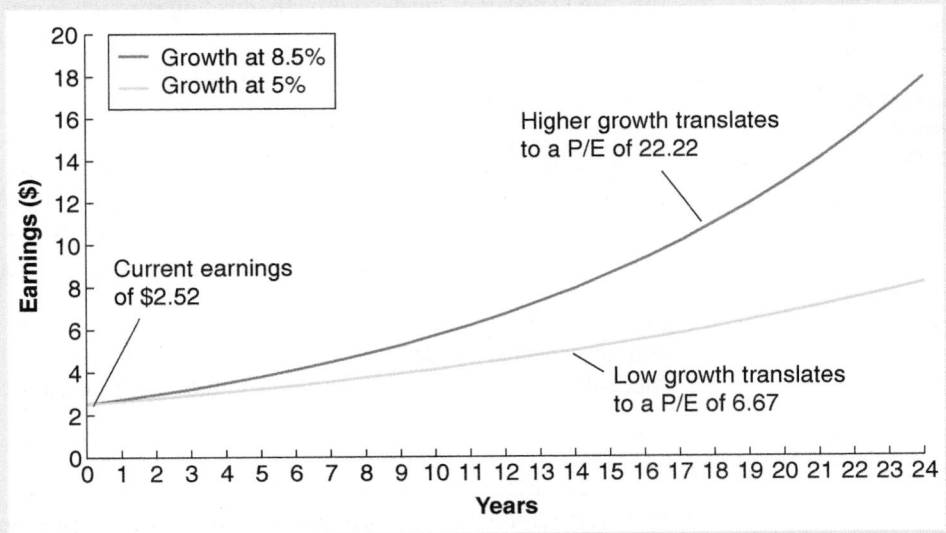

EXAMPLE 7.9 Growth Prospects and the Price-Earnings Ratio

PROBLEM

Amazon.com and Sears are both retailers based in the United States. In 2010, Amazon stock had a price of $138.71 and a forward earnings per share of $2.61. Sears had a price of $20.87 and forward earnings per share of $1.87. Calculate their forward P/E ratios and explain the difference.

SOLUTION

■ Plan

We can calculate their P/E ratios by dividing each company's price per share by its forward earnings per share. The difference is most likely due to different growth expectations.

■ Execute

The forward P/E for Amazon = $138.71/$2.61 = 53. The forward P/E for Sears = $20.87/$1.87 = 11.16. Amazon's P/E ratio is higher because investors expect its earnings to grow more than those of Sears.

■ Evaluate

Although both companies are retailers, they have very different growth prospects, as reflected in their P/E ratios. Investors in Amazon.com are willing to pay 53 times that year's expected earnings because they are also buying the present value of high future earnings created by expected growth. Given the information reported by Bloomberg on May 7, 2018, it seems investors were correct. Forward earnings per share had risen to about $12 for Amazon and its stock price was about $1600 per share. Unfortunately for Sears, forward earnings per share had dropped to a negative amount of –$11.91 and its stock price had dropped to $3.12 per share.

Enterprise Value Multiples. The P/E ratio has the same limitations as the dividend-discount model—because it relates exclusively to equity, it ignores the effect of debt. Consequently, it is also common practice to use valuation multiples based on the firm's enterprise value. By representing the total value of the firm's underlying business rather than just the value of equity, the enterprise value allows us to compare firms with different amounts of leverage.

Because the enterprise value represents the entire value of the firm before the firm pays its debt, to form an appropriate multiple, we divide it by a measure of earnings or cash flows before interest payments are made. Common multiples to consider are enterprise value to EBIT, EBITDA (earnings before interest, taxes, depreciation, and amortization), and free cash flow. However, because capital expenditures can vary substantially from period to period (e.g., a firm may need to add capacity and build a new plant one year, but then may not need to expand further for many years), most practitioners rely on enterprise value to EBITDA multiples. From Equation 7.21, if expected free cash flow growth is constant, then

$$\frac{V_0}{EBITDA_1} = \frac{\dfrac{FCF_1}{r_{wacc} - g_{FCF}}}{EDITDA_1} = \frac{FCF_1/EBITDA_1}{r_{wacc} - g_{FCF}} \tag{7.23}$$

As with the P/E multiple, this valuation multiple is higher for firms with high growth rates and low capital requirements (which means that free cash flow is high in proportion to EBITDA).

EXAMPLE 7.10 Valuation Using the Enterprise Value Multiple

PROBLEM

Westcoast Port Inc. is an ocean transport company with EBITDA of $50 million, cash of $20 million, debt of $100 million, and 10 million shares outstanding. The ocean transport industry as a whole has an average enterprise value to EBITDA (EV/EBITDA) ratio of 8.5. What is one estimate of Westcoast's enterprise value? What is a corresponding estimate of its stock price?

SOLUTION

Plan

To estimate Westcoast's enterprise value, we multiply its EBITDA by the average EV/EBITDA ratio of its industry. From there, we can subtract Westcoast's debt and add its cash to calculate its equity value. Finally, we can divide by the number of shares outstanding to arrive at its stock price.

Execute

Westcoast's enterprise value estimate is $50 million × 8.5 = $425 million.

Next, subtract the debt from its enterprise value and add in its cash:

$425 million − $100 million + $20 million = $345 million, which is an estimate of the equity value.

Its stock price estimate is equal to its equity value estimate divided by the number of shares outstanding:

$345 million/10 million = $34.50.

Evaluate

If we assume that Westcoast should be valued similarly to the rest of the industry, then $425 million is a reasonable estimate of its enterprise value, and $34.50 is a reasonable estimate of its stock price. However, we are relying on the assumption that Westcoast's expected free cash flow growth is similar to the industry average. If that assumption is wrong, so is our valuation.

Other Multiples. Many other valuation multiples are possible. Looking at the enterprise value as a multiple of sales can be useful if it is reasonable to assume that the firm will maintain a similar margin in the future. For firms with substantial tangible assets, the ratio of price to book value of equity per share is sometimes used as a valuation multiple. Some multiples are specific to an industry. In the cable TV industry, for example, it is natural to consider enterprise value per subscriber.

Limitations of Multiples

If comparables were identical to those of the firms being valued, the firms' multiples would match precisely. Of course, firms are not identical, so the usefulness of a valuation multiple will inevitably depend on the nature of the differences between firms and the sensitivity of the multiples to these differences.

Table 7.2 lists several valuation multiples, as of July 2013, for firms in the footwear industry that could be used as comparables for Nike. Also shown in the table is the average for each multiple, together with the range around the average (in percentage terms). The bottom rows showing the range make it clear that the footwear industry has a lot of dispersion for all of the multiples. (For example, Wolverine has a price-to-book (P/B) ratio of 4.13, while Rocky Brands, Inc. has a P/B of only 0.89.) While the enterprise value/sales multiple shows the smallest variation, even with it we cannot expect to obtain a precise estimate of a firm's value.

TABLE 7.2 Stock Prices and Multiples for the Footwear Industry, July 2013

Name	Market Capitalization ($ million)	Enterprise Value ($ million)	P/E	Price/Book	Enterprise Value/Sales	Enterprise Value/EBITDA
Nike, Inc.	55,970	54,023	23.29	5.07	2.03	15.71
Adidas AG	23,105	23,317	32.33	3.06	1.20	11.88
Puma AG	4,330	4,085	70.56	1.96	0.96	9.34
Wolverine World Wide	2,910	3,981	37.6	4.13	1.22	9.28
Steven Madden, Ltd.	2,320	2,140	18.4	3.68	1.74	10.70
Deckers Outdoor Corp.	1,990	1,923	16.74	2.67	1.36	8.73
Crocs, Inc.	1,470	1,240	11.46	2.4	1.10	6.74
Skechers U.S.A.	1,340	1,213	67.41	1.54	0.78	18.16
Weyco Group	301	325	16.53	1.71	1.11	9.69
R. G. Barry Corp.	197	174	14.92	2.31	1.19	6.44
Rocky Brands, Inc.	113	132	12.46	0.89	0.58	6.61
		Average (excluding Nike)	**29.84**	**2.44**	**1.12**	**9.76**
		Maximum (excluding Nike)	136%	70%	55%	86%
		Minimum (excluding Nike)	–62%	–63%	–48%	–34%

All ratios as of July 2013.

The differences in these multiples most likely reflect differences in expected future growth rates, risk (and therefore costs of capital), and, in the case of Puma and Adidas, differences in the accounting conventions used in Germany, where Puma and Adidas are based, and in the United States, where other firms to which they are being compared are based. As with Puma and Adidas, differences in accounting conventions are especially problematic for Canadian firms. This is due to the lack of many comparable companies (that match based on industry and size) in Canada; the comparables are often chosen from the United States, where the accounting rules sometimes differ in important ways. Investors in the market understand that these differences exist, so the stocks are priced accordingly. When valuing a firm using multiples, however, there is no clear guidance about how to adjust for these differences other than by narrowing the set of comparables used and being very careful in interpreting the accounting information given.

Another limitation of comparables is that they provide only information regarding the value of the firm *relative to* the other firms in the comparison set. Using multiples will not help us determine whether an entire industry is overvalued, for example. This issue became especially important during the internet boom of the late 1990s. Because many of these firms did not have positive cash flows or earnings, new multiples were created to value them (e.g., price to "page views"). While these multiples could justify the value of these firms in relation to one another, it was much more difficult to justify the stock prices of many of these firms using a realistic estimate of cash flows and the discounted free cash flow approach.

Comparison with Discounted Cash Flow Methods

The use of a valuation multiple based on comparables is best viewed as a shortcut to the discounted cash flow methods of valuation. Rather than separately estimate the firm's cost of capital and future earnings or free cash flows, we rely on the market's assessment of the value of other firms with similar future prospects. In addition to its simplicity, the multiples approach has the advantage of being based on actual stock prices of real firms, rather than on what may be unrealistic forecasts of future cash flows.

The most important shortcoming of the comparables approach is that it does not take into account the important differences among firms. For example, the approach ignores the fact that some firms have exceptionally talented managers, others have developed more efficient manufacturing processes, and still others might hold a patent on a new technology. Discounted cash flows methods have an advantage in this respect, in that they allow us to incorporate specific information about the firm's cost of capital or future growth. Thus, because the true driver of value for any firm is its ability to generate cash flows for its investors, using the discounted cash flow methods has the potential to be more accurate than using a valuation multiple.

Stock Valuation Techniques: The Final Word

In the end, no single technique provides a final answer regarding a stock's true value. Indeed, all approaches inevitably require assumptions or forecasts that are too uncertain to provide a definitive assessment of the firm's value. Most real-world practitioners use a combination of these approaches and gain confidence in the outcome if the results are consistent across a variety of methods.

Figure 7.5 compares the ranges of values for Nike stock using the different valuation methods discussed in this chapter. The firm's stock price of $60.39 on June 25, 2013, was within the range estimated by some methods, but higher than the range suggested by

FIGURE 7.5 **Range of Valuations for Nike Stock Using Various Valuation Methods**

Valuations from multiples are based on the low, high, and average values of the comparable firms from Table 7.2. The constant dividend growth model is based on a 10% equity cost of capital and dividend growth rates of 6% to 9%, as discussed at the beginning of Section 7.4. The discounted free cash flow model is based on Example 7.7, with the range of parameters in Problem 8 at the end of this chapter. Midpoints are based on average multiples or base case assumptions. Red and blue regions show the variation between the lowest-multiple/worst-case scenario and the highest-multiple/best-case scenario. Nike's actual share price of $60.39 is indicated by the gray line.

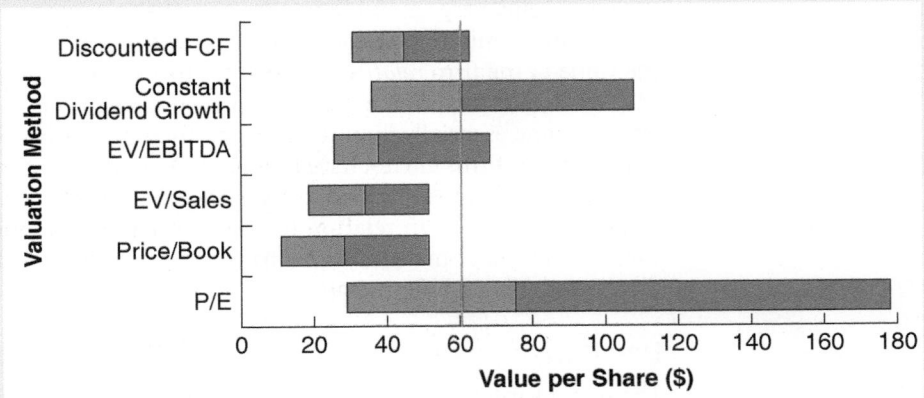

INTERVIEW WITH MARILYN FEDAK

Marilyn Fedak

Marilyn G. Fedak is the vice chair, investment services, and was formerly head of global value equities at AllianceBernstein, a publicly traded global asset management firm with approximately $450 billion in assets.

Q What valuation methods do you use to identify buying opportunities for value stocks?

A We use both a dividend-discount model (DDM) and a proprietary quantitative return model called the Global Edge Model (GEM). For our non-U.S. portfolios, we use the GEM model; in the United States, we use a combination of GEM and the DDM.

At its most basic level, the DDM provides a way to evaluate how much we need to pay today for a company's future earnings and cash flow.* All things being equal, we are looking to buy as much earnings power as cheaply as we can. It is a very reliable methodology *if* you have the right forecasts for companies' future earnings. Our GEM model encompasses a variety of valuation measures, such as P/E and price-to-book ratios and selected success factors—for example, ROE and price momentum.

In both the U.S. and non-U.S. portfolios, we use these valuation tools to rank companies from the most undervalued to the most expensive. We focus on the stocks that rank the highest. Our decision-making bodies, the investment policy groups, meet with analysts to quality-control the forecasts for the highest-ranked group of stocks. Once the forecasts are approved, we add risk tools to construct optimal portfolios.

Q Are there drawbacks to these models?

A Both models have advantages and drawbacks. The DDM is a very reliable valuation methodology. However, its focus on forecasts of cash flow or earnings over some future period requires a large, highly skilled body of research analysts. And, it is oriented to the long term, so the timing of purchases and sales can be too early.

The GEM is very useful for efficiently evaluating investments within large universes. However, it is very oriented to current profitability and valuation metrics—not the future. As such, judgment has to be applied to determine if a company is likely to sustain similar characteristics going forward.

Q Did the precipitous decline in stock prices in late 2008 and early 2009 cause you to retool your valuation methodology?

A In 2006, we began studying the interaction of the DDM and the GEM, and determined that combining the two models gives us superior results to a single methodology when evaluating U.S. securities. The DDM focuses on forecasts of a company's future, whereas the quant [quantitative] return model captures a company's history and current status. This new methodology was very helpful to us in 2008, when the GEM signalled caution for certain sectors that looked inexpensive based on the DDM.

We have also broadened our research to incorporate more external inputs and have assigned a higher probability to unlikely events, such as the recent government intervention in the financial and auto industries. On the risk side, we have added a refinancing risk tool and are tracking short interest in various equities.

*Because of historical usage, many practitioners use the term "dividend-discount model" to refer to the entire class of cash flow discount models.

some multiples. Hence, based on this evidence alone, we would not conclude that the stock is obviously under- or overpriced. But what if this were not the case—what if these valuation techniques produce valuations markedly different to what the stock is trading at in the market? In the next section, we tackle this question.

CONCEPT CHECK

11. What are some common valuation multiples?

12. What implicit assumptions are made when valuing a firm using multiples based on comparable firms?

7.8 Information, Competition, and Stock Prices

As shown in Figure 7.6, the models described in this chapter link the firm's expected future cash flows, its cost of capital (determined by its risk), and the value of its shares. But what conclusions should we draw if the actual market price of a stock does not appear to be consistent with our estimate of its value? Is it more likely that the stock is mispriced or that we are mistaken about its risk and future cash flows?

FIGURE 7.6 The Valuation Triad

Valuation models determine the relationship among the firm's future cash flows, its cost of capital, and the value of its shares. The stock's expected cash flows and cost of capital can be used to assess its market price (share value). Conversely, the market price can be used to assess the firm's future cash flows or cost of capital.

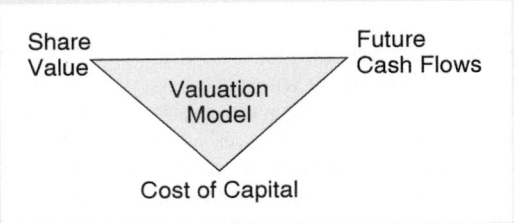

Information in Stock Prices

Suppose you are a new junior analyst assigned to research Nike's stock and assess its value. You scrutinize the company's recent financial statements, look at the trends in the industry, and forecast the firm's future earnings, dividends, and free cash flows. After you carefully crunch the numbers, you estimate the stock's value to be $85 per share. On your way to present your analysis to your boss, you run into a slightly more experienced colleague in the elevator. It turns out that your colleague has been researching the same stock. But according to her analysis, the value of Nike stock is only $65 per share. What would you do?

Although you could just assume your colleague is wrong, most of us would reconsider our own analysis. The fact that someone else who has carefully studied the same stock has come to a very different conclusion is powerful evidence that we might be mistaken. In the face of this information from our colleague, we would probably adjust our assessment of the stock's value downward. Of course, our colleague might also revise her opinion upward based on our assessment. After sharing our analyses, we would probably end up with a consensus estimate somewhere between $65 and $85 per share.

This type of encounter happens millions of times every day in the stock market. When a buyer seeks to buy a stock, the willingness of other parties to sell the same stock suggests that they value the stock differently. This information should lead both buyers and sellers to revise their valuations. Ultimately, investors trade until they reach a consensus regarding the value (market price) of the stock. In this way, stock markets aggregate the information and views of many different investors.

Thus, if your valuation model suggests a stock is worth $30 per share when it is trading for $20 per share in the market, the discrepancy is equivalent to knowing that thousands of investors—many of them professionals who have access to the best information about the stock available—disagree with your assessment. This knowledge should make you reconsider your original analysis. You would need a very compelling reason to trust your own estimate in the face of such contrary opinions.

What conclusion can we draw from this discussion? Recall Figure 7.6 in which a valuation model links the firm's future cash flows, its cost of capital, and its share price. In other words, given accurate information about any two of these variables, a valuation model allows us to make inferences about the third variable. Thus, the way we use a valuation model will depend on the quality of our information; the model will tell us the most about the variable for which our prior information is the least reliable.

The market price of a publicly traded firm should already provide very accurate information, aggregated from a multitude of investors, regarding the true value of its shares. In most situations, a valuation model is best applied to tell us something about the firm's future cash flows or cost of capital, based on its current stock price. Only in the relatively rare case in which we have some superior information that other investors lack regarding the firm's cash flows and cost of capital would it make sense to second-guess the stock price.

EXAMPLE 7.11 Using the Information in Market Prices

PROBLEM

Suppose Tecnorth Industries will have free cash flows next year of $40 million. Its WACC is 11%, and you expect its free cash flows to grow at a rate of approximately 4% per year, though you are somewhat unsure of the precise growth rate. Tecnorth has 10 million shares outstanding, no debt, and $20 million in cash. If Tecnorth's stock is currently trading at $55.33 per share, how would you update your beliefs about its dividend growth rate?

SOLUTION

■ Plan

If we apply the growing perpetuity formula for the growing FCF based on a 4% growth rate, we can estimate a stock price using Equations 7.18 and 7.19. If the market price is higher than our estimate, it implies that the market expects higher growth in FCF than 4%. Conversely, if the market price is lower than our estimate, the market expects FCF growth to be less than 4%.

■ Execute

Applying the growing perpetuity formula, we have $PV(FCF) = 40/(0.11 - 0.04) = \$571.43$ million. Applying Equation 7.18, the price per share would be ($571.43 million − 0 + $20 million)/10 million shares = $59.14 per share. The market price of $55.33, however, implies that most investors expect FCF to grow at a somewhat slower rate.

■ Evaluate

Given the $55.33 market price for the stock, we should lower our expectations for the FCF growth rate from 4% unless we have very strong reasons to trust our own estimate.

Competition and Efficient Markets

The notion that market prices reflect the information of many investors is a natural consequence of investor competition. If information were available that indicated that buying a stock had a positive NPV, investors with that information would choose to buy the stock; their attempts to purchase it would then drive up the stock's price. By a similar logic, investors with information that selling a stock had a positive NPV would sell it, and so the stock's price would fall.

The idea that competition among investors works to eliminate *all* positive-NPV (or value creating) trading opportunities is referred to as the **efficient markets hypothesis**. It implies that securities will be fairly priced, based on their future cash flows, given all information that is available to investors. Figure 7.7 indicates three forms of market efficiency— weak, semistrong, and strong.

efficient markets hypothesis The idea that competition among investors works to eliminate all positive-NPV trading opportunities. It implies that securities will be fairly priced, based on their future cash flows, given all information that is available to investors.

FIGURE 7.7 Forms of Market Efficiency

The type of market efficiency we describe here, where all publicly available information is incorporated very quickly into stock prices, is often called semistrong-form market efficiency. The term "semistrong" indicates that it is not as complete as strong-form market efficiency, where prices immediately incorporate all information, including private information known, for example, only to managers. Finally, the term "weak-form market efficiency" means that only the history of past prices is already reflected in the stock price. It helps to think of the different forms of market efficiency as meaning that prices incorporate a steadily increasing set of information, and that each of these forms encompasses all the lower forms. For example, since the history of past prices is public information, semistrong-form efficiency encompasses weak-form. The diagram illustrates the idea. In the diagram, the information sets of weak-form, semistrong-form, and strong-form efficiency are represented by the blue, green, and yellow circles, respectively.

Not all market participants believe that the stock market is semistrong-form efficient. Technical analysts, who look for patterns in stock prices, do not believe the market is even weak-form efficient. Mutual fund managers and fundamental analysts, such as those who work for brokerages and make stock recommendations, believe that mispricing can be uncovered by careful analysis of company fundamentals. There is evidence that traders with inside information about an upcoming merger or earnings announcements can make abnormal returns by trading (illegally) on that information, so the market is clearly not strong-form efficient.

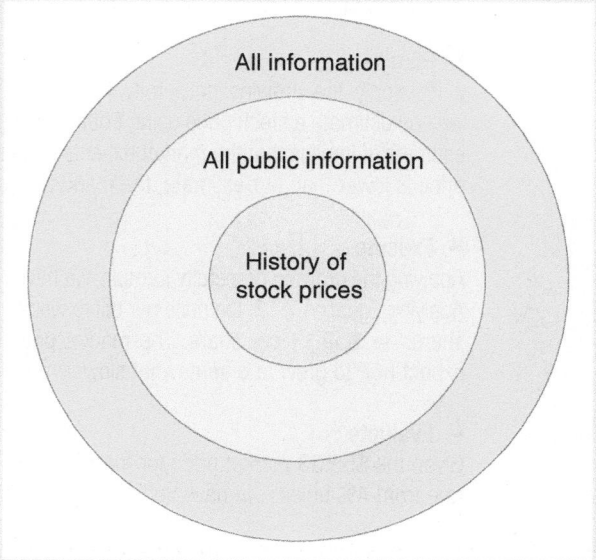

What happens if new information about a stock arrives? The answer depends on the degree of competition; that is, on the number of investors who have access to this new information. Consider two important cases.

Public, Easily Interpretable Information. Information that is available to all investors includes information in news reports, financial statements, corporate press releases, or other public data sources. If investors can readily ascertain the effects of this information on the firm's future cash flows, then all investors can determine how this information will change the firm's value.

In this situation, we expect competition among investors to be fierce and the stock price to react nearly instantaneously to such news. A few lucky investors might be able to trade a small quantity of shares before the price has fully adjusted. Most investors, however, would find that the stock price already reflected the new information before they were able to trade on it. In other words, the efficient markets hypothesis holds very well with respect to this type of information.

EXAMPLE 7.12 Stock Price Reactions to Public Information

PROBLEM

Suppose Pfizer announced it is pulling Viagra from the market due to newly discovered negative side effects. As a result, Pfizer's future expected free cash flow will decline by $850 million per year for the next 10 years. Assume Pfizer has 500 million shares outstanding, no debt, and an equity cost of capital of 8%. If this news came as a complete surprise to investors, what should happen to Pfizer's stock price upon the announcement?

SOLUTION

■ Plan

In this case, we can use the discounted free cash flow method. With no debt, $r_{wacc} = r_E = 8\%$. The effect on the Pfizer's enterprise value will be the loss of a 10-year annuity of $850 million. We can compute the effect today as the present value of that annuity.

■ Execute

Using the annuity formula, the decline in expected free cash flow will reduce Pfizer's enterprise value by

$$\$850 \text{ million} \times \frac{1}{0.08}\left(1 - \frac{1}{1.08^{10}}\right) = \$5.704 \text{ billion}$$

Thus, the share price should fall by $5.704 billion/500 million shares = $11.41 per share.

■ Evaluate

Because this news is public and its effect on the firm's expected free cash flow is clear, we would expect the stock price to drop by $11.41 per share nearly instantaneously.

Private or Difficult-to-Interpret Information. Of course, some information is not publicly available. For example, an analyst might spend considerable time and effort gathering information from a firm's employees, competitors, suppliers, or customers that is relevant to the firm's future cash flows. This information is not available to other investors who have not devoted a similar effort to gathering it.

Even when information is publicly available, it may be difficult to interpret. Non-experts in the field may find it difficult to evaluate research reports on new technologies, for example. It may take a great deal of legal and accounting expertise and effort to understand the full consequences of a highly complicated business transaction. Certain consulting experts may have greater insight into consumer tastes and the likelihood of a product's acceptance. In these cases, while the fundamental information may be public, the *interpretation* of how that information will affect the firm's future cash flows is itself private information.

As an example, imagine that Snowy Pharmaceuticals has just announced the development of a new drug for which the company is seeking approval from Health Canada. If the drug is approved and subsequently launched in the Canadian market, the future profits from the new drug will increase Snowy's market value by $750 million, or $15 per share, given its 50 million shares outstanding. Assume that the development of this drug comes as a surprise to investors, and that the average likelihood of Health Canada approval is 10%. In that case, because many investors probably know that the chance of Health Canada approval is 10%, competition should lead to an immediate jump in Snowy's stock price of $10\% \times \$15 = \$1.50$ per share. Over time, however, analysts and experts in the field will probably make their own assessments of the probable efficacy of the drug. If they conclude that the drug looks more promising than average, they will begin to trade on their private information and buy the stock, and the firm's price will tend to drift higher over time. If the experts conclude that the drug looks less promising than average, however, they will tend to sell the stock, and the firm's price will drift lower over time. Of course, at the time of the announcement, uninformed investors do not know which way it will go. Examples of possible price paths are shown in Figure 7.8.

FIGURE 7.8 Possible Stock Price Paths for Snowy Pharmaceuticals

Snowy's stock price jumps on the announcement based on the average likelihood of Health Canada approval. The stock price then drifts up (green path) or down (orange path) as informed traders trade on their more accurate assessment of the drug's likelihood of approval and, hence, entry into the Canadian market. At the time of the announcement, uninformed investors do not know which way the stock will go.

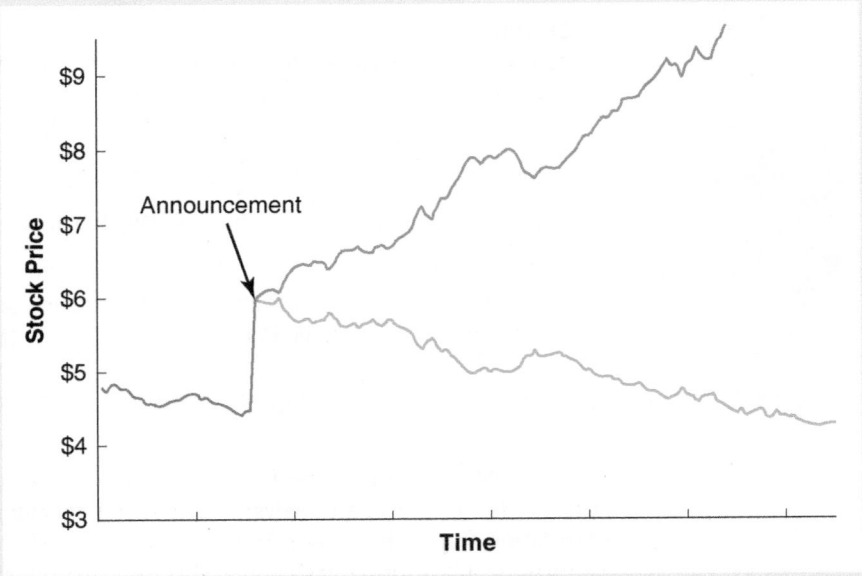

When private information is in the hands of only a relatively small number of investors, these investors may be able to profit by trading on their information.[11] In this case, the efficient markets hypothesis will not hold in the strict sense. However, as these informed traders begin to trade, their actions will tend to move prices, so over time prices will begin to reflect their information as well.

If the profit opportunities from having this type of information are large, other individuals will attempt to gain the expertise and devote the resources needed to acquire it. As more individuals become better informed, competition to exploit this information will increase. Thus, in the long run, we should expect that the degree of "inefficiency" in the market will be limited by the costs of obtaining the information.

Lessons for Investors and Corporate Managers

The effect of competition based on information about stock prices has important consequences for both investors and corporate managers.

Consequences for Investors. Investors should be able to identify positive-NPV trading opportunities in securities markets, as in other markets, only if some barrier or restriction to free competition exists. An investor's competitive advantage may take several forms. For instance, the investor may have expertise or access to information that is known to only a few people. Alternatively, the investor may have lower trading costs than other market participants and so can exploit opportunities that others would find unprofitable. In all cases, the source of the positive-NPV trading opportunity must be something that is difficult to replicate; otherwise, any gains would be competed away in short order.

While the fact that positive-NPV trading opportunities are hard to come by may be disappointing, there is some good news as well. If stocks are fairly priced according to our valuation models, then investors who buy stocks can expect to receive future cash flows that fairly compensate them for the risk of their investment. In such cases, the average investor can invest with confidence, even if he is not fully informed.

Implications for Corporate Managers. If stocks are fairly valued according to the models we have described, then the value of a firm is determined by the cash flows that it can pay to its investors. This result has several key implications for corporate managers:

- *Focus on* NPV *and free cash flow.* A manager seeking to boost the price of her firm's stock should make investments that increase the present value of the firm's free cash flow. Thus, the capital budgeting methods outlined in Chapter 9 are fully consistent with the objective of maximizing the firm's share price.
- *Avoid accounting illusions.* Many managers make the mistake of focusing on accounting earnings as opposed to free cash flows. According to the efficient markets hypothesis, the accounting consequences of a decision do not directly affect the value of the firm and should not drive decision making.
- *Use financial transactions to support investment.* With efficient markets, a firm can sell its shares at a fair price to new investors. As a consequence, the firm should not be constrained from raising capital to fund positive-NPV investment opportunities.

---

[11]Even with private information, informed investors may find it difficult to profit from that information, because they must find others who are willing to trade with them; that is, the market for the stock must be sufficiently *liquid.* A liquid market requires that other investors in the market have alternative motives to trade (e.g., selling shares of a stock to purchase a house) and so be willing to trade even when facing the risk that other traders may be better informed.

The Efficient Markets Hypothesis versus No Arbitrage

There is an important distinction between the efficient markets hypothesis and the notion of a normal market that we introduced in Chapter 3. An arbitrage opportunity is a situation in which two securities (or portfolios) with *identical* cash flows have different prices. Because anyone can earn a sure profit in this situation by buying the low-priced security and selling the high-priced one, we expect investors to immediately exploit and eliminate these opportunities. Thus, arbitrage opportunities will not be found.

The efficient markets hypothesis states that the best estimate of the value of a share of stock is its market price. That is, investors' own estimates of value are not as accurate as the market price. But that does not mean that the market price always correctly estimates the value of a share of stock. There is a difference between the best estimate and being correct. Thus, there is no reason to expect the market price to always assess value accurately; rather, the price is best viewed as an approximation. However, because the price is the best estimate, the efficient market hypothesis implies that you cannot tell which prices overestimate and which underestimate the true value of a stock.

CONCEPT CHECK

13. State the efficient markets hypothesis.

14. What are the implications of the efficient markets hypothesis for corporate managers?

7.9 Individual Biases and Trading

Efficient markets imply that positive-NPV trading opportunities will be hard to come by, especially for most individual investors, who are unlikely to have superior information. Yet investors are people and as such are subject to a range of the behavioural biases that affect their investing behaviour. Here we discuss a few of those biases and how they can harm investors.

Excessive Trading and Overconfidence

Trading is expensive; you must pay commissions on top of the difference between the bid and ask, or the spread. Given how hard it should be to identify over- and undervalued stocks, you might then expect individual investors to take a conservative approach to trading. However, in an influential study of the trading behaviour of individual investors that held accounts at a discount brokerage, researchers Brad Barber and Terrance Odean found that individual investors tend to trade very actively, with average turnover almost 50% above the overall rates during the time period of their study.[12]

overconfidence hypothesis The tendency of individual investors to trade too much, based on the mistaken belief that they can pick winners and losers better than investment professionals.

What might explain this trading behaviour? Psychologists have known since the 1960s that uninformed individuals tend to overestimate the precision of their knowledge. For example, many sports fans sitting in the stands confidently second-guess the coaching decisions on the field, truly believing that they can do a better job. In finance, we call investors' presumption of their ability to beat the market by overtrading the **overconfidence hypothesis**. Barber and Odean hypothesized that this kind of behaviour also characterizes individual investment decision making. Like sports fans, individual investors believe they can pick winners and losers when, in fact, they cannot; this overconfidence leads them to trade too much.

[12]B. Barber and T. Odean, "Trading Is Hazardous to Your Wealth: The Common Stock Investment Performance of Individual Investors," *Journal of Finance* 55 (2000): 773–806.

An implication of this overconfidence hypothesis is that, assuming they have no true ability, investors who trade more will not earn higher returns. Instead, their performance will be worse once we take into account the costs of trading (due to both commissions and bid-ask spreads). Figure 7.9 documents precisely this result, showing that much investor trading appears not to be based on rational assessments of performance.

FIGURE 7.9 Individual Investor Returns versus Portfolio Turnover

The graph shows the average annual return (net of commissions and trading costs) for individual investors at a large discount brokerage from 1991 to 1997. Investors are grouped into quintiles based on their average annual turnover. While the least-active investors had slightly (but not significantly) better performance than the S&P 500, performance declined with the rate of turnover.

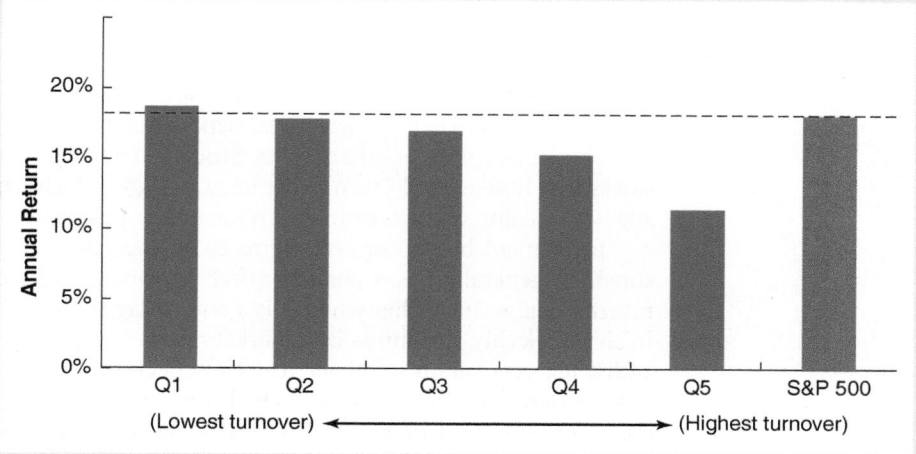

Source: B. Barber and T. Odean, "Trading Is Hazardous to Your Wealth: The Common Stock Investment Performance of Individual Investors," *Journal of Finance* 55 (2000): 773–806.

Hanging on to Losers and the Disposition Effect

disposition effect The tendency to hold on to stocks that have lost value and sell stocks that have risen in value since the time of purchase.

Investors tend to hold on to stocks that have lost value and sell stocks that have risen in value since the time of purchase. We call this tendency to keep losers and sell winners the **disposition effect**. Researchers Hersh Shefrin and Meir Statman, building on the work of psychologists Daniel Kahneman and Amos Tversky, suggest that this effect arises due to investor's increased willingness to take on risk in the face of possible losses.[13] It may also reflect a reluctance to admit a mistake by taking the loss.

Researchers have verified the disposition effect in many studies. For example, in a study of all trades in the Taiwanese stock market from 1995 to 1999, investors in aggregate were twice as likely to realize gains as they were to realize losses. Also, nearly 85% of individual investors were subject to this bias.[14] On the other hand, mutual funds and

[13]H. Shefrin and M. Statman, "The Disposition to Sell Winners Too Early and Ride Losers Too Long: Theory and Evidence," *Journal of Finance* 40 (1985): 777–790; and D. Kahneman and A. Tversky, "Prospect Theory: An Analysis of Decision Under Risk," *Econometrica* 47 (1979): 263–291.

[14]B. Barber, Y.T. Lee, Y.J. Liu, and T. Odean, "Is the Aggregate Investor Reluctant to Realize Losses? Evidence from Taiwan," *European Financial Management* 13 (2007): 423–447.

foreign investors did not exhibit the same tendency, and other studies have shown that more sophisticated investors appear to be less susceptible to the disposition effect.[15]

This behavioural tendency to sell winners and hang on to losers is costly from a tax perspective. Because capital gains are taxed only when the asset is sold, it is optimal for tax purposes to postpone taxable gains by continuing to hold profitable investments; delaying the tax payment reduces its present value. On the other hand, investors should capture tax losses by selling their losing investments, especially near the year's end, in order to accelerate the tax write-off.

Of course, keeping losers and selling winners might make sense if investors forecast that the losing stocks would ultimately "bounce back" and outperform the winners going forward. While investors may in fact have this belief, it does not appear to be justified—if anything, the losing stocks that investors continue to hold tend to underperform the winners they sell. According to one study, losers underperformed winners by 3.4% over the year after the winners were sold.[16]

Investor Attention, Mood, and Experience

Individual investors generally are not full-time traders. As a result, they have limited time and attention to spend on their investment decisions and may be influenced by attention-grabbing news stories or other events. Studies show that individuals are more likely to buy stocks that have recently been in the news, engaged in advertising, experienced exceptionally high trading volume, or had extreme (either positive or negative) returns.[17]

Investment behaviour also seems to be affected by investors' moods. For example, sunshine generally has a positive effect on mood, and studies have found that stock returns tend to be higher when it is a sunny day at the location of the stock exchange. In New York City, the annualized market return on perfectly sunny days is approximately 24.8% per year versus 8.7% per year on perfectly cloudy days.[18] Further evidence of the link between investor mood and stock returns comes from the effect of major sports events on returns. One recent study estimates that a loss in the World Cup elimination stage lowers the next day's stock returns in the losing country by about 0.50%, presumably due to investors' poor moods.[19]

Finally, investors appear to put too much weight on their own experience rather than considering all the historical evidence. As a result, people who grow up and live during a time of high stock returns are more likely to invest in stocks than people who grow up and live during a time of low stock returns.[20]

Why would investors continue to make such mistakes? Even if they started with such misconceptions, wouldn't they be able to learn, over time, the cost of these

---

[15]R. Dhar and N. Zhu, "Up Close and Personal: Investor Sophistication and the Disposition Effect," *Management Science* 52 (2006): 726–740.

[16]T. Odean, "Are Investors Reluctant to Realize Their Losses?" *Journal of Finance* 53 (1998): 1775–98.

[17]See G. Grullon, G. Kanatas, and J. Weston, "Advertising, Breadth of Ownership, and Liquidity," *Review of Financial Studies* 17 (2004): 439–461; M. Seasholes and G. Wu, "Predictable Behavior, Profits, and Attention," *Journal of Empirical Finance* 14 (2007): 590–610; and B. Barber and T. Odean, "All That Glitters: The Effect of Attention and News on the Buying Behavior of Individual and Institutional Investors," *Review of Financial Studies* 21 (2008): 785–818.

[18]Based on data from 1982 to 1997; see D. Hirshleifer and T. Shumway, "Good Day Sunshine: Stock Returns and the Weather," *Journal of Finance* 58 (2003): 1009–1032.

[19]A. Edmans, D. Garcia, and O. Norli, "Sports Sentiment and Stock Returns," *Journal of Finance* 62 (2007): 1967–1998.

[20]U. Malmendier and S. Nagel, "Depression Babies: Do Macroeconomic Experiences Affect Risk-Taking?" NBER working paper no. 14813.

errors? The challenge is that stock returns are extremely volatile, and this volatility masks the small differences in returns from different trading strategies. We will start the next chapter with a review of the historical evidence on average stock returns and their volatility. There you will see how variable returns are and how there have been long stretches of good returns, as in the 1990s, but also stretches when the total return was negative, as in the 2000s.

CONCEPT CHECK

15. What are several systematic behavioural biases that individual investors fall prey to?

16. Why would excessive trading lead to lower realized return?

MyLab Finance

Here is what you should know after reading this chapter. MyLab™ Finance will help you identify what you know, and where to go when you need to practice.

KEY POINTS AND EQUATIONS	TERMS	ONLINE PRACTICE OPPORTUNITIES
7.1 Stock Basics ■ Ownership in a corporation is divided into shares of stock. These shares carry rights to share in the profits of the firm through future dividend payments.	annual meeting, p. 205 common stock, p. 203 cumulative preferred stock, p. 206 cumulative voting, p. 205 non-cumulative preferred stock, p. 206 preferred stock, p. 206 proxy, p. 205 proxy contest, p. 205 straight voting, p. 205 ticker symbol, p. 203	MyLab Study Plan 7.1
7.2 The Dividend-Discount Model ■ The Valuation Principle states that the value of a stock is equal to the present value of the dividends and future sale price the investor will receive. Because these cash flows are risky, they must be discounted at the equity cost of capital, which is the expected return of other securities available in the market with risk equivalent to that of the firm's equity. ■ The total return of a stock is equal to the dividend yield plus the capital gain rate. The expected total return of a stock should equal its equity cost of capital: $r_E = \frac{Div_1 + P_1}{P_0} - 1 = \underbrace{\frac{Div_1}{P_0}}_{\text{Dividend Yield}} + \underbrace{\frac{P_1 - P_0}{P_0}}_{\text{Capital Gain Rate}}$ (7.2)	capital gain, p. 208 capital gain rate, p. 208 dividend-discount model, p. 210 dividend yield, p. 208 equity cost of capital, p. 207 total return, p. 208	MyLab Study Plan 7.2 Using Excel: Building a Dividend-Discount Model

KEY POINTS AND EQUATIONS | TERMS | ONLINE PRACTICE OPPORTUNITIES

- When investors have the same beliefs, the DDM states that, for any horizon, n, the stock price satisfies the following equation:

$$P_0 = \frac{Div_1}{1 + r_E} + \frac{Div_2}{(1 + r_E)^2} + \cdots + \frac{Div_n}{(1 + r_E)^n} + \frac{P_n}{(1 + r_E)^n} \quad (7.4)$$

- If the stock eventually pays dividends and is never acquired, the DDM implies that the stock price equals the present value of all future dividends.

7.3 Estimating Dividends in the Dividend-Discount Model

- The constant dividend growth model assumes that dividends grow at a constant expected rate, g. In that case, g is also the expected capital gain rate, and

$$P_0 = \frac{Div_1}{r_E - g} \quad (7.6)$$

- Future dividends depend on earnings, shares outstanding, and the dividend payout rate:

$$Div_t = \underbrace{\frac{\text{Earnings}_t}{\text{Share Outstanding}_t}}_{EPS_t} \times \text{Dividend Payout Rate}_t \quad (7.8)$$

- If the dividend payout rate and the number of shares outstanding are constant, and if earnings change only as a result of new investment from retained earnings, then the growth rate of the firm's earnings, dividends, and share price is calculated as follows:

$$g = \text{Retention Rate} \times \text{Return on New Investment} \quad (7.12)$$

- Cutting the firm's dividend to increase investment will raise the stock price if, and only if, the new investments have a positive NPV.
- If the firm has a long-term growth rate of g after the period $n + 1$, then we can apply the dividend-discount model and use the constant dividend growth formula to estimate the terminal stock value, P_n.

constant dividend growth model, p. 211
dividend payout rate, p. 212
retention rate, p. 213

MyLab Study Plan 7.3

KEY POINTS AND EQUATIONS	TERMS	ONLINE PRACTICE OPPORTUNITIES
7.4 Limitations of the Dividend-Discount Model ■ The DDM is sensitive to the dividend growth rate, which is difficult to estimate accurately. ■ Some companies do not pay cash dividends, making the model inappropriate for valuation in such cases.		MyLab Study Plan 7.4
7.5 Share Repurchases and the Total Payout Model ■ If the firm undertakes share repurchases, it is more reliable to use the total payout model to value the firm. In this model, the value of equity equals the present value of future total dividends and repurchases. To determine the stock price, we divide the equity value by the initial number of shares outstanding of the firm: $P_0 = \frac{PV\text{(Future Total Dividends and Repurchases)}}{\text{Shares Outstanding}_0}$ (7.15)	share repurchase, p. 220 total payout model, p. 220	MyLab Study Plan 7.5 Interactive Discounted Cash Flow Valuation
7.6 The Discounted Free Cash Flow Model ■ The growth rate of the firm's total payout is governed by the growth rate of earnings, not earnings per share. ■ When a firm has leverage, it is more reliable to use the discounted free cash flow model. In this model, the enterprise value of the firm equals the present value of the firm's future free cash flow: $V_0 = PV\text{(Future Free Cash Flow of Firm)}$ (7.18) ■ We discount cash flows using the WACC, which is the expected return the firm must pay to investors to compensate them for the risk of holding the firm's debt and equity together. ■ We can estimate a terminal enterprise value by assuming free cash flow grows at a constant rate (typically equal to the rate of long-run revenue growth). ■ We determine the stock price by subtracting debt and adding cash to the enterprise value, and then dividing by the initial number of shares outstanding of the firm: $P_0 = \frac{V_0 + \text{Cash}_0 - \text{Debt}_0}{\text{Shares Outstanding}_0}$ (7.19)	discounted free cash flow model, p. 221 weighted average cost of capital (WACC), p. 222	MyLab Study Plan 7.6

KEY POINTS AND EQUATIONS	TERMS	ONLINE PRACTICE OPPORTUNITIES
7.7 Valuation Based on Comparable Firms ■ We can also value stocks by using valuation multiples based on comparable firms. Multiples commonly used for this purpose include the P/E ratio and the ratio of enterprise value to EBITDA. When we use multiples, we assume that comparable firms have the same risk and future growth as the firm being valued. ■ No valuation model provides a definitive value for the stock. It is best to use several methods to identify a reasonable range for the value.	forward earnings, p. 227 forward P/E, p. 227 method of comparables, p. 226 trailing earnings, p. 227 trailing P/E, p. 227 valuation multiple, p. 227	MyLab Study Plan 7.7
7.8 Information, Competition, and Stock Prices ■ Stock prices aggregate the information of many investors. Therefore, if our valuation disagrees with the stock's market price, it is most likely an indication that our assumptions about the firm's cash flows are wrong. ■ Competition among investors tends to eliminate positive-NPV trading opportunities. Competition will be strongest when information is public and easy to interpret. Privately informed traders may be able to profit from their information, which is reflected in prices only gradually. ■ The efficient markets hypothesis states that competition eliminates all positive-NPV trades, which is equivalent to stating that securities with equivalent risk have the same expected returns. ■ In an efficient market, investors will not find positive-NPV trading opportunities without some source of competitive advantage. By contrast, the average investor will earn a fair return on his or her investment. ■ In an efficient market, to raise the stock price, corporate managers should focus on maximizing the present value of the free cash flow from the firm's investments, rather than accounting consequences or financial policy.	efficient markets hypothesis, p. 236	MyLab Study Plan 7.8
7.9 Individual Biases and Trading ■ Individual investors display many biases including overconfidence, disposition effect, limited attention, and mood affects. ■ In an efficient market, these biases can lead to trading losses through excessive trading or biases in valuations	disposition effect, p. 241 overconfidence hypothesis, p. 240	

REVIEW QUESTIONS

1. What rights come with a share of stock?
2. Which two components make up the total return to an investor in a share of stock?
3. What does the DDM say about valuing shares of stock?
4. What is the relationship between the NPV of reinvesting cash flows and the change in the price of the stock?
5. How can the DDM be used with changing growth rates in future dividends?
6. What are some drawbacks of the DDM?
7. What are share repurchases, and how can they be incorporated into the valuation of a stock?
8. What are the advantages of valuing a stock based on discounted free cash flows?
9. Explain the connection between the FCF valuation model and capital budgeting.
10. What is the reasoning behind valuation by multiples and what are the major assumptions?
11. What are the limitations of valuation by multiples?
12. What is an efficient market?
13. How do interactions in a market lead to information being incorporated into stock prices?
14. Why does market efficiency lead a manager to focus on NPV and free cash flow?
15. Why don't investors always trade rationally?
16. What are some of the major behavioural trading biases?

PROBLEMS

All problems in this chapter are available in MyLab Finance. An asterisk (*) indicates problems with a higher level of difficulty.

Stock Basics

1. If you own 15,000 shares of stock of Brookfield Asset Management and it pays a dividend of $0.18 per share, then what is the total dividend you will receive?
2. You own 20% of the stock of a company with 10 directors on its board. How much representation can you get on the board if the company has cumulative voting? How much representation can you ensure if the company has straight voting?
3. Anzio Inc. has two classes of shares. Class B has 10 times the voting rights of Class A. If you own 10% of the Class A shares and 20% of the Class B shares, what percentage of the total voting rights do you hold?

#4-11, 13-16
17-21, 36, 39 ab

The Dividend-Discount Model

4. Assume Evco, Inc. has a current stock price of $50 and will pay a $2 dividend in one year; its equity cost of capital is 15%. To justify its current price, what price must you expect Evco stock to sell for immediately after the firm pays the dividend in one year?

5. You just purchased a share of Northstar Sports for $100. You expect to receive a dividend of $5 in one year. If you expect the price after the dividend is paid to be $110, what total return do you expect to earn over the year? What do you expect to be your dividend yield? What do you expect to be your capital gain rate?

6. Assume Coleco pays an annual dividend of $1.50 and has a share price of $37.50. It announces that its annual dividend will increase to $1.75. If its dividend yield is to stay the same, what should its new share price be?

7. Anle Corporation has a current stock price of $20 and is expected to pay a dividend of $1 in one year. Its expected stock price right after paying that dividend is $22.
a. What is Anle's equity cost of capital?
b. How much of Anle's equity cost of capital is expected to be satisfied by dividend yield and how much by capital gain?

8. Achi Corp has preferred stock with an annual dividend of $3. If the required return on Achi's preferred stock is 8%, what is its price? (*Hint:* For a preferred stock, the dividend growth rate is zero.)

9. Ovit, Inc. has preferred stock with a price of $20 and a dividend of $1.50 per year. What is its dividend yield?

ML PROJECT

10. Suppose Acap Corporation will pay a dividend of $2.80 per share at the end of this year and a dividend of $3.00 per share next year. You expect Acap's stock price to be $52.00 in two years. Assume that Acap's equity cost of capital is 10%.
a. What price would you be willing to pay for a share of Acap stock today if you planned to hold the stock for two years?
b. Suppose, instead, you plan to hold the stock for one year. For what price would you expect to be able to sell a share of Acap stock in one year?
c. Given your answer to part (b), what price would you be willing to pay for a share of Acap stock today if you planned to hold the stock for one year? How does this price compare to your answer in part (a)?

11. Krell Industries has a share price of $22.00 today. If Krell is expected to pay a dividend of $0.88 this year and its stock price is expected to grow to $23.54 at the end of the year, what is Krell's dividend yield and equity cost of capital?

Estimating Dividends in the Dividend-Discount Model

12. NoGrowth Corporation currently pays a dividend of $0.50 per quarter, and it will continue to pay this dividend forever. What is the price per share of NoGrowth stock if the firm's equity cost of capital is 15% (effective annual rate)?

13. Summit Systems just paid an annual dividend of $1.50. If you expect Summit's dividend to grow by 6% per year, what is its price per share if the firm's equity cost of capital is 11%?

14. Dorpac Corporation has a dividend yield of 1.5%. Its equity cost of capital is 8%, and its dividends are expected to grow at a constant rate.
a. What is the expected growth rate of Dorpac's dividends?
b. What is the expected growth rate of Dorpac's share price?

15. Laurel Enterprises pays annual dividends and the next dividend is expected to be in one year. Laurel expects earnings next year of $4 per share and has a 70% retention rate, which it plans to keep constant. Its equity cost of capital is 10%, which is also its expected return on new investment; this is expected to continue forever. What do you estimate the firm's current stock price to be?

***16.** DFB, Inc. expects earnings at the end of this year of $5 per share, and it plans to pay a $3 dividend to shareholders at that time (one year from now). DFB will retain $2 per share of its earnings to reinvest in new projects that have an expected return of 15% per year. Suppose DFB will maintain the same dividend payout rate, retention rate, and return on new investments in the future and will not change its number of outstanding shares.

a. What growth rate of earnings would you forecast for DFB?
b. If DFB's equity cost of capital is 12%, what price would you estimate for DFB stock today?
c. Suppose, instead, that DFB paid a dividend of $4 per share this year and retained only $1 per share in earnings. If DFB maintains this higher payout rate in the future, what stock price would you estimate for the firm now? Should DFB raise its dividend?

17. Cooperton Mining just announced it will cut its dividend from $4 to $2.50 per share and use the extra funds to expand. Prior to the announcement, Cooperton's dividends were expected to grow at a 3% rate, and its share price was $50. With the planned expansion, Cooperton's dividends are expected to grow at a 5% rate. What share price would you expect after the announcement? (Assume that the new expansion does not change Cooperton's risk.) Is the expansion a positive-NPV investment?

18. Gillette Corporation will pay an annual dividend of $0.65 one year from now. Analysts expect this dividend to grow at 12% per year thereafter until the fifth year. Thereafter, growth will level off at 2% per year. According to the DDM, what is the value of a share of Gillette stock if the firm's equity cost of capital is 8%?

19. CX Enterprises has the following expected dividends: $1 in one year, $1.15 in two years, and $1.25 in three years. After that, its dividends are expected to grow at 4% per year forever (so that year four's dividend will be 4% more than $1.25 and so on). If CX's equity cost of capital is 12%, what is the current price of its stock?

20. Colgate-Palmolive Company has just paid an annual dividend of $0.96. Analysts are predicting an 11% per year growth rate in earnings over the next five years. After that, Colgate's earnings are expected to grow at the current industry average of 5.2% per year. If Colgate's equity cost of capital is 8.5% per year and its dividend payout ratio remains constant, for what price does the DDM predict Colgate stock should sell?

***21.** Halliford Corporation expects to have earnings this coming year of $3 per share. Halliford plans to retain all of its earnings for the next two years. Then, for the subsequent two years, the firm will retain 50% of its earnings. It will retain 20% of its earnings from that point onward. Each year, retained earnings will be invested in new projects with an expected return of 25% per year. Any earnings that are not retained will be paid out as dividends. Assume Halliford's share count remains constant and all earnings growth comes from the investment of retained earnings. If Halliford's equity cost of capital is 10%, what price would you estimate for Halliford stock?

The Total Payout and Free Cash Flow Valuation Models

22. Shatin Intl. has 10 million shares, an equity cost of capital 13% and is expected to pay a total dividend of $20 million each year forever. It announces that it will increase its payout to shareholders. Instead of increasing its dividend, it will keep it constant and will start repurchasing $10 million of stock each year as well. How much will its stock price increase?

23. Zoom Enterprises expects that one year from now it will pay a total dividend of $5 million and repurchase $5 million worth of shares. It plans to spend $10 million on dividends and repurchases every year after that forever, although it may not always be an even split between dividends and repurchases. If Zoom's cost of equity capital is 13% and it has 5 million shares outstanding, what is its share price today?

24. AFW Industries has 200 million shares outstanding and expects earnings at the end of this year of $700 million. AFW plans to pay out 60% of its earnings in total, paying 40% as a dividend and using 20% to repurchase shares. If AFW's earnings are expected to grow by 8% per year and these payout rates remain constant, determine AFW's share price assuming an equity cost of capital of 12%.

25. Suppose Cisco Systems pays no dividends but spent $5 billion on share repurchases last year. If Cisco's equity cost of capital is 12%, and if the amount spent on repurchases is expected to grow by 8% per year, estimate Cisco's market capitalization. If Cisco has 6 billion shares outstanding, to what stock price does this correspond?

***26.** Stelco Steel plans to pay a dividend of $3 this year. The company has an expected earnings growth rate of 4% per year and an equity cost of capital of 10%.

a. Assuming that Stelco's dividend payout rate and expected growth rate remain constant, and that the firm does not issue or repurchase shares, estimate Stelco's share price.

b. Suppose Stelco decides to pay a dividend of $1 this year and to use the remaining $2 per share to repurchase shares. If Stelco's total payout rate remains constant, estimate Stelco's share price.

c. If Stelco maintains the dividend and total payout rate given in part (b), at what rates are Stelco's dividends and earnings per share expected to grow?

27. This year, FCF Inc. has EBIT of $10 million, depreciation expense of $1 million, and capital expenditures of $1.5 million, and has increased its net working capital by $500,000. If its tax rate is 35%, what is its free cash flow?

28. Victoria Enterprises expects free cash flows next year of $1 million. Its depreciation and capital expenditures will both be $300,000, and it expects its capital expenditures to always equal its depreciation. Its working capital will increase by $50,000 over the next year. The year-over-year increase in its net working capital will increase by 4% in perpetuity, and its FCFs are also expected to increase at 4% per year in perpetuity. If its tax rate is 40% and its WACC is 10%, what is its enterprise value?

29. The present value of JECK Co.'s expected free cash flows is $100 million. If JECK has $30 million in debt, $6 million in cash, and 2 million shares outstanding, what is its share price?

30. Portage Bay Enterprises has no debt and is expected to have free cash flow of $10 million next year. It is then expected to grow at a rate of 3% per year forever. If Portage Bay's equity cost of capital is 11% and it has 5 million shares outstanding, what should the price of Portage Bay's stock be?

31. Saskatchewan River Enterprises (SRE) has $500 million in debt and 20 million shares of equity outstanding. Its excess cash reserves are $15 million. SRE is expected to generate $200 million in free cash flows next year with a growth rate of 2% per year in perpetuity. SRE's cost of equity capital is 12%.

a. What is SRE's stock price?

b. After analyzing the company, you believe that the growth rate should be 3% instead of 2%. Assume debt and cash values do not change. What should the stock price be given the higher growth rate?
c. Given the growth rate change from 2% to 3%, how can you calculate the change in stock price without calculating the amounts in (a) or (b) above?

32. Heavy Metal Corporation is expected to generate the following free cash flows over the next five years:

Year	1	2	3	4	5
FCF ($ million)	53	68	78	75	82

Thereafter, the free cash flows are expected to grow at the industry average of 4% per year. Use the discounted free cash flow model and a WACC of 14% to estimate the following:
a. The enterprise value of Heavy Metal
b. Heavy Metal's share price if the company has no excess cash, debt of $300 million, and 40 million shares outstanding.

33. Covan, Inc. is expected to have the following free cash flows:

Year	1	2	3	4	...
FCF	10	12	13	14	grow by 4% per year

a. Covan has 8 million shares outstanding, $3 million in excess cash, and it has no debt. If its cost of capital is 12%, what should its stock price be?
b. Covan reinvests all its FCF. If you plan to sell Covan at the beginning of year two, what should you expect its price to be?
c. Assume you bought Covan stock at the beginning of year one. What is your return expected to be from holding Covan stock until year two?

***34.** Sora Industries has 60 million outstanding shares, $120 million in debt, $40 million in cash, and the following projected free cash flow for the next four years (see MyLab Finance for the data in Excel format):

1	Year	0	1	2	3	4
2	**Earnings and FCF Forecast ($ million)**					
3	Sales	433.0	468.0	516.0	547.0	574.3
4	*Growth versus Prior Year*		8.1%	10.3%	6.0%	5.0%
5	Cost of Goods Sold		−313.6	−345.7	−366.5	−384.8
6	**Gross Profit**		154.4	170.3	180.5	189.5
7	Selling, General, and Administrative		−93.6	−103.2	−109.4	−114.9
8	Depreciation		−7.0	−7.5	−9.0	−9.5
9	**EBIT**		53.8	59.6	62.1	65.2
10	Less: Income Tax at a 40%		−21.5	−23.8	−24.8	−26.1
11	Plus: Depreciation		7.0	7.5	9.0	9.5
12	Less: Capital Expenditures		−7.7	−10.0	−9.9	−10.4
13	Less: Increase in NWC		−6.3	−8.6	−5.6	−4.9
14	**Free Cash Flow**		25.3	24.6	30.8	33.3

a. Suppose Sora's revenues and free cash flow are expected to grow at a 5% rate beyond year four. If Sora's WACC is 10%, what is the value of Sora's stock based on this information?
b. Sora's cost of goods sold was assumed to be 67% of sales. If its cost of goods sold is actually 70% of sales, how would the estimate of the stock's value change?
c. Return to the assumptions of part (a) and suppose Sora can maintain its cost of goods sold at 67% of sales. However, the firm reduces its selling, general, and administrative expenses from 20% of sales to 16% of sales. What stock price would you estimate now? (Assume no other expenses, except taxes, are affected.)
*d. Sora's net working capital needs were estimated to be 18% of sales (their current level in year zero). If Sora can reduce this requirement to 12% of sales starting in year one, but all other assumptions remain as in part (a), what stock price do you estimate for Sora? (*Hint*: This change will have the largest effect on Sora's free cash flow in year one.)

35. Consider the valuation of Nike given in Example 7.7.
a. Suppose you believe Nike's initial revenue growth rate will be between 7% and 11% (with growth slowing linearly to 5% by year 2018). What range of prices for Nike stock is consistent with these forecasts?
b. Suppose you believe Nike's initial revenue EBIT margin will be between 9% and 11% of sales. What range of prices for Nike stock is consistent with these forecasts?
c. Suppose you believe Nike's WACC is between 9.5% and 12%. What range of prices for Nike stock is consistent with these forecasts?
d. What range of stock prices is consistent if you vary the estimates as in parts (a), (b), and (c) simultaneously?

Valuation Based on Comparable Firms

36. You notice that Dell Computers has a stock price of $27.85 and EPS of $1.26. Its competitor Hewlett-Packard has EPS of $2.47. What is one estimate of the value of a share of Hewlett-Packard stock?

37. CSH has EBITDA of $5 million. You feel that an appropriate EV/EBITDA ratio for CSH is 9. CSH has $10 million in debt, $2 million in cash, and 800,000 shares outstanding. What is your estimate of CSH's stock price?

38. After researching the competitors of EJH Enterprises, you determine that most comparable firms have the following valuation ratios:

	Comp 1	Comp 2	Comp 3	Comp 4
EV/EBITDA	12	11	12.5	10
P/E	19	18	20	17

EJH Enterprises has EPS of $2, EBITDA of $300 million, $30 million in cash, $40 million in debt, and 100 million shares outstanding. What range of prices is consistent with both sets of multiples?

39. Suppose that in July 2013, Nike had EPS of $2.52 and a book value of equity of $12.48 per share.
a. Using the average P/E multiple in Table 7.2, estimate Nike's share price.
b. What range of share prices do you estimate based on the highest and lowest P/E multiples in Table 7.2?

c. Using the average price to book value multiple in Table 7.2, estimate Nike's share price.
d. What range of share prices do you estimate based on the highest and lowest price to book value multiples in Table 7.2?

40. Suppose that in July 2013, Nike had sales of $25,313 million, EBITDA of $3,254 million, excess cash of $3,337 million, $1,390 million of debt, and 893.6 million shares outstanding.
a. Using the average enterprise value to sales multiple in Table 7.2, estimate Nike's share price.
b. What range of share prices do you estimate based on the highest and lowest enterprise value to sales multiples in Table 7.2?
c. Using the average enterprise value to EBITDA multiple in Table 7.2, estimate Nike's share price.
d. What range of share prices do you estimate based on the highest and lowest enterprise value to EBITDA multiples in Table 7.2?

***41.** Suppose Rocky Shoes and Boots has earnings per share of $2.30 and EBITDA of $30.7 million. The firm also has 5.4 million shares outstanding and debt of $125 million (net of cash). You believe Deckers Outdoor Corporation is comparable to Rocky Shoes and Boots in terms of its underlying business, but Deckers has no debt. If Deckers has a P/E of 13.3 and an enterprise value to EBITDA multiple of 7.4, estimate the value of Rocky Shoes and Boots stock using both multiples. Which estimate is likely to be more accurate?

42. Consider the following data for the airline industry for December 2015 (EV = enterprise value, Book = equity book value). Discuss the potential challenges of using multiples to value an airline.

Company Name	Market Capitalization	Enterprise Value (EV)	EV/Sales	EV/EBITDA	EV/EBIT	P/E	P/Book
Delta Air Lines (DAL)	40,857	45,846	1.1x	6.0x	7.6x	15.0x	4.0x
American Airlines (AAL)	27,249	38,937	0.9x	4.5x	5.5x	6.2x	7.5x
United Continental (UAL)	22,000	28,522	0.7x	4.2x	5.6x	3.4x	2.6x
Southwest Airlines (LUV)	28,499	28,125	1.5x	6.0x	7.4x	16.1x	4.1x
Alaska Air (ALK)	10,396	9,870	1.8x	6.3x	7.9x	13.4x	4.4x
JetBlue Airways (JBLU)	7,338	8,189	1.3x	6.1x	7.9x	13.8x	2.4x
SkyWest (SKYW)	1,039	2,590	0.8x	5.2x	11.1x	21.2x	0.7x
Hawaiian (HA)	1,974	2,281	1.0x	5.3x	6.9x	15.1x	5.3x

Source: Capital IQ and Yahoo! Finance.

43. Suppose Hawaiian Airlines (HA) has 53 million shares outstanding. Estimate Hawaiian's share value using each of the five valuation multiples in Problem 42, based on the median valuation multiple of the other seven airlines shown.

Information, Competition, and Stock Prices

44. Summit Systems (see Problem 13) has an equity cost of capital of 11% and will pay a dividend of $1.50 in one year, and its dividends had been expected to grow by 6% per year. You read in the paper that Summit Systems has revised its growth prospects and now expects its dividends to grow at a rate of 3% per year forever.

a. What is the new value of a share of Summit Systems stock based on this information?
b. If you tried to sell your Summit Systems stock after reading this news, what price would you be likely to get? Why?

45. Assume that Coca-Cola Company has a share price of $43. The firm will pay a dividend of $1.24 in one year, and you expect Coca-Cola to raise this dividend by approximately 7% per year in perpetuity.
a. If Coca-Cola's equity cost of capital is 8%, what share price would you expect based on your estimate of the dividend growth rate?
b. Given Coca-Cola's share price, what would you conclude about your assessment of Coca-Cola's future dividend growth?

46. Roybus, Inc., a manufacturer of flash memory, just reported that its main production facility in Taiwan was destroyed in a fire. Although the plant was fully insured, the loss of production will decrease Roybus's free cash flow by $180 million at the end of this year and by $60 million at the end of next year.
a. If Roybus has 35 million shares outstanding and a WACC of 13%, what change in Roybus's stock price would you expect upon this announcement? (Assume the value of Roybus's debt is not affected by the event.)
b. Would you expect to be able to sell Roybus's stock on hearing this announcement and make a profit? Explain.

***47.** Apnex, Inc. is a biotechnology firm that is about to announce the results of its clinical trials of a potential new cancer drug. If the trials are successful, Apnex stock will be worth $70 per share. If the trials are unsuccessful, Apnex stock will be worth $18 per share. Suppose that the morning before the announcement is scheduled, Apnex shares are trading for $55 per share.
a. Based on the current share price, what sort of expectations do investors seem to have about the success of the trials?
b. Suppose hedge fund manager Paul Kliner has hired several prominent research scientists to examine the public data on the drug and make their own assessment of the drug's promise. Would Kliner's fund be likely to profit by trading the stock in the hours prior to the announcement?
c. Which factors would limit the ability of Kliner's fund to profit on its information?

***48.** Let's revisit Problem 16 in the end-of-chapter problems of Chapter 1. This morning, SPB Ltd., a solar panel and battery manufacturing company, paid a dividend of $2 per share. At 10 a.m. SPB announced its latest earnings results (which were unexpectedly good) and management seems very happy.

Background information:

> One year ago, SPB paid for and implemented the Stealth Disposal (SD) project for handling its toxic waste. Only SPB's management is aware of the SD project; it has reduced SPB's expenses related to toxic waste disposal, but there is a 25% chance of toxic contamination of the drinking water for the nearest city. SPB management has no intention of publicly disclosing that the SD project exists.

Following this morning's 10 a.m. quarterly earnings announcement, SPB's earnings growth prospects look very good based upon substantial cost savings (although investors don't know it, these cost saving are due to the SD project). SPB's earnings announcement has caused investors to reassess SPB's dividend growth with the new expectation that dividends will grow by 0.5% each quarter. Prior to the announcement, dividends were expected to grow by 0.3% each quarter. In addition, given investors' perceived risk of SPB, the equity cost of capital for SPB is 12% (effective annual rate).

a. Refer to Figure 7.7 and assume the market is semi-strong form efficient. What was the price of SPB's stock at 9:30 a.m.?
b. Continue to assume the market is semi-strong form efficient. What was the price of SPB's stock at 10:30 a.m.?
c. By what percent did SPB's stock price change between 9:30 and 10:30 a.m.? Is this consistent with the efficient markets hypothesis?
d. Suppose an analyst is doing a site visit at SPB today and discovers the SD project. At noon, the analyst releases a public announcement about her findings, indicating that the SD project exists and that there is a 25% probability of a catastrophic disaster. This information causes investors to reassess SPB's future dividends as follows: 25% probability of no dividends in the future because SPB would go bankrupt if the water contamination occurred; 75% probability of dividends, but with a growth rate of only 0.3% per quarter. What happens to SBP's stock price after the announcement? Is this consistent with the efficient markets hypothesis?
e. The SD project did result in increased earnings this quarter, so was implementing the SD project consistent with shareholder wealth maximization?
f. Why might the CEO of SPB have implemented the SD project knowing that there could be an adverse market reaction if SD became public? What kind of problem is this?

Individual Biases and Trading

49. You have a $100,000 portfolio made up of 15 stocks. You trade each stock five times this year, and each time you trade you pay about $30 in commissions and spread. You have no special knowledge, so you earn only the average market return of 12% on your investments. How much lower will your total return be because of your trades?

50. Assume the annual return for the lowest turnover portfolio is 18% and the annual return for the highest turnover portfolio is 12%. If you invest $100,000 and have the highest turnover, how much lower will the value of your portfolio be at the end of 10 years than if you had had the lowest turnover?

DATA CASE

As a new junior analyst for a large brokerage firm, you are excited to demonstrate the skills you learned in college and prove that you are worth your attractive salary. Your first assignment is to analyze Johnson & Johnson stock. Your boss recommends determining prices based on both the discounted free cash flow valuation method and the comparable P/E ratio method. You are a little concerned about your boss's recommendation because your finance professor explained that these two valuation methods can result in widely differing estimates when applied to real data. You are really hoping the two methods will reach similar prices. Good luck with that!

1. Go to Reuters (http://www.reuters.com) and enter the symbol for Johnson & Johnson (JNJ) in the "Search" box; then select Johnson and Johnson. From the main page for JNJ, gather the following information, and enter it into a spreadsheet:
   a. The current stock price (on the left side of the page)
   b. The EPS (TTM)
   c. The number of shares of stock outstanding
   d. The industry P/E (TTM) ratio

2. Click the "Analysts" tab. On the Analyst page, scroll down to find the LT (Long-Term) Growth Rate and enter the Mean value into your spreadsheet.
3. Go to Morningstar (http://www.morningstar.com) and enter "JNJ" into the "Quote" box.
4. Under "Financials," Click Income Statement. Copy and paste (or use the Export to Excel button to create a new file with the data) the most recent three years' worth of income statements into a new worksheet in your existing Excel file. Repeat this process for both the balance sheet and the cash flow statement for Johnson and Johnson. Keep all of the different statements in the same Excel worksheet. *Note*: Make sure you are collecting annual data, rather than quarterly or interim data.
5. To determine the stock value based on the discounted free cash flow method:
   a. Forecast the free cash flows. Start by using the historical data from the financial statements downloaded from Morningstar to compute the three-year average of the following ratios:
      i. EBIT/sales
      ii. Tax rate (income tax expense/income before tax)
      iii. Property plant and equipment/sales
      iv. Depreciation/property plant and equipment
      v. Net working capital/sales
   b. Create an empty timeline for the next five years.
   c. Forecast future sales based on the most recent year's total revenue growing at the LT growth rate from Reuters for the first five years.
   d. Use the average ratios computed in part (a) to forecast EBIT, property, plant and equipment, depreciation, and net working capital for the next five years.
   e. Forecast the free cash flow for the next five years using Equation 7.17.
   f. Determine the horizon enterprise value for year 5 using Equation 7.21 and a long-run growth rate of 4% and a cost of capital for JNJ of 11%.
   g. Determine the enterprise value of the firm as the present value of the free cash flows using Equation 7.20.
   h. Determine the stock price using Equation 7.19. Note that your enterprise value is in $ thousands and the number of shares outstanding is in billions.
6. To calculate an estimate of JNJ price based on a comparable P/E ratio, multiply the industry average P/E ratio by JNJ's EPS.
7. Compare the stock prices produced by the two methods to the actual stock price. What recommendations can you make as to whether clients should buy or sell JNJ stock based on your price estimates?
8. Explain to your boss why the estimates from the two valuation methods differ. Specifically address the assumptions implicit in the models themselves as well as the assumptions you made in preparing your analysis. Why do these estimates differ from the actual stock price of JNJ?

PART

Integrative Case 2

This case draws on material from this and earlier chapters.

Adam Rust looked at his mechanic and sighed. The mechanic had just pronounced a death sentence on his road-weary car. The car had served him well—at a cost of $500 it had lasted through four years of university with minimal repairs. Now, he desperately needs wheels. He has just graduated and has a good job at a decent starting salary. He hopes to purchase his first new car. The car dealer seems very optimistic about his ability to afford the car payments, another first for him.

The car Adam is considering is a $35,000 Audi. The dealer has given him three payment options:

1. *Zero-percent financing.* Make a $4000 down payment from his savings and finance the remainder with a 0% annual percentage rate (APR) loan for 48 months. Adam has more than enough cash for the down payment, thanks to generous graduation gifts.
2. *Rebate with no money down.* Receive a $4000 rebate, which he would use for the down payment (and leave his savings intact), and finance the rest with a standard 48-month loan, with an 8% APR with monthly compounding.
3. *Pay cash.* Get the $4000 rebate and pay the rest with cash. While Adam doesn't have $35,000, he wants to evaluate this option. His parents always paid cash when they bought a family car; Adam wonders if this really was a good idea.

Adam's fellow graduate, Jenna Hawthorne, was lucky. Her parents gave her a car for graduation. Okay, it was a little Hyundai, and definitely not her dream car, but it was serviceable, and Jenna didn't have to worry about buying a new car. In fact, Jenna has been trying to decide how much of her new salary she could save. Adam knows that with a hefty car payment, saving for retirement would be very low on his priority list. Jenna believes she could easily set aside $3000 of her $45,000 salary. She is considering putting her savings in a stock fund. She just turned 22 and has a long way to go until retirement at age 65, and she considers this risk level reasonable. The fund she is looking at has earned an average of 9% over the past 15 years and could be expected to continue earning this amount, on average. While she has no current retirement savings, five years ago Jenna's grandparents gave her a new 30-year Government of Canada bond with a $10,000 face value.

Jenna wants to know her retirement income if she both (1) sells her bond at its current market value and invests the proceeds in the stock fund and (2) saves an additional $3000 at the end of each year in the stock fund from now until she turns 65. Once she retires, Jenna wants those savings to last for 25 years until she is 90.

Both Adam and Jenna need to determine their best options.

CASE QUESTIONS

1. What are the cash flows associated with each of Adam's three car financing options?
2. Suppose that, similar to his parents, Adam had plenty of cash in the bank so that he could easily afford to pay cash for the car without running into debt now or in the foreseeable future. If his cash earns interest at a 5.4% APR (based on monthly compounding) at the bank, what would be his best purchase option for the car?
3. In fact, Adam doesn't have sufficient cash to cover all his debts including his (substantial) student loans. The loans have a 10% APR with monthly compounding, and any money spent on the car could not be used to pay down the loans. What is the best option for Adam now?
   (*Hint*: Note that having an extra $1 today allows Adam to pay down the student loans. So, the 10% student loan rate is Adam's opportunity cost of capital in this case.)
4. Suppose, instead, Adam has a lot of credit card debt, with an 18% APR with daily compounding, and he doubts he will pay off this debt completely before he pays off the car. What is Adam's best option now?
5. Suppose Jenna's bond has a coupon rate of 6.5%, paid semi-anually, while current Government of Canada bonds with the same maturity date have a yield to maturity of 5.4435% (expressed as an APR with semi-annual compounding). If she has just received the bond's 10th coupon, for how much can Jenna sell her bond?
6. Suppose Jenna sells the bond, reinvests the proceeds, and then saves as she planned. If, indeed, Jenna earns a 9% effective annual return on her savings, how much could she withdraw each year in retirement? (Assume she begins withdrawing the money from the account in equal amounts at the end of each year once her retirement begins.)
7. Jenna expects her salary to grow regularly. While there are no guarantees, she believes an increase of 4% a year is reasonable. She plans to save $3000 the first year, and then increase the amount she saves by 4% each year as her salary grows. Unfortunately, prices will also grow due to inflation. Suppose Jenna assumes there will be 3% inflation every year. In retirement, she will need to increase her withdrawals each year to keep up with inflation. In this case, how much can she withdraw at the end of the first year of her retirement? What amount does this correspond to in today's dollars? (*Hint*: Build a spreadsheet in which you track the amount in her retirement account each year.)
8. Should Jenna sell her bond and invest the proceeds in the stock fund? Give at least one reason for and against this plan.
9. At the last minute, Jenna considers investing in Coca-Cola stock at a price of $55.55 per share instead. The stock just paid an annual dividend of $1.76 and she expects the dividend to grow at 4% annually. If the next dividend is due in one year, what expected return is Coca-Cola stock offering?

PART

Investment Decisions

3

CHAPTER 8 Investment Decision Rules
CHAPTER 9 Fundamentals of Capital Budgeting

Valuation Principle Connection. One of the most important decisions facing a financial manager is the choice of which investments the corporation should make. These decisions fundamentally drive value in the corporation. We introduced the concept of benefits and costs in Chapter 3 as an application of the Valuation Principle. Now, in Chapter 8, we describe the net present value (NPV) methodology and show the usefulness of the NPV rule for making investment decisions. We also discuss alternative rules found in practice and discuss their drawbacks. The process of allocating the firm's capital for investment is known as capital budgeting. In Chapter 9, we outline how to estimate a project's incremental cash flows, which then become the inputs to the NPV rule. Chapter 9 also provides a practical demonstration of the power of the discounting tools that were introduced in Chapters 4 and 5.

CHAPTER

8 Investment Decision Rules

LEARNING OBJECTIVES

- Define and use the NPV rule to make investment decisions
- Understand alternative decision rules and their drawbacks
- Choose between mutually exclusive alternatives
- Rank projects when a company's resources are limited so that it cannot take all positive-NPV projects

NOTATION

C_n	cash flow that arrives at date n
I	initial investment or initial capital committed to the project
IRR	internal rate of return
NPV	net present value
PV	present value
r	discount rate

In 2000, Toshiba and Sony began experimenting with new DVD technology, leading to Sony's decision to develop and produce Blu-ray high-definition DVD players and Toshiba's decision to develop and produce the HD-DVD player and format. So began an eight-year format war that ended in February 2008 when Toshiba decided to stop producing HD-DVD players and abandon the format. How did Toshiba and Sony managers arrive at the decision to invest in new DVD formats? How did Toshiba managers conclude that the best decision was to stop producing HD-DVD? We focus in this chapter on the decision-making tools managers use to evaluate investment decisions. Examples of these decisions include new products, equipment purchases, and marketing campaigns.

We begin by introducing the net present value (NPV) rule. Although the NPV investment rule maximizes the value of the firm, some firms nevertheless use other techniques to evaluate investments and decide which projects to pursue. As a result, it is important to understand those techniques, so we will explain some commonly used alternative techniques—namely, the payback rule and the internal rate of return (IRR) rule. In each case, we define the decision rule and compare decisions based on this rule to decisions based on the NPV rule. We also illustrate the circumstances in which each of the alternative rules is likely to lead to bad investment decisions. After establishing these rules in the context of a single, stand-alone project, we broaden our perspective to include evaluation of multiple opportunities in order to select the best one. We conclude with a look at project selection when the firm faces limits in capital or on managers' time.

8.1 The NPV Rule

In the previous chapters, we learned how to convert between cash today and cash in the future using the discount rate. As long as we convert costs and benefits to the same point in time, we can use the Valuation Principle to make a decision. In practice, most corporations prefer to measure values in terms of their present value—that is, in terms of cash today. In this section, we apply the Valuation Principle to derive the concept of the *net present value*, or NPV, which we can use to define the "golden rule" of financial decision making, the NPV *rule*.

Net Present Value

net present value (NPV)
The difference between the present value of its benefits and the present value of its costs.

When the value of a cost or benefit is computed in terms of cash today, we refer to it as the present value (PV). Similarly, we define the **net present value (NPV)** of a project or investment as the difference between the present value of its benefits and the present value of its costs:

$$\text{Net Present Value}$$
$$NPV = PV(\text{Benefits}) - PV(\text{Costs}) \tag{8.1}$$

Let's consider a simple example. Suppose your firm is offered the following investment opportunity: In exchange for \$500 today, you will receive \$550 in one year. If the interest rate is 8% per year, then

$$\begin{aligned} PV(\text{Benefit}) &= (\$550 \text{ in one year}) \div (\$1.08 \text{ in one year}/\$1 \text{ today}) \\ &= \$509.26 \text{ today} \end{aligned}$$

This PV is the amount you would need to put in the bank today to generate \$550 in one year (\$509.26 × 1.08 = \$550). In other words, the *present value is the amount you need to invest at the current interest rate to recreate the cash flow*. We can think of this as the cash cost today of generating the cash flow ourselves. Once the costs and benefits are in present value terms, we can compare them by computing the investment's NPV:

$$NPV = \$509.26 - \$500 = \$9.26 \text{ today}$$

The NPV is positive, so the benefits outweigh the costs, which means the firm should undertake this investment opportunity.

But what if you don't have the \$500 needed to cover the initial cost of the project? Does the project still have the same value? Because we computed the value using competitive market prices, it should not depend on your tastes or the amount of cash you have in the bank. If you don't have the \$500, suppose you borrow \$509.26 from the bank at the 8% interest rate and then take the project. What are your cash flows in this case?

Today: \$509.26 (loan) − \$500 (invested in the project) = \$9.26

In one year: \$550 (from project) − \$509.26 × 1.08 (loan balance) = \$0

This transaction leaves you with exactly $9.26 extra cash in your pocket today and no future net obligations. So, taking the project is similar to having an extra $9.26 in cash up front. Thus, the NPV expresses the value of an investment decision as an amount of cash received today. *As long as the NPV is positive, the decision increases the value of the firm and is a good decision regardless of your current cash needs or preferences regarding when to spend the money.*

EXAMPLE 8.1 The NPV Is Equivalent to Cash Today

PROBLEM

After saving $1500 by waiting tables, you are about to buy a 50-inch TV. You notice that the store is offering a "one year same as cash" deal. You can take the TV home today and pay nothing until one year from now, when you will owe the store the $1500 purchase price. If your savings account earns 5% per year, what is the NPV of this offer? Show that its NPV represents cash in your pocket.

SOLUTION

Plan

You are getting something worth $1500 today (the TV), and in exchange will need to pay $1500 in one year. Think of it as getting back the $1500 you thought you would have to spend today to get the TV. We treat it as a positive cash flow.

Cash flows:

Today	In one year
+$1500	−$1500

The discount rate for calculating the present value of the payment in one year is your interest rate of 5%. You need to compare the present value of the cost ($1500 in one year) to the benefit today (a $1500 TV).

Execute

$$NPV = +1500 - \frac{1500}{(1.05)} = 1500 - 1428.57 = \$71.43$$

You could take $1428.57 of the $1500 you had saved for the TV and put it in your savings account. With interest, in one year it would grow to $1428.57 × (1.05) = $1500, enough to pay the store. The extra $71.43 is money in your pocket to spend as you like (or put toward the speaker system for your new media room).

Evaluate

By taking the delayed payment offer, we have extra net cash flows of $71.43 today. If we put $1428.57 in the bank, it will be just enough to offset our $1500 obligation in the future. Therefore, this offer is equivalent to receiving $71.43 today, without any future net obligations.

Making Decisions: The NPV Rule

As shown in Example 8.1, the Valuation Principle implies that we should undertake projects with a positive NPV because undertaking those projects increases wealth. That is, good projects are those for which the present value of the benefits exceeds the present value of the costs. As a result, the value of the firm increases and investors are wealthier.

Projects with negative NPVs have costs that exceed their benefits. Accepting them is equivalent to losing money today.

NPV rule When choosing among investment alternatives, take the alternative with the highest NPV. Choosing this alternative is equivalent to receiving its NPV in cash today.

We capture this logic in the **NPV rule**: *when making an investment decision, take the alternative with the highest NPV. Choosing this alternative is equivalent to receiving its NPV in cash today.*

Because NPV is expressed in terms of cash today, using the NPV decision rule is a simple way to apply the Valuation Principle. Decisions that increase wealth are superior to those that decrease wealth. We don't need to know anything about the investor's preferences to reach this conclusion. As long as we have correctly captured all the cash flows of a project and applied the appropriate discount rate, we can determine whether the project makes us wealthier. Being wealthier increases our options and makes us better off, whatever our preferences are.

A common way companies apply the NPV rule in financial practices is when deciding whether to accept or reject a project. Because rejecting the project generally has $NPV = 0$ (there are no new costs or benefits from not doing the project), the NPV rule implies that we should

- accept positive-NPV projects; accepting them is equivalent to receiving their NPV in cash today, and
- reject negative-NPV projects; accepting them would reduce the value of the firm, whereas rejecting them has no cost ($NPV = 0$)

If the NPV is exactly zero, then you will neither gain nor lose by accepting the project instead of rejecting it, which also has an NPV of zero. It is not a bad project because it does not reduce the firm's value, but it does not add value to the firm either.

CONCEPT CHECK

1. What is the NPV decision rule? How is it related to the Valuation Principle?
2. Why doesn't the NPV decision rule depend on the investor's preferences?

8.2 Using the NPV Rule

We continue our discussion of investment decision rules by considering a take-it-or-leave-it decision about a single, stand-alone project. By undertaking this project, the firm does not constrain its ability to take other projects. In the case of a stand-alone project, the alternatives we are considering are to accept or reject a project. The NPV rule then implies that we should compare the project's NPV to zero (the NPV of rejecting the project and doing nothing). Thus, we should accept the project if its NPV is positive.

Organizing the Cash Flows and Computing the NPV

Researchers at Saskatchewan Fertilizer Ltd. (SFL) have made a breakthrough. They believe that they can produce a new, environmentally friendly fertilizer at a substantial cost saving over the company's existing line of fertilizer. The fertilizer will require a new plant that can be built immediately at a cost of $81.6 million. Financial managers estimate that the benefits of the new fertilizer will be $28 million per year, starting at the end of the first year and lasting for four years, as shown by the following timeline:

Month:	0	1	2	3	4
Cash flow:	−$81.60	+$28	+$28	+$28	+$28

Thus, the cash flows are an immediate $81.6 million outflow followed by an annuity inflow of $28 million per year for four years. Therefore, given a discount rate, r, the NPV of this project is

$$NPV = -81.6 + \frac{28}{1+r} + \frac{28}{(1+r)^2} + \frac{28}{(1+r)^3} + \frac{28}{(1+r)^4} \tag{8.2}$$

We can also use the annuity formula from Chapter 4 to write the NPV as

$$NPV = -81.6 + \frac{28}{r}\left(1 - \frac{1}{(1+r)^4}\right) \tag{8.3}$$

To apply the NPV rule, we need to know the cost of capital to use as the discount rate. The financial managers responsible for this project estimate a cost of capital of 10% per year. If we replace r in Equation 8.2 or 8.3 with the project's cost of capital of 10%, we get an NPV of $7.2 million, which is positive. Recall that an NPV tells us the present value of the benefits (positive cash flows) net of the costs (negative cash flows) of the project. By putting everything into present values, the NPV puts all the costs and benefits on an equal footing for comparison. In this case, the benefits outweigh the costs by $7.2 million in present value. The NPV investment rule indicates that by making the investment, SFL will increase the value of the firm today by $7.2 million, so SFL should undertake this project.

The NPV Profile

NPV profile A graph of a project's NPV over a range of discount rates.

The NPV of the project depends on its appropriate cost of capital. Often, there may be some uncertainty regarding the project's cost of capital. In that case, it is helpful to compute an **NPV profile**, which graphs the project's NPV over a range of discount rates. It is easiest to prepare the NPV profile using a spreadsheet such as Excel. We simply repeat our calculation of the NPV above using a range of different discount rates instead of only 10%. Figure 8.1 presents the NPV profile for SFL's project by plotting the NPV as a function of the discount rate, r.[1]

internal rate of return (IRR) The interest rate that sets the NPV of the cash flows equal to zero.

Notice that the NPV is positive only for discount rates that are less than 14% (the green shaded area in Figure 8.1). Referring to the graph and the accompanying data table, we see that at 14%, the NPV is zero. The discount rate that sets the NPV of the cash flows equal to zero is an investment's **internal rate of return (IRR)**. Thus, by constructing the NPV profile, we have determined that SFL's project has an IRR of 14%. We can also compute the IRR without graphing the NPV by using a financial calculator or a spreadsheet's IRR function. (See the Appendix to Chapter 4. The calculator instructions for solving for the rate of return can be used to solve for the IRR.)

	N	I/Y	PV	PMT	FV
Given:	4		−81.6	28	0
Solve for:		14			

Excel Formula: =RATE(NPER,PMT,PV,FV)=RATE(4,28,−81.6,0)

Measuring Sensitivity with IRR

In our SFL example, the firm's managers provided the cost of capital. If you are unsure of your cost of capital estimate, it is important to determine how sensitive your analysis

[1]In the Appendix to this chapter, we show you how to create an NPV profile in Excel.

FIGURE 8.1 NPV Profile of SFL's New Project

The graph in panel (b) shows the NPV as a function of the discount rate based on the data in panel (a). The NPV is positive, represented by the green-shaded area, only for discount rates that are less than 14%, the IRR. Given the cost of capital of 10%, the project has a positive NPV of $7.2 million. The red-shaded area indicates discount rates above 14% IRR with negative NPVs.

Panel (a)

Discount Rate	NPV ($ millions)
0%	$30.4
2%	$25.0
4%	$20.0
6%	$15.4
8%	$11.1
10%	$7.2
12%	$3.4
14%	**$0.0**
16%	−$3.3
18%	−$6.3
20%	−$9.1
22%	−$11.8
24%	−$14.3

Panel (b)

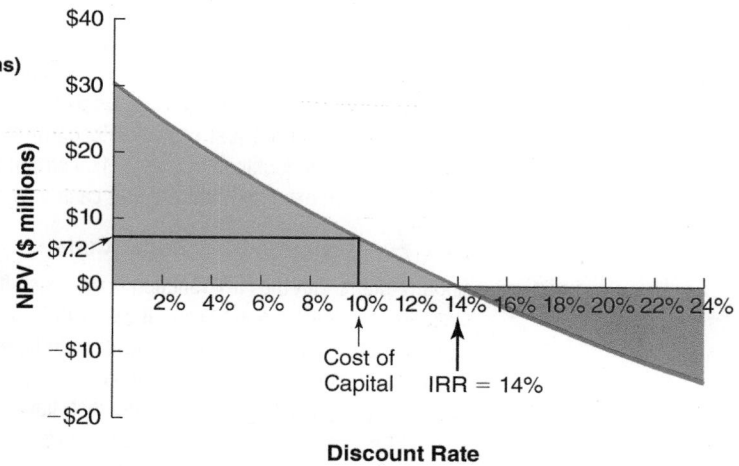

is to errors in this estimate. The IRR can provide this information. IRR measures the return of the project and is the discount rate that equates the PV of the project's inflows to the PV of the project's outflows (i.e., it is the discount rate that makes NPV = 0). For SFL, if the cost of capital estimate is more than the 14% IRR, the NPV will be negative (see the red shaded area in Figure 8.1). Therefore, as long as our estimate of the cost of capital of 10% is within 4% of the true cost of capital, our decision to accept the project is correct. In general, what the difference between the cost of capital and the IRR tells us is the amount of estimation error in the cost of capital estimate that can exist without altering the original decision.

Alternative Rules versus the NPV Rule

The NPV rule indicates that SFL should undertake the investment in fertilizer technology. As we evaluate alternative rules for project selection in the subsequent sections, keep in mind that sometimes other investment rules may give the same answer as the NPV rule, but at other times they may disagree. When the rules conflict, always base your decision on the NPV rule, which is the most accurate and reliable decision rule.

amount of estimation error in the cost of capital estimate that can exist without altering the original decision

- compare it to zero and accept the project if its positive

CONCEPT CHECK

3. Explain the NPV rule for stand-alone projects.
4. How can you interpret the difference between the cost of capital and the IRR?

↳ If the cost of capital estimate is more than IRR the project is negative

Computing NPV and IRR

Here we discuss how to use Microsoft Excel to solve for NPV and IRR. We also identify some pitfalls to avoid when using Excel.

NPV Function: Leaving Out Date 0

Excel's NPV function has the format NPV (rate, value1, value2,...), where "rate" is the interest rate per period used to discount the cash flows, and "value1," "value2," etc., are the cash flows (or ranges of cash flows). The NPV function computes the present value of the cash flows assuming the first cash flow occurs at date 1. Therefore, if a project's first cash flow occurs at date 0, we cannot use the NPV function by itself to compute the NPV. We can use the NPV function to compute the present value of the cash flows from date 1 onward, and then we must add the date 0 cash flow to that result to calculate the NPV. The screenshot below shows the difference. The first NPV calculation (outlined in blue) is correct; we used the NPV function for all of the cash flows occurring at time 1 and later, and then added on the first cash flow occurring at time 0 since it is already in present value. The second calculation (outlined in green) is incorrect; we used the NPV function for all of the cash flows, but the function assumed that the first cash flow occurs in period 1 instead of immediately.

NPV Function: Ignoring Blank Cells

Another pitfall with the NPV function is that cash flows that are left blank are treated differently from cash flows that are equal to zero. If the cash flow is left blank, both the cash flow and the period are ignored. For example, the second set of cash flows below is equivalent to the first—we have simply left the cash flow for date 2 blank instead of entering a "0." However, the NPV function ignores the blank cell at date 2 and assumes the cash flow is 10 at date 1 and 110 at date 2, which is clearly not what is intended and produces an incorrect answer (outlined in red).

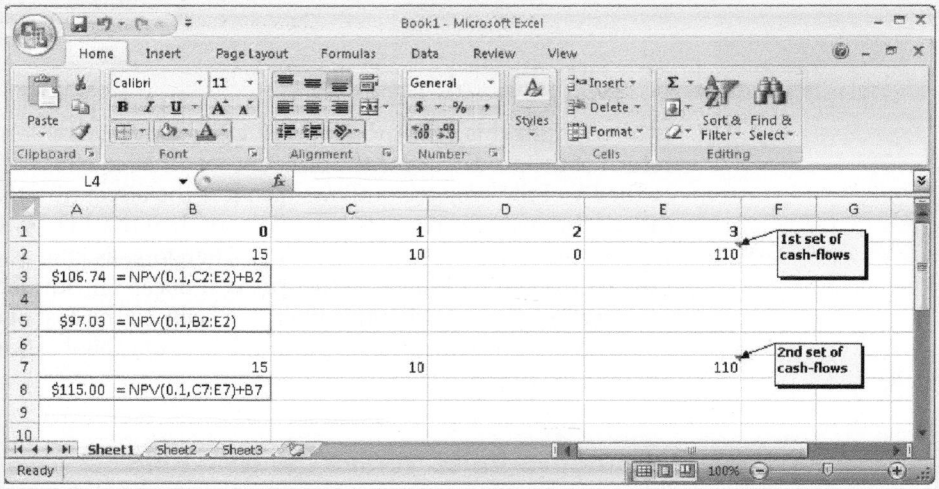

Because of these idiosyncrasies, we avoid using Excel's NPV function. It is more reliable to compute the present value of each cash flow separately in Excel, and then sum them to determine the NPV.

IRR Function

Excel's IRR function has the format IRR (values, guess), where "values" is the range containing the cash flows and "guess" is an optional starting guess where Excel begins its search for an IRR. Two things to note about the IRR function:

1. The values given to the IRR function should include all of the cash flows of the project, including the one at date 0. In this sense, the IRR and NPV functions in Excel are inconsistent.
2. Like the NPV function, the IRR ignores the period associated with any blank cells.

8.3 Alternative Decision Rules

Even though the NPV rule is the most accurate and reliable rule, in practice a wide variety of rules are applied, often in tandem with the NPV rule. In a 2001 study, John Graham and Campbell Harvey[2] found that 74.9% of the firms they surveyed used the NPV rule for making investment decisions. In a 1995 study, Vijay Jog and Ashwani Srivastava[3] found less than 50% of Canadian firms used NPV, but about 75% used some form of discounted cash flow (DCF) analysis. These results are substantially different from those found in a similar study in 1977 by L. J. Gitman and J. R. Forrester,[4] who found that only 9.8% of firms used the NPV rule. Business students in recent years have been listening to their finance professors! Even so, the two more recent studies indicate that over one-quarter of corporations do not use the NPV rule. Exactly why other capital budgeting techniques are used in practice is not always clear. Figure 8.2 summarizes the top three decision rules given in the Graham and Harvey survey. Because you may encounter these techniques in the business world, you should know what they are, how they are used, and how they compare to using the *NPV rule*. In this section, we examine alternative decision rules for single, stand-alone projects within the firm. The focus here is on the *payback rule* and the *IRR rule*.

FIGURE 8.2 **The Most Popular Decision Rules Used by CFOs**

The bar graph shows the most popular decision rules used by CFOs in the Graham and Harvey 2001 survey. Many CFOs used more than one method, but no other methods were mentioned by more than half of CFOs.

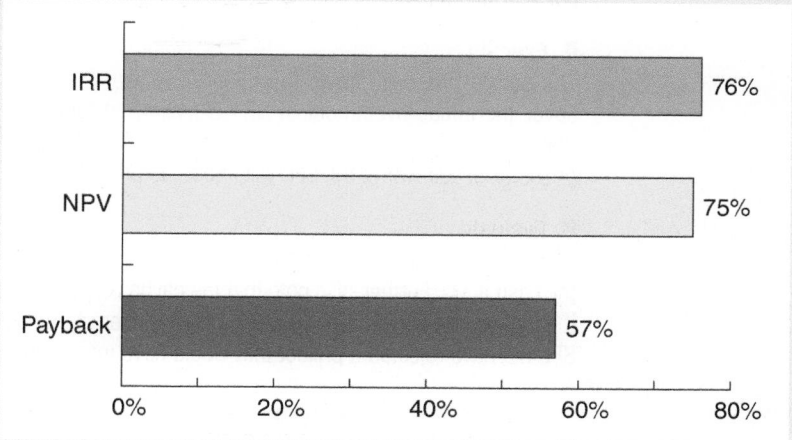

[2]John Graham and Campbell Harvey, "The Theory and Practice of Corporate Finance: Evidence from the Field," *Journal of Financial Economics* 60 (2001): 187–243.

[3]Vijay Jog and Ashwani Srivastava, "Capital Budgeting Practices in Corporate Canada," *Financial Practice and Education* 5 (1995): 37–43.

[4]L. J. Gitman and J. R. Forrester, Jr., "A Survey of Capital Budgeting Techniques Used by Major U.S. Firms," *Financial Management* 6 (1977): 66–71.

The Payback Rule

payback rule Only projects that pay back their initial investment within the payback period are undertaken.

payback period The amount of time until the cash flows from a project offset the initial investment. The time it takes to pay back the initial investment.

The simplest investment rule is the **payback rule**, which states that you should accept a project only if its cash flows pay back its initial investment within a pre-specified period. The rule is based on the notion that an opportunity that pays back its initial investment quickly is a good idea. To apply the payback rule,

1. Calculate the amount of time it takes to pay back the initial investment, called the **payback period**.
2. Accept the project if the payback period is less than a prespecified length of time—usually a few years.
3. Reject the project if the payback period is greater than that prespecified length of time.

For example, a firm might adopt any project with a payback period of less than two years.

EXAMPLE 8.2 Using the Payback Rule

PROBLEM

Assume SFL requires all projects to have a payback period of two years or less. Would the firm undertake the fertilizer project under this rule?

SOLUTION

■ Plan

To implement the payback rule, we need to know whether the sum of the inflows from the project will exceed the initial investment before the end of two years. The project has inflows of $28 million per year and an initial investment of $81.6 million.

■ Execute

The sum of the cash flows from year 1 to year 2 is $28 × 2 = $56 million, which will not cover the initial investment of $81.6 million. In fact, it will not be until year 3 that the cash flows exceed the initial investment ($28 × 3 = $84 million). Because the payback period for this project exceeds two years, SFL will reject the project.

■ Evaluate

While simple to compute, the payback rule requires us to use an arbitrary cutoff period in summing the cash flows. Further, also note that the payback rule does not discount future cash flows. Instead it simply sums the cash flows and compares them to a cash outflow in the present. In this case, SFL will have rejected a project that would have increased the value of the firm.

Relying on the payback rule analysis in Example 8.2, SFL will reject the project. However, as we saw earlier, with a cost of capital of 10%, the NPV is $7.2 million. Following the payback rule would be a mistake because SFL will pass up a project worth $7.2 million.

discounted payback rule Accept only projects where the sum of the discounted cash flows within the payback period is greater than or equal to the initial investment.

The payback rule is not as reliable as the NPV rule because it (1) ignores the time value of money, (2) ignores cash flows after the payback period, and (3) lacks a decision criterion grounded in economics (what is the right number of years to require for a payback period?). Some companies have addressed the first failing by computing the payback period using discounted cash flows (leading to the **discounted payback rule**).

However, this does not solve the fundamental problem, because the other two failings remain. Despite these failings, Graham and Harvey found that about 57% of the firms they surveyed reported using the payback rule as part of the decision-making process.

Why do some companies consider the payback rule? The answer probably relates to its simplicity. This rule is typically used for small investment decisions—for example, whether to purchase a new copy machine or to service the old one. In such cases, the cost of making an incorrect decision might not be large enough to justify the time required to calculate the NPV. The appeal of the payback rule is that it favours short-term projects. Some firms are unwilling to commit capital to long-term investments. Also, if the required payback period is short (one to two years), then most projects that satisfy the payback rule will have a positive NPV. So, firms might save effort by first applying the payback rule, and only if the rule rejects the project will they then take the time to compute the project's NPV.

The Internal Rate of Return Rule

internal rate of return (IRR) rule A decision rule that accepts any investment opportunity where the IRR exceeds the opportunity cost of capital and otherwise rejects the opportunity.

Like the NPV rule, the **internal rate of return (IRR) rule** is based on the concept that if the return on the investment opportunity you are considering is greater than the return on other alternatives in the market with equivalent risk and maturity (i.e., the project's cost of capital), you should undertake the investment opportunity. We state the rule formally as follows:

> *IRR Rule: take any investment opportunity where IRR exceeds the opportunity cost of capital. Turn down any opportunity whose IRR is less than the opportunity cost of capital.*

The IRR rule will give the correct answer (that is, the same answer as the NPV rule) in many—but not all—situations. For instance, it gives the correct answer for SFL's fertilizer opportunity. From Figure 8.1, whenever the cost of capital is in the green area below the IRR (14%), the project has a positive NPV and you should undertake the investment. Table 8.1 summarizes our analysis of SFL's new project. The NPV and IRR rules agree, but using the payback rule with a required payback period of two years or less would cause SFL to reject the project.

TABLE 8.1 Summary of NPV, IRR, and Payback for SFL's New Project

NPV at 10%	\$7.2 million	Accept (\$7.2 million > 0)
Payback period	3 years	Reject (3 years > 2 year required payback)
IRR	14%	Accept (14% > 10% cost of capital)

In general, the IRR rule works for a stand-alone project if all of the project's negative cash flows precede its positive cash flows. In other cases, though, the IRR rule may disagree with the NPV rule and thus be incorrect. Let's examine several situations in which the IRR fails.

Unconventional Cash Flows. Star hockey player Maurice Lafleur is graduating from university with a degree in finance and is preparing for the NHL draft. Several companies have already approached him with endorsement contracts. Two competing sports drink companies are trying to sign him. QuenchIt offers him a single upfront payment of \$1 million to exclusively endorse its sports drink for three years. PowerUp offers \$500,000 per year, payable at the end of each of the next three years, to endorse its product exclusively. Which offer is better? One direct way to compare the two contracts is to realize that signing with QuenchIt causes Maurice to forgo the PowerUp contract, or $500,000 per year. Considering the risk of his alternative income sources and available investment opportunities, Maurice estimates his opportunity cost of capital to be 10%. The timeline of Maurice's investment opportunity is

0	1	2	3
$1,000,000	−$500,000	−$500,000	−$500,000

The NPV of Maurice's investment opportunity is

$$NPV = 1{,}000{,}000 - \frac{500{,}000}{1 + r} - \frac{500{,}000}{(1 + r)^2} - \frac{500{,}000}{(1 + r)^3}$$

By setting the NPV equal to zero and solving for r, we find the IRR. We can use either a financial calculator or a spreadsheet to find the IRR:

	N	I/Y	PV	PMT	FV
Given:	3		1,000,000	−500,000	0
Solve for:		23.38			

Excel Formula: = *RATE(NPER,PMT,PV,FV)* = *RATE*(3,−500000,1000000,0)

The 23.38% IRR is larger than the 10% opportunity cost of capital. According to the IRR rule, Maurice should sign the deal. But what does the NPV rule say?

$$NPV = 1{,}000{,}000 - \frac{500{,}000}{1.1} - \frac{500{,}000}{1.1^2} - \frac{500{,}000}{1.1^3} = -\$243{,}426$$

At a 10% discount rate, the NPV is negative, so signing the deal would reduce Maurice's wealth. He should not sign the endorsement deal with QuenchIt; he should sign with PowerUp instead.

To resolve this conflict, we can prepare an NPV profile for the QuenchIt contract. Figure 8.3 plots the NPV of the investment opportunity for a range of discount rates. It shows that, no matter what the cost of capital is, the IRR rule and the NPV rule will give exactly opposite recommendations. That is, the NPV is positive only when the opportunity cost of capital is *above* 23.38% (the IRR). Maurice should accept the investment only when the opportunity cost of capital is greater than the IRR, the opposite of what the IRR rule recommends.

Figure 8.3 also illustrates the problem with using the IRR rule in this case. For most investment opportunities, expenses occur initially and cash is received later. In this case, Maurice gets cash *up front* from QuenchIt, but the foregone cash flows from PowerUp occurred later. It is as if Maurice borrowed money, and when you borrow money you prefer as *low* a rate as possible. Maurice's optimal rule is to borrow money as long as the rate at which he borrows is *less* than the cost of capital. Thus, the IRR rule must be reversed for projects with unconventional cash flows (or borrowing-type cash flows).

Even though the conventional IRR rule fails to give the correct answer in this case, the IRR itself still provides useful information *in conjunction* with the NPV rule. As mentioned earlier, the IRR provides information on how sensitive the investment decision is to uncertainty in the cost of capital estimate. In this case, the difference

FIGURE 8.3 NPV Profile of Maurice Lafleur's $1 Million QuenchIt Deal

When the benefits of an investment occur before the costs, the NPV is an increasing function of the discount rate. The NPV is positive in the green-shaded areas and negative in the red-shaded areas. Notice that the NPV is positive when the cost of capital is above 23.38%, the IRR, so the NPV and IRR rules conflict.

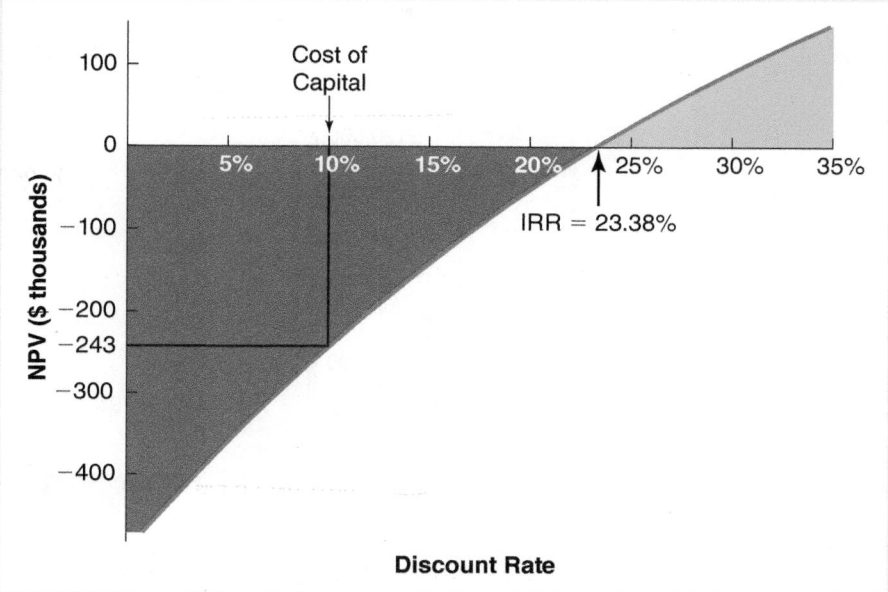

between the cost of capital and the IRR is large—10% versus 23.38%. Maurice would have had to underestimate the cost of capital by 13.38% to make the NPV positive.

Multiple IRRs. Maurice has informed QuenchIt that it needs to sweeten the deal before he will accept it. In response, the company has agreed to make an additional payment of $600,000 in 10 years as deferred compensation for the long-term increase in sales that even a short-term endorsement by Maurice would bring. Should he accept or reject the new offer?

We begin with the new timeline:

0	1	2	3	4	...	9	10
+$1,000,000	−$500,000	−$500,000	−$500,000	0		0	+$600,000

The NPV of Maurice's new investment opportunity is

$$NPV = 1{,}000{,}000 - \frac{500{,}000}{1+r} - \frac{500{,}000}{(1+r)^2} - \frac{500{,}000}{(1+r)^3} + \frac{600{,}000}{(1+r)^{10}}$$

We can find the IRR for this investment opportunity by creating an NPV profile and noting where it crosses zero. Figure 8.4 plots the NPV of the opportunity at different discount rates. In this case, there are two IRRs—that is, there are two values of r that set the NPV equal to zero. You can verify this fact by substituting IRRs of 5.79% and 13.80%

FIGURE 8.4 **NPV Profile of Maurice Lafleur's Sports Drink Deal with Additional Deferred Payments**

The graph in panel (b) shows the NPV of Maurice's deal with additional deferred payment based on the data in panel (a). In this case, there are two IRRs, invalidating the IRR rule. If the opportunity cost of capital is either below 5.79% or above 13.80%, Maurice should accept the deal because the NPV is then positive, as indicated by the green-shaded areas. At any point between the two IRRs, the NPV is negative (see the red-shaded area).

panel (a)

0%	100,000
1%	72,680
2%	50,267
3%	32,151
4%	17,793
5%	6724
6%	−1469
7%	−7148
8%	−10,632
9%	−12,201
10%	−12,100
11%	−10,547
12%	−7732
13%	−3823
14%	1030
15%	6698
16%	13,065
17%	20,030
18%	27,502
19%	35,403
20%	43,663
21%	52,219
22%	61,019
23%	70,014
24%	79,161

panel (b)

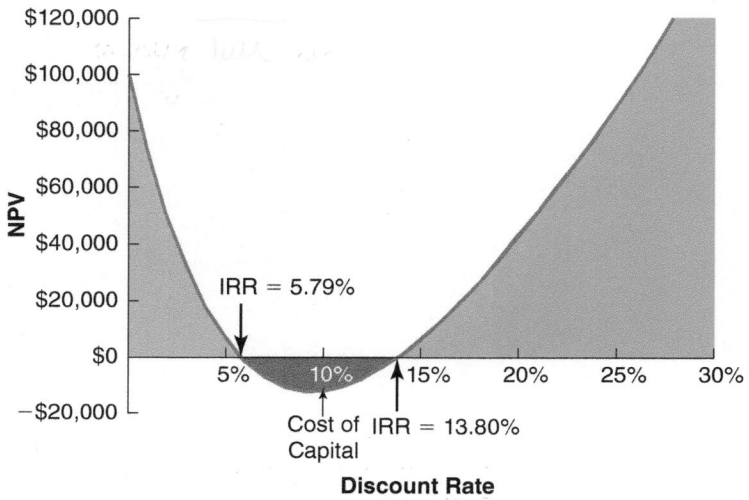

for r into the equation. Because there is more than one IRR, we cannot apply the IRR rule. It is also worth noting that you should take special care when using a spreadsheet or financial calculator to determine the IRR. Recall that both solve for the IRR through trial and error. In cases where there is more than one IRR, the spreadsheet or calculator will simply produce the first one that it finds, with no mention that there could be others! Thus, it always pays to create the NPV profile.

For guidance, let's turn to the NPV rule. If the cost of capital were *either* below 5.79% or above 13.80%, Maurice should undertake the opportunity. But given his cost of capital of 10%, he should still turn it down. Notice that even though the IRR rule fails in this case, the two IRRs are still useful as bounds on the cost of capital estimate. If the cost of capital estimate is wrong, and it is actually smaller than 5.79% or larger than 13.80%, the decision not to pursue the project will change because it will have a positive NPV.

COMMON MISTAKE

IRR versus the IRR Rule

Throughout this subsection, we have distinguished between the IRR itself and the IRR rule. While we have pointed out the shortcomings of using the IRR rule to make investment decisions, *the* IRR *itself remains a very useful tool.* The IRR measures the average return of the investment and indicates the sensitivity of the NPV to estimation error in the cost of capital. Thus, knowing the IRR can be very useful, but relying on it to make investment decisions can be hazardous.

FIGURE 8.5 NPV Profile Profile for a Project with Multiple IRRs

The graph shows the NPV profile for a multiple-IRR project with cash flows of −$1000, $2500, and −$1540 in years 0, 1, and 2, respectively. As the NPV profile shows, the project has two IRRs: 10% and 40%.

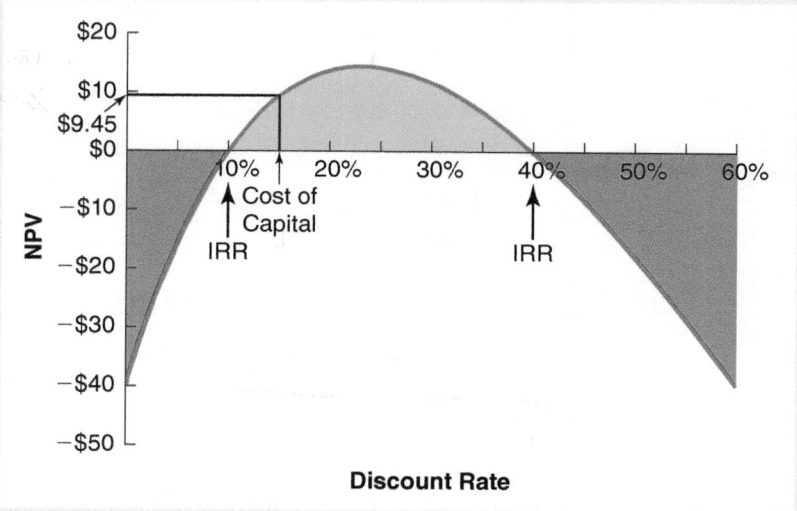

There is no easy fix for the IRR rule when there are multiple IRRs. Although the NPV is negative between the IRRs in this example, the reverse is also possible (see Figure 8.5). In that case, the project would have a positive NPV for discount rates between the IRRs rather than for discount rates lower or higher than the IRRs. Furthermore, there are

WHY DO RULES OTHER THAN THE NPV RULE PERSIST?

Professors Graham and Harvey found that a sizable minority of firms (25%) in their study do not use the NPV rule at all. In addition, about 50% of firms surveyed used the payback rule. Furthermore, it appears that most firms use both the NPV rule and the IRR rule. Why do firms use rules other than NPV if these can lead to erroneous decisions?

One possible explanation for this phenomenon is that Graham and Harvey's survey results might be misleading. CFOs who were using the IRR as a sensitivity measure in conjunction with the NPV rule might have checked both the IRR box and the NPV box on the survey. The question they were asked was, "How frequently does your firm use the following techniques when deciding which projects or acquisitions to pursue?" By computing the IRR and using it in conjunction with the NPV rule to estimate the sensitivity of their results, they might have felt they were using both techniques. Nevertheless, a significant minority of managers surveyed replied that they used only the IRR rule, so this explanation cannot be the whole story.

One common reason that managers give for using the IRR rule exclusively is that you do not need to know the opportunity cost of capital to calculate the IRR. On a superficial level, this is true: the IRR does not depend on the cost of capital. You may not need to know the cost of capital to calculate the IRR, but you certainly need to know the cost of capital when you apply the IRR rule. Consequently, the opportunity cost is as important to the IRR rule as it is to the NPV rule.

Nonetheless, part of the appeal of the IRR rule is that the IRR seems to sum up the attractiveness of an investment without requiring an assumption about the cost of capital. However, a more useful summary is the project's NPV profile, showing the NPV as a function of the discount rate. The NPV profile also does not require knowing the cost of capital, but it has the distinct advantage of being much more informative and reliable.

situations in which more than two IRRs exist.[5] It is not uncommon for projects to have cash flows that can result in multiple IRRs. For instance, in many resource extraction projects (such as mining or oil extraction) there are upfront outflows required to get the project going, followed by inflows as the resource is extracted and sold, but then followed by outflows as the site is cleaned up and the land is restored to its original condition. This pattern of outflows, inflows, outflows may result in more than one IRR. In such situations, our only choice is to rely on the NPV rule.

CONCEPT CHECK

5. How do you apply the payback rule?
6. Under what conditions will the IRR rule lead to the same decision as the NPV rule?

8.4 Choosing Between Projects

Thus far, we have considered only decisions in which the choice is either to accept or to reject a single, stand-alone project. Sometimes, however, a firm must choose just one project from among several possible projects. For example, a manager may be evaluating alternative package designs for a new product. The manager must choose only one of the designs. When choosing any one project excludes us from taking the other projects, we are facing **mutually exclusive projects**.

mutually exclusive projects Projects that compete with one another; by accepting one, you exclude the others.

When projects, such as the package designs, are mutually exclusive it is not enough to determine which projects have positive NPVs. With mutually exclusive projects, the manager's goal is to rank the projects and choose only the best one. In this situation, the NPV rule provides a straightforward answer: *pick the project with the highest NPV*.

Because the IRR is a measure of the expected return of investing in the project, you might be tempted to extend the IRR investment rule to the case of mutually exclusive projects by picking the project with the highest IRR. Unfortunately, picking one project over another simply because it has a larger IRR can lead to mistakes. Problems arise when the mutually exclusive investments have differences in scale (require different initial investments) and when they have different cash flow patterns. We discuss each of these situations in turn.

Differences in Scale

Would you prefer a 200% return on $1 or a 10% return on $1 million? The former return certainly sounds impressive and gives you great bragging rights, but at the end of the day you make only $2. The latter opportunity may sound much more mundane, but you make $100,000. This comparison illustrates an important shortcoming of IRR; because it is a return, you cannot tell how much value has actually been created without knowing the basis for the return—a 10% IRR can have very different value implications for an initial investment of $1 million versus an initial investment of $100 million.

If a project has a positive NPV, then if we can double its size, its NPV will double; according to the Valuation Principle, doubling the cash flows of an investment opportunity

[5]In general, there can be as many IRRs as the number of times the project's cash flows change signs over time. So, if you are analyzing a project and the signs of the cash flows change more than once, beware that there can be more than one IRR.

must make it worth twice as much. However, the IRR rule does not have this property—it is unaffected by the scale of the investment opportunity because the IRR measures the average return of the investment. Hence, the IRR rule cannot be used to compare projects of different scales. Let's illustrate this concept in the context of an example.

EXAMPLE 8.3 NPV and Mutually Exclusive Projects

PROBLEM

You own a small piece of commercial land near a university. You are considering what to do with it. You have recently received an offer to buy it for $220,000. You are also considering using the land for three possible alternatives: a bar, a coffee shop, and an apparel store. You assume that you would operate your choice indefinitely, eventually leaving the business to your children. You have collected the following information about the uses. What should you do?

	Initial Investment	Cash flow in the First Year	Growth Rate	Cost of Capital
Bar	$400,000	$60,000	3.5%	12%
Coffee shop	$200,000	$40,000	3%	10%
Apparel store	$500,000	$75,000	3%	13%

SOLUTION

■ Plan

Since you can do only one project (you have only one piece of land), these are mutually exclusive projects. To decide which project is most valuable, you need to rank them by NPV. Each of these projects (except for selling the land) has cash flows that can be valued as a growing perpetuity, so from Chapter 4, the present value of the inflows is $CF_1/(r - g)$. The NPV of each investment will be

$$\frac{CF_1}{r - g} - \text{Initial Investment}$$

■ Execute

The NPVs are

$$\text{Bar: } \frac{\$60{,}000}{0.12 - 0.035} - \$400{,}000 = \$305{,}882$$

$$\text{Coffee Shop: } \frac{\$40{,}000}{0.10 - 0.03} - \$200{,}000 = \$371{,}429$$

$$\text{Apparel Store: } \frac{\$75{,}000}{0.13 - 0.03} - \$500{,}000 = \$250{,}000$$

So, the ranking is

Alternative	NPV
Coffee shop	$371,429
Bar	$305,882
Apparel store	$250,000
Sell the land	$220,000

and you should choose the coffee shop. ▶

■ Evaluate

All of the alternatives have positive NPVs, but you can take only one of them, so you should choose the one that creates the most value. Even though the coffee shop has the lowest cash flows, its lower start-up cost, coupled with its lower cost of capital (it is less risky), make it the best choice. It is important in our analysis of the three alternatives to also consider the possibility of selling the land. Otherwise, we may end up choosing an option that looks like a positive NPV alternative but is actually inferior to selling the land. In the next chapter we will see that the market value of the land should actually be included as an opportunity cost (as an additional initial cash outflow) for each of the three alternatives.

Identical Scale. We begin by considering two mutually exclusive projects with the same scale. Marek is evaluating two investment opportunities. If he went into business with his girlfriend, he would need to invest $10,000 and the business would generate incremental cash flows of $6000 per year for three years. Alternatively, he could start a two-machine gaming-café where patrons could play old pinball and video games while having a coffee. The gaming-setup will cost $10,000 and will generate $5000 for three years. The opportunity cost of capital for both opportunities is 12%, and both will require all his time, so Marek must choose between them. How valuable is each opportunity, and which one should Marek choose?

Let's consider both the NPV and IRR of each project. The timeline for the investment with Marek's girlfriend is

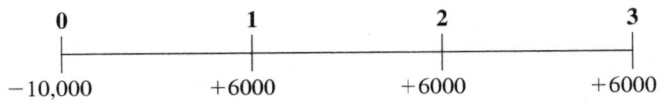

The NPV of the investment opportunity when $r = 12\%$ is

$$NPV = -10{,}000 + \frac{6000}{1.12} + \frac{6000}{1.12^2} + \frac{6000}{1.12^3} = \$4411$$

We can determine the IRR of this investment by using a financial calculator or spreadsheet:

	N	I/Y	PV	PMT	FV
Given:	3		−10,000	6000	0
Solve for:		36.3			
Excel Formula: = *RATE(NPER,PMT,PV,FV)*= *RATE*(3,6000,−10000,0)					

Thus, the IRR for Marek's investment in his girlfriend's business is 36.3%.

The timeline for his investment in the gaming café is

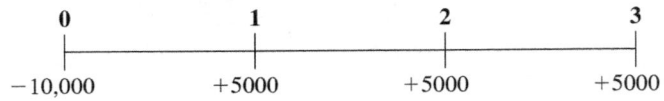

The NPV of the investment opportunity is

$$NPV = -10{,}000 + \frac{5000}{1.12} + \frac{5000}{1.12^2} + \frac{5000}{1.12^3} = \$2009$$

The $2009 NPV of the gaming café is lower than the $4411 NPV for his girlfriend's business, so Marek should join his girlfriend in business. Luckily, it appears that Marek does not need to choose between his chequebook and his relationship!

We could also compare IRRs. For the gaming café, we would find that the IRR is 23.4%. The gaming café has a lower IRR than the investment in his girlfriend's business. As Figure 8.6 shows, in this case the project with the higher IRR has the higher NPV.

FIGURE 8.6 **NPV Profiles of Marek's Investment Opportunities with the Two-Machine Gaming Café**

The NPV of his girlfriend's business is always larger than the NPV of the two-machine gaming café. The same is true for the IRR; the IRR of his girlfriend's business is 36.3%, while the IRR for the gaming café is 23.4%.

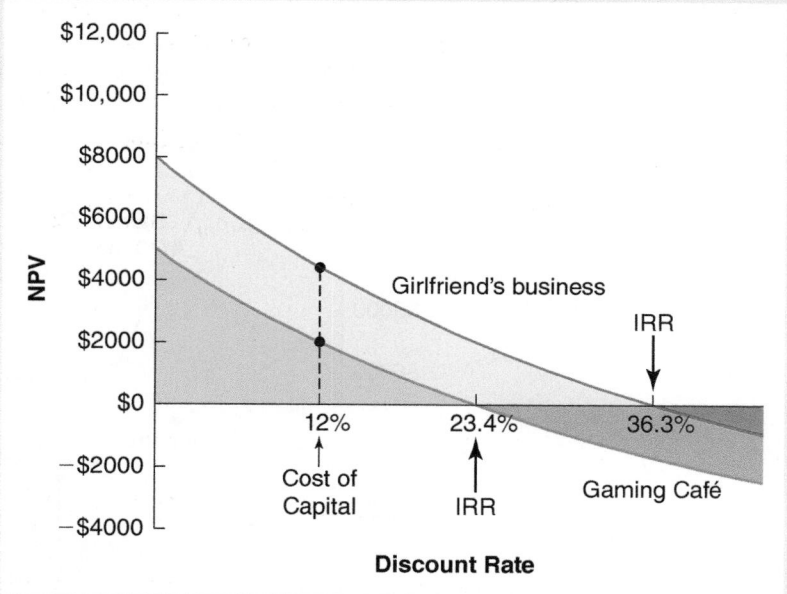

Change in Scale. What happens if we change the scale of one of the projects? Marek's finance professor points out that, given the space available in the facility, he could just as easily install five times as many machines in the gaming café. His setup cost would now be $50,000, and his annual cash flows would be $25,000. What should Marek do now?

Note that the IRR is unaffected by the scale. Because we are scaling all the cash flows up by a factor of 5, a 10-machine gaming café has exactly the same IRR as a 2-machine gaming café, so his girlfriend's business still has a higher IRR than the gaming café:

	N	I/Y	PV	PMT	FV
Given:	3		−50,000	25,000	0
Solve for:		36.3			

Excel Formula: = *RATE*(*NPER*,*PMT*,*PV*,*FV*) = *RATE*(3,25000,−50000,0)

However, the NPV of the gaming café does grow by the scale. It is five times larger:

$$NPV = -50{,}000 + \frac{25{,}000}{1.12} + \frac{25{,}000}{1.12^2} + \frac{25{,}000}{1.12^3} = \$10{,}046$$

Now Marek should invest in the 10-machine gaming café. As Figure 8.7 shows, the NPV of the 10-machine gaming café exceeds the NPV of going into business with his girlfriend whenever the cost of capital is less than 20%. In this case, even though the IRR of going into business with his girlfriend exceeds the IRR of the gaming café, picking the investment opportunity with the higher IRR does not result in taking the opportunity with the higher NPV.

FIGURE 8.7 **NPV Profiles of Marek's Investment Opportunities with the 10-Machine Gaming Café**

As in Figure 8.6, the IRR of his girlfriend's business is 36.3%, while the IRR for the gaming café is 23.4%. But in this case, the NPV of his girlfriend's business is larger than the NPV of the 10-machine gaming café only for discount rates over 20%.

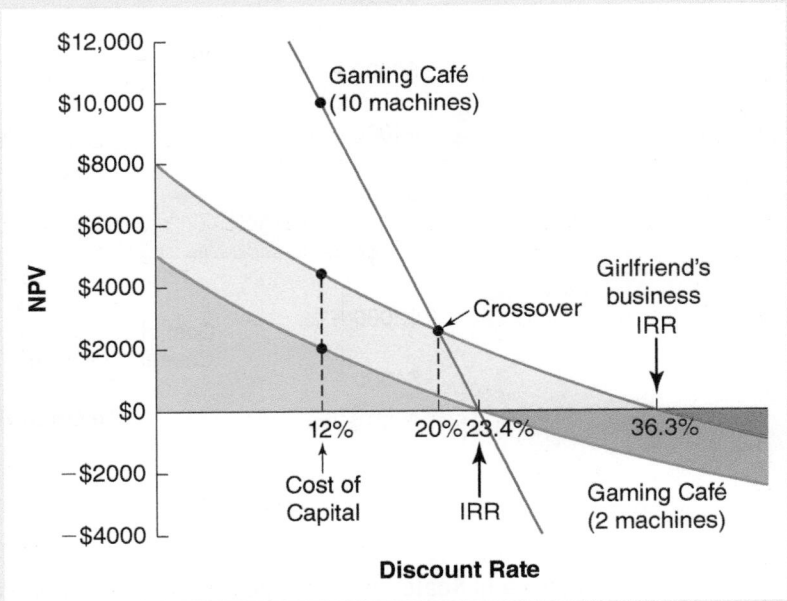

Percentage Return versus Dollar Impact on Value. This result might seem counterintuitive, and you can imagine Marek having a difficult time explaining to his girlfriend why he is choosing a lower return over going into business with her. Why would anyone turn down an investment opportunity with a 36.3% return (IRR) in favour of one with only a 23.4% return? The answer is that the latter opportunity, the gaming café, makes more money. Recall the comparison at the beginning of this section: a 200% return on $1 versus a 10% return on $1 million. We agreed that ranking the returns was not the same as ranking the value created. The IRR is a measure of the average return, which can be valuable information. When you are comparing mutually exclusive projects of different scale, however, you need to know the dollar impact on value—the NPV.

EXAMPLE 8.4 IRR of Incremental Cash Flows and Computing the Crossover Point

PROBLEM

Solve for the crossover point for Marek from Figure 8.7.

SOLUTION

■ Plan

The crossover point is the discount rate that makes the NPV of the two alternatives equal. We can find the discount rate by setting the equations for the NPV of each project equal to each other and solving for the discount rate. If we take the cash flows of the larger project and subtract the cash flows of the smaller project, we have the incremental cash flows of doing the large project instead of the small project. The crossover point is the IRR of these incremental cash flows, and at this IRR the difference in NPVs is 0.

■ Execute

Setting the difference equal to 0:

$$NPV = -50{,}000 + \frac{25{,}000}{1+r} + \frac{25{,}000}{(1+r)^2} + \frac{25{,}000}{(1+r)^3}$$

$$-\left(-10{,}000 + \frac{6000}{(1+r)} + \frac{6000}{(1+r)^2} + \frac{6000}{(1+r)^3}\right) = 0$$

$$-40{,}000 + \frac{19{,}000}{(1+r)} + \frac{19{,}000}{(1+r)^2} + \frac{19{,}000}{(1+r)^3} = 0$$

As you can see, solving for the crossover point is just like solving for the IRR, so we will need to use a financial calculator or spreadsheet:

	N	I/Y	PV	PMT	FV
Given:	3		−40,000	19,000	0
Solve for:		**20.04**			
Excel Formula: = *RATE*(*NPER*,*PMT*,*PV*,*FV*) = *RATE*(3,19000,−40000,0)					

We find that the crossover occurs at a discount rate of 20% (20.04%, to be exact).

■ Evaluate

Just as the NPV of a project tells us the value impact of taking the project, so the difference of the NPVs of two alternatives tells us the *incremental* impact of choosing one project over another. The crossover point is the IRR of the incremental cash flows determined by taking the larger project instead of the smaller project. It is the discount rate at which we would be indifferent about which of the two projects to take, because the incremental value of choosing one over the other would be zero.

We can use the IRR of the incremental cash flows as an alternative to comparing the NPVs of the large and small projects. Effectively, if we apply the IRR rule to the incremental cash flows, we are analyzing whether the decision to switch from the small to the large project is correct. If the IRR of the incremental cash flows exceeds our hurdle rate (in this case, the cost of capital of 12%), then the decision is correct. Given that the IRR of the incremental cash flows is 20.04%, our IRR rule applied to the incremental cash flows agrees with our analysis of comparing the NPVs for the small and large projects.

INTERVIEW WITH DICK GRANNIS

Dick Grannis

Dick Grannis is senior vice-president and treasurer of Qualcomm Incorporated, a world leader in digital wireless communications technology and semiconductors. Qualcomm technologies are used in many mobile phones, including some BlackBerries and iPhones. He joined the company in 1991 and oversees its $10 billion cash investment portfolio. He works primarily on investment banking, capital structure, and international finance. Here, he talks about project evaluation within Qualcomm and the discount rates Qualcomm uses for the project's forecasted incremental cash flows.

Q Qualcomm has a wide variety of products in different business lines. How does your capital budgeting process for new products work?

A Qualcomm evaluates new projects (such as new products, equipment, technologies, research and development, acquisitions, and strategic investments) by using traditional financial measurements, including DCF models, IRR levels, the time needed to reach cumulative positive cash flows, the short-term impact of the investment on our reported net earnings, and tracking the maximum amount of funding the project will require. For strategic investments, we consider the possible value of financial, competitive, technology, and/or market value enhancements to our core businesses—even if those benefits cannot be quantified. Overall, we make capital budgeting decisions based on a combination of objective analyses and our own business judgment.

We do not engage in capital budgeting and analysis if the project represents an immediate and necessary requirement for our business operations. One example is new software or production equipment to start a project that has already received approval.

We are also mindful of the opportunity costs of allocating our internal engineering resources on one project versus another project. We view this as a constantly challenging but worthwhile exercise, because we have many attractive opportunities but limited resources to pursue them.

Q How often does Qualcomm evaluate its discount rates and what factors does it consider in setting them? How do you allocate capital across areas and regions and assess the risk of international investments?

A Qualcomm encourages its financial planners to utilize hurdle (or discount) rates that vary according to the risk of the particular project. We expect a rate of return commensurate with the project's risk. Our finance staff considers a wide range of discount rates and chooses one that fits the project's expected risk profile and time horizon. The range can be from 6% to 8% for relatively safe investments in the domestic market to 50% or more for equity investments in foreign markets that may be illiquid and difficult to predict. We reevaluate our hurdle rates at least every year.

We analyze key factors including (1) market adoption risk (whether or not customers will buy the new product or service at the price and volume we expect), (2) technology development risk (whether or not we can develop and patent the new product or service as expected), (3) execution risk (whether we can launch the new product or service cost effectively and on time), and (4) dedicated asset risk (the amount of resources that must be consumed to complete the work).

Q How are projects categorized and how are the hurdle rates for new projects determined? What would happen if Qualcomm simply evaluated all new projects against the same hurdle rate?

A We primarily categorize projects by risk level, but we also categorize projects by the expected time horizon. We consider short-term and long-term projects to balance our needs and achieve our objectives. For example, immediate projects and opportunities may demand a great amount of attention, but we also stay focused on long-term projects because they often create greater long-term value for stockholders.

If we were to evaluate all new projects against the same hurdle rate, then our business planners would, by default, consistently choose to invest in the highest risk projects, because those projects would appear to have the greatest expected returns in DCF models or IRR analyses. That approach would probably not work well for very long.

Timing of the Cash Flows

Even when projects have the same scale, the IRR may lead you to rank them incorrectly due to differences in the timing of the cash flows. The reason for this is that the IRR is expressed as a return, but the dollar value of earning a given return—and therefore the NPV—depends on how long the return is earned. Consider a high-IRR project with cash flows paid back quickly. It may have a lower NPV than a project with a lower IRR whose cash flows are paid back over a longer period. This sensitivity to timing is another reason why you cannot use the IRR to choose between mutually exclusive investments. To see this in the context of an example, let's return to Marek's gaming café.

Marek believes that after starting the gaming café, he may be able to sell his stake in the business at the end of the first year for $40,000. (He will continue to stay on and manage the business after he sells.) Thus, counting his first-year profit of $25,000, he would earn a total of $65,000 after one year. In that case, the timeline is

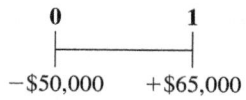

Figure 8.8 plots the NPV profile for the café with and without selling it after one year. If Marek sells, *the NPV* profile crosses the horizontal axis at 30%, which is its IRR.

FIGURE 8.8 NPV Profiles with and without Selling

The IRR from selling after one year (30%) is larger than the IRR without selling (23.4%). However, the NPV from selling after one year exceeds the NPV without selling only for discount rates that are in excess of 16.3% (see the yellow-shaded area vs. the blue-shaded area). Thus, given a cost of capital of 12%, it is better not to sell the gaming café after one year, despite the higher IRR. You should also notice that the short-term project (selling after one year) has a flatter NPV profile than the long-term project. This is typical in that longer-term projects have later cash flows that are more sensitive to changes in the discount rate than are earlier cash flows. We saw the same effect with bonds in Chapter 6 in that longer duration bonds had greater interest rate sensitivity.

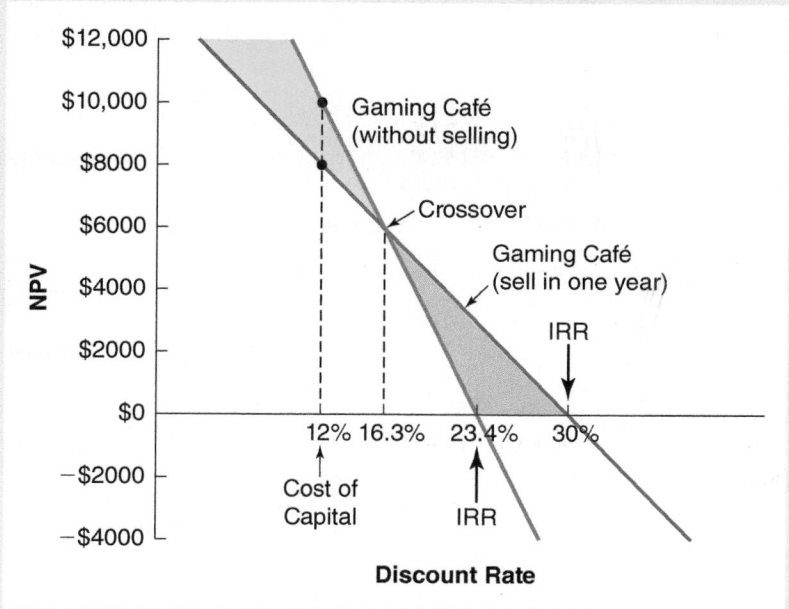

The IRR for the café if he does not sell is still 23.4%. Therefore, if Marek picks the alternative with the higher IRR, he will sell. However, since the height of each line indicates the NPV of that decision, we can see that his NPV, given a 12% cost of capital, is higher if he chooses not to sell. (In fact, the NPV is higher as long as the cost of capital is less than 16.3%.) The intuition is as follows. While the 30% IRR from selling is high, this return is earned only in the first year. While the 23.4% IRR from not selling is not as high, it is still attractive relative to the cost of capital, and it is earned over a longer period. Again, only by comparing the NPV can we determine which option is truly more valuable.

The Bottom Line on IRR. As these examples make clear, picking the investment opportunity with the largest IRR can lead to a mistake. In general, it is dangerous to use the IRR in cases where you are choosing between projects or any time when your decision to accept or reject one project would affect your decision on another project. In such a situation, always rely on NPV.

$\frac{CF_1}{r-g}$ - Investment

CONCEPT CHECK

7. What is the most reliable way to choose between mutually exclusive projects?
8. For mutually exclusive projects, explain why picking one project over another because it has a larger IRR can lead to mistakes.

↳ not a clear decision, picking on high IRR is not always useful when choosing between 2 Project or this situation NPV

8.5 Evaluating Projects with Different Lives

Often, a company will need to choose between two solutions to the same problem. A complication arises when those solutions last for different periods of time. For example, a firm could be considering two vendors for its internal network servers. Each vendor offers the same level of service, but they use different equipment. Vendor A offers a more expensive server with lower per-year operating costs that it guarantees to last for three years. Vendor B offers a less expensive server with higher per-year operating costs that it will guarantee for only two years. The costs are shown in Table 8.2 along with the present value of the costs of each option, discounted at the 10% cost of capital for this project.

TABLE 8.2 Cash Flows ($ Thousands) for Network Server Options

Year	PV at 10%	0	1	2	3
A	−12.49	−10	−1	−1	−1
B	−10.47	−7	−2	−2	-

Note that all of the cash flows are negative, and so is the present value. This is a choice of an internal server, where the project must be taken and the benefits are diffuse. (The company could not function effectively without an internal network.) Thus, we are trying to minimize the cost of providing this service for the company. Table 8.2 shows that option A is more expensive on a present value basis (−$12,490 versus −$10,470). However, the comparison is not that simple; option A lasts for three years while option B only lasts for two. The decision comes down to whether it is worth paying $2000 more for option A to get the extra year. One method that is used to evaluate alternatives such

equivalent annual annuity The level annual cash flow that has the same present value as the cash flows of a project. It is used to evaluate alternative projects with different lives.

as these that have different lives is to compute the **equivalent annual annuity** for each project, which is the level annual cash flow with the same present value as the cash flows of the project. The intuition is that we can think of the cost of each solution as the constant annual cost that gives us the same present value of the lumpy cash flows of buying and operating the server.

When you have a level cash flow at a constant interval, you are dealing with an annuity, and that is exactly how to approach this problem. We know the present value (−$12.49), the number of years (3), and the discount rate (10%). We need to solve for the cash flow of an equivalent annuity. Recall from Chapter 4 that the formula (Equation 4.8) for solving for the cash flow in an annuity is

$$\text{Cash Flow} = \frac{\text{Present Value}}{\frac{1}{r}\left(1 - \frac{1}{(1+r)^n}\right)} = \frac{-12.49}{\frac{1}{0.10}\left(1 - \frac{1}{(1.10)^3}\right)} = -5.02$$

So, buying and operating server A is equivalent to spending $5020 per year to have a network server. We can repeat the calculation for server B, but for a two-year annuity because server B has only a two-year life, the number of years is changed to 2, so the smaller present results in a higher equivalent annual annuity amount:

$$\text{Cash Flow} = \frac{\text{Present Value}}{\frac{1}{r}\left(1 - \frac{1}{(1+r)^n}\right)} = \frac{-10.47}{\frac{1}{0.10}\left(1 - \frac{1}{(1.10)^2}\right)} = -6.03$$

Therefore, we can reinterpret the cost of each alternative as shown in Table 8.3:

TABLE 8.3 **Cash Flows ($ Thousands) for Network Server Options, Expressed as Equivalent Annual Annuities**

Year	PV at 10%	0	1	2	3
A	−12.49	0	−5.02	−5.02	−5.02
B	−10.47	0	−6.03	−6.03	

Now we are ready to choose between the two servers. Server A is equivalent to spending $5020 per year, and server B is equivalent to spending $6030 per year to have a network server. Seen in this light, server A appears to be the less expensive solution.

EXAMPLE 8.5 Computing an Equivalent Annual Annuity

PROBLEM

You are about to sign the contract for server A from Table 8.2 when a third vendor approaches you with another option that lasts for four years. The cash flows for server C are given below. Should you choose the new option or stick with server A?

	0	1	2	3	4
Server C	−14	−1.2	−1.2	−1.2	−1.2

SOLUTION

■ **Plan**

To compare this new option to server A, we need to put server C on an equal footing by computing its annual cost. We can do this by

1. Computing its NPV at the 10% discount rate we used above.
2. Computing the equivalent four-year annuity with the same present value.

■ **Execute**

$$PV = -14 - 1.2\left[\frac{1}{0.10} - \frac{1}{0.10(1.10)^4}\right] = -17.80$$

$$\text{Cash Flow} = \frac{PV}{\left[\frac{1}{0.10} - \frac{1}{0.10(1.10)^4}\right]} = \frac{-17.80}{\left[\frac{1}{0.10} - \frac{1}{0.10(1.10)^4}\right]} = -5.62$$

Server C's annual cost of 5.62 is greater than the annual cost of server A (5.02), so we should still choose server A.

■ **Evaluate**

In this case, the additional cost associated with purchasing and maintaining server C is not worth the extra year we get from choosing it. By putting all of these costs into an equivalent annuity, the equivalent annual annuity tool allows us to see that.

Important Considerations When Using the Equivalent Annual Annuity

Although server A appears to be the lowest-cost alternative, there are a number of factors to consider before making our decision.

Required Life. We computed the equivalent annual cost of server A, assuming we would use it for three years. But suppose it is likely that we will not need the server in the third year. Then we would be paying for something that we would not use. In that case, it may be cheaper to purchase server B, which provides coverage for the years we will need it at a lower total cost.[6]

Replacement Cost. When we compare servers A and B based on their equivalent annual cost, we are assuming that the cost of servers will not change over time. But suppose we believe a dramatic change in technology will reduce the cost of servers by the third year to an annual cost of $2000 per year. Then, server B has the advantage that we can upgrade to the new technology sooner. The cost of three years of service from either server in this case can be represented as follows:

Year	PV at 10%	0	1	2	3
A	−12.49	0	−5.02	−5.02	−5.02
B	−11.97	0	−6.03	−6.03	−2.00

[6]In this scenario, we should also consider any salvage value that server A might have if we sold it after two years.

Therefore, when cost or performance is expected to change significantly over time, it may be cheaper to purchase server B despite its higher equivalent annual cost, because it gives us the option to switch to the new technology sooner.

CONCEPT CHECK

9. Explain why choosing the option with the highest NPV is not always correct when the options have different lives.

10. What issues should you keep in mind when choosing among projects with different lives?

↳ Required life: How many years we would actually use the project for

↳ Replacement cost: any change in technology

8.6 Choosing Among Projects When Resources Are Limited

In the previous sections, we compared projects that had *identical* resource needs. For example, in Marek's case, we assumed that both the gaming café and his girlfriend's business demanded 100% of his time. In this section, we develop an approach for situations in which the choices have differing resource needs.

Evaluating Projects with Different Resource Requirements

In some situations, different investment opportunities demand different amounts of a particular resource. If there is a fixed supply of the resource so that you cannot undertake all possible opportunities, simply picking the highest NPV opportunity might not lead to the best decision.

We usually assume that you will be able to finance all positive-NPV projects that you have. In reality, managers work within the constraint of a budget that restricts the amount of capital they may invest in a given period. Such a capital rationing constraint would force a manager to choose among positive-NPV projects to maximize the total NPV while staying within her budget. For example, assume you are considering the three projects in Table 8.4, and that you have a budget of $200 million. Table 8.4 shows the NPV of each project and the initial investment that each project requires. Project A has the highest NPV but uses up the entire budget. Projects B and C can *both* be undertaken (together they use the entire budget), and their combined NPV exceeds the NPV of project A; thus, you should initiate them both. Together, their NPV is $145 million compared with just $100 million for project A alone.

TABLE 8.4 Possible Projects for $200 Million Budget

Project	NPV ($ millions)	Initial Investment ($ millions)	NPV/Initial Investment
A	100	200	0.500
B	75	120	0.625
C	70	80	0.875

Profitability Index. Note that in the last column of Table 8.4 we included the ratio of the project's NPV to its initial investment. We can interpret this as telling us that for every dollar invested in project A, we will generate 50 cents in value (over and above the dollar investment).[7] Both projects B and C generate higher NPVs per dollar invested than

[7]Sometimes practitioners add 1 to this ratio such that the interpretation for Project A would be that every dollar invested returned $1.50. Leaving off the additional 1 allows the ratio to be applied to resources other than budgets, as we show in Example 8.5.

project A, consistent with the fact that, given our budget of $200 million, projects B and C together created a higher NPV than just project A.

In this simple example, identifying the optimal combination of projects to undertake is straightforward. In actual situations replete with many projects and resources, finding the optimal combination can be difficult. Practitioners often use the **profitability index** to help identify the optimal combination of projects to undertake in such situations:

profitability index
Measures the NPV per unit of resource consumed.

Profitability Index

$$\text{Profitability Index} = \frac{\text{Value Created}}{\text{Resource Consumed}} = \frac{NPV}{\text{Resource Consumed}} \tag{8.4}$$

The profitability index measures the "bang for your buck"—that is, the value created in terms of NPV per unit of resource consumed. After computing the profitability index, we can rank projects based on it. Starting with the project with the highest index, we move down the ranking, taking all projects until the resource is consumed. In Table 8.4, the ratio in the last column is the profitability index. Note how the profitability index rule would correctly select projects B and C.

EXAMPLE 8.6 Profitability Index with a Human Resource Constraint

PROBLEM

Your division at NetIt, a large networking company, has put together a project proposal to develop a new home networking router. The expected NPV of the project is $17.7 million, and the project will require 50 software engineers. NetIt has a total of 190 engineers available and is unable to hire additional qualified engineers in the short run. Therefore, the router project must compete with the following other projects for these engineers' attention:

Project	NPV ($ millions)	Engineering Headcount
Router	17.7	50
Project A	22.7	47
Project B	8.1	44
Project C	14.0	40
Project D	11.5	61
Project E	20.6	58
Project F	12.9	32
Total	107.5	332

How should NetIt prioritize these projects?

SOLUTION

■ Plan

The goal is to maximize the total NPV that we can create with 190 engineers (at most). We can use Equation 8.4 to determine the profitability index for each project. In this case, since engineers are our limited resource, we will use the engineering headcount in the denominator. Once we have the profitability index for each project, we can sort them based on the index. ▶

■ **Execute**

Project	NPV ($ millions)	Engineering Headcount (EHC)	Profitability Index (NPV per EHC)	Cumulative EHC Required
Project A	22.7	47	0.483	47
Project F	12.9	32	0.403	79 (47 + 32)
Project E	20.6	58	0.355	137 (79 + 58)
Router	17.7	50	0.354	187 (137 + 50)
Project C	14.0	40	0.350	
Project D	11.5	61	0.189	
Project B	8.1	44	0.184	

We now assign the resource to the projects in descending order according to the profitability index. The final column shows the cumulative use of the resource as each project is taken on until the resource is used up. To maximize NPV within the constraint of 190 engineers, NetIt should choose the first four projects on the list.

■ **Evaluate**

By ranking projects in terms of their NPV per engineer, we find the most value we can create, given our 190 engineers. There is no other combination of projects that will create more value without using more engineers than we have. This ranking also shows us exactly what the engineering constraint costs us—this resource constraint forces NetIt to forgo three otherwise valuable projects (C, D, and B) with a total NPV of $33.6 million.

Shortcomings of the Profitability Index. Although the profitability index is simple to compute and use, in some situations it does not give an accurate answer. For example, suppose in Example 8.5 that NetIt has an additional small project with an NPV of only $100,000 that requires three engineers. The profitability index in this case is $0.1/3 = 0.03$, so this project would appear at the bottom of the ranking. However, notice that three of the 190 employees are not being used after the first four projects are selected. As a result, it would make sense to take on this project even though it would be ranked last, because it would exactly use up our constraint. When choosing projects based on the profitability index ranking leaves some of the resource unused, it becomes necessary to evaluate all feasible combinations of projects that can be accepted given the resource constraint. The feasible combination that results in the highest combined NPV is the combination of projects that should be chosen.

In general, because the profitability index already includes the cost of capital (in computing the NPV), it would be better if the firm could raise additional funds to relieve a funding (or capital rationing) constraint. If the constraint is something else (such as engineers or physical capacity), there may be no way to relieve the constraint quickly enough to avoid having to choose among projects. Nonetheless, because all of the projects being ranked are value-increasing, positive-NPV projects, it is still better to focus on relieving the constraint.

A more serious problem occurs when multiple resource constraints apply. In this case, the profitability index can break down completely. The only surefire way to find the best combination of projects is to search through all of them. Although this process may sound exceedingly time-consuming, there are more advanced techniques that can tackle this specific kind of problem.[8] By using these techniques on a computer, the solution can usually be obtained almost instantaneously.

[8]Specifically, there are techniques called integer and linear programming that can be used to find the combination with the highest NPV when there are multiple constraints that must be satisfied. These methods are available, for example, in many spreadsheet programs.

CONCEPT CHECK

11. Explain why picking the project with the highest NPV might not be optimal when you evaluate projects with different resource requirements. → Could it would not be optimal you would not get the amount back

12. What does the profitability index tell you?

↳ measures the NPV Per unit of resources consumed

8.7 Putting It All Together

In Table 8.5, we summarize the decision rules outlined in this chapter. As a financial manager, you are likely to run into many different types of investment decision rules in your career. In fact, in the interview in this chapter, the treasurer of Qualcomm mentions five different decision rules his company uses when evaluating investments. We have demon-

TABLE 8.5 Summary of Decision Rules

NPV	
Definition	• The difference between the present value of an investment's benefits and the present value of its costs
Rule	• Take any investment opportunity where the NPV is positive; turn down any opportunity where it is negative
Advantages	• Corresponds directly to the impact of the project on the firm's value • Direct application of the Valuation Principle
Disadvantages	• Relies on an accurate estimate of the discount rate • Can be time-consuming to compute
IRR	
Definition	• The interest rate that sets the NPV of the cash flows equal to zero; the average return of the investment
Rule	• Take any investment opportunity where IRR exceeds the opportunity cost of capital; turn down any opportunity whose IRR is less than the opportunity cost of capital
Advantages	• Related to the NPV rule and usually yields the same (correct) decision for conventional projects
Disadvantages	• Hard to compute • Multiple IRRs or no IRR leads to ambiguity • Special care must be taken to choose among projects. • Rule must be reversed for unconventional (borrowing-type) projects
Payback Period	
Definition	• The amount of time it takes to pay back the initial investment
Rule	• Accept the project if the payback period is less than a prespecified length of time (usually a few years); otherwise, reject it
Advantages	• Simple to compute • Favours liquidity
Disadvantages	• No guidance as to correct payback cutoff period • Ignores cash flows after the cutoff completely • Often an incorrect decision will result
Profitability Index	
Definition	• NPV/resource consumed
Rule	• Rank projects according to their profitability index based on the constrained resource and move down the list accepting value-creating projects until the resource is exhausted
Advantages	• Uses the NPV to measure the benefit • Allows projects to be ranked on value created per unit of resource consumed
Disadvantages	• Breaks down when there is more than one constraint • Requires careful attention to make sure the constrained resource is completely used

strated that while alternative decision rules may sometimes (or even often) agree with the NPV rule, only the NPV decision rule is always correct. This is because the NPV provides you with a dollar-value measure of the impact of the project on shareholder wealth. Thus, it is the only rule that is directly tied to your goal of maximizing shareholder wealth. Computing the IRR can be a useful supplement to the NPV because knowing the IRR allows you to gauge how sensitive your decision is to errors in your discount rate. Some decision metrics are much simpler to calculate, such as the payback period. However, you should never rely on an alternative rule to make investment decisions.

If you are employed by a firm that uses the IRR rule (or another rule) exclusively, our advice is to always calculate the NPV. If the two rules agree, you can feel comfortable reporting the IRR rule recommendation. If they do not agree, you should investigate—by using the concepts in this chapter—why the IRR rule failed. Once you have identified the problem, you can alert your superiors to it and perhaps persuade them to adopt the NPV rule.

MyLab Finance

Here is what you should know after reading this chapter. MyLab™ Finance will help you identify what you know, and where to go when you need to practice.

KEY POINTS AND EQUATIONS	TERMS	ONLINE PRACTICE OPPORTUNITIES
8.1 The NPV Rule ■ If your objective is to maximize wealth, the NPV rule always gives the correct answer.	net present value (NPV), p. 261 NPV rule, p. 263	MyLab Study Plan 8.1
8.2 Using the NPV Rule ■ The difference between the cost of capital and the IRR is the maximum amount of estimation error that can exist in the cost of capital estimate without altering the original decision.	NPV profile, p. 264 internal rate of return (IRR), p. 264	MyLab Study Plan 8.2 Using Excel: Making an NPV Profile
8.3 Alternative Decision Rules ■ Payback investment rule: Calculate the amount of time it takes to pay back the initial investment (the payback period). If the payback period is less than a prespecified length of time, accept the project. Otherwise, turn it down. ■ IRR investment rule: Take any investment opportunity whose IRR exceeds the opportunity cost of capital. Turn down any opportunity whose IRR is less than the opportunity cost of capital. ■ The conventional IRR rule may give the wrong answer if used to analyze a project with unconventional cash flows (a borrowing-type project with an upfront inflow). When there are multiple IRRs or the IRR does not exist, the IRR rule cannot be used to make a decision.	discounted payback rule, p. 268 internal rate of return (IRR) rule, p. 269 payback period, p. 268 payback rule, p. 268	MyLab Study Plan 8.3 Interactive IRR Analysis

KEY POINTS AND EQUATIONS	TERMS	ONLINE PRACTICE OPPORTUNITIES
8.4 Choosing Between Projects ■ When choosing among mutually exclusive investment opportunities, pick the opportunity with the highest NPV. Do not use IRR to choose among mutually exclusive investment opportunities.	mutually exclusive projects, p. 274	MyLab Study Plan 8.4
8.5 Evaluating Projects with Different Lives ■ When choosing among projects with different lives, you need a standard basis of comparison. First compute an annuity with a present value equivalent to the NPV of each project. Then the projects can be compared on their cost or value created *per year*.	equivalent annual annuity, p. 283	MyLab Study Plan 8.5
8.6 Choosing Among Projects When Resources Are Limited ■ When choosing among projects competing for the same resource, rank the projects by their profitability indices and pick the set of projects with the highest profitability indices that can still be undertaken given the limited resource. $\text{Profitability Index} = \frac{\text{Value Created}}{\text{Resource Consumed}} = \frac{NPV}{\text{Resource Consumed}}$ (8.4)	profitability index, p. 286	MyLab Study Plan 8.6

REVIEW QUESTIONS

1. How is the NPV rule related to the goal of maximizing shareholder wealth?
2. What is the intuition behind the payback rule? What are some of its drawbacks?
3. What is the intuition behind the IRR rule? What are some of its drawbacks?
4. Under what conditions will the IRR rule and the NPV rule give the same accept/reject decision?
5. When is it possible to have multiple IRRs?
6. Why is it generally a bad idea to use IRR to choose between mutually exclusive projects?
7. When should you use the equivalent annual annuity?
8. What is the intuition behind the profitability index?

PROBLEMS

1-10

All problems in this chapter are available in MyLab Finance. An asterisk (*) indicates problems with a higher level of difficulty.

The NPV Rule

1. You have an opportunity to invest $50,000 now in return for $60,000 in one year. If your cost of capital is 8%, what is the NPV of this investment?

2. You have an opportunity to invest $100,000 now in return for $80,000 in one year and $30,000 in two years. If your cost of capital is 9%, what is the NPV of this investment?

3. Your storage firm has been offered $100,000 in one year to store some goods for one year. Assume your costs are $95,000, payable immediately, and the cost of capital is 8%. Should you take the contract?

4. You are preparing to produce some goods for sale. You will sell them in one year and you will incur costs of $80,000 immediately. If your cost of capital is 7%, what is the minimum dollar amount you need to expect to sell the goods for in order for this to be a non-negative NPV?

5. You run a construction firm. You have just won a contract to build a government office building. Building it will require an investment of $10 million today and $5 million in one year. The government will pay you $20 million in one year upon the building's completion. Assume the cost of capital is 10%.
   a. What is the NPV of this opportunity?
   b. How can your firm turn this NPV into cash today?

ML PROJECT

6. You have been offered a unique investment opportunity. If you invest $10,000 today, you will receive $500 one year from now, $1500 two years from now, and $10,000 in 10 years.
   a. What is the NPV of the opportunity if the cost of capital is 6% per year? Should you take the opportunity?
   b. What is the NPV of the opportunity if the cost of capital is 2% per year? Should you take it now?

ML PROJECT

7. Marian Plunket owns her own business and is considering an investment. If she undertakes the investment, it will pay $4000 at the end of each of the next three years. The opportunity requires an initial investment of $1000 plus an additional investment at the end of the second year of $5000. What is the NPV of this opportunity if the cost of capital is 2% per year? Should Marian take it?

Using the NPV Rule

8. Your factory has been offered a contract to produce a part for a new printer. The contract would last for three years, and your cash flows from the contract would be $5 million per year. Your upfront setup costs to be ready to produce the part would be $8 million. Your discount rate for this contact is 8%.
   a. What does the NPV rule say you should do?
   b. If you take the contract, what will be the change in the value of your firm?

9. You are considering opening a new plant. The plant will cost $100 million up front and will take one year to build. After that, it is expected to produce profits of $30 million at the end of every year of production (starting two years from now). The cash flows are expected to last forever. Calculate the NPV of this investment opportunity if your cost of capital is 8%. Should you make the investment? Calculate the

1-10, 13, 14, 17
19, 20, 23-26
33, 34, 36

IRR and use it to determine the maximum deviation allowable in the cost of capital estimate to leave the decision unchanged.

10. Bill Clinton reportedly was paid $10 million to write his book *My Way*. The book took three years to write. In the time he spent writing, Clinton could have been paid to make speeches. Given his popularity, assume that he could earn $8 million per year (paid at the end of the year) speaking instead of writing. Assume his cost of capital is 10% per year.

a. What is the NPV of agreeing to write the book (ignoring any royalty payments)?
b. Assume that, once the book is finished, it is expected to generate royalties of $5 million in the first year (paid at the end of the year), and these royalties are expected to decrease at a rate of 30% per year in perpetuity. What is the NPV of the book with the royalty payments?

PROJECT

***11.** FastTrack Bikes, Inc. is thinking of developing a new composite road bike. Development will take six years, and the cost is $200,000 per year. Once in production, the bike is expected to make $300,000 per year for 10 years.

Assume the cost of capital is 10% for parts (a) and (b) below.

a. Calculate the NPV of this investment opportunity. Should the company make the investment?
b. Calculate the IRR and use it to determine the maximum deviation allowable in the cost of capital estimate to leave the decision unchanged.
c. With costs remaining at $200,000 per year, how long must development last to change the decision?

Assume the cost of capital is 14%.

d. Calculate the NPV of this investment opportunity. Should the company make the investment?
e. How much must this cost of capital estimate deviate to change the decision?
f. With costs remaining at $200,000 per year, how long must development last to change the decision?

PROJECT

12. OpenSeas, Inc. is evaluating the purchase of a new cruise ship. The ship would cost $500 million but would operate for 20 years. OpenSeas expects annual cash flows from operating the ship to be $70 million and its cost of capital is 12%.

a. Prepare an NPV profile of the purchase.
b. Identify the IRR on the graph.
c. Should OpenSeas go ahead with the purchase?
d. How far off could OpenSeas' cost of capital estimate be before your purchase decision would change?

Alternative Decision Rules

13. You are a real estate agent thinking of placing a sign advertising your services at a local bus stop. The sign will cost $5000 and will be posted for one year. You expect that it will generate additional revenue of $500 per month. What is the payback period?

PROJECT

14. Does the IRR rule agree with the NPV rule in Problem 8

PROJECT

15. How many IRRs are there in part (a) of Problem 10? Does the IRR rule give the right answer in this case?

16. How many IRRs are there in part (b) of Problem 10? Does the IRR rule work in this case?

PROJECT

17. Professor Wendy Smith has been offered the following deal. A law firm would like to retain her for an upfront payment of $50,000. In return, for the next year the firm would have access to eight hours of her time every month. Smith's rate is $550 per hour and her opportunity cost of capital is 15% per year. What does the IRR rule advise regarding this opportunity? What about the NPV rule?

18. Innovation Company is thinking about marketing a new software product. Upfront costs to market and develop the product are $5 million. The product is expected to generate profits of $1 million per year for 10 years. The company will have to provide product support expected to cost $100,000 per year in perpetuity. Assume all profits and expenses occur at the end of the year.

a. What is the NPV of this investment if the cost of capital is 6%? Should the firm undertake the project? Repeat the analysis for discount rates of 2% and 11%.

b. How many IRRs does this investment opportunity have?

c. What does the IRR rule indicate about this investment?

19. You own a coal mining company and are considering opening a new mine. The mine itself will cost $120 million to open. If this money is spent immediately, the mine will generate $20 million every year for the next 10 years. After that, the coal will run out and the site must be cleaned and maintained at environmental standards. The cleaning and maintenance are expected to cost $2 million per year in perpetuity. What does the IRR rule say about whether you should accept this opportunity? If the cost of capital is 8%, what does the NPV rule say?

20. Your firm is considering a project that will cost $4.55 million up front, generate cash flows of $3,500,000 per year for three years, and then have a cleanup and shutdown cost of $6,000,000 in the fourth year.

a. How many IRRs does this project have?

b. Create an NPV profile for this project. (Plot the NPV as a function of the discount rate—see the Appendix.)

c. Given a cost of capital of 10%, should this project be accepted? Justify your answer.

21. You have just been offered a contract worth $1 million per year for five years. However, to take the contract, you will need to purchase some new equipment. Your discount rate for this project is 12%. You are still negotiating the purchase price of the equipment. What is the most you can pay for the equipment and still have a positive NPV?

***22.** You are considering investing in a new gold mine in South Africa. Gold in South Africa is buried very deep, so the mine will require an initial investment of $250 million. Once this investment is made, the mine is expected to produce revenues of $30 million per year for the next 20 years. It will cost $10 million per year to operate the mine. After 20 years, the gold will be depleted. The mine must then be stabilized on an ongoing basis, which will cost $5 million per year in perpetuity. Calculate the IRR of this investment. (*Hint:* Plot the NPV as a function of the discount rate.)

23. You are evaluating a project that will cost $500,000, but is expected to produce cash flows of $125,000 per year for 10 years, with the first cash flow in one year. Your cost of capital is 11% and your company's preferred payback period is three years or less.

a. What is the payback period of this project?

b. Should you take the project if you want to increase the value of the company?

24. You are considering making a movie. The movie is expected to cost $10 million up front and take a year to make. After that, it is expected to make $5 million in the year it is released and $2 million for the following four years. What is the payback period of this investment? If you require a payback period of two years, will you make the movie? Does the movie have positive NPV if the cost of capital is 10%?

Choosing Between Projects

25. You are choosing between two projects but can only take one. The cash flows for the projects are given in the following table:

	0	1	2	3	4
A	−$50	25	20	20	15
B	−$100	20	40	50	60

a. What are the IRRs of the two projects?
b. If your discount rate is 5%, what are the NPVs of the two projects?
c. Why do IRR and NPV rank the two projects differently?

26. You are deciding between two mutually exclusive investment opportunities. Both require the same initial investment of $10 million. Investment A will generate $2 million per year (starting at the end of the first year) in perpetuity. Investment B will generate $1.5 million at the end of the first year, and its revenues will grow at 2% per year for every year after that.
a. Which investment has the higher IRR?
b. Which investment has the higher NPV when the cost of capital is 7%?
c. In this case, when does picking the higher IRR give the correct answer as to which investment is the best opportunity?

27. You are considering the following two projects and can only take one. Your cost of capital is 11%.

	0	1	2	3	4
A	−100	25	30	40	50
B	−100	50	40	30	20

a. What is the NPV of each project at your cost of capital?
b. What is the IRR of each project?
c. At what cost of capital do you become indifferent about which project to choose?
d. What should you do?

28. You need a particular piece of equipment for your production process. An equipment leasing company has offered to lease you the equipment for $10,000 per year if you sign a guaranteed five-year lease. The company would also maintain the equipment for you as part of the lease. Alternatively, you could buy and maintain the equipment yourself. The cash flows (in thousands) from doing so are listed below. (The equipment has an economic life of five years.) If your discount rate is 7%, what should you do?

0	1	2	3	4	5
−40	−2	−2	−2	−2	−2

29. Your boss hands you the following information about two mutually exclusive projects:

Projects	Cost of Capital	IRR	Initial Cash Flow	Cash Flow in One Year
A	10%	560%	− $2000	$13,200
B	10%	21%	− $150,000	$181,500

She adds the following: "Our discount rate is 10% and both projects have IRRs over 20%. Unfortunately, we are unable to implement both, so we will go with Project A since it has the highest IRR of the two."

How would you respond? Give a supporting numerical analysis.

30. The CEO of Garneau Cinemas is considering making a movie and must decide between a comedy or a thriller—it doesn't have the production space to make both. The comedy is expected to cost $20 million up front (at $t = 0$). After that, it is expected to make $12 million in the first year (at $t = 1$) and $4 million in each of the following two years (at $t = 2$ and $t = 3$). In the fourth year (at $t = 5$) is it expected the movie can be sold into syndication for $2 million with no further cash flows back to Garneau Cinemas. The thriller is expected to cost $40 million up front (at $t = 0$). After that, it is expected to make $20 million in the first year (at $t = 1$) and $5 million in each of the following four years (at $t = 2, 3, 4$ and 5). In the sixth year (at $t = 6$) is it expected the movie can be sold into syndication for $25 million with no further cash flows back to Garneau Cinemas. The cost of capital is 10% and Garneau usually requires projects to have a payback within four years. Determine each project's payback and NPV and advise the CEO what she should do.

31. You are faced with two projects and have the opportunity to invest in either one or both of them. The cash flows are as follows:

Project	Year 0	Year 1
Project	−$200	$100
B	$200	−$100

Your cost of capital is 8%. Evaluate both projects with IRR and NPV and determine what to do.

32. Your boss hands you the following information for a pair of mutually exclusive projects and asks for your recommendation:

Project	Cost of Capital	IRR	Years			
			0	1	2	3
			Cash Flows			
A	12%	29%	−$10,000	$8000	$4000	$3000
B	12%	25%	−$10,000	$2600	$6000	$8000

What should you do?

Evaluating Projects with Different Lives

33. You are trying to decide between two mobile phone carriers. Carrier A requires you to pay $200 for the phone and monthly charges of $60 for 24 months. Carrier B wants you to pay $100 for the phone and monthly charges of $70 for 12 months. Assume you will keep replacing the phone after your contract expires. Your cost of capital is 4%. Based on cost alone, which carrier should you choose?

34. Gateway Tours is choosing between two bus models. One is more expensive to purchase and maintain but lasts much longer than the other. Its discount rate is 11%. The company plans to continue with one of the two models for the foreseeable future. Which one should it choose? Based on the costs of each model shown below, which should it choose?

Model	0	1	2	3	4	5...	7
Old Reliable	−200	−4	−4	−4	−4	−4...	−4
Short and Sweet	−100	−2	−2	−2	−2		

35. Hassle-Free Web is bidding to provide webpage hosting services for Hotel Lisbon. Hotel Lisbon pays its current provider $10,000 per year for hosting its webpage and handling transactions on it. Hassle-Free figures that it will need to purchase equipment worth $15,000 up front and then spend $2000 per year on monitoring, updates, and bandwidth to provide the service for three years. If Hassle-Free's cost of capital is 10%, can it bid less than $10,000 per year to provide the service and still increase its value by doing so?

36. You have to buy a new copier. The cost of the copier is $2000, plus $400 per year in maintenance costs. The copier will last for five years. Alternatively, a local company offers to lease the copier to you and do the maintenance as well. If your discount rate is 6%, what is the most you would be willing to pay per year to lease the copier? (Your first lease payment is due in one year.)

Choosing Among Projects When Resources Are Limited

37. Fabulous Fabricators needs to decide how to allocate space in its production facility this year. It is considering the following contracts:

	NPV	Use of Facility
A	$2 million	100%
B	$1 million	60%
C	$1.5 million	40%

a. What are the profitability indexes of the projects?
b. What should Fabulous Fabricators do?

38. Kartman Corporation is evaluating four real estate investments. Management plans to buy the properties today and sell them three years from today. The annual discount rate for these investments is 15%. The following table summarizes the initial cost and the sale price in three years for each property:

	Cost Today	Sale Price in Year
Parkside Acres	$500,000	$900,000
Real Property Estates	800,000	1,400,000
Lost Lake Properties	650,000	1,050,000
Overlook	150,000	350,000

Kartman has a total capital budget of $800,000 to invest in properties. Which properties should it choose?

39. Orchid Biotech Company is evaluating several development projects for experimental drugs. Although the cash flows are difficult to forecast, the company has come up with the following estimates of the initial capital requirements and NPVs for the projects. Given a wide variety of staffing needs, the company has also estimated the number of research scientists required for each development project. (All cost values are given in millions of dollars.)

Project Number	Initial Capital	Number of Research Scientists	NPV
I	$10	2	$10.1
II	15	3	19.0
III	15	4	22.0
IV	20	3	25.0
V	30	10	60.2

a. Suppose that Orchid has a total capital budget of $60 million. How should it prioritize these projects?
b. Suppose that Orchid currently has 12 research scientists and does not anticipate being able to hire any more in the near future. How should Orchid prioritize these projects?

DATA CASE

After the close of trading on May 6, 2009, Vanda Pharmaceuticals (VNDA) announced that the Food and Drug Administration had approved its drug, Fanapt, for the treatment of schizophrenia. Imagine that you are working as a stock analyst for a large investment firm and Vanda is one of the firms you track. On May 7, 2009, Vanda's stock price increased substantially and your boss wants to you to issue a statement about the size of the cash flows necessary to support the stock price reaction. Therefore, she wants you to estimate the net cash flows the market had anticipated from sales of the new drug. She advises that you treat the value anticipated by the market as the NPV of selling the drug, then work backward from the NPV to determine the annual cash flows necessary to generate that value. Your boss advises that the best way to capture the value is to take the change in stock price from closing on May 6, 2009, to closing on May 7, 2009. You nod your head in agreement, trying to look like you understand how to proceed. You are relatively new to the job and the term NPV is somewhat familiar to you.

1. To determine the change in stock price over this period, go to Yahoo! Finance (http://finance.yahoo.com) and enter the stock symbol for Vanda (ticker symbol: VNDA). Then, click on "Historical Data" and enter the appropriate dates. Use the adjusted closing prices for the two dates.

2. To determine the change in value, multiply the change in stock price by the number of shares outstanding. The number of shares outstanding around those dates can be found by going to the company's investor relations website. Start at http://www.vandapharma.com and then click "Investor Relations." Next, select the "SEC Filings" link on the left side of the screen, and locate the 10-Q from May 11, 2009. The fastest way to do this is to select "Quarterly Filings" from the drop-down menu under "Groupings Filter" and then click "Search." Next, click the "Excel" symbol in the row 5/11/09 10-Q and open the Excel spreadsheet. In the "Balance Sheet" tab, under the March 31, 2009, column, you will find the number of shares of common stock (in thousands) as of March 31, 2009. Because the change in value represents the "expected" NPV of the project, you will have to find the annual net cash flows that would provide this NPV. For this analysis, you will need to estimate the cost of capital for the project. We

show how to calculate the cost of capital in subsequent chapters; for now, use the New York University (NYU) cost of capital website (http://pages.stern.nyu.edu/~adamodar/New_Home_Page/datafile/wacc.htm). Locate the cost of capital in the far-right column for the biotechnology industry.

3. Use the cost of capital from the NYU website and the NPV you computed to calculate the constant annual cash flow that provides this NPV. Compute cash flows for 5-, 10-, and 15-year horizons.

Constructing an NPV profile of a project is a very useful way to really see the project's IRR(s) and how the NPV of the project changes with the discount rate. Consider SFL's fertilizer project from Section 8.2. In the Excel screen shot below, the cash flows from that project are in black in cells D2 to H2. Cell B5 shows the NPV, taking the contents of cell B1 as the discount rate. The formula for doing this is shown just to the left of cell B5. Note that in order to make the NPV a dynamic function of whatever discount rate is entered into cell B1, you enter "B1" instead of "10%" where the formula takes this discount rate. For reference, we also compute the IRR in cell B3, and the formula for doing so is given just to the left of B3.

With the cash flows set up and the NPV entered in cell B5 as a dynamic function of the discount rate, we are ready to use the data table function of Excel to calculate the NPV for a range of different discount rates. A data table shows us how the outcome of a formula (such as NPV) changes when we change one of the cells in the spreadsheet (such as the discount rate). To do this

1. Enter the range of discount rates down a column, as shown below in cells A6 to A30. The placement of these rates is important. They must start in the cell below and to the left of the cell with the NPV. (Cell A6 is immediately below and to the left of cell B5.)
2. Highlight the area containing your range of discount rates and the NPV cell, as shown in the screen shot (cells A5 to B30).

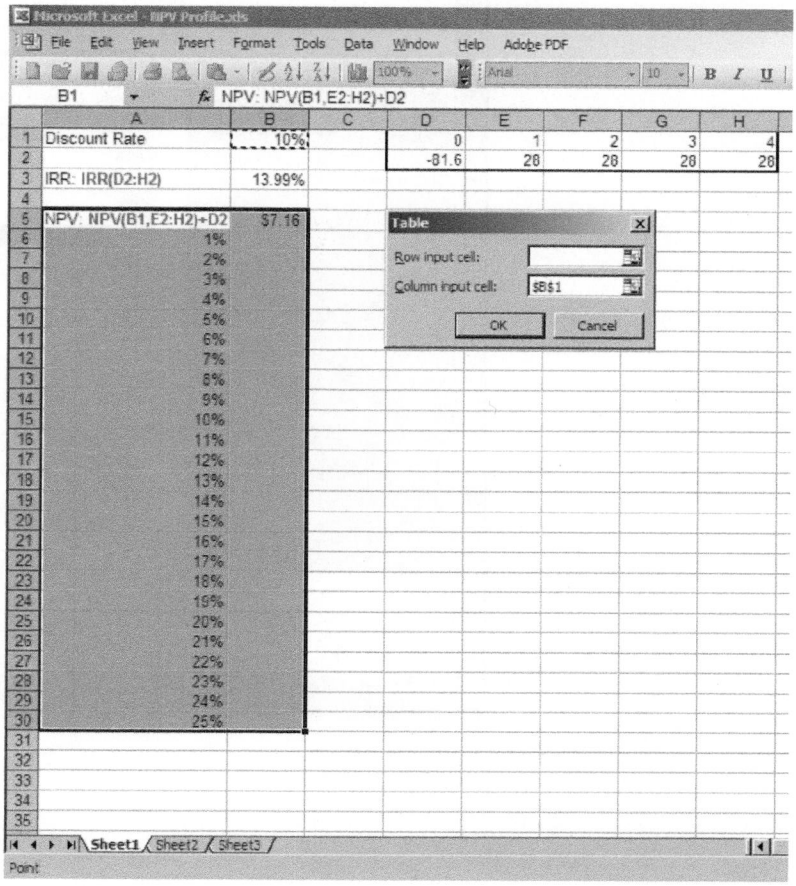

3. From the Data pull-down menu, select "Table."
4. Since our discount rates are in a column, we are using a "Column input cell" instead of a "Row input cell." In the Column input cell box, enter B1 or click on the B1 cell. By doing this, you are telling Excel to recalculate the NPV by substituting the numbers running down the column into cell B1, which contains the discount rate.
5. Click "OK."

After clicking OK, the cells next to the range of discount rates will fill with the NPVs corresponding to each of the discount rates, as shown in the screen shot below. To create an NPV profile graphing these NPVs as a function of the discount rates,

1. Highlight the discount rates and NPVs: cells A6 to B30.
2. Click on the "Chart" icon or select "Chart" from the Insert pull-down menu.
3. Choose "XY(Scatter)" as your Chart type and click on the Chart sub-type shown below in the screen shot.
4. Click "Next" to customize your chart further or click "Finish" to display the chart.

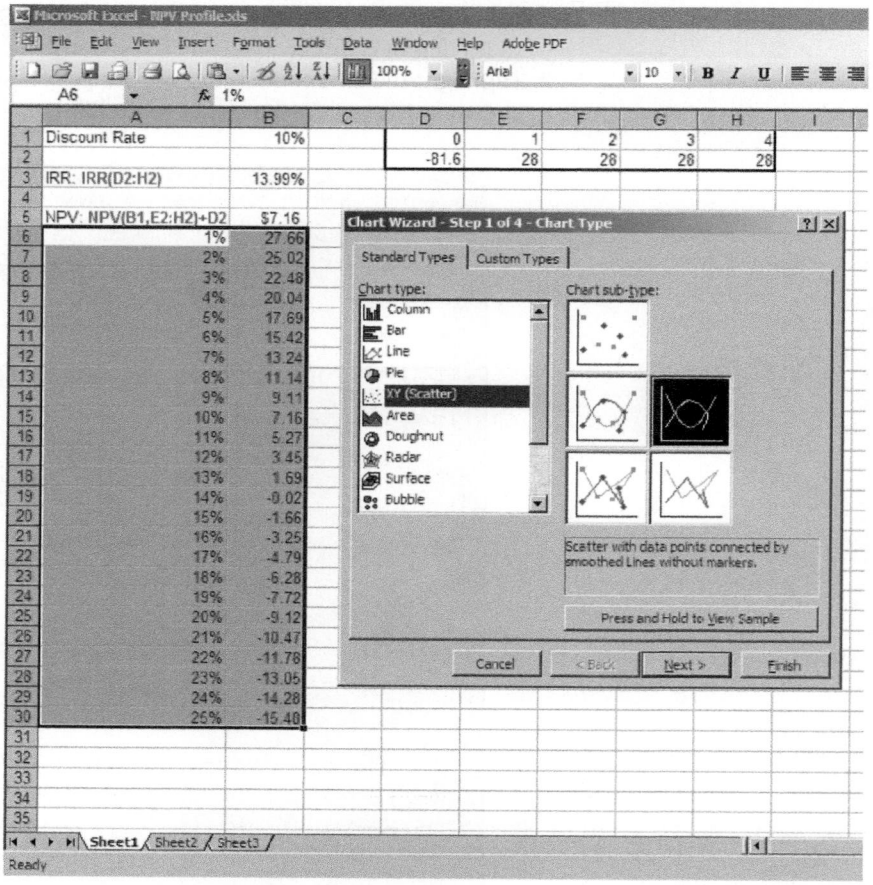

CHAPTER

Fundamentals of Capital Budgeting

9

LEARNING OBJECTIVES

- Identify the types of cash flows needed in the capital budgeting process
- Forecast incremental earnings in a pro forma earnings statement for a project
- Convert forecasted earnings to free cash flows and compute a project's NPV
- Recognize common pitfalls that arise in identifying a project's incremental free cash flows
- Assess the sensitivity of a project's NPV to changes in your assumptions
- Identify the most common options available to managers in projects, and understand why these options can be valuable

NOTATION

CapEx	capital expenditures
CCA	capital cost allowance
EBIT	earnings before interest and taxes
FCF_t	free cash flow in year t
IRR	internal rate of return
NPV	net present value
NWC_t	net working capital in year t
PV	present value
r	projected cost of capital
UCC	undepreciated capital cost

An important responsibility of corporate financial managers is determining which projects or investments a firm should undertake. Capital budgeting, the focus of this chapter, is the process of analyzing investment opportunities and deciding which ones to accept. In doing so, we are allocating the firm's funds to various projects—we are budgeting its capital. Chapter 8 covered the various methods for evaluating projects and proved that NPV will be the most reliable and accurate method for doing so. In retrospect, this may not be surprising, as it is the only rule directly tied to the Valuation Principle. To implement the NPV rule, we must compute the NPV of our projects and accept only those projects for which the NPV is positive. We spoke in the last chapter about Sony and Toshiba each using investment decision rules to pursue competing high definition DVD standards (and eventually Toshiba deciding to abandon HD-DVD). To implement the investment decision rules, financial managers from Toshiba, for example, had first to forecast the incremental cash flows associated with the investments and later to forecast the incremental cash flows associated with the decision to stop investing in HD-DVD. The process of forecasting those cash flows, crucial inputs in the investment decision process, is our focus in this chapter. We begin by estimating the project's expected cash flows by forecasting the project's revenues and costs. Using these cash flows, we can compute the project's NPV—its contribution to shareholder value. Then, because the cash flow forecasts almost always contain uncertainty, we demonstrate how to compute the sensitivity of the NPV to the uncertainty in the forecasts. Finally, we examine the relationship between a project's flexibility and its NPV.

9.1 The Capital Budgeting Process

capital budget A list of the projects that a company plans to undertake during the next period.

capital budgeting The process of analyzing investment opportunities and deciding which ones to accept.

The first step in analyzing various investment opportunities is compiling a list of potential projects. A **capital budget** lists the projects and investments that a company plans to undertake during future years. To create this list, firms analyze alternative projects and decide which ones to accept through a process called **capital budgeting**. This process begins with forecasts of each project's future consequences for the firm. Some of these consequences will affect the firm's revenues; others will affect its costs. Our ultimate goal is to determine the effect of the decision to accept or reject a project on the firm's cash flows, and evaluate the NPV of these cash flows to assess the consequences of the decision for the firm's value. Figure 9.1 depicts the types of cash flows found in a typical project. We will examine each of these as we proceed through our discussion of capital budgeting.

FIGURE 9.1 Cash Flows in a Typical Project

The diagram shows some typical cash flows in project analysis and their timing.

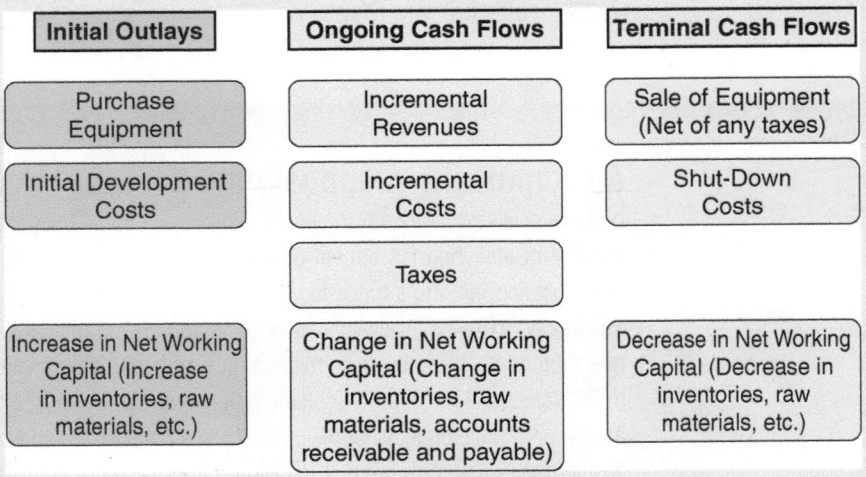

Of course, forecasting these cash flows is frequently challenging. We will often need to rely on different experts within the firm to obtain estimates for many of these cash flows. For example, the marketing department may provide sales forecasts, the operations manager may provide information about production costs, and the firm's engineers may estimate the upfront research and development expenses that are required to launch the project. Another important source of information comes from looking at past projects of the firm, or those of other firms in the same industry. In particular, practitioners often base their assessments of a project's revenues and costs on information on revenues and costs that can be learned from the historical financial statements of the firm or its competitors.

incremental earnings The amount by which a firm's earnings are expected to change as a result of an investment decision.

Once we have these estimates, how do we organize them? One common starting point is first to consider the consequences of the project for the firm's earnings. Thus, we will *begin* our analysis in Section 9.2 by determining the **incremental earnings** of a project—that is, the amount by which the firm's earnings are expected to change as a result of the investment decision. The incremental earnings forecast tells us how the decision will affect the firm's reported profits from an accounting perspective. However, as we emphasized in Chapter 2, *earnings are not actual cash flows*. We need to estimate the project's cash flows to determine its NPV and decide whether it is a good project for the firm. Therefore, in Section 9.3, we demonstrate how to use the incremental earnings to forecast the actual cash flows of the project. Understanding how to compute the cash flow consequences of an investment based on its earning consequences is important for a number of reasons. First, as a practical matter, financial managers often begin by forecasting earnings. Second, if we are looking at historical data, accounting information is often the only information that is readily available.

CONCEPT CHECK

1. What is capital budgeting, and what is its goal?
2. Why is computing a project's effect on the firm's earnings insufficient for capital budgeting?

9.2 Forecasting Incremental Earnings

Let's consider a capital budgeting decision faced by managers of a hypothetical company: Spy Peripherals Incorporated (SPI) located in Waterloo, Ontario. SPI is considering the development of the SPI Phone 86, an advanced micro-sized smartphone with superior features for data encryption, an ultra-high-definition camera, exceptional audio reception, and lightning-fast communication speed. We need to forecast all the cash flows relevant to this project; often this starts with revenue and cost estimation.

Revenue and Cost Estimates

Forecasting future revenues and costs is challenging. The most successful practitioners collect as much information as possible before tackling this task—they will talk to members of marketing and sales teams as well as company economists to develop an estimate of sales, and they will talk to engineering and production teams to refine their estimate of costs.

There are several factors to consider when estimating a project's revenues and costs, including the following:

1. A new product typically has lower sales initially, as customers gradually become aware of the product. Sales will then accelerate, plateau, and ultimately decline as the product nears obsolescence, or increased competition is encountered.

2. The average selling price of a product and its cost of production will generally change over time. Prices and costs tend to rise with the general level of inflation in the economy. The prices of technology products, however, often fall over time as newer, superior technologies emerge and production costs decline.
3. For most industries, competition tends to reduce profit margins over time.

Our focus here is on how to get from these forecasts to incremental earnings and then to cash flows; Chapter 18 discusses forecasting methods in more detail.

All our revenue and cost estimates should be *incremental*, meaning that we account only for additional sales and costs generated by the project. For example, if we are evaluating the purchase of a faster manufacturing machine, we are concerned only with how many additional units of the product we will be able to sell (and at what price) and any additional costs created by the new machine. We do not forecast total sales and costs, because those include our production using the old machine. *Remember, we are evaluating how the project will change the cash flows of the firm. That is why we focus on incremental revenues and costs.*

Let's return to our SPI Phone 86 example. The target market for SPI Phone 86 includes business and government personnel who engage in covert activities. Based on extensive marketing surveys, the sales forecast for SPI Phone 86 is 100,000 units per year. Given the pace of technological change, SPI expects that the product will have a four-year life. It will be sold through a network of private dealers. The expected wholesale price is $260 per unit.

Developing the new hardware will be relatively inexpensive, as existing technologies can be simply modified and repackaged in the newly designed SPI Phone 86. SPI expects total engineering and design costs to amount to $5 million. Once the design is finalized, actual production will be outsourced at a cost (including packaging) of $110 per unit.

In addition to the hardware requirements, SPI must build a new software application to allow full functionality of the advanced camera and audio reception capabilities of the SPI Phone 86. This software development project is expected to take a dedicated team of 50 software engineers a full year to complete. The cost of a software engineer (including benefits and related costs) is $200,000 per year.

The software and hardware design will be completed at the end of one year. At that time, the SPI Phone 86 will be ready to ship. SPI expects to spend $2.8 million per year on marketing and support for this product.

capital cost allowance (CCA) The CRA method of depreciation for income tax purposes.

tax year The fiscal year relevant for tax and CCA calculations for the CRA.

asset class One of a series of categories defined by the CRA to indicate types of depreciable property that will be given the same treatment for CCA calculations.

CCA rate The proportion of UCC that can be claimed as CCA in a given tax year.

Capital Expenditures and Capital Cost Allowance. To verify the compatibility of the SPI Phone 86 with the various software and hardware combinations, SPI must also build a new lab for testing purposes. This lab will occupy existing facilities but will require $7.5 million of new equipment. Recall from Chapter 2 that while investments in plant, property, and equipment are cash outflows, they are not directly listed as expenses when calculating *earnings*. Instead, the firm deducts a fraction of the cost of these items each year for tax purposes as **capital cost allowance (CCA)**—the Canada Revenue Agency (CRA) version of depreciation. Different methods can be used to compute depreciation. For financial reporting purposes, CCA is usually *not* used. For tax purposes, though, CCA is required. It is thus very important when doing capital budgeting to use CCA, the method specified by the CRA, because it affects the company's taxable income, the actual amount of tax paid, and the firm's cash flows. To calculate the annual CCA deductions, SPI must first determine the **tax year** in which the purchase takes place. We will assume that an asset purchased at date 0 is actually purchased at the beginning of the first tax year relevant to the project. Thus, the first CCA deduction affects the taxable income and taxes for date 1 (the end of the first year). To calculate the CCA amounts, SPI must determine the **asset class** for the computer equipment and the relevant **CCA rate**, denoted as d, for the asset class. We will assume the computer equipment falls under asset class 45

COMMON MISTAKE

Using the Wrong CCA Asset Class

CRA has many different asset classes for different types of assets purchased over different time periods. A few of the most common asset classes and rates are shown below. Note that for computers, depending on when they were purchased, they could fall under asset class 10, 46, or 50. As each asset class has a different CCA rate, it is important to use the applicable asset class and its correct rate. Since the Canada Revenue Agency updates CCA Asset Classes and rates frequently it is best to visit the CRA's website rather than other non-official sites to verify the latest and most accurate information.

Asset Class	Examples of Assets within Class	CCA Rate, *d*
1	Most buildings acquired after 1987.	4%
3	Most buildings acquired before 1988.	5%
8	Furniture, appliances, tools, fixtures, machinery, outdoor advertising signs, photocopiers, fax machines, electronic telephone equipment.	20%
10	Computer hardware and systems software acquired before 2005 and motor vehicles, automobiles, and some passenger vehicles.	30%
12	China, cutlery, linen, uniforms, dies, jigs, moulds, cutting or shaping parts of a machine, tools, computer software (except systems software).	100%
43	Machinery and equipment used for manufacturing and processing.	30%
46	Data network infrastructure equipment and systems software for that equipment if acquired after March 22, 2004.	30%
50	General-purpose electronic data processing equipment and systems software for that equipment, including ancillary data processing equipment acquired after March 18, 2007.	55%

Source: Canada Revenue Agency www.cra-arc.gc.ca/tx/bsnss/tpcs/slprtnr/rprtng/cptl/dprcbl-eng.html

half-year rule A rule stating that, as assets may be purchased at any time throughout a year, it can be assumed that on average an asset is owned for half a year during the first tax year of its ownership. Thus, the CRA allows only half of the CapEx to generate CCA in the first tax year (the year in which a purchase takes place).

undepreciated capital cost (UCC) The balance, at a point in time, calculated by deducting an asset's current and prior CCA amounts from the original cost of the asset (the CapEx).

asset pool The sum of all assets in one class.

and has a CCA rate of $d = 45\%$ (always consult the Canada Revenue Agency website to verify the correct asset class and CCA rate. See the Common Mistake Box above). CRA has a "**half-year rule**" that is meant to compensate for the fact that sometimes assets are bought at the beginning of the year and other times they are bought at the end of the year. CRA assumes assets qualify for half a year's worth of CCA in the first tax year. Thus, when an asset is purchased, one-half of its cost, denoted CapEx, is added to the **undepreciated capital cost (UCC)** for the **asset pool** (the collection of assets) in the same class. We denote this addition to the UCC as UCC_1. Thus $UCC_1 = 0.5 \times \text{CapEx}$. For a particular asset, the incremental CCA deduction that can be claimed at the end of the tax year is equal to the incremental UCC associated with that asset multiplied by the CCA rate, d:

$$CCA_t = UCC_t \times d \tag{9.1}$$

where CCA_t is the incremental CCA deduction for an asset taken in tax year t; UCC_t is the incremental UCC for an asset in tax year t prior to the asset's CCA deduction in year t, and d is the CCA rate that determines the proportion of UCC that can be claimed as a CCA deduction.

After a CCA deduction is claimed, the UCC is reduced for the next year. However, for the second tax year we must also remember to add in the other half of CapEx into the incremental UCC. In general, we can determine the incremental UCC for an asset as follows:

Year t Incremental UCC used for calculating the CCA for tax year, t:

$$t = 1 \quad UCC_1 = 0.5 \times CapEx \tag{9.2}$$

$$t \geq 2 \quad UCC_t = CapEx \times \left(1 - \tfrac{d}{2}\right) \times (1 - d)^{t-2}$$

TABLE 9.1 The SPI Phone 86's Schedule of CCA and UCC for the First Five Years

Year		0	1	2	3	4	5
Capital Expenditure, CCA, and UCC Forecasts ($000s)							
1	CapEx (half added into UCC_1, half added into UCC_2)	7500	–	–	–	–	–
2	UCC_t	–	3750	5813	3197	1758	967
3	$CCA_t = UCC_t \times d$	–	1688	2616	1439	791	435
4	CCA rate, d	45%					

Notes: $UCC_1 = 0.5 \times CapEx$
$UCC_2 = UCC_1 - CCA_1 + (0.5 \times CapEx)$
For the yellow cells, $UCC_t = UCC_{t-1} - CCA_{t-1}$
Since $CCA_5 < UCC_5$, there will be a positive balance remaining for UCC_6

We assume the asset is purchased sometime during the first tax year, so the first CCA deduction affects the end-of-year calculation of taxable income. The UCC calculation above is the UCC remaining in year t just before the CCA deduction of year t.

SPI's calculation of the CCA amounts for the first five years of the SPI Phone 86 project is shown in the spreadsheet in Table 9.1. There will still be a positive UCC balance after the CCA deduction in year 5. This means that SPI can claim CCA deductions in future years too. In fact, because the CCA calculation always deducts a proportion of the UCC, UCC will never fall to zero (as long as the asset is not sold), so *CCA deductions can continue forever*. For now we will ignore the CCA deductions beyond year 5. In Section 9.4, we will address how to properly deal with all the CCA effects.

Deducting CCA from the Table 9.1 spreadsheet completes the forecast for the SPI Phone 86's earnings before interest and taxes (EBIT) shown in line 7 of the Table 9.2 spreadsheet. Since the capital expenditures do not show up as a cash outflow in the earnings calculation and the non-cash CCA deduction does, we can see why earnings are not an accurate representation of cash flows.

Incremental Revenue and Cost Estimates

Given the revenue and cost estimates, we can forecast the SPI Phone 86's incremental earnings, as shown in Table 9.2. After the product is developed in year 0, it will generate sales of 100,000 units × $260/unit = $26 million each year for the next four years. The cost of producing these units is 100,000 units × $110/unit = $11 million per year. Thus, the SPI Phone 86 will produce a gross profit of $26 million – $11 million = $15 million per year, as shown in line 3 of the spreadsheet in Table 9.2.[1]

The project's operating expenses include $2.8 million per year in marketing and support costs, which are listed as selling, general, and administrative expenses. In year 0, SPI will spend $5 million on design and engineering, together with 50 × $200,000 = $10 million on software, for a total of $15 million in research and development expenditures.

[1]While revenues and costs occur throughout the year, the standard convention, which we adopt here, is to list revenues and costs in the year in which they occur. Thus, cash flows that occur at the end of one year will be listed in the same column as those that occur seven months into the year, even though they occur five months apart. When additional precision is required, cash flows are often estimated on a quarterly or monthly basis. If the analysis uses quarterly or monthly cashflows, then the discount rate used to calculate NPV should be an effective quarterly or monthly rate too.

EBIT - earnings before income tax

TABLE 9.2 The SPI Phone 86's Incremental Earnings Forecast

Year		0	1	2	3	4	5
Incremental Earnings Forecast ($000s)							
1	Sales	–	26,000	26,000	26,000	26,000	–
2	Cost of Goods Sold	–	(11,000)	(11,000)	(11,000)	(11,000)	–
3	Gross Profit	–	15,000	15,000	15,000	15,000	–
4	Selling, General, and Administrative	–	(2800)	(2800)	(2800)	(2800)	
5	Research and Development	(15,000)	–	–	–	–	–
6	Capital Cost Allowance (CCA)	–	(1688)	(2616)	(1439)	(791)	(435)
7	**EBIT**	(15,000)	10,513	9584	10,761	11,409	(435)
8	Income Tax at 40%	6000	(4205)	(3834)	(4305)	(4564)	174
9	**Unlevered Net Income**	(9000)	6308	5751	6457	6845	(261)

We can calculate the incremental EBIT by using Equation 9.3:

$$\text{Incremental EBIT} = \text{Incremental Revenue} - \text{Incremental Costs} - CCA \tag{9.3}$$

marginal corporate tax rate The tax rate a firm will pay on an incremental dollar of pre-tax income.

Taxes. The final expense we must account for is corporate taxes. The correct tax rate to use is the firm's **marginal corporate tax rate**, which is the tax rate it will pay on an *incremental* dollar of pre-tax income, such as what will be earned in a new project. In Table 9.2, we assume the marginal corporate tax rate for the SPI Phone 86 project is 40% each year. The incremental income tax expense is calculated in line 8 as

$$\text{Income Tax} = EBIT \times \tau_c \tag{9.4}$$

where τ_c is the firm's marginal corporate tax rate.

In year 1, the SPI Phone 86 will contribute an additional $10.513 million to SPI's EBIT, which will result in an additional $10.513 million × 40% = $4.205 million in corporate tax that SPI will owe. We deduct this amount to determine the SPI Phone 86's after-tax contribution to net income.

Taxes and Negative EBIT. Notice that in year 0 the SPI Phone 86's EBIT is negative. Are taxes relevant in this case? Yes. The SPI Phone 86 will reduce SPI's taxable income in year 0 by $15 million. As long as SPI earns taxable income elsewhere in year 0 against which it can offset the SPI Phone 86's losses, SPI will owe $15 million × 40% = $6 million *less* in taxes in year 0 than if it were not undertaking the project. Because the credits come from the research and development expense for the SPI Phone 86 project, the firm should credit this tax savings to the SPI Phone 86 project.

EXAMPLE 9.1 Taxing Losses for Projects in Profitable Companies

PROBLEM

Suppose Loblaw Companies Ltd. plans to launch a new line of high-fibre, zero trans fat breakfast pastries. The heavy advertising expenses associated with the new product launch will generate operating losses of $15 million next year for the product. Loblaw expects to earn pre-tax income of $460 million from operations other than the new pastries next year. If Loblaw pays a 40% tax rate on its pre-tax income, what will it owe in taxes next year without the new pastry product? What will it owe with the new product?

SOLUTION

Plan

We need Loblaw's pre-tax income with and without the new product losses and its tax rate of 40%. We can then compute the tax without the losses and compare it to the tax with the losses.

Execute

Without the new product, Loblaw will owe \$460 million × 40% = \$184 million in corporate taxes next year. With the new product, Loblaw's pre-tax income next year will be only \$460 million − \$15 million = \$445 million, and it will owe \$445 million × 40% = \$178 million in tax.

Evaluate

Thus, launching the new product reduces Loblaw's taxes next year by \$184 million − \$178 million = \$6 million. Because the losses on the new product reduce Loblaw's taxable income dollar for dollar, it is the same as if the new product had a tax bill of negative \$6 million.

unlevered net income Net income that does not include interest expenses associated with debt.

Unlevered Net Income Calculation. We can express the data in Table 9.2 by combining Equations 9.3 and 9.4 as the following shorthand formula for **unlevered net income**:

$$\begin{aligned}\text{Incremental Unlevered Net Income} &= EBIT \times (1 - \tau_c) \\ &= (\text{Incremental Revenue} - \text{Incremental Costs} - CCA) \times (1 - \tau_c)\end{aligned} \tag{9.5}$$

Note: The EBIT calculated in Table 9.2 used CCA instead of accounting depreciation. When you see EBIT numbers in financial reports, those numbers are normally based on accounting depreciation. If this is the case, then the EBIT in Equation 9.4 must be replaced with (*EBIT* + Depreciation − *CCA*).

pro forma statement A statement that is not based on actual data but rather depicts a firm's financials under a given set of hypothetical assumptions.

Pro Forma Statement. Table 9.2 shows the incremental unlevered net income for our SPI Phone 86 project. This is often referred to as a **pro forma statement**, because it is not based on actual data but rather depicts the firm's financials under a given set of hypothetical assumptions. In our SPI example, the firm's forecasts of revenues and costs were assumptions that allowed SPI to forecast incremental earnings in a pro forma statement.

What about Interest Expenses? In Chapter 2, we saw that to compute a firm's net income, we must first deduct interest expenses from EBIT. When evaluating a capital budgeting decision, however, we generally *do not include interest expenses*. Any incremental interest expenses will be related to the firm's decision regarding how to finance the project, which is a separate decision. Here, we wish to evaluate the earnings contributions from the project on its own, separate from the financing decision. Ultimately, managers may also look at the additional earnings consequences associated with different methods of financing the project.

Thus, we evaluate a project *as if* the company will not use any debt to finance it (whether or not that is actually the case), and we postpone the consideration of alternative financing choices until Part 5 of this book. Because we calculate the net income assuming no debt (no leverage), we refer to the net income we compute in Table 9.2 using Equation 9.5, the unlevered net income of the project, to indicate that it does not include any interest expenses associated with debt.

CONCEPT CHECK

3. How are operating expenses and capital expenditures treated differently when calculating incremental earnings?
4. Why do we focus only on incremental revenues and costs rather than all revenues and costs of the firm?

9.3 Determining Incremental Free Cash Flow

As discussed in Chapter 2, earnings are an accounting measure of the firm's performance. They do not represent real profits—the firm cannot use its earnings to buy goods, pay employees, fund new investments, or pay dividends to shareholders. To do those things, the firm needs cash. Thus, to evaluate a capital budgeting decision, we must determine its consequences for the firm's available cash. The incremental effect of a project on the firm's available cash is the project's incremental **free cash flow.**

free cash flow The incremental effect of a project on a firm's available cash.

Calculating Free Cash Flow from Earnings

As discussed in Chapter 2, there are important differences between earnings and cash flow. Earnings include non-cash charges, such as CCA (or depreciation for financial reporting purposes) but do not include the cost of capital investment (the capital expenditures). To determine a project's free cash flow from its incremental earnings, we must adjust for these differences.

Capital Expenditures and Capital Cost Allowance. CCA is not a cash expense that the firm pays. Rather, it is a method used for tax purposes to allocate the original purchase cost of the asset over its life. Because CCA is not a cash flow, we do not include it in the cash flow forecast. However, that does not mean we can ignore CCA. The CCA deduction reduces our taxable earnings and in doing so reduces our taxes. Taxes are cash flows, so because CCA affects our cash flows, it still matters. Our approach for handling CCA is to add it back to the incremental earnings to recognize the fact that we still have the cash flow associated with it.

For example, a project has incremental gross profit (revenues minus costs) of \$1 million and a \$200,000 CCA deduction. If the firm's tax rate is 40%, then the incremental earnings will be (\$1,000,000 − \$200,000) × (1 − 0.40) = \$480,000. However, the firm will still have \$680,000 because the \$200,000 CCA deduction is not an actual cash outflow. Table 9.3 shows the calculation to get the incremental free cash flow in this case. Blue boxes surround all of the actual cash flows in the column labelled "Correct." A good way to check to make sure the incremental free cash flow is correct is to sum the actual cash flows. In this case, the firm generated \$1,000,000 in gross profit (a positive cash flow), paid \$320,000 in taxes (a negative cash flow), and was left with \$1,000,000 − \$320,000 = \$680,000, which is the amount shown as the incremental free cash flow. In the last column, labelled "Incorrect," we show what would happen if you just ignored CCA altogether. Because EBIT would be too high, the taxes would be too high as well,

TABLE 9.3 Deducting and Then Adding Back CCA

	Correct	Incorrect
Incremental Gross Profit	\$1,000,000	\$1,000,000
CCA	−\$200,000	
EBIT	\$800,000	\$1,000,000
Tax at 40%	−\$320,000	−\$400,000
Incremental Earnings	\$480,000	\$600,000
Add Back CCA	\$200,000	
Incremental Free Cash Flow	\$680,000	\$600,000

EXAMPLE 9.2 Incremental Free Cash Flows

PROBLEM

Let's return to the SPI Phone 86 example. In Table 9.2, we computed the incremental earnings for the SPI Phone 86, but we need the incremental free cash flows to decide whether SPI should proceed with the project.

SOLUTION

Plan

The difference between the incremental earnings and incremental free cash flows in the SPI Phone 86 example will be driven by the equipment purchased for the lab. We need to recognize the $7.5 million cash outflow associated with the purchase in year 0 and add back the CCA deductions from years 1 to 5, as they are not actually cash outflows.

Execute

Year		0	1	2	3	4	5
Incremental Earnings Forecast ($000s)							
1	Sales	–	26,000	26,000	26,000	26,000	–
2	Cost of Goods Sold	–	(11,000)	(11,000)	(11,000)	(11,000)	–
3	Gross Profit	–	15,000	15,000	15,000	15,000	–
4	Selling, General, and Administrative	–	(2800)	(2800)	(2800)	(2800)	–
5	Research and Development	(15,000)	–	–	–	–	–
6	Capital Cost Allowance (CCA)	–	(1688)	(2616)	(1439)	(791)	(435)
7	**EBIT**	(15,000)	10,513	9584	10,761	11,409	(435)
8	Income Tax at 40%	6000	(4205)	(3834)	(4305)	(4564)	174
9	**Unlevered Net Income**	(9000)	6308	5751	6457	6845	(261)
	Free Cash Flow ($000s)						
10	Plus: CCA	–	1688	2616	1439	791	435
11	Less: Capital Expenditures	(7500)					
13	**Free Cash Flow**	(16,500)	7995	8366	7895	7636	174

Evaluate

By recognizing the outflow from purchasing the equipment in year 0, we account for the fact that $7.5 million left the firm at that time. By adding back the CCA deductions in years 1 to 5, we adjust the incremental earnings to reflect the fact that CCA deductions are not cash outflows.

and consequently the incremental free cash flow would be too low. (Note that the difference of $80,000 between the two cases is entirely due to the difference in tax payments.)

Net Working Capital. Another way that incremental earnings and free cash flows can differ is if there are changes in net working capital. We defined net working capital (NWC) in Chapter 2 as the difference between current assets and current liabilities. The main components of net working capital are cash, inventory, receivables, and payables:

$$\begin{aligned} NWC &= \text{Current Assets} - \text{Current Liabilities} \\ &= \text{Cash} + \text{Inventory} + \text{Receivables} - \text{Payables} \end{aligned} \tag{9.6}$$

Most projects will require the firm to invest in NWC. Firms may need to maintain a minimum cash balance[2] to meet unexpected expenditures, and inventories of raw materials and finished product to accommodate production uncertainties and demand fluctuations. Also, customers might not pay for the goods they purchase immediately. While sales are immediately counted as part of earnings, the firm does not receive any cash until the customers actually pay. In the interim, the firm includes the amount that customers owe in its receivables. Thus, the firm's receivables measure the total credit that the firm has extended to its customers. In the same way, payables measure the credit the firm has received from its suppliers. The difference between receivables and payables is the net amount of the firm's capital that is consumed as a result of these credit transactions, known as **trade credit**.

trade credit The difference between receivables and payables that is the net amount of a firm's capital consumed as a result of those credit transactions; the credit that a firm extends to its customers.

As discussed in Chapter 2, we do not include short-term financing items, such as notes payable or short-term debt, because those represent financing decisions that we keep separate from our investment decisions.

We care about NWC because it reflects a short-term investment that ties up cash flow that could be used elsewhere. For example, when a firm holds a lot of unsold inventory or has a lot of outstanding receivables, cash flow is tied up in the form of inventory or in the form of credit extended to customers. It is costly for the firm to tie up that cash flow, because it delays the time until the cash flow is available for reinvestment or distribution to shareholders. Since we know that money has time value, we cannot ignore this delay in our forecasts for the project. Thus, whenever NWC increases, reflecting additional investment in working capital, it represents a reduction in cash flow that year.

It is important to note that only changes in NWC affect cash flows. For example, consider a three-year project that causes the firm to build up initial inventory by $20,000 and maintain that level of inventory in years 1 and 2, before drawing it down as the project ends and the last product is sold. It is often necessary for the initial increase in inventory to occur prior to the first sale so that the higher level of inventory would be achieved by the end of year 0. The level of the incremental NWC in each year, the associated change in NWC, and the cash flow implications would be as shown in the spreadsheet below:

1	Year	0	1	2	3
2	Level of Incremental NWC	20,000	20,000	20,000	0
3	*Change* in Incremental NWC	+20,000	0	0	−20,000
4	Cash Flow from Change in NWC	−20,000	0	0	+20,000

Note that the cash flow effect from a change in NWC is always equal and opposite in sign to the change in NWC. For example, an increase in inventory represents an investment or cash outflow, while a reduction in that inventory frees up that investment of capital and represents a cash inflow. Thus, in capital budgeting we subtract changes in NWC to arrive at the cash flows. Also, notice that since the level of incremental NWC did not change in years 1 and 2, there was no new cash flow effect. Intuitively, as the firm is using up inventory and replenishing the same amount, the net new investment in inventory is zero, so no additional cash outflow is required. Finally, note that over the life of the project, the incremental NWC returns to zero so that the changes (in year 0 and in year 3) sum to zero: when the project is over, the inventory accumulated over

[2]The cash included in net working capital is cash that is *not* invested to earn a market rate of return. It includes cash held in the firm's chequing account, in a company safe or cash box, in cash registers (for retail stores), and other sites. This is cash that must be kept on hand for the operation of the project.

its lifespan will be sold, accounts receivable will be collected. This process of working capital recapture ensures that the initial cash outflows are exactly offset by cash inflows as the project winds down.

More generally, we define the change in NWC in year t as

$$\text{Change in NWC in year } t = NWC_t - NWC_{t-1} \tag{9.7}$$

When a project causes a change in NWC, that change must be subtracted from incremental earnings to arrive at incremental free cash flows.

EXAMPLE 9.3 Incorporating Changes in Net Working Capital

PROBLEM

Suppose that the SPI Phone 86 will have no incremental cash or inventory requirements (products will be shipped directly from the contract manufacturer to customers). However, receivables related to the SPI Phone 86 are expected to account for 15% of annual sales, and payables are expected to be 15% of the annual cost of goods sold (COGS). Fifteen percent of $26 million in sales is $3.9 million, and 15% of $11 million in COGS is $1.65 million. SPI Phone 86's NWC requirements are shown in the following table:

1	Year	0	1	2	3	4	5
2	**Net Working Capital Forecast ($000s)**						
3	Cash Requirements	0	0	0	0	0	0
4	Inventory	0	0	0	0	0	0
5	Receivables (15% of Sales)	0	3900	3900	3900	3900	0
6	Payables (15% of COGS)	0	−1650	−1650	−1650	−1650	0
7	**Net Working Capital**	0	2250	2250	2250	2250	0

How does this requirement affect the project's free cash flow?

SOLUTION

Plan

Any increases in NWC represent an investment that reduces the cash available to the firm and so reduces free cash flow. We can use our forecast of the SPI Phone 86's NWC requirements to complete our estimate of SPI Phone 86's free cash flow. In year 1, NWC increases by $2.250 million. This increase represents a cost to the firm. This reduction of free cash flow corresponds to the fact that $3.900 million of the firm's sales in year 1, and $1.625 million of its costs, have not yet been paid.

In years 2 to 4, NWC does not change, so no further contributions are needed. In year 5, when the project is shut down, NWC falls by $2.250 million as the payments of the last customers are received and the final bills are paid. We add this $2.250 million to free cash flow in year 5.

Execute (in $000s)

1	Year	0	1	2	3	4	5
2	Net Working Capital	0	2250	2250	2250	2250	0
3	Change in NWC		+2250	0	0	0	−2250
4	Cash Flow Effect		−2250	0	0	0	+2250

The incremental free cash flows would then be

Year		0	1	2	3	4	5
Incremental Earnings Forecast ($000s)							
1	Sales	–	26,000	26,000	26,000	26,000	–
2	Cost of Goods Sold	–	(11,000)	(11,000)	(11,000)	(11,000)	–
3	Gross Profit	–	15,000	15,000	15,000	15,000	–
4	Selling, General, and Administrative	–	(2800)	(2800)	(2800)	(2800)	–
5	Research and Development	(15,000)	–	–	–	–	–
6	Capital Cost Allowance (CCA)	–	(1688)	(2616)	(1439)	(791)	(435)
7	**EBIT**	(15,000)	10,513	9584	10,761	11,409	(435)
8	Income Tax at 40%	6000	(4205)	(3834)	(4305)	(4564)	174
9	**Unlevered Net Income**	(9000)	6308	5751	6457	6845	(261)
	Free Cash Flow ($000s)						
10	Plus: CCA	–	1688	2616	1439	791	435
11	Less: Capital Expenditures	(7500)					
12	Less: Increases in NWC	–	(2250)	–	–	–	2250
13	**Free Cash Flow**	(16,500)	5745	8366	7895	7636	2424

Evaluate

The free cash flows differ from unlevered net income by reflecting the cash flow effects of capital expenditures on equipment, CCA, and changes in NWC. Note that in the first two years, free cash flow is lower than unlevered net income, reflecting the upfront investment in equipment and NWC required by the project. In later years, free cash flow exceeds unlevered net income because depreciation is not a cash expense. In the last year, the firm ultimately recovers the investment in NWC, further boosting the free cash flow.

Calculating Free Cash Flow Directly

As we noted at the outset of this chapter, because practitioners usually begin the capital budgeting process by first forecasting earnings, we have chosen to do the same. However, we can calculate a project's free cash flow directly by using the following formula:

$$\text{Free Cash Flow} = \overbrace{(\text{Revenues} - \text{Costs} - CCA) \times (1 - \text{tax rate})}^{\text{Unlevered Net Income}} + CCA - CapEx - \text{Change in } NWC \tag{9.8}$$

Note that we first deduct CCA when computing the project's incremental earnings and then add it back (because it is a non-cash expense) when computing free cash flow. Thus, the only effect of CCA is to reduce the firm's taxable income. Indeed, we can rewrite Equation 9.8 as

$$\text{Free Cash Flow} = (\text{Revenues} - \text{Costs}) \times (1 - \text{tax rate}) - CapEx - \text{Change in } NWC + \text{tax rate} \times CCA \tag{9.9}$$

CCA tax shield The tax savings that results from the ability to deduct depreciation.

The last term in Equation 9.9, tax rate × CCA, is called the **CCA tax shield**, which is the tax savings that results from the ability to deduct CCA. As a consequence, CCA deductions have a *positive* impact on free cash flow. Returning to our example in Table 9.3, if the firm ignored CCA, its taxes were $400,000 instead of $320,000, leaving it with incremental free cash flow of $600,000 instead of $680,000. Notice that the $80,000 difference is exactly equal to the tax rate (40%) multiplied by the CCA deduction ($200,000). Every dollar of CCA deducted saves the firm 40 cents in taxes, so the $200,000 CCA deduction translates into an $80,000 tax savings.

Firms often report a different depreciation expense for accounting purposes and use CCA deductions for tax purposes. Because only the tax consequences of CCA are relevant for free cash flow, we should use the CCA deductions that the firm will use for tax purposes in our forecast.

Calculating the NPV

The goal of forecasting the incremental free cash flows is to have the necessary inputs to calculate the project's NPV. To compute a project's NPV, we must discount its free cash flow at the appropriate cost of capital. As discussed in Chapter 5, the cost of capital for a project is the expected return that investors could earn on their best alternative investment with similar risk and maturity. We will develop the techniques needed to estimate the cost of capital in Part 4 of this text, when we discuss risk and return. For now, we take the cost of capital as given.

We compute the present value of each free cash flow in the future by discounting it at the project's cost of capital. As explained in Chapter 5, using r to represent the cost of capital, the present value of the free cash flow in year t (or FCF_t) is

$$PV(FCF_t) = \frac{FCT_t}{(1+r)^t} = FCF_t \times \underbrace{\frac{1}{(1+r)^t}}_{\substack{t\text{-year} \\ \text{discount} \\ \text{factor}}} \tag{9.10}$$

EXAMPLE 9.4 Calculating the Project's NPV

PROBLEM

Assume that SPI's managers believe that the SPI Phone 86 project has risks similar to those of SPI's existing projects, for which it has a cost of capital of 12%. Compute the NPV of the SPI Phone 86 project.

SOLUTION

■ Plan

From Example 9.3, the incremental free cash flows for the SPI Phone 86 project are (in $000s):

1	Year	0	1	2	3	4	5
2	Incremental Free Cash Flows	(16,500)	5745	8366	7895	7636	2424

To compute the NPV, we sum the present values of all of the cash flows, noting that the year 0 cash outflow is already a present value.

■ Execute

Using Equation 9.10,

$$NPV = -16{,}500 + \frac{5745}{(1.12)^1} + \frac{8366}{(1.12)^2} + \frac{7895}{(1.12)^3} + \frac{7636}{(1.12)^4} + \frac{2424}{(1.12)^5} = 7147$$

▶

■ **Evaluate**

Based on our estimates, the SPI Phone 86's NPV is $7.147 million. While the SPI Phone 86's upfront cost is $16.5 million, the present value of the additional free cash flow that SPI will receive from the project is $23.647 million. Thus, taking the SPI Phone 86 project is equivalent to SPI having an extra $7.147 million in the bank today.

CONCEPT CHECK

5. If depreciation or CCA expense is not a cash flow, why do we have to subtract it and add it back? Why not just ignore it?
6. Why does an increase in NWC represent a cash outflow?

9.4 Other Effects on Incremental Free Cash Flows

When computing the incremental free cash flows of an investment decision, we should include *all* changes in the firm's free cash flows with the project versus without the project. These include opportunities foregone due to the project and effects of the project on other parts of the firm. In this section, we discuss these other effects, some of the pitfalls and common mistakes to avoid, and finally the complications that can arise when forecasting incremental free cash flows.

Opportunity Costs

opportunity cost The value a resource could have provided in its best alternative use.

Many projects in the company use a resource that it already owns. Because the firm does not need to pay cash to acquire this resource for a new project, it is tempting to assume that the resource is available for free. However, in many cases the resource could provide value for the firm in another opportunity or project. The **opportunity cost** of using a resource is the value it could have provided in its best alternative use.[3] Because this value is lost when the resource is used by another project, we should include the opportunity cost as an incremental cost of the project. For example, your company may be considering building a retail store on some land that it owns. Even though it already owns the land, it is not free to the store project. If it did not put its store on the land, the company could sell the land, for example. This foregone market price for the land is an opportunity cost of the retail store project.

COMMON MISTAKE

The Opportunity Cost of an Idle Asset

A common mistake is to conclude that if an asset is currently idle, its opportunity cost is zero. For example, the firm might have a warehouse that is currently empty or a machine that is not being used. Often, the asset may have been idled in anticipation of taking on the new project, and would have otherwise been put to use by the firm. Even if the firm has no alternative use for the asset, the firm could choose to sell or rent the asset. The value obtained from the asset's alternative use, sale, or rental represents an opportunity cost that must be included as part of the incremental cash flows.

[3]In Chapter 5, we defined the opportunity cost of capital as the rate you could earn on an alternative investment with equivalent risk. We similarly define the opportunity cost of using an existing asset in a project as the cash flow generated by the next-best alternative use for the asset.

Project Externalities

project externalities Indirect effects of a project that may increase or decrease the profits of other business activities of a firm.

cannibalization The displacement of the sales of one of a firm's existing products by the sales of the firm's new product.

Aflo Co. Ltd./Alamy

Project externalities are indirect effects of a project that may increase or decrease the profits of other business activities of the firm. For instance, some purchasers of Apple's iPhone 6+, Apple's first larger-screen iPhone, would otherwise have bought Apple's iPad Mini. When sales of a new product displace sales of an existing product, the situation is often referred to as **cannibalization**. The lost sales of the existing project are an incremental cost to the company of going forward with the new product.

Sunk Costs

sunk cost Any unrecoverable cost for which a firm is already liable.

A **sunk cost** is any unrecoverable cost for which the firm is already liable. Sunk costs have been or will be paid regardless of whether or not the decision is made to proceed with the project. Therefore, they are not incremental with respect to the current decision and should not be included in its analysis. You may hire a market research firm to do market analysis to determine whether there is demand for a new product you are considering and the analysis may show that there is not enough demand, so you decide not to go forward with the project. Does that mean you do not have to pay the research firm's bill? Of course you still have to pay the bill, emphasizing that the cost was sunk and incurred whether you went forward with the project or not.

A good rule to remember is that *if your decision does not affect a cash flow then the cash flow should not affect your decision*. If the cash flow is the same regardless of the decision, then it is not relevant to your decision. Following are some common examples of sunk costs you may encounter.

overhead expenses Those expenses associated with activities that are not directly attributable to a single business activity but instead affect many different areas of a corporation.

Fixed Overhead Expenses. **Overhead expenses** are associated with activities that are not directly attributable to a single business activity but, instead, affect many different areas of the corporation. Examples include the cost of maintaining the company's headquarters and the salary of the CEO. These expenses are often allocated to the different business activities for accounting purposes. To the extent that these overhead costs are fixed and will be incurred in any case, they are not incremental to the project and should not be included. Include as incremental expenses only the *additional* overhead expenses that arise because of the decision to take on the project.

Past Research and Development Expenditures. A pharmaceutical company may spend tens of millions of dollars developing a new drug, but if it fails to produce an effect in trials (or worse, has only negative effects), should it proceed? The company cannot get its development costs back, and the amount of those costs should have no bearing on whether to continue developing a failed drug.

When a firm has already devoted significant resources to develop a new product, there may be a tendency to continue investing in the product even if market conditions have changed and the product is unlikely to be viable. The rationale that is sometimes given is that if the product is abandoned, the money that has already been invested will be "wasted." In other cases, a decision is made to abandon a project because it cannot possibly be successful enough to recoup the investment that has already been made. In fact, neither argument is correct—any money that has already been spent is a sunk cost and therefore irrelevant. The decision to continue or abandon should be based only on the incremental costs and benefits of the product going forward.

Unavoidable Competitive Effects. As discussed earlier, when developing a new product, managers often worry about the cannibalization of their existing products. However, if competitors' products would have reduced the sales of the company's existing product anyway and the company introduces a new product to maintain or grow its market share, then the lost sales of the existing product should not be counted as an incremental cost of the new product because these lost sales would have occurred regardless of the new product's introduction. In essence, the lost sales of the existing product would be counted as a sunk cost as they are unavoidable.

COMMON MISTAKE

The Sunk Cost Fallacy

Being influenced by sunk costs is such a widespread mistake that it has a special name: sunk cost fallacy. The most common problem is that people "throw good money after bad." That is, people sometimes continue to invest in a project that has a negative NPV because they have already invested a large amount in the project and feel that by not continuing it, the prior investment will be wasted. The sunk cost fallacy is also sometimes called the "Concorde effect," a term that refers to the British and French governments' decision to continue funding the joint development of the Concorde aircraft even after it was clear that sales of the plane would fall far short of those necessary to justify its continued development. The British government viewed the project as a commercial and financial disaster. However, the political implications of halting the project—and thereby publicly admitting that all past expenses on the project would result in nothing—ultimately prevented either government from abandoning the project.

Adjusting Free Cash Flow

Here, we describe a number of complications that can arise when estimating a project's free cash flow.

Timing of Cash Flows. For simplicity, we have treated the cash flows in our examples as if they occur at annual intervals. In reality, cash flows will be spread throughout the year. While it is common to forecast at the annual level, we can forecast free cash flow on a quarterly or monthly basis when greater accuracy is required. In practice, firms often choose shorter intervals for riskier projects so that they might forecast cash flows at the monthly level for projects that carry considerable risk. For example, cash flows for a new facility in Europe may be forecasted at the quarterly or annual level, but if that same facility were located in a politically unstable country, the forecasts would probably be at the monthly level.

Perpetual CCA Tax Shields. The free cash flows we estimated over the five years of the project will miss the value of CCA tax shields that occur after the project has ended. This may be a very important omission that needs to be corrected. If an asset is not sold, it will generate CCA expenses and the resulting tax shields every year into perpetuity. Since the CCA deducted each year is a proportion of the UCC, UCC never falls to zero. In Table 9.1 we have the CCA deductions for the first five years. You may not see an obvious pattern in the CCA deductions, but there is one, and it relates to the way the CRA requires CCA to be calculated. Recall that one-half of the CapEx is added into the UCC initially, and the second half of the CapEx is added into the UCC in the second year. In effect, one-half of the CapEx starts having CCA applied initially and the other half of the CapEx starts having CCA applied in the second year. Table 9.4 shows the CCA calculated in this way.

Line 7 of the Table 9.4 spreadsheet shows the sum of the CCAs calculated from line 2 and line 6. If you compare the CCAs in line 7 to those shown in Table 9.1, you will see that they are the same. Why is this useful? Because it will help us calculate the present value of the CCA tax shields, including those that continue perpetually.

TABLE 9.4 Breaking Down the CCA Deductions into Two Perpetuities

Equivalent CCA calculation using $CCA_t = UCC_t \times d$ and splitting CapEx across two years							
Year		**0**	**1**	**2**	**3**	**4**	**5**
Capital Expenditure, CCA, and UCC Forecasts ($000s)							
1	CapEx added to UCC_1	3750					
2	UCC_t	–	3750	2063	1134	624	343
3	$CCA_t = UCC_t \times d$	–	1688	928	510	281	154
4	CapEx added to UCC_2	3750					
5	UCC_t		–	3750	2063	1134	624
6	$CCA_t = UCC_t \times d$		–	1688	928	510	281
7	*CCA* (line 3) + *CCA* (line 6)		1688	2616	1439	791	435
8	CCA rate, d	45%					

Notes: For the yellow cells, $UCC_t = UCC_{t-1} - CCA_{t-1}$
Since $CCA_5 < UCC_5$, there will be a positive balance remaining for UCC_6)

Recall that each year we can determine the CCA tax shield as $\tau_c \times CCA$. Following the CCA calculations in Table 9.4, Table 9.5 spreadsheet shows the calculations of the CCA tax shields.

The CCA tax shields in line 4 are nothing more than a growing perpetuity with growth rate equal to -45% (thus, growth $= -d$). The first cash flow of this perpetuity occurs in one year, and the cash flow amount is

$$0.5 \times CapEx \times d \times \tau_c$$

The CCA tax shields in line 8 are identical, except they are delayed one additional year. To determine the present value of the total CCA tax shields, we can use the Law of One Price and add the present value of the perpetuity in line 4 to the present value of the perpetuity in line 8. We use the formula for the present value of a growing perpetuity and insert $-d$ for the growth rate.

TABLE 9.5 Breaking Down the CCA Tax Shields into Two Perpetuities

Equivalent CCA, calculation using $CCA_t = UCC_t \times d$ and splitting CapEx across two years									
Year		**0**	**1**	**2**	**3**	**4**	**5**	**6**	**...**
Capital Expenditure, CCA, and UCC Forecasts ($000s))									
1	CapEx added to UCC_1	3750							
2	UCC_t		3750	2063	1134	624	343	189	...
3	$CCA_t = UCC_t \times d$		1688	928	510	281	154	85	...
4	***CCA* tax shield** $= \tau_c \times$ ***CCA***		675	371	204	112	62	34	...
5	CapEx added to UCC_2	3750							
6	UCC_t			3750	2063	1134	624	343	...
7	$CCA_t = UCC_t \times d$			1688	928	510	281	154	...
8	***CCA* tax shield** $= \tau_c \times$ **CCA**			675	371	204	112	62	...
9	Total *CCA* = *CCA* (line 3) + *CCA* (line 7)		1688	2616	1439	791	435	239	...
10	**Total *CCA* tax shield** $= \tau c \times$ **Total *CCA***		675	1046	575	316	174	96	...
11	CCA rate, d	45%							
12	Tax rate, τ_c	40%							

PV of CCA tax shields from line 4: $PV = \dfrac{0.5 \times CapEx \times d \times \tau_c}{r + d}$

PV of CCA tax shields from line 8: $PV = \dfrac{0.5 \times CapEx \times d \times \tau_c}{r + d} \times \dfrac{1}{(1 + r)}$

Summing these two amounts together and simplifying, we get the following:

$$PV = \frac{0.5 \times CapEx \times d \times \tau_c}{r + d} \times \frac{(1 + r)}{(1 + r)} + \frac{0.5 \times CapEx \times d \times \tau_c}{r + d} \times \frac{1}{(1 + r)}$$
$$= \frac{0.5 \times CapEx \times d \times \tau_c}{r + d} \times \frac{(2 + r)}{(1 + r)}$$

This results in our formula for the present value of the CCA tax shield in perpetuity:

$$PV_{CCA \text{ tax shields}} = \frac{CapEx \times d \times \tau_c}{r + d} \times \frac{(1 + \frac{r}{2})}{(1 + r)} \tag{9.11}$$

If the asset is not sold, then Equation 9.11 gives the present value of all the CCA tax shields, including those that continue beyond the end of the project.

If we use Equation 9.11 to get the present value of all the CCA tax shields, then we must adjust our calculation of free cash flows so that we do not count any CCA tax shields twice. The free cash flows we estimated for the SPI Phone 86 in Table 9.2 include the CCA tax shields for the first five years. To remove the CCA tax shields, we can adjust Equation 9.8 and 9.9 by removing all references to CCA. Equation 9.12, below, shows the calculation of free cash flows, excluding CCA tax shields.

$$FCF_{\text{excluding } CCA \text{ tax shield}} = (\text{Revenues} - \text{Costs}) \times (1 - \tau_c) - CapEx - \Delta NWC \tag{9.12}$$

Equation 9.12 can be used only when we account for the value of CCA tax shields separately (as done with Equation 9.11 above or Equation 9.16 below). The Table 9.6 spreadsheet shows the free cash flows and NPV recalculated when we separate the CCA tax shields in the analysis.

The PV of CCA tax shields shown in line 17 is calculated as follows:

$$PV_{CCA \text{ tax shields}} = \frac{7500 \times 0.45 \times 0.40}{0.12 + 0.45} \times \frac{(1 + \frac{0.12}{2})}{(1 + 0.12)} = 2242$$

The NPV shown in line 18 of the Table 9.6 spreadsheet is the sum of the present values of the free cash flows (excluding CCA tax shields) shown in line 16 and the PV of the CCA tax shield perpetuity shown in line 17:

$$NPV = -16{,}500 + 4527 + 5835 + 5210 + 4652 + 1277 + 2242 = 7243$$

As you can see, the NPV rises from \$7.147 million to \$7.243 million when we include all the CCA tax shield effects. If we were to forget to include the CCA tax shields after year 5, then we would underestimate the NPV by about \$96,000.

Liquidation or Salvage Value. Assets that are no longer needed often have a resale value or some salvage value if the parts are sold for scrap. Some assets may have a negative liquidation value. For example, it may cost money to remove and dispose of the used equipment.

capital gain tax A tax collected on the profit (the amount by which the *sale price* exceeds the original purchase price) from assets in the year in which the assets are sold.

In the calculation of expected free cash flow for date t, we include the expected liquidation value of any assets that are expected to be sold during year t. In addition, we need to include the expected tax effects from selling the asset. There are two main tax effects. First, there will be a **capital gain tax** if the asset is sold for an amount greater

TABLE 9.6 The SPI Phone 86's Free Cash Flows and NPV with CCA Tax Shields Treated Separately

Year		0	1	2	3	4	5
Incremental Earnings Forecast ($000s)							
1	Sales	–	26,000	26,000	26,000	26,000	–
2	Cost of Goods Sold	–	(11,000)	(11,000)	(11,000)	(11,000)	–
3	Gross Profit	–	15,000	15,000	15,000	15,000	–
4	Selling, General, and Administrative	–	(2800)	(2800)	(2800)	(2800)	–
5	Research and Development	(15,000)	–	–	–	–	–
6	Capital Cost Allowance (CCA)	not included, as analyzed separately					
7	**EBIT**	(15,000)	12,200	12,200	12,200	12,200	–
8	Income Tax at 40%	6000	(4880)	(4880)	(4880)	(4880)	–
9	**Unlevered Net Income**	(9000)	7320	7320	7320	7320	–
	Free Cash Flow ($000s)						
10	Plus: CCA	not included, as analyzed separately					
11	Less: Net Capital Expenditures	(7500)					
12	Less: Increases in NWC	–	(2250)	–	–	–	2250
13	**Free Cash Flow$_{\text{excluding CCA tax shields}}$**	(16,500)	5070	7320	7320	7320	2250
14	Project Cost of Capital	12%					
15	Discount Factor	1.0000	0.8929	0.7972	0.7118	0.6355	0.5674
16	**PV of Free Cash Flow$_{\text{excluding CCA tax shield}}$**	(16,500)	4527	5835	5210	4652	1277
17	**PV of CCA tax Shields (Equation 9.11)**	2242					
18	**NPV: sum of amounts in rows 16 and 17**	7243					

than its original purchase price, denoted by CapEx. CRA taxes one-half of the gain at the corporate tax rate:

$$\text{Capital Gains Tax} = \frac{1}{2} \times (\textit{Sale Price} - \textit{CapEx}) \times \tau_c \tag{9.13}$$

The capital gain tax will be paid in the tax year the asset is sold and will be included in the free cash flow for that year as a negative effect. When we discussed purchasing an asset at date 0, we assumed the tax effect (the CCA tax shield) would occur at date 1 because the asset was purchased just after the year 0 end-of-year for tax purposes. To be consistent, we will assume that an asset sale at date t is actually at the beginning of the tax year $t + 1$. Thus, given an asset sale at date t, the capital gain tax should be deducted from the free cash flow for date $t + 1$.[4]

The second tax effect from selling an asset is that the subsequent CCA deductions and tax shields will change. The UCC for the asset will be reduced by the asset sale in the tax year of the asset sale. The minimum of the *Sale Price* and the original purchase price, CapEx, is subtracted from the UCC to get the post-sale UCC. If the asset is sold at date t, we will continue our assumption that the sale is at the beginning of tax year $t + 1$.

$$\text{Post-Sale } UCC_{t+1} = UCC_{t+1} - \text{minimum of } (\textit{Sale Price}_t, \textit{CapEx}) \tag{9.14}$$

[4]Other assumptions can be made about the timing of the asset sale. If the asset sale occurs within tax year t rather than at the beginning of tax year $t + 1$, then the capital gain tax would reduce the free cash flow for date t.

Post-sale UCC_{t+1} will be used as the basis to determine CCA_{t+1} and subsequent CCA deductions.

The way post-sale CCA deductions are calculated depends on whether post-sale UCC_{t+1} for the asset pool is positive or negative, whether or not the firm still owns any assets in that asset pool, and whether or not the firm will be buying additional assets in that pool with value greater than the asset's expected *Sale Price*. We will assume that other assets remain in the asset pool, and post-sale UCC_{t+1} for the asset pool remains positive. With this assumption we have what is called a **continuing pool**. We will also assume that in the tax year of the asset sale, future purchases of assets (for other projects) will be less than the asset's expected *Sale Price*; this is referred to as **negative net additions**.[5]

continuing pool An asset pool in which there exists positive UCC for which the company still own assets.

negative net additions A situation in which a continuing asset pool has asset purchases less than asset sales in the same tax year. (The UCC of the pool will decline but still remain positive.)

Continuing Pool, Negative Net Additions. With a continuing pool and negative net additions, adjustments must be made to the post-sale CCA amounts and resulting tax shields. The effect of the asset sale is fully recognized in the tax year of the sale and the UCC is reduced accordingly. Utilizing what we know from deriving Equation 9.11, the present value of the reduction in CCA tax shields can be calculated as follows:

$$PV_{\text{lost } CCA \text{ tax shields}} = \frac{\min(Sale\ Price_t, CapEx) \times d \times \tau_c}{r + d} \times \frac{1}{(1 + r)^t} \tag{9.15}$$

In Equation 9.15, the first reduction in CCA tax shields is in year $t + 1$. The growing perpetuity formula discounts the lost CCA tax shields back to date t; the last term on Equation 9.15 discounts from date t to date 0.

We can combine Equations 9.11 and 9.15 to get the overall present value of expected CCA tax shields under the condition of an expected continuing pool of assets and negative net additions when the asset is sold:

$$\begin{aligned} PV_{CCA \text{ tax shields}} = {} & \frac{CapEx \times d \times \tau_c}{r + d} \times \frac{(1 + \frac{r}{2})}{(1 + r)} \\ & - \frac{\min(Sale\ Price_t, CapEx) \times d \times \tau_c}{r + d} \times \frac{1}{(1 + r)^t} \end{aligned} \tag{9.16}$$ [6]

Remember to consider all the effects of the asset sale. Given our assumptions about the timing of the asset purchase and sale with respect to the relevant tax years, we consider the *Sale Price*, CCA tax shield effects, and capital gain tax as follows. We add the *Sale Price* to the free cash flow for year t. We use Equation 9.16 instead of Equation 9.11 in order to calculate the present value of all the expected CCA tax shields. If there is a capital gain, we subtract the capital gain tax (Equation 9.13) from the free cash flow for year $t + 1$.

---

[5]If purchases of other assets are less than the disposed asset's expected *Sale Price*, they are referred to as positive net additions. The formula for calculating the present value of lost CCA tax shields when positive net additions exist is the same as for negative net additions, except that the half-year rule is applied to the calculation. Further complications arise when the asset pool does not continue, giving rise to either terminal loss or recaptured CCA tax effects. These topics are reserved for intermediate-level corporate finance textbooks.

[6]Alternative assumptions about the timing of the asset purchase or sale can be easily accommodated. For instance, if the asset is purchased at the end of tax year 0 rather than the beginning of tax year 1, the first term of Equation 9.16 would have to be multiplied by $(1 + r)$. If the asset is expected to be sold at the end of tax year t rather than the beginning of tax year $t + 1$, then the last term of Equation 9.16 would be multiplied by $(1 + r)$. Often business reasons (rather than just the tax implications) drive the timing of the asset sale, so it is important to understand how to adjust these formulas.

EXAMPLE 9.5 Adding Salvage Value and CCA Effects to the Analysis

PROBLEM

SPI is expected to sell the specialized computer equipment at date 4 (or the beginning of tax year 5), as the lab will be shut down at that point. The expected Sale Price is high, $8 million, because of the expected appreciation of precious minerals used within the computer equipment. It is expected that SPI will still own other computer equipment at that time but will not be making such purchases in excess of $8 million in tax year 5. Redo the NPV calculation for the SPI Phone 86 project, given this new information.

SOLUTION

Plan

In order to compute the after-tax cash flow, you will need to incorporate the effects on cash flows of the salvage value, the capital gains tax (using Equation 9.13), and the lost CCA tax shields (using Equation 9.16).

Execute

Add in the $8 million to the free cash flow for year 4 and replace Equation 9.11 with Equation 9.16 to take into account how CCA tax shields will be changed by the asset sale. Since there is a capital gain, calculate the capital gain tax and deduct it from the free cash flow for year 5. The results are shown in the spreadsheet below.

Year		0	1	2	3	4	5
Incremental Earnings Forecast ($000s)							
1	Sales	–	26,000	26,000	26,000	26,000	–
2	Cost of Goods Sold	–	(11,000)	(11,000)	(11,000)	(11,000)	–
3	Gross Profit	–	15,000	15,000	15,000	15,000	–
4	Selling, General, and Administrative	–	(2800)	(2800)	(2800)	(2800)	–
5	Research and Development	(15,000)	–	–	–	–	–
6	Capital Cost Allowance (CCA)	not included, as analyzed separately					
7	**EBIT**	(15,000)	12,200	12,200	12,200	12,200	–
8	Income Tax at 40%	6000	(4880)	(4880)	(4880)	(4880)	–
9	**Unlevered Net Income**	(9000)	7320	7320	7320	7320	–
	Free Cash Flow ($000s)						
10	Plus: CCA	not included, as analyzed separately					
11	Less: Net Capital Expenditures	(7500)	–	–	–	8000	–
12	Less: Increases in NWC	–	(2250)	–	–	–	2250
13	Less: Capital Gain Tax	–	–	–	–	–	(100)
14	Free Cash Flow$_{\text{excluding CCA tax shields}}$	(16,500)	5070	7320	7320	15320	2150
15	Project Cost of Capital	12%					
16	Discount Factor	1.0000	0.8929	0.7972	0.7118	0.6355	0.5674
17	**PV of Free Cash Flow$_{\text{excluding CCA tax shield}}$**	(16,500)	4527	5835	5210	9736	1220
18	**PV of CCA tax Shields (Equation 9.16)**	736					
19	**NPV: sum of amounts in rows 17 and 18**	10,765*					

Note that the $8 million from the asset sale is the same as a negative capital expenditure. It is reflected in line 11 of the spreadsheet and is added into the free cash flow for year 4. The capital gain tax shown in line 13 is calculated using Equation 9.13 as follows:

$$\text{Capital Gain Tax} = \frac{1}{2} \times (8000 - 7500) \times 0.40 = 100$$

Since the asset is sold at the beginning of tax year 5, the capital gain tax reduces free cash flow for year 5. The present value of CCA tax shields, using Equation 9.16, in line 18 is calculated as follows:

$$PV_{CCA\ tax\ shields} = \frac{7500 \times 0.45 \times 0.40}{0.12 + 0.45} \times \frac{(1 + \frac{0.12}{2})}{(1 + 0.12)} - \frac{7500 \times 0.45 \times 0.40}{0.12 + 0.45} \times \frac{1}{(1 + 0.12)^4}$$

The NPV (line 19) is the sum of the present values of the free cash flows (excluding CCA tax shields) plus the PV of CCA tax shields calculated with Equation 9.16.

$$NPV = -16{,}500 + 4527 + 5835 + 5210 + 9736 + 1220 + 736$$
$$= 10{,}764 \text{ (*difference is due to rounding)}$$

Evaluate

You should notice that the NPV is much higher than what was calculated in the Table 9.6 spreadsheet. The reason it is higher is because of the large asset *sale price*. Also note that the PV of CCA tax shields is lower and there is a capital gain; these are the other effects of the asset sale.

tax loss carryforwards and **carrybacks** Two features of the Canadian tax code that allow corporations to take losses during a current year and offset them against gains in nearby years. In Canada, companies can "carry back" losses for three years and, for tax years after 2005, "carry forward" losses for 20 years.

Tax Carryforwards. A firm generally identifies its marginal tax rate by determining the tax bracket that it falls into based on its overall level of pre-tax income. Two additional features of the tax code, called **tax loss carryforwards** and **carrybacks**, allow corporations to take losses during a current year and offset them against gains in nearby years. In Canada, companies can "carry back" losses for three years and, for tax years after 2005, companies can "carry forward" losses for 20 years. This tax rule means that a firm can offset losses during one year against income for the past three years, or save the losses to be offset against income during the next 20 years. When a firm can carry back losses, it receives a refund for back taxes in the current year. Otherwise, the firm must carry forward the loss and use it to offset future taxable income. When a firm has tax loss carryforwards well in excess of its current pre-tax income, then additional income it earns today will simply increase the taxes it owes after it exhausts its carryforwards.

Replacement Decisions

Often the financial manager must decide whether to replace an existing piece of equipment. The new equipment may allow increased production, resulting in incremental revenue, or it may simply be more efficient, lowering costs. The typical incremental effects associated with such a decision are salvage value from the old machine, purchase of the new machine, cost savings and revenue increases, and depreciation effects.

EXAMPLE 9.6 Replacing an Existing Machine

PROBLEM

You are trying to decide whether to replace a machine on your production line. The new machine will cost $1.25 million but will be more efficient than the old machine, reducing costs by $500,000 per year. Your old machine could be sold for $50,000. You expect to sell the new machine for $100,000 after five years. While the company does not intend to add any more assets into the pool in five years, it does have many assets in the pool, so the pool will continue indefinitely. The new machine will not change your working capital needs. The CCA rate is 45%. The tax rate is 40%, and the firm expects a 12% return on this project.

SOLUTION

Plan

Incremental revenues: 0

Incremental costs: –$500,000 (It is important to note that a reduction in costs will appear as a positive number in the costs line of our analysis.)

Incremental capital expenditure: $1.25 million – $50,000 = $1.2 million. This is the net change to the asset pool upon replacement.

Cash flow from salvage value: +$100,000

Execute

Year		0	1	2	3	4	5
Incremental Earnings Forecast ($000s)							
1	Sales	–	–	–	–	–	–
2	Cost of Goods Sold	–	500,000	500,000	500,000	500,000	500,000
3	Gross Profit	–	500,000	500,000	500,000	500,000	500,000
6	Capital Cost Allowance (CCA)	not included, as analyzed separately					
7	**EBIT**	–	500,000	500,000	500,000	500,000	500,000
8	Income Tax at 40%	–	(200,000)	(200,000)	(200,000)	(200,000)	(200,000)
9	**Unlevered Net Income**	–	300,000	300,000	300,000	300,000	300,000
	Free Cash Flow ($000s)						
10	Plus: CCA	not included, as analyzed separately					
11	Less: Net Capital Expenditures	(1,200,000)	–	–	–	–	100,000
14	**Free Cash Flow** $_{\text{excluding CCA tax shields}}$	(1,200,000)	300,000	300,000	300,000	300,000	400,000
15	Project Cost of Capital	12%					
16	Discount Factor	1.0000	0.8929	0.7972	0.7118	0.6355	0.5674
17	**PV of Free Cash Flow** $_{\text{excluding CCA tax shield}}$	(1,200,000)	267,857	239,158	213,534	190,655	226,971
18	**PV of CCA tax Shields (Equation 9.16)**	340,727.87					
19	**NPV: sum of amounts from rows 17 and 18**	276,753					

▶

■ **Evaluate**

Even though the decision has no impact on revenues, it still matters for cash flows because it reduces costs. Just as important are the tax implications of both selling the old machine and buying the new machine. Notice that the PV of the CCA tax shields is greater than the NPV. Had we not considered these tax implications, the replacement opportunity would not have looked like a good one.

CONCEPT CHECK

7. Should we include sunk costs in the cash flows of a project? Why or why not?
8. Explain why it is advantageous for a firm to use the most accelerated depreciation schedule possible for tax purposes.

9.5 Analyzing the Project

When evaluating a capital budgeting project, financial managers should make the decision that maximizes NPV. As we have discussed, to compute the NPV for a project you need to estimate the incremental free cash flows and choose a discount rate. Given these inputs, the NPV calculation is relatively straightforward. The most difficult part of capital budgeting is deciding how to estimate the cash flows and cost of capital. These estimates are often subject to significant uncertainty. In this section, we look at methods that assess the importance of this uncertainty and identify the drivers of value in the project.

Sensitivity Analysis

sensitivity analysis An important capital budgeting tool that shows how the NPV varies as a single underlying assumption is changed.

An important capital budgeting tool for assessing the effect of uncertainty in forecasts is sensitivity analysis. **Sensitivity analysis** breaks the NPV calculation into its component assumptions and shows how the NPV varies as the underlying assumptions change. In this way, sensitivity analysis allows us to explore the effects of errors in our NPV estimates for a project. By conducting a sensitivity analysis, we learn which assumptions are the most important; we can then invest further resources and effort to refine these assumptions. Such an analysis also reveals which aspects of a project are most critical when we are actually managing the project.

In fact, we have already performed a type of sensitivity analysis in Chapter 8 when we constructed an NPV profile. By graphing the NPV of a project as a function of the discount rate, we are assessing the sensitivity of our NPV calculation to uncertainty about the correct cost of capital to use as a discount rate. In practice, financial managers explore the sensitivity of their NPV calculation to many more factors than just the discount rate.

To illustrate, consider the assumptions underlying the calculation of the SPI Phone 86's NPV in Example 9.4. There is likely to be significant uncertainty surrounding each revenue and cost assumption. In addition to the base-case assumptions about units sold, *sale price*, cost of goods sold, NWC, and cost of capital, SPI's managers would also identify best and worst-case scenarios for each. For example, assume that they identified the best- and worst-case assumptions listed in Table 9.7. Note that these are best- and worst-case scenarios for each parameter rather than representing one worst-case scenario and one best-case scenario.

TABLE 9.7 Best- and Worst-Case Assumptions for Each Parameter in the SPI Phone 86 Project

Parameter	Initial Assumption	Worst Case	Best Case
Units Sold (thousands)	100	70	130
Sale Price ($/unit)	260	240	280
Cost of Goods ($/unit)	110	120	100
NWC ($ thousands)	2250	3050	1450
Cost of Capital	12%	15%	10%

To determine the importance of this uncertainty, we recalculate the NPV of the SPI Phone 86 project under the best- and worst-case assumptions for each parameter. For example, if the number of units sold is only 70,000 per year, the NPV of the project falls to −$1.053 million. We repeat this calculation for each parameter. The result is shown in Figure 9.2, which reveals that the parameter assumptions with the largest effect on NPV are the number of units sold and the *sale price* per unit. As a result, these assumptions deserve the greatest scrutiny during the estimation process. In addition, as the most important drivers of the project's value, these factors deserve close attention when managing the project after it starts. The Appendix to Chapter 9 shows how sensitivity analysis can be efficiently implemented using Excel.

FIGURE 9.2 SPI Phone 86's NPV under Best- and Worst-Case Parameter Assumptions

Bars show the change in NPV going from the best-case assumption to the worst-case assumption for each parameter. For example, the NPV of the project ranges from −$1.053 million if only 70,000 units are sold, to $15.348 million if 130,000 units are sold. Under the initial assumptions, SPI Phone 86's NPV is $7.147 million.

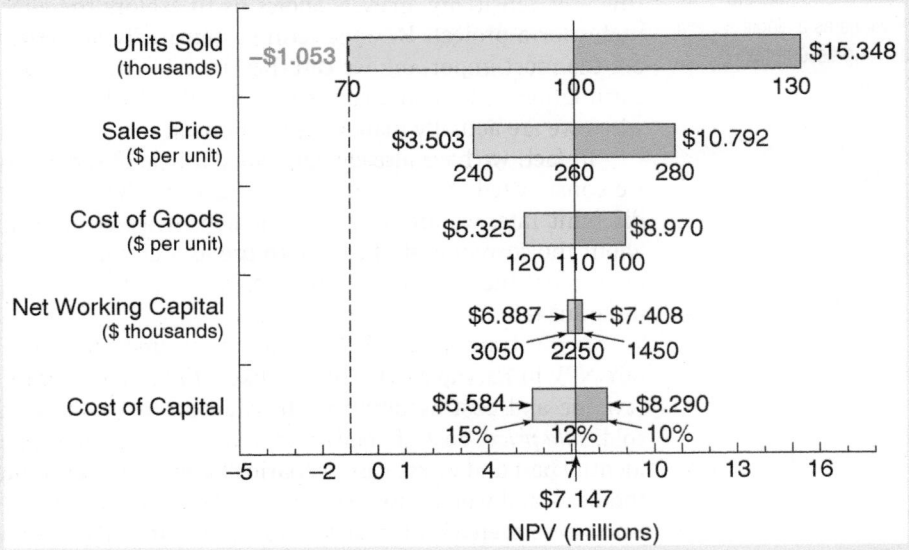

Break-Even Analysis

break-even The level for which an investment has an NPV of zero.

A natural extension of the sensitivity analysis is to ask at what level of each parameter the project would just break even, that is, the level—or **break-even**—for which the investment has an NPV of zero. One example that we have already considered is the calculation of the internal rate of return (IRR). Recall from Chapter 8 that the difference between the IRR of a project and the cost of capital tells you how much error in the cost of capital it would take to change the investment decision. By either graphing the NPV profile or using the Excel function IRR, we would find that the incremental cash flows of the SPI Phone 86 given in Example 9.4 imply an IRR of 29.3%. Hence, the true cost of capital can be as high as 29.3% and the project will still have a positive NPV.

break-even analysis A calculation of the value of each parameter for which the NPV of the project is zero.

We can determine the uncertainty of other parameters as well. In a **break-even analysis**, for each parameter we calculate the value at which the NPV of the project is zero. This would be tedious to do by hand, so in practice it is always done with a spreadsheet. As with the NPV profile for the discount rate, we can graph the NPV as a function of each of the critical assumptions. In each case, we keep all of the other parameters fixed at their base-case values and vary only the parameter in question. Figure 9.3 does this for the SPI Phone 86.

EBIT break-even The level of a particular parameter for which a project's EBIT is zero.

Accounting Break-Even. We have examined the break-even levels in terms of the project's NPV, which is the most useful perspective for decision making. Other accounting notions of break-even are sometimes considered, however. For example, we could compute the **EBIT break-even** for sales, which is the level of sales for which the project's EBIT is zero.

Recall from Equation 9.3 that the project's EBIT is Revenues − Costs − *CCA*. Costs include cost of goods sold; selling, general, and administrative expense (SG&A); and research and development (R&D). Revenues equal Units Sold × *Sale Price*, and cost of goods sold equals Units Sold × Cost Per Unit, so we have *EBIT* = (Units Sold × *Sale Price*) − (Units Sold × Cost Per Unit) − SG&A − R&D − *CCA*. Setting this equal to zero and solving for units sold,

$$\text{Units Sold} \times (\text{Sales Price} - \text{Cost Per Unit}) - \text{SG\&A} - \text{R\&D} - CCA = 0$$

$$\text{Units Sold} = \frac{\text{SG\&A} + \text{R\&D} + CCA}{\text{Sales Price} - \text{Cost Per Unit}} = \frac{\$2{,}800{,}000 + 0 + 1{,}688{,}500}{260 - 110} = 29{,}923$$

However, this EBIT break-even number is misleading. First, it is difficult to derive much use from the year 1 break-even unit sales as the break-even number would change each year due to the fact that CCA deductions will differ each year. Additionally, while SPI Phone 86's EBIT break-even level of sales in the first year is only 29,923 units per year, given the large upfront investment and research and development (incurred in year 0) required in the SPI Phone 86 project, its NPV, −$12.011 million, is at that sales level.

Scenario Analysis

scenario analysis An important capital budgeting tool that shows how the NPV varies as a number of the underlying assumptions are changed simultaneously.

In the analysis thus far, we have considered the consequences of varying only one parameter at a time. In reality, certain factors may affect more than one parameter. **Scenario analysis** considers the effect on NPV of changing multiple project parameters. For example, lowering the SPI Phone 86's price may increase the number of units sold. We can use scenario analysis to evaluate alternative pricing strategies for the SPI Phone 86 product in Table 9.8. In this case, the current strategy is optimal. Figure 9.4 shows the combinations of price and volume that lead to the same NPV of $7.147 million for the SPI Phone 86 as the current strategy. Only strategies with price and volume combinations above the line will lead to a higher NPV.

FIGURE 9.3 Break-Even Analysis Graphs

The graphs in panels (a) and (b) relate two of the key parameters to the project's NPV to identify the parameters' break-even points. For example, based on the initial assumptions, the SPI Phone 86 project will break even with a sales level of just under 74,000 units per year. Similarly, holding sales and the other parameters constant at their initial assumed values, the project will break even at a cost of goods sold of just over $149 per unit.

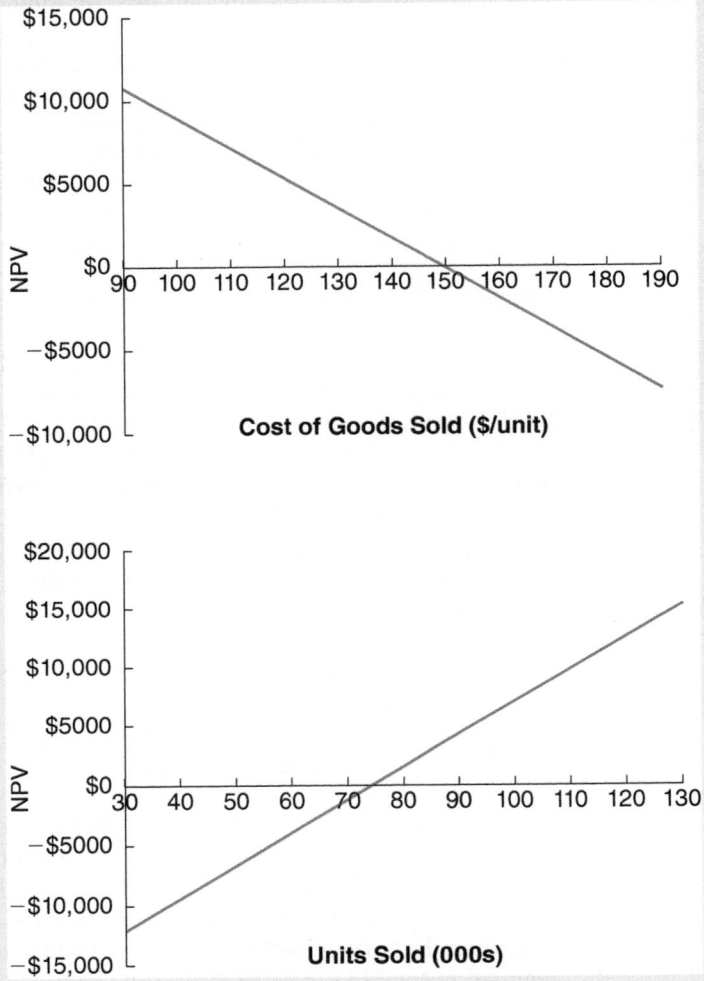

TABLE 9.8 Scenario Analysis of Alternative Pricing Strategies

Strategy	Sale Price ($/unit)	Expected Units Sold (thousands)	NPV ($ thousands)
Current Strategy	260	100	7147
Price Reduction	245	110	6874
Price Increase	275	90	6874

FIGURE 9.4 **Price and Volume Combinations for SPI Phone 86 with Equivalent NPV**

The graph shows alternative price per unit and annual volume combinations that lead to an NPV of $7.147 million. Pricing strategies with combinations above this line will lead to a higher NPV and are superior. For example, if SPI managers think they will be able to sell 90,000 units at a price of $300, this strategy would yield a higher NPV ($10,974 million).

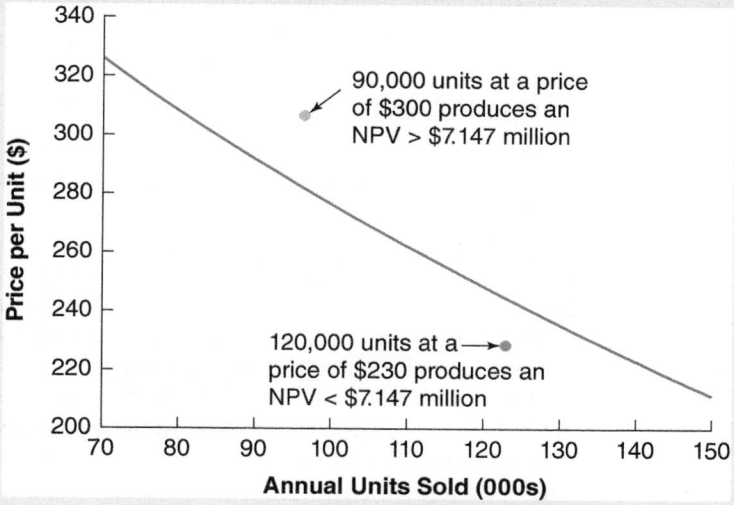

CONCEPT CHECK

9. What is sensitivity analysis?
10. How does scenario analysis differ from sensitivity analysis?

9.6 Real Options in Capital Budgeting

Our approach to capital budgeting thus far has focused on the initial investment decision without explicitly considering future decisions that may need to be made over the life of a project. Rather, we assumed that our forecast of a project's expected future cash flows already incorporated the effect of future decisions that would be made. In truth, most projects contain *real options*. A **real option** is the right, but not the obligation, to make a particular business decision. Because you are not obligated to take the action, you will do so only if it increases the NPV of the project. In particular, because real options allow a decision maker to choose the most attractive alternative after new information has been learned, the presence of real options adds value to an investment opportunity. The tools to estimate the actual value created by real options are beyond the scope of this chapter and are provided later in the book. However, we introduce the concept here to give you a sense of the types of real options you may encounter and establish the idea that flexibility (more options) is valuable. Let's look at some of the most common real options in the context of SPI's SPI Phone 86 project.

real option The right to make a particular business decision, such as a capital investment.

Option to Delay

option to delay commitment The option to time a particular investment, which is almost always present.

The **option to delay commitment** (the option to time the investment) is almost always present. SPI could wait to commit to the SPI Phone 86 project. Waiting could be valuable if SPI expects prices of the components—for example, soon-to-be-released new technology that will make the existing components obsolete—to decrease substantially. In addition, SPI may simply want more time to gather information about the potential market for the SPI Phone 86. As with any other capital budgeting decision, SPI would choose to delay only if doing so would increase the NPV of the project by more than the cost of capital over the time of delay.

Option to Expand

option to expand The option to start with limited production and expand only if the project is successful.

In the section on sensitivity analysis, we looked at changes in our assumptions about units sold. All of the analysis was performed, however, under the assumption that SPI would fully commit to and roll out the SPI Phone 86 worldwide. We did not consider the option to expand, which is the option to start with limited production and expand only if the product is successful. SPI could, instead, testmarket the product in limited release before committing to it fully. Doing so would create an **option to expand** worldwide only if the SPI Phone 86 were successful in limited release. It is possible that, by reducing its upfront commitment and choosing to expand only if the product is successful, SPI will increase the NPV of the SPI Phone 86 product. However, in this particular case, there are large costs of development that would be paid whether SPI sells one or hundreds of thousands of units, so limiting the initial market does not reduce the financial commitment substantially. Thus, in the case of the SPI Phone 86, it is unlikely that SPI would choose a limited release with an option to expand.

Option to Abandon

abandonment option An option for an investor to cease making investments in a project. Abandonment options can add value to a project because a firm can drop a project if it turns out to be unsuccessful.

An **abandonment option** is the option to walk away. Abandonment options can add value to a project because a firm can drop a project if it turns out to be unsuccessful. Imagine that a competitor developed new technology that allowed it to introduce a competing product priced at $170. At that price, SPI would produce substantially lower cash flows every year. Would SPI continue to sell the SPI Phone 86 if it had to do so at a loss? Probably not. SPI has an option to abandon the project. It could stop producing the SPI Phone 86 and sell the equipment. Depending on how much SPI believes the equipment would sell for if it abandoned the project, the abandonment option could make the SPI Phone 86 attractive even if there was a substantial risk of a competing product.

Many industries regularly make use of real options. For example, most movie producers build in an option for a sequel if the first movie does well. Pharmaceutical developers such as Merck develop new drugs in stages, allowing the company to abandon development if tests do not go well. All these options point to the same conclusion: *if you can build greater flexibility into your project, you will increase the NPV of the project.* In Chapter 13, we will discuss how to value options so that you can estimate just how much more valuable the project is with greater flexibility.

CONCEPT CHECK

11. What are real options?

12. Why do real options increase the NPV of the project?

MyLab Finance

Here is what you should know after reading this chapter. MyLab™ Finance will help you identify what you know, and where to go when you need to practice.

KEY POINTS AND EQUATIONS	TERMS	ONLINE PRACTICE OPPORTUNITIES
9.1 The Capital Budgeting Process ■ Capital budgeting is the process of analyzing investment opportunities and deciding which ones to accept. A capital budget is a list of all projects that a company plans to undertake during the next period. ■ We use the NPV rule to evaluate capital budgeting decisions, making decisions that maximize NPV. When deciding to accept or reject a project, we accept projects with a positive NPV.	capital budget, p. 302 capital budgeting, p. 302 incremental earnings, p. 303	MyLab Plan 9.1
9.2 Forecasting Incremental Earnings ■ The incremental earnings of a project comprise the amount by which the project is expected to change the firm's earnings. ■ Incremental earnings should include all incremental revenues and costs associated with the project. ■ Interest and other financing-related expenses are excluded to determine the project's unlevered net income. Incremental Unlevered Net Income $= EBIT \times (1 - \tau_c)$ $=$ (Incremental Revenue − Incremental Costs − CCA) $\times (1 - \tau_c)$ (9.5)	asset class, p. 304 asset pool, p. 305 capital cost allowance (CCA), p. 304 CCA rate, p. 304 half-year rule, p. 305 marginal corporate tax rate, p. 307 pro forma statement, p. 308 tax year, p. 304 undepreciated capital cost (UCC), p. 305 unlevered net income, p. 308	MyLab Study Plan 9.2
9.3 Determining Incremental Free Cash Flow ■ We compute free cash flow from incremental earnings by eliminating all non-cash expenses and including all capital investment. ■ Depreciation (CCA) is not cash expense, so it is added back. ■ Actual capital expenditures are deducted. ■ Increases in NWC are deducted and decreases are added. NWC is defined as Cash + Inventory + Receivables − Payables (9.6) ■ The basic calculation for free cash flow is Free Cash Flow $= \overbrace{(\text{Revenues} - \text{Costs} - CCA) \times (1 - \tau_c)}^{\text{Unlevered Net Income}}$ $+ CCA - CapEx$ $-$ Change in NWC (9.8)	CCA tax shield, p. 313 free cash flow, p. 309 trade credit, p. 311	MyLab Study Plan 9.3

KEY POINTS AND EQUATIONS	TERMS	ONLINE PRACTICE OPPORTUNITIES
9.4 Other Effects on Incremental Free Cash Flows ■ An opportunity cost is the cost of using an existing asset. ■ Project externalities are cash flows that occur when a project affects other areas of the company's business. ■ A sunk cost is an unrecoverable cost that has already been incurred or will be incurred regardless of the project's acceptance. ■ Depreciation expenses affect free cash flow only through the depreciation tax shield. ■ The discount rate for a project is its cost of capital: the expected return of securities with comparable risk and horizon. ■ When you sell an asset, the portion of the proceeds above its original price (CapEx) is taxed: Capital Gains Tax = $\frac{1}{2} \times (\text{Sale Price} - CapEx) \times \tau_c$ (9.13)	cannibalization, p. 316 capital gain tax, p. 319 continuing pool, p. 321 negative net additions, p. 321 opportunity cost, p. 315 overhead expenses, p. 316 project externalities, p. 316 sunk cost, p. 316 tax loss carryforwards and carrybacks, p. 323	MyLab Study Plan 9.4
9.5 Analyzing the Project ■ Sensitivity analysis breaks the NPV calculation down into its component assumptions, showing how the NPV varies as the values of the underlying assumptions change. ■ Break-even analysis computes the level of a parameter that makes the project's NPV equal zero. ■ Scenario analysis considers the effect of changing multiple parameters simultaneously.	break-even, p. 327 break-even analysis, p. 327 EBIT break-even, p. 327 scenario analysis, p. 327 sensitivity analysis, p. 325	MyLab Study Plan 9.5 Interactive Sensitivity Analysis, Using Excel: Performing Sensitivity Analysis
9.6 Real Options in Capital Budgeting ■ Real options are options to make a business decision, often after gathering more information. The presence of real options in a project increases the project's NPV.	abandonment option, p. 330 option to expand, p. 330 option to delay commitment, p. 330 real option, p. 329	MyLab Study Plan 9.6

REVIEW QUESTIONS

1. What are pro forma incremental earnings?
2. What is the difference between pro forma incremental earnings and pro forma free cash flow?
3. Why do we convert from incremental earnings to free cash flow when performing capital budgeting?

4. What is the role of NWC in projects?
5. How does NWC affect the cash flows of a project?
6. Why is it important to adjust project sales and costs for externalities?
7. How is sensitivity analysis performed and what is its purpose?

PROBLEMS

All problems in this chapter are available in MyLab Finance. An asterisk (*) indicates problems with a higher level of difficulty.

The Capital Budgeting Process

1. Daily Enterprises is purchasing a $10 million machine. It will cost $50,000 to transport and install the machine. The machine has a depreciable life of five years and will have no salvage value. Assume that CCA deductions are the same as depreciation expenses. If Daily uses straight-line depreciation, what are the depreciation expenses associated with this machine?
2. The machine in Problem 1 will generate incremental revenues of $4 million per year along with incremental costs of $1.2 million per year. If Daily's marginal tax rate is 35%, what are the incremental earnings associated with the new machine?
3. You are upgrading to better production equipment for your firm's only product. The new equipment will allow you to make more of your product in the same amount of time. Thus, you forecast that total sales will increase next year by 20% over the current amount of 100,000 units. If your sales price is $20 per unit, what are the incremental revenues next year from the upgrade?
4. Pisa Pizza, a seller of frozen pizza, is considering introducing a healthier version of its pizza that will be low in cholesterol and contain no trans fats. The firm expects that sales of the new pizza will be $20 million per year. While many of these sales will be to new customers, Pisa Pizza estimates that 40% will come from customers who switch to the new, healthier pizza instead of buying the original version.
   a. Assume that customers will spend the same amount on either version. What level of incremental sales is associated with introducing the new pizza?
   b. Suppose that 50% of the customers who would switch from Pisa Pizza's original pizza to its healthier pizza will switch to another brand if Pisa Pizza does not introduce a healthier pizza. What level of incremental sales is associated with introducing the new pizza in this case?
5. Kokomochi is considering the launch of an advertising campaign for its latest dessert product, the Mini Mochi Munch. Kokomochi plans to spend $5 million on TV, radio, and print advertising this year for the campaign. The ads are expected to boost sales of the Mini Mochi Munch by $9 million this year and by $7 million next year. In addition, the company expects that new consumers who try the Mini Mochi Munch will be more likely to try Kokomochi's other products. As a result, sales of other products are expected to rise by $2 million each year.

   Kokomochi's gross profit margin for the Mini Mochi Munch is 35%, and its gross profit margin averages 25% for all other products. The company's marginal corporate tax rate is 35% both this year and next year. What are the incremental earnings associated with the advertising campaign?

6. Hyperion, Inc. currently sells its latest high-speed colour printer, the Hyper 500, for $350. It plans to lower the price to $300 next year. Its cost of goods sold for the Hyper 500 is $200 per unit, and this year's sales are expected to be 20,000 units.
   a. Suppose that if Hyperion drops the price to $300 immediately it can increase this year's sales by 25%, to 25,000 units. What would be the incremental impact on this year's EBIT of such a price drop?
   b. Suppose that for each printer sold, Hyperion expects additional sales of $75 per year on ink cartridges for the next three years, and Hyperion has a gross profit margin of 70% on ink cartridges. What is the incremental impact on EBIT for the next three years of a price drop this year?

Determining Incremental Free Cash Flow

7. You are forecasting incremental free cash flows for Daily Enterprises. Based on the information in Problems 1 and 2, what are the incremental free cash flows associated with the new machine?

8. Royal Mount Games would like to invest in a division to develop software for video games. To evaluate this decision, the firm first attempts to project the working capital needs for this operation. Its chief financial officer has developed the following estimates (in millions of dollars):

1	Year	1	2	3	4	5
2	Cash	6	12	15	15	15
3	Accounts Receivable	21	22	24	24	24
4	Inventory	5	7	10	12	13
5	Accounts Payable	18	22	24	25	30

Assuming that Royal Mount Games currently does not have any working capital invested in this division, calculate the cash flows associated with changes in working capital for the first five years of this investment.

9. Anola Inc.'s projected receivables are 15% of sales and its payables are 15% of cost of goods sold (COGS). Forecast the required investment in NWC for Anola Inc. assuming that sales and COGS will be

1	Year	0	1	2	3	4
2	Sales		23,500	26,438	23,794	8566
3	COGS		9500	10,688	9619	3483

10. Etobicoke Enterprises is deciding whether to expand its production facilities. Although long-term cash flows are difficult to estimate, management has projected the following cash flows for the first two years (in millions of dollars):

1	Year	1	2
2	Revenues	125	160
3	Operating Expenses (other than depreciation)	40	60
4	CCA	25	36
5	Increase in Net Working Capital	2	8
6	Capital Expenditures	30	40
7	Marginal Corporate Tax Rate	35%	35%

   a. What are the incremental earnings for this project for years 1 and 2?
   b. What are the free cash flows for this project for the first two years?

11. Atlantic Telecom reported net income of $250 million for the most recent fiscal year. The firm had CCA deductions of $100 million (assume reported depreciation was equal to this CCA), capital expenditures of $200 million, and no interest expenses. NWC increased by $10 million. Calculate the free cash flow for Atlantic Telecom for the most recent fiscal year.

12. Recall the SPI Phone 86 example from this chapter. Suppose the SPI Phone 86s will be housed in warehouse space that the company could have otherwise rented out for $200,000 per year during years 1 to 4. How does this opportunity cost affect the SPI Phone's incremental earnings?

***13.** One year ago, your company purchased a machine used in manufacturing for $110,000. You have learned that a new machine is available that offers many advantages, and you can purchase it for $150,000 today. The CCA rate applicable to both machines is 40%; neither machine will have any long-term salvage value. You expect that the new machine will produce earnings before interest, taxes, depreciation, and amortization (EBITDA) of $40,000 per year for the next 10 years. The current machine is expected to produce EBITDA of $20,000 per year. All other expenses of the two machines are identical. The market value today of the current machine is $50,000. Your company's tax rate is 45%, and the opportunity cost of capital for this type of equipment is 10%. Should your company replace its year-old machine?

***14.** Big Rock Brewery currently rents a bottling machine for $50,000 per year, including all maintenance expenses. The company is considering purchasing a machine instead and is comparing two options:

a. Purchase for $150,000 the machine it is currently renting. This machine will require $20,000 per year in ongoing maintenance expenses.
b. Purchase a new, more advanced machine for $250,000. This machine will require $15,000 per year in ongoing maintenance expenses and will lower bottling costs by $10,000 per year. Also, $35,000 will be spent up front in training the new operators of the machine.

Suppose the appropriate discount rate is 8% per year and the machine is purchased today. Maintenance and bottling costs are paid at the end of each year, as is the rental of the machine. Assume also that the machines are subject to a CCA rate of 25% and will have negligible salvage value in 10 year's time (the end of each machine's life). The marginal corporate tax rate is 35%. Should Big Rock Brewery continue to rent, purchase its current machine, or purchase the advanced machine?

Other Effects on Incremental Free Cash Flows

15. Home Builder Supply, a retailer in the home improvement industry, currently operates seven retail outlets in the Maritimes. Management is contemplating building an eighth retail store across town from its most successful retail outlet. The company already owns the land for this store, which currently has an abandoned warehouse located on it. Last month, the marketing department spent $10,000 on market research to determine the extent of customer demand for the new store. Now Home Builder Supply must decide whether to build and open the new store.

Which of the following should be included as part of the incremental earnings for the proposed new retail store?

a. The original purchase price of the land where the store will be located.
b. The cost of demolishing the abandoned warehouse and clearing the lot.
c. The loss of sales in the existing retail outlet if customers who previously drove from Dartmouth to Halifax to shop at the existing outlet become customers of the new store instead.

d. The $10,000 in market research spent to evaluate customer demand.
e. Construction costs for the new store.
f. The value of the land if sold.
g. Interest expense on the debt borrowed to pay the construction costs.

16. Spherical Manufacturing recently spent $15 million to purchase some equipment used in the manufacture of disk drives. This equipment has a CCA rate of 25%, and Spherical's marginal corporate tax rate is 35%.

a. What are the annual CCA deductions associated with this equipment for the first five years?
b. What are the annual CCA tax shields for the first five years?
c. What is the present value of the first five CCA tax shields if the appropriate discount rate is 10% per year?
d. What is the present value of all the CCA tax shields, assuming the equipment is never sold and the appropriate discount rate is 10% per year?
e. How might your answer to part (d) change if Spherical anticipates that its marginal corporate tax rate will increase substantially over the next five years?

17. You are a manager at Northern Fibre, which is considering expanding its operations in synthetic fibre manufacturing. Your boss comes into your office, drops a consultant's report on your desk, and complains, "We owe these consultants $1 million for this report, and I am not sure their analysis makes sense. Before we spend the $25 million on new equipment needed for this project, look it over and give me your opinion." You open the report and find the following estimates (in thousands of dollars):

1	Year	1	2	. . .	9	10
2	Sales Revenue	30,000	30,000		30,000	30,000
3	Costs of Goods Sold	18,000	18,000		18,000	18,000
4	**Gross Profit**	12,000	12,000		12,000	12,000
5	General, Sales, and Administrative Expenses	2000	2000		2000	2000
6	Depreciation	2500	2500		2500	2500
7	**Net Operating Income**	7500	7500		7500	7500
8	Income Tax	2625	2625		2625	2625
9	**Net Income**	4875	4875		4875	4875

All of the estimates in the report seem correct. You note that the consultants used straight-line depreciation for the new equipment that will be purchased today (year 0), which is what the accounting department recommended. CRA allows a CCA rate of 30% on the equipment for tax purposes. The report concludes that because the project will increase earnings by $4.875 million per year for 10 years, the project is worth $48.75 million. You think back to your glory days in finance class and realize there is more work to be done!

First, you note that the consultants have not factored in that the project will require $10 million in working capital up front (year 0), which will be fully recovered in year 10. Next, you see they have attributed $2 million of selling, general, and administrative expenses to the project, but you know that $1 million of this amount is overhead that will be incurred even if the project is not accepted. Finally, you know that accounting earnings are not the right thing to focus on!

a. Given the available information, what are the free cash flows in years 0 through 10 that should be used to evaluate the proposed project?
b. If the cost of capital for this project is 14%, what is your estimate of the value of the new project?

Analyzing the Project

***18.** Buhler Industries is a farm implement manufacturer. Management is currently evaluating a proposal to build a plant that will manufacture lightweight tractors. Buhler plans to use a cost of capital of 12% to evaluate this project. Based on extensive research, it has prepared the following incremental free cash flow projections (in millions of dollars):

	Year 0	Years 1–9	Year 10
Revenues		100.0	100.0
− Manufacturing expenses (other than depreciation)		−35.0	−35.0
− Marketing expenses		−10.0	−10.0
− CCA		?	?
= EBIT		?	?
− Taxes (35%)		?	?
= Unlevered net income		?	?
+ CCA		?	?
− Increases in net working capital		−5.0	−5.0
− Capital expenditures	−150.0		
+ Continuation value			+12.0
= Free cash flow	−150.0	?	?

The relevant CCA rate for capital expenditures is 10%. Assume assets are never sold.

a. For this base-case scenario, what is the NPV of the plant to manufacture lightweight tractors?

b. Based on input from the marketing department, Buhler is uncertain about its revenue forecast. In particular, management would like to examine the sensitivity of the NPV to the revenue assumptions. What is the NPV of this project if revenues are 10% higher than forecast? What is the NPV if revenues are 10% lower than forecast?

c. Rather than assuming that cash flows for this project are constant, management would like to explore the sensitivity of its analysis to possible growth in revenues and operating expenses. Specifically, management would like to assume that revenues, manufacturing expenses, and marketing expenses are as given in the table for year 1 and grow by 2% per year every year starting in year 2. Management also plans to assume that the initial capital expenditures (and therefore CCA), additions to working capital, and continuation value remain as initially specified in the table. What is the NPV of this project under these alternative assumptions? How does the NPV change if the revenues and operating expenses grow by 5% per year rather than by 2%?

d. To examine the sensitivity of this project to the discount rate, management would like to compute the NPV for different discount rates. Create a graph, with the discount rate on the x-axis and the NPV on the y-axis, for discount rates ranging from 5% to 30%. For what ranges of discount rates does the project have a positive NPV?

***19.** Buckingham Packaging is considering expanding its production capacity by purchasing a new machine, the XC-750. The cost of the XC-750 is $2.75 million. Unfortunately, installing this machine will take several months and will partially disrupt production. The firm has just completed a $50,000 feasibility study to analyze the decision to buy the XC-750, resulting in the following estimates:

- *Marketing:* Once the XC-750 is operational next year, the extra capacity is expected to generate $10 million per year in additional sales, which will continue for the 10-year life of the machine.
- *Operations:* The disruption caused by the installation will decrease sales by $5 million this year. As with Buckingham's existing products, the cost of goods for the products produced by the XC-750 is expected to be 70% of their *sale price*. The increased production will also require increased inventory on hand of $1 million during the life of the project, including year 0.
- *Human Resources:* The expansion will require additional sales and administrative personnel at a cost of $2 million per year.
- *Accounting:* The XC-750 has a CCA rate of 30%, and no salvage value is expected. The firm expects receivables from the new sales to be 15% of revenues and payables to be 10% of the cost of goods sold. Buckingham's marginal corporate tax rate is 35%.
  a. Determine the incremental earnings (using CCA) from the purchase of the XC-750.
  b. Determine the free cash flow from the purchase of the XC-750.
  c. If the appropriate cost of capital for the expansion is 10%, compute the NPV of the purchase (including all CCA tax shield effects).
  d. While the expected new sales will be $10 million per year from the expansion, estimates range from $8 million to $12 million. What is the NPV in the worst case? In the best case?
  e. What is the break-even level of new sales from the expansion? What is the break-even level for the cost of goods sold?
  f. Buckingham could instead purchase the XC-900, which offers even greater capacity. The cost of the XC-900 is $4 million. The extra capacity would not be useful in the first two years of operation, but would allow for additional sales in years 3 to 10. What level of additional sales (above the $10 million expected for the XC-750) per year in those years would justify purchasing the larger machine?

Real Options in Capital Budgeting

20. Why is it that real options must have positive value?

21. What kind of real option does the XC-900 machine (see Problem 19) provide to Buckingham?

22. If Buckingham (see Problem 19) knows that it can sell the XC-750 to another firm for $2 million in two years, what kind of real option would that provide?

DATA CASE

You have just been hired by Intel in its finance division. Your first assignment is to determine the net cash flows and NPV of a proposed new generation of mobile chips.

Capital expenditures to produce the new chips will initially require an investment of $1.2 billion. The R&D that will be required to finish the chips is $500 million this year. Any ongoing R&D for upgrades will be covered in the margin calculation in Question 2(a) below. The product family is expected to have a life of five years. First-year revenues for the new chip are expected to be $2,000,000,000 ($2,000 million). The chip family's revenues are expected to grow by 20% for the second year, decrease by 10% for the third, decrease by 20% for the fourth, and finally decrease by 50% for the fifth (final) year of sales. Your job is to determine the rest of the cash flows associated with this project. Your boss has indicated that the operating costs and net working capital requirements are similar.

1. Obtain Intel's financial statements. Download the annual income statements and balance sheets for the last four fiscal years from Yahoo! Finance (https://finance.yahoo.com/). Enter Intel's ticker symbol (INTC) and then go to "Financials." Click "Annual," to ensure you're getting annual, instead of quarterly, data. Next, copy and paste the income statements and balance sheets into Excel.
2. You are now ready to determine the free cash flow. Compute the free cash flow for each year using Eq. 9.8 from this chapter (with depreciation replacing CCA for the U.S. company):

$$\text{Free Cash Flow} = \overbrace{(\text{Revenues} - \text{Costs} - \text{Depreciation}) \times (1 - \text{tax rate})}^{\text{Unlevered Net Income}} + \text{Depreciation} - \text{CapEx} - \text{Change in NWC}$$

   Set up the timeline and computation of the free cash flow in separate, contiguous columns for each year of the project life. Be sure to make outflows negative and inflows positive.

   a. Assume that the project's profitability will be similar to Intel's existing projects in 2015 and estimate costs each year by using the 2015 ratio of non-depreciation costs to revenue:

   (Cost of Revenue + SG&A + R&D)/ Total Revenue

   You should assume that this ratio will hold for this project as well. You do not need to break out the individual components of operating costs in your forecast. Simply forecast the total of Cost of Revenue + SG&A + R&D for each year.

   b. Determine the annual depreciation by assuming Intel depreciates these assets by the straight-line method over a 5-year life.

   c. Determine Intel's tax rate as [1 - (Income After Tax/Income Before Tax)] in 2015. Note that on Intel's income statement on Google Finance, there is a difference between operating income and income before tax. That difference is due to small adjustments. Ignore this issue and simply focus on the Income Before Tax line.

   d. Calculate the net working capital required each year by assuming that the level of NWC will be a constant percentage of the project's sales. Use Intel's 2015 NWC/Sales to estimate the required percentage. (Use only accounts receivable, accounts payable, and inventory to measure working capital. Other components of current assets and liabilities are harder to interpret and are not necessarily reflective of the project's required NWC—e.g., Intel's cash holdings.)

   e. To determine the free cash flow, calculate the additional capital investment and the change in net working capital each year.

3. Determine the IRR of the project and the NPV of the project at a cost of capital of 12% using the Excel functions. For the calculation of NPV, include cash flows 1 through 5 in the NPV function and then subtract the initial cost

   (i.e., = NPV(rate, CF_1:CF_5) + CF_0). For IRR, include cash flows 0 through 5 in the cash flow range.

CHAPTER 9 APPENDIX USING EXCEL FOR CAPITAL BUDGETING

In this appendix, we illustrate how to build a pro forma statement and perform a sensitivity analysis in Excel.

Building a Pro Forma Statement

The key to frustration-free capital budgeting is to base your analysis on a spreadsheet containing a flexible model of the project's pro forma free cash flows.

List Assumptions

Start by creating a box in the spreadsheet with all of your assumptions, shown here shaded in grey:

D18 =B2*B3

	A	B	C	D
1	**Assumptions**			
2	Unit Sales (thousands)	100		
3	Sales Price ($/unit)	260		
4	Cost of Goods ($/unit)	110		
5	NWC ($ thousands)	2250		
6	Selling, General, and Ac	2800		
7	Research and Developı	15000		
8	Cost of Capital	12%		
9				

Although this step will take you a little more time up front, it has two advantages. First, you are forced to present all of your major assumptions clearly, so you can see the drivers of your analysis. Second, setting them apart this way makes it far easier to change your assumptions later and quickly see the impact on the incremental free cash flows.

Base Cell Formulas on Assumptions

Once you have listed all of your assumptions, it is time to build the pro forma statement by referring back to the cells containing your assumptions. Here, we will show how to build the first year's pro forma cash flows. For example, rather than entering $26,000 into the Sales line of year 1, you will enter the formula shown in the screen shot.

D18 ⇕ × ✓ *fx* =B2*B3

	A	B	C	D
1	**Assumptions**			
2	Unit Sales (thousands)	100		
3	Sales Price ($/unit)	260		
4	Cost of Goods ($/unit)	110		
5	NWC ($ thousands)	2250		
6	Selling, General, and A(	2800		
7	Research and Develop	15000		
8	Cost of Capital	12%		
9				

This formula is simply the cell-referenced version of our calculation from the initial SPI Phone 86 information earlier in this chapter: Unit Sold × Price Per Unit = 100 × $260 = $26,000. As you can see from the screen shot, we have referred back to our assumptions box for each of these inputs (unit sales and sales price). Look at the formula bar at the top of the screen shot to see the cell references. Later, if we want to change the assumption for price per unit, we can change it in our assumptions box and it will automatically change the calculation for Sales in year 1.

To complete the pro forma statement for year 1, we continue down the column. Each time we need to draw on an assumed number, we refer back to our assumptions box. For calculations such as gross profit, we simply refer to the cells in the column: summing sales and the negative cost of goods sold. Formulas used in column D to calculate year 1 amounts are displayed in column E.

As you can imagine, building a pro forma statement like this greatly eases our analysis of the effects of changes in our assumptions. In the next section, we will show how to use a spreadsheet similar to the one we just constructed to perform sensitivity analysis.

	A	B	C	D	E
1	**Assumptions**				
2	Unit Sales (thousands)	100			
3	Sales Price ($/unit)	260			
4	Cost of Goods ($/unit)	110			
5	NWC ($ thousands)	2250			
6	Selling, General, and Admin ($ thousands)	2800			
7	Research and Development ($ thousands)	15000			
8	Cost of capital	12%			
9					
10					
11					
12					
13					
14					
15					
16		Year	0	1	Formula in Year 1
17					
18	Sales		-	26,000	=+$B$2*$B$3
19	Cost of Goods Sold		-	(11,000)	=+$B$2*-$B$4
20	Gross Profit		-	15,000	=E18+E19
21	Selling, General, and Administrative		-	(2,800)	=-$B$6
22	Research and Development		(15,000)	-	-
23	Capital Cost Allowance (CCA)		-	(1,688)	=-$C$29*.50*.45
24	EBIT		(15,000)	10,513	=SUM(E20:E23)
25	Income Tax at 40%		6,000	(4,205)	=-0.4*E24
26	Unlevered Net Income		(9,000)	6,308	=SUM(E24:E25)
27					
28	Plus: CCA		-	1,688	=-E23
29	Les: Capital Expenditures		(7,500)		
30	Less: Increases in NWC		-	(2,250)	=-C5
31	Free Cash Flow		(16,500)	5,745	=SUM(E26:E30)
32					

Performing Sensitivity Analysis

Rather than recalculating the SPI Phone 86's NPV for each possible number of units sold, we can use Excel's Data Table tool. In Chapter 8, we used the Data Table tool to construct an NPV profile. Recall that a data table shows us how the outcome of a formula (such as the NPV of the SPI Phone 86) changes when we change one of the cells in the spreadsheet (such as the number of units sold). Previously, we showed how to build a pro forma statement of the SPI Phone 86 using Excel that would make it easy to change our assumptions later. That is exactly what we do in sensitivity analysis:

	A	B	C	D	E	F	G	H
1	**Assumptions**			**Sensitivity:**	**Units Sold**	**7,147**		
2	Unit Sales (thousands)	100			60	(3,787)		
3	Sales Price ($/unit)	260			70	(1,053)		
4	Cost of Goods ($/unit)	110			80	1,680		
5	NWC ($ thousands)	2250			90	4,414		
6	Selling, General, and Admin ($ thousands)	2800			100	7,147		
7	Research and Development ($ thousands)	15000			110	9,881		
8	Cost of capital	12%			120	12,615		
9					130	15,348		
10								
11								
12								
13								
14								
15								
16		Year	0	1	2	3	4	5
17								
18	Sales		-	26,000	26,000	26,000	26,000	-
19	Cost of Goods Sold		-	(11,000)	(11,000)	(11,000)	(11,000)	-
20	Gross Profit		-	15,000	15,000	15,000	15,000	-
21	Selling, General, and Administrative		-	(2,800)	(2,800)	(2,800)	(2,800)	-
22	Research and Development		(15,000)	-	-	-	-	-
23	Capital Cost Allowance (CCA)		-	(1,688)	(2,816)	(1,439)	(791)	(435)
24	EBIT		(15,000)	10,513	9,584	10,761	11,409	(435)
25	Income Tax at 40%		6,000	(4,205)	(3,834)	(4,305)	(4,564)	174
26	Unlevered Net Income		(9,000)	6,308	5,751	6,457	6,845	(261)
27								
28	Plus: CCA		-	1,688	2,816	1,439	791	435
29	Les: Capital Expenditures		(7,500)					
30	Less: Increases in NWC		-	(2,250)	-	-	-	2,250
31	Free Cash Flow		(16,500)	5,745	8,366	7,895	7,636	2,424
32								
33	NPV		7,147					

change our assumptions and see how the NPV changes. This screen shot shows a completed Excel pro forma statement of the incremental free cash flows of the SPI Phone 86 project. It also shows the NPV calculation and a data table (outlined in red) for our assumption on Units Sold:

To set up the data table, we first create a cell that simply repeats the NPV. In this case, cell F1 is set to equal cell C33 to create a new NPV column. Next, we create the column that will contain the different assumptions of Units Sold. This column must be directly to the left of the NPV cell (F1). We fill in the different values we want to incorporate into the NPV calculation directly below the "Units Sold" heading. Finally, we highlight the Units Sold and NPV columns (at this point, the NPV column is blank with the exception of the first row in our table), and select "Table" from the "Data" menu.

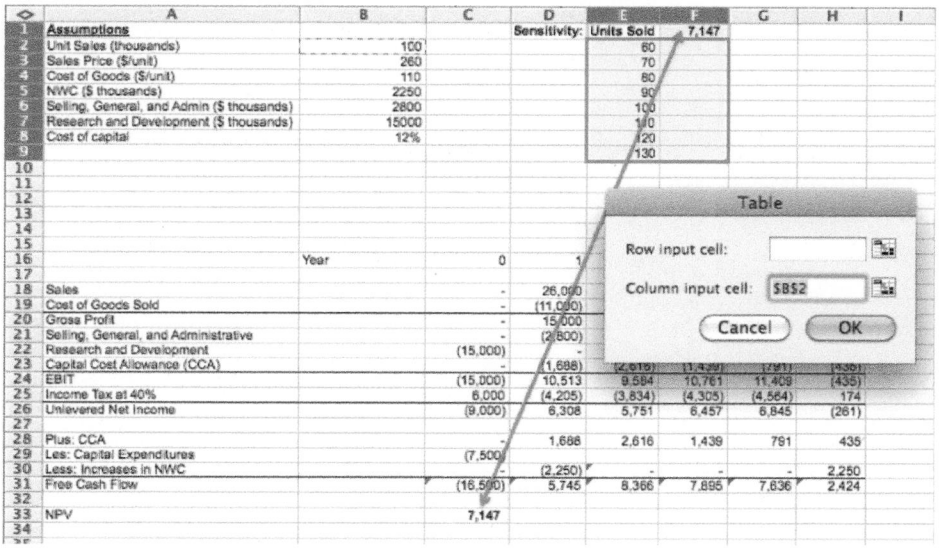

As the screen shot shows, the Table input box will appear. Since our Units Sold assumptions are in a column, we enter, into the column input cell (not the row input cell), the cell in our spreadsheet containing the base-case Units Sold assumption (B2). Once we do this and hit "Enter", Excel will create the sensitivity table shown in the first screen shot. We could now create an NPV profile based on the differing quantities of units sold.

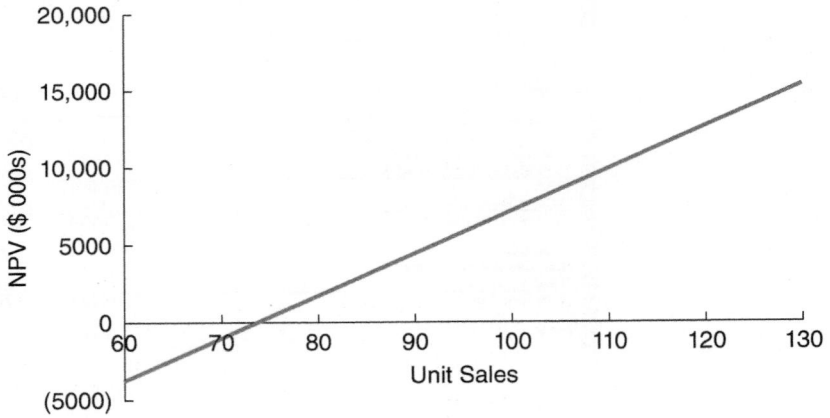

PART

Integrative Case 3

This case draws on material from this and earlier chapters.

CASE 1

Nanovo, Inc., is a manufacturer of low-cost micro batteries for use in a wide variety of compact electronic devices such as children's toys, wireless transmitters, and sensors. Growth in the use of these devices has steadily increased, leading to an ever greater demand for Nanovo's products. Nanovo has responded to this increase in demand by expanding its production capacity, more than doubling the firm's size over the past decade. Despite this growth, however, Nanovo does not have sufficient capacity to meet the current demand for its ultra-long-life, low-voltage batteries. You have been asked to evaluate two proposals to expand one of Nanovo's existing plants, and to make a recommendation.

Proposal 1

The current plant has a capacity of 25,000 cases per month. The first proposal is for a major expansion that would double the plant's current capacity to 50,000 cases per month. After talking with the firm's design engineers, sales managers, and plant operators, you have prepared the following estimates:

- Expanding the plant will require the purchase of $3.6 million in new equipment, and entail upfront design and engineering expenses of $3.9 million. These costs will be paid immediately when the expansion begins.
- Installing the new equipment and redesigning the plant to accommodate the higher capacity will require shutting down the plant for nine months. During that time, the plant's production will cease. After the expansion is finished, the plant will operate at double its original capacity.
- Marketing and selling the additional volume will lead to $1 million per year in additional sales, marketing, and administrative costs. These costs will begin in the first year (even while the plant is under construction and shut down).

Proposal 2

The engineers have put forth a second proposal for a minor expansion that will increase the firm's capacity by only 50%, to 37,500 cases per month. While the capacity is smaller, such an expansion would be cheaper and less disruptive:

- The smaller expansion will require only $2.4 million in new equipment and $1.5 million in design and engineering expenses.

- The existing plant will need to be shut down for only four months.
- Sales, marketing, and administrative costs will increase by only $500,000.

Nanovo believes that with or without any expansion, the technology used at the plant will be obsolete after six years and will have no salvage value, and the plant itself will need to be completely overhauled at that time. You also have the following additional general information:

- With or without either proposed expansion, Nanovo will be able to sell all it can produce at an average wholesale price of $80 per case. This price is not expected to change during the next six years.
- Nanovo has a gross profit margin of 55% on these batteries.
- Nanovo's average net working capital at the end of each year will equal 15% of its annual revenue.
- Nanovo pays a 40% corporate tax rate.
- While all design and engineering costs are immediately deductible as operating expenses, all capital expenditures will be straight-line depreciated for tax purposes over the subsequent six years.

Management believes the risk of the expansion is similar to the risk of Nanovo's existing projects, and because Nanovo is all equity financed, the risk of the expansion is also similar to the risk of Nanovo stock. You have the following additional information about the stock:

- Nanovo has no debt and has 2 million shares outstanding. The firm's current share price is $75 per share.
- Analysts are expecting Nanovo to pay a $3 dividend at the end of this year and to raise its dividend at an average rate of 8% per year in the future.

Based on this information, you have been tasked with preparing expansion recommendations for Nanovo. (Using Excel is optional but recommended.)

CASE QUESTIONS

1. Determine the annual incremental free cash flow associated with each expansion proposal relative to the status quo (no expansion).
2. Compute the IRR and payback period of each expansion proposal. Which plan has a higher IRR? Which has a shorter payback period?
3. Estimate Nanovo's equity cost of capital. Use it to determine the NPV associated with each expansion proposal. Which plan has a higher NPV?
4. Should Nanovo expand the plant? If so, which proposal should Nanovo adopt? Explain.
5. Suppose Nanovo decides to do the major expansion. If investors are not expecting this expansion, and if they agree with the forecasts above, how will the stock price change when the expansion is announced?
6. Suppose Nanovo announces the major expansion and the stock price reacts as in Question 5. Nanovo then issues new shares at this price to cover the upfront free cash flow required to launch the expansion, and thereafter pays out as dividends the total amount it expected to pay prior to the expansion plus the additional free cash flow associated with the expansion. What dividend per share will Nanovo pay over the next eight years? What is the fair price today for Nanovo stock given these dividends?

PART

Return, Risk, and the Cost of Capital

4

CHAPTER 10 Risk and Return in Capital Markets
CHAPTER 11 Systematic Risk and the Equity Risk Premium
CHAPTER 12 Determining the Cost of Capital
CHAPTER 13 Risk and the Pricing of Options

Valuation Principle Connection. To apply the Valuation Principle, we must be able to discount the future costs and benefits of a decision. To do so, we need a discount rate that should reflect the risk, or uncertainty, surrounding those future costs and benefits. Our objective in this part of the book is to explain how to measure and compare risks across investment opportunities and use that knowledge to determine a discount rate, or cost of capital, for each investment opportunity. Chapter 10 introduces the key insight that investors demand a risk premium only for risk they cannot remove themselves without cost by diversifying their portfolios. Hence, only non-diversifiable risk will matter when comparing investment opportunities. In Chapter 11, we quantify this idea, leading to the Capital Asset Pricing Model (CAPM), the central model of financial economics that quantifies what an equivalent risk is and in doing so provides the relationship between risk and return. In Chapter 12, we apply what we have learned to estimate a company's overall cost of capital. In Chapter 13, we discuss options, their pricing, and what affects their value.

CHAPTER

10 Risk and Return in Capital Markets

LEARNING OBJECTIVES

- Identify which types of securities have historically had the highest returns and which have been the most volatile
- Compute the average return and volatility of returns from a set of historical asset prices
- Understand the trade-off between risk and return for large portfolios versus individual stocks
- Describe the difference between common and independent risk
- Explain how diversified portfolios remove independent risk, leaving common risk as the only risk requiring a risk premium

NOTATION

Div_t	dividend paid on date t
P_t	price on date t
R_t	realized or total return of a security from date $t-1$ to t
$\overline{R}$	average return
$SD(R)$	standard deviation of return R
$Var(R)$	variance of return R

Between January 2012 and December 2017, investors in Barrick Gold Corporation earned a total return of –60.6%, which equates to a compounded annual return of about –14.4%. Within this period there was significant variation in Barrick's stock price changes, with the one-month stock price change ranging from –33.45% in April 2013 to 37.70% in April 2016. Over the same period, WestJet Airlines' total return was 124.15%, and this equates to about 14.40% per year. WestJet's monthly stock price changes ranged from a low of –12.78% in July 2015 to a high of 15.35% in March 2016. Finally, investors in three-month Government of Canada treasury bills earned a total return of 4.54% over that six-year period, or an effective annual return of about 0.74%. The treasury bill monthly returns were as low as 0.02% in September 2017 and as high as 0.13% in January 2015. Clearly, these three investments offered returns that were very different in terms of their average level and their variability.[1] What accounts for these differences?

[1]Returns for fixed income securities gathered from the Canadian Financial Markets Research Centre (CFMRC) Database. Returns for Barrick Gold Corporation and WestJet Airlines gathered from Thomson Reuters Datastream.

In this chapter, our goal is to develop an understanding of how risk relates to return. In the previous three chapters, we established that value in projects, and hence in the firm, is determined by the present value of free cash flows. Up until now, we have focused on how to forecast and discount those cash flows. In this chapter and the two that follow, we turn our attention to the discount rate. As we have emphasized, the discount rate should be our cost of capital, and our cost of capital is determined by the risk of the project. But how exactly do we measure risk, and how does a particular level of risk imply a specific cost of capital?

We will see how holding many assets together affects our risk exposure. In the next chapter, we will build on this foundation to develop a theory that explains how to determine the cost of capital for any investment opportunity. Finally, in Chapter 12, we will apply what we have learned about the relationship between risk and return to the cost of capital for a company as a whole.

We begin our investigation of the relationship between risk and return by looking at historical data for publicly traded securities. We will see, for example, that while stocks are riskier investments than bonds, stocks have also earned higher average annual returns. We interpret the higher average return on stocks versus bonds as compensation to investors for the greater risk they are taking. But we will also find that not all risk needs to be compensated. By holding a portfolio of many different investments, investors can eliminate risks that are specific to individual securities. Only risks that cannot be eliminated by holding a large portfolio determine the risk premium investors will require.

10.1 A First Look at Risk and Return

Suppose your great-grandparents had invested only $100 on your behalf at the beginning of 1957, and they instructed their broker to reinvest any dividends or interest earned in the account until the end of 2017. How would that $100 have grown if it were invested in one of the following investments?

1. S&P/TSX Composite Index: A portfolio, constructed by Standard & Poor's (S&P), of the largest, most-liquid stocks and income trust units traded on the Toronto Stock Exchange (TSX). As of January 2018, the index comprises 250 firms with market capitalizations averaging about $9.74 billion and ranging from about $335 million to over $153 billion.
2. Standard & Poor's 500 (S&P 500) Index: A portfolio, constructed by Standard & Poor's, including 90 U.S. stocks up to 1957 and 500 U.S. stocks after that. The firms represented are leaders in their respective industries and are among the largest firms in terms of market capitalization (share price times the number of shares in the hands of the shareholders) traded on U.S. markets. At the end of January 31, 2018, the average market capitalization of each firm was about $50.1 billion and ranged from about $2.6 billion to $859.6 billion. The CAD$100 initial investment is first converted into U.S. dollars and then invested in the S&P 500 index. The value of the investment is converted back into Canadian dollars each month in order to calculate returns from the perspective of a Canadian investor.[2]
3. Long-term Government of Canada bonds: These bonds have maturities of approximately 30 years.
4. Government of Canada treasury bills: These represent an investment in three-month Government of Canada Treasury Bills.

[2]Information for the S&P indices (S&P/TSX and S&P500) is drawn from McGraw-Hill index fact sheets.

FIGURE 10.1 **Value of $100 Invested at the Beginning of 1957 in the S&P/TSX Composite Index, the S&P 500, Long-Term Government of Canada Bonds, and Canadian Treasury Bills**

Note that the investments that performed the best in the long run also had the greatest fluctuations from year to year. The change in the consumer price index (CPI) is shown as a reference point.

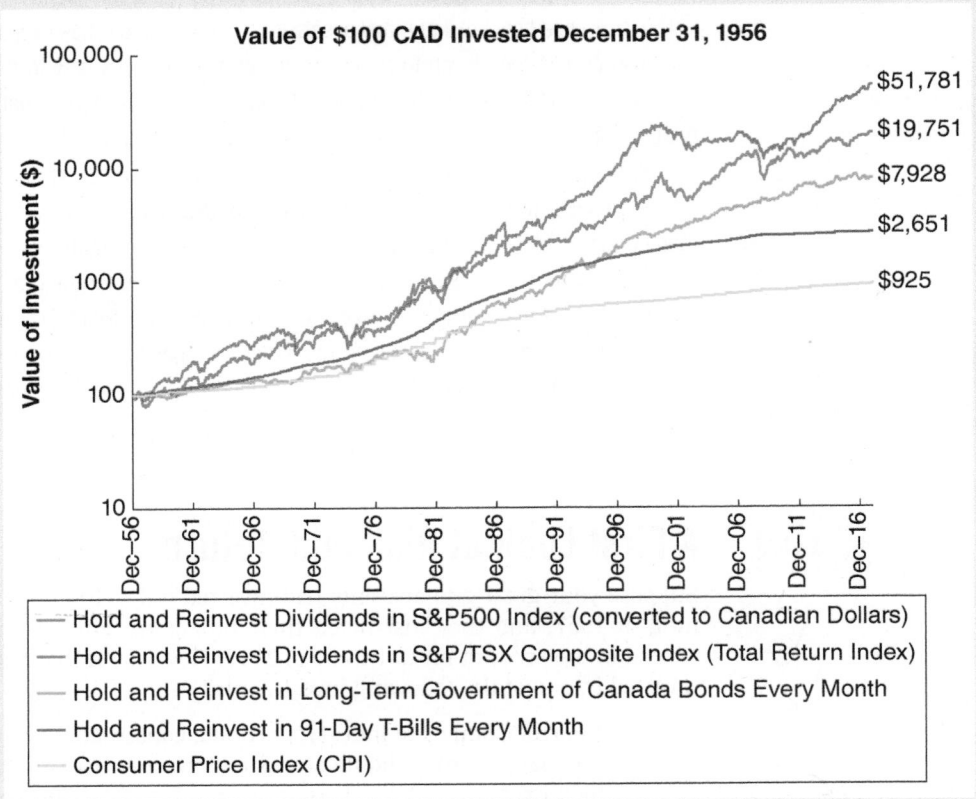

Source: Canadian Financial Markets Research Centre (CFMRC) Database, Center for Research in Security Prices (CRSP), and Statistics Canada.

Figure 10.1 shows the result, through the end of 2017, of investing $100 at the beginning of 1957 for each of these four different investment portfolios. The results are striking—had your grandparents invested $100 in the S&P/TSX portfolio, the investment would have been worth over $19,751 at the end of 2017! On the other hand, if they had invested in treasury bills, the investment would have been worth only $2651.

For comparison, consider how prices have changed during the same period relative to the CPI, the bottom line in Figure 10.1. Over some of the period from 1957 to 2017, smaller stocks (represented by the S&P/TSX Composite Index) experienced higher returns. However, the S&P/TSX is less diversified than the S&P 500 Index and we see that the U.S. index, S&P 500, had higher returns and lower risk (measured by standard deviation of returns) than Canada's S&P/TSX Composite Index. Treasury bills have the smallest fluctuations in value, but their growth over the period was also the least. All of the investments grew faster than inflation (as measured by the CPI).

There is a second pattern evident in Figure 10.1. While the stock indices (S&P/TSX Composite Index and S&P 500 Index) performed the best in the long run, their values also experienced large fluctuations. For example, if your parents had invested $2000 in the S&P/TSX Composite Index in August 1987 the investment would have grown to about $ 17,544 by the end of 2017. In contrast, had your parents invested in long-term Government of Canada bonds, the $2000 investment would have grown to almost $25,672 by the end of 2017 because it would have avoided the major drops caused by the market crash of October 1987 and the downturns in 1998 and 2008. Over the entire time frame from 1957 to 2017, there were some months when the S&P/TSX Composite Index dropped by as much as 22.5% and rose by as much as 16.5% (in one month); its average return was about 0.82% per month. Compare this to Canadian treasury bills that at their worst returned about 0% in a month but at their best returned about 1.9% in a month; their average return was about 0.45% per month.

Because investors are averse to fluctuations in the value of their investments, riskier investments offer higher expected returns. But even more importantly, when times are bad, investors do not like to have their problems further compounded by experiencing losses on their investments. In fact, even if your grandparents had actually put the $100 into the S&P/TSX Composite Index in 1957 it is unlikely you would have received the proceeds. More likely, in the depths of various recessions, your grandparents would have turned to their investments to supplement their income. Recessions occurred in the early 1980s and early 1990s. The S&P/TSX Composite Index dropped over 30% between 1980 and 1982, and declined over 20% in the first 10 months of 1990. So, to make matters worse, at the time your grandparents would need to draw on their investments the value of them had dropped significantly.

During the financial crisis of 2008, many people faced similar difficulties. The S&P/TSX dropped over 37% in the final seven months of 2008. Many investors who had all their retirement money invested in stocks saw close to half their retirement income evaporate in a matter of months. Over the previous years, these individuals enjoyed large gains in their retirement portfolios. However, these high returns came at a cost—the risk of large losses in a downturn. Many investors faced a double whammy: an increased risk of being unemployed (as firms started laying off employees) precisely when the value of their savings eroded.

We have established the general principle that investors do not like risk and, therefore, demand a risk premium to bear it. Our goal in this chapter is to further understand that because investors can eliminate some risk by holding large portfolios of stocks, not all risk is entitled to a risk premium. To show this, we must first develop tools that will allow us to measure risk and return.

- Portfolio investments higher risk higher return

CONCEPT CHECK

1. Historically, which types of investments have had the highest average returns, and which have been the most volatile from year to year? Is there a relation?
2. Why do investors demand a higher return when investing in riskier securities?

↳ because they want a risk premium if the investor high risk

10.2 Historical Risks and Returns of Stocks

In this section, we explain how to compute average returns and a measure of risk, or volatility, using historical stock market data. The distribution of past returns can be useful in estimating the possible future returns for investors. We start by first explaining how to compute historical returns.

Computing Historical Returns

realized return The total return on an investment that occurs over a particular time period.

We begin with *realized returns* for an individual investment and a portfolio. The **realized return** is the total return that occurs over a particular time period.

Individual Investment Realized Return. Suppose you invested $10 in a stock a month ago. Today, it paid a dividend of $0.50 and you then sold it for $11. What was your return? Your return came from two sources: the dividend and the change in price. You earned $0.50 on your \$10 investment through the dividend for a return of \$0.50/\$10 = 5%, and you earned \$1 from the increase in price for a return of \$1/\$10, or 10%. Your total return was 15%:

$$\text{Return} = \frac{\$0.50}{\$10} + \frac{(\$11 - \$10)}{\$10} = 5\% + 10\% = 15\%$$

In general, assume you buy a stock on date t for the price on that date, P_t. If the stock pays a dividend, Div_{t+1}, on date $t + 1$, and you sell the stock at that time for price P_{t+1}, then the timeline of your cash flows for the stock looks like this:

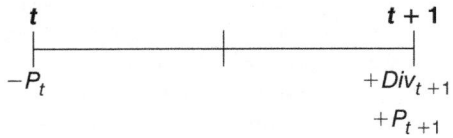

The realized return from your investment in the stock from t to $t + 1$ is

$$R_{t+1} = \frac{Div_{t+1} + P_{t+1} - P_t}{P_t} = \frac{Div_{t+1}}{P_t} + \frac{P_{t+1} - P_t}{P_t} \tag{10.1}$$

$$= \text{Dividend Yield} + \text{Capital Gain Yield}$$

EXAMPLE 10.1 Realized Return

PROBLEM

Barrick Gold Corp. stock (ticker symbol: ABX.TO) paid a dividend of \$0.03 on February 24, 2017. (*Note*: Barrick pays dividends in U.S. dollars [USD], but Canadian financial websites such as Yahoo!Finance Canada (ca.finance.yahoo.com) report the dividends in Canadian dollars [CAD] when one uses Barrick's Toronto Stock Exchange ticker symbol ABX.TO instead of the New York Stock Exchange symbol ABX.) Suppose you bought Barrick stock for \$21.49 on December 30, 2016, and sold it immediately after the dividend was paid for \$25.59. What was your realized return from holding the stock?

SOLUTION

Plan

We can use Equation 10.1 to calculate the realized return. Knowing the purchase price (\$21.49), the selling price (\$25.59), and the dividend (\$0.03), we are ready to proceed.

Execute

Using Equation 10.1, the return from December 30, 2016, until February 24, 2017, is equal to

$$R_{t+1} = \frac{Div_{t+1} + P_{t+1} - P_t}{P_t} = \frac{0.03 + 25.59 - 21.49}{21.49} = 0.192, \quad \text{or} \quad 19.2\%$$

This 19.2% can be broken down into the dividend yield and the capital gain yield:

$$\text{Div Yield} = \frac{Div_{t+1}}{P_t} = \frac{0.03}{21.49} = 0.001, \quad \text{or} \quad 0.1\%$$

$$\text{Capital Gain Yield} = \frac{P_{t+1} - P_t}{P_t} = \frac{(25.59 - 21.49)}{21.49} = 0.191, \text{ or } 19.1\%$$

Evaluate

These returns include both the capital gain (or in some cases, a capital loss) and the return generated from receiving dividends. Both dividends and capital gains contribute to the total realized return—ignoring either one would give a very misleading impression of Barrick's performance.

Your realized return for the period from t to $t + 1$ is the total of the dividend yield and the capital gain (as a percentage of the initial price); as discussed in Chapter 7, it is also called the total return. For each dollar invested at date t, you will have $1 + R_{t+1}$ at date $t + 1$. We can compute the total return for any security in the same way by replacing the dividend payments with any cash flows paid by the security (e.g., with a bond, coupon payments would replace dividends).

If you hold the stock beyond the date of the first dividend, then to compute your return we must specify how you invest any dividends you receive in the interim. To focus on the returns of a single security, we assume that *all dividends are immediately reinvested and used to purchase additional shares of the same stock or security*. In this case, we can use Equation 10.1 to compute a stock's return between dividend payments and then compound the returns from each dividend interval to compute the return over a longer horizon. If a stock pays dividends at the end of each quarter, with realized returns $R_1, \ldots, R_4$ each quarter, then we show the four quarterly returns for this stock as

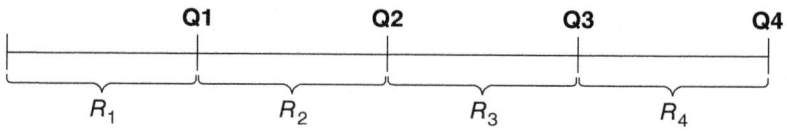

Its annual realized return, R_{annual}, is

$$1 + R_{annual} = (1 + R_1)(1 + R_2)(1 + R_3)(1 + R_4) \tag{10.2}$$

EXAMPLE 10.2 Compounding Realized Returns

PROBLEM

Suppose you purchased Barrick Gold Corp. stock (ticker symbol: ABX.TO, we will use ABX for short) on December 30, 2016, and held it for one year, selling on January 2, 2018. What was your realized return?

SOLUTION

Plan

We need to analyze the cash flows from holding ABX stock for each quarter. In order to obtain the cash flows, we must look up ABX stock price data at the start and end of both years, as well as at any dividend dates. (See Chapter 7 and the textbook's website for online sources of stock price and dividend data.) From the data, we can construct the following table to fill out our cash flow timeline:

Date	Price ($)	Dividend ($)
30-Dec-16	$21.49	
24-Feb-17	$25.59	$0.03
29-May-17	$22.07	$0.03
29-Aug-17	$22.27	$0.03
29-Nov-17	$18.05	$0.03
02-Jan-18	$19.01	

Source: Barrick Gold Corp. and Yahoo!Finance Canada.

Next, compute the return between each set of dates using Equation 10.1. Then, determine each annual return in a way similar to that shown in Equation 10.2, by compounding the returns for all of the periods in that year.

Execute

In Example 10.1, we already computed the realized return for December 30, 2016, to February 24, 2017, as 19.2%. We continue as in that example, using Equation 10.1 for each period until we have a series of realized returns. For example, from August 29, 2017, to November 29, 2017, the realized return is

$$R_{t+1} = \frac{Div_{t+1} + P_{t+1} - P_t}{P_t} = \frac{0.03 + (18.05 - 22.27)}{22.27} = -0.188, \quad \text{or} \quad -18.8\%$$

We then determine the one-year return by compounding.

Note that to use the method in Equation 10.2, we must have an investment to compound, so just as in Chapter 4, when we compounded interest, we add 1 as if we are computing the outcome of investing $1. The first return is 19.2%, giving us 1 + (0.192), or 1.192. The same is true when the return is negative: the second to last return (see table below) is −18.8%, giving us 1 + (−0.188), or 0.812. To compute our final compound return, we simply subtract the initial $1, leaving only the return:

$$1 + R_{Annual} = (1 + R_1)(1 + R_2)(1 + R_3)(1 + R_4)(1 + R_5)$$

$$1 + R_{Annual} = (1.192)(0.864)(1.010)(0.812)(1.053) = 0.89$$

$$R_{Annual} = 0.89 - 1 = -0.11 \quad \text{or} \quad -11\%$$

The table below includes the realized return in each period.

Date	Price ($)	Dividend ($)	Return
30-Dec-16	$21.49		
24-Feb-17	$25.59	$0.03	19.2%
29-May-17	$22.07	$0.03	−13.6%
29-Aug-17	$22.27	$0.03	1.0%
29-Nov-17	$18.05	$0.03	−18.8%
02-Jan-18	$19.01		5.3%
Annual Return over 2017:			−11.0%

Evaluate

By repeating these steps, we have successfully computed the realized annual returns for an investor holding ABX stock over this period. From this exercise, we can see that returns are risky: ABX lost 11% of its value in a single year.

It is unlikely that anyone investing in Barrick on December 30, 2016, expected to receive exactly the realized return we calculated in Example 10.2. In any given year, we observe only one actual realized return from all of the possible returns that could have been realized. However, we can observe realized returns over many years. The realized returns for the S&P/TSX Composite Index are shown in Table 10.1, which for comparison purposes also lists the returns for Barrick Gold Corp. and for treasury bills.

Once we have calculated the realized annual returns, we can compare them to see which investments performed better in a given year. From Table 10.1, we can see that Barrick stock outperformed the S&P/TSX Composite Index in 2008, 2010, and 2016.

TABLE 10.1 Realized Return for the S&P/TSX Composite Index, Barrick Gold Corp., and Treasury Bills, 2008–2017

Year End	S&P TSX Composite Index	Barrick Gold Corp. Return	Treasury Bill Return
2008	–33.00%	7.01%	3.11%
2009	35.05%	–7.27%	0.53%
2010	17.61%	28.12%	0.39%
2011	–8.71%	–13.12%	0.95%
2012	7.19%	–24.55%	0.92%
2013	12.99%	–46.27%	0.98%
2014	10.55%	–33.08%	0.89%
2015	–8.32%	–18.21%	0.60%
2016	21.08%	109.86%	0.50%
2017	9.10%	–15.40%	0.56%
Average	6.35%	–1.29%	0.94%
Variance	0.0359	0.1947	0.0001
Standard Deviation	18.94%	44.13%	0.79%

Source: Canadian Financial Markets Research Centre (CFMRC) Database., Yahoo!Finance Canada.

In 2011 and 2015, treasury bills performed better than both Barrick stock and the S&P/TSX Composite Index.

Over any particular period, we observe realized returns for different types of securities. By counting the number of times the realized return falls within a particular range, we can start to graph the distribution of possible returns. Let's illustrate this process with the data in Figure 10.1.

To arrive at Figure 10.2, we plot the monthly returns for each investment in Figure 10.1 in a histogram. In this histogram, the height of each bar represents the number of months that the returns were in each range indicated on the x-axis. Notice how much more variable stock returns are compared with Canada treasury bills.

Average Annual Returns

average annual return
The arithmetic average of an investment's realized returns for each year.

Out of the distribution of possible returns for each security depicted in Figure 10.2, we want to know the most likely return, represented by the average. The **average annual return** of an investment during some historical period is simply the average of the realized returns for each year. That is, if R_t is the realized return of a security in each year, t, then the average annual return for years 1 through T is

Average Annual Return of a Security

$$\overline{R} = \frac{1}{T}(R_1 + R_2 + \cdots + R_T) \tag{10.3}$$

If we assume that the distribution of possible returns is the same over time, the average return provides an estimate of the return we should expect in any given year—the expected return. This idea is not unique to returns. For example, a Tim Hortons manager cannot know exactly how many customers will come in today, but by looking at the average number of customers who have come in historically, the manager can form an expectation to use in staffing and stocking.

FIGURE 10.2 **The Distribution of Monthly Returns for Canadian Treasury Bills, Long-Term Government of Canada Bonds, U.S. Stocks (S&P 500) Expressed in Canadian Dollars (CAD), and Canadian Stocks (S&P/TSX Composite Index), 1957–2017**

The height of each bar represents the number of months that the monthly returns were in each 1% range. Note the greater variability of stock returns (especially smaller Canadian stocks) compared to the returns of Government of Canada bonds or treasury bills.

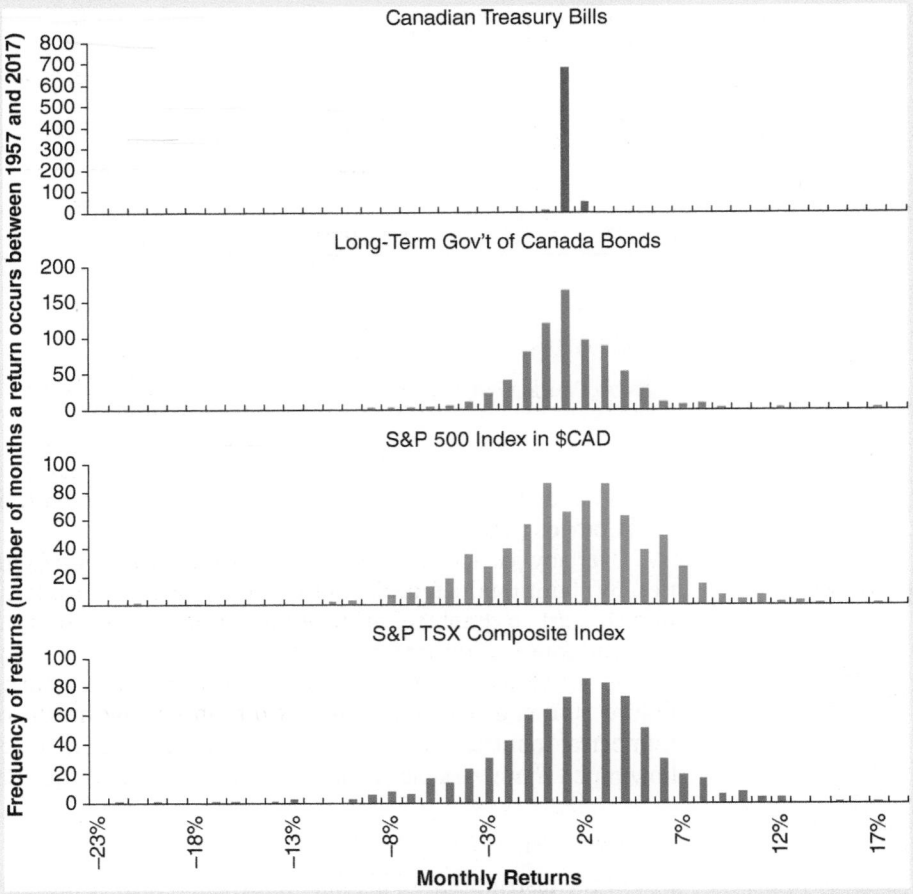

Source: Canadian Financial Markets Research Centre (CFMRC) Database, and Center for Research in Security Prices (CRSP).

Using the S&P/TSX Composite realized returns from Table 10.1, the average return for the S&P/TSX Composite for the years 2008 to 2017 is

$$\frac{1}{10}(-33.00\% + 35.05\% + 17.61\% + -8.71\% + \cdots + 9.10\%) = 6.35\%$$

The average Canada treasury bill return during the same period was 0.94%. Therefore, during this period investors earned 5.41% (6.35% − 0.94%) more, on average, by holding the S&P/TSX Composite Index than by investing in Canadian three-month treasury bills. This average is computed over just 10 years of data. Naturally, our estimate of the true average of the distribution is more precise the more data we use. We display the average returns for different investments from 1957 to 2017 in Figure 10.3.

FIGURE 10.3 **Average Annual Returns in Canada for S&P/TSX Composite Index, S&P 500 in CAD, Long-Term Government of Canada Bonds, and Canadian Treasury Bills, 1957–2017**

Each bar represents an investment's average return.

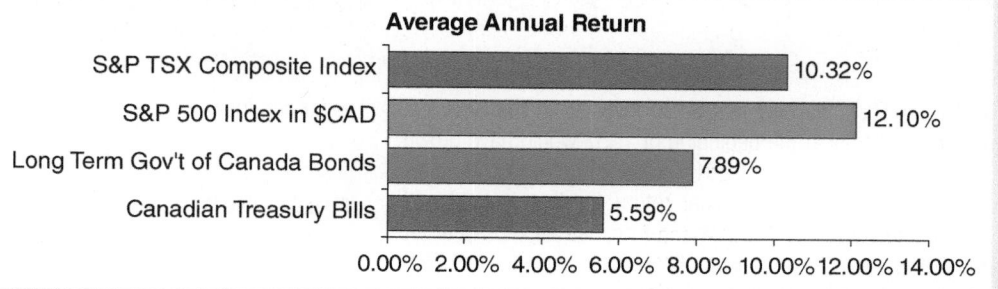

Source: Canadian Financial Markets Research Centre (CFMRC) Database, and Center for Research in Security Prices (CRSP).

The Variance and Volatility of Returns

Looking at Figure 10.2, we can see that the variability of the returns is very different for each investment. The returns of both stock market indices (the S&P 500 and the Canadian S&P/TSX Composite) vary much more than those of Government of Canada bonds or treasury bills. While we can see these differences in variability in Figure 10.2, we need a way to formally quantify them. To determine the variability of returns, we calculate the *standard deviation* of the distribution of realized returns. The **standard deviation** is the square root of the *variance* of the distribution of realized returns. **Variance** measures the variability in returns by taking the differences of the returns from the average return and squaring those differences. We have to square the difference of each return from the average because, by definition, the unsquared differences from an average must sum to zero. Because we square the returns, the variance is in units of "$\%^2$," or percentage squared. That is not very useful to us, so we take the square root to get the standard deviation in units of %.

standard deviation A common method used to measure the risk of a probability distribution—the square root of the variance.

variance A method to measure the variability of returns—the expected squared deviation of returns from the mean.

While that sounds a bit abstract, standard deviation simply indicates the tendency of the historical returns to be different from their average and how far from the average they tend to be. Standard deviation, therefore, captures our intuition of risk: how often will we miss the mark and how far off will we be? Formally, we calculate the variance with the following equation:[3]

Variance Estimate Using Realized Returns

$$Var(R) = \frac{1}{T-1}\left((R_1 - \overline{R})^2 + (R_2 - \overline{R})^2 + \cdots + (R_T - \overline{R})^2\right) \tag{10.4}$$

[3]You may wonder why we divide by $T - 1$ rather than T here. It is because we are not computing deviations from the true expected return; instead, we are computing deviations from the estimated average return $\overline{R}$. Because the average return is derived from the same data, we lose a degree of freedom (in essence, we have used up one of the data points) so that when computing the variance there are really only $T - 1$ additional data points on which to base it.

The standard deviation, which we will call the volatility, is the square root of the variance:[4]

$$SD(R) = \sqrt{Var(R)} \tag{10.5}$$

ARITHMETIC AVERAGE RETURNS VERSUS COMPOUND ANNUAL RETURNS

In Figure 10.1, we saw that $100 invested in the S&P/TSX Composite Index at the beginning of 1957 would have grown to $19,751 by the end of 2017. What if we wanted to know the average compound annual return for that investment? That is the same as asking what return, earned each year for 61 years, would have caused our $100 to grow to $19,751. We know that the formula for future value tells us that

$$FV = PV(1 + R)^n$$

Thus,

$$\$19{,}751 = \$100(1 + R)^{61}$$

Solving for R, we get 9.05%.

However, using the same data, we find the average annual return for the S&P/TSX Composite Index for this period was 10.32%. How can the two answers be different?

The difference is due to the fact that returns are volatile. To see the effect of volatility, suppose an investment has annual returns of +20% one year and −20% the next. The average annual return is

$$\frac{20\% + (-20\%)}{2} = 0\%$$

But the value of $1 invested after two years is

$$\$1 \times (1 + 0.20) \times (1 - 0.20) = \$0.96$$

This tells us that an investor would have lost money. Why? Because the 20% gain happens on a $1 investment for a total of 20 cents, whereas the 20% loss happens on a larger investment of $1.20. The loss is 20% of $1.20, or 24 cents.

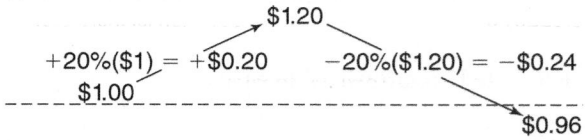

In this case, the compound annual return is

$$0.96 = 1(1 + R)^2$$

so solving for R,

$$R = (0.96)^{1/2} - 1 = -2\%$$

We calculated the 10.32% average for the S&P/TSX Composite Index as a simple arithmetic average of the realized returns, while we calculated 9.05% as the average annual compound return that corresponds to the total gain on our $100 investment (called the *geometric* average).

Which is a better description of an investment's return? The compound annual return is a better description of the long-term *historical performance* of an investment. It describes the average annual compound return for that particular history of returns. The ranking of the long-term performance of different investments coincides with the ranking of their compound annual returns. Thus, the compound annual return is the return that is most often used for comparison purposes. For example, mutual funds generally report their compound annual returns over the last 5 or 10 years.

On the other hand, the arithmetic average return should be used when trying to estimate an investment's *expected* return over a *future* horizon based on its past performance. If we view past annual returns as independent realizations of actual returns from the same set of possible returns, then we know from statistics that the arithmetic average provides the best estimate of the true mean. If the investment above is equally likely to have annual returns of +20% and −20% in the future, then the payoff from a $1 investment after two years will be

25% of the time: $\$1 \times (1.20) \times (1.20) = \$1.44$

50% of the time: $\$1 \times (1.20) \times (0.80)$

$= (0.80) \times (1.20) = \$0.96$

25% of the time: $\$1 \times (0.80) \times (0.80) = \$0.64$

The expected payoff is 25% (1.44) + 50%(0.96) + 25%(0.64) = $1, which is consistent with the arithmetic average return of 0%.

[4]If the returns used in Equation 10.4 are not annual returns, it is conventional to convert the variance to annual terms by multiplying the number of returns per year. Thus, when using monthly returns, we multiply the variance by 12, and equivalently, the standard deviation by $\sqrt{12}$.

EXAMPLE 10.3 Computing Historical Volatility

PROBLEM

Using the data from Table 10.1, what is the standard deviation of the S&P/TSX Composite Index returns for the years 2008 to 2017?

SOLUTION

Plan

With the 10 returns, compute the average return using Equation 10.3 because it is an input to the variance equation. Next, compute the variance using Equation 10.4 and then take its square root to determine the standard deviation.

2008	2009	2010	2011	2012	2013	2014	2015	2016	2017
−33.00%	35.05%	17.61%	−8.71%	7.19%	12.99%	10.55%	−8.32%	21.08%	9.10%

Execute

In the previous section, we already computed the average annual return of the S&P/TSX Composite Index during this period as 6.35%, so we have all of the necessary inputs for the variance calculation.

Applying Equation 10.4, we have

$$\begin{aligned} Var(R) &= \frac{1}{T-1}\left((R_1 - \bar{R})^2 + (R_2 - \bar{R})^2 + \cdots + (R_T - \bar{R})^2\right) \\ &= \frac{1}{10-1}\left((-0.3300 - 0.0635)^2 + (0.3505 - 0.0635)^2 + \cdots + (0.0910 - 0.0635)^2\right) \\ &= 0.0359 \end{aligned}$$

Alternatively, we can break the calculation of this equation out as follows:

	2008	2009	2010	2011	2012	2013	2014	2015	2016	2017
Return	−0.3300	0.3505	0.1761	−0.0871	0.0719	0.1299	0.1055	−0.0832	0.2108	0.0910
Average	0.0635	0.0635	0.0635	0.0635	0.0635	0.0635	0.0635	0.0635	0.0635	0.0635
Difference	−0.3935	0.2870	0.1126	−0.1506	0.0084	0.0664	0.0420	−0.1467	0.1473	0.0275
Squared	0.1548	0.0824	0.0127	0.0227	0.0001	0.0044	0.0018	0.0215	0.0217	0.0008

Summing the squared differences in the last row, we get 0.3228.

Finally, dividing by $(10 - 1 = 9)$ gives us $0.3228/9 = 0.0359$. The standard deviation is, therefore,

$$SD(R) = \sqrt{Var(R)} = \sqrt{0.0359} = 0.1894, \text{ or } 18.94\%$$

Evaluate

Our best estimate of the expected return for the S&P/TSX Composite Index is its average return, 6.35%, but it is risky, with a standard deviation of 18.94%.

COMMON MISTAKE

Mistakes When Computing Standard Deviation

Example 10.3 highlights two missteps often made in computing standard deviations.

1. Remember to divide by *one less* than the number of returns you have ($T - 1$, *not* T).
2. Don't forget to take the square root of the variance to obtain the standard deviation. You are not done when you calculate the variance—you have one more step to go.

USING EXCEL

Computing the Standard Deviation of Historical Returns

1. Enter or import the historical returns into Excel.
2. Next, highlight the cell where you want to produce the standard deviation and select "Function" from the "Insert" pull-down menu.
3. Select the "STDEV.S" function, highlight the returns for which you want to compute the standard deviation, and click "Done."
4. *Make sure that you use the STDEV.S function and not the STDEV.P function.* STDEV.S calculates the sample standard deviation as in Equation 10.4 and 10.5, by dividing by $T - 1$. STDEV.P assumes that you know with certainty the true mean and calculates the standard deviation by dividing by T. See Footnote 3 for more discussion of this important distinction.

STDEV | =STDEV.S(B6:B15)

	A	B	C	D
1	Table 10.1			
2				
3	Realized Return for the S&P/TSX Composite Index, Barrick Gold Corp., and Treas			
4				
5	Year End	S&P TSX Total Return Index	Barrick Gold Corp. Return	Treasury B Return
6	2008	-33.00%	7.01%	3.1
7	2009	35.05%	-7.27%	0.5
8	2010	17.61%	28.12%	0.3
9	2011	-8.71%	-13.12%	0.9
10	2012	7.19%	-24.55%	0.9
11	2013	12.99%	-46.27%	0.9
12	2014	10.55%	-33.08%	0.8
13	2015	-8.32%	-18.21%	0.6
14	2016	21.08%	109.86%	0.5
15	2017	9.10%	-15.40%	0.5
16	Average	6.35%	-1.29%	0.9
17	Variance	0.03587	0.19472	0.000
18	Standard Deviation	=STDEV.S(B6:B15)	44.13%	0.7
19	Source: Canadian Financial Markets Research Centre (CFMRC) Database, YahooFin			

Formula Builder

Show All Functions

STDEV.S

Number1 = {-0.33003484300230 3;0.3505497...

B6:B15

Result: 0.189396788

Done

fx STDEV.S

Courtesy of Microsoft corporation.

FIGURE 10.4 **Volatility (Standard Deviation) of S&P/TSX Composite Index, S&P 500 in CAD, Long-Term Government of Canada Bonds, and Government of Canada Treasury Bills, 1957–2017**

Each bar represents the standard deviation of the investment's returns.

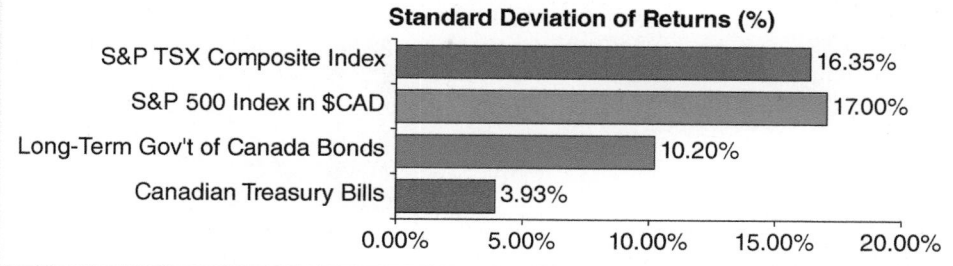

Source: Canadian Financial Markets Research Centre (CFMRC) Database, Yahoo!Finance Canada.

We began our review of statistics with the goal of being able to quantify the difference in the variability of the distributions that we observed over long periods of time, such as those shown in Figure 10.2. We can now do so by computing the standard deviation of the annual returns on the investments from 1957 to 2017. These results are shown in Figure 10.4.

Comparing the standard deviations in Figure 10.4, we see that, as expected, Canadian stocks and larger U.S. companies had the most variable historical returns. The returns of long-term Government of Canada bonds and treasury bills are much less variable than those of stocks, with treasury bills being the least volatile investment category.

normal distribution
A symmetric probability distribution that is completely characterized by its average and standard deviation. Ninety-five percent of all possible outcomes fall within two standard deviations above and below the average.

95% confidence interval
A range of values that is likely to include an unknown parameter. If independent samples are taken repeatedly from the same population, then the true parameter will lie outside the 95% confidence interval 5% of the time.

The Normal Distribution

The standard deviations that we compute in Figure 10.4 are useful for more than just ranking the investments from most to least risky. The standard deviation also plays an important role in describing a **normal distribution**, shown in Figure 10.5, which is a symmetric probability distribution that is completely characterized by its average and standard deviation. Importantly, about two-thirds of all possible outcomes fall within one standard deviation above or below the average, and about 95% of all possible outcomes fall within two standard deviations above and below the average. Figure 10.5 shows these outcomes for the S&P/TSX Composite Index.

Because we can be about 95% confident that next year's return will be within two standard deviations of the average, we say that the **95% confidence interval** runs from

$$\text{Average} \pm (2 \times \text{standard deviation})$$

$$\bar{R} \pm (2 \times SD(R)) \tag{10.6}$$

FIGURE 10.5 Normal Distribution

The height of the line reflects the likelihood of each return occurring. Using the data from Figure 10.3 and Figure 10.4, if the returns of the S&P/TSX Composite Index are normally distributed, then two-thirds of all possible outcomes should lie within one standard deviation of the average return of 10.32% (given in Figure 10.3), and 95% should lie within two standard deviations. Figure 10.4 shows the standard deviation to be 16.35%, so that puts 95% of possible outcomes between −22.38% and +43.02% (the shaded area of the distribution).

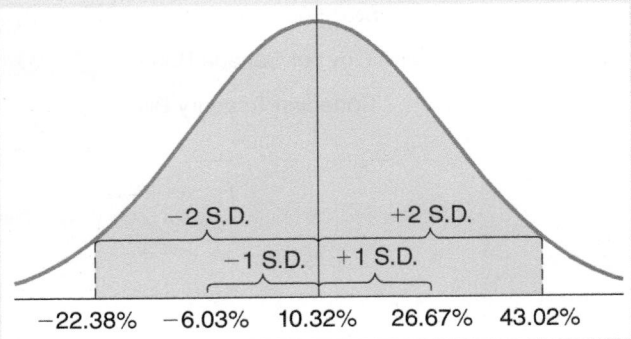

EXAMPLE 10.4 Confidence Intervals

PROBLEM

In Example 10.3, we found the average return for the S&P/TSX Composite Index from 2008 to 2017 to be 6.35% with a standard deviation of 18.94%. What is a 95% confidence interval for 2018's return?

SOLUTION

■ **Plan**

We can use Equation 10.6 to compute the confidence interval.

■ **Execute**

Using Equation 10.6, we have

$$\text{Average} \pm 2 \times \text{standard deviation} = 6.35\% - 2 \times 18.94\% \text{ to } 6.35\% + 2 \times 18.94\%$$
$$= -31.53\% \text{ to } 44.23\%.$$

■ **Evaluate**

Even though the average return from 2008 to 2017 was 6.35%, the S&P/TSX Composite Index was volatile, so if we want to be 95% confident of 2018's return, the best we can say is that it will lie between −31.53% and +44.23%.

Table 10.2 summarizes the central concepts and equations that we developed in this section. Calculating historical averages and volatilities indicates how investments performed in the past and might perform in the future. Of course, using the past to predict the future is fraught with uncertainty. In the next section, we discuss that uncertainty.

TABLE 10.2 Summary of Tools for Working with Historical Returns

Concept	Definition	Formula
Realized Returns	Total return earned over a particular period of time	$R_{t+1} = \frac{Div_{t+1} + P_{t+1} - P_t}{P_t}$
Average Annual Return	Average of realized returns for each year	$\overline{R} = \frac{1}{T}(R_1 + R_2 + \cdots + R_T)$
Variance of Returns	A measure of the variability of returns	$Var(R) = \frac{1}{T-1}\left((R_1 - \overline{R})^2 + (R_2 - \overline{R})^2 + \cdots + (R_T - \overline{R})^2\right)$
Standard Deviation or Volatility of Returns	The square root of the variance (which puts it in the same units as the average—namely "%")	$SD(R) = \sqrt{Var(R)}$
95% Confidence Interval	The range of returns within which we are 95% confident that next period's return will lie	$\overline{R} \pm (2 \times SD(R))$

measure the variability of returns

measure the risk of a first business

CONCEPT CHECK

3. For what purpose do we use the average and standard deviation of historical stock returns? -> calculate risk
4. How does the standard deviation of historical returns affect our confidence in predicting the next period's return? -> helps us plan for the future

look at the last 10 years

10.3 The Historical Trade-Off between Risk and Return

Would you intentionally choose to accept additional risk without additional reward? In other words, are you willing to pursue riskier investments if they do not have the potential to generate higher returns? The answer to both of these questions is most likely "no." In this section, we will examine the historical trade-off between risk (as measured by price volatility) and reward (as measured by returns) to see if, historically, investors behaved as you would.

The Returns of Large Portfolios

In Figures 10.3 and 10.4, we showed the historical average returns and volatilities for a number of different types of investments. In Figure 10.6, we plot the average return versus the volatility of each type of investment for the same investments. Note that the investments with higher volatility, measured here with standard deviation, have rewarded investors with higher average returns.

Figure 10.6 is consistent with our view that investors are risk-averse. Riskier investments must offer investors higher average returns to compensate them for the risk they are taking.

The Returns of Individual Stocks

Figure 10.6 suggests the following simple model of the risk premium: investments with higher volatility should have a higher risk premium and, therefore, higher returns.

FIGURE 10.6 The Historical Trade-Off between Risk and Return in Large Portfolios, 1950–2016

Note the general increasing relationship between historical volatility (standard deviation) and average return for these large portfolios. For comparison purposes, Canadian treasury bills, long-term Government of Canada bonds, the S&P 500 in CAD, and the TSX/S&P Composite Index are included. Unlike the case for large portfolios, there is no precise relationship between volatility and average return for individual stocks. (Individual stock information is based on monthly returns, using 120 months of data ending on March 29, 2017. The annualized historical volatilities and returns of large portfolios are based on monthly returns between 1950 and 2016.)

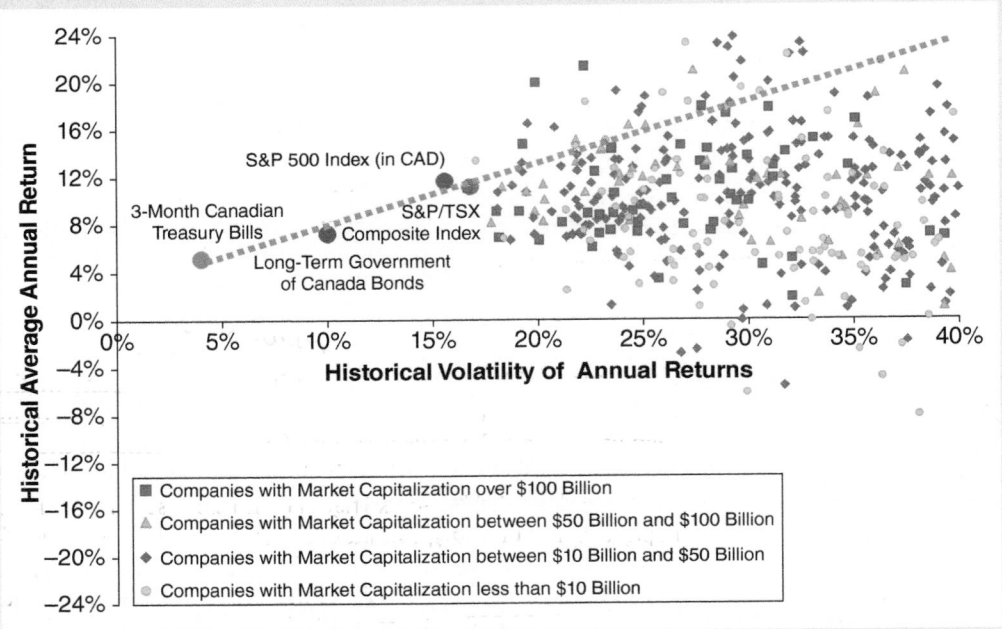

Source: Bloomberg, Bank of Canada, Canadian Financial Markets Research Centre, Passport Financial Services Inc., and Statistics Canada.

Indeed, looking at Figure 10.6, it is tempting to draw a line through the portfolios and conclude that all investments should lie on or near this line—that is, expected return should rise proportionately with volatility. This conclusion appears to be approximately true for the large portfolios we have looked at so far. Is it correct? Does it apply to individual stocks?

Actually, the answer to both questions is "no." There is no clear relationship between volatility and returns for individual stocks. Although it will take more work to establish the relationship between risk and return for individual stocks, the following is true:

1. There is a relationship between size and risk—on average, larger stocks have lower volatility than smaller stocks.
2. Even the largest stocks are typically more volatile than a portfolio of large stocks, such as the S&P 500. The same can be said for stocks of smaller companies in comparison with a portfolio of these companies.
3. Most individual stocks have lower returns and/or higher risk than the portfolios in Figure 10.6. With very few exceptions, the individual stocks in Figure 10.6 all lie below the line.

Thus, while volatility (standard deviation) seems to be a reasonable measure of risk when evaluating a large portfolio, the volatility of an individual security does not explain the size of its average return. What are we to make of this? Why wouldn't investors demand a higher return from stocks with a higher volatility? And how is it that portfolios such as the S&P/TSX Composite Index or the S&P 500 Index are so much less risky than almost all of the 500 stocks individually? To answer these questions, we need to think more carefully about how to measure risk for an investor.

CONCEPT CHECK

5. What is the relationship between risk and return for large portfolios? How are individual stocks different?
6. Do portfolios or the stocks in the portfolios tend to have the lower volatility?

10.4 Common versus Independent Risk

In this section, we explain why the risk of an individual security differs from the risk of a portfolio composed of similar securities. We begin with an example from the insurance industry to understand how the portfolio of insurance products performs for the insurance company offering them.

Theft versus Earthquake Insurance: An Example

Consider two types of home insurance an insurance company might offer: theft insurance and earthquake insurance. Let us assume, for the purpose of illustration, that the risk of each of these two hazards is similar for a given home in the San Francisco area—each year there is about a 1% chance the home will be robbed and also a 1% chance that the home will be damaged by an earthquake. In this case, the chance the insurance company will pay a claim for a single home is the same for the two types of insurance policies. Suppose an insurance company writes 100,000 policies of each type for homeowners in San Francisco. We know the risks of the individual policies are similar, but are the risks of the portfolios of 100,000 policies similar?

First consider theft insurance. Because the chance of a theft for any given home is 1%, we would expect about 1% of the 100,000 homes to be robbed. Thus, the number of theft claims will be about 1000 per year. The actual number of claims may be a bit higher or lower each year, but not much. In this case, if the insurance company holds reserves sufficient to cover 1200 claims, it will almost certainly have enough to cover its obligations on its theft insurance policies.

Now consider earthquake insurance. There is a 99% chance that an earthquake will not occur. All the homes are in the same city, so if an earthquake does occur, all homes are likely to be affected and the insurance company can expect 100,000 claims. As a result, the insurance company can expect either zero claims or 100,000 claims. Because it may have 100,000 claims, it will have to hold reserves of cash (or other investments) sufficient to cover claims on all 100,000 policies it wrote in order to meet its obligations if an earthquake occurs.

Thus, earthquake and theft insurance lead to portfolios with very different risk characteristics. For earthquake insurance, the percentage of claims is very risky—it will most likely be 0, but there is a 1% chance that the insurance company will have to pay claims on *all* the policies it wrote. So the risk of the portfolio of earthquake insurance policies is no different from the risk of any single policy. On the other hand, we have seen that for theft insurance the number of claims in a given year is quite predictable. Year in and year out, it will be very close to 1% of the total number of policies, or 1000 claims. The portfolio of theft insurance policies has almost no risk! That is, the insurance company's payouts are quite stable and predictable over time.

TABLE 10.3 Summary of Types of Risk

Type of Risk	Definition	Example	Risk Diversified in Large Portfolio?
Common Risk	Risks that are linked across outcomes	Risk of earthquake	No
Independent Risk	Risks that bear no relation to each other	Risk of theft	Yes

Types of Risk

Why are the portfolios of insurance policies so different when the individual policies themselves are quite similar? Intuitively, the key difference between them is that an earthquake affects all houses simultaneously, and so the risk is linked across homes, meaning either all homes are damaged or all homes are not damaged. We call risk that is linked in this way **common risk**. In contrast, we have assumed that thefts in different houses are not related to each other—whether one house is burglarized has no effect on another house's chance of being burglarized. **Independent risk**, such as the risk of theft, is not linked across homes. When risks are independent, some individual homeowners are unlucky, others are lucky, but overall the number of claims is similar. The averaging out of risks in a large portfolio is called **diversification**.[5] Table 10.3 summarizes our discussion of common and independent risk.

common risk Risk that is linked across outcomes.

independent risk Risk that bears no relation to other risks. If risks are independent, then knowing the outcome of one provides no information about the other.

diversification The averaging of independent risks in a large portfolio.

The principle of diversification is used routinely in the insurance industry. In addition to theft insurance, many other forms of insurance (life, health, auto) rely on the fact that the number of claims is relatively predictable in a large portfolio. Even in the case of earthquake insurance, insurers can achieve some diversification by selling policies in different geographical regions, or by combining different types of policies. Diversification is used to reduce risk in many other settings. For example, many systems are designed with redundancy to decrease the risk of a disruption. Firms often add redundancy to critical parts of the manufacturing process: NASA puts more than one antenna on its space probes, and automobiles contain spare tires.

In many settings, the risks lie somewhere in between the common risks and independent risks. For example, you may have applied to more than one school. Your chances of being accepted (or rejected) at any one school are not perfectly linked across schools, because schools have different admissions criteria and are looking for different types of students. However, your risk of rejection is not completely independent, either; all schools look at your high school grades, so the schools' decisions will be related.

EXAMPLE 10.5 Diversification

PROBLEM

You are playing a very simple gambling game with your friend: a $1 bet based on a coin flip. That is, you each bet $1 and flip a coin—heads you win your friend's $1, tails you lose and your friend takes your dollar. How is your risk different if you play this game 100 times in a row versus just betting $100 (instead of $1) on a single coin flip?

[5]Harry Markowitz was the first to formalize the benefits from diversification. See H. M. Markowitz, "Portfolio Selection," *Journal of Finance* 7(1) (1952): 77–91.

SOLUTION

Plan

The risk of losing one coin flip is independent of the risk of losing the next one; each time you have a 50% chance of losing, and one coin flip does not affect any other coin flip. We can compute the expected outcome of any flip as a weighted average by weighting your possible winnings (+$1) by 50% and your possible losses (–$1) by 50%. We can then compute the probability of losing all $100 under either scenario.

Execute

If you play the game 100 times, you should lose 50% of the time and win 50% of the time, so your expected outcome is $50 \times (+\$1) + 50 \times (-\$1) = \$0$. You should break even. But even if you don't win exactly half of the time, the probability that you would lose all 100 coin flips (and thus lose $100) is exceedingly small (in fact, it is 0.50^{100}, which is far less than even 0.0001%). If it happens, you should take a very careful look at the coin!

If instead you make a single $100 bet on the outcome of one coin flip, you have a 50% chance of winning $100 and a 50% chance of losing $100, so your expected outcome will be the same: break even. However, there is a 50% chance you will lose $100, so your risk is far greater than it would be for 100 one-dollar bets.

Evaluate

In each case, you put $100 at risk, but by spreading out that risk across 100 different bets rather than placing a single $100 bet, you have diversified much of your risk away.

everyone effected

CONCEPT CHECK

7. What is the difference between common and independent risk? -> everyone not effected

8. How does diversification help with independent risk?

↳ reduces risk in many other ways

10.5 Diversification in Stock Portfolios

As the insurance example indicates, the degree of risk related to a portfolio depends on whether the individual risks within it are common or independent. Independent risks are diversified in a large portfolio, whereas common risks are not. Our goal is to understand the relationship between risk and return in the capital markets, so let's consider the implication of this distinction for the risk of stock portfolios.

Unsystematic versus Systematic Risk

Over any given time period, the risk of holding a stock is that the dividends plus the final stock price will be higher or lower than expected, which makes the realized return risky. What causes dividends or stock prices, and therefore returns, to be higher or lower than we expect? Usually, stock prices and dividends fluctuate due to two types of news:

1. *Company- or industry-specific news:* This is good or bad news about a company (or industry) itself. For example, a firm might announce that it has been successful in gaining market share within its industry. Or the home-building industry may be damaged by a real estate slowdown.
2. *Market-wide news:* This is news that affects the economy as a whole and therefore affects all stocks. For instance, the Bank of Canada might announce that it will lower interest rates in an attempt to boost the economy.

unsystematic risk
Fluctuations of a stock's return that are due to company- or industry-specific news and are independent risks unrelated across stocks.

systematic risk
Fluctuations of a stock's return that are due to market-wide news representing common risk.

Fluctuations of a stock's return that are due to company- or industry-specific news are independent risks. Similar to theft at different homes, these are unrelated across stocks. This type of risk is also referred to as **unsystematic risk**.

On the other hand, fluctuations of a stock's return that are due to market-wide news represent common risk. As with earthquakes, all stocks are affected simultaneously. This type of risk is also called **systematic risk**.

When we combine many stocks in a large portfolio, the unsystematic risks for each stock will average out and be eliminated by diversification. Good news will affect some stocks and bad news will affect others, but the amount of good or bad news overall will be relatively constant. The systematic risk, however, will affect all firms—and therefore the entire portfolio—and will not be eliminated by diversification.

Let's consider a hypothetical example. Suppose type S firms are affected *only* by the systematic risk of the strength of the economy, which has a 50–50 chance of being either strong or weak. If the economy is strong, type S stocks will earn a return of 40%, and if the economy is weak, their return will be −20%. Because the risk these firms face (the strength of the economy) is systematic risk, holding a large portfolio of type S stocks will not diversify the risk. When the economy is strong, the portfolio will have the same return of 40% as each type S firm. When the economy is weak, the portfolio will also have a return of –20%.

Now consider type U firms, which are affected only by unsystematic risks. Their returns are equally likely to be 35% or −25%, based on factors specific to each firm's local market. Because these risks are firm-specific, if we hold a portfolio of many type U stocks, the risk is diversified. About half of the firms will have returns of 35%, and half will have returns of −25%. The return of the portfolio will be the average return of 50% (0.35) + 50% (−0.25) = 0.05, or 5%, no matter whether the economy is strong or weak.

Figure 10.7 illustrates how volatility, measured by standard deviation, declines with the size of the portfolio for type S and U firms. Type S firms have only systematic risk.

FIGURE 10.7 Volatility of Portfolios of Type S and U Stocks

Because type S firms have only systematic risk, the volatility of the portfolio does not change. Type U firms have only unsystematic risk, which is diversified and eliminated as the number of firms in the portfolio grows. Typical stocks carry a mix of both types of risk, so that the risk of the portfolio declines as unsystematic risk is diversified, but systematic risk remains.

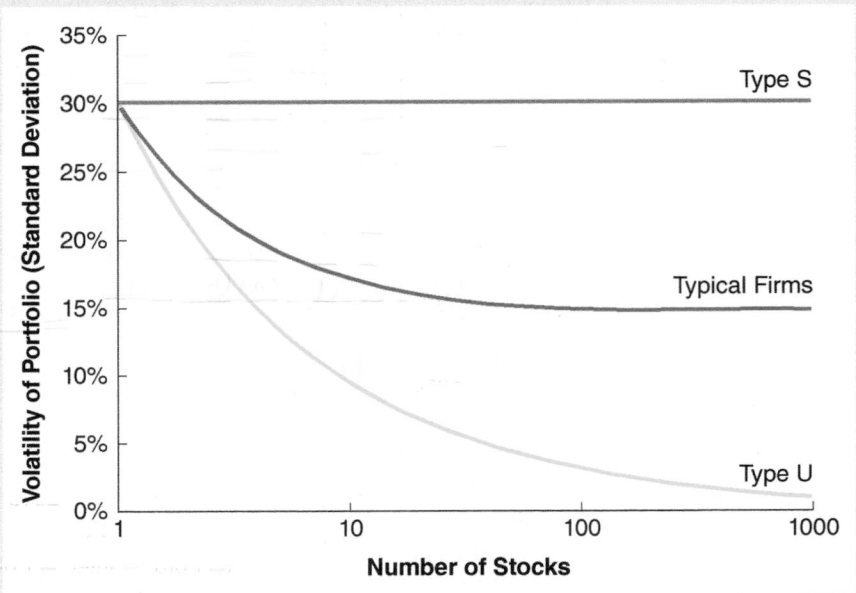

Similar to earthquake insurance, the volatility of the portfolio does not change as we increase the number of firms. Type U firms have only unsystematic risk. As with theft insurance, the risk is diversified as the number of firms increases, and volatility declines. As is evident from Figure 10.7, with a large number of firms, type U firms' risk is, essentially, completely eliminated.

Of course, actual firms are not similar to type S or U firms. Firms are affected by both systematic, market-wide risks, as well as unsystematic risks. Figure 10.7 also shows how the volatility changes with the number of stocks in a portfolio of typical firms. *When firms carry both types of risk, only the unsystematic risk will be eliminated by diversification when we combine many firms into a portfolio. The volatility will, therefore, decline until only the systematic risk, which affects all firms, remains.*

This example explains one of the puzzles from Section 10.3. There we saw that the S&P/TSX Composite Index and the S&P 500 had much lower volatility than most individual stocks. Now we can see why—the individual stocks each contain unsystematic risk, which is eliminated when we combine them into a large portfolio. Thus, the portfolio can have lower volatility than each of the stocks within it. Figure 10.8 illustrates this fact. The dotted lines show the extremes of the range of returns of a portfolio of Ford and Intel. The returns of each of the two stocks in the portfolio cross at least one of these extremes. Thus, the volatility of the portfolio is lower than the volatility of both of the stocks in the portfolio.

FIGURE 10.8 The Effect of Diversification on Portfolio Volatility

While Ford and Intel are each very volatile, some of their movements offset each other. If they are in a portfolio together, as represented by the blue bars, the total movement of the portfolio is muted relative to the movement of either of the individual stocks. The dotted lines show the highest and lowest return of the portfolio—note that the portfolio's worst return is better than the worst return of either stock on its own.

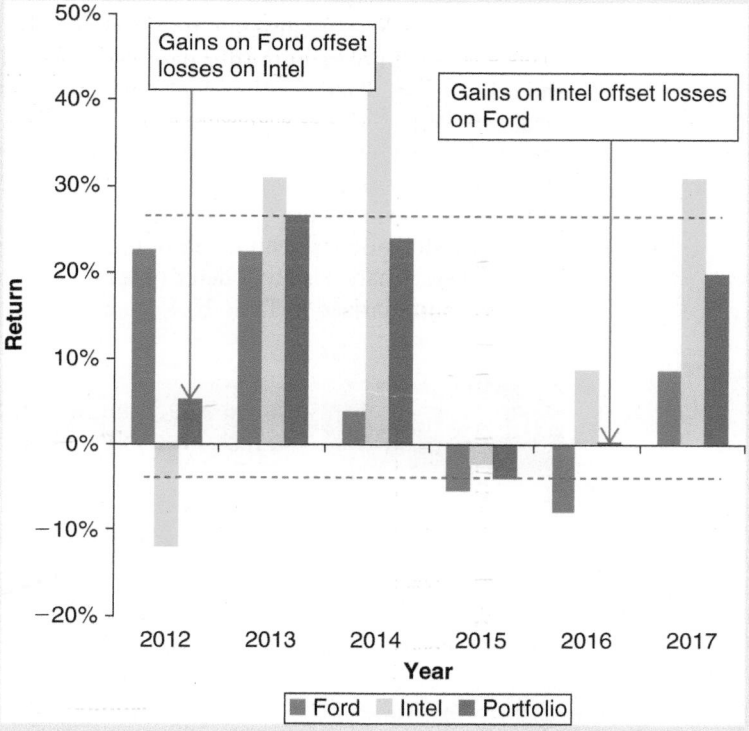

Diversifiable Risk and the Risk Premium

What if you hold only one or two stocks—wouldn't you be exposed to unsystematic risk and demand a premium for it? If the market compensated you with an additional risk premium for choosing to bear diversifiable risk, then other investors could buy the same stocks and earn the additional premium, while putting them in a portfolio so that they could diversify and eliminate the unsystematic risk. By doing so, investors could earn an additional premium without taking additional risk!

This opportunity to earn something for nothing is an arbitrage opportunity as we discussed in Chapter 3, and so it is something investors would find very attractive. As more and more investors take advantage of this situation and purchase shares that pay a risk premium for diversifiable, unsystematic risk, the current share price of those firms would rise, lowering their expected return—recall that the current share price P_t is the denominator when computing the stock's return as in Equation 10.1. This trading would stop only when the risk premium for diversifiable risk dropped to zero. Competition among investors ensures that no additional return can be earned for diversifiable risk. The result:

The risk premium of a stock is not affected by its diversifiable, unsystematic risk.

The argument above is essentially an application of the Valuation Principle's Law of One Price. Imagine a large portfolio of type U firms, which have no systematic risk. As depicted in Figure 10.7, a large portfolio of type U firms eliminates all unsystematic risk, leaving no additional risk. Since that portfolio has no risk, it cannot earn a risk premium and, instead, must earn the risk-free interest rate. This line of reasoning suggests the following, more general, principle:

The risk premium for diversifiable risk is zero. Thus, investors are not compensated for holding unsystematic risk.

The Importance of Systematic Risk

Because investors can eliminate unsystematic risk "for free" by diversifying their portfolios, they will not require (nor deserve) a reward or risk premium for bearing it. On the other hand, diversification does not reduce systematic risk—even when holding a large portfolio, an investor will be exposed to risks that affect the entire economy and, therefore, affect all securities. We can reduce the systematic risk of a portfolio by selling stocks and investing in risk-free bonds, but at the cost of giving up the higher expected return of stocks. Because unsystematic risk can be eliminated for free by diversifying, whereas systematic risk can be eliminated only by sacrificing expected returns, it is a security's systematic risk that determines the risk premium investors require to hold it. This fact, summarized in Table 10.4, leads to the second key principle:

TABLE 10.4 The Expected Return of Type S and Type U Firms, Assuming the Risk-Free Rate Is 5%

	S Firm	U Firm
Volatility (standard deviation)	30%	30%
Risk-Free Rate	5%	5%
Risk Premium	5%	0%
Expected Return	10%	5%

TABLE 10.5 Systematic Risk versus Unsystematic Risk

	Diversifiable?	Requires a Risk Premium?
Systematic Risk	No	Yes
Unsystematic Risk	Yes	No

The risk premium of a security is determined by its systematic risk and does not depend on its diversifiable risk.

This principle implies that a stock's volatility, which is a measure of total risk (that is, systematic risk + unsystematic risk), is not useful in determining the risk premium that investors will earn. For example, consider again type S and U firms. As shown in Figure 10.7, the volatility (standard deviation) of a single type S or U firm is 30%. However, as Table 10.4 shows, although they have the same volatility, type S firms have an expected return of 10% and type U firms have an expected return of 5%.

The difference in expected returns is due to the difference in the kind of risk each firm bears. Type U firms have only unsystematic risk, which does not require a risk premium, and so the expected return of 5% for type U firms equals the risk-free interest rate. Type S firms have only systematic risk. Because investors will require compensation for this risk, the expected return of 10% for type S firms provides investors with a 5% risk premium above the risk-free interest rate. Table 10.5 summarizes the main points about systematic and unsystematic risk.

COMMON MISTAKE

A Fallacy of Long-Run Diversification

We have seen that investors can greatly reduce risk by dividing their investment dollars over many different investments, eliminating the diversifiable risk in their portfolios. It is sometimes argued that the same logic applies over time; by investing for many years, we can also diversify the risk we face during any particular year. Thus, young investors should choose risky portfolios because they have more time to make up their losses. Is this correct? In the long run, does risk still matter?

It is true that if returns each year are independent, the volatility of the average annual return does decline with the number of years that we invest. But, as long-term investors, we don't care about the volatility of our average return; instead we care about the volatility of our cumulative return over the period. This volatility grows with the investment horizon, as illustrated in the following example.

Consider an investor who invested $100 in the S&P/TSX Index at the beginning of 1956. We see from Figure 10.1 that $100 invested at the beginning of 1957 would have grown to about $19,751 by the end of 2017. Suppose that mining and transportation strikes had caused stocks to drop by 50% in 1956. Then, our investor's initial $100 investment would be worth only $100 × (1 – 50%) = $50.0 at the start of 1957. If returns from then on were unchanged, the investment would be worth half as much in 2017, or $9875.5.

Thus, if future returns are not affected by today's return, then an increase or decline in the value of our portfolio today will translate into the same percentage increase or decrease in the value of our portfolio in the future, so there is no diversification over time. The only way the length of the time horizon can reduce risk is if a below-average return this year implies that returns are more likely to be above average in the future (and vice versa). If this were true, past low returns can be used to predict future high returns in the stock market.

For short horizons of a few years, there is no evidence of this predictability in the stock market. For longer horizons, there is some evidence of this historically, but it is not clear how reliable this evidence is (there are not enough decades of accurate stock market data available) or whether the pattern will continue. But even if there is long-run reversal in stock returns, a buy-and-hold diversification strategy is still not optimal; if past returns can be used to predict future returns, it is optimal to invest more in stocks when returns are predicted to be high, and less when they are predicted to be low. Note that this strategy is very different from the diversification we achieve by holding many stocks, where we cannot predict which stocks will have good or bad unsystematic shocks.

We now have an explanation for the second puzzle from Section 10.3. While volatility or standard deviation might be a reasonable measure of risk for a large portfolio, it is not appropriate for an individual security.

Thus, there is no relationship between volatility and average returns for individual securities.

Consequently, to estimate a security's expected return we need to find a measure of a security's systematic risk.

We began this chapter by showing in Figure 10.1 that your grandparents' and parents' investment in the S&P/TSX Composite Index would have lost a lot of money in periods such as the recessions of the early 1980s and early 1990s. Thus, risk-averse investors will demand a premium to invest in securities that will do poorly in bad times. This idea coincides with the notion of systematic risk we have defined in this chapter. Economy-wide risk, the risk of recessions and booms, is systematic risk that cannot be diversified. Therefore, an asset that moves with the economy contains systematic risk and so requires a risk premium. In the next chapter, we will discuss how to measure an investment's systematic risk and then use that measure to compute its expected return. We can then apply that return expected by investors as our cost of capital.

CONCEPT CHECK

9. Why is the risk of a portfolio usually less than the average risk of the stocks in the portfolio?

10. Is systematic or unsystematic risk priced? Why?

1/ systematic is priced, because investors could easily eliminate unsystematic risk

MyLab Finance

Here is what you should know after reading this chapter. MyLab™ Finance will help you identify what you know, and where to go when you need to practice.

KEY POINTS AND EQUATIONS	TERMS	ONLINE PRACTICE OPPORTUNITIES
10.1 A First Look at Risk and Return ■ While in hindsight some investments have had very high returns, they have also had the most volatility over time.		MyLab Study Plan 10.1
10.2 Historical Risks and Returns of Stocks ■ The realized return from investing in a stock from time t to $t + 1$ is $R_{t+1} = \frac{Div_{t+1} + P_{t+1} - P_t}{P_t} = \frac{Div_{t+1}}{P_t} + \frac{P_{t+1} - P_t}{P_t}$ $= \text{Dividend Yield} + \text{Capital Gain Yield} \quad (10.1)$ ■ We can calculate the average annual return and variance of realized returns: $\overline{R} = \frac{1}{T}(R_1 + R_2 + \cdots + R_T) \quad (10.3)$ $Var(R) = \frac{1}{T-1}[(R_1 - \overline{R})^2 + (R_2 - \overline{R})^2 + \cdots + (R_T - \overline{R})^2] \quad (10.4)$ ■ The square root of the estimated variance is the standard deviation, an estimate of the volatility of returns. ■ Based on historical data, small stocks have had higher volatility and higher average returns than large stocks, which have higher volatility and higher average returns than bonds. ■ About 95% of possible outcomes lie within two standard deviations above or below the average outcome.	average annual return, p. 355 realized return, p. 351 standard deviation, p. 357 variance, p. 357 95% confidence interval, p. 361 normal distribution, p. 361	MyLab Study Plan 10.2 Using Excel: Standard Deviation of Historical Returns
10.3 The Historical Trade-Off between Risk and Return ■ There is no clear relationship between the volatility (standard deviation) and return of individual stocks. ■ Larger stocks tend to have lower overall volatility, but even the largest stocks are typically more risky than a portfolio of large stocks. ■ All stocks seem to have higher risk and lower returns than would be predicted based on extrapolation of data for large portfolios.		MyLab Study Plan 10.3

KEY POINTS AND EQUATIONS	TERMS	ONLINE PRACTICE OPPORTUNITIES
10.4 Common versus Independent Risk ■ Common risk is risk that is perfectly linked across investments. ■ Independent risks are unrelated across investments. ■ Diversification is the averaging of risks in a large portfolio.	common risk, p. 366 diversification, p. 366 independent risk, p. 366	MyLab Study Plan 10.4
10.5 Diversification in Stock Portfolios ■ The total risk of a security represents both unsystematic risk and systematic risk. ■ Variation in a stock's return due to company- or industry-specific news is called unsystematic risk. ■ Systematic risk is risk due to market-wide news that affects all stocks simultaneously. ■ Diversification eliminates unsystematic risk but does not eliminate systematic risk. ■ Because investors can eliminate unsystematic risk, they do not require a risk premium for it. ■ Because investors cannot eliminate systematic risk, they must be compensated for it. So, the risk premium for a stock depends on the amount of its systematic risk rather than its total risk.	systematic risk, p. 368 unsystematic risk, p. 368	MyLab Study Plan 10.5 Interactive Risk and Portfolio Diversification Analysis

REVIEW QUESTIONS

1. What does the historical relationship between volatility and return tell us about investors' attitude toward risk?
2. What are the components of a stock's realized return?
3. What is the reasoning behind using the average annual return as a measure of expected return?
4. How does standard deviation relate to the general concept of risk?
5. How does the relationship between the average return and the historical volatility of individual stocks differ from the relationship between the average return and the historical volatility of large, well-diversified portfolios?
6. What is meant by diversification, and how does it relate to common versus independent risk?
7. Which of the following risks of a stock are likely to be unsystematic, diversifiable risks and which are likely to be systematic risks? Which risks will affect the risk premium that investors will demand?
   a. The risk that the founder and CEO retires.
   b. The risk that oil prices rise, increasing production costs.

c. The risk that a product design is faulty and the product must be recalled.
d. The risk that the economy slows, reducing demand for the firm's products.
e. The risk that your best employees will be hired away.
f. The risk that the new product you expect your R&D division to produce will not materialize.

8. What is the difference between systematic and unsystematic risk?

9. There are three companies working on a new approach to customer-tracking software. You work for a software company that thinks this could be a good addition to its software line. If you invest in one of them versus all three of them,
a. Is your systematic risk likely to be very different?
b. Is your unsystematic risk likely to be very different?

10. If you randomly select 10 stocks for a portfolio and 20 other stocks for a different portfolio, which portfolio is likely to have the lower standard deviation? Why?

11. Why doesn't the risk premium of a stock depend on its diversifiable risk?

12. Your spouse works for Southwest Airlines and you work for a grocery store. Is your company or your spouse's company likely to be more exposed to systematic risk?

PROBLEMS

All problems in this chapter are available in MyLab Finance.

Historical Risks and Returns of Stocks

1- 4, 10,
11a, 12acd
18

1. You bought a stock one year ago for $50 per share and sold it today for $55 per share. It paid a $1 per share dividend today.
a. What was your realized return?
b. How much of the return came from dividend yield and how much came from capital gain?

2. Repeat Problem 1 assuming instead that the stock fell $5 to $45.
a. Is your capital gain different? Why or why not?
b. Is your dividend yield different? Why or why not?

3. Your portfolio consists of 100 shares of CSH and 50 shares of EJH, which you just bought at $20 and $30 per share, respectively.
a. What fraction of your portfolio is invested in CSH? In EJH?
b. If CSH increases to $23 and EJH decreases to $29, what is the return on your portfolio?

4. You have just purchased a share of stock for $20. The company is expected to pay a dividend of $0.50 per share in exactly one year. If you want to earn a 10% return on your investment, what price do you need if you expect to sell the share immediately after it pays the dividend?

5. You expect KStreet Co's to trade at $100 per share right after paying a $2 dividend per share in one year. What is the most you would pay to buy the stock now if you want to earn at least a 15% return?

6. The table below contains prices and dividends for a stock. All prices are after the dividend has been paid (ex-dividend). If you bought the stock on January 1 and sold it on December 31, what is your realized return?

	Price	Div
Jan 1	10.00	
Mar 31	11.00	0.20
June 30	10.50	0.20
Sep 30	11.10	0.20
Dec 31	11.00	0.20

7. Using the data in the following table, calculate the return for investing in Boeing stock (BA) from January 2, 2008, to January 2, 2009, and also from January 3, 2011, to January 3, 2012, assuming all dividends are reinvested in the stock immediately.

Historical Stock and Dividend Data for Boeing

Date	Price	Dividend	Date	Price	Dividend
1/2/2008	86.62		1/3/2011	66.40	
2/6/2008	79.91	0.40	2/9/2011	72.63	0.42
5/7/2008	84.55	0.40	5/11/2011	79.08	0.42
8/6/2008	65.40	0.40	8/10/2011	57.41	0.42
11/5/2008	49.55	0.40	11/8/2011	66.65	0.42
1/2/2009	45.25		1/3/2012	74.22	

8. Using the data in the table below, calculate the return for investing in this stock from January 1 to December 31.

Stock and Dividend Data for Boeing

Date	Price	Dividend
Jan 1	33.88	
Feb 5	30.67	0.17
May 14	29.49	0.17
Aug 13	32.38	0.17
Nov 12	39.07	0.17
Dec 31	41.99	

9. What was your dividend yield from investing in the stock in Problem 8? What was your capital gain?

10. The last four years of returns for a stock are as follows:

1	2	3	4
−4%	+28%	+12%	+4%

a. What is the average annual return?
b. What is the variance of the stock's returns?
c. What is the standard deviation of the stock's returns?

11. Ten annual returns are listed below.

−19.9%	16.6%	18.0%	−50.0%	43.3%	1.2%	−16.5%	45.6%	45.2%	−3.0%

a. What is the arithmetic average return over the 10-year period?
*b. What is the geometric average return over the 10-year period?
c. If you invested $100 at the beginning of the period, how much would you have at the end?

12. Consider the following five monthly returns:

5%	−2%	4%	8%	−1%

a. Calculate the arithmetic average return over this period and express your answer as a percentage per month.
*b. Calculate the geometric average monthly return over this period.
c. Calculate the monthly variance over this period.
d. Calculate the monthly standard deviation over this period.

13. Explain the difference between the arithmetic average return you calculated in Problem 12a and the geometric average return you calculated in Problem 12b. Are both numbers useful? If so, explain why.

14. Calculate the 95% confidence intervals for the S&P/TSX Composite Index, the S&P 500 in CAD, long-term Government of Canada bonds, and treasury bills included in Figures 10.3 and 10.4.

15. You are choosing between the four investments from Problem 14, and you want to be 95% certain that you do not lose more than 18% on your investment. Which investments should you choose?

16. You observe a portfolio for five years and determine that its average return is 12% and the standard deviation of its returns is 20%. Can you be 95% confident that this portfolio will not lose more than 40% of its value next year?

Common versus Independent Risk and Diversification

***17.** Consider two local banks. Bank A has 100 loans outstanding, each for $1 million, that it expects will be repaid today. Each loan has a 5% probability of default, in which case the bank is not repaid anything. The chance of default is independent across all the loans. Bank B has only one loan of $100 million outstanding, which it also expects will be repaid today. It also has a 5% probability of not being repaid.
a. What is the expected payoff of each bank's loans?
b. How risky are each bank's loans? What is the standard deviation of the payoff of bank A's portfolio of loans? (*Hint*: the risk of default is independent across loans, so the variance of the payoff of the 100-loan portfolio is simply 100 times the variance of the payoff of a single loan.) What is the standard deviation of the payoff of bank B's loan? Which bank faces less risk? Why?

18. You are a risk-averse investor who is considering investing in one of two economies. The expected return and volatility of all stocks in both economies is the same. In the first economy, all stocks move together—in good times all prices rise together and in bad times they all fall together. In the second economy, stock returns are independent—one stock increasing in price has no effect on the prices of other stocks. Which economy would you choose to invest in? Explain.

19. Consider the following six months of returns for two stocks and a portfolio of those two stocks.

	Jan	Feb	Mar	Apr	May	Jun
Stock A	2%	5%	−6%	3%	−2%	4%
Stock B	0%	−3%	8%	−1%	4%	−2%
Portfolio	1%	1%	1%	1%	1%	1%

a. What is the expected return and standard deviation of returns for each of the two stocks?

b. What is the expected return and standard deviation of return for the portfolio?

c. Is the portfolio more or less risky than the two stocks? Why?

DATA CASE

Today is December 31, 2017, and you have just started your new job with a financial planning firm. In addition to studying for all your licensing exams, you have been asked to review a portion of a client's stock portfolio to determine the risk-return profiles of 12 stocks in the portfolio. Unfortunately, your small firm cannot afford the expensive databases that would provide all this information with a few simple keystrokes, but that's why they hired you. Specifically, you have been asked to determine the monthly average returns and standard deviations for the 12 stocks for the past five years.

The stocks (with their symbols in parentheses) are as follows:

Archer Daniels Midland (ADM)
Boeing (BA)
Caterpillar (CAT)
Deere & Co. (DE)
General Mills Inc. (GIS)
eBay Inc. (EBAY)
Hershey (HSY)
International Business Machines Corporation (IBM)
JPMorgan Chase & Co. (JPM)
Microsoft (MSFT)
Procter & Gamble (PG)
Walmart (WMT)

1. Collect price information for each stock from Yahoo! Finance (finance.yahoo.com) as follows:
   - **a.** Enter the stock symbol. On the page for that stock, click "Historical Data."
   - **b.** Under "Time Period," enter the start date as December 1, 2012, and the end date as December 31, 2017, in order to have enough data to cover the five-year period. Make sure you choose "Monthly" next to "Frequency."
   - **c.** After hitting "Apply," click "Download Data."
   - **d.** Open the downloaded file in Excel, and delete all the columns except the date and the adjusted close (the first and next-to-last) columns. When you save the file, select "Save As" from the "File" pull-down menu and then choose "Excel Workbook."
   - **e.** Keep the Excel file open and go back to the Yahoo! Finance webpage. In the address bar of your browser you will see something similar to this web address: https://finance.yahoo.com/quote/ADM/history?period1=1354345200&period2=1514703600&interval=1mo&filter=history&frequency=1mo
   - **f.** In the browser's address bar, find the symbol for Archer Daniels (ADM) and replace it with the symbol for the next company (BA, for Boeing). Hit "Enter" and the page for Boeing will appear. Click "Download Data" to download the file with Boeing's historical prices and open it in Excel. Copy the next-to-last column, "Adj. Close," and paste it into the original Excel file that already has ADM's data. In order to keep track of each stock, change "Adj. Close" at the top of each column to the stock symbol. Make sure that the first and last prices are in the same rows as they are for the first stock. [Note that editing the information in the address bar of your browser is the fastest and least error prone method

to find the data, but you could also repeat steps (a.), (b.), and (c.) for Boeing instead.]

g. Repeat these steps for the remaining 10 stocks, pasting each adjusted closing price right next to those of the other stocks, again making sure that the correct prices on the correct dates all appear on the same rows.

2. Convert these prices to monthly returns by calculating the percentage change in the monthly prices. (*Hint*: Create a separate worksheet within the Excel file.) Note that to compute a return for each month, you need a beginning and ending price, so you will be able to compute 60 monthly returns from the 61 closing prices that you have collected. (The "adjusted close" series from Yahoo! Finance already incorporates dividends, so we may compute returns based on the percentage change in monthly adjusted prices: there is no need to calculate returns using prices *and* dividends as we had done when we used Equation 10.1 earlier.)

3. Compute the mean monthly returns and standard deviations for the monthly returns of each of the stocks. Convert the monthly statistics to annual statistics for easier interpretation (multiply the mean monthly return by 12, and multiply the monthly standard deviation by $\sqrt{12}$).

4. Add a column in your Excel worksheet with the average return across stocks for each month: start with the average return for January 2013 and finish with the average return for December 2017. When you are done, you will have a 13th column of returns: this is the monthly return series of an equally weighted portfolio of these 12 stocks. Compute the mean and standard deviation of monthly returns for the equally weighted portfolio. Since you already calculated the average return of all of the individual stocks, you can also calculate the average of those 12 averages: this should be equal to the average return on the equally weighted portfolio. Convert the monthly statistics for the equally weighted portfolio to annual statistics (as described in step 3) for ease of interpretation.

5. Using the annual statistics, create an Excel chart with standard deviation (volatility) on the x-axis and average return on the y-axis as follows:

a. Create three columns on your spreadsheet with the statistics you created in Questions 3 and 4 for each of the individual stocks and the equally weighted portfolio. The first column will contain the 13 ticker symbols (you can use EWP for the equally weighted portfolio). The second and the third columns will have the annual standard deviation and annual average return for each of the 13 investments. In the end, you will have 13 rows of data, from ADM to EWP.

b. Highlight the data in the last two columns (standard deviation and mean), choose > Insert > Chart > XY Scatter Plot. Complete the chart wizard to finish the plot.

6. What do you notice about the average of the volatilities (standard deviations) of the individual stocks, compared to the volatility of the equally weighted portfolio?

CHAPTER

Systematic Risk and the Equity Risk Premium

11

LEARNING OBJECTIVES

- Calculate the expected return and volatility (standard deviation) of a portfolio
- Understand the relationship between systematic risk and the market portfolio
- Measure systematic risk
- Use the Capital Asset Pricing Model (CAPM) to compute the cost of equity capital for a stock

NOTATION

β_i	beta of security *i* with respect to the market portfolio
$Corr(R_i, R_j)$	correlation between the returns of security *i* and security *j*
$E[R_i]$	expected return of security *i*
$E[R_{Mkt}]$	expected return of the market portfolio
MV_i	total market value (market capitalization) of security *i*
N_i	number of shares outstanding of security *i*
P_i	price per share of security *i*
r_f	risk-free interest rate
R_P	return of portfolio *P*
$SD(R_i)$	standard deviation (volatility) of the return of security *i*
$Var(R_i)$	variance of the return of security *i*
w_i	fraction of the portfolio invested in security *i* (its relative *weight* in the portfolio)

In Chapter 10, we started our exploration of the trade-off between risk and return. We found that investors should expect to experience higher returns for higher risk for large portfolios; the same does not hold true for individual stocks. Stocks have both unsystematic, diversifiable risk and systematic, undiversifiable risk; only the systematic risk is rewarded with higher expected returns. With no reward for bearing unsystematic risk, rational investors should choose to diversify.

Put yourself in the role of a financial manager at a company, such as Canadian Natural Resources. One part of your job would be to calculate Canadian Natural Resources' cost of equity capital so that its managers know what return its equity investors require. Recall that in Chapter 5 we defined the cost of capital as the best available expected return offered in the market on an investment of comparable risk and term. Since only systematic risk contributes to expected returns, we need to measure the systematic risk of Canadian Natural Resources and map it into an expected return for the company. To do so, we need to think about Canadian Natural Resources' stock the way our investors would—as part of a portfolio. As a result, we begin where we left off in the last chapter: with portfolios. After learning how to calculate the risk and expected return of a portfolio, we will focus on the biggest portfolio of them all—the portfolio of *all* risky securities. This portfolio has no diversifiable risk left and can be used as a baseline for measuring systematic risk. From there, we will develop a simple, powerful model that relates the systematic risk of an investment to its expected return. In other words, the model says that the return we should expect on any investment is equal to the risk-free rate of return plus a risk premium proportional to the amount of systematic risk in the investment.

11.1 The Expected Return of a Portfolio

In the last chapter, we learned the important role that portfolios play in reducing unsystematic risk. As financial managers, we have to be mindful that investors hold our company's stock as part of a larger portfolio. Thus, it is important to understand how portfolios work and the implications for the return our investors expect on the stock of our company and the projects we undertake in that company.

Portfolio Weights

We begin by calculating the return and expected return of a portfolio. For example, consider a portfolio with 2000 shares of WestJet worth $20 per share ($40,000 total), and 1000 shares of Barrick worth $60 per share ($60,000 total). The total value of the portfolio is $100,000, so WestJet is 40% of the portfolio and Barrick is 60% of the portfolio. More generally, we can describe a portfolio by its **portfolio weights**, which are the fractions of the total investment in the portfolio held in each individual investment in the portfolio:

portfolio weight The fraction of the total investment in a portfolio held in each individual investment in the portfolio.

$$w_i = \frac{\text{Value of investment } i}{\text{Total value of portfolio}} \tag{11.1}$$

These portfolio weights add up to 100% (that is, $w_1 + w_2 + \cdots + w_n = 100\%$), so that they represent the way we have divided our money between the different individual investments in the portfolio. We can confirm the portfolio weights for our portfolio of WestJet and Barrick:

$$w_{WestJet} = \frac{2000 \times \$20}{100{,}000} = 40\% \quad \text{and} \quad w_{Barrick} = \frac{1000 \times \$60}{100{,}000} = 60\%$$

Portfolio Returns

Once you know the portfolio weight, you can calculate the return on the portfolio. For example, take the portfolio of WestJet and Barrick. If WestJet earns a 10% return and Barrick earns a 15% return, then 40% of the portfolio earns 10% and 60% of the portfolio earns 15%, so the portfolio as a whole earns $(0.40)(10\%) + (0.60)(15\%) = 13\%$.

return on a portfolio The weighted average of the returns on the investments in a portfolio, where the weights correspond to the portfolio weights.

The **return on a portfolio** is the weighted average of the returns on the investments in the portfolio, where the weights correspond to portfolio weights.

Formally, suppose $w_1, \ldots, w_n$ are the portfolio weights of the n investments in a portfolio and these investments have returns $R_1, \ldots, R_n$, then the formula for the return on the portfolio is

$$R_P = w_1 R_1 + w_2 R_2 + \cdots + w_n R_n \tag{11.2}$$

EXAMPLE 11.1 Calculating Portfolio Returns

PROBLEM

Suppose you invest $100,000 and buy 2000 shares of WestJet at $20 per share ($40,000) and 1000 shares of Barrick at $60 per share ($60,000). If WestJet's stock goes up to $24 per share and Barrick stock falls to $57 per share and neither paid dividends, what is the new value of the portfolio? What return did the portfolio earn? Show that Equation 11.2 is true by calculating the individual returns of the stocks and multiplying them by their weights in the portfolio. If you don't buy or sell any shares after the price change, what are the new portfolio weights?

SOLUTION

Plan

Your portfolio: 2000 shares of WestJet: $20 → $24 ($4 capital gain)

1000 shares of Barrick: $60 → $57 ($3 capital loss)

A. To calculate the return on your portfolio, compute its value using the new prices and compare it to the original $100,000 investment.
B. To confirm that Equation 11.2 is true, compute the return on each stock individually using Equation 10.1 from Chapter 10, multiply those returns by their original weights in the portfolio, and compare your answer to the return you just calculated for the portfolio as a whole.

Execute

The new value of your WestJet stock is 2000 × $24 = $48,000, and the new value of your Barrick stock is 1000 × $57 = $57,000. So, the new value of your portfolio is $48,000 + 57,000 = $105,000, for a gain of $5000, or a 5% return on your initial $100,000 investment.

Since neither stock paid any dividends, we calculate their returns simply as the capital gain or loss divided by the purchase price. The return on WestJet stock was $4/$20 = 20%, and the return on Barrick stock was −$3/$60 = −5%.

The initial portfolio weights were $40,000/$100,000 = 40% for WestJet and $60,000/$100,000 = 60% for Barrick, so we can also compute the return of the portfolio from Equation 11.2 as

$$R_P = w_{WestJet} R_{WestJet} + w_{Barrick} R_{Barrick} = 0.40(20\%) + 0.60(-5\%) = 5\%$$

After the price change, the new portfolio weights are equal to the value of your investment in each stock divided by the new portfolio value:

$$w_{WestJet} = \frac{2000 \times \$24}{105{,}000} = 45.71\% \quad \text{and} \quad w_{Barrick} = \frac{1000 \times \$57}{105{,}000} = 54.29\%$$

As a check on your work, always make sure that your portfolio weights sum to 100%!

Evaluate

The $3000 loss on your investment in Barrick was offset by the $8000 gain in your investment in WestJet, for a total gain of $5000, or 5%. The same result comes from giving a 40% weight to the 20% return on WestJet and a 60% weight to the −5% loss on Barrick—you have a total net return of 5%.

After a year, the portfolio weight on WestJet has increased and the weight on Barrick has decreased. Note that without trading, the portfolio weights will increase for the stock(s) in the portfolio whose returns are above the overall portfolio return.

Expected Portfolio Return

expected return of a portfolio The weighted average of expected returns of the investments in a portfolio, where the weights correspond to the portfolio weights.

As we showed in Chapter 10, you can use the historical average return of a security as its expected return. With these expected returns, you can compute the **expected return of a portfolio**, which is simply the weighted average of the expected returns of the investments within it, using the portfolio weights:

$$E[R_P] = w_1E[R_1] + w_2E[R_2] + \cdots + w_nE[R_n] \tag{11.3}$$

We started by stating that you can describe a portfolio by its weights. These weights are used in computing both a portfolio's return and its expected return. Table 11.1 summarizes these concepts.

TABLE 11.1 Summary of Portfolio Concepts

Term	Concept	Equation
Portfolio Weight	The relative investment in your portfolio	$w_i = \dfrac{\text{Value of investment } i}{\text{Total value of portfolio}}$
Portfolio Return	The total return earned on your portfolio, accounting for the returns of all of the securities in the portfolio and their weights	$R_P = w_1R_1 + w_2R_2 + \cdots + w_nR_n$
Portfolio Expected Return	The return you can expect to earn on your portfolio, given the expected returns of the securities in that portfolio and the relative amount you have invested in each	$E[R_P] = w_1E[R_1] + w_2E[R_2] + \cdots + w_nE[R_n]$

EXAMPLE 11.2 Portfolio Expected Return

PROBLEM

Suppose you invest $10,000 in Loblaw Companies Limited (ticker symbol: L) stock, and $30,000 in TransCanada Corp. (ticker symbol: TRP) stock. You expect a return of 10% for Loblaw and 16% for TransCanada. What is the expected return for your portfolio?

SOLUTION

Plan

You have a total of $40,000 invested:

$10,000/$40,000 = 25% in Loblaw: $E[R_L] = 10\%$

$30,000/$40,000 = 75% in TransCanada: $E[R_{TRP}] = 16\%$

Using Equation 11.3, compute the expected return on your whole portfolio by weighting the expected returns of the stocks in your portfolio by their portfolio weights.

■ **Execute**

The expected return on your portfolio is

$$E[R_P] = w_L\, E[R_L] + w_{TRP}\, E[R_{TRP}]$$

$$E[R_P] = 0.25 \times 10\% + 0.75 \times 16\% = 14.5\%$$

■ **Evaluate**

The importance of each stock for the expected return of the overall portfolio is determined by the relative amount of money you have invested in it. Most (75%) of your money is invested in TransCanada, so the overall expected return of the portfolio is much closer to TransCanada's expected return than it is to Loblaw's.

CONCEPT CHECK

1. What do the weights in a portfolio tell us?
2. How is the expected return of a portfolio related to the expected returns of the stocks in the portfolio?

11.2 The Volatility of a Portfolio

Investors in a company such as Canadian Tire care not only about the return but also about the risk of their portfolios. Understanding how Canadian Tire's investors think about risk requires us to understand how to calculate the risk of a portfolio. As explained in Chapter 10, when we combine stocks in a portfolio, some of their risk is eliminated through diversification. The amount of risk that will remain depends on the degree to which the stocks share common risk. The **volatility of a portfolio** is the total risk, measured as standard deviation, of the portfolio. In this section, we describe the tools to quantify the degree to which two stocks share risk and to determine the volatility of a portfolio.

volatility of a portfolio
The total risk, measured as standard deviation, of a portfolio.

Diversifying Risks

Let's begin with a simple example of how risk changes when stocks are combined in a portfolio. Table 11.2 shows returns for three hypothetical stocks, along with their average returns and volatilities. Note that while the three stocks have the same volatility and average return, the pattern of returns differs. In years when the airline stocks performed well, the oil stock tended to do poorly (see 2012 to 2013), and when the airlines did poorly, the oil stock tended to do well (see 2015 to 2016).

Table 11.2 also shows the returns for two portfolios of the stocks. The first portfolio is an equal investment in the two airlines, North Jet and South Jet. The second portfolio is equal investments in South Jet and Alberta Oil. The bottom two rows display the average return and volatility for each stock and portfolio of stocks. Note that the 10% average return of both portfolios is equal to the 10% average return of the stocks, consistent with Equation 11.3. However, as Figure 11.1 illustrates, their volatilities (standard deviations)—12.1% for portfolio 1 and 5.1% for portfolio 2—are very different from the 13.4% volatility for the individual stocks *and* from each other.

TABLE 11.2 Returns for Three Stocks, and Portfolios of Pairs of Stocks

	Stock Returns			Portfolio Returns	
				(1)	(2)
Year	North Jet	South Jet	Alberta Oil	Half N.J. and Half S.J.	Half S.J. and Half A.O.
2012	21%	9%	−2%	15.0%	3.5%
2013	30%	21%	−5%	25.5%	8.0%
2014	7%	7%	9%	7.0%	8.0%
2015	−5%	−2%	21%	−3.5%	9.5%
2016	−2%	−5%	30%	−3.5%	12.5%
2017	9%	30%	7%	19.5%	18.5%
Avg. Return	10.0%	10.0%	10.0%	10.0%	10.0%
Volatility	13.4%	13.4%	13.4%	12.1%	5.1%

This example demonstrates two important things that we learned in the previous chapter. First, *by combining stocks into a portfolio, we reduce risk through diversification.* Because the stocks do not move identically, some of the risk is averaged out in a portfolio. As a result, both portfolios have lower risk than the individual stocks.

Second, *the amount of risk that is eliminated in a portfolio depends on the degree to which the stocks face common risks and move together.* Because the two airline stocks tend to perform well or poorly at the same time, the portfolio of airline stocks has a volatility that is only slightly lower than the volatility of the individual stocks. The airline and oil stocks, on the other hand, do not move together. Indeed, they tend to move in opposite directions. As a result, more risk is cancelled out, making that portfolio much less risky.

Measuring Stocks' Co-movement: Correlation

Figure 11.1 emphasizes the fact that to find the risk of a portfolio, we need to know more than just the risk of the component stocks: we need to know the degree to which the stocks' returns move together. The stocks' *correlation* is such a measure, ranging from −1 to +1.[1]

correlation A measure of the degree to which returns share common risk, calculated as the covariance of the returns divided by the standard deviation of each return.

As Figure 11.2 shows, **correlation** is a barometer of the degree to which the returns share common risk. The closer the correlation is to +1, the more the returns tend to move together as a result of common risk. When the correlation equals 0, the returns are *uncorrelated*; that is, they have no tendency to move together or in opposite directions. Independent risks are uncorrelated. Finally, the closer the correlation is to −1, the more the returns tend to move in opposite directions.

When will stock returns be highly correlated with each other? Stock returns will tend to move together if they are affected similarly by economic events. Thus, stocks in the same industry tend to have more highly correlated returns than stocks in different industries.

[1]Correlation is scaled covariance and is defined as

$$Corr(R_i, R_j) = \frac{Cov(R_i, R_j)}{SD(R_i)SD(R_j)}$$

FIGURE 11.1 **Volatility of Airline and Oil Portfolios**

The figures graph the portfolio returns from Table 11.2. In panel (a), we see that the airline stocks move in synch with each other, so that a portfolio made up of the two airline stocks does not achieve much diversification. In panel (b), because the airline and oil stocks often move in opposite directions, a portfolio of South Jet and Alberta Oil achieves greater diversification and lower portfolio volatility. Because both stocks have an average return of 10%, so does the portfolio, but it achieves that return with much less volatility than either of the stocks.

Panel (a): Portfolio split equally between South Jet and North Jet

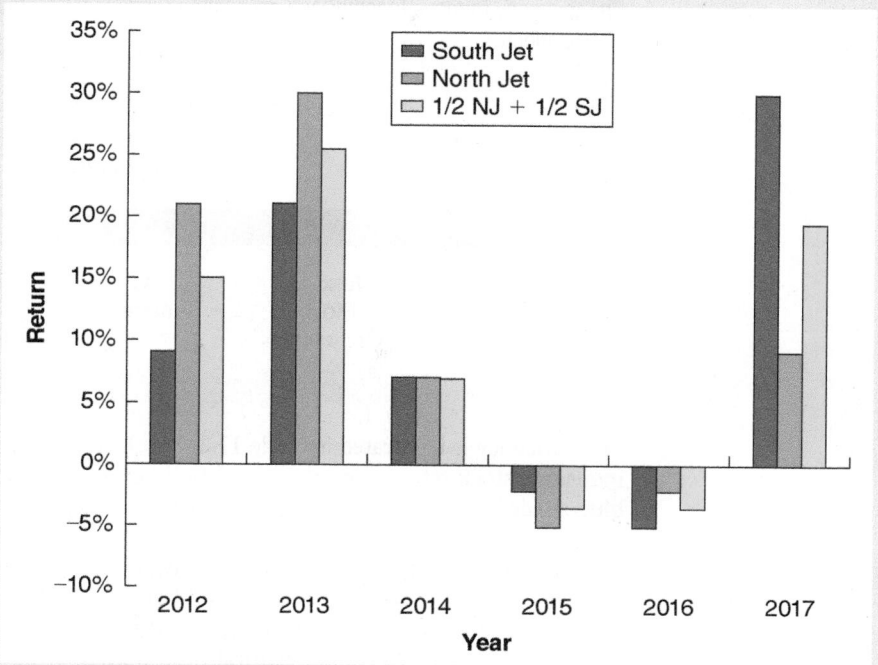

Panel (b): Portfolio split equally between South Jet and Alberta Oil

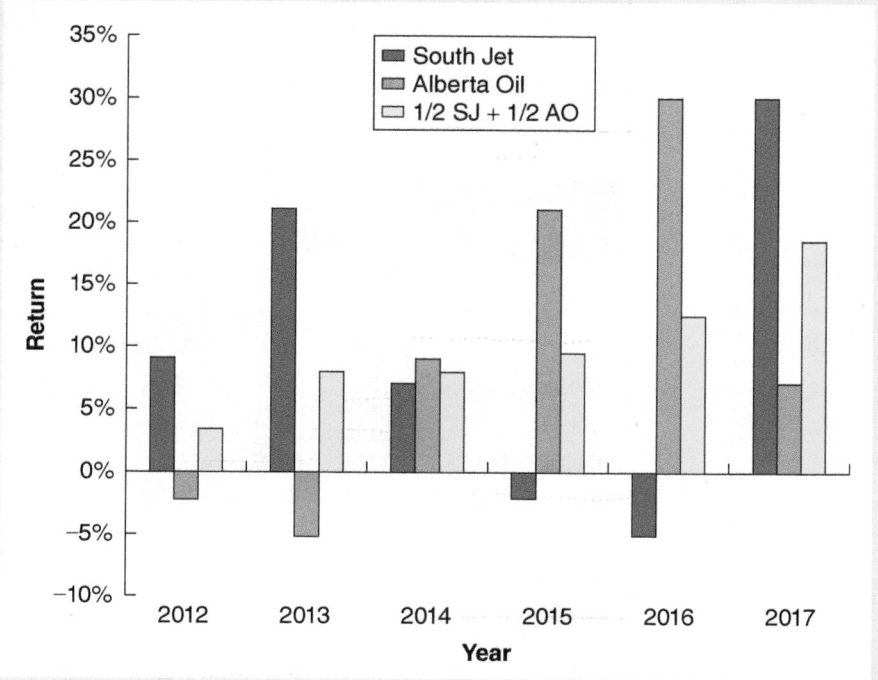

FIGURE 11.2 Correlation

The correlation measures how returns move in relation to each other. The correlation is between +1 (returns always move together) and −1 (returns always move oppositely). Independent risks have no tendency to move together and have zero correlation. See Table 11.3 for more examples of correlations.

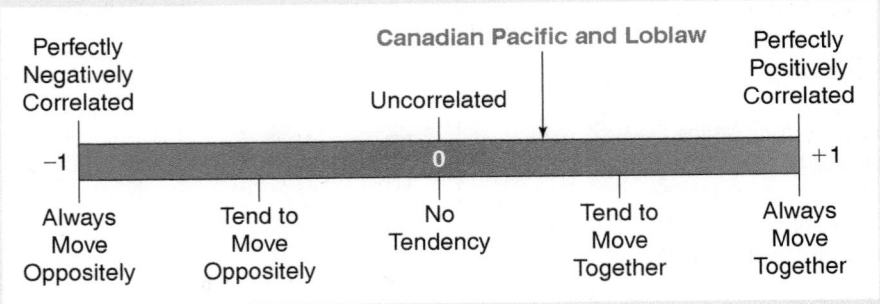

This tendency is illustrated in Table 11.3, which shows the volatility (standard deviation) of individual stock returns and the correlation between them for several common stocks. The blue-shaded boxes along the diagonal show the correlation of a stock with itself—which has to be 1 (a stock is perfectly correlated with itself). The table can be read across the rows or down the columns. Each correlation is shown twice. For example, reading across the Stantec row, the correlation between Stantec and Canadian Natural Resources (yellow box) is 0.44, which you could also find by reading across the Canadian Natural Resources row for the correlation between Canadian Natural Resources and Stantec. These two companies have the highest correlation in the table. Stantec is a technical services company and Canadian Natural Resources is an energy company: it would seem to make sense that customers would spend more (or less) during the same economic circumstances for both of these companies' products and services. None of the correlations are negative, showing the general tendency of stocks to move together. The lowest correlations are shown in the green boxes for example, for OpenText and WestJet, which is 0.00, implying that there is no relationship between

TABLE 11.3 Estimated Annual Volatilities and Correlations for Selected Stocks (Based on Monthly Returns, 2013–2017)

	Stantec	Canadian Tire	Canadian Pacific	OpenText	Loblaw	Canadian Natural Resources	WestJet Airlines
STANDARD DEVIATION	24%	18%	22%	22%	17%	24%	22%
Stantec	1.00	0.18	0.41	0.12	0.12	0.44	0.24
Canadian Tire	0.18	1.00	0.25	0.02	0.35	0.12	0.00
Canadian Pacific	0.41	0.25	1.00	0.29	0.28	0.27	0.19
OpenText	0.12	0.02	0.29	1.00	0.21	0.09	0.00
Loblaw	0.12	0.35	0.28	0.21	1.00	0.07	0.05
Canadian Natural Resources	0.44	0.12	0.27	0.09	0.07	1.00	0.18
WestJet Airlines	0.24	0.00	0.19	0.00	0.05	0.18	1.00

Source: Data from Yahoo!Finance Canada.

firms in the computer software sector and transportation firms. Figure 11.3 shows scatter plots for the returns of Stantec and Canadian Natural Resources, and OpenText and WestJet. While there is a clear relationship between the returns of Stantec and Canadian Natural Resources, the plot for OpenText and WestJet looks like an unrelated cloud of returns.

FIGURE 11.3 Scatter Plots of Returns

The two panels show plots of pairs of monthly returns for Stantec and Canadian Natural Resources, and OpenText and WestJet. Notice the positive relationship between Stantec and Canadian Natural Resources, which move up and down together, versus the lack of a relationship between OpenText and WestJet.

Panel a: Monthly Returns for Stantec and Canadian Natural Resources

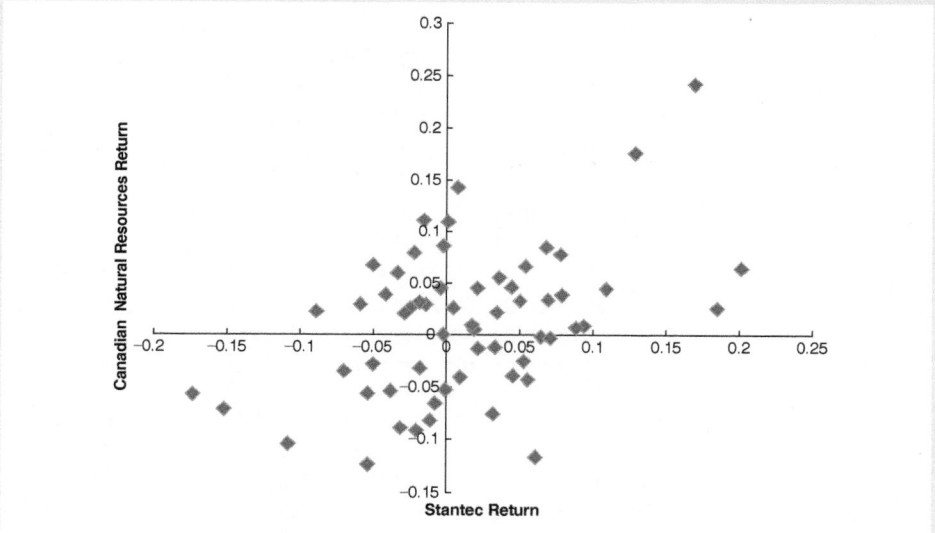

Panel b: Monthly Returns for OpenText and WestJet

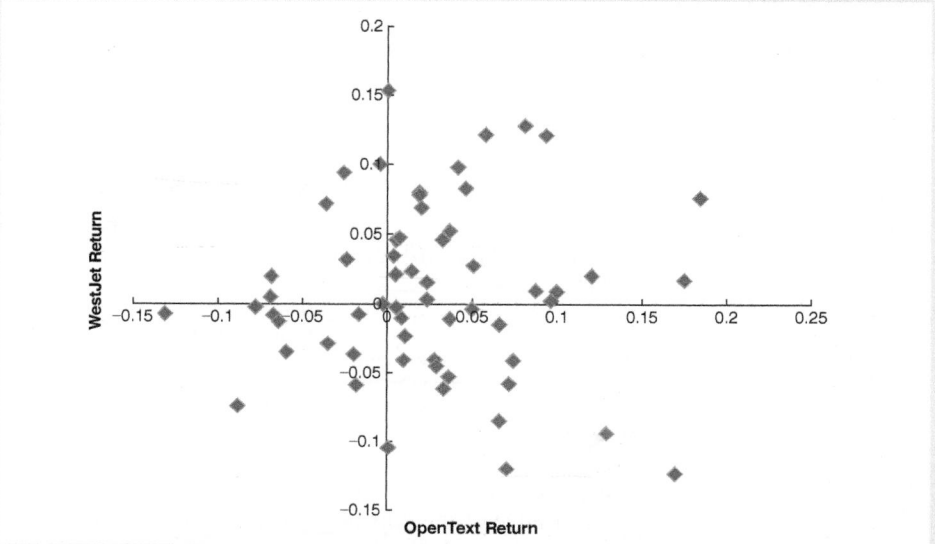

Source: Data from Yahoo!Finance Canada.

USING EXCEL

Calculating the Correlation between Two Sets of Returns

The correlations presented in Table 11.3 were all calculated by comparing the returns of two stocks. Here we describe how you can use Excel to calculate these correlations.

1. Enter or import the historical returns for the two stocks into Excel.
2. Next, highlight the cell where you want to produce the correlation coefficient, and select Function from the Insert pull-down menu.
3. Select the "CORREL" function, highlight the returns for which you want to compute the correlation (first choose "Array1" then "Array2"), and click "Done."

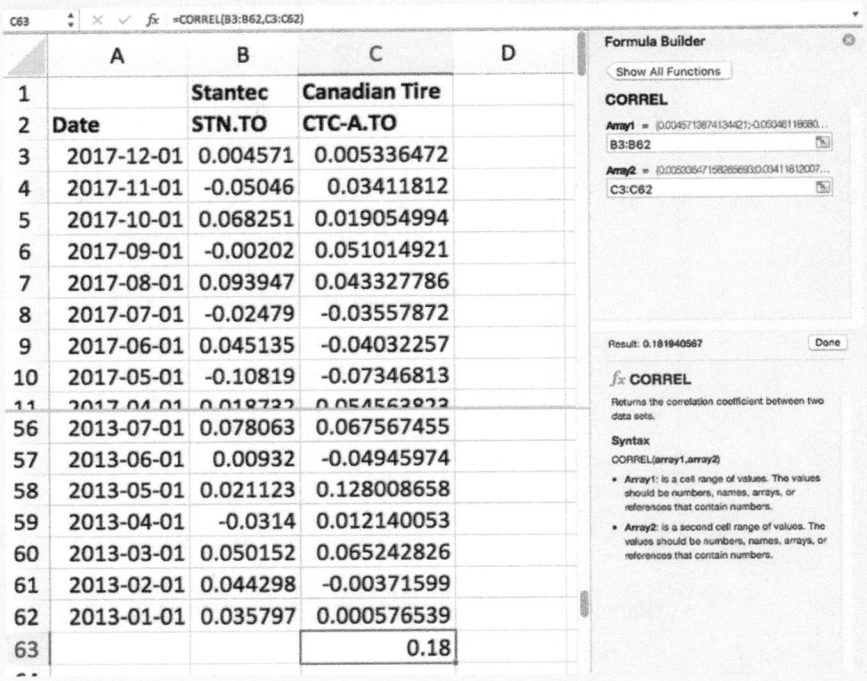

	A	B	C	D
1		Stantec	Canadian Tire	
2	Date	STN.TO	CTC-A.TO	
3	2017-12-01	0.004571	0.005336472	
4	2017-11-01	-0.05046	0.03411812	
5	2017-10-01	0.068251	0.019054994	
6	2017-09-01	-0.00202	0.051014921	
7	2017-08-01	0.093947	0.043327786	
8	2017-07-01	-0.02479	-0.03557872	
9	2017-06-01	0.045135	-0.04032257	
10	2017-05-01	-0.10819	-0.07346813	
11	2017-04-01	0.018732	0.054563823	
56	2013-07-01	0.078063	0.067567455	
57	2013-06-01	0.00932	-0.04945974	
58	2013-05-01	0.021123	0.128008658	
59	2013-04-01	-0.0314	0.012140053	
60	2013-03-01	0.050152	0.065242826	
61	2013-02-01	0.044298	-0.00371599	
62	2013-01-01	0.035797	0.000576539	
63			0.18	

Courtesy of Microsoft corporation

Computing a Portfolio's Variance and Standard Deviation

We now have the tools to formally compute portfolio variance. The formula for the variance of a two-stock portfolio is

$$Var(R_P) = \overbrace{w_1^2 SD(R_1)^2}^{\text{Accounting for the risk of stock 1}} + \overbrace{w_2^2 SD(R_2)^2}^{\text{Accounting for the risk of stock 2}} + \overbrace{2w_1 w_2 Corr(R_1, R_2) SD(R_1) SD(R_2)}^{\text{Adjustment for how much the two stocks move together}} \quad (11.4)$$

The three parts of Equation 11.4 each account for an important determinant of the overall variance of the portfolio—the risk of stock 1, the risk of stock 2, and an adjustment for how much the two stocks move together (their correlation, given as *Corr*

(R_1, R_2)).[2] The equation demonstrates that with a positive amount invested in each stock, the more the stocks move together and the higher their correlation, the more volatile the portfolio will be. The portfolio will have the greatest variance if the stocks have a perfect positive correlation of +1. In fact, when combining stocks into a portfolio, unless the stocks all have a perfect positive correlation of +1 with each other, the risk of the portfolio will be lower than the weighted average volatility of the individual stocks (as shown in Figure 11.1). Contrast this fact with a portfolio's expected return. *The expected return of a portfolio is equal to the weighted average expected return of its stocks, but the volatility of a portfolio is less than the weighted average volatility. As a result, it's clear that we can eliminate some volatility by diversifying.* Equation 11.4 formalizes the concept of diversification introduced in the last chapter. In Example 11.3, we use Equation 11.4 to compute the volatility of a portfolio.

EXAMPLE 11.3 Computing the Volatility of a Two-Stock Portfolio

PROBLEM

Using the data from Table 11.3, what is the volatility (standard deviation) of a portfolio with equal amounts invested in Stantec (ticker symbol: STN) and Canadian Pacific (ticker symbol: CP) stock? What is the standard deviation of a portfolio with equal amounts invested in Loblaw (ticker symbol: L) and Canadian Natural Resources (ticker symbol: CNQ)?

SOLUTION

Plan

	Weight	Volatility	Correlation with Stantec
Stantec	0.5	0.24	1.00
Canadian Pacific	0.5	0.22	0.41

	Weight	Volatility	Correlation with Loblaw
Loblaw	0.5	0.17	1.00
Canadian Natural Resources	0.5	0.24	0.07

A. With the portfolio weights, volatility, and correlations of the stocks in the two portfolios, we have all the information we need to use Equation 11.4 to compute the variance of each portfolio.
B. After computing the portfolio's variance, we can take the square root to get the portfolio's standard deviation.

[2]For three stocks, the formula is

$$Var(R_P) = w_1^2 SD(R_1)^2 + w_2^2 SD(R_2)^2 + w_3^2 SD(R_3)^2 + 2w_1w_2 Corr(R_1, R_2)SD(R_1)SD(R_2) + 2w_2w_3 Corr(R_2, R_3)SD(R_2)SD(R_3) + 2w_1w_3 Corr(R_1, R_3)SD(R_1)SD(R_3)$$

and for n stocks, it is

$$\sum_{i=1}^{n}\sum_{j=1}^{n} w_i w_j \, Corr(R_i, R_j)SD(R_i)SD(R_j)$$

■ **Execute**

For Stantec and Canadian Pacific, from Equation 11.4 the portfolio's variance is

$$\begin{aligned} Var(R_P) &= w^2_{STN} SD(R_{STN})^2 + w^2_{CP} SD(R_{CP})^2 \\ &\quad + 2w_{STN}w_{CP}\, Corr(R_{STN}, R_{CP}) SD(R_{STN}) SD(R_{CP}) \\ &= (0.50)^2(0.24)^2 + (0.50)^2\,(0.22)^2 + 2(0.50)(0.50)(0.41)(0.24)(0.22) \\ &= 0.037 \end{aligned}$$

The standard deviation is, therefore,

$$SD(R_P) = \sqrt{Var(R_P)} = \sqrt{0.037} = 0.193 \text{ or } 19.3\%$$

For the portfolio of Loblaw and Canadian Natural Resources,

$$\begin{aligned} Var(R_P) &= w^2_L SD(R_L)^2 + w^2_{CNQ} SD(R_{CNQ})^2 \\ &\quad + 2w_L w_{CNQ}\, Corr(R_L, R_{CNQ}) SD(R_L) SD(R_{CNQ}) \\ &= (0.50)^2(0.17)^2 + (0.50)^2\,(0.24)^2 + 2(0.50)(0.50)(0.07)(0.17)(0.24) \\ &= 0.023 \end{aligned}$$

The standard deviation in this case is

$$SD(R_P) = \sqrt{Var(R_P)} = \sqrt{0.023} = 0.152 \text{ or } 15.2\%$$

■ **Evaluate**

The weights, standard deviations, and correlation of the two stocks are needed to compute the variance and then the standard deviation of the portfolio. Here, we computed the standard deviation of the portfolio of Stantec and Canadian Pacific to be 19.3% and of Loblaw and Canadian Natural Resources to be 15.2%. Note that the both portfolios are less volatile than either of the individual stocks. The portfolio of Loblaw and Canadian Natural Resources is also less volatile than the portfolio of Stantec and Canadian Pacific: the much lower correlation between Loblaw and Canadian Natural Resources leads to greater diversification benefits in that portfolio.

Risk versus Return: Choosing an Efficient Portfolio with Two Stocks

Now that we understand how to calculate the expected return and volatility of a portfolio, we can return to one of the main goals of the chapter—how an investor can create an efficient portfolio. We will discuss only the simplest case—an investor who can choose between only two stocks.

Consider a portfolio of Intel and Coca-Cola stock. Suppose an investor believes these stocks will perform as follows:

			Correlation with...	
Stock	**Expected Return**	**Volatility**	**Intel**	**Coca-Cola**
Intel	26%	50%	1.0	0.0
Coca-Cola	6%	25%	0.0	1.0

How should the investor choose a portfolio of these two stocks? Are some portfolios preferable to others?

Let's compute the expected return and volatility for different combinations of the stocks. Consider a portfolio with 40% invested in Intel stock and 60% invested in Coca-Cola stock. We can compute the expected return from Equation 11.3 as

$$E[R_{40-60}] = w_I E[R_I] + w_C E[R_C] = 0.40(26\%) + 0.60(6\%) = 14\%$$

We can compute the variance using Equation 11.4,

$$\begin{aligned} Var(R_{40-60}) &= w_1^2 SD(R_1)^2 + w_C^2 SD(R_C)^2 + 2w_I w_C Corr(R_I, R_C) SD(R_I) SD(R_C) \\ &= 0.40^2(0.50)^2 + 0.60^2(0.25)^2 + 2(0.40)(0.60)(0)(0.50)(0.25) \\ &= 0.0625 \end{aligned}$$

so that the volatility is $SD(R_{40-60}) = \sqrt{0.0625} = 25\%$. Table 11.4 shows the results for different portfolio weights.

TABLE 11.4 Expected Returns and Volatility for Different Portfolios of Two Stocks

Portfolio Weights		Expected Return (%)	Volatility (%)
w_I	w_C	$E[R_P]$	$SD[R_P]$
1.00	0.00	26.0	50.0
0.80	0.20	22.0	40.3
0.60	0.40	18.0	31.6
0.40	0.60	14.0	25.0
0.20	0.80	10.0	22.3
0.00	1.00	6.0	25.0

Due to diversification, it is possible to find a portfolio with even lower volatility than either stock. Investing 20% in Intel stock and 80% in Coca-Cola stock, for example, has a volatility of only 22.3%. But knowing that investors care about volatility *and* expected return, we must consider both simultaneously. To do so, we plot the volatility and expected return of each portfolio in Figure 11.4. We labelled the portfolios from Table 11.4 with the portfolio weights. The curve (a hyperbola) represents the set of portfolios that we can create using arbitrary weights.

inefficient portfolio A portfolio is inefficient if it is possible to find another portfolio that is better in terms of both expected return and volatility. An inefficient portfolio is dominated by (i.e., is inferior to) another portfolio with higher return and lower volatility.

efficient frontier A portfolio is efficient if it offers the highest possible expected return for a given level of volatility. The set of all efficient portfolios is known as the efficient frontier.

Faced with the choices in Figure 11.4, which ones make sense for an investor who is concerned with both the expected return and the volatility of her portfolio? Suppose the investor considers investing 100% in Coca-Cola stock. As we can see from Figure 11.4, other portfolios—such as the portfolio with 20% in Intel stock and 80% in Coca-Cola stock—make the investor better off in *both* ways: (1) they have a higher expected return and (2) they have lower volatility. As a result, investing solely in Coca-Cola stock is not a good idea.

Identifying Inefficient Portfolios. More generally, we say a portfolio is an **inefficient portfolio** whenever it is possible to find another portfolio that is better in terms of both expected return and volatility. Looking at Figure 11.4, a portfolio is inefficient if there are other portfolios above and to the left—that is, to the northwest—of it. Investing solely in Coca-Cola stock is inefficient, and the same is true of all portfolios with more than 80% in Coca-Cola stock (the blue part of the curve). Inefficient portfolios are not optimal for an investor.

Identifying Efficient Portfolios. By contrast, portfolios with at least 20% in Intel stock are efficient (the red part of the curve): there is no other portfolio of the two stocks that offers a higher expected return with lower volatility. The **efficient frontier** is the set of all efficient

FIGURE 11.4 Volatility versus Expected Return for Portfolios of Intel and Coca-Cola Stock

Labels indicate portfolio weights (w_I, w_C) for Intel and Coca-Cola stocks. Portfolios on the red portion of the curve, with at least 20% invested in Intel stock, are efficient. Those on the blue portion of the curve, with less than 20% invested in Intel stock, are inefficient—an investor can earn a higher expected return with lower risk by choosing an alternative portfolio.

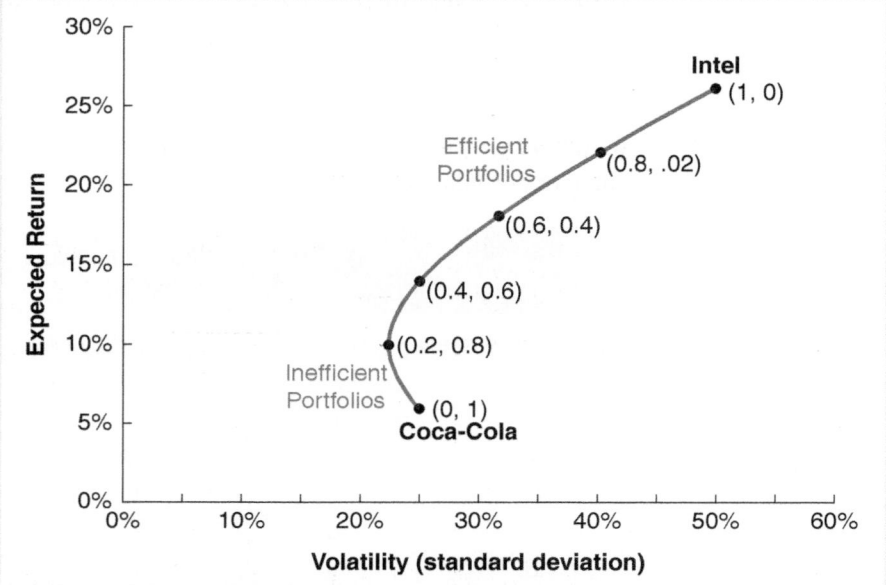

portfolios; this is the red portion of the curve in Figure 11.4. While we can rule out inefficient portfolios as inferior investment choices as they are clearly dominated by one or more of the efficient portfolios, we cannot easily rank the efficient ones; investors will choose among them (along the efficient frontier) based on their own preferences for return versus risk. For example, an extremely conservative investor who cares only about minimizing risk would choose the lowest-volatility portfolio (20% Intel, 80% Coca-Cola). An aggressive investor might choose to invest 100% in Intel stock—even though that approach is riskier, the investor may be willing to take that chance to earn a higher expected return.

EXAMPLE 11.4 Improving Returns with an Efficient Portfolio

PROBLEM

Emily Ashley has invested 100% of her money in Coca-Cola stock and is seeking investment advice. She would like to earn the highest expected return possible without increasing her volatility. Which portfolio would you recommend?

SOLUTION

In Figure 11.4, we can see that Emily can invest up to 40% in Intel stock without increasing her volatility. Because Intel stock has a higher expected return than Coca-Cola stock, she will earn higher expected returns by putting more money in Intel stock. Therefore, you should recommend that Emily put 40% of her money in Intel stock, leaving 60% in Coca-Cola stock. This portfolio has the same volatility of 25%, but an expected return of 14% rather than the 6% she has now.

if cor = 1, no diversification

The Effect of Correlation

In Figure 11.4, we assumed that the returns of Intel and Coca-Cola stocks are uncorrelated. Let's consider how the risk and return combinations in the figure would change if the correlations were different.

Correlation has no effect on the expected return of a portfolio. For example, a 40–60 portfolio will still have an expected return of 14%. However, the volatility of the portfolio will differ depending on the correlation. In particular, the lower the correlation, the lower the volatility we can obtain. In terms of Figure 11.4, as we lower the correlation and, therefore, the volatility of the portfolios, the curve showing the portfolios will bend to the left to a greater degree. This effect is illustrated in Figure 11.5.

When the stocks are perfectly positively correlated, the set of portfolios is identified by the straight line between them. In this extreme case (the red line in Figure 11.5), the volatility of the portfolio is equal to the weighted average volatility of the two stocks—there is no diversification. When the correlation is less than 1, however, the volatility of the portfolios is reduced due to diversification, and the curve bends to the left. The reduction in risk (and the bending of the curve) becomes greater as the correlation decreases. At the other extreme of perfect negative correlation (blue line), the line again becomes straight, this time reflecting off the vertical axis. In particular, when the two stocks are perfectly negatively correlated, it becomes possible to hold a portfolio that bears absolutely no risk.

The Volatility of a Large Portfolio

We can gain additional benefits of diversification by holding more than two stocks in our portfolio. As we add more stocks to our portfolio, the diversifiable firm-specific risk

FIGURE 11.5 **Effect on Volatility and Expected Return of Changing the Correlation between Intel and Coca-Cola Stock**

This figure illustrates correlations of 1, 0.5, 0, − 0.5, and − 1. The lower the correlation, the lower the risk of the portfolios.

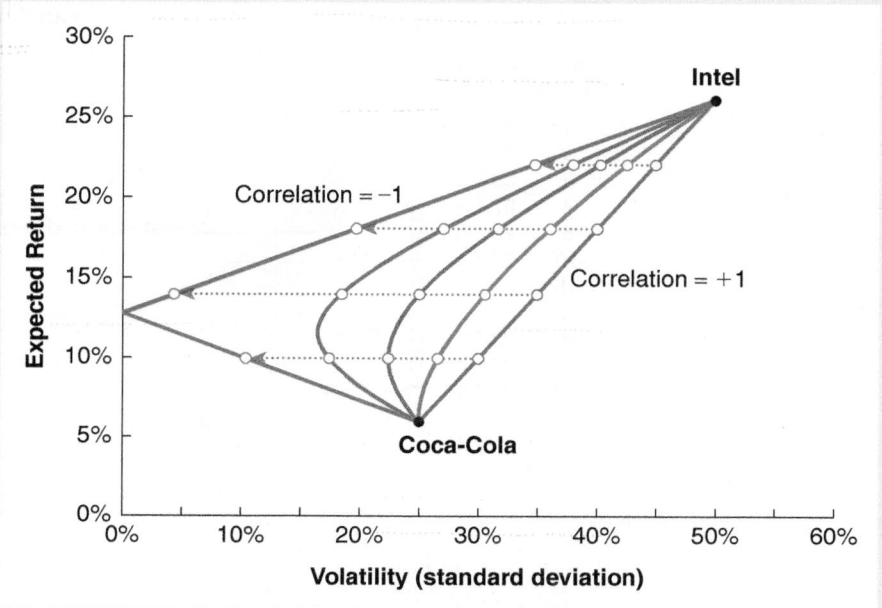

NOBEL PRIZE

Harry Markowitz

The techniques that allow an investor to find the portfolio with the highest expected return for any level of standard deviation (or volatility) were developed in an article, "Portfolio Selection," published in the *Journal of Finance* in 1952 by Harry Markowitz. Markowitz's approach has become one of the main methods of portfolio optimization used on Wall Street. In recognition of his contribution, Markowitz was the co-winner of the Nobel Prize for Economics in 1990.

for each stock matters less and less. Only risk that is common to all of the stocks in the portfolio continues to matter.

equally weighted portfolio A portfolio in which the same dollar amount is invested in each stock.

In Figure 11.6, we graph the volatility for an *equally weighted portfolio* with different numbers of stocks. In an **equally weighted portfolio**, the same amount of money is invested in each stock. Note that the volatility declines as the number of stocks in the portfolio grows. In fact, nearly half the volatility of the individual stocks is eliminated in a large portfolio by diversification. The benefit of diversification is most dramatic

FIGURE 11.6 Volatility of an Equally Weighted Portfolio versus the Number of Stocks

The graph in panel (b) is based on the data in panel (a). Note that the volatility declines as we increase the number of stocks in the portfolio. Yet even in a very large portfolio, systematic (market) risk remains. Also, note that the volatility declines at a decreasing rate. (The effect of going from one to two stocks, an 8 percentage point decrease in volatility, is bigger than the effect of going from four to five stocks, a 1.1 percentage point decrease.) The graph is formed based on the assumption that each stock has a volatility of 40% and a correlation with other stocks of 0.28. Both are average for large stocks.

Panel (a)

No. Stocks	Portfolio Volatility
1	40.0%
2	32.0%
3	28.8%
4	27.1%
5	26.0%
10	23.7%
15	22.9%
20	22.5%
25	22.2%
30	22.1%
50	21.7%
100	21.5%
1000	21.2%

Panel (b)

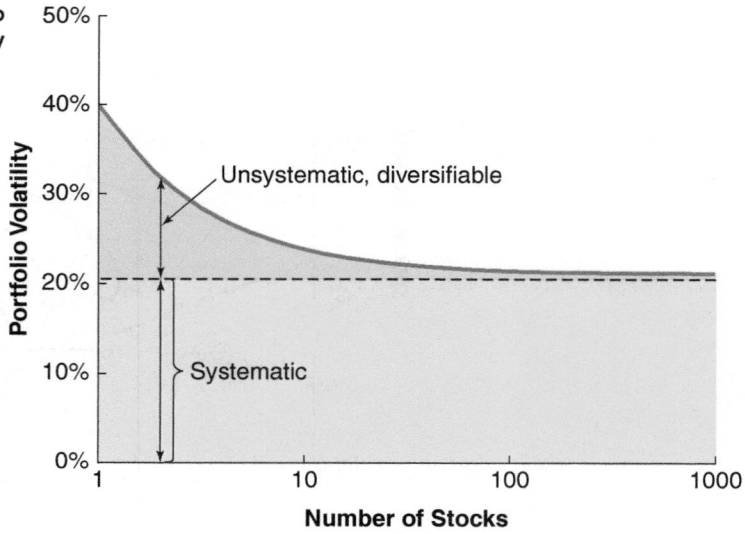

initially—the decrease in volatility going from one to two stocks is much larger than the decrease going from 100 to 101 stocks. Even for a very large portfolio, however, we cannot eliminate all of the risk—the systematic risk remains.

CONCEPT CHECK

3. What determines how much risk will be eliminated by combining stocks in a portfolio?
4. When do stocks have more or less correlation?

11.3 Measuring Systematic Risk

Our goal is to understand the impact of risk on the firm's investors. By understanding how they view risk, we can quantify the relationship between risk and required return to produce a discount rate for our present value calculations. In Chapter 10, we established that the only risk that is related to return is systematic risk, but standard deviation measures *total* risk, including the unsystematic part. We need a way to measure just the systematic risk of an investment opportunity. The previous section contains two important insights that we will now build on to determine the sensitivity of individual stocks to risk. To recap,

1. *The amount of a stock's risk that is removed by diversification depends on its correlation with other stocks in the portfolio.* For example, we showed in Example 11.3 that much less risk is diversified away in a portfolio combining Stantec and Canadian Pacific than in a portfolio consisting of Loblaw and Canadian Natural Resources.
2. *If you build a large enough portfolio, you can remove all unsystematic risk by diversification, but you will still be left with systematic risk.* Figure 11.4 shows that as the number of stocks in your portfolio grows, the unsystematic positive and negative events affecting only a few stocks will cancel out, leaving systematic events as the only source of risk for the portfolio.

Role of the Market Portfolio

As we explained in the previous chapter, investors should diversify their portfolios in order to reduce their risk. If investors choose their portfolios optimally, they will do so until no further diversifiable risk is present, and only systematic risk remains. Let's assume that all investors behave in this way:

Suppose all investors hold portfolios that contain only systematic risk.

If that is the case, then consider the portfolio we obtain by combining the portfolios of every investor. Because each investor's portfolio contains only systematic risk, the same is true for this "aggregate" portfolio. So, the aggregate portfolio held by all investors is a fully diversified, optimal portfolio. Moreover, we can identify this portfolio; because all securities are held by someone, the aggregate portfolio contains all shares outstanding of every risky security. We call this portfolio the **market portfolio**.

market portfolio The portfolio of all risky investments, held in proportion to their value.

To illustrate, imagine that there are only two companies in the world, each with 1000 shares outstanding:

	Number of Shares Outstanding	Price per Share	Market Capitalization
Company A	1000	$40	$40,000
Company B	1000	$10	$10,000

In this simple setting, the market portfolio consists of 1000 shares of each stock and has a total value of $50,000. Stock A's portfolio weight is, therefore, 80% ($40,000/$50,000) and B's is 20% ($10,000/$50,000). Because all of the shares of A and all of the shares of B must be held by someone, the sum of all investors' portfolios must equal this market portfolio. Note from this example that the portfolio weight of each stock is proportional to the total market value of its outstanding shares, which is called its **market capitalization**:

market capitalization The total market value of equity; equals the market price per share times the number of shares.

$$\text{Market Capitalization} = (\text{Number of Shares Outstanding}) \times (\text{Price per Share}) \quad (11.5)$$

More generally, the market portfolio will consist of all risky securities in the market, with portfolio weights proportional to their market capitalization. Thus, for example, if Canadian Tire's market capitalization were equal to 3% of the total market value of all securities, then it would have a 3% weight in the market portfolio. Because stocks are held in proportion to their market capitalization (value), we say that the market portfolio is a **value-weighted portfolio**.

value-weighted portfolio A portfolio in which each security is held in proportion to its market capitalization.

Because the market portfolio contains only systematic risk, we can use it to measure the amount of systematic risk of other securities in the market. In particular, any risk that is correlated with the market portfolio must be systematic risk. Therefore, by looking at the sensitivity of a stock's return to the overall market, we can calculate the amount of systematic risk the stock has.

Stock Market Indexes as the Market Portfolio

While the market portfolio is easy to identify, actually constructing it is a different matter. Because it should contain all risky securities, we need to include all stocks, bonds, real estate, commodities, and so on, both in Canada and around the word. Clearly, it would be impractical if not impossible to collect and update returns on all risky assets everywhere. In practice, we use a **market proxy**—a portfolio whose return should track the underlying, unobservable market portfolio. The most common proxy portfolios are *market indexes*, which are broadly used to represent the performance of the stock market. A **market index** reports the value of a particular portfolio of securities.

market proxy A portfolio whose return is believed to closely track the true market portfolio.

market index The market value of a broad-based portfolio of securities.

S&P/TSX Composite Index. The most familiar index in Canada is the S&P/TSX Composite Index. The weights of the components of the index are determined by the market capitalization of the companies in it. Even though the index includes 250 (as of March 2018) of the over 5000 public firms in Canada, because the index includes the largest stocks, it represents about 95% of Canada's equity market capitalization.

S&P/TSX 60 Index. Another popular index is the S&P/TSX 60. The weights of the 60 companies' stocks are determined partially by their industry sectors that make up the broader composite index. The companies that make up the S&P/TSX 60 Index are large and very liquid. Because of the market capitalization and liquidity of the stocks, investors and portfolio managers consider the S&P/TSX 60 Index easier to replicate than the S&P/TSX Composite Index.

Dow Jones Industrial Average. Most Canadian media also report on the U.S. stock market. The most widely quoted stock index in the United States is the Dow Jones Industrial Average, or DJIA. This index consists of a portfolio of 30 large, industrial stocks. While these stocks are chosen to be representative of different sectors of the economy, they clearly do not represent the entire market. Despite being non-representative of the entire market, the DJIA remains widely cited because it is one of the oldest stock market indexes (first published in 1884).

INDEX FUNDS AND EXCHANGE TRADED FUNDS

One easy way investors can buy (an approximation of) the market portfolio is to invest in an index fund or exchange traded fund (ETF), which, in turn, invests in stocks and other securities with the goal of matching the performance of a particular market index. Many mutual fund companies offer index funds and ETFs. For example, BlackRock Asset Management Canada Limited has several funds called iShares that trade on the TSX. Other subsidiaries of BlackRock Inc. have funds that trade on exchanges around the world. For Canadian investors, iShares are available that replicate the Canadian indexes and the different industry sectors for Canada. Also traded on the TSX are iShares that replicate the S&P 500 and other international stock indices.

The Vanguard Group, which specializes in index funds, became the largest mutual fund company in 2012. Vanguard was founded in 1975 by John Bogle, who advocates the benefits of index funds for individual investors. Comparing index funds to the strategy of trying to pick hot stocks, Bogle reportedly said, "What's the point of looking for the needle in the haystack? Why not own the haystack?"

In August of 1976, Vanguard created its well-known S&P 500 Index Fund, which tries to match the performance of the S&P 500 index as closely as possible. As of March 2018, this fund had $270 billion in assets. Vanguard's Total Stock Market Index Fund is designed to track the performance of the CRSP US Total Market index, an index that measures the performance of all U.S. stocks with available price data.

S&P 500. A better representation of the entire U.S. stock market is the S&P 500, a value-weighted portfolio of 500 of the largest U.S. stocks.[3] The S&P 500 was the first widely publicized, value-weighted index (S&P began publishing its index in 1923), and it is a standard benchmark for professional investors. This index is the most commonly cited index when evaluating the overall performance of the U.S. stock market. It is also the standard portfolio used to represent "the market" in practice. Even though the S&P 500 includes only 500 of the over 4000 individual U.S. stocks, because the S&P 500 includes the largest stocks, it represents approximately 80% of the U.S. stock market in terms of market capitalization.

Market Risk and Beta

Now that we have established that the market portfolio is a good basis for measuring systematic risk, we can use the relationship between an individual stock's returns and the market portfolio's returns to measure the amount of systematic risk present in that stock. The reasoning is that if a stock's returns are highly sensitive to the market portfolio's returns, then that stock is highly sensitive to systematic risk. That is, events that are systematic and affect the whole market also are strongly reflected in its returns. If a stock's returns do not depend on the market's returns, then it has little systematic risk—when systematic events happen, they are not strongly reflected in its returns. So stocks whose returns are volatile *and* are highly correlated with the market's returns are the riskiest in the sense that they have the most systematic risk.

beta (β) The expected percent change in the return of a security for a 1% change in the return of the market (or other benchmark) portfolio.

Specifically, we can measure a stock's systematic risk by estimating the stock's sensitivity to the market portfolio, which we refer to as its **beta (β)**:

A stock's beta (β) is the percentage change in its return that we expect for each 1% change in the market's return.

[3]There is no precise formula for determining which stocks will be included in the S&P 500. Standard & Poor's periodically replaces stocks in the index (on average about seven or eight stocks per year). While size is one criterion, Standard & Poor's also tries to maintain appropriate representation of different segments of the economy and chooses firms that are leaders in their industries.

There are many data sources that provide estimates of beta based on historical data. Typically, these data sources estimate betas using two to five years of weekly or monthly returns, and use the S&P/TSX Composite Index as the market portfolio for Canadian stocks or the S&P 500 as the market portfolio for U.S. stocks. Table 11.5 shows estimates of betas for a number of large stocks and their industries. You can find the betas of other companies by going to the Yahoo! Canada Finance website, ca.finance.yahoo.com.

As we explain below, the beta of the overall market portfolio is 1, so you can think of a beta of 1 as representing average exposure to systematic risk. However, as Table 11.5 demonstrates, many industries and companies have betas much higher

TABLE 11.5 Average Betas for Stocks by Industry (Based on Weekly Data from 2013–2017)

Industry	Industry Beta	Company Ticker Symbol	Company Name	Company Beta
Energy	1.08	CNQ	Canadian Natural Resources Limited	2.25
		HSE	Husky Energy Inc.	1.69
Materials	0.16	AEM	Agnico-Eagle Mines Ltd.	0.32
Industrials	0.88	CP	Canadian Pacific Railway	1.32
		STN	Stantec Inc.	0.92
		WJA	WestJet Airlines Ltd.	0.50
		AC	Air Canada	0.69
Consumer Discretionary	0.71	CTC.A	Canadian Tire Corporation	0.28
		GIL	Gildan Activewear Inc.	0.54
		CGX	Cineplex Inc.	0.31
Consumer Staples	0.38	L	Loblaw Companies Limited	0.58
		MFI	Maple Leaf Foods Inc.	0.72
		PJC.A	Jean Coutu Group (PJC) Inc.	0.63
Healthcare	0.39	VRX	Valeant Pharmaceuticals International, Inc.	1.04
Financials	0.78	GWO	Great-West Lifeco Inc.	0.76
		MFC	Manulife Financial Corporation	1.31
		TD	The Toronto-Dominion Bank	0.93
Information Technology	0.63	BB	BlackBerry	1.51
		OTEXT	OpenText Corporation	0.70
Telecommunications Services	0.23	BCE	BCE Inc.	0.40
		T	TELUS Corporation	0.49
Utilities	0.41	EMA	Emera Inc.	0.55
		FTS	Fortis Inc.	0.59

Source: Bloomberg

COMMON MISTAKE

Standard Deviation versus Beta

Remember that a stock's beta is the percentage change in its return that we expect for each 1% change in the market's return; it is not a direct measure of the part of a stock's volatility that is caused by systematic risk. Therefore, if a stock has a beta of 0.3 and standard deviation of 0.4, it is not correct to divide the 0.4 total volatility into 0.3 systematic risk and 0.1 nonsystematic risk. In fact, even though total risk (volatility) is equal to the sum of systematic risk and firm-specific risk, our measure of volatility does not have to be a bigger number than our measure for beta. To illustrate, consider Loblaw. It has total risk (volatility), measured as standard deviation, of 17%, or 0.17 (see Table 11.3), but Table 11.5 shows that it has systematic risk, measured as a beta of 0.58, which is greater than 0.17. For the same reason, it is possible for Loblaw to have a lower standard deviation than WestJet (17% vs. 22%), but a higher beta (0.58 vs. 0.50). Figure 11.7 illustrates one possible breakdown of total risk for Loblaw and WestJet that would be consistent with these data.

or lower than 1. The differences in betas by industry are related to the sensitivity of each industry's profits to the general health of the economy. For example, Canadian Natural Resources and other energy stocks have high betas (near or above 1.5), because demand for their products usually varies with the business cycle (cyclical stocks); both

FIGURE 11.7 **Systematic versus Firm-Specific Risk in Loblaw and WestJet**

Beta, measuring systematic risk, and standard deviation, measuring total risk, are in different units. Even though Loblaw total risk (standard deviation) is 0.17 (17%), its beta, measuring only systematic risk, is 0.58. In this case, the beta of 0.58 corresponds to a breakdown in total risk as depicted in the figure. Formally, the portion of Loblaw total risk that is in common with the market is calculated by multiplying the correlation between Loblaw and the market by the standard deviation (total risk) of Loblaw. We can do a similar breakdown of WestJet risk. Note that WestJet has more total, but less systematic, risk than Loblaw.

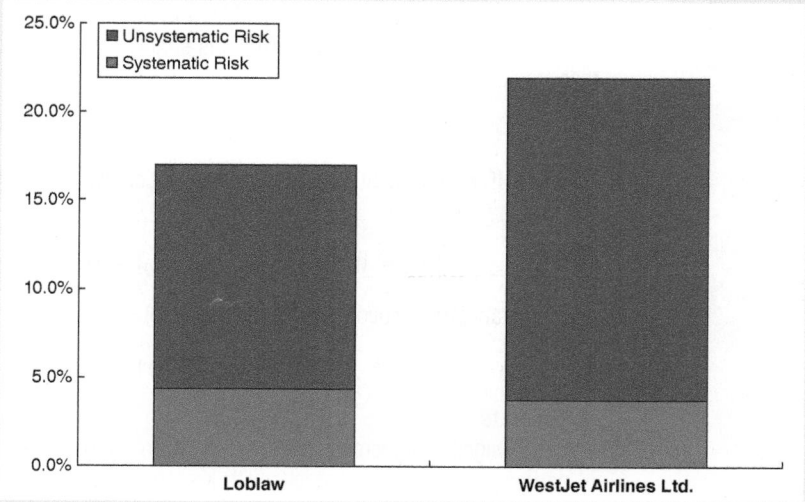

Source: Data from Yahoo!Finance Canada

consumers and companies increase their demand for oil and natural gas when times are good, but cut back on these expenditures when the economy slows. Thus, systematic events have a greater-than-average impact on these firms, and their exposure to systematic risk is greater than average. On the other hand, the demand for personal and household products such as shampoo has very little relationship to the state of the economy. (Stocks of companies providing these types of products are often called defensive stocks.) Firms producing or retailing these consumer staples, such as Loblaw Companies Limited, tend to have low betas (near 0.5). Note also that even within an industry, each company's specific strategy and focus can lead to different exposures to systematic events, so there is variation in beta even within industries (for example, Canadian Natural Resources Limited and Husky Energy Inc.).

EXAMPLE 11.5 Total Risk versus Systematic Risk

PROBLEM

Suppose that in the coming year your expected annual return for Loblaw is 6% and for Canadian Natural Resources is 12%. What is the expected return and risk (standard deviation) of your portfolio if you hold only Loblaw? If you split your money evenly between Loblaw (ticker symbol: L) and Canadian Natural Resources (ticker symbol: CNQ) what is the expected return and risk of your portfolio?

SOLUTION

Plan

We calculated the standard deviation of the 50% Loblaw, 50% Canadian Natural Resources portfolio in Example 11.3. From Table 11.3, we can get the standard deviation of Loblaw:

$$SD(R_P) = 0.15 \text{ (rounded down to two decimals from 0.152) and } SD(R_L) = 0.17$$

With this information and the information from the problem, we can compute the expected return of the portfolio using Equation 11.3. (Recall that we used Equation 11.4 when we calculated the portfolio variance in Example 11.3).

Execute

For the all-Loblaw portfolio, we have 100% of our money in Loblaw stock, so the expected return and standard deviation of our portfolio is simply the expected return and standard deviation of that stock:

$$E[R_L] = 0.06,\ SD(R_L) = 0.17$$

However, if we invest 50% of our money in Loblaw and 50% in Canadian Natural Resources, the expected return is

$$E[R_P] = w_L E[R_L] + w_{CNQ} E[R_{CNQ}] = 0.5(0.06) + 0.5(0.12) = 0.09$$

and the standard deviation (from Example 11.3) is

$$SD(R_P) = 0.15$$

Evaluate

Despite a significant increase in expected return, we gain a reduction in risk. This is the advantage of portfolios—by selecting stocks with low correlation, we achieve our target expected return at the lowest possible risk.

Estimating Beta from Historical Returns

A security's beta is the expected percentage change in the return of the security for a 1% change in the return of the market portfolio. That is, beta represents the amount by which risks that affect the overall market are amplified or dampened in a given stock or investment. Securities whose returns tend to move one for one with the market on average have a beta of 1. Securities that tend to move more than the market have higher betas, while those that move less than the market have lower betas.

Let's look at Canadian Natural Resources' stock as an example. Figure 11.8 shows the monthly returns for Canadian Natural Resources and the monthly returns for the S&P/TSX Composite Index from the beginning of 2013 to 2017. Note the overall tendency for Canadian Natural Resources to have a high return when the market is up and a low return when the market is down. Indeed, Canadian Natural Resources tends to move in the same direction as the market, but Canadian Natural Resources' movements are larger. The pattern suggests that Canadian Natural Resources' beta is greater than 1.

We can see Canadian Natural Resources' sensitivity to the market even more clearly by plotting the company's return as a function of the S&P/TSX Composite Index return, as shown in Figure 11.9. Each point in this figure represents the returns of Canadian Natural Resources and the S&P/TSX Composite Index for one of the months in Figure 11.8. For example, in March 2016, Canadian Natural Resources' return was 24.2% and the S&P/TSX Composite Index's was 5.3%

FIGURE 11.8 **Monthly Returns for Canadian Natural Resources Stock and for the S&P/TSX Composite Index, 2013–2017**

Note that Canadian Natural Resources' returns tend to move in the same direction but farther than those of the S&P/TSX Composite Index.

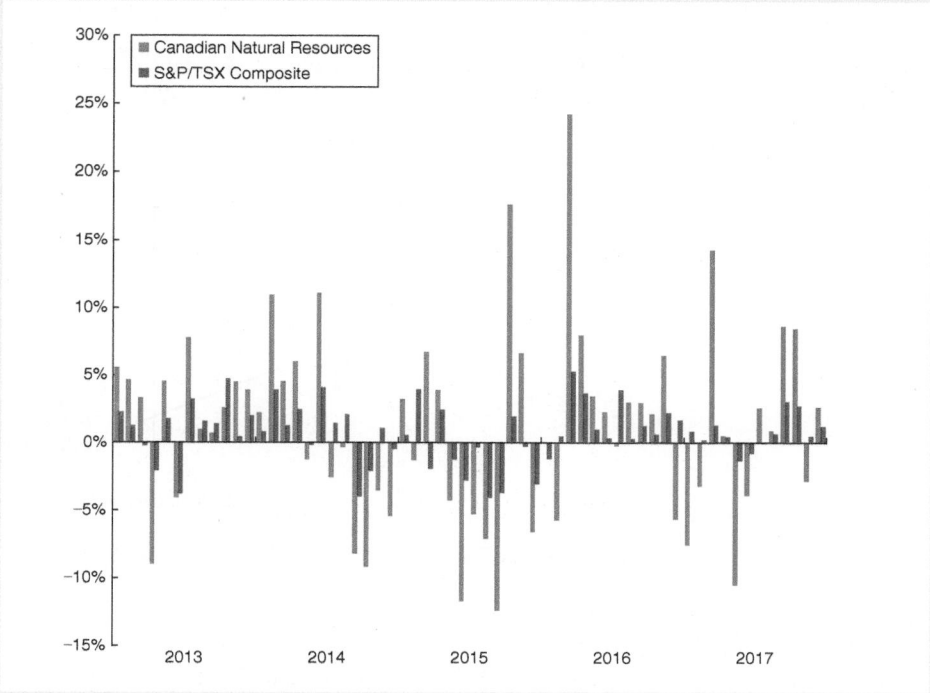

Source: Canadian Financial Markets Research Centre (CFMRC) and Yahoo!Finance Canada.

FIGURE 11.9 **Scatter Plot of Monthly Returns for Canadian Natural Resources versus the S&P/TSX Composite Index, 2013–2017**

Beta corresponds to the slope of the best-fitting line. Beta measures the expected change in Canadian Natural Resources' return per 1% change in the market's return. Deviations from the line of best fit, such as in June 2013, correspond to diversifiable, unsystematic risk.

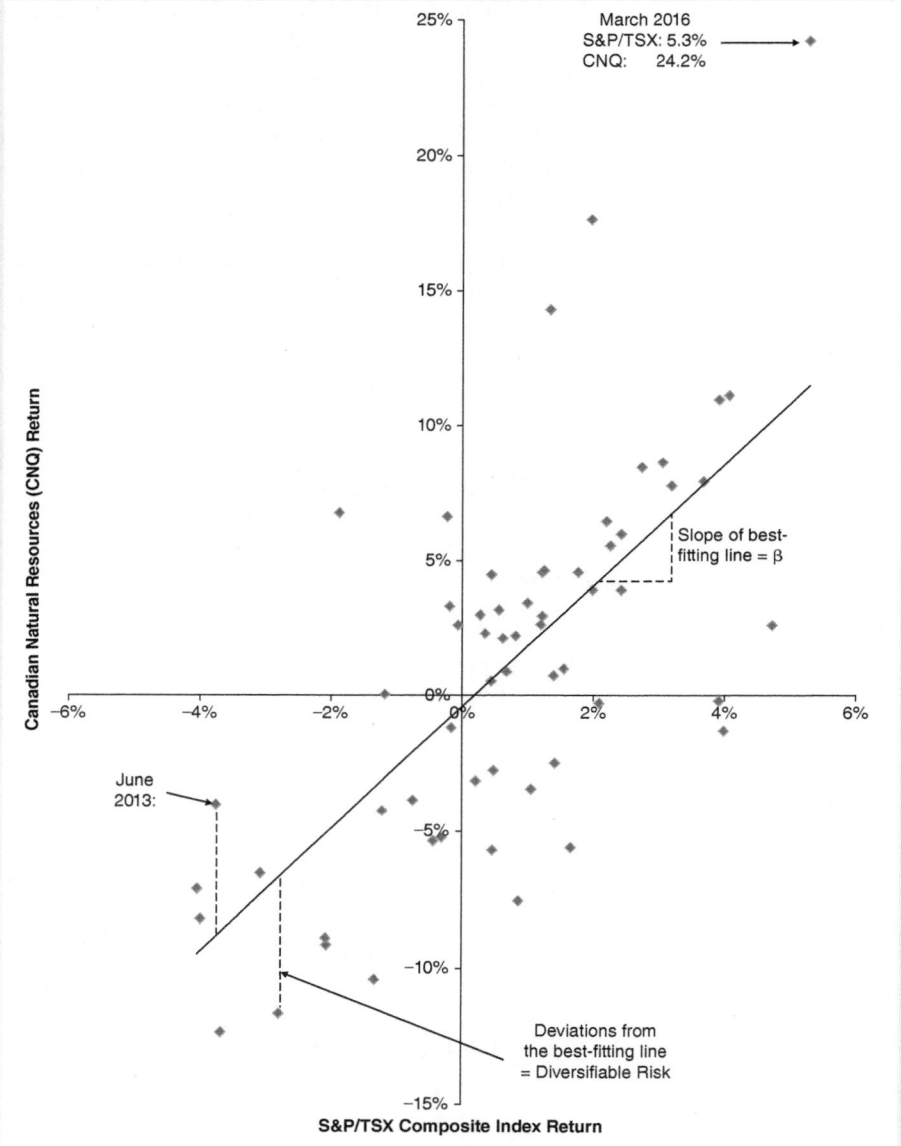

Source: Canadian Financial Markets Research Centre (CFMRC) and Yahoo!Finance Canada.

As the scatter plot makes clear, Canadian Natural Resources' returns have a positive correlation with the market: Canadian Natural Resources tends to be up when the market is up, and vice versa. In practice, we use linear regression to estimate the relationship between Canadian Natural Resources' returns and the market's return. The output of the

USING EXCEL

Calculating a Stock's Beta

1. Enter or import the historical returns for the stock and the S&P/TSX Composite Index into Excel.
2. Next, select the "Data" tab and then choose "Data Analysis." A new window will open; scroll down to find "Regression" and click "OK." (If you are unable to find "Data Analysis," you may not have activated it yet. If you use Excel 2016 for Mac, click on "Tools," select "Add-ins," select the "Analysis ToolPak" check box, and then click "OK." To activate in Excel 2016 for Windows, first click the "File" tab, select "Options" and then "Add-Ins." In the "Manage" box, select "Excel Add-ins" and click "Go." Select the "Analysis ToolPak" check box, and then click "OK.")
3. For the "Input Y Range" box, highlight the stock's returns.
4. For the "Input X Range" box, highlight the S&P/TSX Composite Index's returns, as shown in the screen capture.
5. Click "OK."

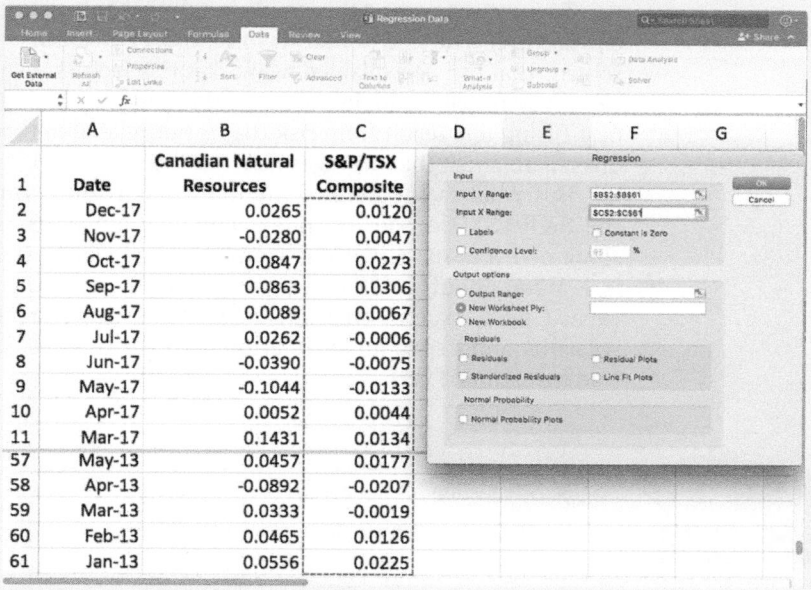

	A	B	C
1	Date	Canadian Natural Resources	S&P/TSX Composite
2	Dec-17	0.0265	0.0120
3	Nov-17	-0.0280	0.0047
4	Oct-17	0.0847	0.0273
5	Sep-17	0.0863	0.0306
6	Aug-17	0.0089	0.0067
7	Jul-17	0.0262	-0.0006
8	Jun-17	-0.0390	-0.0075
9	May-17	-0.1044	-0.0133
10	Apr-17	0.0052	0.0044
11	Mar-17	0.1431	0.0134
57	May-13	0.0457	0.0177
58	Apr-13	-0.0892	-0.0207
59	Mar-13	0.0333	-0.0019
60	Feb-13	0.0465	0.0126
61	Jan-13	0.0556	0.0225

Courtesy of Microsoft corporation

6. The output will appear in a separate sheet. The stock's beta is the coefficient on "X Variable 1." In this case, the beta is 2.25, shown in the screen capture.

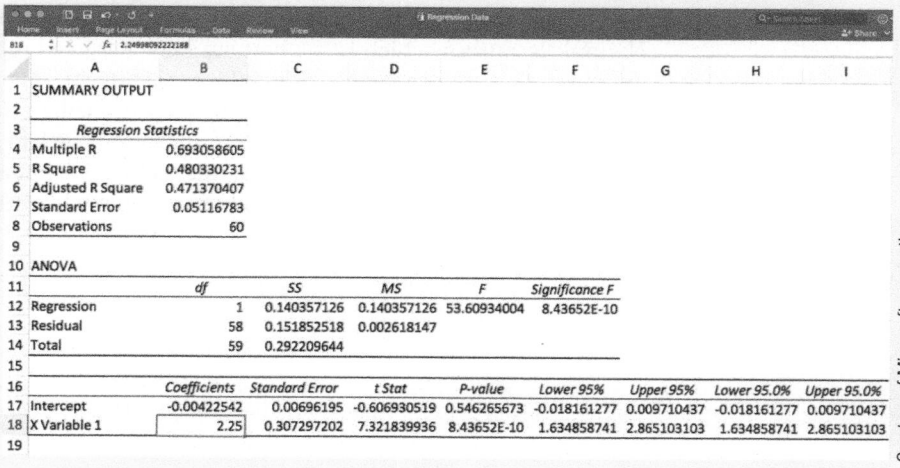

	A	B	C	D	E	F	G	H	I
1	SUMMARY OUTPUT								
2									
3	*Regression Statistics*								
4	Multiple R	0.693058605							
5	R Square	0.480330231							
6	Adjusted R Square	0.471370407							
7	Standard Error	0.05116783							
8	Observations	60							
9									
10	ANOVA								
11		*df*	*SS*	*MS*	*F*	*Significance F*			
12	Regression	1	0.140357126	0.140357126	53.60934004	8.43652E-10			
13	Residual	58	0.151852518	0.002618147					
14	Total	59	0.292209644						
15									
16		*Coefficients*	*Standard Error*	*t Stat*	*P-value*	*Lower 95%*	*Upper 95%*	*Lower 95.0%*	*Upper 95.0%*
17	Intercept	-0.00422542	0.00696195	-0.606930519	0.546265673	-0.018161277	0.009710437	-0.018161277	0.009710437
18	X Variable 1	2.25	0.307297202	7.321839936	8.43652E-10	1.634858741	2.865103103	1.634858741	2.865103103
19									

Courtesy of Microsoft corporation

linear regression analysis is the best-fitting line (or line of best fit) that represents the historical relationship between the stock and the market. The slope of this line is our estimate of its beta. That slope tells us how much, on average, the stock's return changes for a 1% change in the market's return.

Formally, the beta of an investment is defined as

$$\beta_i = \frac{\overbrace{SD(R_i) \times Corr(R_i, R_{Mkt})}^{\text{Volatility of } i \text{ that is Common with the Market}}}{SD(R_{Mkt})} = \frac{Cov(R_i, R_{Mkt})}{Var(R_{Mkt})} \tag{11.6}$$

For example, in Figure 11.9 the line of best fit shows that a 5% change in the market's return corresponds to about a 11.2% change in Canadian Natural Resources' return. That is, Canadian Natural Resources' return moves about 2.2 times (11.2/5) the overall market's movement, and so Canadian Natural Resources' beta is about 2.2.

To fully understand this result, recall that beta measures the systematic market risk of a security. The line of best fit in Figure 11.9 captures the components of a security's returns that can be explained by market risk factors. In any individual month, the security's returns will be higher or lower than the best-fitting line. Such deviations from the best-fitting line result from risk that is not related to the market as a whole. This risk is diversifiable risk that averages out in a large portfolio.

But what is the beta of the market portfolio? Imagine plotting the returns of the S&P/TSX Composite Index against themselves. You would have a line with a slope of 1 and no deviations from that line. Thus, the beta of the market portfolio is 1. What about a risk-free investment? Because the risk-free return is the return earned on Canadian treasury bills and is therefore known in advance, it has no volatility and hence no correlation with the market. Therefore, the beta of the risk-free investment is 0.

CONCEPT CHECK

5. What is the market portfolio?
6. What does beta (β) tell us?

11.4 Putting It All Together: The Capital Asset Pricing Model

One of our goals in this chapter is to compute the cost of equity capital for Canadian Natural Resources, which is the best available expected return offered in the market on an investment of comparable risk and term. Thus, in order to compute the cost of capital, we need to know the relationship between Canadian Natural Resources' risk and its expected return. Over the past three sections, we have laid the foundation for a practical way of measuring this relationship. In this section, we put all the pieces together to build a model for determining the expected return of any investment.

The CAPM Equation Relating Risk to Expected Return

As we have learned, only common, systematic risk determines expected returns—firm-specific risk is diversifiable and does not warrant extra return. In the introduction to this chapter, we stated that, intuitively, the expected return on any investment should come from two components:

1. A baseline risk-free rate of return that we would demand to compensate for inflation and the time value of money, even if there were no risk of losing our money.
2. A risk premium that varies with the amount of systematic risk in the investment.

Expected Return = Risk-Free Rate + Risk Premium for Systematic Risk

We devoted the last section to measuring systematic risk. Beta is our measure of the amount of systematic risk in an investment:

Expected Return for Investment =
Risk-Free Rate + $\beta_i \times$ Risk Premium per Unit of Systematic Risk (per unit of β).

But what is the risk premium per unit of systematic risk? Well, we know that the market portfolio, by definition, has exactly one unit of systematic risk (it has a beta of 1). So, a natural estimate of the risk premium per unit of systematic risk is the historical average excess return on the market portfolio, also known as the **market risk premium (equity risk premium)**. Historically, the average excess return of the S&P/TSX Composite Index over the return on Government of Canada bonds (the risk-free rate) has been 4% to 6% depending on the period of measurement. (We'll discuss this more in the next chapter.) With this last piece of the puzzle, we can write down the equation for the expected return of an investment:

market risk premium (equity risk premium) The historical average excess returns on the market portfolio.

Capital Asset Pricing Model (CAPM) An equilibrium model of the relationship between risk and return that characterizes a security's expected return based on its beta with the market portfolio.

required return The expected return of an investment that is necessary to compensate for the risk of undertaking the investment.

Capital Asset Pricing Model

$$E[R_i] = r_f + \underbrace{\beta_i(E[R_{Mkt}] - r_f)}_{\text{Risk Premium for Security } i} \tag{11.7}$$

This equation for the expected return of any investment is the **Capital Asset Pricing Model (CAPM)**. In words, the CAPM simply says that the return we should expect on any investment is equal to the risk-free rate of return plus a risk premium proportional to the amount of systematic risk in the investment. Specifically, the risk premium of an investment is equal to the market risk premium ($E[R_{Mkt}] - r_f$) multiplied by the amount of systematic (market) risk present in the investment, measured by its beta with the market (β_i). Because investors will not invest in this security unless they can expect at least the return given in Equation 11.7, we also call this return the investment's **required return**.

WHY NOT ESTIMATE EXPECTED RETURNS DIRECTLY?

If we have to use historical data to estimate beta and determine a security's expected return (or an investment's cost of capital), why not just use the security's historical average return as an estimate for its expected return instead? This method would certainly be simpler and more direct.

The answer is that it is extremely difficult to infer the average return of individual stocks from historical data. Because stock returns are so volatile, with even 100 years of data we would have little confidence in our estimate of the true average. (Imagine drawing 100 numbers from a swimming pool full of widely ranging numbers and being asked to guess the average of all of the numbers in the pool). Worse, few stocks have existed for 100 years, and those that have probably bear little resemblance today to what they were like 100 years ago. If we use less than 10 years of data, we would have very little confidence in our estimate at all. In fact, if the volatility of the stock's return is 20%, it turns out that we would need 1600 years of data to be 95% confident that our estimate of its true average return was within +/−1% of being correct!

On the other hand, the linear regression technique allows us to infer beta from historical data reasonably accurately with just a few years of data. Thus, in theory at least, using beta and the CAPM can provide much more accurate estimates of expected returns for stocks than we could obtain from their historical average return.

The CAPM is the main method used by most major corporations to determine the equity cost of capital. In a survey of CFOs, Graham and Harvey found that over 70% rely on the CAPM, and Bruner, Eades, Harris, and Higgins report that 85% of a sample of large firms rely on it.[4] It has become the most important model of the relationship between risk and return, and for his contributions to the theory, William Sharpe was awarded the Nobel Prize for Economics in 1990.

EXAMPLE 11.6 Computing the Expected Return for a Stock

PROBLEM

Suppose the risk-free return is 3% and you measure the market risk premium to be 6%. Canadian Natural Resources (CNQ) has a beta of 2.25. According to the CAPM, what is its expected return?

SOLUTION

Plan

We can use Equation 11.7 to compute the expected return according to the CAPM. For that equation, we will need the market risk premium, the risk-free return, and the stock's beta. We have all of these inputs, so we are ready to go.

Execute

Using Equation 11.7,

$$E[R_{CNQ}] = r_f + \beta_{CNQ}(E[R_{Mkt}] - r_f) = 3\% + 2.25(6\%)$$
$$= 16.50\%$$

Evaluate

Because of Canadian Natural Resources' beta of 2.25, investors will require a risk premium of 13.50% over the risk-free rate for investments in its stock to compensate for the systematic risk of Canadian Natural Resources stock. This leads to a total expected return of 3% + 13.50% = 16.50%.

[4] J. Graham and C. Harvey, "The Theory and Practice of Corporate Finance: Evidence from the Field," *Journal of Financial Economics* 60 (2001): 187–243; and F. Bruner, K. Eades, R. Harris, and R. Higgins, "Best Practices in Estimating the Cost of Capital: Survey and Synthesis," *Financial Practice and Education* 8 (1998): 13–28.

The Security Market Line

Figure 11.10 graphs the relationships between expected return and both total risk and systematic risk (beta) for the stocks in Table 11.5. Recall from Chapter 10 that there is no clear relationship between a stock's standard deviation (total risk) and its expected return, as shown in panel (a). However, the CAPM equation (Equation 11.7) implies that there is a linear relationship between a stock's beta and its expected return. This line is graphed in panel (b) as the line through the risk-free investment (with a beta of 0) and the market (with a beta of 1); it is called the **security market line (SML)**. We see that the relationship between risk and return for individual securities is evident only when we measure market risk as in panel (b), rather than total risk as in panel (a).

security market line (SML) The pricing implication of the CAPM, specifying a linear relationship between the risk premium of a security and its beta with the market portfolio.

The security market line in Figure 11.10 raises the subject of negative beta stocks. While the vast majority of stocks have a positive beta, it is possible to have returns that co-vary negatively with the market. Firms that provide goods or services in greater demand during economic contractions than in booms fit this description.

The CAPM and Portfolios

Because the security market line applies to all securities, we can apply it to portfolios as well. For example, the market portfolio is on the SML, and according to the CAPM, other portfolios (such as mutual funds) are also on the SML. Therefore, the expected return of a portfolio should correspond to the portfolio's beta. We calculate the beta of a portfolio made up of securities each with weight w_i as follows:

$$\beta_P = w_1\beta_1 + w_2\beta_2 + \cdots + w_n\beta_n \tag{11.8}$$

That is, *the beta of a portfolio is the weighted average beta of the securities in the portfolio.*

EXAMPLE 11.7 A Negative Beta Stock

PROBLEM

Suppose the stock of George Weston Limited (ticker symbol: WN) has a negative beta of −0.15. How does its required return compare to the risk-free rate, according to the CAPM? Does your result make sense?

SOLUTION

■ Plan

We can use the CAPM equation, Equation 11.7, to compute the expected return of this negative beta stock just as we would with a positive beta stock. We don't have the risk-free rate or the market risk premium, but the problem doesn't ask us for the exact expected return, just whether or not it will be more or less than the risk-free rate. Using Equation 11.7, we can answer that question.

■ Execute

Because the expected return of the market is higher than the risk-free rate, Equation 11.7 implies that the expected return of WN will be *below* the risk-free rate. As long as the market risk premium is positive (as long as people demand a higher return for investing in the market than for a risk-free investment), then the second term in Equation 11.7 will have to be negative if the beta is negative. For example, if the risk-free rate is 3% and the market risk premium is 6%,

$$E[R_{WN}] = 3\% - 0.15(6\%) = 2.1\%$$

(See Figure 11.10: the SML drops below r_f for $\beta < 0$.) ▶

Evaluate

This result seems odd—why would investors be willing to accept a 2.1% expected return on this stock when they can invest in a safe investment and earn 3%? The answer is that a savvy investor will not hold WN alone; instead, the investor will hold it in combination with other securities as part of a well-diversified portfolio. These other securities will tend to rise and fall with the market. But because WN has a negative beta, its correlation with the market is negative, which means that WN tends to perform well when the rest of the market is doing poorly. Therefore, by holding WN, an investor can reduce the overall market risk of the portfolio. In a sense, WN is "recession insurance" for a portfolio, and investors will pay for this insurance by accepting a lower expected return.

FIGURE 11.10 Expected Return, Volatility, and Beta

Panel (a) Expected Return and Total Risk (Standard Deviation)
The graph compares the standard deviation and expected returns of the stocks in Table 11.5. There is no relationship between total risk and expected return. Some of the stocks are identified. It is clear that we could not predict Canadian Natural Resources' expected return using its total risk (volatility).

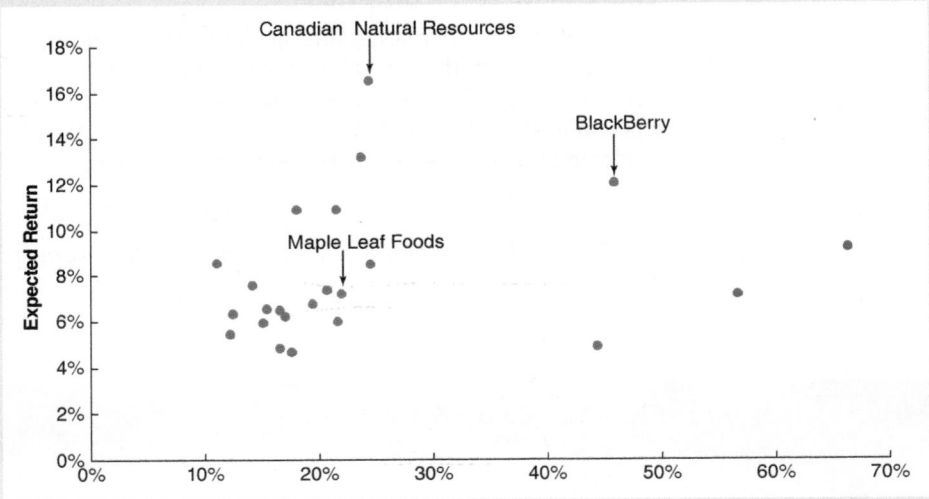

Panel (b) Expected Return and Beta
The security market line shows the expected return for each security in Table 11.5 as a function of its beta with the market. According to the CAPM, all stocks and portfolios (including the market portfolio) should lie on the security market line. Thus, Canadian Natural Resources' expected return can be determined by its beta, which measures its systematic risk.

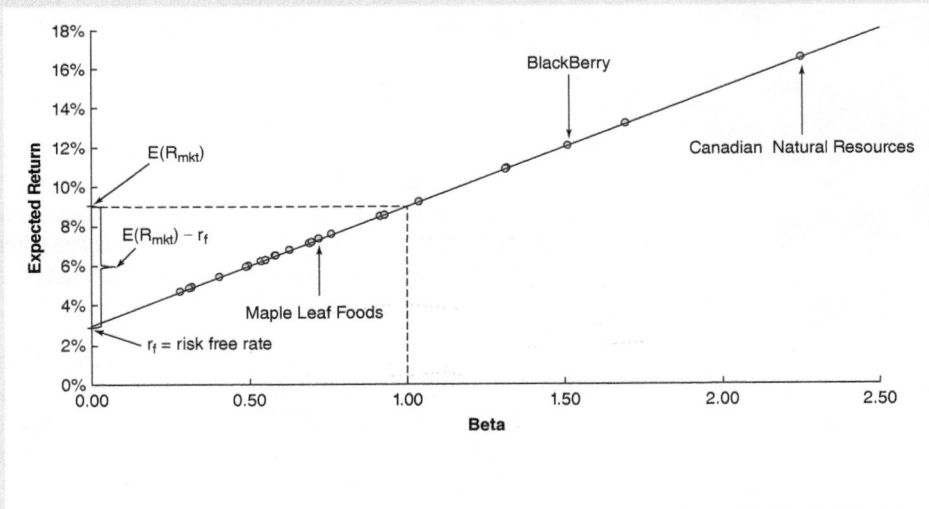

Source: Canadian Financial Markets Research Centre (CFMRC) and Yahoo! Finance Canada.

EXAMPLE 11.8 The Expected Return of a Portfolio

PROBLEM

Suppose the Canadian Pacific Railway (ticker symbol: CP) has a beta of 1.32, whereas the beta of Loblaw Companies Limited (ticker symbol: L) is 0.58. If the risk-free interest rate is 3%, and the market risk premium is 6%, what is the expected return of an equally weighted portfolio of Canadian Pacific and Loblaw, according to the CAPM?

SOLUTION

Plan

We have the following information:

$r_f = 3\%$	$E[R_{Mkt}] - r_f = 6\%$
CP: $\beta_{CP} = 1.32$	$w_{CP} = 0.50$
L: $\beta_L = 0.58$	$w_L = 0.50$

We can compute the expected return of the portfolio in two ways. First, we can use the CAPM (Equation 11.7) to compute the expected return of each stock and then compute the expected return for the portfolio using Equation 11.3.

Or, we could compute the beta of the portfolio using Equation 11.8 and then use the CAPM (Equation 11.7) to find the portfolio's expected return.

Execute

Using the first approach, we compute the expected return for CP and L:

$$E[R_{CP}] = r_f + \beta_{CP}(E[R_{Mkt}] - r_f) \qquad E[R_L] = r_f + \beta_L(E[R_{Mkt}] - r_f)$$
$$E[R_{CP}] = 3\% + 1.32(6\%) = 10.92\% \qquad E[R_L] = 3\% + 0.58(6\%) = 6.48\%$$

Then the expected return of the equally weighted portfolio P is

$$E[R_P] = 0.5(10.92\%) + 0.5(6.48\%) = 8.70\%$$

Alternatively, we can compute the beta of the portfolio using Equation 10.7:

$$\beta_P = w_{CP}\beta_{CP} + w_L\beta_L$$
$$\beta_P = (0.5)(1.32) + (0.5)(0.58) = 0.95$$

We can then find the portfolio's expected return from the CAPM:

$$E[R_P] = r_f + \beta_P(E[R_{Mkt}] - r_f)$$
$$E[R_P] = 3\% + 0.95(6\%) = 8.70\%$$

Evaluate

The CAPM is an effective tool for analyzing securities and portfolios of those securities. You can compute the expected return of each security using its beta and then compute the weighted average of those expected returns to determine the portfolio expected return. Or, you can compute the weighted average of the securities' betas to get the portfolio beta and then compute the expected return of the portfolio using the CAPM. Either way, you will get the same answer.

Summary of the Capital Asset Pricing Model

The CAPM is a powerful tool that is widely used to estimate the expected return on stocks and on investments within companies. The model and its use are summarized below:

- Investors require a risk premium proportional to the amount of *systematic* risk they are bearing.
- We can measure the systematic risk of an investment by its beta, which is the sensitivity of the investment's return to the market's return. For each 1% change in the market portfolio's return, the investment's return is expected to change by beta percent due to risks that it has in common with the market.
- The most common way to estimate a stock's beta is to regress its historical returns on the market's historical returns. The stock's beta is the slope of the line that best explains the relationship between the market's return and the stock's return.
- The CAPM says that we can compute the expected, or required, return for any investment using the following equation:

$$E[R_i] = r_f + \beta_i (E[R_{Mkt}] - r_f)$$

  which when graphed is called the *security market line*.

The Big Picture

The CAPM marks the culmination of our examination of how investors in capital markets trade off risk and return. It provides a powerful and widely used tool to quantify the return that should accompany a particular amount of systematic risk. We have already reached our goal (in Example 11.6) of estimating the cost of equity capital for Canadian Natural Resources. While our finding that equity investors in Canadian Natural Resources should reasonably expect (and therefore require) a return of 16.50% on their investments is an important piece of information to Canadian Natural Resources' managers, it is not the whole picture. While some firms have only equity investors, most have bond investors as well. In the next chapter we will apply what we have learned here and in Chapters 6 and 7 on bonds and stocks to develop the overall cost of capital for a company. The Valuation Principle tells us to use this cost of capital to discount the future expected cash flows of the firm to arrive at the value of the firm. Thus, the cost of capital is an essential input to the financial manager's job of analyzing investment opportunities, so knowing this overall cost of capital is critical to the company's success at creating value for its investors.

Problems with the CAPM in Practice

Researchers have found that using only the S&P 500, or some other simple proxy for the true market portfolio, has led to consistent pricing errors from the CAPM. That is, some stocks and portfolios of stocks earn consistently higher or lower returns than the CAPM would predict. For example, researchers have found that small stocks, stocks with high ratios of book-to-market value of equity, and stocks that have recently performed very well have consistently earned higher returns than the CAPM would predict using a simple stock market proxy for the market portfolio. Despite these so-called anomalies, the CAPM remains the most commonly used approach for estimating the cost of capital. See the Appendix to the chapter for alternative models of systematic risk that may represent an improvement over the CAPM.

NOBEL PRIZE

William Sharpe

The CAPM was proposed as a model of risk and return by William Sharpe in a 1964 paper and in related papers by Jack Treynor (1961), John Lintner (1965), and Jan Mossin (1966).*

Below is an excerpt from a 1998 interview with William Sharpe:

> Portfolio Theory focused on the actions of a single investor with an optimal portfolio. I said what if everyone was optimizing? They've all got their copies of Markowitz and they're doing what he says. Then some people decide they want to hold more IBM, but there aren't enough shares to satisfy demand. So they put price pressure on IBM and up it goes, at which point they have to change their estimates of risk and return, because now they're paying more for the stock. That process of upward and downward pressure on prices continues until prices reach an equilibrium and everyone collectively wants to hold what's available. At that point, what can you say about the relationship between risk and return? The answer is that expected return is proportionate to beta relative to the market portfolio.
>
> The CAPM was and is a theory of equilibrium. Why should anyone expect to earn more by investing in one security as opposed to another? You need to be compensated for doing badly when times are bad. The security that is going to do badly just when you need money when times are bad is a security you have to hate, and there had better be some redeeming virtue or else who will hold it? That redeeming virtue has to be that in normal times you expect to do better. The key insight of the Capital Asset Pricing Model is that higher expected returns go with the greater risk of doing badly in bad times. Beta is a measure of that. Securities or asset classes with high betas tend to do worse in bad times than those with low betas.

Source: Jonathan Burton, "Revisiting the Capital Asset Pricing Model," *Dow Jones Asset Manager* (May/June 1998): 20–28.

---

*W. F. Sharpe, "Capital Asset Prices: A Theory of Market Equilibrium Under Conditions of Risk," *Journal of Finance* 19 (September 1964): 425–442.

Jack Treynor, "Toward a Theory of the Market Value of Risky Assets," unpublished manuscript (1961).

J. Lintner, "The Valuation of Risk Assets and the Selection of Risky Investments in Stock Portfolios and Capital Budgets," *Review of Economics and Statistics* 47 (February 1965): 13–37.

J. Mossin, "Equilibrium in a Capital Asset Market," *Econometrica* 34 (4) (1966): 768–783.

CONCEPT CHECK

7. What does the CAPM say about the required return of a security?
8. What is the security market line?

MyLab Finance

Here is what you should know after reading this chapter. MyLab Finance™ will help you identify what you know, and where to go when you need to practice.

KEY POINTS AND EQUATIONS	TERMS	ONLINE PRACTICE OPPORTUNITIES
11.1 The Expected Return of a Portfolio ■ The portfolio weight is the initial fraction w_i of an investor's money invested in each asset. Portfolio weights add up to 1: $$w_i = \frac{\text{Value of investment } i}{\text{Total value of portfolio}} \quad (11.1)$$ ■ The expected return of a portfolio is the weighted average of the expected returns of the investments within it, using the portfolio weights: $$E[R_P] = w_1E[R_1] + w_2E[R_2] + \cdots + w_nE[R_n] \quad (11.3)$$	expected return of a portfolio, p. 384 portfolio weight, p. 382 return on a portfolio, p. 383	MyLab Study Plan 11.1
11.2 The Volatility of a Portfolio ■ To find the risk of a portfolio, we need to know the degree to which stock returns move together. Correlation measures the co-movement of returns. The correlation is always between −1 and +1. It represents the fraction of the volatility due to risk that is common to the securities. ■ The variance of a portfolio depends on the correlation of the stocks. For a portfolio with two stocks, the portfolio variance is $$Var(R_P) = w_1^2SD(R_1)^2 + w_2^2SD(R_2)^2 + 2w_1w_2\,Corr(R_1, R_2)SD(R_1)\,SD(R_2) \quad (11.4)$$ ■ As we lower the correlation between the two stocks in a portfolio, we lower the portfolio variance. ■ Diversification eliminates independent, firm-specific risks, and the volatility of a large portfolio results from the common systematic risk among the stocks in the portfolio.	correlation, p. 386 efficient frontier, p. 393 equally weighted portfolio, p. 396 inefficient portfolio, p. 393 volatility of a portfolio, p. 385	MyLab Study Plan 11.2 Using Excel: Correlation Between Two Sets of Returns

KEY POINTS AND EQUATIONS	TERMS	ONLINE PRACTICE OPPORTUNITIES
11.3 Measuring Systematic Risk ■ The market portfolio in theory is a value-weighted index of all risky investments. In practice, we often use a stock market index such as the S&P 500 to represent the market. ■ A stock's beta is the percentage change in its return that we expect for each 1% change in the market's return. ■ To estimate beta, we often use historical returns. Most data sources use five years of monthly returns to estimate beta. ■ Beta also corresponds to the slope of the best-fitting line in the plot of a security's returns versus the market's returns. We use linear regression to find the best-fitting line. ■ The beta of a portfolio is the weighted average beta of the securities in the portfolio.	beta (β), p. 399 market capitalization, p. 398 market index, p. 398 market portfolio, p. 397 market proxy, p. 398 value-weighted portfolio, p. 398	MyLab Study Plan 11.3 Interactive Beta Calculation, Using Excel: Calculating a Stock's Beta
11.4 Putting It All Together: The Capital Asset Pricing Model ■ According to the CAPM, the risk premium of any security is equal to the market risk premium multiplied by the beta of the security. This relationship is called the security market line (SML), and it determines the expected or required return for an investment: $$E[R_i] = r_f + \underbrace{\beta_i(E[R_{Mkt}] - r_f)}_{\text{Risk Premium for Security } i} \quad (11.7)$$	Capital Asset Pricing Model (CAPM), p. 407 market risk premium (equity risk premium), p. 407 required return, p. 407 security market line (SML), p. 409	MyLab Study Plan 11.4
Appendix: Alternative Models of Systematic Risk $$E[R_i] = r_f + \beta_i^{Mkt}(E[R_{Mkt}] - r_f) + \beta_i^{SMB}E[R_{SMB}] + \beta_i^{HML}E[R_{HML}] + \beta_i^{PR1YR}E[R_{PR1YR}] \quad (11.9)$$	Arbitrage Pricing Theory (APT), p. 422 Fama-French-Carhart (FFC) factor specification p. 422 multi-factor model, p. 422 risk factors, p. 422	

REVIEW QUESTIONS

1. What information do you need to compute the expected return of a portfolio?
2. What does correlation tell us?
3. Why isn't the total risk of a portfolio simply equal to the weighted average of the risks of the securities in the portfolio?
4. What does beta measure? How do we use beta?
5. What, intuitively, does the CAPM say drives expected return?
6. What relationship is described by the security market line?

PROBLEMS

All problems in this chapter are available in MyLab Finance. An asterisk (*) indicates problems with a higher level of difficulty.

The Expected Return of a Portfolio

1. You buy 100 shares of Tidepool Co. for $40 each and 200 shares of Madfish Inc. for $15 each. What are the weights in your portfolio?
2. Fairmont Enterprises has an expected return of 15%, and Laval News has an expected return of 20%. If you put 70% of your portfolio in Laval and 30% in Fairmont, what is the expected return of your portfolio?
3. HNL has an expected return of 18% and KOA has an expected return of 22%. If you create a portfolio that is 60% HNL and 40% KOA, what is the expected return of the portfolio?
4. You are considering how to invest part of your retirement savings. You have decided to put $200,000 into three stocks: 50% of the money into GoldFinger (currently $25/share), 25% of the money into Moosehead (currently $80/share), and the remainder into Venture Associates (currently $2/share). Suppose that GoldFinger stock goes up to $30/share, Moosehead stock drops to $60/share, and Venture Associates stock rises to $3 per share.
   a. What is the new value of the portfolio?
   b. What return did the portfolio earn?
   c. If you don't buy or sell shares after the price change, what are your new portfolio weights?
5. You have $70,000. You put 20% of your money into a stock with an expected return of 12%, $30,000 into a stock with an expected return of 15%, and the rest into a stock with an expected return of 20%. What is the expected return of your portfolio?
6. There are two ways to calculate the expected return of a portfolio: calculate the expected return using the value and dividend stream of the portfolio as a whole, or calculate the weighted average of the expected returns of the individual stocks that make up the portfolio. Which return is higher?

The Volatility of a Portfolio

7. If the returns of two stocks have a correlation of 1, what does this imply about the relative movements in the stock prices?

8. Download the data for Table 11.3 from MyLab Finance.

a. Compute the correlation of monthly returns between Stantec and Canadian Tire.

b. Compute the annual standard deviation of Stantec and Canadian Tire.

c. Compute the annual variance and standard deviation of a portfolio of 30% Stantec stock and 70% Canadian Tire stock.

9. Stock A and B have the following returns:

	Stock A	Stock B
1	0.10	0.06
2	0.07	0.02
3	0.15	0.05
4	−0.05	0.01
5	0.08	−0.02

a. What are the expected returns of the two stocks?

b. What are the standard deviations of the two stocks?

c. If their correlation is 0.46, what is the expected return and standard deviation of a portfolio of 70% stock A and 30% stock B?

10. Using the data in the following table, estimate the average return and volatility for each stock.

	Realized Returns	
Year	Stock A	Stock B
1998	−10%	21%
1999	20%	30%
2000	5%	7%
2001	−5%	−3%
2002	2%	−8%
2003	9%	25%

11. Using your estimates from Problem 9 and the fact that the correlation of A and B is 0.48, calculate the volatility (standard deviation) of a portfolio that is 70% invested in stock A and 30% invested in stock B.

12. The following spreadsheet contains monthly returns for Cola Co. and Gas Co. for 2010. Using these data, estimate the average monthly return and volatility for each stock.

Date	Cola Co	Gas Co
Jan	−10.84%	−6.00%
Feb	2.36%	1.28%
Mar	6.60%	−1.86%
Apr	2.01%	−1.90%

Date	Cola Co	Gas Co
May	18.36%	7.40%
Jun	−1.22%	−0.26%
Jul	2.25%	8.36%
Aug	−6.89%	−2.46%
Sep	−6.04%	−2.00%
Oct	13.61%	0.00%
Nov	3.51%	4.68%
Dec	0.54%	2.22%

13. Using the spreadsheet from Problem 11 and the fact that Cola Co. and Gas Co. have a correlation of 0.6083, calculate the volatility (standard deviation) of a portfolio that is 55% invested in Cola Co. stock and 45% invested in Gas Co. stock. Calculate the volatility by

a. using Equation 11.4, and
b. calculating the monthly returns of the portfolio and computing its volatility directly.
c. How do your results compare?

14. Using the data in Table 11.2,

a. Compute the annual returns for a portfolio with 25% invested in North Jet, 25% invested in South Jet, and 50% invested in Alberta Oil.
b. What is the lowest annual return for your portfolio in part (a)? How does it compare with the lowest annual return of the individual stocks or portfolios in Table 11.2?

15. Using the data from Table 11.3, what is the volatility of an equally weighted portfolio of Stantec and OpenText stock?

16. Suppose Johnson & Johnson and the Walgreen Company have the expected returns and volatilities shown below, with a correlation of 22%.

	$E[R]$	$SD[R]$
Johnson & Johnson	7%	16%
Walgreen Company	10%	20%

For a portfolio that is equally invested in Johnson & Johnson's and Walgreen's stock, calculate the following:

a. The expected return
b. The volatility (standard deviation)

17. Arbor Systems and Gencore stocks both have a volatility of 40%. Compute the volatility of a portfolio with 50% invested in each stock if the correlation between the stocks is (a) +1, (b) 0.50, (c) 0, (d) −0.50, and (e) −1.0. In which cases is the volatility lower than that of the original stocks?

18. Suppose Wesley Publishing stock has a volatility of 60%, while Addison Printing stock has a volatility of 30%. If the correlation between these stocks is 25%, what is the volatility of the following portfolios of Addison and Wesley: (a) 100% Addison, (b) 75% Addison and 25% Wesley, and (c) 50% Addison and 50% Wesley?

19 - 21, 23, 25, 29-36

19. You have a portfolio with a standard deviation of 30% and an expected return of 18%. You are considering adding one of the two stocks in the table below. If after adding the stock you will have 20% of your money in the new stock and 80% of your money in your existing portfolio, which one should you add?

	Expected Return	Standard Deviation	Correlation with Your Portfolio's Returns
Stock A	15%	25%	0.2
Stock B	15%	20%	0.6

20. Your client has $100,000 invested in stock A. She would like to build a two-stock portfolio by investing another $100,000 in either stock B or C. She wants a portfolio with an expected return of at least 14% and as low a risk as possible, but the standard deviation must be no more than 40%. What do you advise her to do, and what will be the portfolio expected return and standard deviation?

	Exp Return	Std Dev	Correlation with A
A	15%	50%	1
B	13%	40%	0.2
C	13%	40%	0.3

Measuring Systematic Risk

21. Suppose all possible investment opportunities in the world are limited to the five stocks listed in the table below. What are the market portfolio weights?

Stock	Price/Share ($)	Number of Shares Outstanding (millions)
A	10	10
B	20	12
C	8	3
D	50	1
E	45	20

22. Given the information below, construct a value-weighted portfolio of the four stocks if you have $500,000 to invest. That is, how much of your $500,000 would you invest in each stock?

Stock	Market Cap
OGG	$50 million
HNL	$75 million
KOA	$20 million
LIH	$10 million

23. Given $100,000 to invest, construct a value-weighted portfolio of the four stocks listed below.

Stock	Price/Share ($)	Number of Shares Outstanding (millions)
Golden Seas	13	1.00
Jacobs and Jacobs	22	1.25

Stock	Price/Share ($)	Number of Shares Outstanding (millions)
MAG	43	30.00
PDJB	5	10.00

24. If one stock in a value-weighted portfolio goes up in price and all other stock prices remain the same, what trades are necessary to keep the portfolio value weighted?

25. You hear on the news that the S&P/TSX Composite Index was down 2% today (the market's return was −2%). You are thinking about your portfolio and your investments in BlackBerry and WestJet.

a. If BlackBerry's beta is 1.5, what is your best guess as to BlackBerry's return today?

b. If WestJet's beta is 0.5, what is your best guess as to WestJet's return today?

26. Go to Chapter Resources on MyLab Finance and use the data in the spreadsheet provided to estimate the beta of Nike stock using linear regression.

27. The Chapter Resources section of MyLab Finance has data on Microsoft and the S&P 500 from 1987 to 2006.

a. Estimate Microsoft's beta using linear regression over the periods 1987–1991, 1992–1996, 1997–2001, and 2002–2006.

b. Compare the four estimated betas. What do you conclude about how Microsoft's exposure to systematic risk has changed over time? What do you think explains the change?

Putting It All Together: The Capital Asset Pricing Model

28. Suppose the risk-free return is 4% and the market portfolio has an expected return of 10% and a standard deviation of 16%. Suppose Loblaw Companies Limited stock has a beta of 0.32. What is its expected return?

29. What is the sign of the risk premium of a negative beta stock? Explain. (Assume the risk premium of the market portfolio is positive.)

30. EJH has a beta of 1.2, CSH has a beta of 0.6, and KMS has a beta of 1.0. If you put 25% of your money in EJH, 25% in CSH, and 50% in KMS, what is the beta of your portfolio?

31. Suppose Intel stock has a beta of 1.6, whereas Boeing stock has a beta of 1. If the risk-free interest rate is 4% and the expected return of the market portfolio is 10%, according to the CAPM,

a. what is the expected return of Intel stock?

b. what is the expected return of Boeing stock?

c. what is the beta of a portfolio that consists of 60% Intel stock and 40% Boeing stock?

d. what is the expected return of a portfolio that consists of 60% Intel stock and 40% Boeing stock? (Solve this in two ways.)

***32.** You are thinking of buying a stock priced at $100 per share. Assume that the risk-free rate is about 4.5% and the market risk premium is 6%. If you think the stock will rise to $117 per share by the end of the year, at which time it will pay a $1 dividend, what beta would it need to have for this expectation to be consistent with the CAPM?

***33.** You are analyzing a stock that has a beta of 1.2. The risk-free rate is 5% and you estimate the market risk premium to be 6%. If you expect the stock to have a return of 11% over the next year, should you buy it? Why or why not?

34. You have risen through the ranks of a coffee company, from the lowly green-apron barista to the coveted black apron, and all the way to CFO. A quick internet check shows you that your company's beta is 0.6. The risk-free rate is 5% and you believe the market risk premium to be 5.5%. What is your best estimate of investors' expected return on your company's stock (its cost of equity capital)?

35. At the beginning of 2014, Apple's beta was 1.4 and the risk-free rate was about 4.5%. Apple's price was $84.84. Apple's price at the end of 2014 was $198.08. If you estimate the market risk premium to have been 6%, did Apple's managers exceed their investors' required return as given by the CAPM?

36. You want to invest $50,000 in a portfolio with a beta of no more than 1.4 and an expected return of 12.4%. Bay Corp has a beta of 1.2 and an expected return of 11.2%; City Corp has a beta of 1.8 and an expected return of 14.8%. The risk-free rate is 4%. You can invest in Bay Corp, City Corp, and the risk-free asset. How much will you invest in each?

While the CAPM is the most widely used model for estimating the cost of capital in practice, recently some practitioners have tried to improve on the CAPM.

Multi-factor Models

Researchers added new portfolios to the CAPM pricing equation in an attempt to construct a better proxy for the true market portfolio that captures the components of systematic risk that just using a market proxy, such as the S&P 500, alone misses. Although we might not be able to identify a perfect proxy for the true market portfolio, the market portfolio can be constructed from other portfolios. This observation implies that as long as the market portfolio can be constructed from a collection of portfolios, the collection itself can be used to measure risk. *Thus, it is not actually necessary to identify the market portfolio itself.* All that is required is to identify a collection of portfolios from which it can be constructed.

We can use a collection of portfolios to capture the components of systematic risk, referred to as **risk factors**. A model with more than one portfolio to capture risk is known as a **multi-factor model**. Each portfolio can be thought of as either the risk factor itself or a portfolio of stocks correlated with an unobservable risk factor. This particular form of the multi-factor model was originally developed by Professor Stephen Ross, but Professor Robert Merton developed an alternative multi-factor model earlier.[5] The model is also referred to as the **Arbitrage Pricing Theory (APT)**.

risk factors Different components of systematic risk (used in a multi-factor model).

multi-factor model A model that uses more than one portfolio to capture systematic risk. Each portfolio can be thought of as either the risk factor itself or a portfolio of stocks correlated with an unobservable risk factor.

Arbitrage Pricing Theory (APT) One of the earliest multi-factor models, relying on the absence of arbitrage to price securities.

Fama-French-Carhart Factor Specification

Practitioners have added portfolios specifically to address the CAPM pricing errors. The first portfolio is one that is constructed by buying small firms and selling large firms. This portfolio is widely known as the small-minus-big (SMB) portfolio. The second portfolio buys firms with a high book-to-market ratio and sells firms with a low book-to-market ratio, and we call it the high-minus-low (HML) portfolio. Finally, the third portfolio buys stocks that have recently done extremely well and sells those that have done extremely poorly. Since this portfolio addresses the problem that this extremely good and bad performance continues in the short run, it is called the prior one-year momentum (PR1YR) portfolio.

The collection of these four portfolios—the stock market (Mkt), SMB, HML, and PR1YR—is the most popular collection of portfolios used as an alternative model to the CAPM and is one example of a multi-factor model. The average monthly returns of these portfolios are shown in Table 11.6. Using this collection, the expected return of security i is given by Equation 11.9:

$$E[R_i] = r_f + \beta_i^{Mkt}(E[R_{Mkt}] - r_f) + \beta_i^{SMB}E[R_{SMB}] + \beta_i^{HML}E[R_{HML}] + \beta_i^{PR1YR}E[R_{PR1YR}] \tag{11.9}$$

where β_i^{Mkt}, β_i^{SMB}, β_i^{HML}, and β_i^{PR1YR} are the factor betas of stock i and measure the sensitivity of the stock to each portfolio. Because the collection of portfolios (Mkt, SMB, HML, and PR1YR) was identified by Professors Eugene Fama, Kenneth French, and Mark Carhart, we refer to this collection of portfolios as the **Fama-French-Carhart (FFC) factor specification**.

Fama-French-Carhart (FFC) factor specification A multi-factor model of risk and return in which the factor portfolios are the market, small-minus-big, high-minus-low, and PR1YR portfolios identified by Fama, French, and Carhart.

[5]See Stephen A. Ross, "The Arbitrage Theory of Capital Asset Pricing," *Journal of Economic Theory* 3 (December 1976): 343–62; and Robert C. Merton "An Intertemporal Capital Asset Pricing Model," *Econometrica* 41(1973): 867–887.

TABLE 11.6 FFC Portfolio Average Monthly Returns (1927–2007)

Factor Portfolio	Average Monthly Return (%)
Mkt $- r_f$	0.65
SMB	0.23
HML	0.39
PR1YR	0.68

Source: http://mba.tuck.dartmouth.edu/pages/faculty/ken.french/data_library.html

EXAMPLE 11.9 Using the FFC Factor Specification to Calculate the Cost of Capital

PROBLEM

You are currently considering making an investment in a project in the food industry. You determine the project has the same riskiness as investing in McDonald's. You use data over the 2005–2015 time period to estimate the factor betas of McDonald's (ticker symbol: MCD). Specifically, you regress the monthly excess return (the realized return in each month minus the risk-free rate) of McDonald's stock on the return of each of the four-factor portfolios. You determine that the factor betas for MCD are as follows:

$$\beta_{MCD}^{Mkt} = 0.62$$
$$\beta_{MCD}^{SMB} = -0.47$$
$$\beta_{MCD}^{HML} = -0.10$$
$$\beta_{MCD}^{PR1YR} = 0.12$$

The current risk-free monthly rate is 1.2%/12 = 0.10%. Determine the cost of capital by using the FFC factor specification.

SOLUTION

■ Plan

First, gather the information you have. Combining the information in the problem with the data in Table 11.6, you have

	Average Monthly Return (%)	MCD's β with Factor
Mkt $- r_f$	0.65	0.62
SMB	0.23	− 0.47
HML	0.39	− 0.10
PR1YR	0.68	0.12

Using the information you have collected along with the monthly risk-free rate of 0.10%, you can use Equation 11.9 to calculate the monthly expected return for investing in McDonald's. From there, you can multiply by 12 to get the annual expected return, represented as an annual percentage rate. ▶

Execute

Using Equation 11.9, the monthly expected return of investing in McDonald's is

$$\begin{aligned} E[R_{MCD}] &= r_f + \beta_{MCD}^{Mkt}(E[R_{Mkt}] - r_f) + \beta_{MCD}^{SMB}E[R_{SMB}] + \beta_{MCD}^{HML}E[R_{HML}] + \beta_{MCD}^{PR1YR}E[R_{PR1YR}] \\ &= 0.10\% + 0.62 \times 0.65\% - 0.47 \times 0.23\% - 0.10 \times 0.39\% + 0.12 \times 0.68\% \\ &= 0.44\% \end{aligned}$$

The annual expected return is $0.44\% \times 12 = 5.25\%$.

Evaluate

By gathering all of the inputs and applying the FFC specification in the same way we would apply the CAPM, we can calculate this alternative estimate of the equity cost of capital for McDonald's.

According to this approach, we would conclude that the annual cost of capital of the investment opportunity is about 5.25%. This is lower than the cost of capital we would have estimated using the CAPM: $12 \times (0.10\% + 0.62 \times 0.65\%) = 6.04\%$.

CHAPTER

Determining the Cost of Capital

12

LEARNING OBJECTIVES

- Understand the drivers of the firm's overall cost of capital
- Measure the costs of debt, preferred stock, and common stock
- Compute a firm's overall, or weighted average, cost of capital
- Apply the weighted average cost of capital to value projects
- Adjust the cost of capital for the risk associated with the project
- Account for the direct costs of raising external capital

NOTATION

D	market value of debt
Div_1	dividend due in one year
Div_{pfd}	dividend on preferred stock
E	market value of (levered) equity
FCF_t	incremental free cash flow in year t
g	expected growth rate for dividends
P	market value of preferred stock
P_E	price of common stock
P_{pfd}	price of preferred stock
r_D	required return (cost of capital) for debt
r_E	required return (cost of capital) of levered equity
r_{pfd}	required return (cost of capital) for preferred stock
r_U	required return (cost of capital) of unlevered equity
r_{wacc}	weighted average cost of capital
T_c	marginal corporate tax rate
V_0^L	initial levered value

In Chapter 11, we learned how to determine a firm's equity cost of capital. In reality, most firms are financed with a combination of equity, debt, and other securities, such as preferred stock. As a result, financial managers must determine their firm's overall cost of capital based on all sources of financing. This overall cost of capital is a critical input into the capital budgeting process. The Valuation Principle tells us that the value of a project is the present value of its benefits net of the present value of its costs. In capital budgeting, we implement this important concept with net present value (NPV). To calculate a project's NPV, we need a cost of capital to use as a discount rate.

In this chapter, we will learn how to calculate and use the firm's overall cost of capital, which is typically referred to as its weighted average cost of capital (WACC). We will see that the WACC is a weighted average of the costs of capital from each of the firm's different financing sources. After we have learned how to estimate the WACC, we will apply it in capital budgeting. As part of that discussion, we will learn the conditions under which we can use the firm's overall cost of capital as a discount rate, and identify those situations in which we will instead need to determine a cost of capital specific to a project or division of the firm.

12.1 A First Look at the Weighted Average Cost of Capital

Most firms draw on some combination of equity, debt, and other securities to raise the funds they need for investment. In this section, we examine the role of financing sources in determining the firm's overall cost of capital. We begin by stepping back to assess these financing sources in the context of the firm's balance sheet.

The Firm's Capital Structure

capital A firm's sources of financing—debt, equity, and other securities that it has outstanding.

capital structure The relative proportions of debt, equity, and other securities that a firm has outstanding.

A firm's sources of financing, which usually consist of debt and equity, represent its **capital**. The typical firm raises funds to invest by selling shares to shareholders (its equity) and borrowing from lenders (its debt). Recall the most basic form of the balance sheet, as represented in Figure 12.1. The left side of the balance sheet lists the firm's assets, and the right side describes the firm's capital.

The relative proportions of debt, equity, and other securities that a firm has outstanding constitute its **capital structure**. When corporations raise funds from outside investors, they must choose which type of security to issue. The most common choices are financing through equity alone and financing through a combination of debt and equity. The pie charts in panels (a) and (b) of Figure 12.2 show the capital structures of Shopify and Canadian Natural Resources. Capital structures vary widely across firms. In Chapter 16, we will discuss how a firm sets its capital structure.

FIGURE 12.1 A Basic Balance Sheet

This figure provides a very basic balance sheet for reference. As discussed in Chapter 2, the two sides of the balance sheet must equal each other: Assets = Liabilities + Equity. The right side represents the way the assets are financed. In this chapter, we will focus on the required returns for the different forms of financing found on the right side of the balance sheet.

Assets	Liabilities and Equity
Current Assets	Debt (D)
Long-Term Assets	Preferred Stock (P) Equity (E)

FIGURE 12.2 Two Capital Structures

This figure shows the capital structures of two Canadian firms. Shopify is financed 100% with common equity, shown in blue (Panel A), while Canadian Natural Resources is financed 73% with common equity and 27% with debt, shaded in red (Panel B).

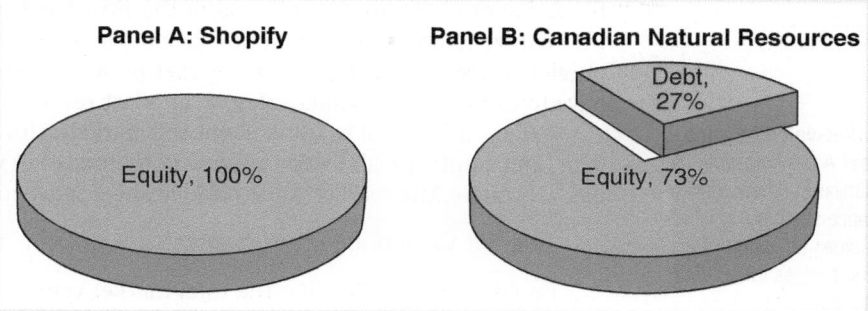

Source: Bloomberg, author's calculations.

Opportunity Cost and the Overall Cost of Capital

Financial managers take into account each component of the firm's capital structure when determining the firm's overall cost of capital. Throughout the discussion that follows, keep in mind the reasoning behind the term "cost of capital." When investors buy the stock or bonds of a company, they forgo the opportunity to invest that money elsewhere. The expected return from those alternative investments constitutes an opportunity cost to them. Thus, to attract their investments as capital to the firm, the firm must offer potential investors an expected return equal to that they could expect to earn elsewhere for assuming the same level of risk. Providing this return is the cost a company bears in exchange for obtaining capital from investors.

Weighted Averages and the Overall Cost of Capital

Intuitively, the firm's overall cost of capital should be a blend of the costs of the different sources of capital. In fact, we calculate the firm's overall cost of capital as a weighted average of its equity and debt costs of capital, known as the firm's **weighted average cost of capital (WACC)**.

weighted average cost of capital (WACC) The average of a firm's equity and debt costs of capital, weighted by the fractions of the firm's value that correspond to equity and debt, respectively.

But what should the weights be? Imagine you owned all of the stock and all of the debt of the firm. If that was all you had in your portfolio, the return on your portfolio would be the total return of the firm. As we showed in Chapter 11, a portfolio return is the weighted average of the returns of the securities in the portfolio. In this case, the return on your portfolio—the total return of the firm—is a weighted average of the return you earn holding all the stock of the firm and the return you earn holding all of the debt. Since you hold all of each, your portfolio weights are just the relative amount of debt and equity issued by the firm. Thus, the weights we use in the WACC are the proportions of debt and equity used in the firm's capital structure. For example, if the firm is financed 30% by debt and 70% by equity, then the weights used in its WACC would be 30% on the debt cost of capital and 70% on the equity cost of capital.

This example suggests that you can determine the weights by looking at the right side of the firm's balance sheet. That assumption is correct, with one important modification—you must use the *market values* of the debt and equity to determine the proportions, not the accounting-based *book values* listed on the balance sheet. Recall from Chapter 2 that book values reflect historical costs, but market values are forward-looking, based on what the assets are expected to produce in the future. Holders of the firm's financial claims—equity and, if the firm has it, debt—assess the firm based on the market value of its assets, not the book value. (If a company's equity or debt is not publicly traded, then there is no market price available for its securities, and we may have to estimate the market value or, as a last resort, use book values instead.)

market-value balance sheet A balance sheet that is similar to an accounting balance sheet but in which all values are current market values rather than historical costs.

In fact, it is useful to think about the **market-value balance sheet**, where the assets, debt, and equity are all listed in terms of their market values, instead of their book values. Of course, the market-value balance sheet must still balance:

$$\text{Market Value of Equity} + \text{Market Value of Debt} = \text{Market Value of Assets} \quad (12.1)$$

Equation 12.1 states that the total market value of all the claims (equity and debt) issued by the firm must be equal to the total market value of all its assets. This equality drives home the point that the equity and debt issued by the firm derive their value from the underlying assets they claim. The risk, and hence the required return, of the debt and equity of the firm are determined by the risk of the firm's assets. This point will be useful as we derive the firm's WACC.

Weighted Average Cost of Capital Calculations

In this section, we will explore the reasoning behind the use of market-value weights, as well as the link between the risk of the assets and the risk of the debt and equity claims on those assets.

unlevered A firm that does not have debt outstanding.

levered A firm that has debt outstanding.

leverage The relative amount of debt on a firm's balance sheet.

We begin with the straightforward case of the firm that does not issue debt—the **unlevered** firm that pays out all of the free cash flows generated by its assets to its equity holders. When some of a firm's financing comes from debt, we say the firm is **levered**. Just as a lever allows you to lift a heavy object by exerting relatively little force, so borrowing money through debt allows equity holders to control highly valued assets with relatively little investment of their own money. We refer to the relative amount of debt on the balance sheet as the firm's **leverage**.

The Weighted Average Cost of Capital: Unlevered Firm. If a firm is unlevered—so it has no debt—all of the free cash flows generated by its assets are ultimately paid out to its equity holders. Because the free cash flows to the equity holders are the same as the free cash flows from the assets, the Valuation Principle tells us that the market value, risk, and cost of capital for the firm's equity are equal to the corresponding amounts for its assets. Given this relationship, we can estimate the firm's equity cost of capital using the Capital Asset Pricing Model (CAPM). The resulting estimate is the cost of capital for the firm as a whole. For example, Shopify does not issue debt, so the cost of capital for Shopify's assets is the same as the firm's costs of equity.

The Weighted Average Cost of Capital: Levered Firm. But what if the firm has debt? How should we incorporate the cost of this debt to determine the cost of capital for the firm's assets as a whole? The market-value balance sheet provides the answer. We can interpret the equality in Equation 12.1 in terms of a portfolio—by holding a portfolio of the firm's equity and debt, we can get the same cash flows as if we held the assets directly. Because the return of a portfolio is equal to the weighted average of the returns of the securities in it, this equality implies the following relationship between the required returns (costs) of equity, debt, and assets:

$$\begin{aligned} r_{wacc} &\equiv \begin{pmatrix}\text{Fraction of Firm Value}\\ \text{Financed by Equity}\end{pmatrix}\begin{pmatrix}\text{Equity}\\ \text{Cost of Capital}\end{pmatrix} \\ &\quad + \begin{pmatrix}\text{Fraction of Firm Value}\\ \text{Financed by Debt}\end{pmatrix}\begin{pmatrix}\text{Debt}\\ \text{Cost of Capital}\end{pmatrix} \\ &= \begin{pmatrix}\text{Asset}\\ \text{Cost of Capital}\end{pmatrix} \end{aligned} \tag{12.2}$$

Weighted Average Cost of Capital (Pre-tax)

We now have the justification for our reasoning that the overall cost of capital for a firm should be a weighted average of its equity and debt costs of capital. Equation 12.2 shows that we can calculate the cost of capital of the firm's assets by computing the weighted average of the firm's equity and debt cost of capital. In the next section, we explore how to estimate the firm's costs of equity and debt capital.

EXAMPLE 12.1 Calculating the Weights in the WACC

PROBLEM

Suppose Great Lakes Corp. has debt with a book (face) value of $10 million, trading at 95% of face value. It also has book equity of $10 million, and one million shares of common stock trading at $30 per share. What weights should Great Lakes use in calculating its WACC?

SOLUTION

Plan

Equation 12.2 tells us that the weights are the fractions of Great Lakes financed with debt and financed with equity. Furthermore, these weights should be based on market values, because the cost of capital is based on investors' current assessment of the value of the firm, not on accounting-based book values. As a consequence, we can ignore the book values of debt and equity.

Execute

Ten million dollars in debt trading at 95% of face value is $9.5 million in market value. One million shares of stock at $30 per share is $30 million in market value. So, the total market value of the firm is $39.5 million. The weights are 9.5 ÷ 39.5 = 24.1% for debt and 30 ÷ 39.5 = 75.9% for equity.

Evaluate

When calculating its overall cost of capital, Great Lakes will use a weighted average of the cost of its debt capital and the cost of its equity capital, giving a weight of 24.1% to its cost of debt and a weight of 75.9% to its cost of equity.

CONCEPT CHECK

1. Why does a firm's capital have a cost?
2. Why do we use market-value weights in the weighted average cost of capital?

12.2 The Firm's Costs of Debt and Equity Capital

Section 12.1 made it clear that to measure the firm's overall cost of capital, we need to start by determining the cost of each type of capital a firm might use. We now turn to how a company measures the costs of its debt, preferred stock, and common stock. We will use BCE Inc. (formerly Bell Canada Enterprises), Canada's largest communications company, as an example.

Cost of Debt Capital

We will start at the top of the right side of the balance sheet with the cost of the firm's debt. A firm's cost of debt is the interest rate it would have to pay to refinance its existing debt, such as through new bond issues. This rate differs from the coupon rate on the firm's existing debt, which reflects the interest rate the firm had to offer at the time the debt was issued.

Yield to Maturity and the Cost of Debt. Existing debt trades in the marketplace, so its price fluctuates to reflect both changes in the overall credit environment and changes in the risk specifically associated with the firm. As we learned in Chapter 6, the market price of the firm's existing debt implies a yield to maturity, which is the return that current purchasers of the debt would earn if they held the debt to maturity and received all of the payments as promised. So, we can use the yield to maturity to estimate the firm's current cost of debt; it is the yield that investors demand to hold the firm's debt (new or existing).[1]

Suppose BCE has debt due in March 2023 with a coupon rate of 3.35% priced at \$1009.70 per \$1000 face value. Because the market price of the debt is above its face value, bondholders earn a yield that is lower than the 3.35% coupon rate. In fact, this price implies a yield to maturity of 3.14%, which is an estimate of BCE's current cost of debt (students can confirm this using Equation 6.4 in Chapter 6; for your calculations, assume that today's date is March 31, 2018, and the last payment on the semi-annual coupon bond will be made on March 31, 2023). In reality, you would not need to actually compute the yield to maturity yourself, because prices and their implied yields to maturity are always quoted together in the bond market.[2]

Taxes and the Cost of Debt. In the case of debt, the return paid to the debt holders is not the same as the cost to the firm. How could this be? The difference arises because interest paid on debt is a tax-deductible expense. When a firm uses debt financing, the cost of the interest it must pay is offset to some extent by the tax savings from the tax deduction.

For example, suppose a firm with a 35% tax rate borrows \$100,000 at 10% interest per year. Then, its net cost at the end of the year is calculated as follows:

		Year-End
Interest expense	$r_D \times \$100{,}000 =$	10,000
Tax savings	$-\text{Tax Rate} \times r_D \times \$100{,}000 =$	−3500
Effective after-tax interest expense	$r_D \times (1 - \text{Tax Rate}) \times \$100{,}000 =$	\$6500

[1]In fact, the yield to maturity is the *most* the firm will pay, because there is some risk the firm may not repay its debt.

[2]Chapter 6 demonstrated how to find current prices and yields to maturity for corporate bonds. Websites such as those of CanadianFixedIncome.ca (www.canadianfixedincome.ca) and the Financial Industry Regulatory Authority (FINRA) (http://finra-markets.morningstar.com/MarketData/Default.jsp) provide current information on corporate and government debt securities.

COMMON MISTAKE

Using the Coupon Rate as the Cost of Debt

A common mistake in estimating a company's overall cost of capital is to use the coupon rate on its existing debt as its debt cost of capital. The company's cost of capital is forward-looking and based on current conditions. By contrast, the coupon rate on existing debt is historical and set under potentially very different conditions. A better estimate of the firm's debt cost of capital is the yield to maturity of its existing debt, which is the promised return its lenders currently demand.

Consider the effects of the collapse of the U.S. real estate market on companies that build homes, such as KB Homes. KB had bonds that were originally issued in 2004 and were due in 2014; these bonds had a coupon rate of 5.75%. When the markets turned downward, KB's performance suffered, and the risk that it might not be able to meet all of its debt obligations increased. By mid-2010, those 5.75% coupon bonds were rated BB (below investment grade) and trading at a yield to maturity of about 8.6%. Therefore, to be willing to take a creditor position in KB, investors demanded a yield to maturity of 8.6%. Taking into account the probability of default and the expected loss in default, the BB-rated bonds had an average expected loss of 1.3%. The true expected return was closer to 7.3% (8.6% promised minus 1.3% expected loss).

In order to estimate the cost of debt capital for KB in 2010, should one rely on the 5.75% coupon rate or the 8.6% yield to maturity? It would be a mistake to use the 5.75% rate, which was set under different circumstances and is not a relevant measure of KB's debt holders' required return in 2010. Because of the increase in default risk, the 7.3% we calculated would be a much better estimate of KB's cost of debt capital. (Note that the increase in default risk affected not just KB's cost of debt capital but also its capital structure due to the decline in the market value of KB's coupon bonds.)

effective cost of debt A firm's net cost of interest on its debt after accounting for the interest tax deduction.

The **effective cost of debt**—the firm's net cost of interest on the debt after taxes—is only \$6500/\$100,000 = 6.50% of the loan amount, rather than the full 10% interest, because the tax deductibility of interest lowers the effective cost of debt financing for the firm. More generally, with tax-deductible interest and denoting the corporate tax rate as T_C, the effective after-tax borrowing rate is

$$r_D(1 - T_C) \tag{12.3}$$

EXAMPLE 12.2 Effective Cost of Debt

PROBLEM

By using the yield to maturity on BCE's debt, we found that its pre-tax cost of debt is 3.14%. If BCE's tax rate is 20%, what is its effective cost of debt?

SOLUTION

Plan

We can use Equation 12.3 to calculate BCE's effective cost of debt: $r_D(1 - T_C)$.

$$r_D = 3.14\% \text{ (pre-tax cost of debt)}$$

$$T_C = 20\% \text{ (corporate tax rate)}$$

Execute

BCE's effective cost of debt is $0.0314(1 - 0.2) = 0.0251 = 2.51\%$. ▶

Evaluate

For every \$1000 it borrows, BCE pays its bondholders 0.0314(\$1000) = \$31.40 in interest every year. Because it can deduct that \$31.40 in interest from its income, every dollar in interest saves BCE 20 cents in taxes, so the interest tax deduction reduces the firm's tax payment to the government by 0.2(\$31.40) = \$6.28. Thus, BCE's net cost of debt is the \$31.40 it pays minus the \$6.28 in reduced tax payments, which is \$25.12 per \$1000, or 2.51%.

We have used corporate bonds as an example in estimating the cost of debt. Many smaller companies do not have access to the bond market and use bank debt instead. In their case, they typically have a good sense of their cost of debt from discussions with their banker about interest rates on new loans.

Cost of Preferred Stock Capital

Firms may also raise capital by issuing preferred stock. Typically, holders of the preferred stock are promised a fixed dividend, which must be paid "in preference to" (i.e., before) any dividends can be paid to common stockholders.

If the preferred dividend is known and fixed, we can estimate the preferred stock's cost of capital using Equation 7.7 in Chapter 7,

$$r_E = \frac{Div_1}{P_0} + g$$

where the growth rate $g = 0$. Thus,

$$\text{Cost of Preferred Stock Capital} = \frac{\text{Preferred Dividend}}{\text{Preferred Stock Price}} = \frac{Div_{pfd}}{P_{pfd}} \tag{12.4}$$

For example, suppose BCE's preferred stock has a price of \$20.80 and an annual dividend of \$1.0325. Its cost of preferred stock, therefore, is 1.0325/20.80 = 4.96%.[3]

Cost of Common Stock Capital

As we learned in Chapter 11, a company cannot directly observe its cost of common stock (equity) but must instead estimate it. We now present and compare the two major methods for doing so.

Capital Asset Pricing Model. The most common approach is to use the CAPM as presented in Chapter 11. That approach is summarized below:

1. Estimate the firm's beta of equity, typically by regressing 60 months of the company's returns against 60 months of returns for a market proxy, such as the S&P/TSX Composite Index. (Practitioners tend to avoid using more than five years of data because firms and their betas change over time: a beta estimated using ten years of monthly returns may not be representative of the riskiness of new projects the firm plans to implement.)

[3]BCE has multiple classes of preferred shares. These calculations were based on information regarding BCE's Class R preferred shares; see http://www.bce.ca/investors/preferredshares.

2. Determine the risk-free rate, typically by using the yield on Government of Canada treasury bills or bonds.
3. Estimate the market risk premium, typically by comparing historical returns on a market proxy to contemporaneous risk-free rates.
4. Apply the CAPM:

$$\text{Cost of Equity} = \text{Risk-Free Rate} + \text{Equity Beta} \times \text{Market Risk Premium}$$

For example, suppose the equity beta of BCE is 0.75 and the yield on 10-year Government of Canada bonds is 2.35%, and you estimate the market risk premium to be 6%. BCE's cost of equity is 2.35% + 0.75 × 6% = 6.85%.

Constant Dividend Growth Model. Another way to estimate a company's cost of equity comes from the Constant Dividend Growth Model (CDGM) introduced in Chapter 7. Equation 7.7 from Chapter 7 shows that

$$\text{Cost of Equity} = \frac{\text{Dividend (in one year)}}{\text{Current Price}} + \text{Dividend Growth Rate} = \frac{Div_1}{P_E} + g \quad (12.5)$$

Thus, to estimate the cost of equity, we need the current price of the stock, the expected dividend in one year, and an estimate of the dividend growth rate. The current price of the stock is easy to obtain online. We may even have a reasonable estimate of next year's dividend. However, as we discussed in Chapter 7, estimating the future dividend growth rate can be very difficult. For example, BCE's dividend was $1.32 per share per year in 2005 and 2006 and then increased to $1.46 in 2007, only to decline to $0.73 in 2008 when dividends were temporarily suspended for two quarters. Dividends were reinstated in 2009 and by early 2019 the dividend is expected to reach $3.02 per year. What about the dividend's long-term growth rate? The historical growth rate has been uneven.

Rather than looking backward at historical growth, one common approach is to use estimates produced by stock analysts, as these estimates are forward-looking. As discussed in Chapter 7, if BCE keeps its dividend payout rate constant, then the long-run growth in dividends will equal the long-run growth in earnings. In early 2018, the average forecast for BCE's long-run earnings growth rate was 3.5%. Thus, with an expected dividend in one year of $3.02, a price of $53.72, and long-run dividend growth of 3.5%, Equation 12.5 estimates BCE's cost of equity as follows:[4]

$$\text{Cost of Equity} = \frac{Div_1}{P_E} + g = \frac{\$3.02}{\$53.72} + 0.035 = 0.0912, \quad \text{or} \quad 9.12\%$$

We should not be surprised that the two estimates of BCE's cost of equity (6.85% and 9.12%) do not match, because each was based on different assumptions. Further, even given an estimate of future growth of dividends, Equation 12.5 makes an assumption that future dividend growth will continue at a constant rate. This assumption is unlikely to be valid for most firms. Looking again at BCE, its dividend initially grew at double-digit rates following the 2009 reinstatement, but its growth rate fell to around

[4]Note that, in practice, companies pay quarterly rather than annual dividends on their common and preferred shares (and semi-annual rather than annual coupons on their bonds). In Chapter 5 we learned how to convert an APR-type rate, such as BCE's 9.12% cost of equity, into an effective annual rate. Given BCE's quarterly dividends, we could obtain a more accurate estimate of BCE's cost of equity capital using Equation 5.3: EAR = $(1 + 0.0912/4)^4 = 9.44\%$. In this chapter, rather than converting all cost of capital figures into *EAR*s, we assume annual dividend (and annual coupon) payments for the sake of simplicity.

TABLE 12.1 Estimating the Cost of Equity

	Capital Asset Pricing Model	Constant Dividend Growth Model
Inputs	Equity beta	Current stock price
	Risk-free rate	Expected dividend next year
	Market risk premium	Future dividend growth rate
Major Assumptions	Estimated beta is correct	Dividend estimate is correct
	Market risk premium is accurate	Growth rate matches market expectations
	CAPM is the correct model	Future dividend growth is constant

5% by 2013 and remained at that level since then. Also note that many young, growing firms do not pay a dividend and have no plans to do so in the near future.

We could use any model relating a firm's stock price to its future cash flows to estimate its cost of equity—the CDGM is just one of the possible models. For example, we could use the discounted free cash flow model from Chapter 7 to solve for the firm's cost of equity.

CAPM and CDGM Comparison. Because of the difficulties with the CDGM, the CAPM is the most popular approach for estimating the cost of equity. Table 12.1 above compares the two approaches.

EXAMPLE 12.3 Estimating the Cost of Equity

PROBLEM

Assume the equity beta for Telus Corp is 0.78. The yield on 10-year Government of Canada bonds is 2%, and you estimate the market risk premium to be 6%. Further, suppose Telus is expected to issue an annual dividend of $2.1 in one year. Its current stock price is $46.5, and you expect dividends to increase at a constant rate of 4% per year. Estimate Telus's cost of equity in two ways.

SOLUTION

■ Plan

The two ways to estimate Telus's cost of equity are to use the CAPM and the CDGM.

1. The CAPM requires the risk-free rate, an estimate of the equity's beta, and an estimate of the market risk premium. We can use the yield on 10-year Government of Canada bonds as the risk-free rate.
2. The CDGM requires the current stock price, the expected dividend next year, and an estimate of the constant future growth rate for the dividend:

Risk-free rate: 2%	Current price: $46.5
Equity beta: 0.78	Expected dividend: $2.1
Market risk premium: 6%	Estimated future dividend growth rate: 4%

We can use the CAPM from Chapter 11 to estimate the cost of equity using the CAPM approach and Equation 12.5 to estimate it using the CDGM approach.

■ Execute

1. The CAPM says that

$$\text{Cost of Equity} = \text{Risk-Free Rate} + \text{Equity Beta} \times \text{Market Risk Premium}$$

▶

For Telus, this implies that its cost of equity is 2% + 0.78 × 6% = 6.7%.

2. The CDGM says

$$\text{Cost of Equity} = \frac{\text{Dividend (in one year)}}{\text{Current Price}} + \text{Dividend Growth Rate} = \frac{\$2.1}{\$46.5} + 4\% = 8.5\%$$

■ **Evaluate**

According to the CAPM, the cost of equity capital is $6.7%; the CDGM produces a result of 8.5%. Because of the different assumptions we make when using each method, the two methods do not have to produce the same answer—in fact, it would be highly unlikely that they would. When the two approaches produce different answers, we must examine the assumptions we made for each approach and decide which set of assumptions is more realistic.

We can also see what assumption about future dividend growth would be necessary to make the answers converge. By rearranging the CDGM and using the cost of equity we estimated from the CAPM, we have

$$\text{Dividend Growth Rate} = \text{Cost of Equity} - \frac{\text{Dividend (in one year)}}{\text{Current Price}} = 6.7\% - 4.5\% = 2.2\%$$

Thus, if we believe that Telus's dividends will grow at a rate of 2.2% per year, the two approaches would produce the same cost of equity estimate.

CONCEPT CHECK

3. How can you measure a firm's cost of debt?
4. What are the major trade-offs in using the CAPM versus the CDGM to estimate the cost of equity?

12.3 A Second Look at the Weighted Average Cost of Capital

Now that we have estimated the costs of BCE's different sources of capital, we are ready to calculate the firm's overall WACC. The weights are the percentage of firm value financed by equity, preferred stock, and debt. We can represent these as $E/(E + P + D)$, $P/(E + P + D)$, and $D/(E + P + D)$, respectively, and note that they must sum to 100% (i.e., we must account for all the sources of financing).

WACC Equation

Formally, denoting the cost of equity, preferred stock, and debt capital as r_E, r_{pfd}, and r_D, respectively, and the corporate tax rate as T_C, the WACC is as follows:

Weighted Average Cost of Capital

$$r_{wacc} = r_E \frac{E}{E + P + D} + r_{Pfd} \frac{P}{E + P + D} + r_D(1 - T_C) \frac{D}{E + P + D} \tag{12.6}$$

For a company that does not have preferred stock, the WACC condenses to

$$r_{wacc} = r_E \frac{E}{E + D} + r_D(1 - T_C) \frac{D}{E + D} \tag{12.7}$$

For example, in early 2018, the market values of BCE's common stock, preferred stock, and debt were $48,333 million, $3,331 million, and $19,321 million, respectively. Its total value was, therefore, \$48,333 million + \$3,331 million + \$19,321 million = \$70,985 million. Given the costs of common stock, preferred stock, and debt we have already computed, BCE's WACC in early 2018 was

$$r_{wacc} = r_E \frac{E}{E + P + D} + r_{Pfd} \frac{P}{E + P + D} + r_D(1 - T_C) \frac{D}{E + P + D}$$

$$r_{WACC} = 6.85\% \left(\frac{\$48{,}333}{\$70{,}985}\right) + 4.96\% \left(\frac{\$3{,}331}{\$70{,}985}\right) + 3.14\% \ (1 - 0.20) \left(\frac{\$19{,}321}{\$70{,}985}\right)$$

$$r_{WACC} = 5.58\%$$

EXAMPLE 12.4 Computing the WACC

PROBLEM

The expected return on Target's equity is 11.5%, and the firm has a yield to maturity on its debt of 6%. Debt accounts for 18% and equity for 82% of Target's total market value. If its tax rate is 35%, what is this firm's WACC?

SOLUTION

Plan

We can compute the WACC using Equation 12.7. To do so, we need to know the costs of equity and debt, their proportions in Target's capital structure, and the firm's tax rate. We have all that information, so we are ready to proceed.

Execute

$$r_{wacc} = r_E \frac{E}{E + D} + r_D(1 - T_C) \frac{D}{E + D} = (0.115)(0.82) + (0.06)(1 - 0.35)(0.18)$$

$$= 0.101, \text{ or } 10.1\%$$

Evaluate

Even though we cannot observe the expected return of Target's investments directly, we can use the expected return on its equity and debt and the WACC formula to estimate it, adjusting for the tax advantage of debt. Target needs to earn at least a 10.1% return on its investment in current and new stores to satisfy both its debt and equity holders.

Weighted Average Cost of Capital in Practice

The WACC is driven by the risk of a company's line of business and, because of the tax effect of interest, its leverage. As a result, WACCs vary widely across industries and companies. Figure 12.3 presents the WACC for several real companies to provide a sense of the degree to which the cost of capital can vary. Some lines of business are clearly riskier than others. For example, being an electric utility, such as Hydro One, is a fairly low-risk proposition, but operating an e-commerce business (as Shopify does) is much riskier.

Methods in Practice

We now turn to some issues that arise for financial managers when they are estimating the WACC in practice.

FIGURE 12.3 WACCs for Real Companies

The cost of equity is computed using the company's equity beta, a risk-free rate of 2%, and a market risk premium of 6%. The cost of debt is based on market yield to maturities of the debt. The percent equity and percent debt are determined from the company's market capitalization and balance sheet. The WACC is computed using Equation 12.7 with a 30% tax rate and is shown in the accompanying bar graph. "N/A" means that the cost of debt is not applicable and refers to companies that have no debt. All data as of April 24, 2018.

Company Name	Beta	Cost of Equity	Cost of Debt	Wt. Of Equity	Wt. Of Debt	WACC
Hydro One	0.52	5.1%	3.1%	54%	46%	3.8%
Capital Power Corp	0.62	5.7%	4.2%	48%	52%	4.3%
Brookfield Asset Management Inc	1.09	8.5%	3.6%	36%	64%	4.7%
Shaw Communications Inc	0.63	5.8%	3.0%	75%	25%	4.8%
Enbridge Inc	0.95	7.7%	3.1%	48%	52%	4.8%
Telus Corp	0.78	6.7%	3.3%	69%	31%	5.3%
Canadian Tire Corporation	0.71	6.2%	4.0%	79%	21%	5.5%
Great-West Lifeco Inc	0.74	6.5%	3.0%	80%	20%	5.6%
Saputo Inc	0.71	6.3%	2.9%	91%	9%	5.9%
Loblaw Cos Ltd	0.92	7.5%	3.5%	72%	28%	6.1%
Rogers Communications Inc	0.93	7.6%	3.5%	71%	29%	6.1%
Altagas Ltd	1.14	8.9%	4.1%	58%	42%	6.4%
Husky Energy	1.00	8.0%	3.2%	76%	24%	6.6%
Canadian National Railway Co	0.92	7.5%	3.5%	89%	11%	7.0%
Cameco Corp	1.31	9.9%	2.9%	78%	22%	8.1%
Canadian Natural Resources Ltd	1.39	10.4%	3.3%	73%	27%	8.2%
Shopify Inc	1.63	11.8%	N/A	100%	0%	11.8%

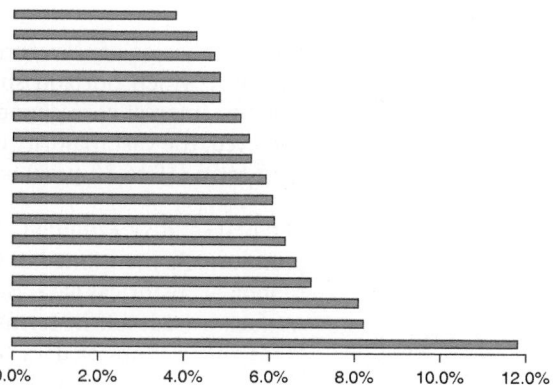

Source: Bloomberg, CanadianFixedIncome.ca, and authors' calculations.

net debt Total debt outstanding minus any cash balances.

Net Debt. When calculating the weights for the WACC, it is increasingly common practice to make an adjustment to the debt. Many practitioners now use **net debt**, the total debt outstanding minus any cash balances:

$$\text{Net Debt} = \text{Debt} - \text{Cash and Risk-Free Securities} \tag{12.8}$$

Why subtract a company's cash from its debt? The assets on a firm's balance sheet include any holdings of cash or risk-free securities. If a firm holds $1 in cash and has $1 of risk-free debt, then the interest earned on the cash will equal the interest paid on the debt. The cash flows from each source cancel each other, just as if the firm held no cash and no debt. In fact, we can view cash as being equivalent to negative debt. Significant excess cash on a firm's balance sheet can complicate the assessment of the risk (and, hence, the cost of capital) of the assets the firm actually uses in the course of business. Thus, when trying to evaluate a firm's business assets separately from any cash holdings, practitioners often measure the leverage of the firm in terms of its net debt and measure the market value of a firm's business assets using its enterprise value. Recall from Chapter 2 the definition of enterprise value as the market value of a firm's equity plus its net debt.

Using this approach, the weights in the WACC would then be

$$\left(\frac{\text{Market Value of Equity}}{\text{Enterprise Value}}\right) \text{ and } \left(\frac{\text{Net Debt}}{\text{Enterprise Value}}\right)$$

For firms with substantial excess cash reserves, this adjustment could be important. For firms with relatively low levels of cash, it will not have a large effect on the overall WACC estimate.

The Risk-Free Interest Rate. Estimating the equity cost of capital using the CAPM requires the risk-free interest rate. The risk-free interest rate is generally determined

TABLE 12.2 Historical *Excess* Returns of the S&P/TSX Composite Index Compared with Three-Month Canadian Treasury Bills and Long-Term Government of Canada Bonds

Risk-Free Security	Period	S&P/TSX Composite Index *Excess* Return
Three-month Canadian treasury bills	1950–2017	6.00%
Long-term Government of Canada bonds	1950–2017	3.94%

Source: Passport Financial Services Inc. 1996–2018.

using the yields of Government of Canada debt securities, which are free from default risk. But which horizon should we choose? The CAPM states that we should use the risk-free interest corresponding to the investment horizon of the firm's investors. When surveyed, the vast majority of large firms and financial analysts report using the yields of long-term (10 to 30-year) bonds to determine the risk-free rate.[5]

The Market Risk Premium. Using the CAPM also requires an estimate of the market risk premium. As mentioned in Chapter 10, one way to estimate the market risk premium is to look at historical data. Because we are interested in the *future* market risk premium, we face a trade-off in terms of the amount of data we use. As noted in Chapter 10, it takes many years of data to produce even moderately accurate estimates of expected returns—yet data that are very old may have little relevance for investors' expectations of the market risk premium today.

Table 12.2 reports excess returns of the S&P/TSX Composite Index versus three-month Canadian treasury bills and long-term Government of Canada bonds. Since 1950, the S&P/TSX Composite Index has produced an average return of 6% above the rate for three-month Canadian treasury bills. In the U.S. markets, a comparison of the S&P 500 Index and short-term U.S. Treasury bills from 1926 until 2015 shows an excess return of 7.7%. An interesting change can be seen when comparing the same two U.S. measures over a more recent period of time. Excess returns of the S&P 500 over short-term U.S. Treasury bills from 1965 to 2015 are only 5.0%. The evidence indicates that the market risk premium has declined over time.

How can we explain this decline? One reason may be that as more investors have begun to participate in the stock market and the costs of constructing a diversified portfolio have declined, investors have tended to hold less-risky portfolios. As a result, the return they require as compensation for taking on that risk has diminished. In addition, the overall volatility of the market has declined over time. Some researchers believe that the future expected returns for the market are likely to be even lower than these historical numbers, in a range of 3% to 5% over treasury bills.[6] Consequently, many financial managers currently use market risk premiums closer to 5%, rather than 7%.

CONCEPT CHECK

5. Why do different companies have different WACCs?
6. What are the trade-offs in estimating the market risk premium?

[5]See Robert Bruner et al., "Best Practices in Estimating the Cost of Capital: Survey and Synthesis," *Financial Practice and Education* 8 (1998): 13–28.

[6]See Ivo Welch, "The Equity Premium Consensus Forecast Revisited," Cowles Foundation Discussion Paper 1325 (2001); and John Graham and Campbell Harvey, "The Long-Run Equity Risk Premium," SSRN working paper (2005).

12.4 Using the WACC to Value a Project

A project's cost of capital depends on its risk. When the market risk of the project is similar to the average market risk of the firm's investments, then its cost of capital is equivalent to the cost of capital for a portfolio of all the firm's securities. In other words, the project's cost of capital is equal to the firm's WACC. As shown in Equation 12.6, the WACC incorporates the benefit of the interest tax deduction by using the firm's *after-tax* cost of capital for debt.

Because the WACC incorporates the tax savings from debt, we can compute the value of an investment, including the benefit of the interest tax deduction, given the firm's leverage policy, sometimes called the investment's **levered value**. To do so, we discount the firm's future incremental free cash flow using the WACC, a process we refer to as the **WACC method**. Specifically, if FCF_t is the expected incremental free cash flow of an investment at the end of year t, then the Valuation Principle tells us that the investment's levered value, V_0^L, is

levered value The value of an investment, including the benefit of the interest tax deduction, given the firm's leverage policy.

WACC method Discounting future incremental free cash flows using the firm's WACC. This method produces the levered value of a project.

$$V_0^L = \frac{FCF_1}{1 + r_{wacc}} + \frac{FCF_2}{(1 + r_{wacc})^2} + \frac{FCF_3}{(1 + r_{wacc})^3} + \cdots \tag{12.9}$$

The reasoning behind the WACC method is that the firm's WACC represents the average return the firm must pay to its investors (both debt and equity holders) on an after-tax basis. Thus, to have a positive NPV, a project with the same risk as the average risk for the firm's projects should generate an expected return of at least the firm's WACC.

EXAMPLE 12.5 The WACC Method

PROBLEM

Suppose Big Rock Brewery is considering introducing a new ultra-light beer with zero calories, to be called BigZero. The firm believes that the beer's flavour and appeal to calorie-conscious drinkers will make it a success. The cost of bringing the beer to market is $200 million, but Big Rock expects first-year incremental free cash flows from BigZero to be $10 million and to grow at 3% per year thereafter. If Big Rock's WACC is 5.7%, should it go ahead with the project?

SOLUTION

Plan

We can use the WACC method shown in Equation 12.9 to value BigZero and then subtract the upfront cost of $200 million. We will need Big Rock's WACC, which is 5.7%.

Execute

The cash flows for BigZero are a growing perpetuity. Applying the growing perpetuity formula with the WACC method, we have

$$NPV = FCF_0 + V_0^L = FCF_0 + \frac{FCF_1}{r_{wacc} - g} = -\$200 + \frac{\$10}{0.057 - 0.03} = \$170.4 \text{ million}$$

Evaluate

The BigZero project has a positive NPV because it is expected to generate a return on the $200 million far in excess of Big Rock's WACC of 5.7%. As discussed in Chapter 8, taking positive-NPV projects adds value to the firm. Here, we can see that the value is created by exceeding the required return of the firm's investors.

Key Assumptions

While it is common practice to use the WACC as the discount rate in capital budgeting, it is important to be aware of the underlying assumptions. We examine the critical assumptions here and then explore these assumptions further in the context of an application.

Assumption 1: Average Risk. We assume initially that the market risk of the project is equivalent to the average market risk of the firm's investments. In that case, we assess the project's cost of capital based on the risk of the firm.

Assumption 2: Constant Debt-Equity Ratio. We assume that the firm adjusts its leverage continuously to maintain a constant ratio of the market value of debt to the market value of equity—a relationship referred to as the **debt-equity ratio**. This policy determines the amount of debt the firm will take on when it accepts a new project. It also implies that the risk of the firm's equity and debt, and therefore its WACC, will not fluctuate owing to leverage changes.

debt-equity ratio A ratio of the market value of debt to the market value of equity.

Assumption 3: Limited Leverage Effects. We assume initially that the main effect of leverage on valuation follows from the interest tax deduction. We assume that any other factors (such as possible financial distress) are not significant at the level of debt chosen. We discuss these other factors in detail in Chapter 16.

Assumptions in Practice. These assumptions are reasonable for many projects and firms. The first assumption is likely to fit typical projects of firms with investments concentrated in a single industry. In that case, the market risk of both the project and the firm will primarily depend on the sensitivity of the industry to the overall economy. The second assumption, while unlikely to hold exactly, reflects the fact that firms tend to increase their levels of debt as they grow larger; some may even have an explicit target for their debt-equity ratio (we discuss the trade-off between debt and equity and the concept of a target debt-equity ratio in Chapter 16). Finally, for firms without very high levels of debt, the interest tax deduction is likely to be the most important factor affecting the capital budgeting decision. Hence, the third assumption is a reasonable starting point to begin our analysis.

Of course, while these three assumptions may be a reasonable approximation in many situations, there are certainly projects and firms for which they do not apply. In the following section, we apply the WACC method under all three assumptions. In Section 12.5, we relax the first assumption, which states that the project has average risk. (We will relax the other two assumptions in later chapters.)

WACC Method Application: Extending the Life of Facilities at BCE

Let's apply the WACC method to value a project. Suppose BCE is considering an investment that would extend the life of one of its facilities for four years. The project would require upfront costs of $6.67 million plus a $24 million investment in equipment. Assume that the equipment will be obsolete in four years and will be depreciated for tax purposes via the straight-line method over that period.[7] During the next four years, however, BCE expects annual sales of $60 million per year from this facility. Cost of sales and operating expenses are expected to total $25 million and $9 million, respectively, per year. Finally, BCE expects no net working capital requirements for the project, and it pays a corporate tax rate of 20%.

[7]Straight-line method of depreciation is used for simplification purposes. Assets would normally be depreciated for tax purposes using rates and methods prescribed by the Canada Revenue Agency.

TABLE 12.3 Expected Free Cash Flow from BCE's Facility Project

1	Year	0	1	2	3	4
2	Incremental Earnings Forecast ($ million)					
3	Sales	—	60.00	60.00	60.00	60.00
4	Cost of Sales	—	−25.00	− 25.00	− 25.00	− 25.00
5	Gross Profit	—	35.00	35.00	35.00	35.00
6	Operating Expenses	− 6.67	− 9.00	− 9.00	− 9.00	− 9.00
7	Depreciation	—	− 6.00	− 6.00	− 6.00	− 6.00
8	EBIT	− 6.67	20.00	20.00	20.00	20.00
9	Income Tax at 20%	1.33	− 4.00	− 4.00	− 4.00	− 4.00
10	Unlevered Net Income	− 5.34	16.00	16.00	16.00	16.00
11	Incremental Free Cash Flow ($ million)					
12	Plus: Depreciation	—	6.00	6.00	6.00	6.00
13	Less: Capital Expenditures	− 24.00	—	—	—	—
14	Less: Increases in NWC	—	—	—	—	—
15	Incremental Free Cash Flow	− 29.34	22.00	22.00	22.00	22.00

Using this information, the spreadsheet in Table 12.3 forecasts the project's expected free cash flow. The market risk of the project of extending the life of the facility is the same as that for BCE's overall business. As a consequence, we can use BCE's WACC to compute the NPV of the project.

We can determine the value of the project, including the present value of the interest tax deduction from the debt, by calculating the present value of its future free cash flows, V_0^L using the WACC method and BCE's WACC of 5.58%, which we computed in Section 12.3:

$$V_0^L = \frac{22}{1.0558} + \frac{22}{1.0558^2} + \frac{22}{1.0558^3} + \frac{22}{1.0558^4} = \$76.97 \text{ million}$$

Because the upfront cost of extending the facility's life is only $29.34 million, this project is a good idea. Taking the project results in an NPV of $76.97 million − $29.34 million = $47.63 million for the firm.

Summary of the WACC Method

To summarize, the key steps in the WACC valuation method are as follows:

1. Determine the incremental free cash flow of the investment.
2. Compute the weighted average cost of capital using Equation 12.6.
3. Compute the value of the investment, including the tax benefit of leverage, by discounting the incremental free cash flow of the investment using the WACC.

In many firms, the corporate treasurer performs the second step, calculating the firm's WACC. This rate can then be used throughout the firm as the company-wide cost of capital for new investments *that are of comparable risk to the rest of the firm and that will not alter the firm's debt-equity ratio.* Employing the WACC method in this way is very simple and straightforward. As a result, this method is the most commonly used in practice for capital budgeting purposes.

CONCEPT CHECK

7. What are the main assumptions you make when you use the WACC method?

8. What inputs do you need to be ready to apply the WACC method?

12.5 Project-Based Costs of Capital

Up to this point, we have assumed that both the risk and the leverage of the project under consideration matched those characteristics for the firm as a whole. This assumption allowed us, in turn, to assume that the cost of capital for a project matched the firm's cost of capital.

In reality, specific projects often differ from the average investment made by the firm. Consider General Electric Company (GE), a large firm with many divisions that operate in completely different lines of business. Projects in GE's health care division are likely to have different market risk than projects in its air transportation equipment division or at NBC Universal. Projects may also vary in terms of the amount of leverage they will support—for example, acquisitions of real estate or capital equipment are often highly levered, while investments in intellectual property are not. We will study the effect of leverage on the cost of capital when we cover the leverage decision in Chapter 16. In this section, we show how to calculate the cost of capital for the project's cash flows when a project's risk differs from the firm's overall risk.

COMMON MISTAKE

Using a Single Cost of Capital in Multidivisional Firms

Many firms combine business units with widely different market risk. Yet some of them use a single cost of capital to evaluate projects throughout the organization. Using the same cost of capital for projects that have different riskiness is, of course, a mistake, and will result in the firm taking on too many risky projects and too few safer projects. That is, when the same cost of capital is used for all investment opportunities, regardless of their riskiness, riskier projects will be discounted at too low a cost of capital, making negative NPV investments appear to be positive NPV and be accepted. Similarly, less risky projects will be discounted at too high a cost of capital, and so may be erroneously rejected.

Survey evidence suggests that this mistake is quite common; Professors Philipp Krüger, Augustin Landier, and David Thesmar* looked at the behaviour of conglomerates and found evidence that they were making this mistake. For each conglomerate, they identified the most important division, what they termed the "core-division." They then demonstrated that, on average, conglomerates invest relatively less in divisions that are less risky than the core-division, and relatively more in divisions that are more risky than the core-division.

*"The WACC Fallacy: The Real Effects of Using a Unique Discount Rate," *Journal of Finance*, 70 (2015): 1253–1285.

Cost of Capital for a New Acquisition

We begin by explaining how to calculate the cost of capital of a project with market risk that is different from the risk for the rest of the firm. Suppose BCE wants to enter the discount retail business. To do so, it is considering acquiring Canadian Tire Corporation (CTC), a company that offers a range of retail goods and services, including general merchandise, clothing, sporting goods and automotive parts. CTC faces different market risks than BCE does in its communications business. What cost of capital should BCE use to value a possible acquisition of CTC?

Because the risks are different, BCE's WACC would be inappropriate for valuing CTC. Instead, BCE should calculate and use CTC's WACC when assessing the acquisition. In Figure 12.3, we find the following information for CTC:

	Beta	Cost of Equity	Cost of Debt	$E/(E + D)$	$D/(E + D)$	WACC
Canadian Tire Corporation	0.71	6.2%	4.0%	79%	21%	5.5%

Assuming that after the acquisition BCE will find it appropriate to continue to finance CTC with the same mix of debt and equity that CTC uses currently, we can use

CTC's WACC as the cost of capital for acquiring it. (We consider what to do if BCE wants to change CTC's financing mix in Chapter 16.) Thus, BCE would use a cost of capital of 5.5% to value CTC for purchase.

Divisional Costs of Capital

Now, assume BCE makes a different decision; it decides to create a discount retail division internally, rather than buying CTC. What should the cost of capital for the new division be? If BCE plans to finance the division with the same proportion of debt as is used by CTC, then BCE would use CTC's WACC as the WACC for its new division. Because CTC's WACC is the right cost of capital given the risks of the discount retail business and 21% debt financing, it has to be the right cost of capital for an internally created discount retail division that is financed 21% with debt.

In reality, firms with more than one division rarely use a single, company-wide WACC to evaluate projects. More typically, they perform analyses similar to BCE's analysis of CTC. Multidivisional firms benchmark their own divisions on the basis of publicly

EXAMPLE 12.6 A Project in a New Line of Business

PROBLEM

You are working for Telus Corporation, evaluating the possibility of entering the e-commerce business. Telus's WACC is 5.3% (see Figure 12.3). E-commerce would be a new line of business for Telus, however, so the systematic risk of this business would probably differ from the systematic risk of Telus's current business. As a result, this new business should have a different cost of capital. You need to find the cost of capital for the e-commerce business. Assuming that the risk-free rate is 2% and the market risk premium is 6%, how would you estimate the cost of capital for this type of investment?

SOLUTION

■ Plan

The first step is to identify a company operating in Telus's targeted line of business. Shopify (ticker symbol: SHOP) is a well-known e-commerce company. In fact, that is all SHOP does. Thus, the cost of capital for SHOP would be a good estimate of the cost of capital for Telus's proposed e-commerce business. Many websites are available that provide betas for traded stocks, including the Yahoo! website, ca.finance.yahoo.com. Suppose you visit that site and find that the beta of SHOP stock is 1.63. With this beta, the risk-free rate, and the market risk premium, you can use the CAPM to estimate the cost of equity for SHOP. Fortunately for us, SHOP has no debt, so its cost of equity is the same as its WACC. (This will be a correct cost of capital for the proposed investment as long as Telus does not plan to use any debt to fund its new e-commerce business. Many technology businesses do rely exclusively on equity financing. We will discuss financing choices in more detail in Chapter 16.)

■ Execute

Using the CAPM, we have

$$\begin{aligned}\text{SHOP's Cost of Equity} &= \text{Risk-Free Rate} + \text{SHOP's Equity Beta} \times \text{Market Risk Premium}\\ &= 2\% + 1.63 \times 6\% = 11.8\%\end{aligned}$$

Because SHOP has no debt, its WACC is equivalent to its cost of equity.

■ Evaluate

Suppose Telus's newly created e-commerce division has a project available with an internal rate of return (IRR) of 8%. Telus should reject this project since its IRR is lower than 11.8%, the correct cost of capital for evaluating an e-commerce investment opportunity. Had Telus used the 5.3% cost of capital that is associated with its *existing* business, the company would have mistakenly approved the project and would have implemented a negative-NPV investment.

INTERVIEW WITH SHELAGH GLASER

Shelagh Glaser

Shelagh M. Glaser is vice-president of Finance and Group Controller of the Client Computing Group at Intel Corporation. Her responsibilities include profit and loss forecasting, reporting and controls.

Q Does Intel set the discount rate at the corporate or project level?

A We typically set the discount rate at the corporate level. As a company, Intel makes a broad set of products that sell into similar markets, so one hurdle rate makes sense for our core business. To justify an investment, every project has to earn or exceed that level of return for our shareholders.

We may use a different discount rate for mergers and acquisitions. For example, recently we've done more software acquisitions. That industry is very different from semiconductors and has different risk factors, so we take those considerations into account to set the hurdle rate.

Q How does Intel compute the cost of capital for new investment opportunities?

A We reexamine our weighted average cost of capital (WACC) each year to see that we have the right inputs and if any have changed: What is the current market risk premium? Are we using the right risk-free rate? How should we weight historical data? We use the CAPM to determine beta but consider whether to continue using the five-year weekly beta or to change to a daily or monthly beta in the calculation. We also look at the latest studies from academia on what the inputs should be.

Once we have estimated the WACC, we think about the appropriate hurdle rate for our circumstances. We have not changed the hurdle rate in recent years—even though the WACC may have changed—and continue to use a hurdle rate that is above the WACC. This higher hurdle rate reflects our ability to time our investments and helps us choose projects that maximize our expected returns. Intel has more projects with returns above our hurdle than we can invest in, so assessing opportunity cost is a significant aspect of decision making. We may invest in some projects with NPVs below the hurdle rate if they are of strategic importance.

Q How do project-specific considerations affect Intel's cost of capital calculation?

A When deciding whether to invest billions in wafer fabrication plants, Intel considers both the physical plant and the product line. We calculate the margin we would need from the product and develop a comprehensive set of metrics to justify the large capital investment. Typically we use our standard hurdle rate and also look at risk factors and the timing of the product launch. Intel's business is driven by the economics of Moore's Law, allowing us to double transistors every two years. Each generation of new technology creates cost reductions that enable new fabrication plants to clear the hurdle rate. These plants produce our leading edge product, which earn our highest margins. To get a premium price, our customers require a product that takes advantage of the performance and power efficiency of the latest technology.

Q Did the 2008 financial crisis affect how you evaluate investment opportunities?

A In 2008, the market was very depressed. We continued making R&D investments and reduced spending in other areas, such as marketing and short-term promotion. Cutting R&D would have left us with a gap in our product line in several years, because product development cycles typically run four years. In this industry, not keeping the R&D machine flowing, to boost short-term earnings, will harm the company's long-term viability. R&D is critical to our fundamental business model, which may require long-term decisions that negatively impact short-term results.

Intel has a long history of investing to maintain performance leadership during downturns. Intel carries almost no debt. Our capital policy is to maintain sufficient cash for fabrication plants and multiple years of R&D expenses, to avoid depending on capital markets to finance ongoing operations. A painful experience in the 1980s, when Intel's access to capital markets was curtailed, highlighted how this conservative capital policy pays off. Going into this crisis with no debt and an extremely strong cash position has served us well.

traded companies that compete with their division and are focused in that single line of business. By performing the same analysis as we did in Figure 12.3, the multidivisional firm can estimate the WACCs of its divisions' competitors—adjusting for different financing if necessary—to estimate the cost of capital for each division. Multidivisional firms are not the only ones that rely on this method—private companies (companies without publicly traded shares and often without publicly traded debt) can use the same process to determine their cost of capital. Estimating the WACC can be challenging if none of the competing firms have publicly traded shares. In such cases, management may resort to making subjective adjustments, adding a premium to the discount rate used in evaluating projects with sales, cash flows, and profits that are more cyclical (fluctuate more closely with the rest of the economy) than the firm's typical activities. On the other hand, the WACC would be lowered for projects with below average market risk.

CONCEPT CHECK

9. When evaluating a project in a new line of business, which assumptions about the WACC method are most likely to be violated?

10. How can you estimate the WACC to be used in a new line of business?

12.6 When Raising External Capital Is Costly

So far, we have assumed that there are no important factors, other than taxes, to consider in seeking capital. Among other things, this implies that we can raise external capital without any extra costs associated with the capital-raising transaction. As a consequence, we have no reason to treat a project financed with new external funds any differently than a project financed with internal funds (retained earnings).

In reality, issuing new equity or bonds carries a number of costs. These costs include the costs of filing and registering with a provincial regulator (e.g., the Ontario Securities Commission) and the fees charged by investment bankers to place the securities. We will discuss the process for issuing equity and bonds in detail in Chapters 14 and 15. Here, we mention it briefly in the context of the cost of capital.

Because of these issuing costs, a project that can be financed from internal funds will be less costly overall than the same project if it were financed with external funds. One approach would be to adjust the costs of equity and debt capital in the WACC to incorporate the issuing costs. A better and far more direct route is to simply treat the issuing costs as what they are—cash outflows that are necessary to the project. We can then incorporate this additional cost as a negative cash flow in the NPV analysis.

EXAMPLE 12.7 Evaluating an Acquisition with Costly External Financing

PROBLEM

You are analyzing BCE's potential acquisition of Canadian Tire Corporation (CTC). BCE plans to offer $9 billion as the purchase price for CTC and will need to issue additional debt and equity to finance such a large acquisition. You estimate that the issuance costs will be $350 million and will be paid as soon as the transaction closes. You also estimate that the incremental free cash flows from the acquisition will be $0.4 billion in the first year and will grow at 1.5% per year thereafter. What is the NPV of the proposed acquisition?

SOLUTION

■ **Plan**

We know from Section 12.5 that the correct cost of capital for this acquisition is CTC's WACC. We can value the incremental free cash flows as a growing perpetuity:

$$PV = FCF_1/(r - g)$$

where

$$FCF_1 = \$0.4 \text{ billion}$$
$$r = \text{CTC's } WACC = 0.055$$
$$g = 0.015$$

▶

The NPV of the transaction, including the costly external financing, is the present value of this growing perpetuity net of both the purchase cost and the transaction costs of using external financing.

■ **Execute**

Noting that $350 million is $0.35 billion,

$$NPV = -\$9 - \$0.35 + \frac{\$0.4}{0.055 - 0.015} = \$0.65 \text{ billion, or } \$650 \text{ million}$$

■ **Evaluate**

It is not necessary to try to adjust CTC's WACC for the issuance costs of debt and equity. Instead, we can subtract the issuance costs from the NPV of the acquisition to confirm that the acquisition remains a positive-NPV project even if it must be financed externally.

The role of capital budgeting is to identify positive-NPV projects that allow a firm to cover the costs of its various types of capital. In this chapter, we learned what a firm's weighted average cost of capital is, its relationship to systematic risk, and how it is used in capital budgeting. Later, in Chapters 14, 15 and 16, we explore another aspect of capital financing—how a firm raises equity and debt capital and how it decides the proportion of each to have in its capital structure. Next, we turn to options, an important risk-management tool used by financial managers.

CONCEPT CHECK

11. What types of additional costs does a firm incur when accessing external capital?

12. What is the best way to incorporate these additional costs into capital budgeting?

MyLab Finance

Here is what you should know after reading this chapter. MyLab™ Finance will help you identify what you know, and where to go when you need to practice.

KEY POINTS AND EQUATIONS	TERMS	ONLINE PRACTICE OPPORTUNITIES
12.1 A First Look at the Weighted Average Cost of Capital ■ A firm's debt and equity represent its capital. The relative proportions of debt, equity, and other securities that a firm has outstanding constitute its capital structure. ■ Investors of each type of capital have a required return. Providing this return is the cost a company bears to obtain capital from investors. ■ We calculate the firm's overall cost of capital as a weighted average of its equity and debt costs of capital, referred to as the firm's weighted average cost of capital. ■ The weights in the WACC must be based on the market values of each of the firm's debt and equity, not the book values.	capital, p. 426 capital structure, p. 426 leverage, p. 428 levered, p. 428 market-value balance sheet, p. 428 unlevered, p. 428 weighted average cost of capital (WACC), p. 427	MyLab Study Plan 12.1

KEY POINTS AND EQUATIONS	TERMS	ONLINE PRACTICE OPPORTUNITIES
12.2 The Firm's Costs of Debt and Equity Capital ■ To estimate the cost of capital for a company as a whole, we usually start by estimating the cost of each of the company's sources of capital. ■ The cost of debt is the interest a firm would need to pay on *new* debt. It will generally differ from the coupon rate on existing debt but can be estimated from the yield to maturity on existing debt. ■ The cost of preferred stock is straightforward to estimate because of its constant and known dividend: $$\text{Cost of Preferred Stock Capital} = \frac{Div_{pfd}}{P_{pfd}} \quad (12.4)$$ ■ The Capital Asset Pricing Model (CAPM) is the most common approach for estimating the cost of equity capital. To apply the CAPM, we need an estimate of the firm's equity beta, the market risk premium, and the risk-free rate: Cost of Equity = Risk-Free Rate + Equity Beta × Market Risk Premium ■ Another approach to estimating the cost of equity is to use the Constant Dividend Growth Model (CDGM). To apply this model, we need the current stock price, the expected future dividend, and an estimate of the dividend's constant growth rate: $$\text{Cost of Equity} = \frac{Div_1}{P_E} + g \quad (12.5)$$	effective cost of debt, p. 431	MyLab Study Plan 12.2
12.3 A Second Look at the Weighted Average Cost of Capital ■ The WACC equation is $$r_{wacc} = r_E\frac{E}{E+P+D} + r_{Pfd}\frac{P}{E+P+D} + r_D(1-T_C)\frac{D}{E+P+D} \quad (12.6)$$ ■ For a company that does not have preferred stock, the WACC equation condenses to $$r_{wacc} = r_E\frac{E}{E+D} + r_D(1-T_C)\frac{D}{E+D} \quad (12.7)$$ ■ The WACC is driven by the risk of a company's line of business and, because of the tax effect of interest, its leverage. As a result, WACCs vary widely across industries and companies.	net debt, p. 437	MyLab Study Plan 12.3

KEY POINTS AND EQUATIONS	TERMS	ONLINE PRACTICE OPPORTUNITIES
12.4 Using the WACC to Value a Project ■ Assuming that a project has average risk for the firm, that the firm will maintain its current leverage ratio, and that a firm's leverage affects its value only through taxes, the WACC can be used to value the cash flows from a new project.	debt-equity ratio, p. 440 levered value, p. 439 WACC method, p. 439	MyLab Study Plan 12.4 Spreadsheet Table 12.3
12.5 Project-Based Costs of Capital ■ If the project's risk differs from the average risk for the firm, the WACC will not be the appropriate discount rate for the project. Instead, you must estimate the WACC from the WACC of other firms operating in the same line of business as the new project.		MyLab Study Plan 12.5
12.6 When Raising External Capital Is Costly ■ The WACC is calculated without accounting for the direct costs of raising external financing. Rather than adjusting the WACC, the correct way to account for these costs is to subtract their present value from the NPV of the project.		MyLab Study Plan 12.6

REVIEW QUESTIONS

1. What does the WACC measure?
2. Why are market-based weights important?
3. Why is the coupon rate of existing debt irrelevant for finding the cost of debt capital?
4. Why is it easier to determine the costs of preferred stock and of debt than it is to determine the cost of common equity?
5. Describe the steps involved in the CAPM approach to estimating the cost of equity.
6. Why would the CDGM and CAPM produce different estimates of the cost of equity capital?
7. Under what assumptions can the WACC be used to value a project?
8. What are some possible problems that might be associated with the assumptions used in applying the WACC method?
9. How should you value a project in a line of business with risk that is different from the average risk of your firm's projects?
10. What is the right way to adjust for the costs of raising external financing?

PROBLEMS

All problems in this chapter are available in MyLab Finance. An asterisk (*) indicates problems with a higher level of difficulty.

A First Look at the Weighted Average Cost of Capital

1. MV Corporation has debt with market value of $100 million, common equity with a book value of $100 million, and preferred stock worth $20 million outstanding. Its common equity trades at $50 per share, and the firm has 6 million shares outstanding. What weights should MV Corporation use in its WACC?

2. Andyco Inc. has the following balance sheet and an equity market-to-book ratio of 1.5. Assuming the market value of debt equals its book value, what weights should it use for its WACC calculation?

Assets	Liabilities and Equity	
1000	Debt	400
	Equity	600

3. Book Co. has one million shares of common equity with a par (book) value of $1 and retained earnings of $30 million, and its shares have a market value of $50 per share. It also has debt with a par value of $20 million that is trading at 101% of par.
a. What is the market value of its equity?
b. What is the market value of its debt?
c. What weights should it use in computing its WACC?

***4.** Consider a simple firm that has the following market-value balance sheet:

Assets	Liabilities and Equity	
1000	Debt	400
	Equity	600

Next year, there are two possible values for its assets, each equally likely: $1200 and $960. Its debt will be due with 5% interest. Because all of the cash flows from the assets must go to either the debt or the equity, if you hold a portfolio of the debt and equity in the same proportions as the firm's capital structure, your portfolio should earn exactly the expected return on the firm's assets. Show that a portfolio invested 40% in the firm's debt and 60% in its equity will have the same expected return as the assets of the firm. That is, show that the firm's pre-tax WACC is the same as the expected return on its assets.

The Firm's Costs of Debt and Equity Capital

5. Aluminum maker Alcoa has a beta of about 2.0, whereas Hormel Foods has a beta of 0.45. If the expected excess return of the marker portfolio is 5%, which of these firms has a higher equity cost of capital, and how much higher is it?

6. Avicorp has a $10 million debt issue outstanding, with a 6% coupon rate. The debt has semi-annual coupons, the next coupon is due in six months, and the debt matures in five years. It is currently priced at 95% of par value.
a. What is Avicorp's pre-tax cost of debt (expressed as an EAR)?
b. If Avicorp faces a 40% tax rate, what is its after-tax cost of debt?

7. Laurel Inc. has debt outstanding with a coupon rate of 6% and a yield to maturity of 7%. Its tax rate is 35%. What is Laurel's effective (after-tax) cost of debt?

8. Dewyco has preferred stock trading at $50 per share. The next preferred dividend of $4 is due in one year. What is Dewyco's cost of capital for preferred stock?

9. Steady Company's stock has a beta of 0.20. If the risk-free rate is 6% and the market risk premium is 7%, what is an estimate of Steady Company's cost of equity?

10. Wild Swings Inc.'s stock has a beta of 2.5. Given the information in Problem 8, what is an estimate of Wild Swings' cost of equity?

11. HighGrowth Company has a stock price of $20. The firm will pay a dividend next year of $1, and its dividend is expected to grow at a rate of 4% per year thereafter. What is your estimate of HighGrowth's cost of equity capital?

12. Slow'n Steady Inc. has a stock price of $30, will pay a dividend next year of $3, and has expected dividend growth of 1% per year. What is your estimate of Slow 'n Steady's cost of equity capital?

13. Mackenzie Company has a price of $36 and will issue a dividend of $2 next year. It has a beta of 1.2, the risk-free rate is 5.5%, and the market risk premium is estimated to be 5%.
    a. Use the CAPM to estimate the equity cost of capital for Mackenzie.
    b. Under the CGDM, at what rate do you need to expect Mackenzie's dividends to grow to get the same equity cost of capital as in part (a)?

A Second Look at the Weighted Average Cost of Capital

14. CoffeeCarts has a cost of equity of 15%, has an effective cost of debt of 4%, and is financed 70% with equity and 30% with debt. What is this firm's WACC?

15. AllCity Inc. is financed 40% with debt, 10% with preferred stock, and 50% with common stock. Its pre-tax cost of debt is 6%, its preferred stock pays an annual dividend of $2.50 and is priced at $30. It has an equity beta of 1.1. Assume the risk-free rate is 2%, the market risk premium is 7% and AllCity's tax rate is 35%. What is its after-tax WACC?

16. Pfd Company has debt with a yield to maturity of 7%, a cost of equity of 13%, and a cost of preferred stock of 9%. The market values of its debt, preferred stock, and equity are $10 million, $3 million, and $15 million, respectively, and its tax rate is 40%. What is this firm's WACC?

17. Growth Company's current share price is $20 and is expected to pay a $1 dividend per share next year. After that, the firm's dividends are expected to grow at a rate of 4% per year.
    a. What is an estimate of Growth Company's cost of equity?
    b. Growth Company also has preferred stock outstanding that pays a $2 per share fixed dividend. If this stock is currently priced at $28, what is Growth Company's cost of preferred stock?
    c. Growth Company has existing debt issued three years ago with a coupon rate of 6%. The firm just issued new debt at par with a coupon rate of 6.5%. What is Growth Company's cost of debt?
    d. Growth Company has 5 million common shares outstanding and 1 million preferred shares outstanding, and its equity has a total book value of $50 million. Its debt has a market value of $20 million. If Growth Company's common and preferred shares are priced at $20 and $28, respectively, what is the market value of Growth Company's assets?
    e. Growth Company faces a 35% tax rate. Given the information in parts (a) through (d), and your answers to those problems, what is Growth Company's WACC?

Using the WACC to Value a Project

18. A retail coffee company is planning to open 100 new coffee outlets that are expected to generate, in total, $15 million in free cash flows per year, with a growth rate of 3% in perpetuity. If the coffee company's WACC is 10% and the cost of the expansion is $200 million, what is the NPV of this expansion?

19. RiverRocks Inc. is considering a project with the following projected free cash flows:

0	1	2	3	4
–50	10	20	20	15

The firm believes that, given the risk of this project, the WACC method is the appropriate approach to valuing the project. RiverRocks' WACC is 12%. Should it take on this project? Why or why not?

Project-Based Costs of Capital

20. RiverRocks (see Problem 19), whose WACC is 12%, is considering an acquisition of Raft Adventures (whose WACC is 15%). What is the appropriate discount rate for RiverRocks to use to evaluate the acquisition? Why?

21. RiverRocks' purchase of Raft Adventures (see Problem 20) will cost $100 million but will generate cash flows that start at $15 million in one year and then grow at 4% per year forever. What is the NPV of the acquisition?

22. Your firm is planning to invest in an automated packaging plant. Harburtin Industries is an all-equity firm that specializes in this business. Suppose Harburtin's equity beta is 0.85, the risk-free rate is 4%, and the market risk premium is 5%. If your firm's project is all equity financed, estimate its cost of capital.

23. CoffeeStop primarily sells coffee. It recently introduced a premium coffee-flavoured liquor. Suppose the firm faces a tax rate of 35% and collects the following information:

	Beta	Equity %	Debt %
CoffeeStop	0.61	96%	4%
Brown-Forman Liquors	0.26	89%	11%

If the company plans to finance 11% of the new liquor-focused division with debt and the rest with equity, what WACC should it use for its liquor division? Assume a cost of debt of 4.8%, and a risk-free rate of 4.5%, and a market risk premium of 5.5%.

24. Your company has two divisions. One division sells software and the other division sells computers through a direct sales channel, primarily taking orders over the internet. You have decided that HP Inc. is very similar to your computer division, in terms of both risk and financing. You go online and find the following information. HP's beta is 1.21, the risk-free rate is 4.5%, its market value of equity is $67 billion, and it has $700 million worth of debt with a yield to maturity of 6%. Your tax rate is 35%, and you use a market risk premium of 5% in your WACC estimates.

a. What is an estimate of the WACC for your computer sales division?

b. If your overall company WACC is 12% and the computer sales division represents 40% of the value of your firm, what is an estimate of the WACC for your software division?

When Raising External Capital Is Costly

25. RiverRocks realizes that it will have to raise the financing for the acquisition of Raft Adventures (described in Problems 20 and 21) by issuing new debt and equity. RiverRocks estimates that the direct issuing costs will amount to $7 million. How should it account for these costs in evaluating the project? Should RiverRocks go ahead with the project?

26. You are planning to issue debt to finance a new project. The project will require $20 million in debt financing and you estimate its NPV to be $15 million. The issue costs for the debt will be 3% of face value. Taking into account the costs of external debt financing, what is the NPV of the project?

27. You work for HydroTech, a large manufacturer of high-pressure industrial water pumps. You report directly to the CFO and she has asked you to calculate HydroTech's WACC. You have gathered the following information about HydroTech: its market capitalization (its market value of equity) is $100 million, its beta is 1.2, the total book value of its debt is $50 million, it has $10 million cash and its cost of debt (using the quoted yields on HydroTech's outstanding bond issues) is 5%. In addition, the yield of the 10-year government bond (the risk-free rate) is 3%, the market risk premium is 5%, and the marginal corporate tax rate is 35%. Using the above inputs, calculate HydroTech's WACC. When is it appropriate to use this WACC to evaluate a new project?

DATA CASE

You work in Walt Disney Company's corporate finance and treasury department and have been assigned to the team estimating Disney's WACC. You must estimate this WACC in preparation for a team meeting later today. You realize that the information you need is readily available online.

1. Go to the Yahoo! Finance website, http://finance.yahoo.com. Under "Markets" you will find the yield to maturity for 10-year treasury bonds listed as "10-Yr Bond." Collect this number as your risk-free rate.
2. In the search box at the top of the page, type Walt Disney's ticker symbol (DIS) and click "Search." Once you see the basic information for Disney, find and click on "Statistics" on the left side of the screen. From the statistics, collect the information for Disney's market capitalization (its market value of equity), enterprise value (market-value equity + net debt), cash, and beta.
3. To get Disney's cost of debt and the market value of its long-term debt, you will need the price and yield to maturity on the firm's existing long-term bonds. Go to the Financial Industry Regulatory Authority's website, http://finra-markets.morningstar.com/BondCenter/Default.jsp?, click "Search," click "Corporate," type Disney's ticker symbol (DIS), and click "Show Results." A list of Disney's outstanding bond issues will appear. Assume that Disney's policy is to use the yield to maturity on non-callable, 10-year obligations as its cost of debt. Find the non-callable bond issue that is as close to 10 years from maturity as possible. (*Hint:* You will see a column titled "Callable"; make sure the issue you choose does not have "Yes" in this column.) You may have to choose a bond issued by one if its subsidiaries, such as ABC. Find the yield to maturity for your chosen bond issue (it is in the column titled "Yield") and enter that yield as your pre-tax cost of debt into your spreadsheet. Next, copy and paste the data in the entire table into Excel.

4. You now have the price for each bond issue, but you need to know the size of the issue. From the current Web page, go to the row of the bond you choose and click "Issuer Name" in the first column. (This will either be Walt Disney Company or ABC or another subsidiary.) This brings up a Web page with all of the information about the bond issue. Scroll down until you find "Amount Outstanding" on the right side. Noting that this amount is quoted in thousands of dollars (e.g., $60,000 means $60 million = $60,000,000), record the issue amount in the appropriate row of your spreadsheet. Repeat this step for all of the bond issues.
5. The price for each bond issue in your spreadsheet is reported as a percentage of the bond's par value. For example, 104.50 means that the bond issue is trading at 104.5% of its par value. You can calculate the market value of each bond issue by multiplying the amount outstanding by (Price ÷ 100). Do so for each issue and then calculate the total of all the bond issues. This is the market value of Disney's debt.
6. Compute the weights for Disney's equity and debt based on the market value of equity and Disney's market value of debt, computed in step 5.
7. Calculate Disney's cost of equity capital using the CAPM, the risk-free rate you collected in step 1, the beta you found in step 2, and a market risk premium of 5%.
8. Assuming that Disney has a tax rate of 35%, calculate its after-tax cost of debt capital.
9. Calculate Disney's WACC.
10. Calculate Disney's net debt by subtracting its cash (collected in step 2) from its debt. Recalculate the weights for the WACC using the market value of equity, net debt, and enterprise value. Recalculate Disney's WACC using the weights based on the net debt. How much does it change?
11. How confident are you of your estimate? Which implicit assumptions did you make during your data collection efforts?

CHAPTER

13 Risk and the Pricing of Options

LEARNING OBJECTIVES

- Understand basic option terminology
- Explain the difference between calls and puts; determine the payoffs and profits from holding each to expiration
- Analyze the factors that affect option prices
- Understand and use the Binomial Option Pricing Model
- Be familiar with the Black-Scholes Option Pricing Formula
- Describe the relation that must hold between the prices of similar *calls* and *puts* on the same stock
- Demonstrate how options are applied in corporate finance

NOTATION

PV	present value
Div	dividend
NPV	net present value
C	call option price
P	put option price
S	stock price
r_f	risk-free interest rate

Since the introduction of publicly traded options on the Chicago Board Options Exchange (CBOE) in 1973, financial options have become one of the most important and actively traded financial assets. The Montreal Exchange was the first to trade stock options in Canada in 1975. Over time, the Montreal Exchange added options on other products: fixed income securities (1991), stock indexes (1999), exchange-traded funds (2000), and the U.S. dollar (2005). In May 2008, the Montreal Exchange merged with the TSX Group to become the TMX Group. Options have become important tools for corporate financial managers. For example, options are often embedded in other securities and transactions, so the material in this chapter will be helpful when we discuss the greenshoe provision in Chapter 14 or convertible bonds in Chapter 15. Many large corporations with operations in different parts of the world use options to control their exposure to exchange rate risk. We will study corporate risk management practices in Chapter 21.

In this chapter, we introduce the financial option: a financial contract between two parties. In Chapter 9, we briefly discussed the idea of real options, or the value of flexibility when managing projects. Here, we delve further into understanding what options are and what factors affect their value. To start, we provide an overview of the basic types of financial options, introduce important terminology, and describe the payoffs of various option-based strategies. We next discuss the factors that affect option prices. Finally, we model the equity of the firm as an option to gain insight into the conflicts of interest between equity holders and debt holders.

13.1 Option Basics

financial option A contract that gives its owner the right (but not the obligation) to purchase or sell an asset at a fixed price at some future date.

call option A financial option that gives its owner the right to buy an asset.

put option A financial option that gives its owner the right to sell an asset.

option writer The seller of an option contract.

derivatives Securities whose cash flows depend solely on the prices of other marketed assets.

warrant A call option written by a company itself on new stock.

exercising the option The enforcement, by the holder of an option, of the agreement to buy or sell a share of stock at the agreed-upon price.

strike price (or exercise price) The price at which an option holder buys or sells a share of stock when the option is exercised.

A **financial option** contract gives its owner the right (but not the obligation) to purchase or sell an asset at a fixed price at some future date. There are two distinct kinds of option contracts: *call options* and *put options*. A **call option** gives the owner the right to *buy* the asset; a **put option** gives the owner the right to *sell* the asset. An option is a contract between two parties. For every owner of a financial option, there is also an **option writer**, the seller and originator of an option contract, who is the person who takes the other side of the contract. Options are part of a broader class of securities called **derivatives**, because they derive their value solely from the price of another asset.

The most common option contracts are options on shares of stock. A stock option gives the holder the option to buy or sell a share of stock on or before a given date for a given price. For example, a call option on Telus Corporation stock might give the holder the right to purchase a share of Telus for $45.00 per share at any time up to, for example, January 18, 2019. Similarly, a put option on Telus stock might give the holder the right to sell a share of Telus stock for $40.00 per share at any time up to, say, February 15, 2019.

When a company writes a call option on *new* stock to be issued by the company, it is called a **warrant**. A regular call option is written by a third party on existing stock. When a holder of a warrant exercises it and thereby purchases stock, the company delivers this stock by issuing new stock. In all other respects, a warrant is identical to a call option.

Option Contracts

Practitioners use specific words to describe the details of option contracts. When a holder of an option enforces the agreement and buys or sells a share of stock at the agreed-upon price, he is **exercising the option**. The price at which the option holder buys or sells the share of stock when the option is exercised is called the **strike price** (or **exercise price**).

There are two kinds of options. **American options**, the most common kind, allow their holders to exercise the option on any date up to and including a final date called the **expiration date**. **European options** allow their holders to exercise the option only on the expiration date—that is, holders cannot exercise the option before the expiration date. The terms "American" and "European" have nothing to do with the location where the options are traded: both types are traded worldwide.

As with other financial assets, options can be bought and sold. Standard stock options are traded on organized exchanges, while more specialized options are sold through dealers. The oldest and largest options exchange is the CBOE. By convention, all traded options can be exercised up to and including the third Friday of the month. The market price of the option is also called the option premium.

American options The most common kind of option, which allow the holder to exercise the option on any date up to and including the expiration date.

expiration date The last date on which an option holder has the right to exercise the option.

European options Options that allow the holder to exercise the option only on the expiration date.

payoff The amount received or paid at the time the exercise/don't exercise decision is made.

profit An option buyer's profit is the payoff minus the price (premium) paid for the option. An option seller's profit is the payoff plus the price (premium) received.

The option buyer, also called the option holder, holds the right to exercise the option and has a *long* position in the contract. The option seller, also called the option writer, sells (or writes) the option and has a *short* position in the contract. Because the long side has the option to exercise, the short side has an *obligation* to fulfill the contract. For example, suppose you own a call option on Cenovus stock with an exercise price of $10. Cenovus stock is currently trading for $15, so you decide to exercise the option. The person holding the short position in the contract is obligated to sell you a share of Cenovus stock for $10. Your positive **payoff** of $5—the difference between the price you pay for the share of stock and the price at which you can sell the share in the market—implies the person short in the option has a negative payoff of –$5.

Investors make the decision to exercise options only when they will have a positive payoff; this decision is made by the person who has the long position in the option. Consequently, whenever an option is exercised, the person holding the short position has a negative payoff that funds the positive payoff of the long party. That is, the obligation will be costly. Why, then, do people write options? The answer is that when you sell an option you get paid for it. This upfront payment (the option price, or premium) compensates the seller for the risk of loss in the event that the option holder chooses to exercise the option. So, for the buyer of an option, the **profit** consists of the payoff minus the price (premium) paid for the option. For the seller of an option, the profit consists of the payoff plus the amount received when the option was originally sold. If all this new terminology is confusing, rest assured that you will become comfortable with it as you proceed through the chapter. We provide a summary of the new terms in Table 13.1.

Stock Option Quotations

Table 13.2 shows near-term options on Bow.com in a format similar to the option tables available on the CBOE website (www.cboe.com) on July 31, 2017. Call options are listed on the left and put options on the right. Each line corresponds to a particular option, identified by its expiration date and exercise price. The first two digits refer to the year of expiration, followed by the month of expiration and the strike (or exercise) price. The first line in the left column of Table 13.2 is a call option with an exercise price of $45 that can be exercised up to and including the third Friday of August 2017 (August 18, 2017).

TABLE 13.1 The Language of Options

Call option	Option to buy the stock at a prespecified price
Put option	Option to sell the stock at a prespecified price
Strike (exercise) price	The prespecified price in the option contract
Write an option	Sell an option
Exercise an option	Enforce the option holder's right to buy or sell the stock as specified in the option contract
American option	An option that can be exercised any time on or before the expiration date
European option	An option that can be exercised only on the expiration date
Warrant	A call option written by the firm whereby new stock will be issued if the warrant is exercised
Payoff	The amount received or paid at the time the exercise/don't exercise decision is made
Profit	Payoff minus (plus) the price paid (received) for the option by the option buyer (seller)

TABLE 13.2 Option Quotes for Bow.com Stock

Bow													48.35–
Jul 31, 2017 @ 11:35 ET (Data 15 Minutes Delayed)							Bid 48.35	Ask 48.37					Vol 3831766
Calls	Last Sale	Net	Bid	Ask	Vol	Open Int	Puts	Last Sale	Net	Bid	Ask	Vol	Open Int
17 Aug 45.00	4.00	pc	3.70	3.90	0	16021	17 Aug 45.00	0.30	−0.05	0.30	0.40	30	20788
17 Aug 47.50	2.20	−0.25	1.90	2.00	86	18765	17 Aug 47.50	0.75	−0.15	0.95	1.05	292	13208
17 Aug 50.00	0.80	—	0.75	0.85	144	9491	17 Aug 50.00	2.30	+0.20	2.30	2.40	177	5318
17 Aug 55.00	0.15	pc	0.05	0.10	0	2497	17 Aug 55.00	6.10	pc	6.60	6.80	0	895
17 Sep 45.00	4.93	pc	4.80	5.00	0	18765	17 Sep 45.00	1.20	−0.10	1.20	1.30	8	29717
17 Sep 47.50	3.70	+0.10	3.20	3.30	5	8068	17 Sep 47.50	1.95	+0.15	2.05	2.15	10	6632
17 Sep 50.00	2.15	+0.15	1.95	2.05	208	27416	17 Sep 50.00	3.30	+0.20	3.30	3.50	162	6668
17 Sep 55.00	0.70	+0.10	0.60	0.70	65	8475	17 Sep 55.00	6.90	−2.50	7.00	7.10	67	5621

Source: Bow.com is a hypothetical stock, but the quotes are based on those from the Chicago Board Options Exchange website, www.cboe.com.

The adjacent columns to the right display market data for the option. The first of these columns shows the last sales price, followed by the net change from the previous day's last reported sales price ("pc" indicates that no trade has occurred on this day, so the last sales price is the previous day's last reported sales price), the current bid and ask prices, and the daily volume. The final column is the **open interest**—the total number of contracts of that particular option that have been written and not yet repurchased by a writer so as to close the short position.

open interest The total number of contracts of a particular option that have been written and not yet closed.

The top line of the option quote displays information about the stock itself. In this case, Bow's stock last traded at a price of $48.35 per share. We also see the current bid and ask prices for the stock, as well as the volume of trade.

When the exercise price of an option is equal to the current price of the stock, the option is said to be **at-the-money**. Notice that much of the trading occurs in options that are closest to being at-the-money—that is, calls and puts with exercise prices of either $47.50 or $50. Notice how the August 50 calls have high volume. They last traded for 80 cents, midway between the current bid price (75 cents) and the ask price (85 cents), which indicates that the trade probably occurred recently, because the last traded price is a current market price.

at-the-money A term describing options whose exercise prices are equal to the current stock price.

Stock option contracts are always written on 100 shares of stock. If, for instance, you decided to purchase one August 47.50 call contract, you would be purchasing an option to buy 100 shares at $47.50 per share. Option prices are quoted on a per-share basis, so the ask price of $2.00 implies that you would pay $100 \times \$2 = \$200$ for the contract. Similarly, if you decide to buy an August 45 put contract, you would pay $100 \times \$0.40 = \$40$ for the option to sell 100 shares of Bow.com stock for $45 per share.

Note from Table 13.2 that, for each expiration date, call options with lower strike prices have higher market prices—the right to buy the stock at a lower price is more valuable than the right to buy it for a higher price. Conversely, because the put option gives the holder the right to sell the stock at the strike price, puts with higher strikes are more valuable (for the same expiration date). On the other hand, holding fixed the strike price, both calls and puts are more expensive for a longer time to expiration. Because these are American-style options that can be exercised at any time, having the right to buy or sell for a longer period is valuable.

in-the-money A term describing an option whose payoff, if exercised immediately, would be positive.

If the payoff from exercising an option immediately is positive, the option is said to be **in-the-money**. Call options with strike prices below the current stock price are

out-of-the-money A term describing an option whose payoff, if exercised immediately, would be negative.

deep in-the-money A term describing options that are in-the-money and for which the strike price and the stock price are very far apart.

in-the-money, as are put options with strike prices above the current stock price. Conversely, if the payoff from exercising the option immediately is negative, the option is **out-of-the-money**. Call options with strike prices above the current stock price are out-of-the-money, as are put options with strike prices below the current stock price. Of course, someone long in an option would not choose to exercise an out-of-the-money option, so the actual payoff at the time the exercise/don't exercise decision is made will be zero for out-of-the-money options. Options for which the strike price and the stock price are very far apart are referred to as **deep in-the-money** or **deep out-of-the-money**.

EXAMPLE 13.1 Purchasing Options

PROBLEM

It is midday on July 31, 2017, and you have decided to purchase 10 September call contracts on Bow.com stock with an exercise price of $50. Because you are buying, you must pay the ask price. How much money will this purchase cost you? Is this option in-the-money or out-of-the-money?

SOLUTION

Plan

From Table 13.2, the ask price of this option is $2.05. Remember that the price quoted is per share and that each contract is for 100 shares.

Execute

You are purchasing 10 contracts and each contract is on 100 shares, so the transaction will cost $10 \times 100 \times \$2.05 = \$2050$ (ignoring any commission fees). Because this is a call option and the exercise price is above the current stock price ($48.35), the option is currently out-of-the-money.

Evaluate

Even though the option is currently out-of-the-money, it still has value. During the time left to expiration, the stock could rise above the exercise (strike) price of $50.

deep out-of-the-money A term describing options that are out-of-the-money and for which the strike price and the stock price are very far apart.

hedging The practice of reducing risk by holding contracts or securities whose payoffs are negatively correlated with some risk exposure.

speculate The practice of using securities to place a bet on the direction in which the investor believes the market is likely to move.

Options on Other Financial Securities

Although the most commonly traded options are written on stocks, options on other financial assets do exist. Perhaps the most well-known are options on stock indexes in the United States, such as the S&P 100 index, the S&P 500 index, the Dow Jones Industrial index, and the NYSE index. These options have become very popular because they allow investors to protect the value of their investments from adverse market changes. In Canada, the Montreal Exchange's only broad index option is on the S&P TSX 60. In addition, Montreal offers options on exchange-traded funds (such as iShares) that track the S&P TSX 60, various industry sectors, fixed income products, and selected commodity prices.

As we will see shortly, a stock index put option can be used to offset the losses on an investor's portfolio in a market downturn; this is an example of *hedging*. In general, **hedging** is accomplished by holding contracts or securities whose payoffs are negatively correlated with some risk exposure that already exists. Options also allow investors to **speculate**, or place a bet on the direction in which they believe the market is likely to move. By purchasing a call, for example, investors can bet on a market rise with a much smaller investment than they could by investing in the market index itself.

OPTIONS ARE FOR MORE THAN JUST STOCKS

Although the examples in this chapter are mainly about options on stocks, there are options on a wide variety of other assets. For example, options are also traded on government debt securities and bankers' acceptances. These options allow investors to bet on or hedge interest-rate risk. There are also options on currencies, gold, platinum, and other commodities such as copper and oil. In Montreal, there is an option contract on 10,000 U.S. dollars. The main markets for options on agricultural commodities, metals, and energy are either in Chicago or New York. Some of these include options on wheat, soybeans, livestock, cotton, orange juice, and sugar. These options allow both farmers and large agribusinesses to hedge their risks from fluctuations in production and prices.

CONCEPT CHECK

1. Does the holder of an option have to exercise it?
2. What is the difference between an American option and a European option?

13.2 Option Payoffs and Profits at Expiration

With our new understanding of the basics of puts and calls, we are now prepared to examine their values. From the Valuation Principle, the value of any security is determined by the future cash flows an investor receives from owning it. Therefore, before we can assess what an option is worth, we must determine an option's payoff at the time of expiration.

The Long Position in an Option Contract

Assume you own a call option with a strike price of \$20. If, on the expiration date, the stock price is greater than the strike price, say \$30, you can make money by exercising the call (by paying \$20, the strike price for the stock) and immediately selling the stock in the open market for \$30. The \$10 difference is the option's payoff at expiration and is what it is worth one moment before it expires. Consequently, when the stock price on the expiration date exceeds the strike price, the value of the call is the difference between the stock price and the strike price. When the stock price is less than the strike price at expiration, the holder will not exercise the call, so the option is worth nothing. In other words, the value of an option just as it is about to expire is simply the payoff, assuming the optimal exercise/don't exercise decision is made. These payoffs are plotted in Figure 13.1.

Thus, the value of the call at expiration is as follows:

Long Call Value (Payoff) at Expiration

$$\begin{aligned} \text{Long Call Value} &= \text{Stock Price} - \text{Strike Price}, && \text{if Stock Price} > \text{Strike} \\ &= 0, && \text{if Stock Price} \leq \text{Strike} \end{aligned} \tag{13.1}$$

The holder of a put option will exercise the option if the stock price is below the strike price. Because the holder receives the strike price when he or she exercises the put, the holder's payoff is equal to Strike Price – Stock Price. If the stock price is above the exercise price, the optimal decision is to not exercise and receive a \$0 payoff. Thus, the value of a put at expiration is as follows:

Long Put Value (Payoff) at Expiration

$$\begin{aligned} \text{Long Put Value} &= \text{Strike Price} - \text{Stock Price}, && \text{if Stock Price} < \text{Strike} \\ &= 0, && \text{if Stock Price} \geq \text{Strike} \end{aligned} \tag{13.2}$$

FIGURE 13.1 Payoff of a Call Option with a Strike Price of $20 at Expiration

If the stock price is greater than the strike price ($20), the call will be exercised and the holder's payoff is the difference between the stock price and the strike price. If the stock price is less than the strike price, the call will not be exercised and so has no value.

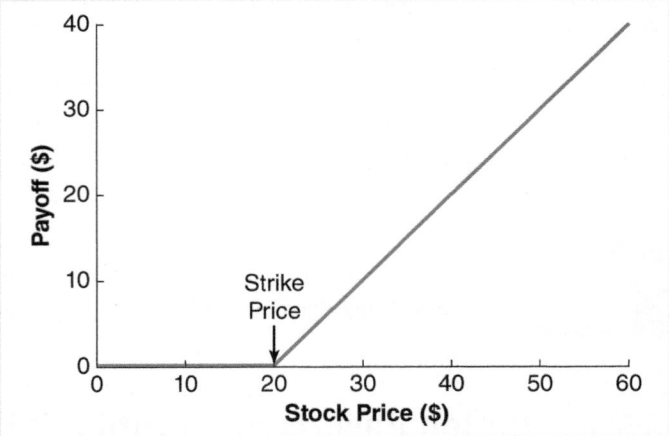

EXAMPLE 13.2 Payoff of a Put Option at Maturity

PROBLEM

You own a put option on Tim Hortons Inc. stock with an exercise price of $20 that expires today. Plot the value of this option as a function of the stock price.

SOLUTION

■ **Plan**

From Equation 13.2, and the fact that the strike price is $20, we see that the value of the put option is as follows:

$$\text{Put Value} = 20 - \text{Stock Price, if Stock Price} < 20$$

$$\text{Put Value} = 0\text{, if Stock Price} \geq 20$$

■ **Execute**

Plotting this function gives the following:

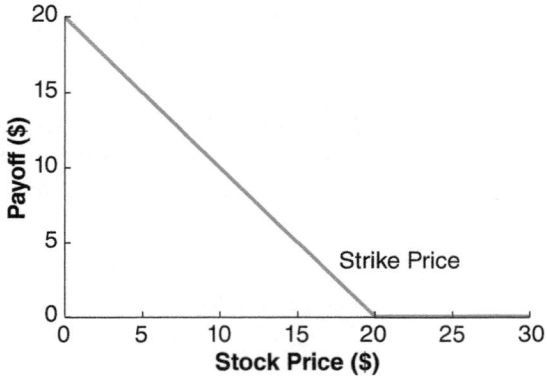

■ **Evaluate**

Because the put option allows you (the long party) to force the put writer to buy the stock for $20, regardless of the current market price, we can see that the put option payoff increases as Tim Hortons' stock price decreases. For example, if Tim Hortons' price were $10, you could buy a share of Tim Hortons in the market for $10 and then sell it to the put writer for $20, generating a payoff of $10.

The Short Position in an Option Contract

An investor with a short position in an option, the option writer, has an obligation to fulfill the contract if the long party (i.e., the option buyer) exercises the option. Therefore, the short position's cash flows are the negative of the long position's cash flows. Because an investor who is long in an option will not exercise an option that is out-of-the-money, a short investor will never receive a positive payoff.

Short Call Payoff at Expiration

$$\begin{aligned} \text{Short Call Payoff} &= -(\text{Stock Price} - \text{Strike Price}), && \text{if Stock Price} > \text{Strike} \\ &= 0, && \text{if Stock Price} \leq \text{Strike} \end{aligned}$$

To demonstrate, assume you have a short position in a call option with an exercise price of $20 and the option is about to expire. If the stock price is greater than the strike price of a call—for example, $25—the holder will exercise the option. You then have the obligation to sell the stock to the option holder for the strike price of $20. Because the market price of the stock is $25, you receive a negative payoff equal to the difference between the two prices, or −$5. (Notice that the higher the stock price, the more negative the payoff, making the sale of call options a risky proposition. Since there is no clear upper limit on how high the stock price can rise there is also no limit on how low the call option seller's payoff could drop.) However, if the stock price is less than the strike price at the expiration date, the holder will not exercise the option, so in this case your payoff is zero. These payoffs are plotted in Figure 13.2.

FIGURE 13.2 Short Position in a Call Option at Expiration

If the stock price is greater than the strike price, the call will be exercised, and the person on the short side of a call will receive a negative payoff equal to the difference between the strike price and the stock price. If the stock price is less than the strike price, the call will not be exercised, and the seller's payoff will be zero.

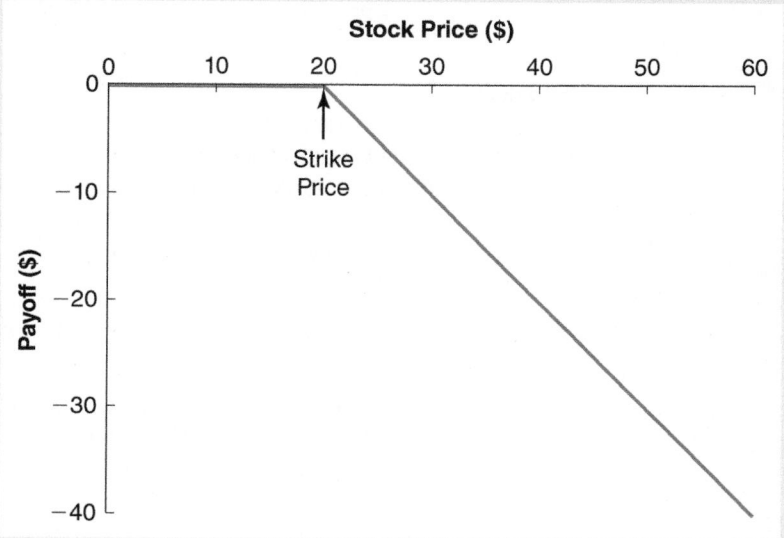

EXAMPLE 13.3 Payoff of a Short Position in a Put Option

PROBLEM

You are short in a put option on Tim Hortons stock with an exercise price of $20 that expires today. What is your payoff at expiration as a function of the stock price?

SOLUTION

Plan

Again, the strike price is $20, and in this case your cash flows will be opposite of those from Equation 13.2, as depicted in the previous example:

Short Put Payoff at Expiration

$$\begin{aligned} \text{Short Put Payoff} &= -(\text{Strike Price} - \text{Stock Price}), && \text{if Stock Price} < \text{Strike} \\ &= 0, && \text{if Stock Price} \geq \text{Strike} \end{aligned}$$

Thus, your cash flows will be as follows:

$$\begin{aligned} -(20 - \text{Stock Price}) &= -20 + \text{Stock Price}, && \text{if Stock Price} < 20 \\ &= 0, && \text{if Stock Price} \geq 20 \end{aligned}$$

Execute

The graph below plots your cash flows:

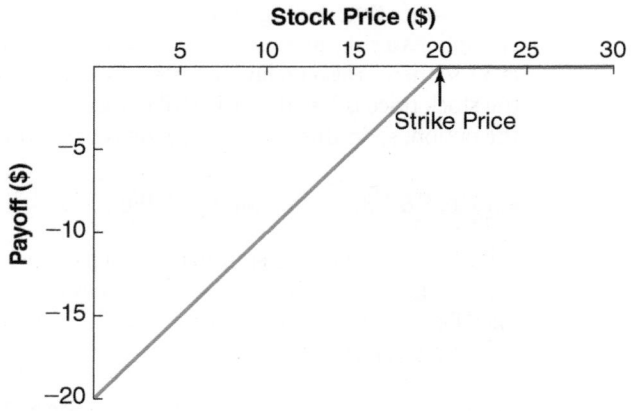

Evaluate

Because the put option allows the put option holder to force you, the put writer, to buy the stock for $20 regardless of the current market price, we can see that the put option payoff for the writer decreases as Tim Hortons' stock price decreases. For example, if Tim Hortons' price were $10, the option owner could buy a share of Tim Hortons in the market for $10 and then sell it to you, the put writer, for $20, making the writer's payoff equal to –$10 (the writer acquires something worth $10 but pays $20 for it).

Notice that because the stock price cannot fall below zero, the downside for a short position in a put option is limited to the strike price of the option. A short position in a call, however, has no limit on the downside (see Figure 13.2).

Profit from Holding an Option to Expiration

Although payoffs on a long position in an option contract are never negative, the *profit* from purchasing an option and holding it to expiration could be negative. That is, the payout at expiration might be less than the initial cost of the option.

To illustrate, let's consider the potential profits from purchasing one of the call options on Bow.com stock quoted in Table 13.2. Suppose C is the price of a call option on July 31. Then, the profit of the call option holder at expiration is as follows. (Note that it is customary to ignore the time value of money when determining option profits.)

$$\text{Long Call Profit} = (\text{Stock Price} - \text{Strike Price}) - \text{C}, \quad \text{if Stock Price} > \text{Strike},$$
$$\text{or} = 0 - \text{C}, \quad \text{if Stock Price} \leq \text{Strike}$$

For example, the 17 September 50 option costs \$2.05. The profit is the call payoff minus the \$2.05 spent when purchasing the option. Once the cost of the position is taken into account, you make a positive profit only if the stock price exceeds the \$50 + \$2.05 = \$52.05 break-even point. (See Figure 13.3) As we can see from Table 13.2, the further in-the-money a call option is, the higher its initial price and thus the larger your potential loss. An out-of-the-money option has a smaller initial cost and hence a smaller potential loss. The probability of a profit, however, is also smaller because the stock price where profits become positive is higher.

Because a short position in an option is the other side of a long position, the profits from a short position in an option are the negative of the profits of a long position:

$$\text{Short Call Profit} = -(\text{Stock Price} - \text{Strike Price}) + \text{C}, \quad \text{if Stock Price} > \text{Strike},$$
$$\text{or} = 0 + \text{C}, \quad \text{if Stock Price} \leq \text{Strike}$$

A short position in the 17 September 50 Bow.com call in Figure 13.3 produces a small positive profit if Bow.com's stock is below \$52.05 but leads to losses if the stock price is above \$52.05.

FIGURE 13.3 **Profit from Holding a Call Option to Expiration**

The diagram shows the profit per share from purchasing the 17 September 50 call option in Table 13.2. Note that the payoff diagram is shifted down by the amount of the option's premium. Thus, even if the payoff is positive, if it is not enough to offset the premium you paid to acquire the option, your profit will be negative.

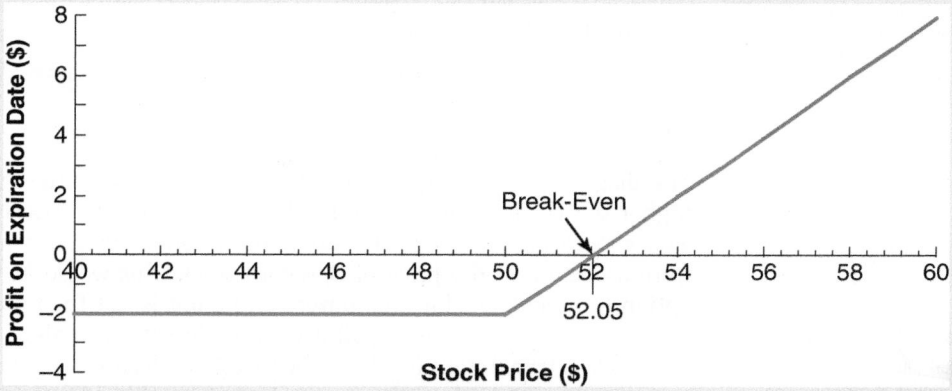

EXAMPLE 13.4 Profit from Holding a Position in a Put Option Until Expiration

PROBLEM

Assume you decided to purchase the 17 September 50 put option quoted in Table 13.2. Plot the profit of each position as a function of the stock price on expiration.

SOLUTION

Plan

Suppose P is the price of a put option on July 31. Then your profit on the expiration date will be as follows:

$$\text{Long Put Profit} = (\text{Strike Price} - \text{Stock Price}) - P, \quad \text{if Stock Price} < \text{Strike Price},$$
$$\text{or} = 0 - P, \quad \text{if Stock Price} \geq \text{Strike Price}$$

Execute

The 17 September 50 option costs \$3.50. The profit is the put payoff minus the \$3.50 spent when purchasing the option. You make a positive profit only if the stock price exceeds the \$50.00 – \$3.50 = \$46.50 break-even point. The graph below plots your profits:

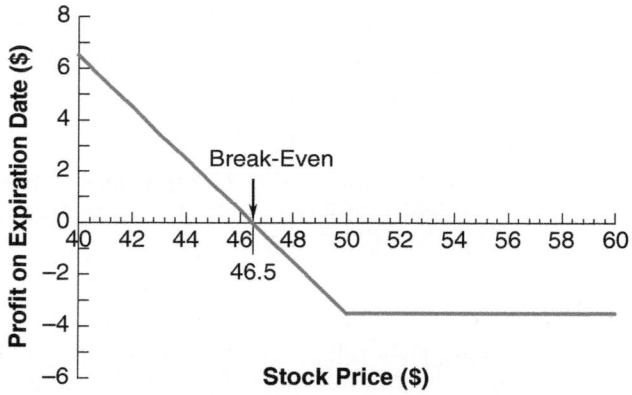

Evaluate

The graph shows the profit per share from purchasing the 17 September 50 put option in Table 13.2. Note that the payoff diagram is shifted down by the amount of the option's premium. Thus, even if the payoff is positive, if it is not enough to offset the premium you paid to acquire the option your profit will be negative.

Short Sales

The diagram accompanying Example 13.4 shows that the lower the stock price, the higher the profit of the put option holder. Consider an investor who thinks that Bow.com's stock price will fall. Buying a put option would allow such an investor to profit from a decline in the price of Bow.com stock; this would be an example of using an option to speculate. However, purchasing a put is not the only way to place a bet that the value of a certain stock will decrease: investors can also engage in a **short sale** of the stock, a transaction in which the investor sells a stock that he or she does not own and then buys it back in the future. In order to be able to sell a stock he or she does not own, the short-seller must first borrow the stock from someone who already owns it, later buying the stock back and returning it to the lender. Just like purchasing a put

short sale A transaction in which the investor sells a stock that he or she does not own and then buys it back in the future.

option, short selling is profitable if the stock price declines in the future. In the profit diagram below, a stock is sold short for $20 and then bought back one period later. If, for example, the stock is bought back for $15, the short seller will turn a $20 − $15 = $5 profit. In Figure 13.4, we see how a lower stock price when the borrowed stock is bought back results in a higher profit for the short seller:

FIGURE 13.4 **Profit from Selling a Stock Short**

Profit diagram for short sale when a stock is sold short for $20 and then bought back one period later. The short seller's profit increases as the future stock price becomes lower.

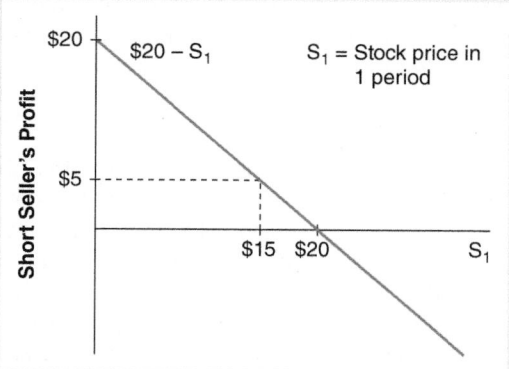

At this point, we have discussed the cost (premium) of buying an option, the payoffs at expiration, and the profits. It is a lot to keep track of, but it is usually helpful to remember that there are only three things being exchanged: (1) the option premium, (2) the strike price, and (3) the share of stock. Further, because an option is a contract between two parties, the losses of one party are the gains of the other. We summarize these relationships in Table 13.3 for the 17 September 50 calls and puts on Bow.com stock from Table 13.2. When reading the table, keep in mind that if you own the option, and exercising it would create a negative payoff, you will choose not to exercise, so the payoff will be zero (see Equations 13.1 and 13.2).

CONCEPT CHECK

3. How are the profits from buying an option different from the payoff to the option at expiration?
4. How are the payoffs to buying a call option related to the payoffs from writing a call option?

TABLE 13.3 **Payoffs and Profits to Buying or Writing Options in Table 13.2**

	At Purchase	At Expiration If Stock Price = 40		At Expiration If Stock Price = 60	
		Payoff	Profit	Payoff	Profit
Buy a "17 September 50" Call	Pay $2.05	$0	0 – 2.05 = –$2.05	$10	10 – 2.05 = $7.95
Write a "17 September 50" Call	Receive $2.05*	$0	2.05 – 0 = $2.05	–$10	2.05 – 10 = –$7.95
Buy a "17 September 50" Put	Pay $3.50	50 – 40 = $10	10 – 3.50 = $6.50	$0	0 – 3.50 = –$3.50
Write a "17 September 50" Put	Receive $3.50*	40 – 50 = –$10	3.50 – 10 = –$6.50	$0	3.50 – 0 = $3.50

Option contracts are for 100 shares. Payoff and profits shown are per share.
*Assumes written options were sold at the ask price.

13.3 Factors Affecting Option Prices

When we discussed Table 13.2, we noted some relationships between the option prices and different characteristics of the options. In this section, we identify and explain all the factors that affect the price of an option.

Strike Price and Stock Price

As we noted earlier for the Bow.com option quotes in Table 13.2, the value of an otherwise identical call option is higher if the strike price the holder must pay to buy the stock is lower. Because a put is the right to sell the stock, puts with a lower strike price are less valuable.

For a given strike price, the value of a call option is higher if the current price of the stock is higher, as there is a greater likelihood the option will end up in-the-money. Conversely, put options increase in value as the stock price falls.

Option Prices and the Expiration Date

For American options, the longer the time to the expiration date, the more valuable the option. To see why, let's consider two options: an option with one year until the expiration date and an option with six months until the expiration date. The holder of the one-year option can turn the option into a six-month option by simply exercising it early. That is, the one-year option has all the same rights and privileges as the six-month option, so by the Valuation Principle, it cannot be worth less than the six-month option. That is, *an American option with a later expiration date cannot be worth less than an otherwise identical American option with an earlier expiration date*. Usually the right to delay exercising the option is worth something, so the option with the later expiration date will be more valuable.

What about European options? The same argument will not work for European options because a one-year European option cannot be exercised early, at six months. As a consequence, a European option with a later expiration date may potentially trade for less than an otherwise identical option with an earlier expiration date. For example, think about a European call on a stock that pays a liquidating dividend in six months (a liquidating dividend is paid when a corporation chooses to go out of business, sells off all of its assets, and pays out the proceeds as a dividend). A one-year European call option on this stock would be worthless, but a six-month call would have value.

Option Prices and the Risk-Free Rate

The value of a call option is increasing in the risk-free rate and the value of a put option is decreasing in the risk-free rate. The intuition is that a higher discount rate reduces the present value of the strike price. Remember that a call gives the owner the right to buy the stock and a put gives the owner the right to sell the stock. Because you must *pay* the strike price to exercise a call option, reducing the present value of your payment increases the value of the option. However, because you *receive* the strike price when you exercise a put, reducing the present value decreases the value of the put option. We note, however, that given normal swings in the risk-free rate, they would be unlikely to change enough over the life of an option to have a substantial impact on the price of the option—that is, option values are not particularly sensitive to changes in the risk-free rate.

Option Prices and Volatility

An important criterion that determines the price of an option is the volatility of the underlying stock. In fact, *the value of an option generally increases with the volatility of the stock.* The reasoning behind this result is that an increase in volatility increases the likelihood of very high and very low returns for the stock. The holder of a call option benefits from a higher payoff when the stock goes up and the option is in-the-money,

TABLE 13.4 How an Increase in Each Factor Affects Option Values

	American		European	
	Call	Put	Call	Put
Stock price	Increases value	Decreases value	Increases value	Decreases value
Strike price	Decreases value	Increases value	Decreases value	Increases value
Time to expiration	Increases value	Increases value	Uncertain	Uncertain
Risk-free rate	Increases value	Decreases value	Increases value	Decreases value
Volatility of stock price	Increases value	Increases value	Increases value	Increases value

but earns the same (zero) payoff no matter how far the stock drops once the option is out-of-the-money. *Because of this asymmetry of the option's payoff, an option holder gains from an increase in volatility.* Consider Example 13.5.

Example 13.5 confirms our supposition that the value of a call option is increasing in the volatility of the underlying stock. The same holds for puts. Recall that adding a put option to a portfolio is equivalent to buying insurance against a decline in value. Insurance is more valuable when there is higher volatility—hence, put options on more volatile stocks are also worth more. Table 13.4 summarizes the factors that affect option values and how an increase in each factor affects those values.

EXAMPLE 13.5 Option Value and Volatility

PROBLEM

Three European call options with a strike price of \$50 are written on three different stocks. Suppose that tomorrow, the lowest-volatility stock (Stock A) will have a price of \$50 for certain. The medium-volatility stock (Stock B) will be worth either \$60 or \$40, with each price having equal probability. The high-volatility stock (Stock C) will be worth either \$80 or \$20, with each price having equal probability. If the expiration date of all options is tomorrow, which option will be worth more today?

SOLUTION

■ Plan

The value of the options will depend on the value of the stocks at expiration. The value of the options at expiration will be the stock price tomorrow minus \$50 if the stock price is greater than \$50, and \$0 otherwise.

■ Execute

The lowest-volatility stock, Stock A, will be worth \$50 for certain, so its option will be worth \$0 for certain. The medium-volatility stock, Stock B, will be worth either \$40 or \$60, so its option will pay off either \$0 or \$60 – \$50 = \$10. The call option on Stock B will have an expected payoff of $\left(\frac{1}{2} \times 0\right) + \left(\frac{1}{2} \times 10\right) = \$5$ and, ignoring the time value of money, its value today would be \$5. The high-volatility stock, Stock C, will be worth either \$20 or \$80, so its option will pay off either \$0 or \$80 – \$50 = \$30. The call option on Stock C will have an expected payoff of $\left(\frac{1}{2} \times 0\right) + \left(\frac{1}{2} \times 30\right) = \$15$ and, ignoring the time value of money, its value today would be \$15. Because options have no chance of a negative payoff, the one that has a 50% chance of a \$30 payoff has to be worth more than the one that has a 50% chance of a \$10 payoff, and that has to be worth more than the option on the lowest-volatility stock (with no chance of a positive payoff at all). ▶

■ **Evaluate**

Because volatility increases the chance that an option will have higher payoffs, the options have very different values even though the expected value of all three stocks tomorrow is \$50—the lowest-volatility stock will be worth this amount for sure, and the medium-volatility stock, Stock B, also has an expected value of $\left(\frac{1}{2} \times 40\right) + \left(\frac{1}{2} \times 60\right) = \$50$, as does the high-volatility stock, Stock C, with expected value of $\left(\frac{1}{2} \times 20\right) + \left(\frac{1}{2} \times 80\right) = \$50$.

CONCEPT CHECK

5. Can a European option with a later expiration date be worth less than an identical European option with an earlier expiration date?
6. Why are options more valuable when there is increased uncertainty about the value of the stock?

13.4 The Binomial Option Pricing Model

Binomial Option Pricing Model An option valuation model based on the simplifying assumption that the stock price can take only two possible values at the end of the next period.

We continue our study of option pricing with the **Binomial Option Pricing Model.**[1] This model prices options by making the simplifying assumption that at the end of the next period the stock price has only two possible values. This approach allows us a to demonstrate the key insight of Black and Scholes—that option payoffs can be replicated exactly by constructing a portfolio out of a risk-free bond and the underlying stock.

The Two-State Single-Period Model: An Example

Consider a European call option that expires in one period and has an exercise price of \$52. Assume that the price of the underlying non-dividend–paying stock is $S_0 = \$52$ today. The one-period risk-free rate is 5%. In one period, the stock price will either go up to $S_U = \$62$ or go down to $S_D = \$42$, with the subscripts U (up) and D (down) indicating the state of the economy and the corresponding direction of the price move. (We will use the same subscripts to identify the option payoffs that correspond to each price move.) We can summarize the information about the stock and the call option using a binomial tree—a timeline with two branches—as follows:

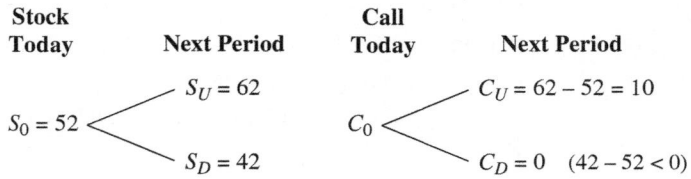

In order to determine the value of the option using the Valuation Principle, we must show that we can replicate it using investments whose prices are known; that is, we need to combine the stock with the risk-free investment into a portfolio with identical payoffs to those of the call option. Let Δ be the number of shares of stock we purchase and let B be our investment in the risk-free asset. (B can be negative; $B < 0$ simply means that, rather than investing in the risk-free asset, the replicating portfolio requires borrowing

[1]This model is also known as the Cox-Ross-Rubinstein (CRR) Model and it is often used to price real assets, callable and putable debt, exotic options, and other financial instruments you will likely learn about in later finance courses. See J.C. Cox, S. Ross, and M. Rubinstein, "Option pricing: A simplified approach," *Journal of Financial Economics* 7 (3) (1979): 229–263.

B at the risk-free rate.) In the "up state," the value of the portfolio must be \$10 in order to perfectly match the C_U payoff of the call option:

$$\Delta 62 + 1.05B = 10 \tag{13.3}$$

In the "down state," the value of the portfolio must be zero (the value of the call in that state):

$$\Delta 42 + 1.05B = 0 \tag{13.4}$$

Subtracting Equation 13.4 from Equation 13.3 produces $\Delta 20 = 10$, which tells us that Δ equals 0.5. Then, substituting $\Delta = 0.5$ into Equation 13.4 we get $21 + 1.05B = 0$ and find that $B = -21/1.05 = -20$. We can easily verify that buying 0.5 shares of stock and borrowing \$20 at a 5% interest rate today will indeed be worth exactly as much in one period as the call option, regardless of the future state of the economy:

$$0.5 \times 62 - 1.05 \times 20 = 10$$
$$0.5 \times 42 - 1.05 \times 20 = 0$$

The Valuation Principle (and the Law of One Price) requires that the price of the call option today, C_0, must equal the current market value of the replicating portfolio, which is the value of 0.5 shares less the amount borrowed:

$$C_0 = \text{Value of Replicating Portfolio} = 0.5 \times 52 - 20 = 6$$

Thus, the price of the call today is \$6.[2]

The Binomial Pricing Formula

Now that we have seen the basic idea, our next step will be to derive a general formula for the replicating portfolio of the binomial model, using the same notation we have just introduced for the stock and the call, and r_f denoting risk-free rate. As before, the payoff of the replicating portfolio must be equal to the value of the option in both states of the economy:

$$\Delta S_U + (1 + r_f)B = C_U \quad \text{and} \quad \Delta S_D + (1 + r_f)B = C_D$$

Solving these two equations for the two unknowns Δ and B we get

$$\Delta = \frac{C_U - C_D}{S_U - S_D} \quad \text{and} \quad B = \frac{C_D - \Delta S_D}{1 + r_f} \tag{13.5}$$

Once we know the composition of the replicating portfolio, we can calculate the value C_0 of the call option today as the cost of purchasing this portfolio:

$$C_0 = \text{Value of Replicating Portfolio} = \Delta S_0 + B \tag{13.6}$$

Equations 13.5 and 13.6 summarize the Binomial Option Pricing Model. These simple formulas are remarkably powerful; we can use them to value *any* security whose payoff depends on the stock price. For example, we can use them to price a put, as in the next example. While the two-state, one-period setting may seem overly simplistic, binomial trees can be easily extended to cover multiple periods. Increasing the number of periods will also increase the number of possible outcomes, making the multi-period binomial model sufficiently realistic to price real life options.[3]

---

[2]If the price of the call was different, there would be an arbitrage opportunity. For example, if the call price was \$7, we could earn an immediate riskless profit of \$1 by selling the call for \$7 and buying the replicating portfolio for \$6. The strategy is risk free because the future payoffs of the option and the replicating portfolio are the same.

[3] We can also use the binomial approach to demonstrate the impact of various factors on options values (summarized earlier in Table 13.4). For instance, in the earlier example, if we increase volatility by changing S_U to \$72 and S_D to \$32 (from the original \$62 and \$42), the value of the option will increase from \$6 to \$10.76.

EXAMPLE 13.6 Valuing a Put Option

PROBLEM

Suppose a stock is currently trading for \$53, and in one period it will either increase to \$63 or decrease to \$43. If the one-period risk-free rate is 5%, what is the price of a European put option that expires in one period and has an exercise price of \$49?

SOLUTION

Plan

We begin by constructing a binomial tree:

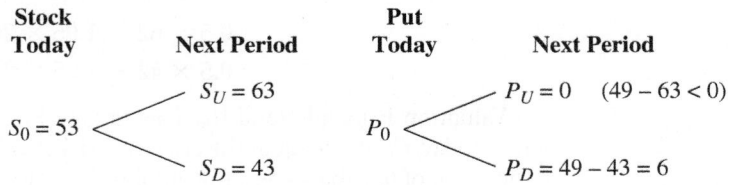

Execute

We can solve for the value of the put by using Equations 13.5 and 13.6 and replacing C_U with P_U and C_D with P_D. Note that $P_U = 0$ is the put option payoff when the value of the stock goes up and $P_D = 6$ is the put payoff when the stock price goes down. Therefore,

$$\Delta = \frac{P_U - P_D}{S_U - S_D} = \frac{0 - 6}{63 - 43} = -0.3 \text{ and } B = \frac{P_D - \Delta S_D}{1 + r_f} = \frac{6 - (-0.3)43}{1.05} = 18.$$

This portfolio is short 0.3 shares of stock and has \$18 invested at the risk-free rate.

Evaluate

Let's check that it replicates the put if the stock price goes up or down:

$$-0.3 \times 63 + 1.05 \times 18 = 0 \text{ and } -0.3 \times 43 + 1.05 \times 18 = 6$$

Thus, the value of the put is the initial cost of this portfolio. Using Equation 13.6,

$$\text{Put Value} = P_0 = \Delta S_0 + B = -0.3 \times 53 + 18 = 2.1$$

CONCEPT CHECK

7. What is the key assumption of the Binomial Option Pricing Model?
8. Why don't we need to know the probabilities of the states in the binominal tree in order to solve for the price of the option?
9. What is a replicating portfolio?

13.5 The Black-Scholes Option Pricing Formula

In Nobel Prize-winning research, Professors Fischer Black and Myron Scholes derived a formula for the price of a European-style call option for a non-dividend–paying stock. The formula now serves as the basis of pricing for options contracts traded worldwide. Their formula is as follows:

Black-Scholes Price of a Call Option on a Non–Dividend-Paying Stock

$$\text{Call Price} = \text{Stock Price} \times N(d_1) - PV(\text{Strike Price}) \times N(d_2) \tag{13.7}$$

The present value is calculated using the risk-free rate, and $N(d_1)$ and $N(d_2)$ are probabilities. The expressions for d_1 and d_2 are complicated, and explaining them is better left to your later finance courses.[4] However, we note here that they contain only the stock price, strike price, risk-free rate, time to expiration of the option, and volatility of the stock. Thus, Black and Scholes confirmed our discussion from the last section, that these five factors are the only ones relevant to the value of an option. What is just as notable is what is not relevant; we do not need to know the expected return of the stock. You might wonder how it is possible to compute the value of a security such as an option that appears to depend critically on the future stock price without knowing the expected return of the stock. In fact, the expected return of the stock is already incorporated into the current stock price, and the value of the option today depends on the stock price today.

Fortunately, you do not need to know the Black-Scholes formula to use it. There are many online option pricing calculators and even add-ins for Excel based on the formula. In Figure 13.5, we show one such calculator from the Bourse de Montréal Inc.

FIGURE 13.5 Online Option Pricing Calculator

This calculator is based on the Black-Scholes option pricing formula. Here, we selected a "European" option using the radio button, "Stock/ETF" as the "Type of Underlying" and "Call" as "Option Type." We then proceeded to enter 60 as the days to expiration, a strike price of $45, an underlying (stock) price of $46, annual volatility (standard deviation) of the stock return of 25%, a risk-free interest rate of 1%, and no dividends. At the bottom of the screen the calculator displays the call price: $2.42 (change the "Option Type" to "Put" and the calculator will show the put option price instead: $1.35). The other outputs at the bottom of the screen are called "the Greeks" because they are mostly Greek letters (vega is not a real Greek letter). Interested students can refer to the Option Calculator Quick Guide for an explanation of what each Greek letter means: https://www.m-x.ca/f_publications_en/calc_guide_en.pdf (see pages 10–12).

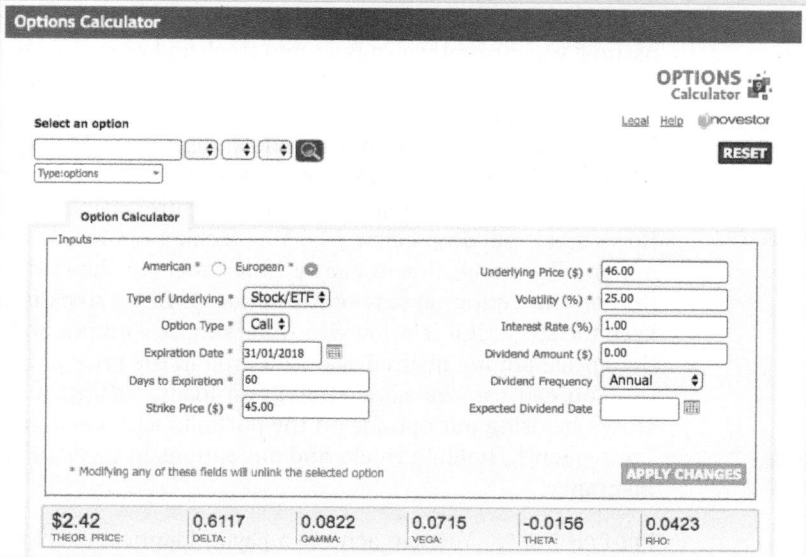

Source: Courtesy of Bourse de Montréal Inc., www.m-x.ca/marc_options_calc_en.php. Reprinted with permission.

[4]For the curious student, they are, $d_1 = \dfrac{\ln[\text{Stock Price}/PV(\text{Strike Price})]}{\sigma\sqrt{T}} + \dfrac{\sigma\sqrt{T}}{2}$ and $d_2 = d_1 - \sigma\sqrt{T}$, where σ is the annual standard deviation of the stock return and T is the time to expiration of the option (in years). We also note that $N(\cdot)$ in Equation 13.7 refers to the cumulative standard normal distribution function.

So far, we have discussed the factors affecting the prices of individual calls and puts. You may have noticed that in Figure 13.5 the prices of both the put and call for the stock are displayed. In fact, those prices cannot move independently of each other. In the next section, we will demonstrate a powerful relationship that links the price of a put to the price of a call on the same stock.

CONCEPT CHECK

10. What factors are used in the Black-Scholes formula to price a call option?

11. How can the Black-Scholes formula not include the expected return on the stock?

13.6 Put-Call Parity

As we have seen, the payoffs to both puts and calls depend on the price of the underlying stock. The expected payoffs determine the prices of the options, so the prices of puts and calls depend partly on the price of the underlying stock. Because the prices of both a put and a call on a given stock are influenced by the price of that same stock, their prices are related to each other. In this section, we develop that relationship by showing that both puts and calls can be packaged in different ways to achieve the same objective—to provide insurance against a drop in the price of a stock. Then we use the Valuation Principle's Law of One Price to show that if the two packages provide exactly the same payoffs, they must have the same price.

Portfolio Insurance

Let's see how we can use combinations of options to insure a stock against a loss. Assume you currently own Bow.com stock and you would like to insure the stock against the possibility of a price decline. To do so, you could simply sell the stock, but you would also give up the possibility of making money if the stock price increases. How can you insure against a loss without relinquishing the upside? You can purchase a put option while still holding the stock, sometimes known as a **protective put**.

protective put The purchasing of a put option on a stock you already own.

For example, suppose you want to insure against the possibility that the price of Bow's stock will drop below $45. You decide to purchase a September 45 European put option. The orange line in Figure 13.6, panel (a), shows the value of the combined position on the expiration date of the option. If Bow's stock is above $45 in September, you keep the stock. If it is below $45, you exercise your put and sell it for $45. Thus, you get the upside but are insured against a drop in the price of Bow's stock.

You can use the same strategy to insure against a loss on an entire portfolio of stocks by using put options on the portfolio as a whole rather than just a single stock. Consequently, holding stocks and put options in this combination is known as **portfolio insurance**.

portfolio insurance A protective put written on a portfolio.

Put-Call Parity. You can achieve a payoff identical to that of the protective put by purchasing a bond and a call option. Let's return to the insurance we purchased on Bow's stock. Bow's stock does not pay dividends, so there are no cash flows before the expiration of the option. Thus, instead of holding a share of Bow's stock and a put, you could get the same payoff by purchasing a risk-free zero-coupon bond with a face value of $45 and a European call option with a strike price of $45. In this case, if Bow is below $45, you receive the payoff from the bond. If Bow is above $45, you can exercise the call and use the payoff from the bond to buy the stock for the strike price of $45. The orange line

FIGURE 13.6 Portfolio Insurance

The plots show two different ways to insure against the possibility of the price of Bow.com stock falling below $45. The orange line in panel (a) indicates the value on the expiration date of a protective put position that is long one share of Bow.com stock and one European put option with a strike price of $45 (the blue dashed line is the payoff of the stock itself). The orange line in panel (b) shows the value on the expiration date of a position that is long a zero-coupon risk-free bond with a face value of $45 and a European call option on Bow.com with a strike price of $45 (the green dashed line is the bond payoff).

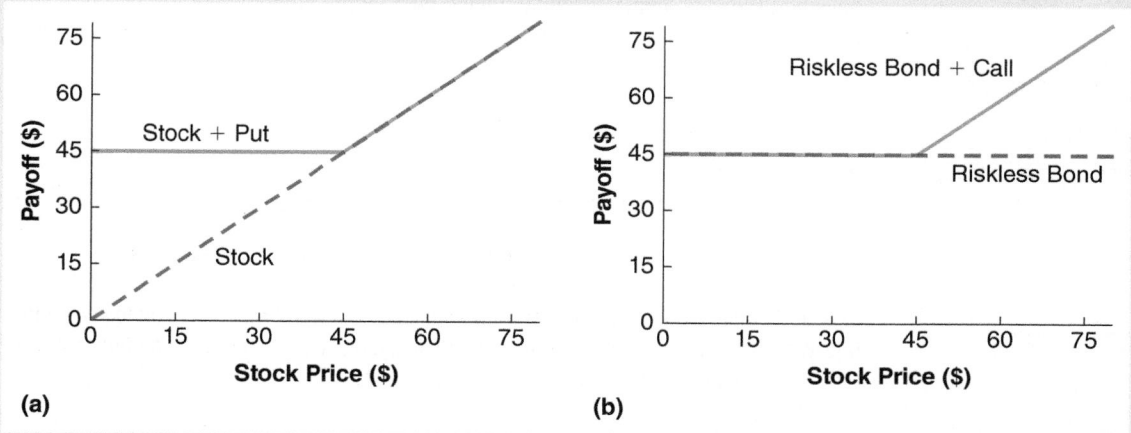

in Figure 13.6, panel (b), shows the value of the combined position on the expiration date of the option; it achieves exactly the same payoffs as owning the stock itself and a put option.

Consider the two different ways to construct portfolio insurance illustrated in Figure 13.6: (1) purchase the stock and a put or (2) purchase a bond and a call. Because both positions provide exactly the same payoff, the Valuation Principle and, in particular, the Law of One Price require that they must have the same price:

$$\text{Stock Price} + \text{Put Price} = PV(\text{Strike Price}) + \text{Call Price}$$

The left side of this equation is the cost of buying the stock and a put; the right side is the cost of buying a zero-coupon bond with face value equal to the strike price of the put and a call option (with the same strike price and expiration date as the put). Recall that the price of a zero-coupon bond is the present value of its face value, which we have denoted by PV (Strike Price). Rearranging terms gives an expression for the price of a European call option for a non-dividend–paying stock:

$$\text{Call Price} = \text{Put Price} + \text{Stock Price} - PV(\text{Strike Price}) \tag{13.8}$$

put-call parity (for non-dividend–paying stocks) The relationship that gives the price of a call option in terms of the price of a put option plus the price of the underlying stock minus the present value of the strike price.

This relationship between the value of the stock, the bond, and the call and put options is known as **put-call parity**. It says that the price of a European call equals the price of the underlying non-dividend–paying stock, plus an otherwise identical put, minus the price of a bond with a face value equal to the strike price that matures on the expiration date of the option. In other words, you can think of a call as a combination of a levered position in the stock, Stock Price – PV(Strike Price), plus insurance against a drop in the stock price, the put.

EXAMPLE 13.7 Using Put-Call Parity

PROBLEM

You are an options dealer who deals in non-publicly traded options. One of your clients wants to purchase a one-year European call option on HAL Computer Systems stock with a strike price of $20. Another dealer is willing to write a one-year European put option on HAL stock with a strike price of $20, and sell you the put option for a price of $2.50 per share. If HAL pays no dividends and is currently trading for $18 per share, and if the risk-free interest rate is 6%, what is the lowest price you can charge for the call option and still guarantee yourself a profit?

SOLUTION

Plan

We can use put-call parity to determine the price of the option:

$$\text{Call Price} = \text{Put Price} + \text{Stock Price} - PV(\text{Strike Price})$$

In order to price a one-year European call with a strike price of $20, we need to know the price of a one-year European put with the same strike price, the current stock price, and the risk-free interest rate. We have all of that information, so we're ready.

$$\begin{aligned}\text{Call Price} &= \text{Put Price} + \text{Stock Price} - PV(\text{Strike Price})\\ &= \$2.50 + \$18 - \$20/1.06 = \$1.632\end{aligned}$$

Evaluate

Put-call parity means that we can replicate the payoff of the one-year call option with a strike price of $20 by holding the following portfolio: buy the one-year put option with a strike price of $20 from the dealer, buy the stock, and sell a one-year, risk-free zero-coupon bond with a face value of $20. With this combination, we have the following final payoff, depending on the final price of HAL stock in one year, S_1:

		Payoff in one year	
		Final HAL Stock Price	
		$S_1 < \$20$	$S_1 \geq 20$
	Long put payoff	$20 - S_1$	0
+	Long stock payoff	S_1	S_1
+	Repay bond	−20	−20
=	Portfolio payoff	0	$S_1 - 20$
+	Short call payoff	0	$-(S_1 - 20)$
=	Total payoff	0	0

Note that the final payoff of the portfolio of the three securities matches the payoff of a call option. Therefore, we can sell the call option to our client and have future payoff of zero no matter what happens. Doing so is worthwhile as long as we can sell the call option for more than the cost of the portfolio, which we found to be $1.632.

Dividend-Paying Stock. What happens if the stock pays a dividend? In that case, the two different ways to construct portfolio insurance do not have the same payout, because the stock will pay a dividend while the zero-coupon bond will not. Thus, the two strategies will cost the same to implement only if we add the present value of future dividends to the combination of the bond and the call, as follows:

$$\text{Stock Price} + \text{Put Price} = PV(\text{Strike Price}) + PV(\text{Dividends}) + \text{Call Price}$$

The left side of this equation is the value of the stock and a put; the right side is the value of a zero-coupon bond, a call option, and the future dividends paid by the stock during the life of the options. Rearranging terms gives the general put-call parity formula:

Put-Call Parity

$$\text{Call Price} = \text{Put Price} + \text{Stock Price} - PV(\text{Strike Price}) - PV(\text{Dividends}) \quad (13.9)$$

In this case, the call is equivalent to having a levered position in the stock without dividends plus insurance against a fall in the stock price.

CONCEPT CHECK

12. Explain put-call parity.

13. If a put option trades at a higher price from the value indicated by the put-call parity equation, what action should you take?

13.7 Options and Corporate Finance

We briefly explored real options in capital budgeting in Chapter 9. We will also note in Chapter 15 that the ability to retire (or call) a bond early is a valuable option for the firm, and that the ability to convert the bond into shares of stock is an option for the bondholders—when a firm issues a convertible bond, it is essentially issuing a package of a straight bond and warrants on its stock.

One other very important corporate finance application of options is interpreting the capital structure of the firm as options on the firm's assets. Specifically, a share of stock can be thought of as a call option on the assets of the firm with a strike price equal to the face value of debt outstanding.[5] To illustrate, consider a single-period world in which at the end of the period the firm is liquidated. If the firm's asset value does not exceed the value of debt outstanding at the end of the period, the firm must declare bankruptcy and the equity holders receive nothing. (Their payoff cannot be negative due to limited liability.) Conversely, if the asset value exceeds the value of debt outstanding, the equity holders get whatever is left once the debt has been repaid. Figure 13.7 illustrates this payoff. Note how the payoff to equity looks exactly the same as the payoff of a call option.

Viewed this way, a share of equity is a call option on the firm's assets. In fact, debt holders can be thought of as owning the firm, but they have written to equity holders a call option on the firm's assets with a strike price equal to the required debt payment. Recall that the price of an option increases with the volatility level of the underlying security. That means equity holders benefit from high-volatility investments. Because the price of equity is increasing with the volatility of the firm's assets, equity holders benefit from a zero-NPV project that increases the volatility of the firm's assets. However,

[5]This insight has been known at least since Black and Scholes wrote their groundbreaking option valuation paper. See F. Black and M. Scholes, "The Pricing of Options and Corporate Liabilities," *Journal of Political Economy* 81 (3) (1973): 637–654.

FIGURE 13.7 Equity as a Call Option

If the value of the firm's assets exceeds the required debt payment, the equity holders receive the value that remains after the debt is repaid. Otherwise, the firm is bankrupt and its equity is worthless. Thus, the payoff to equity is equivalent to a call option on the firm's assets with a strike price equal to the required debt payment.

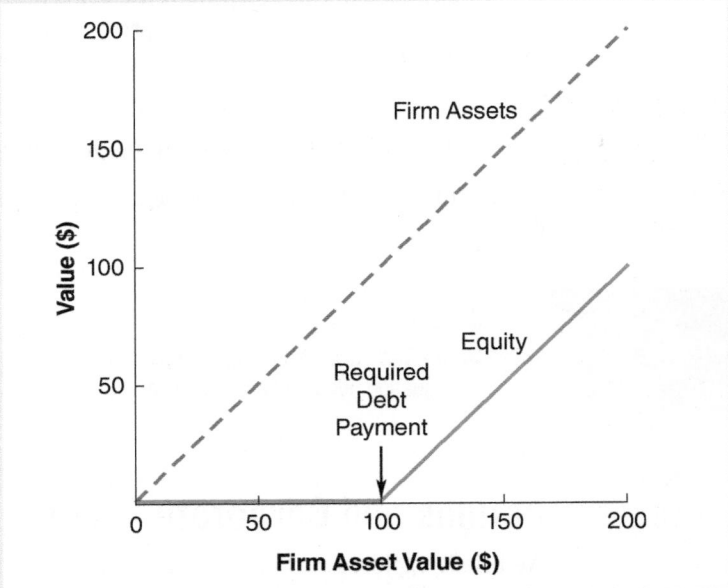

debt holders, as lenders to the firm, do not benefit from an increase in the risk of the firm's assets. Thus, the project increases the value of equity but decreases the value of the debt claims. In fact, because the project is a zero-NPV one, taking it on does not change the value of the firm as a whole. The value of the debt claims decreases by exactly the amount the value of the equity increases. This effect creates a conflict of interest between equity holders and debt holders. Options pricing theory helps us understand why this conflict of interest arises.

The option price is more sensitive to changes in volatility for at-the-money options than it is for in-the-money options. In the context of corporate finance, equity is at-the-money when a firm is close to bankruptcy. In this case, the loss in equity value that results from taking on a negative-NPV investment might be outweighed by the gain in equity value from the increase in volatility. Hence, equity holders have an incentive to take on negative-NPV, high-volatility investments. As we will see in Chapter 16, this excessive risk-taking problem is of concern to debt holders, who bear its cost.

CONCEPT CHECK

14. Explain how equity can be viewed as a call option on the firm.

15. Under what circumstances would equity holders have a possible incentive to take on negative-NPV investments?

MyLab Finance

Here is what you should know after reading this chapter. MyLab™ Finance will help you identify what you know, and where to go when you need to practice.

KEY POINTS AND EQUATIONS	TERMS	ONLINE PRACTICE OPPORTUNITIES
13.1 Option Basics ■ An option that gives the holder the right (but not the obligation) to purchase an asset at some future date is known as a call option. ■ An option that gives the holder the right to sell an asset at some future date is known as a put option. ■ When a holder of an option enforces the agreement and buys or sells the share of stock at the agreed-upon price, the holder is exercising the option. ■ The price at which the holder agrees to buy or sell the share of stock when the option is exercised is known as the strike price or exercise price. ■ The last date on which the holder has the right to exercise the option is known as the expiration date. ■ An American option can be exercised on any date up to, and including, the expiration date. A European option can be exercised only on the expiration date. ■ The option is in-the-money if exercising it immediately would lead to a positive payoff. Conversely, the option is out-of-the-money if exercising it immediately would lead to a negative payoff.	American options, p. 455 at-the-money, p. 457 call option, p. 455 deep in-the-money, p. 458 deep out-of-the-money, p. 458 derivatives, p. 455 European options, p. 455 exercising the option, p. 455 expiration date, p. 455 financial option, p. 455 hedging, p. 458 in-the-money, p. 457 open interest, p. 457 option writer, p. 455 out-of-the-money, p. 458 payoff, p. 456 profit, p. 456 put option, p. 455 speculate, p. 458 strike price (or exercise price), p. 455 warrant, p. 455	MyLab Study Plan 13.1
13.2 Option Payoffs and Profits at Expiration ■ The value of a call option at expiration = Stock Price – Strike Price, if Stock Price > Strike; = 0, if Stock Price ≤ Strike (13.1) ■ The value of a put option at expiration = Strike Price – Stock Price, if Stock Price < Strike; = 0, if Stock Price ≥ Strike (13.2) ■ An investor holding a short position in an option has an obligation; he or she takes the opposite side of the contract to the investor who holds the long position.	short sale, p. 464	MyLab Study Plan 13.2

KEY POINTS AND EQUATIONS	TERMS	ONLINE PRACTICE OPPORTUNITIES
13.3 Factors Affecting Option Prices ■ Call options with lower strike prices are more valuable than otherwise identical calls with higher strike prices. Conversely, put options are more valuable with higher strike prices. ■ Call options increase in value, and put options decrease in value, when the stock price rises. ■ The value of an option generally increases with the volatility of the stock.		MyLab Study Plan 13.3
13.4 The Binomial Option Pricing Model ■ Using a simplified approach, the Binomial Option Pricing Model shows that the price of an option on a non-dividend–paying stock is a function of only the current stock price, the strike price, the time to expiration, the volatility of the stock, and the risk-free rate. $\Delta = \frac{C_U - C_D}{S_U - S_D}$ and $B = \frac{C_D - \Delta S_D}{1 + r_f}$ $C_0 = \Delta S_0 + B$	Binomial Option Pricing Model, 468	MyLab Study Plan 13.4
13.5 The Black-Scholes Option Pricing Formula ■ The Black-Scholes option pricing formula shows that the price of an option on a non-dividend–paying stock is a function of only the current stock price, the strike price, the time to expiration, the volatility of the stock, and the risk-free rate.		MyLab Study Plan 13.5
13.6 Put-Call Parity ■ Put-call parity relates the value of the European call to the value of the European put and the stock: Call Price = Put Price + Stock Price $- PV$(Strike Price) $- PV$(Dividends) (13.9)	portfolio insurance, p. 472 protective put, p. 472 put-call parity, p. 473	MyLab Study Plan 13.6
13.7 Options and Corporate Finance ■ Equity can be viewed as a call option on the firm. ■ The debt holders can be viewed as owning the firm and having sold a call option with a strike price equal to the required debt payment.		MyLab Study Plan 13.7

REVIEW QUESTIONS

1. Explain what the following financial terms mean:
   a. Option – gives the holder the right to buy/sell but not
   b. Expiration date – the price when the holder buy or sell the option/obligation
   c. Strike price
   d. Call – Buyer
   e. Put – sell
2. What is the difference between a European option and an American option?
3. Explain the difference between a long position in a put and a short position in a call.
4. What position has more downside exposure: a short position in a call or a short position in a put? That is, in the worst case, in which of these two positions would your losses be greater?
5. If you own a call option at expiration and the stock price equals the strike price, is your profit zero?
6. Is an increase in a stock's volatility good for the holder of a call option? Is it good for the holder of a put option?
7. Why are the prices of puts and calls on the same stock related?
8. Explain why an option can be thought of as an insurance contract.
9. Explain why equity can be viewed as a call option on a firm.

PROBLEMS

All problems in this chapter are available in MyLab Finance. An asterisk (*) indicates problems with a higher level of difficulty.

Option Basics

1. See the option quote on IBM from the CBOE website below.

IBM (INTL BUSINESS MACHINES) 161.36 1.78

Jul 20 2016 @ 17:21 ET Bid 161.11 Ask 161.3 Size 3 × 1 Vol 4372921

Calls	Last Sale	Net	Bid	Ask	Vol	Open Int	Puts	Last Sale	Net	Bid	Ask	Vol	Open Int
16 Aug 155.00 (IBM1619H155-E)	6.45	0.75	6.95	7.25	9	7640	16 Aug 155.00 (IBM1619T155-E)	1.18	−0.75	1.17	1.25	61	4505
16 Aug 160.00 (IBM1619H160-E)	3.3	0.85	3.15	3.3	101	12811	16 Aug 160.00 (IBM1619T160-E)	2.76	−1.24	2.71	2.84	61	2114
16 Aug 165.00 (IBM1619H165-E)	1.05	0.3	0.96	1.06	178	27064	16 Aug 165.00 (IBM1619T165-E)	7.1	−0.4	5.7	5.9	1	332
16 Aug 170.00 (IBM1619H170-E)	0.21	−0.01	0.21	0.27	20	6086	16 Aug 170.00 (IBM1619T170-E)	12.25	0	9.95	10.3	0	393
16 Sep 155.00 (IBM1616I155-E)	7.77	1.58	7.5	7.7	2	122	16 Sep 155.00 (IBM1616U155-E)	2.34	−0.59	2.13	2.22	3	251
16 Sep 160.00 (IBM1616I160-E)	4.05	0.76	4	4.2	6	380	16 Sep 160.00 (IBM1616U160-E)	4	−1.09	3.8	4	1	476
16 Sep 165.00 (IBM1616I165-E)	1.87	0.47	1.76	1.88	161	297	16 Sep 165.00 (IBM1616U165-E)	6.65	−2.1	6.55	6.75	1	27
16 Sep 170.00 (IBM1616I170-E)	0.65	0.07	0.63	0.71	2	498	16 Sep 170.00 (IBM1616U170-E)	12.35	0	10.4	10.7	0	47

Source: Chicago Board Options Exchange at www.cboe.com.

option write – the seller of the option writer

2-7 9-11

a. Which option contract had the most trades today?
b. Which option contract is being held the most overall?
c. Suppose you purchase one option with symbol IBM1616I155-E. How much will you need to pay your broker for the option (ignoring commissions)?
d. Suppose you sell one option with symbol IBM1619H165-E. How much will you receive for the option (ignoring commissions)?
e. The calls with which strike prices are currently in-the-money? Which puts are in-the-money?

Option Payoffs and Profits at Expiration

2. You own a call option on Intuit stock with a strike price of $40. When you purchased the option, it cost you $5. The option will expire in exactly three months' time.
a. If the stock is trading at $55 in three months, what will be the payoff of the call? What will be the profit of the call?
b. If the stock is trading at $35 in three months, what will be the payoff of the call? What will be the profit of the call?
c. Draw a payoff diagram showing the value of the call at expiration as a function of the stock price at expiration.
d. Redo (c), but instead of showing payoffs, show profits.

3. Assume that you have shorted the call option in Problem 2; when you originally sold (wrote) the option, you received $5.
a. If the stock is trading at $55 in three months, what will your payoff be? What will your profit be?
b. If the stock is trading at $35 in three months, what will your payoff be? What will your profit be?
c. Draw a payoff diagram showing the payoff at expiration as a function of the stock price at expiration.
d. Redo (c), but instead of showing payoffs, show profits.

4. You own a put option on Ford stock with a strike price of $10. When you bought the put, its cost to you was $2. The option will expire in exactly six months' time.
a. If the stock is trading at $8 in six months, what will be the payoff of the put? What will be the profit of the put?
b. If the stock is trading at $23 in six months, what will be the payoff of the put? What will be the profit of the put?
c. Draw a payoff diagram showing the value of the put at expiration as a function of the stock price at expiration.
d. Redo (c) but instead of showing payoffs, show profits.

5. Assume that you have shorted the put option in Problem 4. When you sold (wrote) the put, you received $2.
a. If the stock is trading at $8 in three months, what will your payoff be? What will your profit be?
b. If the stock is trading at $23 in three months, what will your payoff be? What will your profit be?
c. Draw a payoff diagram showing the amount you owe at expiration as a function of the stock price at expiration.
d. Redo (c), but instead of showing payoffs, show profits.

6. You own a share of Costco stock. You are worried that its price will fall and would like to insure yourself against this possibility. How can you purchase insurance against a fall in the price of the stock?

Factors Affecting Option Prices

7. What is the maximum payoff that a long put option can have? How about a long call option?

***8.** A *forward contract* is a contract to purchase an asset at a fixed price on a particular date in the future. Both parties are obligated to fulfill the contract. Explain how to construct a forward contract on a share of stock from a position in options.

***9.** Can a call option be more valuable than the stock it is written on?

10. Why is an American option with a longer time to expiration generally worth more than an otherwise identical option with a shorter time to expiration?

The Binomial Option Pricing Model

11. The current price of Estelle Corporation stock is $25. Its stock price will either go up by 20% or go down by 20% in one year. The stock pays no dividends. The one-year risk-free interest rate is 6%. Using the binomial model, calculate the price of a one-year call option on Estelle stock with a strike price of $25.

12. Using the information in Problem 11, use the binomial model to calculate the price of a one-year put option on Estelle stock with a strike price of $25.

Put-Call Parity

13. Dynamic Energy Systems stock is currently trading for $33 per share. The stock pays no dividends. A one-year European put option on Dynamic with a strike price of $35 is currently trading for $2.10. If the risk-free interest rate is 10% per year, what is the price of a one-year European call option on Dynamic with a strike price of $35?

14. You happen to be checking the newspaper and notice an arbitrage opportunity. The current stock price of Intrawest is $20 per share and the one-year, risk-free interest rate is 8%. A one-year put on Intrawest with a strike price of $18 sells for $3.33, while the identical call sells for $7. Explain what you must do to exploit this arbitrage opportunity.

Options and Corporate Finance

***15.** We know that equity in a company that borrows is analogous to a call option. Using put-call parity, express the position of equity holders in terms of a portfolio that includes put options.

DATA CASE

Your uncle owns 10,000 shares of Walmart stock. He is concerned about the short-term outlook for Walmart's stock due to an impending "major announcement." This announcement has received much attention in the press, so he expects the stock price will change significantly in the next month but is unsure whether it will be a profit or a loss. He hopes the price will increase, but he also doesn't want to suffer if the price were to fall in the short term. He is optimistic about Walmart's long term prospects, so he does not want to sell his shares, but he is willing to consider an option strategy that would protect him from downside risk over the short term.

His broker recommended a "protective put" strategy, but your uncle has never traded options and he is not sure how the strategy would work. You have already explained that the strategy would involve purchasing put options that would allow him to sell his 10,000 Walmart shares at a fixed price at a future date, but he is not convinced.

You decide to show him the profits he could obtain from the strategy suggested by his broker.

1. Download option quotes on options that expire in approximately one month on Walmart from the Chicago Board Options Exchange website (www.cboe.com) into an Excel spreadsheet. If you choose to download "near-term at-the-money" options you will get a range of options expiring in about a month. You can get active quotes only while the exchange is open; bid or ask prices are not available when it is closed.
2. Determine your uncle's protective put profits.
   a. Identify the near-term put with an exercise price closest to, but not below, the current stock price. Determine the investment required to protect all 10,000 shares. For the sake of simplicity, perform all subsequent calculations on a per share basis (i.e., calculate protective put profits for a single share rather than calculating profits using all 10,000 shares).
   b. Determine the put option payoff at expiration for each stock price at $5 increments from $50 to $110 using Equation 13.2. (You can use a different range of prices if the current price of Walmart stock falls far from the centre of the $50 to $110 range. For example, use the $30 to $90 range if Walmart's share price is about $60.)
   c. Compute the profit (or loss) on the put for each stock price used in part (b). You can use Example 13.4 as a blue print for these calculations.
   d. Compute the profit on the stock from the current price for each stock price used in part (b). For example, if the price of Wal-Mart stock is $80 today and then it increased to $85, your uncle would earn $5 profit per share. If the future price is $70 on the other hand, your uncle would lose $10.
   e. Compute his overall profit (or loss) of the protective put (on a per share basis); that is, combine the profits from the put and the stock for each price used in parts (c) and (d).
   f. Draw a profit diagram for the protective put. Your graph should have the same shape as the protective put payoff shown in Figure 13.4 Panel (a), but your diagram is shifted down by the amount of the option's premium and the stock price.
3. Was the broker correct that the protective put would prevent your uncle from taking a huge loss if the announcement caused a large decrease in the stock value? What is your uncle's maximum possible loss per share using the protective put? What is your uncle's maximum possible loss per share when holding Walmart stock on its own (i.e., without the put)? *Hint*: for both alternatives, examine the worst-case scenario by assuming that Walmart shares become worthless and the stock price drops to zero.
4. Which strategy, the protective put or holding Walmart stock on its own, provides the maximum upside potential for your uncle? Why does this occur?

PART

Financing Decisions

5

CHAPTER 14 Raising Equity Capital
CHAPTER 15 Debt Financing
CHAPTER 16 Capital Structure
CHAPTER 17 Payout Policy

Valuation Principle Connection. How should a firm raise the funds it needs to undertake its investments? In this part of the book, we explain the mechanics of raising equity and issuing debt. Chapter 14 describes the process a company goes through when it raises equity capital. In Chapter 15, we review firms' use of debt markets to raise capital. In Chapter 16 we discuss the financial manager's choice between these two major categories of financing. A firm's ability to raise capital depends on the value the market applies to its securities. The Valuation Principle tells us that the price of any securities issued by the firm will be the present value of the cash flows accruing to them. In Chapter 17 we discuss the financial managers' decision as to whether cash should be paid out to stockholders and how this might be done. While we discuss the process for raising capital—choosing between equity and debt financing and deciding on a payout policy—it is important to remember that the price that investors are willing to pay for a firm's securities depends on the financial manager making investment decisions that maximize the value of the firm.

CHAPTER

14 Raising Equity Capital

LEARNING OBJECTIVES

- Contrast the different ways to raise equity capital for a private company
- Understand the process of taking a company public
- Gain insight into puzzles associated with initial public offerings
- Explain how to raise additional equity capital once the company is public

As we pointed out in Chapter 1, most Canadian businesses are small sole proprietorships and partnerships. That said, we found that these firms as a whole are responsible for only about 32% of total Canadian profit generation before tax. Sole proprietorships are not allowed to access outside equity capital, so these businesses have relatively little capacity for growth. Sole proprietors are also forced to hold a large fraction of their wealth in a single asset—the company—and therefore are likely to be undiversified. By incorporating, businesses can gain access to capital, and founders can reduce the risk of their portfolios by selling some of their equity and diversifying. Consequently, even though corporations make up the minority of Canadian businesses, we found that they account for 62% of profit generation before tax in the Canadian economy. The situation is similar in most developed countries.

In this chapter, we discuss how companies raise equity capital. To illustrate this concept, we follow the case of an actual company, Facebook, Inc. (ticker: FB). Facebook is a leading social network company whose products include Instagram, WhatsApp, and Oculus. Facebook was founded in 2004. Using the example of Facebook, we first discuss the alternative ways new companies can raise capital and then examine the impact of these funding alternatives on current and new investors.

14.1 Equity Financing for Private Companies

The initial capital that is required to start a business is usually provided by the entrepreneur and his or her immediate family. Few families, however, have the resources to finance a growing business, so growth almost always requires outside capital. In this section, we examine the sources that can provide this capital to a private company and the effect of the infusion of outside capital on the control of the company.

Sources of Funding

When a private company decides to raise outside equity capital, it can seek funding from several potential sources: *angel investors, venture capital firms, institutional investors, sovereign wealth funds*, and *corporate investors*. Any of these investors may be referred to as a **private equity investor** if they invest in the stock of a private company (a company with non-publicly traded equity).

private equity investor An investor that owns shares of a non-publicly traded company.

angel investors Individual investors who buy equity in small private firms (often start-up firms).

Angel Investors. Individual investors who buy equity in small private firms (often start-ups) are called **angel investors**. For many start-ups, often the first round of outside private equity financing is obtained from angels. The term originated 100 years ago in New York when wealthy investors came to the rescue of new Broadway productions by providing critical funding. These investors are frequently friends or acquaintances of the entrepreneur. Because their capital investment is often large relative to the amount of capital already in place at the firm, they typically receive a sizeable equity share in the business in return for their funds. As a result, these investors may have substantial influence in the business decisions of the firm. Angels may also bring expertise to the firm that the entrepreneur lacks.

In most cases, firms need more capital than what a few angels can provide. Finding angels is difficult—often it is a function of how well connected the entrepreneur is in the local community. Most entrepreneurs, especially those launching their first start-up company, have few relationships with people who have substantial capital to invest. At some point, many firms that require equity capital for growth must turn to the *venture capital* industry.

venture capital firm A business that specializes in raising money to invest in the private equity of young firms.

Venture Capital Firms. A **venture capital firm** is a business that specializes in raising money to invest in the private equity of young firms. Table 14.1 lists the most active venture capital firms in Canada in 2016.

TABLE 14.1 Most Active Venture Capital Investors in Canada in 2016

Venture Capital Firm Name	Location	Number of Companies Financed
Business Development Bank of Canada	Montreal, QC	30
Innovacorp	Halifax, NS	17
Real Ventures	Montreal, QC	14
iNovia Capital	Montreal, QC	9
Relay Ventures	Toronto, ON	9
Y Combinator	Mountain View, CA	8
OMERS Ventures	Toronto, ON	7
Export Development Canada	Ottawa, ON	7
Desjardins	Montreal, QC	6
Anges Quebec	Montreal, QC	6
Globalive Capital	Toronto, ON	6

Source: PwC Canada & CB Insights, "Money Tree Canada Report," Q4 and Full-Year 2016.

INTERVIEW WITH KEVIN LAWS

Kevin Laws

Kevin Laws is an active angel investor, partner at Maiden Lane Ventures, and Chief Operating Officer of AngelList,an online platform where start-up companies can meet investors and recruit talent.

Q How has angel investing changed over the last decade?

A Historically, angel investors typically grouped together in regions and markets not well covered by venture capital (VC) or dispensed cash along with advice at the earliest stages of a few technology companies. Often, investors viewed funding start-ups as a sideline rather than as a full-time business.

The cost of starting a technology company today has dropped significantly. Cloud services, social marketing, search engine optimization, and other platforms and tools allow entrepreneurs to launch for $500,000 rather than $5 million. Because venture investors prefer to invest several million dollars, angels are now the dominant form of fundraising for the earliest (seed stage) cash needs of the company.

Q How has angel investing affected the venture capital industry?

A The lines between angel investing and venture capital are blurring. Today's angels ask for terms they didn't when angel investing was more of a hobby—for example, pro rata investment rights (to maintain their level of percentage ownership during later financing rounds) and information rights. The venture industry is adjusting to a host of new players and is responding primarily by ceding the earliest-stage markets to angel investors and engaging at Series A (the first round of financing after seed capital) and beyond.

Q How do the returns from angel investing compare with other investment classes?

A Historically, angel investing encompassed a wide range of investments (from investing in your nephew's doomed dry cleaner to early Google investors), making it hard to define the returns. An Angel Capital Association's study found that returns of more "professional" angel investors outstripped venture capital investor returns. It is too early to say whether that will continue as angel investing in technology jumps dramatically, because most investments take 7 to 10 years to come to fruition. Early indicators are that it will likely converge with early stage venture returns.

Q Is angel investing only for wealthy investors with domain expertise? Or is it accessible/attractive even for smaller investors?

A Currently, active angel investing with large cheques is still for wealthy investors with domain expertise. Although a typical angel cheque is $25,000, the risk profile of each individual investment is such that you want 30 to 50 investments in a good portfolio. You also need domain expertise to recognize good deals and be familiar enough with the management team and markets to move quickly.

While angel investing is still an asset class for sophisticated investors, it no longer requires as much wealth or start-up experience to participate. Services like AngelList allow investors to invest as little as $1000 per company across hundreds of companies behind the wealthy, experienced investors. This means that the standard for wealth has dropped (because your friends can combine their money with yours to make the appropriate cheque size), plus, by investing behind experienced investors, you can get access without having the same expertise. That has broadened the investor base significantly.

Q On what basis do angel investors make the decision to invest?

A Team, traction, and social proof, in that order, based on a recent study I co-authored with several economists. The characteristics of the founding team were the most important factor, followed by how much progress the company had made (which varies by industry—downloads, paying customers, pre-orders, etc.). The third factor, social proof, is who else is involved as investor or advisor to the company. When you are writing small cheques for companies whose most likely failure reason is "running out of cash too soon," you want to be sure you're investing with many other investors. A successful investor is a lot more likely to be followed by other investors than is an unknown one, much as investors buy a stock after Warren Buffett does. Investing in a company that only manages to raise your $25,000 will lose you money for certain, no matter how "right" you were about its product or market.

venture capitalists The general partners who work for and run a venture capital firm.

Many venture capital firms are structured as limited partnerships. Typically, institutional investors, such as pension funds, are the limited partners. The general partners are known as **venture capitalists** and they work for and run the venture capital firm. Venture capital firms offer limited partners a number of advantages over investing directly in start-ups themselves as angel investors. Because these firms invest in many start-ups, limited partners are more diversified than if they invested on their own. They also benefit from the expertise of the general partners. However, these advantages come at a cost. General partners usually charge substantial fees, taken mainly as a percentage of the positive returns they generate. Most firms charge 20% of any positive returns they make, but the successful firms may charge more than 30%. They also generally charge an annual management fee of about 2% of the fund's committed capital.

Venture capital firms can provide substantial capital for young companies. As you can see in Figure 14.1, in 2009 and 2010, the two years hardest hit by the financial crisis, only 753 financing deals were provided by venture capital firms in Canada, and about $2 billion was raised by venture capitalists. As impressive as this might seem, though, it pales compared to the peak years of 2000 and 2001.

Paul Gompers and Josh Lerner[1] report that venture capitalists typically control about one-third of the seats on a start-up's board of directors and often represent the single largest voting block on the board. Although entrepreneurs generally view this control as a necessary cost of obtaining venture capital, it can actually be an important benefit of accepting venture financing. Venture capitalists use their control to protect their investments, so they may therefore perform a key nurturing and monitoring role for the firm.

FIGURE 14.1 **Venture Capital Funding in Canada, 1995–2016**

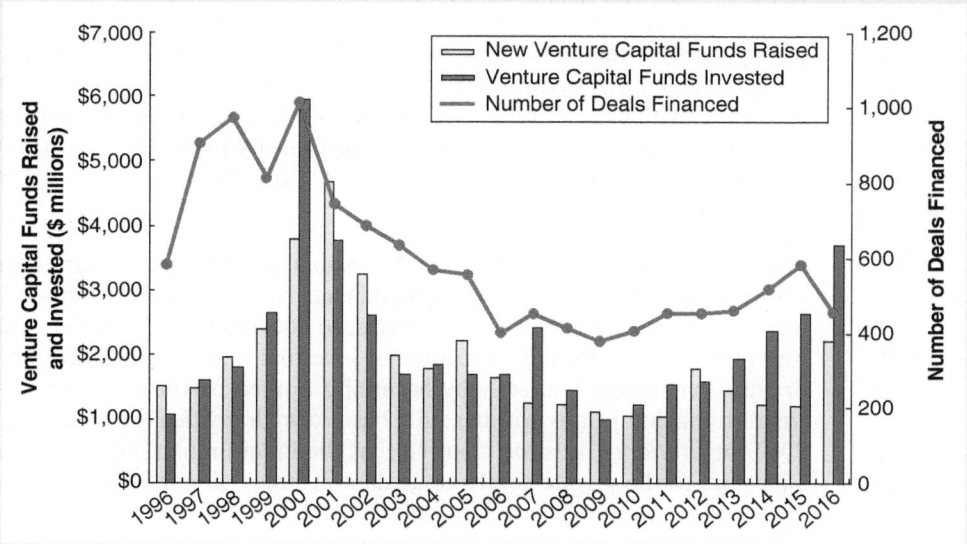

The line indicates the total number of venture capital deals by year. The bars show the total dollar amount of venture capital funds raised and invested.
Source: Data from Canadian Venture Capital Association, Macdonald and Associates Ltd, McKinsey and Company, Thomson Reuters Canada, and Industry Canada.

[1]Paul A. Gompers and Josh Lerner, *The Venture Capital Cycle* (Cambridge, MA: MIT Press, 1999).

Crowdfunding: The Wave of the Future?

The last 10 years has seen growth in an entirely new kind of funding for start-ups, known as crowdfunding, in which the firm raises very small amounts of money from a large number of people. Investment levels can be minute, in some cases less than $100.

Historically, in Canada and the U.S., regulators have enforced strict rules allowing only accredited investors (investors with annual income over $200,000 or net worth over $5 million) to invest in private equity issues. These rules effectively barred crowdfunding sites from offering equity to investors. As a result, companies like Kickstarter and Indiegogo offered investors other payoffs such as the products the company would ultimately produce. In many cases, these "financing" contracts looked more like advanced purchase orders.

However, in 2012 the landscape changed dramatically when the U.S. Congress passed the JOBS Act that exempted crowdfunding from the historical restrictions on private equity investments. In 2015 and 2016, similar relaxation of regulations occurred in various Canadian provinces. The relaxed regulations allow equity investment by non-accredited investors. Specific restrictions on the size of an equity investment via crowdfunding vary depending on jurisdiction. For example, in Ontario and Quebec, companies may raise no more than $1.5 million through crowdfunding, and non-accredited investors can invest no more than $2500 in one crowdfunding-based equity offering and no more than $10,000 in any crowdfunding-based equity offerings per year.

private equity firm A business that specializes in investing in existing privately held firms.

leveraged buyout (LBO) When a group of private investors purchases all the equity of a public company and finances the purchase primarily with debt.

Private Equity Firms. A **private equity firm** is organized very similarly to venture capital firms, but these firms invest in the equity of existing privately held firms rather than start-up companies. Often, private equity firms initiate their investment by finding a publicly traded firm and purchasing all the outstanding equity, thereby taking the company private in a transaction called a **leveraged buyout (LBO)** because in most cases the private equity firms use debt as well as equity to finance the purchase.

Private equity firms share the advantages of venture capital firms and also charge similar fees. One key difference between private equity and venture capital is the magnitude invested. Because private equity firms are buying existing mature businesses, the investment is often over 100 times the size of a typical venture capital investment.

Institutional Investors. Institutional investors, such as pension funds, insurance companies, endowments, and foundations, manage large quantities of money. They are major investors in many different types of assets, so not surprisingly, they are also active investors in private companies. Institutional investors may invest directly in private firms, or they may invest indirectly by becoming limited partners in venture capital firms. Institutional interest in private equity has grown dramatically in recent years. In fact, in 2017, *Institutional Investor* reported that the Preqin ranking of the world's 100 largest allocators to the private equity asset class included 43 public pension funds. The largest investor was the Canada Pension Plan Investment Board with $44.4 billion invested. The sixth and seventh largest investors in the world were the Ontario Teachers' Pension Plan ($21 billion invested) and the Caisse de dépôt et placement du Québec ($20 billion invested).

sovereign wealth funds (SWFs) Pools of money controlled by a government, usually raised from royalty or resource revenue or from taxes collected.

Sovereign Wealth Funds. **Sovereign wealth funds (SWFs)** are pools of money controlled by a government, usually raised from royalty or resource revenue or from taxes collected. SWFs have been in existence for many years. For example, the Kuwait Investment Board was founded in 1953 and is now called the Kuwait Investment Authority. The Alberta Heritage Savings Trust Fund, founded in 1976, is another example. In 2007, SWFs became increasingly newsworthy as they invested in troubled financial institutions. SWFs are also the largest limited partners in global private equity markets. According to the SWF Institute (www.swfinstitute.org), as of March 31, 2017, the largest SWF was the Norway Government Pension Fund with assets of $922 billion. In 2017, the top 10 SWFs in terms of assets came from Norway, UAE/Abu Dhabi, China (four funds), Kuwait, Saudi Arabia, Singapore, and Qatar.

corporate investor, corporate partner, strategic partner, and **strategic investor** A corporation that invests in private companies.

Corporate Investors. Many established corporations purchase equity in younger, private companies. A corporation that invests in private companies is referred to by many different names, including **corporate investor, corporate partner, strategic partner,** and **strategic investor**. Most of the other types of investors in private firms that we have considered so far are primarily interested in the financial return that they will earn on their investments. Corporate investors, by contrast, might invest for corporate strategic objectives in addition to the desire for investment returns. For example, on November 3, 2010, Panasonic Corporation announced that it had invested $30 million in Tesla Motors to help build a multi-year collaboration to accelerate the market expansion of electric vehicles.

Securities and Valuation

preferred stock Stock issued by mature companies, such as banks, that usually has a preferential dividend and seniority in any liquidation, and sometimes special voting rights; when issued by young companies, it has seniority in any liquidation but typically does not pay cash dividends and contains a right to convert to common stock.

convertible preferred stock A preferred stock that gives the owner an option to convert it into common stock on some future date.

When a private company founder decides to sell equity to outside investors for the first time, it is common practice to issue preferred stock rather than common stock to raise capital. **Preferred stock** issued by mature companies, such as banks, usually has a preferential dividend and seniority in any liquidation, and sometimes special voting rights. Conversely, while retaining its seniority, the preferred stock issued by young companies typically does not pay regular cash dividends. However, this preferred stock usually gives the owner an option to convert it into common stock on some future date, so it is often called **convertible preferred stock**. In short, it will have all of the future rights and benefits of common stock if things go well. On the other hand, if the company runs into financial difficulties, the preferred stockholders have a senior claim on the assets of the firm relative to any common stockholders (who are often the employees of the firm).

To illustrate, let's consider Facebook, which was founded by Mark Zuckerberg, Dustin Moskovitz, Chris Hughes, and Eduardo Saverin from their dorm room in 2004. Facebook's initial funding came from $15,000 (Saverin) and another $85,000 (Zuckerberg and his father). By July of 2004, Facebook had caught the attention of angel investors Peter Thiel (co-founder of Paypal), Mark Pincus (co-founder of Zynga) and Reid Hoffman (co-founder of LinkedIn). They invested about $500,000 of new capital into the young firm in return for 10% ownership. As Facebook grew rapidly (reaching over 1 million users by the end of 2004), it needed more capital. Its first round of venture capital financing came in May 2005 with $12.7 million worth of Series A preferred stock sold to Accel Partners (Facebook's angel investors also invested more capital at this point). A year later, in April 2006, Facebook closed its series B funding round with $27.5 million from a group of five venture capital firms.[2] It is important to understand that Facebook remained a private company after this transaction. Simply selling equity to outside investors does not cause a company to be public. Companies may remain private, meaning their shares are not listed on an exchange and they are not required to file their financial statements with the SEC, as long as the number of shareholders remains small. (Later in this chapter, we discuss the process of offering shares to the general

[2]The information given here for this and subsequent funding comes from the IPO prospectus (available on EDGAR at www.sec.gov/edgar/searchedgar/webusers.htm).

public and thereby transitioning to public status.) After this funding round, Facebook's distribution of ownership was

Funding Round	Date	Capital Raised	Ownership Sold to Investors	Founder Ownership	Implied Valuation of Facebook
Angel	Mid-2004	$500,000	10%	90%	$5,000,000
Series A	May 2005	$12,700,000	12.7%	77.3%	$100,000,000
Series B	April 2006	$27,500,000	5%	72.3%	$550,000,000

The Series B preferred shares were new shares of stock being sold by Facebook. At the price the new shares were sold for, Series A and the founders' shares were now worth 397.65 million and represented 72.3% of the shares of the $550 million company. It is important to note that the increase in the value of Zuckerberg's and the other founders' shares was very uncertain when they founded the company. The value of the prior shares outstanding at the funding-round price ($397.65 million in this example) is called the **pre-money valuation**. The value of the whole firm (old plus new shares) at the funding-round price ($550 million) is known as the **post-money valuation**. The difference between the pre- and post-money valuation is the amount invested. In other words,

pre-money valuation
The value of a firm's prior shares outstanding at the price in the funding round.

post-money valuation
The value of the whole firm (old plus new shares) at the price at which the new equity is sold.

$$\text{Post-Money Valuation} = \text{Pre-Money Valuation} + \text{Amount Invested} \tag{14.1}$$

In addition, the fractional ownership held by the new investors is equal to

$$\text{Percentage Ownership} = \text{Amount invested} / \text{Post-money Valuation} \tag{14.2}$$

EXAMPLE 14.1 Funding and Ownership

PROBLEM

You founded your own firm two years ago. Initially you contributed $100,000 of your own money and, in return, received 1.5 million shares of stock. Since then, you have sold an additional 500,000 shares to angel investors. Now you are considering raising even more capital from a venture capitalist (VC). This VC would invest $6 million and would receive 3 million newly issued shares. What is the post-money valuation? Assuming that this is the VC's first investment in your company, what percentage of the firm will she end up owning? What percentage will you own? What is the value of your shares?

SOLUTION

Plan

After this funding round, there will be a total of 5 million shares outstanding:

Your shares	1,500,000
Angel investors' shares	500,000
Newly issued shares	3,000,000
Total	5,000,000

The VC would be paying $6,000,000/3,000,000 = $2 per share. The post-money valuation will be ▶

the total number of shares multiplied by the price paid by the VC. The percentage of the firm owned by the VC is the number of her shares divided by the total number of shares. Your percentage will be the number of your shares divided by the total number of shares, and the value of your shares will be the number of shares you own multiplied by the price the VC paid.

Execute

There are 5 million shares and the VC paid $2 per share. Therefore, the post-money valuation would be 5,000,000 × $2 = $10 million, which, by Equation 14.1, equals the pre-money valuation ($4 million) plus the amount invested ($6 million).

Because she is buying 3 million shares, and there will be 5 million total shares outstanding after the funding round, the VC will end up owning 3,000,000/5,000,000 = 60% of the firm.

You will own 1,500,000/5,000,000 = 30% of the firm, and the post-money valuation of your shares is 1,500,000 × $2 = $3,000,000.

Evaluate

Funding your firm with new equity capital, whether it is from an angel or a venture capitalist, involves a trade-off—you must give up part of the ownership of the firm in return for the money you need to grow. If you can negotiate a higher price per share, the percentage of your firm that you will have to give up for a specified amount of capital will be smaller.

Over the next few years, Facebook raised several more rounds of outside equity in addition to the Series B funding round[3]

Funding Round	Date	Capital Raised	Ownership Sold to Investors	Founder/ Employee Ownership	Implied Valuation of Facebook
Series C	Oct 2007–April 2008	$375,000,000	2.5%	69.8%	$15,000,000,000
Series C	May–Nov 2009	$290,000,000	2.9%	66.9%	$10,000,000,000
Series C	June 2010	$120,000,000	0.6%	66.1%	$20,000,000,000
Common	Jan 2011	$1,500,000,000	3.0%	63.1%	$50,000,000,000

In each case, investors bought preferred stock in the private company. These investors were very similar to the profile of typical investors in private firms that we described earlier. Angel investors invested early and some continued to invest in later rounds as well. The other investors were primarily venture capital funds and wealthy individuals, like Li Ka-shing and Bono. Microsoft purchased most of the Series C stock as a corporate investor.

Exiting an Investment in a Private Company

exit strategy An important consideration for investors in private companies, it details how they will eventually realize the return from their investment.

Like any relationship, the one between a firm and its investors is subject to change as needs and resources develop. An important consideration for investors in private companies is their **exit strategy**—how they will eventually realize the return from their investment. Investors exit in two main ways: through an acquisition or through a public offering. Often, large corporations purchase successful start-up companies. In such a case, the acquiring company purchases the outstanding stock of the private company, allowing all investors to cash out. Roughly 86% of venture capital exits from 2011 to 2015

[3]Funding terms were private. Details are authors' estimates based on media reporting.

occurred through mergers or acquisitions with typical deal sizes in the range of $100 million to $150 million.[4] The alternative way for the company to allow its investors to liquidate their investment is to become a publicly traded company.

Over time, the value of a share of Facebook's stock and the size of its funding rounds increased. Because Goldman Sachs and its investors were willing to pay $1.5 billion for just 3% of the company in January 2011, the valuation of existing stock had increased significantly, representing a substantial capital gain for early investors. Because Facebook was still a private company, however, investors could not realize this gain by selling their stock in the public stock markets. In the next section, we discuss the process a firm goes through to sell shares to the public and have its shares traded on a public market.

CONCEPT CHECK

1. What are the main sources of funding for private companies to raise outside equity capital?
2. What is a venture capital firm?

14.2 Taking Your Firm Public: The Initial Public Offering

initial public offering (IPO) The process of selling stock to the public for the first time.

The process of selling stock to the public for the first time is called an **initial public offering (IPO)**. Headline-grabbing IPOs by Facebook, Alibaba, and Twitter have highlighted this stage in a company's growth. In this section, we look at the mechanics of IPOs in two cases—the traditional setup and recent innovations.

Advantages and Disadvantages of Going Public

Going public provides companies with greater liquidity and better access to capital. By going public, companies give their private equity investors the ability to diversify. In addition, public companies typically have access to much larger amounts of capital through the public markets, both in the IPO and in subsequent offerings. The average size of an IPO in Canada in 2016 was about $155 million. This may seem small compared to the largest IPOs in recent history. For example, the 29 largest equity issues in the world each raised $7 billion or more, as shown in Table 14.2. In Facebook's case, its last round of private equity funding raised about $1.5 billion in January 2011. It sold $16 billion in shares in its May 2012 IPO, with $6.8 billion in new financing and $9 billion to selling shareholders. Thus, as a public company, Facebook was able to raise substantially more money than when it was a private company.

The major advantage of undertaking an IPO is also one of the major disadvantages of an IPO: when investors sell their stake and thereby diversify their holdings, the equity holders of the corporation become more widely dispersed. This undermines investors' ability to monitor the company's management and thus represents a loss of control. Furthermore, once a company goes public, it must satisfy all of the requirements of public companies. Several high-profile corporate scandals during the early part of the twenty-first century prompted tougher regulations designed to address corporate abuses. Organizations such as the SEC in the United States, the provincial securities commissions in Canada, the securities exchanges (including the TSX, New York Stock Exchange, and NASDAQ), the U.S. Congress (through the Sarbanes-Oxley Act of 2002), and the Parliament of Canada adopted new standards that focused on more thorough financial disclosure, greater accountability, and more stringent requirements for the board of directors. In general, these standards were designed to provide better protection for investors. However, compliance with the new standards is costly and time-consuming for public companies.

[4]The National Venture Capital Association.

TABLE 14.2 Top 29 Global IPOs by Capital Raised as of 2016

Company Name	Offer Date	Exchange	Industry	Underwriter	Deal Size (Millions of $ USD)
Alibaba Group Holding	09/18/2014	NYSE	Technology	Credit Suisse	$21,767
ABC Bank	07/07/2010	Hong Kong / Shanghai	Financial	Goldman Sachs (Asia)	$19,228
ICBC Bank	10/20/2006	Hong Kong / Shanghai	Financial	Merrill Lynch	$19,092
NTT Mobile	10/22/1998	Tokyo Stock Exchange	Communications	Goldman Sachs (Asia)	$18,099
Visa	03/18/2008	NYSE	Financial	J.P. Morgan	$17,864
AIA	10/21/2010	Hong Kong	Financial	Citi	$17,816
ENEL SpA	11/01/1999	NYSE	Utilities	Merrill Lynch	$16,452
Facebook	05/17/2012	NASDAQ	Technology	Morgan Stanley	$16,007
General Motors	11/17/2010	NYSE	Capital Goods & Services	Morgan Stanley	$15,774
Nippon Tel	02/09/1987	Tokyo Stock Exchange	Communications	Nomura Securities	$15,301
Deutsche Telekom	11/17/1996	NYSE	Communications	Goldman, Sachs & Co	$13,034
Bank of China	05/24/2006	Hong Kong/Shanghai	Financial	Goldman, Sachs & Co.	$11,186
Dai-ichi Mutual Life Insurance	03/23/2010	Tokyo Stock Exchange	Financial	BofA Merrill Lynch	$10,986
AT&T Wireless Group	04/26/2000	NYSE	Communications	Goldman Sachs & Co.	$10,620
Rosneft Oil Company	07/13/2006	Russian Trading System	Energy	ABN AMRO	$10,421
Glencore International	05/19/2011	LSE Main/Hong Kong	Basic Resources	Citi	$10,316
Japan Tobacco Inc. (JT)	10/27/1994	Tokyo Stock Exchange	Consumer	Nomura Securities	$9,576
China Construction Bank	10/20/2005	Hong Kong/Shanghai	Financial	Morgan Stanley	$9,227
Kraft Foods	06/12/2001	NYSE	Consumer	Credit Suisse	$8,680
Electricite De France	11/18/2005	Euronext/Paris	Utilities	ABN AMRO	$8,328
Water Holding Co	11/22/1989	LSE Main	Utilities	Credit Suisse	$8,199
VTB Bank	05/10/2007	LSE Main	Financial	Citi	$7,988
Banader Hotels Co	11/20/2005	Bahrain Stock Exchange	Consumer	KPMG Corporate	$7,958
Telia AB	06/13/2000	OMX Nordic Exchange	Communications	Morgan Stanley	$7,728
British Gas PLC	12/08/1986	LSE Main	Energy	Goldman Sachs & Co.	$7,610
DDI Corp	09/03/1993	Tokyo Stock Exchange	Communications	Daiwa Securities	$7,592
China Engineering	07/23/2009	Shanghai	Capital Goods & Services	China International Capital	$7,343
France Telecom	10/17/1997	NYSE	Communications	Merrill Lynch	$7,289
Banco Santander Brasil	10/06/2009	NYSE/Bovespa	Financial	Santander Investment	$7,026

Source: Renaissance Capital, www.renaissancecapital.com, June 2016.

TABLE 14.3 Top Investment Banking Firms in Canada and Internationally

2016 Top 10 Canadian Equity and Equity-Related Issuers		
Bookrunner	**Proceeds (Millions of $ CAD)**	**# of Deals**
TD Securities	9,723.2	56
RBC Capital Markets	9,155.3	58
BMO Capital Markets	6,469.1	56
CIBC World Markets	5,825.8	45
Scotiabank	4,103.0	32
National Bank of Canada Financial	2,348.6	46
JP Morgan	1,718.6	2
Credit Suisse	1,598.3	5
Peters & Co. Ltd.	1,552.4	17
GMP Capital Corp.	1,063.1	28
2016 Top 10 International Equity and Equity-Related Issuers		
Bookrunner	**Proceeds (Millions of $ USD)**	**# of Deals**
JP Morgan	56,128.3	335
Morgan Stanley	47,789.1	264
Goldman Sachs & Co.	47,304.1	256
Bank of America Merril Lynch	32,702.9	222
Citi	29,864.7	234
Credit Suisse	27,747.4	206
Deutsche Bank	26,940.0	156
UBS	22,798.7	172
Barclays	20,266.9	145
CITIC	12,592.8	62

Source: Data from Thompson Reuters, "*Global Equity Capital Markets Review, Full Year 2016*" and "*Canada Capital Markets Review, Full Year 2016*".

Primary and Secondary IPO Offerings

underwriter An investment banking firm that manages a security issuance and designs its structure.

primary offering New shares available in a public offering that raise new capital.

secondary offering An equity offering of shares sold by existing shareholders (as part of their exit strategy).

lead underwriter The primary investment banking firm responsible for managing a security issuance.

After deciding to go public, managers of the company work with an **underwriter**, an investment banking firm that manages the security issuance and designs its structure. In this case, the underwriter is managing the company's offering of securities to the public. Choices for the offering's structure include the type of shares to be sold and the mechanism the underwriter will use to sell the stock.

At an IPO, a firm offers a large block of shares for sale to the public for the first time. The shares that are sold in the IPO may either be new shares that raise new capital, known as a **primary offering**, or existing shares that are sold by current shareholders (as part of their exit strategy), known as a **secondary offering**.

The traditional IPO process follows a standardized form. We will explore the steps that underwriters go through during an IPO.

Underwriters and the Syndicate. Many IPOs, especially the larger offerings, are managed by a group of underwriters. The **lead underwriter** is the primary investment banking firm responsible for managing the security issuance. The lead underwriter provides most of the advice on the sale and arranges for a group of other underwriters, called the **syndicate**, to help market and sell the issue. Table 14.3 shows the major underwriters of equity products (including IPOs) in Canada and globally during 2016.

syndicate A group of underwriters who jointly underwrite and distribute a security issuance.

Underwriters market the IPO and help the company with all the necessary filings. More importantly, as we discuss below, underwriters actively participate in determining the offer price. In many cases, the underwriter will also commit to making a market in the stock by matching buyers and sellers after the issue, thereby guaranteeing that the stock will be liquid.

Regulatory Filings. The relevant securities commissions (each provincial securities commission in Canada and the SEC in the United States) require that companies file certain legal documents that provide financial and other information about the company to investors, prior to an IPO. In the United States, this step is the preparation of the **registration statement**. Company managers work closely with the underwriters to prepare this registration statement and submit it to the securities commission. Part of the registration statement, called the **preliminary prospectus (red herring)**, circulates to investors before the stock is offered. In Canada, this first step is the preparation of the preliminary prospectus; there is no separate registration statement. The reason a preliminary prospectus is also called a red herring is because of the red writing on the prospectus, which indicates that the prospectus is not yet final, the information may not be complete, and the securities may not be sold until a receipt for the final prospectus is obtained from the relevant securities regulators. (Interestingly, the term "red herring" originates from the sport of fox hunting, where traditionally a red herring was used to distract the dogs and throw them off the scent of their prey.)

registration statement A legal document that provides financial and other information about a company to investors prior to a security issuance.

preliminary prospectus (red herring) Part of the registration statement prepared by a company prior to an IPO; it is circulated to investors before the stock is offered.

The securities regulators review the preliminary prospectus to make sure that the company has disclosed all of the information necessary for investors to decide whether to purchase the stock. Once the company has satisfied the regulators' disclosure requirements, the regulators approve the stock for sale to the general public. In Canada, the Ontario Securities Commission usually takes the lead in reviewing and approving the preliminary prospectus, and the other provincial securities commissions usually follow Ontario's decision. The company prepares the **final prospectus** containing all the details of the IPO, including the number of shares offered and the offer price.[5] It should be noted that both Canada and the U.S. allow for expedited processes to bring securities to the market; certain requirements must be fulfilled, such as continuous disclosure of required documents, minimums on market value of the issuer, or, for debt securities, minimum rating requirements. In Canada this system is called the Prompt Offering Qualification System, or POP System; in the U.S. it is SEC Rule 415, commonly called "shelf registration." The U.S. also allows Canadian firms relatively quick access to U.S. markets through the Multijurisdictional Disclosure System (MJDS).

final prospectus Part of the final registration statement prepared by a company prior to an IPO; it contains all the details of the offering, including the number of shares offered and the offer price.

To illustrate this process, let's return to Facebook. Figure 14.2 shows the cover page for the final prospectus for Facebook's IPO. This cover page includes the name of the company, the list of lead underwriters (with the co-lead underwriters shown first), and summary information about the pricing of the deal. This was a primary offering of 180 million shares and a secondary offering of 241 million shares.

Valuation. Before the offer price is set, the underwriters work closely with the company to come up with a price range that they believe provides a reasonable valuation for the firm using the techniques described in Chapter 7. As we pointed out in that chapter, there are two ways to value a company: estimate the future cash flows and compute the present value, or estimate the value by examining comparable companies. Most

[5]Canadian prospectuses may be found at SEDAR, the website for Canadian Securities Administrators: www.sedar.com. For U.S. registration statements, you can check EDGAR, the SEC website providing registration information to investors: www.sec.gov/edgar/searchedgar/webusers.htm.

road show The time, during an IPO, when a company's senior management and its lead underwriters travel to promote the company and explain their rationale for an offer price to institutional investors such as mutual funds and pension funds.

underwriters use both techniques. However, when these techniques give substantially different answers, underwriters often rely on comparables based on recent IPOs.

Once an initial price range is established, the underwriters try to determine what the market thinks of the valuation. They begin by arranging a **road show**, in which senior management and the lead underwriters travel around the country (and sometimes around the world) promoting the company and explaining their rationale for the offer price to the underwriters' largest customers—mainly institutional investors, such as mutual funds and pension funds.

FIGURE 14.2 **The Cover Page of Facebook's IPO Prospectus**

The cover page includes the name of the company, a list of lead underwriters, and summary information about the pricing of the offering.

PROSPECTUS

421,233,615 Shares

facebook

CLASS A COMMON STOCK

Facebook, Inc. is offering 180,000,000 shares of its Class A common stock and the selling stockholders are offering 241,233,615 shares of Class A common stock. We will not receive any proceeds from the sale of shares by the selling stockholders. This is our initial public offering and no public market currently exists for our shares of Class A common stock.

We have two classes of common stock, Class A common stock and Class B common stock. The rights of the holders of Class A common stock and Class B common stock are identical, except voting and conversion rights. Each share of Class A common stock is entitled to one vote. Each share of Class B common stock is entitled to ten votes and is convertible at any time into one share of Class A common stock. The holders of our outstanding shares of Class B common stock will hold approximately 96.0% of the voting power of our outstanding capital stock following this offering, and our founder, Chairman, and CEO, Mark Zuckerberg, will hold or have the ability to control approximately 55.9% of the voting power of our outstanding capital stock following this offering.

Our Class A common stock has been approved for listing on the NASDAQ Global Select Market under the symbol "FB."

We are a "controlled company" under the corporate governance rules for NASDAQ-listed companies, and our board of directors has determined not to have an independent nominating function and instead to have the full board of directors be directly responsible for nominating members of our board.

Investing in our Class A common stock involves risks. See "Risk Factors" beginning on page 12.

PRICE $38.00 A SHARE

	Price to Public	Underwriting Discounts and Commissions	Proceeds to Facebook	Proceeds to Selling Stockholders
Per share	$38.00	$0.418	$37.582	$37.582
Total	$16,006,877,370	$176,075,651	$6,764,760,000	$9,066,041,719

We and the selling stockholders have granted the underwriters the right to purchase up to an additional 63,185,042 shares of Class A common stock to cover over-allotments.

The Securities and Exchange Commission and state regulators have not approved or disapproved of these securities, or determined if this prospectus is truthful or complete. Any representation to the contrary is a criminal offense.

The underwriters expect to deliver the shares of Class A common stock to purchasers on May 22, 2012.

MORGAN STANLEY *J.P. MORGAN* *GOLDMAN, SACHS & CO.*

BofA MERRILL LYNCH *BARCLAYS* *ALLEN & COMPANY LLC*

CITIGROUP *CREDIT SUISSE* *DEUTSCHE BANK SECURITIES*

RBC CAPITAL MARKETS *WELLS FARGO SECURITIES*

Source: Securities and Exchange Commision

EXAMPLE 14.2 Valuing an IPO Using Comparables

PROBLEM

Wagner Inc. is a private company that designs, manufactures, and distributes branded consumer products. During its most recent fiscal year, Wagner had revenues of $325 million and earnings of $15 million. Wagner has filed a registration statement with the SEC for its IPO. Before the stock is offered, Wagner's investment bankers would like to estimate the value of the company using comparable companies. The investment bankers have assembled the following information based on data for other companies in the same industry that have recently gone public. In each case, the ratios are based on the IPO price.

Company	Price-Earnings	Price-Revenues
Ray Products Corp.	18.8×	1.2×
Byce-Frasier Inc.	19.5×	0.9×
Fashion Industries Group	24.1×	0.8×
Recreation International	22.4×	0.7×
Average	21.2×	0.9×

After the IPO, Wagner will have 20 million shares outstanding. Estimate the IPO price for Wagner using the price-earnings (P/E) ratio and the price-revenues ratio.

SOLUTION

Plan

If the IPO price of Wagner is based on a P/E ratio that is similar to those for recent IPOs, then this ratio will equal the average of recent deals. Thus, to compute the IPO price based on the P/E ratio, we will first take the average P/E ratio from the comparison group and multiply it by Wagner's total earnings. This will give us a total value of equity for Wagner. To get the per-share IPO price, we need to divide the total equity value by the number of shares outstanding after the IPO (20 million). The approach will be the same for the price-revenues ratio.

Execute

The average P/E ratio for recent deals is 21.2. Given earnings of $15 million, the total market value of Wagner's stock will be $15 million × 21.2 = $318 million. With 20 million shares outstanding, the price per share should be $318 million/20 million = $15.90.

Similarly, if Wagner's IPO price implies a price-revenues ratio equal to the recent average of 0.9, then using its revenues of $325 million, the total market value of Wagner will be $325 million × 0.9 = $292.5 million, or $14.63 per share ($292.5/20).

Evaluate

As we found in Chapter 7, using multiples for valuation always produces a range of estimates—you should not expect to get the same value from different ratios. Based on these estimates, the underwriters will probably establish an initial price range for Wagner stock of $13 to $17 per share to take on the road show.

At the end of the road show, customers inform the underwriters of their interest by telling the underwriters how many shares they may want to purchase. Although these commitments are nonbinding, the underwriters' customers value their long-term relationships with the underwriters, so they rarely go back on their word. The underwriters then add up the total demand and adjust the price until it is unlikely that the issue will fail. This process for coming up with the offer price based on customers' expressions of interest is called **book building**.

book building A process used by underwriters for coming up with an offer price based on customers' expressions of interest.

firm commitment An agreement between an underwriter and an issuing firm in which the underwriter guarantees that it will sell all of the stock at the offer price that is set at a time shortly before the final prospectus is issued.

bought deal An agreement between an underwriter and an issuing firm in which the underwriter guarantees that it will sell all of the stock at a contracted price, but where the price is agreed upon prior to the preliminary prospectus being issued.

spread The fee a company pays to its underwriters that is a percentage of the issue price of a share of stock.

Pricing the Deal and Managing Risk. In the most common arrangement, an underwriter and an issuing firm agree to a **firm commitment** IPO, in which the underwriter guarantees that it will sell all of the stock at the offer price (which is set a short time prior to the final prospectus being issued). The underwriter purchases the entire issue (at a slightly lower price than the offer price) and then resells it at the offer price. If the entire issue does not sell out, the underwriter is on the hook: the remaining shares must be sold at a lower price, and the underwriter must take the loss. The most notorious loss happened when the British government privatized British Petroleum. In a highly unusual deal, the company was taken public gradually. The British government sold its final stake in British Petroleum at the time of the October 1987 stock market crash. The offer price was set just before the crash, but the offering occurred after the crash.[6] At the end of the first day's trading, the underwriters were facing a loss of $1.29 billion. The price then fell even further, until the Kuwaiti Investment Office stepped in and started purchasing a large stake in the company. In Canada, public offerings may also be structured under what is called the Bought Deal Exemption whereby the underwriter enters into an enforceable contract with the issuer to purchase the securities from the issuer at a set price *prior* to the filing of the preliminary prospectus. When structured as a **bought deal**, the underwriter is allowed to do earlier pre-marketing of the offering than in a firm commitment offering; this helps ensure that there will be a market for the securities when issued and thus helps to mitigate the risk the underwriter has taken by providing an earlier guarantee to the issuer of the funds to be raised.

In the Facebook IPO, the final offer price was $38.00 per share. The company agreed to pay the underwriters a fee, called a **spread**, which is a percentage of the issue price of a share of stock, in this case $0.418 per share—1.1% of the issue price. Because this was a firm commitment deal, the underwriters bought the stock from Facebook and the selling shareholders for $38.00 − $0.418 = $37.582 per share and then resold it to their customers for $38.00 per share. A spread of 1.1% is quite low for such an IPO, we will see later in the chapter that more typical spreads are around 7%.

Recall that when an underwriter provides a firm commitment, it is potentially exposing itself to the risk that the investment banking firm might have to sell the shares at less than the offer price and take a loss. However, according to Tim Loughran and Jay Ritter, between 1990 and 1998, just 9% of U.S. IPOs experienced a fall in share price on the first day.[7] For another 16% of firms, the price at the end of the first day was the same as the offer price. Therefore, the vast majority of IPOs experienced a price increase on the first day of trading, indicating that the initial offer price was generally lower than the price that stock market investors were willing to pay.

---

[6]This deal was exceptional in that the offer price was determined more than a week before the issue date. Typically, the underwriter usually sets the final offer price within a day of the IPO date.

[7]Tim Loughran and Jay Ritter, "Why Don't Issuers Get Upset About Leaving Money on the Table in IPOs?" *Review of Financial Studies* 15 (2) (2002): 413–443.

Underwriters appear to use the information they acquire during the book-building stage to intentionally underprice the IPO, thereby reducing their exposure to losses. Furthermore, once the issue price (or offer price) is set, underwriters may invoke another mechanism that allows them to sell extra shares of more successful offerings—the **over-allotment allocation (greenshoe provision)**.[8] This option allows the underwriter to issue more stock, amounting to 15% of the original offer size, at the IPO offer price. In the case of Facebook, the underwriters had the option to purchase additional shares to cover over-allotments, up to 63 million shares, at the underwriter discount price of $37.582 for 30 days after the stock started trading.

over-allotment allocation (greenshoe provision) In an IPO, an option that allows the underwriter to issue more stock, usually amounting to 15% of the original offer size, at the IPO offer price.

Once the IPO process is complete, the company's shares trade publicly on an exchange. The lead underwriter usually makes a market in the stock by matching buyers and sellers, and assigns an analyst to cover it. By doing so, the underwriter increases the liquidity of the stock in the secondary market. This service is of value to both the issuing company and the underwriter's customers. A liquid market ensures that investors who purchased shares via the IPO are able to trade those shares easily. If the stock is actively traded, the issuer will have continued access to the equity markets in the event that the company decides to issue more shares in a new offering. In most cases, the existing shareholders are subject to a **lockup**, a restriction that prevents them from selling their shares for some period (usually 180 days) after the IPO. Once the lockup period expires, they are free to sell their shares.

lockup A restriction that prevents existing shareholders from selling their shares for some period (usually 180 days) after an IPO.

Other IPO Types

Now that we have established the traditional method for IPOs, we will discuss three other ways shares may be sold during an IPO.

Best-Efforts Basis. For smaller IPOs, the underwriter commonly accepts the deal on a **best efforts** basis. In this case, the underwriter does not guarantee that the stock will be sold but instead tries to sell the stock for the best possible price. Often, such deals have an all-or-none clause: either all of the shares are sold in the IPO, or the deal is called off.

best efforts For smaller IPOs; a situation in which the underwriter does not guarantee that the stock will be sold but instead tries to sell the stock for the best possible price.

Auction IPO. In the late 1990s, the investment banking firm of W. R. Hambrecht and Company attempted to change the IPO process by selling new issues directly to the public using an online **auction IPO** mechanism called OpenIPO. Rather than setting the price itself in the traditional way, Hambrecht's method lets the market determine the price of the stock by auctioning off the company.[9] Investors place bids over a set period of time. An auction IPO then sets the highest price such that the number of bids at or above that price equals the number of offered shares. All winning bidders pay this price, even if their bids were higher. The first OpenIPO was the $11.55 million IPO for Ravenswood Winery, completed in 1999.

auction IPO An online method for selling new issues directly to the public, which lets the market determine the price through bids from potential investors.

It's easier to understand how an auction IPO works by considering an example. Your firm is planning an auction IPO for 3 million shares. Potential buyers submit bids at various prices and their bids are then aggregated. Table 14.4 summarizes those bids. The column "Shares Sought at This Price" shows the total number of shares from investors' bids at each price. The last column contains the total number of shares bid at *or above* each price. Because investors are willing to buy at prices lower than the amount they bid, this total represents the number of shares that can be sold at each price. For example, while investors were willing to buy a total of only 75,000 shares at a price of $19.50, at a price of $19.00 a total of 225,000 (150,000 + 75,000) can be sold.

---

[8]The name derives from the Green Shoe Company, the first issuer to have an over-allotment option in its IPO.

[9]You can find details about Hambrecht's auction IPO process at the following website: www.wrhambrecht.com/ind/auctions/openipo/.

TABLE 14.4 Bids Received to Purchase Shares in a Hypothetical Auction IPO

Price	Shares Sought at This Price (in thousands)	Total Shares Sought at or above This Price (in thousands)
$16.50	3200	11,800
$17.00	2900	8600
$17.50	2700	5700
$18.00	1925	3000
$18.50	850	1075
$19.00	150	225
$19.50	75	75

You are interested in selling a total of 3 million shares at the highest price possible. This suggests that you should look in the left column of Table 14.4 to find the highest price at which the total demand is at least 3 million shares. In this case, the highest price at which we can sell 3 million shares is $18. Figure 14.3 shows this graphically.

Although the auction IPO mechanism seems to represent an attractive alternative to traditional IPO procedures, it has not been widely adopted either in Canada, the United States, or abroad. Between 1999 and 2010, Hambrecht completed only 19 auction IPOs (the last two in 2007). This represents less than 1% of the number of IPOs brought to market during that time period. However, in 2004, Google went public using

FIGURE 14.3 Aggregating the Shares Sought in the Hypothetical Auction IPO

The figure graphs the last column in Table 14.4, which indicates the total number of shares that can be sold at each price. In this case, investors are willing to buy a total of 3 million shares at or above a price of $18. So, you would set your IPO price at $18 to give you the highest price at which you could place 3 million shares.

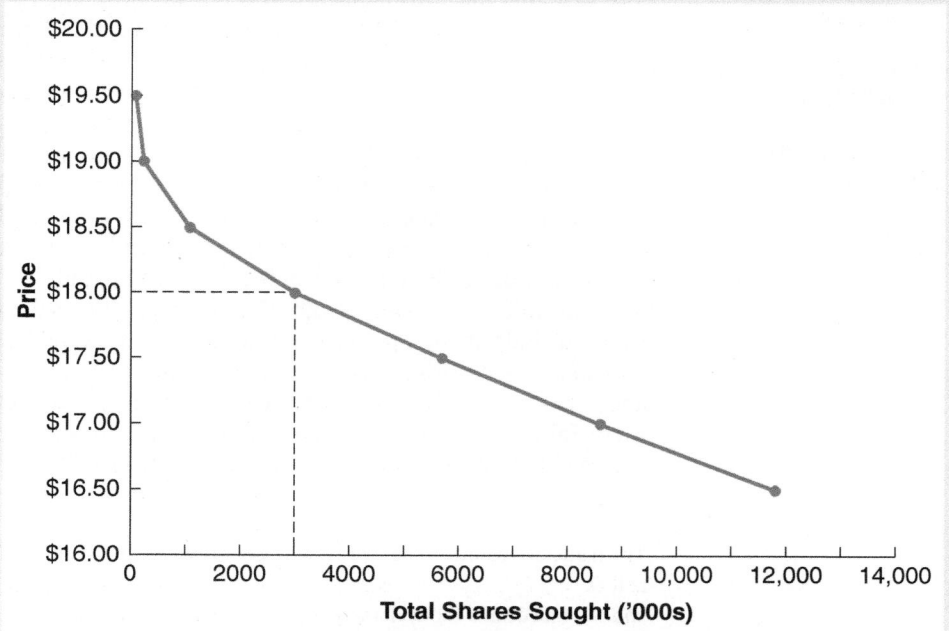

EXAMPLE 14.3 Auction IPO Pricing

PROBLEM

Fleming Educational Software, Inc. is selling 500,000 shares of stock in an auction IPO. At the end of the bidding period, Fleming's investment bank has received the following bids:

Price ($)	Number of Shares Bid
8.00	25,000
7.75	100,000
7.50	75,000
7.25	150,000
7.00	150,000
6.75	275,000
6.50	125,000

What will the offer price of the shares be?

SOLUTION

Plan

First, we must compute the total number of shares demanded at or above any given price. Then, we pick the highest price that will allow us to sell the full issue (500,000 shares).

Execute

Converting the table of bids into a table of cumulative demand, we have

Price ($)	Cumulative Demand
8.00	25,000
7.75	125,000
7.50	200,000
7.25	350,000
7.00	500,000
6.75	775,000
6.50	900,000

For example, the company has received bids for a total of 125,000 shares at $7.75 per share or higher (25,000 + 100,000 = 125,000).

Fleming is offering a total of 500,000 shares. The winning auction price would be $7 per share, because investors have placed orders for a total of 500,000 shares at a price of $7 or higher. All investors who placed bids of at least this price will be able to buy the stock for $7 per share, even if their initial bid was higher.

In this example, the cumulative demand at the winning price exactly equals the supply. If the total demand at this price were greater than the supply, all auction participants who bid prices higher than the winning price would receive their full bid (at the winning price). Shares would be awarded on a pro rata basis to bidders who bid exactly the winning price.

Evaluate

Although the auction IPO does not provide the certainty of the firm commitment, it has the advantage of using the market to determine the offer price. It also reduces the underwriter's role and, consequently, fees.

the auction mechanism (see the box describing Google's IPO), which generated temporarily renewed interest in this alternative. In May 2007, Interactive Brokers Group raised $1.2 billion in its IPO using a Hambrecht OpenIPO auction.

Because no offer price is set in an auction IPO, book building is not as important in that venue as it is in traditional IPOs. In a recent paper, Professors Ravi Jagannathan and Ann Sherman examine why auctions have failed to become a popular IPO method and why they have been plagued by inaccurate pricing and poor performance following the issue. They suggest that because auctions do not use the book-building process, which aids in collecting large investors' valuations of the stock, investors are discouraged from participating in auctions.[10] Table 14.5 summarizes the methods a firm can use for an IPO of its stock.

TABLE 14.5 Summary of IPO Methods

Firm Commitment	Best Efforts	Auction IPO
Underwriter purchases the entire issue at an agreed price and sells it to investors at a higher price.	Underwriter makes its "best effort" to sell the issue to investors at an agreed price.	Firm or underwriter solicits bids (price and quantity) from investors, and chooses the highest price at which there is sufficient demand to sell the entire issue.

GOOGLE'S IPO

On April 29, 2004, Google, Inc. announced plans to go public. Breaking with tradition, Google startled Wall Street by declaring its intention to rely heavily on the auction IPO mechanism for distributing its shares. Google had been profitable since 2001, so according to Google executives, access to capital was not the only motive for going public. The company also wanted to provide employees and private equity investors with liquidity.

One of the major attractions of the auction mechanism was the possibility of allocating shares to more individual investors. Google also hoped to set an accurate offer price by letting market bidders set the IPO price. After the internet stock market boom, there were many lawsuits related to the way underwriters allocated shares. Google hoped to avoid the allocation scandals by letting the auction allocate shares.

Investors who wanted to bid opened a brokerage account with one of the deal's underwriters and then placed their bids with the brokerage house. Google and its underwriters identified the highest bid that allowed the company to sell all of the shares being offered. They also had the flexibility to choose to offer shares at a lower price.

On August 18, 2004, Google sold 19.6 million shares at $85 per share. The $1.67 billion raised was easily the largest auction IPO ever. Google stock (ticker symbol: GOOG) opened trading on the NASDAQ market the next day at $100 per share. Although the Google IPO sometimes stumbled along the way, it represents the most significant example of the use of the auction mechanism as an alternative to the traditional IPO mechanism.

Source: Kevin Delaney and Robin Sidel, "Google IPO Aims to Change the Rules," *Wall Street Journal*, April 30, 2004, p. C1; Ruth Simon and Elizabeth Weinstein, "Investors Eagerly Anticipate Google's IPO," *Wall Street Journal*, April 30, 2004, p. C1; Gregory Zuckerman, "Google Shares Prove Big Winners—for a Day," *Wall Street Journal*, August 20, 2004, p. C1.

CONCEPT CHECK

3. What services does the underwriter provide in a traditional IPO?
4. Explain the mechanics of an auction IPO.

[10]Ravi Jagannathan and Ann Sherman, "Why Do IPO Auctions Fail?" NBER working paper 12151, March 2006.

14.3 IPO Puzzles

Four characteristics of IPOs puzzle financial economists, and all are relevant to the financial manager:

1. On average, IPOs appear to be underpriced; the price at the end of trading on the first day is often substantially higher than the IPO price.
2. The number of IPOs is highly cyclical. When times are good, the market is flooded with IPOs; when times are bad, the number of IPOs dries up.
3. The transaction costs of the IPO are very high, and it is unclear why firms willingly incur such high costs.
4. The long-run performance of a newly public company (three to five years from the date of issue) is poor. That is, on average, a three- to five-year buy-and-hold strategy appears to be a bad investment.

We will now examine each of these puzzles that financial economists seek to understand.

Underpriced IPOs

For Facebook, the underwriters offered the stock at an IPO price of $38.00 per share on May 18, 2012. Facebook stock opened trading on the NASDAQ at a price of $42.05 per share, and traded as high as $45 before closing at $38.23. This lack of underpricing is not at all typical. For example, when Twitter had its IPO, its stock closed more than 72% above its offer price on its first day of trading. As is evident in Figure 14.4, the one-day average return for IPOs has historically been very large around the world. Note that although underpricing is a persistent and global phenomenon, it is generally smaller in more developed capital markets.

Who benefits from the offer price being set below the market price at the end of the first day of trading (underpricing)? We have already explained how the underwriters benefit by controlling their risk—it is much easier to sell the firm's shares if the price is set low. Of course, investors who are able to buy stock from underwriters at the IPO price also gain from the first-day underpricing. Who bears the cost? The pre-IPO shareholders of the issuing firms do. In effect, these owners are selling stock in their firm for less than they could get in the aftermarket.

"Hot" and "Cold" IPO Markets

Figure 14.5 shows the number of U.S. IPOs by year from 1975 to 2015. As the figure makes clear, the volume of IPOs has grown significantly, reaching a peak in 1999–2000. An even more important feature of the data is that the trends related to the number of issues are cyclical. Sometimes, as in 1996, the volume of IPOs is unprecedented by historical standards, yet within a year or two the volume of IPOs may decrease significantly.

This cyclicality by itself is not particularly surprising. We would expect there to be a greater need for capital in times with more growth opportunities than in times with fewer growth opportunities. What is surprising is the magnitude of the swings. For example, it is difficult to explain the almost seven-fold increase in IPOs from the early to mid-1990s, and the nearly 75% drop from 2000 to 2001 and a 45% drop from 2014 to 2015. It appears that the number of IPOs is not solely driven by the demand for capital. Sometimes, firms and investors seem to favour IPOs; at other times, firms appear to rely on alternative sources of capital.

FIGURE 14.4 International Comparison of First-Day IPO Returns

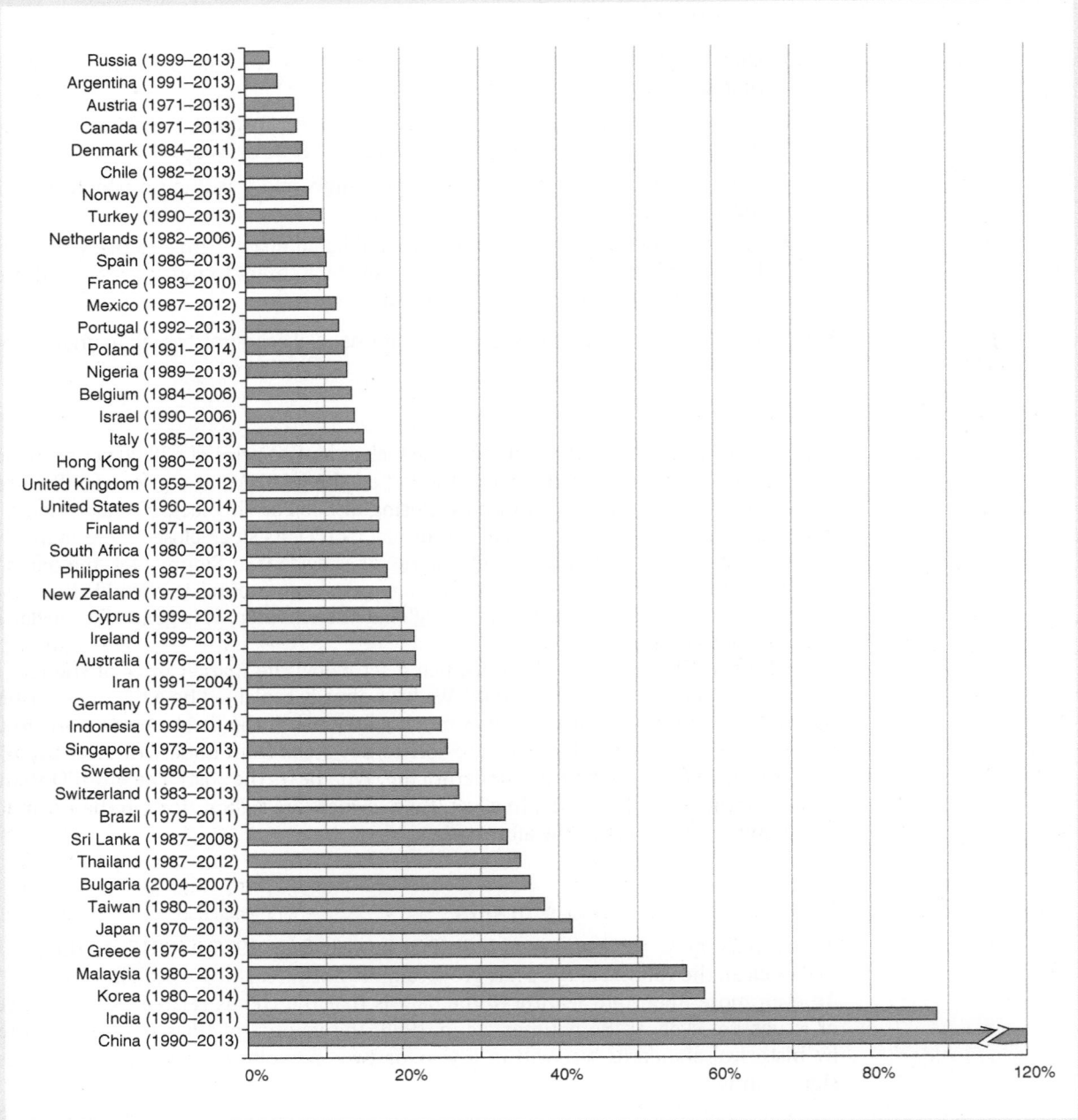

The bars show the average intial returns from the offer price to the first closing market proce. For China, the bar shows the average initial return on A share IPOs, available only to residents of China. The date in parantheses indicates the sample period for each country.
Source: Adapted courtesy of Jay Ritter (https://site.warrington.ufl.edu/ritter/ipo-data/).

FIGURE 14.5 **Cyclicality of Initial Public Offerings in the United States (1975–2012)**

The graph shows the number of IPOs by year. The number of IPOs reached a peak in 1996, demonstrating that trends related to the number of issues are highly cyclical.

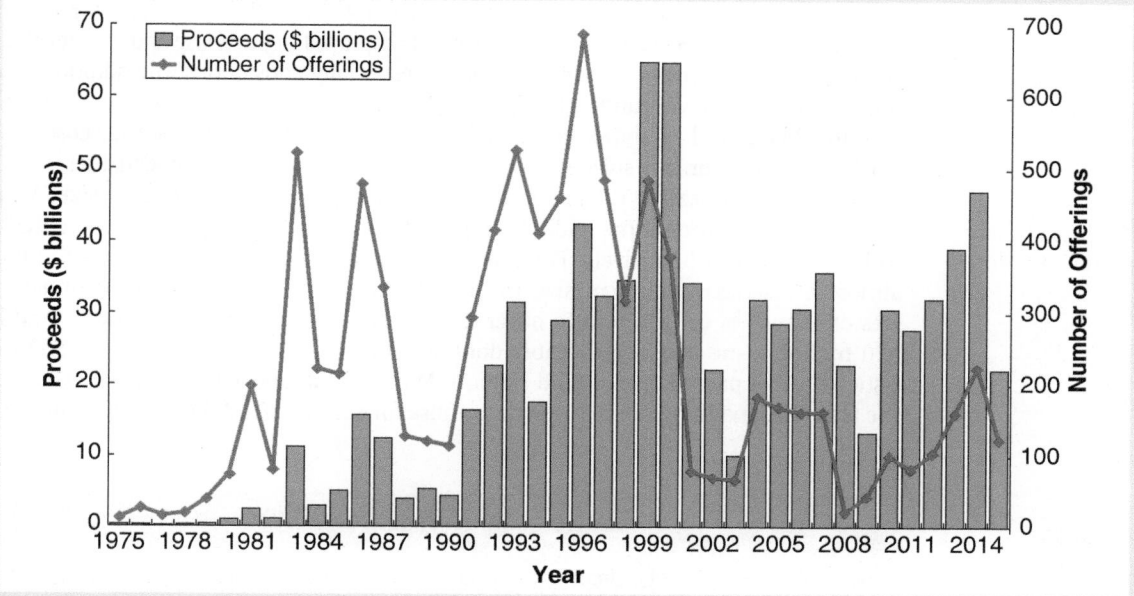

Source: Adapted courtesy of Jay Ritter (http://site.warrington.ufl.edu/ritter/ipo-data/).

GLOBAL FINANCIAL CRISIS 2008–2009: A VERY COLD IPO MARKET

The drop in IPO issues during the 2008 financial crisis was both global and dramatic. The bar graph shows the total, worldwide dollar volume of IPO proceeds in billions of dollars (blue bars) and number of deals (red line), by quarter, from the last quarter of 2006 to the first quarter of 2009. Comparing the fourth quarter of 2007 (a record quarter for IPO issues) to the fourth quarter of 2008, dollar volume dropped a stunning 97% from $102 billion to just $3 billion. Things got even worse in the first quarter of 2009 with just $1.4 billion raised. The market for IPOs essentially dried up altogether.

During the 2008 financial crisis, IPO markets were not the only equity issue markets that saw a collapse in volume. Markets for seasoned equity offerings and leveraged buyouts also collapsed. The extreme market uncertainty at the time created a "flight to quality." Investors, wary of taking risk, sought to move their capital into risk-free investments like U.S. Treasury securities. The result was a crash in existing equity prices and a greatly reduced supply of new capital to risky asset classes.

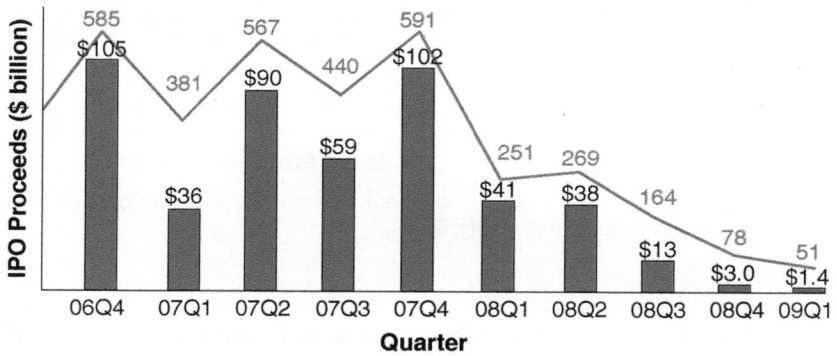

High Cost of Issuing an IPO

In the United States, a typical spread—that is, the discount below the issue price at which the underwriter purchases the shares from the issuing firm—is about 7% of the issue price. For an issue size of $50 million, this amounts to $3.5 million. This fee covers the cost to the underwriter of managing the syndicate and helping the company prepare for the IPO, as well as providing it with a return on the capital employed to purchase and market the issue. By most standards, however, this fee is large, especially considering the additional cost to the firm associated with underpricing. Internationally, spreads are generally about half this amount. As Figure 14.6 shows, compared with other security issues, the total cost of issuing stock for the first time is substantially larger than the costs for other securities.

Even more puzzling is the seeming lack of sensitivity of fees to issue size. Although a large issue requires some additional effort, one would not expect the increased effort to be rewarded as lucratively. For example, Hsuan-Chi Chen and Jay Ritter found that almost all issues ranging in size from $20 million to $80 million paid underwriting fees of about 7% (in addition to other direct costs).[11] It is difficult to understand how a $20 million issue can be profitably done for "only" $1.4 million, while an $80 million issue requires paying fees of $5.6 million. Maher Kooli and Jean-Marc Suret found that the fees for Canadian IPOs are less than those for *similar-sized* IPOs in the United States.

FIGURE 14.6 Relative Costs of Issuing Securities

This figure shows the total direct costs (all underwriting, legal, and auditing costs) of issuing securities as a percentage of the amount of money raised. The figure reports results for IPOs, seasoned equity offerings (subsequent equity offerings), convertible bonds, and standard bonds for issues of different sizes from 1990 to 1994.

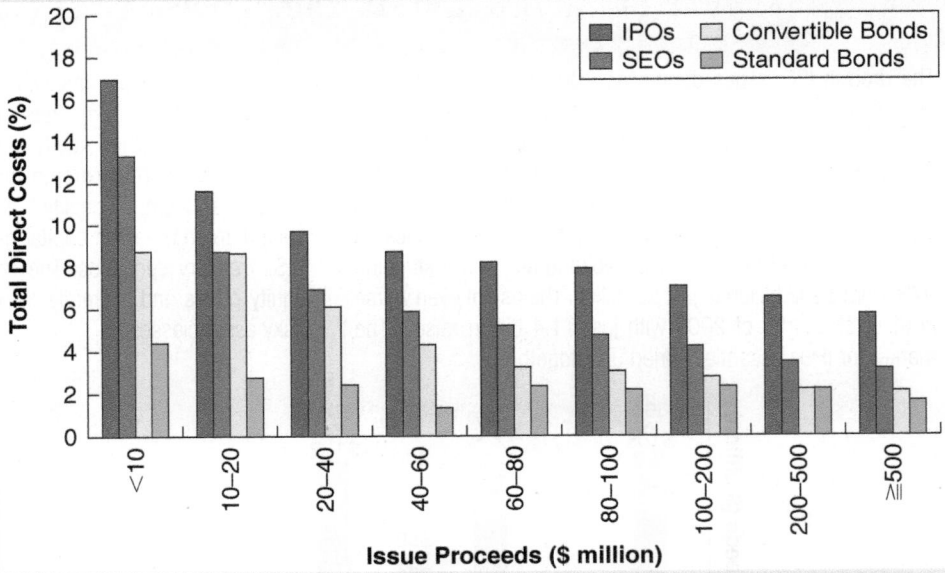

Source: Adapted from I. Lee, S. Lochhead, J. Ritter, and Q. Zhao, "The Costs of Raising Capital," *Journal of Financial Research* 19 (1) (1996): 59–74.

[11]Hsuan-Chi Chen and Jay R. Ritter, "The Seven Percent Solution," *Journal of Finance* 55 (3) (2000): 1105–1131.

For a $50 million IPO, the Canadian spread is only about 6%, compared to 7% in the United States. However, most Canadian IPOs are much smaller than U.S. IPOs. The average Canadian IPO is only about one-fifteenth as large as the average U.S. IPO. For very small IPOs, there is sensitivity of fees to issue size. The total fee, as a percentage of the IPO size, is substantially higher than for large IPOs. As a result, Kooli and Suret also found that when the total fee as a percentage of the IPO size is calculated for every IPO, the average percentage spread across all IPOs in Canada is higher than the average percentage spread across all IPOs in the United States.[12]

Poor Post-IPO Long-Run Stock Performance

We know that the shares of IPOs generally perform very well immediately following the public offering. It's perhaps surprising, then, that Jay Ritter found that newly listed firms subsequently appear to perform relatively poorly over the three to five years following their IPOs.[13] Vijay Jog and A. Srivastava found similar results in Canada. Between 1972 and 1993, IPOs underperformed the TSE 300 market index by 17.9%.[14] This creates a puzzle as to why investors are willing to pay as much as they do for the shares when they begin trading after the IPO.

As we will see in the next section, underperformance is not unique to an initial public issuance of equity; it is associated with subsequent issuances as well. Recently, researchers have begun to explore the possibility that underperformance might not result from the issue of equity itself, but rather from the conditions that motivated the equity issuance in the first place. We will explain this idea in more detail in the next section after we explain how a public company issues additional equity.

CONCEPT CHECK

5. List and discuss four characteristics about IPOs that are puzzling.
6. For each characteristic, identify its relevance to financial managers.

14.4 Raising Additional Capital: The Seasoned Equity Offering

seasoned equity offering (SEO) A public company's return to the equity markets with an offer of new shares for sale.

A firm's need for outside capital rarely ends at the IPO. Usually, profitable growth opportunities occur throughout the life of the firm, and in some cases it is not feasible to finance these opportunities out of retained earnings. Thus, a public company more often than not returns to the equity markets and offers new shares for sale in a type of offering called a **seasoned equity offering (SEO)**.

---

[12]Maher Kooli and Jean-Marc Suret, "How Cost-Effective are Canadian IPO Markets?" *Canadian Investment Review* (Winter) (2003): 20–28.

[13]Jay R. Ritter, "The Long-Run Performance of Initial Public Offerings," *Journal of Finance* 46 (1) (1991): 3–27.

[14]Vijay Jog and Ashwani Srivastava, "Underpricing of Canadian Initial Public Offerings 1971–1992—an Update," *FINECO* (1994): 81–89.

SEO Process

primary shares New shares issued by a company in an equity offering.

secondary shares Shares sold by existing shareholders in an equity offering.

When issuing stock using an SEO, a firm follows many of the same steps as for an IPO. The main difference is that a market price for the stock already exists, so the price-setting process is not necessary.

Facebook has conducted one SEO as of mid-2016. On December 19, 2013, the firm offered 70 million shares in an SEO at a price of $55.05 per share. Of these shares, 27 million were **primary shares** —new shares issued by the company. The remaining 43 million shares were **secondary shares** —shares sold by existing shareholders, including the company's founder, Mark Zuckerberg, who sold 41 million of his 485 million shares. Figure 14.7 shows the cover page of the prospectus for the Facebook SEO.

FIGURE 14.7 Tombstone Advertisement for a Facebook SEO

PROSPECTUS

70,000,000 Shares

facebook

Class A Common Stock

Facebook, Inc. is offering 27,004,761 shares of its Class A common stock and the selling stockholders are offering 42,995,239 shares of Class A common stock. We will not receive any proceeds from the sale of shares by the selling stockholders.

We have two classes of common stock, Class A common stock and Class B common stock. The rights of the holders of Class A common stock and Class B common stock are identical, except voting and conversion rights. Each share of Class A common stock is entitled to one vote. Each share of Class B common stock is entitled to ten votes and is convertible at any time into one share of Class A common stock. The holders of our outstanding shares of Class B common stock will hold approximately 75.4% of the voting power of our outstanding capital stock following this offering, and our Chairman and CEO, Mark Zuckerberg, will hold or have the ability to control approximately 62.8% of the voting power of our outstanding capital stock following this offering.

Our Class A common stock is listed on the NASDAQ Global Select Market under the symbol "FB." On December 20, 2013, the reported closing sale price of our Class A common stock on the NASDAQ Global Select Market was $55.10 per share.

Investing in our Class A common stock involves risks. See "Risk Factors" beginning on page 4.

PRICE $55.05 A SHARE

	Price to Public	Underwriting Discounts and Commissions (1)	Proceeds to Facebook	Proceeds to Selling Stockholders
Per share	$55.05	$0.2752	$54.7748	$54.7748
Total	$3,853,500,000	$19,264,000	$1,479,180,383	$2,355,055,617

(1) See "Underwriting."

The Securities and Exchange Commission and state regulators have not approved or disapproved of these securities, or determined if this prospectus is truthful or complete. Any representation to the contrary is a criminal offense.

The underwriters expect to deliver the shares of Class A common stock to purchasers on December 26, 2013.

J.P. MORGAN BofA MERRILL LYNCH MORGAN STANLEY BARCLAYS

BNP PARIBAS CITIGROUP RBC CAPITAL MARKETS

CREDIT SUISSE HSBC

RBS STANDARD CHARTERED PIPER JAFFRAY

ALLEN & COMPANY LLC

Source: Securities and Exchange Commision

tombstone Newspaper advertisement in which underwriters advertise a security issuance.

cash offer A type of seasoned equity offering (SEO) in which a firm offers the new shares to investors at large.

rights offer A type of seasoned equity offering (SEO) in which a firm offers the new shares only to existing shareholders.

Historically, underwriters would advertise the sale of stock (both IPOs and SEOs) by taking out a newspaper advertisements called a **tombstone**. Through these ads, investors would know who to call to buy stock. Today, investors become informed about the impending sale of stock by the news media, via a road show, or through the book-building process, so these tombstones are purely ceremonial.

Two types of SEOs exist: a cash offer and a rights offer. In a **cash offer**, the firm offers the new shares to investors at large. In a **rights offer**, the firm offers the new shares only to existing shareholders. In Canada and the United States, most offers are cash offers, but the same is not true elsewhere. For example, in the United Kingdom, most seasoned offerings of new shares are rights offers.

Rights offers protect existing shareholders from underpricing. To illustrate, suppose a company holds $100 in cash as its sole asset and has 50 shares outstanding. Each share is worth $2. The company announces a cash offer for 50 shares at $1 per share. Once this offer is complete, the company will have $150 in cash and 100 shares outstanding. The price per share is now $1.50 to reflect the fact that the new shares were sold at a discount. The new shareholders therefore receive a $0.50 per-share windfall at the expense of the old shareholders.

The old shareholders would be protected if, instead of a cash offer, the company did a rights offer. In this case, rather than offer the new shares for general sale, every shareholder would have the right to purchase an additional share for $1 per share. If all shareholders chose to exercise their rights, then after the sale the value of the company would be the same as with a cash offer: it would be worth $150 with 100 shares outstanding and a price of $1.50 per share. In this case, however, the $0.50 windfall accrues to existing shareholders, which exactly offsets the drop in the stock price. Thus, if a firm's management is concerned that its equity may be underpriced in the market, by using a rights offer the firm can continue to issue equity without imposing a loss on its current shareholders.

EXAMPLE 14.4 Raising Money with Rights Offers

PROBLEM

You are the CFO of a company that has a market capitalization of $1 billion. The firm has 100 million shares outstanding, so the shares are trading at $10 per share. You need to raise $200 million and have announced a rights issue. Each existing shareholder is sent one right for every share he or she owns. You have not decided how many rights you will require to purchase a share of new stock. You will require either four rights to purchase one share at a price of $8 per share, or five rights to purchase two new shares at a price of $5 per share. Which approach will raise more money?

SOLUTION

■ Plan

In order to know how much money will be raised, we need to compute how many total shares would be purchased if all shareholders exercise their rights. Then we can multiply it by the price per share to calculate the total amount of capital raised.

■ Execute

There are 100 million shares, each with one right attached. In the first case, four rights will be needed to purchase a new share, so 100 million/4 = 25 million new shares will be purchased. At a price of $8 per share, that would raise $8 × 25 million = $200 million. ▶

In the second case, for every five rights, two new shares can be purchased, so there will be $2 \times (100 \text{ million}/5) = 40$ million new shares. At a price of \$5 per share, that would also raise \$200 million. If all shareholders exercise their rights, both approaches will raise the same amount of money.

Evaluate

In both cases, the value of the firm after the issue is \$1.2 billion. In the first case, there are 125 million shares outstanding after the issue, so the price per share after the issue is \$1.2 billion/125 million = \$9.60. This price exceeds the issue price of \$8, so the shareholders will exercise their rights. Because exercising will yield a profit of (\$9.60 − \$8.00)/4 = \$0.40 per right), the total value per share to each shareholder is \$9.60 + 0.40 = \$10.0. In the second case, the number of shares outstanding will grow to 140 million, resulting in a post-issue stock price of \$1.2 billion/140 million shares = \$8.57 per share (also higher than the issue price). Again, the shareholders will exercise their rights, and receive a total value per share of \$8.57 + 2(\$8.57 − \$5.00)/5 = \$10.0. Thus, in both cases the same amount of money is raised and shareholders are equally well off.

SEO Price Reaction

Researchers have found that, on average, the market greets the news of an SEO with a price decline. Often, the value lost due to the price decline can be a significant fraction of the new money raised. Figure 14.8 shows the typical stock price reaction when an SEO is announced. To see why the market price of the stock drops when an SEO is announced,

FIGURE 14.8 Price Reaction to an SEO Announcement

The figure shows the typical stock price reaction to the announcement of an SEO. The days are relative to the announcement day, so that day 0 is the announcement day. Notice that the stock price is typically increasing prior to the announcement—managers do not like to issue stock when its price has been dropping. Also note that the stock drops by about 1.5% when the SEO is announced and remains relatively flat afterward. The data include all SEOs from 2004 to 2007.

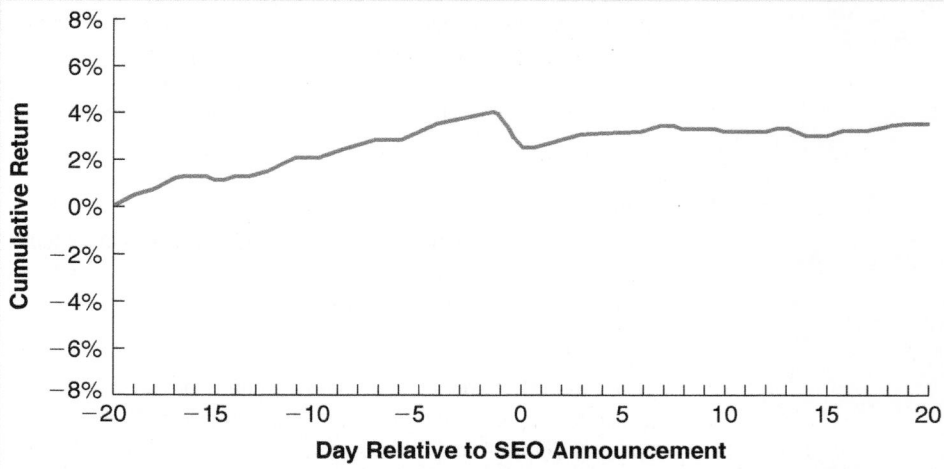

Source: © 2011 CRSP®, Center for Research in Security Prices, Booth School of Business, The University of Chicago and authors' calculations. Used with permission. All rights reserved. www.crsp.chicagobooth.edu.

consider the following situation. Suppose a used-car dealer tells you he is willing to sell you a nice-looking sports car for $5000 less than its typical price. Rather than feel lucky, perhaps your first thought is that there must be something wrong with the car—it is probably a "lemon." Buyers will be skeptical of a seller's motivation for selling, because the seller has private information about the quality of the car. Thus, his *desire to sell* reveals the car is probably of low quality. Buyers are therefore reluctant to buy except at heavily discounted prices. Owners of high-quality cars are reluctant to sell because they know buyers will think they are selling a lemon and offer only a low price. Consequently, the quality and prices of cars sold in the used-car market are both low. This lemons principle—that when quality is hard to judge, the average quality of goods being offered for sale will be low—is referred to as **adverse selection**.

adverse selection The idea, reflecting the lemons principle, that when quality is hard to judge, the average quality of goods being offered for sale will be low.

The lemons problem is very real for financial managers contemplating selling new equity. Because managers concerned about protecting their existing shareholders will tend to sell only at a price that correctly values or overvalues the firm, investors infer from the decision to sell that the company is likely to be overvalued. As a result, the price drops with the announcement of the SEO.

As with IPOs, there are several puzzles surrounding SEOs. First, by offering a rights issue, a company can mitigate the problem leading to the price decline. (Because it is offering the shares directly to its existing shareholders, the firm will not benefit its shareholders by issuing shares that are overvalued.) It is not clear, at least in Canada and the United States, why companies do not initiate more rights issues. Second, as with IPOs, evidence suggests that companies underperform following a seasoned offering. This underperformance appears to suggest that the stock price decrease is not large enough, because underperformance implies that the price following the issue was too high.

SEO Costs

Although not as costly as IPOs, seasoned offerings are still expensive, as Figure 14.6 shows. In addition to the price drop when the SEO is announced, the firm must pay direct costs too. Underwriting fees amount to 5% of the proceeds of the issue and, as with IPOs, the variation across issues of different sizes is relatively small. Furthermore, rights offers have lower costs than cash offers.[15] Given the other advantages of a rights offer, it is a puzzle why the majority of offers in Canada and the United States are cash offers. The one advantage of a cash offer is that the underwriter takes on a larger role and, therefore, can credibly attest to the issue's quality.

CONCEPT CHECK

7. What is the difference between a cash offer and a rights offer for an SEO?

8. What is the typical stock price reaction to an SEO?

[15]In the United Kingdom, Myron Slovin, Marie Sushka, and Kam Wah Lai found that the average fee for a cash offer is 6.1% versus 4.6% for an underwritten rights offer ("Alternative Flotation Methods, Adverse Selection, and Ownership Structure: Evidence from Seasoned Equity Issuance in the U.K.," *Journal of Financial Economics* 57 [2] [2000]).

MyLab Finance

Here is what you should know after reading this chapter. MyLab™ Finance will help you identify what you know, and where to go when you need to practice.

KEY POINTS	TERMS	ONLINE PRACTICE OPPORTUNITIES
14.1 Equity Financing for Private Companies ■ Private companies can raise outside equity capital from angel investors, venture capital firms, institutional investors, sovereign wealth funds, or corporate investors. ■ When a company founder sells stock to an outsider to raise capital, the founder's ownership share and control over the company are reduced. ■ Venture capital investments in private firms are often negotiated in terms of the pre-money valuation of the firm, which is the number of prior shares outstanding times the share price used in the funding round. ■ Given the pre-money valuation and the amount invested, we have: Post-money Valuation = Pre-money Valuation + Amount Invested (14.1) ■ In addition, the fractional ownership held by the new investors is equal to: Percentage Ownership = Amount Invested / Post-money Valuation (14.2) ■ Venture capital investments in private firms are often negotiated in terms of the pre-money valuation of the firm, which is the number of prior shares outstanding times the share price used in the funding round. ■ Equity investors in private companies plan to sell their stock eventually through one of two main exit strategies: an acquisition or a public offering.	angel investors, p. 485 convertible preferred stock, p. 489 corporate investor, corporate partner, strategic partner, strategic investor, p. 489 exit strategy, p. 491 leveraged buyout (LBO), p. 488 post-money valuation, p. 490 preferred stock, p. 489 pre-money valuation, p. 490 private equity firm, p. 488 private equity investor, p. 485 sovereign wealth funds (SWFs), p. 488 venture capital firm, p. 485 venture capitalists, p. 486	MyLab Study Plan 14.1
14.2 Taking Your Firm Public: The Initial Public Offering ■ An initial public offering (IPO) is the first time a company sells its stock to the public. ■ The main advantages of going public are greater liquidity and better access to capital. Disadvantages include regulatory and financial reporting requirements, and the undermining of the investors' ability to monitor the company's management.	auction IPO, p. 499 best efforts p. 499 book building, p. 498 bought deal, p. 498 final prospectus, p. 495 firm commitment, p. 498 initial public offering (IPO), p. 492 lead underwriter, p. 494 lockup, p. 499	MyLab Study Plan 14.2

KEY POINTS	TERMS	ONLINE PRACTICE OPPORTUNITIES
■ During an IPO, the shares sold may represent either a primary offering (if the shares are being sold to raise new capital) or a secondary offering (if the shares are sold by earlier investors). ■ An underwriter is an investment bank that manages the IPO process and helps the company sell its stock. ■ The lead underwriter is responsible for managing the IPO. ■ The lead underwriter forms a group of underwriters, called the syndicate, to help sell the stock. ■ The securities regulators require that a company file a preliminary prospectus (in Canada) or a registration statement (in the United States) prior to an IPO. The preliminary prospectus (which is part of the registration statement in the United States) circulates to investors before the stock is offered. After the deal is completed, the company files a final prospectus and the shares can be sold to the public. ■ Underwriters value a company before an IPO, using valuation techniques and by book building. ■ Stock may be sold during an IPO on a best-efforts basis, as a firm commitment IPO, or using an auction IPO. The firm commitment process is the most common practice for large firms in Canada and the United States.	over-allotment allocation (greenshoe provision), p. 499 preliminary prospectus (red herring), p. 495 primary offering, p. 494 registration statement, p. 495 road show, p. 496 secondary offering, p. 494 spread, p. 498 syndicate, p. 494 underwriter, p. 494	
14.3 IPO Puzzles ■ IPOs are underpriced on average. ■ New issues are highly cyclical. ■ The transaction costs of an IPO are very high. ■ Long-run performance (three to five years) after an IPO is poor on average.		MyLab Study Plan 14.3
14.4 Raising Additional Capital: The Seasoned Equity Offering ■ A seasoned equity offering (SEO) is the sale of stock by a company that is already publicly traded. ■ Two kinds of SEOs exist: a cash offer (when new shares are sold to investors at large) and a rights offer (when new shares are offered only to existing shareholders). ■ The stock price reaction to an SEO is negative on average.	adverse selection, p. 511 cash offer, p. 509 primary shares, p. 508 rights offer, p. 509 seasoned equity offering (SEO), p. 507 secondary shares, p. 508 tombstone, p. 509	MyLab Study Plan 14.4

REVIEW QUESTIONS

1. What are some of the alternative sources from which private companies can raise equity capital?
2. What are the advantages and the disadvantages to a private company of raising money from a corporate investor?
3. What are the main advantages and disadvantages of going public?
4. What are the main differences between a firm commitment IPO and an auction IPO?
5. Do underwriters face the most risk from a best-efforts IPO, a firm commitment IPO, or an auction IPO?
6. How is the price set in an auction IPO?
7. Why should a financial manager be concerned about underpricing?
8. IPOs are very cyclical. In some years, there are large numbers of IPOs; in other years, there are very few. Why is this cyclicality a puzzle?
9. What are the advantages of a rights offer?
10. What are the advantages to a company of selling stock in an SEO using a cash offer?
11. Why does the stock price typically decrease when a firm announces an SEO?

PROBLEMS

All problems in this chapter are available in MyLab Finance. An asterisk (*) indicates problems with a higher level of difficulty.

Equity Financing for Private Companies

1. You have started a company and are in luck—a venture capitalist has offered to invest. You own 100% of the company with 5 million shares. The VC offers $1 million for 800,000 new shares.
   a. What is the implied price per share?
   b. What is the post-money valuation?
   c. What fraction of the firm will you own after the investment?
2. Starware Software was founded last year to develop software for gaming applications. The founder initially invested $800,000 and received 8 million shares of stock. Starware now needs to raise a second round of capital, and it has identified a venture capitalist who is interested in investing. This venture capitalist will invest $1 million and wants to own 20% of the company after the investment is completed.
   a. How many shares must the venture capitalist receive to end up with 20% of the company? What is the implied price per share of this funding round?
   b. What will the value of the whole firm be after this investment (the post-money valuation)?
3. Your start-up company needs capital. Right now, you own 100% of the firm with 10 million shares. You have received two offers from venture capitalists. The first

offers to invest $3 million for 1 million new shares. The second offers $2 million for 500,000 new shares.

a. What is the first offer's post-money valuation of the firm?
b. What is the second offer's post-money valuation of the firm?
c. What is the difference in the percentage dilution caused by each offer?

4. Three years ago, you founded your own company. You invested $100,000 of your money and received 5 million shares of Series A preferred stock. Your company has since been through three additional rounds of financing.

Round	Price ($)	Number of Shares
Series B	0.50	1,000,000
Series C	2.00	500,000
Series D	4.00	500,000

a. What is the pre-money valuation for the Series D funding round?
b. What is the post-money valuation for the Series D funding round?

5. Based on the information in Problem 4 (and that each share of all series of preferred stock is convertible into one share of common stock), what fractions of the firm do the Series B, C, and D investors each own in the your firm?

6. Assuming that you own only the Series A preferred stock in Problem 4 (and that each share of all series of preferred stock is convertible into one share of common stock), what percentage of the firm do you own after the last funding round?

Taking Your Firm Public: The Initial Public Offering

7. Roundtree Software is going public using an auction IPO. The firm has received the following bids:

Price ($)	Number of Shares
14.00	100,000
13.80	200,000
13.60	500,000
13.40	1,000,000
13.20	1,200,000
13.00	800,000
12.80	400,000

Assuming Roundtree would like to sell 1.8 million shares in its IPO, what will be the winning auction offer price?

8. If Roundtree (see Problem 7) decides to issue an extra 500,000 shares (for a total of 2.3 million shares), how much total money will it raise?

9. In 2016, you founded Outdoor Recreation, Inc., a retailer specializing in the sale of equipment and clothing for recreational activities such as camping, skiing, and hiking. So far, your company has gone through three funding rounds:

Round	Date	Investor	Shares	Share Price ($)
Series A	Feb. 2016	You	500,000	1.00
Series B	Aug. 2017	Angels	1,000,000	2.00
Series C	Sept. 2018	Venture capital	2,000,000	3.50

It is now 2019, and you need to raise additional capital to expand your business. You have decided to take your firm public through an IPO. You would like to issue an additional 6.5 million new shares through this IPO. Assuming that your firm successfully completes its IPO, you forecast that 2019 net income will be $7.5 million.

a. Your investment banker advises you that the prices of other recent IPOs have been set such that the P/E ratios based on 2019 forecasted earnings average 20.0. Assuming that your IPO is set at a price that implies a similar multiple, what will your IPO price per share be?

b. What percentage of the firm will you own after the IPO?

10. Your investment bankers price your IPO at $15 per share for 10 million shares. If the price at the end of the first day of trading is $17 per share,

a. What was the percentage return on the first day of trading?

b. How much money did the firm miss out on due to underpricing?

11. Margoles Publishing recently completed its IPO. The stock was offered at a price of $14 per share. On the first day of trading, the stock closed at $19 per share.

a. What was the initial return on Margoles?

b. Who benefited from this underpricing? Who lost, and why?

12. If Margoles Publishing (see Problem 11) paid an underwriting spread of 7% for its IPO and sold 10 million shares, what was the total cost (exclusive of underpricing) to the company of going public?

13. Chen Brothers, Inc. sold 4 million shares in its IPO, at a price of $18.50 per share. Management negotiated a fee (the underwriting spread) of 7% on this transaction. What was the dollar cost of this fee?

14. You are negotiating with your underwriters in a firm commitment offering of 10 million primary shares. You have two options: set the IPO price at $20.00 per share with a spread of 7%, or set the price at $19.50 per share with a spread of 4%. Which option raises more money for your firm?

15. Your firm is selling 3 million shares in an IPO. You are targeting an offer price of $17.25 per share. Your underwriters have proposed a spread of 7%, but you would like to lower it to 5%. However, you are concerned that if you do so, they will argue for a lower offer price. Given the potential savings from a lower spread, how much lower can the offer price go before you would have preferred to pay 7% to get $17.25 per share?

Use the following information for Problems 16 through 18: The firm you founded currently has 12 million shares, of which you own 7 million. You are considering an IPO in which you would sell 2 million shares for $20 each.

16. If all of the shares sold are primary shares, how much will the firm raise? What will your percentage ownership of the firm be after the IPO?

17. If all of the shares sold are from your holdings, how much will the firm raise? What will your percentage ownership of the firm be after the IPO?

18. What is the maximum number of secondary shares you could sell and still retain more than 50% ownership of the firm? How much would the firm raise in that case?

Raising Additional Capital: The Seasoned Equity Offering

19. YVR, Inc. just announced a 10 million share SEO at $50 per share. If all of the SEO shares are primary shares and its underwriter charges 7% of the gross proceeds, how much new capital will YVR raise?

20. On January 20, Metropolitan, Inc. sold 8 million shares of stock in an SEO. The market price of Metropolitan at the time was $42.50 per share. Of the 8 million shares sold, 5 million shares were primary shares being sold by the company, and the remaining 3 million shares were being sold by the venture capital investors. Assume the underwriter charges 5% of the gross proceeds as an underwriting fee.
a. How much money did Metropolitan raise?
b. How much money did the venture capitalists receive?
c. If the stock price dropped 3% on announcement of the SEO and the new shares were sold at that price, how much money would Metropolitan receive?

***21.** Foster Enterprises' stock is trading for $50 per share and there are currently 10 million shares outstanding. It would like to raise $100 million. Assume its underwriter charges 5% of gross proceeds.
a. How many shares must it sell?
b. If it expects the stock price to drop by 2% upon announcement of the SEO, how many shares should it plan to sell?
c. If all of the shares are primary shares and are sold to new investors, what percentage reduction in ownership will all of the existing shareholders experience?

22. MacKenzie Corporation currently has 10 million shares of stock outstanding at a price of $40 per share. The company would like to raise money and has announced a rights issue. Every existing shareholder will be sent one right per share of stock that he or she owns. The company plans to require 10 rights to purchase one share at a price of $40 per share. How much money will it raise if all rights are exercised?

DATA CASE

Few IPOs have garnered as much attention as social media giant Facebook's public offering on May 18, 2012. It was the biggest IPO in internet history, easily topping Google's initial public offering eight years earlier. Let's take a closer look at the IPO itself, as well as the payoffs to some of Facebook's early investors.

1. Begin by navigating to the SEC EDGAR website, which provides access to company filings: (http://www.sec.gov/edgar.shtml). Choose "Search for Company Filings" and pick search by company name. Enter "Facebook" and then search for its IPO prospectus, which was filed on the date of the IPO and is listed as filing "424B4" (this acronym derives from the rule number requiring the firm to file a prospectus, Rule 424(b)(4)).

From the prospectus, calculate the following information:
a. The underwriting spread in percentage terms. How does this spread compare to a typical IPO?
b. The fraction of the offering that comprised primary shares and the fraction that comprised secondary shares.
c. The size, in number of shares, of the greenshoe provision. What percent of the deal did the greenshoe provision represent?

2. Next, navigate to Yahoo Finance and search for "Facebook." Determine the closing price of the stock on the day of the IPO (use the "Historical prices" link). What was the first day return? How does this return compare to the typical IPO?

3. Using the data provided by Yahoo Finance, calculate the performance of Facebook in the three-month post-IPO period. That is, calculate the annualized return an investor would have received if he had invested in Facebook at the closing price on the IPO day and sold the stock three months later. What was the return for a one-year holding period?

4. Prior to the public offering, Facebook was able to raise capital from all the sources mentioned in the chapter. Let's concentrate on one particular source, Microsoft Corporation.
   a. Microsoft made one investment in Facebook, during October 2007. Go to Facebook's corporate news website (http://newsroom.fb.com) and locate the press release announcing this investment. Using the information in that press release and the number of shares owned by Microsoft listed in the IPO prospectus, calculate the per share price Microsoft paid.
   b. Calculate the return (expressed on an annual basis) Microsoft earned on its investment up to the IPO (using the IPO price).
   c. How much money did Microsoft receive from the IPO?
5. Facebook had only one angel investor, Peter Thiel (the founder of PayPal). Mr. Thiel invested more than once in Facebook, both as an angel and, in later rounds, on behalf of investors in his venture capital firm, Founders Fund. As an angel, Mr. Thiel invested $500,000 in September 2004. Assuming that all the shares he received in the angel round were registered under the name Rivendell One LLC, use the information in the prospectus to calculate:
   a. The per share price he paid as an angel.
   b. The annualized return (using the IPO price) he made on his investment.
   c. The amount of angel money Mr. Thiel received from the proceeds of the IPO (that is, from his Rivendell investments alone).

CHAPTER

Debt Financing

15

LEARNING OBJECTIVES

- Identify different types of debt financing available to a firm
- Understand limits within bond contracts that protect the interests of bondholders
- Describe the various options available to firms for the early repayment of debt

NOTATION

YTC	yield to call on a callable bond
YTM	yield to maturity on a bond
PV	present value

In Chapter 14, we discussed the process a firm uses to raise equity capital, starting with angel investors for a young private firm and continuing through to seasoned equity offerings for an established public firm. We noted that each round of new equity financing dilutes the founder's ownership of the firm. An alternative financing source is to borrow the money—debt financing. In fact, debt is the most important source of financing; as we discovered in Chapter 6, there was over $3.3 *trillion* of Canadian bonds outstanding and this does not include bank loans and other forms of debt. While debt financing does not dilute the ownership of the firm, the disadvantage is that loans must be repaid. That is, the firm is legally obligated to make interest and principal payments on its debt. If it fails to do so, it is in default and can be forced into bankruptcy. We discuss the relative advantages and disadvantages of debt versus equity financing in Chapter 16. Here, we focus on the process for financing part of the firm with debt and on the features of corporate debt. Corporations are not the only entities that use debt financing. Governments and quasi-government entities (such as Crown corporations) are also major users of debt markets to raise capital. As reported in Chapter 6, by the end of 2017, 1.4 trillion bonds were issued by various forms of government in Canada with the federal government surpassing $1 trillion in debt for the first time in history. Hence, while this chapter is directly applicable to corporations, much of it is also relevant to organizations other than corporations.

In mid-2005, Ford Motor Company decided to put one of its subsidiaries, Hertz Corporation, up for competitive bid. On September 13, 2005, the Wall Street Journal reported that a group of private investors led by Clayton, Dubilier & Rice (CDR), a private equity firm, had reached a deal with Ford to purchase Hertz's outstanding equity for $5.6 billion. In addition, Hertz had $9.1 billion in existing debt that it needed to refinance as part of the deal. CDR planned to finance the transaction in part by raising over $11 billion in new debt. We will examine the details of this transaction throughout this chapter to illustrate debt financing.

When companies raise capital by issuing debt, they have several potential sources from which to seek funds. To complete the Hertz purchase, the group led by CDR relied on at least four different kinds of debt: domestic- and foreign-denominated high-yield bonds, bank loans, and asset-backed securities. In addition, each debt issue has its own specific terms determined at the time of issue. Building on the discussion of bond valuation in Chapter 6, we begin our exploration of debt financing by explaining the process of issuing debt and the types of debt available to companies. We continue by discussing restrictions on company actions in the debt agreement. Finally, we discuss some of the more advanced features of bonds, such as the call provision.

15.1 Corporate Debt

Corporate debt can be private debt, which is negotiated directly with a bank or a small group of investors, or public debt, which trades in a public market. As we will see, the Hertz example described in the introduction included both.

Private Debt

private debt Debt that is not publicly traded.

The first debt financing many young firms undertake is a bank loan. However, even very large, established firms use bank loans as part of their debt financing. Bank loans are an example of **private debt**, debt that is not publicly traded. The private debt market is larger than the public debt market. Private debt has the advantage that it avoids the cost and delay of registration with a securities commission, such as the Ontario Securities Commission (OSC) in Ontario or the Securities and Exchange Commission (SEC) in the United States. The disadvantage is that because private debt is not publicly traded, it is illiquid, meaning that it is hard for a holder of the firm's private debt to sell it in a timely manner.

There are several segments of the private debt market: *bank loans* (*term loans* and *lines of credit*) and *private placements*.

DEBT FINANCING AT HERTZ: BANK LOANS

As part of the transaction with CDR, Hertz took out more than $2 billion in bank loans. Hertz negotiated a $1.7 billion syndicated term loan with a seven-year term. Deutsche Bank AG negotiated the loan and then sold portions of it to other banks—mostly smaller regional banks that had excess cash but lacked the resources to negotiate a loan of this magnitude alone. In addition to the term loan, Hertz negotiated an asset-backed revolving line of credit (for five years and $1.6 billion), which it could use as needed. Hertz's initial draw on the line of credit was $400 million.

term loan A bank loan that lasts for a specific term.

syndicated bank loan A single loan that is funded by a group of banks rather than just a single bank.

revolving line of credit A credit commitment for a specific time period, typically two to three years, which a company can use as needed.

asset-backed line of credit A type of credit commitment in which the borrower secures a line of credit by pledging an asset as collateral.

private placement A bond issue that does not trade on a public market but rather is sold to a small group of investors.

indenture A formal contract between a bond issuer and a trust company that specifies the firm's obligations to the bondholders.

Bank Loans. A **term loan** is a bank loan that lasts for a specific term. When a single loan is funded by a group of banks rather than just a single bank, it is called a **syndicated bank loan**. Usually, one member of the syndicate (the lead bank) negotiates the terms of the bank loan. Many companies establish a **revolving line of credit**, a credit commitment for a specific time period up to some limit, typically two to three years, which a company can use as needed. A company may be able to get a larger line of credit or a lower interest rate if it secures the line of credit by pledging an asset as collateral. Such a line of credit is referred to as an **asset-backed line of credit**.

Private Placements. Recall from Chapter 6 that corporate bonds are securities issued by corporations. They account for a significant amount of invested capital. At the end of 2017, Canadian corporate bonds accounted for about 39% of all bonds outstanding in Canada. Bonds can be issued publicly or placed privately. A **private placement** is a bond issue that does not trade on a public market but, rather, is sold to a small group of investors. Because a private placement does not need to be registered with the securities commission, it is less costly to issue and often a simple promissory note is sufficient. Privately placed debt also need not conform to the same standards as public debt; as a consequence, it can be tailored to the particular situation.

Public Debt

The Prospectus. A public bond issue is similar to a stock issue. A prospectus or offering memorandum must be produced that describes the details of the offering. Figure 15.1 shows the front page of the Hertz offering memorandum. In addition, the prospectus for a public offering must include an **indenture**, a formal contract that specifies the firm's obligations to the bondholders. This contract is actually written between the bond issuer and a trust company that represents the bondholders and makes sure that the terms of the indenture are enforced. In the case of default, the trust company represents the bondholders' interests. In Chapter 6 we discussed several aspects of the public bond markets for debt. In particular we discussed default risk, bond ratings and the role of ratings agencies. Here we expand our discussion to include the different types of public corporate debt and the markets in which they are offered.

DEBT FINANCING AT HERTZ: PRIVATE PLACEMENTS

Hertz privately placed an additional $4.2 billion of U.S. asset-backed securities and $2.1 billion of international asset-backed securities. In this case, the assets backing the debt were the fleet of rental cars Hertz owned; hence, this debt was termed "fleet debt."

Hertz had an additional $2.7 billion bond issue that it issued under U.S. SEC Rule 144A.* As part of the offering, it agreed to publicly register the bonds within 390 days. Because the debt was marketed and sold with the understanding that it would become public debt, we classified that issue as public debt.

*In 1990, the U.S. SEC issued Rule 144A, which significantly increased the liquidity of certain privately placed debt. Private debt issued under this rule can be traded by large financial institutions among themselves. The rule was motivated by a desire to increase the access of foreign corporations to U.S. debt markets. Bonds that are issued under this rule are nominally private debt, but because they are tradable between financial institutions, they are only slightly less liquid than public debt. Many firms issue debt under Rule 144A with the explicit promise to publicly register the debt within a certain time frame. The advantage of this approach to debt financing is that companies can raise the capital quickly and then spend the time it takes to comply with all of the filing requirements.

FIGURE 15.1 Front Cover of the Offering Memorandum for the Hertz Junk Bond Issue

OFFERING MEMORANDUM CONFIDENTIAL

CCMG Acquisition Corporation
to be merged with and into The Hertz Corporation
$1,800,000,000 8.875% Senior Notes due 2014
$600,000,000 10.5% Senior Subordinated Notes due 2016
€225,000,000 7.875% Senior Notes due 2014

The Company is offering $1,800,000,000 aggregate principal amount of its 8.875% Senior Notes due 2014 (the "Senior Dollar Notes"), $600,000,000 aggregate principal amount of its 10.5% Senior Subordinated Notes due 2016 (the "Senior Subordinated Notes" and, together with the Senior Dollar Notes, the "Dollar Notes"), and €225,000,000 aggregate principal amount of its 7.875% Senior Notes due 2014 (the "Senior Euro Notes"). The Senior Dollar Notes and the Senior Euro Notes are collectively referred to as the "Senior Notes," and the Dollar Notes and the Senior Euro Notes are collectively referred to as the "Notes."

The Senior Notes will mature on January 1, 2014 and the Senior Subordinated Notes will mature on January 1, 2016. Interest on the Notes will accrue from December 21, 2005. We will pay interest on the Notes on January 1 and July 1 of each year, commencing July 1, 2006.

We have the option to redeem all or a portion of the Senior Notes and the Senior Subordinated Notes at any time (1) before January 1, 2010 and January 1, 2011, respectively, at a redemption price equal to 100% of their principal amount plus the applicable make-whole premium set forth in this offering memorandum and (2) on or after January 1, 2010 and January 1, 2011, respectively, at the redemption prices set forth in this offering memorandum. In addition, on or before January 1, 2009, we may, on one or more occasions, apply funds equal to the proceeds from one or more equity offerings to redeem up to 35% of each series of Notes at the redemption prices set forth in this offering memorandum. If we undergo a change of control or sell certain of our assets, we may be required to offer to purchase Notes from holders.

The Senior Notes will be senior unsecured obligations and will rank equally with all of our senior unsecured indebtedness. The Senior Subordinated Notes will be unsecured obligations and subordinated in right of payment to all of our existing and future senior indebtedness. Each of our domestic subsidiaries that guarantees specified bank indebtedness will guarantee the Senior Notes with guarantees that will rank equally with all of the senior unsecured indebtedness of such subsidiaries and the Senior Subordinated Notes with guarantees that will be unsecured and subordinated in right of payment to all existing and future senior indebtedness of such subsidiaries.

We have agreed to make an offer to exchange the Notes for registered, publicly tradable notes that have substantially identical terms as the Notes. The Dollar Notes are expected to be eligible for trading in the Private Offering, Resale and Trading Automated Linkages (PORTAL℠) market. This offering memorandum includes additional information on the terms of the Notes, including redemption and repurchase prices, covenants and transfer restrictions.

Investing in the Notes involves a high degree of risk. See "Risk Factors" beginning on page 23.

We have not registered the Notes under the federal securities laws of the United States or the securities laws of any other jurisdiction. The Initial Purchasers named below are offering the Notes only to qualified institutional buyers under Rule 144A and to persons outside the United States under Regulation S. See "Notice to Investors" for additional information about eligible offerees and transfer restrictions.

Price for each series of Notes: 100%

We expect that (i) delivery of the Dollar Notes will be made to investors in book-entry form through the facilities of The Depository Trust Company on or about December 21, 2005 and (ii) delivery of the Senior Euro Notes will be made to investors in book-entry form through the facilities of the Euroclear System and Clearstream Banking, S.A. on or about December 21, 2005.

Joint Book-Running Managers

Deutsche Bank Securities **Lehman Brothers**

Merrill Lynch & Co. **Goldman, Sachs & Co.** **JPMorgan**

Co-Lead Managers

BNP PARIBAS **RBS Greenwich Capital** **Calyon**

The date of this offering memorandum is December 15, 2005.

Source: © 2013 Hertz System, Inc. Courtesy of Hertz Corporation.

TABLE 15.1 Types of Corporate Debt

Secured	Unsecured
Mortgage bonds (secured with real property)	Notes (original maturity less than 10 years)
Asset-backed bonds (secured with any asset)	Debentures

original issue discount (OID) bond A coupon bond issued at a discount.

unsecured debt A type of corporate debt that, in the event of a bankruptcy, gives bondholders a claim to only the assets of the firm that are not already pledged as collateral on other debt.

notes A type of unsecured corporate debt with maturities shorter than 10 years.

debentures A type of unsecured corporate debt with maturities of 10 years or longer.

secured debt A type of corporate loan or debt security in which specific assets are pledged as a firm's collateral that bondholders have a direct claim to in the event of a bankruptcy.

mortgage bonds A type of secured corporate debt in which real property is pledged as collateral.

asset-backed bonds A type of secured corporate debt in which specific assets are pledged as collateral.

While corporate bonds almost always pay coupons semi-annually, a few corporations (for instance, Coca-Cola) have issued zero-coupon bonds. Corporate bonds have historically been issued with a wide range of maturities. Most corporate bonds have maturities of 30 years or less, although in the past there have even been perpetual bonds (that never mature). In July 1993, for example, Walt Disney Company issued $150 million in bonds with a maturity of 100 years; these bonds soon became known as the "Sleeping Beauty" bonds. Air Canada had several issues of perpetual bonds; however, these defaulted when the company went bankrupt in 2003.

The face value, or principal amount, of the bond is denominated in standard increments, usually $1000. The face value does not always correspond to the actual money raised because of underwriting fees and the possibility that the bond might not actually sell for its face value when it is offered for sale initially. If a coupon bond is issued at a discount, it is called an **original issue discount (OID) bond**.

Secured and Unsecured Corporate Debt. Four types of corporate debt are typically issued: *notes, debentures, mortgage bonds*, and *asset-backed bonds* (see Table 15.1). These types of debt fall into two categories: *unsecured* and *secured debt*. With **unsecured debt**, in the event of a bankruptcy bondholders have a claim to only the assets of the firm that are not already pledged as collateral on other debt. **Notes** are a type of unsecured debt, typically with maturities of less than 10 years, and **debentures** are a type of unsecured debt with maturities of 10 years or longer. With **secured debt**, specific assets are pledged as collateral that bondholders have a direct claim to in the event of a bankruptcy. **Mortgage bonds** are secured by real property, but **asset-backed bonds** can be secured by any kind of asset. Although the word "bond" is commonly used to mean any kind of debt security, technically a corporate bond must be secured.

Seniority. Debentures and notes are unsecured. Because more than one debenture might be outstanding, the bondholder's priority in claiming assets in the event of default, known as the bond's **seniority**, is important. As a result, most debenture issues contain clauses restricting the company from issuing new debt with priority equal to or higher than that of existing debt.

When a firm conducts a subsequent debenture issue that has lower priority than its outstanding debt, the new debt is known as a **subordinated debenture**. In the event of

DEBT FINANCING AT HERTZ: PUBLIC DEBT

As part of the transaction's financing, Hertz planned to issue $2.7 billion worth of unsecured debt—in this case, high-yield notes known as junk bonds. Recall from Chapter 6 that bonds rated below investment grade are called junk bonds. Further, remember that companies such as Standard & Poor's and Moody's rate the creditworthiness of bonds and make this information available to investors (see Table 6.5 for the specific ratings). The high-yield issue for the Hertz transaction was divided into three kinds of debt, or tranches—different classes of securities that make up a single bond issue and are paid from the same cash flow source (see Table 15.2), all of which made semi-annual coupon payments and were issued at par. The largest tranche was a $1.8 billion face-value note maturing in eight years. It paid a coupon of 8.875%, which at the time represented a 4.45% spread over Treasuries.

TABLE 15.2 Hertz's December 2005 Junk Bond Issues

	Tranche 1: Senior Dollar-Denominated Note	Tranche 2: Senior Euro-Denominated Note	Tranche 3: Senior Subordinated Dollar-Denominated Note
Face value	$1.8 billion	€ 225 million	$600 million
Maturity	December 1, 2014	December 1, 2014	December 1, 2016
Coupon	8.875%	7.875%	10.5%
Issue price	Par	Par	Par
Yield	8.875%	7.875%	10.5%
Rating			
Standard and Poor's	B	B	B
Moody's	B1	B1	B3
Fitch	BB–	BB–	BB+

seniority A bondholder's priority, in the event of a default, in claiming assets not already securing other debt.

subordinated debenture A debenture issue that has a lower-priority claim to the firm's assets than other outstanding debt.

tranche Any one of the different classes of securities that make up a single bond issuance.

domestic bonds Bonds issued by a local entity, denominated in the local currency, and traded in a local market but purchased by foreigners.

foreign bonds Bonds issued by a foreign company in a local market and intended for local investors. They are also denominated in the local currency.

Eurobonds International bonds that are not denominated in the local currency of the country in which they are issued.

global bonds Bonds that are offered for sale in several different markets simultaneously.

default, the assets not pledged as collateral for outstanding bonds cannot be used to pay off the holders of subordinated debentures until all more senior debt has been paid off. In Hertz's case, one **tranche** of the junk bond issue is a note that is subordinated to the other two tranches. In the event of bankruptcy, this note has a lower-priority claim on the firm's assets. Because holders of this tranche are likely to receive less in the event Hertz defaults, the yield on this debt is higher than that of the other tranches—10.5% compared with 8.875% for the first tranche.

International Bond Markets. The second tranche of Hertz's junk bond issue is a note that is denominated in euros rather than Hertz's home currency, the U.S. dollar. This is one type of an international bond. International bonds are classified into four broadly defined categories.

1. **Domestic bonds** are bonds issued by a local entity and traded in a local market, but purchased by foreigners. They are denominated in the local currency of the country in which they are issued.
2. **Foreign bonds** are bonds issued by a foreign company in a local market and are intended for local investors. They are also denominated in the local currency. Foreign bonds in Canada are known as Maple bonds; in the United States, foreign bonds are known as Yankee bonds. In other countries, foreign bonds also have special names; for example, in Japan they are called Samurai bonds; in the United Kingdom, they are known as Bulldogs.
3. **Eurobonds** are international bonds that are not denominated in the local currency of the country in which they are issued. Consequently, there is no connection between the physical location of the market on which they trade and the location of the issuing entity. Eurobonds can be denominated in any number of currencies that might or might not be connected to the location of the issuer. The trading of these bonds is not subject to any particular nation's regulations.
4. **Global bonds** combine the features of domestic, foreign, and Eurobonds, and are offered for sale in several different markets simultaneously. Unlike Eurobonds, global bonds can be offered for sale in the same currency as the country of issuance. The Hertz junk bond issue is an example of a global bond issue; it was simultaneously offered for sale in the United States and Europe.

TABLE 15.3 Summary of New Debt Issued as Part of the Hertz Leveraged Buyout

Type of Debt	Amount ($ millions)
Public Debt	
Senior dollar-denominated	1800.0
Senior euro-denominated (€ 225 million)	268.9
Subordinated dollar-denominated	600.0
Private Debt	
Term loan	1707.0
Asset-backed revolving line of credit	400.0
Asset-backed "fleet debt"*	6348.0
Total	$11,123.9

*The collateral of this debt was Hertz's fleet of rental cars.

A bond that makes its payments in a foreign currency contains the risk of holding that currency and, therefore, is priced on the basis of the yields of similar bonds in that currency. Hence, the euro-denominated note of the Hertz junk bond issue has a different yield than the dollar-denominated note, even though both bonds have the same seniority and maturity. While they have the same default risk, they differ in their exchange rate risk—the risk that the foreign currency will depreciate in value relative to the local currency. (For further discussion of exchange rate risk, see Chapter 22.)

Table 15.3 summarizes Hertz's debt after the leveraged buyout transaction. About $2.7 billion of the $11.1 billion total was public debt and the rest was private debt consisting of a term loan, a revolving line of credit, and fleet debt. Both the fleet debt and the line of credit were backed by specific assets of the firm.

CONCEPT CHECK

1. List the four types of corporate public debt that are typically issued.
2. What are the four categories of international bonds?

15.2 Other Types of Debt

Corporations are not the only entities that use debt. We begin with the largest debt sector, loans to government entities.

Sovereign Debt

Sovereign debt is debt issued by national governments. In 1998, the Government of Canada had about $360 billion of bonds outstanding. By the end of 2007, this amount dropped to only $267 billion following several years of budget surpluses being used to pay down the federal government debt. Since that time, the amount has risen as the Government of Canada, under pressure from all political parties in 2008, began to run deficits in order to attempt to mitigate the economic downturn resulting from the global economic crisis; by the beginning of 2017, the Government of Canada had about $552 billion of bonds outstanding of over $705 billion of the government's net debt.

The Canadian government sells its domestic debt to financial market distributors and dealers through auctions run by the Bank of Canada. Four kinds of domestic debt securities and three types of foreign debt securities are used by the Government of

Canada (see Table 15.4). In addition to these tradeable securities, the government also borrows directly from individuals through Canada Savings Bonds and Canada Premium Bonds (available through financial institutions). Cash management bills are pure discount bonds that are issued with very short maturities: as short as one day and less than three months. Treasury bills are the most common form of pure discount bonds and they are issued with original maturities of either 3, 6, or 12 months. Fixed-coupon marketable bonds (more commonly known as Government of Canada bonds) are semiannual coupon bonds with original maturities of between 2 and 40 years.

The last type of domestic security that the Government of Canada is currently issuing is the real return bond with maturities of up to 30 years. These bonds are standard coupon bonds with one difference: The outstanding principal is adjusted for inflation. Thus, although the coupon rate is fixed, the dollar coupon varies because the semi-annual coupon payments are a fixed rate of the inflation-adjusted principal. Thus, the dollar amounts of both the coupons and the final repayment are adjusted for the effects of inflation.

Government of Canada securities are initially sold to the public by auction. Two kinds of auctions are used by the Bank of Canada. For treasury bills and fixed-coupon marketable bonds, a multiple-price auction (also called a discriminatory price auction) is used. In this type of auction, the Bank of Canada receives bids from government securities distributors and sells the securities to these dealers at their bid prices. Starting with the highest bidder (in dollar terms) or lowest bidder (in yield terms) the securities are allocated until all are sold. The result is that each successful bidder may pay a different price for the security being sold. The second type of auction is the Dutch auction (or single-price auction), which is used for real return bonds. In this system, bidders submit their bid prices and the number of securities they desire. The bids are ranked from the highest price down. The lowest price that results in all securities being sold becomes the price charged to all bidders.[1] All income from Government of Canada securities is taxable at the federal and provincial levels. If an investor sells a security before it matures, there may be taxes on both interest income and capital gains.[2]

Zero-coupon government securities with maturities longer than one year also trade in the bond market. They are called STRIP bonds (Separate Trading of Registered Interest and Principal). The Government of Canada itself does not issue STRIP bonds. Instead, investors (or, more usually, investment banks) purchase fixed-coupon notes and bonds and then resell each coupon and principal payment separately as a zero-coupon bond.

TABLE 15.4 Existing Government of Canada Securities

Security Name	Type	Currency of Denomination*	Original Maturity
Cash Management Bills	Discount	CAD	1 day to less than 3 months
Treasury Bills	Discount	CAD	3, 6, or 12 months
Fixed-Coupon Marketable Bonds (Government of Canada Bonds)	Coupon	CAD	2 to 40 years
Real Return Bonds	Coupon	CAD	up to 30 years
Canada Bills	Discount	USD	up to 270 days
Canada Notes	Coupon	USD	up to 5 years
Euro Medium-Term Notes	Coupon	Various (not CAD or USD)	up to 5 years

*CAD refers to the Canadian dollar; USD refers to the U.S. dollar.
Sources: Bank of Canada, Government of Canada (Department of Finance), and Investopedia.com.

[1]See the Bank of Canada's glossary for further information: www.bankofcanada.ca/en/glossary/.

[2]See the Canada Revenue Agency (CRA) website for more information on the taxation of interest and capital gains.

EXAMPLE 15.1 Coupon Payments on Real Return Bonds

PROBLEM

Suppose that in January 2000 the Government of Canada issued a 30-year real return bond with a coupon rate of 4%. On the date of issue, the consumer price index (CPI) was 93.5. In July 2008, the CPI had increased to 116.1. What coupon payment was made in July 2008? What coupon payment was made in January 2017 when the CPI was 129.0?

SOLUTION

Between the issue date and July 2008, the CPI appreciated by a factor of $116.1 \div 93.5 = 1.24171$. Consequently, the principal amount of the bond increased by this amount; that is, the original face value of \$1000 increased to \$1241.71. Because the bond pays semi-annual coupons, the coupon payment was $\$1241.17 \times 0.04 \div 2 = \$24.83$. In January 2017, the coupon payment was $\$1000 \times 129 \div 93.5 \times 0.04 \div 2 = \$27.59$.

Agency Securities

Agency securities are issued by Crown corporations of the Canadian federal government. Canada Mortgage and Housing Corporation (CMHC) bonds are an example, as are Business Development Bank of Canada (BDC) bonds and Export Development Canada (EDC) bonds. These bonds are either a direct obligation of the Government of Canada (this is the case for the BDC) or are fully guaranteed by the Government of Canada (e.g., the CMHC's bonds). Agency securities are issued in a variety of types and maturities. By far, the largest fraction of the issues consists of mortgage-backed securities (MBS). Mortgage-backed securities, such as those guaranteed by the CMHC, are one type of asset-backed securities. In the case of an MBS, each security is backed by an underlying portfolio or pool of mortgages. (Other asset-backed securities may be backed by a portfolio of credit card receivables, consumer loans, car loans, etc.—these would not be considered agency securities if they were created by financial institutions rather than government agencies.) When homeowners in the pool make their mortgage payments, this cash is passed through (minus servicing fees) to the holders of the mortgage-backed securities. Consequently, the cash flows of mortgage-backed securities mirror the cash flows of home mortgages: They are annuities that pay fixed monthly payments over the term of the mortgages in the pool (the most common term is five years) plus a final principal repayment at the end of the term. As most Canadian mortgages have an amortization period longer than the mortgage term, there is normally a substantial amount of principal outstanding at the end of the term. As with most mortgages, the entire principal is not returned at maturity; instead, part of it is also paid back gradually over the life of the bond.

A mortgage borrower usually has an option to repay some or all of the mortgage loan early and this early repayment of principal is also passed through to owners of mortgage-backed securities. Thus, holders of CMHC guaranteed mortgage-backed securities face prepayment risk—the risk that the bond will be partially (or wholly) repaid earlier than expected.

Provincial and Municipal Bonds

Provincial and municipal bonds are issued by provincial and local governments and their Crown corporations (e.g., Manitoba Hydro or Hydro Quebec). Their interest is treated as taxable income by the Canada Revenue Agency. In the United States, so-called "munis" (issued by U.S. states or municipalities) are not taxable at the federal level and some are also exempt from state and local taxes.

general obligation bonds Bonds backed by the full faith and credit of a local government.

double-barrelled bonds Bonds with payments tied to a particular revenue source in addition to the full faith and credit of the local government.

revenue bonds Bonds backed by the revenues generated by projects initially financed by the bond issue but not backed by the full faith and credit of the local government.

Most provincial and municipal bonds pay semi-annual coupons. A single issue will sometimes contain a number of different maturity dates. Such issues are often called serial bonds because the bonds are scheduled to mature serially over a number of years. The coupons on municipal bonds can be either *fixed* or *floating*. A fixed-coupon bond has the same coupon over the life of the bond. In a floating-rate issue, the coupon of the bond is adjusted periodically. The reset formula is a spread over a reference rate like the rate on treasury bills that is established when the bond is first issued.

Bonds backed by the full faith and credit of a local government are known as **general obligation bonds** and are not as secure as bonds backed by the full faith and credit of the federal government. Sometimes local governments strengthen the commitment further by tying the promise to a particular revenue source, such as a special fee. Because a local government can always use its general revenue to repay such bonds, this commitment is over and above the usual commitment, so these bonds are called **double-barrelled bonds**. Not all municipal bonds are backed by the full faith and credit of the local government, however. Instead, the local government can pledge specific revenues generated by projects that were initially financed by the bond issue. These bonds are called **revenue bonds**.

FINANCIAL CRISIS

Subprime Mortgage-Backed Securities

The Canada Mortgage and Housing Corporation (CMHC) restricts the types of mortgages that it is prepared to securitize into mortgage-backed securities. For example, CMHC will only securitize mortgages below a certain face value and, more importantly, that meet certain credit criteria. Mortgages that have a high default probability are known as subprime mortgages, and the CMHC will not insure these. Nevertheless, subprime mortgages do get written by financial institutions and they are often pooled into mortgage-backed securities and sold to other investors. We can attribute part of the U.S. housing boom in the mid-2000s to the increased availability of subprime mortgages. As the number of subprime mortgages exploded, so too, did the incentives to securitize them.

Unlike the CMHC, private organizations do not carry a government guarantee. Investors looked to credit rating agencies to assess the credit worthiness of the privately issued subprime mortgage-backed securities.* While housing prices in the United States rose, default rates on subprime mortgages remained low and the credit rating agencies came under intense pressure to issue the highest credit ratings to subprime mortgage-backed securities. Issuers naturally wanted the high ratings to be able to sell the bonds for high prices, but regulated investors, such as banks, also wanted the bonds highly rated so that they would be able to hold them as reserve capital.

When the U.S. housing market turned for the worse in 2007, increased default rates on mortgages resulted in defaults of the securities backed by these mortgages—the subprime mortgage-backed securities did not live up to their high credit rating. A vicious cycle ensued as the credit rating companies dropped the ratings on the bonds, forcing the banks to sell them at a loss (the prices of the bonds dropped as their ratings dropped). As more and more holders of these bonds moved to sell them, the prices dropped further. These losses ate away at the banks' capital base, causing them to pull back from lending. The end result was a near collapse of the financial system and a severe lack of credit availability.

*In addition, private asset-backed securities can be backed by other asset backed securities. When banks re-securitize other asset-backed securities the new asset-backed security is known as a collateralized debt obligation (CDO). CDO cash flows are usually divided into different tranches that are assigned different priority. For example, investors in the junior tranche of a CDO do not receive any cash flows until investors in the senior tranche have received their promised cash flows.

CONCEPT CHECK

3. What are the seven kinds of securities issued by the Canadian government?
4. What is an asset-backed security?
5. What is the major difference between U.S. municipal bonds and Canadian municipal bonds?

15.3 Bond Covenants

covenants Restrictive clauses in a bond contract that limit the issuer from taking actions that may undercut its ability to repay the bonds.

Now that we have established the main types of debt, we are prepared to take a closer look at the bond contract provisions. **Covenants** are restrictive clauses in a bond contract that limit the issuer from taking actions that may undercut its ability to repay the bonds. Why are such covenants necessary? After all, why would managers voluntarily take actions that increase the firm's default risk? Remember—managers work for the equity holders, and sometimes there are actions managers can take that benefit the equity holders at the expense of debt holders. For example, in Chapter 13 we saw how equity could be viewed as a call option on the firm's assets (Section 13.7) and we know from that chapter that options become more valuable, all else equal, when the underlying assets are riskier. For bondholders, though, an increased risk of the firm's assets results in greater default risk for the bondholders. Covenants are there to protect debt holders from actions managers might take that benefit the equity holders at the expense of debt holders.

Types of Covenants

Once bonds are issued, equity holders have an incentive to increase dividends at the expense of debt holders. Think of an extreme case in which a company issues a bond and then immediately liquidates its assets, pays out the proceeds (including those from the bond issue) in the form of a dividend to equity holders, and declares bankruptcy. In this case, the equity holders receive the value of the firm's assets plus the proceeds from the bond, while bondholders are left with nothing. Consequently, bond agreements often contain covenants that restrict the ability of management to pay dividends. Other covenants may restrict how much more debt the firm can issue, or they may specify that the firm must maintain a minimum amount of working capital. If the firm fails to live up to any covenant, the bond goes into technical default and the bondholder can demand immediate repayment or force the company to renegotiate the terms of the bond. Table 15.5 summarizes typical bond covenants. All of the covenants are designed to limit the company's (the borrower's) ability to increase the risk of the bond. For example, without restrictions on the issuance of new debt, the company could issue new debt with seniority equal to or greater than that of the existing bonds, thus increasing the risk that the firm will not repay the existing bonds.

TABLE 15.5 Typical Bond Covenants

Type of Action Restricted	Typical Restrictions
Issuance of new debt	New debt must be subordinate to existing debt.
	No new debt may be issued unless the firm maintains specific leverage or interest coverage ratios.
Dividends and share repurchases	Payouts can be made only from earnings generated after the bond issue.
	Payouts can be made only if earnings exceed some threshold.
Mergers and acquisitions	Mergers are allowed only if the combined firm has a minimum ratio of net tangible assets to debt.
Asset disposition	The maximum amount of assets that can be sold and/or the minimum amount of assets that must be maintained is set.
	Restrictions are placed on making loans or any other provision of credit.
Maintenance Required	
Accounting measures	Minimum retained earnings, working capital, and/or net assets are set.
	Maximum leverage ratios are set.

Source: Adapted from the American Bar Association's Commentaries on Debentures

Advantages of Covenants

You might expect that equity holders would try to include as few covenants as possible in a bond agreement. In fact, this is not necessarily the case. The stronger the covenants in the bond contract, the less likely the firm will be to default on the bond, and thus the lower the interest rate will be that investors will require to buy the bond. That is, by including more covenants, firms can reduce their costs of borrowing. The reduction in the firm's borrowing costs can more than outweigh the cost of the loss of flexibility associated with covenants.

Application: Hertz's Covenants

Covenants in the Hertz junk bond issue limited Hertz's ability to incur more debt, make dividend payments, redeem stock, make investments, transfer or sell assets, and merge or consolidate. They also included a requirement that Hertz offer to repurchase the bonds at 101% of face value if the corporation experiences a change in control.

CONCEPT CHECK

6. What happens if an issuer fails to live up to a bond covenant?
7. Why can bond covenants reduce a firm's borrowing costs?

15.4 Repayment Provisions

A firm repays its bonds by making coupon and principal payments as specified in the bond contract. However, this is not the only way a firm can repay bonds. For example, the firm can repurchase a fraction of the outstanding bonds in the market, or it can make a tender offer for the entire issue, as Hertz did on its existing bonds. In this section, we explain the three main bonds features affecting the repayment of the bond: *call provisions, sinking funds,* and *convertible provisions.*

Call Provisions

callable bonds Bonds containing a call provision that allows the issuer to repurchase the bonds at a predetermined price.

call date The date in the call provision on or after which the bond issuer has the right to retire the bond.

call price A price, specified at the issuance of a bond, for which the issuer can redeem the bond.

Firms can repay bonds by exercising a *call* provision. **Callable bonds** allow the issuer of the bond to repurchase the bonds at a predetermined price; in effect, with callable bonds, the firm has a call option on those bonds. The call feature allows the issuer the right (but not the obligation) to retire all outstanding bonds on (or after) a specific date known as the **call date**, for the **call price** that is specified at the issuance of the bond. The call price is expressed as a percentage of the bond's face value and is generally set at or above the face value. The difference (in percent) between the call price and the par value is the call premium. For example, a bond might have a call price of 105%, implying a call premium of 5%.

Hertz's Callable Bonds. Hertz's junk bonds are examples of callable bonds. Table 15.6 lists the call features in each tranche. In Hertz's case, the call dates of the two senior tranches are at the end of the fourth year. For the duration of 2010, the first tranche has a call price of 104.438% of the bond's face value. In the following years, the call price is gradually reduced until, in 2012, the bond becomes callable at par (100% of face value). The euro-denominated bond has similar terms at slightly different call prices. The subordinated tranche's call date is a year later and has a different call-price structure.

The Hertz bonds are also partially callable in the first three years. Hertz has the option to retire up to 35% of the outstanding principal at the call prices listed in Table 15.6, as long as the funds needed to repurchase the bonds are derived from the proceeds of an equity issuance.

TABLE 15.6 Call Features of Hertz's Bonds

	Tranche 1: Senior Dollar-Denominated Note	Tranche 2: Senior Euro-Denominated Note	Tranche 3: Senior Subordinated Dollar-Denominated Note
Call Features	Up to 35% of the outstanding principal callable at 108.875% in the first three years.	Up to 35% of the outstanding principal callable at 107.875% in the first three years.	Up to 35% of the outstanding principal callable at 110.5% in the first three years.
	After four years, fully callable at • 104.438% in 2010. • 102.219% in 2011. Par thereafter.	After four years, fully callable at • 103.938% in 2010. • 101.969% in 2011. Par thereafter.	After five years, fully callable at • 105.25% in 2011. • 103.50% in 2012. • 101.75% in 2013.

Call Provisions and Bond Prices. When would a financial manager choose to exercise the firm's right to call the bond? A firm can always retire one of its bonds early by repurchasing the bond in the open market. If the call provision offers a cheaper way to retire the bond, however, the firm will forgo the option of purchasing the bond in the open market and call the bond instead. Thus, when the market price of the bond exceeds the call price, the firm will call the bond.

We know from Chapter 6 that bond prices rise when market interest rates fall. If market interest rates have decreased since the bond was issued and are now less than the bond's coupon rate, the bond will be trading at a premium. If the firm has the option to call the bond at less than the premium, it could do so and refinance its debt at the new, lower market interest rates.

Given the flexibility a call provision provides to a financial manager, you might expect all bonds to be callable. However, that is not the case; to see why, we must consider how the investor views the call provision. The financial manager will choose to call the bonds only when the coupon rate the investor is receiving exceeds the market interest rate. By calling the bond, the firm is forcing the investor to relinquish the bond at a price below the value it would have were it to remain outstanding. Naturally, investors view this possibility negatively and pay less for callable bonds than for otherwise identical non-callable bonds. Suppose that the only difference between two bonds is that one of them is callable. If the two bonds have the same maturity, coupon rate, repayment provisions (except for the call provision), and were issued by the same company, then the bond that is callable will sell at a lower price. The difference in the price between the two bonds will reflect the value of the call option retained by the issuing firm when it uses a callable bond. This means that a firm raising capital by issuing callable bonds instead of non-callable bonds will have to either pay a higher coupon rate or accept lower proceeds. A firm will choose to issue callable bonds despite their higher yield if it finds the option to refinance the debt in the future particularly valuable.

yield to call (YTC) The yield of a callable bond calculated under the assumption that the bond will be called on the earliest call date.

Yield to Call. A financial manager needs to understand how investors are evaluating the firm's callable bonds. For callable bonds, the **yield to call (YTC)**, the annual yield of a callable bond calculated under the assumption that the bond is called on the earliest call date, is most often quoted. In Chapter 6, we learned how investors evaluate a firm's bonds by computing their yield to maturity. The yield to maturity is always calculated on the assumption that the bond will remain outstanding until maturity and make all of its promised payments. In the case of a callable bond, that assumption is not realistic. Thus, the yield to maturity of a callable bond is the interest rate the bondholder receives if the

TABLE 15.7 Bond Calls and Yields

Bond Coupons Relative to Market Yields	Bond Price	Likelihood of Call	Yield to Worst
Coupons are higher	At a premium	High	Yield to call
Coupons are lower	At a discount	Low	Yield to maturity

yield to worst Quoted by bond traders, the lower of the yield to call or yield to maturity.

bond is not called and repaid in full. When the bond's coupon rate is above the yield for similar securities, the yield to call is less than the yield to maturity. However, when the bond's coupon rate is below the yield for similar securities, the bond is unlikely to be called (the firm would not call a bond when it is paying a below-market interest rate). In that case, calling would actually be good for the bondholders, and the yield to call would be above the yield to maturity. To keep all this straight, most bond traders quote **yield to worst**, which is the lower of the yield to call or yield to maturity. Table 15.7 summarizes the yield to call and yield to worst.

EXAMPLE 15.2 Calculating the Yield to Call

PROBLEM

Suppose BCE Inc. (BCE) has just issued a callable (at par) five-year, 8% coupon bond with annual coupon payments. The bond can be called at par in one year or any time thereafter on a coupon payment date. It has a price of $103 per $100 face value, implying a yield to maturity of 7.26%. What is the bond's yield to call?

SOLUTION

■ Plan

The timeline of the promised payments for this bond (if it is not called) is

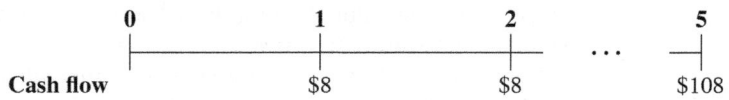

If BCE calls the bond at the first available opportunity, it will call the bond at year 1. At that time, it will have to pay the coupon payment for year 1 ($8 per $100 of face value) and the face value ($100). The timeline of the payments if the bond is called at the first available opportunity (at year 1) is

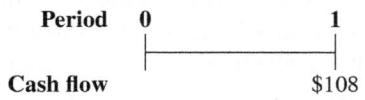

To solve for the yield to call, we use these cash flows and proceed as shown in Chapter 6, setting the price equal to the discounted cash flows and solving for the discount rate.

■ Execute

For the yield to call, setting the present value of these payments equal to the current price gives

$$103 = \frac{108}{(1 + YTC)}$$

▶

Solving for the yield to call gives

$$YTC = \frac{108}{103} - 1 = 4.85\%$$

We can use a financial calculator to derive the same result:

	N	I/Y	PV	PMT	FV
Given:	1		−103	8	100
Solve for:		**4.85**			

Excel Formula: =RATE(NPER,*PMT*,*PV*,*FV*)=RATE(1,8,−103,100)

■ Evaluate

The yield to maturity is higher than the yield to call because the yield to maturity assumes that you will continue receiving your coupon payments for five years, even though interest rates have dropped below 8%. Under the yield to call assumptions, since you are repaid the face value sooner, you are deprived of the extra four years of coupon payments, resulting in a lower total return.

The Canada Call or Make-Whole Call Provision

Canada call or **make-whole call** A callable bond with the call price set equal to the present value of the bond's remaining payments, calculated with a rate adjusted for prevailing interest rates in the economy.

Rather than a standard call provision as just described, many companies have adopted the **Canada call** or **make-whole call** provision instead. This call provision sets the call price as the present value of all remaining payments of the bond, which is calculated using a rate that adjusts with changes in prevailing interest rates in the economy. Thus, if interest rates fall, the call price rises, and the incentive to call the bond in order to refinance at lower rates is eliminated due to the higher call price that would need to be paid. Gady Jacoby and David Stangeland describe how, in 1993, 41% of Canadian corporate bonds had the standard call provision, while only 23% had the Canada call provision; by 1999, however, only 8% of Canadian corporate bonds had the standard call provision while 47% had the Canada call provision. Why do corporations bother with the Canada call provision instead of just leaving the bonds as non-callable? Perhaps management would like to retire a bond issue for reasons other than a drop in interest rates. For example, if a change in capital structure is desired (see Chapter 16) or if a bond covenant becomes troublesome, then management may prefer retiring the bond issue. It may be less costly to call the bond rather than repurchase it on the open market through a tender offer. This benefit may outweigh the fact that, under a Canada call provision, the call price is greater than the present value of the remaining payments of the bond.[3]

[3]See Gady Jacoby and David Stangeland's article, "The Make-Whole, Doomsday, and Canada Call Provisions," *Northern Finance Association Conference Proceedings*, September, 2004. Note that the rate specified to calculate the present value of the remaining payments so as to get the call price is set so it is actually slightly less than the market rate that would otherwise determine the bond's current value. Thus, the call price will be greater than market value of the bond's future cash flows.

Sinking Funds

sinking fund A method for repaying a bond in which a company makes regular payments into a fund administered by a trustee over the life of the bond. These payments are then used to repurchase bonds, usually at the lower of the bond's par value or market price.

Some bonds are repaid through a **sinking fund**, a provision that allows the company to make regular payments into a fund administered by a trustee over the life of the bond, instead of repaying the entire principal balance on the maturity date. These payments are then used to repurchase bonds, usually at the lower of the bond's par value or market price. In this way, the company can reduce the amount of outstanding debt without affecting the cash flows of the remaining bonds.

Sinking fund provisions usually specify a minimum rate at which the issuer must contribute to the fund. In some cases, the issuer has the option to accelerate these payments. Because the sinking fund allows the issuer to repurchase the bonds at par, the option to accelerate the payments is another form of a call provision. As with all call provisions, this option is not free—including this provision lowers the price the company would get for the bonds initially.

The manner in which an outstanding balance is paid off using a sinking fund depends on the issue. Some issues specify equal payments over the life of the bond, ultimately retiring the issue on the maturity date of the bond. In other cases, the sinking fund payments are not sufficient to retire the entire issue, and the company must make a large payment on the maturity date, known as a **balloon payment**. Sinking fund payments often start only a few years after the bond issue. Bonds can be issued with both a sinking fund and a call provision.

balloon payment A large payment that must be made on the maturity date of a bond when the sinking fund payments are not sufficient to retire the entire bond issue.

Convertible Provisions

convertible bonds Corporate bonds with a provision that gives the bondholder an option to convert each bond owned into a fixed number of shares of common stock.

conversion ratio The ratio used to convert a convertible bond into a fixed number of shares, usually stated per $1000 face value.

conversion price The face value of a convertible bond divided by the number of shares received if the bond is converted.

Another way to retire bonds is by converting them into equity. **Convertible bonds** are corporate bonds with a provision that gives the bondholder an option to convert each bond owned into a fixed number of shares of common stock at a ratio called the **conversion ratio**. The provision usually gives bondholders the right to convert the bond into stock at any time up to the maturity date for the bond.[4] The conversion ratio is usually stated per $1000 of face value. Essentially, the conversion feature gives the bondholder a call option (see Chapter 13) on the firm's shares.

Convertible Bond Pricing. Consider a convertible bond with a $1000 face value and a conversion ratio of 20. If you converted the bond into stock on its maturity date, you would receive 20 shares. If you did not convert, you would receive $1000. Hence, by converting the bond you essentially "paid" $1000 for 20 shares, implying a price per share of $1000 ÷ 20 shares = $50 per share. This implied price per share equal to the face value of the bond divided by the number of shares received in conversion is called the **conversion price**; this is similar to the exercise price of a call option on the firm's stock except, rather than paying cash to exercise the option, the bondholder returns the bond to the firm and receives the fixed number of shares. If the price of the stock exceeds $50, you would choose to convert; otherwise, you would take the cash. Thus, as shown in Figure 15.2, the value of the bond on its maturity date is the maximum of its face value ($1000) and the value of 20 shares of stock.

Often companies issue convertible bonds that also have a standard call feature. With these bonds, if the issuer calls them, the holder can choose to convert rather than let the bonds be called. When the bonds are called, the holder faces exactly the same decision as he or she would face on the maturity date of the bonds: the holder will choose to

[4]Some convertible bonds do not allow conversion for a specified amount of time after the issue date.

FIGURE 15.2 Convertible Bond Value

At maturity, the value of a convertible bond is the maximum of the value of a $1000 straight bond (a non-convertible, non-callable bond) and 20 shares of stock, and it will be converted if the stock is above the conversion price. Prior to maturity, the value of the convertible bond will depend on the likelihood of conversion and will be above that of a straight bond or 20 shares of stock. More specifically, the convertible bond's value will equal the straight bond value plus the value of the call option embedded in the convertible bond.

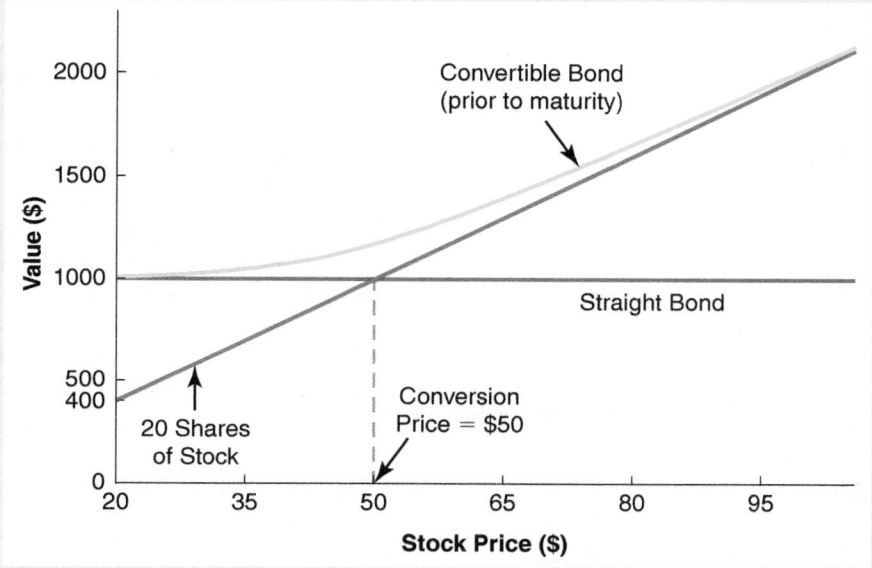

convert if the stock price exceeds the conversion price and otherwise will let the bonds be called. Thus, by calling the bonds, a company can force bondholders to make their decision to convert earlier than they would otherwise have preferred. The possibility of forced conversion reduces the value of the embedded option in a convertible bond since, as discussed in Section 13.3 of Chapter 13, American options with less time until expiration have lower value.

The option (which is not an obligation) to convert the bonds into equity is worth something to a bondholder. Thus, prior to the bond maturity date, a convertible bond is worth more than an otherwise identical **straight bond**, a non-callable, non-convertible bond (also called a plain-vanilla bond). Consequently, if both bonds are issued at par, the straight bond must offer a higher interest rate. Similarly, the option to receive the bond's face value means the convertible bond is also worth more than 20 shares of stock. This relationship is illustrated in Figure 15.2, where the convertible bond's value prior to maturity (the yellow curve) exceeds the value of both the straight bond (red line) and the stock (blue line). More specifically, we can think of the value of the convertible bond as being composed of the straight bond value plus the value of the call option embedded in the convertible bond. The company's management (on behalf of its existing shareholders) must weigh the benefit of the lower interest rate on the convertible bond against the cost of giving those bondholders the call option to buy new shares of stock at a fixed price.

straight bond A non-callable, non-convertible bond (also called a plain-vanilla bond).

Convertible Bonds and Stock Prices. Note that the likelihood of eventually converting a convertible bond depends on the current stock price. When the stock price is low, conversion is unlikely, and the value of the convertible bond is close to that of a straight bond. When the stock price is much higher than the conversion price, conversion is very likely, and the convertible bond's price is close to the price of the converted shares. Finally, when the stock price is in the middle range, near the conversion price, there is the greatest uncertainty about whether it will be optimal to convert or not. In this case, the bondholder's option to decide later whether to convert is most valuable, and the value of the convertible bond exceeds the value of straight debt or equity by the greatest amount.

Combining Features. Companies have flexibility in setting the features of the bonds they issue. As we mentioned above, companies will often add a call provision to convertible bonds or bonds with sinking funds. Another example of flexibility is to add convertibility to subordinated bonds. Subordinated bonds typically have a higher yield because of their riskier position relative to senior bonds. But if the subordinated bond contains a convertibility feature that the senior bonds do not have, the yield on the subordinated bond could be lower than that of the senior bonds. One example is RealNetworks, which issued $100 million in subordinated convertible debt in 2003 with a zero coupon rate. As described in Table 15.8, the debt also contained a provision allowing the company to call the debt at par anytime after July 1, 2008. RealNetworks exercised its option to call the debt in 2008, paying $100 million to repurchase the debt from the debtholders.

leveraged buyout (LBO)
The purchase by a group of private investors of all the equity of a public corporation, primarily through debt financing.

Leveraged Buyouts. Recall from Chapter 14 our discussion of how private companies become public companies. The deal in which CDR bought Hertz is an example of the opposite transition—a public company becoming private, in this case through a *leveraged buyout*. In a **leveraged buyout (LBO)**, a group of private investors purchases all the equity of a public corporation and finances the purchase primarily with debt.[5]

TABLE 15.8 RealNetworks' 2003 Convertible Debt Issue

Convertible Subordinated Notes	
Issued Under U.S. SEC Rule 144A	
Aggregate principal amount	$100 million
Proceeds net of offering costs	$97.0 million
Coupon	0%
Conversion ratio	107.5650 shares per $1000 principal amount
Call date	July 1, 2008
Call price	100%
Maturity	July 1, 2010

[5]At the time of the deal, Hertz was a wholly owned subsidiary of Ford Motor Company, which itself is a public company. Prior to Ford's acquisition of Hertz's outstanding shares in 2001, Hertz was publicly traded.

Damian Creber is an investment banking analyst with RBC Capital Markets. A graduate of the University of Toronto in 2010, he works in the leveraged financing group, helping clients with acquisitions. "My role is to work with the acquirer, to help them with the valuation of the target and, in particular, to help them structure and syndicate the debt used in the transaction."

Firms looking to use debt financing have many different options available to them. "For example, we had a recent client who wanted to do an all cash deal, with no equity. They needed to raise a large amount of debt, in this case preferring long-term debt rather than bank debt," Damian explains. "Possible options are to use revolving credit, or a bridge loan that would eventually become bonds."

Choosing the most suitable loan depends on the firm's current situation, what it will do with the loan proceeds, and how it plans to repay the loan. "I work with the company and the rating agencies to find the optimal structure of debt, and determine whether the debt is secured," Damian says. For him, the key is to strike the right balance between the costs and benefits of taking on additional debt: "I need to minimize their cost of capital while maximizing their flexibility."

INTERVIEW WITH DAMIAN CREBER, RBC CAPITAL MARKETS

Damian Creber

University of Toronto, 2010

"I work with the company and the rating agencies to find the optimal structure of debt, and determine whether the debt is secured."

With a total value of $15.2 billion,[6] the LBO of Hertz was the second-largest transaction of its kind at the time of its announcement. This left Hertz with a substantial amount of debt on its balance sheet. As with most LBOs, Hertz's long-term plan was to reduce its leverage through continued profitability. In November 2006, Hertz went public again by selling new stock through an IPO. In 2012, Hertz increased its debt to acquire Dollar Thrifty, and refinanced some of its senior debt from the LBO by calling the notes due in 2014. In June 2016, the parent company spun off the rental car business so that it trades under HTZ and the equipment rental business trades as a separate company under HRI. Recent LBOs include Michael Dell's purchase of Dell Computer in 2013 and Carlyle Group's buyout of Symantec in 2015. In Chapter 16, we will examine the trade-offs a financial manager faces in deciding how much of a company to finance with debt and how much to finance with equity.

CONCEPT CHECK

8. Do bonds with a standard call feature have a higher or lower yield than otherwise identical bonds without a call feature? Why?
9. Will a drop in interest rates make it advantageous for a company to call a bond with a Canada call feature?
10. What is a sinking fund?
11. Why does a convertible bond have a lower yield than an otherwise identical bond without the option to convert?

[6]The total value includes $14.7 billion for Hertz and $0.5 billion in fees and expenses. In addition to $11.1 billion in new debt, the transaction was financed using $1.8 billion of Hertz's own cash and securities (including a $1.2 billion obligation from Ford, which was forgiven as part of the payment to Ford). The remaining $2.3 billion in private equity was contributed by Clayton, Dubilier & Rice, The Carlyle Group, and Merrill Lynch Global Private Equity.

MyLab Finance

Here is what you should know after reading this chapter. MyLab™ Finance will help you identify what you know, and where to go when you need to practice.

KEY POINTS	TERMS	ONLINE PRACTICE OPPORTUNITIES
15.1 Corporate Debt ■ Companies can raise debt using different sources. Typical kinds of debt are public debt, which trades in a public market, and private debt, which is negotiated directly with a bank or a small group of investors. The securities that companies issue when raising debt are called corporate bonds. ■ Private debt can be in the form of term loans or private placements. A term loan is a bank loan that lasts for a specific term. A private placement is a bond issue that is sold to a small group of investors. ■ For public offerings, the bond agreement takes the form of an indenture, a formal contract between the bond issuer and a trust company. The indenture lays out the terms of the bond issue. ■ Four types of corporate bonds are typically issued: notes, debentures, mortgage bonds, and asset-backed bonds. Notes and debentures are unsecured. Mortgage bonds and asset-backed bonds are secured. ■ Corporate bonds differ in their level of seniority. In case of bankruptcy, senior debt is paid in full before subordinated debt is paid. ■ International bonds are classified into four broadly defined categories: domestic bonds purchased by foreign investors, foreign bonds that are issued in a local market by a foreign entity, Eurobonds that are not denominated in the local currency of the country in which they are issued, and global bonds that trade in several markets simultaneously.	asset-backed bonds, p. 523 asset-backed line of credit, p. 521 debentures, p. 523 domestic bonds, p. 524 Eurobonds, p. 524 foreign bonds, p. 524 global bonds, p. 524 indenture, p. 521 mortgage bonds, p. 523 notes, p. 523 original issue discount (OID) bond, p. 523 private debt, p. 520 private placement, p. 521 revolving line of credit, p. 521 secured debt, p. 523 seniority, p. 523 subordinated debenture, p. 523 syndicated bank loan, p. 521 term loan, p. 521 tranche, p. 524 unsecured debt, p. 523	MyLab Study Plan 15.1
15.2 Other Types of Debt ■ Governments, provinces, and other government-sponsored enterprises issue bonds too.	general obligation bonds, p. 528 double-barrelled bonds, p.528 revenue bonds, p.528	MyLab Study Plan 15.2

KEY POINTS	TERMS	ONLINE PRACTICE OPPORTUNITIES
■ The Government of Canada has issued four kinds of domestic securities: cash management bills, treasury bills, fixed-coupon marketable bonds (also known as Government of Canada bonds), and real return bonds. ■ Agency securities are issued by agencies of the Canadian government or by Canadian government Crown corporations. Examples include bonds issued by the Canada Mortgage and Housing Corporation (CMHC), Business Development Bank of Canada (BDC), and Export Development Canada (EDC). ■ An asset-backed security (ABS) is a security that is made up of other financial securities; that is, the security's cash flows come from the cash flows of the underlying financial securities that "back" it. The underlying financial securities could be mortgages, credit card receivables, consumer loans, etc. ■ Holders of mortgage-backed securities (MBS) guaranteed by the CMHC face prepayment risk, which is the risk that they will find that the bond will be partially (or wholly) repaid earlier than expected. However, an MBS issued by the CMHC does not have default risk, unlike an MBS issued by a financial institution. ■ A collateralized debt obligation is an asset-backed security that is backed by other asset-backed securities. Provincial and municipal bonds are issued by Canadian provinces, their Crown corporations, and municipalities. In the United States, "munis" are issued by state and local governments. U.S. munis have a distinguishing characteristic in that the income on municipal bonds is not taxable at the federal level in the United States.		
15.3 Bond Covenants ■ Covenants are restrictive clauses in the bond contract that help investors by limiting the issuer's ability to take actions that will increase its default risk and reduce the value of the bonds.	covenants, p. 529	MyLab Study Plan 15.3

KEY POINTS	TERMS	ONLINE PRACTICE OPPORTUNITIES
15.4 Repayment Provisions ■ A call provision gives the issuer of the bond the right (but not the obligation) to retire the bond after a specific date (but before maturity). ■ A callable bond will generally trade at a lower price than an otherwise equivalent non-callable bond. ■ The yield to call is the yield of a callable bond, assuming that the bond is called at the earliest opportunity. ■ With a Canada call or make-whole call, the call price is the present value of the bond's remaining payments calculated with a rate adjusted for prevailing interest rates in the economy. ■ Another way in which a bond is repaid before maturity is by periodically repurchasing part of the debt through a sinking fund. ■ Some corporate bonds, known as convertible bonds, have a provision that allows the holder to convert them into equity. ■ Convertible debt carries a lower interest rate than other comparable non-convertible debt.	balloon payment, p. 534 call date, p. 530 call price, p. 530 callable bonds, p. 530 Canada call or make-whole call, p. 533 conversion price, p. 534 conversion ratio, p. 534 convertible bonds, p. 534 leveraged buyout (LBO), p. 536 sinking fund, p. 534 straight bond, p. 535 yield to call (YTC), p. 531 yield to worst, p. 532	MyLab Study Plan 15.4

REVIEW QUESTIONS

1. What are the different types of corporate debt and how do they differ?
2. Explain some of the differences between a public debt offering and a private debt offering.
3. Explain the difference between a secured corporate bond and an unsecured corporate bond.
4. Why do bonds with lower seniority have higher yields than equivalent bonds with higher seniority?
5. What is the difference between a foreign bond and a Eurobond?
6. Why would companies voluntarily choose to put restrictive covenants into a new bond issue?
7. Why would a call feature be valuable to a company issuing bonds?
8. What is the effect of including a standard call feature on the price a company can receive for its bonds?
9. When will the yield to maturity be higher than the yield to call for a bond with a standard call feature?

10. Why might a company's management want to issue a bond with the Canada call provision?

11. How does a sinking fund provision affect the cash flows associated with a bond issue from the company's perspective? From a single bondholder's perspective?

12. Why is the yield on a convertible bond lower than the yield on an otherwise identical bond without a conversion feature?

PROBLEMS

All problems in this chapter are available in MyLab Finance.

Corporate Debt

1. You are finalizing a bank loan for $200,000 for your small business, and the closing fees payable to the bank are 2% of the loan. After paying the fees, what will be the net amount of funds from the loan available to your business?

2. Your firm is considering two one-year loan options for a $500,000 loan. The first carries fees of 2% of the loan amount and charges interest of 4% of the loan amount. The other carries fees of 1% of the loan amount and charges interest of 4.5% of the loan amount.
   a. What is the net amount of funds from each loan?
   b. Based on the net amount of funds, what is the true interest rate of each loan?

3. Your firm is issuing $100 million in straight bonds at par with a coupon rate of 6% and paying total fees of 3%. What is the net amount of funds that the debt issue will provide for your firm?

4. Describe the kinds of domestic securities the Canadian government uses to finance the federal debt.

5. Suppose that on January 15, 2010, the Canadian government issued a five-year inflation indexed note with a coupon of 3%. On the date of issue, the consumer price index (CPI) was 250. By January 15, 2015, the CPI had increased to 300. What principal and coupon payment was made on January 15, 2015?

6. Suppose that on January 15, 2020, the Canadian government issued a 10-year inflation-indexed note with a coupon of 6%. On the date of issue, the CPI was 400. By January 15, 2030, the CPI had decreased to 300. What principal and coupon payment was made on January 15, 2030? Assume that the principal payment is protected against falling below par value (but the coupon payment is not similarly protected).

7. Describe the prepayment risk in a mortgage-backed bond guaranteed by the CMHC.

8. What is the distinguishing feature of how U.S. municipal bonds are taxed?

Repayment Provisions

9. General Electric has just issued a callable (at par) 10-year, 6% coupon bond with annual coupon payments. The bond can be called at par in one year or any time thereafter on a coupon payment date. It has a price of $102.
   a. What is the bond's yield to maturity?
   b. What is its yield to call?
   c. What is its yield to worst?

10. Boeing Corporation has just issued a callable (at par) three-year, 5% coupon bond with semi-annual coupon payments. The bond can be called at par in two years or any time thereafter on a coupon payment date. It has a price of $99.
a. What is the bond's yield to maturity?
b. What is its yield to call?
c. What is its yield to worst?

11. You own a bond with a face value of $10,000 and a conversion ratio of 450. What is the conversion price?

12. A $1000 face value convertible bond has a conversion ratio of 40 and is about to mature. Ignoring any transaction costs, what price must the stock surpass in order for you to convert?

13. You are the CFO of RealNetworks on July 1, 2008. The company's stock price is $9.70 and its convertible debt (as shown in Table 15.8) is now callable.
a. What is the value of the shares the bondholders would receive per $1000 bond if they convert?
b. What is the value per $1000 bond they would receive under the call?
c. If you call the bonds, will the bondholders convert into shares or accept the call price?

DATA CASE

You are working for Home Depot and have been asked to help explore the impact of a potential debt issue. The CFO and other top managers in the finance division are all aware that increasing the debt load will have ramifications in the credit markets. Specifically, they realize that the firm's debt rating could change, which will raise the cost of borrowing as well as possibly lower the value of the existing debt. No one is exactly sure what the impact will be, but they all agree that it deserves investigation.

You have been summoned to an executive-level meeting and asked to estimate the impact of increasing the debt of the firm. You are to consider four different scenarios: issuing $1 billion, $10 billion, $20 billion, and $30 billion in new debt. In each case, proceeds from the debt will be used to repurchase stock (so the total amount of financing for the firm will not change, just the balance between debt and equity). The CFO believes that the $1 billion level will not affect the firm's credit rating. However, each larger increase in debt will cause the debt to be downgraded one letter grade (e.g., from Baa to Ba). For example, the $10 billion scenario will lower the current debt rating one level, the $20 billion scenario would lower the rating still another level, and so on. Your job is to determine the impact of additional debt on borrowing costs at each debt level. Assume the new debt will be raised by issuing 10-year bonds.

1. Determine the current debt rating for The Home Depot.

Research the current bond rating at FINRA (finra-markets.morningstar.com/BondCenter/).

Select the "Corporate" toggle, enter the symbol for Home Depot (HD), and click "Show Results."

What is the Moody's bond rating on the Home Depot bond with the maturity closest to 10 years from today? What is the yield on this bond?

2. Because lower bond ratings will lead to higher interest costs, you will need to determine those costs. Go to **MyLab Finance**. You will see a table of bond spreads prepared by Reuters and the date the table was prepared right below it. These spreads represent the increased yield a bond must pay over the U.S. Treasury of the same maturity. Choose the 10-year spread for Home Depot's current rating and the three ratings below it. The spreads are in basis points; a basis point is 1/100th of a percentage point (thus, 50 basis points is 0.5%). We will adjust these old spreads to estimate the current spread.

   a. Because these spreads are dated, you will need to create new yield spreads for the various ratings. Use the current difference between the Home Depot bonds' yield and the 10-year Treasury as the true spread for the rating. Using Excel, compute the spreads for the other ratings by adding the difference in spreads from the table to the new true spread for Home Depot's rating. Finally, determine the yield for each rating by adding the new spread to the yield on the 10-year Treasury bond.

   b. Compute the required yields on 10-year bonds at each of the new debt levels requested.

3. What factors cause the bond rating to fall, and the bond yields to increase, as Home Depot increases its debt levels?

Note: Updates to this data case may be found on **MyLab Finance**.

CHAPTER 15 APPENDIX USING A FINANCIAL CALCULATOR TO CALCULATE YIELD TO CALL

Calculate the yield to call of the bond from Example 15.1. In the example, the bond is called at year 1; however, this can be generalized and solved for periods longer than one year.

HP-10BII

[ ] [C]	Press [Orange Shift] and then the [C] button to clear all previous entries.
[1] [N]	Enter the number of periods.
[8] [PMT]	Enter the payment amount per period.
[1] [0] [0] [FV]	Enter the price you would receive when it is called.
[1] [0] [3] [+/−] [PV]	Enter the present value or price of the bond.
[I/YR]	Solve for yield to call.

TI-BAII Plus Professional

[2ND] [FV]	Press [2nd] and then the [FV] button to clear all previous entries.
[1] [N]	Enter the number of periods.
[8] [PMT]	Enter the payment amount per period.
[1] [0] [0] [FV]	Enter the price you would receive when it is called.
[1] [0] [3] [+/−] [PV]	Enter the present value or price of the bond.
[CPT] [I/Y]	Solve for yield to call.

If the bond were called after two years, you would simply use 2 instead of 1 for the number of periods.

PART 5

Integrative Case

This case draws on material from Chapters 14 and 15.

On May 8, 1984, Hannah Eisenstat graduated from Louisiana State University. She set to work opening a coffee shop in Baton Rouge called HannaH and found a perfect location in a new development. Using a $50,000 inheritance to finance the venture, together with her own sweat equity, she started the business on August 1, 1984, as a sole proprietorship. The shop was profitable in the first year. Hannah found, however, that the quality of her coffee was not as high as she had initially envisioned. She discussed this issue with one of her regular customers, Natasha Smith. On the spot, Natasha offered to help finance the purchase of a roasting machine. By roasting the beans herself, Hannah could produce higher-quality coffee and, in addition, expand the business by offering beans for sale.

Expansion

After looking carefully at the financials, Hannah determined that she would need an investment of $75,000 from Natasha to undertake this expansion. In exchange for this investment, Hannah offered her a 40% share in the business. Natasha accepted the offer and the business was incorporated with two owners. The equity consisted of 1,000,000 shares in total, with Natasha owning 400,000 shares and Hannah owning 600,000 shares. By the end of the second year, the business was doing extremely well. Revenue from the sale of beans soon began to rival beverage sales. In response to this success, Hannah and Natasha decided to expand to five stores over the next two years. Rather than using equity financing, they decided to seek bank financing. Each new store required an investment of $100,000. Opening the stores took longer than planned, but by the end of 1999, there were five HannaHs in Baton Rouge employing 30 people. As planned, this expansion was financed solely with debt that was ultimately consolidated into a $500,000 term loan due in 2004.

Venture Capital

In early 2000, the two owners decided to take a weekend retreat and reevaluate their initial business plan. Perhaps the biggest surprise was the popularity of beans; almost 80% of revenue was attributable to bean sales alone. Furthermore, a buyer from a local supermarket chain had approached HannaH with a proposal to sell the beans in the chain's stores. However, HannaH was currently at its capacity limits—it could barely roast enough coffee for its five stores. More importantly, to enhance the coffee quality further, Hannah proposed that they buy beans directly from coffee farmers in Costa Rica, where she would be able to monitor quality closely. However, the supermarket proposal would require a significant increase in the production of roasted beans. By the end of the retreat, Hannah and Natasha had decided to change the focus of the business from retail beverage and bean sales to wholesale roasted coffee beans. Rather than build new stores, they decided to invest in a state-of-the-art roasting facility.

In the next few weeks, Hannah approached Dixie Partners, a local venture capital firm. On the strength of the commitment from the supermarket chain to carry the coffee, Dixie agreed to invest $3 million to finance the construction of a high-capacity roasting facility in exchange for a 50% share of the company. To accomplish this, 1,000,000 new shares in HannaH were issued to Dixie.

Further Expansion

Hannah's intuition was correct—the quality of the coffee increased significantly. Within eight years, the company had grown to almost 200 employees and its strong reputation allowed it to sell its coffee for a 50% premium over other brands. To finance the expansion, Dixie made two more equity investments: It paid $4 million for 1,200,000 shares in 2003 and $8 million for 1,500,000 shares in 2006. Furthermore, the term loan was renewed for another five years when it came due in 2004, and in 2007 an additional 400,000 shares were issued to employees as part of their compensation.

IPO

At the beginning of 2008, the board of directors decided to expand the distribution of the coffee throughout the United States and finance this expansion from the proceeds of an IPO. The plan was to initially raise $20 million in new capital at the IPO and then, within a year or two, raise an additional $20 million in an SEO. Dixie planned on selling 10% of its stake in HannaH at the IPO and subsequently liquidating the rest of its investment by the end of 2009. The IPO was successfully undertaken in August 2008. All told, the company sold 2,000,000 shares for $12 per share at the IPO, including 10% of Dixie's stake (no other existing shareholder sold any shares at the IPO).

SEO

A year later, in August 2009, the company did a cash offer SEO, selling an additional 4,000,000 shares for $20 per share, which included 400,000 shares from each original owner, Hannah and Natasha, and 2,000,000 of Dixie's shares. Thus, of the shares sold, 2,800,000 shares were existing shares and the rest were new shares. Some of the proceeds were used to repay the term loan that matured at the same time as the SEO and the remaining proceeds were used to finance the continued national expansion. Dixie had been selling additional shares in the secondary market over the prior year, so that issue represented the liquidation of Dixie's final stake—after the sale, Dixie no longer owned shares in HannaH. During this time, an additional 50,000 shares were issued to employees as part of their compensation.

LBO

By 2010, the fortunes of the company had changed. Although HannaH coffee still had a strong brand name and sales continued to grow the company, it was experiencing significant growing pains. Hannah herself was no longer directly involved in operations. Soon after the SEO a new CEO, Luke Ignion, was hired to take over the day-to-day running of the company, but he proved to be a poor fit. By late 2010, the company's share price had dropped to $5 per share. Hannah was distressed to see the value of her remaining stake drop to this level, so she decided to take advantage of what she saw as a buying opportunity.

Together with six other key employees, she undertook an LBO of HannaH. At the time of the LBO, the firm had 8,000,000 shares outstanding because an additional 20,000 shares had been given to key employees. Hannah and the other key employees had already started purchasing shares, so by the time of the LBO announcement Hannah owned 500,000 shares and the other key employees together owned an additional 100,000 shares. The group issued a tender offer to repurchase the remaining 7,400,000 shares for $7.50 per share. To finance the repurchase, the group combined an additional equity investment of $7,000,000, bank debt, and a (rule 144A) private placement of a $30 million, semi-annual, 10-year coupon bond. The plan was to register this privately placed debt publicly within a year. The debt was convertible and callable (at par) in five years. It had a conversion ratio of 50, a face value of $1000, and coupon rate of 5%.

CASE QUESTIONS

1. Natasha is an example of what kind of an investor?

2. At each funding stage prior to the IPO (i.e., 1985, 2000, 2003, and 2006), calculate the pre-money and post-money valuation of the equity of the company.

3. What fraction of the IPO was a primary offering and what fraction was a secondary offering?

4. Immediately following the IPO, the shares traded at $14.50.

a. At this price, what was the value of the whole company? Expressed in percent, by how much was the deal underpriced?

b. In dollars, how much did this underpricing cost existing shareholders?

c. Assuming that none of the owners purchased additional shares at the IPO, what fraction of the equity did Hannah own and what was it worth immediately following the IPO?

d. What was the company's debt-equity ratio—the ratio of the book value of debt outstanding to the market value of equity—immediately following the IPO?

5. Address the following questions related to the SEO:

a. What fraction of the SEO was a primary offering and what fraction was a secondary offering?

b. Assuming that the underwriters charged a 5% fee, what were the proceeds that resulted from Hannah's sale of her stock? How much money did the company raise that would be available to fund future investments and repay the term loan?

6. Immediately following the SEO, the stock price remained at $20 per share.

a. Once the term loan was repaid, what was the value of the whole company?

b. What fraction of the equity did Hannah own?

7. Assume the LBO was successful.

a. How much bank debt was required?

b. What was the debt-equity ratio immediately following the LBO?

8. A year after the LBO, just after the second payment was made, the convertible debt traded for a price of $950.

a. What was its yield to maturity?

b. What was the yield to call?

9. Assume that in the five years following the LBO Hannah was able to turn the company around. Over the course of this period, all the bank debt was repaid and the company went public again. The price per share was now $60/share. Predict what the holders of the convertible debt would do. What would their investment be worth?

CHAPTER

Capital Structure

16

LEARNING OBJECTIVES

- Examine how capital structures vary across industries and companies
- Understand why investment decisions, rather than financing decisions, fundamentally determine the value and cost of capital of the firm
- Describe how leverage increases the risk of the firm's equity
- Demonstrate how debt can affect the firm's value through taxes and bankruptcy costs
- Show how the optimal mix of debt and equity trades off the costs (including financial distress costs) and benefits (including the tax advantage) of debt
- Analyze how debt can alter the incentives managers have for choosing different projects and can be used as a signal to investors
- Weigh the many costs and benefits to debt that a manager must balance when deciding how to finance the firm's investments

NOTATION

D	market value of debt
E	market value of levered equity
EPS	earnings per share
NPV	net present value
PV	present value
r_D	expected return (cost of capital) of debt
r_E	expected return (cost of capital) of levered equity
r_f	risk-free interest rate
r_U	expected return (cost of capital) of unlevered equity
r_{wacc}	weighted average cost of capital
T_c	marginal corporate tax rate
V^L	value of the firm with leverage
V^U	value of the unlevered firm

When a firm needs to raise new funds to undertake its investments, it must decide which type of financing security it will issue to investors. What considerations should guide this decision, and how does this decision affect the value of the firm?

Consider the case of Facebook, from Chapter 14, issuing new equity in a seasoned equity offering, or Hertz from Chapter 15 substantially increasing its leverage through its leveraged buyout. In January of 2012, Finning International acquired the Bucyrus distribution and support subsidiary of Caterpillar for $465 million. The deal was financed through debt. What led managers at Facebook to rely on equity for its expansion and Hertz and Finning to choose to increase their debt instead? How might such capital structure decisions affect the value of these firms?

In this chapter, we first explore these questions in a setting of *perfect capital markets* in which all securities are fairly priced, there are no taxes or transaction costs, and the total cash flows of the firm's projects are not affected by how the firm finances them. Although, in reality, capital markets are not perfect, this setting provides an important benchmark.

We devote the remainder of the chapter to exploring how violations of our perfect capital markets assumptions affect our conclusions. We further explore how the tax advantage of debt that we briefly discussed in Chapter 12 makes debt a potentially attractive financing source. We then discuss the costs of financial distress and bankruptcy that firms with debt face. This discussion leads us to the insight that managers choose debt by balancing the tax advantages against the distress costs of debt. After discussing other influences on capital structure, including agency problems and differences in information between managers and investors, we conclude with some recommendations for a financial manager making capital structure decisions.

16.1 Capital Structure Choices

Recall that the relative proportions of debt, equity, and other securities that a firm has outstanding constitute its *capital structure*. When they raise funds from outside investors, corporations must choose which type of security to issue and what type of capital structure to have. The most common choices are financing through equity alone and financing through a combination of debt and equity. How do firms arrive at their capital structures, and what factors should a financial manager consider when choosing among financing alternatives?

First and foremost, various financing choices will promise different future amounts to each security holder in exchange for the cash that is raised today. But beyond that, the firm may also need to consider whether the securities it issues will receive a fair price in the market, have tax consequences, entail transactions costs, or even change its future investment opportunities. A firm's capital structure is also affected by decisions on whether to accumulate cash, pay off debt or pay dividends, or conduct share repurchases. Before exploring the theory underpinning this analysis, we place these financing decisions in the context of actual firm practices.

Capital Structure Choices Across Industries

Figure 16.1 shows the average debt-to-value ratios across industries for Canadian stocks. A firm's **debt-to-value ratio**, $D/(E + D)$, is the fraction of the firm's total value that corresponds to debt. Notice that the debt levels financial managers choose differ across industries. For example, software companies, such as OpenText, are far less levered (have less debt relative to their equity) than are banks, such as CIBC.

debt-to-value ratio The fraction of a firm's total value that corresponds to debt.

FIGURE 16.1 Debt-to-Value Ratios, $D/(D + E)$, for 30 Canadian Industries as of December 2017

Debt levels are determined by book values, and equity by market values. The average debt financing for all Canadian publicly traded companies was about 28%.

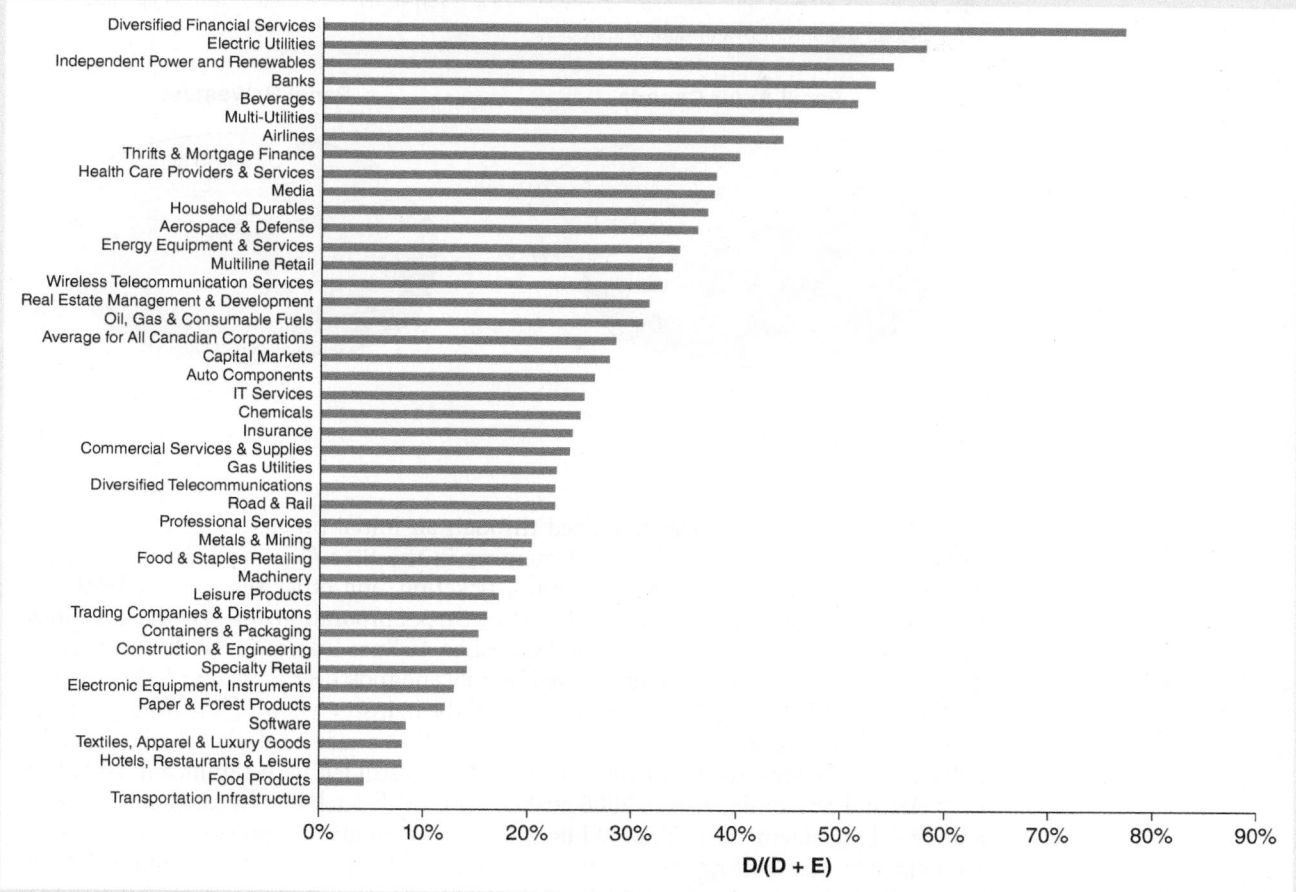

Source: Bloomberg and authors' calculations.

Capital Structure Choices within Industries

The differences in capital structures across industries are striking. However, even within industries, two competing firms may make different choices about their debt-to-value ratios. For example, Air Canada and WestJet, both members of the airline industry, have different capital structures, as depicted in panels (a) and (b) of Figure 16.2. Air Canada has approximately the same amount of debt as equity, as shown in panel (a), and WestJet has much less debt than equity, as shown in panel (b). Even though Air Canada and WestJet are direct competitors, they have very different assets and histories.

Air Canada (formerly Trans-Canada Air Lines) was legislated into existence in 1936 as a subsidiary of the government-owned Canadian National Railway. Through government regulation, Air Canada enjoyed a favourable position in the industry. In the early 1980s, Air Canada borrowed heavily to update its fleet of aircraft, but in the late 1980s, the government deregulated the airline industry, thus allowing for increased

FIGURE 16.2 Capital Structures of Air Canada and WestJet Airlines

The pie charts in panels (a) and (b) show the split between debt and equity in two competing firms, Air Canada and WestJet Airlines, as of December 2017. Both are part of the airline industry, which has an average debt-to-value ratio of 44%. Even within an industry, two companies can choose a different mix of debt and equity.

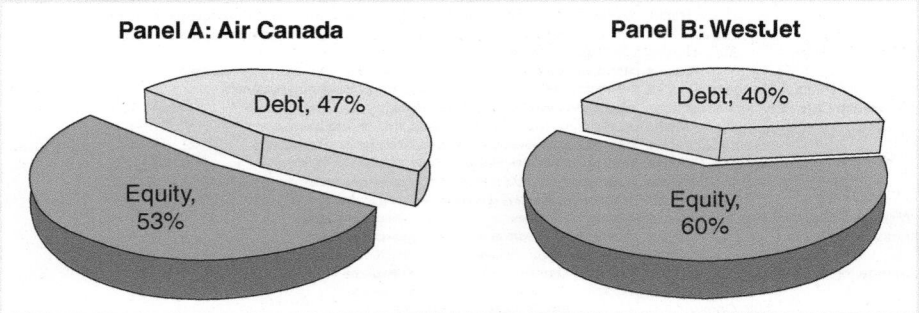

Source: Bloomberg, and author's calculations.

competition. Air Canada was privatized through an initial public offering in 1988. In 1997, Air Canada became a founding member in the Star Alliance, a group of international airlines that cooperated in routes, ticketing, and other services. In 1999, Air Canada was the target of a takeover attempt by Onex Corporation and American Airlines that would have merged Air Canada and Canadian Airlines International. In response to the hostile takeover, Air Canada borrowed heavily and took over Canadian Airlines itself. Air Canada's high debt level and the downturn in the industry following the September 11, 2001, terrorist attacks were two factors that led Air Canada to declare bankruptcy in 2003. After its restructuring in 2004, Air Canada was still left with significant debt. The financial and economic crisis of 2008 pushed Air Canada back into negative net income, and its debt problems resurfaced. While the company gradually recovered from the crisis, helped by cost cutting and the strengthening world economy, it was not until 2013 that Air Canada turned a profit. Since then, Air Canada's performance has continued to improve and its debt-to-value ratio has declined from over 60% to below 50%.

WestJet was founded in 1996 by Clive Beddoe and his partners, and began operations as a discount airline. Management grew the airline slowly and carefully, used one type of aircraft, the Boeing 737, and kept a much more conservative route structure and financial structure. In recent years WestJet has become more similar to Air Canada: it has increased its international flights, joined alliances with other airlines, and increased its debt-to-value ratio from around 20% to 40% over the past four years.

In this chapter, we will learn why these differences in assets and business plans would naturally lead to the different capital structures we observe today. In the next section, we start by developing the critical theoretical foundation of any capital structure analysis. Then we move on to important real-world factors that managers must trade off when considering capital structure decisions.

CONCEPT CHECK

1. What constitutes a firm's capital structure?
2. What are some factors a manager must consider when making a financing decision?

16.2 Capital Structure in Perfect Capital Markets

When a firm issues debt, equity, or other securities to fund a new investment, its decision has many potential consequences. By far the most important question for a financial manager is whether different choices will affect the value of the firm and, thus, the amount of capital it can raise. We begin by considering this question in a simple environment—a perfect capital market. A **perfect capital market** has these characteristics:

perfect capital market
A set of conditions in which investors and firms can trade the same set of securities at competitive market prices; in such a market, there are no tax consequences or transactions costs, and the firm's financing decisions do not change the cash flows that its investments generate.

1. *Securities are fairly priced.* Investors and firms can trade the same set of securities at competitive market prices equal to the present value of their future cash flows.
2. *No tax consequences or transactions costs.* There are no tax consequences, transaction costs, or other issuance costs associated with financing decisions or security trading.
3. *Investment cash flows are independent of financing choices.* A firm's financing decisions do not change the cash flows its investments generate, nor do those decisions reveal new information about those cash flows.

The assumption of perfect capital markets may seem narrow and unrealistic. We will see, however, that by starting with them we will gain important insight into the true benefits and costs of leverage.

Application: Financing a New Business

Let's begin with an example of a possible financing decision in a perfect capital market. Imagine you have one year left in university and you want to earn some extra money before graduation. You have been offered the opportunity to run the coffee shop in the lobby of a nearby office building. The owner of the building is willing to grant you this right on a one-year basis prior to a major remodelling of the building.

Your research indicates that you will need to make an upfront investment of $24,000 to start the business. After covering your operating costs, including paying yourself a nice wage, you expect to generate a cash flow of $34,500 at the end of the year. The current risk-free interest rate is 5%. You believe, however, that your profits will be somewhat risky and sensitive to the overall market (which will affect the level of activity in the building and demand for your business), so a 10% risk premium is appropriate, for a total discount rate of 15% (5% + 10%). You therefore calculate the NPV of this investment in the coffee shop as follows:

$$\begin{aligned} NPV &= -\$24{,}000 + \frac{\$34{,}500}{1.15} = -\$24{,}000 + \$30{,}000 \\ &= \$6000 \end{aligned}$$

Thus, the investment has a positive NPV.

Even though the investment looks attractive, you still need to raise the money for the upfront investment. How should you raise the funds, and what is the amount you will be able to raise?

Equity Financing. First, you consider raising money solely by selling equity in the business to your friends and family. Given the cash flow estimates, how much would they be willing to pay for those shares? Recall that the value of a security equals the present value of its future cash flows. In this case, equity holders in your firm will expect to receive the payoff of $34,500 at the end of the year, with the same risk as the cash flows generated by the coffee shop. Therefore, your firm's equity cost of capital will be 15% and the value of its equity today will be as follows:

$$PV(\text{equity cash flows}) = \frac{\$34{,}500}{1.15} = \$30{,}000$$

unlevered equity Equity in a firm with no debt.

Recall that the absence of debt means the absence of financial leverage. Equity in a firm with no debt is, therefore, called **unlevered equity**. Because the present value of the equity cash flows is $30,000, you can raise $30,000 by selling all the unlevered equity in your firm. Doing so allows you to keep the NPV of $6000 as profit after paying the investment cost of $24,000. In other words, the project's NPV represents the value to the initial owner of the firm (in this case, you, the entrepreneur) that the project creates.

Levered Financing. As an alternative, you also consider borrowing some of the money you will need to invest. Suppose the business's cash flow is certain to be at least $16,000. Then you can borrow $15,000 at the current risk-free interest rate of 5%. You will be able to pay the debt of $15,000 × 1.05 = $15,750 at the end of the year without any risk of defaulting.

levered equity Equity in a firm with outstanding debt.

How much can you raise selling equity in your business now? Equity in a firm that also has outstanding debt is called **levered equity**. After the debt is repaid, equity holders can expect to receive $34,500 − 15,750 = $18,750. What discount rate should we use to value levered equity? What expected return will investors demand?

It's tempting to use the same 15% equity cost of capital as before. In that case, by selling levered equity, you could raise $18,750/1.15 = $16,304. If this result were correct, then using leverage would allow you to raise a total amount, including the debt, of $15,000 + 16,304 = $31,304, or $1304 more than in the case without leverage.

Thus, it would seem that simply financing a project with leverage can make it more valuable. *But if this sounds too good to be true, it is*. Our analysis assumed that your firm's equity cost of capital remained unchanged at 15% after adding leverage. But as we will see shortly, this will not be the case—leverage will increase the risk of the firm's equity and raise its equity cost of capital. To see why, and to understand what will actually happen, we turn to the hallmark work of researchers Franco Modigliani and Merton Miller.

Leverage and Firm Value

In an important paper, researchers Modigliani and Miller (or simply "M&M") considered whether leverage would increase the total value of the firm. Their answer to this question surprised researchers and practitioners at the time.[1] M&M argued that with perfect capital markets, the total value of a firm should *not* depend on its capital structure. Their reasoning: your firm's total cash flows—those paid to both debt and equity holders—still equal the cash flows of the coffee shop, with the same expected value of $34,500 and the same total risk as before, as shown in Figure 16.3.

Because the total cash flows of the debt and equity equal the cash flows of the unlevered firm, the Valuation Principle tells us that their market values must be the same. Specifically, we calculated earlier that the value of the unlevered firm, V^U, is

$$V^U = \$34{,}500/1.15 = \$30{,}000$$

Thus, the total value of the levered firm, V^L, which is the combined value of its debt, D, and levered equity, E, must be the same:

$$V^L = D + E = \$30{,}000$$

[1]Franco Modigliani and Merton Miller, "The Cost of Capital, Corporation Finance and the Theory of Investment," *American Economic Review,* 48(3) (1958): 261–297.

FIGURE 16.3 Unlevered versus Levered Cash Flows with Perfect Capital Markets

When the firm has no debt, as shown in panel (a), the cash flows paid to equity holders correspond to the free cash flows the firm's assets generate. When the firm has the debt shown in panel (b), these cash flows are divided between debt and equity holders. However, with perfect capital markets, the total amount paid to all investors still corresponds to the free cash flows the firm's assets generate. Therefore, the value of the unlevered firm, V^U, must equal the total value of the levered firm, V^L, which is the combined value of its debt D and levered equity E.

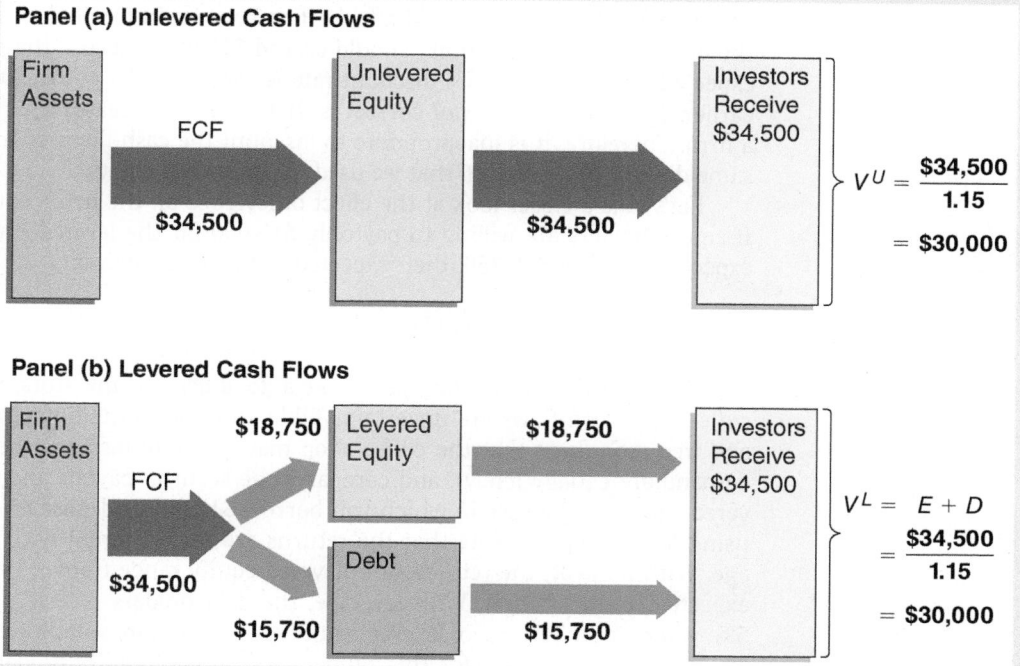

Therefore, if the initial market value of the debt is $D = \$15{,}000$ (the amount borrowed), the initial market value of the levered equity must be $E = \$30{,}000 - \$15{,}000 = \$15{,}000$.

Thus, M&M argued that leverage merely changes the allocation of cash flows between debt and equity without altering the total cash flows of the firm in a perfect capital market. As a result, they concluded the following:

> ***M&M Proposition I:*** *In a perfect capital market, the total value of a firm is equal to the market value of the free cash flows generated by its assets and is not affected by its choice of capital structure.*

We can write this result in an equation as follows:

$$V^L = E + D = V^U \tag{16.1}$$

This equation states that the total value of the firm is the same with or without leverage.

Note that in our example the cash flows of levered equity are smaller than those of unlevered equity; therefore, levered equity will sell for a lower price than unlevered equity ($15,000 versus $30,000). However, the fact that the equity is less valuable with leverage does not mean that you are worse off. You will still raise a total of $30,000 by issuing both debt and levered equity, just as you did with unlevered equity alone, and still keep as profit the $6000 difference between the $30,000 you raise and your $24,000 cost. As a consequence, you will be indifferent about which of these two options to choose for the firm's capital structure.

The Effect of Leverage on Risk and Return

Modigliani and Miller's conclusion went against the common view that even with perfect capital markets, leverage would affect a firm's value. In particular, it was thought that the value of the levered equity should exceed $15,000, because the present value of its expected cash flow at a 15% discount rate is $18,750/1.15 = $16,304, as we calculated earlier. The reason this is *not* correct is that leverage increases the risk of the equity of a firm. Therefore, it is inappropriate to discount the cash flows of levered equity at the same discount rate of 15% that we used for unlevered equity.

Let's take a closer look at the effect of leverage on the firm's equity cost of capital. If equity holders are willing to pay only $15,000 for the levered equity, then given its expected payoff of $18,750, their expected return is as follows:

$$\text{Expected return of levered equity} = \$18{,}750/\$15{,}000 - 1 = 25\%$$

Although this return may seem like a good deal for investors, remember that the coffee shop cash flows are uncertain. Table 16.1 shows the different levels of demand and free cash flows that the coffee shop may generate (assume that weak and strong demand are equally likely), and compares the security payoffs and returns with unlevered equity to the case in which you borrow $15,000 and raise an additional $15,000 using levered equity. Note that the returns are very different with and without leverage. With no debt, the returns of unlevered equity range from −10% to 40%, with an expected return of 15%. With leverage, the debt holders receive a risk-free return of 5%, whereas the returns of levered equity are much more volatile, ranging from −25% to 75%. To compensate for this higher risk, levered equity holders receive a higher expected return of 25%.

We further illustrate the effect of leverage on returns in Figure 16.4. By adding leverage, the returns of the unlevered firm are effectively "split" between low-risk debt and much higher risk levered equity. Note that the returns of levered equity fall twice as fast as those of unlevered equity if the coffee shops cash flows decline. This doubling of the risk justifies a doubling of the risk premium, which is 15% − 5% = 10% for unlevered equity and 25% − 5% = 20% for levered equity. As this example shows, *leverage increases the risk of equity even when there is no risk that the firm will default.*

TABLE 16.1 Returns to Equity in Different Scenarios with and without Leverage

Coffee Shop		Security Cash Flows			Security Returns		
Demand	Free cash flows	Unlevered equity	Debt	Levered equity	Unlevered equity	Debt	Levered equity
Weak	$27,000	$27,000	$15,750	$11,250	−10%	5%	−25%
Expected	$34,500	$34,500	$15,750	$18,750	15%	5%	25%
Strong	$42,000	$42,000	$15,750	$26,250	40%	5%	75%

FIGURE 16.4 **Unlevered versus Levered Returns with Perfect Capital Markets**

Leverage splits the firm's return between low-risk debt and high-risk levered equity compared with the equity of an unlevered firm. In this example, the returns of levered equity are twice as sensitive to the firm's cash flows as the returns of unlevered equity are. This doubling of risk implies a doubling of the risk premium from 10% to 20%.

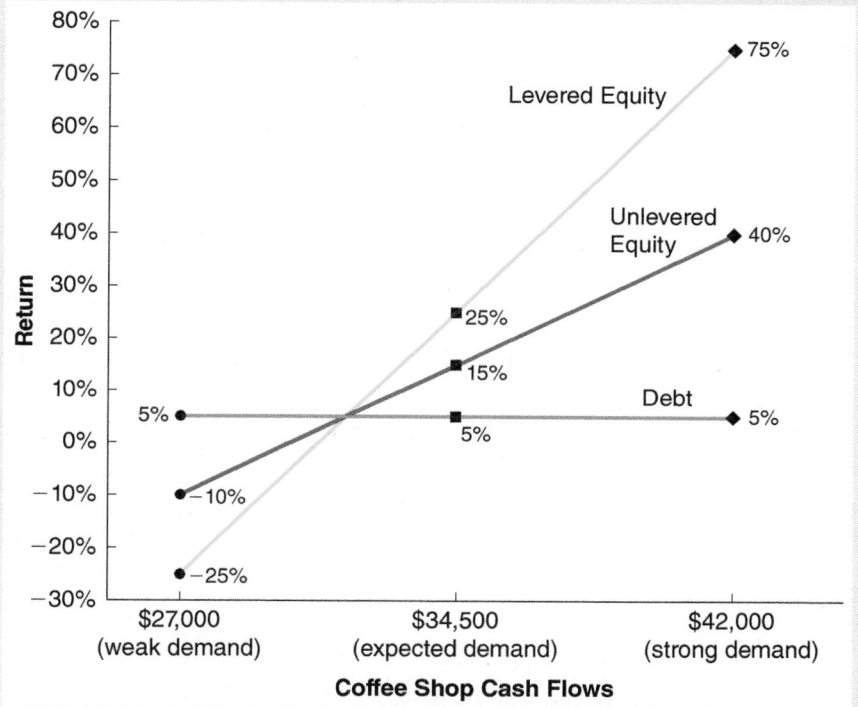

EXAMPLE 16.1 The Risk and Return of Levered Equity

PROBLEM

Suppose you borrow only $6000 when financing your coffee shop. According to M&M, what should the value of the equity be? What is the expected return? Use the three hypothetical demand scenarios from Table 16.1.

SOLUTION

■ Plan

The value of the firm's total cash flows does not change: it is still $30,000. Thus, if you borrow $6000, your firm's equity will be worth $24,000. To determine the equity's expected return, we will compute the cash flows to equity under the two scenarios. The cash flows to equity are the cash flows of the firm net of the cash flows to debt (repayment of principal plus interest).

■ Execute

The firm will owe debt holders $6000 × 1.05 = $6300 in one year. Thus, the expected payoff to equity holders is $34,500 − $6300 = $28,200, for a return of $28,200/$24,000 − 1 = 17.5%. ▶

■ **Evaluate**

While the total value of the firm is unchanged, the firm's equity in this case is more risky than it would be without debt, but less risky than if the firm borrowed $15,000. To illustrate, note that if demand is weak, the equity holders will receive $27,000 − $6300 = $20,700, for a return of $20,700/$24,000 − 1 = −13.75%. Compare this return to −10% without leverage and −25% if the firm borrowed $15,000. As a result, the expected return of the levered equity is higher in this case than for unlevered equity (17.5% versus 15%), but not as high as in the previous example (17.5% versus 25%).

Homemade Leverage

Suppose investors would prefer an alternative capital structure to the one the firm has chosen. M&M demonstrated that in this case, investors can borrow or lend on their own and achieve the same result. For example, an investor who would like more leverage than the firm has chosen can borrow and thus add leverage to his or her own portfolio. Adding leverage in this way will lower the out-of-pocket cost of the security, but increase the risk of the portfolio. When investors use leverage in their own portfolios to adjust the leverage choice the firm has made, we say that they are using **homemade leverage**. As long as investors can borrow or lend at the same interest rate as the firm, which is true in perfect capital markets, homemade leverage is a perfect substitute for the firm's use of leverage. Thus, because different choices of capital structure offer no benefit to investors in perfect capital markets, those choices do not affect the value of the firm.

homemade leverage Leverage that investors use in their own portfolios to adjust the leverage choice a firm has made.

Leverage and the Cost of Capital

We can use the insight of M&M to understand the effect of leverage on the firm's cost of capital. Recall from Figure 16.3 and Equation 16.1 that if we look at a portfolio of the equity and debt of a levered firm together, that portfolio has the same value and cash flows as the unlevered firm. Therefore, the expected return of the portfolio should equal the expected return of the unlevered firm. Recall from Chapter 11 that the expected return of the portfolio of equity and debt is simply the weighted average of the expected returns of each security. Thus, with r_E representing the expected return of the levered equity, r_D the expected return of the debt, and r_U the expected return of the unlevered equity, we have the following:

Weighted Average Cost of Capital (Pre-Tax)

$$\underbrace{r_E \frac{E}{E+D} + r_D \frac{D}{E+D}}_{\text{pre-tax WACC}} = r_U \tag{16.2}$$

The amounts $\frac{E}{E+D}$ and $\frac{D}{E+D}$ represent the fraction of the firm's value financed by equity and debt, respectively. Thus, the left side of Equation 16.2 is the weighted average cost of capital (WACC) of the firm, which we defined in Chapter 12. Note that the cost of debt is not adjusted for taxes, because we are assuming "perfect capital markets" and thus ignoring taxes. When we compute the weighted average cost of capital without taxes, we refer to it as the firm's **pre-tax WACC**. Equation 16.2 states that for any choice

pre-tax WACC The weighted average cost of capital computed using the pre-tax cost of debt.

of capital structure, the firm's pre-tax WACC is unchanged and remains equal to the firm's unlevered cost of capital.

Let's check this result for our coffee shop example. With leverage, the firm's debt cost of capital was $r_D = 5\%$, and its equity cost of capital rose to $r_E = 25\%$. What about the portfolio weights? In this case, the firm borrowed $D = 15{,}000$, and issued equity worth $E = 15{,}000$, for a total value $V^L = E + D = 30{,}000$. Therefore, its pre-tax WACC is as follows:

$$r_E \frac{E}{E+D} + r_D \frac{D}{E+D} = 25\%\left(\frac{15{,}000}{30{,}000}\right) + 5\%\left(\frac{15{,}000}{30{,}000}\right) = 15\%$$

Thus, the pre-tax WACC does indeed equal the firm's unlevered cost of capital, $r_U = 15\%$.

How is it that the firm's WACC stays the same even after adding leverage? There are two offsetting effects of leverage; we finance a larger fraction of the firm with debt, which is a lower-cost source of capital, but at the same time, adding leverage raises the firm's equity cost of capital. Because the firm's total risk has not changed (it has just been split between these two securities), these two effects should exactly cancel out and leave the firm's WACC unchanged.[2] In fact, we can use Equation 16.2 to determine the precise impact of leverage on the firm's equity cost of capital. Solving the equation for r_E, we have

M&M Proposition II: The Cost of Capital of Levered Equity

$$r_E = r_U + \frac{D}{E}(r_U - r_D) \tag{16.3}$$

Or, in words,

> ***M&M Proposition II:*** *The cost of capital of levered equity is equal to the cost of capital of unlevered equity plus a premium that is proportional to the debt-equity ratio (measured using market values).*

Let's check M&M Proposition II for the coffee shop example. In this case,

$$r_E = r_U + \frac{D}{E}(r_U - r_D) = 15\% + \frac{15{,}000}{15{,}000}(15\% - 5\%) = 25\%$$

This result matches the expected return for levered equity we calculated in Table 16.1.

Figure 16.5 illustrates the effect of increasing the amount of leverage in a firm's capital structure on its equity cost of capital, its debt cost of capital, and its WACC. In the figure, the firm's leverage is measured in terms of its debt-to-value ratio, $D/(E + D)$. With no debt, the WACC is equal to the unlevered equity cost of capital. As the firm borrows at the low cost of capital for debt its equity cost of capital rises, according to Equation 16.3. The net effect is that the firm's WACC is unchanged. Of course, as the amount of debt increases, the debt becomes riskier, because there is a chance the firm will default; as a result, the debt cost of capital also rises. With close to 100% debt, the debt would be almost as risky as the assets themselves (similar to unlevered equity).

---

[2]Note that a change in the WACC would also imply a change in the value of the firm, since we would be discounting the same future cash flows using a different discount rate. Therefore, a change in the WACC as a result of changing leverage would lead to a violation of M&M Proposition I.

FIGURE 16.5 WACC and Leverage with Perfect Capital Markets

Panel (a) represents the data in panel (b) for the coffee shop example. As the fraction of the firm that is financed with debt increases, both the equity and the debt become riskier, and their cost of capital rises. Yet, because more weight is put on the lower-cost debt, the WACC remains constant.

Panel (a) Equity, Debt, and WACC for Different Amounts of Leverage

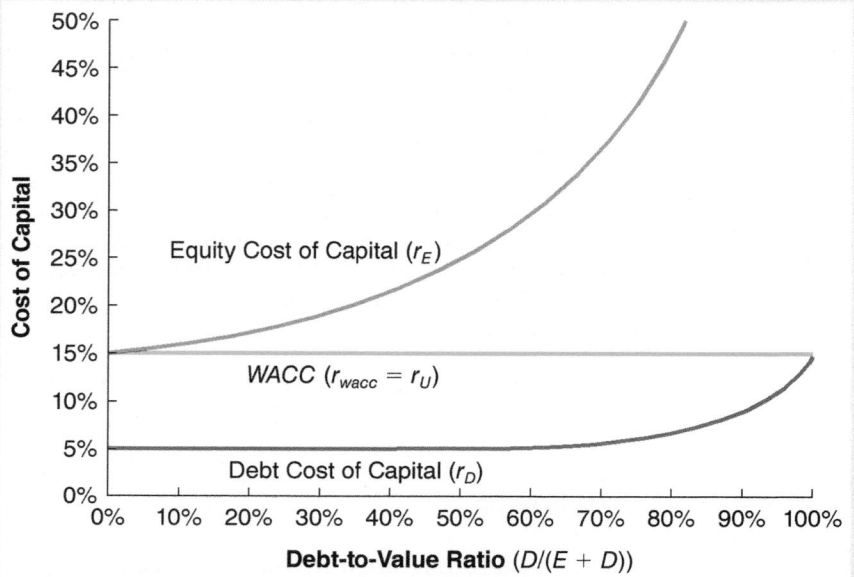

Panel (b) WACC Data for Alternative Capital Structures

E	D	r_E	r_D	$r_E \frac{E}{E+D} + r_D \frac{D}{E+D}$	$= r_{wacc}$
30,000	0	15.0%	5.0%	15.0% × 1.0 + 5.0% × 0.0	= 15%
24,000	6000	17.5%	5.0%	17.5% × 0.8 + 5.0% × 0.2	= 15%
15,000	15,000	25.0%	5.0%	25.0% × 0.5 + 5.0% × 0.5	= 15%
3000	27,000	75.0%	8.3%	75.0% × 0.1 + 8.3% × 0.9	= 15%

But even though the debt and equity costs of capital both rise when leverage is high, because more of the firm is financed with debt (which has lower cost), the WACC remains constant.

M&M and the Real World

Our conclusions so far may seem striking at first; in perfect capital markets, leverage does not affect either the cost of capital or firm value, and so the firm's choice of capital structure would be irrelevant! However, capital markets are not perfect in the real world. What then are we to make of M&M's results?

COMMON MISTAKE

Capital Structure Fallacies

Here, we take a critical look at two incorrect arguments that are sometimes cited in favour of leverage.

Leverage and Earnings per Share

Fallacy 1: Leverage can increase a firm's expected earnings per share; by doing so, leverage should also increase the firm's stock price.

Consider the coffee shop example. In the all-equity case, if you issued 1000 shares, they would each be worth $30 and the expected earnings per share (EPS) would be $34,500/1000 = $34.50. EPS would vary from $27 per share to $42 per share in the case of weak or strong demand. In the case with debt, as shown in Table 16.1, you only need to raise $15,000 in equity and so could issue only 500 shares, each worth $30. In this case, your expected EPS will be $18,750/500 = $37.50, with a range from $22.50 to $52.50. Thus, although the expected EPS is greater with leverage, the variation in EPS is also much greater, as shown in the blue and yellow bars in the figure below. With leverage, EPS falls to $22.50 when cash flows are low, which is much further than EPS would have dropped without leverage ($27). Although EPS increases on average, this increase is necessary to compensate shareholders for the additional risk they are taking. As a result, the entrepreneur's share price does not increase as a result of issuing debt.

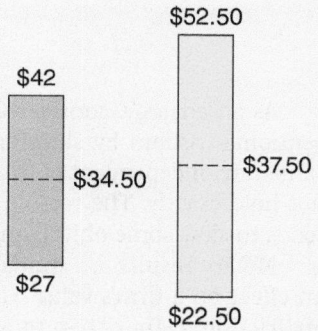

Equity Issuances and Dilution

Fallacy 2: Issuing equity will *dilute* existing shareholders' ownership, so debt financing should be used instead. *Dilution* means that if the firm issues new shares the cash flows generated by the firm must be divided among a larger number of shares, thereby reducing the value of each individual share.

This line of reasoning ignores the fact that the cash raised by issuing new shares will increase the firm's assets. Consider Google's September 2005 seasoned equity offering of 14,159,265 Class A shares at $295 apiece. Google priced the shares to match the market price of Class A shares on NASDAQ at the time of the offer. The amount raised was then $4,176,983,175, so the total value of Google increased to $60,560,157,355, which, when divided by the new total number of shares (205,288,669), still results in a price of $295 per share.

In general, as long as the firm sells the new shares of equity *at a fair price*, there will be no gain or loss to shareholders associated with the equity issue itself. The money taken in by the firm as a result of the share issue exactly offsets the dilution of the shares. *Any gain or loss associated with the transaction will result from the NPV of the investments the firm makes with the funds raised.*

EXAMPLE 16.2 Computing the Equity Cost of Capital

PROBLEM

Suppose you borrow only $6000 when financing your coffee shop. According to M&M Proposition II, what will your firm's equity cost of capital be?

SOLUTION

Plan

Because your firm's assets have a market value of $30,000, according to M&M Proposition I, the equity will have a market value of $24,000 = $30,000 − $6000. We can use Equation 16.3 to compute the cost of equity. We know the unlevered cost of equity is $r_u = 15\%$. We also know that r_D is 5%.

Execute

$$r_E = 15\% + \frac{6000}{24{,}000}(15\% - 5\%) = 17.5\%$$

Evaluate

This result matches the expected return calculated in Example 16.1, where we also assumed debt of $6000. The equity cost of capital should be the expected return of the equity holders.

As an analogy, consider Galileo's law of falling bodies. Galileo overturned the conventional wisdom by showing that without friction, free-falling bodies will fall at the same rate, independent of their mass. If you test this law, you will likely find that it does not hold exactly. The reason, of course, is that unless we are in a vacuum, air friction tends to slow some objects more than others.

M&M's results are similar. In practice, we will find that capital structure can have an effect on a firm's value. Galileo's law of falling bodies reveals that we must look to air friction, rather than to any underlying property of gravity, to explain differences in the speeds of falling objects. M&M's propositions reveal that any effects of capital structure must similarly be due to frictions that exist in capital markets. We explore the important sources of these frictions, and their consequences, in the remainder of this chapter.

NOBEL PRIZE Franco Modigliani and Merton Miller

Franco Modigliani and Merton Miller, the authors of the Modigliani & Miller propositions, have each won the Nobel Prize in Economics for their work in financial economics, including their capital structure propositions. Modigliani won the Nobel Prize in 1985 for his work on personal savings and for his capital structure theorems with Miller. Miller earned his prize in 1990 for his analysis of portfolio theory and capital structure.

In an interview, Miller once described the M&M propositions this way:

> People often ask, "Can you summarize your theory quickly?" Well, I say, you understand the M&M theorem if you know why this is a joke: The pizza delivery man comes to Yogi Berra after the game and says, "Yogi, how

do you want this pizza cut, into quarters or eighths?" And Yogi says, "Cut it in eight pieces. I'm feeling hungry tonight."

Everyone recognizes that's a joke because obviously the number and shape of the pieces don't affect the size of the pizza. And similarly, the stocks, bonds, warrants, etc., issued don't affect the aggregate value of the firm. They just slice up the underlying earnings in different ways.*

Modigliani and Miller each won the Nobel Prize in large part for their observation that the value of a firm should be unaffected by its capital structure in perfect capital markets. Whereas the intuition underlying the M&M propositions may be as simple as slicing pizza, their implications for corporate finance are far-reaching. The propositions imply that the true role of a firm's financial policy is to deal with (and potentially exploit) financial market imperfections such as taxes and transaction costs. M&M's work began a long line of research into these market imperfections, which we will look at in the rest of the chapter.

**Source:* Peter J. Tanous, *Investment Gurus* (New York: Institute of Finance, 1997)

GLOBAL FINANCIAL CRISIS

Bank Capital Regulation and the ROE Fallacy

In banking jargon, a "capital requirement" obligates a bank to finance itself with a certain minimum amount of equity to ensure that its debt-to-equity ratio will stay below a set level. The permitted level of leverage is very high—international standards allow common equity to represent as little as 2% of a bank's total funding.* To put this number in perspective, the equity of a typical non-financial firm exceeds 50% of firm value. Such extreme leverage makes bank equity very risky.

These extreme levels of bank leverage were an important contributing factor to the financial meltdown in 2008 and the subsequent recession: With such a small equity cushion, even a minor drop in asset values can lead to insolvency. Post-crisis, banks have come under increased pressure to reduce leverage with new international rules more than doubling the required proportion of equity financing. Many policymakers believe capital requirements should be increased much more to reduce the risk of the financial sector and the consequent spillovers to the broader economy.

Bankers counter that decreased leverage will lower their return on equity, limiting their ability to compete effectively. According to Josef Ackermann, then CEO of Deutsche Bank, new capital requirements would "depress ROE to levels that make investment into the banking sector unattractive relative to other business sectors."** The return on equity is indeed a function of the firm's leverage. As with EPS, lower leverage will tend to decrease the firm's ROE on average, though it will raise the ROE in bad times. But this decrease in average ROE is compensated for by a reduction in the riskiness of equity and therefore the required risk premium. Thus, from an investor's perspective, the reduction in ROE that results solely from a decrease in leverage does not make investing in the firm any less attractive. Franco Modigliani and Merton Miller were awarded the Nobel Prize for pointing out that in a perfect market the bank's capital structure cannot affect its competitiveness.

The only way a change in leverage can affect the "attractiveness" of equity (and the competitiveness of banks) is if there is a market imperfection. The most important imperfections come from deposit insurance, too-big-to-fail policies, and the tax deductibility of interest, giving banks a strong incentive to maximize their leverage. These imperfections derive from government subsidies, so the banks' gains from leverage come largely at taxpayer expense.

*Two percent was the Tier 1 Common Equity Requirement of the Basel II Accord, the global regulatory standard for bank capital. Starting in 2013, the Basel III Accord raised this requirement to 4.5% by 2015.

**J. Ackermann, "The new architecture of financial regulation: Will it prevent another crisis?" Special Paper 194, FMG Deutsche Bank Conference, London School of Economics, October 2010.

CONCEPT CHECK

3. How does leverage affect the risk and cost of equity for the firm?
4. In a perfect capital market, can you alter the firm's value or WACC by relying more on debt capital?

16.3 Debt and Taxes

So far, we have used the perfect capital markets setting to focus on the fundamental point that the firm's choice of projects and investments is the primary determinant of its value and risk, and hence its overall cost of capital. But in the real world, markets are imperfect, and these imperfections can create a role for the firm's capital structure. In this section, we focus on one important market friction—corporate taxes—and show how the firm's choice of capital structure can affect the taxes that it must pay and, therefore its value to investors.

The Interest Tax Deduction and Firm Value

As we discussed in Chapter 12, corporations can deduct interest expenses from their taxable income. The deduction reduces the taxes they pay and thereby increases the amount available to pay investors. In this way the interest tax deduction increases the value of the corporation.

To illustrate, let's consider the impact of interest expenses on the taxes paid by Loblaw Companies Limited, a grocery store chain. In 2016, Loblaw had earnings before interest and taxes of $2.092 billion, and interest expenses of $653 million. Given a corporate tax rate of 26%, we can compare Loblaw's actual net income with what it would have been without debt, as shown in Table 16.2.

As we can see from Table 16.2, Loblaw's net income in 2016 was lower with leverage than it would have been without leverage. Thus, Loblaw's debt obligations reduced the value of its equity. But more importantly, the *total* amount available to *all* investors was higher with leverage, as can be seen in the last row of the table. With leverage, Loblaw was able to pay out $2317.26 million in total to its investors, versus only $2147.48 million without leverage, representing an increase of $169.78 million.

It might seem odd that a firm can be better off with leverage even though its earnings are lower. But recall from Section 16.1 that the value of a firm is the total amount it can raise from all investors, not just equity holders who receive the earnings. Thus, if the firm can pay out more in total with leverage, it will be able to raise more total capital initially.

TABLE 16.2 Loblaw's Income with and without Leverage and the Effect on Payouts Available to Investors, 2016 ($ millions)

	With Leverage (Actual)	Without Leverage
EBIT	2902.00	2902.00
Interest expense	653.00	0.00
Income before tax	2249.00	2902.00
Taxes 26%	584.74	754.52
Net income	1664.26	2147.48
Interest paid to debt holders	653.00	0.00
Inc available to equity holders	1664.26	2147.48
Total available to all investors	2317.26	2147.48

Where does the additional $169.78 million come from? Looking at Table 16.2, we can see that this gain is equal to the reduction in taxes with leverage: $754.52 million − $584.74 million = $169.78 million. Because Loblaw does not owe taxes on the $653 million of pre-tax earnings it used to make interest payments, this $653 million is *shielded* from the corporate tax, providing the tax savings of 26% × $653 million = $169.78 million.

interest tax shield The reduction in taxes paid due to the tax deductibility of interest payments.

In general, the gain to investors from the tax deductibility of interest payments is referred to as the **interest tax shield**. The interest tax shield is the additional amount a firm can pay to investors by saving the taxes it would have paid if it did not have leverage. We can calculate the amount of the interest tax shield each year as follows:

$$\text{Interest Tax Shield} = \text{Corporate Tax Rate} \times \text{Interest Payments} \tag{16.4}$$

EXAMPLE 16.3 Computing the Interest Tax Shield

PROBLEM

Shown below is the income statement for Delta Farm Buildings (DFB). Given its marginal corporate tax rate of 35%, what is the amount of the interest tax shield for DFB in years 2014 through 2017?

1	**DFB Income Statement ($ million)**	**2014**	**2015**	**2016**	**2017**
2	Total sales	$3369	$3706	$4077	$4432
3	Cost of sales	−2359	−2584	−2867	−3116
4	Selling, general, and administrative expense	−226	−248	−276	−299
5	Depreciation	−22	−25	−27	−29
6	**Operating income**	762	849	907	988
7	Other income	7	8	10	12
9	**EBIT**	769	857	917	1000
10	Interest expense	−50	−80	−100	−100
11	**Income before tax**	719	777	817	900
12	Taxes (35%)	−252	−272	−286	−315
13	**Net income**	$467	$505	$531	$585

SOLUTION

Plan

From Equation 16.4, the interest tax shield is the tax rate of 35% multiplied by the interest payments in each year.

Execute

1	($ million)	2011	2012	2013	2014
2	Interest expense	50	80	100	100
3	Interest tax shield (35% × interest expense)	17.5	28	35	35

Evaluate

By using debt, DFB is able to reduce its taxable income and, therefore, decrease its total tax payments by $115.5 million over the four-year period. Thus, the total amount of cash flows available to all investors (debt holders and equity holders) is $115.5 million higher over the four-year period.

Value of the Interest Tax Shield

When a firm uses debt, the interest tax shield provides a corporate tax benefit each year. To determine the benefit of leverage for the value of the firm, we must compute the present value of the stream of future interest tax shields the firm will receive.

As we saw in the previous example, each year a firm makes interest payments, the cash flows it pays to investors will be higher than they would be without leverage by the amount of the interest tax shield:

$$\begin{pmatrix}\text{Cash Flows to Investors}\\ \text{with Leverage}\end{pmatrix} = \begin{pmatrix}\text{Cash Flows to Investors}\\ \text{without Leverage}\end{pmatrix} + (\text{Interest Tax Shield})$$

Figure 16.6 illustrates this relationship. Notice how each dollar of pre-tax cash flows is divided. The firm uses some fraction to pay taxes, and it pays the rest to investors. By increasing the amount paid to debt holders through interest payments, the amount of the pre-tax cash flows that must be paid as taxes decreases. The gain in total cash flows to investors is the interest tax shield.[3]

Because the cash flows of the levered firm are equal to the sum of the cash flows from the unlevered firm plus the interest tax shield, according to the Valuation Principle the same must be true for the present values of these cash flows. Thus, letting V^L and V^U represent the value of the firm with and without leverage, respectively, we have the following change to M&M Proposition I in the presence of taxes:

$$V^L = V^U + PV(\text{Interest Tax Shield}) \tag{16.5}$$

FIGURE 16.6 The Cash Flows of the Unlevered and Levered Firm

By increasing the cash flows paid to debt holders through interest payments, a firm reduces the amount paid in taxes. The increase in total cash flows paid to investors is the interest tax shield. (The figure assumes a 40% marginal corporate tax rate.)

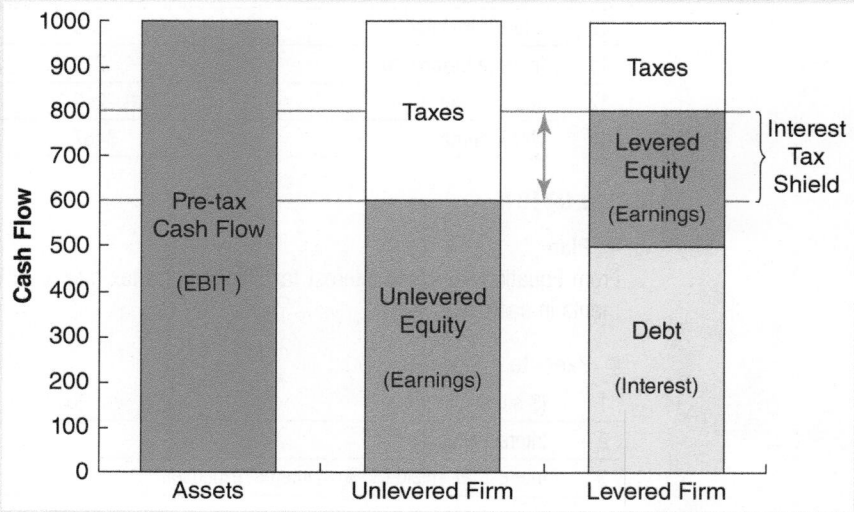

[3]If investors are taxed on interest income at a higher rate than they are on capital gains, this personal tax *disadvantage* of debt will partly offset the corporate tax advantage of debt.

The total value of the levered firm exceeds the value of the firm without leverage due to the present value of the tax savings from debt.

Clearly, there is an important tax advantage to the use of debt financing. But how large is this tax benefit? To compute the increase in the firm's total value associated with the interest tax shield, we need to forecast how a firm's debt—and therefore its interest payments—will vary over time. Given a forecast of future interest payments, we can determine the interest tax shield and compute its present value by discounting it at a rate that corresponds to its risk.

The Interest Tax Shield with Permanent Debt

Many factors can affect the future tax savings from interest. Typically, the level of future interest payments varies due to the following:

- Changes the firm makes in the amount of debt outstanding
- Changes in the interest rate on that debt
- Changes in the firm's marginal tax rate
- The risk that the firm may default and fail to make an interest payment

Rather than attempting to account for all possibilities here, we will consider the special case in which the firm issues debt and plans to keep the dollar amount of debt constant forever.

For example, the firm might issue a perpetual consol bond, making only interest payments but never repaying the principal. More realistically, suppose the firm issues a five-year coupon bond. When the principal is due, the firm raises the money needed to pay it by issuing new debt. In this way, the firm never pays off the principal but simply refinances it whenever it comes due. In this situation, the debt is effectively permanent.

Many large firms have a policy of maintaining a certain amount of debt on their balance sheets. As old bonds and loans mature, they take out new loans and issue new bonds. Note that we are considering the value of the interest tax shield with a *fixed* dollar amount of outstanding debt, rather than an amount that changes with the size of the firm.

If the firm's debt is fairly priced and permanent, the Valuation Principle implies that the market value of the debt today must equal the present value of all the interest payments the firm will make in the future:[4]

$$\text{Market Value of Permanent Debt} = D = PV(\text{Future Interest Payments}) \tag{16.6}$$

If the firm's marginal tax rate (T_c) is constant, then we have the following general formula:

Value of the Interest Tax Shield of Permanent Debt

$$\begin{aligned} PV(\text{Interest Tax Shield}) &= PV(T_c \times \text{Future Interest Payments}) \\ &= T_c \times PV(\text{Future Interest Payments}) \qquad (16.7) \\ &= T_c \times D \end{aligned}$$

[4]Equation 16.6 is valid even if interest rates fluctuate and the debt is risky, as long as any new debt is also fairly priced. It requires only that the firm never repay the principal on the debt (it either refinances or defaults on the principal).

This formula shows the magnitude of the interest tax shield. Given a 35% corporate tax rate, it implies that for every $1 in new permanent debt that the firm issues, the value of the firm increases by $0.35.

EXAMPLE 16.4 Recapitalizing to Capture the Tax Shield

PROBLEM

When a firm makes a significant change to its capital structure, the transaction is called a recapitalization. Let's see how such a transaction might benefit current shareholders.

Midco Industries has 20 million shares outstanding with a market price of $15 per share and no debt. Midco generates stable profits and pays a 35% tax rate. Management plans to borrow $100 million on a permanent basis and use the borrowed funds to repurchase $100 million worth of their outstanding shares. Their expectation is that the tax savings from this transaction will benefit shareholders. Is this expectation realistic?

SOLUTION

Plan

In this case, the debt is permanent so we can use Equation 16.7 to value the interest tax shields. The value of the levered firm is the value of the unlevered company plus the present value of the tax shields, and the value of equity equals the value of the levered firm minus the company's debt.

Execute

Without leverage, Midco's total market value is the value of its unlevered equity, which is the total value of all 20 million shares:

$$V^U = 20 \text{ million} \times \$15 = \$300 \text{ million}$$

With leverage, Midco will reduce its annual tax payments. If Midco borrows $100 million using permanent debt, the present value of the firm's future tax savings is

$$PV(\text{Interest Tax Shield}) = T_C \times D = 35\% \times \$100 \text{ million} = \$35 \text{ million}$$

Thus, the total value of the levered firm will be

$$V^L = V^U + T_C \times D = \$300 \text{ million} + \$35 \text{ million} = \$335 \text{ million}$$

This total value represents the combined value of the debt and the equity after the recapitalization. Because the value of the debt is $100 million, the value of the equity is

$$E = V^L - D = \$335 \text{ million} - \$100 \text{ million} = \$235 \text{ million}$$

Evaluate

While total firm value has increased, the value of equity dropped after the recap. How do shareholders benefit from this transaction? In addition to holding $235 million worth of shares, shareholders will also receive $100 million cash that Midco will pay out through the share repurchase. In total, they will receive $335 million, a gain of $35 million over the value of their shares without leverage.

Leverage and the WACC with Taxes

There is another way we can incorporate the benefit of the firm's future interest tax shield. Recall from Chapter 12 that we defined the WACC with taxes as

WACC with Taxes

$$r_{wacc} = r_E \frac{E}{E + D} + r_D(1 - T_C)\frac{D}{E + D} \tag{16.8}$$

In Equation 16.8, we incorporate the benefit of the interest tax shield by adjusting the cost of debt to the firm. If the firm pays interest rate r_D on its debt, then because it receives a tax shield of $T_C \times r_D$, the effective after-tax cost of debt is reduced to $r_D\,(1 - T_C)$. Comparing Equation 16.8 with Equation 16.2 for the pre-tax WACC, we can see that corporate taxes lower the effective cost of debt financing, which translates into a reduction in the WACC. In fact, Equation 16.8 implies the following:

$$r_{wacc} = \underbrace{r_E \frac{E}{E + D} + r_D \frac{D}{E + D}}_{\text{Pre-tax } WACC} - \underbrace{r_D T_C \frac{D}{E + D}}_{\text{Reduction Due to Interest Tax Shield}} \tag{16.9}$$

Thus, the reduction in the WACC increases with the amount of debt financing. The higher the firm's leverage, the more the firm exploits the tax advantage of debt and the lower its WACC. Figure 16.7 illustrates this decline in the WACC with leverage. The figure also shows the pre-tax WACC, as shown in Figure 16.5.

Debt and Taxes: The Bottom Line

In this section, we have seen that the deductibility of interest expenses for corporate taxes creates an advantage for debt financing. We can calculate the value of this benefit to the firm in two ways. First, we can forecast the firm's future interest tax shields and determine their present value. This approach is especially simple when the amount of debt is fixed permanently, in which case the value of the tax shield is equal to $T_C \times D$.

A second way to calculate the benefit of the interest tax shield is to incorporate it into the firm's cost of capital by using the WACC. Unlike the pre-tax WACC, the WACC with taxes declines with leverage because of the interest tax shield. If we use this lower discount rate to compute the present value of the firm's or an investment's free cash flow, the present value will be higher by an amount that reflects the benefit of the future interest tax shields. This approach is simplest to apply when the firm adjusts its debt to keep the fraction of debt financing (its debt-to-value ratio) constant over time.

To summarize, we can include the interest tax shield when assessing the value of a firm or an investment by *either* of these methods:

1. Discounting its free cash flow using the pre-tax WACC, and adding the present value of expected future interest tax shield
2. Discounting its free cash flow using the WACC (with taxes)

Using either of these methods, we will find the value of the firm will increase with leverage. Thus, unlike the setting with perfect capital markets, capital structure matters. But now we face a new puzzle; given the tax benefit, why don't firms use debt financing almost exclusively?

FIGURE 16.7 The WACC with and without Corporate Taxes

We compute the WACC as a function of leverage using Equation 16.9. Whereas the pre-tax WACC remains constant, with taxes the WACC declines as the firm increases its reliance on debt financing and the benefit of the interest tax deduction grows. The figure assumes a marginal corporate income tax rate of 35%.

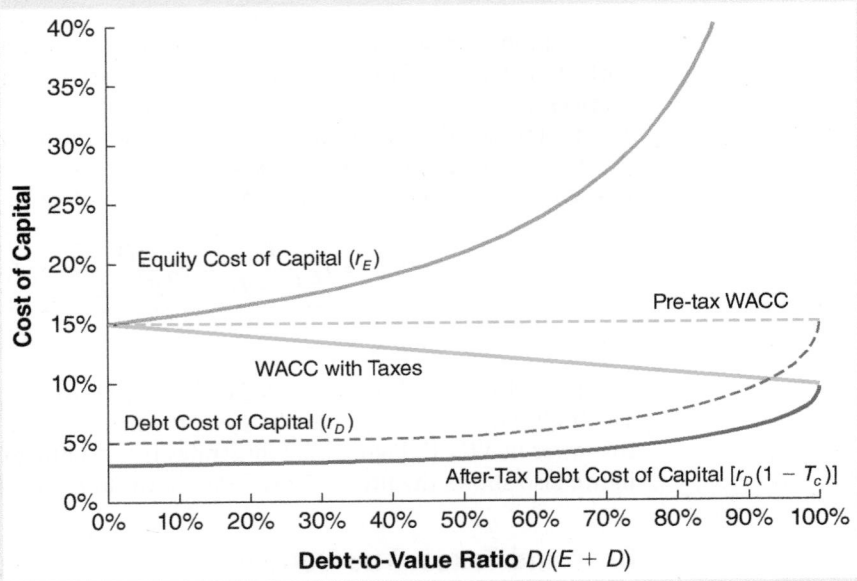

CONCEPT CHECK

5. How does the interest tax deduction affect firm value?
6. How does the firm's WACC change with leverage?

16.4 The Costs of Bankruptcy and Financial Distress

The previous section presents us with an interesting question; if increasing debt increases the value of the firm, why not shift to nearly 100% debt? One part of the answer comes from bankruptcy costs. With more debt, there is a greater chance that the firm will be unable to make its required interest payments and will default on its debt obligations. A firm that has trouble meeting its debt obligations is in **financial distress**. When we assume that capital markets are perfect, we ignore that bankruptcy is a long and complicated process that imposes both direct and indirect costs on the firm and its investors.

financial distress The situation that arises when a firm has difficulty meeting its debt obligations.

Direct Costs of Bankruptcy

Each country has a bankruptcy code that details the process for dealing with a firm in default of its debt obligations (see the Appendix to this chapter). The bankruptcy code is designed to provide an orderly process for settling a firm's debts. However, the process is still complex, time-consuming, and costly. When a corporation becomes financially distressed, outside professionals, such as legal and accounting experts, consultants, appraisers, auctioneers, and others with experience selling distressed assets, are generally hired. Investment bankers may also assist with a potential financial restructuring.

In addition to the money spent by the firm, the creditors may incur costs during the bankruptcy process. In the case of reorganization, creditors must often wait several years for a reorganization plan to be approved and to receive payment. To ensure that their rights and interests are respected, and to assist in valuing their claims in a proposed reorganization, creditors may seek separate legal representation and professional advice.

Studies, typically, report that the average direct costs of bankruptcy are approximately 3% to 4% of the pre-bankruptcy market value of total assets. The costs are likely to be higher for firms with more complicated business operations and for firms with larger numbers of creditors, because reaching agreement among many creditors regarding the final disposition of the firm's assets may be more difficult. Because many aspects of the bankruptcy process are independent of the size of the firm, the costs are typically higher, in percentage terms, for smaller firms.

Indirect Costs of Financial Distress

Aside from the direct legal and administrative costs of bankruptcy, many other *indirect* costs are associated with financial distress (whether or not the firm has formally filed for bankruptcy). Whereas these costs are difficult to measure accurately, they are often much larger than the direct costs of bankruptcy.

Indirect bankruptcy costs often occur because the firm may renege on both implicit and explicit commitments and contracts when in financial distress. For example, a bankrupt software manufacturer need not fulfill an obligation to support one of its products. Knowing this, customers who rely on such support might choose to buy software from companies that have a low chance of bankruptcy; that is, companies with lower leverage. Importantly, many of these indirect costs may be incurred even if the firm is not yet in financial distress but simply faces a significant possibility of bankruptcy in the future. Consider the following examples:

> *Loss of Customers.* Because bankruptcy may enable firms to walk away from future commitments to their customers, those customers may be unwilling to purchase products whose value depends on future support or service from the firm.

BANKRUPTCY CAN BE EXPENSIVE

Outside experts that specialize in aiding distressed firms are costly. At the time Enron entered bankruptcy, it reportedly spent a record $30 million per month on legal and accounting fees, and the total cost ultimately exceeded $750 million. WorldCom paid its advisors $657 million as part of its reorganization to become MCI. Between January 2009 and June 2010, it is estimated that Nortel paid over $290 million in bankruptcy professional fees, or over $16 million per month.*

Whether paid by the firm or its creditors, these direct costs of bankruptcy reduce the value of the assets that the firm's investors will ultimately receive. In the case of Enron, reorganization costs were expected to approach 10% of the value of the assets.

**Source:* Diane A. Urquhart, Consolidated and Updated Report—Bankruptcies and Employee Claims—Nortel Case, January 4, 2010.

Loss of Suppliers. Suppliers may be unwilling to provide a firm with inventory if they fear they will not be paid. For example, Swiss Air was forced to shut down in 2001 because financial concerns caused its suppliers to refuse to fuel its planes.

Cost to Employees. One important cost that often receives a great deal of press coverage is the cost of financial distress to employees. Most firms offer their employees explicit long-term employment contracts or an implicit promise regarding job security. However, during bankruptcy these contracts and commitments are often ignored, and significant numbers of employees may be laid off. In anticipation of this, employees will be less willing to work for firms with significant bankruptcy risk and so will demand a higher compensation to do so. Thus, hiring and retaining key employees may be costly for a firm with high leverage; Nortel implemented a retention and bonus program costing over $92 million to retain key employees while it was in bankruptcy in 2010.

Fire Sales of Assets. A company in distress may be forced to sell assets quickly to raise cash, possibly accepting a lower price than the assets are actually worth to the firm. This cost is likely to be large when creditors are more pessimistic than management regarding the value of the assets, so creditors will try to force liquidation even at low prices.

In total, the indirect costs of financial distress may be substantial. A study of highly levered firms by Gregor Andrade and Steven Kaplan estimated a potential loss due to financial distress of 10% to 20% of firm value.[5] Importantly, many of these indirect costs may be incurred even if the firm is not yet in financial distress but simply faces a significant possibility that it may occur in the future.

CONCEPT CHECK

7. What are the direct costs of bankruptcy?
8. Why are the indirect costs of financial distress likely to be more important than the direct costs of bankruptcy?

16.5 Optimal Capital Structure: The Trade-off Theory

We can now combine our knowledge of the benefits of leverage from the interest tax shield with the costs of financial distress to determine the amount of debt that a firm should issue to maximize its value. The analysis presented in this section is called the *trade-off theory* because it weighs the benefits of debt that result from shielding cash flows from taxes against the costs of financial distress associated with leverage. This theory is also sometimes referred to as the *static trade-off theory*

trade-off theory The theory that the total value of a levered firm equals the value of the firm without leverage, plus the present value of the tax savings from debt, less the present value of financial distress costs.

According to the **trade-off theory**, the total value of a levered firm equals the value of the firm without leverage plus the present value of the tax savings from debt, less the present value of financial distress costs, as follows:

$$V^L = V^U + PV(\text{Interest Tax Shield}) - PV(\text{Financial Distress Costs}) \qquad (16.10)$$

[5]G. Andrade, and S. Kaplan, "How Costly Is Financial (Not Economic) Distress? Evidence from Highly Leveraged Transactions that Became Distressed," *Journal of Finance* 53 (1998): 1443–1493.

Equation 16.10 shows that leverage has costs as well as benefits. Firms have an incentive to increase leverage to exploit the tax benefits of debt. But with too much debt, they are more likely to risk default and incur financial distress costs.

Differences across Firms

Whereas we have seen in Section 16.3 how to calculate the benefits of the interest tax shield, calculating the precise present value of financial distress costs is very difficult, if not impossible. Two key factors determine the present value of financial distress costs: (1) the probability of financial distress and (2) the magnitude of the direct and indirect costs related to financial distress that the firm will incur.

What determines each of these factors? The magnitude of the financial distress costs will depend on the relative importance of the sources of these costs and is likely to vary by industry. For example, software firms are likely to incur high costs associated with financial distress due to the potential for loss of customers and key personnel, as well as a lack of tangible assets that can be easily liquidated. In contrast, power companies are likely to have low costs of financial distress, as much of their value derives from tangible assets (land, buildings, power lines) that can be sold if necessary. Not surprisingly, by reviewing Figure 16.1 we can see that these two industries have very different leverage policies; software firms have very low debt, whereas power companies tend to be highly levered. Similarly, in Figure 16.2 we saw that Air Canada has a higher ratio of debt compared to WestJet. Part of this is historical and part is a difference in assets. The companies have similarities in most of their assets, like airplanes, but Air Canada owns the rights to more international routes, and these rights could potentially be sold to meet the demands of creditors.

The probability of financial distress depends on the likelihood that a firm will be unable to meet its debt commitments and, therefore, default. This probability increases with the amount of a firm's liabilities (relative to its assets). It also increases with the volatility of a firm's cash flows and asset values. Thus, firms with steady, reliable cash flows, such as power companies, are able to use high levels of debt and still have a very low probability of default. Firms whose value and cash flows are very volatile (for example, software firms) must have much lower levels of debt to avoid a significant risk of default.

Optimal Leverage

Figure 16.8 shows how the value of a levered firm, V^L, varies with the level of permanent debt, D, according to Equation 16.10. With no debt, the value of the firm is V^U. For low levels of debt, the risk of default remains low, and the main effect of an increase in leverage is an increase in the interest tax shield, which has present value $T_C \times D$, as shown in Equation 16.7. If there were no costs of financial distress, the value would continue to increase at this rate until the interest on the debt exceeds the firm's earnings before interest and taxes (EBIT), and the tax shield is exhausted.

The costs of financial distress reduce the value of the levered firm, V^L. The amount of the reduction increases with the probability of default, which in turn increases with the level of the debt, D. The trade-off theory states that firms should increase their leverage until it reaches the level D^* for which V_L is maximized. At this point, the tax savings that result from increasing leverage are just offset by the increased probability of incurring the costs of financial distress.

Figure 16.8 also illustrates the optimal debt choices for two types of firms. The optimal debt choice for a firm with low costs of financial distress is indicated by D^*_{low} and the optimal debt choice for a firm with high costs of financial distress is indicated by D^*_{high}. Not surprisingly, with higher costs of financial distress, it is optimal for the firm to choose lower leverage.

FIGURE 16.8 Optimal Leverage with Taxes and Financial Distress Costs

As the level of debt increases, the tax benefits of debt increase until the interest expense exceeds the firm's EBIT. However, the probability of default, and hence the present value of financial distress costs, also increases. The optimal level of debt, D^*, occurs when these effects balance out and the value of the levered firm is maximized. D^* will be lower for firms with higher costs of financial distress.

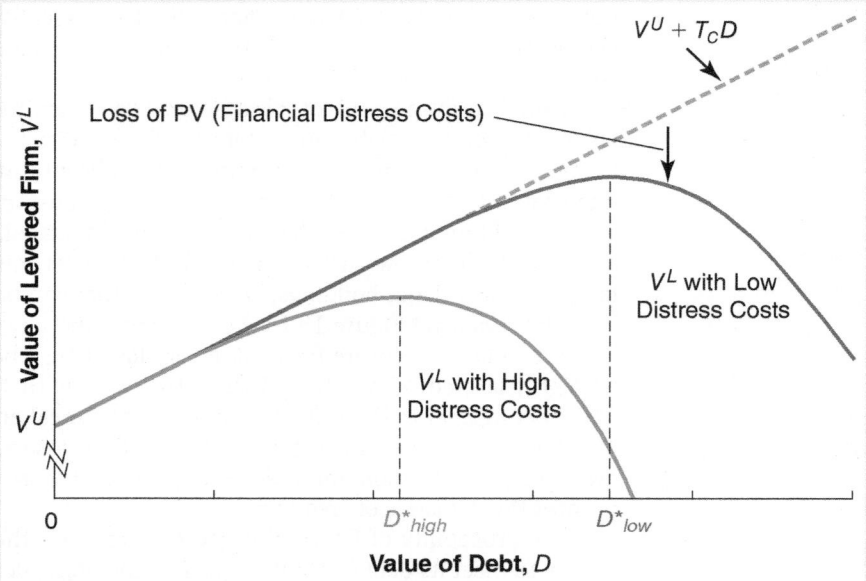

The trade-off theory helps to resolve two important facts about leverage:

1. The presence of financial distress costs can explain why firms choose debt levels that are too low to fully exploit the interest tax shield.
2. Differences in the magnitude of financial distress costs and the volatility of cash flows can explain the differences in the use of leverage across industries.

CONCEPT CHECK

9. According to the trade-off theory, how should a financial manager determine the right capital structure for a firm?
10. Why would managers in one industry choose different capital structures than those in another industry?

16.6 Additional Consequences of Leverage: Agency Costs and Information

Taxes and financial distress costs are not the only capital market imperfections that arise in practice. In this section, we continue to relax the assumption of perfect capital markets to see other ways in which capital structure can affect firm value. We begin by discussing how leverage alters managers' incentives and changes their investment decisions. We then address the complexities of stakeholders in the firm having different information.

Agency Costs

agency costs The costs that arise when there are conflicts of interest between stakeholders.

Agency costs are costs that arise when there are conflicts of interest between stakeholders. In Chapter 1, we briefly mentioned the principal-agent problem that arises when managers put their own interests ahead of shareholders' interest. Here, we discuss how debt can mitigate this problem. However, it may also distort equity holders' preferences for the types of projects the firm pursues.

Managerial Entrenchment. Although managers often do own shares of the firm, in most large corporations they own only a very small fraction of the outstanding shares. Shareholders, through the board of directors, have the power to fire managers. In practice, they rarely do so unless the firm's performance is exceptionally poor.

management entrenchment A situation arising as a result of the separation of ownership and control, in which managers may make decisions that benefit themselves at investors' expense.

agency costs of equity Costs that occur when managers make decisions that benefit themselves at the expense of shareholder value.

This separation of ownership and control creates the possibility of **management entrenchment**; facing little threat of being fired and replaced, managers are free to run the firm in their own best interests. As a result, managers may make decisions that benefit themselves at investors' expense. Managers may reduce their effort (shirk), spend excessively on perquisites such as corporate jets, or undertake wasteful projects that increase the size of the firm (and their pay cheques) at the expense of shareholder value, often called "empire building." If these decisions have negative NPV for the firm, they are a form of agency cost—the **agency costs of equity**.

These agency costs of equity are most likely to arise when equity ownership is highly dispersed (so that no individual shareholder has an incentive to monitor management closely) and when the firm has a great deal of free cash flow available for managers to spend on wasteful projects. Debt can therefore help in two ways. First, by borrowing rather than raising funds by issuing shares, ownership of the firm may remain more concentrated, improving the monitoring of management. Second, by forcing the firm to pay out cash to meet interest and principal payments, debt reduces the funds available to management to spend on wasteful investment. When cash is tight, managers will be much more motivated to run the firm as efficiently as possible. Restraining the agency costs of equity is an additional benefit of using debt rather than equity financing.

AIRLINES USE FINANCIAL DISTRESS TO THEIR ADVANTAGE

The need to generate cash flows sufficient to make interest payments may also tie managers' hands and commit them to pursue sound business strategies with greater vigour than they would without the threat of financial distress. For example, in 2004 when Air Canada was in bankruptcy and attempting to reorganize, the firm was able to win wage concessions from all its unions by explaining such concessions were necessary for Air Canada to receive new financing so it could come out of bankruptcy and avoid liquidation. (A similar situation enabled Delta Airlines to persuade its pilots to accept a 33% wage cut in November 2004.) Without the threat of financial distress and possible liquidation (which would have meant all jobs would have been lost), these airlines might not have reached agreements with their unions as quickly or achieved the same wage concessions.

A firm with greater leverage may also become a fiercer competitor and act more aggressively in protecting its markets, because it cannot risk the possibility of bankruptcy. This commitment to aggressive behaviour can scare off potential rivals. (However, such a high leverage strategy can also backfire, as a firm weakened by too much leverage might become so financially fragile that it crumbles in the face of competition, allowing other firms to erode its markets.)

Equity–Debt Holder Conflicts. When a firm has leverage, a conflict of interest exists if investment decisions have different consequences for the value of equity and the value of debt. Such a conflict is most likely to occur when the risk of financial distress is high. In some circumstances, managers may take actions that benefit shareholders but harm the firm's creditors and lower the total value of the firm. This is an **agency cost of debt**.

agency cost of debt A cost that occurs when managers take actions that benefit shareholders but harm the firm's creditors and lower the total value of the firm.

To illustrate, put yourself in the place of the shareholders of a company in distress that is likely to default on its debt. You could continue as normal, in which case you will very likely lose the value of your shares and hand control of the firm to the bondholders. Alternatively, you could do the following:

1. Roll the dice and take on a risky project that could save the firm, even though its expected outcome is so poor that you normally would not take it on.
2. Conserve funds rather than invest in new, promising projects.
3. Cash out by distributing as much of the firm's capital as possible to the shareholders before the bondholders take over.

Why would you roll the dice? Even if the project fails, you are no worse off because you were headed for default anyway. If it succeeds, then you avoid default and retain ownership of the firm. This incentive leads to **excessive risk-taking**, a situation that occurs when a company is near distress and shareholders have an incentive to invest in risky negative-NPV projects that will destroy value for debt holders and the firm overall. Anticipating this behaviour, security holders will pay less for the firm initially. This cost is likely to be highest for firms that can easily increase the risk of their investments.

excessive risk-taking A situation that occurs when a company is near distress and shareholders have an incentive to invest in risky negative-NPV projects that will destroy value for debt holders and the firm overall.

On the other hand, when default is very likely, a firm may pass up a good project before default, because some or most of the benefit will go to bondholders (by reducing the risk or extent of default). For example, if a firm can invest \$100 in a project that will increase the value of its debt by \$30 and the value of its equity by \$90, then the project has a positive NPV of \$30 + \$90 − \$100 = \$20. Equity holders will not want to fund it, as their gain (\$90) is less than the project's cost of \$100. In this case, there is an **underinvestment problem**: shareholders choose not to invest in a positive-NPV project because the firm is in financial distress and the value of undertaking the investment opportunity will accrue to bondholders rather than themselves. This failure to invest is costly for debt holders and for the overall value of the firm, because it is giving up the NPV of the missed opportunities. The cost is highest for firms that are likely to have profitable future growth opportunities requiring large investments.

underinvestment problem A situation in which shareholders choose not to invest in a positive-NPV project because the firm is in financial distress and the value of undertaking the investment opportunity will accrue to bondholders rather than to shareholders.

We can easily interpret the conflict of interest between equity holders and debt holders and the resulting distortion of investment incentives in an option valuation framework. As seen in Chapter 13, a share of equity is equivalent to a call option on the firm's assets. Recall that the value of a call option increases with the volatility of the underlying investment, implying that equity holders could benefit from excessive risk-taking. Debt holders have a fixed claim on the firm's cash flows and have, therefore, nothing to gain from an increase in risk. Thus, a zero-NPV project that makes the firm riskier increases the value of equity but decreases the value of the debt claims. Further, the loss in equity value that results from taking on a high-risk negative-NPV investment might be outweighed by the gain in equity value from the increase in volatility. Hence, equity holders of distressed firms may have an incentive to take on negative-NPV high-volatility investments. (The fact that the value of a call option decreases if the volatility of the underlying investment is reduced explains why a distressed firm might simultaneously also *underinvest* in low-risk positive-NPV projects.)

The ultimate form of underinvestment is cashing out. Knowing that they are likely to lose the firm to the bondholders, shareholders have an incentive to withdraw as much capital from the firm as possible before it enters bankruptcy and transfers to the debt holders. An extreme example of this would be to sell all the assets of the firm and

MORAL HAZARD AND GOVERNMENT BAILOUTS

The term "moral hazard" refers to the idea that individuals will change their behaviour if they are not fully exposed to its consequences. The agency costs described in this chapter represent a form of moral hazard, as equity holders may take excessive risks or pay excessive dividends if the negative consequences will be borne by bondholders. How are such abuses by equity holders normally held in check? Bondholders will either charge equity holders for the risk of this abuse by increasing the cost of debt, or, more likely, equity holders will credibly commit not to take on excessive risk by, for example, agreeing to very strong bond covenants and other monitoring.

Ironically, despite the potential immediate benefits of the government bailouts in response to the 2008 financial crisis, by protecting the bondholders of many large corporations, the government may have simultaneously weakened this disciplining mechanism and thereby increased the likelihood of future crises. With this precedent in place, all lenders to corporations deemed "too big to fail" may presume they have an implicit government guarantee, thus lowering their incentives to insist on strong covenants and to monitor whether those covenants are being satisfied.[6] Without this monitoring, the likelihood of future abuses by equity holders and managers has likely been increased, as has the government's liability.

distribute the proceeds to shareholders as a special dividend. The firm would then enter bankruptcy as a worthless shell. As we discussed in Chapter 15, bondholders can anticipate this problem and often require restrictions on the size of dividends and source of funds for those dividends.

Our discussion suggests that we can create a more complete trade-off model of capital structure by incorporating the possible agency costs and benefits of debt in addition to tax benefits and financial distress costs. This trade-off model representing optimal leverage is illustrated in Figure 16.9. When debt is too low, adding leverage increases the value of the firm by providing tax benefits and reducing the agency costs of equity by motivating managers to run the firm more efficiently (and avoid wasteful investment). But if debt is too high, the firm will incur financial distress costs and suffer from the agency costs of debt through excessive risk-taking and underinvestment. The optimal level of debt, D^*, is the point that maximizes firm value by balancing these positive and negative consequences of leverage.

Debt and Information

Our final market imperfection is related to the role of information. Throughout this chapter, we have assumed that managers, stockholders, and creditors have the same information. We have also assumed that securities are fairly priced: the firm's shares and debt are priced according to their true underlying value. These assumptions may not always be accurate in practice. Due to **asymmetric information**, managers' information about the firm and its future cash flows is likely to be superior to that of outside investors. This asymmetric information may motivate managers to alter a firm's capital structure.

asymmetric information The varying information that different parties have; for example, when managers have superior information to that of outside investors regarding the firm's future cash flows.

Leverage as a Credible Signal. To convince the stock market that it has great projects, a firm may commit to large future debt payments. If the projects are great, then the firm will have no trouble making the debt payments. But if the firm is making false claims

[6]As an example, a number of large banks continued to pay dividends during the crisis even after receiving bailout funds. Had the funds been raised from outside investors without any government guarantee, it is very likely the new investors would have restricted such payouts.

FIGURE 16.9 Optimal Leverage with Taxes, Financial Distress, and Agency Costs

As the level of debt increases, the value of the firm increases from the interest tax shield ($T_C \times D$) as well as improvements in managerial incentives that reduce the agency costs of equity. If leverage is too high, however, the present value of financial distress costs and the agency costs of debt dominate and reduce firm value. The optimal level of debt, D^*, balances these benefits and costs of leverage.

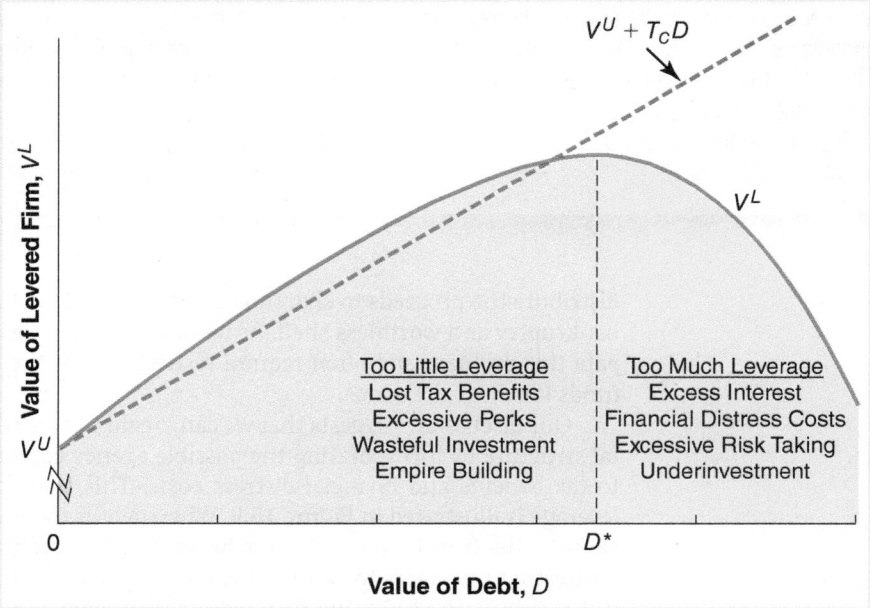

and then does not grow, it will have trouble paying its creditors and will experience financial distress. This distress will be costly for the firm and also for its managers, who will probably lose their jobs. Thus, the managers can use leverage as a way to convince investors that they, the managers, have information that the firm will grow, even if they cannot provide verifiable details about the sources of growth. Investors will interpret the additional leverage as a credible signal of the managers' confidence. The use of leverage as a way to signal good information to investors is known as the **signalling theory of debt**.

signalling theory of debt The use of leverage as a way to signal good information to investors.

Market Timing. When they have better information than outside investors regarding the value of the firm, managers may attempt to engage in **market timing** by selling new shares when they believe the stock is overvalued, and relying on debt and retained earnings (and possibly repurchasing shares) if they believe the stock is undervalued. Managers who successfully time the market in this way benefit long-term shareholders by trading the firm's shares whenever they are mispriced. The firm's capital structure would change as the managers issued new equity (decreasing the leverage) or new debt (increasing the leverage) while attempting to time the market. As a result, the firm's capital structure may deviate above or below the optimal level described by the trade-off theory, depending on management's view of the share price relative to its true value.

market timing The selling of new shares by managers because they believe the stock is overvalued, and managers' reliance on debt and retained earnings (and possibly repurchasing of shares) if they believe the stock is undervalued.

Adverse Selection and the Pecking Order Hypothesis. Suppose managers do try to issue equity when it is overpriced relative to its true value. Knowing this, how would investors react? Recall from Chapter 14 the adverse selection, or "lemon," effect in seasoned equity offerings. Fearful that they are being sold a "lemon," investors will discount the price they are willing to pay for the stock.

The adverse selection problem has implications for capital structure. Managers do not want to sell equity if they have to discount it to find buyers. Therefore, managers may seek alternative forms of financing. Debt issues may also suffer from adverse selection. Because the value of low-risk debt is not very sensitive to managers' private information about the firm (but is instead determined mainly by interest rates), the discount needed to attract buyers will be smaller for debt than for equity. Of course, a firm can avoid underpricing altogether by financing investment using its cash (retained earnings) when possible. The **pecking order hypothesis** states what managers will do to avoid this "lemons cost":

pecking order hypothesis The idea that managers will have a preference to fund investment using retained earnings followed by debt, and will choose to issue equity only as a last resort.

> *Managers will have a preference to fund investment using retained earnings followed by debt, and will choose to issue equity only as a last resort.*

This hypothesis has implications for firms' capital structure. When firms are profitable and generate sufficient cash to fund their investments, they will not issue debt or equity, but rather rely on retained earnings. Thus, highly profitable firms will have little debt in their capital structure. Only firms that need to raise external capital will have significant debt financing. According to the pecking order hypothesis, firms should almost never issue equity. In reality, it is likely that multiple forces will shape the firm's capital structure and firms will issue equity when the agency costs or financial distress costs of debt are too great.

CONCEPT CHECK

11. How can too much debt lead to excessive risk-taking?

12. What is the pecking order hypothesis?

EXAMPLE 16.5 The Pecking Order of Financing Alternatives

PROBLEM

Axon Industries needs to raise $9.5 million for a new investment project. If the firm issues one-year debt, it may have to pay an interest rate of 8%, although Axon's managers believe that 6% would be a fair rate, given the level of risk. However, if the firm issues equity, the managers believe the equity may be underpriced by 5%. What is the cost to current shareholders of financing the project out of retained earnings, debt, and equity?

SOLUTION

■ Plan

We can evaluate the financing alternatives by comparing what the firm would have to pay to get the financing versus what its managers believe it should pay if the market had the same information they do.

■ Execute

If the firm spends $9.5 million out of retained earnings rather than paying that money out to shareholders as a dividend, the cost of financing the project is $9.5 million.

Using one-year debt costs the firm $9.5 × (1.08) = $10.26 million in one year, which has a present value based on management's view of the firm's risk of $10.26 ÷ (1.06) = $9.68 million. ▶

If equity is underpriced by 5%, then to raise $9.5 million the firm will need to issue shares that are actually worth $10 million. (For example, if the firm's shares are each worth $50, but it sells them for 0.95 × $50 = $47.50 per share, it will need to sell $9.5 million ÷ $47.50/share = 200,000 shares. These shares have a true value of 200,000 shares × $50/share = $10 million.) Thus, the cost of financing the project with equity will be $10 million.

Evaluate

Comparing the three options, retained earnings are the cheapest source of funds, followed by debt, and finally by equity. The ranking reflects the effect of differences in information between managers and investors that result in a lemons problem when they issue new securities, particularly when they issue new equity.

16.7 Capital Structure: Putting It All Together

In this chapter, we have examined a number of factors that might influence a firm's choice of capital structure. What is the bottom line for a financial manager devising the optimal capital structure for a firm? The optimal capital structure depends on market imperfections such as taxes, financial distress costs, agency costs, and asymmetric information, as follows:

1. *Make use of the interest tax shield if your firm has consistent taxable income.* The interest tax shield allows firms to repay investors and avoid the corporate tax.
2. *Balance the tax benefits of debt against the costs of financial distress when determining how much of the firm's income to shield from taxes with leverage.* Whereas the risk of default is not itself a problem, financial distress may lead to other consequences that reduce the value of the firm.
3. *Consider more debt for external financing when agency costs of equity are significant.* When free cash flows are high, too little leverage may encourage wasteful spending and shirking. Beware, though, of too much debt, which can motivate managers and equity holders to take excessive risks or under invest in a firm and thus cause the agency costs of debt.
4. *Increase leverage to signal managers' confidence in the firm's ability to meet its debt obligations.* Investors understand that bankruptcy is costly for managers.
5. *Be mindful that investors are aware that you have an incentive to issue securities that you know are overpriced.* Thus, when an issue is announced, investors will lower their valuation of that security. This effect is most pronounced for equity issues, because the value of equity is most sensitive to the manager's private information.
6. *Rely first on retained earnings, then debt, and finally equity.* This pecking order of financing alternatives will be most important when managers are likely to have a great deal of private information regarding the value of the firm.
7. *Do not change the firm's capital structure unless it departs significantly from the optimal level.* Actively changing a firm's capital structure (e.g., by selling or repurchasing shares or bonds) entails transactions costs. Most changes to a firm's debt-equity ratio are likely to occur passively, as the market value of the firm's equity fluctuates with changes in the firm's stock price.

MyLab Finance

Here is what you should know after reading this chapter. MyLab™ Finance will help you identify what you know, and where to go when you need to practice.

KEY POINTS AND EQUATIONS	TERMS	ONLINE PRACTICE OPPORTUNITIES
16.1 Capital Structure Choices ■ The collection of securities that a firm issues to raise capital from investors is called the firm's capital structure. Equity and debt are the securities most commonly used by firms. ■ Various financing choices will promise different future amounts to each security holder in exchange for the cash that is raised today. ■ Managers also need to consider whether the securities that the firm issues will receive a fair price in the market, have tax consequences, entail transactions costs, or even change its future investment opportunities.	debt-to-value ratio, p. 550	MyLab Study Plan 16.1
16.2 Capital Structure in Perfect Capital Markets ■ When equity is used without debt, the firm is said to be unlevered. Otherwise, the amount of debt determines the firm's leverage. ■ The owner of a firm should choose the capital structure that maximizes the total value of the securities issued. ■ According to M&M Proposition II, the cost of capital for levered equity is $$r_E = r_U + \frac{D}{E}(r_U - r_D) \quad (16.3)$$ ■ Debt is less risky than equity and so has a lower cost of capital. Leverage increases the risk of equity, however, raising the equity cost of capital. The benefit of debt's lower cost of capital is offset by the higher equity cost of capital, leaving a firm's weighted average cost of capital (WACC) unchanged with perfect capital markets. ■ According to M&M Proposition I, with perfect capital markets the value of a firm is independent of its capital structure. With perfect capital markets, homemade leverage is a perfect substitute for firm leverage.	homemade leverage, p. 558 levered equity, p. 554 perfect capital market, p. 553 pre-tax WACC, p. 558 unlevered equity, p. 554	MyLab Study Plan 16.2 Interactive Leverage Effect Analysis
16.3 Debt and Taxes ■ Because interest expense is tax deductible, leverage increases the total amount of income available to all investors. The gain to investors	interest tax shield, p. 565	MyLab Study Plan 16.3

KEY POINTS AND EQUATIONS	TERMS	ONLINE PRACTICE OPPORTUNITIES
from the tax deductibility of interest payments is called the interest tax shield. Interest Tax Shield = Corporate Tax Rate × Interest Payments (16.4) ■ When we consider corporate taxes, the total value of a levered firm equals the value of an unlevered firm plus the present value of the interest tax shield. $V^L = V^U + PV(\text{Interest Tax Shield})$ (16.5) ■ When securities are fairly priced the original shareholders of a firm capture the full benefit of the interest tax shield from an increase in leverage. ■ When we introduce corporate taxes, the weighted average cost of capital is $r_{wacc} = r_E \frac{E}{E+D} + r_D(1 - T_C)\frac{D}{E+D}$ (16.8) ■ Absent other market imperfections, the WACC declines with a firm's leverage, because interest expense is tax deductible. ■ To capture the effect of the interest tax deduction on firm value, you can either compute the PV of the future tax shields or use the WACC with taxes to discount the firm's free cash flows, but not both!		
16.4 The Costs of Bankruptcy and Financial Distress ■ Bankruptcy is a costly process that imposes both direct and indirect costs on a firm and its investors. ■ Some direct costs are fees paid to lawyers and bankruptcy experts. ■ Some indirect costs are loss of customers, suppliers, or employees, or being forced to sell assets at a deep discount to raise money.	financial distress, p. 570	MyLab Study Plan 16.4
16.5 Optimal Capital Structure: The Trade-Off Theory ■ According to the trade-off theory, the total value of a levered firm equals the value of the firm without leverage plus the present value of the tax savings from debt minus the present value of financial distress costs: $V^L = V^U + PV(\text{Interest Tax Shield}) - PV(\text{Financial Distress Costs})$ (16.10) ■ The optimal leverage is the level of debt that maximizes V^L.	trade-off theory, p. 572	MyLab Study Plan 16.5

3abc, 4-6, 12, 13, 15-19, 21

KEY POINTS AND EQUATIONS	TERMS	ONLINE PRACTICE OPPORTUNITIES
16.6 Additional Consequences of Leverage: Agency Costs and Information ■ Leverage can reduce the agency costs of equity by improving the incentives for managers to run a firm more efficiently and effectively. However, when a firm enters financial distress, agency cost of debt may occur, as leverage can create incentives to forgo good projects or to take excessive risk. ■ When managers have better information than investors, it is asymmetric information. Given asymmetric information, managers may use leverage as a credible signal to investors of the firm's ability to generate future free cash flow. ■ Managers who perceive that the firm's equity is underpriced will have a preference to fund investment using retained earnings, or debt, rather than equity. This is called the pecking order hypothesis.	agency costs, p. 575 agency cost of debt, p. 576 agency costs of equity, p. 575 asymmetric information, p. 577 excessive risk-taking, p. 576 management entrenchment, p. 575 market timing, p. 578 pecking order hypothesis, p. 579 signalling theory of debt, p. 578 underinvestment problem, p. 576	MyLab Study Plan 16.6

REVIEW QUESTIONS

1. Absent tax effects and market imperfections, why can't we change the cost of capital of the firm by using more debt financing and less equity financing?
2. Explain what is wrong with the following argument: "If a firm issues debt that is risk free because there is no possibility of default, the risk of the firm's equity does not change. Therefore, risk-free debt allows the firm to get the benefit of a low cost of capital of debt without raising its cost of capital of equity."
3. What are the channels through which financing choices can affect firm value?
4. How do taxes affect the choice of debt versus equity?
5. What is meant by "indirect costs of financial distress"?
6. Which type of firm is more likely to experience a loss of customers in the event of financial distress:
   a. Campbell Soup Company or Intuit Inc. (a maker of accounting software)?
   b. Allstate Corporation (an insurance company) or Reebok International (a footwear and clothing firm)?
7. According to the trade-off theory, how is capital structure determined?
8. For each pair below, which type of asset is more likely to be liquidated for close to its full market value in the event of financial distress:
   a. An office building or a brand name?
   b. Product inventory or raw materials?
   c. Patent rights or engineering "know-how"?

3abc, 4-6, 12, 13, 15-19, 21

9. Which of the following industries have low optimal debt levels according to the trade-off theory? Which have high optimal levels of debt?
   a. Tobacco firms
   b. Accounting firms
   c. Established restaurant chains
   d. Lumber companies
   e. Smartphone manufacturers

10. How can leverage alter the incentives of managers?

PROBLEMS

All problems in this chapter are available in MyLab Finance.

Capital Structure in Perfect Capital Markets

For problems in this section, assume there are no taxes or distress costs.

1. Consider a project with free cash flows in one year of either $130,000 or $180,000, with either outcome being equally likely. The initial investment required for the project is $100,000, and the project's cost of capital is 20%. The risk-free interest rate is 10%.
   a. What is the NPV of this project?
   b. Suppose that to raise the funds for the initial investment, the project is sold to investors as an all-equity firm. The equity holders will receive the cash flows of the project in one year. How much money can be raised in this way—that is, what is the initial market value of the unlevered equity?
   c. Suppose the initial $100,000 is instead raised by borrowing at the risk-free interest rate. What are the cash flows of the levered equity, and what is its initial value according to M&M?

2. You are an entrepreneur starting a biotechnology firm. If your research is successful, the technology can be sold for $30 million. If your research is unsuccessful, it will be worth nothing. To fund your research, you need to raise $2 million. Investors are willing to provide you with $2 million in initial capital in exchange for 50% of the unlevered equity in the firm.
   a. What is the total market value of the firm without leverage?
   b. Suppose you borrow $1 million. According to M&M, what fraction of the firm's equity will you need to sell to raise the additional $1 million you need?
   c. What is the value of your share of the firm's equity in cases (a) and (b)?

3. Acort Industries owns assets that will have an 80% probability of having a market value of $50 million in one year. There is a 20% chance that the assets will be worth only $20 million. The current risk-free rate is 5%, and Acort's assets have a cost of capital of 10%.
   a. If Acort is unlevered, what is the current market value of its equity?
   b. Suppose instead that Acort has debt with a face value of $20 million due in one year. According to M&M, what is the value of Acort's equity in this case?
   c. What is the expected return of Acort's equity without leverage? What is the expected return of Acort's equity with leverage?
   d. What is the lowest possible realized return of Acort's equity with and without leverage?

4. Suppose there are no taxes. Firm ABC has no debt, and firm XYZ has debt of $5000 on which it pays interest of 10% each year. Both companies have identical projects that generate a free cash flow of $800 or $1000 each year. After paying any interest on debt, both companies use all remaining free cash flows to pay dividends each year.

	ABC		XYZ	
FCF	Interest Payments	Equity Dividends	Interest Payments	Equity Dividends
$800	0	800	500	300
$1000	0	1000	500	500

a. In the table above, fill in the payments debt and equity holders of each firm will receive, given each of the two possible levels of free cash flows.
b. Suppose you hold 10% of the equity of ABC. What is another portfolio you could hold that would provide the same cash flows?
c. Suppose you hold 10% of the equity of XYZ. If you can borrow at 10%, what is an alternative strategy that would provide the same cash flows?

5. Hardmon Enterprises is currently an all-equity firm with an expected return of 12%. It is considering borrowing money to buy back some of its existing shares, thus increasing its leverage. Buying debt
a. Suppose Hardmon borrows to the point that its debt-equity ratio is 0.50. With this amount of debt, the debt cost of capital is 6%. What will the expected return of equity be after this transaction?
b. Suppose instead Hardmon borrows to the point that its debt-equity ratio is 1.50. With this amount of debt, Hardmon's debt will be much riskier. As a result, the debt cost of capital will be 8%. What will the expected return of equity be in this case?
c. A senior manager argues that it is in the best interest of the shareholders to choose the capital structure that leads to the highest expected return for the stock. How would you respond to this argument?

6. Microsoft has no debt and a WACC of 9.2%. The average debt-to-value ratio for the software industry is 13%. What would its cost of equity be if it took on the average amount of debt for its industry at a cost of debt of 6%?

7. Your firm is financed 100% with equity and has a cost of equity capital of 12%. You are considering your first debt issue, which would change your capital structure to 30% debt and 70% equity. If your cost of debt is 7%, what will be your new cost of equity?

8. One of your new employees notes that your debt has a lower cost of capital (5%) than your equity (15%). So, he suggests that the firm swap its capital structure from 30% debt and 70% equity to 70% debt and 30% equity instead. He estimates that after the swap, your cost of equity would be 20%.
a. What would be your new cost of debt?
b. Have you lowered your overall cost of capital?

Debt and Taxes

9. Pelamed Pharmaceuticals had EBIT of $325 million in 2006, interest expenses of $125 million, and a corporate tax rate of 40%.
a. What was Pelamed's 2006 net income?
b. What was the total of Pelamed's 2006 net income and interest payments?
c. If Pelamed had no interest expenses, what would its 2006 net income have been? How does it compare to your answer in part (b)?
d. What was the amount of Pelamed's interest tax shield in 2006?

12, 13, 15-19, 21

10. Grommit Engineering expects to have net income next year of $20.75 million and free cash flow of $22.15 million. Grommit's marginal corporate tax rate is 35%.
a. If Grommit increases leverage so that its interest expense rises by $1 million, how will its net income change?
b. For the same increase in interest expense, how will free cash flow change?

11. Braxton Enterprises currently has debt outstanding of $35 million and an interest rate of 8%. Braxton plans to reduce its debt by repaying $7 million in principle at the end of each year for the next five years. If Braxton's marginal corporate tax rate is 40%, what is the interest tax shield from Braxton's debt in each of the next five years?

12. Assume that Microsoft has a total market value of $300 billion and a marginal tax rate of 35%. If it permanently changes its leverage from no debt by taking on new debt in the amount of 13% of its current market value, what is the present value of the tax shield it will create?

13. Suppose the corporate tax rate is 40%. Consider a firm that earns $1000 before interest and taxes each year with no risk. The firm's capital expenditures equal its depreciation expenses each year, and it will have no changes to its net working capital. The risk-free interest rate is 5%.
a. Suppose the firm has no debt and pays out its net income as a dividend each year. What is the value of the firm's equity?
b. Suppose instead the firm makes interest payments of $500 per year. What is the value of equity? What is the value of debt?
c. What is the difference between the total value of the firm with leverage and without leverage?
d. To what percentage of the value of the debt is the difference in part (c) equal?

14. Your firm currently has $100 million in debt outstanding with a 10% interest rate. The terms of the loan require the firm to repay $25 million of the balance each year. Suppose that the marginal corporate tax rate is 40% and that the interest tax shields have the same risk as the loan. What is the present value of the interest tax shields from this debt?

15. Arnell Industries has $10 million in permanent debt outstanding. The firm will pay interest only on this debt. Arnell's marginal tax rate is expected to be 35% for the foreseeable future.
a. Suppose Arnell pays interest of 6% per year on its debt. What is its annual interest tax shield?
b. What is the present value of the interest tax shield, assuming its risk is the same as the loan?
c. Suppose instead that the interest rate on the debt is 5%. What is the present value of the interest tax shield in this case?

16. Rogot Instruments makes fine violins and cellos. It has $1 million in debt outstanding and equity valued at $2 million, and pays corporate income tax at rate 35%. Its cost of equity is 12% and its cost of debt is 7%.
a. What is Rogot's pre-tax WACC?
b. What is Rogot's (effective after-tax) WACC?

17. Rumolt Motors has 30 million shares outstanding with a price of $15 per share. In addition, Rumolt has issued bonds with a total current market value of $150 million. Suppose Rumolt's equity cost of capital is 10% and its debt cost of capital is 5%.
a. What is Rumolt's pre-tax WACC?
b. If Rumolt's corporate tax rate is 35%, what is its after-tax WACC?

18. Summit Builders has a market debt-equity ratio of 0.65 and a corporate tax rate of 40%, and pays 7% interest on its debt. By what amount does the interest tax shield from its debt lower Summit's WACC?

19. Milton Industries expects free cash flows of $5 million each year. Milton's corporate tax rate is 35%, and its unlevered cost of capital is 15%. The firm also has outstanding debt of $19.05 million and expects to maintain this level of debt permanently.

a. What is the value of Milton Industries without leverage?
b. What is the value of Milton Industries with leverage?

20. NatNah, a builder of acoustic accessories, has no debt and an equity cost of capital of 15%. Suppose NatNah decides to increase its leverage and maintain a market debt-to-value ratio of 0.5. Suppose its debt cost of capital is 9% and its corporate tax rate is 35%. If NatNah's pre-tax WACC remains constant, what will its (effective after-tax) WACC be with the increase in leverage?

***21.** Kurz Manufacturing is currently an all-equity firm with 20 million shares outstanding and a stock price of $7.50 per share. Although investors currently expect Kurz to remain an all-equity firm, Kurz plans to announce that it will borrow $50 million and use the funds to repurchase shares. Kurz will pay interest only on this debt, and it has no further plans to increase or decrease the amount of debt. Kurz is subject to a 40% corporate tax rate.

a. What is the market value of Kurz's existing assets before the announcement?
b. What is the market value of Kurz's assets (including any tax shields) just after the debt is issued but before the shares are repurchased?
c. What is Kurz's share price just before the share repurchase? How many shares will Kurz repurchase?
d. What are Kurz's market value balance sheet and share price after the share repurchase?

22. Kohwe Corporation plans to issue equity to raise $50 million to finance a new investment. After making the investment, Kohwe expects to earn free cash flows of $10 million each year. Kohwe currently has 5 million shares outstanding, and it has no other assets or opportunities. Suppose the appropriate discount rate for Kohwe's future free cash flows is 8% and the only capital market imperfections are corporate taxes and financial distress costs.

a. What is the NPV of Kohwe's investment?
b. What is Kohwe's share price today?

23. Suppose Kohwe borrows the $50 million instead. The firm will pay interest only on this loan each year and will maintain an outstanding balance of $50 million on the loan. Suppose that Kohwe's corporate tax rate is 40% and expected free cash flows are still $10 million each year. What is Kohwe's share price today if the investment is financed with debt?

24. Now suppose that with leverage Kohwe's expected free cash flows will decline to $9 million per year due to reduced sales and other financial distress costs. Assume that the appropriate discount rate for Kohwe's future free cash flows is still 8%. What is Kohwe's share price today, given the financial distress costs of leverage?

***25.** Rally Inc. is an all-equity firm with assets worth $25 billion and 10 billion shares outstanding. Rally plans to borrow $10 billion and use these funds to repurchase shares. The firm's corporate tax rate is 35%, and Rally plans to keep its outstanding debt equal to $10 billion permanently.

a. Without the increase in leverage, what would Rally's share price be?
b. Suppose Rally offers $2.75 per share to repurchase its shares. Would shareholders sell for this price?
c. Suppose Rally offers $3.00 per share and shareholders tender their shares at this price. What will Rally's share price be after the repurchase?
d. What is the lowest price Rally can offer and have shareholders tender their shares? What will its stock price be after the share repurchase in that case?

Optimal Capital Structure: The Trade-Off Theory

26. With its current leverage, Impi Corporation will have net income next year of $4.5 million. If Impi's corporate tax rate is 35% and it pays 8% interest on its debt, how much additional debt can Impi issue this year and still receive the benefit of the interest tax shield next year?

27. Now that your firm has matured, you are considering adding debt to your capital structure for the first time. Your all-equity firm has a market value of $20 million and you are considering issuing $2 million in debt with an interest rate of 7% and using it to repurchase shares. You pay a corporate tax rate of 40%. Assume taxes are the only imperfection and the debt is expected to be permanent.
a. What will be the total value of the firm after the change in capital structure?
b. What will be the value of the remaining equity after the change in capital structure?

28. Hawar International is a shipping firm with a current share price of $5.50 and 10 million shares outstanding. Suppose that Hawar announces plans to lower its corporate taxes by borrowing $20 million and repurchasing shares, that Hawar pays a corporate tax rate of 30%, and that shareholders expect the change in debt to be permanent.
a. If the only imperfection is corporate taxes, what will the share price be after this announcement?
b. Suppose the only imperfections are corporate taxes and financial distress costs. If the share price rises to $5.75 after this announcement, what is the PV of financial distress costs Hawar will incur as the result of this new debt?

29. Marpor Industries has no debt and expects to generate free cash flows of $16 million each year. Marpor believes that if it permanently increases its level of debt to $40 million, the risk of financial distress may cause it to lose some customers and receive less favourable terms from its suppliers. As a result, Marpor's expected free cash flows with debt will be only $15 million per year. Suppose Marpor's tax rate is 35%, the risk-free rate is 5%, the expected return of the market is 15%, and the beta of Marpor's free cash flows is 1.10 (with or without leverage).
a. Estimate Marpor's value without leverage.
b. Estimate Marpor's value with the new leverage.

***30.** Colt Systems will have EBIT this coming year of $15 million. It will also spend $6 million on total capital expenditures and increases in net working capital and have $3 million in depreciation expenses. Colt is currently an all-equity firm with a corporate tax rate of 35% and a cost of capital of 10%.
a. If Colt's free cash flows are expected to grow by 8.5% per year, what is the market value of its equity today?
b. If the interest rate on its debt is 8%, how much can Colt borrow now and still have non-negative net income this coming year?
c. Is there a tax incentive today for Colt to choose a debt-to-value ratio that exceeds 50%? Explain.

Additional Consequences of Leverage: Agency Costs and Information

31. Dynron Corporation's primary business is natural gas transportation using its vast gas pipeline network. Dynron's assets currently have a market value of $150 million. The firm is exploring the possibility of raising $50 million by selling part of its pipeline network and investing the $50 million in a fibre-optic network to generate revenues by selling high-speed network bandwidth. Whereas this new investment is expected to increase profits, it will also substantially increase Dynron's risk. If Dynron is levered, would this investment be more or less attractive to equity holders than if Dynron had no debt?

32. Consider a firm whose only asset is a plot of vacant land and whose only liability is debt of $15 million due in one year. If left vacant, the land will be worth $10 million in one year. Alternatively, the firm can develop the land for an upfront cost of $20 million. The developed land will be worth $35 million in one year. Suppose the risk-free interest rate is 10%, all cash flows are risk free, and there are no taxes.

a. If the firm chooses not to develop the land, what is the value of the firm's equity today? What is the value of the debt today?
b. What is the NPV of developing the land?
c. Suppose the firm raises $20 million from equity holders to develop the land. If the firm develops the land, what is the value of the firm's equity today? What is the value of the firm's debt today?
d. Given your answer to part (c), would equity holders be willing to provide the $20 million needed to develop the land?

***33.** Zymase is a biotechnology start-up firm. Researchers at Zymase must choose one of three different research strategies. The payoffs (after taxes) and their likelihood for each strategy are shown below. The risk of each project is diversifiable.

Strategy	Probability (%)	Payoff ($ millions)
A	100	75
B	50	140
	50	0
C	10	300
	90	40

a. Which project has the highest expected payoff?
b. Suppose Zymase has debt of $40 million due at the time of the project's payoff. Which strategy has the highest expected payoff for equity holders?
c. Suppose Zymase has debt of $110 million due at the time of the strategy's payoff. Which strategy has the highest expected payoff for equity holders?
d. If management chooses the strategy that maximizes the payoff to equity holders, what is the expected agency cost to the firm from having $40 million in debt due? What is the expected agency cost to the firm from having $110 million in debt due?

***34.** You own a firm, and you want to raise $30 million to fund an expansion. Currently, you own 100% of the firm's equity, and the firm has no debt. To raise the $30 million solely through equity, you will need to sell two-thirds of the firm. However, you would prefer to maintain at least a 50% equity stake in the firm to retain control.

a. If you borrow $20 million, what fraction of the equity will you need to sell to raise the remaining $10 million? (Assume perfect capital markets.)
b. What is the smallest amount you can borrow to raise the $30 million without giving up control? (Assume perfect capital markets.)

***35.** Empire Industries forecasts net income this coming year as shown below (in thousands of dollars):

EBIT	$1000
Interest expense	$0
Income before tax	$1000
Taxes	–$350
Net income	$650

Approximately $200,000 of Empire's earnings will be needed to make new, positive-NPV investments. Unfortunately, Empire's managers are expected to waste 10% of its net income on needless perks, pet projects, and other expenditures that do not contribute to the firm. All remaining income will be distributed to shareholders.

a. What are the two benefits of debt financing for Empire?
b. By how much would each $1 of interest expense reduce Empire's distributions to shareholders?
c. What is the increase in the *total* funds Empire will pay to investors for each $1 of interest expense?

***36.** Info Systems Technology (IST) manufactures microprocessor chips for use in appliances and other applications. IST has no debt and 100 million shares outstanding. The correct price for these shares is either $14.50 or $12.50 per share. Investors view both possibilities as equally likely, so the shares currently trade for $13.50.

IST must raise $500 million to build a new production facility. Because the firm would suffer a large loss of both customers and engineering talent in the event of financial distress, managers believe that if IST borrows the $500 million, the present value of financial distress costs will exceed any tax benefits by $20 million. At the same time, because investors believe that managers know the correct share price, IST faces a lemons problem if it attempts to raise the $500 million by issuing equity.

a. Suppose that if IST issues equity, the share price will remain $13.50. To maximize the long-term share price of the firm once its true value is known, would managers choose to issue equity or borrow the $500 million if
   i. they know the correct value of the shares is $12.50?
   ii. they know the correct value of the shares is $14.50?
b. Given your answer to part (a), what should investors conclude if IST issues equity? What will happen to the share price?
c. Given your answer to part (a), what should investors conclude if IST issues debt? What will happen to the share price in that case?
d. How would your answers change if there were no distress costs, but only the tax benefits of leverage?

When a firm fails to make a required payment to debt holders, it is in default. Debt holders can then take legal action against the firm to collect payment by seizing the firm's assets. Because most firms have multiple creditors, coordination is required to guarantee that each creditor will be treated fairly. Moreover, because the assets of the firm might be more valuable if kept together, creditors seizing assets in a piecemeal fashion might destroy much of the remaining value of the firm.

Canadian bankruptcy law was created to organize this process so that creditors are treated fairly and the value of the assets is not needlessly destroyed. There are two relevant acts for financially distressed firms in Canada: the Bankruptcy and Insolvency Act (BIA) and the Companies' Creditors Arrangement Act (CCAA).

The BIA applies to businesses and individuals. Usually smaller companies use the BIA, and liquidation is often the result. Under the BIA, a firm may put forth a proposal that can either be accepted or rejected by its creditors. To be accepted, each class of creditor must vote and pass the proposal, and the court must also give its approval. A creditor class is said to pass the proposal if at least a majority of the creditors in number and two-thirds in value agree to the proposal. If a proposal does not pass, a trustee is appointed to oversee the liquidation of the firm's assets through an auction. The proceeds from the liquidation are used to pay the firm's creditors, and the firm ceases to exist.

The CCAA applies to firms that owe $5 million or more to creditors. It allows a company to pre-empt going into formal bankruptcy under the BIA and, instead, propose a formal plan of arrangement (or reorganization). Once the company has applied to the court for protection against its creditors—a stay, under the CCAA—all pending collection attempts are automatically suspended and the firm's existing management is given the opportunity to propose a reorganization plan. While developing the plan, management continues to operate the business under the watch of a monitor (often the company's auditor). The plan of arrangement specifies the treatment of each creditor of the firm. In addition to cash payment, creditors may receive new debt or equity securities of the firm. The value of cash and securities is generally less than the amount each creditor is owed but more than the creditors would receive if the firm were shut down immediately and be liquidated. The creditors must vote to accept the plan, and it must be approved by the court.[7] If an acceptable plan is not put forth, the company loses its protection under the CCAA and the stay is lifted. The company is not automatically forced to enter into bankruptcy but will likely do so under the BIA, either voluntarily or by petition of its creditors. At this point, liquidation is the likely eventual outcome.

U.S. firms can file for bankruptcy protection under the provisions of the 1978 Bankruptcy Reform Act. In the United States, the main bankruptcy laws for corporations fall under two chapters. "Chapter 7" is for liquidation of firms. "Chapter 11" is for reorganization and is similar to the CCAA in Canada. A notable difference between the CCAA and Chapter 11 is that, under the latter, the bankruptcy court can impose a plan (in a process commonly known as a "cram down") even if not all creditor classes approve it.

---

[7]Specifically, management holds the exclusive right to propose a plan of arrangement during the initial stay (which is 30 days), and the stay may be extended indefinitely by the court. Thereafter, any interested party may propose a plan. Creditors who will receive full payment or have their claims fully reinstated under the plan are deemed unimpaired and do not vote on the plan of arrangement. All impaired creditors are grouped according to the nature of their claims. If the plan is approved by creditors holding two-thirds of the claim amount in each group and a majority in the number of the claims in each group, the court may sanction the plan. If a class of creditors or the court does not approve the plan of arrangement, the stay is lifted.

CHAPTER

17 Payout Policy

LEARNING OBJECTIVES

- Identify the different ways in which corporations can make distributions to shareholders
- Understand why the way in which they distribute cash flow does not affect value, absent market imperfections
- Indicate how taxes can create an advantage for share repurchases versus dividends
- Explain how increased payouts can reduce principal-agent problems but potentially reduce financial flexibility
- Describe alternative non-cash methods for payouts

NOTATION

P_{cum}	cum-dividend stock price	P_{rep}	stock price with share repurchase
P_{ex}	ex-dividend stock price	PV	present value

When a firm's investments generate free cash flow, the firm must decide how to use that cash. If the firm has new positive-NPV investment opportunities, it can reinvest the cash and increase the value of the firm. Many young, rapidly growing firms reinvest 100% of their cash flows in this way. But mature, profitable firms often find that they generate more cash than they need to fund all of their attractive investment opportunities. When a firm has excess cash, it can hold those funds as part of its cash reserves or pay the cash out to shareholders. If the firm decides to follow the latter approach, it has two choices: it can pay a dividend or it can repurchase shares from current owners. These decisions represent the firm's payout policy.

For many years, Microsoft Corporation chose to distribute cash to investors primarily by repurchasing its own stock. During the five fiscal years ending June 2004, for example, Microsoft spent an average of $5.4 billion per year on share repurchases. Microsoft began paying dividends to investors in 2003, with what CFO John Connors called "a starter dividend" of $0.08 per share. Then, on July 20, 2004, Microsoft stunned financial markets by announcing plans to pay the largest single cash dividend payment in history, a one-time dividend of $32 billion, or $3 per share, to all shareholders of record on November 17, 2004. In addition to this dividend, Microsoft announced plans to repurchase up to $30 billion worth of its stock over the next four years and pay regular quarterly dividends at an annual rate of $0.32 per share. What considerations led financial managers at Microsoft to make this payout? What are the implications of such actions for shareholders and the value of the firm?

In this chapter, we show that, as with capital structure, a firm's payout policy is shaped by market imperfections such as taxes, agency costs, transaction costs, and asymmetric information between managers and investors. We look at why some firms prefer to pay dividends, while others pay no dividends at all and rely exclusively on share repurchases. In addition, we explore why some firms retain cash and build up large reserves, while others tend to pay out their excess cash.

17.1 Distributions to Shareholders

Figure 17.1 illustrates the alternative uses of free cash flow.[1] A firm that chooses to retain free cash flow will invest in new projects or increase cash reserves. The firm pays out free cash flow through distributions to shareholders by repurchasing shares or paying dividends. The way a firm chooses between these alternatives is referred to as its **payout policy**. We begin our discussion of a firm's payout policy by considering the choice between paying dividends and repurchasing shares. In this section, we examine the details of these methods of paying cash to shareholders.

payout policy The way a firm chooses between the alternative ways to pay cash out to shareholders.

FIGURE 17.1 Uses of Free Cash Flow

A firm can retain its free cash flow, either investing or accumulating it, or pay out its free cash flow through a dividend or share repurchase. The choice between these options is determined by the firm's payout policy.

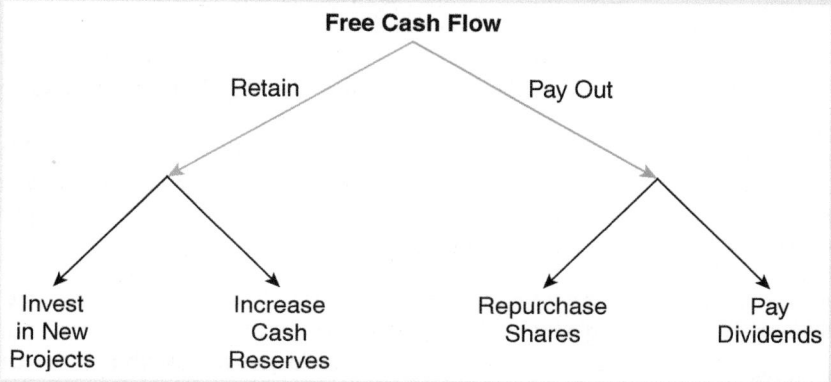

[1]Strictly speaking, Figure 17.1 is for an all-equity firm. For a levered firm, we would begin with the firm's free cash flows to equity, which is free cash flows less after-tax payments to debt holders.

declaration date The date on which a public company's board of directors authorizes the payment of a dividend.

record date The specific date set by a public company's board of directors on which a shareholder must be on record as owning the shares in order to qualify to be paid the upcoming dividend.

ex-dividend date A date, two days prior to a dividend's record date, on or after which anyone buying the stock will not be eligible for the dividend.

payable date (distribution date) A date, generally within a month after the record date, on which a firm mails dividend cheques to its registered stockholders.

Dividends

A public company's board of directors determines the amount of the firm's dividend. The board sets the amount per share that will be paid and decides when the payment will occur. The date on which the board authorizes the dividend is the **declaration date**. After the board declares the dividend, the firm is legally obligated to make the payment.

The firm will pay the dividend to all shareholders of record on a specific date set by the board called the **record date**. Because it takes three business days for shares to be registered, only shareholders who purchase the stock at least three days prior to the record date receive the dividend. As a result, the date two business days prior to the record date is known as the **ex-dividend date**. Anyone who purchases the stock on or after the ex-dividend date will not receive the dividend. Finally, on the **payable date (distribution date)**, which is generally within a month after the record date, the firm mails dividend cheques to the registered shareholders. Figure 17.2 shows these dates for Microsoft's $3 dividend.

Microsoft declared the dividend on July 20, 2004, payable on December 2 to all shareholders of record on November 17. Because the record date was November 17, the ex-dividend date was two days earlier, or November 15, 2004.

FIGURE 17.2 Important Dates for Microsoft's Special Dividend

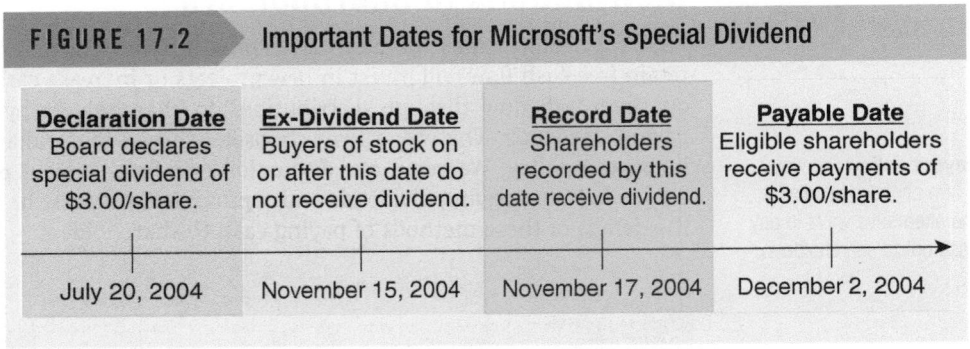

Special Dividend. Most companies that pay dividends pay them at regular quarterly intervals. Companies usually do not adjust the amount of their dividends, and the amount of the dividend varies little from quarter to quarter. Occasionally, a firm may pay a one-time **special dividend** that is usually much larger than a regular dividend, like Microsoft's $3 dividend in 2004. Figure 17.3 shows the dividends paid by General Motors (GM) from 1983 to 2008. In addition to regular dividends, GM paid special dividends in December 1997 and again in May 1999 (associated with spinoffs of subsidiaries, discussed further in Section 17.6).

special dividend A one-time dividend payment a firm makes that is usually much larger than a regular dividend.

return of capital The payment by a firm of dividends from sources such as paid-in capital or the liquidation of assets instead of from current earnings (or accumulated retained earnings).

liquidating dividend A return of capital to shareholders from a business operation that is being terminated.

While GM raised its dividends throughout the 1980s, it cut its dividends during the recession in the early 1990s. GM raised its dividends again in the late 1990s but was forced to cut its dividends again in early 2006 and suspend them altogether in July 2008 in response to financial difficulties.

Accounting Implications. Dividends are a cash outflow for the firm. From an accounting perspective, dividends generally reduce the firm's current (or accumulated) retained earnings. In some cases, dividends are attributed to other accounting sources, such as paid-in capital or the liquidation of assets. In this case, the dividend is known as a **return of capital** or a **liquidating dividend**. Although the source of the funds makes little difference to a firm or to investors directly, there is a difference in tax treatment: a return of capital is taxed as a capital gain rather than as a dividend for the investor.

FIGURE 17.3 Dividend History for GM Stock, 1983–2008

Until suspending its dividends in July 2008, GM had paid a regular dividend each quarter since 1983. GM paid additional special dividends in December 1997 and May 1999, and had a 2-for-1 stock split in March 1989. GM ultimately filed for bankruptcy in June of 2009.

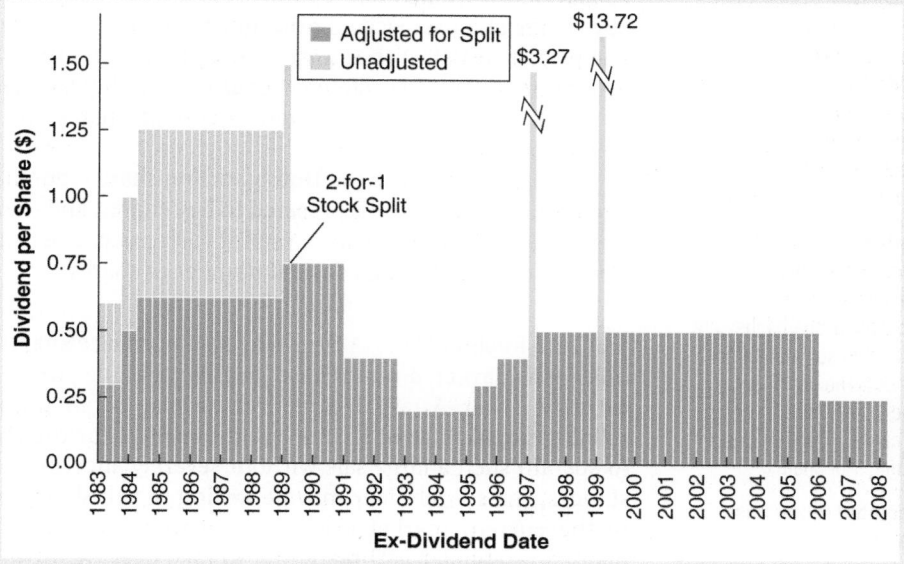

Share Repurchases

An alternative way to pay cash to investors is through a share repurchase or buyback. In this kind of transaction, the firm uses cash to buy shares of its own outstanding stock. In Canada, these shares are generally cancelled or restored to authorized but unissued shares; in the U.S., these shares may also be held in the corporate treasury as treasury shares. Repurchasing shares does not preclude the firm from issuing shares to raise money in the future. We now examine three possible transaction types for a share repurchase.

open market repurchase The repurchasing by a firm of its own shares by buying them on the open market over time.

Open Market Repurchase. With an **open market repurchase**, the most common way that firms repurchase shares, a firm announces its intention to buy its own shares on the open market and then proceeds to do so over time, just as any other investor. The firm may take a year or more to buy the shares, and it is not obligated to repurchase the full amount it originally stated. Also, the firm must not buy its shares in a way that might appear to manipulate the price. For example, both the Toronto Stock Exchange (TSX) and the U.S. Securities and Exchange Commission (SEC) guidelines recommend that the firm not purchase more than 25% of the average daily trading volume in its shares on a single day, nor make purchases at the market open or within 30 minutes of the close of trade.[2]

[2]SEC Rule 10b-18, introduced in 1983, defines guidelines for open market share repurchases in the United States. *The TSX Company Manual*, Part VI, Section 629 defines the guidelines for such repurchases known in Canada as a Normal Course Issuer Bid.

While open market share repurchases represent about 95% of all repurchase transactions,[3] other methods are available to a firm that wants to buy back its stock. These methods are used when a firm wishes to repurchase a substantial portion of its shares, often as part of a recapitalization.

tender offer A public announcement by a firm of an offer to all existing security holders to buy back a specified amount of outstanding securities at a prespecified price over a short time period, generally 20 days.

Dutch auction A share repurchase method in which shareholders indicate how many shares they are willing to sell at different prices. The firm then pays the lowest price at which it can buy back its desired number of shares.

Tender Offer. A firm can repurchase shares through a **tender offer** in which it offers to buy shares at a prespecified price during a short time period, generally within 20 days. The price is usually set at a substantial premium (10%–20% is typical) to the current market price. The offer often depends on shareholders tendering a sufficient number of shares. If shareholders do not tender enough shares, the firm may cancel the offer and no buyback occurs.

A related method is the **Dutch auction** share repurchase, in which the firm lists different prices at which it is prepared to buy shares, and shareholders in turn indicate how many shares they are willing to sell at each price. The firm then pays the lowest price at which it can buy back its desired number of shares.

targeted repurchase The repurchasing of shares by a firm directly from a specific shareholder; the purchase price is negotiated directly with the seller.

Targeted Repurchase. A firm may also purchase shares directly from a major shareholder in a **targeted repurchase**. In this case, the purchase price is negotiated directly with the seller. A targeted repurchase may occur if a major shareholder desires to sell a large number of shares but the market for the shares is not sufficiently liquid to sustain such a large sale without severely affecting the price. Under these circumstances, the shareholder may be willing to sell shares back to the firm at a discount to the current market price. Alternatively, targeted repurchases may be used if a major shareholder is threatening to take over the firm and remove its management. In a repurchasing tactic known as **greenmail**, the firm may decide to eliminate the threat by buying out the shareholder—often at a large premium over the current market price.

CONCEPT CHECK

1. How is a stock's ex-dividend date determined, and what is its significance?
2. What is an open market share repurchase?

17.2 Dividends versus Share Repurchases in a Perfect Capital Market

greenmail A firm's avoidance of a threat of takeover and removal of its management by a major shareholder by buying out the shareholder, often at a large premium over the current market price.

If a corporation decides to pay cash to shareholders, it can do so through either dividend payments or share repurchases. How do firms choose between these alternatives? In this section, we show that in the perfect capital markets setting of Modigliani and Miller, the method of payment does not matter.

Consider the case of Genron Corporation, a hypothetical firm. Genron has $20 million in excess cash and no debt. The firm expects to generate additional free cash flows of $48 million per year in subsequent years. If Genron's unlevered cost of capital is 12%, then the enterprise value of its ongoing operations is as follows:

$$\text{Enterprise Value} = PV(\text{Future } FCF) = \frac{\$48 \text{ million}}{12\%} = \$400 \text{ million}$$

[3] G. Grullon and D. Ikenberry, "What Do We Know About Stock Repurchases?" *Journal of Applied Corporate Finance* 13 (1) (2000): 31–51.

Including the cash, Genron's total market value is $420 million.

Genron's board is meeting to decide how to pay out its $20 million in excess cash to shareholders. The board is considering three options:

1. Use the $20 million to pay a $2 cash dividend for each of Genron's 10 million outstanding shares.
2. Repurchase shares instead of paying a dividend.
3. Raise additional cash to pay an even larger dividend today and in the future.

Will the amount of the current dividend affect Genron's share price? Which policy would shareholders prefer?

To provide a baseline for our discussion of payout policy, we will analyze the consequences of each of these three alternative policies in the next section and compare them in a setting of perfect capital markets. We will also explore how market imperfections such as taxes and transaction costs affect payout policy.

Alternative Policy 1: Pay a Dividend with Excess Cash

Suppose the board opts for the first alternative and uses all excess cash to pay a dividend. With 10 million shares outstanding, Genron will be able to pay a $2 dividend immediately. Because the firm expects to generate future free cash flows of $48 million per year, it anticipates paying a dividend of $4.80 per share each year thereafter. The board declares the dividend and sets the record date as December 14, so that the ex-dividend date is December 12. To determine the impact of this decision, let's compute Genron's share price just before and after the stock goes ex-dividend.

Recall from Chapter 7 and the Valuation Principle that the fair price for the shares is the present value of the expected dividends, given Genron's equity cost of capital. Because Genron has no debt, its equity cost of capital equals its unlevered cost of capital of 12%. Just before the ex-dividend date, the stock is said to trade **cum-dividend** ("with the dividend") because anyone who buys the stock will be entitled to the dividend. In this case,

cum-dividend A modifier indicating that the stock is trading before the ex-dividend date, entitling anyone who buys the stock to the dividend.

$$P_{cum} = \text{Current Dividend} + PV(\text{Future Dividends}) = 2 + \frac{4.80}{0.12} = 2 + 40 = \$42$$

After the stock goes ex-dividend, new buyers will not receive the current dividend. At this point, the share price will reflect only the dividends in subsequent years:

$$P_{ex} = PV(\text{Future Dividends}) = \frac{4.80}{0.12} = \$40$$

The share price will drop on the ex-dividend date, December 12, from $42 to $40. The amount of the price drop is equal to the amount of the current dividend, $2. We can also determine this change in the share price using the market value balance sheet:

	December 11 (Cum-Dividend)	December 12 (Ex-Dividend)
Cash	$20,000,000	$0
Other assets	$400,000,000	$400,000,000
Total market value of assets	$420,000,000	$400,000,000
Shares	10,000,000	10,000,000
Share price	$42	$40

As the market value balance sheet shows, the share price falls when a dividend is paid, because the reduction in cash decreases the market value of the firm's assets. Although the stock price falls, holders of Genron stock do not incur a loss overall. Before the dividend, their stock was worth $42. After the dividend, their stock is worth $40 and they hold $2 in cash from the dividend, for a total value of $42. Our analysis of both the stock price and the market value balance sheet leads to the following conclusion:

In a perfect capital market, when a dividend is paid, the share price drops by the amount of the dividend when the stock begins to trade ex-dividend.

Alternative Policy 2: Share Repurchase (No Dividend)

Suppose that Genron does not pay a dividend this year, but instead uses the $20 million to repurchase its shares on the open market. How will the repurchase affect the share price?

With an initial share price of $42, Genron will repurchase $20 million ÷ $42 per share = 0.476 million shares, leaving only 10 million − 0.476 million = 9,523,810 shares outstanding. Once again, we can use Genron's market value balance sheet to analyze this transaction:

	December 11 (Before Repurchase)	December 12 (Ex-Dividend)
Cash	$20,000,000	$0
Other assets	$400,000,000	$400,000,000
Total market value of assets	$420,000,000	$400,000,000
Shares	10,000,000	9,523,810
Share price	$42	$42

In this case, the market value of Genron's assets falls when the company pays out cash, but the number of shares outstanding also falls from 10 million to 9.524 million. The two changes offset each other, so the share price remains the same, at $42.

Genron's Future Dividends. We can also see why the share price does not fall after the share repurchase by considering the effect on Genron's future dividends. In future years, Genron expects to have $48 million in free cash flow, which can be used to pay a dividend of $48 million ÷ 9.524 million shares = $5.04 per share each year. Thus, with a share repurchase, Genron's share price today is as follows:

$$P_{rep} = \frac{5.04}{0.12} = \$42$$

In other words, by not paying a dividend today and repurchasing shares instead, Genron is able to raise its dividends *per share* in the future. The increase in future dividends compensates shareholders for the dividend they give up today. This example illustrates the following general conclusion about share repurchases:

In perfect capital markets, an open market share repurchase has no effect on the stock price, and the stock price is the same as the cum-dividend price if a dividend were paid instead.

Investor Preferences. Would an investor prefer that Genron issue a dividend or repurchase its stock? Both policies lead to the same *initial* share price of $42. But is there a difference in shareholder value *after* the transaction? Consider an investor who currently holds 2000 shares of Genron stock. Assuming the investor does not trade the stock, the investor's holdings after a dividend or share repurchase are as follows:

Dividend	Repurchase
$40 × 2000 = $80,000 stock	$42 × 2000 = $84,000 stock
$2 × 2000 = $4000 cash	

In either case, the value of the investor's portfolio is $84,000 immediately after the transaction. The only difference is the distribution between cash and stock holdings. Thus, it might seem the investor would prefer one approach or the other depending on whether she needs the cash.

But if Genron repurchases shares and the investor wants cash, she can raise cash by selling shares. For example, she can sell 95 shares to raise 95 × $42 per share = $3990 in cash. She will then hold 1905 shares, or 1905 × $42 = $80,010 in stock. Thus, in the case of a share repurchase, by selling shares an investor can create a *homemade dividend.*

Similarly, if Genron pays a dividend and the investor does not want the cash, she can use the $4000 proceeds of the dividend to purchase 100 additional shares at the ex-dividend share price of $40 per share. As a result, she will hold 2100 shares, worth 2100 × $40 = $84,000. In fact, many firms allow investors to register for a dividend reinvestment program, or *DRIP,* that automatically reinvests any dividends into new shares of the stock.

We summarize these two cases below:

Dividend 1 Buy 100 Shares	Repurchase 1 Sell 95 Shares
$40 × 2100 = $84,000 stock	$42 × 1905 = $80,010 stock
	$42 × 95 = $3990 cash

By selling shares or reinvesting dividends, the investor can create any combination of cash and stock desired. As a result, the investor is indifferent between the various payout methods the firm might employ:

> *In perfect capital markets, investors are indifferent between the firm distributing funds via dividends versus share repurchases. By reinvesting dividends or selling shares, investors can replicate either payout method on their own.*

COMMON MISTAKE

Repurchases and the Supply of Shares

There is a misconception that when a firm repurchases its own shares, the price rises due to the decrease in the supply of shares outstanding. This reasoning follows naturally from the standard supply and demand analysis taught in microeconomics. Why does that analysis not apply here?

When a firm repurchases its own shares, two things happen. First, the supply of shares is reduced. At the same time, however, the value of the firm's assets declines when it spends its cash to buy the shares. If the firm repurchases its shares at their market price, these two effects offset each other, leaving the share price unchanged.

This result is similar to the dilution fallacy discussed in Chapter 16: when a firm issues shares at their market price, the share price does not fall due to the increase in supply. The increase in supply is offset by the increase in the firm's assets that results from the cash it receives from the issuance.

Alternative Policy 3: High Dividend (Equity Issue). Let's look at a third possibility for Genron. Suppose the board wishes to pay an even larger dividend than $2 per share right now. Is that possible and, if so, will the higher dividend make shareholders better off?

Genron plans to pay $48 million in dividends starting next year. Suppose the firm wants to start paying that amount today. Because it has only $20 million in cash today, Genron needs an additional $28 million to pay the larger dividend now. It could raise cash by scaling back its investments. But if the investments have positive NPV, reducing them would lower the firm's value. An alternative way to raise more cash is to borrow money or sell new shares. Let's consider an equity issue. Given a current share price of $42, Genron could raise $28 million by selling $28 million ÷ $42 per share = 0.67 million shares. Because this equity issue will increase Genron's total number of shares outstanding to 10.67 million, the amount of the dividend per share each year will be as follows:

$$\frac{\$48 \text{ million}}{10.67 \text{ million shares}} = \$4.50 \text{ per share}$$

Under this new policy, Genron's cum-dividend share price is:

$$P_{cum} = 4.50 + \frac{4.50}{0.12} = 4.50 + 37.50 = \$42$$

As in the previous examples, the initial share value is unchanged by this policy, and increasing the dividend has no benefit to shareholders.

EXAMPLE 17.1 Homemade Dividends

PROBLEM

Suppose Genron does not adopt the third alternative policy and instead pays a $2 dividend per share today. Show how an investor holding 2000 shares could create a homemade dividend of $4.50 per share × 2000 shares = $9000 per year on her own.

SOLUTION

Plan

If Genron pays a $2 dividend, the investor receives $4000 in cash and holds the rest in stock. She can raise $5000 in additional cash by selling 125 shares at $40 per share just after the dividend is paid.

Execute

The investor creates her $9000 this year by collecting the $4000 dividend and then selling 125 shares at $40 per share. In future years, Genron will pay a dividend of $4.80 per share. Because she will own 2000 − 125 = 1875 shares, the investor will receive dividends of 1875 × $4.80 = $9000 per year from then on.

Evaluate

Again, the policy that the firm chooses is irrelevant—the investor can transact in the market to create a homemade dividend policy that suits her preferences.

Modigliani and Miller and Dividend Policy Irrelevance

In our analysis, we considered three possible dividend policies for the firm: (1) pay out all cash as a dividend; (2) pay no dividend and use the cash instead to repurchase shares; or (3) issue equity to finance a larger dividend. These policies are illustrated in Table 17.1.

TABLE 17.1 Genron's Dividends per Share Each Year Under the Three Alternative Policies

		Dividend Paid ($ per share)			
	Initial Share Price	Year 0	Year 1	Year 2	...
Policy 1	$42.00	2.00	4.80	4.80	...
Policy 2	$42.00	0	5.04	5.04	...
Policy 3	$42.00	4.50	4.50	4.50	...

Table 17.1 shows an important trade-off. If Genron pays a higher *current* dividend per share, it will pay lower *future* dividends per share. For example, if the firm raises the current dividend by issuing equity, it will have more shares and therefore smaller free cash flows per share to pay dividends in the future. If the firm lowers the current dividend and repurchases its shares, it will have fewer shares in the future, so it will be able to pay a higher dividend per share. The net effect of this trade-off is to leave the total present value of all future dividends, and hence the current share price, unchanged at $42.

The logic of this section matches that in our discussion of capital structure in Chapter 16. There, we explained that in perfect capital markets, buying and selling equity and debt are zero-NPV transactions that do not affect firm value. Moreover, any choice of leverage by a firm could be replicated by investors using homemade leverage. As a result, the firm's choice of capital structure is irrelevant. Here, we have established the same principle for a firm's choice of a dividend. Regardless of the amount of cash the firm has on hand, it can pay a smaller dividend (and use the remaining cash to repurchase shares) or a larger dividend (by selling equity to raise cash). Because buying or selling shares is a zero-NPV transaction, such transactions have no effect on the initial share price. Furthermore, shareholders can create a homemade dividend of any size by buying or selling shares themselves.

M&M Dividend Irrelevance proposition
The proposition that, in perfect capital markets, holding fixed the investment policy of a firm, the firm's choice of dividend policy is irrelevant and does not affect the initial share price.

Modigliani and Miller developed this idea in another influential paper published in 1961.[4] As with their result on capital structure, it went against the conventional wisdom that dividend policy could change a firm's value and make its shareholders better off even absent market imperfections. We state here their important proposition.

***M&M Dividend Irrelevance proposition**: In perfect capital markets, holding fixed the investment policy of a firm, the firm's choice of dividend policy is irrelevant and does not affect the initial share price.*

COMMON MISTAKE

The Bird in the Hand Fallacy

"A bird in the hand is worth two in the bush."

The bird in the hand hypothesis states that firms choosing to pay higher current dividends will enjoy higher stock prices because shareholders prefer current dividends to future ones (with the same present value). According to this view, alternative Policy 3 above would lead to the highest share price for Genron.

This view is a misconception. Modigliani and Miller showed that with perfect capital markets, shareholders can generate an equivalent homemade dividend at any time by selling shares. Thus, the dividend choice of the firm should not matter.

[4]See M. Modigliani and M. Miller, "Dividend Policy, Growth, and the Valuation of Shares," *Journal of Business* 34 (4) (1961): 411–433. See also J.B. Williams, *The Theory of Investment Value* (Cambridge, MA: Harvard University Press, 1938).

Dividend Policy with Perfect Capital Markets

The examples in this section illustrate the idea that by using share repurchases or equity issues a firm can easily alter its dividend payments. Because these transactions do not alter the value of the firm, neither does dividend policy.

This result may at first seem to contradict the idea that the price of a share should equal the present value of its future dividends. As our examples have shown, however, a firm's choice of dividend today affects the dividends it can afford to pay in the future in an offsetting fashion. Thus, although dividends *do* determine share prices, a firm's choice of dividend policy does not.

As Modigliani and Miller made clear, the value of a firm ultimately derives from its underlying free cash flows. A firm's free cash flows determine the level of payouts that it can make to its investors. In a perfect capital market, whether these payouts are made through dividends or share repurchases does not matter. Of course, in reality capital markets are not perfect. As with capital structure, it is the imperfections in capital markets that should determine the firm's payout policy. The main imperfection we will discuss is taxes: repurchases and dividends have different tax implications, and investors also face different tax rates. In addition, when managers have information investors do not, payout policy decisions can help signal that information. We start with taxes.

CONCEPT CHECK

3. Explain the misconception that when a firm repurchases its own shares, the price rises due to the decrease in the supply of shares outstanding.
4. In a perfect capital market, how important is the firm's decision to pay dividends versus repurchase shares?

17.3 The Tax Disadvantage of Dividends

As with capital structure, taxes are an important market imperfection that influence a firm's decision to pay dividends or repurchase shares.

Taxes on Dividends and Capital Gains

Shareholders typically must pay taxes on the dividends they receive. They must also pay capital gains taxes when they sell their shares. Historically, the taxes applied to dividend income have been higher than taxes applied to capital gains income. The actual difference in tax rates on dividend income and capital gains income has changed over the years in both Canada and the United States. (Since 2003, they have been equal in the United States.) Table 17.2 shows the marginal tax rates in Canada on personal income for a taxpayer in the top tax bracket in 2018. In all provinces and territories, the tax rates on capital gains income are less than the tax rates on dividend income. In addition, taxes on capital gains income are deferred until the stock is sold; thus, the present value of the taxes on capital gains is substantially less than the taxes on dividends (which must be paid in the year of the dividend payment).

Do taxes affect investors' preferences for dividends versus share repurchases? When a firm pays a dividend, shareholders are taxed according to the dividend tax rate. If the firm repurchases shares instead, and shareholders sell shares to create a homemade dividend, the homemade dividend will be taxed according to the capital gains tax rate. If dividends are taxed at a higher rate than capital gains, shareholders will prefer share repurchases to dividends. Recent changes to the tax code in the United States have equalized the tax

TABLE 17.2 **2018 Canadian Personal Income Tax Rates for a Taxpayer in the Top Tax Bracket**

Province	Marginal Rate on Regular Income	Marginal Rate on Capital Gains Income	Marginal Rate on Dividend Income
B.C	49.80%	24.90%	34.20%
Alberta	48.00%	24.00%	31.71%
Saskatchewan	47.50%	23.75%	29.64%
Manitoba	50.40%	25.20%	37.78%
Ontario	53.53%	26.76%	39.34%
Quebec	53.31%	26.65%	39.83%
N.B.	53.30%	26.65%	33.51%
N.S	54.00%	27.00%	41.58%
P.E.I.	51.37%	25.69%	34.22%
Nfld	51.30%	25.65%	42.61%
Yukon	48.00%	24.00%	28.93%
N.W.T	47.05%	23.53%	28.33%
Nunavut	44.50%	22.25%	33.08%

Source: Canada Revenue Agency, KPMG Combined Top Marginal Tax Rates for Individuals, taxtips.ca, 2018.

rates on dividends and capital gains. It is probably not coincidental that Microsoft started paying dividends shortly after these changes. Nonetheless, because long-term investors can defer the capital gains tax until they sell, *there is still a tax advantage for share repurchases over dividends.*

Not all countries tax dividends at a higher rate than capital gains. Figure 17.4 shows the dividend and capital gains tax rates for different countries. In Finland, for example, capital gains are taxed at a 33% rate, while dividends are taxed at 28.9%. A similar tax preference for dividends exists in Greece, Hungary, Spain, Estonia, and Slovakia—with the last two countries having no tax on dividends at all.

Optimal Dividend Policy with Taxes

When the tax rate on dividends exceeds the tax rate on capital gains, shareholders will pay lower taxes if a firm uses share repurchases for all payouts rather than dividends.

FIGURE 17.4 Dividend and Capital Gains Tax Rates around the World

The capital gains tax rate (red bar) and dividend tax rate (blue bar) for different countries are shown. A missing bar indicates that the distribution is exempt from taxation in that country. Whereas most countries tax dividends at rates greater than or equal to the rate for capital gains, providing a tax preference for share repurchases, some countries, such as Finland, tax capital gains at a higher rate. Several countries, including Singapore and Hong Kong (not pictured), do not tax either.

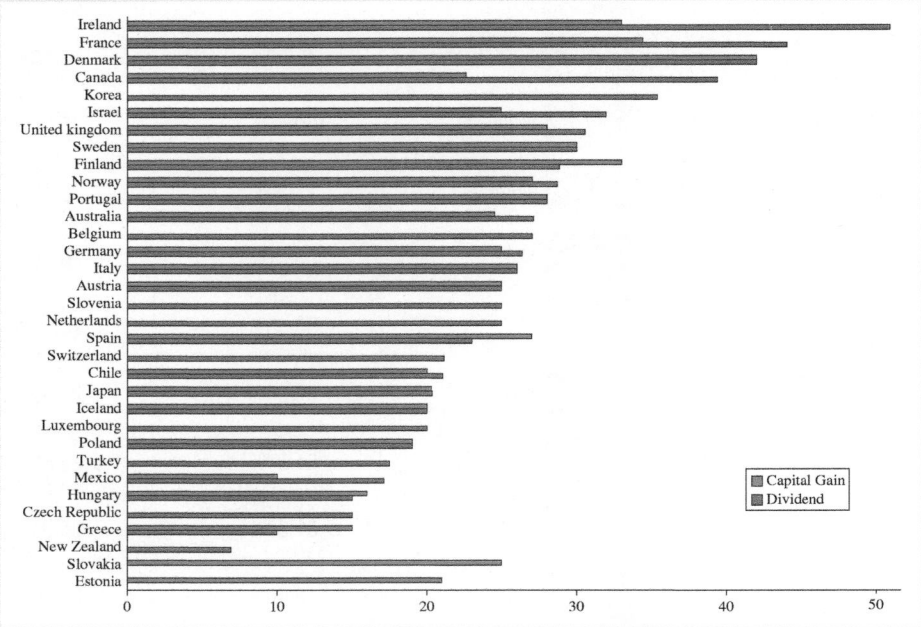

Source: OECD 2015, www.oecd.org; capital gains rates based on marginal rate for an investor with $100,000 in income exceeding any initial exemption.

This tax savings will increase the value of a firm that uses share repurchases rather than dividends. We can also express the tax savings in terms of a firm's equity cost of capital. Firms that use dividends will have to pay a higher pre-tax return (and thus a higher equity cost of capital) to offer their investors the same after-tax return as firms that use share repurchases. As a result, the optimal dividend policy when the dividend tax rate exceeds the capital gain tax rate is to *pay no dividends at all.*

Dividends in Practice. While firms do still pay dividends, substantial evidence shows that many firms have recognized their tax disadvantage. For example, prior to 1980, most U.S. firms used dividends exclusively to distribute cash to shareholders (see Figure 17.5). But by 2000, only about 20% of U.S. firms relied exclusively on dividends. Starting in the early 2000's, this trend has partially reversed. By 2015 the fraction of firms that relied exclusively on dividends rose to about 40%, most likely driven by the Bush administration's dramatic lowering of the dividend tax rate in 2003. A relatively stable 30% of all firms (and more than half of firms making payouts to shareholders) used share repurchases exclusively or in combination with dividends.

FIGURE 17.5 The Rise of Repurchases

This figure shows the percentage of U.S. firms making payouts to shareholders. The shaded regions show the firms that used dividends exclusively (*blue*), repurchases exclusively (*green*), or both (*red*). Because firms that repurchase shares do not usually do so every year, we classify a firm as using repurchases if it repurchased that year or the previous year. Note that after steadily declining for more than 20 years, dividend use has been on the rise since 2000. However, as Figure 17.6 shows, repurchases now account for the largest part of the total value of distributions.

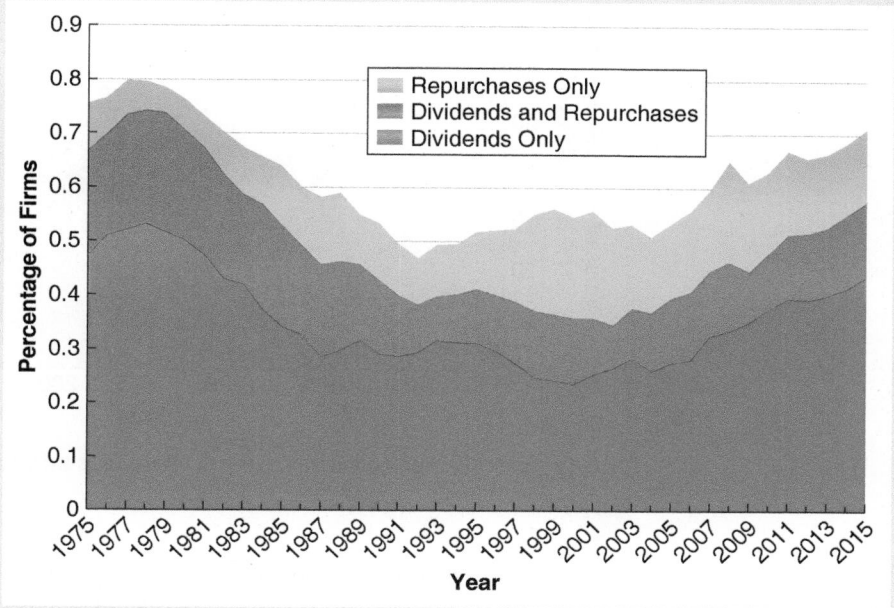

Source: Compustat.

We see a more dramatic trend if we consider the relative magnitudes of both forms of corporate payouts. Figure 17.6 shows the relative importance of share repurchases as a proportion of total payouts to shareholders of U.S. firms. Although dividends accounted for more than 80% of corporate payouts until the early 1980s, the importance of share repurchases grew dramatically in the mid-1980s. Repurchase activity slows during recessions (see 1990–91, 2001–02, and 2009). This fact highlights the flexibility companies have to adjust repurchase payouts as their profits fluctuate. At the same time, there is a strong expectation that companies will maintain dividend payouts unless they are near distress. Partly due to this flexibility and the tax advantages, by the end of the 1990s distributions through repurchasing surpassed those through dividends.

While the data shown in Figures 17.5 and 17.6 are for U.S. companies, a similar pattern is found for Canadian firms. Luke Schmidt, in his 2006 master's thesis at the University of Saskatchewan, found that in 1995 the dollar amount of dividends was more than four times the dollar amount of share repurchases by Canadian corporations. The dollar amount of dividends fluctuated and rose slightly over time; however, the dollar amount of repurchases grew substantially and eclipsed dividends by 2004.[5]

[5]See L. Schmidt, "Credibility of Corporate Announcements and Market Reaction: Evidence from Canadian Share Repurchase Programs," master's thesis, University of Saskatchewan, 2006.

FIGURE 17.6 The Changing Composition of Shareholder Payouts

This figure shows the value of share repurchases as a percentage of total payouts to shareholders (dividends and repurchases). Although initially small, the total dollar amount of share repurchases has grown faster than dividends, so that by the late 1990s share repurchases surpassed dividends to become the largest form of corporate payouts for U.S. industrial firms.

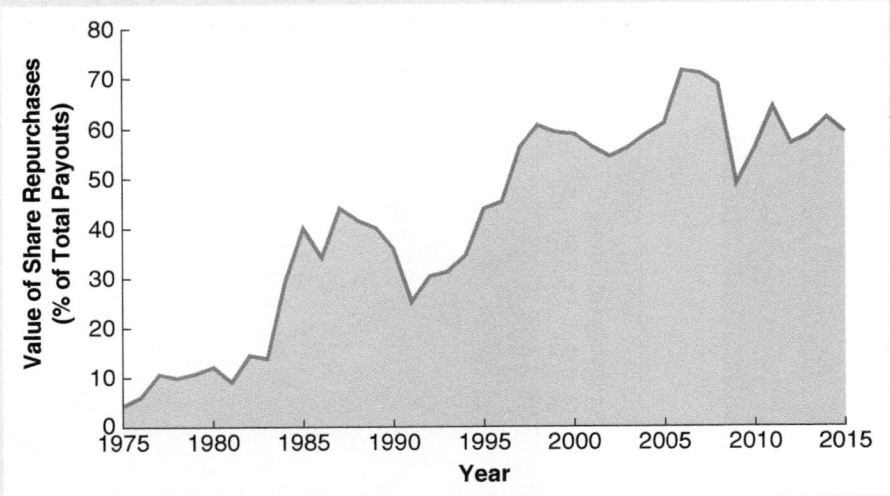

Source: Compustat/CRSP data for U.S. firms, excluding financial firms and utilities.

While this evidence is indicative of the growing importance of share repurchases as a part of firms' payout policies, it also shows that dividends remain a key form of payouts to shareholders. The fact that firms continue to issue dividends despite their tax disadvantage is often referred to as the **dividend puzzle**.[6] Table 17.3 summarizes dividends versus repurchases, highlighting the differences between the two ways to distribute cash to shareholders. In the next section, we consider some factors that may mitigate this tax disadvantage. In Section 17.5, we examine alternative motivations for using dividends based on differences in information between managers and investors.

dividend puzzle A firm's continuing issuance of dividends despite their tax disadvantage.

TABLE 17.3 Summary of Dividends versus Repurchases

	Dividends	Share Repurchases
How cash is distributed to shareholders	Cash payment made on a per-share basis to all shareholders	Shares repurchased
Participation	Involuntary (everyone with a share receives a dividend)	Voluntary (shareholders choose whether to sell their shares)
Taxation for ordinary investors	Taxed less than regular income (see Table 17.2, as relative rates vary by province or territory)	Taxed as capital gains, which are taxed less than regular income (see Table 17.2, as relative rates vary by province or territory)
Effect on share price	Share price drops by the amount of the dividend	Share price is unaffected as long as shares are repurchased at a fair (market) price

[6]See F. Black, "The Dividend Puzzle," *Journal of Portfolio Management* 2 (1976): 5–8.

Tax Differences across Investors

Even though many investors have a tax preference for share repurchases rather than dividends, the strength of that preference depends on the difference between the dividend tax rate and the capital gains tax rate that they face. Tax rates vary by income, by jurisdiction, and by whether the stock is held in a retirement account or tax-free savings account. Because of these differences, firms may attract different groups of investors, depending on their dividend policy. In this section, we highlight the differences in the tax treatment of dividends across investors and discuss how that leads different groups of investors to prefer different payout policies.

Dividend Tax Rate Factors. Tax rates on dividends and capital gains differ across investors for a variety of reasons:

Income Level. Investors with different levels of income fall into different tax brackets and face different tax rates.

Investment Horizon. Long-term investors can defer the payment of capital gains taxes (lowering their effective capital gains tax rate even further). An investor who never intends to sell her shares effectively pays no capital gains tax. For example, an investor who holds her shares for a long time period and then plans to donate her shares to a Canadian charity will not have to pay any capital gains tax, and the full amount of the donation will be eligible for a charitable tax credit.

Tax Jurisdiction. Canadian investors are subject to provincial taxes that differ by province. U.S. investors in Canadian stocks and Canadian investors in U.S. stocks are subject to a 15% withholding tax for dividends they receive. Other foreign investors may be subject to a higher withholding tax on dividends they receive. There is no similar withholding for capital gains.

Type of Investor or Investment Account. Stocks held by individual investors in a registered retirement savings plan (RRSP), registered retirement income fund (RRIF), or tax-free savings account (TFSA) are not subject to taxes on dividends or capital gains.[7] Similarly, stocks held through pension funds or nonprofit endowment funds are not subject to dividend or capital gains taxes. Corporations that hold stocks are able to exclude 100% of dividends they receive from corporate taxes, but are unable to exclude capital gains.

As a result of their different tax rates, these investors have varying preferences regarding dividends:

1. Long-term investors are more heavily taxed on dividends, so they would prefer share repurchases to dividend payments.
2. Pension funds, and other non-taxed investors have no tax preference for share repurchases over dividends; they would prefer a payout policy that most closely matches their cash needs. For example, a non-taxed investor who desires current income would prefer high dividends so as to avoid the brokerage fees and other transaction costs of selling the stock.
3. Corporations enjoy a tax *advantage* associated with dividends due to the 100% exclusion allowance. For this reason, a corporation that chooses to invest its cash will prefer to hold stocks with high-dividend yields.

clientele effects
The effects of the tax preferences of a firm's investor clientele on the firm's dividend policy.

Clientele Effects. Table 17.4 summarizes the different preferences across investor groups. These differences in tax preferences create clientele effects, in which the dividend policy of a firm is optimized for the tax preference of its investor clientele. Individuals in

[7]While taxes may be owed when the money is withdrawn from the retirement account, these taxes do not depend on whether the money came from dividends or capital gains.

the highest tax brackets have a preference for stocks that pay no or low dividends, whereas tax-free investors and corporations have a preference for stocks with high dividends. So if a firm has a particular type of clientele for its investors, it will set its dividend policy in accordance with its investors' preferences.

TABLE 17.4 Differing Dividend Policy Preferences across Investor Groups

Investor Group	Dividend Policy Preference	Proportion of Investors
Individual investors	Tax disadvantage for dividends; prefer share repurchase	~53%
Institutions, pension funds, retirement accounts	No tax preference; prefer dividend policy that matches income needs	~46%
Corporations	Tax advantage for dividends	~1%

Source: Proportions based on Federal Reserve Flow of Funds Accounts, 2007.

Evidence supports the existence of tax clienteles. For example, Franklin Allen and Roni Michaely[8] report that, in 1996, individual investors held 54% of all stocks by market value, yet received only 35% of all dividends paid, indicating that individuals tend to hold stocks with low-dividend yields. Of course, the fact that high-tax investors receive any dividends at all implies that the clienteles are not perfect—dividend taxes are not the only determinants of investors' portfolios.

CONCEPT CHECK

5. Under what conditions will investors have a tax preference for share repurchases rather than dividends?
6. What is the dividend puzzle?

17.4 Payout versus Retention of Cash

We have thus far considered only one aspect of a firm's payout policy (shown in Figure 17.1): the choice between paying dividends and repurchasing shares. But how should a firm decide the amount it should pay out to shareholders and the amount it should retain?

To answer this question, we must first consider what the firm will do with cash that it retains. It can invest the cash in new projects or in financial instruments. In the next section, we will examine these options in the context of perfect capital markets.

Retaining Cash with Perfect Capital Markets

Once a firm has taken all positive-NPV projects, it is left with the question of whether to retain any remaining cash or distribute it to shareholders. If the firm retains the cash, it can hold the cash in the bank or use it to purchase financial assets. The firm can then pay the money to shareholders at a future time or invest it when positive-NPV investment opportunities become available.

What are the advantages and disadvantages of retaining cash and investing in financial securities? In perfect capital markets, buying and selling securities is a zero-NPV transaction, so it should not affect the firm's value. On their own, shareholders can

[8]Franklin Allen and Roni Michaely, "Payout Policy," in *Handbook of the Economics of Finance: Corporate Finance*, vol. 1A, G. M. Constantinides, M. Harris, and R. M. Stulz, eds. (Amsterdam, The Netherlands: Elsevier, 2003).

make any investment a firm makes if the firm pays out the cash. Thus, it should not be surprising that, with perfect capital markets, the retention versus payout decision—just like the dividend versus share repurchase decision—is irrelevant.

EXAMPLE 17.2 Payout Decisions in a Perfect Capital Market

PROBLEM

Yellowknife Mining has $100,000 in excess cash. Yellowknife is considering investing the cash in one-year treasury bills paying 6% interest, and then using the cash to pay a dividend next year. Alternatively, the firm can pay a dividend immediately, and shareholders can invest the cash on their own. In a perfect capital market, which option would shareholders prefer?

SOLUTION

■ Plan

We need to compare what shareholders would receive from an immediate dividend ($100,000) to the present value of what they would receive in one year if Yellowknife invested the cash. Note, in a perfect capital market there are no taxes.

■ Execute

If Yellowknife retains the cash, at the end of one year the company would be able to pay a dividend of $100,000 × (1.06) = $106,000. Note that this payoff is the same as if shareholders had invested the $100,000 in treasury bills themselves. In other words, the present value of this future dividend is exactly $106,000 ÷ (1.06) = $100,000, which is the same as the $100,000 shareholders would receive from an immediate dividend. Thus, shareholders are indifferent about whether the firm pays the dividend immediately or retains the cash.

■ Evaluate

Because Yellowknife is not doing anything that the investors could not have done on their own, it does not create any value by retaining the cash and investing it for the shareholders versus simply paying it to them immediately. As we showed with Genron in Example 17.1, if Yellowknife retains the cash, but investors prefer to have the income today, they could sell $100,000 worth of shares.

As Example 17.2 illustrates, there is no difference for shareholders if the firm pays the cash immediately or retains the cash and pays it out at a future date. This example provides yet another illustration of Modigliani and Miller's fundamental insight regarding financial policy irrelevance in perfect capital markets:

M&M Payout Irrelevance proposition The proposition that, in perfect capital markets, if a firm invests excess cash flows in financial securities, the firm's choice of payout versus retention is irrelevant and does not affect the initial value of the firm.

> ***M&M Payout Irrelevance proposition:*** *In perfect capital markets, if a firm invests excess cash flows in financial securities, the firm's choice of payout versus retention is irrelevant and does not affect the initial value of the firm.*

Retaining Cash with Imperfect Capital Markets

Based on M&M's payout irrelevance proposition, it is clear that the decision of whether to retain cash depends on market imperfections, which we now address.

Taxes and Cash Retention. The Yellowknife example assumed perfect capital markets and so ignored the effect of taxes. How would our result change with taxes?

EXAMPLE 17.3 Retaining Cash with Corporate Taxes

PROBLEM

Recall Yellowknife Mining from Example 17.2. Suppose Yellowknife must pay corporate taxes at a 35% rate on the interest it will earn from the one-year treasury bills paying 6% interest. Would pension fund investors (who do not pay taxes on their investment income) prefer that Yellowknife use its excess cash to pay the $100,000 dividend immediately or retain the cash for one year?

SOLUTION

■ Plan

As in Example 17.2, the comparison is between what shareholders could generate on their own and what shareholders will receive if Yellowknife retains and invests the funds for them. The key question then is this—what is the difference between the after-tax return that Yellowknife can earn and distribute to shareholders versus the pension fund's tax-free return on investing the $100,000?

■ Execute

Because the pension fund investors do not pay taxes on investment income, the result still holds from the prior example when the pension fund receives the dividend now; they would get $100,000, invest it, and earn 6% to receive a total of $106,000 in one year.

If Yellowknife retains the cash for one year it will earn the following after-tax return on the treasury bills:

$$6\% \times (1 - 0.35) = 3.90\%$$

Thus, at the end of the year Yellowknife will pay a dividend of $100,000 × (1.039) = $103,900.

■ Evaluate

This amount is less than the $106,000 the investors would have received if they had invested the $100,000 in treasury bills themselves. Because Yellowknife must pay corporate taxes on the interest it earns, there is a tax disadvantage to retaining cash. Pension fund investors will therefore prefer that Yellowknife pays the dividend now.

As Example 17.3 shows, corporate taxes make it costly for a firm to retain excess cash. This effect is the very same effect we identified in Chapter 16 with regard to leverage: when a firm pays interest, it receives a tax deduction for that interest, whereas when a firm receives interest, it owes taxes on the interest. Cash can be thought of as equivalent to *negative* leverage, so the tax advantage of leverage implies a tax disadvantage to holding cash.

Investor Tax Adjustments. The decision to pay out versus retain cash may also affect the taxes paid by shareholders. Although pension and retirement fund investments are tax exempt, individual investors must pay taxes on interest, dividends, and capital gains if their investments are held outside RRSPs, RRIFs, or TFSAs. How do investor taxes affect the tax disadvantage of retaining cash?

Because the dividend tax will be paid whether the firm pays the cash immediately or retains the cash and pays the interest over time, the dividend tax rate does not affect the cost of retaining cash. However, when a firm retains cash, it must pay corporate tax on the interest it earns. In addition, the investor will owe capital gains tax on the increased value of the firm. In essence, the interest on retained cash is taxed twice. If the firm paid the cash to its shareholders instead, they could invest it and be taxed only once on the interest that they earn. The cost of retaining cash therefore depends on the combined effect of the corporate and capital gains taxes, compared to the single tax on interest income. Under most tax regimes there remains a substantial tax *disadvantage* for the firm to retaining excess cash even after adjusting for investor taxes.

Issuance and Distress Costs. If there is a tax disadvantage to retaining cash, why do some firms accumulate large cash balances? Often, they retain cash balances to cover potential future cash shortfalls. For example, if there is a reasonable likelihood that future earnings will be insufficient to fund future positive-NPV investment opportunities, a firm may start accumulating cash to make up the difference. This motivation is especially relevant for firms that may need to fund large-scale research and development projects or large acquisitions.

The advantage of holding cash to cover future potential cash needs is that this strategy allows a firm to avoid the transaction costs of raising new capital (through new debt or equity issues). As we discussed in Chapters 14 and 15, the direct costs of issuance range from 1% to 3% for debt issues and from 3.5% to 7% for equity issues. There can also be substantial indirect costs of raising capital due to the agency and adverse selection (lemons) costs discussed in Chapter 16. A firm must therefore balance the tax costs of holding cash with the potential benefits of not having to raise external funds in the future. Firms with very volatile earnings may also build up cash reserves to enable them to weather temporary periods of operating losses. By holding sufficient cash, these firms can avoid financial distress and its associated costs.

Agency Costs of Retaining Cash. There is no benefit to shareholders when a firm holds cash above and beyond its future investment or liquidity needs. In fact, in addition to the tax cost, there are likely to be agency costs of equity associated with having too much cash in the firm. As discussed in Chapter 16, when firms have excessive cash, managers may use the funds inefficiently by continuing money-losing pet projects, paying excessive executive perquisites (perks), being less diligent in their managing of the firm (shirking), or overpaying for acquisitions. Leverage is one way to reduce a firm's excess cash; dividends and share repurchases perform a similar role by taking cash out of the firm.

Thus, paying out excess cash through dividends or share repurchases can boost the stock price by reducing managers' ability and temptation to waste resources. For example, on April 23, 2004, Value Line announced it would use its accumulated cash to pay a special dividend of $17.50 per share. Value Line's stock increased by roughly $10 on the announcement of its special dividend, very likely due to the perceived tax benefits and reduced agency costs that would result from the transaction.

EXAMPLE 17.4 Cutting Negative-NPV Growth

PROBLEM

OilSand Resources is an all-equity firm with 100 million shares outstanding. OilSand has $150 million in cash and expects future free cash flows of $65 million per year. Management plans to use the cash to expand the firm's operations, which will, in turn, increase future free cash flows to $72.8 million per year. If the cost of capital of OilSand's investments is 10%, how would a decision to use the cash for a share repurchase rather than the expansion change the share price?

SOLUTION

■ Plan

We can use the perpetuity formula to value OilSand under the two scenarios. The repurchase will take place at market prices, so the repurchase itself will have no effect on OilSand's share price. The main question is whether spending $150 million now (instead of repurchasing) to increase cash flows by $7.8 million per year is a positive-NPV project. ▶

Execute

Investment option:

Using the perpetuity formula, if OilSand invests the $150 million to expand, its market value will be $72.8 million ÷ 10% = $728 million, or $7.28 per share with 100 million shares outstanding.

Repurchase option:

If OilSand does not expand, the value of its future free cash flows will be $65 million ÷ 10% = $650 million. Adding the $150 million in cash it currently has, OilSand's market value is $800 million, or $8.00 per share.

If OilSand repurchases shares, there will be no change to the share price; the company will repurchase $150 million ÷ $8.00 per share = 18.75 million shares, so it will have assets worth $650 million with 81.25 million shares outstanding, for a share price of $650 million ÷ 81.25 million shares = $8.00 per share.

In this case, cutting investment and growth to fund a share repurchase increases the share price by $0.72 per share ($8.00 − $7.28).

Evaluate

The share price is higher with the repurchase because the alternative of expansion has a negative NPV; it costs $150 million but increases future free cash flows by only $7.8 million per year forever, for an NPV of

$$-\$150 \text{ million} + \$7.8 \text{ million}/10\% = -\$72 \text{ million, or } -\$0.72 \text{ per share}$$

Thus, by avoiding the expansion, the repurchase keeps the shares from suffering the $0.72 loss.

Ultimately, firms should choose to retain cash for the same reasons they would use low leverage—to preserve financial slack for future growth opportunities and to avoid financial distress costs. These needs must be balanced against the tax disadvantage of holding cash and the agency cost of wasteful investment. It is not surprising, then, that high-tech and biotechnology firms, which typically choose to use little debt, also tend to retain and accumulate large amounts of cash. Table 17.5 shows the non-financial companies in the U.S. and Canada with the largest cash balances as of 2018.

As with capital structure decisions, however, even though a firm's board of directors sets its payout policy, managers whose incentives may differ from those of shareholders may heavily influence that policy. Managers may prefer to retain and maintain control over the firm's cash rather than pay it out. The retained cash can be used to fund investments that are costly for shareholders but have benefits for managers (e.g., pet projects and excessive salaries), or it can simply be held as a means to reduce leverage and the risk of financial distress that could threaten managers' job security. According to the managerial entrenchment theory of payout policy, managers pay out cash only when pressured to do so by the firm's investors.

CONCEPT CHECK

7. Is there an advantage for a firm to retain its cash instead of paying it out to shareholders in perfect capital markets?
8. How do corporate taxes affect the decision of a firm to retain excess cash?

TABLE 17.5 U.S. and Canadian non-financial firms ranked by their holdings of cash and marketable securities based on stock market data and latest annual reports as of May 22, 2018. Currency amounts are in billions of each country's respective domestic dollars.

Country	Rank in Country	Ticker	Company Name	Cash and Marketable Securities	Percentage of Market Capitalization	Market Capitalization
USA	1	AAPL	Apple Inc	268.9	29.2%	922.2
USA	2	MSFT	Microsoft Corp	133.0	17.7%	749.9
USA	3	GOOGL	Alphabet Inc (Google)	101.9	13.6%	751.2
USA	4	GE	General Electric Co	82.0	61.9%	132.5
USA	5	CSCO	Cisco Systems Inc	70.5	33.4%	210.8
USA	6	ORCL	Oracle Corp	66.1	34.3%	192.7
USA	7	T	At&T Inc	50.5	25.2%	200.1
USA	8	FB	Facebook Inc	41.7	7.8%	534.2
Canada	1	WN	Weston (George) Ltd	3.1	23.5%	13.4
Canada	2	BBD	Bombardier Inc	3.0	29.0%	10.3
Canada	3	BB	BlackBerry Ltd	2.3	28.3%	8.0
Canada	4	ABX	Barrick Gold Corp	2.2	11.3%	19.8

Source: Bloomberg, company annual filings, and author's calculations.

17.5 Signalling with Payout Policy

One market imperfection that we have not yet considered is asymmetric information. When managers have better information than investors regarding the future prospects of the firm, managers' payout decisions may signal this information. In this section, we look at managers' motivations when setting a firm's payout policy, and we evaluate what these decisions may communicate to investors.

Dividend Smoothing

Firms can change dividends at any time, but in practice they vary the sizes of their dividends relatively infrequently. For example, General Motors (GM) has changed the amount of its regular dividend only eight times over a 20-year period. Yet, during that same period, GM's earnings varied widely, as shown in Figure 17.7.

The pattern seen with GM is typical of most firms that pay dividends. Firms adjust dividends relatively infrequently, and dividends are much less volatile than earnings. This practice of maintaining relatively constant dividends is called **dividend smoothing**. Firms also increase dividends much more frequently than they cut them. For example, from 1971 to 2001, only 5.4% of dividend changes were decreases.[9] In a classic survey of corporate executives, John Lintner suggested that these observations resulted from (1) management's belief that investors prefer stable dividends with sustained growth and (2) management's desire to maintain a long-term target level of dividends as a fraction

dividend smoothing The practice of maintaining relatively constant dividends.

[9]Franklin Allen and Roni Michaely, "Payout Policy," in *Handbook of the Economics of Finance: Corporate Finance*, vol. 1A, G. M. Constantinides, M. Harris, and R. M. Stulz, eds. (Amsterdam, The Netherlands: Elsevier, 2003).

FIGURE 17.7 GM's Earnings and Dividends per Share, 1985–2008

Compared with GM's earnings, its dividend payments have remained relatively stable. (Data adjusted for splits; earnings exclude extraordinary items.)

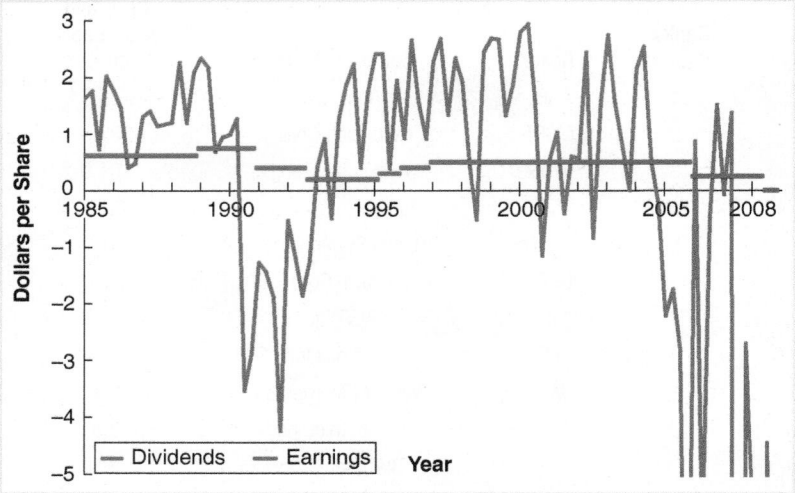

Source: Compustat and Capital IQ.

of earnings.[10] Thus, firms raise their dividends only when they perceive a long-term sustainable increase in the expected level of future earnings, and cut them only as a last resort. While this is perhaps a good description of how firms *do* set their dividends, as we have shown in this chapter there is no clear reason why firms *should* smooth their dividends. One explanation is that it contributes to signalling with dividends, as discussed in the next section.

How can firms keep dividends smooth as earnings vary? As we have already discussed, firms can maintain almost any level of dividend in the short run by adjusting the number of shares they repurchase or issue and the amount of cash they retain. However, due to the tax and transaction costs of funding a dividend with new equity issues, managers do not wish to commit to a dividend that the firm cannot afford to pay out of regular earnings. For this reason, firms generally set dividends at a level they expect to be able to maintain based on the firm's earnings prospects.

Dividend Signalling

If firms smooth dividends, the firm's dividend choice will contain information regarding management's expectations of future earnings.

1. When a firm increases its dividend, it sends a positive signal to investors that management expects to be able to afford the higher dividend for the foreseeable future.
2. When managers cut the dividend, it may signal that they have given up hope that earnings will rebound in the near term and so need to reduce the dividend to save cash.

[10] J. Lintner, "Distribution of Incomes of Corporations Among Dividends, Retained Earnings and Taxes," *American Economic Review* 46 (1956): 97–113.

dividend signalling hypothesis The idea that dividend changes reflect managers' views about a firm's future earnings prospects.

The idea that dividend changes reflect managers' views about a firm's future earnings prospects is called the **dividend signalling hypothesis**.

While an increase of a firm's dividend may signal management's optimism regarding its future cash flows, it might also signal a lack of investment opportunities. For example, Microsoft's move to initiate dividends in 2003 was largely seen as a result of its declining growth prospects as opposed to a signal about its increased future profitability.[11] Conversely, a firm might cut its dividend to exploit new positive-NPV investment opportunities. In this case, the dividend decrease might lead to a positive—rather than negative—stock price reaction (see the box below about Royal & SunAlliance's dividend cut). In general, we must interpret dividends as a signal in the context of the type of new information managers are likely to have.

Signalling and Share Repurchases

Share repurchases, similar to dividends, may also signal managers' information to the market. However, several important differences distinguish share repurchases and dividends:

1. Managers are much less committed to share repurchases than to dividend payments. As we noted earlier, when firms announce authorization for an open market share repurchase, they generally announce the maximum amount they plan to spend on repurchases. The actual amount spent, however, may be far less. Also, it may take several years to complete the share repurchase.
2. Firms do not smooth their repurchase activity from year to year, as they do with dividends. Thus, announcing a share repurchase today does not necessarily represent a long-term commitment to repurchase shares. In this regard, share repurchases may be less of a signal than dividends are about future earnings of a firm.

ROYAL & SUNALLIANCE'S DIVIDEND CUT

In some quarters, Julian Hance must have seemed like a heretic. On November 8, 2001, the finance director of Royal & SunAlliance, a U.K.-based insurance group with £12.6 billion ($20.2 billion) in annual revenue, did the unthinkable—he announced that he would cut the firm's dividend.

Many observers gasped at the decision. Surely, they argued, cutting the dividend was a sign of weakness. Didn't companies cut their dividend only when profits were falling?

Quite the contrary, countered Hance. With insurance premiums rising around the world, particularly following the World Trade Center tragedy, Royal & SunAlliance believed that its industry offered excellent growth opportunities.

"The outlook for business in 2002 and beyond makes a compelling case for reinvesting capital in the business rather than returning it to shareholders," explains Hance.

The stock market agreed with him, sending Royal & SunAlliance's shares up 5% following its dividend news. "Cutting the dividend is a positive move," observed Matthew Wright, an insurance analyst at Credit Lyonnais. "It shows the company expects future profitability to be good."

While a dividend cut can be associated with either good or bad news about a company, the empirical evidence shows that stock prices typically drop around announcements of dividend cuts. What we observed with Royal & SunAlliance's shares was more of an exception, usually dividend cuts are associated with bad news for a company.

Source: Justin Wood, http://CFOEurope.com, December 2001.

[11]See "An End to Growth?" *The Economist* (July 22, 2004): 61.

INTERVIEW WITH JOHN CONNORS

John Connors

John Connors was senior vice-president and chief financial officer of Microsoft. He retired in 2005 and is now a partner at Ignition Partners, a Seattle venture capital firm.

Q Microsoft declared a dividend for the first time in 2003. What goes into the decision of a company to initiate a dividend?

A Microsoft was in a unique position. The company had never paid a dividend and was facing shareholder pressure to do something with its $60 billion cash buildup. The company considered five key questions in developing its distribution strategy:

1. Can the company sustain payment of a cash dividend in perpetuity and increase the dividend over time? Microsoft was confident it could meet that commitment and raise the dividend in the future.
2. Is a cash dividend a better return to stockholders than a stock buyback program? These are capital structure decisions: Do we want to reduce our shares outstanding? Is our stock attractively priced for a buyback, or do we want to distribute the cash as a dividend? Microsoft had plenty of capacity to issue a dividend *and* continue a buyback program.
3. What is the tax effect of a cash dividend versus a buyback to the corporation and to shareholders? From a tax perspective, to shareholders it was largely a neutral decision in Microsoft's case.
4. What is the psychological impact on investors, and how does it fit the story of the stock for investors? This is a more qualitative factor. A regular ongoing dividend put Microsoft on a path to becoming an attractive investment for income investors.
5. What are the public relations implications of a dividend program? Investors don't look to Microsoft to hold cash but to be a leader in software development and provide equity growth. So they viewed the dividend program favourably.

Q How does a company decide whether to increase its dividend, have a special dividend, or repurchase its stock to return capital to investors?

A The decision to increase the dividend is a function of cash flow projections. Are you confident that you have adequate cash flow to sustain this and future increases? Once you increase the dividend, investors expect future increases as well. Some companies establish explicit criteria for dividend increases. In my experience as a CFO, the analytic framework involves a set of relative comparables. What are the dividend payouts and dividend yields of the market in general and of your peer group, and where are we relative to them? We talk to significant investors and consider what is best for increasing shareholder value long-term.

A special dividend is a very efficient form of cash distribution that generally involves a nonrecurring situation, such as the sale of a business division or a cash award from a legal situation. Also, companies without a comprehensive distribution strategy use special dividends to reduce large cash accumulations. For Microsoft, the 2004 special dividend and announcement of the stock dividend and stock buyback program resolved the issue of what to do with all the cash and clarified our direction going forward.

Q What other factors go into dividend decisions?

A Powerful finance and accounting tools help us to make better and broader business decisions. But these decisions involve as much psychology and market thinking as math. You have to consider non-quantifiable factors such as the psychology of investors. Not long ago, everyone wanted growth stocks; no one wanted dividend-paying stocks. Now dividend stocks are in vogue. You must also take into account your industry and what the competition is doing. In many tech companies, employee ownership in the form of options programs represents a fairly significant percentage of fully diluted shares. Dividend distributions reduce the value of options.*

At the end of the day, you want to be sure that your cash distribution strategy helps your overall story with investors.

DISCUSSION QUESTIONS

1. How does Connors's comment about investor preferences for growth versus dividend-paying stocks fit within the framework of the dividend signalling discussion?
2. Does such a preference argument fit the efficient markets hypothesis discussed in Chapter 7?

---

*We discussed options in Chapter 13. The key point here is that employee stock options increase in value when the stock price goes up, but as we learned in this chapter, a dividend reduces the stock price on the ex-dividend day.

3. The cost of a share repurchase depends on the market price of the stock. If managers believe the stock is currently overvalued, a share repurchase will be costly to the firm. That is, buying the stock at its current (overvalued) price is a negative-NPV investment. By contrast, repurchasing shares when managers perceive the stock to be undervalued is a positive-NPV investment. Managers will clearly be more likely to repurchase shares if they believe the stock to be undervalued.

Thus, share repurchases may signal that managers believe the firm to be undervalued (or at least not severely overvalued). Share repurchases are a credible signal that the shares are underpriced, because if they are overpriced a share repurchase is costly for current shareholders (and particularly for long-term investors who do not sell during the share repurchase). If investors believe that managers have better information regarding the firm's prospects and act on behalf of current shareholders, then investors will react favourably to share repurchase announcements.

In a 2004 survey, 87% of CFOs agreed that firms should repurchase shares when their stock price is a good value relative to its true value,[12] implicitly indicating that most CFOs believe that they should act in the interests of the long-term shareholders. Thus, if investors believe that managers have better information regarding the firm's prospects than they do, then investors should react favourably to share repurchase announcements. Indeed they do: the average market price reaction to the announcement of an open market share repurchase program is about 3% (with the size of the reaction increasing with the portion of shares outstanding sought).[13]

CONCEPT CHECK

9. What possible signals does a firm give when it cuts its dividend?

10. Would managers be more likely to repurchase shares if they believe the stock is under- or overvalued?

17.6 Stock Dividends, Splits, and Spinoffs

In this chapter, we have focused on a firm's decision to pay cash to its shareholders. But a firm can pay another type of dividend that does not involve cash: a stock dividend. In this case, each shareholder who owns the stock before it goes ex-dividend receives additional shares of stock of the firm itself (a stock split) or of a subsidiary (a spinoff). Here, we briefly review these two types of transactions.

Stock Dividends and Splits

stock dividend (stock split) The issuing by a company of a dividend in shares of stock rather than cash to its shareholders.

In a **stock dividend (stock split)**, the company issues additional shares rather than cash to its shareholders. If a company declares a 10% stock dividend, each shareholder will receive 1 new share of stock for every 10 shares already owned. Stock dividends of 50% or higher are generally referred to as stock splits. For example, with a 50% stock dividend, each shareholder will receive 1 new share for every 2 shares owned. Because a holder of two shares will end up holding three shares, this transaction is also called a 3:2 ("3-for-2") stock split. Similarly, a 100% stock dividend is equivalent to a 2:1 stock split.

---

[12]A. Brav, J. Graham, C. Harvey, and R. Michaely, "Payout Policy in the 21st Century," *Journal of Financial Economics* 77 (3) (2005): 483–527.

[13]See D. Ikenberry, J. Lakonishok, and T. Vermaelen, "Market Underreaction to Open Market Share Repurchases," *Journal of Financial Economics* 39 (2) (1995): 181–208.

BERKSHIRE HATHAWAY'S A AND B SHARES

Many managers split their stock to keep the price affordable for small investors, making it easier for them to buy and sell the stock. Warren Buffett, chairman and chief executive of Berkshire Hathaway, disagrees. As he commented in Berkshire's 1983 annual report, "We are often asked why Berkshire does not split its stock. . . we want [shareholders] who think of themselves as business owners with the intention of staying a long time. And, we want those who keep their eyes focused on business results, not market prices." In its 40-year history, Berkshire Hathaway has never split its stock.

As a result of Berkshire Hathaway's strong performance and the lack of stock splits, the stock price climbed. By 1996, it exceeded $30,000 per share. Because this price was much too expensive for some small investors, several financial intermediaries created unit investment trusts whose only investment was Berkshire shares. (Unit investment trusts are similar to mutual funds, but their investment portfolio is fixed.) Investors could buy smaller interests in these trusts, effectively owning Berkshire stock with a much lower initial investment.

In response, Buffett announced in February 1996 the creation of a second class of Berkshire Hathaway stock, the Class B shares. Each owner of the original shares (now called Class A shares) was offered the opportunity to convert each A share into 30 B shares. "We're giving shareholders a do-it-yourself split, if they care to do it," Buffett said. Through the B shares, investors could own Berkshire stock with a smaller investment, and they would not have to pay the extra transaction costs required to buy stock through the unit trusts. In 2010, Berkshire Hathaway did a further 50 for 1 split of its B shares.

Meanwhile the value of the A shares has continued to do well. After reaching a peak of $148,000 in late 2007 and dropping to below $75,000 in March 2009 (at the bottom of the financial crisis), the price of one share of Berkshire Hathaway Class A shares was more than $306,000 per share on January 21, 2019.*

*We should note that Buffett's logic for not splitting the stock is a bit puzzling. It is unclear why allowing the stock price to rise to a very high level would attract the kind of investors Buffett wanted. If indeed this was the motivation for Buffett's policies, he could have obtained the desired results much earlier by simply doing a reverse stock split.

With a stock dividend, a firm does not pay out any cash to shareholders. As a result, the total market value of the firm's assets and liabilities, and therefore of its equity, is unchanged. The only thing that is different is the number of shares outstanding. The stock price will therefore fall, because the same total equity value is now divided over a larger number of shares.

Unlike cash dividends, stock dividends are not taxed. Thus, from both the firm's and shareholders' perspectives, there is no real consequence to a stock dividend. The number of shares is proportionally increased and the price per share is proportionally reduced so that there is no change in value.

Stock Splits and Share Price. Why, then, do companies pay stock dividends or split their stock? The typical motivation for a stock split is to keep the share price in a range thought to be attractive to small investors. Stocks generally trade in lots of 100 shares, and in any case do not trade in units of less than one share. As a result, if the share price rises significantly, it might be difficult for small investors to afford one share, let alone 100. Making the stock more attractive to small investors can increase the demand for and the liquidity of the stock, which may in turn boost the stock price. On average, announcements of stock splits are associated with a 2% increase in the stock price.[14]

Most firms use splits to keep their share prices from exceeding $100. From 1990 to 2000, Cisco Systems split its stock nine times, so that one share purchased at the IPO split into 288 shares. Had it not split, Cisco's share price at the time of its last split in March 2000 would have been 288 × $72.19, or $20,790.72.

[14]S. Nayak and N. Prabhala, "Disentangling the Dividend Information in Splits: A Decomposition Using Conditional Event-Study Methods," *Review of Financial Studies* 14 (4) (2001): 1083–1116.

Firms also do not want their stock prices to fall too low. First, a stock price that is very low raises transaction costs for investors. For example, one tick (the minimum spread between the bid and ask price) is $0.01 (for the NYSE and NASDAQ exchanges and for TSX stocks with stock prices greater than $0.50). In percentage terms, the tick size is larger for stocks with a low price than for stocks with a high price. Also, many exchanges require stocks to maintain a minimum price to remain listed on an exchange. (For example, the NYSE and NASDAQ require listed firms to maintain a price of at least $1 per share. The TSX has no such requirement.)

If the price of the stock falls too low a company can engage in a reverse split and reduce the number of shares outstanding. For example, in a 1 for 10 reverse split, every 10 shares of stock are replaced with a single share. As a result, the share price increases tenfold. Reverse splits became necessary for many dot-coms after the dot-com bust in 2000.

Through a combination of splits and reverse splits, firms on major exchanges (like the NYSE and TSX) can keep their share prices in any range they desire. Almost all firms on major exchanges have stock prices below $100 per share, with most firms' prices being between $5 and $60 per share. On August 14, 2014, the average price for shares traded on the TSX was about $13.48 per share. For exchanges like the TSX Venture Exchange, it is more common for firms to have lower stock prices, including many with prices below $1 per share. On August 14, 2014, the average price for shares traded on the TSX Venture Exchange was about $0.36 per share.

Spinoffs

spinoff The situation in which a firm sells a subsidiary by distributing the subsidiary's shares as a non-cash special dividend.

Rather than pay a dividend using cash or shares of its own stock, a firm can also distribute shares of a subsidiary in a transaction referred to as a **spinoff**, where non-cash special dividends are used to spin off assets or a subsidiary as a separate company. For example, after selling 10% of Northern Electric stock in an IPO in 1973, and further reducing ownership over the years, Bell Canada Enterprises (BCE) announced it would spin off its 35% ownership of Nortel in May 2000. The spinoff was accomplished through a special dividend in which each BCE shareholder received 1.570386 shares of Nortel per share of BCE owned. After receiving the Nortel shares, BCE shareholders could trade them separately from the shares of the parent firm.

Alternatively, BCE could have sold the shares of Nortel and distributed the cash to shareholders as a cash dividend. The transaction BCE chose offers two advantages over that strategy: (1) it avoids the transaction costs associated with such a sale, and (2) the special dividend is not taxed as a cash distribution. Instead, BCE shareholders who received Nortel shares are liable for capital gains tax only at the time they sell the Nortel shares.

CONCEPT CHECK

11. What is the difference between a stock dividend and a stock split?

12. What are some advantages of a spinoff as opposed to selling the division and distributing the cash?

17.7 Advice for the Financial Manager

Payout policy decisions are related to the capital structure decisions we discussed in Chapter 16. The amount of debt the firm has determines how much cash flow is pre-committed to debt holders as interest payments and how much will be left for possible distribution to shareholders or reinvestment in the firm. Further, distributing capital to shareholders reduces the equity left in the firm, increasing leverage. When setting the amount of the payout to shareholders, the financial manager needs to carefully weigh the future investment plans of the firm. If the manager expects to make large investment expenditures in the near future, then it does not make sense to make a large distribution to shareholders only to quickly return to the markets for new capital financing (either through debt or additional equity as discussed in Chapters 14 and 15). Overall, as a financial manager you should consider the following when making payout policy decisions:

1. For a given payout amount, try to maximize the after-tax payout to the shareholders. Repurchases and dividends are often taxed differently, and one can have an advantage over the other.
2. Repurchases and special dividends are useful for making large, infrequent distributions to shareholders. Neither implies any expectation of repeated payouts.
3. Starting and increasing a regular dividend is seen by shareholders as an implicit commitment to maintain this level of regular payout indefinitely. Set only regular dividend levels that you are confident the firm can maintain.
4. Because regular dividends are seen as an implicit commitment, they send a stronger signal of financial strength to shareholders than do infrequent distributions such as repurchases. However, this signal comes with a cost, because regular payouts reduce a firm's financial flexibility.
5. Be mindful of future investment plans. There are transaction costs associated with both distributions and raising new capital, so it is expensive to make a large distribution and then raise capital to fund a project. It would be better to make a smaller distribution and fund the project internally.

Table 17.6 briefly summarizes these considerations as a series of questions you should ask yourself when deciding whether to make a distribution and what form it should take.

TABLE 17.6 Navigating the Payout Decision

Payout or Not	Dividend or Repurchase
Do we have any unfunded positive-NPV projects?	What are the tax implications for our shareholder base?
What are our future investment plans?	Do we value the flexibility that repurchases allow?
Do we have sufficient cash reserves to weather a recession without distress?	Do we need to send the stronger signal that dividends would convey?
Would we benefit from signaling financial strength to the market?	

MyLab Finance

Here is what you should know after reading this chapter. MyLab™ Finance will help you identify what you know, and where to go when you need to practice.

KEY POINTS	TERMS	ONLINE PRACTICE OPPORTUNITIES
17.1 Distributions to Shareholders ■ When a firm wants to distribute cash to its shareholders, it can pay a cash dividend or it can repurchase shares. ■ Most companies pay regular, quarterly dividends. Sometimes firms announce one-time, special dividends.	declaration date, p. 594 Dutch auction, p. 596 ex-dividend date, p. 594 greenmail, p. 596 liquidating dividend, p. 594	MyLab Study Plan 17.1

KEY POINTS	TERMS	ONLINE PRACTICE OPPORTUNITIES
■ Firms repurchase shares using an open market repurchase, a tender offer, a Dutch auction repurchase, or a targeted repurchase. ■ On the declaration date, firms announce that they will pay dividends to all shareholders of record on the record date. The ex-dividend date is the first day on which the stock trades without the right to an upcoming dividend; it is usually two trading days prior to the record date. Dividend cheques are mailed on the payment date.	open market repurchase, p. 595 payable date (distribution date), p. 594 payout policy, p. 593 record date, p. 594 return of capital, p. 594 special dividend, p. 594 targeted repurchase, p. 596 tender offer, p. 596	
17.2 Dividends versus Share Repurchases in a Perfect Capital Market		
■ In perfect capital markets, the stock price falls by the amount of the dividend when a dividend is paid. An open market share repurchase has no effect on the stock price, and the stock price is the same as the cum-dividend price if a dividend were paid instead. ■ The Modigliani & Miller Dividend Irrelevance proposition states that, in perfect capital markets, holding fixed the investment policy of a firm, the firm's choice of dividend policy is irrelevant and does not affect the initial share price. ■ In reality, capital markets are not perfect, and market imperfections affect firm dividend policy.	cum-dividend, p. 597 M&M Dividend Irrelevance proposition, p. 601	MyLab Study Plan 17.2
17.3 The Tax Disadvantage of Dividends		
■ Taxes are an important market friction that affects dividend policy. ■ Considering taxes as the only market imperfection, when the tax rate on dividends exceeds the tax rate on capital gains, the optimal dividend policy is for firms to pay no dividends. Firms should use share repurchases for all payouts. ■ The tax impact of a dividend varies across investors for several reasons, including income level, investment horizon, tax jurisdiction, and type of investment account. ■ Different investor taxes create clientele effects, with the result that the dividend policy of a firm is made to suit the tax preference of its investor clientele.	clientele effects, p. 607 dividend puzzle, p. 606	MyLab Study Plan 17.3

KEY POINTS	TERMS	ONLINE PRACTICE OPPORTUNITIES
17.4 Payout versus Retention of Cash ■ The Modigliani & Miller Payout Irrelevance proposition says that, in perfect capital markets, if a firm invests excess cash flows in financial securities, the firm's choice of payout versus retention is irrelevant and does not affect the initial share price. ■ Corporate taxes make it costly for a firm to retain excess cash. Even after adjusting for investor taxes, retaining excess cash is a substantial tax disadvantage for a firm. ■ Even though there is a tax disadvantage to retaining cash, some firms accumulate cash balances. Cash balances help firms minimize the transaction costs of raising new capital when they have future potential cash needs. However, there is no benefit to shareholders from firms holding cash in excess of future investment needs. ■ In addition to the tax disadvantage of holding cash, agency costs may arise, as managers may be tempted to shirk or to spend excess cash on inefficient investments and perks. Without pressure from shareholders, managers may choose to hoard cash to spend in this way or as a means of reducing a firm's leverage and increasing their job security. ■ Dividends and share repurchases help minimize the principal-agent problems of shirking and wasteful spending when a firm has excess cash.	M&M Payout Irrelevance proposition, p. 609	MyLab Study Plan 17.4
17.5 Signalling with Payout Policy ■ Firms typically maintain relatively constant dividends. This practice is called dividend smoothing. ■ The idea that dividend changes reflect managers' views about a firm's future earnings prospects is called the dividend signalling hypothesis. ■ Managers usually increase dividends only when they are confident the firm will be able to afford higher dividends for the foreseeable future. ■ When managers cut the dividend, it may signal that they have lost hope that earnings will improve. ■ Share repurchases may be used to signal positive information, as repurchases are more attractive if management believes the stock is undervalued at its current price.	dividend signalling hypothesis, p. 615 dividend smoothing, p. 613	MyLab Study Plan 17.5

KEY POINTS	TERMS	ONLINE PRACTICE OPPORTUNITIES
17.6 Stock Dividends, Splits, and Spinoffs ■ In a stock dividend or a stock split, a company distributes additional shares rather than cash to shareholders. ■ With a stock dividend, shareholders receive either additional shares of stock of the firm itself (a stock split) or shares of a subsidiary (a spinoff). The stock price generally falls proportionally with the size of the split.	spinoff, p. 619 stock dividend (stock split), p. 617	MyLab Study Plan 17.6

REVIEW QUESTIONS

1. What are the ways in which a corporation can distribute cash to its shareholders?
2. Describe the different mechanisms available to a firm for the repurchase of shares.
3. Without taxes or any other imperfections, why doesn't it matter how the firm distributes cash?
4. What kind of payout preference do tax codes typically create?
5. What are the advantages and disadvantages of retaining excess cash?
6. How can dividends and repurchases be used to signal managers' information about their firms' prospects?
7. Explain under which conditions an increase in the dividend payment can be interpreted as a signal of good news or bad news.
8. Why is an announcement of a share repurchase considered a positive signal?
9. Why do managers split their firms' stock?

PROBLEMS

All problems in this chapter are available in MyLab Finance. An asterisk (*) indicates problems with a higher level of difficulty.

Distributions to Shareholders

1. ABC Corporation announced that it would pay a dividend to all shareholders of record as of Monday, April 3, 2006. It takes three business days after a purchase for the new owners of a share of stock to be registered.
   a. What was the date of the ex-dividend day?
   b. When was the last day an investor could have purchased ABC stock and still received the dividend payment?

2. RFC Corp. has announced a $1 dividend. If RFC's last price cum-dividend is $50, what should its first ex-dividend price be (assuming perfect capital markets)?

3. ECB Co. has 1 million shares outstanding selling at $20 per share. It plans to repurchase 100,000 shares at the market price. What will its market capitalization be after the repurchase? What will its stock price be?

4. KMS corporation has assets of $500 million, $50 million of which are cash. It has debt of $200 million. If KMS repurchases $20 million of its stock,
   a. what changes will occur on its balance sheet?
   b. what will its new leverage ratio be?

5. Suppose that KMS in Problem 4 decides to initiate a dividend instead, but it wants the present value of payout to be the same $20 million. If its cost of equity capital is 10%, to what amount per year in perpetuity should it commit?

Dividends versus Share Repurchases in a Perfect Capital Market

6. EJH Company has a market capitalization of $1 billion and 20 million shares outstanding. It plans to distribute $100 million through an open market repurchase. Assuming perfect capital markets,
   a. what will the price per share of EJH be right before the repurchase?
   b. how many shares will be repurchased?
   c. what will the price per share of EJH be right after the repurchase?

7. Natsam Corporation has $250 million of excess cash. The firm has no debt and 500 million shares outstanding with a current market price of $15 per share. Natsam's board has decided to pay out this cash as a one-time dividend.
   a. What is the ex-dividend price of a share in a perfect capital market?
   b. If the board instead decided to use the cash to do a one-time share repurchase, in a perfect capital market, what is the price of the shares once the repurchase is complete?
   c. In a perfect capital market, which policy in part (a) or (b) makes investors in the firm better off?

8. Suppose the board of Natsam Corporation decided to do the share repurchase in Problem 7(b), but you as an investor would have preferred to receive a dividend payment. How can you leave yourself in the same position as if the board had elected to make the dividend payment instead?

The Tax Disadvantage of Dividends

9. The HNH Corporation will pay a constant dividend of $2 per share, per year, in perpetuity. Assume all investors pay a 20% tax on dividends and that there is no capital gains tax. The cost of capital for investing in HNH stock is 12%.
   a. What is the price of a share of HNH stock?
   b. Assume that management makes a surprise announcement that HNH will no longer pay dividends but will use the cash to repurchase stock instead. What is the price of a share of HNH stock now?

10. You purchased CSH stock for $40 and it is now selling for $50. The company has announced that it plans a $10 special dividend.
    a. Assuming a capital gains and a dividend tax rate of 15%, if you sell the stock or wait and receive the dividend, will you have different after-tax income?
    b. If the capital gains tax rate is 20% and the dividend tax rate is 40%, what is the difference between the two options in part (a)?

Payout versus Retention of Cash

11. Clovix Corporation has $50 million in cash, 10 million shares outstanding, and a current share price of $30. Clovix is deciding whether to use the $50 million to pay an immediate special dividend of $5 per share, or to retain and invest it at the risk-free rate of 10% and use the $5 million in interest earned to increase its regular annual dividend of $0.50 per share. Assume perfect capital markets.

a. Suppose Clovix pays the special dividend. How can a shareholder who would prefer an increase in the regular dividend create it on her own?

b. Suppose Clovix increases its regular dividend. How can a shareholder who would prefer the special dividend create it on her own?

12. You manage a (tax-free) pension fund that is invested in KOA Corporation. KOA's managers have just announced that they unexpectedly generated an extra $50 million in cash flow this year. They are considering paying it out now as a special dividend or investing it in one-year Treasury securities that will earn 1% interest over the next year. They would then distribute the $50 million plus interest earned as a special dividend. If KOA pays a 35 corporate tax rate, would you prefer they pay the $50 million as a special dividend now or wait a year?

13. Assume perfect capital markets. Kay Industries currently has $100 million invested in short-term treasury bills paying 7%, and it pays out the interest payments on these securities as a dividend. The board is considering selling the treasury bills and paying out the proceeds as a one-time dividend payment.

a. If the board went ahead with this plan, what would happen to the value of Kay stock upon the announcement of a change in policy?

b. What would happen to the value of Kay stock on the ex-dividend date of the one-time dividend?

c. Given these price reactions, will this decision benefit investors?

14. Redo Problem 13, but assume that Kay must pay a corporate tax rate of 35%, and that investors pay no taxes.

15. Redo Problem 13, but assume that investors pay a 15% tax on dividends but no capital gains taxes, and that Kay does not pay corporate taxes.

16. AMS Company has unexpectedly generated a one-time extra $5 million in cash-flow this year. After announcing the extra cash flow, AMS stock price was $55 per share (it has 1 million shares outstanding). The managers are considering spending the $5 million on a project that would generate a single cash flow of $5.5 million in one year, which they would then use to repurchase shares. Assume the cost of capital for the project is 12%.

a. If they decide on the investment, what will happen to the price per share?

b. If they instead use the $5 million repurchase stock immediately, what will be the price per share?

c. Which decision is better and why?

Signalling with Payout Policy

Use the following information to answer Problems 17 through 21:

AMC Corporation currently has an enterprise value of $400 million and $100 million in excess cash. The firm has 10 million shares outstanding and no debt. Suppose AMC uses its excess cash to repurchase shares. After the share repurchase, news will come out that will change AMC's enterprise value to either $600 million or $200 million.

17. What is AMC's share price prior to the share repurchase?

18. What would AMC's share price be after the repurchase if its enterprise value goes up? What would AMC's share price be after the repurchase if its enterprise value declines?

***19.** Suppose AMC waits until after the news comes out to do the share repurchase. What would AMC's share price be after the repurchase if its enterprise value goes up? What would AMC's share price be after the repurchase if its enterprise value declines?

20. Suppose AMC management expects good news to come out. Based on your answers to Problems 18 and 19, if management wants to maximize AMC's ultimate share price, will they undertake the repurchase before or after the news comes out? When would management undertake the repurchase if they expect bad news to come out?

***21.** Given your answers to Problem 20, what effect would you expect an announcement of a share repurchase to have on the stock price? Why?

Stock Dividends, Splits, and Spinoffs

22. FCF Co. has 20,000 shares outstanding and a total market value of $1 million, $300,000 of which is debt and the other $700,000 is equity. It is planning a 10% stock dividend.

a. What is the stock price before the dividend, and what will it be after the dividend?
b. If an investor owns 1000 shares before the dividend, what will the total value of her investment in FCF be before and after the dividend?

23. Suppose the stock of Host Hotels & Resorts is currently trading for $20 per share.

a. If Host issues a 20% stock dividend, what would its new share price be?
b. If Host does a 3:2 stock split, what would its new share price be?

24. If Berkshire Hathaway's A shares are trading at $120,000, what split ratio would it need to bring its stock price down to $50?

25. After the market close on May 11, 2001, Adaptec, Inc. distributed a dividend of shares of the stock of its software division, Roxio, Inc. Each Adaptec shareholder received a 0.1646 share of Roxio stock per share of Adaptec stock owned. At the time, Adaptec stock was trading at a price of $10.55 per share (cum-dividend), and Roxio's share price was $14.23 per share. In a perfect market, what would Adaptec's ex-dividend share price be after this transaction?

DATA CASE

In your role as a consultant at a wealth management firm, you have been assigned a very powerful client who holds 1 million shares of Cisco Systems, Inc., purchased on February 28, 2003. In researching Cisco, you discovered that they are holding a large amount of cash. Additionally, your client is upset that the Cisco stock price has been somewhat stagnant as of late. The client is considering approaching the Board of Directors with a plan for half of the cash the firm has accumulated, but can't decide whether a share repurchase or a special dividend would be best. You have been asked to determine which initiative would generate the greatest amount of money after taxes, assuming that with a share repurchase your client would keep the same proportion of ownership. Because both dividends and capital gains are taxed at the same rate (20%), your client has assumed that there is no difference between the repurchase and the dividend. To confirm, you need to "run the numbers" for each scenario.

1. Go to finance.yahoo.com, enter the symbol for Cisco (CSCO), and click "Search" then click on "Statistics".
   a. Record the current price and the number of shares outstanding.
   b. Click "Balance Sheet" under "Financials." Copy and paste the balance sheet data into Excel.
2. Using one-half of the most recent cash and cash equivalents reported on the balance sheet (in thousands of dollars), compute the following:
   a. The number of shares that would be repurchased given the current market price.
   b. The dividend per share that could be paid given the total number of shares outstanding.
3. Go to http:// finance.yahoo.com to obtain the price at which your client purchased the stock on February 28, 2003.
   a. Enter the symbol for Cisco and click "Search."
   b. Click "Historical Data"; enter the date your client purchased the stock as the start date and the end date, and hit "Enter." Record the adjusted closing price.
4. Compute the total cash that would be received by your client under the repurchase and the dividend both before taxes and after taxes.
5. The calculation in step 4 reflects your client's immediate cash flow and tax liability, but it does not consider the final payoff for the client after any shares not sold in a repurchase are liquidated. To incorporate this feature, you first decide to see what happens if the client sells all remaining shares of stock immediately after the dividend or the repurchase. Assume that the stock price will fall by the amount of the dividend if a dividend is paid. What are the client's total after-tax cash flows (considering both the payout and the capital gain) under the repurchase of the dividend in this case?
6. Under which program would your client be better off before taxes? Which program is better after taxes, assuming the remaining shares are sold immediately after the dividend is paid?
7. Because your client is unlikely to sell all 1 million shares today, at the time of dividend/repurchase, you decide to consider two longer holding periods: Assume that under both plans the client sells all remaining shares of stock 5 years later, or the client sells 10 years later. Assume that the stock will return 10% per year going forward. Also assume that Cisco will pay no other dividends over the next 10 years.
   a. What would be the stock price after 5 years or 10 years if a dividend is paid now?
   b. What would be the stock price after 5 years or 10 years if Cisco repurchases shares now?
   c. Calculate the total after-tax cash flows at both points in time (when the dividend payment or the share repurchase takes place, and when the rest of the shares are sold) for your client if the remaining shares are sold in 5 years under both initiatives. Compute the difference between the cash flows under both initiatives at each point in time. Repeat assuming the shares are sold in 10 years.
8. Repeat Question 7 assuming the stock will return 20% per year going forward. What do you notice about the difference in the cash flows under the two initiatives when the return is 20% and 10%?

PART

5 Integrative Case

This case draws on material from Chapters 16 and 17.

Maria Suarez returned to her office after spending the afternoon meeting with her firm's investment bankers. Suarez was CFO of Midco Industries, a mid-sized manufacturing firm, and she was taking a hard look at its capital structure and payout policy. Suarez felt that Midco was underlevered and potentially not taking full advantage of the tax benefits of debt. Further complicating matters, Midco's institutional investors had been clamouring for either a repurchase or a special dividend.

One possibility floated by Suarez's investment bankers was a "leveraged recap," in which Midco would issue debt and use the proceeds to repurchase shares. Midco Industries has 20 million shares outstanding, with a market price of $15 per share and no debt. The firm has had consistently stable earnings and pays a 35% tax rate. Midco's investment bankers proposed that the firm borrow $100 million on a permanent basis through a leveraged recap in which it would use the borrowed funds to repurchase outstanding shares.

As Suarez sat down at her desk, she stared at her notepad. She had written down several questions that she would need to answer before making her decision.

CASE QUESTIONS

1. What are the tax consequences of the recap?
2. Based only on the tax effects and the Valuation Principle, what will the total value of the firm be after the recap?
   a. How much of the new value will be equity?
   b. How much will be debt?
3. At what price should Midco be able to repurchase its shares?
4. Who benefits from the recap? Who loses?
5. What other costs or benefits of the additional leverage should Midco's managers consider?
6. If Midco's managers decide to issue the debt and distribute the tax shield as a special dividend instead of repurchasing shares, what will the dividend per share be?

PART

Financial Planning and Forecasting

6

CHAPTER 18 Financial Modelling and Pro Forma Analysis
CHAPTER 19 Working Capital Management
CHAPTER 20 Short-Term Financial Planning

Valuation Principle Connection. In Part 6, we turn to the details of running the financial side of a corporation and focus on forecasting and short-term financial management. We begin in Chapter 18 by developing the tools to forecast the cash flows and long-term financing needs of a firm. We then turn our attention to the important decisions a financial manager makes about the short-term financing and investments of the firm. In Chapter 19, we discuss how firms manage their working capital requirements, including accounts receivable, accounts payable, and inventory. In Chapter 20, we explain how firms finance their short-term cash needs.

In a perfect capital market, the Valuation Principle—in particular, the Law of One Price—and the Modigliani and Miller propositions imply that how a firm chooses to manage its short-term financial needs does not affect the value of the firm. In reality, short-term financial policy does matter because of the existence of market frictions. In this part of the book, we identify these frictions and explain how firms set their short-term financial policies.

CHAPTER

18 Financial Modelling and Pro Forma Analysis

LEARNING OBJECTIVES

- Understand the goals of long-term financial planning
- Create pro forma income statements and balance sheets using the percent of sales method
- Develop financial models of the firm by directly forecasting capital expenditures, working capital needs, and financing events
- Distinguish between the concepts of sustainable growth and value-increasing growth
- Use pro forma analysis to model the value of the firm under different scenarios, such as expansion

NOTATION

FCF	free cash flow
PV	present value
ROA	return on assets
ROE	return on equity
SGR	sustainable growth rate

Most decisions a financial manager makes have long-term consequences. For example, in the late 1990s, Airbus managers decided to bet the future of the company on the market for mega-jets, giving the green light to development of the 555-seat A380. Shortly thereafter, Boeing managers bet that airlines would favour improvements in fuel efficiency and gave the go-ahead to the all-composite, technologically advanced 787. The outcomes of these decisions are still playing out today. In this chapter, we will learn how to build a financial model to analyze the consequences of our financial decisions well into the future. In particular, we will use these models to forecast when the firm will need to secure additional external funding and to determine how the decision will affect the value of the firm.

We will start by explaining the goals of forecasting through financial modelling and pro forma analysis, and how this analysis relates to the overall goal of maximizing firm value. Then, we will move to a basic forecasting technique based on projections of the firm's future sales. Next, we will develop an improved approach to forecasting that produces a more realistic financial model of the firm. Finally, we will use our financial model to value the firm under the new business plan and discuss value-increasing versus value-decreasing growth. In doing so, we will see the connection between the role of forecasting, NPV analysis, and the Valuation Principle that underlies all of finance.

18.1 Goals of Long-Term Financial Planning

The goal of the financial manager is to maximize the value of the stockholders' stake in the firm. One tool to help with this goal is long-term financial planning and modelling. In the following sections, we will develop specific methods to forecast the financial statements and cash flows for the firm as a whole. For context, in this section we discuss the objectives of long-term planning.

Identify Important Linkages

As you will see in Sections 18.2 and 18.3, when you build a model of the future course of the firm, by necessity you will uncover important linkages between variables—for example, sales, costs, capital investment, and financing. A well-designed spreadsheet model will allow you to examine how a change in your cost structure will affect your future free cash flows, financing needs, and so on. Some links may be obvious, but others are much more difficult to determine without building a forecast of the entire firm's financial statements years into the future. For example, technological improvements leading to reduced costs could allow the firm to reduce prices and sell more product. However, increased production will require more equipment and facilities, and the associated capital expenditures will require financing and create additional depreciation tax shields. None of these links would be easy to see without a careful forecasting model. This is an important outcome of long-term planning, because it allows the financial manager to understand the business and, through that understanding, to increase its value.

Analyze the Impact of Potential Business Plans

Perhaps your firm is planning a big expansion or considering changes in how it manages its inventory. By building a long-term model of your firm's financials, you can examine exactly how such business plans will affect the firm's free cash flows and, hence, its value. In Chapter 9, we developed the tools of capital budgeting, with the goal of deciding whether to invest in a new project. To consider a fundamental change in the firm's business plan, the financial manager models the firm as a whole, rather than just a single project. In Section 18.3, we will analyze the impact of a firm-wide expansion plan, including necessary capital investment, debt financing, changes in free cash flows, and changes in value.

Plan for Future Funding Needs

Building a model for long-term forecasting reveals points in the future at which the firm will need additional external financing—for example, when its retained earnings will not be enough to fund planned capital investment. Identifying the firm's funding needs in advance gives financial managers enough time to plan for them and line up the source of financing that is most advantageous for the firm. In a perfect capital market, this would be unnecessary—you would be able to secure financing instantaneously for any positive-NPV project, and the source of financing would have no effect on the firm's value. However, in reality market frictions mean that you need time to issue debt or new equity and, as we learned in Chapter 16, that financing decisions affect firm value. Thus, identifying and planning for these financing decisions far in advance is a valuable exercise.

CONCEPT CHECK

1. How does long-term financial planning fit into the goal of the financial manager?
2. What are the three main things that the financial manager can accomplish by building a long-term financial model of the firm?

18.2 Forecasting Financial Statements: The Percent of Sales Method

We will illustrate our discussion of forecasting financial statements via an application: the firm KXS Designs. KXS Designs is a boutique women's fashion house specializing in affordable fashionable separates, with its own production facility. KXS Designs is a growing firm, and its financial managers predict that it will need external financing to fuel its growth. In order to predict when KXS will need this financing and the amount the managers will need to secure, we need to prepare a financial model in Excel for KXS that will allow us to produce pro forma income statements and balance sheets. After developing a technique for forecasting, we will turn to the steps involved in preparing the pro forma income statement and balance sheet.

Percent of Sales Method

percent of sales method A forecasting method that assumes that as sales grow many income statement and balance sheet items will grow, maintaning the same percentage of sales.

A common starting point for forecasting is the *percent of sales method*. The **percent of sales method** assumes that as sales grow many income statement and balance sheet items will grow, maintaining the same percentage of sales. For example, Table 18.1 shows that KXS's costs excluding depreciation were 78% of sales in 2018. There were sales of $74,889. If KXS forecasts that sales will grow by 18% in 2019, then

- sales will grow to $74,889 × 1.18 = $88,369.
- costs excluding depreciation will remain at 78% of sales, so costs will be $88,369 × 0.78 = $68,928 in 2019.[1]

We are essentially assuming that KXS will maintain its profit margins as its sales revenues grow. We proceed by making similar assumptions about working capital items on the balance sheet, such as cash, accounts receivable, inventory, and accounts payable. The far-right column of Table 18.1 shows what percentage of sales each of these items was in 2018. We can use those percentages to forecast part of the balance sheet in 2019. For example, if sales grow to $88,369 as we predict, then our inventory will need to grow to $88,369 × 0.20 = $17,674 to support those sales.

Some of the items are marked "NM" for "Not Meaningful" in the percentage of sales column. For example, our assets and accounts payables might reasonably be expected to grow in line with sales, but our long-term debt and equity will not naturally grow in line with sales. Instead, the change in equity and debt will reflect choices we make about dividends and net new financing.

Pro Forma Income Statement

Table 18.2 shows KXS's pro forma income statement for 2019, along with how each line was determined. KXS is forecasting 18% growth in sales from 2018 to 2019. In addition to the sales forecast, we require three other details to prepare the pro forma income statement: costs excluding depreciation in 2018 as a percentage of sales, depreciation as a percentage of sales, and the tax rate. KXS's info from Table 18.1 is as follows:

- Costs excluding depreciation were 78% of sales.
- Depreciation was 7% of sales in 2018.
- KXS pays a 35% tax rate.

[1]For ease of exposition, we will base our forecast on a single year, 2018. Companies often take into account averages and trends over several years in forecasting for the future.

TABLE 18.1 KXS Designs 2018 Income Statement and Balance Sheet

1	**Year**	**2018**	**% of Sales**
2	**Income Statement ($000s)**		
3	Sales	74,889	100%
4	Costs Except Depreciation	−58,413	78%
5	**EBITDA**	16,476	22%
6	Depreciation	−5492	7%
7	**EBIT**	10,984	15%
8	Interest Expense (net)	−306	NM*
9	**Pre-tax Income**	10,678	14%
10	Income Tax (35%)	−3737	NM
11	**Net Income**	6941	9%

** NM indicates that representing the item as a percentage of sales is not meaningful.*

1	**Year**	**2018**	**% of Sales**
2	**Balance Sheet ($000s)**		
3	**Assets**		
4	Cash and Equivalents	11,982	16%
5	Accounts Receivable	14,229	19%
6	Inventories	14,978	20%
7	**Total Current Assets**	41,189	55%
8	Property, Plant, and Equipment	49,427	66%
9	**Total Assets**	90,616	121%
10	**Liabilities and Stockholders' Equity**		
11	Accounts Payable	11,982	16%
12	Debt	4500	NM
13	**Total Liabilities**	16,482	NM
14	**Stockholders' Equity**	74,134	NM
15	**Total Liabilities and Equity**	90,616	121%

TABLE 18.2 KXS Designs Pro Forma Income Statement for 2019

1	**Year**	**2018**	**2019**	**Calculation**
2	**Income Statement ($000s)**			
3	Sales	74,889	88,369	74,889 × 1.18
4	Costs Except Depreciation	−58,413	−68,928	78% of Sales
5	**EBITDA**	16,476	19,441	Lines 3 + 4
6	Depreciation	−5492	−6480	7% of Sales
7	**EBIT**	10,984	12,961	Lines 5 + 6
8	Interest Expense (net)	−306	−306	Remains the same
9	**Pre-tax Income**	10,678	12,655	Lines 7 + 8
10	Income Tax (35%)	−3737	−4429	35% of Line 9
11	**Net Income**	6941	8226	Lines 9 + 10

The one final assumption we need to make is about our interest expense.[2] We assume for now that it will remain the same as in 2018 because we will determine whether our debt needs will change as part of the forecasting process.

Based on our pro forma balance sheet, we are forecasting an increase in net income of \$8226 − \$6941 = \$1285, which represents an 18.5% increase over 2018 net income.[3] We now turn to forecasting the balance sheet to determine whether we will need any new financing in 2019 to pay for our growth. The net income we forecast in Table 18.2 will be one of the inputs to the pro forma balance sheet. The part of that net income not distributed as dividends will add to stockholders' equity on the balance sheet.

EXAMPLE 18.1 Percent of Sales

PROBLEM

KXS has just revised its sales forecast downward. If KXS expects sales to grow by only 10% next year, what are its costs, except for depreciation, projected to be?

SOLUTION

■ Plan

Forecasted 2019 sales will now be \$74,889 × (1.10) = \$82,378. With this figure in hand and the information from Table 18.1, we can use the percent of sales method to calculate KXS's forecasted costs.

■ Execute

From Table 18.1, we see that costs are 78% of sales. With forecasted sales of \$82,378, that leads to forecasted costs except depreciation of \$82,378 × (0.78) = \$64,255.

Pro Forma Balance Sheet

Forecasting the balance sheet using the percent of sales method requires a few iterating steps. In any balance sheet analysis, we know that assets and liabilities + equity must be equal. The assets and liabilities + equity sides of the pro forma balance sheet will not balance, however, until we make assumptions about how our equity and debt will grow with sales. We see this point in Table 18.3, where we have taken a first stab at the pro forma balance sheet (we will explain the details of the calculation below). Our assets are projected to be \$8396 more than our liabilities and equity. The imbalance indicates that we will need \$8396 in *net new financing* to fund our growth. **Net new financing** is the amount of additional external financing we will need to pay for the planned increase in assets. It can be computed as follows:

net new financing The amount of additional external financing a firm needs to pay for the planned increase in assets.

$$\text{Net New Financing} = \text{Projected Assets} - \text{Projected Liabilities and Equity}$$

[2]The interest expense should be interest paid on debt, net of interest earned on any invested cash—just as interest paid is tax deductible, interest earned is taxable—so KXS's tax shield comes from its net interest expense. In order to focus on forecasting, we will assume that all cash held by KXS is a necessary part of its working capital needed for transactions. Thus, we assume that KXS holds all of its cash in a non–interest-bearing account. In Chapter 19, we will discuss alternative ways to invest cash.

[3]This is higher than the sales growth of 18% because we assumed that interest expenses would not increase.

TABLE 18.3 First-Pass Pro Forma Balance Sheet for 2019

1	Year	2018	2019	Calculation
2	**Balance Sheet ($000s)**			
3	**Assets**			
4	Cash and Cash Equivalents	11,982	14,139	16% of Sales
5	Accounts Receivable	14,229	16,790	19% of Sales
6	Inventories	14,978	17,674	20% of Sales
7	**Total Current Assets**	41,189	48,603	Lines 4 + 5 + 6
8	Property, Plant, and Equipment	49,427	58,324	66% of Sales
9	**Total Assets**	90,616	106,927	Lines 7 + 8
10	**Liabilities**			
11	Accounts Payable	11,982	14,139	16% of Sales
12	Debt	4500	4500	Remains the same
13	**Total Liabilities**	16,482	18,639	Lines 11 + 12
14	**Stockholders' Equity**	74,134	79,892	74,134 + 70% of 8226
15	**Total Liabilities and Equity**	90,616	98,531	Lines 13 + 14
16	**Net New Financing**		8396	Line 9 − Line 15

Let's take a closer look at how we arrived at the $8396 figure. Because we are using the percent of sales method, we assume that assets increase in line with sales. Thus, total assets have increased by 18%, the same as sales. The liabilities side of the balance sheet is more complicated. The amount of dividends a company pays will affect the retained earnings it has to finance growth. Further, any increases in debt or equity reflect capital structure decisions and require managers to actively raise capital, as discussed in Chapters 14 and 15. The bottom line is that we cannot simply assume that debt and equity increase in line with sales.

In KXS's case, it has a policy of paying out 30% of its net income as dividends. Thus, $2468 of its forecasted $8226 net income will be distributed to stockholders as dividends:

2019 Net Income	$8226
− 2019 Dividends (30% of NI)	− $2468
= 2019 Retained Earnings	= $5758

The $5758 in retained earnings (the remaining 70% of net income after dividends are paid) adds to stockholders' equity on the balance sheet. As a result, in Table 18.3 stockholders' equity is forecast to increase from $74,134 to $79,892.

2018 Stockholders' Equity	$74,134
+ 2019 Retained Earnings	+ $5758
= 2019 Stockholders' Equity	= $79,892

We also assume that accounts payable will grow along with sales, remaining at 16% of sales as they were in 2018, so they are forecast to grow to $14,139. However, our initial assumption is that debt will remain the same, so our forecasted growth in liabilities and equity falls short of our forecasted growth in assets by $8396.

COMMON MISTAKE

Confusing Stockholders' Equity with Retained Earnings

It is easy to confuse new retained earnings, total retained earnings, and stockholders' equity. As in the example above, new retained earnings are the amount of net income left over after paying dividends. These new retained earnings are then added to the *total* accumulated retained earnings from the life of the firm. Total retained earnings makes up one part of stockholders' equity, which also includes the value of the stock at its original issue price and any paid-in capital.

Making the Balance Sheet Balance: Net New Financing

How do we address this $8396 difference between assets and liabilities? The projected difference between KXS's assets and liabilities in the pro forma balance sheet indicates that KXS will need to obtain new financing from its investors. The net new financing of $8396 in this case is sometimes referred to as **the plug**—the amount we have to add to the liabilities and equity side of the pro forma balance sheet to make it balance.

the plug The amount of net new financing that needs to be added to the liabilities and equity side of the pro forma balance sheet to make it balance.

While KXS definitely has to secure $8396 in new financing, it could come from new debt or new equity. We discussed the issues involved in the equity versus debt decision in Chapter 16. It is a complex decision weighing many factors. Rather than complicating our analysis here, we assume that KXS's financial managers have evaluated these factors and decided that the best way to finance the growth is through additional debt. Table 18.4 shows our second-pass pro forma balance sheet, including the $8396 in additional debt financing that brings the sheet into balance.

We should note that the decision to take on additional debt in 2019 makes our initial assumption that our interest expense would remain constant in 2019 potentially incorrect. If KXS takes on the debt before the end of the year, then there will be a partial-year interest expense from the debt. Thus, any increase in interest expense would result

TABLE 18.4 Second-Pass Pro Forma Balance Sheet for KXS

1	Year	2018	2019	Calculation
2	**Balance Sheet ($000s)**			
3	**Assets**			
4	Cash and Cash Equivalents	11,982	14,139	16% of Sales
5	Accounts Receivable	14,229	16,790	19% of Sales
6	Inventories	14,978	17,674	20% of Sales
7	**Total Current Assets**	41,189	48,603	Lines 4 + 5 + 6
8	Property, Plant, and Equipment	49,427	58,324	66% of Sales
9	**Total Assets**	90,616	106,927	Lines 7 + 8
10	**Liabilities**			
11	Accounts Payable	11,982	14,139	16% of Sales
12	Debt	4500	12,896	4500 + 8396
13	**Total Liabilities**	16,482	27,035	Lines 11 + 12
14	**Stockholders' Equity**	74,134	79,892	74,134 + 70% of 8226
15	**Total Liabilities and Equity**	90,616	106,927	Lines 13 + 14

in a reduction to net income and retained earnings. The balance sheet would still not quite balance, and we would need a bit more financing than first calculated. We would need to adjust the pro forma income statement and iterate with the pro forma balance sheet to get the exact amount of new debt needed. However, we have achieved our primary objective: to identify a future funding need and determine approximately how much we will need and how we will fund it. This will give KXS's managers enough time to begin the debt-issuance process with its bankers. We also note that debt has more than doubled, which justifies our original decision not to assume that it will increase in proportion to sales.

EXAMPLE 18.2 Net New Financing

PROBLEM

If, instead of paying out 30% of earnings as dividends, KXS decides not to pay any dividend and instead retains all of its 2018 earnings, how would its net new financing change?

SOLUTION

Plan

KXS currently pays out 30% of its net income as dividends, so rather than retaining only $5758, it will retain the entire $8226. This will increase stockholders' equity, reducing the net new financing.

Execute

The additional retained earnings are $8226 − $5758 = $2468. In comparison with the amount in Table 18.3, stockholders' equity will be $79,892 + $2468 = $82,360, and total liabilities and equity will also be $2468 higher, rising to $100,999. Net new financing, the imbalance between KXS's assets and liabilities and equity, will decrease to $8396 − $2468 = $5928.

1	**Year**	**2018**	**2019**
2	**Balance Sheet ($000s)**		
3	**Liabilities**		
4	Accounts Payable	11,982	14,139
5	Debt	4500	4500
6	**Total Liabilities**	16,482	18,639
7	**Stockholders' Equity**	74,134	82,360
8	**Total Liabilities and Equity**	90,616	100,999
9	**Net New Financing**		5928

Evaluate

When a company is growing faster than it can finance internally, any distributions to shareholders will cause it to seek greater additional financing. It is important not to confuse the need for external financing with poor performance. Most growing firms need additional financing to fuel that growth, as their expenditures for growth naturally precede their income from that growth. We will revisit the issue of growth and firm value in Section 18.4.

Choosing a Forecast Target

Forecasting by assuming fixed ratios of sales is very common. Another approach is to forecast by targeting specific ratios that the company either wants or needs to maintain. For example, debt covenants (such as those discussed in Chapter 16) often require a company to maintain certain levels of liquidity or minimum interest coverage. The firm does this by specifying a minimum current ratio (current assets/current liabilities) of 1.5, or a minimum cash flow-to-interest ratio of 1.2. The company would then incorporate these target ratios into its forecasts to ensure it will be in compliance with its loan covenants.

The need to consider other target ratios is an example of a larger issue in forecasting—that the firm's investment, payout, and financing decisions are linked together and cannot be treated separately. As we saw in Table 18.4, the balance sheet must balance. So a financial manager must understand that the firm can set an investment budget and a financing plan, but those will then determine what is available to pay out. Alternatively, a firm could decide on an investment budget and payout policy, but those will then determine the firm's financing position—perhaps in unintended ways. The bottom line is that a financial manager must balance all these linked decisions, and a careful forecast allows him or her to see the consequences of decisions.

CONCEPT CHECK

3. What is the basic idea behind the percent of sales method for forecasting?
4. How does the pro forma balance sheet help the financial manager forecast net new financing?

18.3 Forecasting a Planned Expansion

The percent of sales method is a useful starting point and may even be sufficient for mature companies with relatively stable but slow growth. Its shortcoming is handling the realities of fast growth requiring "lumpy" investments in new capacity. The typical firm cannot smoothly add capacity in line with expected sales. Instead, it must occasionally make a large investment in new capacity that it expects to be sufficient for several years. This kind of capacity expansion also implies that new funding will happen in large, infrequent financing rounds, rather than small increments each year as sales grow. However, we can address these realities in our long-term forecasting by modelling our capacity needs and capital expenditures directly. In this section, we consider a planned expansion by KXS and generate pro forma statements that allow us to decide whether the expansion will increase the value of KXS. First, we identify capacity needs and how to finance that capacity. Next, we construct pro forma income statements and forecast future free cash flows. Finally, we use those forecasted free cash flows to assess the impact of the expansion on firm value.

KXS's managers have constructed a detailed sales forecast by first forecasting the size of the market and what market share KXS can expect to capture. While the size of the market is generally based on demographics and the overall economy, KXS's market share will depend on the appeal of its product and its price, which KXS has forecast as well. KXS currently has the capacity to produce a maximum of 1.1 million units (i.e., 1100 thousand units). However, as detailed in Table 18.5, KXS expects both the total market size and its share of the market to grow to the point at which the company will quickly exceed that capacity. Thus, KXS is considering an expansion that will increase its capacity to 2 million units—enough to handle its projected requirements through 2023.

TABLE 18.5 KXS Forecasted Production Capacity Requirements

1	Year	2018	2019	2020	2021	2022	2023
2	**Production Volume (000s units)**						
3	Market Size	10,000	10,500	11,025	11,576	12,155	12,763
4	Market Share	10.0%	11.0%	12.0%	13.0%	14.0%	15.0%
5	Production Volume (3 × 4)	1000	1155	1323	1505	1702	1914
6	**Additional Market Information**						
7	Average Sales Price	$ 74.89	$ 76.51	$ 78.04	$ 79.60	$ 81.19	$ 82.82

KXS Design's Expansion: Financing Needs

The first step in our analysis is estimating KXS's financing needs based on the capital expenditures required for the expansion.

Capital Expenditures for the Expansion. The new equipment to increase KXS's capacity will cost $20 million and will need to be purchased in 2019 to meet the company's production needs. Table 18.6 details KXS's forecasted capital expenditures and depreciation over the next five years. Based on the estimates for capital expenditures and depreciation, this spreadsheet tracks the book value of KXS's plant, property, and equipment, starting from the book value's level at the beginning of 2018.[4] The depreciation entries in Table 18.6 are based on the appropriate depreciation schedule for each type of property. Those calculations are quite specific to the nature of the property and are not detailed here. Assume the depreciation shown will be used for tax purposes.[5] KXS has ongoing capital investment requirements to cover the replacement of existing equipment—these were expected to be $5 million per year without the new equipment. The additional $20 million is reflected in 2019, bringing the total to $25 million for 2019 and increasing expected recurring investment to $8 million per year in years 2020 to 2023.

TABLE 18.6 KXS Forecasted Capital Expenditures

1	Year	2018	2019	2020	2021	2022	2023
2	**Fixed Assets and Capital Investment ($000s)**						
3	Opening Book Value	49,919	49,427	66,984	67,486	67,937	68,344
4	Capital Investment	5000	25,000	8000	8000	8000	8000
5	Depreciation	−5492	−7443	−7498	−7549	−7594	−7634
6	Closing Book Value	49,427	66,984	67,486	67,937	68,344	68,709

[4]In Table 18.6, and elsewhere in the chapter, we display rounded numbers. Calculations such as Closing Book Value are based on the actual numbers in the spreadsheet with all significant digits. As a result, there will occasionally be a small discrepancy between the Excel-calculated value shown and the hand-calculated value using the rounded numbers displayed.

[5]Firms often maintain separate books for accounting and tax purposes, and they may use different depreciation assumptions for each. Because depreciation affects cash flows through its tax consequences, tax depreciation, specifically capital cost allowance, is more relevant for valuation.

Financing the Expansion. While KXS believes it can fund recurring investment from its operating cash flows, as shown in Table 18.7, it will have to seek external financing for the $20 million in new equipment. KXS plans to finance the new equipment by issuing 10-year coupon bonds with a coupon rate of 6.8%. Thus, KXS will pay only interest on the bonds until the repayment of principal in 10 years. The principal on its outstanding debt of $4500 is also not due before 2023.

TABLE 18.7 KXS Planned Debt and Interest Payments

1	Year	2018	2019	2020	2021	2022	2023
2	**Debt and Interest Table ($000s)**						
3	Outstanding Debt	4500	24,500	24,500	24,500	24,500	24,500
4	Net New Borrowing	—	20,000	—	—	—	—
5	Interest on Debt 6.80%	306	306	1666	1666	1666	1666

Given KXS's outstanding debt, its interest expense each year is computed as follows:[6]

$$\text{Interest in Year } t = \text{Interest Rate} \times \text{Ending Balance in Year } (t - 1) \tag{18.1}$$

As we saw in Chapter 16, the interest on the debt will provide a valuable tax shield to offset KXS's taxable income.

KXS Design's Expansion: Pro Forma Income Statement

The value of any investment opportunity arises from the future cash flows it will generate. To estimate the cash flows resulting from the expansion, we begin by projecting KXS's future earnings. We then consider KXS's working capital and investment needs and estimate its free cash flows. With its free cash flows and projected interest tax shields, we can compute the value of KXS with and without the expansion to decide whether the benefit of the new equipment is worth the cost.

Forecasting Earnings. To build the pro forma income statement, we begin with KXS's sales. We calculate sales for each year from the estimates in Table 18.5 as follows:

$$\text{Sales} = \text{Market Size} \times \text{Market Share} \times \text{Average Sales Price} \tag{18.2}$$

For example, in 2019, KXS has projected sales of 10.5 million units × 11% market share × $76.51 average sales price = $88.369 million. We will assume that costs except depreciation will continue to be 78% of sales, so that our projected costs, except depreciation in 2019, will be 78% × $88,369 = $68,928. To arrive at forecasted earnings, we take the following steps:

- Deducting these operating expenses from KXS's sales, we can project EBITDA over the next five years as shown in Table 18.8.
- Subtracting the depreciation expenses we estimated in Table 18.6, we arrive at KXS's earnings before interest and taxes.
- We next deduct interest expenses according to the schedule given in Table 18.7.
- The final expense is the corporate income tax. KXS pays a 35% tax rate, and the income tax is computed as follows:

$$\text{Income Tax} = \text{Pre-tax Income} \times \text{Tax Rate} \tag{18.3}$$

[6]Equation 18.1 assumes that changes in debt occur at the end of the year. If debt changes during the year, computing interest expenses based on the average level of debt during the year provides a more accurate measure.

After subtracting the income tax from the pre-tax income, we arrive at the forecasted net income, as shown in the bottom line in Table 18.8.

TABLE 18.8 Pro Forma Income Statement for KXS Expansion

1	Year	2018	2019	2020	2021	2022	2023
2	**Income Statement ($000s)**						
3	Sales	74,889	88,369	103,247	119,793	138,167	158,546
4	Costs Except Depreciation	−58,413	−68,928	−80,533	−93,438	−107,770	−123,666
5	**EBITDA**	16,476	19,441	22,714	26,354	30,397	34,880
6	Depreciation	−5 492	−7443	−7498	−7549	−7594	−7634
7	**EBIT**	10,984	11,998	15,216	18,806	22,803	27,246
8	Interest Expense (net)	−306	−306	−1666	−1666	−1666	−1666
9	**Pre-tax Income**	10,678	11,692	13,550	17,140	21,137	25,580
10	Income Tax	−3737	−4092	−4742	−5999	−7398	−8953
11	**Net Income**	6941	7600	8807	11,141	13,739	16,627

Working Capital Requirements. We have one more step before we are ready to forecast the free cash flows for KXS. Recall that increases in working capital reduce free cash flows. Thus, we still need to forecast KXS's working capital needs. The spreadsheet in Table 18.9 lists KXS's current working capital requirements and forecasts the firm's future working capital needs. (See Chapter 19 for a further discussion of working capital requirements and their determinants.) We have forecast that the minimum required cash will be 16% of sales, accounts receivable will be 19% of sales, inventory will be 20% of sales, and accounts payable will be 16% of sales, all as they were in 2018.

The minimum required cash represents the minimum level of cash needed to keep the business running smoothly, allowing for the daily variations in the timing of income and expenses. Firms generally earn little or no interest on these balances, which are held in cash or in a chequing or short-term savings account. As a consequence, we account for

TABLE 18.9 KXS Projected Working Capital Needs

1	Year	2018	2019	2020	2021	2022	2023
2	**Working Capital ($000s)**						
3	**Current Assets**						
4	Cash	11,982	14,139	16,520	19,167	22,107	25,367
5	Accounts Receivable	14,229	16,790	19,617	22,761	26,252	30,124
6	Inventory	14,978	17,674	20,649	23,959	27,633	31,709
7	**Total Current Assets**	41,189	48,603	56,786	65,886	75,992	87,201
8	**Current Liabilities**						
9	Accounts Payable	11,982	14,139	16,520	19,167	22,107	25,367
10	**Total Current Liabilities**	11,982	14,139	16,520	19,167	22,107	25,367
11	**Net Working Capital**						
12	Net Working Capital (7–10)	29,207	34,464	40,266	46,719	53,885	61,833
13	Increase in Net Working Capital		5257	5802	6 453	7166	7948

this opportunity cost by including the cash balance as part of the firm's working capital. We will make the assumption that KXS distributes all cash in excess of the minimum required cash as dividends. If our forecast shows that KXS's cash flows will be insufficient to fund the minimum required cash, then we know that we need to plan to finance those cash needs. Again, identifying these future funding needs is one of the advantages of forecasting.

If KXS instead retained some cash above the amount needed for transactions, the company would probably invest it in some short-term securities that earn interest. Most companies choose to do this to provide funds for future investment so that they do not need to raise as much capital externally. In this case, the excess amount of cash would not be included in working capital. We discuss cash management in Chapter 19.

COMMON MISTAKE

Treating Forecasts as Fact

Forecasts, like much of finance, give the illusion of precision—we can produce an answer down to dollars and cents. As a result, it is easy to lose sight of the fact that the answer depends on a number of big assumptions that could easily turn out to be wrong. Although it is the financial manager's job to build the forecast and analyze it, he or she is highly dependent on all the other functional areas for input. Good financial managers will talk to operations, marketing, and sales people to develop reliable estimates of future production costs and potential revenues for each product. However, even the best forecasts can be wrong. That's why it is so important to perform sensitivity and scenario analysis as we did in Chapter 9.

Forecasting the Balance Sheet

We have enough data now to forecast the balance sheet for our planned expansion. Recall from Section 18.2 that with the percent of sales method forecasting the balance sheet helps us identify any future funding needs, because the balance sheet must balance. Here, we have explicitly planned for the funding of the expansion in 2019. Nonetheless, we can check to make sure that our debt issue will be enough and then forecast past the expansion to see if we will need any future financing. Table 18.10 shows the balance sheet for 2018 and 2019 filled in with the information we have so far. The only piece of information we are missing is the dividend amount, so we assume for now that we will not pay any dividends in 2019.

As we can see from the column for 2019 in the pro forma balance sheet, KXS's balance sheet does not initially balance: the liabilities and equity are greater than the assets. In Section 18.2, KXS faced the opposite situation—its assets were greater than its liabilities and equity—and this told KXS's managers that they needed external financing. When liabilities and equity are greater than the assets, we have generated more cash than we had planned to consume, and we need to decide what to do with it. KXS has these options:

- Build up extra cash reserves (which would increase the cash account to bring assets in line with liabilities and equity).
- Pay down (retire) some of its debt.
- Distribute the excess as dividends.
- Repurchase shares.

TABLE 18.10 Pro Forma Balance Sheet for KXS, 2019

1	Year	2018	2019	Source for 2019	2019 Data (Revised)
2	**Balance Sheet ($000s)**				
3	**Assets**				
4	Cash and Cash Equivalents	11,982	14,139	Table 18.9	14,139
5	Accounts Receivable	14,229	16,790	Table 18.9	16,790
6	Inventories	14,978	17,674	Table 18.9	17,674
7	**Total Current Assets**	41,189	48,603	Lines 4 + 5 + 6	48,603
8	Property, Plant, and Equipment	49,427	66,984	Table 18.6	66,984
9	**Total Assets**	90,616	115,587	Lines 7 + 8	115,587
10	**Liabilities**				
11	Accounts Payable	11,982	14,139	Table 18.9	14,139
12	Debt	4500	24,500	Table 18.7	24,500
13	**Total Liabilities**	16,482	38,639	Lines 11 + 12	38,639
14	**Stockholders' Equity**				
15	Starting Stockholders' Equity	69,275	74,134	2018 Line 18	74,134
16	Net Income	6941	7600	Table 18.8	7600
17	Dividends	−2082	0	Assumed	−4786
18	**Stockholders' Equity**	74,134	81,734	Lines 15 + 16 + 17	76,948
19	**Total Liabilities and Equity**	90,616	120,373	Lines 13 + 18	115,587

Let's assume that KXS's managers choose to distribute the excess as dividends. The excess is the amount by which liabilities and equity exceeds assets: $120,373 − $115,587 = $4786. The final column of Table 18.10, labelled "2019 (Revised)," shows the new pro forma balance sheet, including KXS's planned dividend. The balance sheet now balances! We can do this for the full forecast horizon (2019–2023). The completed pro forma balance sheet is shown in the chapter appendix.

The general lesson from the example in Section 18.2, as well as in this section, is summarized in Table 18.11.

TABLE 18.11 Pro Forma Balance Sheets and Financing

Liabilities and equity are. . .	less than assets	greater than assets
	New financing needed—the firm must borrow or issue new equity to fund the shortfall.	Excess cash available—the firm can retain it as extra cash reserves (thus increasing assets), pay dividends, or reduce external financing by retiring debt or repurchasing shares.

CONCEPT CHECK

5. What is the advantage of forecasting capital expenditures, working capital, and financing events directly?
6. What role does minimum required cash play in working capital?

18.4 Growth and Firm Value

We just analyzed an expansion for KXS that involved an expensive capital investment. For KXS, this forecast would be a starting point for the capital budgeting analysis necessary to decide whether the expansion is a positive-NPV project. It is important to remember that not all growth is worth the price. It is possible to pay so much to enable growth that the firm, on net, is worth less. Even if the cost of the growth is not an issue, other aspects of growth can leave the firm less valuable. For example, expansion may strain managers' capacity to monitor and handle the firm's operations, surpass the firm's distribution or quality control capabilities, or even change customers' perceptions of the firm and its brand.

For example, in Starbucks' 2005 annual report, chairman Howard Schultz and CEO Jim Donald wrote to shareholders that Starbucks planned to continue opening new stores—1800 in 2006 alone—and planned revenue growth of approximately 20% for the next five years. Around the time that Starbucks' shareholders were reading this (early 2006), the price of the company's stock was about $36. By the end of 2007, Starbucks' stock price had fallen to $21, Jim Donald had been fired as CEO, and chairman and founder Howard Schultz had written a memo to employees that Starbucks' recent expansion had caused it to "lose its soul," meaning that the Starbucks experience that was the key to its success, and the loyalty of its customers had been watered down. To distinguish between growth that adds to or detracts from the value of the firm, we will discuss two growth rates that factor in financing needs, and revisit our top decision rule: NPV analysis.

Sustainable Growth Rate and External Financing

The Starbucks example makes the point that not all growth is valuable growth. The distinction between value-enhancing and value-destroying growth can be made only through careful NPV analysis. However, this distinction is often confused with the concept of a firm's **internal growth rate**—the maximum growth rate a firm can achieve without resorting to external financing. Intuitively, this is the growth the firm can support by reinvesting its earnings. A closely related and more commonly used measure is the firm's **sustainable growth rate**—the maximum growth rate the firm can sustain without issuing new equity or increasing its debt-equity ratio. Let's discuss each of these in turn.

internal growth rate The maximum growth rate a firm can achieve without resorting to external financing.

sustainable growth rate The maximum growth rate a firm can achieve without issuing new equity or increasing its debt-equity ratio.

Internal Growth Rate Formula. Both of these benchmark growth rates are aimed at identifying how much growth a firm can support based on its existing net income. For a firm that does not pay any dividends, its internal growth rate is its return on assets, because that tells us how fast it could grow its assets using only its net income. If the firm pays some of its net income out as a dividend, then its internal growth rate is reduced to only the growth supported by its retained earnings. This reasoning suggests a more general formula for the internal growth rate:

$$\text{Internal Growth Rate} = \left(\frac{\text{Net Income}}{\text{Beginning Assets}}\right) \times (1 - \text{payout ratio}) \tag{18.4}$$

$$= \text{ROA} \times \text{retention rate}$$

Recall from Chapter 7 that the fraction of net income retained for reinvestment in the firm is called the retention rate. In the context of internal and sustainable growth rates, the retention rate is often called the **plowback ratio**. The internal growth rate is simply the return on assets (*ROA*) multiplied by the retention rate (plowback ratio).

plowback ratio Also called the retention ratio, 1 minus the payout ratio of the firm.

Sustainable Growth Rate Formula. The sustainable growth rate allows for some external financing. It assumes that no new equity will be issued and that the firm's managers want to maintain the same debt-equity ratio. Thus, it tells us how fast the firm can grow by reinvesting its retained earnings and issuing only as much new debt as can be supported by those retained earnings. The formula for the sustainable growth rate is as follows:

$$\text{Sustainable Growth Rate} = \left(\frac{\text{Net Income}}{\text{Beginning Equity}}\right) \times (1 - \text{payout ratio}) \tag{18.5}$$
$$= ROE \times \text{retention rate}$$

Sustainable Growth Rate Versus Internal Growth Rate. Because your return on equity (*ROE*) will be larger than your *ROA* any time you have debt, the sustainable growth rate will be greater than the internal growth rate. While the internal growth rate assumes no external financing, the sustainable growth rate assumes that you will make use of some outside financing equal to the amount of new debt that will keep your debt-equity ratio constant as your equity grows through reinvested net income.

EXAMPLE 18.3 Internal and Sustainable Growth Rates and Payout Policy

PROBLEM

Your firm has $70 million in equity and $30 million in debt and forecasts $14 million in net income for the year. It currently pays dividends equal to 20% of its net income. You are analyzing a potential change in payout policy—an increase in dividends to 30% of net income. How would this change affect your internal and sustainable growth rates?

SOLUTION

We can use Equations 18.4 and 18.5 to compute your firm's internal and sustainable growth rates under the old and new policy. To do so, we'll need to compute its *ROA*, *ROE*, and retention rate (plowback ratio). The company has $100 million (= $70 million in equity + $30 million in debt) in total assets.

$$ROA = \frac{\text{Net Income}}{\text{Beginning Assets}} = \frac{14}{100} = 14\% \quad ROE = \frac{\text{Net Income}}{\text{Beginning Equity}} = \frac{14}{70} = 20\%$$

$$\text{Old Retention Rate} = (1 - \text{payout ratio}) = (1 - 0.20) = 0.80$$
$$\text{New Retention Rate} = (1 - 0.30) = 0.70$$

Execute

Using Equation 18.4 to compute the internal growth rate before and after the change, we have the following:

$$\text{Old Internal Growth Rate} = ROA \times \text{retention rate} = 14\% \times 0.80 = 11.2\%$$
$$\text{New Internal Growth Rate} = 14\% \times 0.70 = 9.8\%$$

Similarly, we can use Equation 18.5 to compute the sustainable growth rate before and after:

$$\text{Old Sustainable Growth Rate} = ROE \times \text{retention rate} = 20\% \times 0.80 = 16\%$$
$$\text{New Sustainable Growth Rate} = 20\% \times 0.70 = 14\%$$

Evaluate

By reducing the amount of retained earnings available to fund growth, an increase in the payout ratio necessarily reduces your firm's internal and sustainable growth rates.

TABLE 18.12 Summary of Internal Growth Rate versus Sustainable Growth Rate

	Internal Growth Rate	Sustainable Growth Rate
Formula	*ROA* × retention rate	*ROE* × retention rate
Maximum growth financed only by:	retained earnings	retained earnings and new debt that keeps the debt-equity ratio constant
To grow faster, a firm must:	reduce payout or raise external capital	reduce payout, or raise new equity, or increase leverage

Whenever you forecast growth greater than the internal growth rate, you will have to either reduce your payout ratio (increase your plowback ratio), plan to raise additional external financing, or both. If your forecasted growth is greater than your sustainable growth rate, you will have to increase your plowback ratio, raise additional equity financing, or increase your leverage (increase your debt faster than keeping your debt-equity ratio constant would allow). Table 18.12 compares internal and sustainable growth rates.

While the internal and sustainable growth rates are useful in alerting you to the need to plan for external financing, they cannot tell you whether your planned growth increases or decreases the firm's value. The growth rates do not evaluate the future costs and benefits of the growth, and the Valuation Principle tells us that the value implications of the growth can be assessed only by doing so. *There is nothing inherently bad or unsustainable about growth greater than the sustainable growth rate as long as that growth is value-increasing. The firm will simply need to raise additional capital to finance the growth.*

For example, in the 1990s Starbucks' average revenue growth was above 60%, even though its average *ROE* was 20%. Until 2010, Starbucks never paid dividends, so its retention rate was 1, making its sustainable growth rate at the time also 20%.

$$SGR = ROE \times \text{retention rate} = 20\% \times 1 = 20\%$$

Despite expanding at three times its sustainable growth rate, Starbucks' value increased almost 10 times (1000%), as shown in Figure 18.1.

Conversely, Starbucks' recent experience illustrates that sustainable growth need not be value-increasing growth, as seen in Figure 18.1. We noted at the beginning of this section that, starting in 2006, Starbucks was aiming for annual growth of 20%. How does this compare with its sustainable growth rate at the time? When Schultz and Donald wrote their letter to shareholders, Starbucks' *ROE* was 20% (based on its 2005 annual report). Again, Starbucks has never paid dividends, so its retention rate is 1, making its sustainable growth rate also 20%. Thus, 20% growth was sustainable—it just wasn't value-increasing.[7]

As we discussed in Chapters 14 and 15, there are costs to seeking external financing—the flotation and issuance costs associated with issuing new equity or new bonds. Thus, the internal growth rate indicates the fastest growth possible without incurring any of these costs. The sustainable growth rate still assumes that some new debt will be sought, so the company reduces, but does not eliminate entirely, its costs of external financing when growing at the sustainable growth rate. Thus, managers, especially those at small firms, concerned with these costs might track these growth rates. However, these costs are generally small relative to the NPV of, for example, an expansion plan.

[7]This text's website contains a spreadsheet with a proposed further expansion of *KXS* Designs that allows you to explore further the differences between sustainable growth, internal growth rate, and value-increasing growth.

FIGURE 18.1 Starbucks' Stock Price During Periods of Growth at, above, and below Its *SGR*

The graph shows Starbucks' stock price since 2000. During most of its early years, Starbucks grew at well above its sustainable growth rate (*SGR*) and its value increased substantially. In 2006, it planned growth at its *SGR* but suffered a share decrease in value. The graph demonstrates that there is not necessarily a relationship between a firm's growth relative to its *SGR* and whether that growth is valuable.

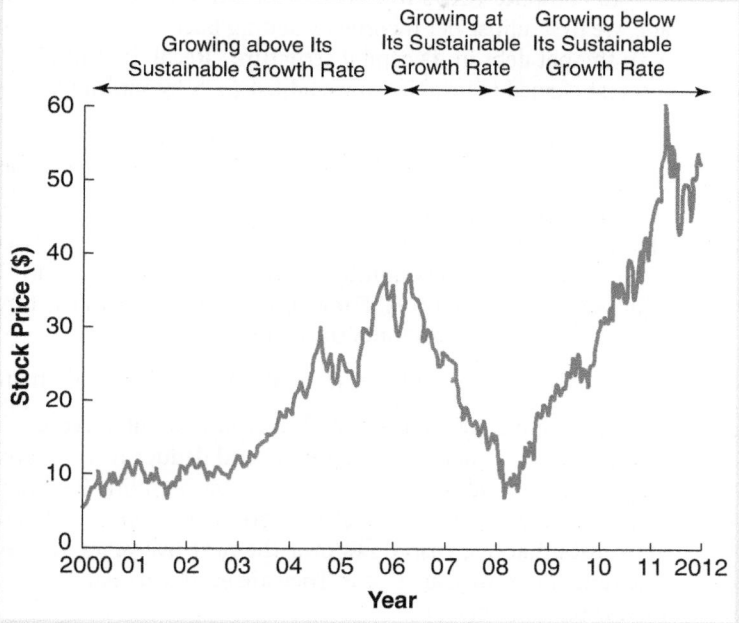

Source: http://finance.yahoo.com, Compustat, and authors' calculations.

While these costs are usually small relative to the NPV of expanding the business, ignoring them completely would be a mistake. The proper way to incorporate them is to calculate the cash outflow associated with these costs and subtract it from the NPV of the expansion. The point remains that growth above a firm's internal or sustainable growth rates is not necessarily bad, but will require external financing and the costs associated with that financing.

CONCEPT CHECK

7. What is the difference between internal growth rate and sustainable growth rate?

8. If a firm grows faster than its sustainable growth rate, is that growth value-decreasing?

18.5 Valuing the Expansion

As the last section made clear, growth can increase or decrease the value of the firm. Planning for and forecasting the impact of growth is just the first step in the analysis of whether the growth will make sense for the shareholders. Our forecasting exercise in Section 18.3 gave us the implications of the planned expansion for the debt, net income, and working capital of KXS. Now we are ready to determine whether the expansion is a good idea. The Valuation Principle guides us here—we need to forecast the cash flows and compute their present value.

Forecasting Free Cash Flows

We now have the data needed to forecast KXS's free cash flows over the next five years. KXS's earnings are available from the income statement (Table 18.8), as are its depreciation and interest expenses. Capital expenditures are available from Table 18.6, and changes in net working capital can be found in Table 18.9. We combine these items to estimate the free cash flows in the spreadsheet shown in Table 18.13.

To compute KXS's free cash flows, which exclude cash flows associated with leverage, we first adjust net income by adding back the after-tax interest payments associated with the net debt in its capital structure. Recall that interest paid is tax deductible, and interest earned is taxable, so we adjust each by multiplying by (1 − Tax Rate):[8]

$$\text{After-Tax Interest Expense} = (1 - \text{Tax Rate}) \times (\text{Interest on Debt} - \text{Interest on Excess Cash}) \tag{18.6}$$

Because KXS has no excess cash, its after-tax interest expense in 2019 is $(1 - 35\%) \times \$306 = \$199$ (thousand), providing unlevered net income of $\$7600 + 199 = \$7799$. We could also compute the unlevered net income in Table 18.13 by starting with EBIT and deducting taxes. For example, in 2019, EBIT is forecasted as \$11.998 million (Table 18.8), which amounts to the following:

$$\$11.998 \times (1 - 35\%) = \$7.799 \text{ million after taxes}$$

To compute KXS's free cash flows from its unlevered net income, we add back depreciation (which is not a cash expense) and deduct KXS's increases in net working capital and capital expenditures. The free cash flows on line 9 of Table 18.13 show the cash the firm will generate for its investors, both debt and equity holders.[9] While KXS will generate substantial free cash flows over the next five years, the level of free cash flows varies substantially from year to year. They are even forecasted to be negative in 2019 (when the expansion takes place).

As we noted, free cash flows are the total cash available to all investors (debt and equity holders). To determine the amount that can be paid out to equity holders, we can adjust the free cash flows to account for all (after-tax) payments to or from debt holders.

TABLE 18.13 KXS Forecasted Free Cash Flows

1	Year	2019	2020	2021	2022	2023
2	**Free Cash Flow ($000s)**					
3	**Net Income**	7600	8807	11,141	13,739	16,627
4	Plus: After-Tax Interest Expense	199	1083	1083	1083	1083
5	**Unlevered Net Income**	7799	9890	12,224	14,822	17,710
6	Plus: Depreciation	7443	7498	7549	7594	7634
7	Less: Increases in NWC	−5257	−5802	−6453	−7166	−7948
8	Less: Capital Expenditures	−25,000	−8000	−8000	−8000	−8000
9	**Free Cash Flow of Firm**	−15,015	3586	5320	7250	9396

[8]If KXS had some interest income or expenses from working capital, we would *not* include that interest here. We adjust only for interest that is related to the firm's *financing*—that is, interest associated with debt and excess cash (cash not included as part of working capital).

[9]While we are maintaining the assumption that, after paying the interest on its debt, KXS will distribute any excess funds to shareholders as dividends, this payout decision has no impact on the amount of free cash flows the firm generates in the first place, and hence has no impact on the value we will compute for KXS.

For example, in 2019 KXS will pay after-tax interest of $199,000 and receive $20 million by issuing new debt as follows:

	2019 ($000s)
Free Cash Flows	−15,015
Less: After-Tax Interest Expense	−199
Plus: Increase in Debt	+20,000
= Free Cash Flows to Equity	= 4786

Note that the free cash flows that are available to equity holders in 2019, $4.786 million, are exactly the amount of dividends we forecasted at the end of Section 18.3. This is no coincidence—we chose in that section to pay out all excess available cash flows as a dividend. This is exactly what the free cash flows to equity tell us—the total amount of excess cash flows that belongs to the equity holders for them to use to pay dividends, repurchase shares, retain in the firm as cash, or retire debt. (See the appendix to this chapter for a forecast of free cash flows to equity and dividends through 2023.)

COMMON MISTAKE

Confusing Total and Incremental Net Working Capital

When calculating free cash flows from earnings, students often make the mistake of subtracting the firm's *total* net working capital each year rather than only the incremental change in net working capital. Remember that only a change in net working capital results in a new cash inflow or outflow for the firm. Subtracting the entire *level* of net working capital will reduce the free cash flows, often even making them negative, and lead the student to understate the NPV of the decision.

KXS Design's Expansion: Effect on Firm Value

We've accomplished a lot by carefully forecasting the impact of the planned expansion on KXS's net income, capital expenditures, and working capital needs. First, we identified future financing needs, allowing us ample time to plan to secure the necessary funding. Next, in order to construct our pro forma statements, we built an Excel model of the interactions between sales growth, costs, capital investment, working capital needs, and financing choices. This model allows us to study how changes in any of these factors will affect the others and our expansion plans.[10] Remember the lesson from sensitivity and scenario analysis in Chapter 9—these numbers are only forecasts, and therefore you need to see how reasonable deviations from the forecast would affect the value of the expansion. Nonetheless, as a starting point, we use these forecasts to provide our best estimate of whether the expansion plan is a good idea—does it increase the value of KXS? There are two ways of doing this: (1) value the whole company with and without the expansion and compare the values or (2) value only the incremental changes to the company caused by the expansion, as we did in Chapter 9's capital budgeting exercise. We will go the first route to provide an example of how to do whole-company valuation. However, you could arrive at the same answer by following the incremental approach.

As we learned in Chapter 16, absent distress costs, the value of a firm with debt is equal to the value of the firm without debt plus the present value of its interest tax

[10]You can download a copy of the forecasting model in Excel from this textbook's website and experiment with changes in these factors yourself.

shields. Our careful forecast of the financing of KXS's expansion allows us to apply the same approach to valuing the expansion; we compute the present value of the *unlevered* free cash flows of KXS and add to it the present value of the tax shields created by our planned interest payments.[11] However, we have forecast cash flows only to 2023, so we will need to account for the remaining value of KXS at that point. We do so using the tools developed in Chapter 7 for valuing common stock.

continuation value
The value of a project's remaining free cash flows beyond the forecast horizon.

Multiples Approach to Continuation Value. Practitioners generally estimate a firm's **continuation value** (also called the terminal value) at the end of the forecast horizon using a valuation multiple. Explicitly forecasting cash flows is useful in capturing those specific aspects of a company that distinguish the firm from its competitors in the short run. However, because of competition between firms, the long-term expected growth rates, profitability, and risk of firms in the same industry should move toward one another. As a consequence, long-term expectations of multiples are likely to be relatively homogeneous across firms in a given sector. Thus, a realistic assumption is that a firm's multiple will eventually move toward the industry average. Because distant cash flows are difficult to forecast accurately, estimating the firm's continuation, or terminal, value based on a long-term estimate of the valuation multiple for the industry is a common (and, generally, reasonably reliable) approach.

Of the different valuation multiples available, the EBITDA (earnings before interest, taxes, depreciation, and amortization) multiple is most often used in practice. In most settings, the EBITDA multiple is more reliable than sales or earnings multiples because it accounts for the firm's operating efficiency and is not affected by leverage differences between firms. We discussed the use of multiples in valuation in Chapter 7. As in that context, here we estimate the continuation value using an EBITDA multiple as follows:

$$\begin{aligned}&\text{Continuation Enterprise Value at Forecast Horizon}\\&\quad = \text{EBITDA at Horizon} \times \text{EBITDA Multiple at Horizon}\end{aligned} \tag{18.7}$$

From the income statement in Table 18.8, KXS's EBITDA in 2023 is forecast to be \$34.880 million. Firms in KXS's industry are valued at an average EBITDA multiple of 9. If we assume that the appropriate EBITDA multiple in 2023 is unchanged from the current value of 9, then KXS's continuation value in 2023 is \$34.880 × 9 = \$313.920 million. This assumption is important—the EBITDA multiple at the horizon will have a large impact on our value calculation. A careful analysis of the prospects for industry growth (which tends to be related to higher multiples) at the horizon is important. Here, we assume that the design and apparel industry is mature and will remain relatively stable, but this assumption can be probed, especially in sensitivity analysis.

KXS Design's Value with the Expansion. Assume that KXS's financial managers have estimated KXS's unlevered cost of capital to be 10% (specifically, 10% is their pre-tax WACC as discussed in Chapter 16; see the details regarding the estimation of the cost of capital in Chapter 12). Now we have all the inputs we need to value KXS with the expansion. Table 18.14 presents the calculation. First, we compute the present value of the forecasted free cash flows of the firm over the next five years. These are the cash flows available to both bondholders and equity holders, so they are free of any effects of leverage. Because they represent cash flows to both debt and equity holders, and because we will account for the benefits of the interest tax shield separately, we discount KXS's free

[11]This approach is called the adjusted present value because it adjusts the present value of the unlevered free cash flows for the effect of the interest tax shields.

TABLE 18.14 Calculation of KXS Firm Value with the Expansion

1	Year	2018	2019	2020	2021	2022	2023
2	Free Cash Flow of Firm ($000s)		−15,015	3586	5320	7250	9396
3	**PV (Free Cash Flow) (at 10%)**	4097					
4	Continuation Value						313,920
5	**PV (Continuation Value) (at 10%)**	194,920					
6	Net Interest Expense		−306	−1666	−1666	−1666	−1666
7	Interest Tax Shield		107	583	583	583	583
8	**PV (Interest Tax Shield) (at 6.8%)**	1958					
9	**Firm Value (3 + 5 + 8)**	200,974					

cash flows at the firm's pre-tax WACC of 10%. Using the free cash flows we forecasted for 2019–2023 in Table 18.13, we get a present value of $4097:

$$PV(FCF) = \frac{-15{,}015}{(1.10)^1} + \frac{3586}{(1.10)^2} + \frac{5320}{(1.10)^3} + \frac{7250}{(1.10)^4} + \frac{9396}{(1.10)^5} = 4097 \qquad (18.8)$$

Even though the PV of the cash flows over the next five years is small, the expansion pays off in the long run by providing higher free cash flows from 2023 onward. This growth results in a higher EBITDA in 2023 than would otherwise be possible, and thus a higher continuation value once that EBIDTA is multiplied by the continuation multiple of 9. The $313,920 continuation value in 2023 that we calculated is included in Table 18.14. However, because it is a 2023 value, we need to discount it to the present as follows:

$$PV(\text{Continuation Value}) = \frac{313{,}920}{(1.10)^5} = 194{,}920 \qquad (18.9)$$

Finally, because we are financing the expansion with debt, we will have additional interest tax shields. The total net interest expense is included in Table 18.14, and the interest tax shield there is calculated as we did in Chapter 16, by multiplying the interest expense by the tax rate (35% for KXS):

$$\text{Interest Tax Shield} = \text{Net Interest Expense} \times \text{Tax Rate} \qquad (18.10)$$

Also as we did in Chapter 16, we calculate the present value of the interest tax shield using the interest rate on debt as the discount rate, *not* using the WACC. Recall that the reason for doing so is that the tax shield is only as risky as the debt that creates it, so the proper discount rate is the debt's interest rate, here at 6.8%:[12]

$$PV = (\text{Interest Tax Shield}) = \frac{107}{(1.068)^1} + \frac{583}{(1.068)^2} + \frac{583}{(1.068)^3} + \frac{583}{(1.068)^4} + \frac{583}{(1.068)^5} = 1958 \qquad (18.11)$$

[12]We have not ignored the rest of the interest tax shields from the new debt. The value of those shields is subsumed in the continuation value of the firm. When we say that the firm will be worth nine times EBITDA, we are saying that the total value at that point, including all unused tax shields, will be nine times EBITDA.

The total value of KXS with the expansion is the sum of the present values of the forecasted unlevered free cash flows, the continuation value of the firm, and the interest tax shields. As shown in Table 18.14, the total firm value is $200.974 million.

KXS Design's Value Without the Expansion. But how do we know if the expansion is a good idea? We can compare KXS's value with the expansion to its value without the expansion. If KXS does not invest in the new equipment, it will be stuck with a maximum capacity of 1100 units. While its sales revenue will grow due to price increases, its main source of growth will be cut off. Table 18.15 shows the sales revenue without the expansion. By 2019, KXS reaches maximum production capacity and can no longer expand. Comparing the sales revenue in Table 18.15 to the sales revenue with the expansion given in Table 18.8, we see how much higher sales are forecasted to be with the expansion.

TABLE 18.15 KXS's Sales Forecast Without Expansion

1	Year	2018	2019	2020	2021	2022	2023
2	Production Volume	1000	1100	1100	1100	1100	1100
3	Sales Price	$74.89	$76.51	$78.04	$79.60	$81.19	$82.82
4	Sales Revenue	$74,889	$84,161	$85,844	$87,561	$89,312	$91,099

We can complete the same process for forecasting the free cash flows of the firm without the expansion as we did for the firm with the expansion. In this case, we would find that the 2019 EBITDA would be only $20,042, so the continuation value would drop to $20,042 × 9 = $180,378. Also, KXS will not be taking on any additional debt, so the interest expense will remain constant at $306 per year. The final result of the valuation is presented in Table 18.16.

TABLE 18.16 KXS's Value Without the Expansion

1	Year	2018	2019	2020	2021	2022	2023
2	Free Cash Flow of Firm ($000s)		5324	8509	8727	8952	9182
3	**PV (Free Cash Flow) (at 10%)**	**30,244**					
4	Continuation Value						180,378
5	**PV (Continuation Value) (at 10%)**	**112,001**					
6	Net Interest Expense			−306	−306	−306	−306
7	Interest Tax Shield			107	107	107	107
8	**PV (Interest Tax Shield) (at 6.8%)**	**441**					
9	**Firm Value (3 + 5 + 8)**	**142,686**					

While the PV of the free cash flows over the next five years is higher because we don't have to spend $20 million for the new equipment, the lower growth substantially reduces our continuation value, and the reduced debt (because we do not need to borrow to fund the equipment) produces a much lower present value of interest tax shields as well. The resulting firm value is almost $60 million lower without the expansion than it is with the expansion. Thus, the expansion is certainly a good idea for KXS.

Optimal Timing and the Option to Delay

We just showed that if the alternative is not to expand at all, KXS should definitely expand in 2019. However, what if it also has the option to simply delay expansion to 2020 or later, rather than not to expand at all? If we repeat the valuation analysis above for expansion in each year from 2019 to 2023, we get the following firm values in 2018:[13]

Expand in. . .	2019	2020	2021	2022	2023
KXS's Firm Value in 2018 ($000s)	200,974	203,553	204,728	204,604	203,277

KXS's firm value is maximized by delaying the expansion to 2021. The reason is that while delaying expansion means that KXS cannot produce enough units to meet demand, the shortfall is not too great until 2021. The value gained from putting off such a large financial outlay is greater than the value lost from forgone sales.

The timing analysis recalls an important point from Chapter 9: managers often have real options embedded in capital budgeting decisions. In this case, it is important for KXS's managers to realize that the alternative is not to expand or do nothing. Rather, it is expand or delay expansion for another year (or more). As we see here, this option is valuable, allowing KXS's managers to add almost $4 million in additional value to the firm.

CONCEPT CHECK

9. What is the multiples approach to continuation value?
10. How does forecasting help the financial manager decide whether to implement a new business plan?

[13]Interested students may perform this analysis for themselves using the spreadsheet that accompanies this chapter on the textbook's website.

MyLab Finance

Here is what you should know after reading this chapter. MyLab™ Finance will help you identify what you know, and where to go when you need to practice.

KEY POINTS AND EQUATIONS	TERMS	ONLINE PRACTICE OPPORTUNITIES
18.1 Goals of Long-Term Financial Planning ■ Building a financial model to forecast the financial statements and free cash flows of a firm allows the financial manager to ■ identify important linkages. ■ analyze the impact of potential business plans. ■ plan for future funding needs.		MyLab Study Plan 18.1
18.2 Forecasting Financial Statements: The Percent of Sales Method ■ One common approach to forecasting is the percent of sales approach, in which you assume that costs, working capital, and total assets will remain a fixed percentage of sales as sales grow. ■ A pro forma income statement projects the firm's earnings under a given set of hypothetical assumptions.	net new financing, p. 634 percent of sales method, p. 632 the plug, p. 636	MyLab Study Plan 18.2 Spreadsheet Tables 18.1–18.4

KEY POINTS AND EQUATIONS	TERMS	ONLINE PRACTICE OPPORTUNITIES
■ A pro forma balance sheet projects the firm's assets, liabilities, and equity under the same assumptions used to construct the pro forma income statement. ■ Forecasting the balance sheet with the percent of sales method requires two passes. ■ The first pass reveals by how much equity and liabilities would fall short of the amount needed to finance the expected growth in assets. ■ The amount by which the financing falls short is called the plug, and indicates the total net new financing needed from external sources. ■ In the second pass, the pro forma balance sheet shows the necessary financing from the planned sources and is in balance.		
18.3 Forecasting a Planned Expansion ■ An improvement over the percent of sales method is to forecast the firm's working capital and capital investment, along with planned financing of those investments directly. ■ Such a financial model will have the correct timing of external financing and capital investment so that we can estimate the firm's future free cash flows.		MyLab Study Plan 18.3 Spreadsheet Tables 18.5–18.10
18.4 Growth and Firm Value ■ Two common concepts are internal growth rate and sustainable growth rate. ■ The internal growth rate identifies the maximum rate at which the firm can grow without external financing: Internal Growth Rate = *ROA* × retention rate (18.4) ■ The sustainable growth rate identifies the maximum rate at which the firm can grow if it wants to keep its D/E ratio constant without any new equity financing: Sustainable Growth Rate = *ROE* × retention rate (18.5) ■ Neither the internal growth rate nor the sustainable growth rate indicates whether planned growth is good or bad. Only an NPV analysis can tell us whether the contemplated growth will increase or decrease the value of the firm.	internal growth rate, p. 644 plowback ratio, p. 644 sustainable growth rate, p. 644	MyLab Study Plan 18.4

KEY POINTS AND EQUATIONS	TERMS	ONLINE PRACTICE OPPORTUNITIES
18.5 Valuing the Expansion ■ In addition to forecasting cash flows for a few years, we need to estimate the firm's continuation value at the end of the forecast horizon. ■ We discussed continuation values in depth in Chapter 7. One method is to use a valuation multiple based on comparable firms. ■ Given the forecasted cash flows and an estimate of the cost of capital, the final step is to combine these inputs to estimate the value of the firm based on the business plan. We can compare this with the value of the firm without the new plan to determine whether to implement the plan.	continuation value, p. 650	MyLab Study Plan 18.5 Interactive Financial Statement Model Spreadsheet Tables 18.12–18.15

REVIEW QUESTIONS

1. What is the purpose of long-term forecasting?
2. What are the advantages and disadvantages of the percent of sales method?
3. What is gained by forecasting capital expenditures and external financing specifically?
4. How can the financial manager use the long-term forecast to decide on adopting a new business plan?
5. What can the sustainable growth rate tell a financial manager and what can it not tell?

PROBLEMS

All problems in this chapter are available in MyLab.

Forecasting Financial Statements: The Percent of Sales Method

1. Your company has sales of $100,000 this year and cost of goods sold of $72,000. You forecast sales to increase to $110,000 next year. Using the percent of sales method, forecast next year's cost of goods sold.

2. For the next fiscal year, you forecast net income of $50,000 and ending assets of $500,000. Your firm's payout ratio is 10%. Your beginning stockholders' equity is $300,000 and your beginning total liabilities are $120,000. Your non-debt liabilities, such as accounts payable, are forecasted to increase by $10,000. What is your net new financing needed for next year?

3. Assume your beginning total liabilities in Problem 2 is $100,000. What amount of equity and what amount of debt would you need to issue to cover the net new financing in order to keep your debt-equity ratio constant?

For Problems 4 to 6, use the following income statement and balance sheet for Jim's Espresso:

Income Statement		**Balance Sheet**	
Sales	200,000	Assets	
Costs Except Depreciation	(100,000)	Cash and Equivalents	15,000
EBITDA	100,000	Accounts Receivable	2000
Depreciation	(6000)	Inventories	4000
EBIT	94,000	Total Current Assets	21,000
Interest Expense (net)	(400)	Property, Plant, and Equipment	10,000
Pre-tax Income	93,600	Total Assets	31,000
Income Tax	(32,760)		
Net Income	60,840	Liabilities and Equity	
		Accounts Payable	1500
		Debt	4000
		Total Liabilities	5500
		Stockholders' Equity	25,500
		Total Liabilities and Equity	31,000

4. Jim's Espresso expects sales to grow by 10% next year. Using the percent of sales method, forecast the following:
   a. Costs
   b. Depreciation
   c. Net income
   d. Cash
   e. Accounts receivable
   f. Inventory
   g. Property, plant, and equipment

5. Assume that Jim's Espresso pays out 90% of its net income. Use the percent of sales method to forecast the following:
   a. Stockholders' equity
   b. Accounts payable

6. What is the amount of net new financing needed for Jim's Espresso?

7. If Jim's Espresso adjusts its payout policy to 70% of net income, how will the net new financing change?

For Problems 8 to 11, use the following income statement and balance sheet for Global Corp.:

Figures in $ millions

Net Sales	186.7	Assets	23.2
Costs Except Depreciation	–175.1	Cash	
EBITDA	11.6	Accounts Receivable	18.5
Depreciation and Amortization	–1.2	Inventories	15.3
EBIT	10.4	Total Current Assets	57
Interest Income (expense)	–7.7		
Pre-tax Income	2.7	Net Property, Plant, and Equipment	113.1
Taxes	–0.7	Total Assets	170.1
Net Income	2.0		

Liabilities and Equity	
Accounts Payable	34.7
Long-Term Debt	113.2
Total Liabilities	147.9
Total Stockholders' Equity	22.2
Total Liabilities and Equity	170.1

8. Global Corp. expects sales to grow by 8% next year. Using the percent of sales method, forecast the following:
a. Costs
b. Depreciation
c. Net income
d. Cash
e. Accounts receivable
f. Inventory
g. Property, plant, and equipment
h. Accounts payable

9. Assume that Global pays out 50% of its net income. Use the percent of sales method to forecast stockholders' equity.

10. What is the amount of net new financing needed for Global?

11. If Global decides that it will limit its net new financing to no more than $9 million, how will this affect its payout policy?

Forecasting a Planned Expansion

For problems in this section, download the KXS spreadsheets available on the text's website.

12. Assume that KXS's market share will increase by 0.25% per year rather than the 1% used in the chapter (see Table 18.5) and that its prices remain as in the chapter. What production capacity will KXS require each year? When will an expansion become necessary (i.e., when will production volume exceed 1100)?

13. Under the assumption that KXS's market share will be 0.25% higher in each subsequent year (e.g., 2018 will be 10.25%, 2019 will be 10.50%, and so on), you determine that the plant will require an expansion in 2020. The expansion will cost $20 million. Assuming that the financing of the expansion will be delayed accordingly, calculate the projected interest payments and the amount of the projected interest tax shields (assuming that KXS still uses a 10-year bond and interest rates remain the same as in the chapter) through 2023.

14. Under the assumption that KXS's market share will increase by 0.25% per year (and the investment and financing will be adjusted as described in Problem 13), you project the following depreciation:

Year	2018	2019	2020	2021	2022	2023
Depreciation ($000s)	5492	5443	7398	7459	7513	7561

Using this information, project net income through 2023 (i.e., reproduce Table 18.8 under the new assumptions).

15. Assuming that KXS's market share will increase by 0.25% per year (implying that the investment, financing, and depreciation will be adjusted as described in

Problems 13 and 14), and that the working capital assumptions used in the chapter still hold, calculate KXS's working capital requirements through 2023 (that is, reproduce Table 18.9 under the new assumptions).

Growth and Firm Value

16. Information for a company is provided in the table below:

Net Income	$50,000
Beginning Total Assets	$400,000
Beginning Stockholders' Equity	$250,000
Payout Ratio	0%

Calculate the following for the company:
a. Internal growth rate
b. Sustainable growth rate
c. Sustainable growth rate if it pays out 40% of its net income as a dividend

17. Did KXS's expansion plan call for it to grow slower or faster than its sustainable growth rate?

18. Your firm has an *ROE* of 12%, a payout ratio of 25%, $600,000 of stockholders' equity, and $400,000 of debt. If you grow at your sustainable growth rate this year, how much additional debt will you need to issue?

19. IZAX Co. has the following items on its balance sheet:

Assets		Liabilities and Equity	
Cash	$50,000	Debt	$100,000
PPE	$350,000	Equity	$300,000

Its net income this year is $20,000 and it pays dividends of $5000. If it grows at its internal growth rate, what will its D/E ratio be next year?

Valuing the Planned Expansion

20. Forecast KXS's free cash flows (reproduce Table 18.13), assuming KXS's market share will increase by 0.25% per year; investment, financing, and depreciation will be adjusted accordingly; and working capital will be as you projected in Problem 15.

21. Calculate the continuation value of KXS using your reproduction of Table 18.8 from Problem 14, and assuming an EBITDA multiple of 8.5.

22. Assuming a cost of capital of 10%, compute the value of KXS under the 0.25% growth scenario.

The information we have calculated so far can be used to project KXS's balance sheet and statement of cash flows through 2023. While these statements are not critical for our valuation of the expansion, they often prove helpful in providing a more complete picture of how a firm will grow during the forecast period. These statements for KXS are shown in the spreadsheets in Table 18.17 and Table 18.18.

The balance sheet (Table 18.17) continues the work we started in Table 18.10. Current assets and liabilities come from the net working capital spreadsheet (Table 18.9). The inventory entry on the balance sheet includes both raw materials and finished goods. Property, plant, and equipment information comes from the forecasted capital expenditure spreadsheet (Table 18.6), and the debt comes from Table 18.7.

TABLE 18.17 Pro Forma Balance Sheet for KXS, 2018–2023

1	**Year**	**2018**	**2019**	**2020**	**2021**	**2022**	**2023**
2	**Balance Sheets ($000s)**						
3	**Assets**						
4	Cash and Cash Equivalents	11,982	14,139	16,520	19,167	22,107	25,367
5	Accounts Receivable	14,229	16,790	19,617	22,761	26,252	30,124
6	Inventories	14,978	17,674	20,649	23,959	27,633	31,709
7	**Total Current Assets**	41,189	48,603	56,786	65,886	75,992	87,201
8	Property, Plant, and Equipment	49,427	66,984	67,486	67,937	68,344	68,709
9	**Total Assets**	90,616	115,587	124,272	133,823	144,335	155,910
10							
11	**Liabilities**						
12	Accounts Payable	11,982	14,139	16,520	19,167	22,107	25,367
13	Debt	4500	24,500	24,500	24,500	24,500	24,500
14	**Total Liabilities**	16,482	38,639	41,020	43,667	46,607	49,867
15							
16	**Stockholders' Equity**						
17	Starting Stockholders' Equity	69,275	74,134	76,948	83,252	90,156	97,729
18	Net Income	6940	7600	8807	11,141	13,739	16,627
19	Dividends	−2082	−4786	−2503	−4237	−6167	−8313
20	**Stockholders' Equity**	74,134	76,948	83,252	90,156	97,729	106,042
21	**Total Liabilities and Equity**	90,616	115,587	124,272	133,823	144,335	155,910

KXS's book value of equity will steadily grow as the company expands and remains profitable, paying out only a portion of its net income each year. Its debt will jump from $4500 to $24,500 in 2019 when it finances its expansion. KXS's other liabilities—accounts payable—will grow steadily with sales. KXS's book debt-equity ratio will jump from $4500/$74,134 = 6% in 2018 to $24,500/$76,948 = 32% in 2019, and then will steadily decline to 23% by 2023.

The statement of cash flows in Table 18.18 starts with net income. Cash from operating activities includes depreciation as well as *changes* to working capital items (other than cash) from Table 18.9. Cash from investing activities includes the capital expenditures in Table 18.6. Cash from financing activities includes net borrowing from Table 18.7, and dividends are equal to free cash flows to equity because we assume KXS

TABLE 18.18 Pro Forma Statement of Cash Flows for KXS, 2018–2023

1	Year	2018	2019	2020	2021	2022	2023
2	**Statement of Cash Flows ($000s)**						
3	Net Income		7600	8807	11,141	13,739	16,627
4	Depreciation		7443	7498	7549	7594	7634
5	Changes in Working Capital						
6	Accounts Receivable		−2561	−2827	−3144	−3491	−3872
7	Inventory		−2696	−2976	−3309	−3675	−4076
8	Accounts Payable		2157	2381	2647	2940	3261
9	**Cash from Operating Activities**		11,942	12,884	14,884	17,107	19,574
10	Capital Expenditures		−25,000	−8000	−8000	−8000	−8000
11	Other Investment		—	—	—	—	—
12	**Cash from Investing Activities**		−25,000	−8000	−8000	−8000	−8000
13	Net Borrowing		20,000	—	—	—	—
14	Dividends		−4786	−2503	−4237	−6167	−8313
15	**Cash from Financing Activities**		15,214	−2503	−4237	−6167	−8313
16							
17	**Change in Cash** (9 + 12 + 15)		2157	2381	2647	2940	3261

pays out all excess cash. We can compute FCF to equity from Table 18.13 using the following equation:

$$\begin{aligned} FCF \text{ to Equity} = {} & FCF \text{ of the Firm} + \text{Net Borrowing} \\ & - \text{After-Tax Interest Expense} \end{aligned} \tag{18.12}$$

KXS is not planning to raise any additional equity financing, so there are no capital contributions on the cash flow statement. As a final check on the calculations, note the change in the minimum cash balance shown on the balance sheet (Table 18.18). For example, in 2019, the change in cash and cash equivalents is $2.157 million, which is the amount by which 2019 cash exceeds 2018 cash on the balance sheet.

CHAPTER

Working Capital Management

19

LEARNING OBJECTIVES

- Understand the cash cycle of the firm and why managing working capital is important
- Use trade credit to the firm's advantage
- Make decisions on extending credit and adjusting credit terms
- Manage accounts payable
- Contrast the different instruments available to a financial manager for investing cash balances

NOTATION

CCC	cash conversion cycle
EAR	effective annual rate
g	perpetuity growth rate
NPV	net present value
r	discount rate

In Chapter 2, we defined a firm's net working capital as its current assets minus its current liabilities. Net working capital is the capital required in the short term to run the business. Thus, working capital management involves short-term asset accounts such as cash, inventory, and accounts receivable, as well as short-term liability accounts such as accounts payable. The level of investment in each of these accounts differs from firm to firm and from industry to industry. It also depends on factors such as the type of business and industry standards. Some firms, for example, require heavy inventory investments because of the nature of their business.

Consider Barrick Gold Corporation, a gold mining company, and Wyndham Worldwide Corporation, an owner and operator of hotels. Inventory amounted to 7.5% of Barrick's total assets at the end of 2017, whereas Wyndham's investment in inventory was less than 3%. A gold mining company maintains a great deal of gold ore in stockpile waiting to be processed and gold ore on leach pad where the precious metal is being extracted. In contrast, a hotel chain's profitability is generated primarily from its investment in plant, property, and equipment—that is, its hotels and furnishings.

There are opportunity costs associated with investing in inventories and accounts receivable, and from holding cash. Excess funds invested in these accounts could, instead, be used to pay down debt or be returned to shareholders in the form of a dividend or share repurchase. This chapter focuses on the tools firms use to manage their working capital efficiently and thereby minimize these opportunity costs. We begin by discussing why firms have working capital and how it affects firm value. In a perfect capital market, many of the working capital accounts would be irrelevant. Not surprisingly, the existence of these accounts for real firms can be traced to market frictions. We discuss the costs and benefits of trade credit and evaluate the trade-offs firms make in managing various working capital accounts. Finally, we discuss the cash balance of a firm and provide an overview of the short-term investments in which a firm may choose to invest its cash.

19.1 Overview of Working Capital

Most projects require the firm to invest in net working capital. The main components of net working capital are cash, inventory, receivables, and payables. Working capital includes the cash that is needed to run the firm on a day-to-day basis. It does not include excess cash, which is cash that is not required to run the business and can be invested at a market rate. As we discussed in Chapter 12, excess cash may be viewed as part of the firm's capital structure, offsetting firm debt. In Chapter 9, we discussed how any increases in net working capital represent an investment that reduces the cash that is available to the firm. The Valuation Principle tells us that the value of the firm is the present value of its free cash flows. Therefore, working capital alters a firm's value by affecting its free cash flows. In this section, we examine the components of net working capital and their effects on the firm's value.

The Cash Cycle

The level of working capital reflects the length of time between when cash goes out of a firm at the beginning of the production process and when it comes back in. Take Intel, for example in 2017. Let's trace the path of $1000 worth of inventory and raw materials through Intel's production process.

- First, Intel buys $1000 of raw materials and inventory from its suppliers, purchasing them on credit, which means that the firm does not have to pay cash immediately at the time of purchase.
- About 39 days later, Intel pays for the materials and inventory, so over a month has passed between when Intel purchased the materials and when the cash outflow occurred.
- After another 57 days, Intel sells the materials (now in the form of finished microprocessors) to a computer manufacturer, but the sale is on credit, meaning that the computer manufacturer does not pay cash immediately. A total of 96 days has passed between when Intel purchased the materials and when it sold them as part of the finished product.
- About 30 days later, the computer manufacturer pays for the microprocessors, producing a cash inflow for Intel.

operating cycle The average length of time between when a firm originally receives its inventory and when it receives the cash back from selling its product.

cash cycle The length of time between when a firm pays cash to purchase its initial inventory and when it receives cash from the sale of the output produced from that inventory.

A total of 39 + 57 + 30 = 126 days have passed from when Intel originally bought the raw materials until it received the cash from selling the finished product. Thus, Intel's *operating cycle* is 110 days: a firm's **operating cycle** is the average length of time between when the firm originally purchases its inventory and when it receives the cash back from selling its product. A firm's **cash cycle** is the length of time between when the firm pays cash to purchase its initial inventory

FIGURE 19.1 The Cash and Operating Cycle for a Firm

The cash cycle is the average time between when a firm pays for its inventory and when it receives cash from the sale of its product. If the firm pays cash for its inventory, this period is identical to the firm's cash cycle. However, most firms buy their inventory on credit, which reduces the amount of time between the cash investment and the receipt of cash from that investment.

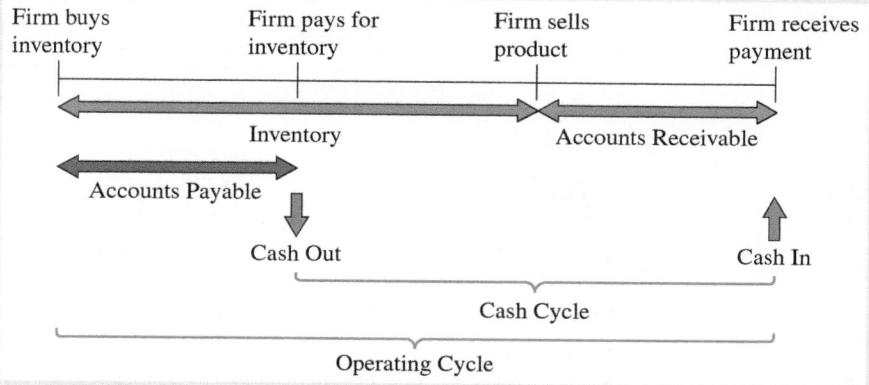

and when it receives cash from the sale of the output produced from that inventory. For Intel, the cash cycle is 87 days: the 57 days it holds the material after paying for it plus the 30 days it waits to receive cash after selling the finished product. Some companies actually have a *negative* cash cycle; that is, they are paid for the product before they have to pay for the cost of producing it! This is generally possible only if companies keep very low inventory and have the size to force their suppliers to wait to be paid. Example 19.1 goes through an example of this for Loblaw Companies Limited. Figure 19.1 illustrates the operating and cash cycle.

cash conversion cycle (CCC) A measure of the cash cycle calculated as the sum of a firm's inventory days and accounts receivable days, less its accounts payable days.

Some practitioners measure the cash cycle by calculating the *cash conversion cycle*. The **cash conversion cycle (CCC)** is defined as follows:

$$CCC = \text{Inventory Days} + \text{Accounts Receivable Days} - \text{Accounts Payable Days} \quad (19.1)$$

where

$$\text{Inventory Days} = \frac{\text{Inventory}}{\text{Average Daily Cost of Goods Sold}}$$

$$\text{Accounts Receivable Days} = \frac{\text{Accounts Receivable}}{\text{Average Daily Sales}}$$

$$\text{Accounts Payable Days} = \frac{\text{Accounts Payable}}{\text{Average Daily Cost of Goods Sold}}$$

All of these ratios can be computed from the firm's financial statements. We discussed how to compute and use them in Chapter 2. Even though the cash conversion cycle is an important metric on its own, a financial manager needs to keep an eye on each of its components, as they all contain valuable information about how efficiently the firm is managing its working capital. Higher accounts receivable days may signal that the firm is having trouble collecting from its customers, and low accounts payable days might suggest that the firm is not taking full advantage of opportunities

EXAMPLE 19.1 Computing the Cash Conversion Cycle

PROBLEM

The following information is from Loblaw's 2013 income statement and balance sheet (numbers are $millions). Use it to compute Loblaw's cash conversion cycle.

Sales	32,371
Cost of Merchandise Inventories Sold	24,696
Accounts Receivable	618
Inventories	2084
Accounts Payable	3797

SOLUTION

Plan

The CCC is defined above as Inventory Days + Accounts Receivable Days − Accounts Payable Days. Thus, we need to compute each of the three ratios in the CCC. In order to do that, we need to convert Sales and Cost of Goods Sold (COGS) into their average daily amounts simply by dividing the total given for the year by 365 days in a year.

Execute

Average Daily Sales = Sales/365 Days = 32,371/365 = 88.69

Average Daily *COGS* = *COGS*/365 Days = 24,696/365 = 67.66

$$\text{Inventory Days} = \frac{\text{Inventory}}{\text{Average Daily Cost of Goods Sold}} = \frac{2084}{67.66} = 30.80$$

$$\text{Accounts Receivable Days} = \frac{\text{Accounts Receivable}}{\text{Average Daily Sales}} = \frac{618}{88.69} = 6.97$$

$$\text{Accounts Payable Days} = \frac{\text{Accounts Payable}}{\text{Average Daily Cost of Goods Sold}} = \frac{3797}{67.66} = 56.12$$

Thus, Loblaw's *CCC* = 30.80 + 6.97 − 56.12 = −18.35!

Evaluate

Loblaw actually has a *negative* cash conversion cycle, meaning that it generally receives cash for its goods *before* it pays its suppliers. Loblaw is able to do this because it sells directly to the consumer, so it charges your credit card or receives cash as soon as you make your purchase. This results in a relatively low receivables balance. At the same time, Loblaw's suppliers allow it to wait over 56 days before paying them. This more than offsets the number of days capital is tied up in inventory and receivables.

to delay payment to suppliers. Finally, high inventory days would focus a manager on why the firm needs to have its inventory on hand so long before it sells the product.

Working Capital Needs by Industry

The longer a firm's cash cycle, the more working capital the firm has, and the more cash it needs to carry to conduct its daily operations. Table 19.1 provides data on the working capital needs for selected firms in a variety of industries. Because of the characteristics of the different industries, working capital levels vary significantly. As illustrated in the previous example, a retail store typically sells on a cash-only basis, so you would expect accounts receivable to be a very small percentage of its sales.[1]

[1]When you use your Visa or MasterCard to pay for your groceries, it is a cash sale for the store. The credit card company pays the store cash on receipt of the credit slip, even if you do not pay your credit card bill on time.

TABLE 19.1 Working Capital in Various Industries

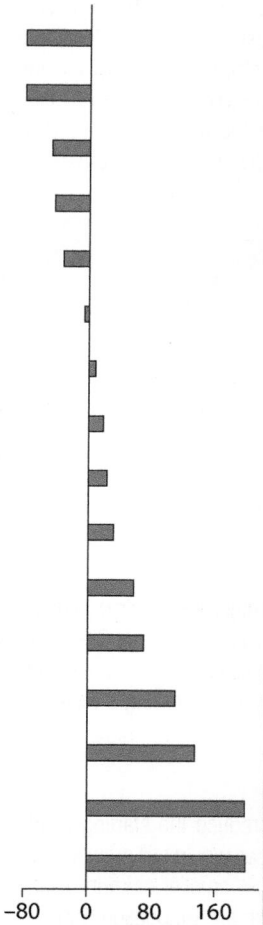

Company	Industry Group	Type of Business	Accounts Receivable Days	Inventory Days	Accounts Payable Days	CCC
TransCanada Corporation	Energy	Natural Gas Transmission and Power Services	62	30	215	–122
Air Canada	Transportation	Mainline Airline	17	19	152	–116
Ritchie Bros Auctioneers	Commercial & Professional Services	Auctioneer	37	154	239	–48
BlackBerry	Software & Services	Infrastructure Software	69	20	133	–44
Cineplex	Media	Movies & Entertainment	27	19	78	–32
BCE	Telecommunication Services	Diversified Telecommunications	48	11	65	–7
Canadian Tire	Retailing	Multiline Retail	17	72	81	8
Sleep Country Canada	Retailing	Furniture Stores	7	32	20	20
Cott Corporation	Food, Beverage & Tobacco	Beverages	45	40	61	24
Magna International	Automobiles & Components	Auto Parts	61	34	63	32
West Fraser Timber Company	Materials	Paper & Forest Products	19	60	21	58
Lundin Mining	Materials	Base Metals	53	74	56	70
Bombardier	Capital Goods	Aircraft and Railroad Rolling Stock	26	150	64	112
Kinross Gold Corporation	Materials	Gold Mining	1	146	11	136
Valeant Pharmaceuticals	Pharmaceuticals & Biotechnology	Pharmaceuticals	97	151	50	199
Canada Goose Holdings	Consumer Durables & Apparel	Apparel & Textile Production	12	233	45	200

Source: Most current fiscal year-end data as of May 28, 2018. Data from company filings, Bloomberg, and author's calculations. Note, numbers shown are rounded to the whole day; the CCC calculation is based on unrounded numbers.

Sleep Country, seen in Table 19.1, also has very low accounts receivable balances as a percentage of sales. Similar results hold for airlines (see Air Canada) because many of its customers pay in advance for airline tickets with cash or credit cards. Inventory represents a large percentage of sales for biotechnology, manufacturing and mining firms (see Valeant Pharmaceuticals, Bombardier and Kinross Gold) which have a long development or production times and long sales cycles. Note also the wide variation in the firms' cash conversion cycles. For example, Air Canada's cash conversion cycle is negative (–116 days), reflecting the fact that it receives cash from its customers before having to pay its suppliers, whereas Canada Goose's cash conversion cycle is quite long (200 days) due to the very long time it has product in inventory and the fact that it is slower to collect from customers than it is in paying suppliers.

Firm Value and Working Capital

To understand why working capital management can increase firm value, recall that any funds your company has from investors need to earn an opportunity cost of capital for those investors. Working capital ties up funds that could be deployed elsewhere in the firm to earn a return. For example, imagine $50,000 in raw materials sitting in a factory waiting to be used. That $50,000 needs to earn a return, so any delay in converting that material into a product that can be sold reduces its return. If you could improve your production process so that at any one time only $30,000 of raw material was waiting to be used, you would have freed up $20,000 to be invested elsewhere or returned to the shareholders. Similarly, when you allow your customers to pay within 30 days, you are giving them a 30-day interest-free loan. However, your investors and banks have not given you interest-free funds! If you can reduce the time it takes customers to pay without reducing sales, you can improve the return your investors earn on the business.

Any reduction in working capital requirements generates a positive free cash flow that the firm can distribute immediately to shareholders. For example, if a firm is able to reduce its

EXAMPLE 19.2 The Value of Working Capital Management

PROBLEM

The projected net income and free cash flows next year for River City Paints are given in the following table (in $thousands):

Net Income	20,000
+ Depreciation	+5000
− Capital Expenditures	−5000
− Increase in Working Capital	−1000
= Free Cash Flow	19,000

River City expects capital expenditures and depreciation to continue to offset each other, and both net income and increase in working capital to grow at 4% per year. River City's cost of capital is 12%. If River City were able reduce its annual increase in working capital by 20% by managing its working capital more efficiently without adversely affecting any other part of the business, what would be the effect on River City's value?

SOLUTION

Plan

A 20% decrease in required working capital from its starting point would reduce the starting point from $1,000,000 per year to $800,000 per year. The working capital increases would still grow at 4% per year, but each increase would then be 20% smaller because of the 20% smaller starting point. We can value River City using the formula for a growing perpetuity from Chapter 4 (Equation 4.7):

$$PV = \frac{\text{Cash Flow}}{r - g}$$

We can calculate River City's free cash flow using the information contained in the table above: Net Income + Depreciation − Capital Expenditures − Increases in Working Capital.

Execute

Currently, River City's value is as follows:

$$\frac{20{,}000{,}000 + 5{,}000{,}000 - 5{,}000{,}000 - 1{,}000{,}000}{0.12 - 0.04} = 237{,}500{,}000$$

If the company can manage its working capital more efficiently, the value will be as follows:

$$\frac{20{,}000{,}000 + 5{,}000{,}000 - 5{,}000{,}000 - 800{,}000}{0.12 - 0.04} = 240{,}000{,}000$$

Evaluate

Although the change will not affect River City's earnings (net income), it will increase the free cash flow available to shareholders and increase the value of the firm by $2.5 million.

required net working capital by $50,000, it will be able to distribute this $50,000 as a dividend to its shareholders immediately, or use it as a source of funds for other productive projects.

Recall that the Valuation Principle implies that the value of the firm is the present value of its free cash flows. Managing working capital efficiently will increase those free cash flows, allowing a manager to maximize firm value. We now turn our attention to some specific working capital accounts.

CONCEPT CHECK

1. What is the difference between a firm's cash cycle and operating cycle?
2. How does working capital affect a firm's value?

19.2 Trade Credit

When a firm allows a customer to pay for goods at some date later than the date of purchase, it creates an account receivable for the firm and an account payable for the customer. Accounts receivable represent the credit sales for which a firm has yet to receive payment. The accounts payable balance represents the amount that a firm owes its suppliers for goods that it has received but for which it has not yet paid. The credit that the firm is extending to its customer is known as **trade credit**; the difference between receivables and payables is the net amount of a firm's capital consumed as a result of those credit transactions. A firm would, of course, prefer to be paid in cash at the time of purchase. A "cash only" policy, however, may cause it to lose its customers to competition. Even after a customer decides to pay a bill, there is a delay before the money is credited to the firm because of processing and mailing the payment. In this section, we demonstrate how managers can compare the costs and benefits of trade credit to determine optimal credit policies.

trade credit The difference between receivables and payables that is the net amount of a firm's capital consumed as a result of those credit transactions; the credit that a firm extends to its customers.

Trade Credit Terms

To see how the terms of trade credit are quoted, let's consider some examples. If a supplier offers its customers terms of "net 30," payment is not due until 30 days from the date of the invoice. Essentially, the supplier is letting the customer use its money for an extra 30 days. (Note that "30" is not a magic number; the invoice could specify "net 40," "net 15," or any other number of days as the payment due date.)

Sometimes the selling firm will offer the buying firm a discount if payment is made early. The terms "2/10, net 30" mean that the buying firm will receive a 2% discount if it pays for the goods within 10 days; otherwise, the full amount is due in 30 days. The **cash discount** is the percentage discount offered if the buyer pays early, in this case 2%. The **discount period** is the number of days the buyer has to take advantage of the cash discount; here it is 10 days. Finally, the **credit period** is the total length of time credit is extended to the buyer—the total amount of time the buyer has to pay. It is 30 days in our example. Firms offer discounts to encourage customers to pay early so that the selling firm gets cash from the sale sooner. However, the amount of the discount also represents a cost to the selling firm, because it does not receive the full selling price for the product. This timeline shows the terms of our 2/10, net 30 example:

cash discount The percentage discount offered on a payment if the buyer pays early.

discount period The number of days a buyer has to take advantage of the cash discount.

credit period The total length of time credit is extended to the buyer.

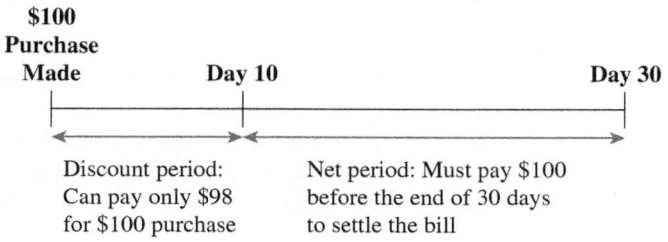

COMMON MISTAKE

Using APR Instead of EAR to Compute the Cost of Trade Credit

Some managers fail to fully recognize the cost of trade credit by using the annual percentage rate (APR, or simple interest) rather than the effective annual rate (EAR) to compute the annual cost for comparison with other financing options. Recall from Chapter 5 that whereas the EAR appropriately accounts for the compounding "interest on interest" effect over the year, the APR ignores compounding. Thus, in our example below with 2.04% interest over 20 days, the corresponding APR would be (365/20) × 2.04 = 37.23%, which is less than the true effective annual cost of this credit: 44.6%.

Trade Credit and Market Frictions

In a perfectly competitive market, trade credit is just another form of financing. As we learned in Chapter 16, financing decisions are irrelevant under the assumptions of perfect capital markets. In reality, product markets are rarely perfectly competitive, so firms can maximize their value by using their trade credit options effectively.

Cost of Trade Credit. Trade credit is, in essence, a loan from the selling firm to its customer. The price discount represents an interest rate. Often, firms offer favourable interest rates on trade credit as a price discount to their customers. Therefore, financial managers should evaluate the terms of trade credit to decide whether to use it.

How do we compute the interest rate on trade credit? Suppose a firm sells a product for $100 but offers its customer terms of 2/10, net 30. The customer doesn't have to pay anything for the first 10 days, so it effectively has a zero-interest loan for this period. If the customer takes advantage of the discount and pays within the 10-day discount period, he or she pays only $98 for the product. The cost of the discount to the selling firm is equal to the discount percentage times the selling price. In this case, it is 0.02 × $100, or $2.

Rather than pay within 10 days, the customer has the option to use the $98 for an additional 20 days (30 − 10 = 20). The interest rate for the 20-day term of the loan is $2/$98 = 2.04%. To compare this 20-day interest rate with interest rates available from other financing sources, we convert it to an EAR using Equation 5.1 from Chapter 5, where n is the number of 20-day periods in a year:

$$EAR = (1 + r)^n - 1$$

With a 365-day year, there are 365/20 (18.25) 20-day periods in a year. Thus, this 2.04% rate over 20 days corresponds to the following EAR:

$$= (1.0204)^{365/20} - 1 = 44.6\%$$

Therefore, by not taking the discount, the firm is effectively paying 2.04% to borrow the money for 20 days, which translates to an EAR of 44.6%! If the firm can obtain a bank loan at a lower interest rate, it would be better off borrowing at the lower rate and using the cash proceeds of the loan to take advantage of the discount offered by the supplier.

Benefits of Trade Credit. For a number of reasons, trade credit can be an attractive source of funds. First, trade credit is simple and convenient to use, and it has lower transaction costs than alternative sources of funds. For example, no paperwork must be completed, as would be the case for a loan from a bank. Second, it is a flexible source of funds and can be used as needed. Finally, it is sometimes the only source of funding available to a firm.

EXAMPLE 19.3 Estimating the Effective Cost of Trade Credit

PROBLEM

Your firm purchases goods from its supplier on terms of 1/15, net 40. What is the effective annual cost to your firm if it chooses not to take advantage of the trade discount offered?

SOLUTION

■ Plan

Using a $100 purchase as an example, 1/15, net 40 means that you get a 1% discount if you pay within 15 days, or you can pay the full amount within 40 days. One percent of $100 is a $1 discount, so you can either pay $99 in 15 days, or $100 in 40 days. The difference is 25 days, so you need to compute the interest rate over the 25 days and then compute the EAR associated with that 25-day interest rate.

■ Execute

The implied interest rate is $1/$99 = 0.0101, or 1.01% for 25 days. There are 365/25 = 15.6 periods of 25 days in a year. Thus, your effective annual rate is $(1.0101)^{14.6} - 1 = 0.158$, or 15.8%.

■ Evaluate

If you really need to take the full 40 days to produce the cash to pay, you would be better off borrowing the $99 from the bank at a lower rate and taking advantage of the discount.

Trade Credit versus Standard Loans. You might wonder why companies would ever provide trade credit. After all, most companies are not banks, so why are they in the business of making loans? Several reasons explain their willingness to offer trade credit. First, providing financing at below-market rates is an indirect way to lower prices for only certain customers. Consider, for example, an automobile manufacturer. Rather than lowering prices on all cars, the financing division may offer specific credit terms that are attractive to customers with bad credit, but unattractive to customers with good credit. In this way, the car manufacturer is able to discount the price only for those customers with bad credit who otherwise might not be able to afford the car.

Second, because a supplier may have an ongoing business relationship with its customer, it may have more information about the credit quality of the customer than a traditional outside lender such as a bank would have. The supplier may also be able to increase the likelihood of payment by threatening to cut off future supplies if payment is not made. Finally, if the buyer defaults, the supplier may be able to seize the inventory as collateral. This inventory is likely to be more valuable to a company within the industry, such as the supplier (which presumably has other customers), than to an outsider.

Managing Float

One factor that contributes to the length of a firm's receivables and payables is the delay between the time a bill is paid and the time the cash is actually received. This delay, or processing float, will affect a firm's working capital requirements.

collection float The amount of time it takes for a firm to be able to use funds after a customer has paid for its goods.

mail float The time it takes a firm to receive a customer's payment cheque after the customer has mailed it.

Collection Float. The amount of time it takes for a firm to be able to use funds after a customer has paid for its goods is referred to as **collection float**. Firms can reduce their working capital needs by reducing their collection float. Collection float is determined by three factors, as shown in Figure 19.2:

- **Mail float:** The time it takes the firm to receive a payment cheque after the customer has mailed it.

FIGURE 19.2 Collection Float

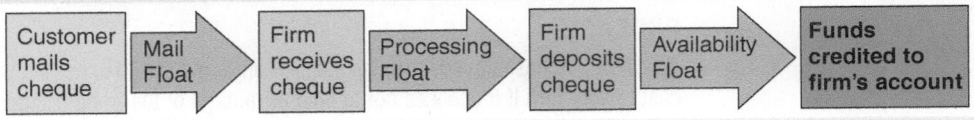

processing float The time it takes a firm to process a customer's payment cheque and deposit it in the bank.

availability float The time it takes a bank to give a firm credit for customer payments the firm has deposited in the bank.

disbursement float The amount of time it takes before a firm's payments to its suppliers actually result in a cash outflow for the firm.

- **Processing float**: The time it takes the firm to process a customer's payment cheque and deposit it in the bank.
- **Availability float**: The time it takes a bank to post the funds from customer payments the firm has deposited in the bank.

Disbursement Float. The amount of time it takes before payments to suppliers actually result in a cash outflow for the firm is referred to as **disbursement float**. Similar to the collection float, it is a function of mail time, processing time, and cheque-clearing time. Although a firm may try to extend its disbursement float in order to lengthen its payables and reduce its working capital needs, it risks making late payments to suppliers. In such a case, the firm may be charged an additional fee for paying late or may be required to pay cash before delivery (CBD) or cash on delivery (COD) for future purchases. In some cases, the supplier may refuse to do business in the future with the delinquent firm.

Electronic Cheque Processing. Firms can employ several methods to reduce their collection and disbursement floats. In addition, many countries have streamlined the way cheques are handled. In the 1980s, Singapore began making electronic images of cheques. By 2001, the cheque-clearing systems in Singapore, Spain, the United Kingdom, and Australia allowed for the clearing of cheques through the use of image transmissions rather than physically moving actual paper cheques. In 2004, the United States adopted such a system. In Canada, the Canadian Payments Association had been working on the "Truncation and Electronic Cheque Presentment" system, with a goal of implementation by 2009. The 11-year-old project was scrapped in October of 2008, and banks have developed and implemented their own imaging projects to try to gain efficiencies. These systems allow for cheques to clear more quickly. As the efficiency increases, it may be possible for financial institutions to reduce the hold period that is sometimes applied when a cheque is deposited. If this occurs, then a firm's collection float would be reduced. So far, though, evidence from the United States shows that even though the funds are taken out of the cheque writer's account almost immediately, the cheque recipient's account is not credited as quickly.

There are, however, several ways that a firm *can* reduce its collection float. For example, the firm may streamline its in-house cheque processing procedures. In addition, with electronic collection, funds are automatically transferred from the customer's bank account to the firm's bank account on the payment date, reducing the collection float to zero. The methods a firm employs to reduce its collection float are not without costs, of course. New cheque-processing systems could be expensive and disruptive, and hiring a collection agency to speed up collections generates costs, such as fees to the agency, and bad will with the firm's customers. Therefore, to decide which method, if any, to employ, the firm must compare the costs and benefits of systems that allow it to use its cash for a longer period.

CONCEPT CHECK

3. What does the term "2/10, net 30" mean?
4. List three factors that determine collection float.

19.3 Receivables Management

So far, we have discussed the costs and benefits of trade credit in general. Next, we look at some issues that arise specifically from the management of a firm's accounts receivables. In particular, we focus on how a firm adopts a policy for offering credit to its customers and how it monitors its accounts receivable on an ongoing basis.

Determining the Credit Policy

Establishing a credit policy involves three steps that we will discuss in turn:

1. Establishing credit standards
2. Establishing credit terms
3. Establishing a collection policy

Establishing Credit Standards. Management must first decide on its credit standards. Will it extend credit to anyone who applies for it? Or will it be selective and extend credit only to those customers who have very low credit risk? Unless the firm adopts the former policy, it will need to assess the credit risk of each customer before deciding whether to grant credit. Large firms perform this analysis in-house with their own credit departments. Small firms purchase credit reports from credit rating agencies such as Dun & Bradstreet.

Many firms will consider additional factors when deciding whether to grant credit to a particular customer. For example, in order to win sales a firm may be more likely to grant credit if the customer is expected to be a repeat customer. If the cost of the credit is small relative to the purchase price, the firm may also adopt a less restrictive policy. Thus, while credit risk is the starting point, the firm's managers may choose to extend credit strategically when dealing with potentially important customers or high-margin sales.

THE 5 C'S OF CREDIT

Lenders have coined the phrase "the 5 C's of Credit" to summarize the qualities they look for before granting credit:

Character: Is the borrower trustworthy, with a history of meeting its debt obligations?
Capacity: Will the borrower have enough cash flow to make its payments?
Capital: Does the borrower have enough capital (net worth) to justify the loan?
Collateral: Does the borrower have any assets that can secure the loan?
Conditions: How are the borrower and the economy performing and how are they expected to perform?

The decision of how much credit risk to assume plays a large role in determining how much money a firm ties up in its receivables. Although a restrictive policy can result in a lower sales volume, the firm will have a smaller investment in receivables. Conversely, a less selective policy will produce higher sales, but the level of receivables will also rise.

Establishing Credit Terms. After a firm decides on its credit standards, it must next establish its credit terms. The firm decides on the length of the period before payment must be made (the "net" period) and chooses whether to offer a discount to encourage early payments. If it offers a discount, it must also determine the discount percentage and the discount period. If the firm is relatively small, it will probably follow the lead of other firms in the industry in establishing these terms.

EXAMPLE 19.4 Evaluating a Change in Credit Policy

PROBLEM

Your company currently sells its product with a 1% discount to customers who pay cash immediately. Otherwise, the full price is due within 30 days. Half of your customers take advantage of the discount. You are considering dropping the discount so that your new terms would just be net 30. If you do that, you expect to lose some customers who were willing to pay only the discounted price, but the rest will simply switch to taking the full 30 days to pay. You estimate that you will sell 20 fewer units per month (compared to 500 units currently). Your variable cost per unit is $60, and your price per unit is $100. If your required return is 1% per month, should you change your policy?

SOLUTION

■ Plan

To decide whether to change your policy, compute the NPV of the change. It costs you $30,000 to make the 500 units. You receive payment for half of the units immediately at a price of $99 per unit (1% discount). The other half of the payment comes in 30 days at a price of $100 per unit. At that point, you are starting over again with the next set of product. Thus, you can think of your cash flows now and in any 30-day period as shown in the table below:

	Now	30 days
Produce first set of 500 units at $60 apiece	−30,000	
Customers pay for 250 units at $99 apiece	+24,750	
Customers pay for 250 units at $100 apiece		+25,000
Produce next set of 500 units at $60 apiece		−30,000
Customers pay for 250 units at $99 apiece		+24,750
Total	**−5250**	**+25,000 − 5250**

Under the new policy, your cash flows would change to the following:

	Now	30 days
Produce first set of 480 units at $60 apiece	28,800	
Customers pay for 480 units at $100 apiece		+48,000
Produce next set of 480 units at $60 apiece		−28,800
Total	**−28,800**	**+48,000 − 28,800**

The "30 days" cash flows repeat every 30 days in perpetuity, so with these cash flows, we are ready to compute the NPV of each alternative by considering the upfront outflow now plus the present value of a perpetuity of inflows. We can then compute the NPV of the policy change.

■ Execute

$$NPV_{current} = -5250 + \frac{25{,}000 - 5250}{0.01} = 1{,}969{,}750$$

$$NPV_{new} = -28{,}800 + \frac{48{,}000 - 28{,}800}{0.01} = 1{,}891{,}200$$

So the NPV of the policy change will be $1,969,750 − $1,891,200 = −$78,550.

■ Evaluate

You shouldn't make the change in credit policy because you will lose too many customers, even though your remaining customers will be paying the full price. The NPV helps us weigh this trade-off—the present value of the costs outweighs the present value of the benefits, so the decision is not a good one.

Establishing a Collection Policy. The last step in the development of a credit policy is to decide on a collection policy. The content of this policy can range from doing nothing if a customer is paying late (generally not a good choice), to sending a polite letter of inquiry, to charging interest on payments extending beyond a specified period, to threatening legal action at the first late payment.

Monitoring Accounts Receivable

After establishing a credit policy, a firm must monitor its accounts receivable to analyze whether its credit policy is working effectively. Two tools that firms use to monitor the accounts receivable are the *accounts receivable days* (or average collection period) and the *aging schedule.*

accounts receivable days The average number of days that a firm takes to collect on its sales.

Accounts Receivable Days. The **accounts receivable days** is the average number of days that it takes a firm to collect on its sales. A firm can compare this number to the payment policy specified in its credit terms to judge the effectiveness of its credit policy. If the credit terms specify "net 30" and the accounts receivable days outstanding is 50 days, the firm can conclude that its customers are paying 20 days late, on average.

The firm should also look at the trend in the accounts receivable days over time. If the accounts receivable days ratio of a firm has been approximately 35 days for the past few years and it is 43 days this year, the firm may want to re-examine its credit policy. Of course, if the economy is sluggish, the entire industry may be affected. Under these circumstances, the increase might have little to do with the firm itself.

Accounts receivable days can be calculated from the firm's financial statement. Outside investors commonly use this measure to evaluate a firm's credit management policy. A major weakness of the accounts receivable days is that it is merely one number and conceals much useful information. Seasonal sales patterns may cause the number calculated for the accounts receivable days to change depending on when the calculation takes place. The number can also look reasonable even when a substantial percentage of the firm's customers are paying late.

aging schedule Categorizes a firm's accounts by the number of days they have been on the firm's books. It can be prepared using either the number of accounts or the dollar amount of the accounts receivable outstanding.

Aging Schedule. An **aging schedule** categorizes accounts by the number of days they have been on the firm's books. It can be prepared using either the number of accounts or the dollar amount of the accounts receivable outstanding. For example, assume that a firm selling on terms of 2/15, net 30 has $530,000 in accounts receivable that has been on the books for 15 or fewer days in 220 accounts. The firm has another $450,000 that has been on the books for 16 to 30 days and is made up of 190 accounts, and $350,000 has been on the books for 31 to 45 days and represents 80 accounts. The firm has $200,000 that has been on the books for 46 to 60 days in 60 accounts. Yet another $70,000 has been on the books for more than 60 days and is made up of 20 accounts. Table 19.2 includes aging schedules based on the number of accounts and dollar amounts outstanding.

In this case, if the firm's average daily sales are $65,000, its accounts receivable days is $1,600,000/$65,000 = 25 days. But on closer examination, using the aging schedules in Table 19.2, we can see that 28% of the firm's credit customers (and 39% by dollar amounts) are paying late.

If the aging schedule gets "bottom-heavy"—that is, if the percentages in the lower half of the schedule, representing late-paying firms, begin to increase—the firm will probably need to revisit its credit policy. The aging schedule is also sometimes augmented by analysis of the **payments pattern**, which provides information on the percentage of monthly sales for which the firm collects payment in each month after the sale. By examining past data, a firm may observe that 10% of its sales are usually collected in the month of the sale, 40% in the month following the sale, 25% two months after the sale, 20% three months after the sale, and 5% four months after the sale. Management can compare this normal payments pattern to the current payments pattern. Knowledge of the payments pattern is also useful for forecasting the firm's working capital requirements.

payments pattern The pattern of the percentage of monthly sales for which the firm collects payment in each month after the sale.

TABLE 19.2 Aging Schedules

(a) Number of Accounts

Days Outstanding	Number of Accounts	Percentage of Accounts (%)
1–15	220	38.6
16–30	190	33.3
31–45	80	14.0
46–60	60	10.5
60+	20	3.5
	570	100.0

(b) Dollar Amounts Outstanding

Days Outstanding	Amount Outstanding ($)	Percentage Outstanding (%)
1–15	530,000	33.1
16–30	450,000	28.1
31–45	350,000	21.9
46–60	200,000	12.5
60+	70,000	4.4
	1,600,000	100.0

EXAMPLE 19.5 Aging Schedules

PROBLEM

Financial Training Systems (FTS) bills its accounts on terms of 3/10, net 30. The firm's accounts receivable include $100,000 that has been outstanding for 10 or fewer days, $300,000 outstanding for 11 to 30 days, $100,000 outstanding for 31 to 40 days, $20,000 outstanding for 41 to 50 days, $10,000 outstanding for 51 to 60 days, and $2000 outstanding for more than 60 days. Prepare an aging schedule for FTS.

SOLUTION

■ Plan

An aging schedule shows the amount and percentage of total accounts receivable outstanding for different lengths outstanding. With the available information, we can calculate the aging schedule based on dollar amounts outstanding.

■ Execute

Days Outstanding	Amount Outstanding ($)	Percentage Outstanding (%)
1–10	100,000	18.8
11–30	300,000	56.4
31–40	100,000	18.8
41–50	20,000	3.8
51–60	10,000	1.9
60+	2000	0.4
	532,000	100.0

■ **Evaluate**

FTS does not have an excessive percentage outstanding at the long-end of the table (only 6% of the company's accounts receivable are more than 40 days outstanding).

CONCEPT CHECK

5. Describe three steps in establishing a credit policy.
6. What is the difference between accounts receivable days and an aging schedule?

19.4 Payables Management

A firm should choose to borrow using accounts payable only if trade credit is the cheapest source of funding. The cost of the trade credit depends on the credit terms. The higher the discount percentage offered, the greater the cost of foregoing the discount. The cost of foregoing the discount is also higher with a shorter loan period. When a company has a choice between trade credit from two different suppliers, it should take the least expensive alternative.

In addition, a firm should always pay on the latest day allowed. For example, if the discount period is 10 days and the firm is taking the discount, payment should be made on day 10, not on day 2. If the discount is not taken and the terms are 2/10, net 30, the full payment should be made on day 30, not on day 16. A firm should strive to keep its money working for it as long as possible without developing a bad relationship with its suppliers or engaging in unethical practices. In this section, we examine two techniques that firms use to monitor their accounts payable.

Determining Accounts Payable Days Outstanding

Similar to the situation with its accounts receivable, a firm should monitor its accounts payable to ensure that it is making its payments at an optimal time. One method is to calculate the accounts payable days outstanding and compare it to the credit terms. The accounts payable days outstanding is the accounts payable balance expressed in terms of the number of days of cost of goods sold. If the accounts payable outstanding is 40 days and the terms are 2/10, net 30, the firm can conclude that it generally pays late and may be risking supplier difficulties. Conversely, if the accounts payable days outstanding is 25 days and the firm has not been taking the discount, the firm is paying too early. It could be earning another five days' interest on its money.

EXAMPLE 19.6 Accounts Payable Management

PROBLEM

The Rowd Company has an average accounts payable balance of $250,000. Its average daily cost of goods sold is $14,000, and it receives terms of 2/15, net 40 from its suppliers. Rowd chooses to forgo the discount. Is the firm managing its accounts payable well?

SOLUTION

Plan

Given Rowd's accounts payable balance and its daily COGS, we can compute the average number of days Rowd takes to pay its vendors by dividing the average balance by the daily costs. Given the terms from its suppliers, Rowd should either be paying on the 15th day (the last possible day to get the discount) or on the 40th day (the last possible day to pay). There is no benefit to paying at any other time.

Execute

Rowd's accounts payable days outstanding is \$250,000/\$14,000 = 17.9 days. If Rowd made payment three days earlier, it could take advantage of the 2% discount. If, for some reason, it chose to forgo the discount, it should not be paying the full amount until the 40th day.

Evaluate

The firm is not managing its accounts payable well. The earlier it pays, the sooner the cash leaves Rowd. Thus, the only reason to pay before the 40th day is to receive the discount by paying before the 15th day. Paying on the 18th day not only misses the discount but also costs the firm 22 days (40 − 18) use of its cash.

Stretching Accounts Payable

stretching the accounts payable A firm's practice of ignoring a payment due period and paying later.

Some firms ignore the payment due period and pay the amount owed later, in a practice referred to as **stretching the accounts payable.** Given terms of 2/10, net 30, for example, a firm may choose not to pay the amount owed until 45 days have passed. Doing so reduces the direct cost of trade credit because it lengthens the time that a firm has use of the funds. Although the interest rate per period remains the same—\$2/\$98 = 2.04%—the firm is now using the \$98 for 35 days beyond the discount period, rather than 20 days as provided by the trade credit terms.

EXAMPLE 19.7 Cost of Trade Credit with Stretched Accounts Payable

PROBLEM

What is the effective annual cost of credit terms of 1/15, net 40 if the firm stretches the accounts payable to 60 days?

SOLUTION

Plan

First, we need to compute the interest rate per period. The 1% discount means that on a \$100 purchase, you can either pay \$99 in the discount period, or keep the \$99 and pay \$100 later. Thus, you pay \$1 interest on the \$99. If you pay on time, then this \$1 in interest is over the 25-day period between the 15th day and the 40th day. If you stretch, then this \$1 in interest is over the 45-day period between the 15th day and the 60th day.

Execute

The interest rate per period is \$1/\$99 = 1.01%. If the firm delays payment until the 60th day, it has use of the funds for 45 days beyond the discount period. There are 365/45 = 8.11 45-day periods in one year. Thus, the effective annual cost is $(1.0101)^{8.11} - 1 = 0.0849$, or 8.49%.

■ **Evaluate**

Paying on time corresponds to a 25-day credit period, and there are 365/25 = 14.6 periods of 25 days in a year. Thus, if the firm pays on the 40th day, the effective annual cost is $(1.0101)^{14.6} - 1 = 0.1580$, or 15.8%. By stretching its payables, the firm substantially reduces its effective cost of credit.

Firms may also make a payment on the 30th day but pay only the discounted price. Some may pay only the discounted price and pay even later than the 30th day. Although all of these actions will reduce the effective annual rate associated with the trade credit, the firm may incur costs as a result of these actions. Suppliers may react to a firm whose payments are always late by imposing terms of cash on delivery (COD) or cash before delivery (CBD). The delinquent firm then bears the additional costs associated with these terms and may have to negotiate a bank loan to have the cash available to pay. The supplier may also discontinue business with the delinquent customer, leaving the customer to find another source, which may be more expensive or of lower quality. A poor credit rating might also result, making it difficult for the firm to obtain good terms with any other supplier. Moreover, when a firm explicitly agrees to the terms of the sale, violating these terms constitutes unethical business behaviour.

CONCEPT CHECK

7. What is the optimal time for a firm to pay its accounts payable?
8. What do the terms "COD" and "CBD" mean?

19.5 Inventory Management

As we discussed earlier, in a perfect capital markets setting, firms would not need to have accounts payable or receivable. Interest rates on trade credit would be competitive, and firms could use alternative sources of financing. However, unlike trade credit, inventory represents one of the required factors of production. Therefore, even in a perfect markets setting, firms still need inventory.

Inventory management receives extensive coverage in a course on operations management. Nevertheless, it is the firm's financial manager who must arrange for the financing necessary to support the firm's inventory policy and who is responsible for ensuring the firm's overall profitability. Therefore, the role of the inventory manager is to balance the costs and benefits associated with inventory. Because excessive inventory uses cash, efficient management of inventory increases firm value.

Benefits of Holding Inventory

For several reasons, a firm needs its inventory to operate. First, inventory helps minimize the risk that the firm will not be able to obtain an input it needs for production. If a firm holds too little inventory, a **stock-out**—running out of inventory—may occur and lead to lost sales. Disappointed customers may switch to one of the firm's competitors.

stock-out The situation in which a firm runs out of inventory.

Second, firms may hold inventory because factors such as seasonality in demand mean that customer purchases do not perfectly match the most efficient production cycle. Consider the case of the Snowdrift Toy Company. As is typical for many toy manufacturers, 80% of Snowdrift's annual sales occur between September and December, in anticipation of the holiday gift season. It is more efficient for Snowdrift to manufacture toys at relatively constant levels throughout the year. If Snowdrift produces its toys at a constant rate, its inventory levels will increase to very high levels by August, in anticipation of the increase in sales beginning in September. In contrast, Snowdrift may consider a seasonal manufacturing strategy, producing more toys between September and December when sales are high. Under this strategy, inventory would not accumulate, freeing up cash flow from working capital and reducing the costs of inventory. However, seasonal manufacturing incurs additional costs, such as increased wear and tear on the manufacturing equipment during peak demand and the need to hire and train seasonal workers. Snowdrift must weigh the costs of the inventory buildup under constant production against the benefits of more efficient production. The optimal choice is likely to involve a compromise between the two extremes, so Snowdrift will carry some inventory.

INVENTORY MANAGEMENT ADDS TO THE BOTTOM LINE AT GAP

In 2003, the apparel chain GAP reduced its investment in inventory significantly by reducing its inventory days outstanding by 24%. This change freed up $344 million for other purposes. GAP invested some of this cash in short-term securities—primarily in U.S. government and agency securities, and in bank certificates of deposit with maturities between three months and one year. The firm reported an increase of *$1.2 million* in interest income in fiscal year 2003 compared with fiscal year 2002. It attributed the increase in interest income to increases in the average cash balances available for investment.

Source: GAP 2003 annual report.

Costs of Holding Inventory

As suggested by the Snowdrift Toy example, tying up capital in inventory is costly for a firm. We can classify the direct costs associated with inventory into three categories:

- *Acquisition costs* are the costs of the inventory itself over the period being analyzed (usually one year).
- *Order costs* are the total costs of placing an order over the period being analyzed.
- *Carrying costs* include storage costs, insurance, taxes, spoilage, obsolescence, and the opportunity cost of the funds tied up in the inventory.

Minimizing these total costs involves some trade-offs. For example, if we assume no quantity discounts are available, the lower the level of inventory a firm carries, the lower its carrying cost but the higher its annual order costs because it needs to place more orders during the year.

"just-in-time" (JIT) inventory management
The practice of acquiring inventory precisely when the firm needs it so that the firm's inventory balance is always zero, or very close to it.

Some firms seek to reduce their carrying costs as much as possible. With **"just-in-time" (JIT) inventory management**, a firm acquires inventory precisely when needed so that its inventory balance is always zero, or very close to it. This technique requires exceptional coordination with suppliers, as well as a predictable demand for the firm's products. In 2007, Boeing established a global production system for its new 787 "Dreamliner." Very little of the new plane is actually produced at its plant in Everett, Washington. Rather, all of the plane's major systems, including the fuselage and wings, are produced elsewhere and are flown to the final assembly plant using a specially modified 747 cargo plane. The pieces arrive very shortly before they are needed in the final assembly of the airplane, so Boeing does not have to incur the carrying costs of maintaining a large inventory. However, such a plan has risks, as Boeing initially had substantial troubles with its contracted producers finishing their parts on time. Consequently, the firm delayed the delivery of the first planes and faced significant financial penalties from doing so.

Even if your company does not practice JIT inventory management, it may be forced to adopt it if a major customer does so. For example, in 1999, Toys"R"Us instituted JIT, which caused one of its suppliers, toy manufacturer Hasbro, to make changes in its production schedule.[2]

CONCEPT CHECK

9. What are the direct costs of holding inventory?

10. Describe "just-in-time" inventory management.

19.6 Cash Management

In the perfect markets setting, the level of cash is irrelevant. With perfect capital markets, a firm is able to raise new money instantly at a fair rate, so it can never be short of cash. Similarly, the firm can invest excess cash at a fair rate to earn an NPV of zero.

In the real world, of course, markets are not perfect. Liquidity has a cost; for example, holding liquid assets may earn a below-market return, and a firm may incur transaction costs if it needs to raise cash quickly. Similarly, recall from Chapter 16 that holding excess cash has a tax disadvantage. In these cases, the optimal strategy for a firm is to hold cash in anticipation of seasonalities in demand for its products and random shocks that affect its business. Risky firms and firms with high-growth opportunities tend to hold a relatively high percentage of assets as cash. Firms with easy access to capital markets (for which the transaction costs of accessing cash are therefore lower) tend to hold less cash.[3] In this section, we examine the firm's motivation for holding cash, tools for managing cash, and the short-term securities in which firms invest.

Motivation for Holding Cash

A firm holds cash for three reasons:

- To meet its day-to-day needs
- To compensate for the uncertainty associated with its cash flows
- To satisfy bank requirements

We will now examine in detail each of these motivations for holding cash.

transactions balance
The amount of cash a firm needs to be able to pay its bills.

Transactions Balance. Just like you, a firm or business must hold enough cash to pay its bills. The amount of cash a firm needs to be able to pay its bills is sometimes referred to as a **transactions balance**. The amount of cash a firm needs to satisfy the transactions balance requirement depends on both the average size of the transactions made by the firm and the firm's cash cycle, discussed earlier in the chapter.

---

[2]Hasbro 1999 annual report.

[3]See T. Opler, L. Pinkowitz, R. Stulz, and R. Williamson, "The Determinants and Implications of Corporate Cash Holdings," *Journal of Financial Economics* 52 (1) (1999): 3–46.

precautionary balance
The amount of cash a firm holds to counter the uncertainty surrounding its future cash needs.

compensating balance
An amount a firm's bank may require the firm to maintain in an account at the bank as compensation for services the bank may perform.

Precautionary Balance. The amount of cash a firm holds to counter the uncertainty surrounding its future cash needs is known as a **precautionary balance.** The size of this balance depends on the degree of uncertainty surrounding a firm's cash flows. The more uncertain future cash flows are, the harder it is for a firm to predict its transactions need, so the larger the precautionary balance must be.

Compensating Balance. A firm's bank may require it to hold a **compensating balance** in an account at the bank as compensation for services that the bank performs. Compensating balances are typically deposited in accounts that either earn no interest or pay a very low interest rate. This arrangement is similar to a bank offering individuals free chequing as long as their balances do not fall below a certain level—say, $1000. Essentially, the customer has $1000 cash that she cannot use unless she is willing to pay a service charge. Similarly, the cash that a firm has tied up to meet a compensating balance requirement is unavailable for other uses.

CASH BALANCES

Corporate liquidity is measured as corporate investments in short-term, marketable securities. In the United States, it rose from $3.6 trillion in 1999 to $5.6 trillion in 2007, an increase of almost 55%. According to a 2004 survey of more than 360 companies conducted by Treasury Strategies Inc., a Chicago consultant, more than half of those firms consider themselves to be net investors, having more short-term investments than short-term debt outstanding.

Why have companies been accumulating more cash? Factors include a shift away from industries such as manufacturing that spend heavily on plant and equipment, strength in sectors such as financial services that have low capital expenditures and high cash flows, and reluctance by companies to invest heavily after the technology spending spree in the late 1990s. As a result, corporate savings have reached an all-time high.

How are companies investing their cash? A 2007 survey by Treasury Strategies indicated that 20% is invested in money market funds and accounts, 18% is invested in bonds and notes, and the remainder is invested directly in commercial paper, certificates of deposit, repurchase agreements, and other investments.

During the 2008 financial crisis, short-term credit markets froze, and many businesses that relied on short-term credit found themselves unable to conduct business. You might expect that businesses that held a lot of cash were in good shape. However, during the crisis, cash-holding firms did not know what to do with the cash. Before it became clear that governments were going to bail out large banks, firms had to worry about how secure their cash was. In the event of a bank bankruptcy, the firm risked losing access to its cash in the short term and perhaps ultimately losing the cash altogether. For firms that relied on cash balances to conduct business, the impact of the breakdown in financial markets was potentially as big as for firms that relied on credit.

Source: Authors' calculations from Federal Reserve Data and Treasury Strategies 2007 Corporate Liquidity Research Overview.

Alternative Investments

In our discussion of collection and disbursement floats, we assumed that the firm will invest any cash in short-term securities. In fact, the firm may choose from a variety of short-term securities that differ somewhat with regard to their default risk and liquidity risk. The greater the risk, the higher the expected return on the investment. The financial manager must decide how much risk she is willing to accept in return for a higher yield. If her firm expects to need the funds within the next 30 days, the manager will probably avoid the less liquid options. Table 19.3 briefly describes the most frequently used short-term investments; these short-term debt securities are collectively referred to as *money market securities.*

TABLE 19.3 Money Market Investment Options

Investment	Description	Maturity	Risk	Liquidity
Cash management bills (CMBs)	Very short-term debt of the Canadian government.	One day up to less than three months when newly issued.	Default risk free.	Very liquid and marketable.
Treasury bills	Short-term debt of the Canadian government. Provincial governments also issue their own treasury bills.	3, 6, or 12 months when newly issued.	Default risk free.	Very liquid and marketable.
Term deposits, certificates of deposit (CDs), guaranteed investment certificates (GICs)	Short-term debt issued by banks.	Term deposits have maturities up to one year. CD maturities are 30 days to five years. GIC maturities are one to five years.	If the issuing bank is insured by the CDIC, any amount up to $100,000 is free of default risk because it is covered by the insurance. Any amount in excess of $100,000 is not insured and is subject to default risk.	These are generally not liquid. CDs from U.S. banks do have a liquid secondary market.
Repurchase agreements	Essentially a loan arrangement wherein a securities dealer is the "borrower" and the investor is the "lender." The investor buys securities, such as treasury bills, from the securities dealer, with an agreement to sell the securities back to the dealer at a later date for a specified higher price.	Very short term, ranging from overnight to approximately three months.	The security serves as collateral for the loan, and therefore the investor is exposed to very little risk. However, the investor needs to consider the creditworthiness of the securities dealer when assessing the risk.	No secondary market exists.
Banker's acceptances	Drafts written by the borrower and guaranteed by the bank on which the draft is drawn. Typically used in international trade transactions. The borrower is an importer who writes the draft in payment for goods.	Typically one to six months.	Because both the borrower and a bank have guaranteed the draft, there is very little risk.	When the exporter receives the draft, he may hold it until maturity and receive its full value, or he may sell the draft at a discount prior to maturity.
Bearer deposit notes	Short-term discount notes issued by banks.	Up to one year.	Guaranteed by the issuing bank, but not by the CDIC, these notes entail very little risk.	Secondary market exists.
Commercial paper	Short-term, unsecured debt issued by large corporations. The minimum denomination is $25,000, but most commercial paper has a face value of $100,000 or more.	Typically one to six months.	Default risk depends on the creditworthiness of the issuing corporation.	Secondary market exists.

Thus, a financial manager who wants to invest the firm's funds in the least risky security will choose to invest in treasury bills. However, if the financial manager wishes to earn a higher return on the firm's short-term investments, she may opt to invest some or all of the firm's excess cash in a riskier alternative, such as commercial paper.

CONCEPT CHECK

11. List three reasons why a firm holds cash.

12. What trade-off does a firm face when choosing how to invest its cash?

MyLab Finance

Here is what you should know after reading this chapter. MyLab™ Finance will help you identify what you know, and where to go when you need to practice.

KEY POINTS	TERMS	ONLINE PRACTICE OPPORTUNITIES
19.1 Overview of Working Capital ■ Working capital management involves managing a firm's short-term assets and short-term liabilities. ■ A firm's cash cycle is the length of time between when the firm pays cash to purchase its initial inventory and when it receives cash from the sale of the output produced from that inventory. The operating cycle is the average length of time between when a firm originally purchases its inventory and when it receives the cash back from selling its product.	cash conversion cycle (CCC), p. 663 cash cycle, p. 662 operating cycle, p. 662	MyLab Study Plan 19.1
19.2 Trade Credit ■ Trade credit is effectively a loan from the selling firm to its customer. The cost of trade credit depends on the credit terms. The cost of not taking a discount that is offered by a supplier implies an interest rate for the loan. ■ Firms provide trade credit to their customers for two reasons: (a) as an indirect way to lower prices and (b) because firms may have advantages in making loans to their customers relative to other potential sources of credit. ■ A firm should compare the cost of trade credit with the cost of alternative sources of financing in deciding whether to use the trade credit offered. ■ Collection float is the amount of time it takes for a firm to be able to use funds after a customer has paid for its goods. Firms can reduce their working capital needs by reducing their collection float.	availability float, p. 670 cash discount, p. 667 collection float, p. 669 credit period, p. 667 disbursement float, p. 670 discount period, p. 667 mail float, p. 669 processing float, p. 670 trade credit, p. 667	MyLab Study Plan 19.2

KEY POINTS	TERMS	ONLINE PRACTICE OPPORTUNITIES
19.3 Receivables Management ■ Establishing a credit policy involves three steps: establishing credit standards, establishing credit terms, and establishing a collection policy. ■ The accounts receivables days and aging schedule are two methods used to monitor the effectiveness of a firm's credit policy.	accounts receivable days, p. 673 aging schedule, p. 673 payments pattern, p. 673	MyLab Study Plan 19.3
19.4 Payables Management ■ Firms should monitor accounts payable to ensure that they are making payments at an optimal time. ■ Paying late, known as stretching accounts payable, can reduce the direct costs of trade credit, but may result in worse terms from suppliers.	stretching the accounts payable, p. 676	MyLab Study Plan 19.4
19.5 Inventory Management ■ Because excessive inventory uses cash, efficient inventory management increases the firm's free cash flow and thus increases firm value. ■ Firms hold inventory to avoid lost sales due to stockouts and because of factors such as seasonal demand. ■ The costs of inventory include acquisition costs, order costs, and carrying costs.	"just-in-time" (JIT) inventory management, p. 678 stock-out, p. 677	MyLab Study Plan 19.5
19.6 Cash Management ■ If a firm's need to hold cash is reduced, the funds can be invested in a number of different short-term securities, including cash management bills, treasury bills, term deposits, certificates of deposit, guaranteed investment certificates, repurchase agreements, banker's acceptances, bearer deposit notes, and commercial paper.	compensating balance, p. 680 precautionary balance, p. 680 transactions balance, p. 679	MyLab Study Plan 19.6

REVIEW QUESTIONS

1. What does a firm's cash cycle tell us?

2. Answer the following:

a. What is the difference between a firm's cash cycle and its operating cycle?

b. How will a firm's cash cycle be affected if a firm increases its inventory, all else being equal?

c. How will a firm's cash cycle be affected if the firm begins to take the discounts offered by its suppliers, all else being equal?

3. Does an increase in a firm's cash cycle necessarily mean that the firm is managing its cash poorly?
4. Why is trade credit important?
5. What are the ways that receivables management can affect a firm's value?
6. What are the three steps involved in establishing a credit policy?
7. What factors determine how a firm should manage its payables?
8. What is meant by "stretching the accounts payable"?
9. What are the trade-offs involved in reducing inventory?
10. What are the different ways you can invest your firm's cash?
11. Which of the following short-term securities would you expect to offer the highest before-tax return: treasury bills, certificates of deposit, short-term tax exempts, or commercial paper? Why?

PROBLEMS

All problems in this chapter are available in MyLab Finance. An asterisk (*) indicates problems with a higher level of difficulty.

Overview of Working Capital

1. Homer Boats has accounts payable days of 20, inventory days of 50, and accounts receivable days of 30. What is its operating cycle?
2. FastChips Semic°nductors has inventory days of 75, accounts receivable days of 30, and accounts payable days of 90. What is its cash conversion cycle?
3. The following financial information is for Westerly Industries:

Sales	$ 100,000
Cost of Goods Sold	$ 80,000
Accounts Receivable	$ 30,000
Inventory	$ 15,000
Accounts Payable	$ 40,000

What is Westerly's cash conversion cycle?

4. Aberdeen Outboard Motors is contemplating building a new plant. The company anticipates that the plant will require an initial investment of $2 million in net working capital today. The plant will last 10 years, at which point the full investment in net working capital will be recovered. Given an annual discount rate of 6%, what is the net present value of this working capital investment?
5. Your firm currently has net working capital of $100,000 that it expects to grow at a rate of 4% per year forever. You are considering some suggestions that could slow that growth to 3% per year. If your discount rate is 12%, how would these changes affect the value of your firm?

6. The Greek Connection had sales of $32 million, and a cost of goods sold of $20 million. A simplified balance sheet for the firm appears below:

The Greek Connection

Balance Sheet ($thousands)

Assets		**Liabilities and Equity**	
Cash	$ 2000	Accounts payable	$ 1500
Accounts receivable	3950	Notes payable	1000
Inventory	1300	Accruals	1220
Total current assets	$ 7250	Total current liabilities	$ 3720
Net plant, property, and equipment	$ 8500	Long-term debt	$ 3000
Total assets	$ 15,750	Total liabilities	$ 6720
		Common equity	$ 9030
		Total liabilities and equity	$ 15,750

a. Calculate the Greek Connection's net working capital.
b. Calculate the cash conversion cycle of the Greek Connection.
c. The industry average accounts receivable days is 30 days. What would the cash conversion cycle for the Greek Connection have been had it matched the industry average for accounts receivable days? (See MyLab Finance for the data in Excel format.)

Trade Credit

7. Assume the credit terms offered to your firm by your suppliers are 3/5, net 30. Calculate the cost of the trade credit if your firm does not take the discount and pays on day 30.

8. Your supplier offers terms of 1/10, net 45. What is the effective annual cost of trade credit if you choose to forgo the discount and pay on day 45?

***9.** The Fast Reader Company supplies bulletin board services to numerous hotel chains nationwide. The owner of the firm is investigating the desirability of employing a billing firm to do her billing and collections. Because the billing firm specializes in these services, collection float will be reduced by 20 days. Average daily collections are $1200, and the owner can earn 8% annually (expressed as an APR with monthly compounding) on her investments. If the billing firm charges $250 per month, should the owner employ the billing firm?

***10.** The Saban Corporation is trying to decide whether to switch to a bank that will accommodate electronic funds transfers from Saban's customers. Saban's financial manager believes the new system would decrease its collection float by as much as five days. The new bank would require a compensating balance of $30,000, whereas its present bank has no compensating balance requirement. Saban's average daily collections are $10,000, and it can earn 8% on its short-term investments. Should Saban make the switch? (Assume the compensating balance at the new bank will be deposited in a non–interest-earning account.)

Receivables Management

11. The Manana Corporation had sales of $60 million this year. Its accounts receivable balance averaged $2 million. How long, on average, does it take the firm to collect on its sales?

12. The Mighty Power Tool Company has the following accounts on its books:

Customer	Amount Owed ($)	Age (days)
ABC	50,000	35
DEF	35,000	5
GHI	15,000	10
KLM	75,000	22
NOP	42,000	40
QRS	18,000	12
TUV	82,000	53
WXY	36,000	90

The firm extends credit on terms of 1/15, net 30. Develop an aging schedule using 15-day increments through 60 days, and then indicate any accounts that have been outstanding for more than 60 days.

Payables Management

13. Simple Simon's Bakery purchases supplies on terms of 1/10, net 25. If Simple Simon's chooses to take the discount offered, it must obtain a bank loan to meet its short-term financing needs. A local bank has quoted Simple Simon's owner an interest rate of 12% on borrowed funds. Should Simple Simon's enter the loan agreement with the bank and begin taking the discount?

14. Your firm purchases goods from its supplier on terms of 3/15, net 40.

a. What is the effective annual cost to your firm if it chooses not to take the discount and makes its payment on day 40?

b. What is the effective annual cost to your firm if it chooses not to take the discount and makes its payment on day 50?

***15.** Use the financial statements supplied below for International Motor Corporation (IMC) to answer the following questions. (See MyLab for the data in Excel format.)

a. Calculate the cash conversion cycle for IMC for both 2017 and 2018. What change has occurred, if any? All else being equal, how does this change affect IMC's need for cash?

b. IMC's suppliers offer terms of net 30. Does it appear that IMC is doing a good job of managing its accounts payable?

International Motor Corporation
Income Statement ($ millions)
for the Years Ending December 31

	2017	2018
Sales	$60,000	$75,000
Cost of goods sold	52,000	61,000
Gross profit	$ 8000	$14,000
Selling, general, and administrative expenses	6000	8000
Operating profit	$ 2000	$ 6000
Interest expense	1400	1300
Earnings before tax	$ 600	$ 4700
Taxes	300	2350
Earnings after tax	$ 300	$ 2350

International Motor Corporation
Balance Sheet ($ millions)
As of December 31

	2017	2018		2017	2018
Assets			**Liabilities**		
Cash	$ 3080	$ 6100	Accounts payable	$ 3600	$ 4600
Accounts receivable	2800	6900	Notes payable	1180	1250
Inventory	6200	6600	Accruals	5600	6211
Total current assets	$12,080	$19,600	Total current liabilities	$10,380	$12,061
Net plant, property, and equipment	$23,087	$20,098	Long-term debt	$ 6500	$ 7000
Total assets	$35,167	$39,698	Total liabilities	$16,880	$19,061
			Equity		
			Common stock	$ 2735	$ 2735
			Retained earnings	$15,552	$17,902
			Total equity	$18,287	$20,637
			Total liabilities and equity	$35,167	$39,698

Inventory Management

16. Your company had $10 million in sales last year. Its cost of goods sold was $7 million and its average inventory balance was $1,200,000. What was its average days of inventory?

17. Happy Valley Homecare Suppliers Inc. (HVHS) had $20 million in sales this past year. Its cost of goods sold was $8 million, and its average inventory balance was $2,000,000.

a. Calculate the average number of days inventory outstanding ratios for HVHS.

b. The average days of inventory in the industry is 73 days. By how much would HVHS reduce its investment in inventory if it could improve its inventory days to meet the industry average?

CHAPTER

20 Short-Term Financial Planning

LEARNING OBJECTIVES

- Forecast cash flows and short-term financing needs
- Understand the principle of matching short-term needs to short-term funding sources
- Know the different types of bank loans and their trade-offs
- Understand the use of commercial paper as an alternative to bank financing
- Use financing secured by accounts receivable or inventory
- Know how to create a short-term financial plan

NOTATION

EAR	effective annual rate
APR	annual percentage rate

Hasbro is a multinational corporation with year-end 2013 assets of $4.4 billion. Hasbro designs and manufactures toys throughout the world; its major product lines include the Playskool, Tonka, and Transformers brands. Typically, the demand for toys is highly seasonal, with demand peaking during the fall in anticipation of December's holiday retailing season. As a result, Hasbro's revenues vary dramatically throughout the calendar year. For example, revenues during the fourth quarter of the calendar year are typically more than twice as high as revenues in the first quarter.

Hasbro's varying business revenues cause its cash flows to be highly cyclical. The firm generates surplus cash during some months; it has a great demand for capital during other months. These seasonal financing requirements are quite different from its ongoing, long-term demand for permanent capital. How does a company such as Hasbro manage its short-term cash needs within each calendar year?

In this chapter, we analyze short-term financial planning. We begin by showing how companies forecast their cash flows to determine their short-term financing needs, and we explore the reasons why firms use short-term financing. Next, we discuss the financing policies that guide these financing decisions. Finally, we compare alternative ways a company can finance a shortfall during periods when it is not generating enough cash, including short-term financing with bank loans, commercial paper, and secured financing.

20.1 Forecasting Short-Term Financing Needs

The first step in short-term financial planning is to forecast the company's future cash flows. This exercise has two distinct objectives. First, a company forecasts its cash flows to determine whether it will have surplus cash or a cash deficit for each period. Second, management needs to decide whether that surplus or deficit is temporary or permanent. If it is permanent, it may affect the firm's long-term financial decisions. For example, if a company anticipates an ongoing surplus of cash, it may choose to increase its dividend payout. Deficits resulting from investments in long-term projects are often financed using long-term sources of capital, such as equity or long-term bonds.

In this chapter, we focus specifically on short-term financial planning. With this perspective, we are interested in analyzing the types of cash surpluses or deficits that are temporary and, therefore, short-term in nature. When a company analyzes its short-term financing needs, it typically examines cash flows at quarterly intervals.

Application: Whistler Snowboards, Inc.

Eric Limon/Shutterstock

To illustrate, let's assume that it is currently December 2019 and consider the case of Whistler Snowboards, Inc. Whistler manufactures snowboarding equipment, which it sells primarily to sports retailers. Whistler anticipates that in 2020 its sales will grow by 10% to $20 million and its total net income will be $1,950,000. Assuming that both sales and production will occur uniformly throughout the year, management's forecast of its quarterly net income and statement of cash flows for 2020 is presented in the spreadsheet in Table 20.1.[1] (Also shown, in grey, is the income statement from the fourth quarter of 2019.)[2]

From this forecast, we see that Whistler is a profitable company. Its quarterly net income is almost $500,000. Whistler's capital expenditures are equal to depreciation. While Whistler's working capital requirements increase in the first quarter due to the increase in sales, they remain constant thereafter and so have no further cash flow consequences. Based on these projections, Whistler will be able to fund projected sales growth from its operating profit and, in fact, will accumulate excess cash on a continuing basis. Given similar growth forecasts for next year and beyond, this surplus is likely to be long term. Whistler could reduce the surplus by paying some of it out as a dividend or by repurchasing shares.

Let's now turn to Whistler's potential short-term financing needs. Firms require short-term financing for three reasons: negative cash flow shocks, positive cash flow shocks, and seasonalities.

---

[1]In this table, and elsewhere in the chapter, we display rounded numbers. Calculations, such as net income, are based on the actual numbers in the spreadsheet with all significant digits. As a result, there will occasionally be a small discrepancy between the Excel-calculated value shown and the hand-calculated value using the rounded numbers displayed.

[2]Given the coverage we have provided in Chapters 2 and 18 on how to construct pro forma financial statements, we do not discuss those details here. For simplicity, we have assumed that Whistler has no debt and earns no interest on retained cash.

TABLE 20.1 Projected Financial Statements for Whistler Snowboards, 2020, Assuming Lel Sales

1	**Quarter**	2019Q4	2020Q1	2020Q2	2020Q3	2020Q4
2	**Income Statement ($000s)**					
3	Sales	4545	5000	5000	5000	5000
4	Cost of Goods Sold	−2955	−3250	−3250	−3250	−3250
5	Selling, General, and Administrative	−455	−500	−500	−500	−500
6	**EBITDA**	1136	1250	1250	1250	1250
7	Depreciation	−455	−500	−500	−500	−500
8	**EBIT**	682	750	750	750	750
9	Taxes	−239	−263	−263	−263	−263
10	**Net Income**	443	488	488	488	488
11	**Statement of Cash Flows**					
12	Net Income		488	488	488	488
13	Depreciation		500	500	500	500
14	Changes in Working Capital					
15	Accounts Receivable		−136	—	—	—
16	Inventory		—	—	—	—
17	Accounts Payable		48	—	—	—
18	**Cash from Operating Activities**		899	988	988	988
19	Capital Expenditures		−500	−500	−500	−500
20	Other Investment		—	—	—	—
21	**Cash from Investing Activities**		−500	−500	500	−500
22	Net Borrowing		—	—	—	—
23	Dividends		—	—	—	—
24	Capital Contributions		—	—	—	—
25	**Cash from Financing Activities**		—	—	—	—
26	**Change in Cash and Equivalents** (lines 18 + 21 + 25)		399	488	488	488

Negative Cash Flow Shocks

Occasionally, a company will encounter circumstances in which cash flows are temporarily negative for an unexpected reason. These situations, which we refer to as *negative cash flow shocks*, can create short-term financing needs.

Returning to the Whistler Snowboards example, assume that during April 2020 management learns that some manufacturing equipment has broken unexpectedly. If replacing the equipment is costly enough, Whistler's cash reserves would be insufficient to pay for a replacement. Whistler will have to borrow (or arrange for another financing source) to cover the shortfall. However, once the equipment is replaced, the company will continue to generate positive cash flow in subsequent quarters, and will have generated enough in cumulative cash flow to repay the loan. Therefore, this negative cash flow shock has created the need for short-term financing.

Positive Cash Flow Shocks

We next analyze a case in which a positive cash flow shock affects short-term financing needs. Although this surprise is good news, it still creates demand for short-term financing.

During the first quarter of 2020, a major sporting goods chain agrees to sell Whistler snowboards exclusively. The opportunity to grow comes with large upfront marketing, working capital, and production capacity expenses.

The unexpected event in this case—the opportunity to grow more rapidly—is positive. It results, however, in a negative net cash flow during the first quarter, due primarily to the new marketing expenses and capital expenditures. Because the company will be even more profitable in subsequent quarters, this financing need is temporary.

Seasonalities

For many firms, sales are seasonal. For example, department store, sporting goods, and toy sales are concentrated during the Christmas holiday season, but, for building materials, sales peak in the spring ahead of the summer building season. When sales are concentrated during a few months, sources and uses of cash are also likely to be seasonal. Firms in this position may find themselves with a surplus of cash during some months that is sufficient to compensate for a shortfall during other months. However, because of timing differences, such firms often have short-term financing needs.

To illustrate, let's return to the example of Whistler Snowboards. In Table 20.1, management assumed that Whistler's sales occur uniformly throughout the year. In reality, for a snowboard manufacturer, sales are likely to be highly seasonal. Assume that 20% of sales occur during the first quarter, 10% during each of the second and third quarters (largely southern hemisphere sales), and 60% of sales during the fourth quarter, in anticipation of the (northern hemisphere) winter snowboarding season. The spreadsheet in Table 20.2 presents the resulting statement of cash flows. (Also shown, in grey, is a revised income statement from the fourth quarter of 2019, reflecting seasonal sales.) These forecasts continue to assume production occurs uniformly throughout the year.

From Table 20.2, we see that Whistler is still a profitable company, and its annual net income still totals $1,950,000. However, the introduction of seasonal sales creates some dramatic swings in Whistler's short-term cash flows. There are two effects of seasonality on cash flows. First, although the cost of goods sold fluctuates proportionally with sales, other costs (such as administrative overhead and depreciation) do not, leading to large changes in the firm's net income by quarter. Second, net working capital changes are more pronounced. In the first quarter, Whistler receives cash by collecting the receivables from last year's high fourth quarter sales. During the second and third quarters, the company's inventory balance increases. Given capacity constraints in its manufacturing equipment, Whistler produces snowboards throughout the year, even though sales during the summer are low. Because production occurs uniformly, accounts payable do not vary over the year. Inventory, however, builds up in anticipation of fourth-quarter sales—and increases in inventory-use cash. As a consequence, Whistler has negative net cash flows during the second and third quarters, primarily to fund its inventory. By the fourth quarter, high sales recover cash for the company.

Seasonal sales create large short-term cash flow deficits and surpluses. During the second and third quarters, the company will need to find additional short-term sources of cash to fund inventory. During the fourth quarter, Whistler will have a large short-term surplus. Given that its seasonal cash flow needs are likely to recur next year, Whistler may choose to invest this cash in one of the short-term investment options discussed in Chapter 19. Management can then use this cash to fund some of its short-term working capital needs during the following year.

The Cash Budget

The statement of cash flows section of Table 20.2 reflects assumptions made by Whistler's managers about the timing of cash receipts and disbursements throughout the year. Once Whistler's managers forecast the sales and production costs for the year,

TABLE 20.2 Projected Financial Statements for Whistler Snowboards, 2020, Assuming Seasonal Sales

1	**Quarter**	**2019Q4**	**2020Q1**	**2020Q2**	**2020Q3**	**2020Q4**
2	**Income Statement ($000s)**					
3	Sales	10,909	4000	2000	2000	12,000
4	Cost of Goods Sold	−7091	−2600	−1300	−1300	−7800
5	Selling, General, and Administrative	−773	−450	−350	−350	−850
6	**EBITDA**	3045	950	350	350	3350
7	Depreciation	−455	−500	−500	−500	−500
8	**EBIT**	2591	450	−150	−150	2850
9	Taxes	−907	−158	53	53	−998
10	**Net Income**	1684	293	−98	−98	1853
11	**Statement of Cash Flows**					
12	Net Income		293	−98	−98	1853
13	Depreciation		500	500	500	500
14	Changes in Working Capital					
15	Accounts Receivable		2073	600	—	−3000
16	Inventory		−650	−1950	−1950	4550
17	Accounts Payable		48	—	—	—
18	**Cash from Operating Activities**		2263	−948	−1548	3903
19	Capital Expenditures		−500	−500	−500	−500
20	Other Investment		—	—	—	—
21	**Cash from Investing Activities**		−500	−500	−500	−500
22	Net Borrowing		—	—	—	—
23	Dividends		—	—	—	—
24	Capital Contributions		—	—	—	—
25	**Cash from Financing Activities**		—	—	—	—
26	**Change in Cash and Equivalents** (lines 18 + 21 + 25)		1763	−1488	−2048	3403

cash budget A forecast of cash inflows and outflows on a quarterly (or sometimes monthly) basis.

they must also forecast when Whistler will actually receive the cash for those sales and when it will need to pay its suppliers. They do this in a **cash budget**, a forecast of cash inflows and outflows on a quarterly (or sometimes monthly) basis used to identify potential cash shortfalls.

For example, based on experience, Whistler assumes that it will receive payment for 70% of its sales in the quarter they are made, with the remaining 30% coming in the following quarter. (This corresponds with an accounts receivable payment period of about one month.) So each quarter, cash receipts will be 30% of last quarter's sales in receivables plus 70% of the current quarter's sales:

$$\text{Whistler's Quarterly Cash Receipts} = 30\% \times \text{Last Quarter's Sales} + 70\% \times \text{This Quarter's Sales}$$

Using this assumption and the sales forecast from Table 20.2, we can forecast Whistler's cash receipts. Note that sales in 2019Q4 were $10,909, so beginning receivables are 30% × $10,909 = $3273. Table 20.3 presents the projected cash receipts.

The next step is to forecast cash disbursements. As we mentioned earlier, although Whistler's sales are seasonal, it produces a constant amount each quarter

TABLE 20.3 Projected Cash Receipts for Whistler Snowboards, Assuming Seasonal Sales

1	Quarter	2020Q1	2020Q2	2020Q3	2020Q4
2	Beginning Receivables ($000s)	3273	1200	600	600
3	Sales	4000	2000	2000	12,000
4	Cash Collections (Line 2 + 70% of Line 3)	6073	2600	2000	9000
5	Ending Receivables (30% of Line 3)	1200	600	600	3600

and simply builds up inventory. Thus, each quarter it pays its suppliers a level amount for materials. These costs are reflected in the income statement when sales occur, but the cash outflow happens when the firm pays its suppliers.

This can be seen by adding the inventory line to the cost of goods sold line in Table 20.2. In 2020Q1 it is −$2600 − $650 = −$3250, and it is in for the rest of the quarters in 2020 as well, reflecting the steady production of snowboards. Whistler's managers forecast that of the $3250 of cost of goods sold in each quarter, they will need to pay $2725 in the quarter, carrying $525 in accounts payable into the next quarter. Each quarter, their cash disbursements on materials will be last quarter's accounts payable plus $2725 of the current quarter's costs. Because Whistler's production was lower in 2019, it had lower costs, so it ended 2019 with lower accounts payable than it will have going forward. Table 20.4 shows that it will have $477 in accounts payable for the first quarter of 2020 only, before it rises to $525 for the rest of the quarters. Using that fact and the assumption we just made, we can forecast their disbursements on materials. The other cash disbursements will be selling, general, and administrative expenses (SG&A), and taxes and interest, as well as any capital expenditures, each of which is forecasted in Table 20.2. The table also shows Whistler's forecasted cash disbursements.

TABLE 20.4 Projected Cash Disbursements for Whistler Snowboards, Assuming Seasonal Sales

Panel (a) Calculating Payments to Suppliers					
1	**Quarter**	**2020Q1**	**2020Q2**	**2020Q3**	**2020Q4**
2	**Payment to Suppliers**				
3	Last Quarter's AP	477	525	525	525
4	This Quarter's Payments	2725	2725	2725	2725
5	**Total Payments**	3202	3250	3250	3250
6					
7	**Ending AP** ($3250 − Line 4)	525	525	525	525
Panel (b) Total Cash Disbursements					
1	**Quarter**	**2020Q1**	**2020Q2**	**2020Q3**	**2020Q4**
2	Cash Collections (from Line 4 of Table 20.3)	6073	2600	2000	9000
3					
4	**Disbursements**				
5	Payments to Suppliers (from Line 5 of panel [a])	−3202	−3250	−3250	−3250
6	SG&A + Taxes + Interest (from Lines 5 and 9 of Table 20.2)	−608	−297	−297	−1848
7	Capital Expenditures (from Line 19 of Table 20.2)	−500	−500	−500	−500
8	**Total Disbursements**	−4310	−4047	−4047	−5598
9					
10	**Net Cash Flow** (Line 2 + Line 8)	1763	−1447	−2047	3402

TABLE 20.5 Cash Budget for Whistler Snowboards, 2020

1	Quarter	2020Q1	2020Q2	2020Q3	2020Q4
2	**Beginning Cash Balance**	1000	2763	1316	−731
3	Net Cash Flow	1763	−1447	−2047	3402
4	**Ending Cash Balance**	2763	1316	−731	2671
5	Minimum Cash Balance	500	500	500	500
6	**Surplus (Deficit)**	2263	816	−1231	2171

Now that we have the quarterly net cash flow, we can generate Whistler's cash budget. We need two more pieces of information: the amount of cash Whistler will start 2020 with and the minimum amount of cash it needs on hand for transactions purposes. Whistler will start 2020 with $1 million in cash, and its managers have set $500,000 as the minimum acceptable cash balance. Putting it all together, we have Whistler's cash budget, shown in Table 20.5.

Looking at the cash budget, we can immediately see that there will be a substantial cash shortfall in the third quarter. Having identified the shortfall, Whistler's managers can prepare external financing to cover it. We discuss the factors that determine how to cover such a shortfall in the next two sections.

CONCEPT CHECK

1. How do we forecast the firm's future cash requirements?
2. What is the effect of seasonalities on short-term cash flows?

20.2 The Matching Principle

In a perfect capital market, the choice of financing is irrelevant; thus, how the firm chooses to finance its short-term cash needs cannot affect the firm's value. In reality, important market frictions exist, including transaction costs. For example, one transaction cost is the opportunity cost of holding cash in accounts that pay little or no interest. Firms also face high transaction costs if they need to negotiate a loan on short notice to cover a cash shortfall. Firms can increase their value by adopting a policy that minimizes these kinds of costs. One such policy is known as the matching principle. The **matching principle** states that short-term cash needs should be financed with short-term debt and long-term cash needs should be financed with long-term sources of funds.

matching principle The principle that states that a firm's short-term cash needs should be financed with short-term debt and long-term cash needs should be financed with long-term sources of funds.

permanent working capital The amount that a firm must keep invested in its short-term assets to support its continuing operations.

Permanent Working Capital

Permanent working capital is the amount that a firm must keep invested in its short-term assets to support its continuing operations. Because this investment in working capital is required as long as the firm remains in business, it constitutes a long-term investment. The matching principle indicates that the firm should finance this permanent investment in working capital with long-term sources of funds. Such sources have lower transaction costs than short-term sources of funds that have to be replaced more often.

Temporary Working Capital

Another portion of a firm's investment in its accounts receivable and inventory is temporary and results from seasonal fluctuations in the firm's business or unanticipated

TABLE 20.6 Projected Levels of Working Capital for Whistler Snowboards, 2020, Seasonal Sales

1	Quarter	2019Q4	2020Q1	2020Q2	2020Q3	2020Q4
2	**Net Working Capital Requirements ($000s)**					
3	Minimum Cash Balance	500	500	500	500	500
4	Accounts Receivable	3273	1200	600	600	3600
5	Inventory	300	950	2900	4850	300
6	Accounts Payable	−477	−525	−525	−525	−525
7	**Net Working Capital**	3596	2125	3475	5425	3875

temporary working capital The difference between the firm's actual level of investment in short-term working capital needs and its permanent working capital requirements.

shocks. This **temporary working capital** is the difference between the firm's actual level of investment in short-term working capital needs and its permanent working capital investment. Because temporary working capital represents a short-term need, the firm should finance this portion of its investment with short-term financing.

Permanent versus Temporary Working Capital

To illustrate the distinction between permanent and temporary working capital, we return to the Whistler Snowboards example. Table 20.2 presented cash flow forecasts assuming seasonal sales. In the spreadsheet in Table 20.6, we report the underlying levels of working capital that correspond to these forecasts.

In Table 20.6, we see that working capital for Whistler varies from a minimum of $2,125,000 in the first quarter of 2020 to $5,425,000 in the third quarter. The minimum level of working capital, or $2,125,000, can be thought of as the firm's permanent working capital. The difference between this minimum level and the higher levels in subsequent quarters (fo r example, $5,425,000 − $2,125,000 = $3,300,000 in the third quarter) reflects Whistler's temporary working capital requirements.

Financing Policy Choices

Following the matching principle should, in the long run, help minimize a firm's transaction costs.[3] But what if, instead of using the matching principle, a firm financed its permanent working capital needs with short-term debt? When the short-term debt comes due, the firm will have to negotiate a new loan. This new loan will involve additional transaction costs, and it will carry whatever market interest rate exists at the time. As a result, the firm is also exposed to interest rate risk.

aggressive financing policy The financing of part or all of a firm's permanent working capital with short-term debt.

Aggressive Financing Policy. Financing part or all of the permanent working capital with short-term debt is known as an **aggressive financing policy**. An ultra-aggressive policy would involve financing even some of the plant, property, and equipment with short-term sources of funds.

When the yield curve is upward sloping, the interest rate on short-term debt is lower than the rate on long-term debt. In that case, short-term debt may appear cheaper than

[3]Some evidence indicates that most firms appear to follow the matching principle. See W. Beranek, C. Cornwell, and S. Choi, "External Financing, Liquidity, and Capital Expenditures," *Journal of Financial Research* (Summer 1995): 207–222; and M. H. Stohs and D. C. Mauer, "The Determinants of Corporate Debt Maturity Structure," *Journal of Business* 69 (3) (1996): 279–312.

FIGURE 20.1 Financing Policy Choices for Whistler Snowboards

Assuming $25,000 in fixed assets, the figure shows the levels of fixed assets (green), permanent working capital ($2125, yellow), and seasonal inventory (grey) for Whistler Snowboards. In panel (a), each quarter shows the mix of long-term financing (purple) and short-term debt (red) used to finance the assets and working capital. In the aggressive policy illustrated in panel (a), Whistler maintains no excess cash reserves and instead finances its working capital entirely through short-term borrowing. The amount of borrowing must match the amount of working capital.

Panel (b) illustrates a conservative policy, in which Whistler maintains enough cash reserves to cover its peak temporary financing needs. The company does this with $30,425 in long-term financing, which is enough to finance its fixed assets, permanent working capital, and peak inventory. Whistler's total working capital is constant at $5425, but the composition of the working capital varies over the year as the company draws down its cash reserves (blue) to build inventory and then replenishes the cash reserves when it sells the inventory.

Panel (a) Aggressive financing policy: All working capital is financed with short-term debt.

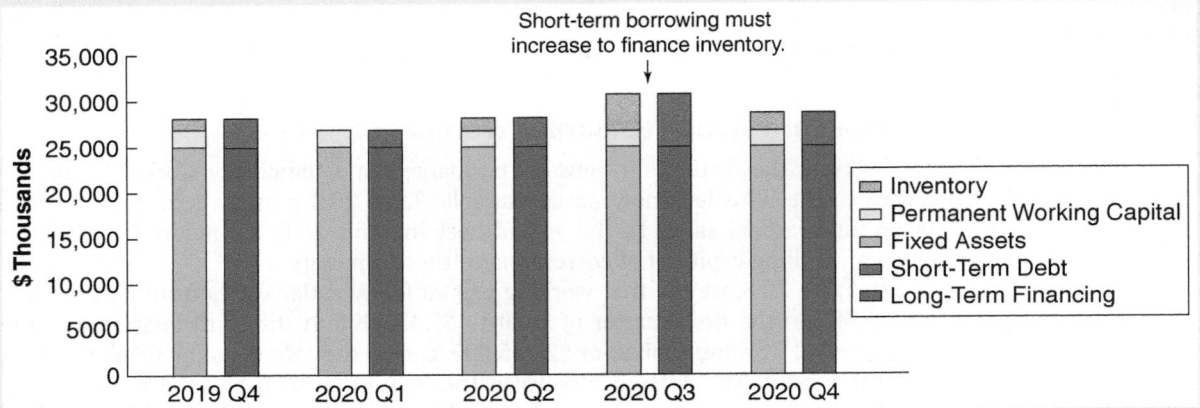

Panel (b) Conservative financing policy: Working capital is financed with long-term debt.

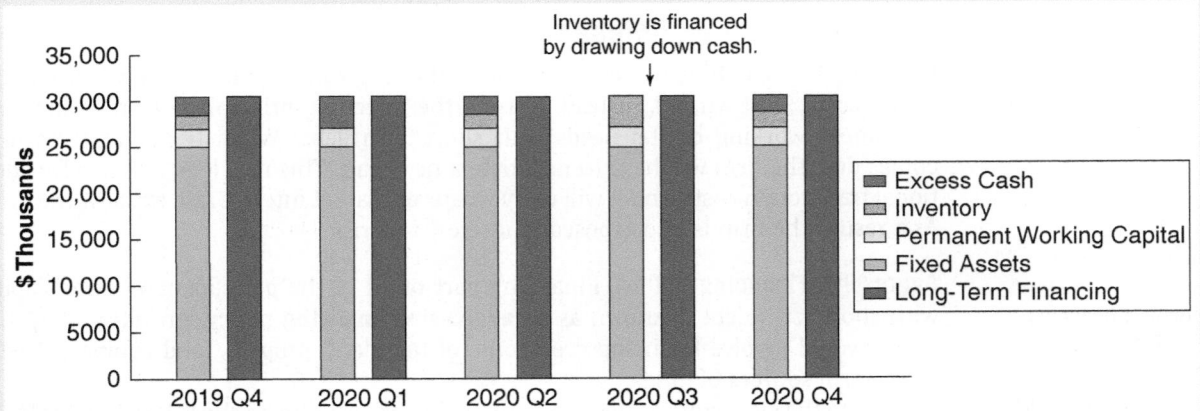

long-term debt. However, we know that with perfect capital markets, Modigliani and Miller's propositions from Chapter 16 apply: the benefit of the lower rate from short-term debt is offset by the risk that the firm will have to refinance the debt in the future at a higher rate. This risk is borne by the equity holders, and so the firm's equity cost of capital will rise to offset any benefit from the lower borrowing rate.

Why, then, might a firm choose an aggressive financing policy? Such a policy might be beneficial if the market imperfections mentioned in Chapter 16, such as agency costs and asymmetric information, are important. The value of short-term debt is less sensitive to the firm's credit quality than long-term debt is; therefore, the value of short-term debt will be less affected by management's actions or information. As a result, short-term debt can have lower agency and lemons costs than long-term debt does, and an aggressive financing policy can benefit shareholders. On the other hand, by relying on short-term debt the firm exposes itself to **funding risk**, which is the risk of incurring financial distress costs should the firm not be able to refinance its debt in a timely manner or at a reasonable rate.

funding risk The risk of incurring financial distress costs should a firm not be able to refinance its debt in a timely manner or at a reasonable rate.

Conservative Financing Policy. Alternatively, a firm could finance its short-term needs with long-term debt, a practice known as a **conservative financing policy**. For example, when following such a policy, a firm would use long-term sources of funds to finance its fixed assets, permanent working capital, and some of its seasonal needs. The firm would use short-term debt very sparingly to meet its peak seasonal needs. To implement such a policy effectively, there will necessarily be periods when excess cash is available—those periods when the firm requires little or no investment in temporary working capital. In an imperfect capital market, this cash will earn a below-market interest rate, thereby reducing the firm's value. It also increases the possibility that managers of the firm will use this excess cash unproductively—for example, on perquisites for themselves.

conservative financing policy The financing of a firm's short-term needs with long-term debt.

In Figure 20.1, we illustrate aggressive and conservative financial policies for Whistler. With an aggressive policy, Whistler relies entirely on short-term financing to fund its inventory buildup, so its borrowing reaches a peak, along with its inventory, in the third quarter. With a conservative policy, the firm uses long-term borrowing to ensure that it will have enough cash to pay for its peak inventory. In this case, Whistler's borrowing does not fluctuate at all, but rather it draws down its cash reserves so that they are at a minimum when its inventory is at its peak.

Once a firm determines its short-term financing needs, it must choose which instruments it will use for this purpose. In the rest of this chapter, we survey the specific financing options that are available: bank loans, commercial paper, and secured financing.

CONCEPT CHECK

3. What is the matching principle?
4. What is the difference between temporary and permanent working capital?

20.3 Short-Term Financing with Bank Loans

One of the primary sources of short-term financing, especially for small businesses, is the commercial bank. Each of Canada's major chartered banks has a commercial banking division. Bank loans are typically initiated with a **promissory note**, which is a written statement that indicates the amount of the loan, the date payment is due, and the interest rate. In this section, we examine three types of bank loans: a single, end-of-period-payment loan; a line of credit; and a bridge loan. In addition, we compare the interest rates of these bank loans and present the common stipulations and fees associated with them.

promissory note A written statement that indicates the amount of a loan, the date payment is due, and the interest rate.

Single End-of-Period-Payment Loan

The most straightforward type of bank loan is a single end-of-period-payment loan. Such a loan agreement requires that the firm pay interest on the loan and pay back the

bank rate The rate at which the Bank of Canada lends to financial institutions.

prime rate The rate banks charge their most creditworthy customers.

London Inter-Bank Offered Rate (LIBOR) The rate of interest at which banks borrow funds from each other in the London interbank market.

line of credit A bank loan arrangement in which a bank agrees to lend a firm any amount up to a stated maximum. This flexible agreement allows the firm to draw upon the line of credit whenever it chooses.

uncommitted line of credit A line of credit that is an informal agreement and does not legally bind a bank to provide the funds a borrower requests.

committed line of credit A legally binding written agreement that obligates a bank to provide funds to a firm (up to a stated credit limit) regardless of the financial condition of the firm (unless the firm is bankrupt) as long as the firm satisfies any restrictions in the agreement.

revolving line of credit A line of credit, which a company can use as needed, that involves a solid commitment from a bank for a longer time period, typically two to three years.

evergreen credit A revolving line of credit with no fixed maturity.

bridge loan A type of short-term bank loan that is often used to "bridge the gap" until a firm can arrange for long-term financing.

principal in one lump sum at the end of the loan. The interest rate may be fixed or variable. With a fixed interest rate, the specific rate that the commercial bank will charge is stipulated at the time the loan is made. With a variable interest rate, the terms of the loan may indicate that the rate will vary with some spread relative to a benchmark rate, such as the **bank rate** (the rate at which the Bank of Canada lends to financial institutions) or the *prime rate*. The **prime rate** is the rate banks charge their most creditworthy customers. However, large corporations can often negotiate bank loans at an interest rate that is *below* the prime rate. For example, in its 2013 annual report, Hasbro indicated that the weighted average interest rate it paid on average short-term borrowings from domestic institutions was 1.46% at the end of 201212 and there were no short-term borrowings at the end of 2013. By comparison, the average prime rate at the end of 2012 was 3.25%.[4] Another common benchmark rate is the **London Inter-Bank Offered Rate (LIBOR)**, which is the rate of interest at which banks borrow funds from each other in the London interbank market. It is quoted for maturities of one day to one year for 10 major currencies. As it is a rate paid by banks with the highest credit quality, most firms will borrow at a rate that exceeds LIBOR.

Line of Credit

Another common type of bank loan arrangement is a **line of credit**, in which a bank agrees to lend a firm any amount up to a stated maximum. This flexible agreement allows the firm to draw upon the line of credit whenever it chooses.

Firms frequently use lines of credit to finance seasonal needs. An **uncommitted line of credit** is an informal agreement that does not legally bind the bank to provide the funds. As long as the borrower's financial condition remains good, the bank is happy to advance additional funds. A **committed line of credit** consists of a legally binding written agreement that obligates the bank to provide funds to a firm (up to a stated credit limit) regardless of the financial condition of the firm (unless the firm is bankrupt) as long as the firm satisfies any restrictions in the agreement. These arrangements are typically accompanied by a compensating balance requirement (i.e., a requirement that the firm maintain a minimum level of deposits with the bank) and restrictions regarding the level of the firm's working capital. The firm pays a commitment fee of 0.25% to 0.5% of the unused portion of the line of credit in addition to interest on the amount that the firm borrowed. The line of credit agreement may also stipulate that at some point in time the outstanding balance must be zero. This policy ensures that the firm does not use the short-term financing to finance its long-term obligations.

Banks usually renegotiate the terms of a line of credit annually. A **revolving line of credit** is a committed line of credit, which a company can use as needed, that involves a solid commitment from the bank for a longer period of time, typically two to three years. A revolving line of credit with no fixed maturity is called **evergreen credit**. In its 2013 annual report, Hasbro reported that it relied on a $700 million revolving credit facility as the primary source of financing for its seasonal working capital requirements.

Bridge Loan

A **bridge loan** is another type of short-term bank loan that is often used to "bridge the gap" until a firm can arrange for long-term financing. For example, a real estate developer may use a bridge loan to finance the construction of a shopping mall. After the mall is completed, the developer will obtain long-term financing. Other firms use bridge loans to finance plant and equipment until they receive the proceeds from the sale of

[4]Hasbro 2013 annual report and the Federal Reserve Statistical Release website.

a long-term debt or an equity issue. After a natural disaster, lenders may provide businesses with short-term loans to serve as bridges until they receive insurance payments or long-term disaster relief.

Bridge loans are often quoted as discount loans with fixed interest rates. With a **discount loan**, the borrower is required to pay the interest at the *beginning* of the loan period. The lender deducts interest from the loan proceeds when the loan is made.

discount loan A type of bridge loan in which the borrower is required to pay the interest at the beginning of the loan period. The lender deducts interest from the loan proceeds when the loan is made.

Common Loan Stipulations and Fees

We now turn to common loan stipulations and fees that affect the effective interest rate on a loan. Specifically, we look at loan commitment fees, loan origination fees, and compensating balance requirements.

Commitment Fees. Various loan fees charged by banks affect the effective interest rate that the borrower pays. For example, the commitment fee associated with a committed line of credit increases the effective cost of the loan to the firm. The "fee" can really be considered an interest charge under another name. Suppose that a firm has negotiated a committed line of credit with a stated maximum of $1 million and an interest rate of 10% (EAR) with a bank. The commitment fee is 0.5% (EAR). At the beginning of the year, the firm borrows $800,000. It then repays this loan at the end of the year, leaving $200,000 unused for the rest of the year. The total cost of the loan is as follows:

Interest on borrowed funds = 0.10($800,000)	$80,000
Commitment fee paid on unused portion = 0.005($200,000)	$ 1000
Total cost	$81,000

loan origination fee The fee a bank charges to cover credit checks and legal fees.

Loan Origination Fee. Another common type of fee is a **loan origination fee**, which a bank charges to cover credit checks and legal fees. The firm pays the fee when the loan is initiated, which makes the loan similar to a discount loan. The loan origination fee reduces the amount of usable proceeds that the firm receives and, like the commitment fee, is effectively an additional interest charge.

To illustrate, assume that Timmons Towel and Diaper Service is offered a $500,000 loan for three months at an APR of 12%. This loan has a loan origination fee of 1%. The loan origination fee is charged on the principal of the loan; thus, the fee in this case amounts to $0.01 \times \$500{,}000 = \$5000$, so the actual amount borrowed is $495,000. The interest payment for three months is $\$500{,}000(0.12/4) = \$15{,}000$. These cash flows are shown here on a timeline:

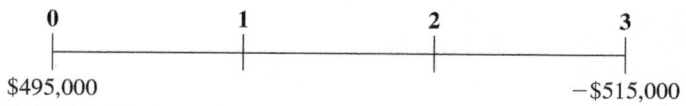

Thus, the actual three-month interest rate paid is as follows:

$$\frac{515{,}000}{495{,}000} - 1 = 4.0404\%$$

Expressing this rate as an EAR gives $1.040404^4 - 1 = 17.17\%$.

Compensating Balance Requirements. Regardless of the loan structure, the bank may include a compensating balance requirement in the loan agreement that reduces the usable loan proceeds. Recall from Chapter 19 that a compensating balance requirement means that the firm must hold a certain percentage of the principal of the loan in an account at the bank. Assume that rather than charging a loan origination fee,

Timmons Towel and Diaper Service's bank requires that the firm keep an amount equal to 10% of the loan principal in a non–interest-bearing account with the bank as long as the loan remains outstanding. The loan is for \$500,000, so this requirement means that Timmons must hold $0.10 \times 500{,}000 = \$50{,}000$ in an account at the bank. Thus, the firm has only \$450,000 of the loan proceeds actually available for use, although it must pay interest on the full loan amount. At the end of the loan period, the firm owes $\$500{,}000 \times (1 + 0.12/4) = \$515{,}000$ and so must pay $\$515{,}000 - 50{,}000 = \$465{,}000$ after applying its compensating balance to the repayment. These cash flows are shown here on a timeline:

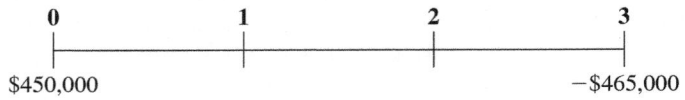

The actual three-month interest rate paid is as follows:

$$\frac{465{,}000}{450{,}000} - 1 = 3.3333\%$$

Expressing this as an EAR gives $1.033333^4 - 1 = 14.01\%$.

We assumed that Timmons's compensating balance is held in a non–interest-bearing account. Sometimes, a bank will allow the compensating balance to be held in an account that pays a small amount of interest to offset part of the interest expense of the loan.

EXAMPLE 20.1 Compensating Balance Requirements and the Effective Annual Rate

PROBLEM

Assume that Timmons Towel and Diaper Service's bank pays 1% (APR with quarterly compounding) on its compensating balance accounts. What is the EAR of Timmons's three-month loan?

SOLUTION

■ Plan

The interest earned on the \$50,000 will reduce the net payment Timmons must make to pay off the loan. Once we compute the final payment, we can determine the implied three-month interest rate and then convert it into an EAR.

■ Execute

The balance held in the compensating balance account will grow to $\$50{,}000(1 + 0.01/4 = \$50{,}125)$. Thus, the final loan payment will be $\$500{,}000 + \$15{,}000 - \$50{,}125 = \$464{,}875$. Notice that the interest on the compensating balance accounts offsets some of the interest that Timmons pays on the loan. The new cash flows are shown here on a timeline:

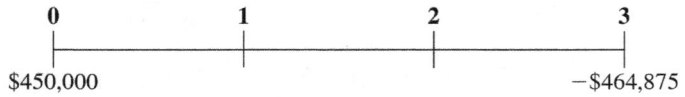

The actual three-month interest rate paid is as follows:

$$\frac{464{,}875}{450{,}000} - 1 = 3.3056\%$$

Expressing this as an EAR gives $1.033056^4 - 1 = 13.89\%$. ▶

■ **Evaluate**

As expected, because the bank allowed Timmons to deposit the compensating balance in an interest-bearing account, the interest earned on the compensating balance reduced the overall interest cost of Timmons for the loan from 14.01% to 13.89%.

CONCEPT CHECK

5. What is the difference between an uncommitted line of credit and a committed line of credit?
6. Describe common loan stipulations and fees.

20.4 Short-Term Financing with Commercial Paper

commercial paper Short-term, unsecured debt issued by large corporations that is usually a cheaper source of funds than a short-term bank loan.

direct paper Commercial paper that a firm sells directly to investors.

dealer paper Commercial paper that dealers sell to investors in exchange for a spread (or fee) for their services.

Commercial paper is short-term, unsecured debt used by large corporations that is usually a cheaper source of funds than a short-term bank loan. The minimum face value is $25,000, and most commercial paper has a face value of at least $100,000. Like long-term debt, commercial paper is rated by credit-rating agencies. The interest on commercial paper is typically paid by selling it at an initial discount.

The average maturity of commercial paper is 30 days, and the maximum maturity is one year. Extending the maturity beyond one year triggers a registration requirement with the relevant provincial securities commission, which increases issue costs and creates a time delay in the sale of the issue. Commercial paper is referred to as either *direct paper* or *dealer paper*. With **direct paper**, the firm sells the security directly to investors. With **dealer paper**, dealers sell the commercial paper to investors in exchange for a spread (or fee) for their services. The spread decreases the proceeds that the issuing firm receives, thereby increasing the effective cost of the paper. Like long-term debt, commercial paper is rated by credit-rating agencies.

EXAMPLE 20.2 The Effective Annual Rate of Commercial Paper

PROBLEM

A firm issues three-month commercial paper with a $100,000 face value and receives $98,000. What effective annual rate is the firm paying for its funds?

SOLUTION

■ **Plan**

First, put the firm's cash flows on a timeline:

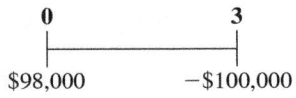

The three-month rate can be computed by comparing the present value ($98,000) with the future value ($100,000). From there, we can convert it into an EAR using Equation 5.1: $EAR =$ equivalent one-year $= (1 + r)^n - 1$, where n is the number of three-month periods in a year.

■ **Execute**

The actual three-month interest rate paid is as follows:

$$\frac{100{,}000}{98{,}000} - 1 = 2.0408\%$$

Expressing this as an EAR gives $1.020408^4 - 1 = 8.42\%$.

■ **Evaluate**

The financial manager needs to know the EAR of all of the firm's funding sources to be able to make comparisons across them and choose the least costly way to finance the firm's short-term needs.

CONCEPT CHECK

7. What is commercial paper?
8. What is the maximum maturity of commercial paper?

20.5 Short-Term Financing with Secured Financing

secured loan A type of corporate loan in which specific assets, most typically a firm's accounts receivable or inventory, are pledged as the firm's collateral.

factors Firms that purchase the receivables of other companies.

pledging of accounts receivable agreement An agreement in which a lender reviews the credit sales of the borrowing firm and decides which credit accounts it will accept as collateral for the loan, based on its own credit standards.

factoring of accounts receivable arrangement An arrangement in which a firm sells receivables to the lender (i.e., the factor), and the lender agrees to pay the firm the amount due from its customers at the end of the firm's payment period.

Businesses can also obtain short-term financing by using a **secured loan**, a type of corporate loan in which specific assets, most typically the firm's accounts receivables or inventory, are pledged as a firm's collateral. Commercial banks, finance companies, and **factors**, which are firms that purchase the receivables of other companies, are the most common sources for secured short-term loans.

Accounts Receivable as Collateral

Firms can use accounts receivable as security for a loan by pledging or factoring. We'll examine these uses of accounts receivable to secure loans in the following sections.

Pledging of Accounts Receivable. In a **pledging of accounts receivable agreement**, the lender reviews the invoices that represent the credit sales of the borrowing firm and decides which credit accounts it will accept as collateral for the loan, based on its own credit standards. The lender then, typically, lends the borrower some percentage of the value of the accepted invoices—say, 75%. If the borrowing firm's customers default on their bills, the firm is still responsible to the lender for the money.

Factoring of Accounts Receivable. In a **factoring of accounts receivable arrangement**, the firm sells receivables to the lender (i.e., the factor), and the lender agrees to pay the firm the amount due from its customers at the end of the firm's payment period. For example, if a firm sells its goods on terms of net 30, then the factor will pay the firm the face value of its receivables, less a factor's fee, at the end of 30 days. The firm's customers are usually instructed to make payments directly to the lender. In many cases, the firm can borrow as much as 80% of the face value of its receivables from the factor, thereby receiving its funds in advance. In such a case, the lender will charge interest on the loan in addition to the factor's fee. The lender charges the factor's fee, which may range from 0.75% to 1.5% of the face value of the accounts receivable, whether or not the firm borrows any of the available funds. Both the interest rate and the factor's fee vary, depending on such issues as the size of the borrowing firm and the dollar volume of its receivables. The dollar amounts involved in factoring agreements may be substantial.

A SEVENTEENTH-CENTURY FINANCING SOLUTION

In recent years, it has become more difficult for small businesses to obtain funding so as to purchase inventory. Several factors have contributed to this trend. First, the largest Canadian chartered banks have acquired many small, regional banks that were traditionally important sources of loans to small businesses. Second, large banks have tightened lending requirements for small borrowers. Third, many small businesses rely increasingly on foreign suppliers that demand payment up front, increasing the immediate demand for capital by small businesses.

Some small businesses have started to rely on a 400-year-old solution: venture merchant financing. This type of financing arrangement began in the 17th century, when groups of investors would provide capital for the voyages of Dutch sea captains. The captains would sail the seas, using the capital to purchase exotic merchandise. On their return, the merchant bankers would take about one-third of the captains' profits when the goods were sold as compensation for the financing.

Now consider the Kosher Depot, which sells exotic kosher foods to restaurants and supermarkets in Westbury, New York. It wanted to grow but lacked access to capital to purchase more specialty-foods inventory. Kosher Depot arranged a two-year, $3.3 million venture merchant financing arrangement with Capstone Business Credit. Kosher Depot would prearrange sales and notify Capstone, which would use its capital to buy the goods for Kosher Depot. Capstone would purchase and import the goods, storing them in its own warehouses. The warehouses then filled the orders received by Kosher Depot. For its services, Capstone received about 30% of the profits.

The cost of this arrangement—the 30% margin charged by the venture merchant—may be expensive relative to some of the alternative financing arrangements discussed in this chapter. However, the price may be worthwhile for a small business with no other short-term alternatives.

Source: Marie Leone, "Capital Ideas: A Little Cash'll Do Ya," http://ww2.cfo.com/accounting-tax/2005/03/capital-ideas-a-little-cashll-do-ya/, March 3, 2005.

In December 2009, for example, Hasbro had approximately $250 million of its accounts receivable under factoring arrangements, but at the end of 2013 there were no such factoring agreements.

with recourse A financing arrangement in which the lender can claim all the borrower's assets—not just explicitly pledged collateral—in the event of a default.

without recourse A financing arrangement in which the lender's claim on the borrower's assets in the event of a default is limited to only explicitly pledged collateral.

A factoring arrangement may be **with recourse**, meaning that the lender can seek payment from the borrower should the borrower's customers default on their bills. Alternatively, the financing arrangement may be **without recourse**, in which case the lender's claim on the borrower's assets in the event of a default is limited to only explicitly pledged collateral. In this latter case, the factor will pay the firm the amount due regardless of whether the factor receives payment from the firm's customers. If the arrangement is with recourse, the lender may not require that it approve the customers' accounts before sales are made. If the factoring agreement is without recourse, the borrowing firm must receive credit approval for a customer from the factor prior to shipping the goods. If the factor gives its approval, the firm ships the goods and the customer is directed to make payment directly to the lender.

Inventory as Collateral

Inventory can be used as collateral for a loan in one of three ways: as a floating lien, as a trust receipt, or in a warehouse arrangement. These options are discussed in the following sections.

floating lien (general lien or blanket lien) A financial arrangement in which all of a firm's inventory is used to secure a loan.

Floating Lien. In a **floating lien (general lien** or **blanket lien)** arrangement, all of the firm's inventory is used to secure the loan. This arrangement is the riskiest setup from the standpoint of the lender, because the value of the collateral used to secure the loan dwindles as inventory is sold. When a firm becomes financially distressed, management may be tempted to sell the inventory without making payments on the loan. In such a case, the firm may not have enough funds to replenish its inventory. As a result, the loan may become under-collateralized. To counter this risk, this type of loan bears a higher interest rate than the next two arrangements discussed. In addition, lenders will lend a low percentage of the value of the inventory.

trust receipts loan (floor planning) A type of loan in which distinguishable inventory items are held in a trust as security for the loan. As these items are sold, the firm remits the proceeds from their sale to the lender in repayment of the loan.

Trust Receipt. With a **trust receipts loan (floor planning)**, distinguishable inventory items are held in a trust as security for the loan. As these items are sold, the firm remits the proceeds from their sale to the lender in repayment of the loan. The lender will periodically have its agent verify that the borrower has not sold some of the specified inventory and failed to make a repayment on the loan. Car dealerships often use this type of secured financing arrangement to obtain the funds needed to purchase vehicles from the manufacturer.

warehouse arrangement An arrangement in which the inventory that serves as collateral for a loan is stored in a warehouse.

public warehouse A business that exists for the sole purpose of storing and tracking the inflow and outflow of inventory, providing the lender tighter control over the inventory.

field warehouse A warehouse arrangement that is operated by a third party but is set up on the borrower's premises in a separate area so that the inventory collateralizing the loan is kept apart from the borrower's main plant.

Warehouse Arrangement. In a **warehouse arrangement**, the inventory that serves as collateral for the loan is stored in a warehouse. A warehouse arrangement is the least risky collateral arrangement from the standpoint of the lender. This type of arrangement can be set up in one of two ways.

The first method is to use a **public warehouse**, which is a business that exists for the sole purpose of storing and tracking the inflow and outflow of the inventory. The lender extends a loan to the borrowing firm, based on the value of the inventory stored. When the borrowing firm needs the inventory to sell, it returns to the warehouse and retrieves it upon receiving permission from the lender. This arrangement provides the lender with the tightest control over the inventory. Public warehouses work well for some types of inventory, such as wine and tobacco products, which must age before they are ready to be sold. It is not practical for items that are subject to spoilage or are bulky and, therefore, difficult to transport to and from the warehouse.

The second option, a **field warehouse**, is operated by a third party but is set up on the borrower's premises in a separate area so that the inventory collateralizing the loan is kept apart from the borrower's main plant. This type of arrangement is convenient for the borrower but gives the lender the added security of having the inventory that serves as collateral controlled by a third party.

Warehouse arrangements are expensive. The business operating the warehouse charges a fee on top of the interest that the borrower must pay the lender for the loan. However, the borrower may also save on the costs of storing the inventory herself. Because the warehouser is a professional at inventory control, little loss due to damaged goods or theft is likely to occur, which in turn lowers insurance costs. Because the control of the inventory remains in the hands of a third party, lenders may be willing to lend a greater percentage of the market value of the inventory than they would under other inventory arrangements.

EXAMPLE 20.3 Calculating the Effective Annual Cost of Warehouse Financing

PROBLEM

The Row Cannery wants to borrow $2 million for one month. Using its inventory as collateral, it can obtain a 12% (APR) loan. The lender requires that a warehouse arrangement be used. The warehouse fee is $10,000, payable at the end of the month. Calculate the effective annual rate of this loan for Row Cannery.

SOLUTION

■ Plan

The monthly interest rate is 12%/12 = 1%. We need to compute the total cash flows Row will owe at the end of the month (including interest and the warehouse fee). By scaling those cash ▶

flows by the amount of the loan, we will have a total monthly cost for the loan that we can then convert to an EAR.

Execute

At the end of the month, Row will owe \$2,000,000 × 1.01 = \$2,020,000 plus the warehouse fee of \$10,000. The cash flows are shown here on a timeline:

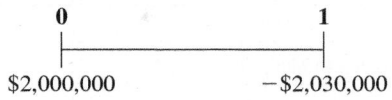

The actual one-month interest rate paid is as follows:

$$\frac{2{,}030{,}000}{2{,}000{,}000} - 1 = 1.5\%$$

Expressing this as an EAR gives $1.015^{12} - 1 = 19.56\%$.

Evaluate

The warehouse arrangement is quite costly: the EAR on the loan itself is $1.01^{12} - 1 = 12.68\%$, but the warehouse arrangement raises it to 19.56%!

The method that a firm adopts when using its inventory to collateralize a loan will affect the ultimate cost of the loan. The blanket lien agreement exposes the lender to the most risk and will, therefore, carry the highest interest rate of the three types of arrangements discussed. Although a warehousing arrangement provides the greatest amount of control over the inventory to the lender, resulting in a lower interest rate on the loan itself, the borrowing firm must pay the additional fees charged by the warehouser and accept the inconvenience associated with the loss of control. Although a trust receipts arrangement may offer a lower interest rate than a blanket lien and allows the firm to avoid the high fees associated with a warehouse arrangement, it can be used only with certain types of inventory.

CONCEPT CHECK

9. What is factoring of accounts receivable?

10. What is the difference between a floating lien and a trust receipt?

20.6 Putting It All Together: Creating a Short-Term Financial Plan

Let's return to Whistler Snowboards. In Table 20.2, we found that, due to the seasonal nature of the company's sales, there would be wide swings in its forecasted cash flows—with large positive cash flows in the first and fourth quarters and big negative ones in the second and third quarters of the year. A financial manager at Whistler would need to plan for how to deal with those cash flow swings, and in particular how to finance any shortfalls. To do so, she would prepare a spreadsheet tracking Whistler's cash balance and short-term financing, such as the one shown in Table 20.7. Whistler will end the fourth quarter of 2019 with \$1 million in cash, and it needs to maintain a minimum

TABLE 20.7 Projected Cash Balance and Short-Term Financing at Whistler Snowboards

1	Quarter	2019Q4	2020Q1	2020Q2	2020Q3	2020Q4
2	**Cash Balance and Short-Term Financing ($000s)**					
3	Starting Cash Balance		1000	2763	1315	500
4	Change in Cash and Equivalents		1763	−1448	−2048	3403
5	Minimum Cash Balance		500	500	500	500
6	**Surplus (Deficit) Relative to Minimum** (3 + 4 − 5)		2263	815	−1233	3403
7	Increase (Decrease) in Short-Term Financing		0	0	1233	−1269
8	Existing Short-Term Financing		0	0	0	1269
9	Total Short-Term Financing (lines 7 + 8)		0	0	1233	0
10	**Ending Cash Balance** (lines 3 + 4 + 7)	1000	2763	1315	500	2633

cash balance of $500,000 to meet its basic transaction needs. Given the cash flows projected in Table 20.2, it will have a cash deficit by the third quarter of 2020.

The analysis identifies two decisions facing the financial manager: what to do with the excess cash generated in the first quarter, and how to finance the third quarter deficit. The analysis currently assumes that the excess cash is held as just that—cash. However, as we discussed in the last chapter, there are many different options for investing excess cash, even over short horizons, which would generate (taxable) interest income. With such investments, the beginning cash in a quarter would be equal to the ending cash in the previous quarter plus the after-tax portion of the interest received.

Turning to the third-quarter deficit, we see that cash flows in the fourth quarter will be large enough to pay off any financing of the third-quarter deficit. After reviewing their options, Whistler's managers decide to obtain a one-quarter bank loan with a single repayment. Their bank charges them 3% interest per quarter, so they will need to repay $1233(1.03) = $1270 in the fourth quarter, which they will easily be able to do, given their excess cash flow at that time. By creating a short-term financial plan, the managers can anticipate upcoming shortfalls, allowing them enough time to investigate the least costly way to finance those shortfalls.

MyLab Finance

Here is what you should know after reading this chapter. MyLab™ Finance will help you identify what you know, and where to go when you need to practice.

KEY POINTS	KEY TERMS	ONLINE PRACTICE OPPORTUNITIES
20.1 Forecasting Short-Term Financing Needs ■ The first step in short-term financial planning is to forecast future cash flows. The cash flow forecasts allow a company to determine whether it has a cash flow surplus or deficit, and whether the surplus or deficit is short term or long term.	cash budget, p. 692	MyLab Study Plan 20.1 Spreadsheet Tables 20.1–20.4

KEY POINTS	TERMS	ONLINE PRACTICE OPPORTUNITIES
■ Firms need short-term financing to deal with seasonal working capital requirements, negative cash flow shocks, or positive cash flow shocks. ■ Using forecasted inflows and outflows of cash, a cash budget allows managers to identify any potential cash shortfalls.		
20.2 The Matching Principle		
■ The matching principle specifies that short-term needs for funds should be financed with short-term sources of funds and long-term needs should be financed with long-term sources of funds.	aggressive financing policy, p. 695 conservative financing policy, p. 697 funding risk, p. 697 matching principle, p. 694 permanent working capital, p. 694 temporary working capital, p. 695	MyLab Study Plan 20.2 Spreadsheet Table 20.5
20.3 Short-Term Financing with Bank Loans		
■ Bank loans are a primary source of short-term financing, especially for small firms. ■ The most straightforward type of bank loan is a single, end-of-period-payment loan. ■ Bank lines of credit allow a firm to borrow any amount up to a stated maximum. The line of credit may be uncommitted, which is a nonbinding, informal agreement, or, more typically, may be committed. ■ A bridge loan is a short-term bank loan that is used to bridge the gap until the firm can arrange for long-term financing. ■ The number of compounding periods and other loan stipulations, such as commitment fees, loan origination fees, and compensating balance requirements, affect the effective annual rate of a bank loan.	bank rate, p. 698 bridge loan, p. 698 committed line of credit, p. 698 discount loan, p. 699 evergreen credit, p. 698 line of credit, p. 698 loan origination fee, p. 699 London Inter-Bank Offered Rate (LIBOR), p. 698 prime rate, p. 698 promissory note, p. 697 revolving line of credit, p. 698 uncommitted line of credit, p. 698	MyLab Study Plan 20.3
20.4 Short-Term Financing with Commercial Paper		
■ Commercial paper is a method of short-term financing that is usually available only to large companies with high-quality credit ratings. It is a low-cost alternative to a short-term bank loan for those firms with access to the commercial paper market.	commercial paper, p. 701 dealer paper, p. 701 direct paper, p. 701	MyLab Study Plan 20.4

KEY POINTS	TERMS	ONLINE PRACTICE OPPORTUNITIES
20.5 Short-Term Financing with Secured Financing ■ Short-term loans may also be structured as secured loans. The accounts receivable and inventory of a firm typically serve as collateral in short-term secured financing arrangements. ■ Accounts receivable may be either pledged as security for a loan or factored. In a factoring arrangement, the accounts receivable are sold to the lender (or factor), and the firm's customers are usually instructed to make payments directly to the factor. ■ Inventory can be used as collateral for a loan in several ways: a floating lien (also called a general or blanket lien), a trust receipts loan (or floor planning), or a warehouse arrangement. These arrangements vary in the extent to which specific items of inventory are identified as collateral; consequently, these arrangements vary in the amount of risk the lender faces.	factoring of accounts receivable arrangement, p. 702 factors, p. 702 field warehouse, p. 704 floating lien (general lien, or blanket lien), p. 703 pledging of accounts receivable agreement, p. 702 public warehouse, p. 704 secured loan, p. 702 trust receipts loan (floor planning), p. 704 warehouse arrangement, p. 704 without recourse, p. 703 with recourse, p. 703	MyLab Study Plan 20.5
20.6 Putting It All Together: Creating a Short-Term Financial Plan ■ A short-term financial plan tracks a firm's cash balance and new and existing short-term financing. The plan allows managers to forecast shortfalls and plan to fund them in the least costly manner.		MyLab Study Plan 20.6 Spreadsheet Table 20.6

REVIEW QUESTIONS

1. What are the objectives of short-term financial planning?
2. What are seasonalities, and what role do they play in short-term financial planning?
3. Which of the following companies are likely to have high short-term financing needs? Why?
   a. A clothing retailer
   b. A professional sports team
   c. An electric utility
   d. A company that operates toll roads
   e. A restaurant chain
4. Why is it important to distinguish between permanent and temporary shortfalls?
5. What is the difference between permanent working capital and temporary working capital?

6. Describe the different approaches a firm could take in preparing for cash flow shortfalls.
7. What are the different bank financing options, and what are their relative advantages?
8. What is the difference between evergreen credit and a revolving line of credit?
9. What is the difference between direct paper and dealer paper?
10. What is the difference between pledging accounts receivable to secure a loan and factoring accounts receivable? What types of short-term secured financing can a firm use to cover shortfalls?
11. What will a short-term financial plan enable a financial manager to do?

PROBLEMS

All problems in this chapter are available in MyLab Finance.

Forecasting Short-Term Financing Needs

1. Sailboats Etc. is a retail company specializing in sailboats and other sailing-related equipment. The following table contains financial forecasts as well as current (month 0) working capital levels.

	Month						
($000s)	**0**	**1**	**2**	**3**	**4**	**5**	**6**
Net Income		10	12	15	25	30	18
Depreciation		2	3	3	4	5	4
Capital Expenditures		1	0	0	1	0	0
Levels of Working Capital							
Accounts Receivable	2	3	4	5	7	10	6
Inventory	3	2	4	5	5	4	2
Accounts Payable	2	2	2	2	2	2	2

a. During which month are the firm's seasonal working capital needs the greatest?
b. When does the firm have surplus cash?

2. Emerald City Umbrellas sells umbrellas and rain gear in Seattle, so its sales are fairly level across the year. However, it is branching out to other markets where it expects demand to be much more variable across the year. Its expected sales in its new market are as follows:

Q1	Q2	Q3	Q4
$20,000	$50,000	$10,000	$50,000

It carries inventory equal to 20% of the next quarter's sales, has accounts payable of 10% of the next quarter's sales, and accounts receivable of 20% of this quarter's sales.

a. Assume that the company starts with $4000 in inventory, $2000 in accounts payable, and no accounts receivable for the new market. Forecast its working capital levels and changes over the four quarters.
b. If Emerald City Umbrellas has net income equal to 20% of sales, what will its financing needs be over the next quarter?

The Matching Principle

The following table includes quarterly working capital levels for your firm for the next year. Use it to answer Problems 3 to 7.

	Quarter			
($000s)	1	2	3	4
Cash	100	100	100	100
Accounts Receivable	200	100	100	600
Inventory	200	500	900	50
Accounts Payable	100	100	100	100

3. What are the permanent working capital needs of your company? What are the temporary needs?

4. If you choose to use only long-term financing, what total amount of borrowing will you need to have on a permanent basis? Forecast your excess cash levels under this scenario.

5. If you hold only $100 in cash at any time, what is your maximum short-term borrowing and when?

6. If you choose to enter the year with $400 total in cash, what is your maximum short-term borrowing?

7. If you want to limit your maximum short-term borrowing to $500, how much excess cash must you carry?

Short-Term Financing with Bank Loans

8. Hand-to-Mouth (H2M) is currently cash-constrained, and must make a decision about whether to delay paying one of its suppliers, or take out a loan. They owe the supplier $10,000 with terms of 2/10 Net 40, so the supplier will give them a 2% discount if they pay today (when the discount period expires). Alternatively, they can pay the full $10,000 in one month when the invoice is due. H2M is considering three options:

Alternative A:	Forgo the discount on its trade credit agreement, wait and pay the full $10,000 in one month.
Alternative B:	Borrow the money needed to pay its supplier today from Bank A, which has offered a one-month loan at an APR of 12% with monthly compounding. The bank will require a (no-interest) compensating balance of 5% of the face value of the loan and will charge a $100 loan origination fee. Because H2M has no cash, it will need to borrow the funds to cover these additional amounts as well.
Alternative C:	Borrow the money needed to pay its supplier today from Bank B, which has offered a one-month loan at an APR of 15% with monthly compounding. The loan has a 1% loan origination fee, which, again, H2M will need to borrow to cover.

Which alternative is the cheapest source of financing for Hand-to-Mouth?

9. Your firm has a committed line of credit with your bank with a commitment fee of 0.5% (EAR) and an interest rate of 6% (EAR). The total line is $500,000 and you borrowed $300,000 at the beginning of the year. If you repay the $300,000 at the end of the year, what is your total cost, in dollars of the interest and commitment fee? What is this cost as a percentage of the amount you borrowed?

10. Your firm's bank has offered you two options for short-term financing in the amount of $400,000. The first option is a committed line of credit with a commitment fee of 0.5% (EAR) and an interest rate of 8% (APR, compounded quarterly). The second option is a loan with a 5% compensating balance and an interest rate of 7.6% (APR, compounded quarterly). If you need $380,000 in financing at the beginning of the year and plan to pay it back at the end of the year, which option has a lower effective annual rate of interest?

11. Consider two loans with one-year maturities and identical face values: an 8% loan with a 1% loan origination fee, and an 8% loan with a 5% (no-interest) compensating balance requirement. Which loan would have the higher effective annual rate? Why?

12. Which of the following one-year, $1000 bank loans offers the lowest effective annual rate?

a. A loan with an APR of 6%, compounded monthly
b. A loan with an APR of 6%, compounded annually, with a compensating balance requirement of 10% (on which no interest is paid)
c. A loan with an APR of 6%, compounded annually, with a 1% loan origination fee

13. The Needy Corporation borrowed $10,000 from Bank Ease. According to the terms of the loan, Needy must pay the bank $400 in interest every three months for the three-year life of the loan, with the principal to be repaid at the maturity of the loan. What effective annual rate is Needy paying?

Short-Term Financing with Commercial Paper

14. The Treadwater Bank wants to raise $1 million using three-month commercial paper. The net proceeds to the bank will be $985,000. What is the effective annual rate of this financing for Treadwater?

15. Magna Corporation has an issue of commercial paper with a face value of $1,000,000 and a maturity of six months. Magna received net proceeds of $973,710 when it sold the paper. What is the effective annual rate of the paper to Magna?

16. Assume that the prime rate is 8% APR, compounded quarterly. How much dollar savings in interest did Treadwater (Problem 14) and Magna (Problem 15) achieve by accessing the commercial paper market?

17. The Signet Corporation has issued four-month commercial paper with a $6 million face value. The firm netted $5,870,850 on the sale. What effective annual rate is Signet paying for these funds?

Short-Term Financing with Secured Financing

18. The Ontario Steel Corporation has borrowed $5 million for one month at a stated annual rate of 9%, using inventory stored in a field warehouse as collateral. The warehouser charges a $5000 fee, payable at the end of the month. What is the effective annual rate of this loan?

19. The Rasputin Brewery is considering using a public warehouse loan as part of its short-term financing. The firm will require a loan of $500,000. Interest on the loan will be 10% (APR, annual compounding) to be paid at the end of the year. The warehouse charges 1% of the face value of the loan, payable at the beginning of the year. What is the effective annual rate of this warehousing arrangement?

Creating a Short-Term Financial Plan

20. Construct a short-term financial plan for Whistler Snowboards based on its expansion opportunity described in the "Positive Cash Flow Shocks" part of Section 20.1. Base the plan on the following table, which forecasts additional capital expenditures, marketing (SG&A), and working capital in Q1 and Q2, along with higher sales in Q2 to Q4. Assume that Whistler ends 2019 with $1 million in cash and that its bank will offer it a short-term loan at the rate 2.5% per quarter. (*See MyLab Finance for the data in Excel format.*)

1	Quarter	2019Q4	2020Q1	2020Q2	2020Q3	2020Q4
2	**Income Statement ($000s)**					
3	Sales	4545	5000	6000	6000	6000
4	Cost of Goods Sold	−2955	−3250	−3900	−3900	−3900
5	Selling, General, and Administrative	−455	−1000	−600	−600	−600
6	EBITDA	1135	750	1500	1500	1500
7	Depreciation	−455	−500	−525	−525	−525
8	EBIT	680	250	975	975	975
9	Taxes	−239	−88	−341	−341	−341
10	Net Income	441	162	634	634	634
11	**Statement of Cash Flows**					
12	Net Income		162	634	634	634
13	Depreciation		500	525	525	525
14	Changes in Working Capital					
15	Accounts Receivable		−136	−300	—	—
16	Inventory		—	—	—	—
17	Accounts Payable		48	105	—	—
18	Cash from Operating Activities		574	964	1159	1159
19	Capital Expenditures		−1500	−525	−525	−525
20	Other Investment		—	—	—	—
21	Cash from Investing Activities		−1500	−525	−525	−525
22	Net Borrowing		—	—	—	—
23	Dividends		—	—	—	—
24	Capital Contributions		—	—	—	—
25	Cash from Financing Activities		—	—	—	—
26	Change in Cash and Equivalents (18 + 21 + 25)		−926	439	634	634

PART

Integrative Case 6

This case draws on material from Chapters 18 to 20.

Idexo Corporation is a privately held designer and manufacturer of licensed college apparel in Ottawa, Ontario. In late 2019, after several years of lacklustre performance by the firm, the firm's owner and founder, Rebecca Ferris, returned from retirement to replace the current CEO, reinvigorate the firm, and plan for its eventual sale or a possible IPO. She has hired you to assist with developing the firm's financial plan for the next five years.

In 2019, Idexo had total assets of about $103 million and annual sales of $100 million (see Table 1). The firm was profitable, with expected 2010 earnings of over $9 million, for a net profit margin of 9.1%.[5] However, revenue growth has slowed dramatically in recent years, and the firm's net profit margin has actually been declining. Ferris is convinced the firm can do better. After only several weeks at the helm, she has already identified a number of potential improvements to drive the firm's future growth.

TABLE 1 Idexo's 2019 Income Statement and Balance Sheet

1	Year	2019		1	Year	2019
2	**Income Statement ($000s)**			2	**Balance Sheet ($000s)**	
3	Sales	100,000		3	**Assets**	
4	Cost of Goods Sold			4	Cash and Cash Equivalents	15,000
5	Raw Materials	−21,333		5	Accounts Receivable	20,000
6	Direct Labour Costs	−24,000		6	Inventories	8219
7	**Gross Profit**	54,667		7	**Total Current Assets**	43,219
8	Sales and Marketing	−15,000		8	Property, Plant, and Equipment	60,000
9	Administration	−18,000		9	Goodwill	—
10	**EBITDA**	21,667		10	**Total Assets**	103,219
11	Depreciation	−6667		11	**Liabilities and Stockholders' Equity**	
12	**EBIT**	15,000		12	Accounts Payable	6205
13	Interest Expense (net)	−1021		13	Debt	20,000
14	**Pre-tax Income**	13,979		14	**Total Liabilities**	26,205
15	Income Tax	−4893		15	**Stockholders' Equity**	77,014
16	**Net Income**	9087		16	**Total Liabilities and Equity**	103,219

[5]See Table 1 for further projected income and balance sheet information for 2010.

Operational Improvements. On the operational side, Ferris is quite optimistic regarding the company's prospects. The market is expected to grow by 6% per year, and Idexo produces a superior product. Idexo's market share has not grown in recent years, because prior management devoted insufficient resources to product development, sales, and marketing. At the same time, Idexo has overspent on administrative costs. Indeed, as shown in Table 1, Idexo's current administrative expenses are $18 million/$100 million = 18% of sales, which exceeds its expenditures on sales and marketing (15% of sales). Competitors spend less on administrative overhead than on sales and marketing.

Ferris plans to cut administrative costs immediately to 15% of sales and redirect resources to new product development, sales, and marketing. By doing so, she believes Idexo can increase its market share from 10% to 14% over the next four years. Using the existing production lines, the increased sales demand can be met in the short run by increasing overtime and running some weekend shifts. The resulting increase in labour costs, however, is likely to lead to a decline in the firm's gross margin to 53%. Table 2 shows sales and operating-cost projections for the next five years based on this plan, including the reallocation of resources from administration to sales and marketing over the five-year period, and an increase in Idexo's average selling price at a 2% inflation rate each year.

TABLE 2 **Idexo's Sales and Operating-Cost Projections**

1	Year		2019	2020	2021	2022	2023	2024
2	***Sales Data***	***Growth/Yr***						
3	Market Size (000s units)	6.0%	20,000	21,200	22,472	23,820	25,250	26,765
4	Market Share	*1.0%	10.0%	11.0%	12.0%	13.0%	14.0%	14.0%
5	Average Sales Price ($/unit)	2.00%	50.00	51.00	2.02	53.06	54.12	55.20
6								
7	**Operating Expense and Tax Data**							
8	Gross Margin		54.7%	53.0%	53.0%	53.0%	53.0%	53.0%
9	Sales and Marketing (% sales)		15.0%	16.5%	18.0%	19.5%	20.0%	20.0%
10	Administration (% sales)		18.0%	15.0%	15.0%	14.0%	13.0%	13.0%
11	Tax Rate		35.0%	35.0%	35.0%	35.0%	35.0%	35.0%

*Market Share growth is expected through 2023 only.

Expansion Plans. Table 3 shows the forecast for Idexo's capital expenditures over the next five years. Based on the estimates for capital expenditures and depreciation, this spreadsheet tracks the book value of Idexo's plant, property, and equipment, starting from its level at the end of 2019. Note that investment is expected to remain relatively low over the next two years—slightly below depreciation. Idexo will expand production during this period by using its existing plant more efficiently.

However, once Idexo's volume grows by more than 50% over its current level, the firm will need to undertake a major expansion to increase its manufacturing capacity. Based on the projections in Table 2, sales growth exceeds 50% of current sales in 2020. Therefore, Table 3 budgets for a major expansion of the plant at that time, leading to a large increase in capital expenditures in 2022 and 2023.

Working Capital Management. To compensate for its weak sales and marketing efforts, Idexo has sought to maintain the loyalty of its retailers, in part through a very lax

TABLE 3 Idexo's Capital Expenditure Forecast

1	Year	2019	2020	2021	2022	2023	2024
2	**Fixed Assets and Capital Investment ($000s)**						
3	Opening Book Value	60,167	60,000	58,500	57,150	73,935	77,341
4	Capital Investment	6500	5000	5000	25,000	12,000	8000
5	Depreciation	−6667	−6500	−6350	−8215	−8594	−8534
6	Closing Book Value	60,000	58,500	57,150	73,935	77,341	76,807

credit policy. This policy affects Idexo's working capital requirements: for every extra day that customers take to pay, another day's sales revenue is added to accounts receivable (rather than received in cash). From Idexo's current income and balance sheet (Table 1), we can estimate the number of days of receivables as follows:

$$\text{Accounts Receivable Days} = \frac{\text{Accounts Receivable (\$)}}{\text{Sales Revenue (\$/yr)}} \times 365 \text{ days/yr}$$
$$= 20 \text{ million}/100 \text{ million} \times 365 = 73 \text{ days}$$

The standard for the industry is 45 days. Ferris believes that Idexo can tighten its credit policy to achieve this goal without sacrificing sales.

Ferris does not foresee any other significant improvements in Idexo's working capital management, and expects inventories and accounts payable to increase proportionately with sales growth. The firm will also need to maintain a minimum cash balance equal to 30 days sales revenue to meet its liquidity needs. It earns no interest on this minimal balance, and Ferris plans to pay out all excess cash each year to the firm's shareholders as dividends.

Capital Structure Changes: Levering Up. Idexo currently has $20 million in debt outstanding with an interest rate of 6.8%, and it will pay interest only on this debt during the next five years. The firm will also obtain additional financing at the end of years 2022 and 2023 associated with the expansion of its manufacturing plant, as shown in Table 4. While Idexo's credit quality will likely improve by that time, interest rates may also increase somewhat. You expect that rates on these future loans will be about 6.8% as well.

Given Idexo's outstanding debt, its interest expense each year is computed as follows:

$$\text{Interest in year } t = \text{Interest Rate} \times \text{Ending Balance in Year } t - 1$$

The interest on the debt will provide a valuable tax shield to offset Idexo's taxable income.

TABLE 4 Idexo's Debt and Interest Forecast

1	Year	2019	2020	2021	2022	2023	2024
2	**Debt and Interest Table ($000s)**						
3	Outstanding Debt	20,000	20,000	20,000	35,000	40,000	40,000
4	Interest on Term Loan 6.80%		−1360	−1360	−1360	−2380	−2720

CASE QUESTIONS

1. Based on the forecasts above, use the spreadsheet below to construct a pro forma income statement for Idexo over the next five years. What is the annual growth rate of the firm's net income over this period?

1	Year	2019	2020	2021	2022	2023	2024
2	**Income Statement ($000s)**						
3	Sales	100,000					
4	Cost of Goods Sold	−45,333					
5	Gross Profit	54,667					
6	Sales and Marketing	−15,000					
7	Administration	−18,000					
8	EBITDA	21,667					
9	Depreciation	−6667					
10	EBIT	15,000					
11	Interest Expense (net)	−1021					
12	Pre-tax Income	13,979					
13	Income Tax	−4893					
14	Net Income	9086					

2. Use the spreadsheet below to project Idexo's working capital needs over the next five years. Why is the increase in net working capital negative in 2020? Why does the increase in net working capital decline from 2023 to 2024?

1	Year	2019	2020	2021	2022	2023	2024
2	**Working Capital ($000s)**						
3	Assets						
4	Accounts Receivable	20,000					
5	Inventories	8219					
6	Minimum Cash Balance	8219					
7	Total Current Assets	36,438					
8	Liabilities						
9	Accounts Payable	6205					
10	Net Working Capital	30,233					
11	Increase in Net Working Capital						

3. Based on the forecasts you have already developed, use the spreadsheet below to project Idexo's free cash flow for 2020 to 2024. Will the firm's free cash flow steadily increase over this period? Why or why not?

1	Year	2019	2020	2021	2022	2023	2024
2	**Free Cash Flow ($000s)**						
3	Net Income						
4	Plus: After-Tax Interest Expense						
5	Unlevered Net Income						
6	Plus: Depreciation						
7	Less: Increases in NWC						
8	Less: Capital Expenditures						
9	Free Cash Flow of Firm						
10	Plus: Net Borrowing						
11	Less: After-Tax Interest Expense						
12	Free Cash Flow to Equity						

4. (Optional) Recall that Idexo plans to maintain only the minimal necessary cash and pay out all excess cash as dividends.

a. Suppose that, at the very end of 2019, Ferris plans to use all excess cash to pay an immediate dividend. How much cash can the firm pay out at this time? Compute a new 2019 balance sheet reflecting this dividend using the spreadsheet below.

b. Forecast the cash available to pay dividends in future years—the firm's *free cash flow to equity*—by adding any new borrowing and subtracting *after-tax* interest expenses from free cash flow each year. Will Idexo have sufficient cash to pay dividends in all years? Explain.

c. Using your forecast of the firm's dividends, construct a pro forma balance sheet for Idexo over the next five years.

1	Year	2019	2020	2021	2022	2023	2024
2	**Balance Sheet ($000s)**						
3	Assets						
4	Cash and Cash Equivalents						
5	Accounts Receivable						
6	Inventories						
7	Total Current Assets						
8	Property, Plant, and Equipment						
9	Goodwill						
10	Total Assets						
11	Liabilities and Stockholders' Equity						
12	Accounts Payable						
13	Debt						
14	Total Liabilities						
15	Stockholders' Equity						
16	Starting Stockholders' Equity						
17	Net Income						
18	Dividends						
19	Capital Contributions						
20	Stockholders' Equity						
21	Total Liabilities and Equity						

5. In late 2019, soon after Ferris's return as CEO, the firm receives an unsolicited offer of $210 million for its outstanding equity. If Ferris accepts the offer, the deal would close at the end of 2019. Suppose Ferris believes that Idexo can be sold at the end of 2024 for an enterprise value equal to nine times its final EBITDA. Idexo's unlevered cost of capital is 10% (specifically, 10% is the pre-tax WACC). Based on your forecast of Idexo's free cash flow in 2020 to 2024 in Question 3, and its final enterprise value in 2024, estimate the following:

a. Idexo's unlevered value at the end of 2019.

b. The present value of Idexo's interest tax shields in 2020 to 2024. (Recall that these tax shields are fixed and so have the same risk level as the debt.)

c. Idexo's enterprise value at the end of 2019. (Add the present value of the interest tax shield in 5b to the unlevered value of the firm in 5a.)

d. Idexo's equity value today. (Adjust the enterprise value in part (c) to reflect the firm's debt and excess cash at the end of 2019.)

e. Based on your analysis, should Ferris sell the company now?

PART

Special Topics

7

CHAPTER 21 Risk Management
CHAPTER 22 International Corporate Finance
CHAPTER 23 Leasing
CHAPTER 24 Mergers and Acquisitions
CHAPTER 25 Corporate Governance

Valuation Principle Connection. In Part 7, the final section of the text, we address special topics in corporate financial management. The Valuation Principle continues to provide a unifying framework as we consider these topics. In Chapter 21, we focus on corporations' use of options and other methods to manage risk. We use the Valuation Principle to evaluate the costs and benefits of risk management. Chapter 22 introduces the issues a firm faces when making a foreign investment, and addresses the valuation of foreign projects. We will see that the Law of One Price generates several important relations that will drive our valuation of foreign cash flows. Chapter 23 introduces an alternative to long-term debt financing, leasing. By presenting leasing as a financing alternative, we apply the Law of One Price to determine that the benefits of leasing must derive from the tax differences, incentive effects, or other market imperfections. The Law of One Price continues to provide a unifying framework as we consider the topics of mergers and acquisitions in Chapter 24 and corporate governance in Chapter 25.

CHAPTER

21 Risk Management

LEARNING OBJECTIVES

- Understand the use of insurance to manage financial risk
- Demonstrate how commodity price changes create risk and how to manage that risk
- Show how a nonfinancial firm can still be at risk from fluctuations in interest rates

NOTATION

r_f	risk-free interest rate	$Pr(\cdot)$	probability of
r_L	cost of capital for an insured loss	$\tilde{r}_t$	floating interest rate on date t
β_L	beta of an insured loss	NPV	net present value

All firms are subject to risk from a variety of sources: changes in consumers' tastes and the cost of raw materials, employee turnover, the entry of new competitors, and countless other uncertainties. Entrepreneurs and corporate managers willingly take on these risks in the pursuit of high returns and accept risk as part of the cost of doing business. But as with any other cost, firms should manage risk to minimize its effect on the value of the firm.

The primary method of risk management is prevention. For example, firms can avoid, or at least reduce, many potential risks by increasing safety standards in the workplace by making prudent investment decisions and by conducting appropriate due diligence when entering into new relationships. But some risks are too costly to prevent and are the inevitable consequences of running a business. As discussed in Part 6 of the text, the firm shares these business risks with its investors through its capital structure. Some of the risk is passed on to debt holders, who bear the risk that the firm will default. Most of the risk is held by equity holders, who are exposed to the volatility of the stock's realized return. Both types of investors can reduce their risk by holding the firm's securities in a well-diversified portfolio.

Not all risks need to be passed on to the firm's debt and equity holders. Insurance and financial markets allow firms to trade risk and shield their debt holders and equity holders from some types of risk. For example, after a fire shut down its processing plant in January 2005, Suncor Energy received more than $200 million in settlements from insurance contracts covering both the damage to the plant and the lost business while the plant was being repaired. Much of the loss from the fire was thus borne by Suncor's insurers rather than by its investors. In 2007, Southwest Airlines received $686 million from financial contracts that compensated it for the rise in the cost of jet fuel. Air Canada received $31 million from financial contracts that protected its fuel prices in 2007 and had contracts that protected 28% of its 2008 fuel needs in the price range of $61 to $68 per barrel while world oil prices surpassed $130 per barrel. In 2011, Cisco held contracts to protect more than $5 billion worth of projected foreign revenues from fluctuations in exchange rates, and General Electric held contracts, with a total market value exceeding $10 billion, designed to reduce its exposure to interest rate fluctuations.

In this chapter, we consider the strategies that firms use to manage and reduce the risk borne by their investors. We begin with the most common form of risk management: insurance. After carefully considering the costs and benefits of insurance, we look at the ways firms can use financial markets to off-load the risks associated with changes in commodity prices and interest rate movements. (We address exchange rate fluctuations in the following chapter.)

21.1 Insurance

property insurance A type of insurance that companies purchase to compensate them for losses to their assets due to fire, storm damage, vandalism, earthquakes, and other natural and environmental risks.

business liability insurance A type of insurance that covers the costs that result if some aspect of a business causes harm to a third party or someone else's property.

business interruption insurance A type of insurance that protects a firm against the loss of earnings if the business is interrupted due to fire, accident, or some other insured peril.

key personnel insurance A type of insurance that compensates a firm for the loss or unavoidable absence of crucial employees in the firm.

Insurance is the most common method firms use to reduce risk. Many firms purchase **property insurance** to insure their assets against hazards such as fire, storm damage, vandalism, earthquakes, and other natural and environmental risks. Other common types of insurance include the following:

- **Business liability insurance**, which covers the costs that result if some aspect of the business causes harm to a third party or someone else's property
- **Business interruption insurance**, which protects the firm against the loss of earnings if the business is interrupted due to fire, accident, or some other insured peril
- **Key personnel insurance**, which compensates the firm for the loss or unavoidable absence of crucial employees in the firm

In this section, we illustrate the role of insurance in reducing risk and examine its pricing and potential benefits, as well as its costs for a firm.

The Role of Insurance: A Simplified Example

To understand the role of insurance in reducing risk, consider an oil refinery with a 1 in 5000, or 0.02%, chance of being destroyed by a fire in the next year. If it is destroyed, the firm estimates that it will lose $150 million in rebuilding costs and lost business. We can summarize the risk from fire with a probability distribution:

Event	Probability	Loss ($ millions)
No fire	99.98%	0
Fire	0.02%	150

Given this probability distribution, the firm's expected loss from fire each year is as follows:

$$(99.98\% \times \$0) + (0.02\% \times \$150 \text{ million}) = \$30{,}000$$

While the expected loss is relatively small, the firm faces a large downside risk if a fire does occur. If the firm could eliminate completely the chance of fire for less than the present value of $30,000 per year, it would do so; such an investment would have a positive NPV. But avoiding *any* chance of a fire is probably not feasible with current technology (or at least would cost far more than $30,000 per year). Consequently, the firm can manage the risk by instead purchasing insurance to compensate its loss of $150 million. In exchange, the firm will pay an annual fee, called an **insurance premium**, to the insurance company. In this way, insurance allows the firm to exchange a random future loss for a certain upfront expense.

insurance premium The fee a firm pays to an insurance company for the purchase of an insurance policy.

Insurance Pricing in a Perfect Market

When a firm buys insurance it transfers the risk of the loss to an insurance company. The insurance company charges an upfront premium to take on that risk. At what price will the insurance company be willing to bear the risk in a perfect market?

In a perfect market without other frictions, insurance companies should compete until they are just earning a fair return and the NPV from selling insurance is zero. The NPV is zero if the price of insurance equals the present value of the expected payment; in that case, we say it is an **actuarially fair price**. Actuaries are professionals who attempt to figure the likelihood and severity of insurance claims. These are the probability and expected payment in the event of a loss, so when we say a price is actuarially fair we mean that the price is fair given the present value of the expected claim. If rL is the appropriate cost of capital given the risk of the loss, we can calculate the actuarially fair premium as follows:[1]

actuarially fair price A price such that the NPV from selling the insurance is zero because the price of the insurance equals the present value of the expected payment.

Actuarially Fair Insurance Premium

$$\text{Insurance Premium} = \frac{Pr(\text{Loss}) \times E[\text{Payment in the Event of Loss}]}{1 + r_L} \tag{21.1}$$

The cost of capital r_L used in Equation 21.1 depends on the risk that is insured. Consider again the oil refinery. The risk of fire is surely unrelated to the performance of the stock market or the economy. Instead, this risk is specific to this firm and, therefore, diversifiable in a large portfolio. As we discussed in Chapter 10, by pooling together the risks from many uncorrelated policies, insurance companies can create very low-risk portfolios whose annual claims are relatively predictable. In other words, the risk of fire has a beta of zero, so it will not command a risk premium. In this case, $r_L = r_f$, the risk-free interest rate.

Not all insurable risks have a beta of zero. Some risks, such as hurricanes and earthquakes, create losses of tens of billions of dollars and may be difficult to diversify completely.[2] Other types of losses may be correlated across firms. Increases in the cost of health care or more stringent environmental regulations raise the potential claims

[1]Equation 21.1 assumes insurance premiums are paid at the start of the year and payments in the event of loss are made at the end of the year. Extending this to alternative timing assumptions is straightforward. An actuarially fair insurance premium will generate a zero NPV from selling the insurance as long as there are no other costs associated with managing the insurance contract (e.g., administration costs).

[2]For example, insured losses from hurricanes Katrina, Rita, and Wilma, which pummelled the southeastern United States in 2005, exceeded $40 billion, with total economic losses topping $100 billion. When insuring large risks such as these, many insurance companies buy insurance on their own portfolios from reinsurance companies. Reinsurance firms pool risks globally from different insurance companies worldwide. For natural disasters, typically one-fourth to one-third of the insured losses are passed on to reinsurers.

from health insurance and liability insurance for all firms. Finally, some risks can have a causal effect on the stock market. The September 11, 2001, terrorist attacks in the United States cost insurers $34 billion[3] and also led to a 12% decline in the S&P 500 in the first week of trading following the attacks.

For risks that cannot be fully diversified, the cost of capital r_L will include a risk premium. By its very nature, insurance for nondiversifiable hazards is generally a negative-beta asset (it pays off in bad times); the insurance payment to the firm tends to be *larger* when total losses are high and the market portfolio is low. Thus, the risk-adjusted rate r_L for losses is *less than* the risk-free rate r_f (in effect, there is a negative risk premium), leading to a *higher* insurance premium, as shown in Equation 21.1 and demonstrated in Example 21.1. Although firms that purchase insurance earn a return $r_L \leq r_f$ on their investment, because of the negative beta of the insurance payoff it is still a zero-NPV transaction.[4]

EXAMPLE 21.1 Insurance Pricing and the CAPM

PROBLEM

As the owner of the CN Tower in Toronto, you decide to purchase insurance that will pay $1 billion in the event the building is destroyed by terrorists. Suppose the likelihood of such a loss is 0.1%, the risk-free interest rate is 4%, and the expected return of the market is 10%. If the risk has a beta of zero, what is the actuarially fair insurance premium? What is the premium if the beta of terrorism insurance is −2.5? Assume the timeframe is one year and that any insurance payout would be one year from now.

SOLUTION

Plan

The expected loss is 0.1% × $1 billion = $1 million.

Given a risk-free rate of 4% and an expected market return of 10%, we can use the Capital Asset Pricing Model (CAPM) to compute the rate of return we would use to compute the fair insurance premium under the two scenarios of a zero beta and a beta of −2.5. Once we have the rate of return, we will divide the expected loss (the cash flow) by 1 + rate of return, as shown in Equation 21.1.

Execute

If the risk has a beta of zero, we compute the insurance premium using the risk-free interest rate:

$$\$1 \text{ million}/1.04 = \$961{,}538$$

Given a beta for the loss, βL, of −2.5, the required return is as follows:

$$r_L = r_f + \beta_L(r_{mkt} - r_f) = 4\% - 2.5(10\% - 4\%) = -11\%$$

In this case, the actuarially fair premium is $1 million/(1 − 0.11) = $1,123,596.

Evaluate

Although this premium exceeds the expected loss when there is a negative beta, it is a fair price given the negative beta of the risk. The insurance pays off exactly when the cash flows from your business operations are likely to be very low.

---

[3]This includes property, life, and liability insurance, as estimated by the Insurance Information Institute, www.iii.org.

[4]Not all insurance must have a zero or negative beta; a positive beta is possible if the amount of the insured loss is higher when market returns are also high.

The Value of Insurance

In a perfect capital market, insurance will be priced so that it has an NPV of zero for both the insurer and the insured. But if purchasing insurance has an NPV of zero, what benefit does it have for the firm?

Modigliani and Miller have already provided us with the answer to this question; in a perfect capital market, there is no benefit to the firm from any financial transaction, *including insurance*. Insurance is a zero-NPV transaction that has no effect on value. Although insurance allows the firm to divide its risk in a new way (e.g., the risk of fire is held by insurers, rather than by debt and equity holders), the firm's total risk—and, therefore, its value—remains unchanged.

Thus, similar to a firm's capital structure, the value of insurance must come from reducing the cost of market imperfections on the firm. Let's consider the potential benefits of insurance with respect to market imperfections considered in Part 6 of the text.

Bankruptcy and Financial Distress Costs. When a firm borrows, it increases its chances of experiencing financial distress. In Chapter 16, we saw that financial distress may impose significant direct and indirect costs on the firm, including agency costs, such as excessive risk taking and underinvestment. By insuring risks that could lead to distress, the firm can reduce the likelihood that it will incur these costs.

For example, for an airline with a large amount of leverage, the losses associated with an accident involving one of its planes may lead to financial distress. While the actual losses from the incident might be $150 million, the costs from distress might

EXAMPLE 21.2 Avoiding Distress and Issuance Costs

PROBLEM

Suppose the risk of an airline accident for a major airline is 1% per year, with a beta of zero. If the risk-free rate is 4%, what is the actuarially fair premium for a policy that pays $150 million in the event of a loss? What is the NPV of purchasing insurance for an airline that would experience $15 million in financial distress costs and $10 million in issuance costs if it were uninsured in the event of a loss?

SOLUTION

■ Plan

The expected loss is 1% × $150 million = $1.5 million, but the total value to the airline is $150 million plus an additional $25 million in distress and issuance costs that it can avoid if it has insurance. The premium is based solely on the expected loss, as the present value of the expected loss shown in Equation 21.1. Because the beta is zero, the appropriate discount rate is 4%.

■ Execute

The actuarially fair premium is $1.5 million/1.04 = $1.44 million.

The NPV of purchasing the insurance is the expected benefit, including avoiding the distress and issuance costs, net of the premium:

$$NPV = -1.44 + 1\% \times (150 + 25)/1.04 = \$0.24 \text{ million}$$

■ Evaluate

The insurance company charges a premium to cover the expected cash flow it must pay, but receiving the insurance payment may be worth more than the amount of the payment. The insurance payment allows the firm to avoid other costs, so it is possible for the premium to be actuarially fair and for the insurance to still be a positive-NPV investment.

be an additional $40 million. The airline can avoid these distress costs by purchasing insurance that will cover the $150 million loss. In this case, the $150 million paid by the insurer is worth $190 million to the firm.

Issuance Costs. When a firm experiences losses, it may need to raise cash from outside investors by issuing securities. Issuing securities is an expensive endeavour. In addition to underwriting fees and transaction costs, there are costs from underpricing due to adverse selection, as well as potential agency costs due to reduced ownership concentration. Because insurance provides cash to the firm to offset losses, it can reduce the firm's need for external capital and thus reduce issuance costs.

Tax Rate Fluctuations. When a firm is subject to graduated income tax rates, insurance can produce a tax savings if the firm is in a higher tax bracket when it pays the premium than the tax bracket it is in when it receives the insurance payment in the event of a loss.

Consider a canola farmer with a 10% chance of a weather-related crop failure. If the risk of crop failure has a beta of zero and the risk-free rate is 4%, the actuarially fair premium per $100,000 of insurance is as follows:

$$\frac{1}{1.04} \times 10\% \times \$100{,}000 = \$9615$$

Suppose the farmer's current tax rate is 35%. In the event of a crop failure, however, the farmer expects to earn much less income and face a lower 15% tax rate. Then the farmer's NPV from purchasing insurance is positive:

$$\begin{aligned} NPV &= -\$9615 \times (1 - 0.35) + \underbrace{\frac{1}{1.04} \times 10\% \times \$100{,}000}_{= \$9615} \times (1 - 0.15) \\ &= \$1923 \end{aligned}$$

The benefit arises because the farmer is able to shift income from a period in which he has a high tax rate (by purchasing insurance) to a period in which he has a low rate (when overall income is reduced and the insurance payout is received). This tax benefit of insurance can be large if the potential losses are significant enough to have a substantial impact on a firm's marginal tax rate.

Debt Capacity. Firms limit their leverage to avoid financial distress costs. Because insurance reduces the risk of financial distress, it can relax this trade-off and allow the firm to increase its use of debt financing. In fact, it is not unusual for creditors to require the firm to carry insurance as part of a covenant. In Chapter 16, we found that debt financing provides several important advantages for the firm, including lower corporate tax payments due to the interest tax shield, lower issuance costs, and lower agency costs (through an increase in equity ownership concentration and a reduction in excess cash flow).

Managerial Incentives. By eliminating the volatility that results from perils outside management's control, insurance turns the firm's earnings and share price into informative indicators of management's performance. The firm can therefore increase its reliance on these measures as part of performance-based compensation schemes, without exposing managers to unnecessary risk. In addition, by lowering the volatility of the stock, insurance can encourage concentrated ownership by an outside director or investor who will monitor the firm and its management.

Risk Assessment. Insurance companies specialize in assessing risk. In many instances, they may be better informed about the extent of certain risks that may affect the firm than the firm's own managers. This knowledge can benefit the firm by improving its investment decisions. Requiring the firm to purchase fire insurance, for example, implies that the firm will consider differences in fire safety, through their effects on the insurance premium, when choosing a warehouse. Otherwise, the managers might overlook such differences. Insurance firms also routinely monitor the firms they insure and can make value-enhancing safety recommendations.

The Costs of Insurance

When insurance premiums are actuarially fair, using insurance to manage the firm's risk can reduce costs and improve investment decisions. But in reality, market imperfections exist that can raise the cost of insurance above the actuarially fair price and offset some of these benefits.

Insurance Market Imperfections. Three main frictions may arise between the firm and its insurer. First, transferring the risk to an insurance company entails administrative and overhead costs. The insurance company must employ sales personnel who seek out clients, underwriters who assess the risks of a given property, appraisers and adjusters who assess the damages in the event of a loss, and lawyers who can resolve potential disputes that arise over the claims from a loss. Insurance companies will include these expenses when setting their premiums. In 2017, expenses for the property and casualty insurance industry amounted to approximately 27.95% of premiums charged.[5]

A second factor that raises the cost of insurance is adverse selection. Recall that a manager's desire to sell equity may signal that the manager knows the firm is likely to perform poorly. Similarly, a firm's desire to buy insurance may signal that it has above-average risk. If firms have private information about how risky they are, insurance companies must be compensated for this adverse selection with higher premiums.

Agency costs are a third factor that contributes to the price of insurance. Insurance reduces the firm's incentive to avoid risk. This change in behaviour that results from the presence of insurance is referred to as **moral hazard**. For example, after purchasing fire insurance, a firm may decide to cut costs by reducing expenditures on fire prevention. The extreme case of moral hazard is insurance fraud, in which insured parties falsify or deliberately cause losses to collect insurance money. Property and casualty insurance companies estimate that moral hazard costs account for more than 11% of premiums.[6]

moral hazard A reduction, due to a firm's purchasing of insurance, of the firm's incentive to avoid risk.

EXAMPLE 21.3 Adverse Selection and Policy Limits

PROBLEM

Your firm faces a potential $100 million loss that it would like to insure. Because of tax benefits and the avoidance of financial distress and issuance costs, each $1 received in the event of a loss is worth $1.50 to the firm. Two policies are available: one pays $55 million and the other pays $100 million if a loss occurs. The insurance company charges 20% more than the actuarially fair premium to cover administrative expenses. To account for adverse selection, the insurance company estimates a 5% probability of loss for the $55 million policy and a 6% probability of loss for the $100 million policy.

[5]Insurance Information Institute, https://www.iii.org/article/2017-commentary-on-year-end-financial-results.

[6]Insurance Research Council estimate (2002).

Suppose the beta of the risk is zero and the risk-free rate is 5%. Which policy should the firm choose if its risk of loss is 5%? Which should it choose if its risk of loss is 6%?

SOLUTION

Plan

The premium for each policy will be based on the expected loss using the insurance company's estimate of the probability of loss:

$55 million policy: 5% chance of loss $100 million policy: 6% chance of loss

Because it is charging 20% more than the actuarially fair premium, the insurance company will set the premium at 1.20 times the present value of expected losses.

However, the value of the policy to you depends on your estimate of the true probability of loss, which is based on your own assessment and does not depend on the size of the policy. Because each $1 of insured loss benefits your firm by $1.50, you are willing to pay 1.50 times the present value of the expected loss.

Because the beta of the risk is 0, the risk-free rate of 5% is the appropriate discount rate for all calculations.

Execute

The premium charged for each policy is as follows:

$$\text{Premium (\$55 million policy)} = \frac{5\% \times \$55 \text{ million}}{1.05} \times 1.20 = \$3.14 \text{ million}$$

$$\text{Premium (\$100 million policy)} = \frac{6\% \times \$100 \text{ million}}{1.05} \times 1.20 = \$6.86 \text{ million}$$

If the true risk of a loss is 5%, the NPV of each policy is as follows:

NPV ($55 million policy):

$$= -\$3.14 \text{ million} + \frac{5\% \times \$55 \text{ million}}{1.05} \times 1.50 = \$0.79 \text{ million}$$

NPV ($100 million policy):

$$= -\$6.86 \text{ million} + \frac{5\% \times \$100 \text{ million}}{1.05} \times 1.50 = \$0.28 \text{ million}$$

Thus, with a 5% risk, the firm should choose the policy with lower coverage. If the risk of a loss is 6%, the policy with higher coverage is superior:

NPV ($55 million policy):

$$= -\$3.14 \text{ million} + \frac{6\% \times \$55 \text{ million}}{1.05} \times 1.50 = \$1.57 \text{ million}$$

NPV ($100 million policy):

$$= -\$6.86 \text{ million} + \frac{6\% \times \$100 \text{ million}}{1.05} \times 1.50 = \$1.71 \text{ million}$$

Evaluate

Note that the insurance company's concerns regarding adverse selection are justified: firms that are riskier will choose the higher-coverage policy.

Addressing Market Imperfections. Insurance companies try to mitigate adverse selection and moral hazard costs in a number of ways. To prevent adverse selection, they screen applicants to assess their risk as accurately as possible. Just as medical examinations are often required for individuals seeking life insurance, plant inspections and reviews of safety procedures are required to obtain large commercial insurance policies. To deter moral hazard, insurance companies routinely investigate losses to look for evidence of fraud or deliberate intent.

Insurance companies also structure their policies to reduce these costs. For example, most policies include both a **deductible**, which is the initial amount of the loss that is not covered by insurance and must be paid by the insured, and **policy limits**, provisions that limit the amount of the loss that is covered regardless of the extent of the damage. These provisions mean that the firm continues to bear some of the risk of the loss even after it is insured. In this way, the firm retains an incentive to avoid the loss, reducing moral hazard. Also, because a risky firm will prefer lower deductibles and higher limits (because it is more likely to experience a loss), insurers can use the firm's policy choice to help identify its risk and reduce adverse selection.

deductible A provision in an insurance policy in which an initial amount of loss is not covered by the policy and must be paid by the insured.

policy limits Provisions in an insurance policy that limit the amount of loss that the policy covers regardless of the extent of the damage.

The Insurance Decision

In a perfect capital market, purchasing insurance does not add value to the firm. It can add value in the presence of market imperfections, but market imperfections are also likely to raise the premiums insurers charge. For insurance to be attractive, the benefit to the firm must exceed the additional premium the insurer charges.

For these reasons, insurance is most likely to be attractive to firms that are currently financially healthy, do not need external capital, and are paying high current tax rates. They will benefit most from insuring risks that can lead to cash shortfalls or financial distress, and that insurers can accurately assess and monitor to prevent moral hazard.

Full insurance is unlikely to be attractive for risks about which firms have a great deal of private information or that are subject to severe moral hazard. Also, firms that are already in financial distress have a strong incentive not to purchase insurance—they need cash today and have an incentive to take risk because future losses are likely to be borne by their debt holders.

CONCEPT CHECK

1. How can insurance add value to a firm?
2. Identify the costs of insurance that arise due to market imperfections.

21.2 Commodity Price Risk

Firms use insurance to protect against the unlikely event that their real assets are damaged or destroyed by hazards such as fire, hurricane, accident, or other catastrophes that are outside their normal course of business. At the same time, many risks that firms face arise naturally as part of their business operations. For many firms, changes in the market prices of the raw materials they use and the goods they produce may be the most important source of risk to their profitability. In the airline industry, for example, the second-largest expense after labour is jet fuel. With oil prices increasing from a low of $17 a barrel in 2001 to nearly $150 a barrel in mid-2008, most major carriers struggled to achieve profitability. Industry analysts estimate that each $1 per barrel increase in the price of oil equates to a $425 million increase in the industry's annual jet fuel expenses. For an airline, the risk from increases in the price of oil is clearly one of the most important risks that it faces.

hedge Risk reduction achieved by using contracts or transactions which provide the firm with cash flows that offset its losses from price changes.

In this section, we discuss the ways firms can reduce, or **hedge**, their exposure to commodity price movements. Like insurance, hedging involves contracts or transactions that provide the firm with cash flows that offset its losses from price changes.

Hedging with Vertical Integration and Storage

Firms can hedge risk by making real investments in assets with offsetting risk. The most common strategies are *vertical integration* and *storage*.

vertical integration The merger of two companies in the same industry that make products required at different stages of the production cycle.

Vertical Integration. The merger of a firm and its supplier (or a firm and its customer) is referred to as **vertical integration**. Because an increase in the price of the commodity raises the firm's costs and the supplier's revenues, these firms can offset their risks by merging. For example, in 2005, Japanese tire maker Bridgestone purchased a large Indonesian rubber plantation to control its costs. As the price of rubber increases, so will the profits of the rubber plantation, offsetting the higher costs of making tires. Similarly, airlines could offset their oil price risk by merging with an oil company.

While vertical integration can reduce risk, it does not always increase value. Recall the key lesson of Modigliani and Miller: firms add no value by doing something investors can do for themselves. Investors concerned about commodity price risk can diversify by "vertically integrating" their portfolios and buying shares of the firm and its supplier. Because the acquiring firm often pays a substantial premium over the current share price of the firm being acquired, the shareholders of the acquiring firm would generally find it cheaper to diversify on their own. Vertical integration can add value if combining the firms results in important synergies. For example, Boeing ultimately decided to purchase a number of its suppliers involved in its 787 "Dreamliner" to improve quality control and coordination, and reduce production delays. In many instances, however, diseconomies would be the more likely outcome, as the combined firm would lack a strategic focus (e.g., airlines combined with oil producers). Finally, vertical integration is not a perfect hedge; a firm's supplier is exposed to many other risks besides commodity prices. By integrating vertically, the firm eliminates one risk but acquires others.

Storage. A related strategy is the long-term storage of inventory. An airline concerned about rising fuel costs could purchase a large quantity of fuel today and store the fuel until it is needed. By doing so, the firm locks in its cost for fuel at today's price plus storage costs. But for many commodities, storage costs are much too high for this strategy to be attractive. Such a strategy also requires a substantial cash outlay upfront. If the firm does not have the required cash, it would need to raise external capital—and consequently would suffer issuance and adverse selection costs. Finally, maintaining large amounts of inventory would dramatically increase working capital requirements, a cost for the firm. Storage of inventory also does not work for firms that produce and sell commodities. Managers at these firms are concerned about the price at which their commodity is *sold*; storage of inventory would actually be counterproductive as a hedging strategy for commodity sellers, as they would have a greater quantity waiting to be sold and would be subject to the commodity price risk on this greater quantity.

HEDGING STRATEGY LEADS TO PROMOTION . . . SOMETIMES

A good example is provided by Southwest Airlines. In early 2000, when oil prices were close to $20 per barrel, CFO Gary Kelly developed a strategy to protect the airline from a surge in oil prices. By the time oil prices soared above $30 per barrel later that year and put the airline industry into a financial crisis, Southwest had already signed contracts guaranteeing a price for its fuel equivalent to $23 per barrel. The savings from its fuel hedge amounted to almost 50% of Southwest's earnings that year, as shown in Figure 21.1. Kelly was promoted to become Southwest's CEO, and Southwest has continued this strategy to hedge fuel costs. Between 1998 and 2008, Southwest saved $3.5 billion over what it would have spent if it had paid the industry's average price for jet fuel, accounting for 83% of the company's profits during that period.

Of course, like insurance, commodity hedging does not always boost a firm's profits. Had oil prices fallen below $23 per barrel in the fall of 2000, Southwest's hedging policy would have reduced the firm's earnings by obligating it to pay $23 per barrel for its oil (and perhaps Kelly might not have gone on to be CEO). Presumably, Southwest felt that it could afford to pay $23 per barrel for oil even if the price fell. While the long-term contracts would have been costly, they would not have led to financial distress. In other words, the long-term contracts stabilized Southwest's earnings at an acceptable level, no matter what happened to oil prices. Figure 21.1 illustrates how hedging stabilizes earnings.

Air Canada also has a history of fuel hedging. From 1994 to 1996, oil prices had increased by about 33%. In 1997, Air Canada signed contracts locking in about one-half of its anticipated 1998 fuel needs at an oil price of $19 per barrel. Unfortunately, in 1998, oil prices dropped to about $12 per barrel, and Air Canada lost the equivalent of $89 million because of these contracts. Nobody was promoted because of this result.

Southwest increased its fuel hedges in the years that followed, but Air Canada hedged a lower proportion of its fuel costs. At the end of 2007, Air Canada had hedges for its anticipated fuel needs of about 20% for 2008, 3% for 2009, and 2% for 2010. At the beginning of 2007, Southwest had 100% of its fuel costs hedged. At the beginning of 2008, Southwest had its anticipated fuel costs hedged as follows: 70% for 2008 at $51 per barrel, 55% for 2009 at $51 per barrel, 30% for 2010 at $63 per barrel, and 15% for each of 2011 and 2012 at $63 to $64 per barrel. Which strategy will be better depends on oil prices. By early July 2008, oil was over $145 per barrel, so Southwest's strategy looked better.

WestJet followed an alternative strategy; at the end of 2007, WestJet had no outstanding fuel hedges. Certainly, the hedging strategy of Southwest helped its earnings in mid-2008, but as oil prices dropped rapidly with the onset of the world financial crisis and fell below $40 per barrel by the end of 2008, Southwest's hedging strategy hurt its earnings. In 2009, Southwest's hedging actually reduced its earnings by about $245 million. Was WestJet the winner in terms of these hedged or unhedged strategies? Again, time will tell. By early 2011, oil prices were again over $100 per barrel. Prices varied between $112 and $53.45 per barrel in the period 2011–2014. In 2014, the price of oil dropped by 50% from June to December, so airlines that entered into hedging strategies in June would have suffered compared to those airlines that remained unhedged. However, after their recent low around $30 per barrel in early 2016, oil prices had more than doubled by early 2018; thus, airlines that hedged over this time period would have benefited significantly.

Predicting the price in the future is always very difficult. Thus, hedging should not be done because of a feeling as to where prices will go; it should be done on the basis of whether benefits besides price stability, such as reducing financial distress costs, will result from the strategy.

Hedging with Long-Term Contracts

An alternative to vertical integration or storage is a long-term supply contract. Firms routinely enter into long-term lease contracts for real estate, fixing the price at which they will obtain office space many years in advance. Similarly, utility companies sign long-term supply contracts with power generators, and steelmakers sign long-term contracts with mining firms for iron ore. Through these contracts, both parties can achieve price stability for their product or input.

Of course, similar to insurance, commodity hedging does not always boost a firm's profits. Consider a steelmaker and an iron ore producer that lock in the iron ore price for future transactions through long-term contracts. The steelmaker agrees to buy the iron ore, and the iron ore producer agrees to sell it; they fix the price today for future transactions. If the market price of iron ore rises, then the steelmaker's profits will be boosted and the iron ore producer's profits will be reduced relative to what would have

FIGURE 21.1 Commodity Hedging Smoothes Earnings

By locking in its fuel costs through long-term supply contracts, Southwest Airlines has kept its earnings stable in the face of fluctuating fuel prices. The figure corresponds to the Southwest hedge described in the "Hedging Strategy ..." box earlier. With a long-term contract at a price of $23 per barrel, Southwest would gain by buying at this price if oil prices go above $23 per barrel. If oil prices fall below $23 per barrel, Southwest would lose from its commitment to buy at a higher price. Note that the figure assumes no changes to the firm's revenues or other costs.

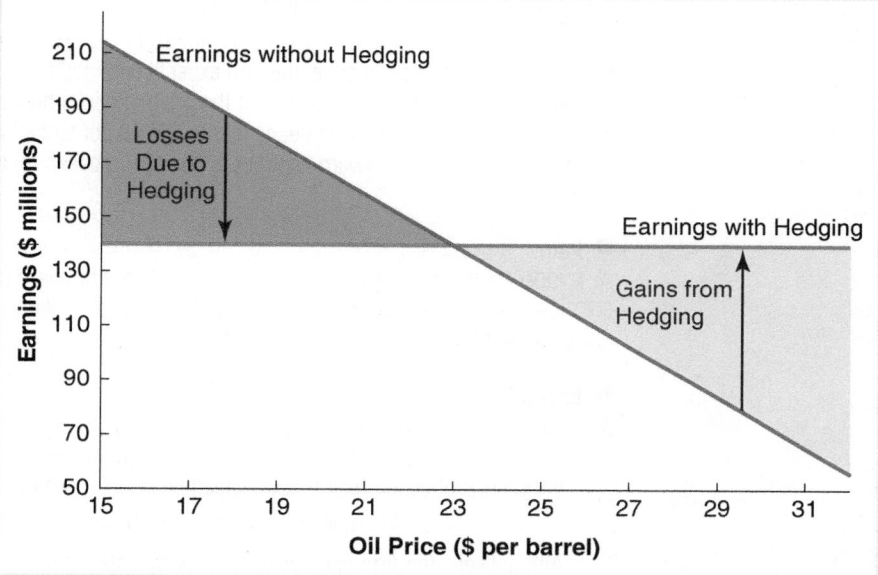

happened without the long-term contracts. On the other hand, if the market price of iron ore falls, then the steelmaker's profits will be reduced while the iron ore producer's profits will be boosted relative to what would have happened without the long-term contracts. In other words, the long-term contracts can be used to stabilize earnings at an acceptable level, no matter what happens to the iron ore prices. Figure 21.1 illustrates how hedging stabilizes earnings for the purchaser of a commodity.

forward contract A customized agreement between two parties who are known to each other, whereby they agree to trade an asset on some future date at a price that is fixed today.

One form of long-term contact is called a **forward contract**. A forward contract is a customized agreement between two parties who are known to each other, whereby they agree to trade a certain quantity of an asset on some future date at a price that is fixed today. Forward contracts and many other types of long-term supply contracts are bilateral contracts negotiated by a buyer and a seller to suit their particular needs. Unfortunately, such contracts have several potential disadvantages:

1. They expose each party to the risk that the other party may default and fail to live up to the terms of the contract. Thus, although long-term contracts insulate the firms from commodity price risk, they expose them to credit (default) risk.
2. Long-term contracts cannot be entered into anonymously; the buyer and seller know each other's identity. This lack of anonymity may have strategic disadvantages, as a party's willingness to enter into the contract reveals information to its rivals about its risk exposures.
3. The market value of the long-term contract at any point in time may not be easy to determine, making it difficult to track gains and losses, and it may be difficult or even impossible to cancel the contract if necessary.

An alternative strategy that avoids these disadvantages is to hedge with futures contracts. In the next section we investigate this strategy.

EXAMPLE 21.4 Hedging with a Forward Contract

PROBLEM

Consider a chocolate maker that will need 10,000 tonnes of cocoa beans next year. Due to political unrest in Ivory Coast where 40% of the world's cocoa beans are produced, there is a lot of uncertainty about cocoa beans supply and future prices. The current market price of cocoa beans is $2900 per tonne. At this price, the firm expects earnings before interest and taxes of $44 million next year. What will the firm's EBIT be if the price of cocoa beans rises to $3500 per tonne? What will EBIT be if the price of cocoa beans falls to $2600 per tonne? What will EBIT be in each scenario if the firm enters into a forward contract to buy cocoa beans for a fixed price of $2950 per tonne?

SOLUTION

Plan

At $2900 per tonne, the firm's EBIT is $44 million. For every dollar above $2900 per tonne, its EBIT will decrease by $10,000 (for 10,000 tonnes) and similarly will increase by $10,000 for every dollar below $2900 per tonne.

Execute

At $3500 per tonne, the firm's costs will increase by ($3500 − $2900) × 10,000 = $6 million. Other things being equal, EBIT will decline to $44 million − $6 million = $38 million.

If the price of cocoa beans falls instead to $2600 per tonne, EBIT will rise to

$$\$44 \text{ million} - (\$2600 - \$2900) \times 10{,}000 = \$47 \text{ million}.$$

Alternatively, the firm can avoid this risk by entering into the forward contract that fixes the price in either scenario at $2950 per tonne, for an EBIT of

$$\$44 \text{ million} - (\$2950 - \$2900) \times 10{,}000 = \$43.5 \text{ million}.$$

Evaluate

The firm can completely reduce its cocoa-price risk by entering into the forward contract. The cost is accepting lower (by $500,000) profits for certain. Note, though, there are still risks of supply disruption and other risks within the firm that could be important if management is concerned about risk management.

Hedging with Futures Contracts

futures contract A standardized agreement between two anonymous parties that is traded on an organized futures exchange and contracts the two parties to trade an asset on some future date at a price that is fixed today.

A commodity *futures contract* is a type of long-term contract designed to avoid the disadvantages cited above. A **futures contract** is a standardized agreement to trade an asset on some future date at a price that is locked in today. Futures contracts are traded anonymously on a futures exchange at a publicly observed market price and generally are very liquid. The party who has entered into a futures contract to buy a commodity is said to be "long" in the futures contract; the party who has entered into a futures contract to sell a commodity is said to be "short" in the futures contract. Both the buyer and the seller can get out of the contract at any time by finding a third party to take over the contract at the current market price. Given that the futures contract trades on an organized futures exchange, and that supply and demand forces determine current market prices, parties will always be standing by to enter into these futures contracts and take over the positions of the original parties. Finally, through a mechanism we will describe shortly, futures contracts are designed to almost completely eliminate credit risk.

FIGURE 21.2 Futures Prices for Light, Sweet Crude Oil, September 2010

Each point represents the futures price per barrel in September 2010 for the delivery of oil in the month indicated.

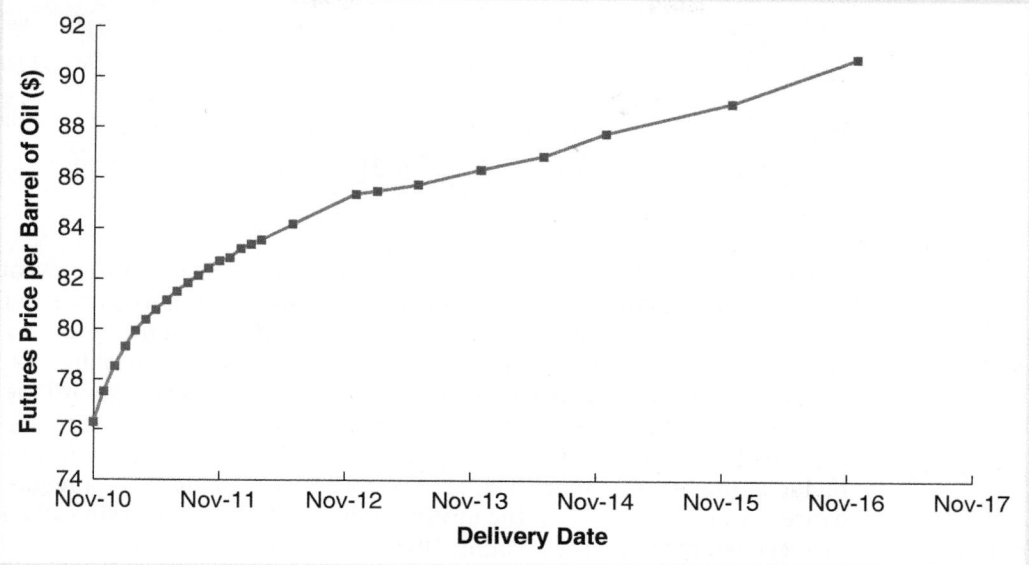

Figure 21.2 shows the prices in September 2010 of futures contracts for light, sweet crude oil traded on the New York Mercantile Exchange (NYMEX). Each contract represents a commitment to trade 1000 barrels of oil at the futures price on its delivery date. For example, by trading the March 2011 contract, buyers and sellers agreed in September 2010 to exchange 1000 barrels of oil in March 2011 at a price of $79.96 per barrel. By doing so, they are able to lock in the price they will pay or receive for oil six months in advance. Buyers and sellers of the December 2016 futures contract locked in a price of $90.80 per barrel for delivery six years and nine months into the future.

The futures prices shown in Figure 21.2 are not prices that are paid on the date the contract is entered. Rather, they are prices *agreed* to on the date the contract is entered but to be paid in the future. The futures prices are determined in the market based on supply and demand for each delivery date. They depend on expectations of future oil prices, adjusted by an appropriate risk premium.

After the passage of time, oil rose to over $100 per barrel in March, 2011; those who originally entered into a contract to buy oil for $79.96 per barrel gained over $20 per barrel (having effectively locked in a price to buy at the lower original futures price instead of the new higher market price), while those who originally entered into a contract to sell for $79.96 lost over $20 per barrel (having effectively locked in a price to sell at the original lower futures price instead of the new higher market price). In contrast, by December 2016, oil dropped to $49 per barrel. Those who contracted to buy for $90.80 lost $41.80 per barrel while those who had contracted to sell gained $41.80 per barrel.

Mitigating Credit Risk in Futures Contracts. If a buyer commits in May 2017 to purchase crude oil for delivery in May 2021 for $50.83 per barrel, how can the seller be assured that the buyer will honour that commitment? If the actual price of oil in December 2021 is only $30 per barrel, the buyer will have a strong incentive to renege and default on the contract. Similarly, the seller will have an incentive to default if the actual price of oil is more than $50.83 in May 2021.

TABLE 21.1 Example of Marking to Market and Daily Settlement for the May 2021 Light, Sweet Crude Oil Futures Contract ($/BBL)

	May 2017						May 2021		
Trading Day	**0**	**1**	**2**	**3**	**4**	**...**	**998**	**999**	**1000**
Futures Price	50.83	48	50	51.7	51.45	...	78.64	79.85	79
Daily Marked-to-Market Profit or Loss		−2.83	2	1.75	−0.3	...	...	1.21	−0.85
Cumulative Profit or Loss		−2.83	−0.83	0.92	0.62	...	27.81	29.02	28.17

margin Collateral that investors are required to deposit into their brokerage account when entering a transaction that could generate losses beyond the initial investment.

marking to market The daily exchange of cash flows based on computing gains and losses due to the daily change in the market price of a futures contract.

margin call A requirement for investors to inject new cash into their brokerage account when their account balance falls below a maintenance margin requirement due to marking to market cash flows.

Default Risk Prevention. Futures exchanges use two mechanisms to prevent buyers or sellers from defaulting. First, investors (both the long and short parties to the futures contract) are required to post collateral, called **margin**, when using futures contracts. This collateral serves as a guarantee that traders will meet their obligations. In addition, cash flows are exchanged on a daily basis, rather than waiting until the end of the contract, through a procedure called **marking to market**. That is, gains and losses are computed each day based on the change in the market price of the futures contract. If, due to the marking to market, an investor's account falls below a required maintenance margin amount, then the investor will be subject to a **margin call** and required to inject new cash into the account. After the marking to market each day, both parties essentially have new futures contracts rewritten with prices based on the new market conditions. The combination of rewritten contracts at the new futures price and the exchange of cash flows through marking to market results in two effects: (1) there is no longer an incentive to default on the futures contract, as it reflects current market conditions, and (2) each party's net purchase or sale price for the commodity (based on a combination of the new futures price and the marking to market cash flows exchanged) is kept at the original futures price that existed when the parties entered the futures contract.

Marking to Market. Consider an example. Suppose that the price of the May 2021 futures contract varies, as shown in Table 21.1, over the 1000 remaining trading days between May 2017 and the delivery date in May 2021. A buyer who enters into the contract on date 0 has committed to pay the futures price of $50.83 per barrel for oil. If the next day the futures price is only $48 per barrel, the buyer has a loss of $2.83 per barrel on her position. This loss is settled immediately by deducting $2.83 from the buyer's margin account. If the price rises to $50 per barrel on day 2, the gain of $2 is added to the buyer's margin account. This process continues until the contract delivery date, with the daily gains and losses shown. The buyer's cumulative loss or gain is the sum of these daily amounts and always equals the difference between the original contract price of $50.83 per barrel and the current contract price

In May 2021, delivery takes place at the final futures price, which is equal to the actual price of oil at that time.[7] In the example in Table 21.1, the buyer ultimately pays $79 per barrel for oil but has gained $28.17 per barrel in her margin account. Thus, her total cost is $79 − $28.17 = $50.83 per barrel, the price for oil she originally committed to. Through this daily marking to market, the contracted futures price is rewritten every day to reflect current market conditions, and buyers and sellers pay for any losses or

[7]At its delivery date, a futures contract is a contract for immediate delivery. Thus, by the Law of One Price, its price must be the actual price of oil in the market.

receive any gains as they occur, rather than waiting until the final delivery date. In this way, the parties to the contract avoid the risk of default.[8]

In essence, the May 2021 futures contract is the same as a forward contract with a set price of $50.83 per barrel of oil. However, with a forward contract that is between two individual parties, there is potential for one party to default if the market price diverges from the forward price. With a futures contract, the buyer and the seller of a futures contract can close their positions at any time (and accept the cumulative losses or gains in their margin accounts), and the contract will then be reassigned to a new buyer or seller, because the contract is continually rewritten to reflect current market conditions. Because of this liquidity and the lack of credit risk, commodity futures contracts are the predominant method by which many firms hedge oil price risk. Similar futures contracts exist for many other commodities, including natural gas, coal, electricity, silver, gold, aluminum, canola, barley, soybeans, corn, wheat, rice, cattle, pork bellies, cocoa, sugar, carbon dioxide emissions, and even frozen concentrated orange juice. In addition, futures contracts exist for many financial products, such as currency exchange, fixed income (interest-rate related) instruments, and stock indices.

Hedging with Options Contracts

In addition to long-term contracts and derivatives such as forward and futures contracts, options are also be very useful for hedging. We described call and put options in detail in Chapter 13; such options exist on a wide variety of commodities.[9] Let's consider how a hedge using futures contracts can be replaced with a hedge using options contracts.

Consider the steel mill and the iron ore companies discussed earlier. They could use futures contracts to hedge against changes in iron ore prices. The steel mill, needing to buy iron ore in the future, would go long in a futures contract on iron ore, and the iron ore producer would go short in a futures contract on iron ore. The steel mill is concerned about iron ore prices increasing and wants to protect itself from that when it comes time to buy the ore. Can the steel mill get protection from increasing iron ore prices using an options contract? The answer is yes. Consider which options contract allows the owner of the contract to buy an asset for a fixed amount even though the price of the asset has risen. Of course, this is a call option contract. So the steel mill company may choose to hedge by buying call options on iron ore rather than hedging through a long futures contract to buy the ore. If iron ore prices rise above the strike price of the call option, the steel mill can exercise the call option and purchase the iron ore at the strike price.

What about the iron ore producer? In the case of a futures contract, the producer would have entered into a short futures contract so as to lock in a price to sell the iron ore in the future. That protects the iron ore producer in case iron ore prices drop. The way to protect against a price drop of iron ore using options is to purchase a put option on iron ore. If the iron ore price drops below the strike price of the put option, the iron ore producer can exercise the put option and sell the iron ore at the strike price. The put option sets a minimum at which the iron ore producer will be able to sell the ore.

---

[8]For this system to work, the buyer's margin account must always have a sufficient balance to cover at least one day's potential loss. If a buyer's remaining margin in the account is too low, below a required maintenance margin amount, then the futures exchange will require the buyer to replenish the account through a margin call. If the buyer fails to do so, the account will be closed and the buyer's contract will be assigned to a new buyer.

[9]In most cases, these options are actually options on futures contracts for the commodity. This distinction is not that important for our purposes, because under the Law of One Price, at the maturity of the options and futures contracts, the futures price becomes a contract for immediate delivery, and thus the futures price will equal the spot price of the commodity.

TABLE 21.2 Alternative Ways for a Firm to Hedge: Futures versus Options Strategies

	Hedge to Protect Against an Unfavourable Price Change	
Firm's Exposure to a Change in the Commodity Price	**Futures Strategy**	**Options Strategy**
Firm intends to buy the commodity in the future: concerned about a price increase	Long futures contract	Purchase a call option
Firm intends to sell the commodity in the future: concerned about a price decrease	Short futures contract	Purchase a put option

To summarize, if a company will need to purchase a commodity in the future, its management can hedge with options by buying a call option on the commodity. If a company will need to sell a commodity in the future, its management can hedge with options by buying a put option on the commodity.

Comparing Futures Hedging with Options Hedging

Table 21.2 shows the alternative ways to hedge using futures or options. These alternatives protect against unfavourable changes in the commodity prices; however, there are important differences between a futures hedging strategy and an options hedging strategy. When an options contract is purchased, the buyer must pay for it (i.e., it is costly). With a futures hedging strategy, there is no cost to enter into the contract. In effect, the party who takes the long futures position does not have to pay the party who takes the short futures position at the time the contract is entered, because both parties are simply signing a contract at a fair market price for a future transaction. (Note that the initial margin requirement is paid by both the long and short parties to a futures contract; the margin is collateral backing up the contract, but it is not a cost of the contract.)

A second difference between hedging with options versus futures is the nature of the final cash flows. With a futures contract, the final price is fixed regardless of whether the market price rises or falls. For example, a firm that has contracted to buy a commodity through a long futures contract is protected against a price rise, but the firm also misses out on the potential savings if the price falls. With an options hedge, the firm is

EXAMPLE 21.5 Hedging: Futures versus Options

PROBLEM

It is April, and Magda Nowak is planting her canola crop on her farm near Trembowla, Manitoba. She expects to grow 1000 tonnes of canola over the season and plans to sell it in November after the harvest is done. Also on this April day, Japan Canola Crushers (JCC) is planning on buying 1000 tonnes of canola in November so that the company can export it to Japan as an input into their canola oil plant. Both Magda and JCC are concerned about the price for canola in November and are considering hedging. The following data about current futures and options contracts are available:

- Futures contracts for delivery in November are available with a futures price of $600 per tonne.
- Call options on canola with expiration in November are available with a strike price of $600 per tonne. These call options cost $34 (per option on one tonne).
- Put options on canola with expiration in November are available with a strike price of $600 per tonne. These put options cost $36 (per option on one tonne).

SOLUTION

Plan

Since Magda will be growing canola, she is concerned about the price dropping by the time she harvests and sells it. She can either enter into short futures contracts on 1000 tonnes of canola or she can purchase put options on 1000 tonnes of canola. JCC, on the other hand, will be buying canola once it is harvested and is concerned that the price will rise before the purchase. JCC can either enter into long futures contracts on 1000 tonnes of canola, or JCC can buy call options on 1000 tonnes of canola.

Execute

Consider the futures hedges of the two parties. Entering into futures contracts for 1000 tonnes at $600 per tonne ensures that, after all futures price changes and marking to market, the net result will be that Magda receives $600,000 and JCC pays $600,000 for the canola in November.

Alternatively, consider the options hedges. First, let's consider Magda's situation. To purchase the put options, she had to pay for puts on 1000 tonnes of canola:

$$\$36 \text{ per put option per tonne} \times 1000 \text{ tonnes} = \$36{,}000$$

If the price of canola in November is less than $600 per tonne, she will exercise her put options and sell her canola at the strike price of $600. In this case, the net amount she receives (after deducting the cost of purchasing the put options) is as follows:

$$\text{Magda's net amount received if puts are exercised} = \$600{,}000 - \$36{,}000 = \$564{,}000$$

On a per tonne basis, Magda's net amount is $564 per tonne whenever the price of canola is $600 or below. If the price of canola is above $600, then Magda will let her put options expire and sell the canola for the more favourable higher market price that exists in November. On a per tonne basis, Magda will net whatever the market price is (over $600) minus the $36 option cost originally paid.

Now consider JCC's situation with the call option hedge. To purchase the call options, JCC had to pay for calls on 1000 tonnes of canola:

$$\$34 \text{ per call option per tonne} \times 1000 \text{ tonnes} = \$34{,}000$$

If the price of canola in November is greater than $600 per tonne, JCC will exercise the call options and buy the canola at the strike price of $600. In this case, the net amount JCC pays (after including the cost of purchasing the call options) is as follows:

$$\text{JCC's net amount paid if calls are exercised} = \$600{,}000 + \$34{,}000 = \$634{,}000$$

On a per tonne basis, JCC's net amount paid is $634 per tonne whenever the price of canola is $600 or above. If the price of canola is below $600, then JCC will let the call options expire and buy the canola for the more favourable lower market price that exists in November. On a per tonne basis, JCC's net cost of the canola will be whatever the market price is (under $600) plus the $34 option cost originally paid.

Evaluate

Both Magda and JCC can completely eliminate canola price risk by using the futures contracts and locking in a price of $600 per tonne. A benefit of using futures is that there is no additional cost of the hedge, but a drawback is that favourable price changes cannot be exploited.

With options hedges, both Magda and JCC can eliminate their exposure to unfavourable price changes. A drawback of options hedges is that they are costly—Magda must pay $36,000 for the put options, and JCC must pay $34,000 for the call options. A benefit of options hedges, though, is that if there is a favourable price change, the party can benefit from it. The graphs below show the net cash flows from the hedges for Magda and JCC:

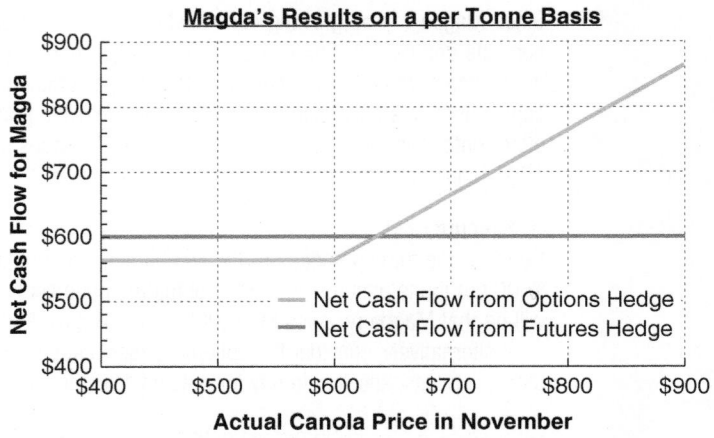

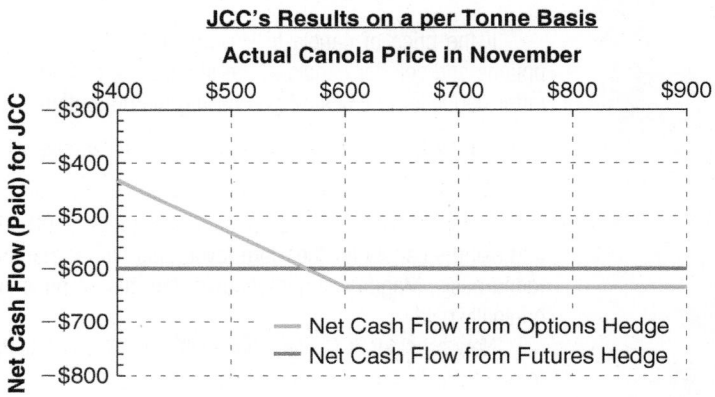

protected against an unfavourable price change, because the option can be exercised; however, if there is a favourable price change, the option can be left to expire unexercised, and the firm can transact at the new favourable price. Example 21.5 shows how the different types of hedges can produce very different net results.

An additional benefit of an options hedge versus a futures hedge arises when there is the possibility that the hedge will not actually be needed. Consider Magda in Example 21.5. She is planting her canola crop and expects to grow 1000 tonnes of canola to sell in November. But what happens if a major hailstorm occurs, resulting in the destruction of her crop and many other farmers' crops and a canola price that jumps to $800 per tonne? Without any canola to sell, Magda no longer needs to hedge against canola price changes. With the put options hedge, she can simply let her put option expire worthless and lose the original $36,000 she paid for the put options. However, with a short futures position, she does not have the canola available that she contracted to deliver. She will have to close out her futures contract on 1000 tonnes of canola at $800 per tonne. The net effect of the marking to market between when she entered into the short futures contracts at $600 and closes out at $800 is as follows:

Magda's loss on short futures position

$$-\$200 \text{ per tonne} \times 1000 \text{ tonnes} = -\$200{,}000$$

With her valuable crop lost, Magda ends up losing an additional $200,000 due to her futures position. Clearly, she would have preferred the put option hedge in this case.

Deciding to Hedge Commodity Price Risk

In a perfect market, commodity supply contracts, futures contracts, and options contracts are zero-NPV investments that do not change the value of the firm. But hedging commodity price risk can benefit the firm by reducing the costs of other frictions. Just as with insurance, the potential benefits include reduced financial distress and issuance costs, tax savings, increased debt capacity, and improved managerial incentives and risk assessment. Commodity futures and options markets, in particular, provide valuable information to commodity producers and users. For example, an oil firm can lock in a future sale price or fix a minimum for the future sale price of oil before it spends millions of dollars on drilling a new well. A canola farmer unsure of future canola prices can lock in the futures price or she can use a put option on canola to ensure her price does not fall below a minimum level. The farmer, knowing her actual costs of seed, fertilizer, and so on, can determine before planting whether she will have a profitable season and can avoid financial distress.

natural hedge The ability of a firm to pass on cost increases to its customers or revenue decreases to its suppliers.

liquidity risk The risk of being forced to liquidate an investment (at a loss) because the cash is required to satisfy another obligation (most often a margin requirement).

Hedging commodity price risk has potential benefits similar to those of buying insurance, but it does not have the same costs. In comparison with the market for hazard insurance, the commodity markets are less vulnerable to the problems of adverse selection and moral hazard. Firms generally do not possess better information than outside investors do regarding the risk of future commodity price changes, nor can they influence that risk through their actions. Also, futures and options contracts are very liquid and do not entail large administrative costs.

COMMON MISTAKE

Mistakes When Hedging Risk

There are several common mistakes to avoid when hedging risk.

Not Accounting for Natural Hedges

Even though purchases of a commodity may be a firm's largest expense, they may not be a source of risk if the firm can pass along those costs to its customers. For example, gas stations do not need to hedge their cost of oil, because the price of gasoline—and thus their revenues—fluctuates with it. When a firm can pass on cost increases to its customers or revenue decreases to its suppliers, it has a **natural hedge** for these risks. A firm should hedge risks to its profits only after such natural hedges are accounted for, lest it over-hedge and increase risk.

Exposing the Firm to Liquidity Risk

When hedging with futures contracts, the firm stabilizes its earnings by offsetting business losses with gains on the futures contracts and by offsetting business gains with losses on the futures contracts. In the latter scenario, the firm runs the risk of receiving margin calls on its futures positions before it realizes the cash flows from the business gains. To hedge effectively, the firm must have, or be able to raise, the cash required to meet these margin calls, or it may be forced to default on its positions. Hence, when hedging with future contracts, the firm is exposed to **liquidity risk**. Such was the case for Metallgesellschaft Refining and Marketing (MGRM), which shut down in 1993 with more than $1 billion in losses in the oil futures market. MGRM had written long-term contracts to supply oil to its customers and hedged its risk that oil prices might rise by buying oil futures. When oil prices subsequently dropped, MGRM faced a cash flow crisis and could not meet the margin calls on its futures positions. Hedging with options contracts does not create the potential for this problem (although options do entail an upfront cost that does not exist with futures contracts).

Mismatching Contracts and Risk Exposure

Futures and options contracts are available only for a set of standardized commodities, with specific delivery dates and locations. Thus, while a futures contract that promises to deliver canola in Saskatchewan in November is a reasonable hedge for canola purchased at the port of Vancouver in December, it will not be a perfect match. **Basis risk** is the risk that arises because the value of the futures contract will not be perfectly correlated with the firm's exposure.

basis risk The risk that arises because the value of a futures contract is not perfectly correlated with a firm's exposure.

speculate The use of securities to place a bet on the direction in which the trader believes the market is likely to move.

Firms that hedge commodity price risk must hire expert traders who understand the nature of the contracts and the various markets in which they trade. Often a firm will allow its traders some leeway to do additional trading (beyond that needed for hedging). In effect, the firm also allows its traders to **speculate** by entering into contracts that do not offset actual risks. Traders who speculate use securities to bet on the direction in which they believe the market price is likely to move. Speculating increases the firm's risk rather than reducing it. Unless a firm monitors traders carefully, when it authorizes traders to trade contracts to hedge, the firm opens the door to the possibility of speculation. The firm must guard against the potential to speculate, which adds risk to the firm, through appropriate governance procedures.

DIFFERING HEDGING STRATEGIES AT U.S. AIRLINES

In mid-2005, oil prices rose to more than $60 per barrel. As a result of its aggressive hedging policy, Southwest Airlines was paying slightly more than $26 per barrel for 85% of its oil at the time. Many of the major U.S. airlines, however, lacked the cash or creditworthiness necessary to enter into long-term contracts. In 2004, Delta was forced to sell its supply contracts to raise cash so as to avoid defaulting on its debt. United Airlines, which filed for bankruptcy protection in December 2002, had only 30% of its fuel hedged in 2005 at a price of $45 per barrel. By 2008, when oil prices were over $130 per barrel, the prices from 2005 looked like a relative bargain. In keeping with its strategy, Southwest had entered into long-term hedges so that most of its fuel costs in 2008 were locked in at $60 per barrel.

These differences in strategy are somewhat understandable given the airlines' differing financial positions. Southwest is currently profitable and would like to reduce its risk of becoming financially distressed by hedging its fuel costs. Delta and United are already in financial distress, so hedging would not avoid these costs. And for equity holders, taking a risk by not hedging may be the best strategy—a sudden drop in oil prices would lead to a windfall for equity holders, while losses from further increases would likely be borne by debt holders in default.

Source: Eric Roston, "Hedging Their Costs," *Time*, June 20, 2005.

CONCEPT CHECK

3. Discuss risk-management strategies that firms use to hedge commodity price risk.
4. What are the potential risks associated with hedging using futures contracts?

21.3 Interest Rate Risk

Firms that borrow must pay interest on their debt. An increase in interest rates raises firms' borrowing costs and can reduce their profitability. In addition, many firms have fixed long-term future liabilities, such as capital leases or pension fund liabilities. A decrease in interest rates raises the present value of these liabilities and can lower the value of the firm. Thus, when interest rates are volatile, interest rate risk is a concern for many firms.

Interest Rate Risk Measurement: Duration

duration The sensitivity to interest rate changes of an asset or a liability.

Financial managers need to know the **duration**—the sensitivity to interest rate changes—of their assets and liabilities. In Chapter 6 on bonds, we saw increased sensitivity of bonds to interest rates for longer maturity bonds. For example, for a 10-year, zero-coupon bond, an increase of one percentage point in the yield to maturity from 5% to 6% causes the bond price per $100 face value to fall from

$$\frac{100}{1.05^{10}} = \$61.39 \text{ to } \frac{100}{1.06^{10}} = \$55.84$$

This represents a price change of (55.84 − 61.39)/61.39 = −9.0%. The price of a five-year bond drops only 4.6% for the same yield change. The interest rate sensitivity of a *single* cash flow is roughly proportional to its maturity. The farther away the cash flow is, the larger the effect of interest rate changes on its present value.

The idea can be expanded to a security or asset that produces multiple cash flows. The specific formula for duration is shown in the online Appendix C of Chapter 6. The idea is that securities whose value comes mostly from later cash flows have a longer duration (higher interest rate sensitivity) than do securities whose value comes mostly from earlier cash flows.

Duration-Based Hedging

A firm's market capitalization (equity) is determined by the difference in the market value of its assets and its liabilities. If changes in interest rates affect these values, they will affect the firm's equity value. Thus, we can assess a firm's sensitivity to interest rates by examining its balance sheet. Moreover, by restructuring the balance sheet to reduce its duration, we can hedge the firm's interest rate risk.

Banks: An Example. Consider a typical bank. These institutions hold short-term deposits, in the form of chequing and savings accounts, as well as guaranteed investment certificates. They also make long-term loans, such as car loans and home mortgages. Most banks face a problem, because the duration of the loans they make is generally longer than the duration of their deposits. When the durations of a firm's assets and liabilities are significantly different, the firm has a **duration mismatch**. This mismatch puts the bank at risk if interest rates change significantly.

duration mismatch A significant difference between the durations of a firm's assets and liabilities.

How can a bank reduce its sensitivity to interest rates? It must reduce the duration of its assets or increase the duration of its liabilities. Because it can't easily increase the duration of its liabilities (it can't force people to leave their money in the bank longer than they want to), it must focus on its assets (mortgage loans). By selling the mortgages to another mortgage servicer in exchange for cash, the bank can reduce its asset interest rate sensitivity to zero. In fact, many banks sell their mortgage loans to reduce their sensitivity to interest rate risk.

Swap-Based Hedging

interest rate swap A contract in which two parties agree to exchange the coupons from two different types of loans.

A bank can reduce its interest rate sensitivity by selling assets. For most firms, selling assets is not an attractive prospect, as those assets are typically necessary to conduct the firms' normal business operations. Interest rate swaps are an alternative means of modifying the firms' interest rate risk exposure without buying or selling assets. An **interest rate swap** is a contract a firm enters into with a bank in which the firm and the

TABLE 21.3 Cash Flows ($ millions) for a $100 Million Fixed-for-Floating Interest Rate Swap

Year	Six-Month LIBOR	Fixed Coupon	Floating-Rate Coupon	New Swap Cash Flow: Fixed-for-Floating
0.0	6.8%			0.0
0.5	7.2%	3.9	3.4	0.5
1.0	8.0%	3.9	3.6	0.3
1.5	7.4%	3.9	4.0	−0.1
2.0	7.8%	3.9	3.7	0.2
2.5	8.6%	3.9	3.9	0.0
3.0	9.0%	3.9	4.3	−0.4
3.5	9.2%	3.9	4.5	−0.6
4.0	8.4%	3.9	4.6	−0.7
4.5	7.6%	3.9	4.2	−0.3
5.0		3.9	3.8	0.1

bank agree to exchange the coupons from two different types of loans. In this section, we describe interest rate swaps and explore how they are used to manage interest rate risk.

In a standard interest rate swap, one party agrees to pay coupons based on a fixed interest rate in exchange for receiving coupons based on the prevailing market interest rate during each coupon period. An interest rate that adjusts to current market conditions is called a *floating rate*. Thus, the parties exchange a fixed-rate coupon for a floating-rate coupon, which explains why this swap is also called a "fixed-for-floating interest rate swap."

To demonstrate how an interest swap works, consider a five-year, $100 million interest rate swap with a 7.8% fixed rate. Standard swaps have semi-annual coupons, so the fixed coupon amounts would be 1/2(7.8% × $100 million) = $3.9 million every six months. The floating-rate coupons are typically based on a six-month market interest rate, such as the six-month treasury bill rate or the six-month London Inter-Bank Offered Rate (LIBOR).[10] This rate varies over the life of the contract. Each coupon is calculated based on the six-month interest rate that prevailed in the market six months prior to the coupon payment date. Table 21.3 calculates the cash flows of the swap under a hypothetical scenario for LIBOR rates over the life of the swap. For example, at the first coupon date in six months, the fixed coupon is $3.9 million and the floating-rate coupon is 1/2(6.8% × $10 million) = $3.4 million, for a net payment of $0.5 million from the fixed- to the floating-rate payer.

Each payment of the swap is equal to the difference between the fixed- and floating-rate coupons. Unlike an ordinary loan, there is no payment of principal. Because the $100 million swap amount is used only to calculate the coupons but is never actually paid, it is referred to as the **notional principal** of the swap. Finally, there is no initial cash flow associated with the swap. That is, the swap contract—like forward and futures contracts—is typically structured as a "zero-cost" security. The fixed rate of the swap contract is set based on current market conditions so that the swap is a fair deal (i.e., it has an NPV of zero) for both sides.

notional principal The calculated amount of the coupon payments in an interest rate swap.

[10]The LIBOR is the rate at which major international banks with offices in London stand ready to accept deposits from one another. It is a common benchmark interest rate for swaps and other financial agreements.

Interest rate forward contracts, futures contracts, and options contracts also exist and can be used to manage interest rate risk. Swaps, however, are by far the most common strategy used by corporations.

Combining Swaps with Standard Loans. Corporations routinely use interest rate swaps to alter their exposure to interest rate fluctuations. The interest rate a firm pays on its loans can fluctuate for two reasons. First, the risk-free interest rate in the market may change. Second, the firm's credit quality, which determines the spread the firm must pay over the risk-free interest rate, can vary over time. By combining swaps with loans, firms can choose which of these sources of interest rate risk they will tolerate and which they will eliminate.

EXAMPLE 21.6 Using Interest Rate Swaps

PROBLEM

Bolt Industries is facing increased competition and wants to borrow $10 million in cash to protect against future revenue shortfalls. Currently, long-term AA rates are 10%. Given its credit rating, Bolt can borrow at 10.5%. The company is expecting interest rates to fall over the next few years, so it would prefer to borrow at short-term rates and refinance after rates drop. However, Bolt's management is afraid that its credit rating may deteriorate as competition intensifies, which may greatly increase the spread the firm must pay on a new loan. How can Bolt benefit from declining interest rates without worrying about changes in its credit rating?

SOLUTION

Plan

Bolt wants to convert its long-term fixed rate into a floating rate (one that will decline if market interest rates decline). It can do this by entering into a swap in which it will receive a fixed rate (which can then be used to pay its fixed long-term obligation) and pay a floating rate $\mathcal{T}_t$. Its net exposure will be the floating rate.

Execute

Bolt can borrow at the long-term rate of 10.5% and then enter into a swap in which it receives the long-term AA fixed rate of 10% and pays the short-term rate $\mathcal{T}_t$. Its net borrowing cost will then be as follows:

Long-Term Loan Rate	+ Floating Rate Due on Swap	− Fixed Rate Received from Swap	= Net Borrowing Cost
10.5%	$+ \mathcal{T}_t$	− 10%	$= \mathcal{T}_t + 0.5$

Evaluate

In this way, Bolt locks in its current credit spread of 0.5% but gets the benefit of lower rates as rates decline. The trade-off is that if rates increase instead, the firm is worse off.

As a financial manager, hedging interest rate risk can help your firm avoid financial distress costs of the types we described in Chapter 16. If the business is performing fundamentally well, you do not want a sudden shift in borrowing costs to cause a cash flow problem that can lead to distress. As we have seen in this section, there are tools such as duration matching and swaps available to help you avoid such costs.

CONCEPT CHECK

5. What is the intuition behind the calculation of duration?
6. How do firms manage interest rate risk?

MyLab Finance

Here is what you should know after reading this chapter. MyLab™ Finance will help you identify what you know, and where to go when you need to practise.

KEY POINTS AND EQUATIONS	TERMS	ONLINE PRACTICE OPPORTUNITIES
21.1 Insurance ■ Insurance is a common method firms use to reduce risk. In a perfect market, the price of insurance is actuarially fair. An actuarially fair insurance premium is equal to the present value of the expected loss: $\frac{Pr(\text{Loss}) \times E[\text{Payment in the Event of Loss}]}{1 + r_L}$ (21.1) ■ Insurance for large risks that cannot be well diversified has a negative beta, which raises its cost. ■ The value of insurance comes from its ability to reduce the cost of market imperfections for the firm. Insurance may be beneficial to a firm because of its effects on bankruptcy and financial distress costs, issuance costs, taxes, debt capacity, and risk assessment. ■ The costs of insurance include administrative and overhead costs, adverse selection, and moral hazard.	actuarially fair price, p. 722 business interruption insurance, p. 721 business liability insurance, p. 721 deductible, p. 728 insurance premium, p. 722 key personnel insurance, p. 721 moral hazard, p. 726 policy limits, p. 728 property insurance, p. 721	MyLab Study Plan 21.1
21.2 Commodity Price Risk ■ Firms use several risk-management strategies to hedge their exposure to commodity price movements. ■ Firms can make real investments in assets with offsetting risk using techniques such as vertical integration and storage. ■ Firms can enter into long-term contracts with suppliers or customers or use forward contacts to achieve price stability. ■ Firms can hedge risk using futures contracts or option contracts that are available in financial markets.	basis risk, p. 740 forward contract, p. 731 futures contract, p. 732 hedge, p. 729 liquidity risk, p. 739 margin, p. 734 margin call, p. 734 marking to market, p. 734 natural hedge, p. 739 speculate, p. 740 vertical integration, p. 729	MyLab Study Plan 21.2
21.3 Interest Rate Risk ■ Firms face interest rate risk when exchange rates are volatile. The interest rate sensitivity of a stream of cash flows is greater if more of the value of the stream comes from later cash flows.	duration, p. 741 duration mismatch, p. 741 interest rate swap, p. 741 notional principal, p. 742	MyLab Study Plan 21.3

KEY POINTS AND EQUATIONS | TERMS | ONLINE PRACTICE OPPORTUNITIES

- Firms can manage interest rate risk by buying or selling assets to match the interest rate sensitivity of their assets to the interest rate sensitivity of their liabilities.
- Interest rate swaps allow firms to separate the risk of interest rate changes from the risk of fluctuations in the firm's credit quality.
- By borrowing long term and entering into an interest rate swap in which the firm receives a fixed-rate coupon and pays a floating-rate coupon, the firm will pay a floating interest rate plus a spread that is fixed, based on its initial credit quality.
- By borrowing short term and entering into an interest rate swap in which the firm receives a floating-rate coupon and pays a fixed-rate coupon, the firm will pay a fixed interest rate plus a spread that will float with its credit quality.
- Firms use interest rate swaps to modify their interest rate risk exposure without buying or selling assets.

REVIEW QUESTIONS

1. Why is it possible for a firm to pay an actuarially fair price for insurance and still have the insurance purchase be a positive-NPV investment?
2. How can an insurance company mitigate adverse selection and moral hazard?
3. What are some common approaches to hedging commodity price risk?
4. Can hedging lead to losses?
5. How can a firm become exposed to interest rate risk?
6. How can a firm use a swap to manage its interest rate risk?

PROBLEMS

All problems in this chapter are available in MyLab Finance. An asterisk (*) indicates problems with a higher level of difficulty.

Insurance

1. The William Companies (WMB) owns and operates natural gas pipelines that deliver 12% of the natural gas consumed in the United States. WMB is concerned that a major hurricane could disrupt its Gulfstream pipeline, which runs 691 miles through the Gulf of Mexico. In the event of a disruption, the firm anticipates a loss of profits of

$65 million. Suppose the likelihood of a disruption is 3% per year, and the beta associated with such a loss is −0.25. If the risk-free interest rate is 5% and the expected return of the market is 10%, what is the actuarially fair insurance premium?

2. Genentech's main facility is located in south San Francisco. Suppose that Genentech would experience a direct loss of $450 million in the event of a major earthquake that disrupted its operations. The chance of such an earthquake is 2% per year, with a beta of −0.5.
   a. If the risk-free interest rate is 5% and the expected return of the market is 10%, what is the actuarially fair insurance premium required to cover Genentech's loss?
   b. Suppose Genentech's insurance company raises the premium by an additional 15% over the amount calculated in part (a) to cover its administrative and overhead costs. What amount of financial distress or issuance costs would Genentech have to suffer if it were not insured to justify purchasing the insurance?

3. Your firm imports manufactured goods from China. You are worried that Canada-China trade negotiations could break down next year, leading to a moratorium on imports. In the event of a moratorium, your firm expects its operating profits to decline substantially and its marginal tax rate to fall from its current level of 40% to 10%. An insurance firm has agreed to write a trade insurance policy that will pay $500,000 in the event of an import moratorium. The chance of a moratorium is estimated to be 10%, with a beta equal to −1.5. Suppose the risk-free interest rate is 5% and the expected return of the market is 10%.
   a. What is the actuarially fair premium for this insurance?
   b. What is the NPV of purchasing this insurance for your firm? What is the source of this gain?

4. Your firm faces a 9% chance of a potential loss of $10 million next year. If your firm implements new policies, it can reduce the chance of this loss to 4%, but these new policies have an upfront cost of $100,000. Suppose the beta of the loss is 0, and the risk-free interest rate is 5%.
   a. If the firm is uninsured, what is the NPV of implementing the new policies?
   b. If the firm is fully insured, what is the NPV of implementing the new policies?
   c. Given your answer to part (b), what is the actuarially fair cost of full insurance?
   d. What is the minimum-size deductible that would leave your firm with an incentive to implement the new policies?
   e. What is the actuarially fair price of an insurance policy with the deductible in part (d)?

Commodity Price Risk

***5.** BHP Billiton is the world's largest mining firm. BHP expects to produce 2 billion pounds of copper next year, with a production cost of $0.90 per pound.
   a. What will be BHP's operating profit from copper next year if the price of copper is $1.25, $1.50, or $1.75 per pound, and the firm plans to sell all of its copper next year at the going price?
   b. What will be BHP's operating profit from copper next year if the firm enters into a contract to supply copper to end users at an average price of $1.45 per pound?
   c. What will be BHP's operating profit from copper next year if copper prices are described as in part (a), and the firm enters into supply contracts as in part (b) for only 50% of its total output?
   d. Describe situations for which each of the strategies in parts (a), (b), and (c) might be optimal.

6. Your utility company will need to buy 100,000 barrels of oil in 10 days' time, and it is worried about fuel costs. Suppose you go long on 100 oil futures contracts, each for 1000 barrels of oil, at the current futures price of $60 per barrel. Suppose futures prices change each day as follows:

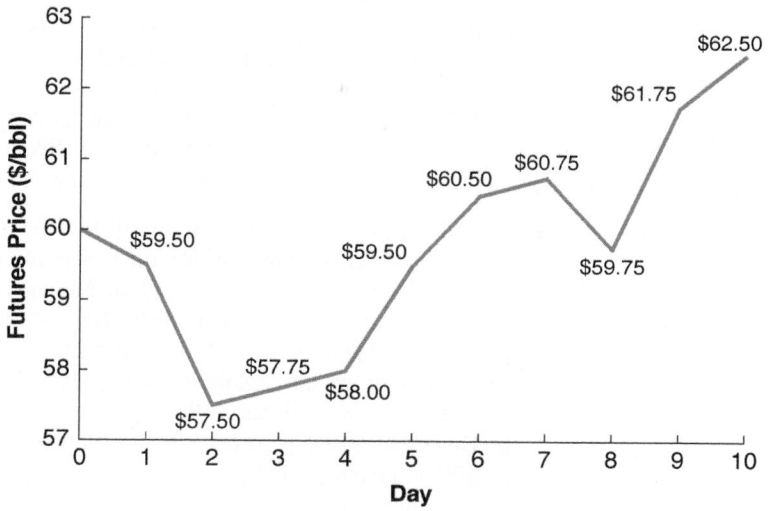

a. What is the marking-to-market profit or loss (in dollars) that you will have on each date?
b. What is your total profit or loss after 10 days? Have you been protected against a rise in oil prices?
c. What is the largest cumulative loss you will experience over the 10-day period? In what case might this be a problem?

7. Suppose Starbucks consumes 100 million pounds of coffee beans per year. As the price of coffee rises, Starbucks expects to pass along 60% of the cost to its customers through higher prices per cup of coffee. To hedge its profits from fluctuations in coffee prices, Starbucks should lock in the price of how many pounds of coffee beans using supply contracts?

***8.** It is April, and Hans Anderson is planting his barley crop near Plunkett, Saskatchewan. He is concerned about losing his farm if his operations result in a loss at the end of the season. He expects to harvest 3000 tonnes of barley and sell it in October. Futures contracts are available for October delivery with a futures price of $200 per tonne. Options with strike price of $200 per tonne are also available; puts cost $15 and calls cost $18.

a. Describe how Hans can fully hedge using futures contracts.
b. Given the strategy in (a), what will be the total net amount received by Hans (for all 3000 tonnes) if the price of barley in October is as follows:
   i. $150 per tonne
   ii. $200 per tonne
   iii. $250 per tonne
c. Describe how Hans can fully hedge using options.
d. Given the strategy in (c), what will be the total net amount received by Hans (for all 3000 tonnes) if the price of barley in October is as follows:
   i. $150 per tonne
   ii. $200 per tonne
   iii. $250 per tonne

e. Hans has asked for your advice regarding hedging. Discuss how the each of the following individually will influence your advice.
   i. Hans does not expect to have much cash available between May and September.
   ii. Hans thinks there is a 25% chance his crop will be destroyed by hail before he has a chance to harvest it.
   iii. Hans's farming business will go bankrupt if his net revenues in October do not cover his costs. He estimates his costs will be $570,000. If his business goes bankrupt, Hans's bank will foreclose and take his house and farm.
   iv. Hans's farming business will go bankrupt if his net revenues in October do not cover his costs. He estimates his costs will be $700,000. If his business goes bankrupt, Hans's bank will foreclose and take his house and farm.

***9.** It is March, and Alberta Oil Refinery Ltd (AOR) has enough crude oil in inventory to continue refinery operations until September. AOR expects to need to purchase 500,000 barrels of oil in September. Management at AOR is concerned about oil price volatility. Futures contracts for September delivery are available with a futures price of $110 per barrel. Options contracts with a strike price of $110 and expiration in September are also available; puts cost $25 and calls cost $20.

a. Describe how AOR can fully hedge using oil futures contracts.
b. Given the strategy in (a), what will be the total net amount paid by AOR (for all 500,000 barrels) if the price of oil in September is as follows:
   i. $60 per barrel
   ii. $110 per barrel
   iii. $160 per barrel
c. Describe how AOR can fully hedge using options.
d. Given the strategy in (c), what will be the total net amount paid by AOR (for all 500,000 barrels) if the price of oil in September is as follows:
   i. $60 per barrel
   ii. $110 per barrel
   iii. $160 per barrel
e. AOR has asked for your advice regarding hedging. Discuss how the each of the following individually will influence your advice.
   i. AOR does not expect to have much cash available between April and August.
   ii. AOR thinks that a drop in oil prices will occur if the economy goes into recession. There is a 33% chance this will happen. In a recession, demand for AOR's refined oil products will drop by half.
   iii. AOR will experience extreme financial distress costs if its net revenues in August do not cover the net costs of oil purchased then. AOR net revenues are estimated to be $60 million.
   iv. AOR will experience extreme financial distress costs if its net revenues in August do not cover the net costs of oil purchased then. AOR net revenues are estimated to be $50 million.
   v. AOR can pass along any price increases in oil by increasing the prices of its refined products.

Interest Rate Risk

***10.** Assume each of the following securities has the same yield to maturity: a five-year zero-coupon bond, a nine-year zero-coupon bond, a five-year annuity, and a nine-year annuity. Rank these securities from lowest to highest duration.

***11.** Your firm needs to raise $100 million in funds. You can borrow short term at a spread of 1.00% over LIBOR. Alternatively, you can issue 10-year fixed-rate bonds at a spread of 2.50% over 10-year treasuries, which currently yield 7.60%. Current 10-year interest rate swaps are quoted at LIBOR versus the 8.00% fixed rate.

Management believes that the firm is currently "underrated" and that its credit rating is likely to improve in the next year or two. Nevertheless, the managers are not comfortable with the interest rate risk associated with using short-term debt.

a. Suggest a strategy for borrowing the $100 million. What is your effective borrowing rate?

b. Suppose the firm's credit rating does improve three years later. It can now borrow at a spread of 0.50% over treasuries, which now yield 9.10% for a seven-year maturity. Also, seven-year interest rate swaps are quoted at LIBOR versus 9.50%. How would you lock in your new credit quality for the next seven years? What is your effective borrowing rate now?

CHAPTER

22 International Corporate Finance

LEARNING OBJECTIVES

- Explain the basics of currency exchange rates
- Identify and hedge exchange rate risk
- Understand integrated capital markets and their implication for prices
- Determine how to handle cash flows in foreign currencies in capital budgeting
- Analyze the impact of different countries' tax rates on investment decisions and firm value
- Show how to exploit opportunities from segmented international markets
- Demonstrate how to address exchange rate risk in your capital budgeting approach

NOTATION

C_{FOC}	foreign currency cash flow
S	spot exchange rate
F	forward exchange rate
r^*_{HOC}	home currency cost of capital
r_{HOC}	home currency risk-free interest rate
r^*_{FOC}	foreign currency cost of capital
r_{FOC}	foreign currency risk-free interest rate
r_{wacc}	weighted average cost of capital
D	market value of debt
E	market value of equity
r_E	required return on equity
r_D	required return on debt
τ_c	corporate tax rate

In the 1990s, Starbucks Coffee Company identified Japan as a potentially lucrative new market for the company's coffee products, and decided to invest as much as 10 million USD[1] in fiscal year 1996 to begin operations there. Because Starbucks realized it needed specialized knowledge of the Japanese market, it established a joint venture with Sazaby Inc., a Japanese retailer and restaurateur. This venture, called Starbucks Coffee Japan Ltd., intended to open as many as 12 stores in this initial phase. Although stores opened more slowly than expected, the venture had more than 200 stores and sales of 29 billion JPY (252 million USD) by 2001, and it opened its 500th store in

November 2003. To finance this growth, Starbucks Coffee Japan Ltd. used the Japanese capital markets. It held an initial public offering of shares on the Osaka Stock Exchange in October 2001 with a market capitalization of 90.88 billion JPY (756 million USD), raising 18.8 billion JPY (156 million USD) in additional capital for expansion. How did Starbucks' managers decide to undertake this investment opportunity? Why did they decide to use the Japanese domestic market to finance it rather than their home markets in the U.S.?

This chapter focuses on some of the special factors a firm faces when making a foreign investment. There are three key issues that arise when considering an investment in a foreign project such as Starbucks Coffee Japan Ltd.:

- The project will most likely generate foreign currency cash flows, although the firm cares about the home-currency value of the project.
- Interest rates and costs of capital will likely be different in the foreign country as a result of the macroeconomic environment.
- The firm will probably face a different tax rate in the foreign country and will be subject to both foreign and domestic tax codes.

We begin this introduction to international finance with an overview of currency exchange rates and markets and the risk that comes from currency exchange rate fluctuations. From there, we extend the discussion of risk management in Chapter 21 to examine how a firm can manage currency exchange rate risk. Next, we discuss how a financial manager should evaluate foreign projects. We begin by examining *internationally integrated capital markets,* which provides a useful benchmark for comparing different methods of valuing a foreign project. We next explain how to value a foreign project and address the three key issues mentioned above. We then value foreign currency cash flows using two valuation methodologies, and consider the implications of foreign and domestic tax codes. Finally, we explore the implications of internationally segmented capital markets.

22.1 Currency Exchange Rates

currency exchange rate
The price of one country's currency in terms of another country's currency.

The price of one country's currency in terms of another country's currency is called a **currency exchange rate**. For example, if a Canadian is planning a trip to the United States and she decides to purchase some U.S. currency, she will have to exchange CAD for USD. Suppose the exchange rate is 1.1825 CAD/USD. That means that the price of 1 USD is 1.1825 CAD. If the Canadian traveller wanted to buy 1000 USD to take on the trip, she would have to pay 1000 USD $\times$ 1.1825 CAD/USD = 1182.50 CAD. As travellers, we often exchange our currencies in our local bank or at a kiosk at an airport. These retail currency exchange providers make up a small portion of what is called the foreign exchange market.

[1]We will use a three-letter currency code to indicate a country's currency; for example: CAD = Canadian dollar, USD = U.S. dollar, JPY = Japanese yen. Using the currency codes avoids the confusion caused by the fact that many countries use the same symbol for their currency (e.g., $ is used in Canada, Australia, the United States, and several other countries). For a list of countries, their three-letter currency codes, and their symbols, see the website maintained by Professor Werner Antweiler at the University of British Columbia's Sauder School of Business: http://fx.sauder.ubc.ca/currencies.html.

The Foreign Exchange Market

foreign exchange (FX or forex) market A market where currencies are traded that has no central physical location.

Imagine a market that is open 24 hours a day during the week, has no central physical location, and experiences *daily* turnover of over 5 trillion USD worth of currencies. The **foreign exchange (FX** or **forex) market**, where currencies are traded, is such a market. There are many reasons to trade currencies, but we will focus on those of a financial manager in a firm doing business in more than one country (a multinational firm). Consider Brookfield Asset Management Inc., headquartered in Toronto. It owns real estate, renewable-power plants, infrastructure, and other assets in 20 countries around the world. Thus, its revenues come in many different currencies. However, because it is a Canadian company, Brookfield's management will eventually want to exchange their profits in the various currencies back into Canadian dollars. In addition to its revenues, Brookfield has costs that are incurred in many currencies, even beyond the 20 countries where it operates; for example, other currencies may be used when Brookfield purchases power generation equipment from suppliers in countries where Brookfield does not have operations. Because of its multinational operations, Brookfield must regularly transact in the FX market. However, the FX market is not just important for large multinational enterprises. Many businesses import or export some of their products from abroad, and the FX market affects them too. Tourists need access to foreign currencies when they travel, so the value of the home currency in relation to other currencies may affect which vacation destination is chosen. Even purely domestic businesses need to be aware of FX markets, because as the value of the home currency appreciates or depreciates relative to other currencies, it affects potential competition from foreign firms.

The top 10 players in the FX market ranked in Euromoney's 2018 survey are JPMorgan, UBS, XTX Markets, Bank of America Merrill Lynch, Citigroup, HSBC, Goldman Sachs, Deutsche Bank, Standard Chartered, and State Street. These banks' trading accounted for over 65% of FX trades; they trade on their own account and for client multinational firms. Some large multinational firms trade for themselves. Other players in the market are government central banks, hedge funds and other investment managers, and retail brokers. Even though there are over 150 currencies in the world, just two of them, the U.S. dollar and the euro, account for more than half of all trading volume in the FX market. Figure 22.1 shows the 10 most-traded currencies in 2016. Note that the total volume sums to 200%, not 100%, because there is a currency on the buy and sell side of every transaction. To put these percentages in context, in April 2016, about 5.1 trillion USD of currencies were exchanged in various types of transactions.

Exchange Rates

Table 22.1 shows seven days of foreign currency noon exchange rates as of January 20, 2015 (reported by the Bank of Canada). Each exchange rate is the CAD price of one unit of the foreign country's currency. Also included is the closing CAD price of the USD for each day. For example, the third line indicates that one Argentine peso (ARS) can be purchased for 0.1404 CAD, or equivalently, 7.1225 ARS buys 1 CAD. This is determined by calculating the inverse of the ARS/CAD exchange rate as follows:

1 ARS is worth 0.1404 CAD,

So the exchange rate is $\dfrac{0.1404 \text{ CAD}}{\text{ARS}}$

Taking the inverse, this is equivalent to $\dfrac{1 \text{ ARS}}{0.1404 \text{ CAD}} = \dfrac{7.1225 \text{ ARS}}{\text{CAD}}$,

so 7.1225 ARS buys 1 CAD

Thus, if we want to convert from 100 ARS to CAD, we multiply the number of ARS by the CAD/ARS exchange rate: 100 ARS $\times$ 0.1404 CAD/ARS = 14.04 CAD. Conversely, if we

FIGURE 22.1 The Most-Traded Currencies

Counting 100% of buying currencies and 100% of selling currencies, for a total of 200%, this table lists the top 10 traded currencies in 2016. Note that these 10 currencies accounted for more than 178% of the total of 200%.

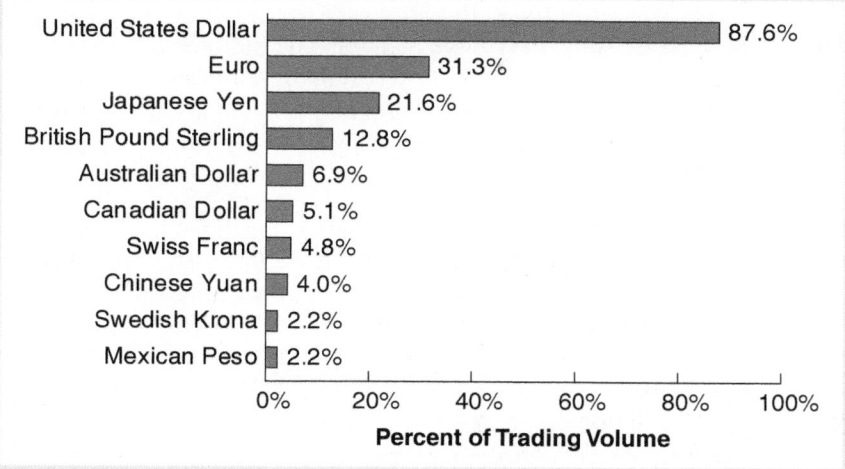

Source: Bank of International Settlements: Triennial Central Bank Survey (December, 2016).

want to convert from 14.04 CAD to ARS, we multiply the number of CAD by the ARS/CAD exchange rate: 14.04 CAD × 7.1225 ARS/CAD = 100 ARS. (Note that this is the same as dividing the number of CAD by the CAD/ARS exchange rate: 14.04 CAD ÷ 0.1404 CAD/ARS = 100 ARS. When you work with exchange rates, it is important to keep track of which currency is in the numerator and which is in the denominator. You can see in the conversions we just did that when we multiply a currency amount by the appropriate exchange rate, the old currency units cancel out and we are left with the new currency units:

$$100 \text{ ARS} \times \frac{0.1404 \text{ CAD}}{\text{ARS}} = 14.04 \text{ CAD}$$

Most exchange rates are market prices, and they change from day to day and even within the day. For instance, in Table 22.1, the CAD/USD exchange rate at noon on January 12, 2015, was 1.1930 CAD/USD, but by the close of business in Ontario that day, the exchange rate had risen to 1.1967 CAD/USD, and as of the close of business on January 20, 2015, the exchange rate had risen to 1.2107 CAD/USD. Since these exchange rates are the CAD price of 1.00 USD, when the exchange rate rises, the USD is appreciating relative to the CAD, and when it drops, the USD is depreciating relative to the CAD. If we took the inverse of each of these exchange rates, we would have USD/CAD, and such an exchange rate would tell us the value of 1.00 CAD in terms of USD. When the USD is appreciating relative to the CAD, as we saw by the change in the CAD/USD between noon, January 12, 2015, and the close of business, January 20, 2015, the inverse exchange rates show that the CAD is depreciating relative to the USD. Looking at the inverse rates, at noon, January 12, 2015, we would have had 0.8382 USD/CAD, and at the close of business on January 20, 2015, we would have had 0.8260 USD/CAD; this change is consistent with the value of the CAD depreciating relative to the USD. Exchange rate fluctuations are not always as small as the fluctuations of rates over the seven days shown in Table 22.1. The USD/CAD rate has moved over a wide range and sometimes very quickly. For example, on January 21, 2002, the rate touched a record

TABLE 22.1 **Canadian Dollar Daily Noon Currency Exchange Rates for the Seven Trading Days Ending January 20, 2015 (also included are USD closing rates)**

Currency	Currency Code	Date						
		2015-01-12	2015-01-13	2015-01-14	2015-01-15	2015-01-16	2015-01-19	2015-01-20
U.S. dollar (noon)	USD	1.193	1.1948	1.1958	1.1932	1.1986	1.1966	1.2085
U.S. dollar (close)	USD	1.1967	1.1954	1.1945	1.1964	1.1968	1.1947	1.2107
Argentine peso	ARS	0.1389	0.1391	0.1392	0.1388	0.1394	0.1392	0.1404
Australian dollar	AUD	0.974	0.9753	0.976	0.9797	0.9821	0.9825	0.988
Bahamian dollar	BSD	1.193	1.1948	1.1958	1.1932	1.1986	1.1966	1.2085
Brazilian real	BRL	0.4472	0.4531	0.4572	0.453	0.457	0.4543	0.4621
CFA franc (African Financial Community)	XAF	0.002152	0.002145	0.002152	0.002109	0.002104	0.00212	0.002129
CFP franc (Pacific Financial Community)	XPF	0.01183	0.01179	0.01183	0.01159	0.01157	0.01165	0.01171
Chilean peso	CLP	0.001938	0.001929	0.001909	0.001907	0.00191	0.001906	0.001922
Chinese renminbi	CNY	0.1923	0.1928	0.193	0.1928	0.1931	0.1924	0.1945
Colombian peso	COP	0.000494	0.00049	0.000491	0.000496	0.000505	0.000508	0.000509
Croatian kuna	HRK	0.1837	0.1831	0.1836	0.1801	0.1795	0.1808	0.1813
Czech Republic koruna	CZK	0.04972	0.05	0.05029	0.04945	0.04947	0.04979	0.04995
Danish krone	DKK	0.1897	0.1892	0.1898	0.1861	0.1858	0.1871	0.1879
East Caribbean dollar	XCD	0.4435	0.4442	0.4445	0.4436	0.4456	0.4448	0.4493
European Euro	EUR	1.4115	1.4072	1.4118	1.3836	1.3804	1.3907	1.3968
Fiji dollar	FJD	0.6025	0.6014	0.6004	0.5987	0.6052	0.6031	0.6058
Ghanaian cedi	GHS	0.3626	0.3693	0.364	0.3671	0.3694	0.3686	0.365
Guatemalan quetzal	GTQ	0.1523	0.1523	0.1525	0.1523	0.1531	0.1528	0.1543
Honduran lempira	HNL	0.05681	0.0569	0.05694	0.05682	0.05708	0.05698	0.05755
Hong Kong dollar	HKD	0.153877	0.154107	0.154207	0.153884	0.154577	0.154339	0.155896
Hungarian forint	HUF	0.00443	0.004421	0.004412	0.004297	0.004319	0.004348	0.004399
Icelandic krona	ISK	0.009165	0.009146	0.009179	0.009043	0.009046	0.009094	0.009146
Indian rupee	INR	0.01922	0.01928	0.01926	0.01923	0.01937	0.01941	0.0196
Indonesian rupiah	IDR	0.000095	0.000095	0.000095	0.000095	0.000095	0.000095	0.000096
Israeli new shekel	ILS	0.3027	0.3035	0.307	0.3037	0.3042	0.3058	0.3073
Jamaican dollar	JMD	0.0104	0.01042	0.01043	0.0104	0.01042	0.0104	0.0105
Japanese yen	JPY	0.01008	0.01011	0.01024	0.0102	0.0102	0.01018	0.0102
Malaysian ringgit	MYR	0.3345	0.3325	0.3327	0.3348	0.3368	0.335	0.3343
Mexican peso	MXN	0.08149	0.08198	0.08204	0.08178	0.08202	0.08168	0.08251
Moroccan dirham	MAD	0.1293	0.1288	0.1294	0.1272	0.1273	0.1276	0.1287
Myanmar (Burma) kyat	MMK	0.00116	0.00116	0.00116	0.00116	0.00116	0.00116	0.00118
Neth. Antilles guilder	ANG	0.6778	0.6789	0.6794	0.678	0.681	0.6799	0.6866

TABLE 22.1 (continued)

Currency	Currency Code	Date						
		2015-01-12	2015-01-13	2015-01-14	2015-01-15	2015-01-16	2015-01-19	2015-01-20
New Zealand dollar	NZD	0.9276	0.9237	0.9262	0.9294	0.9322	0.9303	0.9296
Norwegian krone	NOK	0.1546	0.1542	0.1565	0.1559	0.1576	0.1569	0.1577
Pakistan rupee	PKR	0.01185	0.01187	0.01187	0.01187	0.01192	0.01187	0.012
Panamanian balboa	PAB	1.193	1.1948	1.1958	1.1932	1.1986	1.1966	1.2085
Peruvian new sol	PEN	0.3993	0.4002	0.3992	0.3979	0.3973	0.3968	0.4014
Philippine peso	PHP	0.02658	0.02674	0.0268	0.02677	0.02687	0.02685	0.02711
Polish zloty	PLN	0.3298	0.3287	0.3313	0.3207	0.3201	0.3209	0.3225
Romanian new leu	RON	0.3147	0.3132	0.3139	0.3074	0.3067	0.3089	0.3095
Russian ruble	RUB	0.0189	0.01816	0.01811	0.01843	0.01842	0.01846	0.01847
Serbian dinar	RSD	0.01149	0.01146	0.01151	0.01129	0.01131	0.01141	0.01143
Singapore dollar	SGD	0.8941	0.8955	0.8968	0.8976	0.9033	0.8973	0.9032
South African rand	ZAR	0.1035	0.1038	0.1045	0.1036	0.1035	0.1028	0.104
South Korean won	KRW	0.0011	0.001105	0.001106	0.001106	0.001112	0.001109	0.001111
Sri Lanka rupee	LKR	0.009069	0.009082	0.00909	0.00907	0.009124	0.009074	0.009166
Swedish krona	SEK	0.1478	0.148	0.1484	0.1465	0.1472	0.1473	0.1477
Swiss franc	CHF	1.1753	1.1718	1.1755	1.3333	1.4117	1.3663	1.3807
Taiwanese new dollar	TWD	0.03742	0.03752	0.03762	0.03769	0.03809	0.038	0.03818
Thai baht	THB	0.03629	0.03636	0.03651	0.03643	0.03686	0.03671	0.03692
Trinidad and Tobago dollar	TTD	0.1875	0.1877	0.1876	0.1871	0.1879	0.1888	0.1907
Tunisian dinar	TND	0.631	0.6296	0.6316	0.6235	0.6233	0.6274	0.6307
Turkish lira	TRY	0.5226	0.5232	0.5245	0.5178	0.5127	0.5125	0.514
U.A.E. dirham	AED	0.3248	0.3253	0.3256	0.3249	0.3263	0.3258	0.329
U.K. pound sterling	GBP	1.8094	1.8119	1.8215	1.809	1.8136	1.8109	1.8321
Venezuelan bolivar fuerte	VEF	0.1894	0.1897	0.1898	0.1894	0.1903	0.1899	0.1918
Vietnamese dong	VND	0.000056	0.000056	0.000056	0.000056	0.000056	0.000056	0.000057

Source: http://www.bankofcanada.ca/rates/exchange/noon-rates-5-day/. January 20, 2015.

low of 0.6179 USD/CAD and, less than six years later, on November 7, 2007, it reached its all-time high of 1.1030 USD/CAD; this change represents over a 78.5% appreciation of the CAD relative to the USD. The continual and sometimes large changes in exchange rates mean that just as it will be hard for you to plan your budget for your vacation abroad, companies doing business abroad face considerable risk from changes in exchange rates. We discuss those risks and how to mitigate them in the next section.

CONCEPT CHECK

1. What is an exchange rate?
2. Why would multinational companies need to exchange currencies?

22.2 Exchange Rate Risk

Multinational firms face the risk of exchange rate fluctuations. In this section, we consider two strategies that firms use to hedge this risk: currency forward contracts and currency options.

Exchange Rate Fluctuations

floating rate An exchange rate that changes constantly depending on the supply and demand for each currency in the market.

Like most currencies, the CAD exchange rate with other currencies is a **floating rate**; this means CAD exchange rates change constantly depending on the quantity supplied and demanded for each currency in the market. The supply and demand for each currency is driven by three factors:

- *Firms trading goods:* A Canadian Audi dealer exchanges CAD for EUR to buy cars from the German automaker.
- *Investors trading securities:* A U.S. investor exchanges USD for CAD to buy shares in Canadian oil companies operating in the Alberta tar sands.
- *The actions of central banks in each country:* The Chinese government exchanges CNY for USD to purchase U.S. bonds to hold in China's official reserves in an effort to slow the appreciation of the CNY.

Because the supply and demand for currencies varies with global economic conditions, exchange rates are volatile. Figure 22.2 shows the CAD price of USD from January 1, 2001, through January 20, 2015. Notice that the price of the USD often varies by as much as 10% over periods as short as a few months. From 2002 to 2007, the value of the USD dropped more than 40% relative to the CAD.

FIGURE 22.2 CAD/USD Noon Exchange Rates from January 1, 2001, to January 20, 2015

The exchange rates show the cost of 1 USD in terms of CAD. Note, on January 21, 2002, it took 1.6183 CAD to buy 1 USD due to the depressed value of the CAD. On November 7, 2007, the CAD reached its most valuable point relative to the USD and it only took 0.9066 CAD to buy 1 USD.

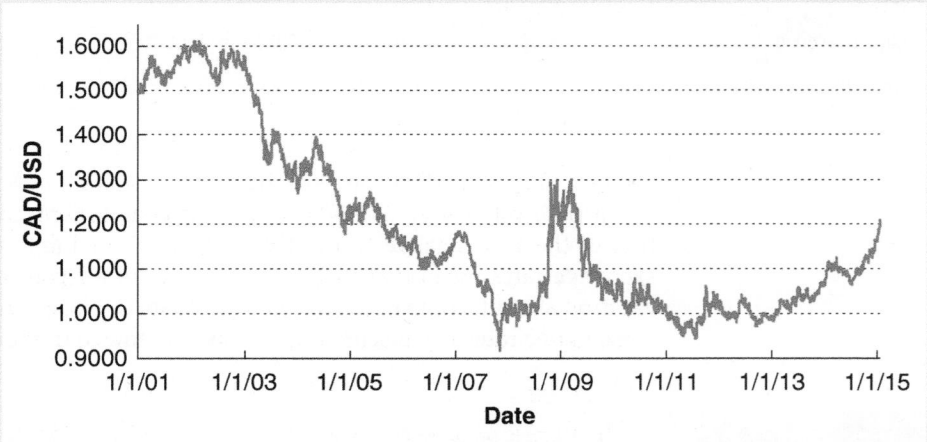

Source: Bank of Canada

Fluctuating exchanges rates cause a problem known as the *importer-exporter dilemma* for firms doing business in international markets. This is particularly important to Canada–U.S. trade, as our two countries are each other's biggest trading partners. To illustrate, consider the problem faced by Modern Bathrooms, a bathroom renovation company. Modern Bathrooms needs to import steam generators from a U.S. supplier, ThermaSol, so it can install steam rooms in customers' homes. If ThermaSol sets the price of its parts in USD, then Modern Bathrooms faces the risk that the CAD may fall, making the USD, and therefore the steam generators, more expensive. If ThermaSol sets its prices in CAD for its Canadian customers, then ThermaSol faces the risk that the CAD may fall and it will receive fewer USD for the steam generators it sells to Canadians.

Exchange rate risk is a general problem in any import-export relationship. If neither company will accept the exchange rate risk, the transaction may be difficult or impossible to negotiate. Example 22.1 demonstrates the potential magnitude of the problem.

EXAMPLE 22.1 The Effect of Exchange Rate Risk

PROBLEM

In March 2009, Whole Foods Market in the United States ordered its 2010 shipment of shampoos from Avalon Natural Products' Canadian manufacturing facility when the exchange rate was 1.3000 CAD per USD. They agreed to a price of 520,000 CAD, to be paid when the shampoos were delivered in one year's time. One year later, the exchange rate was 1.0251 CAD per USD. What was the actual cost in USD for Whole Foods Market when the payment was due? If the price had instead been set at 400,000 USD (which had equivalent value at the time of the agreement), how many CAD would Avalon have received?

SOLUTION

■ Plan

The price is set at 520,000 CAD, but the CAD/USD exchange rate will fluctuate over time, and the problem asks us to consider what would happen if it goes to 1.0251 CAD/USD, which means that USD are worth less (it takes more USD to buy one CAD).

We can always convert between CAD and USD at the going exchange rate by multiplying the CAD/USD exchange rate by the number of USD or by dividing the number of CAD by the CAD/USD exchange rate.

■ Execute

With the price set at 520,000 CAD, Whole Foods Market had to pay 520,000 CAD ÷ 1.0251 CAD/USD = 507,267.58 USD. This cost is 107,267.58 USD, or 26.8% higher than it would have been if the price had been set in USD (400,000 USD, given the original exchange rate of 1.3000 CAD/USD).

If the price had been set in USD, Whole Foods Market would not have had any exchange rate risk. However, from Avalon's point of view, given the original exchange rate of 1.3000 CAD/USD, Whole Foods Market would have paid 400,000 USD, which would have been worth only 400,000 USD × (1.0251 CAD/USD) = 410,040 CAD to Avalon at the actual time of payment. This is more than 21% less than if the price was set at 520,000 CAD.

■ Evaluate

Whether the price was set in CAD or USD, one of the parties would have suffered a substantial loss. Because neither knows which will suffer the loss ahead of time, each has an incentive to hedge.

Brexit

On Thursday, June 23, 2016, voters in the U.K. surprised financial markets by voting to leave the European Union (EU). This vote for a British-Exit, or "Brexit," as it is called, sent the British pound plunging more than 11% in dollar terms when the result was announced. The EU's currency, the euro, dropped at the same time. The large currency swings reflected currency traders' concerns about the uncertainty surrounding future trade, economic activity, and consumer confidence in both regions. The equity markets tumbled as well, reflecting the same concern that future economic growth would be stunted by the decision.

The chart below shows that the pound appreciated leading up to the vote as traders grew confident that the U.K. would stay. It then plunged when the results revealed the decision to leave.

Value of a British Pound in Dollars around Brexit (June 23, 2016)

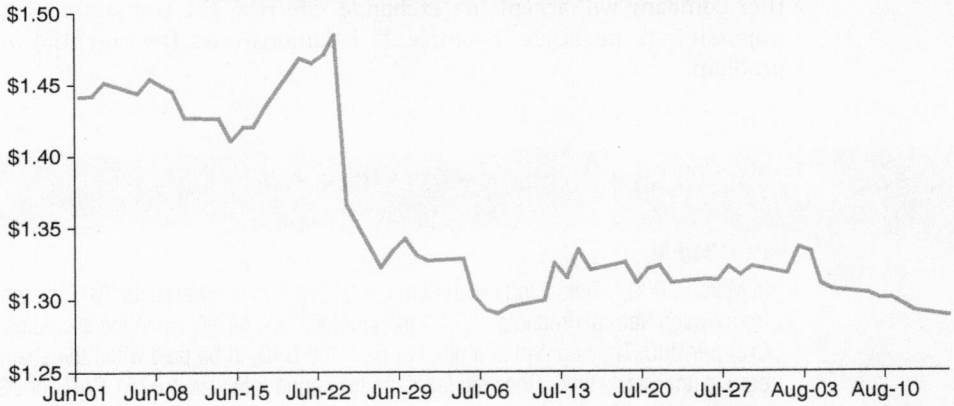

Hedging with Forward Contracts

Exchange rate risk naturally arises whenever transacting parties use different currencies: one of the parties will be at risk if exchange rates fluctuate. The most common method firms use to reduce the risk that results from changes in exchange rates is to hedge the transaction using *currency forward contracts*. These are special cases of forward contracts (discussed in Chapter 21) applied to currency exchange rates.

currency forward contract A contract that sets a currency exchange rate and an amount to exchange in advance.

forward exchange rate The exchange rate set in a currency forward contract that applies to an exchange that will occur in the future.

A **currency forward contract** is a contract that sets the exchange rate and an amount to exchange in advance. It is usually written between a firm and a bank, and it fixes a currency exchange rate for a transaction that will occur at a future date. A currency forward contract specifies (1) an exchange rate, (2) an amount of currency to exchange, and (3) a delivery date on which the exchange will take place. The exchange rate set in the contract is referred to as the **forward exchange rate**, because it applies to an exchange that will occur in the future. By entering into a currency forward contract, a firm can lock in an exchange rate in advance and reduce or eliminate its exposure to fluctuations in a currency's value.

If the forward contract allows the importer to eliminate the risk of a stronger CAD, where does the risk go? At least initially, the risk passes to the bank that has written the forward contract. Because the bank agrees to exchange CAD for USD at a fixed rate, it will experience a loss if the CAD increases in value. In Example 22.2, the bank receives only 393,900 USD in the forward contract but gives up CAD that are worth 507,267.58 USD.

Why is the bank willing to bear this risk? First, the bank is much larger and has more capital than a small importer, so it can bear the risk without being in jeopardy of financial distress. More importantly, in most settings the bank will not even hold the risk. Instead, the bank will find another party willing to trade CAD for USD (such as a Canadian company that imports from the United States). By entering into a second forward contract with offsetting risk, the bank can eliminate its risk altogether.

EXAMPLE 22.2 Using a Forward Contract to Lock in an Exchange Rate

PROBLEM

In March 2009, banks were offering one-year currency forward contracts with a forward exchange rate of 0.7575 USD/CAD. Suppose that at that time Whole Foods Market placed the order with Avalon's Canadian manufacturing facility with a price of 520,000 CAD and simultaneously entered into a forward contract to purchase 520,000 CAD at a forward exchange rate of 0.7575 USD/CAD in one year. What payment would Whole Foods Market be required to make when the shampoo shipment took place in 2010?

SOLUTION

■ Plan

If Whole Foods Market enters into a forward contract locking in an exchange rate of 0.7575 USD/CAD, then it doesn't matter what the actual exchange rate is in March 2010—Whole Foods Market will be able to buy 520,000 CAD for 0.7575 USD/CAD.

■ Execute

Even though the CAD appreciated by March 2010, making the CAD more expensive, Whole Foods Market would obtain the 520,000 CAD using the forward contract at the forward exchange rate of 0.7575 USD/CAD. Thus, in March 2010, Whole Foods must pay

$$520{,}000 \text{ CAD} \times 0.7575 \text{ USD/CAD} = 393{,}900 \text{ USD}.$$

Whole Foods Market would pay this amount to the bank in exchange for 520,000 CAD, which is then paid to Avalon.

■ Evaluate

This forward contract would have been a good deal for Whole Foods Market, because without the hedge, the company would have had to exchange USD for CAD at the prevailing exchange rate. In Example 22.1, we saw that the prevailing exchange rate in March 2010 was 1.0251 CAD/USD (or approximately 0.9755 USD/CAD), and this would have resulted in Whole Foods Market paying 507,267.58 USD for the CAD funds. However, the exchange rate could have moved the other way. If the exchange rate had fallen to 0.7000 USD/CAD, the forward contract still commits Whole Foods to pay 0.7575 USD/CAD. In other words, the forward contract locks in the exchange rate and eliminates the risk—whether the movement of the exchange rate is favourable or unfavourable.

This situation is illustrated in Figure 22.3. A U.S. importer, who must pay for goods with CAD, purchases CAD from the bank through a forward contract with a forward exchange rate of 0.7575 USD per CAD. This transaction locks in the U.S. importer's cost at 393,900 USD. Similarly, a Canadian importer, who must pay for goods in USD, uses a forward contract to sell the CAD to the bank, locking in the Canadian importer's cost at 520,000 CAD. The bank holds both forward contracts—the first to exchange USD for CAD and the second to exchange CAD for USD. The bank bears no exchange rate risk and earns fees from both the U.S. and Canadian importers. Most of the large Canadian banks offer services in both Canada and the United States, so they are able to accommodate clients (such as these importers) in both countries.

Cash-and-Carry and the Pricing of Currency Forwards

An alternative method, the *cash-and-carry strategy*, also enables a firm to eliminate exchange rate risk. Because this strategy provides the same cash flows as the forward contract, we can use it to determine the forward exchange rate using the Law of One

FIGURE 22.3 The Use of Currency Forwards to Eliminate Exchange Rate Risk

In this example, the Canadian importer and the U.S. importer both hedge their exchange rate risk by using currency forward contracts at 0.7575 USD/CAD (circled in red). By writing offsetting contracts, the bank bears no exchange rate risk and earns a fee from each transaction.

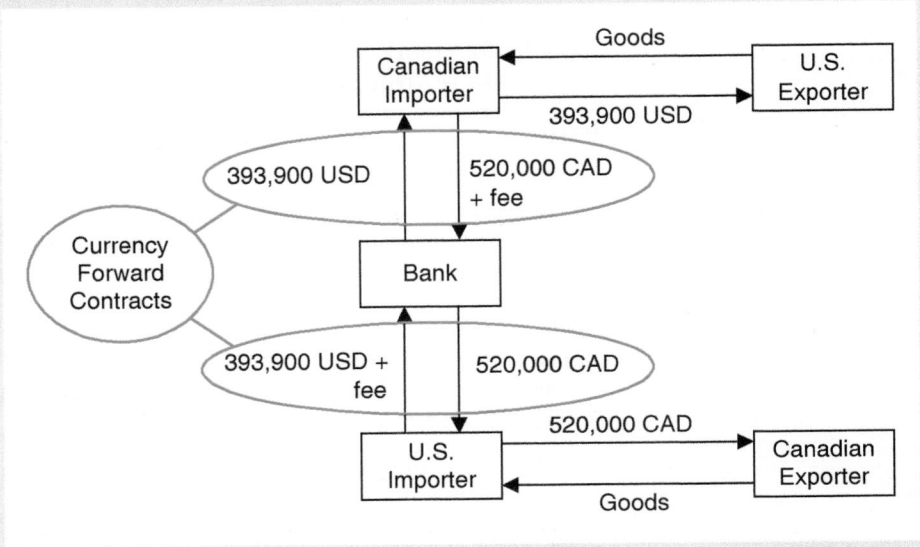

Price. Let's begin by considering the different ways investors can exchange foreign currency in the future for dollars in the future.

currency timeline A diagram that indicates time horizontally by dates (as in a standard timeline) and currencies (as in dollars and euros) vertically.

Currency Timeline. Currency forward contracts allow investors to exchange a foreign currency in the future for dollars in the future at the forward exchange rate. We illustrate such an exchange in the **currency timeline** in Figure 22.4, which indicates time horizontally by dates (as in a standard timeline) and currencies vertically (CAD and USD). Thus "CAD in one year" corresponds to the upper-right point in the timeline, and "USD in one year" corresponds to the lower-right point in the timeline. To convert cash flows between points, we must convert them at an appropriate rate. The forward exchange rate, indicated by $F_{USD/CAD}$, tells us the rate at which we can exchange CAD for USD in one year using a forward contract.

spot exchange rate The current foreign exchange rate.

Figure 22.4 also illustrates other transactions that we can use to move between dates or currencies in the timeline. We can convert CAD to USD today at the current exchange rate, also referred to as the **spot exchange rate**, $S_{USD/CAD}$. By borrowing or lending at the CAD interest rate r_{CAD}, we can exchange CAD today for CAD in one year. Finally, we can convert USD today for USD in one year at the USD interest rate r_{USD}, which is the rate at which banks will borrow or lend on USD-denominated accounts.

cash-and-carry strategy A strategy used to lock in the future cost of an asset by buying the asset for cash today and storing (or "carrying") it until a future date.

Cash-and-Carry Strategy. As Figure 22.4 shows, combining these other transactions provides an alternative way to convert CAD to USD in one year. The **cash-and-carry strategy** consists of the following three simultaneous trades:

1. Borrow CAD today using a one-year loan with the interest rate *rCAD*.
2. Exchange the CAD for USD today at the spot exchange rate *SUSD/CAD*.
3. Invest the USD today for one year at the interest rate r_{USD}.

FIGURE 22.4 Currency Timeline Showing Forward Contract and Cash-and-Carry Strategy

The cash-and-carry strategy (three transactions in red) replicates the forward contract (in blue) by borrowing in one currency, converting to the other currency at the spot exchange rate, and investing in the new currency.

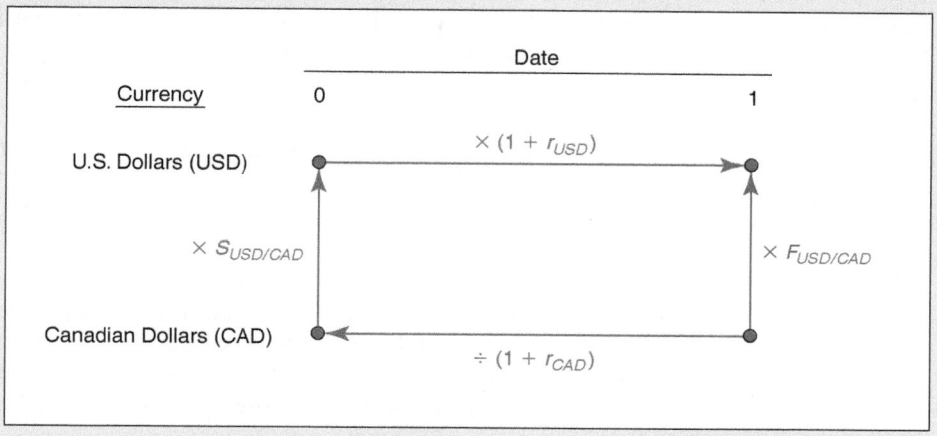

In one year's time, we will owe CAD (from the loan in transaction 1) and receive USD (from the investment in transaction 3). That is, we have converted CAD in one year to USD in one year, just as with the forward contract. This method is called a cash-and-carry strategy because we borrow cash that we then carry (invest) in the future.

Covered Interest Parity. Because the forward contract and the cash-and-carry strategy accomplish the same conversion, by the Law of One Price they must do so at the same rate. Equation 22.1 expresses the forward exchange rate in terms of the spot exchange rate and the interest rates in each currency. Note that on both sides of the equation, the ultimate units are USD/CAD in one year.

$$\underbrace{\text{Forward Rate}}_{\frac{\text{USD in one year}}{\text{CAD in one year}}} = \underbrace{\text{Spot Rate}}_{\frac{\text{USD today}}{\text{CAD today}}} \times \underbrace{\frac{1 + r_{USD}}{1 + r_{CAD}}}_{\frac{\text{USD in one year/USD today}}{\text{CAD in one year/CAD today}}} \tag{22.1}$$

Let's evaluate Equation. 22.1 in light of our assumptions in Examples 22.1 and 22.2. In March 2009, the spot exchange rate was 1.3000 CAD/USD (which is about 0.76923 USD/CAD), and let's suppose one-year interest rates were 1.42925% for USD and 3.00% for CAD. From Equation 22.1, the no-arbitrage forward exchange rate at that time for an exchange to take place one year later was

$$F = S \times \frac{1 + r_{USD}}{1 + r_{CAD}} = \frac{0.76923 \text{ USD}}{\text{CAD}} \times \frac{1.0142925}{1.03} = \frac{0.7575 \text{ USD}}{\text{CAD}}$$

which is the rate offered by the bank in Example 22.2.

covered interest parity equation The equation stating that the difference between the forward and spot exchange rates is related to the interest rate differential between the currencies.

Equation 22.1 is referred to as the **covered interest parity equation**; it states that the difference between the forward and spot exchange rates is related to the interest rate differential between the currencies. When the interest rate differs across countries, investors have an incentive to borrow in the low-interest rate currency and invest in the high-interest rate currency. Of course, there is always the risk that the high-interest rate currency could depreciate while the investment is held. Suppose you try to avoid this risk by locking in the future exchange rate using a forward contract. Equation 22.1 implies that the forward exchange rate will exactly offset any benefit from the higher interest rate, eliminating any arbitrage opportunity.

Equation 22.1 easily generalizes to a forward contract over any time period. Using the same logic, but investing or borrowing for T years rather than one year, the no-arbitrage forward rate for an exchange that will occur T years in the future is

$$\underbrace{\text{Forward Rate}_T}_{\frac{\text{USD in } T \text{ years}}{\text{CAD in } T \text{ years}}} = \underbrace{\text{Spot Rate}}_{\frac{\text{USD today}}{\text{CAD today}}} \times \underbrace{\frac{(1 + r_{USD})^T}{(1 + r_{CAD})^T}}_{\frac{\text{USD in } T \text{ years/USD today}}{\text{CAD in } T \text{ years/CAD today}}} \tag{22.2}$$

In this equation, the spot and forward rates are in units of USD/CAD, and the interest rates are the current risk-free T-year rates from the yield curve for each currency. (A useful rule to remember is that the ratio of interest rates must match the units of the exchange rate. Because the exchange rate is USD/CAD, we multiply by the USD interest rate and divide by the CAD interest rate. We could also solve the problem by converting all the rates to CAD/USD.)

Advantages of Forward Contracts. Why do firms use forward contracts rather than the cash-and-carry strategy? First, the forward contract is simpler, requiring one transaction rather than three, so it may have lower transaction fees. Second, many firms are not able to borrow easily in different currencies and may pay a higher interest rate if their credit quality is poor. Generally speaking, cash-and-carry strategies are used primarily by large banks, which can borrow easily and face low transaction costs. Banks use such a strategy to hedge their currency exposures that result from commitments to forward contracts.

Hedging Exchange Rate Risk with Options

Currency options are another method that firms commonly use to manage exchange rate risk. Currency options, as with the stock options introduced in Chapter 13, give the holder the right—but not the obligation—to exchange currency at a given exchange rate. Currency forward contracts allow firms to lock in a future exchange rate; currency options allow firms to insure themselves against the exchange rate moving beyond a certain level.

Forward Contracts versus Options. To demonstrate the difference between hedging with forward contracts and hedging with options, let's examine a specific situation. Assume it is April and the forward exchange rate is 1.0380 USD/CAD for September delivery. Instead of locking in this exchange rate using a forward contract, a U.S. firm that will need CAD in September can buy a call option on the CAD, giving it the right to buy CAD at a maximum price.[2] Suppose a call option on the CAD with a September expiration and strike price of 1.0350 USD/CAD trades for 0.0255 USD (per call on 1 CAD). That is, for a cost of 0.0255 USD, the firm can buy the right—but not the obligation—to purchase 1 CAD for 1.0350 USD/CAD in September. By doing so, the firm protects itself against a large increase in the value of the CAD but still benefits if the CAD declines.

Table 22.2 shows the outcome from hedging with a call option if the actual exchange rate in September is one of the values listed in the first column. If the spot

[2]Currency options can be purchased over the counter from a bank or on an exchange. The CME Group is one exchange offering currency options.

TABLE 22.2 **Net Cost of CAD (USD/CAD) When Hedging with a Currency Call Option with a Strike Price of 1.0350 USD/CAD and an Initial Premium of 0.0255 USD/CAD**

September Spot Exchange Rate	Exercise Call Option?	Exchange Rate Taken	+	Cost of Option	=	Total
0.9500	No	0.9500		0.0255		0.9755
1.0000	No	1.0000		0.0255		1.0255
1.0500	Yes	1.0350		0.0255		1.0605
1.1000	Yes	1.0350		0.0255		1.0605

exchange rate is less than the 1.0350 USD/CAD strike price of the option, then the firm will not exercise the call option and will convert USD to CAD at the spot exchange rate. If the spot exchange rate is more than 1.0350 USD/CAD, the firm will exercise the call option and convert USD to CAD at the rate of 1.0350 USD/CAD (see the second and third columns). We then add the initial cost of the call option (fourth column) to determine the total USD cost per CAD paid by the firm (fifth column).[3]

FIGURE 22.5 **Comparison of Hedging the Exchange Rate Using a Forward Contract, a Call Option, or No Hedge**

The forward hedge locks in an exchange rate and so eliminates all risk. Not hedging leaves the firm fully exposed. Hedging with a call option allows the firm to benefit if the exchange rate falls and protects the firm from a very large increase.

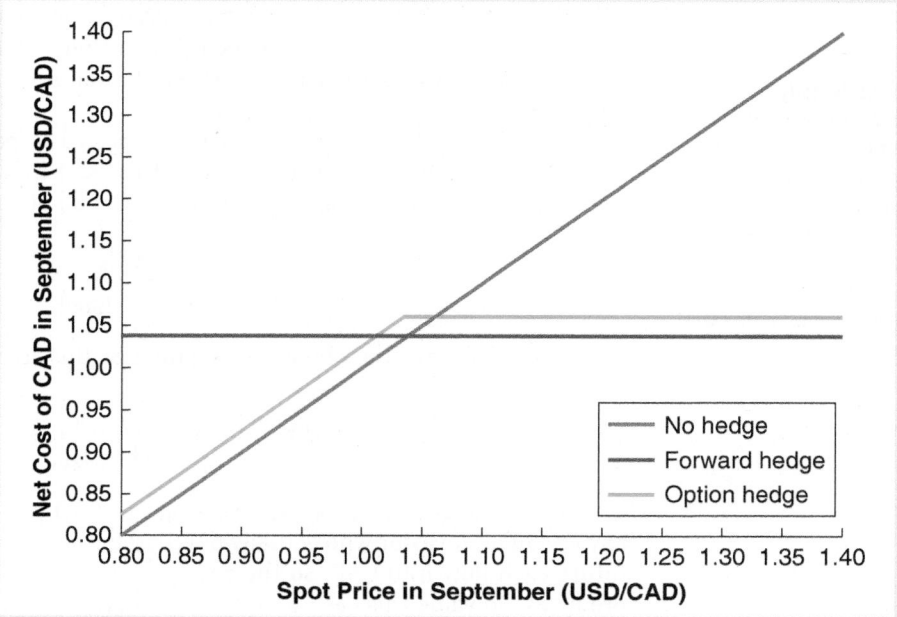

[3]In computing the total cost, we have ignored the small amount of interest that could have been earned on the option premium.

The data from Table 22.2 is plotted in Figure 22.5, where we compare hedging with options to the alternative of hedging with a forward contract or not hedging at all. If the firm does not hedge at all, its cost for CAD is simply the spot exchange rate. If the firm hedges with a forward contract, it locks in the cost of CAD at the forward exchange rate, and the firm's cost is fixed. As Figure 22.5 shows, hedging with options represents a middle ground: the firm puts a *cap* on its potential cost but will benefit if the CAD depreciates in value.

Advantages of Options. Why might a firm choose to hedge with options rather than forward contracts? Many managers want the firm to benefit if the exchange rate moves in its favour, rather than being stuck paying an above-market rate. Firms also prefer options to forward contracts if the transaction they are hedging might not take place. In this case, a forward contract could commit them to making an exchange at an unfavourable rate for currency they do not need, whereas an option allows them to walk away from the exchange. In any case, it is worth noting that an option holder can always sell the position at a gain rather than demanding delivery of the currency, so if the transaction does not take place and the option is in-the-money, the company need not actually demand delivery of the foreign currency.

CONCEPT CHECK

3. How can firms hedge exchange rate risk?
4. Why might a firm prefer to hedge exchange rate risk with options rather than forward contracts?

22.3 Internationally Integrated Capital Markets

Does the value of a foreign investment depend on the currency we use in the analysis? To address this important question, we will develop a conceptual benchmark based on the assumptions that any investor can exchange either currency in any amount at the spot rate or forward rates, and is free to purchase or sell any security in any amount in either country at their current market prices. Under these conditions, which we term **internationally integrated capital markets**, the value of an investment does *not* depend on the currency we use in the analysis.

internationally integrated capital markets Markets in which any investor can exchange currencies in any amount at the spot or forward rates and is free to purchase or sell any security in any amount in any country at its current market prices.

Consider a risky foreign asset that is expected to pay the cash flow, C_{FOC}, in one period.[4] In a normal market, the price of this asset in a foreign market is the present value of this cash flow using r^*_{FOC}, the cost of capital of an investor local to that market:

$$PV_{FOC} = \frac{C_{FOC}}{(1 + r^*_{FOC})} \tag{22.3}$$

A Canadian investor who wants to purchase this asset in CAD will have to pay

$$PV_{CAD} = S \times \frac{C_{FOC}}{(1 + r^*_{FOC})} \tag{22.4}$$

where S is the current spot exchange rate in CAD per FOC (foreign currency). Now any Canadian investor who actually purchased this security would have to convert the future cash flow into CAD, so the payoff to such an investor is the CAD cash flow it produces. To value this cash flow, assume that the Canadian investor contracts today to convert the *expected* cash flow in one period at the forward rate, F, quoted as CAD per FOC. If we assume that spot exchange rates and the foreign currency cash flows of the security are uncorrelated, then this Canadian investor's expected CAD cash flow

[4]FOC is the hypothetical code for the foreign currency.

is $F \times C_{FOC}$.[5] If r^*_{CAD} is the appropriate cost of capital from the standpoint of a Canadian investor, the present value of this expected cash flow is

$$PV_{CAD} = F \times \frac{C_{FOC}}{(1 + r^*_{CAD})} \tag{22.5}$$

By the Law of One Price, this value must be equal to what the Canadian investor paid for the security:

$$S \times \frac{C_{FOC}}{(1 + r^*_{FOC})} = \frac{F \times C_{FOC}}{(1 + r^*_{CAD})}$$

Rearranging terms gives

$$\underbrace{F}_{CAD/FOC} = \underbrace{S}_{CAD/FOC} \times \frac{(1 + r^*_{CAD})}{(1 + r^*_{FOC})} \tag{22.6}$$

This condition ought to look familiar, because Equation 22.6 is simply covered interest parity (Equation 22.1), here derived for risky cash flows rather than riskless cash flows.

EXAMPLE 22.3 Present Values and Internationally Integrated Capital Markets

PROBLEM

You are a Canadian who is trying to calculate the present value of a 10 million JPY cash flow that will occur one year in the future. You know that the spot exchange rate is $S = 110$ JPY/CAD and the one-year forward rate is $F = 105.8095$ JPY/CAD. You also know that the appropriate CAD cost of capital for this cash flow is $r^*_{CAD} = 5\%$ and that the appropriate JPY cost of capital for this cash flow is $r^*_{JPY} = 1\%$. What is the present value of the 10 million JPY cash flow from the standpoint of a Japanese investor, and what is the CAD equivalent of this amount? What is the present value of the 10 million JPY cash flow from the standpoint of a Canadian investor who first converts the 10 million JPY into CAD and then applies the CAD discount rate?

SOLUTION

■ Plan

For the Japanese investor, we can compute the present value of the future JPY cash flow at the JPY discount rate and use the spot exchange rate to convert that amount to CAD.

For the Canadian investor, we can convert the future JPY cash flow to CAD at the forward rate and compute the present value using the CAD discount rate.

■ Execute

For the Japanese investor, the CAD present value of the JPY cash flow is

$$10{,}000{,}000 \text{ JPY}/(1.01) = 9{,}900{,}990 \text{ JPY}$$

▶

[5]The actual cash flow in foreign currency will be $C_{FOC} + e$ where e is the uncertainty in the cash flow and has an expected value of zero. In CAD terms, this cash flow is $F \times C_{FOC} + S_1 \times e$ because the forward contract is only for the amount C_{FOC}; the rest must be converted at the prevailing spot rate in one period, S_1. Taking expectations, $E\,[S_1 \times e] = E[S_1] \times E[e] = 0$ because spot rates are uncorrelated with the project cash flows and $E\,[e] = 0$.

and the CAD equivalent is

$$9{,}900{,}990/110 = 90{,}009 \text{ CAD}$$

(Note that we adjusted the formula in Equation 22.4 because the exchange rate is expressed as JPY per CAD rather than CAD per JPY.)

The present value from the standpoint of a Canadian investor who first converts the 10 million JPY into CAD using the forward rate and then applies the CAD cost of capital is

$$(10{,}000{,}000 \text{ JPY}/105.8095)/1.05 = 90{,}009 \text{ CAD}$$

(Again, we have adjusted the formula in Equation 22.5 because the exchange rate is expressed as JPY per CAD.[6])

■ Evaluate

Because the Canadian and Japanese capital markets are internationally integrated, both methods produce the same result.

CONCEPT CHECK

5. What assumptions are needed to have internationally integrated capital markets?
6. What implication do internationally integrated capital markets have for the value of the same asset in different countries?

22.4 Valuation of Foreign Currency Cash Flows

The most obvious difference between a domestic project and a foreign project is that the foreign project will most likely generate cash flows in a foreign currency. If the foreign project is owned by a domestic corporation, managers and shareholders need to determine the home currency value of the foreign currency cash flows.

In an internationally integrated capital market, two equivalent methods are available for calculating the NPV of a foreign project:

1. Calculate the NPV in the foreign country and convert it to the home currency at the spot rate.
2. Convert the cash flows of the foreign project into the home currency and then calculate the NPV of these cash flows.

The first method is essentially what we have done throughout this book (calculating the NPV of a project in a single currency) with the added step at the end of converting the NPV into the home currency using spot rates. Because this method should be familiar to you at this stage, we will concentrate on the second method. The second valuation method requires converting to the expected CAD value of the foreign currency cash flows and then proceeding to value the project as if it were a domestic project.

[6]It is best to always write down the cash flows along with their currency signs so that you can keep track of them. Then by crossing out currency signs as you go, you can be sure that you will be left with an answer in the correct currency.

Application: Ityesi Inc.

Ityesi Inc., a manufacturer of custom packaging products headquartered in Canada, wants to apply the weighted average cost of capital (WACC) technique to value a project in the United Kingdom. Ityesi is considering introducing a new line of packaging in the United Kingdom that will be the company's first foreign project. The project will be completely self-contained in the United Kingdom, such that all revenues are generated and all costs are incurred there.

Engineers expect the technology used in the new products to be obsolete after four years. The marketing group expects annual sales of 37.5 million GBP per year for this product line. Manufacturing costs and operating expenses are expected to total 15.625 million GBP and 5.625 million GBP per year, respectively. Developing the product will require an upfront investment of 15 million GBP in capital equipment that will be obsolete in four years and an initial marketing expense of 4.167 million GBP. Ityesi pays a corporate tax rate of 40% no matter in which country it manufactures its products. The expected GBP free cash flows of the proposed project are projected in Table 22.3.

TABLE 22.3 Expected Foreign Free Cash Flows from Ityesi's U.K. Project

Year		0	1	2	3	4
	Incremental Earnings Forecast (million GBP)					
1	Sales	—	37.500	37.500	37.500	37.500
2	Cost of Goods Sold	—	(15.625)	(15.625)	(15.625)	(15.625)
3	**Gross Profit**	—	21.875	21.875	21.875	21.875
4	Operating Expenses	(4.167)	(5.625)	(5.625)	(5.625)	(5.625)
5	Depreciation	—	(3.750)	(3.750)	(3.750)	(3.750)
6	**EBIT**	(4.167)	(12.500)	(12.500)	(12.500)	(12.500)
7	Income tax at 40%	1.667	(5.000)	(5.000)	(5.000)	(5.000)
8	**Unlevered Net Income**	(2.500)	7.500	7.500	7.500	7.500
	Free Cash Flow					
9	Plus: Depreciation	—	3.750	3.750	3.750	3.750
10	Less: Capital Expenditures	(15.000)	—	—	—	—
11	Less: Increases in NWC	—	—	—	—	—
12	**GBP Free Cash Flow**	**(17.500)**	**11.250**	**11.250**	**11.250**	**11.250**

Ityesi's managers have determined that there is no correlation between the uncertainty in these cash flows and the uncertainty in the spot CAD/GBP exchange rate. As we explained in the last section, under this condition, the expected value of the future cash flows in CAD is the expected value in GBP multiplied by the forward exchange rate. Obtaining forward rate quotes for as long as four years in the future is difficult, so Ityesi's managers have decided to use the covered interest rate parity formula (the generalized version shown in Equation 22.2) to compute the forward rates.

Forward Exchange Rates. The current spot exchange rate, S, is 2.00 CAD/GBP. Suppose that the yield curve in both countries is flat: the risk-free rate on CAD, r_{CAD}, is 4%, and the risk-free interest rate on pounds, r_{GBP}, is 7%. Using the covered interest parity condition for a multiyear forward exchange rate (Equation 22.2), we have

$$F_1 = S \times \frac{(1 + r_{CAD})}{(1 + r_{GBP})} = (2.00 \text{ CAD/GBP})\frac{(1.04)}{(1.07)} = 1.9439 \text{ CAD/GBP}$$

$$F = S \times \frac{(1 + r_{CAD})^2}{(1 + r_{GBP})^2} = (2.00 \text{ CAD/GBP})\frac{(104)^2}{(107)^2} = 1.8894 \text{ CAD/GBP}$$

$$F = S \times \frac{(1 + r_{CAD})^3}{(1 + r_{GBP})^3} = (2.00 \text{ CAD/GBP})\frac{(104)^3}{(107)^3} = 1.8364 \text{ CAD/GBP}$$

$$F_4 = S \times \frac{(1 + r_{CAD})^4}{(1 + r_{GBP})^4} = (2.00 \text{ CAD/GBP})\frac{(104)^4}{(107)^4} = 1.7850 \text{ CAD/GBP}$$

Free Cash Flow Conversion. Using these forward exchange rates, we can now calculate the expected free cash flows in CAD by multiplying the expected cash flows in GBP by the forward exchange rate, as shown in Table 22.4.

TABLE 22.4 Expected CAD Free Cash Flows from Ityesi's U.K. Project

		0	1	2	3	4
	CAD Free Cash flow (million CAD)					
1	GBP Free Cash Flow (million GBP)	(17.500)	11.250	11.250	11.250	11.250
2	Forward Exchange Rate (CAD/GBP)	2.0000	1.9439	1.8894	1.8364	1.7850
3	**CAD Value of GBP Free Cash Flow**	(35.000)	21.869	21.256	20.660	20.081

The Value of Ityesi's Foreign Project with WACC. With the cash flows of the U.K. project now expressed in CAD, we can value the foreign project as if it were a domestic CAD project. We proceed, as we did in Chapter 12, under the assumption that the market risk of the U.K. project is similar to that of the company as a whole; as a consequence, we can use Ityesi's costs of equity and debt in Canada to calculate the WACC.[7]

Ityesi has built up 20 million CAD in cash for investment needs and has debt of 320 million CAD, so its net debt is $D = 320 - 20 = 300$ million CAD. This amount is equal to the market value of its equity, implying a (net) debt-equity ratio of 1. Ityesi intends to maintain a similar (net) debt-equity ratio for the foreseeable future. The WACC thus assigns equal weights to equity and debt, as shown in Table 22.5.

[7]The risk of the foreign project is unlikely to be *exactly* the same as the risk of domestic projects (or the firm as a whole), because the foreign project contains residual exchange rate risk that the domestic projects often do not contain (e.g., political or macroeconomic risks specific to the foreign country). In Ityesi's case, managers have determined that the additional risk premium for this risk is small, so for practical purposes they have chosen to ignore it and just use the domestic cost of capital. In fact, if the additional risks are all diversifiable (not systematic), then there should be no additional risk premium.

TABLE 22.5 Ityesi's Current Market Value Balance Sheet (million CAD) and Cost of Capital without the U.K. Project

Assets		Liabilities and Equity		Cost of Capital	
Cash	20	Debt	320	Debt	6%
Existing Assets	600	Equity	300	Equity	10%
	620		620		

With Ityesi's cost of equity at 10% and its cost of debt at 6%, we calculate Ityesi's WACC as follows:

$$r_{wacc} = \frac{E}{E+D} r_E + \frac{D}{E+D} r_D(1 - T_C)$$
$$= (0.5)(10.0\%) + (0.5)(6.0\%)(1 - 40\%) = 6.8\%$$

We can now determine the value of the foreign project, including the tax shield from debt, by calculating the present value of the future free cash flows using the WACC:

$$\frac{21.869}{1.068} + \frac{21.256}{1.068^2} + \frac{20.660}{1.068^3} + \frac{20.081}{1.068^4} = 71.506 \text{ million CAD}$$

Because the upfront cost of launching the product line in dollars is only 35 million CAD, the net present value is 71.506 − 35 = 36.506 million CAD. Thus, Ityesi should undertake the U.K. project.

The Law of One Price as a Robustness Check

To arrive at the NPV of Ityesi's project required making a number of assumptions—for example, that international markets are integrated, and that the exchange rate and the cash flows of the project are uncorrelated. The managers of Ityesi will naturally worry about whether these assumptions are justified. Luckily, there is a way to check the analysis.

Recall that there are two ways to compute the NPV of the foreign project. Ityesi could just as easily have computed the foreign NPV by discounting the foreign cash flows at the foreign cost of capital and converting this result to a domestic NPV using the spot rate. Except for the last step, this method requires doing the same calculation we have performed throughout this book—that is, calculate the NPV of a (domestic) project. Determining the NPV requires knowing the cost of capital—in this case, the cost of capital for an investment in the United Kingdom. Recall that to estimate this cost of capital we use return data for publicly traded single-product companies—in this case, U.K. firms. For this method to provide the same answer as the alternative method, the estimate for the foreign cost of capital, r^*_{GBP}, must satisfy the Law of One Price, which from Equation 22.6 implies

$$(1 + r^*_{GBP}) = \frac{S}{F} \times (1 + r^*_{CAD}) \tag{22.7}$$

If it does not, then Ityesi's managers should be concerned that the simplifying assumptions in their analysis are not valid: market frictions exist so that the market integration assumption is not a good approximation of reality, or perhaps there is a significant correlation between spot exchange rates and cash flows.

We can rewrite Equation 22.7 as follows. Using the covered interest rate parity relationship (Equation 22.1), we have

$$\frac{S}{F} = \frac{(1 + r_{GBP})}{(1 + r_{CAD})} \tag{22.8}$$

Here, r_{GBP} and r_{CAD} are the foreign and domestic risk-free interest rates, respectively. Combining Equations 22.7 and 22.8 and rearranging terms gives the foreign cost of capital in terms of the domestic cost of capital and interest rates:

$$r^*_{GBP} = \frac{(1 + r_{GBP})}{(1 + r_{CAD})} \times (1 + r^*_{CAD}) - 1 \tag{22.9}$$

If the simplifying assumptions Ityesi made in calculating the NPV of its U.K. project are valid, then the cost of capital estimate calculated using Equation 22.9 will be close to the cost of the capital estimate calculated directly using comparable single-product companies in the United Kingdom.

EXAMPLE 22.4 Internationalizing the Cost of Capital

PROBLEM

Use the Law of One Price to infer the GBP WACC from Ityesi's CAD WACC. Verify that the NPV of Ityesi's project is the same when its GBP free cash flows are discounted at this GBP WACC and converted at the spot rate.

SOLUTION

■ Plan

We can use Equation 22.9 to compute the GBP WACC. The market data we need is

$$r_{CAD} = 4\%,\ r_{GBP} = 7\%,\ r^*_{CAD} = 6.8\%$$

Finally, we'll need the spot exchange rate (2.00 CAD/GBP) to convert the GBP NPV to CAD.

■ Execute

Applying Equation 22.9, we have

$$r^*_{GBP} = \frac{(1 + r_{GBP})}{(1 + r_{CAD})} \times (1 + r^*_{CAD}) - 1 = \frac{(1.07)}{(1.04)} \times (1.068) - 1 = 0.0988$$

The GBP WACC is 9.88%.

We can now use Ityesi's GBP WACC to calculate the present value of the GBP free cash flows in Table 22.3:

$$\frac{11.250}{1.0988} + \frac{11.250}{1.0988^2} + \frac{11.250}{1.0988^3} + \frac{11.250}{1.0988^4} = 35.754 \text{ million GBP}$$

The NPV in GBP of the investment opportunity is 35.754 − 17.5 = 18.254 million GBP. Converting this amount to CAD at the spot rate gives 18.254 million GBP × 2.00 CAD/GBP = 36.508 million CAD, which is exactly the NPV we calculated before except for a slight difference due to rounding.

■ Evaluate

The Canadian and U.K. markets are integrated, and our simplifying assumptions for the WACC valuation method are valid.

CONCEPT CHECK

7. Explain two methods we use to calculate the NPV of a foreign project.
8. When do these two methods give the same NPV of the foreign project?

22.5 Valuation and International Taxation

In this chapter, we assume that Ityesi pays a corporate tax rate of 40% no matter where its earnings are generated. In practice, determining the corporate tax rate on foreign income is complicated, because corporate income taxes may have to be paid to two national governments: the host government (the United Kingdom in this example) and the home government (Canada). If the foreign project is a separately incorporated subsidiary of the parent company, the amount of taxes a firm pays generally depends on the amount of profits repatriated (brought back to the home country)—the **repatriated earnings** and whether a tax treaty exists between Canada and the foreign country. International taxation is a complex subject to which specialized experts devote considerable time. In this introductory setting, we aim only to provide a broad overview and sense of the issues involved.

repatriated earnings The profits from a foreign project that a firm brings back to its home country.

A Single Foreign Project with Immediate Repatriation of Earnings

We begin by assuming that the firm has a single foreign project and that all foreign profits are repatriated immediately. The general international arrangement prevailing with respect to taxation of corporate profits is that the host country gets the first opportunity to tax income produced within its borders. The home government then gets an opportunity to tax the income to the domestic firm from a foreign project. In particular, the home government must establish a tax policy specifying its treatment of foreign income and foreign taxes paid on that income. In addition, it needs to establish the timing of taxation.

Canadian tax policy requires Canadian corporations to pay taxes on their foreign income at the same rate as profits earned in Canada if the income is passive income (such as rental or royalty income) or if the income is from a country without a tax treaty with Canada. However, a full tax credit is given for foreign taxes paid *up to* the amount of the Canadian tax liability. In other words, if the foreign tax rate is less than the Canadian tax rate, the company pays total taxes equal to the Canadian tax rate on its foreign earnings. In this case, all of the company's earnings are taxed at the same rate no matter where they are earned—the working assumption we used for Ityesi.

If the foreign tax rate exceeds the Canadian tax rate, companies must pay this higher rate on foreign earnings. Because the Canadian tax credit exceeds the amount of Canadian taxes owed, no tax is owed in Canada. Note that Canadian tax policy does not allow companies to apply the part of the tax credit that is not used to offset domestic taxes owed, so this extra tax credit is wasted. In this scenario, companies pay a higher tax rate on foreign income and a lower (Canadian) tax rate on income generated in Canada.

If the Canadian corporation receives active income from a subsidiary located in a country that has a tax treaty with Canada, that income is not taxed in Canada when it is returned to Canada. This is called the **territorial approach** to taxation whereby a government only taxes profits earned within its borders. This is in sharp contrast to the former system used in the United States that also taxed active income earned by U.S.-based multinationals when their subsidiaries remit a dividend back to the parent company. The former U.S. tax system is called the **worldwide approach to taxation** whereby a country taxes profits on companies domiciled in it no matter whether the profit was earned at home or abroad. In the former U.S. system, U.S. taxes on foreign source income were only levied when the income was repatriated to the U.S.. As a result of the former U.S. system, many U.S. multinationals deferred remitting dividends back to the parent company as a way to

territorial approach to taxation where a government only taxes profits earned within its borders.

worldwide approach to taxation where a country taxes profits on companies domiciled in it no matter whether the profit was earned at home or abroad avoid paying U.S. tax. Apple, Alphabet (Google) and Facebook all used this strategy and kept income offshore to avoid U.S. taxes. Under tax reform passed at the end of 2017, U.S. firms will be subject to a one-time tax of their foreign subsidiaries cash holdings and in future years the taxation method will switch to the territorial approach.

Multiple Foreign Projects and Deferral of Earnings Repatriation

Thus far, we have assumed that the firm has only one foreign project and that it repatriates earnings immediately. Neither assumption is realistic. Firms can lower their taxes by pooling multiple foreign projects and deferring the repatriation of earnings. Let's begin by considering the benefits of pooling the income on all foreign projects.

Pooling Multiple Foreign Projects. Under Canadian tax law, Canadian-based multinational corporations may use any excess tax credits generated in high-tax foreign countries to offset their net Canadian tax liabilities on earnings in low-tax foreign countries. Thus, if the Canadian tax rate exceeds the combined tax rate on all foreign income, it is valid to assume that the firm pays the same tax rate on all income no matter where it is earned. Otherwise, the firm must pay a higher tax rate on its foreign income.

Deferring Repatriation of Earnings. Now consider an opportunity to defer repatriation of foreign profits earned by a subsidiary in a non-tax-treaty country. This consideration is important, because a Canadian tax liability is not incurred until the profits are brought back home if the foreign operation is set up as a separately incorporated subsidiary (rather than as a foreign branch). If a company chooses not to repatriate 12.5 million GBP in pre-tax earnings, for example, it effectively reinvests those earnings abroad and defers its Canadian tax liability. When the foreign tax rates exceed the Canadian tax rates, there are no benefits to deferral, because in such a case there is no additional Canadian tax liability.

When the foreign tax rate is less than the Canadian tax rate, deferral can provide significant benefits. Deferring repatriation of earnings lowers the overall tax burden in much the same way as deferring capital gains lowers the tax burden imposed by the capital gains tax. Other benefits from deferral arise because the firm effectively gains a real option to repatriate income at times when repatriation might be cheaper. For example, we have already noted that by pooling foreign income, the firm effectively pays the combined tax rate on all foreign income. Because the income generated across countries changes, this combined tax rate will vary from year to year. In years in which it exceeds the Canadian tax rate, the repatriation of additional income does not incur an additional Canadian tax liability, so the earnings can be repatriated tax free.

CONCEPT CHECK

9. What tax rate should we use to value a foreign project?

10. How can a Canadian firm lower its taxes on foreign projects?

22.6 Internationally Segmented Capital Markets

segmented capital markets Capital markets that are not internationally integrated.

To this point, we have worked under the assumption that international capital markets are integrated. Often, however, this assumption is not appropriate. In some countries, especially in the developing world, all investors do not have equal access to financial securities. In this section, we consider why countries' capital markets might not be integrated—a case called **segmented capital markets**.

Many of the interesting questions in international corporate finance address the issues that result when capital markets are internationally segmented. In this section, we briefly consider the main reasons for segmentation of the capital markets and the implications for international corporate finance.

Differential Access to Markets

In some cases, a country's risk-free securities are internationally integrated, but markets for a specific firm's securities are not. Firms may face differential access to markets if there is any kind of asymmetry with respect to information about them. For example, Ityesi may be well known in Canada and enjoy easy access to CAD equity and debt markets there because it regularly provides information to an established community of analysts tracking the firm. It may not be equally well known in the United Kingdom and, therefore, may have difficulty tapping into the GBP capital markets, because it has no track record there. For this reason, investors in the United Kingdom may require a higher rate of return to persuade them to hold GBP stocks and bonds issued by the Canadian firm.

With differential access to national markets, Ityesi would face a higher GBP WACC than the GBP WACC implied by Equation 22.9. Ityesi would then view the foreign project as less valuable if it raises capital in the United Kingdom rather than in Canada. In fact, to maximize shareholder value, the firm should raise capital at home; the method of valuing the foreign project as if it were a domestic project would then provide the correct NPV. Differential access to national capital markets is common enough that it provides the best explanation for the existence of **currency swaps**, which are like the interest rate swap contracts we discussed in Chapter 21, but with the holder receiving coupons in one currency and paying coupons denominated in a different currency. Currency swaps generally also have final face-value payments, also in different currencies. Using a currency swap, a firm can borrow in the market where it has the best access to capital, and then "swap" the coupon and principal payments to whichever currency it would prefer to make payments in. Thus, swaps allow firms to mitigate their exchange rate risk exposure between assets and liabilities, while still making investments and raising funds in the most attractive locales.

currency swaps A contract in which parties agree to exchange coupon payments and a final face-value payment that are in different currencies.

EXAMPLE 22.5 Risky Government Bonds

PROBLEM

For July 27, 2009, the spot exchange rate between Russian rubles and U.S. dollars was 30.9845 RUB/USD, and the one-year forward exchange rate was 33.7382 RUB/USD. At the time, the yield on short-term Russian government bonds was about 11%, while the comparable one-year yield on U.S. Treasury securities was 0.5%. Using the covered interest parity relationship, calculate the implied one-year forward rate. Compare this rate to the actual forward rate, and explain why the two rates differ.

SOLUTION

Plan

Using the covered interest parity formula, the implied forward rate is

$$F = S \times \frac{(1 + r_{RUB})}{(1 + r_{USD})}$$

Thus, we need the spot exchange rate, 30.9845 RUB/USD, the USD interest rate, 0.5%, and the RUB interest rate, 11%. ▶

■ **Execute**

$$F = S \times \frac{(1 + r_{RUB})}{(1 + r_{USD})} = 30.9845 \frac{\text{RUB}}{\text{USD}} \times \frac{1.110}{1.005} = 34.2217 \frac{\text{RUB}}{\text{USD}}$$

The implied forward rate is higher than the current spot rate because Russian government bonds have higher yields than U.S. government bonds. The difference between the implied forward rate and the actual forward rate probably reflects the default risk in Russian government bonds. (The Russian government defaulted on its debt as recently as 1998.) A holder of 100,000 RUB seeking a true risk-free investment could convert the RUB to USD, invest in U.S. Treasury securities, and convert the proceeds back to RUB at a rate locked-in with a forward contract. By doing so, the investor would earn

$$\frac{100{,}000 \text{ RUB}}{30.9845 \frac{\text{RUB}}{\text{USD}} \text{today}} \times \frac{1.005 \text{ USD in 1 yr}}{1 \text{ USD today}} \times \left(33.7382 \frac{\text{RUB}}{\text{USD}} \text{in 1 yr}\right)$$

$$= 109{,}432 \text{ RUB in 1 yr}$$

for an effective RUB risk-free rate of 9.432%.

■ **Evaluate**

The higher rate of 11% on Russian bonds reflects a credit spread of 11% − 9.432% = 1.568% to compensate bondholders for the additional default risk of the Russian bonds compared to the American bonds.

Macro-Level Distortions

Markets for risk-free instruments may also be segmented. Important macroeconomic reasons for segmented capital markets include capital controls and foreign exchange controls that create barriers to international capital flows and thus segment national markets. Many countries regulate or limit capital inflows or outflows, and many do not allow their currencies to be freely converted into dollars, thereby creating capital market segmentation. Similarly, some countries restrict who can hold financial securities.

Political, legal, social, and cultural characteristics that differ across countries may require compensation in the form of a country risk premium. For example, the rate of interest paid on government bonds or other securities in a country with a tradition of weak enforcement of property rights is not likely to truly be a risk-free rate. Instead, interest rates in the country will reflect a risk premium for the possibility of default, so relations such as covered interest rate parity will likely not hold exactly.

EXAMPLE 22.6 Valuing a Foreign Acquisition in a Segmented Market

PROBLEM

Camacho Enterprises is a U.S. company that is considering expanding by acquiring Xtapa, Inc., a firm in Mexico. The acquisition is expected to increase Camacho's free cash flows by 21 million MXN (Mexican pesos) the first year; this amount is then expected to grow at a rate of 8% per year. The price of the investment is 525 million MXN, which is 52.5 million USD at the current exchange rate of 10 MXN/USD. Based on an analysis in the Mexican market, Camacho has determined that the appropriate after-tax MXN WACC is 12%. If Camacho has also determined that its after-tax USD WACC for this expansion is 7.5%, what is the value of the Mexican acquisition? Assume that the Mexican and U.S. markets for risk-free securities are integrated and that the yield curve in both countries is flat. U.S. risk-free interest rates are 6%, and Mexican risk-free interest rates are 9%.

SOLUTION

Plan

We can calculate the NPV of the expansion in MXN and convert the result into USD at the spot rate. The free cash flows are

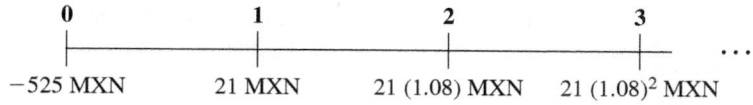

We can also compute the NPV in USD by converting the expected cash flows into USD using forward rates. The N-year forward rate (Equation 22.2) expressed in MXN/USD is

$$F_N = S \times \frac{(1 + r_{MXN})^N}{(1 + r_{USD})^N} = 10 \times \left(\frac{1.09}{1.06}\right)^N = 10 \times 1.0283^N = 1.0283 \times 1.0283^{N-1}$$

Execute

The net present value of the MXN cash flows at the MXN WACC is

$$NPV = \frac{21}{0.12 - 0.08} - 525 = 0$$

Thus, the purchase is a zero-NPV transaction. Presumably, Camacho is competing with other Mexican companies for the purchase.

To compute the NPV using the USD WACC, we need to convert the MXN cash flows to USD cash flows. The USD expected cash flows are the MXN cash flows (from the earlier timeline) converted at the appropriate forward rate (we divide by the forward rate because it is in MXN/USD):

$$C^N_{MXN}/F_N = \frac{21(1.08)^{N-1}}{10.283 \times 1.0283^{N-1}} = 2.0422 \times 1.0503^{N-1}$$

The USD expected cash flows are therefore

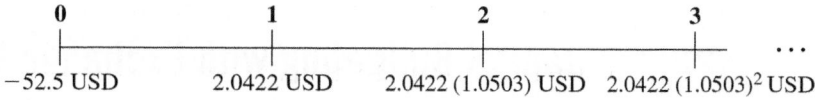

Thus, the USD cash flows grow at about 5.03% per year. The NPV of these cash flows is

$$NPV = \frac{2.0422}{0.075 - 0.0503} - 52.5 = 30.18 \text{ million USD}$$

Evaluate

We calculated two different NPVs, but which NPV more accurately represents the benefits of the expansion? The answer depends on the source of the difference. To compute the USD expected cash flows by converting the MXN expected cash flows at the forward rate, we must accept the assumption that spot rates and the project cash flows are uncorrelated. The difference might simply reflect that this assumption failed to hold. Another possibility is that the difference reflects estimation error in the respective WACC estimates.

If Camacho is relatively confident in its assumptions about spot rates and its WACC estimates, a third possibility is that Mexican and U.S. capital markets are not integrated. In this case, Camacho, because of its access to U.S. capital markets, might have a competitive advantage. Perhaps other companies with which it is competing for the purchase of Xtapa are all Mexican firms that do not have access to capital markets outside of Mexico. Hence, Camacho can raise capital at a cheaper ▶

rate. Of course, this argument also requires that other U.S. companies not be competing for the purchase of Xtapa. Camacho, however, might have special knowledge of Xtapa's markets that other U.S. companies lack. This knowledge would give Camacho a competitive advantage in the product market over other U.S. companies and would put it on an equal footing in the product market with other Mexican companies. Because Camacho would have a competitive advantage in capital markets over other Mexican companies, the NPV of the purchase would be positive for Camacho but zero for the other bidders for Xtapa.

Implications of Internationally Segmented Capital Markets

A segmented financial market has an important implication for international corporate finance: one country or currency has a higher rate of return than another country or currency, when the two rates are compared in the same currency. If the return difference results from a market friction such as capital controls, corporations can exploit this friction by setting up projects in the high-return country/currency and raising capital in the low-return country/currency. Of course, the extent to which corporations can capitalize on this strategy is naturally limited; if such a strategy were easy to implement, the return difference would quickly disappear as corporations competed to use the strategy. Nevertheless, certain corporations might realize a competitive advantage by implementing such a strategy. For example, as an incentive to invest, a foreign government might strike a deal with a particular corporation that relaxes capital controls for that corporation alone.

As Example 22.6 demonstrates, the existence of segmented capital markets makes many decisions in international corporate finance more complicated but potentially more lucrative for a firm that is well positioned to exploit the market segmentation.

CONCEPT CHECK

11. What are the reasons for segmentation of capital markets?

12. What is the main implication for international corporate finance of a segmented financial market?

22.7 Capital Budgeting with Exchange Rate Risk

The final issue that arises when a firm is considering a foreign project is that the cash flows of the project may be affected by exchange rate risk. The risk is that the cash flows generated by the project will depend on the future level of the exchange rate. A large part of international corporate finance addresses this foreign exchange risk. This section offers an overview with respect to valuation of foreign currency cash flows.

The working assumptions made thus far in this chapter are that the project's free cash flows are uncorrelated with the spot exchange rates. Such an assumption often makes sense if the firm operates as a local firm in the foreign market—it purchases its inputs and sells its outputs in that market, and price changes of the inputs and outputs are uncorrelated with exchange rates. However, many firms use imported inputs in their production processes or export some of their output to foreign countries. These scenarios alter the nature of a project's foreign exchange risk and, in turn, change the valuation of the foreign currency cash flows.

Application: Ityesi, Inc.

As an example, let's reconsider what happens if the Ityesi project in the United Kingdom imports some materials from Canada. In this case, the project's GBP free cash flows will be correlated with exchange rates. Assuming the cost of the material in Canada remains stable, if the value of the CAD appreciates against the GBP, the GBP cost of these materials will increase, thereby reducing the GBP free cash flows. The reverse is also true; if the CAD depreciates, then the GBP free cash flows will increase. Hence, our working assumption that changes in the free cash flows are uncorrelated with changes in the exchange rate is violated, and it is no longer appropriate to calculate the expected CAD free cash flows by converting the expected GBP free cash flows at the forward rate.

Whenever a project has cash flows that depend on the values of multiple currencies, the most convenient approach is to separate the cash flows according to the currency they depend on. For example, a fraction of Ityesi's manufacturing costs may be for inputs whose cost fluctuates with the value of the CAD. Specifically, suppose 5.625 million GBP of the costs are denominated in GBP, and an additional 20 million CAD (or 10 million GBP at the current exchange rate of 2.00 CAD/GBP) are for inputs whose price fluctuates with the value of the dollar. In this case, we would calculate Ityesi's GBP-denominated free cash flows excluding these CAD-based costs, as shown in Table 22.6.

TABLE 22.6 Ityesi's GBP-Denominated Free Cash Flows

	Year	0	1	2	3	4
	Incremental Earnings Forecast (million GBP)					
1	**Sales**	—	37.500	37.500	37.500	37.500
2	Cost of Goods Sold	—	(5.625)	(5.625)	(5.625)	(5.625)
3	**Gross Profit**	—	31.875	31.875	31.875	31.875
4	Operating Expenses	(4.167)	(5.625)	(5.625)	(5.625)	(5.625)
5	Depreciation	—	(3.750)	(3.750)	(3.750)	(3.750)
6	**EBIT**	(4.167)	22.500	22.500	22.500	22.500
7	Income tax at 40%	1.667	(9.000)	(9.000)	(9.000)	(9.000)
8	**Unlevered Net Income**	(2.500)	13.500	13.500	13.500	13.500
	Free Cash Flow					
9	Plus: Depreciation	—	3.750	3.750	3.750	3.750
10	Less: Capital Expenditures	(15.000)	—	—	—	—
11	Less: Increases in NWC	—	—	—	—	—
12	**GBP Free Cash Flow**	**(17.500)**	**17.250**	**17.250**	**17.250**	**17.250**

If the revenues and costs in the spreadsheet in Table 22.6 are not affected by changes in the spot exchange rates, it makes sense to assume that changes in the free cash flows are uncorrelated with changes in the spot exchange rates. Hence, we can convert the GBP-denominated free cash flows to equivalent CAD amounts using the forward exchange rate, as we did in Section 22.4. The spreadsheet shown in Table 22.7 performs this calculation, with the CAD value of the GBP-denominated free cash flow shown in line 3.

Next, we add the CAD-based cash flows to determine the project's aggregate free cash flow in CAD terms. This calculation is done in lines 4 through 6 of Table 22.7. Note that we deduct Ityesi's CAD-denominated costs, and then add the tax shield associated with these costs. Even if the taxes will be paid in GBP in the United Kingdom, they will fluctuate with the CAD cost of the inputs and so can be viewed as a CAD-denominated cash flow.

Given the CAD-denominated free cash flow in line 6 of Table 22.7, we can now compute the NPV of the investment using Ityesi's CAD WACC:[8]

[8]We again use the domestic WACC to discount the cash flows, because we continue to assume that any additional risk premium for the exchange rate risk is small. If this assumption does not hold, then the CAD costs and the CAD value of the expected GBP free cash flows would have to be discounted at different rates to reflect the additional exchange rate risk in the GBP free cash flows.

TABLE 22.7 Expected CAD Free Cash Flows from Ityesi's U.K. Project

		0	1	2	3	4
	CAD Free Cash Flow (million CAD)					
1	GBP Free Cash Flow (million GBP)	(17.500)	17.250	17.250	17.250	17.250
2	Forward Exchange Rate (CAD/GBP)	2.0000	1.9439	1.8894	1.8364	1.7850
3	**CAD Value of GBP Free Cash Flow (1 × 2)**	(35.000)	33.533	32.593	31.679	30.791
4	CAD Costs	—	(20.000)	(20.000)	(20.000)	(20.000)
5	Income tax at 40%	—	8.000	8.000	8.000	8.000
6	**Free Cash Flow**	(35.000)	21.533	20.593	19.679	18.791

$$\frac{21.533}{1.068} + \frac{20.593}{1.068^2} + \frac{19.679}{1.068^3} + \frac{18.791}{1.068^4} - 35.000 = 33.814 \text{ million CAD}$$

Conclusion

The Ityesi example was simplified because we could easily isolate the cash flows that would vary perfectly with the CAD/GBP exchange rate from those that would be uncorrelated with the exchange rate. In practice, determining these sensitivities may be difficult. If historical data are available, the tools of regression can be used to identify the exchange rate risk of project cash flows, in much the same way that we used regression to identify the market risk of security returns earlier in the text.

In this chapter, we have endeavoured to provide an introduction to international capital budgeting. This topic is sufficiently complicated that entire textbooks have been devoted to it. Hence, it is difficult to do justice to this issue in a single chapter's treatment. Nonetheless, we have provided a basic framework for approaching the problem.

CONCEPT CHECK

13. What conditions cause the cash flows of a foreign project to be affected by exchange rate risk?

14. How do we make adjustments when a project has inputs and outputs in different currencies?

MyLab Finance

Here is what you should know after reading this chapter. MyLab™ Finance will help you identify what you know, and where to go when you need to practice.

KEY POINTS AND EQUATIONS	TERMS	ONLINE PRACTICE OPPORTUNITIES
22.1 Currency Exchange Rates ■ Currencies are traded on the foreign exchange market. ■ It has very high volume, is dominated by large international banks, and operates 24 hours a day during the week. ■ A currency exchange rate is a price for one currency denominated in another currency.	currency exchange rate, p. 751 foreign exchange (FX or forex) market, p. 752	MyLab Study Plan 22.1

KEY POINTS AND EQUATIONS	TERMS	ONLINE PRACTICE OPPORTUNITIES
22.2 Exchange Rate Risk ■ Firms can manage exchange rate risk in financial markets using currency forward contracts to lock in an exchange rate in advance, and using currency options contracts to protect against an exchange rate moving beyond a certain level. ■ The cash-and-carry strategy is an alternative strategy that provides the same cash flows as the currency forward contract. By the Law of One Price, we determine the forward exchange rate by the cost-of-carry formula, called the covered interest parity equation. Using FOC to represent any foreign currency, for an exchange that will take place in one year, the corresponding forward exchange rate is $\underbrace{\text{Forward Rate}}_{\frac{\text{USD in one year}}{\text{CAD in one year}}} = \underbrace{\text{Spot Rate}}_{\frac{\text{USD today}}{\text{CAD today}}} \times \underbrace{\frac{1 + r_{USD}}{1 + r_{CAD}}}_{\frac{\text{USD in one year/USD today}}{\text{CAD in one year/CAD today}}} \quad (22.1)$ ■ Currency options allow firms to insure themselves against the exchange rate moving beyond a certain level. A firm may choose to use options rather than forward contracts if ▪ it would like to benefit from favourable exchange rate movements but not be obligated to make an exchange at unfavourable rates. ▪ there is some chance that the transaction it is hedging will not take place.	cash-and-carry strategy, p. 760 covered interest parity equation, p. 761 currency forward contract, p. 758 currency timeline, p. 760 floating rate, p. 756 forward exchange rate, p. 758 spot exchange rate, p. 760	MyLab Study Plan 22.2
22.3 Internationally Integrated Capital Markets ■ The condition necessary to ensure internationally integrated capital markets is that the value of a foreign investment does not depend on the currency (home or foreign) used in the analysis. ■ Two methods are used to value foreign currency cash flows when markets are internationally integrated and uncertainty in spot exchange rates are uncorrelated with the foreign currency cash flows: ▪ Compute the expected value of the foreign currency cash flows in the home currency by multiplying the expected value in the foreign currency by the forward exchange rates, and then compute the NPV of these home currency cash flows using the domestic cost of capital.	internationally integrated capital markets, p. 764	MyLab Study Plan 22.3

KEY POINTS AND EQUATIONS	TERMS	ONLINE PRACTICE OPPORTUNITIES
■ Calculate the foreign currency value of a foreign project as the NPV of the expected foreign currency future cash flows discounted at the foreign cost of capital, and then convert the foreign currency NPV into the home currency using the current spot exchange rate.		
22.4 Valuation of Foreign Currency Cash Flows		
■ When markets are internationally integrated and uncertainty in spot exchange rates is uncorrelated with the foreign currency cash flows, the foreign and domestic WACCs are related as follows (using FOC for the foreign currency): $$r^*_{GBP} = \frac{(1 + r_{GBP})}{(1 + r_{CAD})} \times (1 + r^*_{CAD}) - 1 \quad (22.9)$$		MyLab Study Plan 22.4 Spreadsheet Table 22.2
22.5 Valuation and International Taxation		
■ A Canadian corporation pays the higher of the foreign or domestic tax rate on its foreign project, so project valuation should use the higher of these two rates as well. The Canadian corporation may be able to reduce its tax liability by undertaking foreign projects in other countries whose earnings can be pooled with those of the new project or by deferring the repatriation of earnings.	repatriated earnings, p. 771 territorial approach to taxation, p. 771 worldwide approach to taxation, p. 771	MyLab Study Plan 22.5
22.6 Internationally Segmented Capital Markets		
■ Capital markets might be internationally segmented. The implication is that one country or currency has a higher cost of capital than another country or currency, when the two are compared in the same currency.	currency swaps, p. 773 segmented capital markets, p. 772	MyLab Study Plan 22.6
22.7 Capital Budgeting with Exchange Rate Risk		
■ When a project has inputs and outputs in different currencies, the foreign-denominated cash flows are likely to be correlated with changes in spot rates. To correctly value such projects, the foreign and domestic cash flows should be valued separately.		MyLab Study Plan 22.7 Spreadsheet Table 22.5 Spreadsheet Table 22.6

REVIEW QUESTIONS

1. How is an exchange rate used?
2. What are some reasons a financial manager would need to access the foreign exchange market?
3. What are the differences between hedging exchange rate risk with options versus forwards?
4. What does it mean to say that international capital markets are integrated?
5. What assumptions are necessary to value foreign cash flows using the domestic WACC method?
6. How are Canadian firms taxed on their foreign earnings?
7. If international markets are segmented, how does that change the way the financial manager approaches valuation problems?
8. How does exchange rate risk affect our approach to valuation?

PROBLEMS

All problems in this chapter are available in MyLab Finance. An asterisk (*) indicates problems with a higher level of difficulty.

Currency Exchange Rates

1. You have just landed in London with 500 CAD in your wallet. Stopping at the foreign exchange booth, you see that pounds are being quoted at 1.95 CAD/GBP. For how many pounds can you exchange your 500 CAD?
2. Your firm needs to pay its French supplier 500,000 EUR. If the exchange rate is 0.65 EUR/CAD, how many dollars will you need to make the exchange?

Exchange Rate Risk

3. Your start-up company has negotiated a contract to provide a database installation for a manufacturing company in Poland. That firm has agreed to pay you 100,000 CAD in three-month's time when the installation will occur. However, it insists on paying in Polish zloty (PLN). You don't want to lose the deal (the company is your first client!) but are worried about the exchange rate risk. In particular, you are worried the PLN could depreciate relative to the CAD. You contact Fortis Bank in Poland to see if you can lock in an exchange rate for the PLN in advance.
   a. The current spot exchange rate is 2.3117 PLN per CAD. The three-month forward exchange rate is 2.2595 PLN per CAD. How many PLN should you demand in the contract to receive 100,000 CAD in three months if you hedge the exchange rate risk with a forward contract?
   b. Given the bank forward rates in part (a), were short-term interest rates higher or lower in Poland than in Canada? Explain.

*4. You are a broker for frozen seafood products for Choyce Products. You just signed a deal with a Belgian distributor. Under the terms of the contract, in one year you will deliver 4000 kilograms of frozen king crab for 100,000 EUR. Your cost for obtaining the king crab is 110,000 CAD. All cash flows occur in exactly one year.

a. Plot your profits in one year from the contract as a function of the exchange rate in one year, for exchange rates from 0.75 CAD/EUR to 1.50CAD/EUR. Label this line "Unhedged Profits."
b. Suppose the one-year forward exchange rate is 1.25 CAD/EUR. Suppose you enter into a forward contract to sell the EUR you will receive at this rate. In the figure from part (a), plot your combined profits from the crab contract and the forward contract as a function of the exchange rate in one year. Label this line "Forward Hedge."
c. Suppose that instead of using a forward contract, you consider using options. A one-year call option to buy EUR at a strike price of 1.25 CAD/EUR is trading for 0.10 CAD/EUR. Similarly, a one-year put option to sell EUR at a strike price of 1.25 CAD/EUR is trading for 0.10 CAD/EUR. To hedge the risk of your profits, should you buy or sell the call or the put?
d. In the figure from parts (a) and (b), plot your "all in" profits using the option hedge (combined profits of crab contract, option contract, and option price) as a function of the exchange rate in one year. Label this line "Option Hedge." (*Note:* You can ignore the effect of interest on the option price.)
e. Suppose that by the end of the year, a trade war erupts, leading to a European embargo on North American food products. As a result, your deal is cancelled, and you don't receive the EUR or incur the costs of procuring the crab. However, you still have the profits (or losses) associated with your forward or options contract. In a new figure, plot the profits associated with the forward hedge and the options hedge (label each line). When there is a risk of cancellation, which type of hedge has the least downside risk? Explain briefly.

Internationally Integrated Capital Markets

5. You are a Canadian investor who is trying to calculate the present value of a 5 million EUR cash inflow that will occur one year in the future. The spot exchange rate is $S = 1.25$ CAD/EUR and the forward rate is $F_1 = 1.215$ CAD/EUR. You estimate that the appropriate CAD discount rate for this cash flow is 4% and the appropriate EUR discount rate is 7%.

a. What is the present value of the 5 million EUR cash inflow computed by first discounting the EUR and then converting it into CAD?
b. What is the present value of the 5 million EUR cash inflow computed by first converting the cash flow into CAD and then discounting?
c. What can you conclude about whether these markets are internationally integrated, based on your answers to parts (a) and (b)?

6. Mamma Mia Enterprises, a Canadian manufacturer of children's toys, has made a sale in Poland and is expecting a 4 million PLN cash inflow in one year. The current spot rate is 2.040 PLN/CAD and the one-year forward rate is 2.055 PLN/CAD.

a. What is the present value of Mamma Mia's 4 million PLN inflow computed by first discounting the cash flow at the appropriate PLN discount rate of 10% and then converting the result into CAD?
b. What is the present value of Mamma Mia's 4 million PLN inflow computed by first converting the cash flow into CAD and then discounting at the appropriate CAD discount rate of 6%?
c. What can you conclude about whether these markets are internationally integrated, based on your answers to parts (a) and (b)?

Valuation of Foreign Currency Cash Flows

7. Etemadi Amalgamated, a U.S. manufacturing firm, is considering a new project in Portugal. You are in Etemadi's corporate finance department and are responsible for deciding whether to undertake the project. The expected free cash flows, in EUR, are shown here:

Year	0	1	2	3	4
Free Cash Flow (EUR million)	−15	9	10	11	12

You know that the spot exchange rate is $S = 1.15$ USD/EUR. In addition, the risk-free interest rate on USD is 4% and the risk-free interest rate on EUR is 6%.

Assume that these markets are internationally integrated and the uncertainty in the free cash flows is not correlated with uncertainty in the exchange rate. You determine that the USD WACC for these cash flows is 8.5%. What is the USD present value of the project? Should Etemadi Amalgamated undertake the project?

8. Etemadi Amalgamated, the U.S. manufacturing company in Problem 7, is still considering a new project in Portugal. All information presented in Problem 7 is still accurate, except the spot rate is now $S = 0.85$ USD/EUR, about 26% lower. What is the new present value of the project in dollars? Should Etemadi Amalgamated undertake the project?

9. You work for a Canadian firm, and your boss has asked you to estimate the cost of capital for countries using the EUR. You know that $S = 1.20$ CAD/EUR and $F_1 = 1.157$ CAD/EUR. Suppose the CAD WACC for your company is known to be 8%. If these markets are internationally integrated, estimate the EUR cost of capital for a project with free cash flows that are uncorrelated with spot exchange rates. Assume the firm pays the same tax rate no matter where the cash flows are earned.

10. Montreal Light, a Canadian light fixtures manufacturer, is considering an investment in Japan. The CAD cost of equity for Montreal Light is 11%. You are in the corporate treasury department, and you need to know the comparable cost of equity in JPY for a project with free cash flows that are uncorrelated with spot exchange rates. The risk-free interest rates on CAD and JPY are $r_{CAD} = 5\%$ and $r_{JPY} = 1\%$, respectively. Montreal Light is willing to assume that capital markets are internationally integrated. What is the JPY cost of equity?

11. The dollar cost of debt for Javelin Consulting, a Canadian research firm, is 7.5%. The firm faces a tax rate of 30% on all income, no matter where it is earned. Managers in the firm need to know its JPY cost of debt because they are considering launching a new bond issue in Tokyo to raise money for a new investment there. The risk-free interest rates on CAD and JPY are $r_{CAD} = 5\%$ and $r_{JPY} = 1\%$, respectively. Javelin Consulting is willing to assume that capital markets are internationally integrated and that its free cash flows are uncorrelated with the JPY–CAD spot rate. What is Javelin Consulting's after-tax cost of debt in JPY? (*Hint:* Start by finding the after-tax cost of debt in CAD and then find the JPY equivalent.)

12. McCain Foods, a Canadian food processing and distribution company, is considering an investment in Germany. You are in McCain's corporate finance department and are responsible for deciding whether to undertake the project. The expected free cash flows, in EUR, are uncorrelated to the spot exchange rate and are shown here:

Year	0	1	2	3	4
Free Cash Flow (EUR million)	−25	12	14	15	15

The new project has similar dollar risk to McCain's other projects. Management at the company knows that its overall CAD WACC is 9.5% and so is comfortable using this WACC for the project. The risk-free interest rate on CAD is 4.5% and the risk-free interest rate on EUR is 7%.

a. McCain is willing to assume that capital markets in Canada and the European Union are internationally integrated. What is the company's EUR WACC?
b. What is the present value of the project in EUR?

Valuation and International Taxation

13. Tailor Johnson, a U.S. maker of fine menswear, has a subsidiary in Ethiopia. This year, the subsidiary reported and repatriated earnings before interest and taxes (EBIT) of 100 million ETB (Ethiopian birrs). The current exchange rate is 8 ETB/USD or 0.125USD/ETB. The Ethiopian tax rate on this activity is 25%. Tax law in the United States requires Tailor Johnson to pay taxes on the Ethiopian earnings at the same rate as profits earned in the United States, which is currently 45%. However, the United States gives a full tax credit for foreign taxes paid up to the amount of the U.S. tax liability. What is Tailor Johnson's U.S. tax liability on its Ethiopian subsidiary?

***14.** Tailor Johnson, the menswear company with a subsidiary in Ethiopia described in Problem 13 is considering the tax benefits resulting from deferring repatriation of the earnings from the subsidiary. Under U.S. tax law, the U.S. tax liability is not incurred until the profits are brought back home. Tailor Johnson reasonably expects to defer repatriation for 10 years, at which point the ETB earnings will be converted into USD at the prevailing spot rate, S_{10}, and the tax credit for Ethiopian taxes paid will still be converted at the current exchange rate = 0.125 USD/ETB. Tailor Johnson's after-tax cost of debt is 5%.

a. Suppose the exchange rate in 10 years is identical to this year's exchange rate, so $S_{10} = 0.125$ USD/ETB. What is the present value of deferring the U.S. tax liability on Tailor Johnson's Ethiopian earnings for 10 years?
b. How will the exchange rate in 10 years affect the actual amount of the U.S. tax liability? Write an equation for the U.S. tax liability as a function of the exchange rate S_{10}.

15. Qu'Appelle Enterprises, a Canadian real-estate investment firm, is considering its international tax situation. Canadian tax law requires Canadian corporations to pay taxes on their foreign passive income at the same rate as profits earned in Canada; this rate is currently 35%. However, a full tax credit is given for the foreign taxes paid up to the amount of the Canadian tax liability. Qu'Appelle has major operations in Poland, where the tax rate is 20%, and in Sweden, where the tax rate is 60%. The profits, which are fully and immediately repatriated, and foreign taxes paid for the current year are shown here:

	Poland	Sweden
Earnings before interest and taxes (EBIT)	80 million CAD	100 million CAD
Host country taxes paid	16 million CAD	60 million CAD
Earnings before interest and after taxes	64 million CAD	40 million CAD

a. What is the Canadian tax liability on the earnings from the Polish subsidiary assuming the Swedish subsidiary did not exist?
b. What is the Canadian tax liability on the earnings from the Swedish subsidiary assuming the Polish subsidiary did not exist?

c. Under Canadian tax law, Qu'Appelle is able to pool the earnings from its operations in Poland and Sweden when computing its Canadian tax liability on foreign earnings. Total EBIT is thus 180 million CAD, and the total host country taxes paid is $76 million CAD. What is the total Canadian tax liability on foreign earnings? Show how this relates to the answers in parts (a) and (b).

Internationally Segmented Capital Markets

***16.** Suppose the interest on Russian government bonds is 7.5%, and the current exchange rate is 28 RUB per CAD. If the forward exchange rate is 28.5 RUB per CAD, and the current Canadian risk-free interest rate is 4.5%, what is the implied credit spread for Russian government bonds?

Capital Budgeting with Exchange Rate Risk

***17.** Assume that in the original Ityesi example in Table 22.3, all sales actually occur in Canada and are projected to be 75 million CAD per year for four years. Keeping other costs the same, calculate the NPV of the investment opportunity.

DATA CASE

You are a senior financial analyst with IBM in its capital budgeting division. IBM is considering expanding in Australia due to its positive business atmosphere and cultural similarities to the United States.

The new facility would require an initial investment in fixed assets of 5 billion AUD, and an additional capital investment of 3% would be required each year in years 1 to 4. All capital investments would be depreciated straight line over the five years that the facility would operate. First-year revenues from the facility are expected to be 6 billion AUD and grow at 10% per year. Cost of goods sold would be 40% of revenue; the other operating expenses would amount to 12% of revenue. Net working capital requirements would be 11% of sales and would be required the year prior to the actual revenues. All net working capital would be recovered at the end of the fifth year. Assume that the tax rates are the same in the two countries, that the two markets are internationally integrated, and that the cash flow uncertainty of the project is uncorrelated with changes in the exchange rate. Your team manager wants you to determine the NPV of the project in U.S. dollars using a cost of capital of 12%.

1. Go to the NASDAQ website (www.nasdaq.com).
   a. Enter the ticker symbol for IBM (IBM) in the "Enter Symbol" box.
   b. Click on "Income Statement" in the menu on the left. When the income statement appears, place the cursor inside the statement and right-click. Select "Export to Microsoft Excel" from the menu. If this option does not appear, then copy and paste the information.
2. Obtain exchange rates and comparable interest rates for Australia at the Bloomberg website (www.bloomberg.com).
   a. Click on "Currencies" in the drop-down menu. Export the currency table to Excel and paste it into the same spreadsheet as the IBM income statement.
   b. Click back to the prior webpage and click on "Rates & Bonds." Next, click on "Australia" to get the interest rates for Australia. Right-click and export the table to Excel; paste it into the spreadsheet.
   c. Go back to the webpage and click on "U.S." Download the Treasury data and paste it into the spreadsheet.

3. You may have noticed that the one-year and four-year rates are not available at Bloomberg.com for the U.S. Treasury. Go to the U.S. Treasury website (www.treas.gov).
   a. To find the one-year rate, type "yield curve" into the search box at the top of the page and select the second link that appears. Be sure it is *not* the link for the "real" rates. Export the yields into Excel into the same spreadsheet as the other data. Add the one-year yield to the other Treasury rates.
   b. To find an estimate of the four-year yield, calculate the average of the three- and five-year yields from the Treasury yield curve.
4. In your Excel spreadsheet, create a new worksheet with a timeline for the project's expected cash flows.
   a. Compute the tax rate as the four-year average of IBM's annual income tax divided by annual earnings before tax.
   b. Determine the expected free cash flows of the project.
5. Note that the free cash flows you calculated in Question 4 are in Australian dollars. Use Equation 22.2 to determine the forward exchange rates for each of the five years of the project. Then use the forward rates to convert the cash flows to U.S. dollars.
6. Compute the NPV of the project in U.S. dollars using the 12% required return given by your team manager.

CHAPTER

Leasing 23

LEARNING OBJECTIVES

- Know typical lease types and terms
- Understand the accounting, tax, and legal consequences of leasing
- Decide whether to buy or lease an asset
- Evaluate the reasons for leasing

NOTATION

L	lease payments
PV	present value
r_D	debt cost of capital
τ_c	marginal corporate income tax rate

To implement an investment project, a firm must acquire the necessary property, plant, and equipment. As an alternative to purchasing these assets outright, the firm can lease them. You are probably familiar with leases if you have leased a car or rented an apartment. These consumer rentals are similar to the leases used by businesses: the owner retains title to the asset, and the firm pays for its use of the asset through regular lease payments. When firms lease property, plant, or equipment, the leases generally exceed one year. This chapter focuses on such long-term leases.

If you can purchase an asset, you can probably lease it. Commercial real estate, computers, trucks, copy machines, airplanes, and even power plants are examples of assets that firms can lease rather than buy. Equipment leasing is a rapidly growing industry, with more than one-half of the world's leasing now being done by companies in Europe and Asia. More than 25% of the world's jet fleet, by dollar value, is leased.[1] One of the biggest aircraft leasing companies by fleet size is GE Capital Aviation Services. As of 2018, GE owned and managed over 1900 aircraft, the world's largest commercial airplane fleet.[2] GE leases these commercial aircraft to some 250 airline customers in over 75 countries.

---

[1]Beacon Funding (www.beaconfunding.com/vendor_programs/statistics.aspx).

[2]GE Capital Aviation Services website (https://www.gecapital.com/gecas).

As you will learn, leases are not merely an alternative to purchasing; they also function as an important financing method for tangible assets. In fact, long-term leasing is the most common method of equipment financing. How do companies, such as GE Capital Aviation Services, set the terms for their leases? How do their customers—the commercial airlines—evaluate and negotiate these leases? In this chapter, we first discuss the basic types of leases and provide an overview of the accounting and tax treatment of leases. We then show how to evaluate the lease-versus-buy decision. Firms often cite various benefits to leasing as compared to purchasing property and equipment, and we conclude the chapter with an evaluation of their reasoning.

23.1 The Basics of Leasing

lessee The party in a lease who is liable for periodic payments in exchange for the right to use the asset.

lessor The party in a lease who is the owner of the asset and is entitled to the lease payments.

sales-type lease A lease in which the lessor is the manufacturer (or a primary dealer) of the asset.

direct lease A lease in which the lessor is not the manufacturer of the asset but is often an independent company that specializes in purchasing assets and leasing them to customers.

sale and leaseback A lease in which the lessee receives cash from the sale of the asset and then makes lease payments to retain the use of the asset.

leveraged lease A lease in which the lessor borrows from a bank or other lender to obtain the initial capital for the purchase of an asset, using the lease payments to pay the interest and principal on the loan.

A lease is a contract between two parties: the *lessee* and the *lessor*. The **lessee** is liable for periodic payments in exchange for the right to use the asset. The **lessor** is the owner of the asset, who is entitled to the lease payments in exchange for lending the asset.

Most leases involve little or no upfront payment. Instead, the lessee commits to make regular lease (or rental) payments for the term of the contract. At the end of the contract term, the lease specifies who will retain ownership of the asset and at what terms. The lease also specifies any cancellation provisions, the options for renewal and purchase, and the obligations for maintenance and related servicing costs.

Examples of Lease Transactions

Many types of lease transactions are possible, based on the relationship between the lessee and the lessor. In a **sales-type lease**, the lessor is the manufacturer (or a primary dealer) of the asset. For example, IBM both manufactures and leases computers. Similarly, Xerox leases its copy machines. Manufacturers generally set the terms of these leases as part of a broader sales and pricing strategy, and they may bundle other services or goods (such as software, maintenance, or product upgrades) as part of the lease.

In a **direct lease**, the lessor is not the manufacturer but is often an independent company that specializes in purchasing assets and leasing them to customers. For example, Ryder Systems Inc. owns more than 135,000 commercial trucks, tractors, and trailers, which it leases to small businesses and large enterprises throughout Canada, the United States, and the United Kingdom. In many instances of direct leases, the lessee identifies the equipment it needs first and then finds a leasing company to purchase the asset.

If a firm already owns an asset that it would prefer to lease, it can arrange a **sale and leaseback** transaction. In this type of lease, the lessee receives cash from the sale of the asset and then makes lease payments to retain the use of the asset. In 2002, San Francisco Municipal Railway (Muni) used the $35 million in proceeds from the sale and leaseback of 118 of its light-rail vehicles to offset a large operating budget deficit. The purchaser, CIBC World Markets, received a tax benefit from depreciating the rail cars, something Muni could not do as a public transit agency.

With many leases, the lessor provides the initial capital necessary to purchase the asset, and then receives and retains the lease payments. In a **leveraged lease**, however, the lessor borrows from a bank or other lender to obtain the initial capital for the purchase, using the lease payments to pay the interest and principal on the loan. Also, in

special-purpose entity (SPE) An entity created by the lessee for the sole purpose of obtaining the lease.

synthetic lease A lease that is designed to obtain specific accounting and tax treatment.

some circumstances, the lessor is not an independent company but rather a separate business partnership, called a **special-purpose entity (SPE)**, which is created by the lessee for the sole purpose of obtaining the lease. SPEs are commonly used in **synthetic leases**, which are designed to obtain specific accounting and tax treatment (discussed further in Section 23.2).

Lease Payments and Residual Values

Suppose your business needs a new $20,000 electric forklift for its warehouse operations, and you are considering leasing the forklift for four years. In this case, the lessor will purchase the forklift and allow you to use it for four years. At that point, you will return the forklift to the lessor. How much should you expect to pay for the right to use the forklift for the first four years of its life?

residual value The leased asset's market value at the end of the lease.

The cost of the lease will depend on the asset's **residual value**, which is its market value at the end of the lease. Suppose the residual value of the forklift in four years will be $6000. If lease payments of amount L are made monthly, then the lessor's cash flows from the transaction are as follows. (Note that lease payments are typically made at the beginning of each payment period.)

	0	1	2	...	47	48
Purchase price	−$20,000					
Lease payment	$+L$	L	L	...	L	
Residual value						$6000

In a perfect capital market (where lessors compete with one another in initiating leases), the lease payment should be set so that the NPV of the transaction is zero and the lessor breaks even:

$$PV(\text{Lease Payments}) = \text{Purchase Price} - PV(\text{Residual Value}) \tag{23.1}$$

In other words, *in a perfect market, the cost of leasing is equivalent to the cost of purchasing and reselling the asset.* In effect, this is just another example of the application of the Law of One Price.

Thus, the amount of the lease payment will depend on the purchase price, the residual value, and the appropriate discount rate for the cash flows.

EXAMPLE 23.1 Lease Terms in a Perfect Market

PROBLEM

Suppose the purchase price of the forklift is $20,000, its residual value in four years is certain to be $6000, and there is no risk that the lessee will default on the lease. If the risk-free interest rate is a 6% APR with monthly compounding, what would be the monthly lease payment for a four-year lease in a perfect capital market?

SOLUTION

Plan

Because all cash flows are risk free, we can discount them using the risk-free interest rate of 6%/12 = 0.5% per month using Equation 23.1. Once we know the PV of the monthly lease payments, we can solve for the payment as the cash flow in an annuity due. ▶

■ **Execute**

$$PV(\text{Lease Payments}) = \$20{,}000 - \$6000/1.005^{48} = \$15{,}277.41$$

Because the first lease payment starts today, we can view the lease as an initial payment of L plus a 47-month annuity of L. Thus, using the annuity formula, we need to find L so that

$$15{,}277.41 = L + L \times \frac{1}{0.005}\left(1 - \frac{1}{1.005^{47}}\right) = L \times \left[1 + \frac{1}{0.005}\left(1 - \frac{1}{1.005^{47}}\right)\right]$$

Solving for L, we get

$$L = \frac{15{,}277.41}{1 + \frac{1}{0.005}\left(1 - \frac{1}{1.005^{47}}\right)} = \$357.01 \text{ per month}$$

■ **Evaluate**

If the lessee pays $357.01 per month, starting immediately, the PV of the 48 lease payments will equal the price of the forklift less the PV of its residual value at the end of the lease.

Leases versus Loans

Alternatively, you could obtain a four-year loan for the purchase price and buy the forklift outright. If M is the monthly payment for a fully amortizing loan, the lender's cash flows will be as follows:

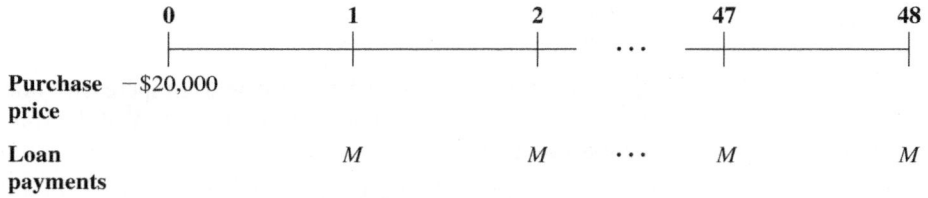

Assuming the loan is fairly priced, the loan payments would be such that

$$PV(\text{Loan Payments}) = \text{Purchase Price} \tag{23.2}$$

Comparing Equation 23.2 with Equation 23.1, we see that while with a standard loan we are financing the entire cost of the asset, with a lease we are financing only the cost of the economic depreciation of the asset during the term of the lease. Because we are getting the entire asset when we purchase it with the loan, the loan payments are higher than the lease payments.

EXAMPLE 23.2 Loan Payments in a Perfect Market

PROBLEM

Suppose you purchase the forklift for $20,000 by borrowing the purchase price using a four-year annuity loan. What would the monthly loan payment be in a perfect capital market where the risk-free interest rate is a 6% APR with monthly compounding, assuming no risk of default? How does this compare with the lease payment of Example 23.1?

SOLUTION

Plan

Because all cash flows are risk free, we can discount them using the risk-free interest rate of 6%/12 = 0.5% per month. Because loan payments are made at the end of each month, we can use the annuity formula to value the loan payments.

Execute

Equation 23.2 becomes the following:

$$M \times \frac{1}{0.005}\left(1 - \frac{1}{1.005^{48}}\right) = 20{,}000$$

Solving for M gives the loan payments:

$$M = \frac{20{,}000}{\frac{1}{0.005}\left(1 - \frac{1}{1.005^{48}}\right)} = \$469.70 \text{ per month}$$

Evaluate

Of course, while the lease payments are lower, with the lease, we have the use of the forklift for four years only. With the loan, we own the forklift for its entire life.

CALCULATING AUTO LEASE PAYMENTS

Rather than use the annuity formula to calculate the lease payments, as we did in Example 23.1, in many cases practitioners use the following approximation to calculate the lease payments, where the purchase price includes any fees charged on the lease (and is net of any down payment), the term is the number of payment periods, and the interest rate is for a payment period:

$$L = \underbrace{\frac{\text{Purchase Price} - \text{Residual Value}}{\text{Term}}}_{\text{Average Depreciation}} + \underbrace{\left(\frac{\text{Purchase Price} + \text{Residual Value}}{2}\right) \times \text{Interest Rate}}_{\text{Financing Cost}}$$

The idea behind this approximation is that the first term is the average depreciation over a payment period and the second term is the interest cost associated with the average value of the asset. The sum is what you have to pay to use the asset over one payment period.

Despite its simplicity, this formula is very accurate for lease terms up to five years and interest rates up to 10%. Using it to calculate the lease payments in Example 23.1 gives the following:

$$\frac{20{,}000 - 6000}{48} + \left(\frac{20{,}000 + 6000}{2}\right) \times 0.005$$

$$= \$356.67$$

This is within \$1 of the amount calculated in Example 23.1.

This approximation for the lease payment is used to calculate the payment on automobile leases. In that case, the formula is often stated as follows:

$$L = \frac{\text{Purchase Price} - \text{Residual Value}}{\text{Term}} + (\text{Purchase Price} + \text{Residual Value}) \times \text{Money Factor}$$

This leaves many first-time car lessees wondering why they have to pay interest on both the purchase price and the residual value. In reality, all that has happened is that the factor of 2 is subsumed into the money factor; that is, the money factor is half the interest rate.

The monthly loan payments in Example 23.2 exceed the lease payments in Example 23.1. This difference does not mean the lease is superior to the loan. While the lease payments are lower, with the lease, we have use of the forklift for four years only. If we purchase the forklift using the loan, we own it after four years and can sell it for its residual value of $6000. Alternatively, if we lease the forklift and want to keep it after the lease terminates, we can purchase it for its fair market value of $6000. Once we consider the benefit of this residual value, by the Law of One Price, the total cost of purchasing with either the loan or the lease is the same. That is, combining Equation 23.1 and Equation 23.2, we have

$$PV(\text{Lease Payments}) + PV(\text{Residual Value}) = PV(\text{Loan Payments}) \tag{23.3}$$

In other words, in a perfect market, the cost of leasing and then purchasing the asset is equivalent to the cost of borrowing to purchase the asset.[3] This is another example of the application of the Law of One Price.

End-of-Term Lease Options

In Example 23.1, we assumed that at the end of the lease the forklift would be returned to the lessor, who would then obtain its residual market value of $6000. In reality, other lease terms are possible. In many cases, the lease allows the lessee to obtain ownership of the asset for some price, as described below and shown in Example 23.3.

fair market value (FMV) lease A lease that gives the lessee the option to purchase the asset at its fair market value at the termination of the lease.

- A **fair market value (FMV) lease** gives the lessee the option to purchase the asset at its fair market value at the termination of the lease. (Depending on the asset, determining its fair market value may be complicated. The lease will typically stipulate a procedure for doing so and often will require that an independent third party provide estimates of the fair market value.) With perfect capital markets, there is no difference between an FMV lease and a lease in which the assets are retained by the lessor, because acquiring the asset at its fair market value is a zero-NPV transaction.

$1.00 out lease (finance lease) A lease in which ownership of the asset transfers to the lessee at the end of the lease for a nominal cost of $1.00.

fixed price lease A lease in which the lessee has the option to purchase the asset at the end of the lease for a fixed price that is set up front in the lease contract.

fair market value cap lease A lease in which the lessee can purchase the asset at the minimum of its fair market value and a fixed price (the "cap").

- In a **$1.00 out lease (finance lease)**, ownership of the asset transfers to the lessee at the end of the lease for a nominal cost of $1.00. Thus, the lessee will continue to have use of the asset for its entire economic life. The lessee has effectively purchased the asset by making the lease payments. As a result, this type of lease is in many ways equivalent to financing the asset with a standard loan.
- In a **fixed price lease**, the lessee has the option to purchase the asset at the end of the lease for a fixed price that is set up front in the lease contract. This type of lease is very common for consumer leases (such as for autos). Notice that this kind of lease gives the lessee an option; at the end of the lease, if the market value of the asset exceeds the fixed price, the lessee can buy the asset at below its market value. If the market value of the asset does not exceed the fixed price, however, the lessee can walk away from the lease and purchase the asset for less money elsewhere. Consequently, the lessor will set a higher lease rate to compensate for the value of this option to the lessee.
- In a **fair market value cap lease**, the lessee can purchase the asset at the minimum of its fair market value and a fixed price (the "cap"). The lessee has the same option as in a fixed price lease, although the option in this case is easier to exercise because the lessee does not have to find a similar asset elsewhere to buy when the fixed price exceeds the market value.

[3]For a theoretical analysis of competitive lease pricing, see M. Miller and C. Upton, "Leasing, Buying, and the Cost of Capital Services," *Journal of Finance* 31(3) (1976): 761–786; and W. Lewellen, M. Long, and J. McConnell, "Asset Leasing in Competitive Capital Markets," *Journal of Finance* 31(3) (1976): 787–798.

EXAMPLE 23.3 Lease Payments and End-of-Lease Options

PROBLEM

Compute the lease payments for the forklift lease of Example 23.1 if the lease is (a) a FMV lease, (b) a $1.00 out lease, or (c) a fixed price lease that allows the lessee to buy the asset at the end of the lease for $4000.

SOLUTION

■ Plan

With the FMV lease, the lessee can buy the forklift for its fair market value of $6000 at the end of the lease. The lessor obtains a residual value of $6000, either from the forklift itself or from the payment from the lessee. Thus, the lease payments will be unchanged from Example 23.1, or $357 per month.

With the $1.00 out lease, the lessor receives essentially no residual value. Thus, the lease payments themselves will have to compensate the lessor for the full $20,000 purchase price.

With the fixed price lease, because the forklift will be worth $6000 for certain, the lessee will exercise the option to purchase it for $4000. As a result, the lessor will receive only $4000 at the end of the lease.

■ Execute

The lease payments for the $1.00 out lease must have a present value of $20,000, so they are

$$L = \frac{20{,}000}{1 + \frac{1}{0.005}\left(1 - \frac{1}{1.005^{47}}\right)} = \$467.36 \text{ per month}$$

For the fixed price lease to have an NPV of zero, the present value of the lease payments must be $\$20{,}000 - \$4000/1.005^{48} = \$16{,}851.61$. Therefore, the lease payment will be

$$L = \frac{16{,}851.61}{1 + \frac{1}{0.005}\left(1 - \frac{1}{1.005^{47}}\right)} = \$393.79 \text{ per month}$$

■ Evaluate

The $1.00 out lease payments are slightly less than the loan payments of $470 per month calculated in Example 23.2, because the lease payments occur at the beginning—rather than the end—of the month. The fixed price lease payment exceeds that of the FMV lease due to the lessee's ability to buy the asset at a discount at the end of the lease.

Other Lease Provisions

Leases are privately negotiated contracts and can contain many more provisions than are described here. For example, they may include early cancellation options that allow the lessee to end the lease early (perhaps for a fee). They may contain buyout options that allow the lessee to purchase the asset before the end of the lease term. Clauses may allow the lessee to trade in and upgrade the equipment to a newer model at certain points in the lease. Each lease agreement can be tailored to fit the precise nature of the asset and the needs of the parties at hand.

These features of leases will be priced as part of the lease payment. Terms giving valuable options to the lessee cause an increase the amount of the lease payments, whereas terms that restrict these options will decrease them. Absent market imperfections, leases represent another form of zero-NPV financing available to a firm, and the

Modigliani & Miller propositions apply: leases neither increase nor decrease firm value, but serve only to divide the firm's cash flows and risks in different ways.[4]

CONCEPT CHECK

1. In a perfect capital market, how is the amount of a lease payment determined?
2. What types of lease options would raise the amount of the lease payment?

23.2 Accounting, Tax, and Legal Consequences of Leasing

We have seen that with perfect capital markets, leasing represents yet another zero-NPV financing alternative for a firm. Thus, the decision to lease is often driven by real-world market imperfections related to leasing's accounting, tax, and legal treatment. In particular, when a firm leases an asset, a number of important questions arise: Should the firm list the asset on its balance sheet and deduct depreciation expenses? Should the firm list the lease as a liability? Can the lease payments be deducted for tax purposes? In the event of bankruptcy, is the leased asset protected from creditors? As we will see in this section, the answers to these questions depend on how the lease is structured.

Lease Accounting

When publicly traded firms disclose leasing transactions in their financial statements, they must follow the recommendations of the Accounting Standards Board (AcSB). As mentioned in Chapter 2, International Financial Reporting Standards (IFRS) have been adopted as Canadian Generally Accepted Accounting Principles (GAAP) for public companies. For lessees, IFRS distinguishes two types of leases based on the lease terms, and this classification determines the lease's accounting treatment:

operating lease A lease that is viewed as a rental for accounting purposes. The lessee reports the entire lease payment as an operating expense.

finance lease A lease that transfers substantially all the risks and rewards incidental to ownership of an asset. It is viewed as an acquisition for accounting purposes. The asset acquired is listed on the lessee's balance sheet.

- An **operating lease** is viewed as a rental for accounting purposes. In this case, the lessee reports the entire lease payment as an operating expense. The lessee does not deduct a depreciation expense for the asset and does not report the asset, or the lease payment liability, on its balance sheet. Operating leases are disclosed in the notes of the lessee's financial statements.
- A **finance lease** is viewed as an acquisition for accounting purposes. The asset acquired is listed on the lessee's balance sheet, and the lessee incurs depreciation expenses for the asset. In addition, the present value of the future lease payments is listed as a liability, and the interest portion of the lease payment is deducted as an interest expense.[5]

The different accounting treatment for each type of lease will affect the firm's balance sheet as well as its debt-equity ratio, as shown in Example 23.4.

---

[4]For an analysis of options embedded in lease contracts, see J. McConnell and J. Schallheim, "Valuation of Asset Leasing Contracts," *Journal of Financial Economics* 12(2) (1983): 237–261; and S. Grenadier, "Valuing Lease Contracts: A Real-Options Approach," *Journal of Financial Economics* 38(3) (1995): 297–331.

[5]The accounting treatment of leases can be more complex when agreements involve sales and leaseback transactions. Special guidelines, not dealt with in this textbook, also exist that are unique to manufacturers and dealers granting finance leases.

EXAMPLE 23.4 Leasing and the Balance Sheet

PROBLEM

Maritime Cruise Lines currently has the following balance sheet (in $ millions):

Assets		Liabilities	
Cash	100	Debt	900
Property, Plant, and Equipment	1500	Equity	700
Total Assets	1600	Total Debt plus Equity	1600

Maritime is about to add a new fleet of cruise ships. The price of the fleet is $400 million. What will Maritime's balance sheet look like if (a) it purchases the fleet by borrowing the $400 million, (b) it acquires the fleet through a $400 million finance lease, or (c) it acquires the fleet through an operating lease?

SOLUTION

■ Plan

For parts (a) and (b), the balance sheet consequences are the same; the fleet becomes a new asset of the firm, and the $400 million becomes an additional liability. If the fleet is acquired through an operating lease, as described in part (c), there is no change in the original balance sheet.

■ Execute

For (a) and (b):

Assets		Liabilities	
Cash	100	Debt	1300
Property, Plant, and Equipment	1900	Equity	700
Total Assets	2000	Total Debt plus Equity	2000

Note that the firm's debt-equity ratio increases in this case (from 900/700 = 1.29 to 1300/700 = 1.86).

For part (c), there is no change to the balance sheet; the fleet is not listed as an asset, and the lease is not viewed as a liability. Thus, the apparent leverage ratio is unchanged.

■ Evaluate

The finance lease has the same effect on the firm's balance sheet and leverage ratio as does buying the asset by borrowing, because the lease provides close to the same benefits as owning the assets. The operating lease, however, does not affect the balance sheet or its leverage.

Because finance leases increase the apparent leverage on the firm's balance sheet, firms sometimes prefer to have a lease categorized as an operating lease to keep it off the balance sheet. IFRS (under International Accounting Standard [IAS] 17) does not provide separate guidance for lessees and lessors when determining the classification of a lease. Instead, examples are provided of situations that individually or in combination would normally lead to a lease being classified as a finance lease.[6]

[6]BDO Dunwoody LLP.

These are as follows:

1. The lease transfers ownership of the asset to the lessee by the end of the lease term.
2. The lessee has the option to purchase the asset at a price that is expected to be sufficiently lower than the fair value at the date the option becomes exercisable for it to be reasonably certain, at the inception of the lease, that the option will be exercised.
3. The lease term is for the major part of the economic life of the asset, even if title is not transferred.
4. At the inception of the lease, the present value of the minimum lease payments amounts to at least substantially all of the fair value of the leased asset.
5. The leased assets are of such a specialized nature that only the lessee can use them without major modifications.

Other indicators that individually, or in combination, could also lead to a lease being classified as a finance lease are as follows:

1. If the lessee can cancel the lease, the lessor's losses associated with the cancellation are borne by the lessee
2. Gains or losses from the fluctuation in the fair value of the residual accrue to the lessee (e.g., in the form of a rent rebate equalling most of the sales proceeds at the end of the lease).
3. The lessee has the ability to continue the lease for a secondary period at a rent that is substantially lower than market rent.

These conditions are designed to identify situations in which the lease provides the lessee with use of the asset for a large fraction of its useful life. For example, a $1.00 out lease satisfies the second condition and so would be ruled a finance lease for accounting purposes. Firms that prefer to keep a lease off the balance sheet will often structure lease contracts to avoid these conditions.

EXAMPLE 23.5 Operating versus Finance Leases

PROBLEM

Consider a seven-year fair market value lease for a $12.5 million Gulfstream jet with a remaining useful life of 10 years. Suppose the monthly lease payments are $175,000 and the appropriate discount rate is a 6% APR with monthly compounding. Would this lease be classified as an operating lease or a finance lease for the lessee? What if the lease contract gave the lessee the option to cancel the contract after five years?

SOLUTION

■ Plan

We compute the present value of the monthly lease payments at the beginning of the lease using the annuity formula with a monthly interest rate of $6\%/12 = 0.5\%$ and $7 \times 12 - 1 = 83$ monthly payments after the initial payment. If the PV of the minimum lease payments is at least substantially all the fair market value of the jet, it will be classified as a capital lease. If the contract can be cancelled after five years, then the lease will be a finance lease only if the PV of the lease payments over the first five years is at least substantially all of the fair market value of the jet. ▶

■ **Execute**

$$PV(\text{Lease Payments}) = 175{,}000 \times \left[1 + \frac{1}{0.005}\left(1 - \frac{1}{1.005^{83}}\right)\right] = \$12.04 \text{ million}$$

Because the present value of the lease payments is 12.04/12.50 − 96.3% of the value of the jet, the lease satisfies situation 4 above and, thus, is a finance lease.

If the lessee can cancel the contract after five years, then the minimum number of lease payments is 60 under the contract. In this case,

$$PV(\text{Lease Payments}) = 175{,}000 \times \left[1 + \frac{1}{0.005}\left(1 - \frac{1}{1.005^{59}}\right)\right] = \$9.10 \text{ million}$$

This is only 9.10/12.5 = 73% of the value of the jet. As no other situations for a finance lease seem to present in this scenario, the lease would be classified as an operating lease.

■ **Evaluate**

Simply by adding a cancellation option, the lease can be classified as an operating lease such that it would have no impact on the balance sheet of the lessee.

The Tax Treatment of Leases

The categories used to report leases on the financial statements affect the values of assets on the balance sheet, but they have no direct effect on the cash flows that result from a leasing transaction. The Canada Revenue Agency (CRA) had its own classification rules under Interpretation Bulletin IT-233R that effectively ruled that leases that resulted in eventual ownership should be treated as a sale transaction and not a lease. However, on June 14, 2001, the CRA cancelled the interpretation bulletin and announced that the legal form of the contract would be central to determining whether the transaction was a sale or lease. A lease contract would be treated as a lease, and a sale contract would be treated as a sale. However, if the contract were designed strictly to avoid tax, the General Anti-Avoidance Rule (GAAR) could be used to reassess the case. In addition, under the Specialized Leasing Property Rules, certain assets held under financial (i.e., finance) leases could be fully treated as a lease for tax purposes. These "exempt assets" allow the lessor to claim the capital cost allowance (CCA) deductions and the lessee to claim rental expense. Exempt assets include rail cars, trucks for hauling freight, office furniture and equipment, personal items such as furniture, appliances, furnaces and hot-water tanks, passenger vehicles, vans, and pickup trucks. Non-exempt items include most other assets.[7]

true tax lease A lease in which the lessor receives the depreciation deductions associated with the ownership of the asset. The lessee can deduct the full amount of the lease payments as an operating expense, and these lease payments are treated as revenue for the lessor.

For the remainder of the discussion, we will refer to operating leases and financial leases of exempt assets as *true tax leases* and other leases as *non-tax leases*. Thus, with a **true tax lease**, the lessor receives the CCA deductions associated with the ownership of the asset. The lessee can deduct the full amount of the lease payments as an operating expense, and these lease payments are treated as revenue for the lessor.

[7]*Sources:* Income Tax Act (Canada); Income Tax Regulations (Canada); Interpretation Bulletin IT-233R; *Income Tax Technical News,* No. 21, June 14, 2001, Canada Customs and Revenue Agency. A reference regarding leasing and taxes in Canada is by John Tobin, Jim Hong, and Richard Johnson, "Canada: Asset/Equipment Finance and Leasing," found in the *2007/2008 Lexpert/CCCA Corporate Counsel Directory and Yearbook,* 6th edition.

non-tax lease A lease in which the lessee receives the depreciation deductions for tax purposes and can also deduct the interest portion of the lease payments as an interest expense. The interest portion of the lease payment is interest income for the lessor.

Although the legal ownership of the asset resides with the lessor, in a **non-tax lease** the lessee receives the CCA deductions. The lessee can also deduct the interest portion of the lease payments as an interest expense. The interest portion of the lease payment is interest income for the lessor.

For example, imagine that a piece of industrial equipment costing $2,000,000 had a CCA rate of 20%. It would take 11 years before the firm could claim 90% of the available CCA on the asset. However, by acquiring the asset through a four-year $1.00 out lease, with payments of $500,000 per year, a firm could receive 100% of the $2,000,000 total deduction at a faster rate as long as the lease is categorized as a true tax lease.[8] The CRA rules prevent this type of transaction by categorizing such a lease as a non-tax lease because it is a non-exempt asset.

Leases and Bankruptcy

When a firm files for bankruptcy under the Companies' Creditors Arrangement Act (CCAA) or the Bankruptcy and Insolvency Act (BIA), the firm's assets are protected from seizure by its creditors while existing management is given the opportunity to propose a reorganization plan. Even secured lenders are prevented from taking the assets that

SYNTHETIC LEASES

Synthetic leases are designed to be treated as an operating lease for accounting purposes and as a non-tax lease for tax purposes. With a synthetic lease, the lessee is able to deduct depreciation and interest expenses for tax purposes, just as if it had borrowed to purchase the asset, but does not need to report the asset or the debt on its balance sheet.

To obtain this accounting and tax treatment, synthetic leases have typically been structured by creating a special-purpose entity (SPE) that will act as the lessor and obtain financing, acquire the asset, and lease it to the firm. To ensure that the lease qualifies as an operating lease, the lease is structured so that it (1) provides a fixed purchase price at the end of the lease term based on an initial appraised value (and so is not a bargain price), (2) has a term less than 75% of the economic life of the asset (which is renewable under certain conditions), and (3) has minimum lease payments with a present value less than 90% of the fair value of the property. In addition, to avoid balance sheet consolidation, the owner of record of the SPE must make an initial minimum equity investment of 3% that remains at risk during the entire lease term. The lease can qualify as a non-tax lease by designating some portion of the lease payments as interest.

A major motivation for such leases appears to be that they allow firms to use debt while avoiding the accounting consequences of debt. In particular, by keeping the debt off the balance sheet, the firm's debt-equity ratio is improved, its return on assets is generally raised, and, if the lease payments are less than the interest and depreciation expenses, the firm's reported earnings per share will be higher.

These types of transactions were used and abused by Enron Corporation to boost its earnings and hide its liabilities prior to its downfall. In the wake of the Enron scandal, the Financial Accounting Standards Board has significantly tightened the requirements for SPEs, raising the at-risk equity investment of the SPE to 10% and requiring that ownership truly be independent from the lessor. With the adoption of International Financial Reporting Standards (IFRS) in Canada, consolidation of the SPE with its related company is necessary if the substance of the relationship is for the SPE mainly to benefit its related company. Thus, the debt of the SPE would no longer be hidden off the balance sheet. Investors have also reacted skeptically to such deals, forcing many firms to avoid synthetic leases or unwind structures that were already in place. For example, in 2002, Krispy Kreme Doughnut Corporation reversed its decision to use a synthetic lease to fund a new $35 million plant after an article critical of the transaction was published in *Forbes* magazine.

[8]This transaction would have the opposite tax consequence for the lessor; the lease payments would be taxed as revenues, but the cost of the asset would be depreciated at the CCA rate. However, there can be an advantage if the lessor is in a lower tax bracket than the lessee.

serve as collateral for their loans during this period, which can last from a few months to several years. Instead, bankruptcy law permits the firm to continue to use the assets in an effort to remain a going concern. When Air Canada filed for protection under the CCAA in 2003, it was still able to use its planes even though most of them were leased.

The treatment of leased property in bankruptcy will depend on whether the lease is classified as a *security interest* or a *true lease* by the bankruptcy judge. If the lease is deemed to be a **security interest**, the firm is assumed to have effective ownership of the asset, and the asset is protected against seizure. The lessor is then treated as any other secured creditor and must await the firm's reorganization or ultimate liquidation.

security interest A lease in which the lessee is assumed to have effective ownership of the asset and the asset is protected against seizure.

true lease A lease in which in bankruptcy the lessor retains ownership rights over the asset.

If the lease is classified as a **true lease** in bankruptcy, then the lessor retains ownership rights over the asset. A special provision exists in the case of aircraft. Within 60 days of filing under the CCAA, the lessee must choose whether to continue or repudiate an aircraft lease. If it continues the lease, it must settle all pending claims and continue to make all promised lease payments (including maintenance and insurance). If it repudiates the lease, the asset must be returned to the lessor (with any pending claims of the lessor becoming unsecured claims against the bankrupt firm). Air Canada had 278 aircraft leased at the beginning of 2003. By the time its CCAA proceedings finished, it had repudiated 29 of the leases, and an additional 19 leases had ended with either consensual returns or lease expirations.

If a lease contract is characterized as a true lease in bankruptcy, the lessor is in a somewhat superior position than the lender if the firm defaults. By retaining ownership of the asset, the lessor has the right to repossess it if the lease payments are not made, even if the firm seeks bankruptcy protection. While a benefit to the lessor, this right of repossession limits the options for the firm in the event of financial distress.[9]

Whether a transaction is classified as a true lease or a security interest will depend on the facts of each case, but the distinction is very similar to the accounting and tax distinctions made earlier. Operating and true tax leases are generally viewed as true leases by the courts, whereas capital and non-tax leases are more likely to be viewed as security interests. In particular, leases for which the lessee obtains possession of the asset for its remaining economic life (either within the contract or through an option to renew or purchase at a nominal charge) are generally deemed security interests.[10]

CONCEPT CHECK

3. How is a $1.00 out lease characterized for accounting and tax purposes?
4. Is it possible for a lease to be treated as an operating lease for accounting purposes and as a non-tax lease for tax purposes?

23.3 The Leasing Decision

How should a firm decide whether to buy or lease an asset? Recall that in a perfect market the decision is irrelevant, so the real-world decision depends on market frictions. In this section, we consider one important market friction—taxes—and evaluate the financial consequences of the leasing decision from the perspective of the lessee. We

[9]For an analysis of the consequences of this treatment of leases for a firm's borrowing capacity, see A. Eisfeldt and A. Rampini, "Leasing, Ability to Repossess, and Debt Capacity," *Review of Financial Studies* 22(4): 1621–1657.

[10]See Article 1 of the Uniform Commercial Code, Section 1-203 at www.law.upenn.edu/bll/ulc/ulc.htm#ucc1.

show how to determine whether it is more attractive to lease an asset or to buy it and (potentially) finance the purchase with debt. First, we consider a true tax lease, then we turn to non-tax leases at the end of the section.

Cash Flows for a True Tax Lease

If a firm purchases a piece of equipment, the expense is a capital expenditure. Therefore, the purchase price can be depreciated over time, generating a CCA tax shield. If the equipment is leased and the lease is a true tax lease, there is no capital expenditure, but the lease payments are an operating expense.

Let's compare the cash flows arising from a true tax lease with those arising from a purchase using an example. Spafax Canada Inc., a magazine publisher, needs new equipment. It can purchase the equipment for $50,000 in cash. The equipment will last five years and will be subject to a CCA rate of 45%. This means that Spafax can deduct CCA as per Table 23.1. For example, in year 1, Spafax can claim a CCA deduction of $11,250. Given its tax rate of 35%, Spafax will therefore save $3937.50 in taxes due to the CCA tax shield.

Alternatively, Spafax can lease the equipment instead of purchasing it. The equipment qualifies as exempt assets (therefore, a true tax lease), and thus the lessor can claim CCA deductions while Spafax will claim rental expense. A five-year lease contract will cost $12,000 per year. Spafax must make these payments at the beginning of each year. Because the lease is a true tax lease, Spafax deducts each lease payment as an operating expense in the year in which it occurs. Thus, an income tax savings of $4200 occurs at the end of each year. The lease contract does not provide for maintenance or servicing of the equipment, so these costs are identical whether the equipment is leased or purchased.

Table 23.1 shows the free cash flow consequences of buying and leasing. Here we consider only the cash flows that differ as a result of leasing versus buying. We do not need to consider cash flows that would be the same in both situations, such as the sales revenues generated by having the equipment and maintenance expenses. We have also assumed that the equipment will have no residual value after five years; thus, if purchased, it will be disposed of for $0. If any of these differences existed, we would include

TABLE 23.1 Cash Flows ($) Consequences from Leasing versus Buying

Buy	Year	0	1	2	3	4	5	6
1	Capital Expenditures	(50,000)	—	—	—	—	—	—
2	CCA Deduction*	—	11,250	17,438	9591	5275	2901	3546
3	CCA Tax Shield	—	3938	6103	3357	1846	1015	1241
4	**Free Cash Flow (Buy)**	(50,000)	3938	6103	3357	1846	1015	1241
Lease								
5	Lease Payments	(12,000)	(12,000)	(12,000)	(12,000)	(12,000)	—	—
6	Income Tax Savings†	—	4200	4200	4200	4200	4200	—
7	**Free Cash Flow (Lease)**	(12,000)	(7800)	(7800)	(7800)	(7800)	4200	—

Notes:

*Equations 9.1 and 9.2 are used to determine UCC and CCA. Assuming disposal for $0 at the beginning of year 6, the remaining UCC is claimed as a terminal loss and is shown as the year 6 CCA deduction amount.

†To keep consistency with the assumption that an asset purchased at the beginning of year 1 (thus year 0 on the timeline) results in a series of CCA tax shields starting at the end of year 1, lease payments made at the beginning of a year are assumed to generate an income tax savings at the end of the year too.

them in the cash flows. Recall from Equation 9.9 of Chapter 9 that free cash flow can be calculated as EBITDA less taxes, capital expenditures, and increases in net working capital, plus the CCA tax shield (i.e., tax rate × *CCA* deduction). Thus, if Spafax buys, the only change to free cash flow is from capital expenditures and the CCA tax shield, and if Spafax leases, the only change is a reduction in EBITDA, and therefore taxes, from the lease payment.

Note that the cash flows of leasing differ from those of buying. A purchase requires a large initial outlay followed by a series of CCA tax shields. In contrast, the cost of leased equipment is more evenly spread out over time.

Lease versus Buy (an Unfair Comparison)

Is it better for Spafax to lease or buy the equipment? To begin to answer this question, let's compare the present value of the cash flows in each transaction (or, equivalently, we can compute the NPV of the difference between the cash flows). To compute the present value, we need to determine the cost of capital.

The appropriate cost of capital depends, of course, on the risk of the cash flows. Lease payments are a fixed obligation of the firm. If Spafax fails to make the lease payments, it will default on the lease. The lessor will seek the remaining lease payments and, in addition, will take back the equipment. In that sense, a lease is similar to a loan secured with the leased asset as collateral. Moreover, as discussed in Section 23.2, in a true lease the lessor is in an even better position than a secured creditor if the firm files for bankruptcy. Thus, *the risk of the lease payments is no greater than the risk of secured debt*, so it is reasonable to discount the lease payments at the firm's secured borrowing rate.

The tax savings from the lease payments and from depreciation expenses are also low-risk cash flows, as they are predetermined and will be realized as long as the firm generates positive income.[11] Therefore, a common assumption in practice is to use the firm's borrowing rate for these cash flows as well.

If Spafax's borrowing rate is 8%, the cost of buying the equipment has the following present value:

$$PV(\text{Buy}) = -50{,}000 + \frac{3938}{1.08} + \frac{6103}{1.08^2} + \frac{3357}{1.08^3} + \frac{1846}{1.08^4} + \frac{1015}{1.08^5} + \frac{1241}{1.08^6} = -\$35{,}627$$

The cost of leasing the equipment has the following present value:

$$PV(\text{Lease}) = -12{,}000 - \frac{7800}{1.08} - \frac{7800}{1.08^2} - \frac{7800}{1.08^3} - \frac{7800}{1.08^4} + \frac{4200}{1.08^5} = -\$34{,}976$$

Thus, leasing is cheaper than buying, with a net savings of \$35,627 − \$34,976.

The preceding analysis ignores an important point, however. When a firm enters into a lease, it is committing to lease payments that are a fixed future obligation of the firm. If the firm is in financial distress and cannot make the lease payments, the lessor can seize the equipment. Moreover, the lease obligations themselves could trigger financial distress. Therefore, when a firm leases an asset, it is effectively adding leverage to its capital structure (whether or not the lease appears on the balance sheet for accounting purposes).

Because leasing is a form of financing, we should compare it to other financing options that Spafax may have. Rather than buy the asset outright, Spafax could borrow funds (or reduce its planned cash balances, and thereby increase its net debt) to finance

[11]Even if income is negative, these tax benefits may still be obtained through carryback or carryforward provisions that allow the firm to apply these credits against income generated in past or future years.

the purchase of the equipment, thus matching the leverage of the lease. If Spafax does borrow, it will also benefit from the interest tax shield provided by leverage. This tax advantage may make borrowing to buy the equipment more attractive than leasing. Thus, to evaluate a lease correctly, we should compare it to purchasing the asset using an equivalent amount of leverage. In other words, the appropriate comparison is not lease versus buy, but rather lease versus borrow.

Lease versus Borrow (the Right Comparison)

lease-equivalent loan
The loan that is required on the purchase of the asset that leaves the purchaser with the same obligations as the lessee would have.

To compare leasing to borrowing, we must determine the amount of the loan that leads to the same level of fixed obligations that Spafax would have with the lease. We call this loan the **lease-equivalent loan**. That is, the lease-equivalent loan is the loan that is required on the purchase of the asset that leaves the purchaser with the same obligations as the lessee would have.[12]

The Lease-Equivalent Loan. To compute the lease-equivalent loan in Spafax's case, we first compute the difference between the cash flows from leasing versus buying, which we refer to as the incremental free cash flow of leasing. As Table 23.2 shows, relative to buying, leasing saves cash up front but results in lower future cash flows. The incremental free cash flow in years 1 through 6 represents the effective leverage the firm takes on by leasing.

Alternatively, Spafax could take on this same leverage by purchasing the equipment and taking on a loan with these same after-tax debt payments. How much could Spafax borrow by taking on such a loan? Because the future incremental cash flows are the after-tax payments Spafax will make on the loan, the initial balance on the lease-equivalent loan is the present value of these cash flows using Spafax's after-tax cost of debt:

$$\text{Loan Balance} = PV(\text{Future } FCF \text{ of Lease versus Buy at } r_D(1-\tau_c)) \tag{23.4}$$

Using Spafax's after-tax borrowing cost of 8% (1 − 35%) = 5.2%, the initial loan balance is

$$\begin{aligned}\text{Loan Balance} &= \frac{11{,}738}{1.052} + \frac{13{,}903}{1.052^2} + \frac{11{,}157}{1.052^3} + \frac{9646}{1.052^4} - \frac{3185}{1.052^5} + \frac{1241}{1.052^6} \\ &= \$39{,}622 \end{aligned} \tag{23.5}$$

Equation 23.5 implies that if Spafax is willing to take on the future obligations implied by leasing, it could instead buy the equipment and borrow $39,622. This exceeds the savings in year 0 from leasing of $38,000 shown in Table 23.2. Thus, by buying and borrowing using the lease-equivalent loan, Spafax saves an additional $39,622 − $38,000 = $1622 initially, and so leasing the equipment is unattractive relative to this alternative.

TABLE 23.2 Incremental Free Cash Flows ($) of Leasing versus Buying

	Year	0	1	2	3	4	5	6
1	FCF Lease (Line 7, Table 23.1)	(12,000)	(7800)	(7800)	(7800)	(7800)	4200	—
2	Less: FCF Buy (Line 4, Table 23.1)	50,000	(3938)	(6103)	(3357)	(1846)	(1015)	(1241)
3	Lease – Buy	38,000	(11,738)	(13,903)	(11,157)	(9646)	3185	(1241)

[12]For a development of this method, see S. Myers, D. Dill, and A. Bautista, "Valuation of Financial Lease Contracts," *Journal of Finance* 31(3) (1976): 799–819.

TABLE 23.3 Cash Flows ($) from Buying and Borrowing Using the Lease-Equivalent Loan

	Year	0	1	2	3	4	5	6
	Lease-Equivalent Loan							
1	Loan Balance (PV at 5.2%)	39,622	29,945	17,599	7358	(1906)	1180	—
	Buy with Lease-Equivalent Loan							
2	Net Borrowing (Repayment)	39,622	(9677)	(12,346)	(10,242)	(9264)	3085	(1180)
3	Interest (at 8%)		(3170)	(2396)	(1408)	(589)	152	(94)
4	Interest Tax Shield at 35%		1109	838	493	206	(53)	33
5	Cash Flows of Loan (After-tax)	39,622	(11,738)	(13,903)	(11,157)	(9646)	3185	(1241)
6	FCF Buy		(50,000)	3938	6103	3357	1846	1015
7	Cash Flows of Borrow + Buy	(10,378)	(7800)	(7800)	(7800)	(7800)	4200	—

We verify this result explicitly in the spreadsheet in Table 23.3. There, we compute the cash flows that result from buying the equipment and borrowing using the lease-equivalent loan. Line 1 shows the lease-equivalent loan balance, which we compute at each date by applying Equation 23.4. Line 2 shows the initial borrowing and principal payments of the loan (computed as the change in the loan balance from the prior year). Line 3 shows the interest due each year (8% of the prior loan balance), and line 4 computes the interest tax shield (35% of the interest amount). Line 5 then totals the after-tax cash flows of the loan, which we combine with the free cash flow from buying the equipment, to compute the total cash flow from buying and borrowing on line 7.

Comparing the cash flows from buying the equipment and financing it with the lease-equivalent loan (line 7 of Table 23.3) with the cash flows of the lease (line 1 of Table 23.2), we see that in both cases Spafax has a net future obligation of $7800 per year for four years followed by an inflow of $4200 in year 5. But while the leverage is the same for the two strategies, the initial cash flow is not. With the lease, Spafax will pay $12,000 initially; with the loan, Spafax will pay the purchase price of the equipment minus the amount borrowed, or $50,000 − $39,622 = $10,378. Again, we see that borrowing to buy the equipment is cheaper than the lease, with a savings of $12,000 − $10,378 = $1622. For Spafax, the lease is not attractive. If Spafax is willing to take on that much leverage, it would be better off doing so by borrowing to purchase the equipment rather than leasing it.

A Direct Method. Now that we have seen the role of the lease-equivalent loan, we can directly compare leasing with an equivalent debt-financed purchase. Because the incremental cash flows from leasing versus borrowing are relatively affordable, it is appropriate to use the cost of debt, adjusted for taxes, as the discount rate. So, $r = r_D(1 - T_c)$. Thus, *we can compare leasing to buying the asset using equivalent leverage by discounting the incremental cash flows of leasing versus buying using the after-tax borrowing rate.*

In Spafax's case, discounting the incremental free cash flow in Table 23.2 at Spafax's after-tax borrowing cost of 8% × (1 − 35%) = 5.2%, we get

$$NPV(\text{Lease versus Borrow}) = 38{,}000 - \frac{11{,}738}{1.052} - \frac{13{,}903}{1.052^2} - \frac{11{,}157}{1.052^3} - \frac{9646}{1.052^4} + \frac{3185}{1.052^5} - \frac{1241}{1.052^6} = -\$1622$$

Note that this is precisely the difference we calculated earlier.

EXAMPLE 23.6 Evaluating New Lease Terms

PROBLEM

Suppose Spafax rejects the lease we analyzed, and the lessor agrees to lower the lease rate to $11,400 per year. Does this change make the lease attractive?

SOLUTION

■ Plan

The incremental cash flows with the lower lease rate are shown in the following table:

Buy	Year	0	1	2	3	4	5	6
1	Capital Expenditures	(50,000)	—	—	—	—	—	—
2	CCA Deduction	—	11,250	17,438	9591	5275	2901	3546
3	CCA Tax S hield	—	3938	6103	3357	1846	1015	1241
4	Free Cash Flow (Buy)	(50,000)	3938	6103	3357	1846	1015	1241
Lease								
5	Lease Payments	(11,400)	(11,400)	(11,400)	(11,400)	(11,400)	—	—
6	Income Tax Savings	—	3990	3990	3990	3990	3990	—
7	Free Cash Flow (Lease)	(11,400)	(7410)	(7410)	(7410)	(7410)	3990	—
	Lease versus Buy							
8	Lease − Buy	38,600	(11,348)	(13,513)	(10,767)	(9256)	2975	(1241)

Note: The following data were used to create this table: asset cost = 50,000; lease payments = 11,400; *CCA* rate $d = 45\%$; $\tau_c = 35\%$.

We can recompute the NPV of leasing versus borrowing using the cash flows from the lower lease rate.

■ Execute

Using Spafax's after-tax borrowing cost of 5.2%, the gain from leasing versus an equivalently leveraged purchase is

$$\begin{aligned} NPV(\text{Lease versus Borrow}) &= 38{,}600 - \frac{11{,}348}{1.052} - \frac{13{,}513}{1.052^2} - \frac{10{,}767}{1.052^3} \\ &\quad - \frac{9256}{1.052^4} + \frac{2975}{1.052^5} - \frac{1241}{1.052^6} \\ &= 38{,}600 - 38{,}409 \\ &= \$191 \end{aligned}$$

Therefore, the lease is attractive at the new terms.

■ Evaluate

By reducing the lease payments by $600 ($390 after tax) each, we can make the lease more attractive than borrowing and buying. It is important to re-evaluate the decision when the lease terms change.

The Effective After-Tax Lease Borrowing Rate. We can also compare leasing and buying in terms of an effective after-tax borrowing rate associated with the lease. This is given by the IRR of the incremental lease cash flows in Table 23.2, which we can calculate as 7%:

$$41{,}875 - \frac{11{,}625}{1.07} - \frac{11{,}625}{1.07^2} - \frac{11{,}625}{1.07^3} - \frac{11{,}625}{1.07^4} - \frac{3500}{1.07^5} = 0$$

Thus, the lease is equivalent to borrowing at an after-tax rate of 7%. This option is not attractive compared to the after-tax rate of only 8% × (1 − 35%) = 5.2% that Spafax pays on its debt. Because we are borrowing (positive followed by negative cash flows), a lower IRR is better. But be careful with this approach—as discussed in Chapter 8, if the cash flows alternate signs more than once, the IRR method cannot be relied upon.

Evaluating a True Tax Lease

In sum, when evaluating a true tax lease, we should compare leasing to a purchase that is financed with equivalent leverage. We suggest the following approach:

1. Compute the *incremental cash flows* for leasing versus buying, as we did in Table 23.2. Include the CCA tax shield (if buying) or the tax deductibility of the lease payments (if leasing).
2. Compute the NPV of leasing versus buying using equivalent leverage by discounting the incremental cash flows at the *after-tax borrowing rate*.

If the NPV computed in step 2 is negative, then leasing is unattractive compared to traditional debt financing. In this case, the firm should not lease but rather should acquire the asset using an optimal amount of leverage (based on the trade-offs and techniques discussed in Part 6).

If the NPV computed in step 2 is positive, then leasing does provide an advantage over traditional debt financing and should be considered. Management should recognize, however, that while it may not be listed on the balance sheet, the lease increases the firm's effective leverage by the amount of the lease-equivalent loan.[13]

Evaluating a Non-tax Lease

Evaluating a non-tax lease is much more straightforward than evaluating a true tax lease. For a non-tax lease, the lessee still receives the CCA deductions (as though the asset were purchased). Only the interest portion of the lease payment is deductible, however. Thus, in terms of cash flows, a non-tax lease is directly comparable to a traditional loan. Therefore, it is attractive if it offers a better interest rate than would be available with a loan. To determine whether it does offer a better rate, we can discount the lease payments at the firm's *pre-tax* borrowing rate and compare it to the purchase price of the asset.

For both the true tax lease and the non-tax lease, we have ignored the residual value of the asset, any differences in the maintenance and service arrangements with a lease versus a purchase, and any cancellation or other lease options. If these features are present, they should also be included when comparing leasing versus a debt-financed purchase.

[13]If financial distress or other costs of leverage are large, the firm may wish to offset some of this increase in leverage by reducing other debt of the firm.

EXAMPLE 23.7 Comparing a Non-tax Lease with a Standard Loan

PROBLEM

Suppose the lease in Example 23.6 is a non-tax lease. Would it be attractive for Spafax in this case?

SOLUTION

Plan

Instead of purchasing the equipment for $50,000, Spafax will pay lease payments of $11,400 per year. That is, Spafax is effectively borrowing $50,000 by making payments of $11,400 per year. Given Spafax's 8% borrowing rate, we can calculate how much Spafax could borrow if it made payments of $11,400 per year on a standard loan. If that amount is more than $50,000, then it would be better off borrowing than leasing.

Execute

$$PV(\text{Lease Payments}) = 11{,}400 + \frac{11{,}400}{1.08} + \frac{11{,}400}{1.08^2} + \frac{11{,}400}{1.08^3} + \frac{11{,}400}{1.08^4} = \$49{,}158$$

Evaluate

By making the same payments on a loan, Spafax could raise less than $50,000. Thus, the lease is attractive at these terms if it is a non-tax lease—Spafax's lease payments are less than the payments that would be required on a $50,000 loan.

CONCEPT CHECK

5. What discount rate should be used for the incremental lease cash flows to compare a true tax lease to borrowing?
6. How can we compare a non-tax lease to borrowing?

23.4 Reasons for Leasing

In Section 23.3, we saw how to determine whether a lease is attractive for the potential lessee. A similar but reverse argument can be used from the standpoint of the lessor. The lessor could compare leasing the equipment to lending the money to the firm so that it can purchase the equipment. Under what circumstances would leasing be profitable for both the lessor and the lessee? If a lease is a good deal for one of the parties, is it a bad deal for the other? Or are there underlying economic sources of value in a lease contract?

Valid Arguments for Leasing

For a lease to be attractive to both the lessee and the lessor, the gains must come from some underlying economic benefits that the leasing arrangement provides. Here, we consider some valid reasons for leasing.

Tax Differences. With a true tax lease, the lessee replaces CCA and interest tax deductions with a deduction for the lease payments. Depending on the timing of the payments, one set of deductions will have a larger present value. A tax gain occurs if the lease shifts the more valuable deductions to the party with the higher tax rate. Generally speaking, if the asset's CCA deductions are more rapid than its lease payments, a true tax lease is advantageous if the lessor is in a higher tax bracket than the lessee. In contrast, if the asset's CCA deductions are slower than its lease payments, there are tax gains from a true tax lease if the lessor is in a lower tax bracket than the lessee.

EXAMPLE 23.8 Exploiting Tax Differences through Leasing

PROBLEM

Suppose Spafax is offered a true tax lease for the equipment at a lease rate of $11,400 per year. Show that this lease is profitable for Spafax as well as for a lessor with a 55% tax rate and an 8% borrowing cost.

SOLUTION

■ Plan

We already evaluated the lease with these terms in Example 23.6. There, we found that the NPV of leasing versus borrowing was $191 for Spafax. Now we need to consider the lease from the standpoint of the lessor. The lessor will buy the equipment and then lease it to Spafax. We can calculate the incremental cash flows for the lessor from buying and leasing, evaluate them at the after-tax rate, and compute the NPV for the lessor. (Using the after-tax rate for the lessor implies that the lessor will borrow against the future free cash flows of the transaction.)

■ Execute

Buy	Year	0	1	2	3	4	5	6
1	Capital Expenditures	(50,000)	—	—	—	—	—	—
2	CCA Deduction	—	11,250	17,438	9591	5275	2901	3546
3	CCA Tax Shield	—	6188	9591	5275	2901	1596	1950
4	Free Cash Flow (Buy)	(50,000)	6188	9591	5275	2901	1596	1950
Lease								
5	Lease Payments	11,400	11,400	11,400	11,400	11,400	—	—
6	Income Tax	—	(6270)	(6270)	(6270)	(6270)	(6270)	—
7	Free Cash Flow (Lease)	11,400	5130	5130	5130	5130	(6270)	—
	Lessor Free Cash Flow							
8	**Buy and Lease**	**(38,600)**	**11,318**	**14,721**	**10,405**	**8031**	**(4674)**	**1950**

Note: The following data were used to create this table: asset cost = 50,000; lease payments = 11,400; *CCA* rate $d = 45\%$; $\tau_c = 55\%$.

Evaluating the cash flows at the after-tax rate of $8\% \times (1 - 55\%) = 3.6\%$, we find the $NPV = \$30.27 > 0$ for the lessor.

■ Evaluate

Both sides gain from the transaction due to the difference in tax rates. The gain comes from the fact that for the lessor, his or her asset's CCA deductions provide more accelerated tax deductions than the taxes the lessor pays on the lease payments. Because the lessor is in a higher tax bracket than Spafax, shifting the faster tax deductions to the lessor is advantageous.

Reduced Resale Costs. Many assets are time consuming and costly to sell. If a firm needs to use the asset for only a short time, leasing it is probably less costly than buying and later reselling the asset. In this case, the lessor is responsible for finding a new user for the asset. Lessors are often specialized in finding new users and so face much lower costs. For example, car dealerships are in a better position to sell a used car at the end of a lease than a consumer is. Some of this advantage can be passed along through a lower lease rate. In addition, while owners of assets are likely to resell them only if the assets are "lemons," a short-term lease can commit the user of an asset to return it regardless of its quality. In this way, leases can help mitigate the adverse selection problem in the used goods market.[14]

Efficiency Gains from Specialization. Lessors often have efficiency advantages over lessees in maintaining or operating certain types of assets. For example, a lessor of office copy machines can employ expert technicians and maintain an inventory of spare parts required for maintenance. Some types of leases may even come with an operator, such as a truck with a driver (in fact, the term "operating lease" originated from such leases). By offering assets together with these complementary services, lessors can achieve efficiency gains and offer attractive lease rates. In addition, if the value of the asset depends on these additional services, then a firm that purchases the asset would be dependent on the service provider, who could then raise the price for services and exploit the firm.[15] By leasing the asset and the services as a bundle, the firm maintains its bargaining power by retaining its flexibility to switch to a competing equipment lessor.

Reduced Distress Costs and Increased Debt Capacity. As noted in Section 23.2, assets leased under a true lease are not afforded bankruptcy protection and can be seized in the event of default. In addition, the lessor may be better able to recover the full economic value of the asset (by re-leasing it) than a lender would. Because of the higher recovery value in the event of default, a lessor may be able to offer more attractive financing through the lease than an ordinary lender could. Recent studies suggest that this effect is important for small firms and firms that are capital constrained.[16]

Transferring Risk. At the beginning of a lease, there may be significant uncertainty about the residual value of the leased asset, and whoever owns the asset bears this risk. Leasing allows the party best able to bear the risk to hold it. For example, small firms with a low tolerance for risk may prefer to lease rather than purchase assets.

Improved Incentives. When the lessor is the manufacturer, a lease in which the lessor bears the risk of the residual value can improve incentives and lower agency costs. Such a lease provides the manufacturer with an incentive to produce a high-quality, durable product that will retain its value over time. In addition, if the manufacturer is a monopolist, leasing the product gives the manufacturer an incentive not to overproduce and lower the product's residual value, as well as an ability to restrict competition from sales of used goods.

---

[14]For evidence of this effect, see T. Gilligan, "Lemons and Leases in the Used Business Aircraft Market," *Journal of Political Economy* 112(5) (2004): 1157–1180.

[15]This concern is often referred to as the *hold-up problem.* The importance of the hold-up problem in determining the optimal ownership of assets was identified by B. Klein, R. Crawford, and A. Alchian, "Vertical Integration, Appropriable Rents, and the Competitive Contracting Process," *Journal of Law and Economics* 21(1978): 297–326.

[16]See S. Sharpe and H. Nguyen, "Capital Market Imperfections and the Incentive to Lease," *Journal of Financial Economics* 39(2–3) (1995): 271–294; J. Graham, M. Lemmon, and J. Schallheim, "Debt, Leases, Taxes, and the Endogeneity of Corporate Tax Status," *Journal of Finance* 53(1) (1998): 131–162; and A. Eisfeldt and A. Rampini, "Leasing, Ability to Repossess, and Debt Capacity," *Review of Financial Studies,* 22(4): 1621–1657.

Despite these potential benefits, significant agency costs may also be associated with leasing. For leases in which the lessor retains a substantial interest in the asset's residual value, the lessee has less of an incentive to take proper care of an asset that is leased rather than purchased.[17]

Suspect Arguments for Leasing

Some reasons that lessees and lessors cite for preferring leasing to purchasing are difficult to justify economically. While they may be important in some circumstances, they deserve careful scrutiny.

Avoiding Capital Expenditure Controls. One reason some managers will choose to lease equipment rather than purchase it is to avoid the scrutiny from superiors that often accompanies large capital expenditures. For example, some companies may place limits on the dollar amounts a manager can invest over a certain period; lease payments may fall below these limits, whereas the cost of the purchase would not. By leasing, the manager avoids having to make a special request for funds. This reason for leasing is also apparent in the public sector, where large assets are often leased to avoid asking the government or the public to approve the funds necessary to purchase the assets. However, the lease may cost more than the purchase, wasting stockholder or taxpayer dollars in the long run.

Preserving Capital. A common argument made in favour of leasing is that it provides "100% financing" because no down payment is required, so the lessee can save cash to use for other needs. Of course, the firm can also borrow to purchase an asset (possibly using the asset as collateral). For most large corporations, the amount of leverage the firm can obtain through a lease is unlikely to exceed the amount of leverage the firm can obtain through a loan. Thus, this benefit is likely to exist only for small or highly capital-constrained firms.

Reducing Leverage Through Off–Balance-Sheet Financing. By carefully avoiding the four criteria that define a capital lease for accounting purposes, a firm can avoid listing the long-term lease as a liability. Because a lease is equivalent to a loan, the firm can increase its actual leverage without increasing the debt-equity ratio on its balance sheet. But whether they appear on the balance sheet or not, lease commitments are liabilities for the firm. As a result, they will have the same effect on the risk and return characteristics of the firm as other forms of leverage do. Most financial analysts and sophisticated investors understand this fact and consider operating leases (which must be listed in the footnotes of the financial statements) to be additional sources of leverage.

CONCEPT CHECK

7. What are some of the potential gains from leasing if the lessee plans to hold the asset for only a small fraction of its useful life?
8. If a lease is not listed as a liability on the firm's balance sheet, does it mean that a firm that leases rather than borrows is less risky?

[17]As an example, auto manufacturers require individuals who lease their cars to provide proper maintenance. Without such requirements, individuals would be tempted to avoid paying for oil changes and other maintenance near the end of the lease term. Of course, there are other ways lessees may abuse their cars (e.g., driving at excessive speeds) that cannot be easily controlled.

MyLab Finance

Here is what you should know after reading this chapter. MyLab™ Finance will help you identify what you know, and where to go when you need to practice.

KEY POINTS	TERMS	ONLINE PRACTICE OPPORTUNITIES
23.1 The Basics of Leasing ■ A lease is a contract between two parties: the lessee and the lessor. The lessee is liable for periodic payments in exchange for the right to use the asset. The lessor, who is the owner of the asset, is entitled to the lease payments in exchange for lending the asset. ■ Many types of lease transactions are possible, depending on the relationship between the lessee and the lessor. ■ In a sales-type lease, the lessor is the manufacturer or primary dealer of the asset. ■ In a direct lease, the lessor is an independent company that specializes in purchasing assets and leasing them to customers. ■ If a firm already owns an asset it would prefer to lease, it can arrange a sale and leaseback transaction. ■ In a perfect market, the cost of leasing is equivalent to the cost of purchasing and reselling the asset. Also, the cost of leasing and then purchasing the asset is equivalent to the cost of borrowing to purchase the asset. ■ In many cases, the lease provides options for the lessee to obtain ownership of the asset at the end of the lease. Some examples include fair market value leases, $1.00 out leases, fixed price leases, and fair market value cap leases.	$1.00 out lease (finance lease), p. 792 direct lease, p. 788 fair market value cap lease, p. 792 fair market value (FMV) lease, p. 792 fixed price lease, p. 792 lessee, p. 788 lessor, p. 788 leveraged lease, p. 788 residual value, p. 789 sale and leaseback, p. 788 sales-type lease, p. 788 special-purpose entity (SPE), p. 789 synthetic lease, p. 789	MyLab Study Plan 23.1
23.2 Accounting, Tax, and Legal Consequences of Leasing ■ Under IFRS, two types of leases are recognized based on the lease terms: operating leases and finance leases. Operating leases are viewed as rentals for accounting purposes. Finance leases are viewed as purchases. ■ The CRA separates leases into two broad categories: true tax leases and non-tax leases. With a true tax lease, the lessee deducts lease payments as an operating expense. With a non-tax lease, the lessee must depreciate the asset and can expense only the interest portion of the lease payments.	finance lease, p. 794 non-tax lease, p. 798 operating lease, p. 794 security interest, p. 799 true lease, p. 799 true tax lease, p. 797	MyLab Study Plan 23.2

KEY POINTS	TERMS	ONLINE PRACTICE OPPORTUNITIES
■ In a true lease, the asset is not protected in the event that the lessee declares bankruptcy, and the lessor can seize the asset if lease payments are not made. If the lease is deemed a security interest by the bankruptcy court, then the asset is protected and the lessor becomes a secured creditor.		
23.3 The Leasing Decision ■ To evaluate the leasing decision for a true tax lease, managers should compare the cost of leasing with the cost of financing using an equivalent amount of leverage. ■ Compute the incremental cash flows for leasing versus buying. ■ Compute the NPV by discounting the incremental cash flows at the after-tax borrowing rate. ■ The cash flows of a non-tax lease are directly comparable to the cash flows of a traditional loan, so a non-tax lease is attractive only if it offers a better interest rate than a loan.	lease-equivalent loan, p. 802	MyLab Study Plan 23.3
23.4 Reasons for Leasing ■ Good reasons for leasing include tax differences, reduced resale costs, efficiency gains from specialization, reduced bankruptcy costs, risk transfer, and improved incentives. ■ Suspect reasons for leasing include avoiding capital expenditure controls, preserving capital, and reducing leverage through off–balance-sheet financing.		MyLab Study Plan 23.4

REVIEW QUESTIONS

1. Why would a firm enter into a sale and leaseback transaction?
2. What are the main differences between fair market value, $1 out, fixed price, and fair market value cap leases?
3. How are operating leases different from capital leases?
4. Which classification of a lease is more important for cash flows and valuation: that of the IFRS or of Canada Revenue Agency?
5. What is the advantage of a synthetic lease?
6. Why does it matter whether the lease is classified as a security interest or as a true lease?
7. Why is comparing leasing versus buying an unfair comparison?
8. What are the main steps in evaluating a true tax lease?
9. Explain why preserving capital and reducing leverage are suspect reasons for leasing

PROBLEMS

All problems in this chapter are available in MyLab Finance.

The Basics of Leasing

1. Suppose an H1200 supercomputer has a cost of $200,000 and will have a residual market value of $60,000 in five years. The risk-free interest rate is 5% APR with monthly compounding.
   a. What is the risk-free monthly lease rate for a five-year lease in a perfect market?
   b. What would be the monthly payment for a five-year $200,000 risk-free loan to purchase the H1200?

2. Suppose the risk-free interest rate is 5% APR with monthly compounding. If a $2 million MRI machine can be leased for seven years for $22,000 per month, what residual value must the lessor recover to break even in a perfect market with no risk?

3. Consider a five-year lease for a $400,000 bottling machine, with a residual market value of $150,000 at the end of the five years. If the risk-free interest rate is 6% APR with monthly compounding, compute the monthly lease payment in a perfect market for the following leases:
   a. A fair market value lease
   b. A $1.00 out lease
   c. A fixed price lease with an $80,000 final price

Accounting, Tax, and Legal Consequences of Leasing

4. Acme Distribution currently has the following items on its balance sheet:

Assets		Liabilities	
Cash	20	Debt	70
Property, Plant, and Equipment	175	Equity	125

How will Acme's balance sheet change if it enters into an $80 million finance lease for new warehouses? What will its book debt-equity ratio be? How will Acme's balance sheet and debt-equity ratio change if the lease is an operating lease?

5. Your firm is considering leasing a $50,000 copier. The copier has an estimated economic life of eight years. Suppose the appropriate discount rate is 9% APR with monthly compounding. Classify each lease below as a finance lease or operating lease:
   a. A four-year fair market value lease with payments of $1150 per month
   b. A six-year fair market value lease with payments of $790 per month
   c. A five-year fair market value lease with payments of $925 per month
   d. A five-year fair market value lease with payments of $1000 per month and an option to cancel after three years with a $9000 cancellation penalty

The Leasing Decision

6. Craxton Engineering will either purchase or lease a new $756,000 fabricator. If purchased, the fabricator will be depreciated for tax purposes on a straight-line basis over seven years. Craxton can lease the fabricator for $130,000 per year for seven years. Craxton's tax rate is 35%. (Assume the fabricator has no residual value at the end of the seven years.)

a. What are the free cash flow consequences of buying the fabricator?
b. What are the free cash flow consequences of leasing the fabricator if the lease is a true tax lease?
c. What are the incremental free cash flows of leasing versus buying?

7. Riverton Mining plans to purchase or lease $220,000 worth of excavation equipment. If purchased, the equipment will be depreciated for tax purposes on a straight-line basis over five years, after which it will be worthless. If leased, the annual lease payments will be $55,000 per year for five years. Assume Riverton's borrowing cost is 8%, its tax rate is 35%, and the lease qualifies as a true tax lease.
a. If Riverton purchases the equipment, what is the amount of the lease-equivalent loan?
b. Is Riverton better off leasing the equipment or financing the purchase using the lease-equivalent loan?
c. What is the effective after-tax lease borrowing rate? How does this compare to Riverton's actual after-tax borrowing rate?

8. Suppose Clorox can lease a new computer data processing system for $975,000 per year for five years. Alternatively, it can purchase the system for $4.25 million. Assume Clorox has a borrowing cost of 7% and a tax rate of 35%, and the system will be obsolete at the end of five years.
a. If Clorox will depreciate (for tax purposes) the computer equipment on a straight-line basis over the next five years, and if the lease qualifies as a true tax lease, is it better to finance the purchase of the equipment or to lease it?
b. Suppose that if the Clorox Canada division buys the equipment, it will use capital cost allowance for depreciation tax purposes. Specifically, the CCA rate will be 45% and any undepreciated capital cost in year 6 will be taken as a terminal loss. Compare leasing with purchase in this case.

9. Suppose Procter and Gamble (P&G) is considering purchasing $15 million in new manufacturing equipment. If it purchases the equipment, P&G will depreciate it for tax purposes on a straight-line basis over five years, after which the equipment will be worthless. P&G will also be responsible for maintenance expenses of $1 million per year. Alternatively, it can lease the equipment for $4.2 million per year for the five years, in which case the lessor will provide necessary maintenance. Assume P&G's tax rate is 35% and its borrowing cost is 7%.
a. What is the NPV associated with leasing the equipment versus financing it with the lease-equivalent loan?
b. What is the break-even lease rate—that is, what lease amount could P&G pay each year and be indifferent about leasing versus financing a purchase?

Reasons for Leasing

10. Suppose Netflix Canada is considering the purchase of special software to facilitate its enhancement of video-on-demand services. In total, the firm will purchase $48 million in new software. This software will qualify for CCA deductions at a rate of 100%. However, because of the firm's substantial loss carryforwards, Netflix estimates its marginal tax rate to be 10% over the next five years, so it will get very little tax benefit from the CCA deductions. Thus Netflix considers leasing the software instead. Suppose Netflix and the lessor face the same 8% borrowing rate, but the lessor has a 40% tax rate. For the purpose of this question, assume the software is worthless after five years, the lease term is five years, and the lease qualifies as a true tax lease.
a. What is the lease rate for which the lessor will break even?
b. What is the gain to Netflix with this lease rate?
c. What is the source of the gain in this transaction?

CHAPTER

24 Mergers and Acquisitions

LEARNING OBJECTIVES

- Discuss the types of mergers and trends in merger activity
- Understand the stock price reactions to takeover announcements
- Critically evaluate the different reasons to acquire
- Follow the major steps in the takeover process
- Discuss the main takeover defences
- Identify factors that determine who gets the value added in a merger

NOTATION

A	pre-merger total value of acquirer
EPS	earnings per share
N_A	pre-merger number of shares of acquirer outstanding
N_T	pre-merger number of shares of target outstanding
P/E	price-earnings ratio
P_A	pre-merger share price of acquirer
P_T	pre-merger share price of target
S	value of all synergies
T	pre-merger total value of target
x	number of new shares issued by acquirer to pay for target

In this chapter, we first provide some historical background about the market for mergers and acquisitions. Next, we discuss some of the reasons why a corporate financial manager may decide to pursue an acquisition. We then review the takeover process. Finally, we address the question of who benefits from the value that is added when a takeover occurs.

24.1 Background and Historical Trends

acquirer (or bidder) A firm that, in a takeover, buys another firm.

target A firm that is acquired by another in a merger or acquisition.

takeover Either a merger or an acquisition, by which ownership and control of a firm can change.

Mergers and acquisitions are part of what is often referred to as "the market for corporate control." When one firm acquires another, there is typically a buyer, the **acquirer (or bidder)**, and a seller, the **target** firm. There are two primary mechanisms by which ownership and control of a public corporation can change: either another corporation or group of individuals can acquire the target firm, or the target firm can merge with another firm. In both cases, the acquiring entity must purchase the stock or existing assets of the target either for cash or for something of equivalent value (such as shares in the acquiring or newly merged corporation). For simplicity, we refer to either mechanism as a **takeover**.

The global takeover market is highly active, averaging more than $1 trillion per year in transaction value. Table 24.1 lists the 20 largest transactions completed during the period from 1998 through fall 2017. As the table indicates, many takeovers happen between well-known companies, and individual transactions can involve huge sums of money.

TABLE 24.1 Twenty Largest Merger Transactions, 1998–2017

Date Announced	Date Completed	Target Name	Acquirer Name	Equity Value ($ billions)
Nov. 1999	June 2000	Mannesmann AG	Vodafone AirTouch PLC	203
Oct. 2004	Aug. 2005	Shell Transport & Trading Co.	Royal Dutch Petroleum Co.	185
Jan. 2000	Jan. 2001	Time Warner	America Online Inc.	182
Apr. 2007	Nov. 2007	ABN-AMRO Holding NV	RFS Holdings BV	98
Mar. 2006	Dec. 2006	BellSouth Corp.	AT&T Inc.	89
Nov. 1999	June 2000	Warner-Lambert Co.	Pfizer Inc.	89
Dec. 1998	Nov. 1999	Mobil Corp.	Exxon Corp.	85
Jan. 2000	Dec. 2000	SmithKline Beecham PLC	Glaxo Wellcome PLC	79
Feb. 2006	July 2008	Suez SA	Gaz de France SA	75
Apr. 1998	Oct. 1998	Citicorp	Travelers Group Inc.	73
July 1998	June 2000	GTE Corp.	Bell Atlantic Corp.	71
May 1998	Oct. 1999	Ameritech Corp.	SBC Communications Inc.	70
June 1998	Mar. 1999	Tele-Communications Inc. (TCI)	AT&T Corp.	70
Nov. 2014	Mar. 2015	Allergan Inc.	Actavis PLC	68
Jan. 2009	Oct. 2009	Wyeth	Pfizer Inc.	67
Jan. 1999	June 1999	AirTouch Communications Inc.	Vodafone Group PLC	66
Jan. 2004	Aug. 2004	Aventis SA	Sanofi-Synthelabo SA	66
Apr. 1998	Sep. 1998	BankAmerica Corp.	NationsBank Corp.	62
July 2002	Apr. 2003	Pharmacia Corp.	Pfizer Inc.	61
June 2008	Nov. 2008	Anheuser-Busch Cos Inc.	InBev NV	60

Source: Data from Thomson Reuters' SDC M&A Database.

Merger Waves

merger waves Peaks of heavy activity followed by quiet troughs of few transactions in the takeover market.

The takeover market is also characterized by **merger waves**—peaks of heavy activity followed by quiet troughs of few transactions. Figure 24.1 displays the time series of takeover activity from 1926 to 2015. Merger activity is greater during economic expansions than during contractions, and correlates with bull markets. Many of the same technological and economic conditions that lead to bull markets

FIGURE 24.1 Fraction of U.S. Public Companies Acquired Each Year, 1926–2015

Shown is the fraction, by number and by value, of U.S. public firms acquired each year. Mergers appear to occur in distinct waves, with the most recent waves occuring in the 1980s, 1990s, and 2000s.

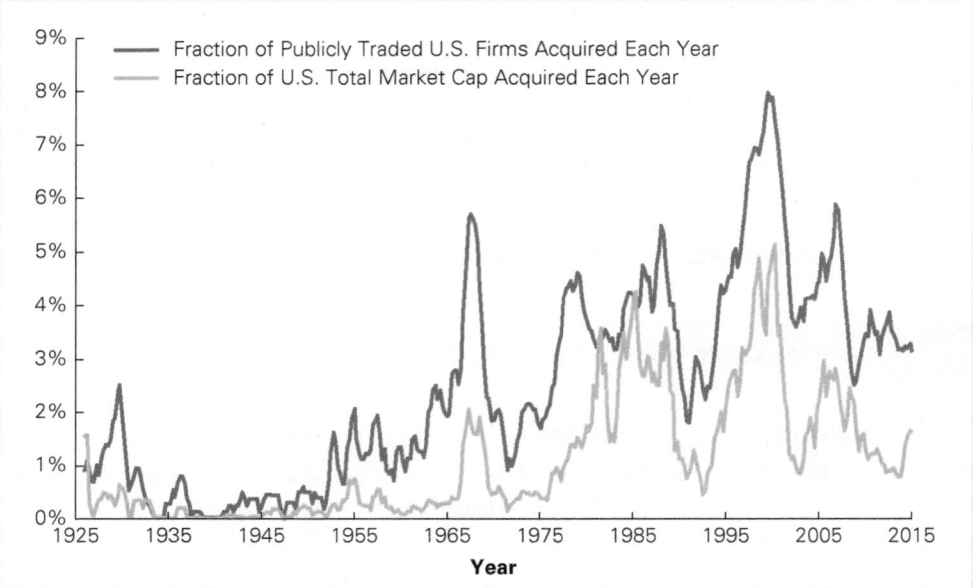

Source: Authors' calculations based on Center for Research in Securities Prices data.

also motivate managers to reshuffle assets through mergers and acquisitions. Thus, the same economic activities that drive expansions most likely also drive peaks in merger activity.[1]

Figure 24.1 shows that the periods of the greatest takeover activity occurred in the 1960s, 1980s, 1990s, and 2000s. Each merger wave was characterized by a typical type of deal. The increase in activity in the 1960s is known as the "conglomerate wave," because firms typically acquired firms in unrelated businesses. At the time, it was thought that managerial expertise was portable across business lines and that the conglomerate business form offered great financial advantages. This conglomerate fad eventually fell out of favour, and the 1980s were known for hostile, "bust-up" takeovers, in which the acquirer purchased a poorly performing conglomerate and sold off its individual business units for more than the purchase price. The 1990s, in contrast, were known for "strategic" or "global" deals that were more likely to be friendly and to involve companies in related businesses; these mergers often were designed to create strong firms on a scale that would allow them to compete globally. At the end of 2004, takeover activity began to pick up again, starting the next big merger wave, marked by consolidation in many industries such as telecommunications and software. In this wave, private equity played a larger role than it had in the past, and some private equity groups, such as KKR, TPG, Blackrock, and Cerberus, took ever-larger firms such as Hertz (see Chapter 15), Chrysler, and Harrah's private. According to Thomson Reuters, 2007 saw the value of merger and

[1]See J. Harford, "What Drives Merger Waves," *Journal of Financial Economics* 77(2005): 529–560, for an analysis of why these waves occur.

acquisition activity hit an all-time high, with over $4.5 trillion worth of deals announced globally. Almost 30% of these transactions involved consolidation in the materials, energy, and power sectors. That merger wave came to a crashing end, though, as the credit crisis of late 2007 and 2008 curtailed the ability to finance mergers. Merger activity picked up again in 2014–2015. In fact, according to data from Thomson Reuters, nearly $5 trillion in global M&A deals were announced in 2015, setting a new record.

horizontal merger A merger in which the target and acquirer are in the same industry.

vertical merger A merger in which the target's industry buys or sells to the acquirer's industry.

conglomerate merger A merger in which the target and acquirer operate in unrelated industries.

stock swap A merger deal in which the target shareholders receive stock as payment for target shares.

term sheet A summary of the structure of a merger transaction that includes details such as who will run the new company, the size and composition of the new board, the location of the headquarters, and the name of the new company.

Types of Mergers

While we tend to talk about merger waves and mergers in general, the term "merger," as commonly used, encompasses several types of transactions that vary by the relationship between the target and the acquirer and by the method of payment used in the transaction. If the target and acquirer are in the same industry, the merger is typically called a **horizontal merger**, whereas if the target's industry buys or sells to the acquirer's industry, it is called a **vertical merger**. Finally, if the target and acquirer operate in unrelated industries, the deal is a **conglomerate merger**. Conglomerate mergers, while popular in the 1960s, have generally fallen out of favour with shareholders because of the difficulty in creating value when combining two unrelated businesses.

Deals also vary based on whether the target shareholders receive stock or cash as payment for target shares. When they receive stock, the deal is often called a **stock swap**, because target shareholders are swapping their old stock for new stock in either the acquirer or a newly created merged firm. The consideration paid to target shareholders can be very complex, including debt instruments, options, and mixes of any of these with cash and/or stock. Commonly, however, target shareholders receive stock, cash, or a mix of the two.

While news reports understandably focus on the price and method of payment, the structure of a merger transaction, summarized in a **term sheet**, can be simple or incredibly complex. The items to negotiate include, among other things, who will run the new company, the size and composition of the new board, the location of the headquarters, and even the name of the new company.

CONCEPT CHECK

1. What are merger waves?
2. What is the difference between a horizontal and a vertical merger?

24.2 Market Reaction to a Takeover

acquisition premium The percentage difference between the acquisition price and the pre-merger price of a target firm that the acquirer in a takeover pays.

In Canada and most U.S. states, the law requires that when existing shareholders of a target firm are forced to sell their shares, they receive a fair value for their shares. Typically, this concept is interpreted as the value exclusive of any value that arises because of the merger itself. For practical purposes, this principle translates into the share price prior to the merger. As a consequence, a bidder is unlikely to acquire a target company for less than its current market value. Instead, most acquirers pay a substantial **acquisition premium**, which is the percentage difference between the acquisition price and the pre-merger price of the target firm.

Table 24.2 lists the average historical premium and market reaction to a takeover.[2] As the table shows, acquirers pay an average premium of 43% over the pre-merger price

[2]The original research done in the 1970s and 1980s documented that shareholders experience significant gains (between 20% and 30%) upon successful takeover of their firms. More recent papers have found combined losses on the order of $240 billion in capitalization at the announcement of takeover bids. This finding appears to be driven by spectacular losses from some large takeovers of public targets, especially in the late 1990s.

TABLE 24.2 Average Acquisition Premium and Stock Price Reactions to Mergers

Premium Paid over Pre-merger Price	Announcement Price Reaction	
	Target	Acquirer
43%	15%	1%

Source: *Handbook of Corporate Finance: Empirical Corporate Finance,* Vol. 2, Chapter 15, pp. 291–430, B. E. Eckbo, ed., Elsevier/North-Holland Handbook of Finance Series, 2008.

of the target. When a bid is announced, the target shareholders enjoy a gain of 15% on average in their stock price. Although acquirer shareholders see an *average* gain of 1%, in half of the transactions the bidder price *decreases* (in effect the median gain is not significantly different from 0%). These facts raise three important questions that we answer in this chapter:

1. Why do acquirers pay a premium over the market value for a target company?
2. Although the price of the target company rises on average on the announcement of the takeover, why does it rise less than the premium offered by the acquirer?
3. If the transaction is a good idea, why does the acquirer not consistently experience a large price increase?

Let's start with the first question—why do acquirers pay a premium over market value? In fact, this question has two parts: (1) why is the target worth a premium over the current market value, and (2) even if the target is worth more than its pre-merger value, why do acquirers pay more than the pre-merger market price? In the next section, we answer the first part of this question. We delay the discussion of the second part until the end of the chapter, when we fully understand the mechanics of the takeover process.

CONCEPT CHECK

3. On average, what happens to the target share price on the announcement of a takeover?

4. On average, what happens to the acquirer share price on the announcement of a takeover?

24.3 Reasons to Acquire

For most investors, an investment in the stock market is a zero-NPV investment. How, then, can an acquirer pay a premium for a target and still satisfy the requirement that the investment be a positive-NPV investment opportunity? The answer is that an acquirer might be able to add economic value, as a result of the acquisition, that an individual investor cannot. The basis of the assumption that the value of the combined companies will be worth more than the sum of the two companies' individual values is the assumption that they will create *synergies*. We discuss some examples of synergies below, but for simplicity in this section we refer to any additional value created as **synergies**.

synergies Value obtained from an acquisition that could not be obtained if the target remained an independent firm; that is, value in excess of the firms' stand-alone value.

Large synergies are by far the most common justification that bidders give for the premium they pay for a target. An extreme example is SBC's acquisition of AT&T in 2005 for more than $15 billion. In interviews immediately after the announcement, SBC's Chairman Ed Whitacre was quick to point out that the projected synergies of $15 billion alone could justify the price SBC agreed to pay for AT&T, let alone AT&T's assets.

Such synergies usually fall into two categories: cost reductions and revenue enhancements. Cost-reduction synergies are more common and easier to achieve, because they generally translate into layoffs of overlapping employees and elimination of redundant resources. This was the case in the SBC/AT&T acquisition, which forecasted 13,000 layoffs in the first year. If the merger will create possibilities to expand into new markets or gain more customers, then the merger partners will predict synergies that enhance their revenue. For example, when Dell and EMC announced their merger agreement in October 2015, they forecasted $1 billion in revenue-enhancement synergiesl; one example was by providing new opportunities for EMC's partially held VMWare to sell its virtualization software.

Let's examine in detail the synergies most often cited by acquirers to justify takeovers.

Economies of Scale and Scope

economies of scale The savings a large company can enjoy from producing goods in high volume. Such savings are not available to a small company.

economies of scope The savings large companies can realize that come from combining the marketing and distribution of different types of related products.

A large company can enjoy **economies of scale**, or savings from producing goods in high volume, that are not available to a small company. For example, in Stride Rite's acquisition of sports shoemaker Saucony in 2005, one motivation was to reduce Saucony's manufacturing costs because, due to its larger size, Stride Rite could negotiate superior manufacturing contracts in China. Larger firms can also benefit from **economies of scope**, which are savings that come from combining the marketing and distribution of different types of related products (e.g., soft drinks and snack foods).

There may also be costs associated with size. Chief among these is that larger firms are more difficult to manage. In a small firm, the CEO is often close to the firm's operations. He or she can keep in touch with the firm's largest customers and most important personnel, thereby keeping abreast of changing market conditions and potential problems. Because they receive information quickly, small firms are often able to react in a timely way to changes in the economic environment.

Vertical Integration

vertical integration The merger of two companies that make products required at different stages of the production cycle for the final good; also, the merger of a firm and its supplier or a firm and its customer.

Vertical integration refers to the merger of two companies that make products required at different stages of the production cycle of the final good. A company might conclude that it can enhance its product if it has direct control of the inputs required to make the product. Similarly, another company might not be happy with how its products are being distributed, so it might decide to take control of its distribution channels.

The principal benefit of vertical integration is coordination. By putting two companies under central control, management can ensure that both companies work toward a common goal. For example, oil companies are often vertically integrated. They generally own all stages of the production process, from the oil fields to the refineries and so on, even down to the gas stations that distribute their primary product—gasoline. Many also have divisions that prospect for new oil.

Vertically integrated companies are large, and as we have already pointed out, large corporations are more difficult to run. Consequently, not all successful corporations are vertically integrated. A good example is Microsoft Corporation. Microsoft has chosen to make the operating system that the vast majority of computers use, but not the computers themselves. Many experts have argued that a key factor in Microsoft's early success over rivals IBM and Apple was its decision not to integrate vertically.

Expertise

Firms often need expertise in particular areas to compete more efficiently. Faced with this situation, a firm can enter the labour market and attempt to hire personnel with the required skills. However, hiring experienced workers with the appropriate talent might be difficult in the case of an unfamiliar, new technology. A more efficient solution may be to purchase the talent as an already functioning unit by acquiring an existing firm. For example, in 2000, Paris-based AXA bought Sanford C. Bernstein, a Wall Street private partnership, to gain expertise and a pre-existing client base in the huge U.S. asset management market. Similarly, U.K. builder Amec bought a large stake in Spie Batignolles, a French contractor, to gain local contacts and expertise in the French building industry. Such mergers are common in high-tech industries. Networking firm Cisco Systems is known for its strategy of buying young start-up firms that have developed promising new networking technologies.

Monopoly Gains

It is often argued that merging with or acquiring a major rival enables a firm to substantially reduce competition within the industry and thereby increase profits. Society as a whole bears the cost of monopoly strategies, so most countries have antitrust laws that limit such activity and protect the free enterprise system.

The extent to which these laws are enforced tends to vary across countries and over time, depending on the policy of current leaders. When General Electric (GE) agreed to buy Honeywell in October 2000, the U.S. Justice Department approved the deal with limited conditions. However, the European Commission (EC) determined that putting GE's aircraft leasing division and Honeywell's extensive avionics product line under the same management would lead to unacceptable anticompetitive effects in the avionics market. Despite substantial concessions by GE and top-level political lobbying by U.S. officials, the EC refused to approve the deal, and it was eventually called off. The GE/Honeywell deal was the first time a merger of two U.S. companies that had been approved by U.S. authorities was blocked by European officials. The EC had no direct jurisdiction over the merger of the companies, but it was in the position to impose crippling restrictions on sales inside the European Union. In 2009, Suncor Energy Inc. and Petro-Canada announced plans to merge. Canada's Competition Bureau indicated that competition would be lessened substantially in some markets—particularly in southern Ontario and the greater Toronto area. Consequently, to receive approval for the merger, the Bureau required Suncor and Petro-Canada to sell over 100 retail gas stations in southern Ontario and commit to sell to other parties for 10 years the following: 98 million litres of gasoline each year, storage, and distribution network capacity.

Monopoly power could be very valuable, and we would expect that in the absence of strong antitrust laws, many companies would merge. However, while all companies in an industry benefit when competition is reduced, only the merging company pays the associated costs (e.g., from integrating the target and managing a larger corporation). Perhaps this reason, along with existing antitrust regulations, accounts for the lack of convincing evidence that monopoly gains result from the reduction of competition following takeovers. For example, financial researchers have found that the share prices of other firms in the same industry did not significantly increase following the announcement of a merger within the industry.[3]

Efficiency Gains

Another justification acquirers cite for paying a premium for a target is efficiency gains, which are often achieved through an elimination of duplication—for example, as in the

[3]See B.E. Eckbo, "Horizontal Mergers, Collusion and Stockholder Wealth," *Journal of Financial Economics* 11(1) (1983): 241–273; and R. Stillman, "Examining Antitrust Policy Toward Horizontal Mergers," *Journal of Financial Economics* 11(1) (1983): 225–240.

SBC/AT&T merger mentioned earlier. Acquirers also often argue that they can run the target organization more efficiently than existing management could.

Although in theory a chief executive of an inefficiently run corporation can be ousted by current shareholders voting to replace the board of directors, very few managers are replaced in this way. Instead, unhappy investors typically sell their stock, so the stock of a corporation with an inept chief executive trades at a discount relative to the price at which it would trade if it had more capable leadership. In such a situation, an acquirer could purchase shares at the discounted price to take control of the corporation and replace the chief executive with a more effective one. Once the benefits of the new management team become obvious to investors, the discount for the old management will likely disappear and the acquirer can resell its shares for a profit.

Although identifying poorly performing corporations is relatively easy, fixing them is another matter entirely. Takeovers relying on the improvement of target management are difficult to complete, and post-takeover resistance to change can be great. Thus, not all inefficiently run organizations necessarily become more efficient following a takeover.

Tax Savings from Operating Losses

When a firm makes a profit, it must pay taxes on the profit. However, when it incurs a loss, the government does not rebate taxes. Thus, it might appear that a conglomerate has a tax advantage over a single-product firm simply because losses in one division can be offset by profits in another division. Let's illustrate this scenario with an example.

EXAMPLE 24.1 Taxes for a Merged Corporation

PROBLEM

Consider two firms, Yin Corporation and Yang Corporation. Both corporations will either make \$50 million or lose \$20 million every year with equal probability. The only difference is that the firms' profits are perfectly negatively correlated. That is, any year Yang Corporation earns \$50 million, Yin Corporation loses \$20 million, and vice versa. Assume that the corporate tax rate is 34%. What are the total expected after-tax profits of both firms when they are two separate firms? What are the expected after-tax profits if the two firms are combined into one corporation called Yin-Yang Corporation but are run as two independent divisions? (Assume it is not possible to carry back or carry forward any losses.)

SOLUTION

■ Plan

We need to calculate the after-tax profits of each firm in both the profitable and unprofitable states by multiplying profits by (1 − tax rate). We can then compute expected after-tax profits as the weighted average of the after-tax profits in the profitable and unprofitable states. If the firms are combined, their total profits in any year would always be \$50 million − \$20 million, so the after-tax profit will always be \$30 × (1 − tax rate).

■ Execute

Let's start with Yin Corporation. In the profitable state, the firm must pay corporate taxes, so after-tax profits are \$50 × (1 − 0.34) = \$33 million. No taxes are owed when the firm reports losses, so the after-tax profits in the unprofitable state are −\$20 million. ▶

Thus, the expected after-tax profits of Yin Corporation are $\$33 \times (0.5) + (-\$20) \times (0.5) = \$6.5$ million. Because Yang Corporation has identical expected profits, its expected profits are also $6.5 million. Thus, the total expected profit of both companies operated separately is $13 million.

The merged corporation, Yin-Yang Corporation, would have after-tax profits of $\$30 \times (1 - 0.34) = \$19.8$ million.

■ **Evaluate**

Yin-Yang Corporation has significantly higher after-tax profits than the total stand-alone after-tax profits of Yin Corporation and Yang Corporation. This is because the losses on one division reduce the taxes on the other division's profits.

Although Example 24.1 is an extreme case, it illustrates a benefit of conglomeration. In Canada and the United States, however, these benefits are mitigated because the tax authorities allow companies to carry losses forward up to 20 years. That is, a company can use losses to offset earnings up to 20 years in the future. Furthermore, companies with current-year losses can also use them to offset earnings for the three prior years in Canada and the two prior years in the United States. These carryback and carryforward provisions deliver most of the tax benefits of conglomeration (except time value differences) to a small firm with volatile earnings. While these rules would reduce the tax benefit in Example 24.1, they also create a motive for profitable firms to acquire targets with large tax loss carryforwards in order to reap the tax savings from them. However, both the CRA in Canada and the IRS in the United States will disallow a tax break if it can show that the principal reason for a takeover is tax avoidance, so it is unlikely that such a tax benefit could, by itself, be a valid reason to acquire another firm.

Diversification

The benefits of diversification are frequently cited as a reason for a conglomerate merger. The justification for these benefits comes in three forms: direct risk reduction, lower cost of debt or increased debt capacity, and liquidity enhancement. We discuss each in turn.

Risk Reduction. Like a large portfolio, large firms bear less idiosyncratic risk, so often mergers are justified on the basis that the combined firm is less risky. The problem with this argument is that it ignores the fact that investors can achieve the benefits of diversification themselves by purchasing shares in the two separate firms. Because most stockholders will already be holding a well-diversified portfolio, they get no further benefit from the firm diversifying through acquisition. Moreover, as we have already pointed out, there are costs associated with merging and with running a large diversified firm. Because it may be harder to measure performance accurately in a conglomerate, agency costs may increase and resources may be inefficiently allocated across divisions. As a result, it is cheaper for investors to diversify their own portfolios than to have the corporation do it through acquisition.

Debt Capacity and Borrowing Costs. All else being equal, larger, more diversified firms have a lower probability of bankruptcy, given the same degree of leverage. Consequently, such firms can increase leverage further and enjoy greater tax savings without incurring significant costs of financial distress. Thus, increased tax benefits and reduction in bankruptcy costs from leverage are potential benefits of diversifying mergers that diversified investors cannot achieve on their own. Of course, to justify a merger, these gains must be large enough to offset any disadvantages of running a larger, less-focused firm.

Liquidity. Shareholders of private companies are often underdiversified; they have a disproportionate share of their wealth invested in the private company. Consequently, when an acquirer buys a private target, it provides the target's owners with a way to reduce their risk exposure by cashing out their investment in the private target and reinvesting in a diversified portfolio. This liquidity that the bidder provides to the owners of a private firm can be valuable and often is an important incentive for the target shareholders to agree to the takeover.

Earnings Growth

It is possible to combine two companies with the result that the earnings per share of the merged company exceed the pre-merger earnings per share of either company, *even when the merger itself creates no economic value.* Let's look at how this can happen.

EXAMPLE 24.2 Mergers and Earnings per Share

PROBLEM

Consider two corporations that both have earnings of $5 per share. The first firm, Upper Canada Enterprises, is a mature company with few growth opportunities. It has 1 million shares that are currently outstanding, priced at $60 per share. The second company, Lower Canada Corporation, is a young company with much more lucrative growth opportunities. Consequently, it has a higher value; although it has the same number of shares outstanding, its stock price is $100 per share. Assume Lower Canada acquires Upper Canada using its own stock, and the takeover adds no value. In a perfect market, what is the value of Lower Canada after the acquisition? At current market prices, how many shares must Lower Canada offer to Upper Canada's shareholders in exchange for their shares? Finally, what are Lower Canada's earnings per share after the acquisition?

SOLUTION

■ Plan

Because the takeover adds no value, the post-takeover value of Lower Canada is just the sum of the values of the two separate companies: $100 per share × 1 million shares + $60 per share × 1 million shares = $160 million. To acquire Upper Canada, Lower Canada must pay $60 million. We need to first calculate how many shares Lower Canada must issue to pay Upper Canada shareholders $60 million. The ratio of Lower Canada shares issued to Upper Canada shares will give us the exchange ratio. Once we know how many new shares will be issued, we can divide the total earnings of the combined company by the new total number of shares outstanding to get the earnings per share.

■ Execute

At its pre-takeover stock price of $100 per share, the deal requires issuing 600,000 shares ($60 million/$100 = 600,000). As a group, Upper Canada's shareholders will then exchange 1 million shares in Upper Canada for 600,000 shares in Lower Canada. The exchange ratio is the ratio of issued shares to exchanged shares: 600,000/1 million = 0.6. Therefore, each Upper Canada shareholder will get 0.6 shares in Lower Canada for each 1 share in Upper Canada. Notice that the price per share of Lower Canada stock is the same after the takeover: the new value of Lower Canada is $160 million, and there are 1.6 million shares outstanding, giving it a stock price of $100 per share. ▶

However, Lower Canada's earnings per share have changed. Prior to the takeover, both companies earned \$5/share × 1 million shares = \$5 million. The combined corporation thus earns \$10 million. There are 1.6 million shares outstanding after the takeover, so Lower Canada's post-takeover earnings per share are

$$EPS = \frac{\$10 \text{ million}}{1.6 \text{ million shares}} = \$6.25/\text{share}$$

By taking over Upper Canada, Lower Canada has raised its earnings per share by \$1.25.

■ Evaluate

Because no value was created, we can think of the combined company as simply a portfolio of Lower Canada and Upper Canada. Although the portfolio has higher total earnings per share, it also has lower growth, because we have combined the low-growth Upper Canada with the high-growth Lower Canada. The higher current earnings per share has come at a price—lower earnings per share growth.

As Example 24.2 demonstrates, by acquiring a company with low growth potential (and thus a low P/E multiple), a company with high growth potential (and high P/E multiple) can raise its earnings per share. In the past, people have cited this increase as a reason to merge. Of course, a savvy investor will see that the merger *adds no economic value*. All that has happened is that the high-growth company, by combining with a low-growth company, has lowered its overall growth rate. As a result, its P/E multiple should fall, which results from its earnings per share rising. Thus, we can draw no conclusion regarding whether a merger was beneficial solely by looking at its impact on the acquirer's earnings per share.

EXAMPLE 24.3 Mergers and the Price-Earnings Ratio

PROBLEM

Calculate Lower Canada's price-earnings ratio before and after the takeover described in Example 24.2.

SOLUTION

■ Plan

The price-earnings ratio is price per share/earnings per share. Lower Canada's price per share is \$100 both before and after the takeover, and its earnings per share is \$5 before and \$6.25 after the takeover.

■ Execute

Before the takeover, Lower Canada's price-earnings ratio is

$$P/E = \frac{\$100/\text{share}}{\$5/\text{share}} = 20$$

After the takeover, Lower Canada's price-earnings ratio is

$$P/E = \frac{\$100/\text{share}}{\$6.25/\text{share}} = 16$$

■ **Evaluate**

The price-earnings ratio has dropped to reflect the fact that after taking over Upper Canada, Lower Canada derives more of its value from earnings from current projects than from its future growth potential.

Managerial Motives to Merge

Most of the reasons given so far are economically motivated, shareholder-driven incentives to merge. However, managers sometimes have their own reasons to merge. Studies have consistently found that the stock price of large bidders drops on average when a bid is announced, especially when the target is publicly traded. Two possible explanations might be conflicts of interest with their shareholders and overconfidence.

Conflicts of Interest. Managers may prefer to run a larger company due to the additional pay and prestige it brings. Because most CEOs hold only a small fraction of their firm's stock, they may not bear enough of the cost of an otherwise bad merger that increases their personal benefits.[4] For example, a CEO who owns 1% of her firm's stock bears 1% of every dollar lost on a bad acquisition but enjoys 100% of the gains in compensation and prestige that come with being the CEO of a larger company. If the acquisition destroys $100 million in shareholder value but increases the present value of her compensation by more than $1 million, she will prefer to execute the merger anyway. Why would the board of directors create these incentives? Either due to poor monitoring of the manager, or belief that the strategy is correct even if the stock market disagrees, boards typically increase the pay of CEOs along with the size of the firm, even if the size comes at the expense of poorly performing acquisitions.[5]

Overconfidence. As explained in Chapter 10, people in general tend to be overconfident about their abilities. Psychological research has shown that it takes repeated failures for people to change their beliefs that they are above-average at some activity. Most CEOs perform, at most, one large acquisition during their tenure as CEO. In a well-known 1986 paper,[6] Richard Roll proposed the "hubris hypothesis" to explain takeovers, which maintains that overconfident CEOs pursue mergers that have a low chance of creating value because they truly believe that their ability to manage is great enough to succeed. The critical distinction between this hypothesis and the incentive conflict discussed above is that overconfident managers believe they are doing the right thing for their shareholders but irrationally overestimate their own abilities.

---

[4]M. Jensen highlighted the agency conflict in acquisition decisions in his 1986 paper, "Agency Costs of Free Cash Flow, Corporate Finance and Takeovers," *American Economic Review* 76(1986): 323–329.

[5]J. Harford and K. Li, "Decoupling CEO Wealth and Firm Performance: The Case of Acquiring CEOs," *Journal of Finance* 62(2007): 917–949, shows that in 75% of mergers where the acquiring shareholders lose money, acquiring CEOs are financially better off.

[6]R. Roll, "The Hubris Hypothesis of Corporate Takeovers," *Journal of Business* 59(2) (1986): 197–216.

Under the incentive conflict explanation, managers know they are destroying shareholder value but personally gain from doing so.

CONCEPT CHECK

5. What are the reasons most often cited for a takeover?
6. Explain why risk-diversification benefits and earnings growth are not good justifications for a takeover intended to increase shareholder wealth.

24.4 Valuation and the Takeover Process

In this section, we explore how the takeover process works. We begin by establishing how a bidder determines the initial offer. We then review the tax and accounting issues specific to a takeover and explain the regulatory approval process. We end by discussing board approval, including defensive strategies that boards implement to discourage takeovers.

Valuation

In Chapter 7, we demonstrated how to value the stock of a company. Recall that there are two broad categories of valuation approaches that can be applied here to valuing a target company. The first—and simplest—approach compares the target to other comparable companies. Although this approach is easy to implement, it gives at best a rough estimate of value. Valuing the target using a multiple based on comparable firms does not directly incorporate the operational improvements and other synergistic efficiencies that the acquirer intends to implement. Purchasing a corporation usually constitutes a very large capital investment decision, so it requires a more accurate estimate of value, including careful analysis of both operational aspects of the firm and the ultimate cash flows the deal will generate. Thus, the second approach to valuation requires making a projection of the expected cash flows that will result from the deal, and valuing those cash flows.

A key issue for takeovers is quantifying and discounting the value added as a result of the merger. As demonstrated in Section 24.3, a takeover can generate many different sources of value, which we can characterize as the takeover synergies.

Conceptually, we can separate the price paid for a target into its pre-bid market value plus a premium:

$$\text{Amount Paid} = \text{Target's Pre-Bid Market Capitalization} + \text{Acquisition Premium} \tag{24.1}$$

From the bidder's standpoint, the benefit from the acquisition includes both the standalone value of the target (what it is worth on its own) and any synergies created:

$$\text{Value Acquired} = \text{Target Stand-Alone Value} + \text{PV(Synergies)} \tag{24.2}$$

Comparing Equations 24.1 and 24.2, if we equate the pre-bid market capitalization with the stand-alone value of the target,[7] then from the bidder's perspective, the takeover is a positive-NPV project only if the premium it pays does not exceed the synergies created. Although the premium that is offered is a concrete number, the synergies are not—investors might well be skeptical of the acquirer's estimate of their magnitude. The bidder's stock price reaction to the announcement of the merger is one way to gauge investors' assessments of

[7]Rumours about a potential bid for the target will often push its share price up in anticipation of the premium offer. Practitioners refer to the "unaffected" target price, meaning the target's share price before it was affected by rumours of a takeover. This price would be used to compute the stand-alone value of the target.

whether the bidder overpaid or underpaid for the target. As Table 24.2 shows, the average stock price reaction is 1%, but as we noted, the median is closer to zero. Thus, the market, on average, believes that the premium is approximately equal to the synergies. Nonetheless, there is a large variation in the premium across deals. One recent large-scale study of the value effects of mergers found that positive reactions to bids are concentrated in smaller bidders. In fact, during the 1990s, 87 large public acquirers announced bids that resulted in $1 billion or more in value reduction at announcement.[8] This finding is likely related to some of the managerial motives discussed in the previous section.

The Offer

tender offer A public announcement of an offer to all existing security holders to buy a specified amount of outstanding securities at a prespecified price over a prespecified period of time.

exchange ratio In a takeover, the number of bidder shares received in exchange for each target share.

Once the acquirer has completed the valuation process, it is in the position to make a **tender offer**—that is, a public announcement of its intention to purchase a large block of shares for a specified price. A bidder can use either of two methods to pay for a target: cash or stock. In a cash transaction, the bidder simply pays for the target, including any premium, in cash. In a stock-swap transaction, the bidder pays for the target by issuing new stock and giving it to the target shareholders; that is, the bidder offers to swap target stock for acquirer stock. The "price" offered is determined by the **exchange ratio**—the number of bidder shares received in exchange for each target share—multiplied by the market price of the acquirer's stock.

A stock-swap merger is a positive-NPV investment for the acquiring shareholders if the share price of the merged firm (the acquirer's share price after the takeover) exceeds the premerger price of the acquiring firm. We can write this condition as follows. Let A be the premerger, or stand alone, value of the acquirer, and T be the premerger (standalone) value of the target. Let S be the value of the synergies created by the merger. If the acquirer has N_A shares outstanding before the merger at share price P_A and issues x new shares to pay for the target, then the acquirer's share price should increase post-acquisition if

$$\frac{A + T + S}{N_A + x} > \frac{A}{N_A} = P_A \tag{24.3}$$

The left side of Equation 24.3 is the share price of the merged firm. The numerator indicates the total value of the merged firm: the stand-alone value of the acquirer and target plus the value of the synergies created by the merger. The denominator represents the total number of shares outstanding once the merger is complete. The ratio is the post-merger share price.

The right side of Equation 24.3 is the premerger share price of the acquirer: the total premerger value of the acquirer divided by the premerger number of shares outstanding. We can rearrange Equation 24.3 to find the following condition for the acquirer to earn a positive NPV:

$$x P_A < T + S \tag{24.4}$$

Equation 24.4 simply states that the value of the shares offered, xPA, must be less than the value of the target plus the synergies created. If we let $P_T = T/N_T$ be the premerger value of the target, then we can rewrite this condition to find the maximum exchange ratio the acquirer should offer:

$$\text{Exchange Ratio} = \frac{x}{N_T} < \frac{P_T}{P_A}\left(1 + \frac{S}{T}\right) \tag{24.5}$$

[8]S. Moeller, R. Stulz, and F. Schlingemann, "Wealth Destruction on a Massive Scale: A Study of Acquiring Firm Returns in the Recent Merger Wave," *Journal of Finance* 60(2) (2005): 757–782.

For example, if the value of synergies equals 20% of the value of the target, you would be willing to pay an exchange ratio 20% higher than the current price ratio.

EXAMPLE 24.4 Maximum Exchange Ratio in a Stock Takeover

PROBLEM

At the time Sprint announced plans to acquire Nextel in December 2004, Sprint stock was trading for $25 per share and Nextel stock was trading for $30 per share. If the projected synergies were $12 billion, and Nextel had 1.033 billion shares outstanding, what is the maximum exchange ratio Sprint could offer in a stock swap and still generate a positive NPV? What is the maximum cash offer Sprint could make?

SOLUTION

■ Plan

We can use Equation 24.5 to compute the maximum shares Sprint could offer and still have a positive NPV. To compute the maximum cash offer, we can calculate the synergies per share and add that to Nextel's current share price.

■ Execute

To use Equation 24.5, we must first calculate T:

$$T = \$30/\text{share} \times 1.033 \text{ billion shares} = \$31 \text{ billion}$$

and thus the Exchange Ratio $< \frac{P_T}{P_A}\left(1 + \frac{S}{T}\right) = \frac{30}{25}\left(1 + \frac{12}{31}\right) = 1.665$

That is, Sprint could offer up to 1.665 shares of Sprint stock for each share of Nextel stock and generate a positive NPV.

For a cash offer, given synergies of $12 billion/1.033 billion shares = $11.62 per share, Sprint could offer up to $30 + 11.62 = $41.62.

■ Evaluate

Both the cash amount and the exchange offer ($25 × 1.665 = $41.62) have the same value. That value is the most that Nextel is worth to Sprint—if Sprint pays $41.62 for Nextel, it is paying full price plus paying Nextel shareholders for all the synergy gains created, leaving none for Sprint shareholders. Thus, at $41.62, buying Nextel is exactly a zero-NPV project.

Merger "Arbitrage"

Once a tender offer is announced, there is no guarantee that, in fact, the takeover will take place at this price. Often acquirers have to raise the price to consummate the deal. Alternatively, the offer may fail. When an acquirer bids for a target, the target firm's board may not accept the bid and may recommend that existing shareholders not tender their shares, even when the acquirer offers a significant premium over the pre-offer share price. Even if the target board supports the deal, there is also the possibility that regulators might not approve the takeover. When the London Stock Exchange (LSE) and the TMX Group (the owner of the TSX in Canada) agreed to merge in 2011, the price of TMX did not reflect what its value would be if the merger succeeded, because of substantial doubt as to whether the needed approval from the provincial and federal authorities would occur. Because of this uncertainty about whether a takeover will succeed, the market price generally does not rise by the amount of the premium when the takeover is announced. In the LSE-TMX case, the merger never went through. The TMX was subsequently bought out by a consortium led by a group of banks.

risk arbitrageurs Traders who, once a takeover offer is announced, speculate on the outcome of the deal.

This uncertainty creates an opportunity for investors to speculate on the outcome of the deal. Traders known as **risk arbitrageurs**, who believe that they can predict the outcome of a deal, take positions based on their beliefs. While the strategies these traders use are sometimes referred to as arbitrage, they are actually quite risky, so they do not represent a true arbitrage opportunity in the sense we have defined in this book. Let's illustrate the strategy using the 2002 stock-swap merger of Hewlett-Packard (HP) and Compaq.

In September 2001, HP announced that it would purchase Compaq by swapping 0.6325 shares of HP stock for each share of Compaq stock. After the announcement, HP traded for \$18.87 per share, so the implied value of HP's offer was $\$18.87 \times 0.6325 = \$11.9353$. Yet, the price of Compaq was only \$11.08 per share after the announcement, \$0.8553 below the value of HP's offer. Thus, a risk arbitrageur who simultaneously purchased 10,000 Compaq shares and sold short 6325 HP shares would net $6325 \times \$18.87 - 10{,}000 \times \$11.08 = \$8553$ immediately. Then, if the takeover was successfully completed on the original terms, the 10,000 Compaq shares would convert into 6325 HP shares, allowing the risk arbitrageur to cover the short position in HP and be left with no net exposure. Thus, the arbitrageur would pocket the original \$8553 as a profit.[9]

merger-arbitrage spread In a takeover, the difference between a target stock's price and the implied offer price.

The potential profit described above arises from the difference between the target's stock price and the implied offer price, and is referred to as the **merger-arbitrage spread**. However, it is not a true arbitrage opportunity, because there is a risk that the deal will not go through. If the takeover did not ultimately succeed, the risk arbitrageur would eventually have to unwind his position at whatever market prices prevailed. In most cases, these prices would have moved against him (in particular, the price of Compaq would be likely to decline if the takeover did not occur), so he would face losses on the position.

The HP-Compaq takeover was distinctive in that the uncertainty about the success of the deal stemmed largely from acquirer discomfort with the deal rather than from target shareholder discomfort. Although initially supportive of the merger, the Hewlett family got cold feet. About two months after the deal was announced, Walter Hewlett disclosed his family's opposition to it. On the day of Walter Hewlett's announcement, the price of HP stock rose to \$19.81, while Compaq's stock price fell to \$8.50, causing the merger-arbitrage spread to widen to $\$19.81 \times 6325 - \$8.5 \times 10{,}000 = \$40{,}298$. We plot the merger-arbitrage spread for the HP-Compaq merger in Figure 24.2. The risk-arbitrage strategy outlined above is effectively a short position on this spread, which pays off if the spread declines. Thus, an arbitrageur who opened the strategy when the deal was announced and closed it after Walter Hewlett announced his opposition would face a loss of $\$40{,}298 - \$8553 = \$31{,}745$.

Although the Hewlett family members were large shareholders of HP, they were not controlling shareholders; they did not have enough shares to block the deal single-handedly. Hence, a battle for control of HP ensued between the Hewlett family and then-

[9]For simplicity, we are ignoring dividend payments made during the period. HP paid \$0.24 and Compaq paid \$0.075 in dividends prior to the completion of the merger, reducing slightly the profit from the trade by $10{,}000 \times \$0.075 - 6325 \times \$0.24 = -\$768$.

FIGURE 24.2 Merger-Arbitrage Spread for the Merger of HP and Compaq

The plot shows the potential profit, given that the merger was ultimately successfully completed, from purchasing 10,000 Compaq shares and short-selling 6325 HP shares on the indicated date. A risk arbitrageur who expects the deal to go through can profit by opening the position when the spread is large and closing the position after it declines.

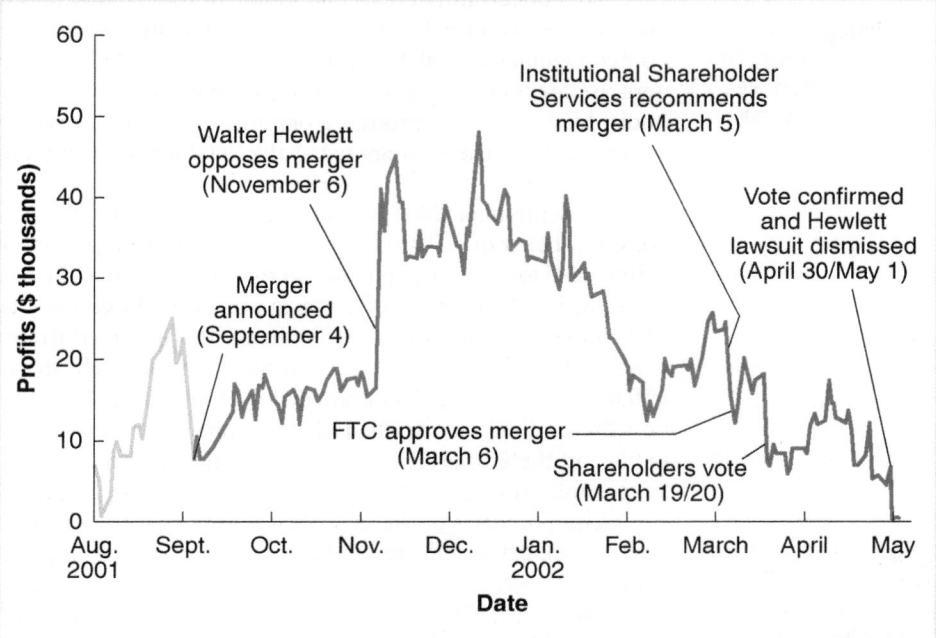

CEO Carly Fiorina, the driving force behind the acquisition of Compaq. This conflict was resolved months later only when HP shareholders, by a slim margin, voted in favour of issuing new shares, thereby effectively approving the merger and netting a profit for any risk arbitrageur who stayed the course. As is clear from Figure 24.2, arbitrageurs who did not have the stomach to hold on would have faced large losses at several points during the roller-coaster ride. And while HP CEO Carly Fiorina survived this early challenge to her authority, the performance of HP following the merger vindicated Hewlett's position. HP's board ultimately fired Fiorina in 2005.

Tax and Accounting Issues

Once the terms of trade have been decided, the tax and accounting implications of a merger can be determined. How the acquirer pays for the target affects the taxes of both the target shareholders and the combined firm. Any cash received in full or partial exchange for shares triggers an immediate tax liability for target shareholders. They will have to pay a capital gains tax on the difference between the price paid for their shares in the takeover and the price they paid when they first bought the shares. If the acquirer pays for the takeover entirely by exchanging bidder stock for target stock, then the tax liability is deferred until the target shareholders actually sell their new shares of bidder stock.

step up Increase the book value of a target's assets to the purchase price when an acquirer purchases those assets directly instead of purchasing the target stock.

If the acquirer purchases the target assets directly (rather than the target stock), then the acquirer can **step up** the book value of the target's assets to the purchase price.

This higher depreciable basis reduces future taxes through larger depreciation charges. The same treatment applies to a *forward cash-out merger*, in which the target is merged into the acquirer and target shareholders receive cash in exchange for their shares.

While the method of payment (cash or stock) affects how the value of the target's assets is recorded for tax purposes, it does not affect the combined firm's financial statements for financial reporting. The combined firm must mark up the value assigned to the target's assets on the financial statements by allocating the purchase price to target assets according to their fair market value. If the purchase price exceeds the fair market value of the target's identifiable assets, then the remainder is recorded as goodwill and is examined annually by the firm's accountants to determine whether its value has decreased. For example, in HP's takeover of Compaq, HP recorded more than $10 billion in goodwill. The footnotes to the statements attributed the goodwill to the value of the Compaq brand name, which is assumed to have an indefinite life.

Even when a merger has a positive NPV, bidding managers are typically very concerned with the effect of the merger on earnings. This is the other side of the earnings-growth argument as a reason to merge. Just as merging two companies can increase earnings without affecting economic value, it can also decrease earnings without affecting economic value. Nevertheless, acquirers are hesitant to commit to a deal that would be dilutive to earnings per share, even if only in the short run.

Board and Shareholder Approval

For a merger to proceed, both the target and the acquiring board of directors must approve the deal and put the question to a vote of the shareholders of the target (and, in some cases, the shareholders of the acquiring firm as well).

friendly takeover A takeover in which the target's board of directors supports a merger, negotiates with potential acquirers, and agrees on a price that is ultimately put to a shareholder vote.

hostile takeover A takeover in which an individual or organization, sometimes referred to as a corporate raider, purchases a large fraction of a target corporation's stock and in doing so gets enough votes to replace the target's board of directors and its CEO.

corporate raider (or **raider)** The acquirer in a hostile takeover.

In a **friendly takeover**, the target board of directors supports the merger, negotiates with potential acquirers, and agrees on a price that is ultimately put to a shareholder vote. Although it is rare for acquiring boards to oppose a merger, target boards sometimes do not support the deal even when the acquirer offers a large premium. In a **hostile takeover**, the board of directors (together with upper-level management) fights the takeover attempt. To succeed, the acquirer must garner enough shares to take control of the target and replace the board of directors. When a takeover is hostile, the acquirer is often called a **corporate raider (**or **raider)**.

If the shareholders of a target company receive a premium over the current market value of their shares, why would a board of directors ever oppose a takeover? There are a number of reasons. The board might legitimately believe that the offer price is too low. In this case, a suitor that is willing to pay more might be found or the original bidder might be convinced to raise its offer. Alternatively, if the offer is a stock swap, target management may oppose the offer because they feel the acquirer's shares are overvalued, and, therefore, that the value of the offer is actually less than the stand-alone value of the target. Finally, managers (and the board) might oppose a takeover because of their own self-interests, especially if the primary motivation for the takeover is efficiency gains. In this case, the acquirer probably plans to undertake a complete change of leadership of the corporation. Upper-level managers could view opposing the merger as a way of protecting their jobs (and the jobs of their employees). In fact, this concern is perhaps the single biggest reason for the negative associations that hostile takeovers generate. Bear in mind that if substantial efficiency gains are indeed possible, current management is not doing an effective job. A takeover, or threat thereof, might be the only recourse investors have to fix the problem.

In theory, the duty of the target board of directors is to choose the course of action that is in the best interests "of the corporation" in Canada or in the best interests "of the target shareholders" in the United States. In practice, the courts in the United States and, more recently, in Canada have given target directors wide latitude under what is called the "business judgment rule" to determine the best course for their companies, including spurning a premium offer if the directors can reasonably argue that more value will eventually be realized for their shareholders by remaining independent. The premise of this rule is that absent evidence of misconduct or self-dealing, the court will not substitute its judgment for that of the elected, informed directors.

In merger transactions, however, there is heightened judicial scrutiny under what is commonly referred to as the "Revlon duties" and "Unocal," named after the U.S. cases in which they were established. The Revlon duties state that if a change of control is going to occur, then directors must seek the highest value (they cannot favour one controlling entity over another based on anything other than value to shareholders). In Canada, the Supreme Court rejected the precedent from the Revlon case and required that no one stakeholder (equity holder or debt holder) be given priority by a target's management in their response to a takeover attempt. The Unocal case, in the United States, established that when the board takes actions deemed as defensive (we discuss these in detail in the next section), its actions are subject to extra scrutiny to ensure that they are not coercive or designed simply to preclude a deal. The board must believe that there is a threat to its corporate strategy, and the board's defences must be proportional to the magnitude of the threat. Rulings similar to the Unocal case have emerged in Canada.

CONCEPT CHECK

7. What are the steps in the takeover process?
8. What do risk arbitrageurs do?

24.5 Takeover Defences

For a hostile takeover to succeed, the acquirer must go around the target board and appeal directly to the target shareholders. The acquirer can do this by making an unsolicited offer to buy target stock directly from the shareholders (a tender offer). The acquirer will usually couple this with a **proxy fight**: the acquirer attempts to convince target shareholders to unseat the target board by using their proxy votes to support the acquirer's candidates for election to the target board. Target companies have a number of strategies available to them to stop this process. These strategies can force a bidder to raise its bid or entrench management more securely, depending on the independence of the target board. We begin with the most effective defensive strategy, the poison pill.

proxy fight In a hostile takeover, the acquirer's attempts to convince the target's shareholders to unseat the target's board by using their proxy votes to support the acquirer's candidates for election to the target's board.

Poison Pills

A **poison pill** is a rights offering that gives existing target shareholders the right to buy shares in the target or the acquirer at a deeply discounted price once certain conditions are met. The acquirer is specifically excluded from this right. Because target shareholders can purchase shares at less than the market price, the rights offering dilutes the value of any shares held by the acquirer. This dilution makes the takeover so expensive for the acquiring shareholders that they choose to pass on the deal.

poison pill A rights offering that gives the target shareholders the right to buy shares in either the target or an acquirer at a deeply discounted price, as a defence against a hostile takeover.

The poison pill was invented in 1982 by a takeover lawyer, Martin Lipton, who successfully warded off a takeover attempt of El Paso Electric by General American Oil.[10] Because the original poison pill goes into effect only in the event of a complete takeover

[10]For a brief history, see Len Costa, "The Perfect Pill," *Legal Affairs* (March 2005), www.legalaffairs.org.

(i.e., a purchase of 100% of the outstanding shares), one way to circumvent it is to not do a complete takeover. The first time this work-around was used was by Sir James Goldsmith, who took control of Crown Zellerbach by purchasing slightly more than 50% of the outstanding stock. Because he did not purchase the rest, Crown Zellerbach's poison pill was ineffective.

In response to the takeover of Crown Zellerbach, corporate lawyers have perfected the original poison pill. Most poison pills now specify that if a raider acquires more than a trigger amount (typically 20%) of the target shares (but chooses not to execute a complete takeover by purchasing all outstanding shares), existing shareholders—with the exception of the acquirer—have the right to buy more shares in the target at a discounted price.

The term *poison pill* comes from the world of espionage. Once caught, a spy is supposed to take his own life by swallowing a poison pill rather than give up important secrets. Poison pills are very effective in stopping takeovers, but where is the suicide analogy? The answer is that by adopting a poison pill, a company effectively entrenches its management by making it much more difficult for shareholders to replace bad managers, thereby potentially destroying value. Financial research has verified this effect. A firm's stock price typically drops when it adopts a poison pill. Furthermore, once firms have adopted poison pills, these same firms have below-average financial performance.[11]

Not surprisingly, companies adopting poison pills are harder to take over, and when a takeover occurs, the premium that existing shareholders receive for their stock is higher. Therefore, because a poison pill increases the cost of a takeover, all else being equal, a target company must be in worse shape (there must be a greater opportunity for profit) to justify the expense of waging a takeover battle.

A poison pill also increases the bargaining power of the target firm when negotiating with the acquirer, because completing the takeover is more difficult without the cooperation of the target board. If used effectively, this bargaining power can allow target shareholders to capture more of the takeover gains by negotiating a higher premium than they would get if no pill existed. Numerous studies on the impact of antitakeover provisions on takeovers have found that such provisions result in higher premiums accruing to existing shareholders of the target company.[12]

Staggered Boards

staggered (classified) board In some public companies, a board of directors whose three-year terms are staggered so that only one-third of the directors are up for election each year.

A determined bidder that faces a poison pill has another available option—get its own slate of directors for the target board, which it can submit at the next annual shareholders meeting. If the target shareholders elect those candidates, then the new directors can cancel the poison pill and accept the bidder's offer. To prevent such a coup from happening, about two-thirds of public companies in the United States have a **staggered (classified) board**. These are less typical in Canada. In a typical staggered board, every director serves a three-year term and the terms are staggered so that only one-third of the directors are up for election each year. Thus, even if the bidder's candidates win board seats, the bidder

[11]P. Malatesta and R. Walkling, "Poison Pill Securities: Stockholder Wealth, Profitability and Ownership Structure," *Journal of Financial Economics* 20(1) (1988): 347–376; M. Ryngaert, "The Effects of Poison Pills Securities on Stockholder Wealth," *Journal of Financial Economics* 20(1) (1988): 377–417; and D. Stangeland, "Why Are Anti-Takeover Devices Being Used?" *Business Quarterly*, 1995.

[12]R. Comment and G. W. Schwert, "Poison or Placebo: Evidence on the Deterrence and Wealth Effects of Modern Antitakeover Measures," *Journal of Financial Economics* 39(1), (1995): 3–43; N. Varaiya, "Determinants of Premiums in Acquisition Transactions," *Managerial and Decision Economics* 8(3) (1987): 175–184; and R. Heron and E. Lie, "On the Use of Poison Pills and Defensive Payouts by Takeover Targets," *Journal of Business* 79(4) (2006): 1783–1807.

will control only a minority of the target board. A bidder's candidate would have to win a proxy fight two years in a row before the bidder had a majority presence on the target board. The length of time required to execute this manoeuvre can deter a bidder from making a takeover attempt when the target board is staggered. Most experts consider a poison pill combined with a staggered board to be the most effective defence available to a target company. While staggered boards and poison pills are an effective defense against hostile takeovers, preventing such takeovers may not be in shareholders' best interest. Indeed, many investors have come to view these mechanisms as fostering management entrenchment, allowing subpar managers to escape market discipline. Increased shareholder activism in the 2000s has led to dramatic decline in the use of these devices.

White Knights

white knight A target company's defence against a hostile takeover attempt, in which the target looks for another, friendlier company to acquire it.

white squire A variant of the white knight defence, in which a large, passive investor or firm agrees to purchase a substantial block of shares in a target with special voting rights.

When a hostile takeover appears to be inevitable, a target company will sometimes look for another, friendlier company to acquire it. This company that comes charging to the target's rescue is known as a **white knight**. The white knight will make a more lucrative offer for the target than the hostile bidder did. Incumbent managers of the target maintain control by reaching an agreement with the white knight to retain their positions.

One variant on the white knight defence is the **white squire** defence. In this case, a large investor or firm agrees to purchase a substantial block of shares in the target with special voting rights. This action prevents a hostile raider from acquiring control of the target. The idea is that the white squire itself will not choose to exercise its control rights.

Golden Parachutes

golden parachute An extremely lucrative severance package that is guaranteed to a firm's senior managers in the event that the firm is taken over and the managers are let go.

A **golden parachute** is an extremely lucrative severance package that is guaranteed to a firm's senior managers in the event that the firm is taken over and the managers are let go. For example, when Procter & Gamble acquired The Gillette Company in 2005, Gillette CEO James Kilts was reported to have received a severence package worth $165 million.

Golden parachutes have been criticized because they are seen both as excessive and a misuse of shareholder wealth. In fact, the empirical evidence does not support this view.[13] If anything, it supports the view that an adoption of a golden parachute actually creates value. If a golden parachute exists, management will be more likely to be receptive to a takeover. Gillette CEO James Kilts is a case in point. He reportedly solicited the offer from Procter & Gamble, which long coveted Gillette. This means the existence of golden parachutes lessens the likelihood of managerial entrenchment. Researchers have found that stock prices rise on average when companies announce that they plan to implement a golden parachute policy, and that the number of firms bidding against one another for the target and the size of the takeover premium are higher if a golden parachute agreement exists.

Recapitalization

Another defence against a takeover is a recapitalization, in which a company changes its capital structure to make itself less attractive as a target. For example, a company with a lot of cash might choose to pay out a large dividend. Companies without a lot of cash might instead choose to issue debt and then use the proceeds to pay a dividend or repurchase stock.

---

[13]M. Narayanan and A. Sundaram, "A Safe Landing? Golden Parachutes and Corporate Behavior," *University of Michigan Business School Working Paper No. 98015* (1998).

Why does increasing leverage make a firm less attractive as a target? In many cases, a substantial portion of the synergy gains that an acquirer anticipates from a takeover are from tax savings from an increase in leverage as well as other cost reductions. By increasing leverage on its own, the target firm can reap the benefit of the interest tax shields. In addition, the need to generate cash to meet the debt service obligations provides a powerful motivation to managers to run a corporation efficiently. In effect, the restructuring itself can produce efficiency gains, often removing the principal motivation for the takeover in the first place.

Other Defensive Strategies

Corporate managers and defence advisors have devised other mechanisms to forestall a takeover. A corporation's charter can require a supermajority (sometimes as much as 80%) of votes to approve a merger. It can also restrict the voting rights of very large shareholders. Finally, a firm can require that a "fair" price be paid for the company, where the determination of what is "fair" is up to the board of directors or senior management. Beauty is always in the eye of the beholder, so "fair" in this case usually implies an optimistic determination of value.

We might expect the presence of defensive strategies to reduce firm value. However, Gregg Jarrell and Annette Poulsen[14] found that, on average, the public announcement of antitakeover amendments by 600 firms in the period 1979 to 1985 had an insignificant effect on the value of announcing firms' shares.

Regulatory Approval

All mergers must be approved by regulators. In Section 24.3, we discussed monopoly gains from takeovers and the use of antitrust regulations to limit them and protect the free enterprise system. In Canada, the Competition Bureau monitors potential monopoly combinations. In the United States, antitrust enforcement is governed by three main statutes: the Sherman Act, the Clayton Act, and the Hart-Scott-Rodino Act. The Sherman Act of 1890, which was passed in response to the formation of huge oil trusts, such as Standard Oil, prohibits mergers that would create a monopoly or undue market control. The Clayton Act, enacted in 1914, strengthened the government's hand by prohibiting companies from acquiring the stock (or, as later amended, the assets) of another company if it would adversely affect competition. Under both the Sherman and Clayton acts, the government had to sue to block a merger. Often by the time a decision was rendered, the merger had taken place and was difficult to undo. The Hart-Scott-Rodino (HSR) Act of 1976 put the burden of proof on the merging parties. Under the HSR Act, all mergers above a certain size (the formula for determining whether a transaction qualifies is complicated, but it comes out to approximately $60 million) must be approved by the government before the proposed takeovers occur. The government cannot delay the deal indefinitely, however, because it must respond with approval or a request for additional information within 20 days of receiving notification of the proposed merger. The U.S. government has been very active in enforcing competition policy and is rated by the Global Competition Review in the "elite" category for enforcement. (The United Kingdom and European Union competition commissions are also rated elite.) Some criticisms have been made regarding Canada's Competition Bureau, because it does not appear to act as vigorously. Canada's Competition Bureau was rated in the "good" category by the Global Competition Review.

---

[14]G. Jarrell and A. Poulsen, "Shark Repellents and Stock Prices: The Effects of Antitakeover Amendments Since 1980," *Journal of Financial Economics* 19(1988): 127–168.

WEYERHAEUSER'S HOSTILE BID FOR WILLAMETTE INDUSTRIES

In November 2000, Weyerhaeuser, a forest products company based in Federal Way, Washington, announced a hostile bid of $48 per share for its smaller neighbour, Willamette Industries, based in Portland, Oregon. Weyerhaeuser had been pursuing Willamette in private since 1998, when Steve Rogel unexpectedly resigned as CEO of Willamette to become CEO of Weyerhaeuser. Each time Rogel approached his old employer in private, he was rebuffed. The response to the hostile tender offer was no different. Despite the fact that the bid represented a substantial premium to the firm's pre-bid stock price, the Willamette board rejected the offer and urged its shareholders not to tender their shares to Weyerhaeuser.

Willamette's defences included a staggered board and a poison pill, so Weyerhaeuser made its tender offer conditional on Willamette's board cancelling the poison pill. Consequently, Weyerhaeuser initiated a proxy fight at the next annual shareholders' meeting in June 2001. One of the directors up for re-election at that time was Duane McDougall, Willamette's CEO. One month before the meeting, Weyerhaeuser increased its offer to $50 per share, but Willamette's board still believed that the offer was too low and worried that too many of its long-time employees would face layoffs after the merger. Nonetheless, at the annual meeting, Weyerhaeuser's slate received 1.4% more votes than Willamette's, thereby removing Willamette's CEO from its board.

The loss of the board seats did not change Willamette's position. Willamette unsuccessfully searched for a white knight to generate a bidding contest that would force Weyerhaeuser to up its bid. It also entered into talks to buy Georgia-Pacific's building products division. Such a deal would have increased its size and added enough debt to its balance sheet to render the firm unattractive to Weyerhaeuser.

In the end, Weyerhaeuser increased its offer to $55.50 per share in January 2002, and Willamette finally agreed to a deal and called off its negotiations with Georgia-Pacific. Even without the presence of other bidders, Willamette's board was able to get what it considered to be a fair price from Weyerhaeuser.

The European Commission has established a process similar to the process under the HSR Act, which requires merging parties to notify the EC, provide additional information if requested about the proposed merger, and wait for approval before proceeding. As discussed in the Honeywell/GE example, even though the EC technically lacks legal authority to block a merger of foreign companies, it can stop a takeover by imposing restrictions on the combined firm's operations and sales in Europe. Although globally a proposed takeover might have to satisfy antitrust rules in more than 80 jurisdictions, practically the most important jurisdictions besides the home jurisdiction of the firm are Europe and the United States.

Another regulatory hurdle may come into play when a merger involves companies in two different countries. Many countries have regulatory authorities that oversee foreign takeovers, and they may prevent foreign takeovers that are not in the best interest of their own country. Canada is one such country. A transaction may require approval under the Investment Canada Act (ICA) if the size of the transaction exceeds a specified threshold ($354 million as of 2014). When a company with assets of $354 million or more will transfer from Canadian control to foreign control, the transaction will be subject to regulatory review.[15] The proposed takeover of Saskatchewan-based PotashCorp (the world's largest fertilizer company by capacity) was a notable example of the importance of this Canadian regulatory feature. Management at PotashCorp lobbied vigorously in the media and with the provincial and federal governments to block the takeover of PotashCorp by BHP Billiton, because PotashCorp was a strategic resource in Canada and the takeover would not be good for Canadians. Eventually the takeover was cancelled following the ruling by Industry Minister Tony Clement that the takeover did not pass the "net benefit assessment" under the ICA.

[15]The threshold of $354 million is applied in cases where the acquiring company is a member of the World Trade Organization (WTO). In cases where the acquirer is not a WTO member, thresholds for review are much lower.

Regulatory approval can block mergers of companies that want to merge or it can be used by a target (with appropriate lobbying) as a method to defend against unwanted takeovers.

CONCEPT CHECK

9. What defensive strategies are available to help target companies resist an unwanted takeover?

10. How can a hostile acquirer get around a poison pill?

24.6 Who Gets the Value Added from a Takeover?

Now that we have explained the takeover process, we can return to the remaining questions posed at the beginning of this chapter—why does the price of the acquiring company not rise at the announcement of the takeover, and why is the bidder forced to pay a premium for the target?

You might imagine that the people who do the work of acquiring the corporation and replacing its management will capture the value created by the merger. Based on the average stock price reaction, it does not appear that the acquiring corporation generally captures this value. Instead, the premium the acquirer pays is approximately equal to the value it adds, which means the *target* shareholders ultimately capture the value added by the acquirer. To see why, we need to understand how market forces react to a takeover announcement.

The Free Rider Problem

Assume you are one of the one million shareholders of HighLife Corporation, all of whom own one share of stock. HighLife has no debt. Its chief executive is not doing a good job, preferring to spend his time using the company's jets to fly to the corporate condo in Whistler, B.C., rather than running the company in Regina. As such, the shares are trading at a substantial discount. They currently have a price of $45 per share, giving HighLife a market value of $45 million. Under a competent manager, the company would be worth $75 million. HighLife's corporate charter specifies that a simple majority is required to make all decisions, so to take control of HighLife a shareholder must purchase half the outstanding shares.

Suppose Mr. T. Boone Icon decides to fix the situation (and make a profit at the same time) by making a tender offer to buy half the outstanding shares for $60 per share in cash. If fewer than 50% of the shareholders tender their shares, the deal is off.

In principle, this idea could land T. Boone a handsome profit. If 50% of shareholders tender their shares, those shares will cost him $\$60 \times 500{,}000 = \$30$ million. Once he has control of the firm, he can replace the managers. When the executive jets and the Whistler condo are sold and the market realizes that the new managers are serious about improving performance, the market value of the firm will rise to $75 million. Hence T. Boone's shares will be worth $75 per share, netting him a profit of $\$15 \times 500{,}000 = \$7.5$ million. But will 50% of the shareholders tender their shares?

The offer price of $60 per share exceeds the value of the firm if the takeover does not go through ($45 per share). Hence, the offer is a good deal for shareholders overall. But if all shareholders tender their shares, as an individual shareholder, you could do better by not tendering your share. Then if T. Boone takes control, each of your shares will be worth $75 rather than the $60 you would get by tendering. In this case, it is wiser to not tender. Of course, if all shareholders think this way, no one will tender their shares, and T. Boone's deal will not get off the ground. The only way to persuade shareholders to tender their shares is to offer them at least $75 per share, which removes any profit opportunity for T. Boone. The problem here is that existing shareholders do not have to invest time and effort but still participate in all the gains from the takeover that Mr. T. Boone Icon generates—hence the term "free rider problem." By sharing the gains in this way, T. Boone Icon is forced to give up substantial profits and thus will likely choose not to bother at all.

Toeholds

One way for Mr. T. Boone Icon to get around the problem of shareholders' reluctance to tender their shares is to buy the shares in the market anonymously. However, Canadian securities laws and the SEC in the United States make it difficult for investors to buy much more than about 10% of a firm in secret.[16] After T. Boone acquires such an initial stake in the target, called a **toehold**, he would have to make his intentions public by informing investors of his large stake. To successfully gain control of HighLife, he would have to announce a tender offer to buy an additional 40% of the shares for $75 per share. Once in control, he would be able to sell his stake for $75 per share. Assuming he accumulated the first 10% for $50 per share, his profits in this case will be $\$25 \times 100{,}000 = \$2.5$ million. Not bad, but substantially less than the value he is adding.

toehold An initial ownership stake in a firm that a corporate raider can use to initiate a takeover attempt.

Why should investors care whether T. Boone's profits are substantially lower than the value he is adding? The answer is that people like T. Boone perform an important service. Because of the threat that such a person might attempt to take over their company and fire them, chief executives are less likely to shirk their duties. Thus, the more profitable we make this activity, the less likely we will have to resort to it. If $2.5 million is not enough to justify T. Boone's time and effort, he will not try to acquire HighLife. Current management will remain entrenched, and T. Boone will think about acquiring the company only if further erosion in the stock price makes the deal lucrative enough for him.

A number of legal mechanisms exist that allow acquirers to avoid the free rider problem and capture more of the gains from the acquisition. Next we describe the two most common, the leveraged buyout and the freezeout merger.

The Leveraged Buyout

The good news for shareholders is that another significantly lower-cost mechanism allows people like T. Boone Icon to take over companies and fire underperforming managers. Recall from Chapter 15 that this mechanism is called the leveraged buyout (LBO). Let's illustrate how it works by returning to HighLife Corporation.

Assume that T. Boone chooses not to buy any shares in the market secretly, but instead announces a tender offer for half the outstanding shares at a price of $50 per share. However, instead of using his own cash to pay for these shares, he borrows the money through a shell corporation (one that is created for the sole purpose of making the acquisition) by *pledging the shares themselves as collateral on the loan*. The only time he will need the money is if the tender offer succeeds, so the banks lending the

[16]In Canada, the rules require an investor to issue a press release once the 10% threshold is reached. If a takeover bid is already outstanding, a 5% threshold triggers the requirement for a press release. In the United States, the rules actually require that any shareholder who owns more than 5% of a firm publicly disclose this fact, but the time delays in the disclosure process allow investors to accumulate more than 5% of the firm before this information is made public.

money can be certain that he will have control of the collateral. Even more important, if the tender offer succeeds, with control of the company, T. Boone can merge the target with the shell corporation, effectively attaching the loans directly to the target—that is, it is as if the target corporation, and not T. Boone, has borrowed the money. At the end of this process, T. Boone still owns half the shares, but the *corporation* is responsible for repaying the loan. T. Boone has effectively acquired half the shares without paying for them!

You might imagine that no shareholder would be willing to tender her shares under these circumstances. Surprisingly, this conclusion is wrong. If you tender your shares, you will receive $50 for each of them. If you do not tender your shares, but enough other shareholders do, then T. Boone will take control of the company. After he replaces the managers, the enterprise value of the company will be $75 million. What will your shares be worth if you did not tender them?

For simplicity, assume that there are no frictions or taxes. To gain control of the firm, T. Boone borrowed $25 million to purchase half the outstanding shares ($50 × 500,000). Because this debt is now attached to HighLife, the total value of HighLife's equity is just the total value of the company, minus the value of debt:

$$\text{Total Value of HighLife Equity} = \$75 \text{ million} - \$25 \text{ million} = \$50 \text{ million}$$

The total number of outstanding shares is the same (remember that T. Boone purchased existing shares), so the price per share is $50 million ÷ 1 million = $50/share. If the tender offer succeeds, you will be indifferent. Whether you tender your shares or keep them, each is always worth $50. If you keep your shares and the tender offer fails, the price per share stays at $45. Clearly, it is always in your best interests to tender your shares, so T. Boone's tender offer will succeed. T. Boone also makes substantially more profits than he would if he used a toehold strategy—his profits are the value of his shares upon completion of the takeover: $50 × 500,000 = $25 million.

EXAMPLE 24.5 Leveraged Buyout

PROBLEM

FAT Corporation stock is currently trading at $40 per share. There are 20 million shares outstanding, and the company has no debt. You are a partner in a firm that specializes in leveraged buyouts. Your analysis indicates that the management of this corporation could be improved considerably. If the managers were replaced with more capable ones, you estimate that the value of the company would increase by 50%. You decide to initiate a leveraged buyout and issue a tender offer for at least a controlling interest—50% of the outstanding shares. What is the maximum amount of value you can extract and still complete the deal?

SOLUTION

■ Plan

Currently, the value of the company is $40 × 20 million = $800 million, and you estimate you can add an additional 50%, or $400 million. If you borrow $400 million and the tender offer succeeds, you will take control of the company and install new management. The total value of the company will increase by 50% to $1.2 billion. You will also attach the debt to the company, so the company will now have $400 million in debt. You can then compute the value of the post-takeover equity and your gain. You can repeat this computation assuming you borrow more than $400 million and confirming that your gain does not change. ▶

Execute

The value of the equity once the deal is done is the total value minus the debt outstanding:

$$\text{Total Equity} = \$1200 \text{ million} - \$400 \text{ million} = \$800 \text{ million}$$

The value of the equity is the same as the pre-merger value. You own half the shares, which are worth $400 million, and paid nothing for them, so you have captured the value you anticipated adding to FAT.

What if you borrowed more than $400 million? Assume you were able to borrow $450 million. The value of equity after the merger would be as follows:

$$\text{Total Equity} = \$1200 \text{ million} - \$450 \text{ million} = \$750 \text{ million}$$

This is lower than the pre-merger value. Recall, however, that in Canada and the United States, existing shareholders must be offered at least the pre-merger price for their shares. Because existing shareholders anticipate that the share price will be lower once the deal is complete, all shareholders will tender their shares. This implies that you will have to pay $800 million for these shares, and so to complete the deal, you will have to pay $800 million − $450 million = $350 million out of your own pocket. In the end, you will own all the equity, which is worth $750 million. You paid $350 million for it, so your profit is again $400 million.

Evaluate

In each case, the most you can gain is the $400 million in value you add by taking over FAT. Thus, you cannot extract more value than the value you add to the company by taking it over.

The examples we have illustrated are extreme in that the acquirer takes over the target without paying any premium and with no initial investment. In practice, premiums in LBO transactions are often quite substantial—while they can avoid the free rider problem, acquirers must still get board approval to overcome other defences such as poison pills, as well as outbid other potential acquirers. Also, lenders typically require that the acquirer have a substantial equity stake as protection for the debt holders, in case the claimed post-acquisition benefits do not materialize. In the $15.2 billion Hertz LBO (at the time, the second largest in history), which we described in Chapter 15, the acquirers contributed $2.3 billion in cash out of a total of $5.6 billion that was paid for Hertz's equity.

From 2003 to 2007, there was a surge in LBO activity, fuelled by a combination of huge flows of capital to buy out (private equity) firms and increased appetite for risk by lenders willing to allow buyout groups to leverage their equity investment at attractive terms. Buyout firms took many companies private with the stated goal of increasing their performance without concern for perceived pressure from public investors to meet short-term earnings targets. They also employed so-called roll-up strategies whereby they would buy many smaller, already private firms in a particular industry and consolidate them into a larger player. The typical LBO has a planned exit in five years, either by taking the firm public again or selling it to an operating firm or another private equity group. In 2008, the financial crisis and contraction of credit put an almost complete halt to private equity activity. Some highly levered private equity transactions from the peak faltered under their debt load during the recession. For example, Chrysler, which had been purchased and taken private from DaimlerChrysler AG by private equity firm Cerberus Group, declared bankruptcy in 2009, wiping out Cerberus's stake in the firm. The LBO market has gradually recovered in the years since the financial crisis, and by 2015 the annual dollar volume of deals was back at 2005 levels.

THE LEVERAGED BUYOUT OF RJR NABISCO BY KKR

By the summer of 1988, Ross Johnson, CEO of RJR Nabisco (RJR) and alumnus of the University of Manitoba, was becoming increasingly worried about the poor stock price performance of the conglomerate. Despite a strong earnings record, management had not been able to shake loose its image as a tobacco company, and the stock price was languishing at $55 per share. In October 1988, Johnson and a small team of RJR's executives, backed by the Wall Street firms of Shearson Lehman Hutton and Salomon Brothers, announced a bid of $75 per share for the company. At this price, the deal would have been valued at $17.6 billion, more than twice as large as the largest LBO completed up to that point. Because this deal involved the current management of the company, it falls into a special category of LBO deals called **management buyout (MBO)**.

The announcement focused Wall Street's attention on RJR. Even at this substantial premium, the MBO appeared to be a good deal for Johnson and his team, because soon after the offer went public, it became hotly contested. Foremost among the contenders was the firm of Kohlberg, Kravis, and Roberts (KKR). KKR launched its own bid with a cash offer of $90 per share. A bidding war ensued in which the offer price ultimately rose to $109 per share, valuing the deal at more than $25 billion. In the end, both Johnson and KKR offered very similar deals, although management's final bid was slightly higher than KKR's. Eventually, RJR's board accepted KKR's bid of $109 per RJR share. The offer price comprised $81 per share in cash, $18 per share in preferred stock, and $10 per share in debenture securities.

From an economic point of view, this outcome is surprising. One would think that, given their inside knowledge of the company, management would be in the best position not only to value it, but also to run it. Why, then, would an outsider choose to outbid an insider for a company? The answer in RJR's case appeared to point to the managers themselves. As the deal proceeded, it became increasingly obvious to investors that executives (and members of the board of directors) enjoyed perks that were unprecedented. For example, Johnson had the personal use of numerous corporate apartments in different cities and literally a fleet of corporate jets that he, the top executives, and members of the corporate board used for personal travel. In their leveraged buyout proposal, they had obtained a 4% equity stake for top executives that was worth almost $1 billion, $52.5 million in golden parachutes, and assurances that the RJR air force (the fleet of corporate jets) and the flamboyant Atlanta headquarters would not be subject to budget cutting.

management buyout (MBO) A leveraged buyout in which the buyer group includes the firm's own management.

freezeout merger A situation in which the laws on tender offers allow an acquiring company to freeze existing shareholders out of the gains from merging by forcing non-tendering shareholders to sell their shares for the tender offer price.

The Freezeout Merger

Although a leveraged buyout is an effective tool for a group of investors to use to purchase a company, it is less well suited to the case of one company acquiring another. An alternative is the **freezeout merger**; the laws on tender offers allow the acquiring company to freeze existing shareholders out of the gains from merging by forcing non-tendering shareholders to sell their shares for the tender offer price. In Canada, it is a requirement that 90% of the target's shares be acquired by the bidder before a freezeout can be implemented. Let's see how this is accomplished.

An acquiring company makes a tender offer at an amount slightly higher than the current target stock price. If the tender offer succeeds, the acquirer gains control of the target and merges its assets into a new corporation, which is fully owned by the acquirer. In effect, the non-tendering shareholders lose their shares because the target corporation no longer exists. In compensation, non-tendering shareholders get the right to receive the tender offer price for their shares. The bidder, in essence, gets complete ownership of the target for the tender offer price.

Because the value the non-tendering shareholders receive for their shares is equal to the tender price (which is more than the pre-merger stock price), the law generally recognizes it as fair value, and non-tendering shareholders have no legal recourse. Under these circumstances, existing shareholders will tender their stock, reasoning that there is no benefit to holding out; if the tender offer succeeds, they get the tender price anyway, and if they hold out, they risk jeopardizing the deal and forgoing the small gain. Hence the acquirer is able to capture almost all the value added from the merger and, as in a leveraged buyout, is able to effectively eliminate the free rider problem.

The freezeout tender offer has a significant advantage over a leveraged buyout because an acquiring corporation need not make an all-cash offer. Instead of paying the target's shareholders in cash, it can use shares of its own stock to pay for the acquisition. In this case, the bidder offers to exchange each shareholder's stock in the target for stock in the acquiring company. As long as the exchange rate is set so that the value in the acquirer's stock exceeds the pre-merger market value of the target stock, the non-tendering shareholders will receive fair value for their shares and will have no legal recourse.

Competition

The empirical evidence in Table 24.2 suggests that, despite the availability of both the freezeout merger and the leveraged buyout as acquisition strategies, most of the value added still appears to accrue to the target shareholders. That is, on average, acquirers do not have a positive price reaction on the announcement of a takeover. Why do acquirers choose to pay so large a premium that they effectively hand the value they create to the target company's shareholders?

In addition to the presence of the takeover defences we have previously discussed, the most likely explanation is the competition that exists in the takeover market. Once an acquirer starts bidding on a target company and it becomes clear that a significant gain exists, other potential acquirers may submit their own bids. The result is effectively an auction in which the target is sold to the highest bidder. Even when a bidding war does not result, most likely it is because, rather than participate in a bidding war, an acquirer offered a large enough initial premium to forestall the process. In essence, it must give up most of the value added to the target shareholders.

CONCEPT CHECK

11. What mechanisms allow corporate raiders to get around the free rider problem in takeovers?

12. Based on the empirical evidence, who gets the value added from a takeover? What is the most likely explanation of this fact?

MyLab Finance

Here is what you should know after reading this chapter. MyLab™ Finance will help you identify what you know, and where to go when you need to practice.

KEY POINTS	TERMS	ONLINE PRACTICE OPPORTUNITIES
24.1 Background Historical Trends ■ Mergers can be horizontal, vertical, or conglomerate. ■ The global takeover market is active, averaging more than $1 trillion per year in transaction value. The periods of greatest activity were the 1960s, 1980s, 1990s, and 2000s.	acquirer (or bidder), p. 815 conglomerate merger, p. 817 horizontal merger, p. 817 merger waves, p. 815 stock swap, p. 817 takeover, p. 815 target, p. 815 term sheet, p. 817 vertical merger, p. 817	MyLab Study Plan 24.1

KEY POINTS	TERMS	ONLINE PRACTICE OPPORTUNITIES
■ During the 1960s, deals were aimed at building conglomerates. In the 1980s, the trend reversed and conglomerates were split into individual businesses. In the 1990s, there was a rise in "strategic" or "global" deals designed to create firms that could compete globally. From 2004 to 2008, further consolidation and global-scale deals contributed to the most recent merger wave.		
24.2 Market Reaction to a Takeover		
■ While on average the shareholders of the acquiring firm obtain small or no gains, shareholders from the acquired firm typically enjoy gains of 15% on the announcement of a takeover bid.	acquisition premium, p. 817	MyLab Study Plan 24.2
24.3 Reasons to Acquire		
■ The most common justifications given for acquiring a firm are the synergies that can be gained through an acquisition. ■ The most commonly cited sources of synergies are economies of scale and scope, the control provided by vertical integration, gaining monopolistic power, the expertise gained from the acquired company, improvements in operating efficiency, and benefits related to diversification, such as increased borrowing capacity and tax savings. ■ Shareholders of a private company that is acquired gain by switching to a more liquid investment. ■ Some mergers are motivated by incentive conflicts or overconfidence of the acquirer management.	economies of scale, p. 819 economies of scope, p. 819 synergies, p. 818 vertical integration, p. 819	MyLab Study Plan 24.3
24.4 Valuation and the Takeover Process		
■ From the bidder's perspective, a takeover is a positive-NPV project only if the premium paid does not exceed the synergies created. The bidder's stock price reaction to the announcement of the merger is one way to gauge investors' assessments of whether the bidder overpaid or underpaid for the target. ■ A tender offer is a public announcement of an intention to purchase a large block of shares for a specified price. Making a tender offer does not guarantee that a deal will take place. ■ Bidders use either of two methods to pay for a target: cash or stock. In a cash transaction, the bidder simply pays for the target in cash. In a	corporate raider (or raider), p. 831 exchange ratio, p. 827 friendly takeover, p. 831 hostile takeover, p. 831 merger-arbitrage spread, p. 829 risk arbitrageurs, p. 829 step up, p. 830 tender offer, p. 827	MyLab Study Plan 24.4

KEY POINTS	TERMS	ONLINE PRACTICE OPPORTUNITIES
stock-swap transaction, the bidder pays for the target by issuing new stock and giving it to the target shareholders. The method used by the bidder to pay for the acquired firm has tax and accounting implications. ■ For a merger to proceed, both the target and the acquiring boards of directors must approve the merger and put the question to a vote of the shareholders of the target (and, in some cases, the shareholders of the acquiring firm as well). ■ In a friendly takeover, the target board of directors supports the merger and negotiates with the potential acquirers. ■ If the target board opposes the merger, then the acquirer must go around the target board and appeal directly to the target shareholders, asking them to elect a new board that will support the merger.		
24.5 Takeover Defences ■ A target board of directors can defend itself in several ways to prevent a merger. The most effective defence strategy is the poison pill, which gives target shareholders the right to buy shares in either the target or the acquirer at a deeply discounted price. The purchase is effectively subsidized by the existing shareholders of the acquirer, making the takeover very expensive. ■ Another effective defence strategy is having a staggered board, which prevents a bidder from acquiring control over the board in a short period of time. ■ Other defences include looking for a friendly bidder (a white knight), making it expensive to replace management, and changing the capital structure of firm.	golden parachute, p. 834 poison pill, p. 832 proxy fight, p. 832 staggered (classified) board, p. 833 white knight, p. 834 white squire, p. 834	MyLab Study Plan 24.5
24.6 Who Gets the Value Added from a Takeover? ■ When a bidder makes an offer for a firm, the target shareholders can benefit by keeping their shares and letting other shareholders sell at a low price. However, because all shareholders have the incentive to keep their shares, no one will sell. This scenario is known as the free rider problem. ■ To overcome this problem, bidders can acquire a toehold in the target; attempt a leveraged buyout; or, if the acquirer is a corporation, offer a freezeout merger.	freezeout merger, p. 841 management buyout (MBO), p. 841 toehold, p. 838	MyLab Study Plan 24.6

REVIEW QUESTIONS

1. What are the two primary mechanisms under which ownership and control of a public corporation can change?
2. Why do you think mergers cluster in time, causing merger waves?
3. What are some reasons why a horizontal merger might create value for shareholders?
4. Why do you think shareholders from target companies enjoy an average gain when acquired, while acquiring shareholders on average often do not gain anything?
5. If you are planning an acquisition that is motivated by trying to acquire expertise, you are basically seeking to gain intellectual capital. What concerns would you have in structuring the deal and the post-merger integration that would be different from the concerns you would have when buying physical capital?
6. Do you agree that the European Union should be able to block mergers between two U.S.-based firms? Why or why not?
7. How do the carryforward and carryback provisions of the Canadian or U.S. tax codes affect the benefits of merging to capture operating losses?
8. Diversification is good for shareholders, so why shouldn't managers acquire firms in different industries to diversify a company?
9. How does a toehold help overcome the free rider problem?

PROBLEMS

All problems in this chapter are available in MyLab Finance. An asterisk (*) indicates problems with a higher level of difficulty.

Reason to Acquire

1. Your company has earnings per share of $4. It has 1 million shares outstanding, each of which has a price of $40. You are thinking of buying TargetCo, which has earnings per share of $2, 1 million shares outstanding, and a price per share of $25. You will pay for TargetCo by issuing new shares. There are no expected synergies from the transaction.
   a. If you pay no premium to buy TargetCo, what will your earnings per share be after the merger?
   b. Suppose you offer an exchange ratio such that, at current pre-announcement share prices for both firms, the offer represents a 20% premium to buy TargetCo. What will your earnings per share be after the merger?
   c. What explains the change in earnings per share in part (a)? Are your shareholders any better or worse off?
   d. What will your price-earnings (P/E) ratio be after the merger (if you pay no premium)? How does this compare to your (P/E) ratio before the merger? How does this compare to TargetCo's pre-merger (P/E) ratio?
2. If companies in the same industry as TargetCo (from Problem 1) are trading at multiples of 14 times earnings, what would be one estimate of an appropriate premium for TargetCo?

3. You are invested in GreenFrame, Inc. The CEO owns 3% of GreenFrame and is considering an acquisition. If the acquisition destroys $50 million of GreenFrame's value, but the present value of the CEO's compensation increases by $5 million, will he be better or worse off?

Valuation and the Takeover Process

4. Loki, Inc. and Thor, Inc. have entered into a stock-swap merger agreement whereby Loki will pay a 40% premium over Thor's pre-merger price. If Thor's pre-merger price per share was $40 and Loki's was $50, what exchange ratio will Loki need to offer?

5. The NFF Corporation has announced plans to acquire LE Corporation. NFF is trading for $35 per share and LE is trading for $25 per share, implying a pre-merger value of LE of $4 billion. If the projected synergies are $1 billion, what is the maximum exchange ratio NFF could offer in a stock swap and still generate a positive NPV?

6. Let's reconsider part (b) of Problem 1. The actual premium that your company will pay for TargetCo when it completes the transaction will not be 20%, because on the announcement the target price will go up and your price will go down to reflect the fact that you are willing to pay a premium for TargetCo without any synergies. Assume that the takeover will occur with certainty and all market participants know this on the announcement of the takeover (ignore time value of money).
   a. What is the price per share of the combined corporation immediately after the merger is completed?
   b. What is the price of your company immediately after the announcement?
   c. What is the price of TargetCo immediately after the announcement?
   d. What is the actual premium your company will pay?

*7. ABC has 1 million shares outstanding, each of which has a price of $20. It has made a takeover offer of XYZ Corporation, which has 1 million shares outstanding and a price per share of $2.50. Assume that the takeover will occur with certainty and all market participants know this. Furthermore, there are no synergies to merging the two firms.
   a. Assume ABC made a cash offer to purchase XYZ for $3 million. What happens to the price of ABC and XYZ on the announcement? What premium over the current market price does this offer represent?
   b. Assume ABC makes a stock offer with an exchange ratio of 0.15. What happens to the price of ABC and XYZ this time? What premium over the current market price does this offer represent?
   c. At current market prices, both offers are to purchase XYZ for $3 million. Does that mean that your answers to parts (a) and (b) must be identical? Explain.

Takeover Defences

*8. BAD Company's stock price is $20, and the firm has 2 million shares outstanding. You believe you can increase the company's value if you buy it and replace the management. Assume that BAD has a poison pill with a 20% trigger. If it is triggered, all BAD's shareholders—other than the acquirer—will be able to buy one new share in BAD for each share they own at a 50% discount. Assume that the price remains at $20 while you are acquiring your shares. If BAD's management decides to resist your buyout attempt, and you cross the 20% threshold of ownership,

a. How many new shares will be issued and at what price?
b. What will happen to your percentage ownership of BAD?
c. What will happen to the price of your shares of BAD?
d. Do you lose or gain from triggering the poison pill? If you lose, where does the loss go (who benefits)? If you gain, from where does the gain come (who loses)?

Who Gets the Value Added from a Takeover?

***9.** You work for a leveraged buyout firm and are evaluating a potential buyout of UnderWater Company. UnderWater's stock price is $20, and it has 2 million shares outstanding. You believe that if you buy the company and replace its management, its value will increase by 40%. You are planning on doing a leveraged buyout of UnderWater, and will offer $25 per share for control of the company.

a. Assuming you get 50% control, what will happen to the price of non-tendered shares?
b. Given the answer in part (a), will shareholders tender their shares, not tender their shares, or be indifferent?
c. What will your gain from the transaction be?

CHAPTER

25 Corporate Governance

LEARNING OBJECTIVES

- See corporate governance as a response to principal-agent problems
- Know the role of the board, employees, lenders, analysts, and regulators in monitoring managers
- Understand how compensation policies can help mitigate principal-agent problems
- Be familiar with the different ways shareholders can act to reduce the agency conflict
- Understand the major regulations and their role in corporate governance
- See similarities and differences in agency conflicts and how they are dealt with around the world
- Evaluate corporate governance as a trade-off among costs and benefits that will not result in a single solution for all firms

Scandals and corruption marked the turn of the twenty-first century. The names of once well-respected companies, like Enron, WorldCom, Tyco, and Adelphia, filled the news. Enron, with stock worth $68 billion at its peak, became almost worthless in a matter of months, wiping out the retirement savings of thousands of employees and other stockholders. The story at WorldCom was similar. The once high-flying stock peaked at a market value of $115 billion after a string of acquisitions that included well-known phone company MCI. In 2002, WorldCom filed what was at the time the largest bankruptcy ever. After building one of the United States' largest cable companies from scratch, the Rigas family of Adelphia was forced to endure the indignity of watching their own cable system carrying the image of Adelphia's demise into millions of homes.

The common theme among these companies is the accusation of fraud, perpetrated by the manipulation of accounting statements. Shareholders, analysts, and regulators were kept in the dark as the companies' financial situations became ever more precarious, resulting, in the end, in total collapse. How did this happen? Aren't managers supposed to act in the interests of shareholders? Why did auditors go along with the fraud? Where were the boards of directors when all of this was happening?

The examples above are well known in the United States and led to a new regulatory environment there. Canada did not escape such problems though. Once the most valuable company in Canada, Nortel accounted for more than a third of the total value of the TSE 300 Index (now the S&P TSX Composite Index). In mid-2000, Nortel's stock was trading at over $120 per share, and the company's market capitalization was almost $400 billion. After a management shakeup, plunging sales, and several profit warnings, Nortel's stock traded at 69 cents by October 2002. In 2007 both the Ontario Securities Commission (OSC) and the Securities and Exchange Commission (SEC) in the United States brought fraud charges against several former Nortel executives. Some of the charges included earnings management fraud, material misstatements, and making securities filings that were materially misleading. Nortel eventually declared bankruptcy on January 14, 2009. Investors who held Nortel's stock at its peak lost over 99% of its value by the time it hit its low.

There is an opportunity cost to bad governance, but by replacing bad governance with good governance it is possible to increase firm *value*—in other words, good governance is a positive-NPV project. We begin by discussing various governance mechanisms that are designed to mitigate the agency conflicts between managers and owners. A firm's governance mechanisms cannot remove agency conflicts completely, so next we discuss regulations that are designed to prohibit managers from taking certain acts that are not in the interests of shareholders. We conclude the chapter with a discussion of corporate governance around the world.

25.1 Corporate Governance and Agency Costs

corporate governance
The system of controls, regulations, and incentives designed to minimize agency conflicts between managers and investors and prevent corporate fraud.

Any discussion of **corporate governance**—the system of controls, regulations, and incentives designed to prevent fraud—is a story of conflicts of interest and attempts to minimize them. As we saw in Chapter 15, the different stakeholders in a firm all have their own interests. When those interests diverge, we may have agency conflicts. That chapter emphasized the sources of conflicts between bondholders and shareholders. In this chapter, we focus on the conflicts between managers and investors.

The conflict of interest between managers and investors derives from the separation of ownership and control in a corporation. As we pointed out in Chapter 1, the separation of ownership and control is perhaps the most important reason for the success of the corporate organizational form. Because any investor can hold an ownership stake in a corporation, investors are able to diversify and thus reduce their risk exposures without cost. This is especially true for the managers of a corporation; because they are not also required to own the firm, their risk exposures are much lower than they would be if ownership and control were not separate.

Once control and ownership are separated, however, a conflict of interest arises between the owners and the people in control of a corporation. For example, in Chapter 24, we talked about mergers that are motivated by managers' desire to manage a larger firm, gaining them more prestige and greater pay, even if that might not be in the best interests of shareholders. Other examples of principal-agent problems are excessive perquisites managers enjoy, such as using corporate jets for family vacations, or not working as diligently as they would if it were their own business. Agency conflicts are likely to arise any time the manager does not internalize the full cost of his or her actions—just think about how you order at a restaurant when you are paying compared to when your parents are paying!

The seriousness of this conflict of interest depends on how closely aligned are the interests of the managers and shareholders (the owners of the firm). Aligning their interests comes at a cost—it increases the risk exposure of the managers. For example, tying managerial compensation to performance aligns managers' incentives with investors' interests, but then managers are exposed to the firm's risk (because the firm might do poorly for reasons unrelated to the managers' performance).

The role of the corporate governance system is to mitigate the conflict of interest that results from the separation of ownership and control without unduly burdening managers with the risk of the firm. The system attempts to align these interests by providing incentives for taking the right action and punishments for taking the wrong action. The incentives come from owning stock in the company and from compensation that is sensitive to performance. Punishment comes when a board fires a manager for poor performance or fraud or when, in the event that the board fails to act, shareholders or raiders launch control contests to replace the board and management. As we will see, these actions interact in complicated ways. For example, as managers own more stock in the firm, their incentives become better aligned, but, in addition to the increase in risk the managers must bear, the managers also become harder to fire because the block of stock they own gives them significant voting rights.

Let's take a closer look at the components of the corporate governance system.

CONCEPT CHECK

1. What is corporate governance?
2. What agency conflict do corporate governance structures address?

25.2 Monitoring by the Board of Directors and Others

At first glance, one might think that there is a simple solution to the conflict of interest problem—monitor the firm's managers closely. The problem with this reasoning is that it ignores the cost of monitoring. When the ownership of a corporation is widely held, no one shareholder has an incentive to bear this cost (because she bears the full cost of monitoring but the benefit is divided among all shareholders). Instead, the shareholders as a group elect a board of directors to monitor managers. The directors themselves, however, have the same conflict of interest—monitoring is costly, and in many cases directors do not get significantly greater benefits than other shareholders from monitoring the managers closely. Consequently, in most cases, shareholders understand that there are reasonable limits on how much monitoring they can expect from the board of directors.

In principle, the board of directors hires the executive team, sets its compensation, approves major investments and acquisitions, and dismisses executives if necessary. In the United States, the board of directors has a clear fiduciary duty to protect the interests of the owners of the firm—the shareholders. In Canada, section 122.1.a of the Canada Business Corporations Act (CBCA) defines the board's duty to act in the best interests of the corporation. While the United States and Canadian board duties may sound equivalent, Canadian courts have sometimes interpreted "the corporation" to include stakeholders (such as bondholders) in addition to shareholders. Most other countries give some weight to the interests of other stakeholders in the firm, such as the employees. In Germany, this concept is formalized through a two-tier board structure that gives half of the seats on the upper board—called the *supervisory board*—to employees.

inside directors Members of a board of directors who are employees, former employees, or family members of employees.

grey directors Members of a board of directors who are not as directly connected to the firm as insiders are but have existing or potential business relationships with the firm.

Types of Directors

Generally, researchers have categorized directors into three groups: inside, grey, and outside (or independent). **Inside directors** are employees, former employees, or family members of employees. **Grey directors** are people who are not as directly connected to the firm as insiders are but have existing or potential business relationships with the firm. For example, bankers, lawyers, and consultants who are already retained by the firm, or who would be interested in being retained, may sit on a board. Thus, their judgment could be compromised by their desire to keep the CEO happy. Finally, all other

outside (or independent) directors Any member of a board of directors other than an inside or grey director.

directors are considered **outside (or independent) directors** and are the most likely to make decisions solely in the interests of the shareholders.

Board Independence

Researchers have hypothesized that boards with a majority of outside directors are better monitors of managerial effort and actions. One early study showed that a board was more likely to fire the firm's CEO for poor performance if the board had a majority of outside directors.[1] Other studies have found that firms with independent boards make fewer value-destroying acquisitions and are more likely to act in shareholders' interests if targeted in an acquisition.[2]

Despite evidence that board independence matters for major activities such as firing CEOs and making corporate acquisitions, researchers have struggled to find a connection between board structure and firm performance. Although the firm's stock price increases on the announcement of its addition of an independent board member, the increased firm value appears to come from the potential for the board to make better decisions on acquisitions and CEO turnover rather than from improvements in the firm's operating performance. Researchers have argued, however, that so many other factors affect firm performance that the effect of a more or less independent board is very difficult to detect.

Another reason why it may be difficult to explicate a relationship between board independence and firm performance is the nature of the role of the independent director. On a board composed of insider, grey, and independent directors, the role of the independent director is really that of a watchdog. But because independent directors' personal wealth is likely to be less sensitive to performance than that of insider and grey directors, they have less incentive to closely monitor the firm. However, there has been a trend toward more equity-based pay for outside directors. As recently as the early 1990s, it was very common for directors to be paid a fixed annual cash fee plus perhaps an extra nominal fee per meeting attended. It is now standard for outside directors to be granted shares of stock and/or options to more closely align their interests with the shareholders they serve.

Incentives notwithstanding, even the most active independent directors spend only one or two days per month on firm business, and many independent directors sit on multiple boards, further dividing their attention. In fact, some studies have found that value decreases when too many of a board's directors are "busy," meaning that they sit on three or more boards.[3]

captured board A board of directors whose monitoring duties have been compromised by connections or perceived loyalties to management.

A board is said to be a **captured board** when its monitoring duties have been compromised by connections or perceived loyalties to management. Theoretical and empirical research supports the notion that the longer a CEO has served, especially when that person is also chair of the board, the more likely the board is to become captured. Over time, most of the independent directors will have been nominated by the CEO. Even though they have no business ties to the firm, they are still likely to be friends, or at least

---

[1]M. Weisbach, "Outside Directors and CEO Turnover," *Journal of Financial Economics* 20(1–2) (1988): 431–460.

[2]J. Byrd and K. Hickman, "Do Outside Directors Monitor Managers? Evidence from Tender Offer Bids," *Journal of Financial Economics* 32(2) (1992): 195–207; and J. Cotter, A. Shivdasani, and M. Zenner, "Do Independent Directors Enhance Target Shareholder Wealth During Tender Offers?" *Journal of Financial Economics* 43(2) (1997): 195–218. H. Ryan and R. Wiggins show that firms with more outsiders on their boards award directors more equity-based compensation, increasing incentives for the board to monitor ("Who Is in Whose Pocket? Director Compensation, Board Independence, and Barriers to Effective Monitoring," *Journal of Financial Economics* 73(2204): 497–525).

[3]E. Fich and A. Shivdasani, "Are Busy Boards Effective Monitors?" *Journal of Finance* 61(2) (2006): 689–724.

acquaintances, of the CEO. The CEO can be expected to stack the board with directors who are less likely to challenge her or him. When the CEO is also chair of the board, the nominating letter offering a seat to a new director comes from the CEO. This process merely serves to reinforce the sense that the outside directors owe their positions to the CEO and work for the CEO rather than for the shareholders.

The Sarbanes-Oxley Act of 2002 (SOX), which we discuss in more depth in Section 25.5, required that the audit committee of the board, charged with overseeing the audit of the firm's financial statements, be composed entirely of independent directors. Following the implementation of SOX, major U.S. exchanges (NYSE and NASDAQ) changed their listing requirements such that firms listed on those exchanges must have a majority of independent directors on their board. More recently, the Dodd-Frank Act of 2010 in the United States further requires that all members of a firm's compensation committee be independent directors. Ideally, these changes will reduce entrenchment and improve governance. However, all such changes come at a cost, because the other major role of the board is to advise managers on strategic issues. Independent directors, while unbiased, are also the least likely to be experts in the firm's business, thus reducing their ability to advise.

Board Size and Performance

Researchers have found the surprisingly robust result that smaller boards are associated with greater firm value and performance.[4] The likely explanation for this phenomenon comes from psychology and sociology research, which finds that smaller groups make better decisions than larger groups. Most firms that have just gone public either as young companies or as older firms returning to public status after a leveraged buyout choose to start with smaller boards. Boards tend to grow over time as members are added for various reasons. For example, boards are often expanded by one or two seats after an acquisition to accommodate the target CEO and perhaps one other target director.

Other Monitors

The board is complemented by other monitors, both inside and outside the firm. We discuss direct shareholder monitoring and action in Section 25.4, but other monitors include security analysts, lenders, employees within the firm itself, and the securities regulators.

Securities analysts produce independent valuations of the firms they cover so that they can make buy and sell recommendations to clients. These analysts collect as much information as they can, becoming experts on the firm and its competitors by poring over a company's financial statements and filings. As a result, they are in a position to uncover irregularities first. Analysts often ask difficult and probing questions of CEOs and CFOs during quarterly earnings releases. Anyone can listen to these conference calls, which are typically simulcast on the company's investor relations website.

Lenders also carefully monitor firms to which they are exposed as creditors. Loans and lines of credit also contain financial covenants designed to provide early warning signs of trouble. These covenants, such as requiring maintenance of a certain quick ratio or profitability level, are primarily designed to capture the firm's ability to repay the loan. Nonetheless, they complement other signals of potential governance problems. A stockholder must keep in mind, however, that the stockholder's interests are not perfectly aligned with the creditors' interests. The creditor, lacking the ability to benefit from the positive side of taking risk, is particularly interested in minimizing risk, even at the expense of some positive-NPV projects.

---

[4]D. Yermack, "Higher Market Valuation of Companies with Small Boards of Directors," *Journal of Financial Economics* 40(2) (1996): 185–211.

Employees of the firm are most likely to detect outright fraud because of their inside knowledge. However, they do not always have strong incentives to report the fraud. They may personally benefit from the fraud, or they may fear retribution from "blowing the whistle." Some jurisdictions have whistle-blower statutes to protect employees who report fraud to the authorities.

The SEC in the United States and the provincial securities commissions in Canada are charged with the task of protecting the investing public against fraud and stock price manipulation in their respective jurisdictions. But while the regulators' enforcement powers are extensive and carry with them the weight of criminal prosecution, their detection resources are limited. Out of necessity, the regulators must rely on the array of other monitors, each with vested interests in detecting governance problems, to alert the regulators to potential wrongdoing.

CONCEPT CHECK

3. What is the difference between grey directors and outside directors?

4. What does it mean for a board to be captured?

25.3 Compensation Policies

In the absence of monitoring, the other way the conflict of interest between managers and owners can be mitigated is by closely aligning their interests through the managers' compensation policy. That is, by tying compensation to performance, the shareholders effectively give the manager an ownership stake in the firm.

Stock and Options

Managers' pay can be linked to the performance of a firm in many ways. The most basic approach is through bonuses based on, for example, earnings growth. During the 1990s, most companies adopted compensation policies that more directly gave managers an ownership stake by including grants of stock or stock options to executives. These grants give managers a direct incentive to increase the stock price to make their stock or options as valuable as possible. Consequently, stock and option grants naturally tie managerial wealth to the wealth of shareholders.

Many studies have examined firms' compensation policies. One of the earlier studies examined the sensitivity of managers' compensation to the performance of their firms.[5] The authors found that for every $1000 increase in firm value, CEO pay changed, on average, by $3.25. Most of this increase came from changes in the value of their stock ownership ($2). The rest was driven by options, bonuses, and other compensation changes. The authors of the study argued that this seemed too small a sensitivity to provide managers with the proper incentives to exert extra effort on the behalf of shareholders. Recall, however, that increasing the pay-for-performance sensitivity comes at the cost of burdening managers with risk. As a consequence, the optimal level of sensitivity depends on the managers' level of risk aversion, which is hard to measure.

[5]M. Jensen and K. Murphy, "Performance Pay and Top-Management Incentives," *Journal of Political Economy* 98(2) (1990): 225–264.

Pay and Performance Sensitivity

Figure 25.1 shows the dramatic rise in CEO pay during the economic expansion of the 1990s. As the figure illustrates, the median cash pay, consisting of salary and bonuses, has fluctuated only moderately. The climb in CEO total compensation has been driven instead by the sharp increase in the value of stock, options, and deferred compensation granted each year. The median value of options granted rose from less than $200,000 in 1993 to more than $1 million in 2001. Not surprisingly, the substantial use of stock and option grants in the 1990s greatly increased managers' pay-for-performance sensitivity. Consequently, recent estimates put this sensitivity at $25 per $1000 change in wealth.[6] While the value of stock and option grants have fluctuated in the 2000s with the performance of the overall stock market, there appears to have been some substitution toward deferred compensation and retirement packages, with median amounts exceeding $2 million in 2014.

Besides increasing managers' risk exposure, increasing the sensitivity of managerial pay and wealth to firm performance has some other negative effects. For example, often options are granted "at the money," meaning that the exercise price is equal to the current stock price. Therefore, managers have an incentive to manipulate the release of financial forecasts so that bad news comes out before options are granted

FIGURE 25.1 CEO Compensation

This figure shows the median cash pay; stock and option grants; and deferred compensation and other pay (for example, long-term incentive payouts and retirement packages) for CEOs of the 1600 largest public companies over the period 1993 through 2014.

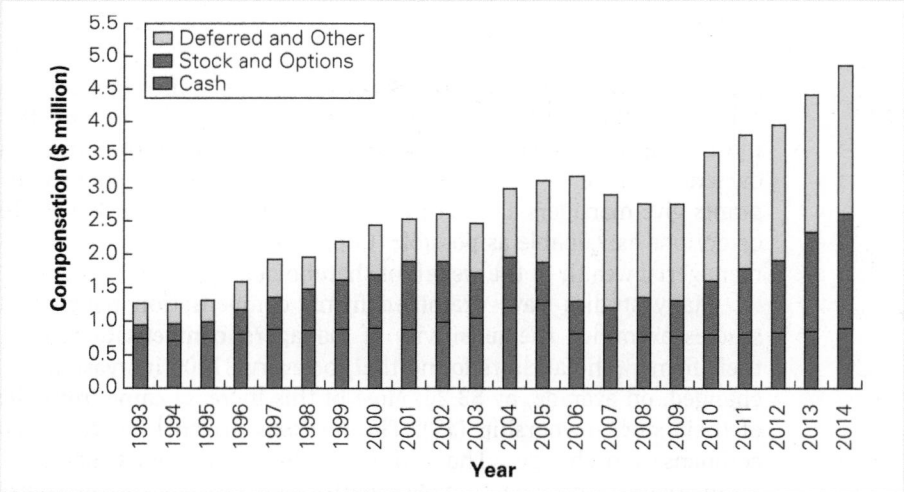

Source: Execucomp.

[6]B. Hall and J. Liebman, "Are CEOs Really Paid Like Bureaucrats?" *Quarterly Journal of Economics* 103(3) (1998): 653–691.

(to drive the exercise price down) and good news comes out after options are granted. Studies have found evidence that the practice of timing the release of information to maximize the value of CEO stock options is widespread.[7]

More recently, Professor Erik Lie has found evidence suggesting that many executives have engaged in a more direct form of manipulating their stock option compensation: backdating their option grants.[8] **Backdating** refers to the practice of choosing the grant date of a stock option retroactively, so that the date of the grant would coincide with a date when the stock price was at its low for the quarter or for the year. By backdating the option in this way, the executive receives a stock option that is already in-the-money, with a strike price equal to the lower price on the supposed grant date.

backdating The practice of choosing the grant date of a stock option retroactively so that the date of the grant would coincide with a date when the stock price was lower than its price at the time the grant was actually awarded.

The use of backdating suggests that some executive stock option compensation may not truly have been earned as the result of good *future* performance of the firm. Furthermore, unless it is reported in a timely manner to the tax authority and to shareholders, and reflected in the firm's financial statements, backdating is illegal. In mid-2006, the SEC and U.S. Justice Department investigations into alleged backdating were ongoing for more than 70 firms. New SEC rules require firms to report option grants within two days of the grant date, which may help prevent further abuses. Canadian rules require firms to report option grants within 10 days of the end of the month the options were granted; this rule was similar to the prior rules in the United States and allows more time for backdating should the share price increase during the time since the option grant. In February 2009, executives at Research In Motion (RIM), now known as BlackBerry, agreed to pay about $77 million in penalties to settle an options-backdating investigation carried out by the Ontario Securities Commission.

CONCEPT CHECK

5. What is the main reason for tying managers' compensation to firm performance?
6. What is the negative effect of increasing the sensitivity of managerial pay to firm performance?

25.4 Managing Agency Conflicts

Even with the benefits of separating ownership and control, there are still examples of corporations in which the top managers have substantial ownership interests (e.g., Google). One might conjecture that such corporations have suffered less from the conflict of interest between managers and shareholders.

Academic studies have supported the notion that greater managerial ownership is associated with fewer value-reducing actions by managers.[9] But while increasing managerial ownership may reduce perquisite consumption, it also makes managers harder

[7]D. Yermack, "Good Timing: CEO Stock Option Awards and Company News Announcements," *Journal of Finance* 52(2) (1997): 449–476. For evidence that the option compensation may induce misreporting, see N. Burns and S. Kedia, "The Impact of Performance-Based Compensation on Misreporting," *Journal of Financial Economics* 79(2006): 35–67.

[8]See E. Lie, "On the Timing of CEO Stock Option Awards," *Management Science* 51 (2005): 802–812. Also, R. Heron and E. Lie show that new rules enacted as part of the Sarbanes-Oxley legislation in 2002 that require grants to be reported within two business days have curbed the practice of backdating ("Does Backdating Explain the Stock Price Pattern Around Executive Stock Option Grants?" *Journal of Financial Economics* 83(2) (2007): 271–295).

[9]See, for example, R. Walkling and M. Long, "Agency Theory, Managerial Welfare, and Takeover Bid Resistance," *Rand Journal of Economics* 15(1) (1984): 54–68.

to fire—thus reducing the incentive effect of the threat of dismissal. Therefore, the relationship between managerial ownership and firm value is unlikely to be the same for every firm, or even for different executives of the same firm. Shareholders will use all of the tools at their disposal to mitigate the agency conflicts. Thus, if managers have small ownership stakes, shareholders may use compensation policies or a stronger board to create the desired incentives. Harold Demsetz and Kenneth Lehn argue that if you look at a group of firms at any time, you should not necessarily see any relationship between ownership and value, unless you are able to control for all of the other, sometimes unobservable, parts of the governance system, including the risk aversion of the manager.[10] More recent studies have supported their position.[11]

Direct Action by Shareholders

If all else fails, the shareholders' last line of defence against expropriation by self-interested managers is direct action. Recall that shareholders elect the board of directors. Typically, these elections look like those in the former Soviet Union—there is only one slate of candidates and you vote "yes" or "no" for the slate as a whole. When shareholders are angry about the management of the company and frustrated by a board unwilling to take action, however, they have at their disposal a variety of options for expressing that displeasure.

Shareholder Voice. First, any shareholder can submit a resolution that is put to a vote at the annual meeting. A resolution could direct the board to take a specific action, such as discontinue investing in a particular line of business or country, or remove a poison pill. Such resolutions rarely receive majority support, but if large shareholders back them, they can be embarrassing for the board.[12] Some large public pension funds, one of the first being the California Public Employees' Retirement System (CalPERS), take an activist role in corporate governance. Typically, these funds target firms that are taking actions without considering the concerns of the stockholders; for example, they may privately approach the board of the firm and ask it to reverse its course. The explicit threat at that stage is that if the board fails to comply, the pension fund will put the issue to a shareholder vote. Studies have reported that such activist investors are usually successful in achieving their goals without having to take matters public.[13]

Recently, shareholders have started organizing "no" votes. That is, when they are dissatisfied with a board, they simply refuse to vote to approve the slate of nominees for the board. The most high-profile example of this type of action occurred in 2004 with the Walt Disney Company. Major shareholders were dissatisfied with the recent performance of Disney under long-time CEO and chairman, Michael Eisner. They

---

[10]H. Demsetz and K. Lehn, "The Structure of Corporate Ownership: Causes and Consequences," *Journal of Political Economy* 93(6) (1985): 1155–1177.

[11]C. Himmelberg, R.G. Hubbard, and D. Palia, "Understanding the Determinants of Managerial Ownership and the Link Between Ownership and Performance," *Journal of Financial Economics* 53(3) (1999): 353–384; and J. Coles, M. Lemmon, and J. Meschke, "Structural Models and Endogeneity in Corporate Finance: the Link Between Managerial Ownership and Corporate Performance," SSRN working paper, 2007.

[12]For a theoretical analysis of the informativeness and effectiveness of such votes, see D. Levit and N. Malenko, "Non-binding Voting for Shareholder Proposals," SSRN working paper (2009).

[13]W. Carleton, J. Nelson, and M. Weisbach, "The Influence of Institutions on Corporate Governance Through Private Negotiations: Evidence from TIAA-CREF," *Journal of Finance* 53(4) (1998): 1335–1362.

began an organized campaign to convince the majority of Disney shareholders to withhold their approval of the re-election of Eisner as director and chairman of the board. When the votes were counted, about 43% of Disney's shareholders had voted to withhold approval of Eisner. While Eisner technically had won re-election, a 43% "no" vote is practically unprecedented in large public companies. The signal was clear, and an embarrassed Eisner and the Disney board decided that Eisner would remain CEO but relinquish the chairman title. Shortly thereafter, Eisner announced plans to retire completely in 2006.

Shareholder Approval. In addition to electing the directors of the company, shareholders must approve many major actions taken by the board. For example, target shareholders must approve merger agreements and, in some cases, so must bidder shareholders. Even in cases where bidder shareholders are not required to approve a merger directly, listing requirements on some exchanges—the NYSE, for example—demand that shareholders approve any large issue of new shares, such as might be necessary in a stock-swap merger. Normally, approval is perfunctory, but it cannot be taken for granted. As we saw in Chapter 24, after Hewlett-Packard CEO Carly Fiorina negotiated the merger of HP and Compaq, the Hewlett family used their board seats and voting bloc to oppose the deal.

A recent movement, which gained momentum and regulators' interest during the 2008 financial crisis, is to let shareholders have a "say-on-pay" vote. Typically, this is a non-binding vote to approve or disapprove of the compensation plan for senior executives each year. In 2009, the SEC moved to require recipients of U.S. federal bailout money to give shareholders an advisory say-on-pay vote, and some legislators planned bills extending this requirement to all public companies. Despite shareholder anger over losses at U.S. corporations during the financial crisis, surprisingly, the first two rejections of executives' pay packages in the United States did not occur until May 2010 (at Motorola and Occidental Petroleum). In February 2010, CIBC became the first Canadian financial firm to conduct a say-on-pay vote. Their proposed compensation package passed with the approval of over 90% of shareholders.

Proxy Contests. Perhaps the most extreme form of direct action that disgruntled shareholders can take is to hold a proxy contest and introduce a rival slate of directors for election to the board (see Figure 25.2). This action gives shareholders an actual choice between the nominees put forth by management and the current board and a completely different slate of nominees put forth by dissident shareholders.

For example, in February 2008, Microsoft made an unsolicited offer to buy Yahoo! For $31 per share. While many shareholders supported the offer, which represented a 60% premium to its stock price, Yahoo!'s management and board of directors resisted and Microsoft eventually withdrew its offer that May. Immediately thereafter, dissident Carl Icahn launched an effort aimed at replacing Yahoo!'s board via a proxy contest. Yahoo! settled the contest in July by agreeing to give board seats to Icahn and two of his supporters. Perhaps because proxy fights can push management to take needed action, one early study of proxy contests found that the incumbents won re-election.[14]

---

[14]P. Dodd and J. Warner, "On Corporate Governance: A Study of Proxy Contests," *Journal of Financial Economics* 11(1) (1983): 401–438.

FIGURE 25.2 Proxy Contest Outcomes

Outcomes of proxy fights involving dissident proposals, showing the fraction of cases management lost or compromised. While dissidents do not often win these fights outright, they are becoming more successful in getting management to settle.

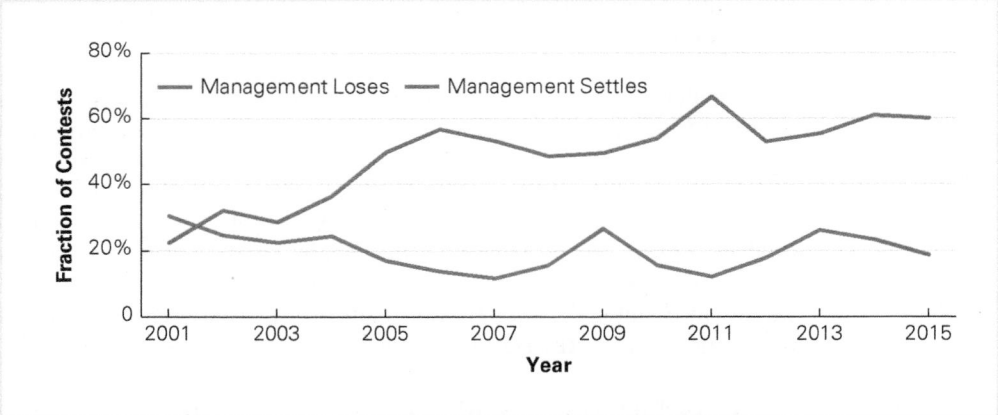

Source: Factset SharkWatch.

Management Entrenchment

Given the importance of shareholder action in corporate governance, researchers and large investors alike have become increasingly interested in measuring the balance of power between shareholders and managers in a firm. Over time, the tools that managers can use to entrench themselves have evolved, including anti-takeover protections such as those discussed in Chapter 24. The Investor Responsibility Research Center (IRRC) collected information on 24 different characteristics that can entrench, or give more power to, managers vis-à-vis shareholders. These provisions include state antitakeover statutes, poison pills, staggered boards, and restrictions on the ability of shareholders to call special meetings themselves.

Researchers have begun using data from the IRRC as a way to measure how entrenched managers are. One study found that, during the 1990s, firms with more restrictions on shareholder power performed worse than firms with fewer restrictions.[15] Other studies have found connections between the degree of entrenchment and the compensation offered to managers, and even to the value of acquisitions made.[16] While the index offered by the IRRC does not capture every aspect of corporate governance, many practitioners are finding it to be a useful summary measure of the degree to which managers are entrenched and less likely to have their actions checked by shareholders.

[15]P. Gompers, J. Ishii, and A. Metrick, "Corporate Governance and Equity Prices," *Quarterly Journal of Economics* 118(1) (2003): 107–155. The cause of this effect, however, is not clear; see J. Core, W. Guay, and T. Rusticus, "Does Weak Governance Cause Weak Stock Returns? An Examination of Firm Operating Performance and Investors' Expectations," *Journal of Finance* 61(2) (2006): 655–687.

[16]G. Garvey and T. Milbourn, "Asymmetric Benchmarking in Compensation: Executives Are Paid for Good Luck but Not Punished for Bad," *Journal of Financial Economics* (2006); and R. Masulis, C. Wang, and F. Xie, "Corporate Governance and Acquirer Returns," *Journal of Finance* 62(4) (2007) 1851–1889.

The Threat of Takeover

Many of the provisions listed in the IRRC index concern protection from takeovers. As we discussed in Chapter 24, one motivation for a takeover can be to replace poorly performing management. When internal governance systems such as ownership, compensation, board oversight, and shareholder activism fail, the one remaining way to remove poorly performing managers is by mounting a hostile takeover. Thus, the effectiveness of the corporate governance structure of a firm depends on how well protected its managers are from removal in a hostile takeover.

An active takeover market is part of the system through which the threat of dismissal is maintained. In fact, some research has suggested that an active takeover market complements a board's own vigilance in dismissing incompetent managers. That research found that boards are actually more likely to fire managers for poor performance during active takeover markets than they are during lulls in takeover activity.[17] This finding also has implications internationally, because some countries have much more active takeover markets than others. In particular, hostile takeovers are far more common in the United States than in other countries.

CONCEPT CHECK

7. Describe and explain a proxy contest.

8. What is the role of takeovers in corporate governance?

25.5 Regulation

So far, we've focused on those parts of the corporate governance system that have evolved over time as economic responses to the need for shareholders to mitigate the conflict of interest between themselves and managers. For example, boards of directors came into being long before there was any regulation of the governance of a company, and CEOs have long appointed independent directors to their boards without being required to do so. Nonetheless, from time to time government has added to existing requirements by passing laws that force minimum standards of governance. A recent significant example is the Sarbanes-Oxley Act of 2002 (SOX) and the Dodd-Frank Act of 2010 in the United States (similar regulations were enacted in some countries, including Canada, in the years that followed).

In the wake of the massive failures of large public companies and corporate fraud scandals mentioned in the introduction to this chapter, the U.S. Congress rushed to enact legislation to fix what it saw as inadequate safeguards against malfeasance by managers of public corporations. The result was the Sarbanes-Oxley Act. Prior to SOX, the largest overhaul of securities markets and introduction of regulation came in response to the stock market crash of 1929 and the Great Depression that followed. The Securities Act of 1933 and the Securities Exchange Act of 1934, among other things, established the Securities and Exchange Commission (SEC) and prohibited trading on private information gained as an insider of a firm.

The Sarbanes-Oxley Act

One of the most critical inputs to the monitoring process is accurate information. If a board of directors has inaccurate information, it cannot do its job. The overall intent of SOX was to improve the accuracy of information given to both boards and shareholders. SOX had

[17]W. Mikkelson and M. Partch, "The Decline of Takeovers and Disciplinary Managerial Turnover," *Journal of Financial Economics* 44(2) (1997): 205–228.

three main components: (1) it overhauled incentives and independence in the auditing process, (2) it stiffened penalties for providing false information, and (3) it required companies to validate their internal financial control processes.

More specifically, to reduce incentive conflicts in auditing, SOX

- put strict limits on the amount of non-audit fees (consulting or otherwise) that an accounting firm can earn from the same firm that it audits.
- required that audit partners rotate every five years.
- called on the SEC to force companies to have audit committees that are dominated by outside directors and required that at least one outside director have a financial background.

SOX also stiffened the criminal penalties for providing false information to shareholders:

- The CEO and the CFO must personally attest to the accuracy of the financial statements.
- Penalties for providing false or misleading financial statements can be as much as $5 million and imprisonment can be a maximum of 20 years.
- CEOs and CFOs must now return bonuses or profits from the sale of stock or the exercise of options during any period covered by statements that are later restated.

Finally, SOX requires senior management and the boards of public companies to be comfortable enough with the process through which funds are allocated and controlled and outcomes monitored throughout the firm and to willing to attest to their effectiveness and validity.

The Cadbury Commission

It is difficult to determine definitively whether the costs of SOX outweigh its benefits. Even if we could measure the total direct and indirect costs of a law, we could never accurately estimate how much fraud is deterred by that law. One place to turn to for guidance is the experiences of other countries. The following quote from *The Independent*[18] sounds like it was written to describe the motivation behind the Sarbanes-Oxley legislation:

> *Prompted by public concern over a string of unexpected collapses of recently audited firms and over big rises in executive pay, exchanges and public officials rode a wave of public outrage to institute corporate governance reforms to strengthen the independence of the board and address the conflicts of interest in the auditing process.*

In actuality, this passage was written near the end of 1991, and it described what happened in the United Kingdom in 1991. Following the collapse of some large public companies, the U.K. government commissioned Sir Adrian Cadbury to form a committee to develop a code of best practices in corporate governance. Sir Cadbury, in introducing his recommendations, reportedly said the following:

---

[18]S. Pincombe, "Accountancy and Management: Auditors Look to Pass the Buck as Pressure for Reform Increases," *The Independent* (London), November 12, 1991, p. 21.

> *The fundamental issue is one of pressure. There is pressure on the company to show the results that the market expects. There is pressure on the auditors who don't want to lose their jobs. The question is whether a structure can emerge out of the dialogue which is robust enough to give the shareholders what they ought to get and what they can rely upon. Internal controls are a part of the legitimate expectations of those who receive accounts.*[19]

The problems that the Cadbury Commission identified are the same as those that SOX attempted to address in the United States 10 years later. Perhaps not surprisingly, the resulting recommendations were quite similar as well. According to the Commission's findings, audit and compensation committees should be made up entirely of independent directors or, at least, have a majority of them. The CEO should not be chair of the board, and at the very least there should be a lead independent director with similar agenda-setting powers. Auditors should be rotated, and there should be fuller disclosure of non-audit work. Unlike SOX, these recommendations were not backed up by the force of law. Rather, companies could adopt them or instead explain in their annual reports why they chose not to adopt them. Some researchers have studied firms that adopted the Cadbury recommendations versus those that did not. The results are mixed. While one study found that those firms that separated the position of CEO and chair performed better, another found no relationship between the independence of key board committees and firm performance in the post-Cadbury era.[20]

Dodd-Frank Act

As the previous cases illustrate, regulatory change is often prompted by crisis. The Dodd-Frank Act of 2010 was spurred by the 2008 financial crisis. Many people believed that poor corporate governance was an important factor that contributed to the crisis, so the act has numerous clauses designed to strengthen governance, including these:

- **Independent Compensation Committee:** All U.S. exchanges must require that the listed firms' compensation committees be composed of only independent board members, and have the authority to hire outside compensation consultants.
- **Nominating Directors:** Large shareholders owning at least 3% of a company's stock for at least three years may nominate candidates for the board of directors, with the candidates listed on the firm's proxy statement alongside the nominees of management.
- **Vote on Executive Pay and Golden Parachutes:** At least once every three years, firms must provide shareholders with a non-binding vote on the compensation of the firm's CEO, CFO, and the three other most highly paid executives. While the vote is nonbinding, companies must formally respond regarding how they have taken into account the results of the vote.
- **Clawback Provisions:** Public companies must establish policies that allow firms to take back up to three years of any executive incentive compensation erroneously awarded in the event of an accounting restatement.

---

[19]Ibid.

[20]J. Dahya, A. Lonie, and D. Power, "The Case for Separating the Roles of Chairman and CEO: An Analysis of Stock Market and Accounting Data," *Corporate Governance* 4(2) (1996): 71–77; and N. Vafeas and E. Theodorou, "The Association Between Board Structure and Firm Performance in the UK," *British Accounting Review* 30(4) (1998): 383–407.

- **Pay Disclosure:** Companies must disclose the ratio of CEO annual total compensation to that of the median employee. Companies are also required to disclose the relationship between executive compensation and the firm's financial performance. Finally, firms are required to disclose whether they permit employees and directors to hedge against decreases in the market value of the company's stock.

President Trump promised to repeal many aspects of the Dodd-Frank Act—at the time of writing, January 2018, a second attempt to appeal was under way; it was not clear which parts would remain enforced.

Insider Trading

insider trading Trading a person does on the basis of privileged information.

One aspect of the conflict of interest between managers and outside shareholders that we have not yet addressed is **insider trading**. Insider trading occurs when a person makes a trade based on privileged information. Managers have access to information that outside investors do not have. By using this information, managers can exploit profitable trading opportunities that are not available to outside investors. If they were allowed to trade on their information, their profits would come at the expense of outside investors and, as a result, outside investors would be less willing to invest in corporations. Insider trading regulation was passed to address this problem.

In the United States, regulation against insider trading traces back to the Great Depression—specifically, to the Securities Exchange Act of 1934. In Canada, insider trading laws exist at both the provincial and federal levels. The Canada Corporation Act of 1970 introduced the first federal provisions regarding insider trading, and this was carried over into the Canada Business Corporations Act, which continues in force today. In addition, the Criminal Code of Canada was amended in 2004 to create tougher insider trading laws and penalties. Insiders of a company are defined broadly to include managers, directors, and anyone else who has access to material non-public information, including temporary insiders—for example, lawyers working on a merger deal or commercial printers contracted to print the merger agreement documents. Whether information is material has been defined in the courts as referring to whether the information would have been a significant factor in an investor's decision about the value of the security. Some examples include knowledge of an upcoming merger announcement, earnings release, or change in payout policy. The law is especially strict with regard to takeover announcements, prohibiting anyone (whether an insider or not) with non-public information about a pending or ongoing tender offer from trading on that information or revealing it to someone who is likely to trade on it.

The penalties for violating insider trading laws include jail time, fines, and civil penalties. In Canada, actions can be brought forward under the provincial securities regulations or, for a federally incorporated firm, under the Canada Business Corporations Act. Penalties can include prison terms less than five years, and fines up to $5 million or four times the profit made by the trade. In addition, a conviction under Canada's Criminal Code could bring imprisonment of up to 10 years. In the United States, only the U.S. Justice Department—on its own or at the request of the SEC—can bring charges that carry the possibility of a prison sentence. However, the SEC can bring civil actions if it chooses. In 1984, Congress stiffened the civil penalties for insider trading by passing the Insider Trading Sanctions Act, which allowed for civil penalties of up to three times the gain from insider trading. Enforcement of insider trading laws is more vigorous in the United States than in Canada. *The Globe and Mail* reported in 2001 that the OSC had won only a "handful of convictions for insider trading in its long history"[21] compared to the U.S. SEC that

[21]"When insiders go bad," *The Globe and Mail*, October 23, 2001, page A.16.

INTERVIEW WITH LAWRENCE E. HARRIS

Lawrence E. Harris

As chief economist of the U.S. Securities and Exchange Commission from 2002 to 2004, Dr. Lawrence E. Harris was the primary advisor to the SEC on all economic issues. He participated extensively in the development of Sarbanes-Oxley (SOX) regulations. Currently Dr. Harris holds the Fred V. Keenan Chair in Finance at the University of Southern California's Marshall School of Business.

Q Why is legislation such as Sarbanes-Oxley necessary to protect shareholders?

A Public investors will supply capital to entrepreneurs seeking to fund new business ventures only if they believe it will be used wisely. Regrettably, history has shown that management too often has violated that trust.

The interests of managers and shareholders often conflict. To solve this principal-agent problem, shareholders rely on information produced by corporate accounting systems. Sarbanes-Oxley mandated accounting and audit standards to improve the quality of corporate financial disclosure.

Opponents of governance regulation believe that shareholders can—and should—take care of themselves. Unfortunately, shareholders often cannot exercise the control necessary to solve principal-agent problems that they could not have anticipated when the firm was first founded. The firm's governance structure, which may have been sensible when the firm was a small company funded primarily by its founders, may no longer be appropriate for a large, widely held corporation operating in the modern economy. Management with little ownership stake may be entrenched, and the directors may be compromised or captured. When shareholders cannot solve their principal-agent problems, the government must intervene with the lightest possible hand.

Q What are the costs and benefits of Sarbanes-Oxley?

A Good corporate disclosure is essential to public finance. SOX improved the quality of disclosure by strengthening accounting and auditing standards. By requiring the CEO and CFO to sign accounts and attest to their accuracy, SOX also put teeth into enforcement if fraud is discovered.

What many people perceive as costs of SOX are really expenditures that weak firms avoided. All well-managed firms must ensure the integrity of their accounting. SOX merely requires that people adopt *existing* best practice. Many companies were already fully compliant with SOX in most essential respects.

Critics claim that SOX made going public more difficult for small firms by increasing the cost of being a public firm. But a public firm *must* have secure control mechanisms to protect shareholders. SOX may decrease the number of firms that go public, but it will also decrease the losses suffered by public investors.

SOX established the Public Company Accounting Oversight Board (PCAOB) to regulate auditors. Previous efforts at self-regulation failed because accountants would not discipline their peers. Following numerous notable failures, Congress stepped in and created the PCAOB.

Q Is SOX a good law?

A Regulators are blamed for failing to regulate when crises occur, but they do not bear the costs of their regulations. This asymmetry often causes them to underestimate the costs of their regulations and thus adopt unnecessary regulations. The problem is greatest when political considerations force Congress to write regulations that would be better written by well-informed specialists in regulatory agencies such as the SEC. Congress wrote SOX in response to the financial accounting crises that greatly offended the public. Although SOX permits the SEC to essentially rewrite any provision that it determines not to be in the public interest, under the circumstances, it could not do so.

SOX is generally good regulation, but it has some notable unintended consequences. The power it gives audit firms over their corporate clients allows them to interpret SOX to their advantage and thereby increase the work necessary to comply with SOX. SOX also imposes unnecessary costs on mutual funds. Investment companies are subject to SOX because they are public corporations, but they do not face the same accounting problems that operating companies face. In its haste to appease the public, Congress failed to be as discriminating as it could have been.

had "prosecuted or settled 550 insider trading cases since 1985."[22] This puts Canadian capital markets at a disadvantage relative to those in the United States, as investors hesitate to commit money to markets where there is a greater chance of being exploited by insiders.

[22]Ibid.

MARTHA STEWART AND IMCLONE

One of the most famous insider trading cases involved Martha Stewart, self-made celebrity, billionaire, and CEO of a media empire built around her name. Stewart sold 3928 shares of ImClone Systems in December 2001, just before the Food and Drug Administration announced that it was rejecting ImClone's application to review a new cancer drug. The SEC investigated, alleging that Stewart sold the shares after receiving a tip from her broker that the ImClone founder and his family had been selling shares. Even though Stewart was not an employee of ImClone, insider trading laws prohibited her from trading on information gained through a tip, as the origin of the information violated the duty of trust. Nonetheless, in the end, Stewart was charged only with lying to a federal officer and conspiracy to obstruct justice (the investigation of her trades). She was convicted and served five months in prison and an additional five months of home confinement. In addition, she was fined $30,000.

While Stewart's case made the headlines, it was relatively minor by SEC standards. From 2009–2015, the SEC has charged over 600 individuals for insider trading, with some of those convicted facing penalties exceeding $100 million and jail terms of up to 11 years. The largest penalty ever imposed was $1.8 billion against hedge fund SAC Capital in 2013, with at least eight individuals at the firm convicted or pleading guilty to a series of violations.

Source: "Stewart Likely to Get Time in Prison Camp," Thomas S. Mulligan, *Los Angeles Times*, July 16, 2004.

CONCEPT CHECK

9. Describe the main requirements of the Sarbanes-Oxley Act of 2002.

10. What is insider trading, and how can it harm investors?

25.6 Corporate Governance Around the World

Most of our discussion in this chapter has focused on corporate governance in the United States and Canada. Yet, both the protection of shareholder rights and the basic ownership and control structure of corporations vary across countries. We explore some of those differences here.

Protection of Shareholder Rights

Recent events notwithstanding, investor protection in the United States is generally seen as being among the best in the world. The degree to which investors are protected against expropriation of company funds by managers and even the degree to which investors' rights are enforced vary widely across countries and legal regimes. In an important study, researchers collected data on aspects of shareholder rights in more than 30 countries.[23] The researchers claimed that the degree of investor protection was largely determined by the legal origin of the country—specifically, whether its legal system was based on British common law (more protection) or French, German, or Scandinavian civil law (less protection). This purported link between legal origin and investor protection has been challenged by other researchers, however, who demonstrate that formal legal protection for investors is a relatively recent development in the United Kingdom itself.[24] In the late nineteenth and early twentieth centuries, there was essentially no formal legal protection of minority investors.

[23]R. La Porta, F. Lopez-de-Silanes, A. Shleifer, and R. Vishny, "Law and Finance," *Journal of Political Economy* 106 (1998): 1113–1155.

[24]J. Franks, C. Mayer, and S. Rossi, "Ownership: Evolution and Regulation," *Review of Financial Studies* 22 (2009): 4009-4056.

Controlling Owners and Pyramids

Much of the focus in the United States is on the agency conflict between shareholders, who own the majority of a firm but are a dispersed group, and managers, who own little of the firm and must be monitored. In many other countries, the central conflict is between what are called "controlling shareholders" and "minority shareholders." In Canada and Europe, many corporations are run by families that own controlling blocks of shares. For most practical purposes, blocks of shares in excess of 20% are considered to be controlling, as long as no one else has any large concentration of shares. The idea is that if you own 20% and the other 80% is dispersed among many different shareholders, you will have considerable say in the operation of the firm; other shareholders would have to coordinate their activities to try to outvote you—a formidable challenge.

In these firms, there is usually little conflict between the controlling family and the management (it is often made up of family members). Instead, the conflict arises between the minority shareholders (those without the controlling block) and the controlling shareholders. Controlling shareholders can make decisions that benefit them disproportionately relative to the minority shareholders, such as employing family members rather than the most talented managers or establishing contracts favourable to other family-controlled firms.

dual class shares One class of a firm's shares that has voting rights which are superior to those of the other class.

Dual Class Shares and the Value of Control. One way for families to gain control over firms even when they do not own more than half the shares is to issue **dual class shares**—a scenario in which companies have more than one class of shares and one class has superior voting rights over the other class. For example, a Class B share might have 10 votes for every one vote of a Class A share. Controlling shareholders—often families—will hold all or most of the shares with superior voting rights and issue the inferior voting class to the public. This approach allows the controlling shareholders to raise capital without diluting their control. Dual class shares are common in Brazil, Canada, Denmark, Finland, Germany, Italy, Mexico, Norway, South Korea, Sweden, and Switzerland. In the United States, they are far less common. Some countries, such as Belgium, China, Japan, Singapore, and Spain, outlaw differential voting rights altogether.

pyramid structure A way for an investor to control a corporation without owning 50% of the equity, whereby the investor first creates a company in which he has a controlling interest. This company then owns a controlling interest in another company. The investor controls both companies but may own as little as 25% of the second company.

Pyramid Structures. Another way families can control a corporation without owning 50% of the equity is to create a pyramid structure. In a **pyramid structure**, a family first creates a company in which it owns more than 50% of the shares and therefore has a controlling interest. This company then owns a controlling interest—that is, at least 50% of the shares—in another company. Notice that the family controls *both* companies, but *owns* only 25% of the second company. Indeed, if the second company purchased 50% of the shares of a third company, then the family would control all three companies, even though it would own only 12.5% of the third company. The farther you move down the pyramid the less ownership the family has, but it still remains in complete control of all the companies. Although this example is stylized, a variety of pyramid structures based on this idea are quite common in Canada and other countries except the United States.

Figure 25.3 details the actual pyramid controlled by the Pesenti family in Italy as of 1995.[25] The Pesenti family effectively controls five companies primarily concentrated in the construction industry—Italmobiliare, Italcementi, Franco Tosi, Cementerie Siciliane, and Cementerie de Sardegna—even though it does not have

[25]P. Volpin, "Governance with Poor Investor Protection: Evidence from Top Executive Turnover in Italy," *Journal of Financial Economics* 64(1) (2002): 61–90.

FIGURE 25.3 Pesenti Family Pyramid, 1995

Each box contains both ownership and voting rights (which can differ when preferred stock with superior voting rights is used). The first set of numbers (in blue) indicates the rights of the preceding company one step up the pyramid. The second set of numbers (in red) shows the effective rights of the Pesenti family in that company. For example, Italmobiliare controls Italcementi through its 54% voting block but owns only 32% of the company. The Pesenti family's investment in Italmobiliare gives it a 10% ownership of Italcementi but, because it is controlled by Italmobiliare, 45% of the effective voting rights in Italcementi.

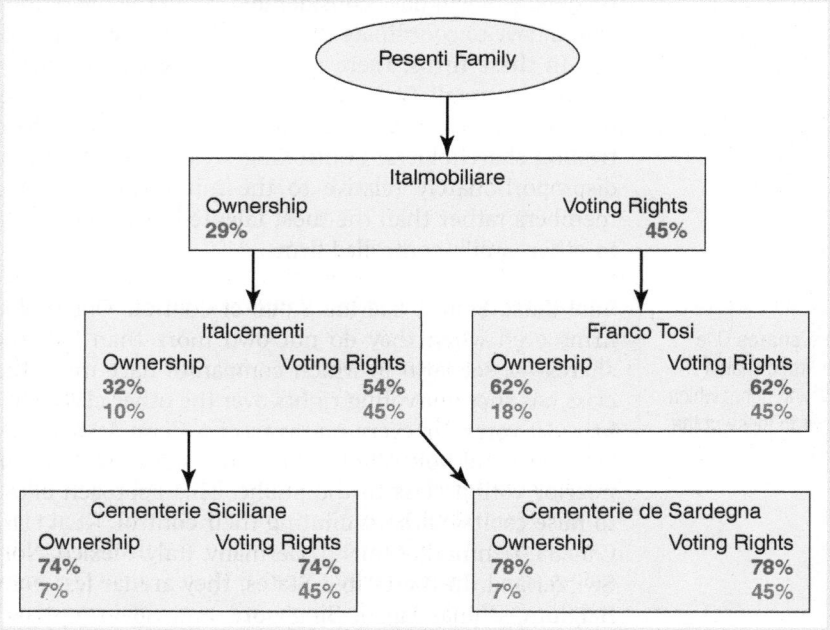

Source: Journal of Financial Economics. Adapted from "Governance with Poor Investor Protection: Evidence from Top Executive Turnover in Italy" Fig. 1. Structure of the Pesenti's group as of 12/31/1995, http://faculty.london.edu/pvolpin/turnover.PDF. Used with permission.

more than 50% ownership of any one of them. In this case, the family uses a pyramid structure plus shares with special voting rights to control companies even when its ownership share is as little as 7%.

A controlling family has many opportunities to expropriate minority shareholders in a pyramid structure. The source of the problem is that, at progressively lower levels of the pyramid, the difference between the family's control and its cash flow rights increases. *Cash flow rights* refer simply to the family's direct ownership stake and, therefore, the portion of the cash flows generated by the firm that the family has a right to. Notice that Italcementi gets 74% of the dividends of Cementerie Siciliane; Italmobiliare gets 32% of the dividends of Italcementi. Finally, the Pesenti family has rights to 29% of the dividends of Italmobiliare. Thus, the family receives only 29% × 32% × 74% = 7% of the dividends of Cementerie Siciliane but still controls it.

tunnelling A conflict of interest that arises when a shareholder who has a controlling interest in multiple firms moves profits (and hence dividends) away from companies in which he has relatively less cash flow rights toward firms in which he has relatively more cash flow rights.

A conflict of interest arises because the family has an incentive to try to move profits (and hence dividends) up the pyramid—that is, away from companies in which it has few cash flow rights and toward firms in which it has more cash flow rights. This process is called **tunnelling**. An example of how this might occur is if the Pesenti family would have Cementerie Siciliane enter into an agreement to be supplied by Italmobiliare at prices that are extremely favourable to Italmobiliare. Such a move would reduce Cementerie Siciliane's profits and increase Italmobiliare's profits.

Of course, if you are a minority shareholder in one of these subsidiaries, you would rationally anticipate this expropriation, so you would pay less for the shares of a firm in which a family has control, especially if the firm is low in the pyramid. In effect, you would factor in your expected loss from being a minority shareholder rather than a controlling shareholder. Many studies have confirmed this reasoning, finding sharp differences between the value of controlling blocks and minority shares.[26] Thus, controlling shareholders pay for their control rights because the firm effectively faces a higher cost of equity for outside capital.

The Stakeholder Model

stakeholder model The explicit consideration most countries (other than the United States) give to other stakeholders besides equity holders, in particular, rank-and-file employees.

The agency costs and the ways to control them that we have discussed are general to all companies anywhere in the world. However, the United States is somewhat of an exception, in that it focuses solely on maximizing shareholder welfare. Most countries follow what is called the **stakeholder model**, giving explicit consideration to other stakeholders—in particular, rank-and-file employees. As noted earlier, countries such as Germany give employees board representation. Others have mandated *works councils*, local versions of labour unions that are to be informed and consulted on major corporate decisions. Finally, some countries mandate employee participation in decision making in their constitutions. Table 25.1 summarizes employee standing in the governance of firms in some Organisation for Economic Co-operation and Development (OECD) countries.

It is important to keep in mind that in countries like the U.S. where other stakeholders are not explicitly considered in the firm's objective, the interests of these stakeholders are not necessarily ignored. Most firms are constrained because they operate in competitive markets. If they mistreat other stakeholders, such as employees or customers, those stakeholders will be tempted to disrupt or sever their relationship with the firm. Thus, an objective that maximizes shareholder value must also implicitly consider stakeholder preferences.

---

[26]For estimates based on research on mergers and acquisitions, see P. Hanouna, A. Sarin, and A. Shapiro, "Value of Corporate Control: Some International Evidence," SSRN working paper (2004). Estimates of the value of control have also been done comparing the value of shares with different voting rights. With respect to the United States, see C. Doidge, "U.S. Cross-Listings and the Private Benefits of Control: Evidence from Dual Class Shares," *Journal of Financial Economics* 72(3) (2004): 519–553. With respect to Italy, a country where the value of control is much larger, Zingales reports a premium of 82% on voting shares, presumably because of lower protection to minority investors. See L. Zingales, "The Value of the Voting Right: A Study of the Milan Stock Exchange Experience," *Review of Financial Studies* 7(1) (1994): 125–148. Other work includes H. Almeida and D. Wolfenzon, "A Theory of Pyramidal Ownership and Family Business Groups," *Journal of Finance* 61(6) (2006): 2637–2680; L. Bebchuk, R. Kraakman, and G. Triantis, "Stock Pyramids, Cross-Ownership, and Dual Class Equity," in R. Morck (ed.), *Concentrated Corporate Ownership* (Chicago: University of Chicago Press, 2000): 295–318; M. Bertrand, P. Mehta, and S. Mullainathan, "Ferreting Out Tunneling: An Application to Indian Business Groups," *Quarterly Journal of Economics* 117(1) (2002): 121–148; and S. Johnson, R. La Porta, F. Lopez-de-Silanes, and A. Shleifer, "Tunneling," *American Economic Review* 90(2) (2000): 22–27.

TABLE 25.1 Employee Participation in Corporate Governance in OECD Countries

Mandated Works Councils	Employee Appointed Board Members	Constitutional Employee Protections	No Explicit Requirements
Austria	Austria	France	Australia
Belgium	Czech Republic	Italy	Canada
Denmark	Denmark	Norway	Ireland
Finland	Germany		Japan
France	Netherlands		Mexico
Germany	Norway		New Zealand
Greece	Sweden		Poland
Hungary			Slovak Republic
Netherlands			Switerzerland
Portugal			Turkey
Spain			United Kingdom
South Korea			United States

Source: Based on Organisation for Economic Co-operation and Development, *Survey of Corporate Governance Developments in OECD Countries* (2004).

Cross Holdings

While in the United States it is rare for one company's largest shareholder to be another company, in many countries, such as Germany, Japan, and South Korea, it is the norm. In Japan, groups of firms connected through cross holdings of each other and a common relation to a bank are known as *keiretsu*. Monitoring of each company comes from others in the group holding blocks of its stock and primarily from the main bank of the group, which as a creditor monitors the financial well-being of the group companies closely. In South Korea, huge conglomerate groups such as Hyundai, Samsung, LG, and SK comprise companies in widely diversified lines of business and are known as *chaebol*. For example, SK Corporation has subsidiary and group companies in energy, chemicals, pharmaceuticals, and telecommunications. An important difference between the South Korean *chaebol* and the Japanese *keiretsu* is that in South Korea the firms do not share a common relationship with a single bank.

CONCEPT CHECK

11. How does shareholder protection vary across countries?

12. How can a minority owner in a business gain a controlling interest?

25.7 The Trade-Off of Corporate Governance

Corporate governance is a system of checks and balances that trades off costs and benefits. As this chapter makes clear, this trade-off is very complicated. No one structure works for all firms. For example, it would be hard to argue that having Larry Page as CEO and a controlling shareholder of Google was bad for minority investors. For Google, the alignment of incentives assured by Larry Page's large stake in Google appeared to outweigh the costs of having such a large shareholder. In other cases, however, this is unlikely to be true.

The costs and benefits of a corporate governance system also depend on cultural norms. Acceptable business practice in one culture is unacceptable in another culture, and thus it is not surprising that there is such a wide variation in governance structures across countries.[27]

It is important to keep in mind that good governance is value enhancing and so, in principle, is something investors in the firm should strive for. Because there are many ways to implement good governance, one should expect firms to display—and firms do display—wide variation in their governance structures.

MyLab Finance

Here is what you should know after reading this chapter. MyLab™ Finance will help you identify what you know, and where to go when you need to practice.

KEY POINTS	TERMS	ONLINE PRACTICE OPPORTUNITIES
25.1 Corporate Governance and Agency Costs ■ Corporate governance refers to the system of controls, regulations, and incentives designed to prevent fraud from happening. ■ The conflicts between those who control the operations of a firm and those who supply capital to the firm are as old as the corporate organizational structure. Shareholders use a combination of incentives and threats of dismissal to mitigate this conflict.	corporate governance, p. 849	MyLab Study Plan 25.1
25.2 Monitoring by the Board of Directors and Others ■ The board of directors hires managers, sets their compensation, and fires them if necessary. Some boards become captured, meaning that they act in the interests of managers rather than shareholders. Boards with strong outside directors who were nominated before the current CEO took the helm of the firm are the least likely to be captured.	captured board, p. 851 grey directors, p. 850 inside directors, p. 850 outside (or independent) directors, p. 851	MyLab Study Plan 25.2

[27]Resources that detail how governance differs across the world include J. Charkham, *Keeping Good Company: A Study of Corporate Governance in Five Countries* (Oxford: Clarendon Press, 1994); J. Franks and C. Mayer, "Corporate Ownership and Control in the U.K., Germany and France," *Journal of Applied Corporate Finance,* 9(4) (1997): 30–45; R. La Porta, F. Lopez-de-Silanes, and A. Shleifer, "Corporate Ownership Around the World," *Journal of Finance,* 54(4) (1999): 471–517; and D. Denis and J. McConnell, "International Corporate Governance," *Journal of Financial and Quantitative Analysis,* 38(1) (2003): 1–38.

KEY POINTS	TERMS	ONLINE PRACTICE OPPORTUNITIES
25.3 Compensation Policies ■ By tying managers' compensation to firm performance, boards can better align managers' interests with shareholders' interests. Care must be taken to make sure managers do not have incentives to try to manipulate the firm's stock price to garner a big compensation payout.	backdating p. 855	MyLab Study Plan 25.3
25.4 Managing Agency Conflicts ■ Ownership of company's stock by management can reduce managers' perquisite consumption. However, moderate holdings of shares can have a negative effect by making the managers harder to fire (reducing the threat of dismissal), without fully aligning their interests with those of shareholders. ■ If a board fails to act, shareholders are not without recourse. They can propose an alternative slate of directors or vote not to ratify certain actions of the board. ■ A board and management can adopt provisions, such as staggered boards and limitations on special shareholder meetings that serve to entrench them. These provisions also have the effect of limiting the efficacy of a hostile takeover bid. ■ Despite the defences that a determined management can erect, one source of the threat of dismissal comes from a hostile acquirer, which can take over a firm and fire the management, even if the board fails to do so.		MyLab Study Plan 25.4
25.5 Regulation ■ Regulation is an important piece of the total corporate governance environment. Regulation can be beneficial by reducing asymmetric information between managers and capital providers and, thus, reducing the overall cost of capital. Regulation also carries with it costs of compliance and enforcement. Good regulation balances these forces to produce a net benefit for society. ■ The most recent overhaul of U.S. governance regulation is the Sarbanes-Oxley Act of 2002. The act was intended to improve shareholder monitoring of managers by increasing the accuracy of their information. The act ■ overhauls incentives and independence in the auditing process,	insider trading, p. 862	MyLab Study Plan 25.5

KEY POINTS	TERMS	ONLINE PRACTICE OPPORTUNITIES
▪ stiffens the penalties for providing false information, and ▪ forces top management of companies to validate their internal financial control process. ▪ The Securities Act of 1933 and the Securities Exchange Act of 1934 are the basis of insider trading regulation. Over time, the SEC and the courts have developed interpretations of the law that prohibit ▪ insiders with a fiduciary duty to their shareholders from trading on material non-public information in that stock, and ▪ anyone with non-public information about a pending or ongoing tender offer from trading on that information or revealing it to someone who is likely to trade on it.		
25.6 Corporate Governance Around the World ▪ Corporate governance, regulations, and practices vary widely across countries. ▪ Some studies suggest that countries with common-law roots generally provide better shareholder protection than countries with civil-law origins. ▪ Ownership structures in Canada, Europe, and Asia often involve pyramidal control of a group of companies by a single family. In these situations, the controlling family has many opportunities for expropriation of minority shareholders through tunnelling. ▪ Dual class shares with differential voting rights allow a controlling shareholder or family to maintain control of a company or group even if their cash flow rights are relatively small. Dual class shares are common outside the United States. ▪ Most countries give employees some role in governing a firm. Employee involvement usually takes the form of board seats or works councils that are consulted before major decisions. ▪ It is common outside the United States for a company's largest shareholder to be another company. These cross holdings create incentives for firms to monitor one another.	dual class shares, p. 865 pyramid structure, p. 865 stakeholder model, p. 867 tunnelling p. 866	MyLab Study Plan 25.6

KEY POINTS | TERMS | ONLINE PRACTICE OPPORTUNITIES

25.7 The Trade-Off of Corporate Governance

- It is important to keep in mind that good governance is value enhancing and so, in principle, is something investors in the firm should strive for. Because there are many ways to implement good governance, one should expect firms to display—and firms do display—wide variation in their governance structures.

REVIEW QUESTIONS

1. Why is governance important in a corporation?
2. Why would a grey director be compromised as a monitor?
3. Why can we not simply rely on regulators to monitor managers?
4. How can compensation design help mitigate principal-agent problems?
5. Why is managerial ownership not always value improving?
6. What are shareholders' options to confront managers who they believe are damaging shareholder value?
7. Should insider trading be illegal?
8. How is it possible for an entity with low cash flow interest in a company to exercise control?

PROBLEMS

All problems in this chapter are available in MyLab Finance.

Corporate Governance and Agency Costs

1. What inherent characteristic of corporations creates the need for a system of checks on manager behaviour?
2. What are some examples of principal-agent problems?
3. What are the advantages and disadvantages of the corporate organizational structure?

Monitoring by the Board of Directors and Others

4. What is the role of the board of directors in corporate governance?
5. How does a board become captured by a CEO?

6. What role do security analysts play in monitoring?
7. How are lenders part of corporate governance?
8. What is a whistle-blower?

Compensation Policies

9. What are the advantages and disadvantages of increasing the options granted to CEOs?

Managing Agency Conflicts

10. Is it necessarily true that increasing managerial ownership stakes will improve firm performance?
11. How can proxy contests be used to overcome a captured board?
12. What is a say-on-pay vote?
13. What are a board's options when confronted with dissident shareholders?

Regulation

14. What is the essential trade-off government faces in designing regulation of public firms?
15. Many of the provisions of the Sarbanes-Oxley Act of 2002 were aimed at auditors. How does this affect corporate governance?
16. What are the costs and benefits of prohibiting insider trading?
17. How do the laws on insider trading differ for merger-related versus non–merger-related trading?

Corporate Governance Around the World

18. Are the rights of shareholders better protected in the United States or in France?
19. How can a controlling family use a pyramidal control structure to benefit itself at the expense of other shareholders?

Index

Note: Page numbers followed by '*f*,' '*t*' and '*n*' denotes figures, tables and notes respectively.

A

abandonment option, 330
Abu Dhabi, 489
Abu Dhabi Investment Authority, 489
accounting break-even, 327
accounting illusions, 237
accounting scandals, 55
  see also corporate governance
accounts payable, 31
  payables management, 675–677
  stretching the accounts payable, 676–677
accounts payable days, 45
accounts payable days outstanding, 675
accounts receivable, 31
  accounts receivable days, 673
  aging schedule, 673–675, 674*t*
  as collateral, 702–703
  factoring of accounts receivable arrangement, 702–703
  factors, 702
  monitoring, 673–675
  pledging of accounts receivable agreement, 702
  receivables management, 671–675
accounts receivable days, 45, 45*n*, 673
acid-test ratio, 43
Ackermann, Josef, 563
acquirer, 815
acquisition costs, 678
acquisition premium, 817, 818*t*
acquisitions, 442–443, 491
  see also mergers and acquisitions
actuarially fair price, 722, 722*n*
Adelphia, 848
Adidas, 231, 231*t*
adjusted present value, 650*n*
adverse selection, 511, 578–579, 726–727
Africa, 29
agency conflicts, 855–859
agency cost of debt, 576
agency costs, 575–577, 849–850
  of cash retention, 611–613
  equity–debt holder conflicts, 576–577
  managerial entrenchment, 575
agency costs of equity, 575
agency securities, 527
aggressive financing policy, 695–697
aging schedule, 673–675, 674*t*
Airbus, 630
Air Canada, 43, 219, 551–552, 552*f*, 573, 575, 665, 721, 730
Alberta Heritage Savings Trust Fund, 488
Alchian, A., 808*n*
Allen, Franklin, 608, 608*n*, 613*n*
AllianceBernstein, 233
Almeida, H., 867*n*
alternative rules, 267–274
  vs. NPV rule, 265
Amazon.com, 33, 229
Amec, 820
American options, 455, 466
amortization, 36*n*
amortizing loan, 140–143, 142*f*
Andrade, Gregor, 572
angel investors, 485, 486
annual meeting, 205
annual percentage rate *(APR)*, 137–140, 668
  conversion to discount rate, 139–140
  conversion to effective annual rate, 139
annual report, 28
annual return, 355–356
annuity, 104–110, 108*n*
  annual percentage rate and, 138
  discount rates, variations in, 150
  effective annual rate and, 138
  equivalent annual annuity, 282–285
  future value of, 105–109, 132–133
  growing annuity, 120–121
  lottery prize annuity, 107–108
  present value of, 104–105
  retirement savings plan annuity, 109–110
annuity due, 108*n*
Antweiler, Werner, 751*n*
Apple, Inc., 10, 11–12, 819
arbitrage, 77, 240
arbitrage opportunity, 77, 370, 469*n*
Arbitrage Pricing Theory (APT), 422
arithmetic average returns, 358
ask price, 17
asset-backed bonds, 523
asset-backed line of credit, 521
asset classes, 304, 305*t*
asset efficiency, 45, 53–54*t*
asset pool, 305
assets, 31
  asset sale, 320–321, 320*n*
  on balance sheet, 31
  book value, 31
  current assets, 31
  defined, 30
  idle asset, 315
  liquidation value, 319–321
  long-term assets, 31
  negative net additions, 321
  salvage value, 319–321
asset turnover, 45
asymmetric information, 577
AT&T, 818, 819
at-the-money, 457
auction IPO, 499–502, 500*t*, 500*f*
auditing firms, 56
auditor, 28
Australia, 10, 29
availability float, 670
average annual return, 355–356, 356*f*
average collection period, 45
average returns, 358
average risk, 440
AXA, 820

B

backdating, 855
bailout funds, 577*n*
balance sheet, 29–35, 426*f*
  acid-test ratio, 43
  assets, 30, 31
  balance, 636–637
  current ratio, 43
  debt-equity ratio, 34–35
  defined, 29
  enterprise value, 34–35
  identity, 30–31
  and leasing, 795
  leverage, 428
  liabilities, 30, 31–32
  market-to-book ratio, 33–34
  market-value balance sheet, 428
  market value *vs.* book value, 32–33
  price-to-book ratio (P/B), 33
  pro forma balance sheet. *See* pro forma balance sheet
  quick ratio, 43
  shareholders' equity, 30, 32
balance sheet identity, 30–31
balloon payment, 534
Bank Capital Regulation, 563
bankers' acceptances, 188*f*, 188*n*, 681*t*
bank loans, 520, 697–701
  amortizing loan, 140–143
  asset-backed line of credit, 521
  bridge loan, 698–699
  collateral, 702–705
  combining swaps with standard loans, 743

bank loans (*continued*)
commitment fees, 699
committed line of credit, 698
common loan stipulations and fees, 699–701
compensating balance requirements, 699–701
defined, 521
discount loan, 699
and discount rates, 140–144
evergreen credit, 698
lease-equivalent loan, 802–803
vs. leases, 790–792
line of credit, 698
loan origination fee, 699
loan payment, 111–112, 140–143
loan payments in perfect market, 790–791
outstanding loan balance, 143–144
revolving line of credit, 521, 698
secured loans, 702
single, end-of-period-payment loan, 697–698
syndicated bank loan, 521
term loan, 521
vs. trade credit, 669
trust receipts loan, 704
uncommitted line of credit, 698
Bank of America, 752
Bank of Canada, 150, 526*n*, 698, 752
bank rate, 698
bankruptcy, 571, 724, 798–799, 848
Bankruptcy and Insolvency Act (BIA), 591, 798
bankruptcy code, 591
1978 Bankruptcy Reform Act, 591
banks, 20*t*, 741
Barber, Brad, 240, 240*n*, 241*n*, 242*n*
Barrick Gold Corporation, 348, 352, 353, 354, 355*t*, 661
basis risk, 740
Bautista, A., 802*n*
BCE Inc. *See* Bell Canada Enterprises Inc.
Beacon Funding, 787*n*
bearer deposit notes, 681*t*
Bebchuk, L., 867*n*
Beddoe, Clive, 552
Bell Canada Enterprises Inc., 430, 619
Beranek, W., 695*n*
Berkshire Hathaway, 618
Bertrand, M., 867*n*
best efforts, 499
beta (β), 410*f*
average betas for stocks by industry, 400*t*
calculating, with Excel, 405
estimating, from historical returns, 403–406
and expected return, 410*f*
and market risk, 399–401
mixing standard deviation and beta, 401
negative beta stock, 409–410
of a portfolio, 409–410
BHP Billiton, 836
bid-ask spread, 17, 18
bidder, 815
bid price, 17
Big Mac (McDonald's), prices of, 77–78, 77–78*t*
Big Rock Brewery, 439
binomial option pricing model, 468–470
binomial pricing formula, 469
bird in the hand fallacy, 601
Black, Fischer, 468, 470, 475*n*, 606*n*
Black, Lisa, 186
BlackBerry, 219
BlackRock Asset Management Canada Limited, 399
BlackRock Inc., 399
Black-Scholes option pricing formula, 470–472
blanket lien, 703
board independence, 851–852
board of directors, 12, 850–853, 861
Boeing, 11, 630
Bogle, John, 399
bond covenants, 529–530, 529*t*
bond indenture, 163
bond market, 19
bond price, 531, 532*t*
changes in, 173–181
computing, from yield to maturity, 172
coupon bonds, 170–171
coupon payment, 163, 175*t*
credit spreads, 187
discount, 175–176
immediately after coupon payment, 175*t*
and interest rate changes, 169–176, 175*t*, 178*t*
interest rate risk, 178–179, 178*t*, 182*t*
Law of One Price, 175
online, 173
par, 173
in practice, 179–181
premium, 173, 175–176
time and, 176–177, 177*f*
trading above par, 175
trading below par, 175
and yield to maturity, 174, 174*f*, 180*f*
zero-coupon bonds, 168–169
bond ratings, 183–185, 184*t*
bonds
see also public debt
bond ratings, 183–185, 184*t*
Business Development Bank of Canada, 527
callable bonds, 530
Canada Mortgage and Housing Corporation, 527
consol, 101
convertible bonds, 37
corporate bonds, 182–188
coupon bonds, 169–173
coupon rate, 163
coupons, 163
domestic bonds, 524
double-barrelled bonds, 528
duration, 178*n*
Eurobonds, 524
Export Development Canada, 527
face value, 163
foreign bonds, 524
general obligation bonds, 528
global bonds, 524
Government of Canada bonds, 169, 525–527
Hertz bonds, 530, 531*t*
high-yield bonds, 183
international bond markets, 524–525
investment-grade bonds, 183, 184*t*
junk bonds, 183
maturity date, 163
municipal bonds, 527–528
par value, 163
perpetual bond, 101, 102
price. *See* bond price
private placement, 521
provincial bonds, 185–188, 185*f*, 527–528
pure discount bonds, 164
real return bonds, 527
revenue bonds, 528
risk-free interest rates, 166
serial bonds, 528
speculative bonds, 183, 184*t*
term, 163
terminology, 163, 164*t*
yields, and credit crisis, 188
yields, on bonds with same maturity, 199–200
yield to maturity *(YTM)*, 164–165, 168
zero-coupon bonds, 164–166
zero-coupon yield curve, 166, 166*f*
book building, 498
book value, 31
of debt, 47*n*
vs. market value, 32–33
book value of equity, 32, 33
see also shareholders' equity
borrowing costs, 822
borrowing money. *See* bank loans; debt financing
bought deal, 498
bourses. *See* stock market
Bow.com, 457, 457*t*, 466
Brav, A., 617*n*
break-even, 327
break-even analysis, 327, 328*f*
bridge loan, 698–699
British Petroleum, 498
Brookfield Asset Management Inc., 752
Bruner, F., 408*n*
Bruner, Robert, 438*n*
Bucyrus, 550
Buffett, Warren, 618
Burns, N., 855*n*
Burton, Jonathan, 413

Business Development Bank of Canada (BDC) bonds, 527
business income trust, 8, 9
business interruption insurance, 721
business judgment rule, 832
business liability insurance, 721
business plans, 631
bust-up takeovers, 816
Byrd, J., 851*n*

C

Cadbury, Adrian, 860–861
Cadbury Commission, 860–861
calculator. *See* financial calculator
California Public Employees' Retirement System (CalPERS), 856
callable bonds, 530
call date, 530
call option, 455, 460*f*, 476*f*
call price, 469*n*, 530
call provisions, 530–532
Canada
  accounting standards, 28
  bond prices online, 173
  cash offers, 509
  dividend tax credit, 10
  financial control processes, 56
  foreign takeovers, 836
  Government of Canada bonds, 169, 525–527
  insider trading, 862, 864
  interest rates and inflation rates, 1960–2014, 147*f*
  IPOs fees, 506–507
  mergers and acquisitions, 838*n*
  mortgage payments, 143
  NPV rule, use of, 267
  open market repurchase, 595–596
  top investment banking firms in, 494*t*
  top ten corporations, 7*t*
Canada Business Corporations Act, 6, 850, 862
Canada Call, 533, 533*n*
Canada Corporation Act, 862
Canada Mortgage and Housing Corporation (CMHC), 527, 528
Canada Revenue Agency (CRA), 8*n*, 8, 36*n*, 304, 526*n*
Canadian Airlines International, 552
Canadian Bond Rating Service, 183
CanadianFixedIncome.ca, 430*n*
Canadian National Railway, 551
Canadian Natural Resources, 382, 388–389, 412
Canadian Pacific, 388*t*, 391–392, 397, 411
Canadian Tire Corporation, 43, 385, 388*t*, 398, 400
Can Deal, 173
cannibalization, 316
capacity expansion. *See* planned expansion
capital, 426
Capital Asset Pricing Model (CAPM), 406–413
  big picture, 412
  CAPM equation relating risk to expected return, 407–408
  cost of common stock capital, 432–433
  defined, 407
  insurance pricing, 723
  and portfolios, 409–410
  problems with, in practice, 412
  security market line (SML), 409, 410*f*
  summary of, 412
capital budget, 302
capital budgeting
  analysis of project, 325–329
  break-even analysis, 327, 328*f*
  defined, 302
  Excel, using, 340–344
  exchange rate risk, 776–778
  forecasting incremental earnings, 303–308
  incremental free cash flow, 309–315
  process, 302–303
  real options, 329–330
  scenario analysis, 327–329
  sensitivity analysis, 325–326, 326*t*
capital cost allowance (CCA), 36*n*, 304–305, 309–310, 309*t*, 318*t*, 639*n*
capital expenditures, 40, 309–310
capital gain rate, 208, 604*f*
capital gains, 207–208, 602–603
capital gains tax, 320
capital market
  internationally integrated, 764–766
  perfect capital markets. *See* perfect capital market
  segmented capital markets, 772–776
capital structure, 426, 427*f*
  agency costs, 574–577
  choices across industries, 550
  choices within industries, 551–552
  debt and information, 577–580
  debt and taxes, 564–570
  debt-to-value ratio, 550, 551*f*
  defined, 550
  fallacies, 561, 570–572
  optimal, 572–574
  in perfect capital markets, 553–564
  summary, 580
  trade-off theory, 572–574, 574*f*
Capstone Business Credit, 703
captured board, 851
Carleton, W., 856*n*
carrying costs, 678
cash, 221*n*
  cash balances, 680
  cash management, 679–682
  compensating balance, 680
  large cash balances, 613*t*
  motivation for holding cash, 679–680
  precautionary balance, 680
  retention of. *See* cash retention
  transactions balance, 679
cash-and-carry strategy, 759–762, 761*f*
cash balances, 680
cash budget, 691–694, 692–694*t*
cash conversion cycle (CCC), 663–664
cash cycle, 662–664, 663*f*
cash discount, 667
cash flow
  CAD-based cash flows, 777–778, 778*t*
  cash flow rights, 866
  common mistake, 84
  coupon bond, 169
  estimate of, 305
  expected cash flows, 206, 226
  foreign currency cash flows, valuation of, 766–771
  free cash flow. *See* free cash flow
  future value, 85
  growing, 118–121
  growing cash flows, 118–121
  interest rate risk, 742*t*
  Ityesi's GBP-denominated free cash flows, 776–777, 777*t*
  leasing *vs.* buying, 800*t*, 801–802
  of levered firm, 566–567, 566*f*
  negative cash flow shocks, 690
  and net working capital, 310–312
  one-year investor, 207
  organization of, 263–264
  from owning a stock, 207
  positive cash flow shocks, 690–691
  present value, 87–88
  rate of return, 112–115
  solving for, 110–112
  stream of cash flows. *See* stream of cash flows
  summing cash flows across time, 84
  timing of, 281–282, 317
  true tax lease, 800–801
  in a typical project, 302*f*
  of unlevered firm, 566–567, 566*f*
  unlevered *vs.* levered, 554–555, 555*f*
  valuation. *See* cash flow valuation
  zero-coupon bond, 164
cash flow statement. *See* statement of cash flows
cash flow valuation, 83–88
  annuities, 104–110
  application of rules of, 89, 89*t*, 96–100
  combination of values, 84
  common mistake, 84
  comparison of values, 84
  compounding, 84–85
  compound interest, 85
  at different points in time, 83–88
  discounting, 86–88
  inflows *vs.* outflows, 83
  monthly cash flows, 136–137
  perpetuities, 101–103
  stream of cash flows, 96–100. *See also* stream of cash flows
  timelines, 82–83
cash inflows, 83
cash in net working capital, 311*n*

cash management, 679–682
cash management bills, 681*t*
cash offers, 509
cash outflows, 83
cash retention
  agency costs, 611–613
  distress costs, 611
  imperfect capital markets, 609–613
  investor tax adjustments, 610–611
  issuance costs, 611
  vs. payout, 608–613
  perfect capital markets, 608–609
  taxes and, 609–610
cash today, 75
  and *NPV* rule, 262
Catholic Church usury laws, 102
CBID, 173
CCA rate, 304–305
CCA tax shield, 313–314, 317–319, 318t, 321*n*
census agreements, 102
CEO compensation, 854–855, 854*f,* 861
certificates of deposit (CDs), 681*t*
Charkham, J., 869*n*
Chen, Hsuan-Chi, 506, 506*n*
Chicago Board Options Exchange (CBOE), 454–455
chief executive officer (CEO), 12, 15
chief financial officer (CFO), 13*f*
China, 489
Choi, S., 695*n*
CIBC, 206, 550, 857
CIBC World Markets, 788
Cisco Systems, 618, 626–627, 721, 820
Citigroup, 752
classified board, 833–834
Clawback provisions, 861
Clayton, Dubilier & Rice, 520, 537*n*
Clayton Act, 835
Clement, Tony, 836
clientele effects, 607–608
CME Group, 762*n*
Coca-Cola, 392–394, 394*f,* 395, 523
"cold" IPO markets, 503–505
Coles, J., 856*n*
collateral
  accounts receivable, 702–703
  margin, 734
collection, 670*f*
collection float, 669–670, 670*f*
collection policy, 673
Comment, R., 833*n*
commercial paper, 188, 188*n,* 681*t,* 701–702
commissions, 74*n*
commitment fees, 699
committed line of credit, 698
commodity price risk, 728–740
  default risk prevention, 734
  forward contract, 731–732
  futures contract, 732–735
  futures hedging *vs.* options hedging, 736–739, 736*t*
  hedging, 729–740
  hedging decision, 739–740
  long-term contracts, 730–732
  options contracts, 735–736
  storage, 729
  vertical integration, 729
common risk, 365–367
common stock, 30, 203, 205–206
common stock capital, 432–434, 434*t*
co-movement of stock, 386–389
Companies' Creditors Arrangement Act (CCAA), 591, 798
Compaq, 829, 830*f,* 831
compensating balance, 680
compensating balance requirements, 699–701
compensation policies, 853–855, 854*f*
competition, 236–239, 842
Competition Bureau, 820
competitive market, 74–75
competitive market prices, 74–75, 77–78
compound annual returns, 358
compounding, 84–85, 137–138
compound interest, 85
confidence intervals, 361–362
conflicts of interest, 576, 825, 849–850
conglomerate merger, 817
conglomerate wave, 816
Connors, John, 616
conservative financing policy, 697
consol, 101
constant dividend growth model, 211–212, 433–434
consumer price index (CPI), 350*f*
continuation value, 650
continuing pool, 321
contracts, financial option, 455–456
controller, 13*f*
conversion price, 534
conversion ratio, 534
convertible bonds, 37, 534, 534*n*
  combining features, 536
  pricing, 534–535, 535*f*
  and stock prices, 536
convertible preferred stock, 489
convertible provisions, 534–537, 535*f*
core-division, 442
Core, J., 858*n*
Cornwell, C., 695*n*
corporate bonds, 182–188
  bond ratings, 183–185, 184*t*
  credit crisis, 188
  credit risk, 182
  credit spreads, 187
  default spread, 185
  defined, 182
  high-yield bonds, 183
  investment-grade bonds, 183, 184*t*
  investment-grade debt, 184*t*
  junk bonds, 183
  liquidity, lack of, 182*n*
  speculative bonds, 183, 184*t*
  yield curve, 185–188, 185*f*
  yields, 183
  yield to maturity, 183
corporate citizenship, 14
corporate debt, 520–525
  asset-backed bonds, 523
  debentures, 523
  and information, 577–580
  mortgage bonds, 523
  notes, 523
  private debt, 520–521
  public debt, 521–525
  secured debt, 523
  seniority, 523–524
  sovereign debt, 525–526
  subordinated debenture, 523–524
  and taxes, 564–570
  types, 523*t*
  unsecured debt, 523
corporate finance, and options, 475–476
corporate governance, 849–850
  see also ethics
  and agency costs, 849–850
  compensation policies, 853–855, 854*f*
  controlling owners, 865–867
  cross-holdings, 868
  defined, 849
  mitigation of agency conflicts, 855–859
  monitoring by board of directors, 850–853, 861
  monitoring by others, 852–853
  pyramid structure, 865–867
  regulation, 859–864
  shareholder rights, protection of, 864
  stakeholder model, 867–868
  trade-off, 868–869
  tunnelling, 866–867
  worldwide, 864–868
corporate investor, 489
corporate management team, 12–13
corporate managers
  implications for, 239
corporate partner, 489
corporate raider, 15, 831
corporate social responsibility, 14
corporation
  board of directors, 12, 850–853
  Canada's top ten corporations, 7*t*
  defined, 5
  double taxation, 7, 8
  ethics, 13–15
  financial functions within, 13*f*
  formation of, 6
  incentives, 13–15
  ownership of, 6–7
  principal-agent problem, 13–15
  taxation around the world, 10
  tax implications, 7–10
correlation, 386–389, 386*n,* 388*f,* 388*t*
  effect of, 395
corruption, 848–849
Costa, Len, 832*n*

cost-benefit analysis, 73–75
competitive market prices and, 74–75
financial manager, role of, 73–74
quantification, 74
cost estimates, 303–308
costly external capital, 445–446
cost of capital, 153–154, 317*n*
common stock capital, 432–434, 434*t*
costly external capital, 445–446
debt capital, 430–432
divisional costs of capital, 443–445
effective cost of debt, 431–432
equity, computation of, 562
equity cost of capital, 207, 209*n*
for Intel, 444
internationalisation, 770
multidivisional firm, 442
new acquisition, 442–443
and opportunity cost, 427
preferred stock capital, 432
project-based costs of capital, 442–445
weighted average cost of capital (WACC). *See* weighted average cost of capital (WACC)
cost of equity, 433–434, 434*t*
costs
acquisition costs, 678
agency costs, 575–577, 611–613, 849–850
bankruptcy, 571
borrowing costs, 822
carrying costs, 678
cost estimates, 303–308
cost of capital. *See* cost of capital
distress costs, 611, 808
financial distress, 571–572, 724
holding inventory, 678–679
initial public offering (IPO), 506–507
issuance costs, 611
liquidity, 679
order costs, 678
resale costs, 807–808
seasoned equity offering (SEO), 511
sunk cost, 316–317
trade credit, 668–669, 676–677
Cotter, J., 851*n*
coupon bonds, 169–173
cash flows, 169
discount, 175–176
premium, 175–176
price, 170–171
price quotes, 171–173
yields, 198–200
yield to maturity *(YTM)*, 170–171
zero-coupon prices, valuation with, 197–198, 197*t*
zero-coupon yields, valuation using, 198
coupon rate, 163, 431
coupons, 163, 181
covenants
advantages of, 530
defined, 529
Hertz's covenants, 530
types of, 529
covered interest parity, 761–762
covered interest parity equation, 761–762
cram down, 591
Crawford, R., 808*n*
Creber, Damian, 537
credible signal, leverage as, 577–578
credit cards, 664*n*
credit crisis, 188
credit period, 667
credit policy, 671–673
credit rating agencies, 671
credit risk, 182, 733
credit spreads, 187, 188*f*
credit standards, 671
credit terms, 671
credit unions, 20*t*
Criminal Code of Canada, 862
Crocs, Inc., 226*t*
cross-holdings, 868
crossover point, 279
Crown Zellerbach, 833
CRSP US Total Market index, 399
5 C's of credit, 671
cum-dividend, 597
cumulative preferred stock, 206
cumulative voting, 205
currency code, 751*n*
currency exchange rates, 751–755, 754–755*t*
exchange rate risk, 756–764
floating rate, 756
fluctuations, 756–758
forward exchange rate, 758–759, 767–768
spot exchange rate, 760
currency forward contract, 758, 759–761
currency swaps, 773
currency timeline, 760, 761*f*
current assets, 31
current liabilities, 31
current ratio, 43

D

Dahya, J., 861*n*
dark pools, 18
dates, identifying, on timelines, 82–83
days sales outstanding, 45
DDM. *See* dividend-discount model (DDM)
dealer paper, 701
debentures, 523
debt. *See* corporate debt
debt capacity, 725, 808, 822
debt capital, cost of, 430–432
debt-equity ratio, 34–35, 47, 440
debt financing
see also bonds
bond covenants, 529–530
corporate debt, 520–525
leveraged buyout (LBO), 536–537
repayment provisions, 530–537
users of, 519
debt-to-capital ratio, 48
debt-to-value ratio, 550, 551*f*
decision making, 73–74
see also valuation principle
NPV rule, 262–263
decision-making tools. *See* investment decision rules
decision rules. *See* investment decision rules
Deckers Outdoor Corp., 231*t*
declaration date, 594
deductible, 728
deep in-the-money, 458
deep out-of-the-money, 458
default risk prevention, 734
default spread, 185
defensive stocks, 402
deferral of earnings repatriation, 771–772
Delaney, Kevin, 502
Dell, 226–227, 819
Delta Airlines, 575
Demsetz, H., 856*n*
Denis, D., 869*n*
depreciation, 31, 40–41, 639, 639*n*
straight-line method of, 440*n*
derivatives, 455
Deutsche Bank AG, 520, 563, 752
Dhar, R., 242*n*
differential access to markets, 773
difficult-to-interpret information, 237–239
Dill, D., 802*n*
diluted EPS, 37
dilution, 37, 561
direct lease, 788
directors, 850–851
see also board of directors
direct paper, 701
disbursement float, 670
disclosure
of financial information, 28–29. *See also* financial statements
initial public offering, 492
notes to the financial statements, 42
discount, 164, 175–176, 175*n*
discounted cash flow (DCF), 267, 268–269
discounted cash flow models, 226*f*, 227*n*, 231–232
discounted free cash flow model, 221–226
and capital budgeting, 224–225
defined, 221
enterprise value, 222
implementation of, 222–223
discounted payback rule, 268
discount factor, 81
discounting, 86–88
discounting too often, 103
discount loan, 699

discount period, 667
discount rate, 81
and annuity formula, 150
conversion from annual percentage rate, 139–140
for future cash flows, 145*n*
and loans, 140–144
meaning of, 153
and yield curve, 147–150
disposition effect, 241–242
distress costs, 611, 808
distribution date, 594
distributions to shareholder, 593–596
see also payout policy
changing composition of shareholder payouts, 606*f*
dividends, 594–595. *See also* dividends
share repurchases, 595–596 (*see also* share repurchases)
diversifiable risk, 370
diversification, 366–367
long-run diversification, 371–372
portfolio, 367–372, 369*f*
risk, 385–386
dividend-discount model (DDM), 203, 206–210, 218*t*
capital gains, 207–208
changing growth rates, 215–217
constant dividend growth model, 211–212
defined, 210
different growth rates, 216–217
vs. discounted cash flows, 227*n*
dividends *vs.* investment and growth, 212–215
dividend yields, 207–208
equation, 210
estimate of dividends, 211–218
limitations, 218–219
multi-year investor, 209–210
non-dividend-paying stocks, 219
one-year investor, 207
share repurchase, 220–221
total payout model, 220–221
total returns, 207–208
value drivers, 217–218
dividend-discount model equation, 210
dividend-paying stock, 475
dividend payments, 6
dividend payout rate, 212
dividend puzzle, 606
dividends, 594
accounting implications, 594
clientele effects, 607–608
cum-dividend, 597
declaration date, 594
differing investor preferences, 608*t*
distribution date, 594
dividend payments, 6
dividend puzzle, 606
dividend signalling hypothesis, 615
dividend smoothing, 613–614
dividend tax credit, 10
dividend yields, 207–208
estimate of, 211–218
with excess cash, 597–598
ex-dividend date, 594
the first dividend, 216
Genron's future dividends, 598
high dividend (equity issue), 601
homemade dividend, 599, 600
vs. investment and growth, 212–215
investor preferences, 598–599
liquidating dividend, 594
M&M Dividend Irrelevance proposition, 600–601
optimal dividend policy with taxes, 603–606
payable date, 594
payout rate, 212
with perfect capital markets, 602
in practice, 604–606
record date, 594
return of capital, 594
vs. share repurchases in perfect capital market, 596–602
special dividend, 594
spinoff, 619
stock dividend, 617–619
summary, 606*t*
tax disadvantage of, 602–608
tax rate factors, 607
tax rates, worldwide, 604*f*
dividend signalling hypothesis, 615
dividend smoothing, 613–614
dividend tax credit, 10
dividend yields, 207–208
divisional costs of capital, 443–445
Dodd-Frank Act, 861–862
Dodd, P., 857*n*
Doidge, C., 867*n*
domestic bonds, 524
Dominion Bond Rating Service (DBRS), 183, 184*t*
double taxation, 7, 8
double-barrelled bonds, 528
Dow Jones Industrial Average, 398
dual class shares, 865
Dun & Bradstreet, 671
DuPont analysis, 52–53
DuPont Identity, 51–52, 52*n*
duration, 178*n*, 741
duration-based hedging, 741
duration mismatch, 741
Dutch auction, 596

E

Eades, K., 408*n*
earnings
see also net income
defined, 35
EBIT (earnings before interest and taxes), 36–37
forward earnings, 227
free cash flow from, 309–313
growth, and mergers, 823–824
incremental earnings. *See* incremental earnings
repatriated earnings, 771–772
trailing earnings, 227
earnings per share *(EPS)*, 36–37, 47, 561, 823–824
easily interpretable information, 237
EBIT break-even, 327
EBIT (earnings before interest and taxes), 37, 46, 47, 306, 308, 573
EBITDA (earnings before interest, taxes, depreciation, and amortization), 37, 46, 47, 650
Eckbo, B.E., 818*n*, 820*n*
economies of scale, 819
economies of scope, 819
EDGAR, 489*n*, 495*n*
Edmans, A., 242*n*
effective annual rate *(EAR)*, 135–137, 139*t*, 668, 700–702
adjusting to effective rate, 136
conversion from annual percentage rate, 139
implied effective interest rate per compounding period, 138
effective cost of debt, 431–432
efficiency gains
mergers and acquisitions, 820–821
from specialization, 808
efficient frontier, 393–394
efficient markets hypothesis, 240
efficient portfolio, 392–394
Eisfeldt, A., 799*n*, 808*n*
Eisner, Michael, 856–857
electronic cheque processing, 670
El Paso Electric, 832
EMC, 819
energy trust, 8, 10
Enron Corporation, 55, 571, 798, 848
enterprise value, 34–35, 222
enterprise value multiples, 229–230
equally weighted portfolio, 396–397, 396*f*
equity, 6, 561
see also stock
agency costs of equity, 575
as call option, 476*f*
financing. *See* equity financing
levered equity, 554
unlevered equity, 554
equity cost of capital, 207, 209*n*
equity–debt holder conflicts, 576–577
equity financing
initial public offering. *See* initial public offering (IPO)
new business financing, 553–554
private companies, 485–492
seasoned equity offering (SEO), 507–511
equity holder. *See* shareholder
equity multiplier, 48
equity risk premium, 407
see also market risk premium
equivalent annual annuity, 282–285

Ernst & Young, 56–57
ethics
accounting scandals, 55
corporate governance. *See* corporate governance
in corporations, 13–15
Enron, 55
principal-agent problem, 13–15
Eurobonds, 524
Euromoney, 752
European Commission, 820, 836
European options, 456, 466
European Union (EU), 29, 820, 835
evergreen credit, 698
Excel
beta, calculation of, 405
capital budgeting, 340–344
correlation between two sets of returns, 390
future value, solving for, 106–107
IRR, computation of, 266
NPV, computation of, 263–264, 266
NPV profile, 299–300
present value, solving for, 106–107
pro forma statement, 340
sensitivity analysis, 342–344
standard deviation of historical returns, 360
excessive risk-taking, 576
excessive trading, 240–241
exchange rate risk, 756–764
capital budgeting, 776–778
cash-and-carry strategy, 760–761, 761*f*
covered interest parity, 761–762
covered interest parity equation, 761–762
currency forward contract, 758, 759–761
currency timeline, 760, 761*f*
effect of, 757
exchange rate fluctuations, 756–758, 756*f*
hedging with forward contracts, 758–759, 760*f*
hedging with options, 762–764
pricing of currency forwards, 759–762
spot exchange rate, 760
exchange rates. *See* currency exchange rates
exchange ratio, 827
ex-dividend date, 594
executive incentive compensation, 861
exercise price, 455
exercising the option, 455
exit strategy, 491–492
expansion. *See* planned expansion
expected cash flows, 206, 226
expected return, 370–371, 370*t*
and beta (β), 410*f*
CAPM equation relating risk to, 407–408
computation of, 408
direct estimate of, 408
and total risk, 410*f*
vs. volatility, 394*f*
expected return of a portfolio, 384–385, 393*t*, 411
expenses
interest expenses, 308, 634*n*
operating expenses, 36
overhead expenses, 316–317
expertise, 819–820
expiration date, 456, 466
Export Development Canada (EDC) bonds, 527

F

Facebook, 219, 484, 489–492, 503, 550
initial public offering (IPO), 495, 496*f*, 498–499
seasoned equity offering (SEO), 508–509, 508*f*
face value, 163
factoring of accounts receivable a rrangement, 702–703
factors, 702
fair market value (FMV) lease, 792
Fama-French-Carhart factor specification (FFC), 422, 423*t*
Fanapt, 297
Fastow, Andrew, 55
Fedak, Marilyn, 233
Fich, E., 851*n*
field warehouse, 704
final prospectus, 495
finance, study, 3
finance lease, 792, 794–797
Financial Accounting Standards Board, 798
financial calculator
decimal places, 131
end-of-period mode, 131
future value of annuity, 132–133
future value, solving for, 88, 106–107
general TVM buttons, 131
number of periods per year, 131
present value, solving for, 88, 106–107
present value of single future cash flow, 132
rate of return, computation of, 113*n*, 114–115, 133
using, 131–133
yield to call (YTC), 544
yield to maturity *(YTM),* 196
financial crisis of 2008, 351, 577
financial crisis of 2008–2009, 505
financial cycle, 19, 20*f*
financial distress, 697
costs, 571–572, 724
defined, 571
factors, 573
Financial Industry Regulatory Authority (FINRA), 173
financial institutions, 19–21
defined, 19
financial cycle, 19, 20*f*
role of, 21
types of, 20–21, 20*t*
financial manager
advice for, 619–620
decision making, 73–74
financing decisions, 11
goal of, 11–12
investment decisions, 11
place in corporation, 12–15
role of, 10–12, 73–74
short-term cash needs, 11
financial markets
bond market, 19
foreign exchange market, 19
other financial markets, 19
stock markets, 16–19
financial option
American options, 455, 466
at-the-money, 457
basics, 455–459
binomial option pricing model, 468–470
binomial pricing formula, 469
Black-Scholes option pricing formula, 470–472
call option, 455, 460*f*, 476*f*
compensation policies, 853
and corporate finance, 475–476
deep in-the-money, 458
deep out-of-the-money, 458
defined, 455
derivatives, 455
dividend-paying stock, 475
European options, 456, 466
exchange rate risk, 762–764
exercise price, 455
exercising the option, 455
expiration date, 456, 466
vs. forward contracts, 762–764
futures hedging *vs.* options hedging, 736–739, 736*t*
hedging, 458
hedging with options contracts, 735–736
in-the-money, 457
language of options, 456*t*
long position, 459–460, 460*f*
non-dividend-paying stock, 470, 473
online option pricing calculator, 471*f*
open interest, 457
option buyer, 456
option contracts, 455–456
option prices, factors affecting, 466–467, 467*t*
options hedging, 736–739, 736*t*
option writer, 455
on other financial securities, 458–459
out-of-the-money, 458
payoff, 456, 465*t*
payoff at expiration, 459–465
portfolio insurance, 472–475, 473*f*
profit, 456, 465*t*
profit at expiration, 463–464, 463*f*

financial option (*continued*)
protective put, 472
purchasing options, 458
put-call parity, 472–475
put option, 455, 460–461
risk-free rate, 466
short position, 461–462, 461*f*
short sales, 464–465, 465*f*
speculating, 458
stock option quotations, 456–458, 457*t*
stock price, 466
strike price, 455, 460*f*, 466
two-state single-period model, 468–469
volatility, 466–468
warrant, 455
financial reporting in practice, 55–57
financial statement analysis
accounts payable days, 45
accounts receivable days, 45, 45*n*
acid-test ratio, 43
asset efficiency, 45, 53–54*t*
asset turnover, 45
average collection period, 45
current ratio, 43
days sales outstanding, 45
debt-equity ratio, 34–35, 47
debt-to-capital ratio, 48
debt-to-enterprise value ratio, 48
DuPont analysis, 52–53
DuPont Identity, 51–52, 52*n*
EBITDA, 46
enterprise value, 34–35
equity multiplier, 48
fixed asset turnover, 45
gross margin, 42–43
interest coverage ratios, 52 *t*, 46–47
inventory days, 45
inventory turnover ratio, 45
leverage ratios, 52 *t*, 47–48
liquidity ratios, 43–44, 53*t*
market-to-book ratio, 33–34
mismatched ratios, 49
net debt, 48, 48*n*
net profit margin, 43
operating margin, 43
operating returns, 50–51, 54*t*
P/E to Growth (PEG) ratio, 49
price-earnings ratio (P/E), 48
price-to-book ratio (P/B), 33
profitability ratios, 42–43, 49–50, 53*t*
quick ratio, 43
return on assets (ROA), 50
return on equity (ROE), 50, 50*n*
return on invested capital (ROIC), 50–51
times interest earned (TIE) ratio, 46
valuation ratios, 52 *t*, 48–50
working capital ratios, 45–46, 53–54*t*
financial statements
analysis. *See* financial statement analysis
annual report, 28
balance sheet, 29–35
defined, 28
financial reporting in practice, 55–57
forecasting, 632–638
income statement, 35–37
interim financial statements, 28
management discussion and analysis (MD&A), 42
notes to the financial statements, 42
preparation, 28
pro forma statement, 308, 342 (*see also* specific pro forma statements)
as starting point, 57
statement of cash flows, 37–41
statement of shareholders' equity, 41
types of, 28
financing
capital structure. *See* capital structure
debt financing. *See* debt financing
equity. *See* equity financing
and interest, 648*n*
levered financing, 554
long-term financial planning, 631
net new financing, 634, 636–637
planned expansion, 638–643
and pro forma balance sheet, 643*t*
short-term financing. *See* short-term financing
sustainable growth rate, 644–647
venture merchant financing, 703
financing activity, 40
financing decisions, 11
Finland, 10
Fiorina, Carly, 829–830, 857
firm commitment, 498
firms
common stock capital, cost of, 432–434, 434*t*
corporation, 5–10
debt capital, cost of, 430–432
differences across, 573
disclosure of financial information, 28–29
levered, 428–429
partnerships, 5
preferred stock capital, cost of, 432
sole partnerships, 4
types of firms, 3–10, 9–10*t*
unlevered, 428
value of. *See* firm value
firm-specific risk, 401*f*
firm value
enterprise value, 222
with expansion, 650–652, 651*t*
and growth, 644–647
and interest tax deduction, 564–565
leverage and, 554–556
planned expansion, effect of, 649–652
Valuation Principle, 662, 667
without expansion, 652, 652*t*
and working capital, 665–667
fixed asset turnover, 45
fixed-for-floating interest rate swap, 742, 742*t*
fixed overhead expenses, 316–317
fixed price lease, 792
fleet debt, 521
floating lien, 703–704
floating rate, 742, 756
float management, 669–670
floor planning, 704
Florida Marlins, 84
flow-through entities, 8
Food and Drug Administration, 297
Ford Motor Company, 32, 520, 536*n*
forecasting
cash budget, 691–694, 692–694*t*
continuation value, 650
financial statements, 632–638
forecast target, 638
free cash flows, 648–649, 648*t*
incremental earnings, 303–308
net new financing, 636–637
percent of sales method, 632
planned expansion, 638–643
the plug, 636
pro forma balance sheet, 634–635, 635*t*, 642–643, 643*t*
pro forma income statement, 632–634, 633*t*
short-term financing needs, 689–694
foreign bonds, 524
foreign currency cash flows, valuation of, 766–771
foreign exchange (FX or forex) market, 19, 752
currency exchange rates, 752–755, 754–755*t*
exchange rate risk, 756–764
most traded currencies, 752, 753*f*
foreign project
deferral of earnings repatriation, 771–772
immediate repatriation of earnings, 771–772
multiple foreign projects, 772
single foreign project, 771–772
valuation, and international taxation, 771–772
value of, 768–769
foreign takeovers, 836
forex market. *See* foreign exchange (FX or forex) market
Forrester, J. R., Jr., 267, 267*n*
forward cash-out merger, 831
forward contract, 731–732
hedging with, 758–759, 760*f*
vs. option, 762–764
forward earnings, 222
forward exchange rate, 758–760, 767–768
forward P/E, 227
France, 102
Franks, J., 864*n*, 869*n*

free cash flow, 307–315
adjusting, 317–323
calculation of, from earnings, 309–315
cannibalization, 316
conversion, 768
defined, 309
direct calculation, 313–314
discounted free cash flow model, 221–226
enterprise valuation, 222
focus on, 239
forecasting, 648–649, 648*t*
incremental, 309–315
leasing *vs.* buying, 800*t*
liquidation value, 319–321
net present value, calculation of, 314–315
opportunity cost, 315
perpetual *CCA* tax shields, 317–319
project externalities, 316
salvage value, 319–321
stock valuation, 223–224
timing of cash flows, 317
free rider problem, 837–838
freezeout merger, 841–842
Frieden, Sue, 56–57
friendly takeover, 831
funding risk, 697
future funding needs, 631
futures contract, 732–735
futures hedging, 736–739, 736*t*
future value, 80, 84
of annuity, 105–109, 132–133
of cash flow, 85
compounding, 84–85
computation of, 97–98
of growing annuity, 121
vs. present value, 81
solving for, with financial calculator, 88, 106–107
FX market. *See* foreign exchange (FX or forex) market

G

GAAP. *See* Generally Accepted Accounting Principles (GAAP)
Garcia, D., 242*n*
Garvey, G., 858*n*
GE Capital Aviation Services, 787–788
General American Oil, 832
General Electric Company (GE), 442, 820
general lien, 703
Generally Accepted Accounting Principles (GAAP), 28, 29
General Motors (GM), 183, 594, 595*f*, 613–614, 614*f*
general obligation bonds, 528
general partnership, 5
Genron's future dividends, 598
George Weston Ltd., 7*t*
Georgia-Pacific, 836
Germany, 850
Gillette Company, 834
Gilligan, T., 808*n*
Gitman, L. J., 267, 267*n*
Glaser, Shelagh M., 444
global bonds, 524
Global Competition Review, 835
global financial crisis, 563
global takeover market, 815
Goetzmann, William, 102
going public. *See* initial public offering (IPO)
golden parachute, 834
Goldman Sachs, 752
Goldsmith, James, 833
Gompers, Paul A., 487, 487*n*, 858*n*
Google, Inc., 219, 502
Google Finance, 203, 204*f*, 227
government bailouts, 577, 577*n*
Government of Canada bonds, 169, 350*f*, 356, 356*f*, 357*f*, 361, 364*f*
Government of Canada bond yield curves, 201
Government of Canada treasury bills, 348, 349, 361*f*, 438*t*
Graham, J., 808*n*
Graham, John, 267, 267*n*, 273, 408*n*, 617*n*
Grannis, Dick, 280
Great Depression, 859, 862
Great-West Lifeco, 7*t*
greenmail, 596
Green Shoe Company, 499*n*
greenshoe provision, 499
Grenadier, S., 794*n*
grey directors, 850
gross margin, 42–43
gross profit, 36
growing annuity, 120–121
growing cash flows, 118–121
growing perpetuity, 118–121, 211*n*
growth, 644–647
changing growth rates, 215–217
different growth rates, 216–217
vs. dividends, 212–215
and firm value, 644–647
internal growth rate, 644, 645, 646*t*
profitable growth, 213–215
simple model of growth, 212–213
sustainable growth rate, 644–647, 646*t*
unprofitable growth, 214–215
growth stocks, 34
Grullon, G., 242*n*, 596*n*
guaranteed investment certificates (GICs), 135, 681*t*
Guay, W., 858*n*

H

half-year rule, 305
Hall, B., 854*n*
Halley, Edmond, 105
Hance, Julian, 615
hanging on to losers, 241–242
Hanouna, P., 867*n*
Harford, J., 816*n*, 825*n*
Harris, Lawrence, 863
Harris, R., 408*n*
Hart-Scott-Rodino Act, 835
Harvey, Campbell, 267, 267*n*, 273, 408*n*, 617*n*
Hasbro, 668, 698, 698*n*, 703
Health Canada, 238
hedge funds, 20*t*
hedging, 458
commodity price risk, 729–740
duration-based hedging, 741
earnings smoothing, 731*f*
exchange rate risk, 758–759, 760*f*, 762–764
forward contract, 731–732, 758–759, 760*f*
futures contract, 732–735
futures hedging *vs.* options hedging, 736–739, 736*t*
long-term contracts, 730–732
mismatching contracts and risk exposure, 740
mistakes when hedging risk, 739–740
natural hedge, 739
options contracts, 735–736, 762–764
storage, 729
swap-based hedging, 741–743
at U.S. airlines, 740
vertical integration, 729
Heron, R., 833*n*, 855*n*
Hertz Corporation, 520, 521, 522*f*, 524–525*t*, 536, 550
callable bonds, 530, 531*t*
covenants, 530
Hewlett-Packard, 226–227, 829–830, 857
Hewlett, Walter, 803, 804
Hickman, K., 851*n*
Higgins, R., 408*n*
high dividend (equity issue), 601
high-yield bonds, 183
Himmelberg, C., 856*n*
Hirshleifer, D., 242*n*
historical returns, 351–363, 403–406, 438*t*
historical tradeoff between risk and return, 363–365, 364*f*
historical volatility, 359
Hoffman, Reid, 489
hold-up problem, 808*n*
Home Depot, 542–543
homemade dividend, 599, 600
homemade leverage, 558
Honeywell, 820, 836
Hong, Jim, 797*n*
Hoogheemraadschap Lekdijk Bovendams, 102
horizontal merger, 817
hostile takeover, 15, 831
"hot" IPO markets, 503–505
HSBC, 752
Hubbard, R.G., 856*n*
hubris hypothesis, 825, 825*n*

Hudson's Bay Company (HBC), 72
Hughes, Chris, 489
human resource constraint, 286–287

I

IBM, 819
idle asset, 315
Ignition Partners, 616
Ikenberry, D., 596*n*, 617*n*
ImClone, 864
imperfect capital markets, and cash retention, 609–613
Imperial Oil, 7*t*
implied effective interest rate per compounding period, 138
importer-exporter dilemma, 757
incentives, 13–15
incentives, improved, 808
income
  net income, 35, 37
  operating income, 36
  pre-tax income, 37
  unlevered net income, 308
income statement, 35–37, 36*t*
  accounts payable days, 45
  accounts receivable days, 45, 45*n*
  asset efficiency, 45, 53–54*t*
  asset turnover, 45
  average collection period, 45
  days sales outstanding, 45
  debt-to-capital ratio, 48
  debt-to-enterprise value ratio, 48
  defined, 35
  DuPont Identity, 51–52, 52*n*
  earnings calculations, 35–37
  EBIT (earnings before interest and taxes), 36–37
  EBITDA, 37, 46
  equity multiplier, 48
  fixed asset turnover, 45
  gross margin, 42–43
  gross profit, 36
  interest coverage ratios, 52 *t*, 46–47
  inventory days, 45
  inventory turnover ratio, 45
  leverage ratios, 52 *t*, 47–48
  liquidity ratios, 43–44, 53*t*
  net income, 35, 37
  net profit margin, 43
  operating expenses, 36
  operating margin, 43
  operating returns, 50–51, 54*t*
  P/E to Growth (PEG) ratio, 49
  pre-tax income, 37
  price-earnings ratio (P/E), 48
  profitability ratios, 42–43, 49–50, 53*t*
  return on assets (ROA), 50
  return on equity (ROE), 50, 50*n*
  return on invested capital (ROIC), 50–51
  times interest earned (TIE) ratio, 46
  valuation ratios, 52 *t*, 48–50
  working capital ratios, 45–46, 53–54*t*
income trusts, 8
incremental earnings
  defined, 303
  forecasting, 303–308
incremental free cash flow, 309–315
  see also free cash flow
incremental net working capital, 649
incremental revenue, 306–308
indenture, 521
Independent Compensation Committee, 861
independent directors, 851
independent risk, 365–367
index funds, 399
individual biases and trading, 240–243
Industry Regulatory Authority (FINRA), 430*n*
inefficient portfolio, 393
inflation, 145–146
inflation rates, 147*f*
information
  adverse selection and pecking order hypothesis, 578–579
  asymmetric information, 577
  and corporate debt, 577–580
  leverage as credible signal, 577–578
  market timing, 578
  private, difficult-to-interpret, 237–239
  public, easily interpretable, 237
  in stock prices, 234–235
initial public offering (IPO), 492–502
  advantages of going public, 492–493
  auction IPO, 499–502, 500*t*, 500*f*
  best efforts, 499
  book building, 498
  bought deal, 498
  "cold" IPO markets, 503–505
  costs, 506–507
  cyclicality of IPOs in United States, 505*f*
  defined, 492
  disadvantages of going public, 492–493
  disclosure, 492
  final prospectus, 495
  firm commitment, 498
  Google, Inc., 502
  greenshoe provision, 499
  high costs of issuing, 506–507
  "hot" IPO markets, 503–505
  international comparison of first-day IPO returns, 504*t*
  lead underwriter, 494
  lockup, 499
  other types of, 499–502
  over-allotment allocation, 499
  poor post-IPO long-run stock performance, 507
  preliminary prospectus, 495
  pricing the deal, 498–499
  primary offering, 494
  puzzles of, 503–507
  red herring, 495
  regulatory filings, 495
  risk management, 498–499
  road show, 496
  secondary offering, 494
  spread, 498
  summary of IPO methods, 502*t*
  syndicate, 494–495
  tombstones, 509
  top twenty nine global IPOs, 493*t*
  traditional method, 494–499
  underpriced IPOs, 503
  underwriter, 494–495, 494*t*
  valuation of, using comparables, 495–496
inside directors, 850
insider trading, 862–864
Insider Trading Sanctions Act, 862
institutional investors, 488
insurance, 721–728
  actuarially fair price, 722, 722*n*
  adverse selection, 726–727
  bankruptcy, 724
  business interruption insurance, 721
  business liability insurance, 721
  Capital Asset Pricing Model (CAPM), 723
  costs of, 726–728
  debt capacity, 725
  deductible, 728
  insurance decision, 728
  insurance market imperfections, 726
  insurance premium, 722, 722*n*
  issuance costs, 724
  key personnel insurance, 721
  moral hazard, 726
  policy limits, 728
  pricing in perfect market, 722–723
  property insurance, 721
  risk assessment, 726
  role of, 721–722
  tax rate fluctuations, 725
  value of, 724–726
insurance companies, 20*t*
Insurance Information Institute, 723*n*, 726*n*
insurance premium, 722, 722*n*
Insurance Research Council, 726*n*
integer programming, 287*n*
integrative case, 257–258, 345–346, 545–548, 628, 713–718
Intel, 338–339, 392–394, 394*f*, 395, 444
interest
  composition, over time, 86*f*
  compound interest, 85
  coupon rate, 163
  coupons, 163
  and financing, 648*n*
  simple interest, 138
interest coverage ratios, 46–47, 54*t*
interest expenses, 308, 634*n*

interest rate, 79–82, 134–154
annual percentage rate *(APR)*, 137–140, 668
bank rate, 698
and bond price, 174–176, 177*t*, 178*t*
coupon rate, 163
defined, 79
determinants, 144–153
determination, 150
discount rate. *See* discount rate
effective annual rate *(EAR)*, 135–137, 668, 700–702
and inflation rates, 147*f*
interest rate factor, 79
and investment, 146–147
London Inter-Bank Offered Rate (LIBOR), 698
market interest rate, 153
nominal, 145–146, 145*n*
overnight rate, 150
prime rate, 698
quotes and adjustments, 135–140
real, 145–146
risk-free interest rates, 148–149, 148*f*, 166
risk-free rate, 466
spot interest rates, 166
term structure, 147, 148*f*, 149
three-year bonds, various borrowers, 182*t*
yield curve, 147–153
interest rate factor, 79
interest rate risk, 178–179, 178*t*, 182*t*, 740–743
cash flow, 742*t*
combining swaps with standard loans, 743
duration, 741
duration-based hedging, 741
fixed-for-floating interest rate swap, 742, 742*t*
interest rate swap, 743
swap-based hedging, 741–743
interest rate swap, 743
interest tax deduction, 564–565
interest tax shield, 651, 651*n*
computation, 565
defined, 565
with permanent debt, 567–568, 567*n*
valuation, 566–567
interim financial statements, 28
internal growth rate, 644, 645, 646*t*
internal rate of return *(IRR)*
computation of, 266
vs. IRR rule, 272
multiple IRRs, 271–274
sensitivity, measurement of, 264–265, 265*f*
internal rate of return (IRR) rule, 269–274, 269*t*
of incremental cash flows, 279
vs. IRR, 28
multiple IRRs, 271–274
mutually exclusive projects, 274–282
vs. NPV rule, 281–282
unconventional cash flows, 269–271
International Accounting Standards, 795
International Accounting Standards Board (IASB), 29
International Accounting Standards Committee, 29
international bond markets, 524–525
International Business Machines Corporation, 27
international corporate finance
capital budgeting with exchange rate risk, 776–778
currency exchange rates, 751–755, 754–755*t*
exchange rate risk, 756–764
foreign currency cash flows, valuation of, 766–771
global takeover market, 815
internationally integrated capital markets, 764–766
segmented capital markets, 772–776
valuation and international taxation, 771–772
International Financial Reporting Standards (IFRS), 28, 29, 794, 798
internationally integrated capital markets, 764–766
in-the-money, 457
inventory, 31
benefits of holding inventory, 677–678
costs of holding inventory, 678–679
floating lien, 703–704
"just-in-time" (JIT) inventory management, 678–679
management, 677–679
stock-out, 677
storage, 729
trust receipts loan, 704
warehouse arrangement, 704–705
inventory days, 45
inventory management, 677–679
inventory turnover ratio, 45
investment
see also trading
alternative investments, 680–681
behaviour, 242–243
competitive advantage, 239
vs. dividends, 212–215
individual biases and trading, 240–243
and interest rate policy, 146–147
levered value, 439
liquid, 16
opportunity cost of capital, 153–154
rate of return, 112–115
retention rate, 213
investment activity, 40
Investment Canada Act, 836
investment decision rules
alternative rules, 269–274
choosing between projects, 274–282
discounted cash flow (DCF), 267, 268–269
internal rate of return (IRR) rule, 269–274
limited resources, 285–288
most popular decision rules, 267, 267*f*
mutually exclusive projects, 274–282
NPV rule, 261–266 (*see also* NPV rule)
payback period, 268
payback rule, 268–269
persistence of other rules, 273
projects with different lives, 282–285
summary of, 288*t*
using NPV rule, 263–266
variety of rules used, 267
investment decisions, 11
investment-grade bonds, 183, 184*t*
investment-grade debt, 184*t*
Investor Responsibility Research Center (IRRC), 858
investors
angel investors, 485
annual returns *vs.* portfolio turnover, 241*f*
attention, mood, and experience, 242–243
consequences for, 239
corporate investor, 489
corporate partner, 489
dividends *vs.* share repurchases, preferences, 607–608, 608*t*
institutional, 488
private equity investor, 485
strategic investor, 489
strategic partner, 489
venture capital firm, 485–487
IPO. *See* initial public offering (IPO)
Ireland, 10
IRR rule. *See* internal rate of return *(IRR)* rule
iShares, 399
Ishii, J., 858*n*
issuance costs, 611, 724
Italy, 102

J

Jacoby, Gady, 533, 533*n*
Jagannathan, Ravi, 502, 502*n*
Japan, 29
Jarrell, Gregg, 835, 835*n*
Jensen, M., 825*n*, 853*n*
Jog, Vijay, 267, 267*n*, 507, 507*n*
Johnson & Johnson, 255
Johnson, Richard, 797*n*
Johnson, Ross, 841
Johnson, S., 867*n*
JP Morgan, 752
junk bonds, 183
"just-in-time" (JIT) inventory management, 678–679

K

Kahneman, Daniel, 241, 241*n*
Kanatas, G., 242*n*
Kaplan, Steven, 572

Kedia, S., 855*n*
keiretsu, 868
Kelly, Gary, 730
Kevin Laws, 486
key personnel insurance, 721
Kilts, James, 834
Klein, B., 808*n*
Kohlberg, Kravis, and Roberts (KKR), 841
Kooli, Maher, 506, 507, 507*n*
Kosher Depot, 703
Kraakman, R., 867*n*
Krispy Kreme Doughnut Corporation, 798
Kroger, John R., 55*n*
Krüger, Philipp, 442
Kuwait, 489
Kuwait Investment Authority, 489
Kuwait Investment Board, 489

L

Lai, Kam Wah, 511*n*
Lakonishok, J., 617*n*
Landier, Augustin, 442
La Porta, R., 864*n*, 867*n*, 869*n*
large portfolios, 363, 364*f*, 395–397
Latin America, 29
Law of One Price, 77
  bond price, 175*n*
  futures contract, 734*n*, 735*n*
  method of comparables, 226–233
  as robustness check, 769–770
  yield curve, 197–201
lead underwriter, 494
lease-equivalent loan, 802–803
leasing
  accounting consequences, 794–797, 794*n*
  and balance sheet, 795
  bankruptcy, 798–799
  basics, 788–794
  vs. buying, 801–802
  calculation of lease payments, 791
  capital, preservation of, 809
  and capital expenditure controls, 809
  cash flows, 800–801
  competitive lease pricing, 792*n*
  debt capacity, increased, 808
  decision, 799–806
  direct lease, 788
  distress costs, reduced, 808
  effective after-tax lease borrowing rate, 804–805
  efficiency gains from specialization, 808
  end-of-term lease options, 792–793
  examples of lease transactions, 788–789
  fair market value cap lease, 792
  fair market value (FMV) lease, 792
  finance lease, 792, 794–797
  fixed price lease, 792
  incentives, improved, 808
  lease-equivalent loan, 802–803
  lease payments and residual values, 789–790
  lease terms in perfect market, 789–790
  lessee, 788
  lessor, 788
  leveraged lease, 788
  vs. loans, 790–792
  new lease terms, evaluation of, 804
  non-tax lease, 798, 805–806
  off-balance-sheet financing, 809
  operating lease, 794, 796–797
  other lease provisions, 793–794
  $1.00 out lease, 792
  reasons, 806–809
  reduced resale costs, 807–808
  residual value, 789
  sale and leaseback, 788
  sales-type lease, 788
  special-purpose entity (SPE), 789, 798
  synthetic lease, 789, 798
  tax differences, 806–807
  tax treatment, 797–798
  transfer of risk, 808
  true lease, 799
  true tax lease, 797, 800–801, 805
Lee, I., 506*n*
Lee, Y.T., 241*n*
Lehn, K., 856*n*
Lemmon, M., 808*n*, 856*n*
Leone, Marie, 703*n*
Lerner, Josh, 485–487, 485*t*
lessee, 788
lessor, 788
leverage, 47, 428, 440, 569
  consequences, 574–580
  as credible signal, 577–578
  and earnings per share, 561
  effect on risk and return, 556–558, 556*t*, 557*f*
  and firm value, 554–556
  homemade leverage, 558
  optimal, 573–574, 574*f*
  unlevered *vs.* levered cash flow, 554–555, 555*f*
leveraged buyout (LBO), 488, 536–537, 838–841
leveraged lease, 788
leverage ratios, 47–48, 54*t*
levered equity, 554
  risk and return of, 557–558
levered financing, 554
levered firm, 428–429
  cash flow of, 566–567, 566*f*
levered value, 439
Levit, D., 856*n*
Lewellen, W., 792*n*
Li, K., 825*n*
liabilities
  on balance sheet, 31–32
  current liabilities, 31
  defined, 30
  long-term liabilities, 32
Liebman, J., 854*n*
Lie, Erik, 833*n*, 855, 855*n*
liens
  blanket lien, 703
  floating lien, 703–704
  general lien, 703
Li, K., 825*n*
limited liability, 5
limited liability partnership (LLP), 5
limited partnership, 5
limited resources, 285–288
linear programming, 287*n*
line of credit, 698
linkages between variables, 631
Lintner, John, 413, 614*n*
Lipton, Martin, 832
liquid, 16
liquidating dividend, 594
liquidation value, 32, 319–321
liquidity, 679, 823
liquidity ratios, 43–44, 53*t*
liquidity risk, 739
liquid market, 239*n*
listing standards, 19
Liu, Y.J., 241*n*
loan origination fee, 699
loans. *See* bank loans
Loblaw Companies Limited, 384–385, 401, 401*f*, 402, 564–565, 565*t*
Lochhead, S., 506*n*
lockup, 499
logarithms, 116
London Inter-Bank Offered Rate (LIBOR), 698, 742, 742*n*
London Stock Exchange, 828
Long, M., 792*n*, 855*n*
long-run diversification, 371–372
long-term assets, 31
long-term contracts, hedging with, 730–732
long-term debt, 32
long-term financial planning
  forecasting. *See* forecasting
  goals, 631
long-term lending, 151–152
long-term liabilities, 32
Lonie, A., 861*n*
Lopez-de-Silanes, F., 864*n*, 867*n*, 869*n*
Los Angeles Angels, 84
losses for projects in profitable companies, 307–308
Loughran, Tim, 498, 498*n*
Lululemon Athletica Inc., 43

M

macro-level distortions, 774
Magna International, 7*t*
mail float, 669
make-whole call, 533
Malatesta, P., 833*n*
Malenko, N., 856*n*
Malmendier, U., 242*n*
management buyout (MBO), 841

management discussion and analysis (MD&A), 42
management entrenchment, 858
managerial decision making, 73–74
managerial entrenchment, 575
managerial incentives, 725
Manulife Financial, 7*t*
margin, 734
gross margin, 42–43
net profit margin, 43
operating margin, 43
margin account, 735*n*
marginal corporate tax rate, 307
margin call, 734
market
bond market, 19
capital markets. *See* capital markets
"cold" IPO markets, 403–405
competitive market, 74–75
financial markets, 16–19
foreign exchange (FX or forex) market. *See* foreign exchange (FX or forex) market
global takeover market, 815
"hot" IPO markets, 403–405
imperfect capital markets, and cash retention, 609–613
international bond markets, 524–525
liquid market, 239*n*
primary market, 16
secondary market, 16
stock market. *See* stock market
marketable securities, 31
market cap, 6
market capitalization, 6, 32, 398
market efficiency, 236*f*
market frictions, and trade credit, 668–669
market index, 398
market interest rate, 153
market makers, 18
market portfolio
defined, 397
market proxy, 398
role of, 397–398
stock market indexes as, 398–399
market prices
valuation principle and, 75–78
market proxy, 398
market risk, 399–401
market risk premium, 407, 438
market timing, 578
market-to-book ratio, 33–34
market value
vs. book value, 32–33
of debt, 47*n*
market-value balance sheet, 428
marking to market, 734–735, 734*t*
Markowitz, Harry, 366*n*, 396, 413
Masulis, R., 858*n*
matching principle, 694–697, 695*n*
maturity date, 163
Mauer, D.C., 695*n*
Mayer, C., 864*n*, 869*n*
McConnell, J., 792*n*, 794*n*, 869*n*
McDonald's Big Mac, prices of, 77–78, 77–78*t*
McDougall, Duane, 836
MCI, 848
Mehta, P., 867*n*
merger "arbitrage," 828–830
merger-arbitrage spread, 829, 830*f*
mergers and acquisitions
accounting issues, 830–831
acquirer, 815
acquisition premium, 817, 818*t*
background, 815–817
bidder, 815
borrowing costs, 822
competition, 842
conflicts of interest, 825
conglomerate merger, 817
diversification, 822–823
earnings growth, 823–824
and earnings per share, 823–824
economies of scale, 819
economies of scope, 819
efficiency gains, 820–821
exchange ratio, 827
expertise, 819–820
foreign takeovers, 836
forward cash-out merger, 831
fraction of U.S. public companies over, 816*f*
free rider problem, 837–838
freezeout merger, 841–842
friendly takeover, 831
historical trends, 815–817
horizontal merger, 817
hostile takeover, 831
leveraged buyout (LBO), 838–841
liquidity, 823
management buyout (MBO), 841
managerial motives, 825–826
market reaction to takeover, 817–818
merger-arbitrage spread, 829, 830*f*
merger waves, 815–817
monopoly gains, 820
and poorly performing management, 859
and price-earnings ratio, 824–825
reasons to acquire, 818–826
recapitalization, 834–835
regulatory approval, 835–837
risk reduction, 822
step up, 830
stock swap, 817
synergies, 818
takeover, 815
takeover defences, 832–837
takeover process, 826–832
target, 815
taxes, 830–831
tax savings from operating losses, 821–822
tender offer, 827
term sheet, 817
toehold, 838
twenty largest merger transactions, 1998–2017, 815*t*
types of mergers, 817
unaffected target price, 826*n*
value added, recipient of, 837–842
vertical integration, 819
vertical merger, 817
merger waves, 815–817
Merrill Lynch, 752
Merton, Robert C., 422*n*
Meschke, J., 856*n*
method of comparables, 226–233
Metrick, A., 858*n*
Mexico, 10
Michaely, Roni, 608, 608*n*, 613*n*, 617*n*
Microsoft Corporation, 592–593, 616, 819
Mikkelson, W., 859*n*
Milbourn, T., 858*n*
Miller, Merton, 554, 556, 562–563, 601*n*, 792*n*
see also M&M (Modigliani & Franco)
mismatched ratios, 49
mitigation of agency conflicts, 855–859
M&M (Modigliani & Franco), 554–555, 562–563
commodity price risk, 729
insurance, 724
M&M Dividend Irrelevance proposition, 600–601
M&M Payout Irrelevance proposition, 609
and real world, 560–562
M&M Dividend Irrelevance proposition, 600–601
M&M Payout Irrelevance proposition, 609
Modigliani, Franco, 554, 556, 562–563, 601*n*
see also M&M (Modigliani & Franco)
Moeller, S., 827*n*
money market securities, 680, 681*t*
monopoly gains, 820
Montreal Exchange, 16, 454
Moody's Investors Service, 183, 184*t*
moral hazard, 577, 726
Morck, R., 867*n*
mortgage
defined, 143
mortgage payments, 143
outstanding loan balance, 144
mortgage bonds, 523
mortgage payments, 143
Moskovitz, Dustin, 489
Mossin, Jan, 413
Motorola, 857
Mullainathan, S., 867*n*
multidivisional firms, in cost of capital, 442
multi-factor model, 422
multiple *IRR*s, 271–274

multi-year investor, 209–210
Murphy, K., 853*n*
mutual funds, 20*t*
mutually exclusive projects, 274–282
  change in scale, 277–278
  defined, 274
  differences in scale, 274–280
  identical scale, 276–277
  internal rate of return *(IRR)* rule, 274–282
  and net present value *(NPV)*, 275–276
  NPV rule, 274–282
  percentage return *vs.* dollar impact on value, 278
  timing of cash flow, 281–282
Myers, S., 802*n*

N

n (number of periods), 88
Nagel, S., 242*n*
Narayanan, M., 834*n*
NASDAQ, 16, 203*n*, 492, 502, 619
natural hedge, 739
Nayak, S., 618*n*
negative beta stock, 409–410
negative cash flow shocks, 690
negative *EBIT*, 307
negative net additions, 321
Nelson, J., 856*n*
net debt, 48, 48*n*, 437
net income, 35, 37
  see also earnings
  defined, 35
net new financing, 634, 636–637
net present value *(NPV)*, 261–262
  see also NPV rule
  computation of, 263–264, 266, 314–316
  focus on, 239
  and free cash flow, 314–316
  and mutually exclusive projects, 275–276
  negative *NPV* growth, 611–612
  sensitivity analysis, 325–326, 326*t*
  of SFL's New Project, 265*f*
  sunk cost fallacy, 316
  with and without selling, 281*f*
net profit margin, 43
net sales, 36
net working capital, 32, 310–312, 649
  changes in, 312–313
New York Stock Exchange (NYSE), 16, 18, 203, 203*n*, 492, 619, 852, 857
New Zealand, 10
Nguyen, H., 808*n*
Nike, Inc., 203–205, 204*f*, 218–219, 219*f*, 223–224, 225, 227, 228, 231, 232–233, 232*f*
95% confidence interval, 362
Nobel Prize, 396, 413, 562–563
nominal interest rates, 145–146, 145*n*
non-callable bonds, 531
non-cumulative preferred stock, 206
non-dividend-paying stocks, 219, 470, 473
non-tax lease, 798, 805–806
Norli, O., 242*n*
normal distribution, 361–362, 362*f*
Nortel, 571, 619, 848–849
Norway, 10, 489
notes, 523
notes payable, 31
notes to the financial statements, 42
notional principal, 742
NPV profile, 264, 299–300
NPV rule, 261–266
  see also net present value (NPV)
  vs. alternative rules, 265
  application of, 263–266
  and cash today, 262
  computation of net present value, 263–265
  cost of capital, 264, 265
  decision-making, 262–263
  defined, 263
  vs. internal rate of return (IRR) rule, 281–282
  mutually exclusive projects, 274–282
  NPV profile, 264
  using the NPV rule, 263–266

O

Occidental Petroleum, 857
Odean, Terrance, 240, 240*n*, 241*n*, 242*n*
Of Compound Interest, 105
off-balance-sheet financing, 809
off-balance sheet transactions, 42, 55*n*
offer price, 17
$1.00 out lease (finance lease), 792
Onex Corp., 7*t*
one-year investor, 207
Ontario Securities Commission (OSC), 495, 520, 849, 855, 862
open interest, 457
open market repurchase, 595–596
OpenText, 388–389, 550
operating activity, 39
operating cycle, 662–663, 663*f*
operating expenses, 36
operating income, 36
operating lease, 794, 796–797
operating losses, 821–822
operating margin, 43
operating returns, 50–51, 54*t*
Opler, T., 679*n*
opportunity cost, 315
  of capital, 150–154, 317*n*
  of idle asset, 315
  and overall cost of capital, 427
option buyer, 456
option prices
  Black-Scholes option pricing formula, 470–472
  and expiration date, 466
  factors affecting, 466–467, 467*t*
  and risk-free rate, 466
  strike price and stock price, 466
  and volatility, 466–468, 475–476
options. *See* financial option
options hedging, 735–739, 736*t*, 762–764
option to delay, 652–653
option to delay commitment, 330
option to expand, 330
option writer, 455
order costs, 678
Organisation for Economic Co-operation and Development (OECD), 10
original issue discount (OID) bond, 523
Osaka Stock Exchange, 751
out-of-the-money, 458
outside directors, 851
outstanding loan balance, 143–144
over-allotment allocation, 499
overconfidence, 240–241, 825–826
overconfidence hypothesis, 240–241
overhead expenses, 316
overnight rate, 150

P

Palia, D., 856*n*
par, 173
Partch, M., 859*n*
partnerships, 5
par value, 163
payable date, 594
payables management, 675–677
payback period, 268
payback rule, 268–269
pay-for-performance sensitivity, 854–855
payments pattern, 673
payoff, 456, 465*t*
  call option, 460*f*
  at expiration, 459–465
  put option, 460–461
  short position in put option, 462
payout policy
  changing composition of shareholder payouts, 606*f*
  defined, 593
  dividends, 594–595 (*see also* dividends)
  dividend signalling hypothesis, 615
  dividend smoothing, 613–614
  dividends *vs.* share repurchases in perfect capital markets, 596–602
  financial manager, advice for, 619–620
  and internal growth rate, 645
  M&M Payout Irrelevance proposition, 609
  payout *vs.* retention of cash, 608–613
  perfect capital market, payout decisions in, 608–609
  share repurchases, 595–596 (*see also* share repurchases)
  signalling, 613–617
  and sustainable growth rate, 645
payout ratio, 40
pecking order hypothesis, 578–579

pension funds, 20*t*
pension plans, 7*n*
percent of sales method, 632
perfect capital market
cash, retaining, 608–609
defined, 553
dividends policy, 602
dividends *vs.* share repurchases in, 596–602
homemade leverage, 558
insurance pricing, 722–723
lease terms, 789–790
leverage and firm value, 554–556
leverage effect on risk and return, 556–557
loan payments, 790–791
M&M Dividend Irrelevance proposition, 600–601
new business financing, 553–554
unlevered *vs.* levered cash flow, 554–555, 555*f*
unlevered *vs.* levered return, 557*f*
WACC and leverage with, 559–560, 560*f*
performance-based compensation schemes, 725
permanent debt
interest tax shield with, 567–568, 567*n*
permanent working capital, 694
perpetual bond, 101, 102
perpetual *CCA* tax shields, 317–319
perpetuities, 101–103
growing perpetuity, 118–119, 211*n*
historical examples, 102
present value of, 102
perquisites, 13
personal finance
computation of future value, 97–98
endowing a growing perpetuity, 119
endowing a perpetuity, 102–103
number of periods, solving for, 116–117
outstanding loan balance on a mortgage, 144
personal financial decisions, 73–74
present value of lottery prize annuity, 107–108
present value of stream of cash flows, 99–100
rate of return, computation of, 113*n*, 114–115
retirement savings plan annuity, 109–110
retirement savings with a growing annuity, 120–121
valuation of monthly cash flows, 136–137
Pesenti family pyramid, 866*f*
P/E to Growth (PEG) ratio, 49
Petro-Canada, 820
Pfizer, 237
Pincombe, S., 860*n*
Pincus, Mark, 489
Pinkowitz, L., 679*n*
planned expansion
financing needs, 639–640
firm value, effect on, 649–652
forecasting, 638
optimal timing, 652–653
option to delay, 652–653
pro forma balance sheet, 642–643, 643*t*
pro forma income statement, 640–642, 641*t*
valuing, 647–653
pledging of accounts receivable agreement, 702
plowback ratio, 644
the plug, 636
poison pill, 832–833
policy limits, 728
portfolio
beta of, 409–410
and Capital Asset Pricing Model (CAPM), 409–410
diversification, 367–372, 369*f*
efficient portfolio, 392–394
equally weighted portfolio, 396–397, 396*f*
expected return of a portfolio, 384–385, 393*t*, 411
inefficient portfolio, 392–394
large portfolios, 363, 364*f*, 395–397
market portfolio, 397–399
return on a portfolio, 382–384
standard deviation, 390–392
value-weighted portfolio, 398
variance, 390–392
volatility, 368–369, 368*f*, 391–392, 393*t*
volatility of a portfolio, 385–390
portfolio insurance, 472–475, 473*f*
portfolio weights, 382
positive beta, 723*n*
positive cash flow shocks, 690–691
positive net additions, 321*n*
post-money valuation, 490
PotashCorp, 836
Poulsen, Annette, 835, 835*n*
Power, D., 861*n*
Power Corp. of Canada, 7*t*
Prabhala, N., 618*n*
precautionary balance, 680
preferred stock, 206, 489
convertible, 489
cumulative, 206
as equity or debt, 206
non-cumulative, 206
preferred stock capital, 432
preliminary prospectus, 495
premium, 173, 175–176, 175*n*
pre-money valuation, 490
present value *(PV)*, 80–81
adjusted present value, 650*n*
of annuity, 104–105
of cash flow, 87–88
of cash flow stream using term structure of discount rates, 149
vs. future value, 81
of growing annuity, 120–121
of growing perpetuity, 119, 211*n*
and internationally integrated capital markets, 765–766
of lost *CCA* tax shields, 321*n*
lottery prize annuity, 107–108
of perpetuity, 102
of single future cash flow, 88, 132
solving for, with financial calculator, 88, 106–107
stream of cash flows of, 99–100
term structure, 149
pre-tax income, 37
pre-tax WACC, 558–559, 569–570
price
actuarially fair price, 722, 723*n*
ask price, 17
bid price, 17
bonds. *See* bond price
call price, 469*n*
competitive market prices, 74–75, 77–78
convertible bonds, 534–535, 535*f*
exercise price, 455
Law of One Price. *See* Law of One Price
McDonald's Big Mac, 77–78, 77–78*t*
offer price, 17
option prices. *See* option prices
of securities, 203
stock. *See* stock prices
strike price, 455, 460*f*, 466
unaffected target price, 826*n*
valuation principle and, 75–78
price-earnings ratio (P/E), 48, 227–229, 228*f*, 824–825
price risk management liabilities, 55*n*
price-to-book ratio (P/B), 33
primary market, 16
primary offering, 494
primary shares, 508
prime rate, 698
principal-agent problem, 13–15, 849–850
Principle of No Arbitrage, 77
Prior one-year momentum (PR1YR) portfolio, 422
private companies
exit strategy, 491–492
securities and valuation, 489–491
sources of funding, 485–491
private debt, 520–521
private equity firm, 488
private equity funds, 20*t*
private equity investor, 485
private or difficult-to-interpret information, 237–239
private placement, 521
processing float, 670
Procter & Gamble, 834

profit, 456, 465*t*
at expiration, 463–464, 463*f*
holding a put option to expiration, 464
holding call option to expiration, 463*f*
net profit margin, 43
profitability index, 285–287
profitability ratios, 42–43, 49–50, 53*t*
profitable growth, 213–215
profit and loss statement, 35
see also income statement
pro forma balance sheet, 634–635, 635*t*, 659–660, 659*t*
and financing, 643*t*
planned expansion, 642–643, 643*t*
pro forma income statement, 632–634, 633*t*
planned expansion, 640–642, 641*t*
pro forma statement of cash flows, 659–660, 660*t*
pro forma statements, 308, 340
see also specific pro forma statements
project-based costs of capital, 442–445
project externalities, 316
projects
analysis of project, 325–329
with different lives, 282–285
different resource requirements, 285–287
limited resources, 285–288
losses for projects in profitable companies, 307–308
mutually exclusive projects, 274–282
in new line of business, 443
WACC method, 439
promissory note, 697
property insurance, 721
prospectus
Facebook, 496*f*
final prospectus, 495
preliminary prospectus, 495
protective put, 472
provincial bonds, 185–188, 185*f*
provincial securities commissions, 492, 495, 853
proxy, 205
proxy contest, 205, 857
Proxy contest outcomes, 858*f*
proxy fight, 832
public, easily interpretable information, 237
public debt, 521–525
see also bonds
public warehouse, 704
Pujols, Albert, 84
Puma, 231
purchasing options, 458
pure discount bonds, 164
put-call parity, 472–475
put option, 455, 460–461
short position in, 462
valuation, 470
pyramid structure, 865–867

Q
Qualcomm Incorporated, 280
quick ratio, 43

R
R. G. Barry Corp., 231*t*
raider, 831
Rampini, A., 799*n*, 808*n*
rate of return, 112–115
computation of, 113*n*, 114–115, 133
defined, 112
financial calculator, 133
ratios, 53–54*t*
accounts payable days, 45
accounts receivable days, 45, 45*n*
acid-test ratio, 43
asset efficiency, 45, 53–54*t*
asset turnover, 45
average collection period, 45
balance sheet, 33–34
current ratio, 43
days sales outstanding, 45
debt-equity ratio, 34–35, 47, 440
debt-to-capital ratio, 48
debt-to-enterprise value ratio, 48
debt-to-value ratio, 550, 551*f*
DuPont Identity, 51–52, 52*n*
EBITDA, 46
equity multiplier, 48
exchange ratio, 827
fixed asset turnover, 45
gross margin, 42–43
interest coverage ratios, 46–47, 54*t*
inventory days, 45
inventory turnover ratio, 45
leverage ratios, 47–48, 54*t*
market-to-book ratio, 33–34
mismatched ratios, 49
net debt, 48, 48*n*
net profit margin, 43
operating margin, 43
operating returns, 50–51, 54*t*
payout ratio, 40
P/E to Growth (PEG) ratio, 49
plowback ratio, 644
price-earnings ratio (P/E), 48, 824–825
price-to-book ratio (P/B), 33
profitability ratios, 42–43, 49–50, 53*t*
quick ratio, 43
retention ratio, 644
return on assets (ROA), 50
return on equity (ROE), 50, 50*n*
return on invested capital (ROIC), 50–51
times interest earned (TIE) ratio, 46
valuation ratios, 48–50, 54*t*
working capital ratios, 45–46, 53–54*t*
RBC Capital Markets, 537
real estate investment trust (REIT), 8–9, 10
real interest rate, 145–146
realized return, 351–355, 355*t*
RealNetworks, Inc., 536, 536*t*
real options, 329–330
recapitalization, 834–835
recaptured *CCA*, 321*n*
receivables management, 671–675
credit policy, 671–673
monitoring accounts receivable, 673–675
record date, 594
recosts, 807–808
red herring, 495
registered education savings plan (RESP), 7*n*
registered retirement income fund (RRIF), 7*n*
registered retirement savings plan (RRSP), 7*n*, 109–110
registration statement, 495
regulatory filings, 495
rentes, 102
repatriated earnings, 771–772
repayment provisions, 530–537
call provisions, 530–532
Canada Call, 533
convertible provisions, 534–537, 535*f*
make-whole call, 533
sinking funds, 534
replacement cost, 284–285
replacement decisions, 323–325
reporting, stock market, 203–205
repurchase agreements, 681*t*
repurchases. *See* share repurchase
required life, 284
required return, 407
resale costs, 807–808
research and development expenditures, 316
residual value, 789
retained earnings, 30
defined, 40
vs. shareholders' equity, 636
retention rate, 213
retention ratio, 644
return
see also risk-return relationship
arithmetic average returns *vs.* compound annual returns, 358
average annual return, 355–356, 356*f*
correlation between two sets of returns, 390
efficient portfolio, 394
expected return. *See* expected return
historical returns, 351–363, 403–406, 438*t*
individual stocks, 363–365
large portfolios, 363, 364*f*
realized return, 351–355, 355*t*
required return, 407
vs. risk, 392–394
scatter plots of, 389*f*
of single security, 353
unlevered *vs.* levered, 557*f*
variance of, 357
volatility of, 357

return of capital, 594
return on a portfolio, 382–384
return on assets (ROA), 50
return on equity (ROE), 50, 50*n*, 52*n*, 563
return on invested capital (ROIC), 50–51
revenues, 36
  bonds, 528
  estimate, 303–306
  incremental revenue, 306–308
reverse splits, 619
Revlon duties, 832
revolving line of credit, 521, 698
rights offer, 509
risk
  see also risk-return relationship
  average risk, 440
  basis risk, 740
  commodity price risk, 728–740
  common risk, 365–367
  credit risk, 182, 733
  default risk prevention, 734
  diversifiable risk, 370
  diversification, 366–367, 369*f*, 385–386
  exchange rate risk, 756–764
  firm-specific risk, 401*f*
  of foreign project, 768*n*
  independent risk, 365–367
  insurance example, 365
  interest rate risk, 740–743
  and leasing, 808
  liquidity risk, 739
  market risk, 399–401
  vs. return, 392–394
  systematic risk. *See* systematic risk
  total risk, 371, 385, 397, 401, 401*f*, 409, 410*f*
  transfer of, 808
  types of, 366, 366*t*
  unsystematic risk, 367–369, 371*t*
risk arbitrageurs, 829
risk assessment, 726
risk factors, 422
risk-free interest rate, 147–149, 148*f*, 166, 437–438
risk-free rate, 466
risk management, 498–499
  commodity price risk, 728–740
  insurance, 721–728
  interest rate risk, 740–743
  mergers and acquisitions, 822
  prevention, 720
risk premium, 370
  equity risk premium, 407
  market risk premium, 407
risk-return relationship, 349–351
  see also return; risk
  diversification, 367–372
  historical risk and returns, 351–363
  historical tradeoff, 363–365, 364*f*
  leverage effect on, 556–558, 556*t*, 557*f*
  levered equity, 557–558
  recessions, 351
risky government bonds, 773–774
Ritter, Jay, 498, 498*n*, 504, 505, 506, 506*n*, 507, 507*n*
RJR Nabisco, 841
road show, 496
Rocky Brands, Inc., 230, 231*t*
Rodriguez, Alex, 82
Rogel, Steve, 836
Roll, R., 825, 825*n*
Ross, Stephan A., 422*n*
Rossi, S., 864*n*
rounded numbers, 689*n*
Rouwenhorst, Geert, 102
Royal Bank of Canada, 7*t*
Royal Dutch Shell, 6
Royal & SunAlliance, 615
Rule of 72, 85
Rusticus, T., 858*n*
Ryan, H., 851*n*
Ryder Systems, Inc., 788
Ryngaert, M., 833*n*

S

Saks Inc., 72
sale and leaseback, 788
sales, 36
sales-type lease, 788
Salomon Brothers, 841
salvage value, 284*n*, 319–321
Sanford C. Bernstein, 820
San Francisco Municipal Railway, 788
Sarbanes-Oxley Act, 55–56,, 492, 852, 859–860
Sarin, A., 867*n*
Saskatchewan Fertilizer Ltd. (SFL), 263
Saudi Arabia, 489
Saverin, Eduardo, 489
say-on-pay vote, 857
Sazaby, Inc., 750
SBC, 818, 819, 821
scaled covariance, 386*n*
scandals, 848–849
scatter plots of returns, 389*f*
scenario analysis, 327–329
Schallheim, J., 794*n*, 808*n*
Schlingemann, F., 827*n*
Schmidt, Luke, 605, 605*n*
Scholes, Myron, 468, 470, 475*n*
Schwert, G. W., 833*n*
Sears, 229
Seasholes, M., 242*n*
seasonalities, 691
seasoned equity offering (SEO), 507–511
  adverse selection, 511
  cash offers, 509
  costs, 511
  defined, 507
  price reaction, 510–511, 510*f*
  primary shares, 508
  process, 508–509
  puzzles of, 511
  rights offer, 509
  secondary shares, 508
  tombstones, 509
secondary market, 16
secondary offering, 494
secondary shares, 508
SEC Rule 10b-18, 595*n*
secured debt, 523
secured loan, 702
securities
  agency, 527
  Government of Canada securities, 526, 526*t*
  price, and Valuation Principle, 203, 206–207
  pricing using Law of One Price, 77
  private companies, 489–491
  return. *See* return
  risk. *See* risk
  subprime mortgage-backed securities, 528
Securities Act, 859
Securities Exchange Act, 859, 862
security interest, 799
security market line (SML), 409, 410*f*
SEDAR (System for Electronic Document Analysis and Retrieval), 28, 495*n*
segmented capital markets, 772–776
semistrong-form market efficiency, 236
seniority, 523–524
sensitivity analysis, 225, 325–326, 326*t*, 342–344
Shapiro, A., 867*n*
shareholder, 6
  activism, 859
  annual meeting, 205
  approval, 857
  board of directors, election of, 11
  direct action by, 856–858
  distributions to. *See* distributions to shareholder
  lockup, 499
  proxy, 205
  rights, 205, 864
  voice, 856–857
  voting, 205
shareholders' equity
  on balance sheet, 32
  common stock, 30
  defined, 30
  retained earnings, 30
  vs. retained earnings, 636
  statement of, 41
shareholder wealth maximization, 11
share repurchases, 220–221, 595–596
  vs. dividends, in perfect capital market, 596–602
  Dutch auction, 596
  greenmail, 596
  with no dividend, 598–600
  open market repurchase, 595–596
  rise of, 605–606, 605*f*
  and signalling, 615–617
  summary, 606*t*

share repurchases (*continued*)
and supply of shares, 599
targeted repurchase, 596
taxes, 603–604, 606, 607–608
tender offer, 596
shares. *See* stock
Sharpe, S., 808*n*
Sharpe, William, 413
Shearson Lehman Hutton, 841
Shefrin, H., 241, 241*n*
Shenzhen Stock Exchange, 18
Sherman, Ann, 502, 502*n*
Sherman Act, 835
Sherritt International, 202–203
Sherwin, Henry, 105
shirking, 13
Shivdasani, A., 851*n*
Shleifer, A., 864*n*, 867*n*, 869*n*
short sales, 464–465, 465*f*
short-term cash needs, 11
short-term debt, 31
short-term financial plan, 705–706
short-term financing
aggressive financing policy, 695–697
bank loans, 697–701
cash budget, 691–694, 692–694*t*
commercial paper, 701–702
conservative financing policy, 697
financing policy choices, 695–697
forecasting needs, 689–694
funding risk, 697
matching principle, 694–697, 695*n*
permanent working capital, 694
secured financing, 702–705
short-term financial plan, 705–706
temporary working capital, 694–695
short-term lending, 151–152
Shumway, T., 242*n*
Sidel, Robin, 502
signalling theory of debt, 578
signalling with payout policy, 613–617
Simon, Ruth, 502
simple interest, 138
Singapore, 489
single, end-of-period-payment loan, 697–698
sinking funds, 534
Skechers U.S.A., 231*t*
Sleep Country, 665
Slovin, Myron, 511*n*
Snowy Pharmaceuticals, 238, 238*f*
sole partnerships, 4
sole proprietorship, 484
Sony, 260
Southwest Airlines, 721, 731*f*, 740
sovereign debt, 525–526
sovereign wealth funds (SWFs), 488–489
S&P 500, 250*f*, 399, 422
Spain, 102
special dividend, 594
specialists, 18
special-purpose entity (SPE), 789, 798
speculation, 458, 740
speculative bonds, 183, 184*t*
Spie Batignolles, 820
S&P 500 Index, 349, 350*f*, 357*f*
spinoff, 619
spot interest rates, 166
spread, 498
S&P/TSX Composite Index, 349, 350, 350*f*, 351, 355*t*, 356*f*, 398, 438*t*
S&P/TSX 60 Index, 398
Srivastava, Ashwani, 267*n*, 507, 507*n*
staggered boards, 833–834
stakeholder model, 867–868
stakeholder satisfaction, 14
Standard Chartered, 752
standard deviation, 357–358, 358*n*, 360, 362*f*, 371, 372
see also volatility
mixing standard deviation and beta, 401
portfolio, 390–392
Standard Oil, 835
Standard & Poor's, 183, 184*t*, 349
Stangeland, David, 533, 533*n*, 833*n*
Stantec, 388–389, 391–392
Stanton, Giancarlo, 84
Star Alliance, 552
Starbucks Coffee Company, 644, 646, 647*f*, 750–751
Starbucks Coffee Japan Ltd., 751
statement of cash flows, 37–41
defined, 38
financing activity, 40
investment activity, 40
operating activity, 39
pro forma statement of cash flows, 659–660, 660*t*
statement of financial position. *See* balance sheet
statement of shareholders' equity, 41
State Street, 752
Statman, M., 241, 241*n*
step up, 830
Steven Madden, Ltd., 231*t*
Stewart, Martha, 864
Stillman, R., 820*n*
stock, 6
see also equity
basics of, 203–206
cash flows from owning, 207
common stock, 203, 205–206
co-movement, 386–389
compensation policies, 853
convertible preferred stock, 489
correlation, 386–389, 386*n*, 388*f*, 388*t*
defensive stocks, 402
dilution, 37
dividend-paying stock, 475
dual class shares, 865
growth stocks, 34
individual biases and trading, 240–243
market capitalization, 32
non-dividend-paying stocks, 219
preferred stock, 206, 489
price. *See* stock price
proxy, 205
repurchases. *See* share repurchase
return. *See* return
risk. *See* risk
share repurchase, 220–221
stock quotes, 203–205, 204*f*
supply of shares, and share repurchases, 599
valuation. *See* stock valuation
value stocks, 34
stock dividend, 617–619
stock exchange. *See* stock market
stockholder. *See* shareholder
stockholders' equity. *See* shareholders' equity
stock market, 16–19
ask price, 17
bid-ask spread, 17
bid price, 17
defined, 16
largest stock markets, 16–18, 17*f*
listing standards, 19
market makers, 18
new competition and market changes, 18–19
offer price, 17
primary market, 16
reporting, 203–205
secondary market, 16
specialists, 18
stock quotes, 203–205, 204*f*
thinly traded, 18
ticker symbol, 203
transaction cost, 18
stock market indexes, 398–399
stock option quotations, 456–458, 457*t*
stock options, 37
stock-out, 677
stock prices
see also stock valuation
competition and efficient markets, 236–239
convertible bonds and, 536
information in, 234–235
public information, reactions to, 237
and returns, 208–209
and stock splits, 618–619
and strike price, 466
stock quotes, 203–205, 204*f*
stock split, 617–619
stock swap, 817
stock valuation
see also stock prices
competition and efficient markets, 236–239
discounted cash flow models, 226*f*, 231–232
discounted free cash flow model, 221–226
dividend-discount model (DDM). *See* dividend-discount model (DDM)
free cash flow, 223–224

individual biases and trading, 240–243
information in stock prices, 234–235
method of comparable, 226–233
non-dividend-paying stocks, 219
post-money valuation, 490
pre-money valuation, 490
private companies, 489–491
sensitivity analysis, 225
with share repurchase, 220–221
valuation multiples, 227–230
valuation triad, 234
Stohs, M. H., 695*n*
storage, 729
straight bond, 535
straight-line method, of depreciation, 440*n*
straight voting, 205
strategic investor, 489
strategic partner, 489
stream of cash flows
see also cash flow
annuities, 104–110
defined, 96
future value, 106–107
growing annuity, 120–121
growing perpetuity, 118–119
perpetuities, 101–103
present value, 106–107
solving for cash flow, 110–112
valuation, 96–100
stretching the accounts payable, 676–677
strike price, 455, 460*f*, 466
STRIP bonds (Separate Trading of Registered Interest and Principal), 526
strong-form market efficiency, 236
Stulz, R., 679*n*, 827*n*
subordinated debenture, 523–524
subprime mortgage-backed securities, 528
summing cash flows across time, 84
Suncor Energy Inc., 7*t*, 16, 721, 820
Sundaram, A., 834*n*
sunk cost, 316–317
sunk cost fallacy, 317
supervisory board, 850
Suret, Jean-Marc, 506, 507, 507*n*
Sushka, Marie, 511*n*
sustainable growth rate, 644–647, 646*t*
swap-based hedging, 741–743
SWF Institute, 488–489
syndicate, 494–495
syndicated bank loan, 521
synergies, 818
synthetic lease, 789, 798
systematic risk, 367–372, 371*t*
alternative models, 422–424
Arbitrage Pricing Theory (APT), 422
Fama-French-Carhart factor specification (FFC), 422, 423*t*
vs. firm-specific risk, 401*f*
market portfolio, role of, 397–399
market risk and beta, 399–401
measurement of, 397–406
multi-factor model, 422
risk factors, 422
stock market indexes, 398–399
vs. total risk, 402
System for Electronic Document Analysis and Retrieval (SEDAR), 28

T

takeover, 815, 817–818
see also mergers and acquisitions
takeover defences
golden parachute, 834
other defensive strategies, 835
poison pill, 832–833
recapitalization, 834–835
regulatory approval, 835–837
staggered boards, 833–834
white knight, 834
white squire, 834
takeover process, 826–832
board and shareholder approval, 831–832
merger "arbitrage," 828–830
offer, 827–828
tax and accounting issues, 830–831
valuation, 826–827
Tanous, Peter J., 563
target, 815
targeted repurchase, 596
taxes
around the world, 10
bottom line, 569–570
Canadian personal income tax rates, top tax bracket, 603*t*
capital cost allowance (CCA), 304–305, 309–310, 309*t*, 318*t*, 321*n*
capital gains rate, 208, 604*f*
capital gains tax, 320, 602–603
and cash retention, 609–610
CCA rate, 304–305
CCA tax shield, 313–314, 317–319, 318*t*
corporate debt and, 564–570
corporate entities, tax implications for, 7–10
cost of debt, 430–431
on dividend income, 7*n*
dividend rates, worldwide, 604*f*
dividends, tax disadvantages of, 602–608
double taxation, 7, 8
half-year rule, 305
insurance, and tax rate fluctuations, 725
interest tax deduction, 564–565
interest tax shield, 565–568, 651, 651*n*
leases, 797–798
losses for projects in profitable companies, 307–308
marginal corporate tax rate, 307
mergers and acquisitions, 830–831
and negative *EBIT*, 307
operating losses, tax savings from, 821–822
perpetual *CCA* tax shields, 317–319
recaptured *CCA*, 321*n*
registered retirement savings plan (RRSP), 7*n*
share repurchase, 603–604, 606, 607–608
tax loss carrybacks, 323
tax loss carryforwards, 323
tax-sheltered investments, 7*n*
terminal loss, 321*n*
true tax lease, 797, 800–801, 805
undepreciated capital cost (UCC), 305
valuation and international taxation, 771–772
WACC with, 569, 570*f*
tax loss carrybacks, 323
tax loss carryforwards, 323
tax-sheltered investments, 7*n*
tax year, 304
Teachers Insurance and Annuity Association, 186
Telus Corporation, 443
temporary working capital, 694–695
tender offer, 596, 827
term (of the bond), 163
term deposits, 681*t*
terminal loss, 321*n*
term loan, 521
term sheet, 817
term structure, 147, 148*f*, 149, 209*n*
Tesla Motors, 489
The Independent, 860
Theodorou, E., 861*n*
Thesmar, David, 442
thinly traded, 18
ticker symbol, 203
time, and bond price, 176–177, 177*f*
timelines, 82–83
cash inflows *vs.* outflows, 83
constructing, 82
defined, 82
identifying dates on, 82–83
representing time periods, 82
times interest earned (TIE) ratio, 47
time value of money, 78–79, 79*f*, 95–121
annuities, 104–110
growing cash flows, 118–121
perpetuities, 101–103
stream of cash flows valuation, 96–100
variables, 110–117
TMX Group, 198*n*, 454, 829
Tobin, John, 797*n*
toehold, 838
tombstones, 509
Toronto-Dominion Bank, 7*t*
Toronto Stock Exchange (TSX), 6, 16–18, 203, 492, 595, 619
Toshiba, 260
total net working capital, 649
total payout model, 220–221

total returns, 207–208
total risk, 371, 385, 397, 401, 401*f*, 409, 410*f*
trade credit, 311, 667–670
  vs. bank loans, 669
  benefits of, 669
  cash discount, 667
  costs of, 668–669, 676–677
  credit period, 667
  defined, 667
  discount period, 667
  electronic cheque processing, 670
  float management, 669–670
  and market frictions, 668–669
  vs. standard loans, 669
  stretched accounts payable, 676–677
  terms, 667
trade-off, 868–869
trade-off theory, 572–574, 574*f*
  differences across firms, 573
  optimal leverage, 573–574, 574*f*
trading
  disposition effect, 241–242
  excessive, 240–241
  hanging on to losers, 241–242
  and individual biases, 240–243
  investor attention, mood, and experience, 242–243
  overconfidence, 240–241
trailing earnings, 227
trailing P/E, 227
tranches, 524
transactions balance, 679
transactions costs, 18, 74*n*
Trans-Canada Air Lines. *See* Air Canada
treasurer, 13*f*
treasury bills, 164, 681*t*
  see also Government of Canada treasury bills
Treasury Strategies, Inc., 680
Treynor, Jack, 413
Triantis, G., 867*n*
true lease, 799
true tax lease, 797, 800–801, 805
trust receipts loan, 704
TSX. *See* Toronto Stock Exchange (TSX)
TSX Venture Exchange, 16, 18
tunnelling, 866–867
Tversky, Amos, 241, 241*n*
two-state single-period model, 468–469
two-stock portfolio
  volatility, computation of, 391–392
Tyco, 848

U

UAE, 489
UBS, 752
unaffected target price, 826*n*
uncommitted line of credit, 698
unconventional cash flows, 269–271
undepreciated capital cost (UCC), 305
underinvestment problem, 576
underpriced IPOs, 503
underwriter, 494–495, 494*t*
United Airlines, 740
United Kingdom, 509, 511*n*
United States
  accounting standards, 29
  airlines, hedging strategies at, 740
  bond prices online, 173
  cash offers, 509
  cyclicality of IPOs in, 505*f*
  EDGAR, 489*n*, 495*n*
  insider trading, 862–863
  IPOs fees, 506
  IRS, 822
  mergers and acquisitions, 838*n*
  open market repurchase, 595*n*
  registration statement, 495
  Sarbanes-Oxley Act. *See* Sarbanes-Oxley Act
unit holders, 8, 10
unlevered equity, 554
unlevered firm, 428
  cash flow of, 566–567, 566*f*
unlevered net income, 308
Unocal, 832
unprofitable growth, 214–215
unsecured debt, 523
unsystematic risk, 367–369, 371*t*
Upton, C., 792*n*
Urquhart, Diane A., 571
U.S. Justice Department, 820, 855
U.S. Securities and Exchange Commission (SEC), 28, 28*n*, 56, 489, 520, 595, 849, 853, 859, 863, 864
  Rule 144A, 521
  SEC Rule 10b-18, 595*n*

V

Vafeas, N., 861*n*
valuation and international taxation, 771–772
valuation multiples, 227–230
  continuation value, 650
  defined, 227
  vs. discounted cash flow models, 231–232
  enterprise value multiples, 229–230
  limitations of multiples, 230–231
  other multiples, 230
  price-earnings ratio (P/E), 227–230, 228*f*
valuation of cash flows. *See* cash flow valuation
valuation of stock. *See* stock valuation
Valuation Principle, 76
  application (example), 76
  arbitrage, 77
  arbitrage opportunity, 77
  cash flows, 83–88
  cash inflows *vs.* outflows, 83
  cost-benefit analysis, 73–75
  defined, 76
  expected cash flows, 206, 226
  financial calculators, 88
  firm value, 662, 667
  growth, value implications of, 645–647
  interest rates, 79–82
  Law of One Price, 77
  market interest rate, 153
  market prices and, 75–78
  NPV rule. *See* NPV rule
  option prices and expiration date, 466
  price of a security, 203, 206–207
  Principle of No Arbitrage, 77
  timelines, 82–83
  time value of money, 78–79, 79*f*
valuation ratios, 46–48, 54*t*
valuation triad, 234
value drivers, 217–218
value stocks, 34
value-weighted portfolio, 398
Vanda Pharmaceuticals (VNDA), 297–298
Vanguard Group, 399
Vanguard's Total Stock Market Index Fund, 399
Varaiya, N., 833*n*
variables, 106
variance, 357, 358*n*, 390–392
venture capital firm, 485–487, 485*t*
venture capital funds, 20*t*, 487*f*
venture capitalists, 486–487
venture merchant financing, 703
Vermaelen, T., 617*n*
vertical integration, 729, 819
vertical merger, 817
Vishny, R., 864*n*
volatility, 357, 368–369, 368*f*, 371, 372, 388*t*, 410*f*
  see also standard deviation
  vs. expected return, 394*f*
  mixing volatility with beta, 401
  and option prices, 466–468, 475–476
  two-stock portfolio, computation of, 391–392
  volatility *vs.* expected return, 394
volatility of a portfolio, 385–397, 393*t*
Volpin, P., 865*n*
voting rights
  cumulative voting, 205
  straight voting, 205

W

WACC method, 439
Walkling, R., 833*n*, 855*n*
Wal-Mart, 481–482
Walt Disney Company, 452–453, 856
Wang, C., 858*n*
warehouse arrangement, 704
warehouse financing, 704–705
Warner, J., 857*n*
warrants, 455
weak-form market efficiency, 236
weighted average cost of capital (WACC), 222–223, 222*n*, 426–429, 435–438
  assumptions, 440
  average risk, 440

calculations, 428–429
computation of, 436
constant debt-equity ratio, 440
defined, 426, 427
discounting cash flows, 777*n*
foreign project, value of, 768–769
levered firm, 428–429
limited leverage effects, 440
market risk premium, 438
net debt, 437
and overall cost of capital, 427
perfect capital markets and, 559–560, 560*f*
in practice, 436, 437*f*
pre-tax WACC, 558–559
risk-free interest rate, 437–438
taxes with, 569, 570
unlevered firm, 428
valuation of project, 439–441
WACC equation, 435–436
WACC method, 439–441
Weinstein, Elizabeth, 502
Weisbach, M., 851*n*, 856*n*
Welch, Ivo, 438*n*
Westcoast Port, Inc., 230
WestJet, 43, 388–389, 401*f*, 551, 552, 552*f*, 573, 730
Weston, J., 242*n*
Weyco Group, 231*t*
Weyerhaeuser, 836
Whitacre, 818
white knight, 834
white squire, 834
Wiggins, R., 851*n*
Willamette Industries, 836
Williams, J.B., 601*n*
Williamson, R., 679*n*
without recourse, 703
with recourse, 703
Wolfenzon, D., 867*n*
Wolverine World Wide, 231*t*
Wood, Justin, 615
working capital, 11*n*
see also working capital management
adjustments, 39
cash cycle, 662–664, 663*f*
and firm value, 665–667
incremental net working capital, 649
needs, by industry, 664–665, 665*t*
net working capital, 32, 312–314, 649
overview of, 662–667
permanent working capital, 694
ratios, 45–46, 53–54*t*
requirements, for planned expansion, 641–642, 641*t*
temporary working capital, 694–695
total net working capital, 649
trade credit, 667–670
working capital management
cash management, 679–682
inventory management, 677–679
payables management, 675–677
receivables management, 671–675
value of, 666
WorldCom, 848
World Trade Organization (WTO), 836*n*
W.R. Hambrecht and Company, 499
Wright, Matthew, 615
Wu, G., 242*n*
Wyndham Worldwide Corporation, 661

X

Xie, F., 858*n*
XTX Markets, 752

Y

Yermack, D., 852*n*, 855*n*
yield curve, 147–153
corporate bonds, 185–188, 185*f*
defined, 147
and discount rate, 147–150
and the economy, 150–153
Government of Canada bond, 201
and Law of One Price, 197–201
provincial bonds, 185–188, 185*f*
shape of, 150–153
zero-coupon yield curve, 166, 166*f*
yield to call (YTC), 531–533
financial calculator, 544
yield to maturity *(YTM)*, 164–165, 168
and bond price, 174, 174*f*, 180*f*
computation of bond price from, 172
corporate bonds, 183
cost of debt, 430, 430*n*
coupon bonds, 170–171
financial calculator, solving with, 196
yield to worst, 532, 532*t*

Z

Zenner, M., 851*n*
zero-coupon bonds, 164–166
cash flows, 164
price, 164–165
risk-free interest rates, 166
yield to maturity *(YTM)*, 164–165
zero-coupon yield curve, 166, 166*f*
Zhao, Q., 506*n*
Zhu, N., 242*n*
Zingales, L., 867*n*
Zuckerberg, Mark, 489, 490, 508
Zuckerman, Gregory, 502

KEY EQUATIONS

EQ. #	EQ. TITLE	PAGE
3.3	Future Value of a Cash Flow	85
3.4	Present Value of a Cash Flow	87
4.3	Present Value of a Cash Flow Stream	99
4.4	Present Value of a Perpetuity	102
4.5	Present Value of an n-Period Annuity	105
4.6	Future Value of an n-Period Annuity	108
4.7	Loan Payment	111
4.8	Present Value of a Growing Perpetuity	119
4.9	Present Value of a Growing Annuity	120
4.10	Future Value of a Growing Annuity	121
5.1	Effective Rate over Different Time Periods	136
5.2	Implied Effective Interest Rate per Compounding Period	138
5.3	Converting an APR to an EAR	138
5.5	The Real Interest Rate	145
5.7	Present Value of a Cash Flow Stream Using a Term Structure of Discount Rates	149
6.1	Coupon Payment	163
6.3	Yield to Maturity for Zero-Coupon Bond	165
6.4	Yield to Maturity of a Coupon Bond	170
6.B1	Price of a Coupon Bond	198
7.2	Total Return	208
7.4	Dividend-Discount Model	210
7.6	Constant Dividend Growth Model	211
7.13	Dividend-Discount Model with Constant Long-Term Growth	215
7.15	Total Payout Model	220
7.17	Free Cash Flow	222
7.19	Share Price based on Enterprise Value	222
8.1	Net Present Value	261
8.4	Profitability Index	286
9.11	Present Value of CCA Tax Shield	319
10.1	Realized Return	352
10.2	Annual Realized Return	353
10.3	Average Annual Return of a Security	355
11.1	Portfolio Weight	382
11.3	Expected Return of a Portfolio	384
11.4	Variance of a Two-Stock Portfolio	390
11.7	Capital Asset Pricing Model	407
11.8	Beta of a Portfolio	409
12.2	Weighted Average Cost of Capital (Pre-tax)	429
12.4	Cost of Preferred Stock Capital	432